THE
CAMBRIDGE ANCIENT HISTORY

VOLUME II
PART 1

THE CAMBRIDGE ANCIENT HISTORY

THIRD EDITION

VOLUME II
PART 1

HISTORY OF THE MIDDLE EAST AND THE AEGEAN REGION *c.* 1800–1380 B.C.

EDITED BY

I. E. S. EDWARDS F.B.A.
Keeper of Egyptian Antiquities, The British Museum

THE LATE C. J. GADD F.B.A.
*Professor Emeritus of Ancient Semitic Languages and Civilizations,
School of Oriental and African Studies, University of London*

N. G. L. HAMMOND F.B.A.
Professor of Greek, University of Bristol

E. SOLLBERGER
Deputy Keeper of Western Asiatic Antiquities, The British Museum

CAMBRIDGE
AT THE UNIVERSITY PRESS

1973

Published by the Syndics of the Cambridge University Press
Bentley House, 200 Euston Road, London NW1 2DB
American Branch: 32 East 57th Street, New York, N.Y.10022

© Cambridge University Press 1973

Library of Congress Catalogue Card Number: 75–85719

ISBN: 0 521 08230 7

Printed in Great Britain
at the University Printing House, Cambridge
(Brooke Crutchley, University Printer)

CONTENTS

CHAPTER I

NORTHERN MESOPOTAMIA AND SYRIA

by J.-R. KUPPER
Professeur à l'Université de Liège

CHAPTER II

EGYPT: FROM THE DEATH OF AMMENEMES III TO SEQENENRE II

by the late WILLIAM C. HAYES
Formerly Curator of the Department of Egyptian Art in the Metropolitan Museum of Art, New York

CHAPTER III

PALESTINE IN THE MIDDLE BRONZE AGE

by KATHLEEN M. KENYON

Principal of St Hugh's College, Oxford

CHAPTER IV

(a) GREECE AND THE AEGEAN ISLANDS IN THE MIDDLE BRONZE AGE

by JOHN L. CASKEY

*Professor of Classical Archaeology and Fellow of the
Graduate School in the University of Cincinnati*

(b) THE MATURITY OF MINOAN CIVILIZATION

by F. MATZ

*Professor Emeritus of Archaeology in the
University of Marburg*

(c) CYPRUS IN THE MIDDLE BRONZE AGE

by H. W. CATLING
Director of the British School of
Archaeology at Athens

CHAPTER V

HAMMURABI AND THE END OF HIS DYNASTY

by the late C. J. GADD
Professor Emeritus of Ancient Semitic Languages and Civilizations,
School of Oriental and African Studies, University of London

CHAPTER VI

ANATOLIA c. 1750–1600 B.C.

by O. R. GURNEY
Reader in Assyriology in the University of Oxford

CHAPTER VII

PERSIA *c.* 1800–1550 B.C.

by WALTHER HINZ
Professor of Iranian History in the University of Göttingen

CHAPTER VIII

EGYPT: FROM THE EXPULSION OF THE HYKSOS TO AMENOPHIS I

by T. G. H. JAMES
Assistant Keeper in the Department of Egyptian Antiquities, British Museum

CHAPTER IX

EGYPT: INTERNAL AFFAIRS FROM TUTHMOSIS I TO THE DEATH OF AMENOPHIS III

by the late WILLIAM C. HAYES

CHAPTER X

SYRIA *c.* 1550–1400 B.C.

by MARGARET S. DROWER
Reader in Ancient History in the University of London

CHAPTER XI

PALESTINE IN THE TIME OF THE EIGHTEENTH DYNASTY

by KATHLEEN M. KENYON

CHAPTER XII

THE ZENITH OF MINOAN CIVILIZATION

by F. MATZ

CHAPTER XIII

THE LINEAR SCRIPTS AND THE TABLES AS HISTORICAL DOCUMENTS

(*a*) LITERACY IN MINOAN AND MYCENAEAN LANDS

by STERLING DOW
Professor of Archaeology, Harvard University

(*b*) THE LINEAR B TABLETS AS HISTORICAL DOCUMENTS

by JOHN CHADWICK
Reader in Classics, University of Cambridge

CONTENTS

CHAPTER XVI

THE ARCHAEOLOGICAL EVIDENCE OF THE SECOND MILLENNIUM B.C. ON THE PERSIAN PLATEAU

by ROBERT H. DYSON, JR.

*The University Museum, University of Pennsylvania,
Philadelphia, Pennsylvania*

BIBLIOGRAPHIES

Chronological Tables

MAPS

TABLES

[xvii]

TEXT-FIGURES

PREFACE

THE second volume of this History begins with events which
occurred at a time when the Amorite dynasties in Western Asia
were vying with each other for supremacy, making and breaking alliances but nevertheless maintaining the great Sumero-
Akkadian culture which they had inherited from the conquered populations. It was the era of the Western Semites and,
in particular, of the most outstanding of the Semitic dynasties,
that of Hammurabi, the 'lawgiver'. The Semites were, however,
not destined to remain in control for long. Foreigners from the
north-east, the Kassites, soon took possession of Babylonia and
held it under their sway for five centuries, thereby establishing
the longest dynastic succession in the history of the land. Meanwhile, in Anatolia, the rise of the Hittites marked the beginning
of the first Indo-European empire which was eventually to deal a
death blow to Amorite rule in Babylon.

Disturbances in Western Asia soon began to affect life in the
Nile Valley. Asiatic elements moved southwards until they
occupied most of the Delta and penetrated into Middle and
Upper Egypt, asserting their authority as they went. Manetho
called these Asiatic settlers the Hyksos, and he claimed that they
achieved their domination 'without a battle'. While there is
nothing in contemporary evidence to suggest that they established their position by any other way than by a process of
gradual infiltration, they were certainly helped by the possession
of superior weapons, notably the horse-drawn chariot, and by
Egypt's political and military weakness at the time. Like other
invaders, both before and after them, they soon adopted Egyptian customs, but they were never accepted by the populace and
were always regarded as foreigners. Their expulsion, after about
150 years, led to the rise of a succession of warrior kings, the
Eighteenth Dynasty, who extended their realm to the banks of
the Euphrates in the north-east and far into the Sudan in the south.
The fruits of their conquests swelled the treasuries of the pharaohs
and their temples for two centuries and raised the standard
of life, at least for the upper classes, to its highest level of prosperity. Under Amenophis III, however, stagnation set in, notwithstanding outward appearances to the contrary, and his reign,
the last period of Egyptian history described in the present part,
marks the end of an epoch.

Within the Aegean region the outstanding civilization of this age was that of Minoan Crete. Its most striking monuments are the great palaces at Cnossus, Mallia and Phaestus, and we learn much of the society and life of the times from the scenes which are so beautifully portrayed on frescoes, gems, sealings and metal objects. Meanwhile on the Greek mainland the Middle Bronze Age began with invasions by people who spoke an Indo-European language which was the remote ancestor of the Greek of the Homeric epics; it ended with the rise of Mycenaean civilization which owed much to the influence of Minoan Crete but finally overthrew the rulers of the island. One of the inventions of Minoan civilization was a linear script, and the Mycenaean conquerors of Crete used a successor to this script which has been deciphered and provides us with the earliest texts in the Greek language.

A number of the contributors to this Part have taken advantage of the invitation of the Syndics of the Cambridge University Press to include in their chapters information which was not available when the chapters were first published as fascicles. No doubt the number would have been larger if Professor Gadd, whose death was mentioned in the Preface to Volume 1, Part 2, and Dr W. C. Hayes had lived until this volume was prepared for the printer. Professor Gadd had begun to gather notes for his chapter on 'Hammurabi and the End of his Dynasty' but his work was only in its initial stage and the Editors decided to leave the text unchanged, apart from making small adjustments necessary for the present publication.

In the Preface to Volume 1, Part 1 an explanation was given of the code used in the footnotes for references to the bibliographies; the same system has been adopted in this Part. References are also given in the footnotes to plates which will be published as a separate volume after the completion of Volume 2, Part 2. In accordance with the intention expressed in the fascicles, sketch maps have been inserted in the text of this edition. Also included here, but not in the fascicles, are text-figures for Chapters III and XI, plans of palaces in Chapter XII, and a genealogical table of Hittite kings, descendants of Tudkhaliash II, in Chapter XV.

Two chapters have been translated by Mr C. E. N. Childs, formerly Assistant Keeper in the Department of Printed Books, British Museum, Chapter I from French and Chapter VII from German. Chapter IV(*b*) and Chapter XII have been translated from German by Mr W. J. Dale, Headmaster of Tettenhall College.

Although, with one exception, all the chapters relating to Western Asia had already been published as fascicles before the death of Professor Gadd, the preparation of a large part of the present volume for the printer involved extra editorial work which required special knowledge of that field. The Syndics of the Press therefore accepted a request from the two surviving Editors and appointed Dr E. Sollberger as an additional Editor.

Professor Sterling Dow wishes to express his gratitude to Mr John Chadwick for his generous help and advice in the writing of Chapter XIII (a); he is also indebted to W. E. McLeod for data about potters' marks from Lerna, and to J. L. Caskey, the excavator, for permission to publish them. Dr R. H. Dyson is indebted to the following scholars for allowing him to include in Chapter XVI some of the results of their excavations and archaeological surveys before they were published: C. A. Burney (northern Azarbāyjān), C. Goff (eastern and southern Luristān, Tepe Bābā Jān, near Nūrābād in Luristān), L. Levine (Kurdistān), J. Meldgaard (western Luristān), O. W. Muscarella (Dinkha Tepe), D. Stronach (Gurgan and Hamadān region, Yarim Tepe), H. Thrane (western Luristān), M. van Loon (Schmidt data on Kamtarlan, Chigha Sabz, Surkh Dom), and T. C. Young, Jr. (southern Azarbāyjān, Kurdistān, north-eastern Luristān, Godin Tepe).

The Editors have continued to receive from the Staff of the Cambridge University Press the utmost help and they wish to record their appreciation both of their friendly cooperation and of their skill and care in the production of this book.

I.E.S.E.
N.G.L.H.
E.S.

CHAPTER I

NORTHERN MESOPOTAMIA
AND SYRIA

I. SHAMSHI-ADAD I

SCARCELY thirty years ago the figure of Hammurabi, the unifier of Babylonia, still stood out in striking isolation. In fact, at the time he ascended the throne another centralized empire already occupied the whole of northern Mesopotamia: it was the personal creation of Shamshi-Adad I, to whom recent discoveries have made it possible to give his place in history.

Whereas Hammurabi had inherited a considerable territory from his father, Shamshi-Adad had more modest beginnings. He belonged to one of the numerous nomad clans which had infiltrated into Mesopotamia after the break-up of the Third Dynasty of Ur. His father, Ila-kabkabu, ruled over a land bordering on the kingdom of Mari, with which he had come into conflict.[1] It is not well known what happened next. According to one version, the authenticity of which is not certain, Shamshi-Adad made his way into Babylonia, while his brother succeeded to Ila-kabkabu. Later on he seized Ekallatum; the capture of this fortress, on the left bank of the Tigris, in the southern reaches of the lower Zab, laid the gates of Assyria open to him.[2] The moment was propitious, for Assyria had only lately regained her independence, having previously had to submit to Naram-Sin of Eshnunna, who had advanced as far as the upper Khabur.[3] But Naram-Sin's conquests had been ephemeral: on his death, Assyria had shaken off the yoke of Eshnunna, only to fall beneath that of Shamshi-Adad. Once installed on the throne of Ashur, the latter soon set about extending his dominion in the direction of the West. Among the archives of the palace of Mari has been found a letter from a prince of the 'High Country' seeking Iakhdunlim's protection.[4] He feels that the encroachments of Shamshi-Adad, who has already taken several of his towns, are a threat to him; until then he had victoriously resisted the attacks of his neighbours from the lands of Aleppo, Carchemish and Urshu. But

---

[1] G, 6, 207 f., 212.   [2] G, 7, 34 f.; G, 6, 211; §1, 5, 26 f.
[3] G, 6, 8 n. 1.   [4] G, 1, vol. 1, 22, no. 1.

Iakhdunlim himself was to pass from the scene, assassinated by his own servants,[1] who perhaps acted on Shamshi-Adad's instigation. At all events, he turned the affair to account by occupying Mari, while the heir to the throne, Zimrilim, took refuge with the king of Aleppo. The annexation of Mari represented a considerable gain in territory, for Iakhdunlim had controlled the middle Euphrates valley at least as far as the mouth of the Balīkh.

In possession, from now onwards, of an empire which stretched from the Zagros hills to the Euphrates, Shamshi-Adad shared his power with his two sons.[2] He installed the eldest, Ishme-Dagan, in Ekallatum, with the onerous task of keeping the warlike inhabitants of the mountains in check and of mounting a vigilant guard against the kingdom of Eshnunna, which was to remain his chief enemy. In Mari he left his younger son, Iasmakh-Adad, who would have to exert himself mostly against incursions of nomads from the Syrian steppe.

The correspondence between the king and his two sons recovered at Mari, along with a small collection of archives coming from Tell Shemshāra, the centre of a district government in southern Kurdistan, make it possible to determine the limits of Shamshi-Adad's authority. In the direction of Eshnunna the frontier—if one may speak of 'frontier' at this date—must have run more or less along the 'Adhaim, at least along the Tigris valley, since the eastern marches remained in dispute. Thus it was that Shamshi-Adad had to struggle with Dadusha, the successor of Naram-Sin, for the possession of Qabrā,[3] in the district of Arbela, while the Turukkians made it impossible to retain Shusharra (Tell Shemshāra).[4] Here it was not only the almost continuous hostility of Eshnunna which had to be faced, but the turbulent inhabitants of the foot-hills of the Zagros as well—the Gutians and Turukkians. These last must have been particularly dangerous opponents. On the occasion of a peace treaty Mut-Ashkur, the son and successor of Ishme-Dagan, married the daughter of a Turukkian chieftain called Zaziya,[5] and even Hammurabi of Babylonia did not disdain to seek this man's alliance.[6]

The whole of Upper Mesopotamia proper was in Shamshi-Adad's hands. The Assyrian 'colonies' in Cappadocia were showing renewed activity at that time, but it is not known how far the new ruler's real authority extended in the direction of the

[1] G, 7, 35 n. 28; §1, 3, 63.   [2] §1, 5, 27.
[3] §1, 7, 441. Cf. below, p. 6.   [4] §1, 6, 31.
[5] G, 1, vol. ii, 90, no. 40.   [6] G, 1, vol. vi, 54, no. 33.

Anatolian plateau. In the west it must have stopped at the Euphrates, where began the kingdom of Iamkhad, with its capital at Aleppo. When Shamshi-Adad boasts of having erected triumphal stelae on the Mediterranean coast, in the Lebanon,[1] it can have been only upon one of those short-lived expeditions, more economic than military, in the tradition established by Sargon of Agade years before. However, Shamshi-Adad did not neglect to extend his influence so as to neutralize Aleppo. He was in alliance with princes of Upper Syria, notably the prince of Carchemish, and he sealed his good relations with Qatna by a marriage: his son Iasmakh-Adad married the daughter of the king of that city, Ishkhi-Adad.[2] In the south, finally, he dominated the middle Euphrates valley almost to the latitude of Eshnunna.

The empire which Shamshi-Adad had carved out for himself in this way was vast and prosperous. Crossed by several great trade routes, it embraced the prolific Assyrian plain, the humid belt bordering on the Anatolian plateau and the fertile valleys of the Khabur and Euphrates. Naturally, it was coveted to an equal degree by all his neighbours—the half-starved plunderers of the mountains and steppes, and the ambitious monarchs of Aleppo, Eshnunna and Babylon. Shamshi-Adad was to manœuvre through these manifold dangers with clear-sightedness and skill, energy and tenacity. We have seen that he gave his sons the duty of watching the two flanks of his realm. On Ishme-Dagan, who was, like himself, a forceful soldier not afraid to risk his own skin, he could rely unhesitatingly. Nor did he omit to hold him up as an example to his second son, who was far from following in his footsteps. Feeble and hesitant, Iasmakh-Adad more often deserved blame than praise:[3] 'Are you a child, not a man,' his father reproached him, 'have you no beard on your chin?' He tells him some blunt home-truths: 'While here your brother is victorious, down there you lie about among the women....' Ishme-Dagan too does not scruple to admonish his younger brother: 'Why are you setting up a wail about this thing? That is not great conduct.'[4] Later, he suggests, either as a political manœuvre or out of a genuine desire to help his brother, that he should not address himself to the king, their father, directly, but use him as intermediary: 'Write me what you are intending to write to the king, so that, where possible, I can advise you myself.' Elsewhere he exclaims: 'Show some sense.' It is under-

[1] §1, 1, 15.   [2] See below, p. 20.
[3] See §1, 3, 68 f.   [4] G, 1, vol. IV, 96 ff., no. 70.

1-2

standable that Shamshi-Adad, whose commendable intention was
to school his son for exercising power, should give him advisers
who had his confidence and were kept informed of the instructions
Iasmakh-Adad received from his father.[1] At the same time, the
latter kept his hand on everything. His letters deal not only with
questions of high policy, with international relations or military
operations, but frequently concern themselves with matters of
lesser importance, such as the appointment of officials, caravans
or messengers passing through, measures to be taken with regard
to fugitives, the watch to be kept on nomads, the despatch of
livestock or provisions, boat-building, the projected movements
of Iasmakh-Adad, not to mention private matters concerning
individuals.

If Shamshi-Adad kept a strict control over things, it was still
not his intention to take all initiative away from his sons or
officials. For instance, it was for Iasmakh-Adad himself to fill the
post of governor of Terqa, or of mayor of the palace at Mari.[2] It
was often the matter of his father's complaints: 'How long will
you not rule in your own house? Do you not see your brother
commanding great armies?'[3] On the other hand, the whole running of affairs did not rest solely on the sovereign's shoulders, for
the administrative service was organized on a sound basis at all
levels. Each district was entrusted to a governor assisted by
other career-officials, all carefully selected on the dual ground of
competence and loyalty.[4] Other high officers were specialized,
like the one concerned with the preparation of censuses, who was
attached to Iasmakh-Adad's 'headquarters'.[5] Chancellery and
accounting services were organized with the same concern for
efficiency. Fast-moving couriers regularly passed through the
land, and Shamshi-Adad often emphasized the urgency of messages which were to be passed. That is why he sometimes dates
his letters, a practice uncommon at that time, in certain cases even
going so far as to specify the time of day.[6] The king and his sons
were always on the move, but the correspondence addressed to
them nevertheless ended by being sorted and catalogued in the
archive rooms of the central administration. There was the same
strictness about the drafting and the keeping of financial docu-

---

[1] G, 6, 194.   [2] G, 1, vol. 1, 38, no. 9; 120, no. 61.
[3] G, 1, vol. 1, 182, no. 108.
[4] G, 1, vol. 1, 38, no. 9; 52 ff., no. 18; 122, no. 62; 200, no. 120.
[5] G, 6, 194.
[6] G, 1, vol. 1, 42, no. 10; 128, no. 67 (cf. A. L. Oppenheim, *J.N.E.S.* 11 (1952), 131 f.).

ments. Thus, Shamshi-Adad required that detailed accounts should be produced concerning the cost of making silver statues.[1]

Military affairs were naturally organized with no less care than the civil administration. Garrisons, no doubt small in numbers, were permanently stationed in the towns, and troops were levied for each campaign, both from the fixed population and the nomads; the Khanaeans, especially, provided valued contingents. On their return, the men were demobilized. It sometimes happened that they were sent to rest in their homes for a few days between two engagements, and for the same reason, measures were taken to relieve fortress garrisons periodically. Before marching, a list of the men taking part in the campaign was drawn up, and the distribution of provisions was settled. Sometimes troops operated in considerable numbers: for the siege of Nurrugum, the capture of which represented, on the evidence of Shamshi-Adad himself, one of the most important military events of his reign, the figure of 60,000 men is mentioned.[2] Censuses, which involved at the same time purificatory rites and the registering of inhabitants on the army muster-rolls, were instituted sometimes at district level, sometimes throughout the kingdom.[3] Although the Mari texts make no mention of it, the army must have included some specialized personnel in its ranks. It was perfectly equipped for siege-warfare, about which previously our only information was derived from Assyrian sources. All the methods which may be called classic were employed—the throwing-up of encircling ramparts to strengthen the blockade of a besieged town, the construction of assault-banks of compacted earth making it possible to reach the top of fortifications, digging of galleries to undermine walls, and the use of two kinds of siege-engines, the assault-tower and the battering-ram.[4] Preparations for conquests were made far in advance: recourse was had to spies, and a propaganda campaign, carried out by natives who had been bought over, opened the way for the military offensive. The aim was to get the populace to come over to the invader's side of its own accord. Finally, the invading columns were preceded by advance guards, whose duty it was to carry out reconnaissance.[5]

Whether it was to lead his troops into battle in person, or to inspect them, to meet foreign princes, or simply to make sure that

[1] G, 1, vol. 1, 138 ff., no. 74.
[2] See J. Læssøe in *Assyriological Studies*, 16 (1965), 193.
[3] G, 6, 23 ff.
[4] See J.-R. Kupper, *R.A.* 45 (1951), 125 f.
[5] *Ibid.* 123 f.

his orders were carried out intelligently and to keep in working-order the bureaucratic machine he had created, Shamshi-Adad was continually on the move. It cannot really be said that he had a capital. To judge from the letters that have come down to us, he was not often at Ashur or at Nineveh, but preferred living in a city on the upper Khabur, which we must probably look for at the site of Chagar Bazar,[1] where a repository of financial archives has been found.

This city was called Shubat-Enlil in honour of the god of Nippur, who pronounced the names of kings and delivered the sceptre to them. The ambition of Shamshi-Adad was in proportion with his success, and he did not hesitate to proclaim himself 'king of all', a title borne of old by Sargon of Agade. In accordance with this claim he invoked the patronage of Enlil, whose lieutenant he was pleased to style himself, and built a new temple for that god at Ashur.[2] It was probably in the same line of conduct that he repaired the ruins of the temple of Ishtar, built in former days at Nineveh by Manishtusu, and that he dedicated a temple to Dagan in his town of Terqa,[3] for Dagan was the god who had once accepted the worship of Sargon, and granted him in return sovereignty over the 'Upper Country'.

It is not yet possible to write a history of Shamshi-Adad's reign. Thanks to the letters from Mari we know some of its outstanding events, but they give us only momentary glimpses. They are not arranged chronologically, and they cover, irregularly no doubt, only part of the reign, which is said to have lasted thirty-three years in all. Texts were dated in two manners,[4] the Assyrian practice of appointing annual eponyms being much more widely used than the Babylonian system of naming years after an event. Nevertheless, the numerous references to military operations in the king's correspondence indicate that his reign was far from peaceful. One of the principal campaigns had the region of the Lesser Zab as its objective. This ended with the capture of several important towns, notably Qabrā, Arrapkha and Nurrugum.[5] Many operations, conducted with varying fortune against the Turukkians, also took place in the mountainous region of the eastern marches.[6] A most carefully organized expedition was made in order to conquer the land of Zalmaqum, the name given to the region of Harran.[7] Only a few echoes reveal

[1] G, 7, 36; G, 6, 2 ff.
[2] §1, 1, 13 f.
[3] §1, 1, 9 f., 17. See §1, 8, 25 f.
[4] §1, 2, 53 f.
[5] §1, 6, 72 ff.
[6] §1, 5, 28 n. 1.
[7] G, 1, vol. 1, 40, no. 10; 72, no. 29; 110, no. 53; 116 ff., no. 60.

the hostilities with Eshnunna; we know, from a year-name of Dadusha's reign, that he defeated an army commanded by Ishme-Dagan.[1] A series of letters deals with another defensive campaign waged against the armies of Eshnunna, but it is composed only of messages exchanged between Iasmakh-Adad and his brother Ishme-Dagan. All the evidence suggests that these events took place only after their father's death.

Shamshi-Adad, in fact, must have passed from the scene at the height of his career. In Eshnunna, Dadusha's son and successor, Ibalpiel II, called the fifth year of his reign 'the year of Shamshi-Adad's death', which suggests that about this time he had become a dependant of the great king. This is confirmed by a letter in which Ishme-Dagan, having ascended the throne, reassures his brother, saying in particular that he has the Elamites on a leash as well as their ally, the king of Eshnunna.[2] However, Iasmakh-Adad's fears were well-founded. Here the testimonies bear one another out. Several letters recovered at Mari indicate the advance of the troops of Eshnunna; they had reached the Euphrates at Rapiqum, three days' march above Sippar, and were moving upstream. The names of the eighth and ninth years of Ibalpiel II, for their part, commemorate the destruction of Rapiqum and the defeat of the armies of Subartu and Khana, by which we should understand Assyria and Mari.[3] Ishme-Dagan had not been able to come to his brother's aid effectively. No doubt he was engaged elsewhere against other adversaries, for the conqueror's death had certainly spurred all his enemies on to attack his dominions. As soon as he was reduced to his own resources, Iasmakh-Adad, a colourless individual, was doomed to be lost from sight in the storm. The precise circumstances accompanying his downfall are not known. A passage in a letter implies that he was driven out of Mari after a defeat inflicted on his elder brother.[4]

The army of Eshnunna did not get as far as Mari, for Ibalpiel makes no reference to the city's capture. But the representative of the dynasty which had been dispossessed, Zimrilim, took advantage of these events in order to regain the throne of his fathers. He could count on the support of King Iarimlim of Aleppo, who had made him welcome during his long years of exile and had given him his daughter in marriage.[5] Perhaps the defeat suffered by Ishme-Dagan was inflicted on him by troops from Aleppo, who had then expelled Iasmakh-Adad in favour of Zimrilim. In

[1] §I, 7, 440 f.   [2] G, I, vol. IV, 36, no. 20.
[3] G, 7, 38 f.; §I, 7, 445 ff.   [4] §V, 4, 981 n. I.
[5] §III, 4, 236 f.

a letter to his father-in-law Zimrilim declares: 'Truly it is my father who has caused me to regain my throne.'[1] It is nevertheless a fact that the king of Eshnunna's campaign had opened the way for Zimrilim's reconquest by invading Shamshi-Adad's former empire from the south.

As for Ishme-Dagan, he succeeded in holding his own, but only in Assyria, losing at one stroke the middle Euphrates and the greater part of Upper Mesopotamia, which either regained its independence or passed under Zimrilim's control.[2] Even the region of the upper Khabur, along with his father's residence Shubat-Enlil, passed out of his hands.[3] He did indeed attempt several counter offensives in this direction, but apparently without success, at least during Zimrilim's reign. We do not know whether he succeeded in regaining a foothold in this portion of his father's heritage after Eshnunna and Mari had fallen under Hammurabi's onslaughts: from that moment our sources fall silent, leaving in obscurity the rest of the reign of Ishme-Dagan, to whom the royal lists give the high total of forty or even fifty years.[4]

To judge from his father's letters Ishme-Dagan seemed nevertheless to have the stature to carry on the work which had been begun. The fact was that the empire Shamshi-Adad bequeathed him was difficult to maintain. It was rich and populous, but lacking in cohesion, formed by a juxtaposition of several quite distinct provinces. Besides, exposed along all its frontiers, its geographical situation made it particularly vulnerable; there was, for example, no direct communication between Mari and Ashur. Hemmed in by powerful and ill-disposed neighbours, Aleppo and Eshnunna, it could not survive the man who had created it by his personal qualities alone, by his unflagging energy, his military genius, and his abilities as an organizer.

II. MARI

Like Shamshi-Adad, Iakhdunlim, his unsuccessful opponent at Mari, was a Western Semite whose forebears had abandoned the nomadic life in order to settle in the Euphrates valley. The origins of his dynasty are obscure. Of his father Iagitlim we know only that he came into conflict with Shamshi-Adad's father, after having been his ally.[5] But it was Iakhdunlim who seems to have laid the foundations of Mari's greatness. In a building-

[1] §III, 4, 235.   [2] §I, 5, 29.   [3] G, 6, 30.
[4] G, 7, 36; §I, 5, 31.   [5] G, 6, 33.

record,[1] which by its flawless material execution and brilliant literary qualities shows how far the sons of the desert had adopted Babylonian culture, Iakhdunlim recalls the triumphant campaign he had waged, as the first of his line, on the Mediterranean coast and in the mountains, from which he had brought back valuable timber, while at the same time forcing the country to pay tribute. It has been seen that Shamshi-Adad boasted that he had done the same thing (above, p. 3), which cannot be considered a real conquest. Moreover, Iakhdunlim's power was not wholly secure in his own territory; he had to withstand both attacks by the petty kings of the middle Euphrates and the incursions of nomads, Benjaminites and Khanaeans. It was against the last of these that he had his most striking successes, imposing his rule on them from that time onwards. Once the country was pacified he was able to build a temple to Shamash and to undertake great irrigation projects, designed, notably, to supply water to a new city. It is a fact, as he himself claimed, that he had strengthened the foundations of Mari.[2] Although his kingdom was shortly to fall into Shamshi-Adad's hands, his work was not in vain, since it was eventually taken up by his son Zimrilim.

The latter did not wait long after the usurper's death to ascend the throne of Mari. We are no more in a position to give an account of the new king's reign than to understand how the reconquest took place. More than thirty year-names have been recovered, but the order of their succession is not known. State correspondence makes it possible to reconstruct certain events, but the constant instability of the political situation in Mesopotamia at this time obliges us to show extreme caution in arranging the letters.

Basically, Zimrilim's kingdom was made up of the middle Euphrates and Khabur valleys. To the south it cannot have reached farther than Hīt. To the north it undoubtedly included the mouth of the Balīkh, but beyond that it is uncertain whether there lay territories directly dependent on Mari and administered by district governors, or simply more or less autonomous vassal princedoms.[3] In his attempts to expand Zimrilim directed the best part of his efforts towards the 'High Country', that is to say Upper Mesopotamia, which in those days was split up into numerous little states. In particular the region, bordering on the upper Khabur, which at Mari was called Idamaraz, appears to have been under his control all the time.[4] But Zimrilim's policy

[1] §II, 2.
[2] G, 6, 33 f.
[3] §II, 4, 163.
[4] G, 1, vol. IX, 348 f.; G, 6, 10.

was to impose his tutelage on the petty monarchs of the 'High Country', or even simply to draw them into alliance with him, rather than to annex their countries—no doubt because he had not the resources to do so. This line of conduct was fairly general. We have only to listen to the report of one of Zimrilim's correspondents: 'No king is powerful by himself: ten or fifteen kings follow Hammurabi, king of Babylon, as many follow Rim-Sin, king of Larsa, as many follow Ibalpiel, king of Eshnunna, as many follow Amutpiel, king of Qatna, twenty kings follow Iarimlim, king of Iamkhad....'[1] Grouping their vassals about them, the 'great powers' of the time entered in their turn into wider coalitions, aiming at supremacy, but these formed and broke up as circumstances and the interests of the moment dictated.

In this changing world, between negotiations and battles, Zimrilim's policy nevertheless kept certain constant factors in view—it remained loyal to the alliances with Babylon and Aleppo. In this the king of Mari obeyed a vital necessity, for his country was above all a line of communication linking Babylon with northern Syria, and he needed to retain the goodwill of the powers which guarded both ends. These powers, for their part, had every interest in protecting the freedom of trade and leaving the burden of doing it to an ally. But once Hammurabi, after unifying Babylonia, felt strong enough to assume control himself and reap the profit from it he did not hesitate to subjugate Mari.

It is understandable that in these conditions political intrigue was extremely vigorous, leading constantly to fresh conflicts. Zimrilim recognizes this in a message which he sends to his father-in-law the king of Aleppo: 'Now, since I regained my throne many days ago, I have had nothing but fights and battles.'[2] The opponents were manifold; first, enemies outside, the most dangerous of whom was Eshnunna, frequently operating in concert with its ally Elam, and not afraid to send its troops into the heart of the High Country.[3] There were also rebellious vassals whose loyalty had to be enforced. Lastly, and perhaps above all, there were the nomads, constantly on watch at the edge of the desert, whom no defeat could disarm once and for all.[4] Zimrilim boasts of having crushed the Benjaminites in the Khabur valley, but a victory like this could, at the most, procure only a momentary respite, for the struggle between nomads and settlers, having its origins in physical conditions, could never cease. Without any respite, new groups came to replace those who had left

[1] G, 3, 117; §III, 4, 230 f. [2] §III, 4, 235.
[3] See below, p. 15. [4] See below, pp. 25 ff.

the desert to install themselves in the sown lands. The threat was there each day. Not content with raiding the flocks or plundering the villages, the nomads became bold enough to attack important localities, whether caravan cities or towns on the banks of the Euphrates. The anxiety to ensure the policing of the desert and to contain the movements of the nomads must have been among Zimrilim's main preoccupations. No negligence could be permitted, lest it should be the start of a catastrophic invasion, for every advance of the nomads brought with it an inevitable process of disintegration. Despite the measures taken, security remained precarious. Sometimes it happened that the nomads infested the whole countryside and were brought to a halt only before the ramparts of the towns. The king himself was advised not to leave the capital. Clearly, a struggle like this must have been a considerable embarrassment to Zimrilim's policy, using up his resources and weakening the country's economy.

This state of affairs was certainly not what the country had known in the time of Shamshi-Adad. Relations with the Benjaminites, in particular, had distinctly deteriorated. Shamshi-Adad was at the head of a powerful, centralized state, making the nomads, whose movements he could control over vast areas of land, acutely aware of his authority. Zimrilim, on the other hand, absorbed in exhausting competition with other sovereigns, had relatively limited means at his disposal and reigned over a smaller territory, entirely surrounded by steppe. However, the archives seem to reflect the image of a prosperous, vigorous country. The palace of Mari enrolled a large staff, in which singing girls, for example, are to be counted in tens.[1] We see executives in movement all the time, hurrying in from all the surrounding countries, while reports pour in addressed to the king by his representatives and by the ambassadors he maintains at the principal foreign courts.[2] The inventories bear witness to the wealth of precious things,[3] and the accounts record the arrival of foodstuffs and luxury products, the latter generally sent by kings of neighbouring lands, to whom Zimrilim replied in kind.

Archaeological discoveries have given this picture material form. We have a message in which the king of Aleppo communicates to Zimrilim the wish expressed to him by the king of Ugarit to visit the palace of Mari.[4] This palace is in fact the most remarkable monument that excavations have found there.[5] It is of gigantic proportions. More than 260 chambers, courtyards and

---

[1] §II, 1, 59.
[2] §II, 3, 585 ff.; G, 1, vol. VII, 333.
[3] G, 2, 104.
[4] §III, 4, 236.
[5] See Plate 65.

corridors have already been counted, arranged according to a plan in the shape of a trapezium, but one part of the building has entirely disappeared; the complete structure must have covered an area of more than six acres. The decoration of the private apartments and some of the reception rooms is up to the standard of this royal architecture. The brilliant art of the fresco-painters is displayed particularly in the great compositions of the central court, leading to the chamber with a *podium* and the throne room. In the scene which has given its name to the main painting, the king is receiving investiture at the hands of the goddess Ishtar, shown in her warlike aspect.[1] The luxurious refinement of the decoration has its counterpart in the comfort of the domestic installations. But the palace was not simply the king's residence; it was also an administrative centre, with a school for training scribes, its archive-repositories, its magazines and workshops.

It is impossible to believe that a building like this could have been the work of a single person. Moreover, the successive stages in the plan or in the construction can be picked out without difficulty. But Zimrilim was responsible for the latest architectural phase and left his mark in the form of bricks inscribed with his name.[2] The occupant of such an imposing palace, which excited the admiration of contemporaries, needed abundant resources, as reading of the records suggests. Hence arises the question of Zimrilim's resources—what did his wealth come from? The reports of his provincial governors reveal the attention paid by the king to agriculture and to the irrigation-works upon which it depended.[3] There was an extensive network of canals, the most important of which (still visible today) had been dug on the orders of Iakhdunlim.[4] These made it possible, at the cost of unremitting efforts, to extend the area under cultivation. But despite their fertility the Euphrates and Khabur valleys, closed in by arid plateaux, are not enough to explain Mari's prosperity, for as a result of a famine, caused no doubt by war, we even find Zimrilim having corn brought from Upper Syria.[5]

The geographical position of Mari provides the answer to our question: the city controlled the caravan-route linking the Persian Gulf with Syria and the Mediterranean coast. Merely to trace the main destinations of trade on the map establishes how much it followed this route. Along it Babylonia received the timber,

---

[1] See Plate 66.
[2] §II, 10, 169 f.; §II, 8, part I, 18, 47, 52, and *passim*.
[3] §II, 3, 583 f.; §II, 4, 175 ff.   [4] G, 1, vol. III, 112; G, 6, 33 f.
[5] §III, 4, 235. See also A, 1, 40 f.

stone and resinous substances of Lebanon and the Amanus mountains, the wine and olive-oil of Syria.[1] Other products too reached Mari from more distant countries, perhaps to be re-exported. Thus Zimrilim sends Hammurabi of Babylon some object, or a piece of cloth, coming from Crete.[2] On the other hand the Cypriot copper which is several times mentioned in the accounts,[3] no doubt remained at Mari, because Babylonia had other sources of supply. In any case, the city kept up close relations with the Mediterranean ports of Ugarit and Byblos,[4] and even with Palestine. Babylonian messengers went through Mari on their return from a long stay at Hazor in Galilee.[5] In the other direction, Babylonia had little to export. But she kept up a vigorous flow of trade with Tilmun, the island of Baḥrain, from which she got notably copper and precious stones. An embassage from Tilmun to Shubat-Enlil has been observed returning home by way of Mari—this was in the reign of Shamshi-Adad.[6] Moreover there were other routes, bringing the products of central Asia, which ran into Babylonia. Along one of these lay Susa, another came down the Diyālā valley. It was no doubt by this route that lapis-lazuli, quarried in Afghanistan, was brought. One text does in fact mention lapis-lazuli as coming from Esh-nunna.[7] It was also through Mari that the tin imported by Babylonia from Elam passed westwards towards Aleppo, Qatna, Carchemish and Hazor.[8]

The chamber of commerce (kārum) of Sippar had good reason to keep a mission in the capital of the middle Euphrates,[9] which was one of the cross-roads of international trade. The numerous stores and repositories of the palace, in which even now rows of enormous jars have been found, bear witness perhaps to Zimri-lim's direct participation in this profitable business, without taking into account the revenue he got from it to swell his treasury. In spite of the struggles caused by inter-state rivalries the whole of western Asia at that time shared a common civilization. There was no splitting up into compartments, and despite temporary restrictions men and merchandise could move about from the Persian Gulf to Upper Syria, and from Elam to the Mediterranean coast.

[1] §II, 5, 102 ff.; A, 2, 73 ff.; A, 6, 115.   [2] G, 2, 111.
[3] Ibid.   [4] Ibid.
[5] G, I, vol. VI, 110, no. 78.
[6] G, I, vol. I, 50, no. 17. See §II, 5, 141.
[7] G, I, vol. IX, 209, no. 254.   [8] G, I, vol. VII, 337 f.; §II, 5, 123 f.
[9] §II, 5, 106 ff.

It was the prominent part played by Mari in these exchanges which guaranteed its material prosperity and placed Zimrilim on a level footing with the principal sovereigns of his time, permitting him to finance expensive campaigns or to act as intermediary between the kings of Aleppo and Babylon. But in the last analysis, this power was artificial and could give only a false security. The glamour is deceptive, the wonders of Mari more brilliant than solid. Without natural defences and without hinterland, spread out along the Euphrates and Khabur valleys, and plagued by the disturbing proximity of the nomads, the country could not put up any serious resistance to the pressure of a real military power. So long as Hammurabi was kept occupied on other frontiers, he played Zimrilim skilfully, leaving him the profit he gained from his situation as well as the duty of protecting the route to the west. But as soon as his hands were free he changed his policy. Mari was eliminated in two stages, the second ending in the city's occupation and final ruin.[1] Here is the palpable weakness of its position: the middle Euphrates would never again seem a political factor of any importance. Mari's prosperity was vulnerable because it depended to a large extent upon external circumstances. Its high point coincided with a moment of equilibrium, the fortunate conditions of which did not recur. Zimrilim had the merit of turning it to the best possible account.

III. ESHNUNNA, IAMKHAD, QATNA AND OTHER STATES

Among the chief powers of the day enumerated by one of Zimrilim's correspondents[2] are two Syrian kingdoms, Qatna and Iamkhad, and at the other extremity of the Fertile Crescent, in the region beyond the Tigris, the kingdom of Eshnunna. There is good reason for the last of these states figuring on the list: the best proof of this is found in the direct interference of its kings in the affairs of Upper Mesopotamia. Naram-Sin, the first of them, who had gained a foothold in Assyria, penetrated far into the region and seized Ashnakkum, a locality in the district of Upper Idamaraz.[3] This exploit was to have no lasting result for Eshnunna, because Naram-Sin was shortly to be driven out of Ashur by Shamshi-Adad. During the latter's reign relations with Eshnunna were not good,[4] but the theatre of military operations was

---

[1] See below, p. 28.
[2] See above, p. 10.
[3] See above, pp. 1 and 9.
[4] See above, p. 7.

on the eastern frontiers of Assyria. Ishme-Dagan guarded Ekallatum strongly, and in spite of a defeat inflicted on him by Dadusha, Naram-Sin's brother and successor, he barred the way into Upper Mesopotamia. It has been seen that on Shamshi-Adad's death, Ishme-Dagan reassured his brother Iasmakh-Adad, declaring that he held Elam and Eshnunna on a leash (above, p. 7). The alliance of these two powers was of long standing, for it is frequently recalled in the correspondence of Zimrilim, who seems to credit Elam with the leading role.[1] However, Dadusha's son, Ibalpiel II, who occupied the throne of Eshnunna at that time, was not long in opening hostilities by attacking the weak spot. His troops pushed on as far as the Euphrates, then moved up the valley in the direction of Mari. The campaign ended with the expulsion of Iasmakh-Adad and with Zimrilim's return to the throne of Mari.[2]

It is hard to believe that this was all that Ibalpiel intended, yet the king of Eshnunna does not seem to have exploited his success in any other way. But the dismembering of Shamshi-Adad's empire had freed Upper Mesopotamia. It is in this direction that Eshnunna once again set its sights, managing from time to time to get the co-operation of its former enemy: Ishme-Dagan had held on to Assyria only, and was naturally trying to regain the lands he had lost. The troops of Elam and Eshnunna took again the road to Idamaraz and to the town of Ashnakkum.[3] They laid siege to Razama, a town not yet located; it was in the hands of one of Zimrilim's vassal princes. The prize was important, for Hammurabi of Babylon got reinforcements through to his ally in Mari.[4] Zimrilim's correspondence seldom names the king of Eshnunna, we do not know when Silli-Sin succeeded to Ibalpiel II.[5] But the days of the dynasty were numbered. The 32nd year of Hammurabi's reign takes its name from a great victory won against Eshnunna and its allies. Zimrilim, who was to be the future victim of Babylonian expansion, advised Hammurabi to set himself on the throne of Eshnunna or to designate one of his adherents.[6]

If the armies despatched by Eshnunna were able to advance so far into Upper Mesopotamia, it was no doubt because they had met with support, but also because they had not come up against any organized force. Apart from the time when it was unified under the sceptre of Shamshi-Adad, Upper Mesopotamia

[1] §ii, 6, 333 ff.
[2] See above, p. 7.
[3] G, 6, 10 n. 2.
[4] G, 6, 86; §ii, 6, 338 ff.
[5] G, 2, 109; §iii, 6, 140, 200.
[6] G, 3, 120.

was split up into a series of small principalities. The Mari letters contain references to the kings of Subartu and Zalmaqum and the princes of Idamaraz.[1] The most influential of them, like the kings of Kurda or Nakhur must, at the most, have ruled over a few towns. The humid belt of higher country between the Tigris and Euphrates is rich in agricultural resources, and the numerous *tells* scattered across it, especially in the Khabur 'triangle', reveal how densely it was populated in ancient times. But this proliferation of towns close together is unfavourable to the formation of wide territorial units. Moreover this was a corridor zone, open to migratory movements and to the armies of conquerors.

The Mari documents name some of these petty kings; the majority of them have 'West Semitic' names, the rest Hurrian.[2] About the people themselves we have no information, except at Chagar Bazar, the possible site of Shubat-Enlil.[3] Here the Akkadian element is foremost, exceeding by a clear margin the Hurrians, who themselves outnumber the 'Western Semites'. It is therefore likely that a double stream, originating in the mountainous periphery and the Syrian steppe, had come in and mingled with the old element under Babylonian influence, supplanting it in the political structure.

To find a country which has a place in international relations, even in the second rank, one has to go as far as the Euphrates: this was the kingdom of Carchemish. Hemmed in between the important kingdom of Iamkhad in the south, and that of Urshu in the north, the territory under the sway of Carchemish cannot have been very extensive. But its situation on the great bend of the Euphrates, where the mountains open out, was highly favourable for large-scale trade: it was the gateway to the Taurus and to the Anatolian plateau. That is why its princes sent to Mari not only local products such as wine, honey and olive-oil, and also manufactured articles—clothing and vases—of unknown provenance, but cedar-wood from the Amanus mountains and horses bred in Anatolia.[4]

In the interests of both cities relations between Mari and Carchemish were always friendly, although the two participants cannot have dealt with one another as equals. It is known that exchanges of gifts between sovereigns were only a form of trade, but Aplakhanda of Carchemish showed himself remarkably atten-

---

[1] G, 1, vol. II, 80, no. 35; vol. III, 60, no. 37; G, 3, 109; §II, 10, 173; §V, 4, 986, 992. See also G, 1, vol. IX, 346 ff.

[2] G, 6, 230 n. 1.   [3] G, 6, 229.

[4] G, 1, vol. VII, 337; vol. IX, 346; §III, 1, 119 f.; §III, 2, 48; §II, 5, 103.

tive in fulfilling the wishes of Iasmakh-Adad. He calls Shamshi-
Adad his father, and, on the latter's evidence, joined in his
alliance.[1] The change of régime at Mari did not make any difference to the good relations. On Aplakhanda's death his son
Iatar-ami made a declaration of fidelity to Zimrilim, which reveals
his position as a vassal.[2]

In fact, the position of Carchemish on the borders of one of the
most important states of the time, the kingdom of Iamkhad, or of
Aleppo, from the name of its capital, was peculiarly delicate.
While other sovereigns could reckon between ten and fifteen vassals, twenty princes followed Iarimlim, the first king of Iamkhad
whose memory has been preserved in the letters of Zimrilim.
Little is known of his country's history before him. A certain
Sumuepu' of Iamkhad is named among the opponents of Zimrilim's father Iakhdunlim. He is referred to several times in the
correspondence of Shamshi-Adad, who launched an attack on
him with the help of the princes of Khashshum, Urshu and Carchemish. Some have therefore proposed to see in him a king of
Iamkhad preceding Iarimlim,[3] but neither Iakhdunlim nor
Shamshi-Adad gives him the royal title, and the latter does not
even mention the land of Iamkhad in connection with him.

At all events, the Aleppo monarchy was well-established before
Zimrilim's return to Mari, for it was in Aleppo that the latter
found sanctuary during his exile, and it was owing to the support
of Iarimlim, who had become his father-in-law in the meantime,
that he was able to reconquer his paternal throne. The letters of
Shamshi-Adad's time practically ignore Aleppo and the land of
Iamkhad, but this was not on account of the distance, for Shamshi-
Adad maintained excellent relations with the king of Qatna, who
was another Syrian prince. It is probable that there was some
hostility between Iarimlim—or his predecessor—and Shamshi-
Adad. As the latter did not seek to enlarge his empire on the
right bank of the Euphrates at the expense of his western neighbour, one may conclude that he had there a serious opponent.
Perhaps it was as much in order to contain this neighbour as to
find an opening on to the Mediterranean that Shamshi-Adad had
concluded an alliance with Qatna.

It would seem that the kingdom of Iamkhad was at the height
of its power under Iarimlim, although it is often difficult for us to
make a distinction between his reign and that of his successor
Hammurabi. As regards Iarimlim there is no lack of evidence

---

[1] §III, 8, 28. [2] §III, 1, 120.
[3] §III, 8, 44 ff.; §VII, 4, 114.

to bear witness to his prestige and power. We need only observe the marked deference Zimrilim shows him,[1] the report already quoted in which he appears as the foremost sovereign of his age (above, p. 10), and a letter addressed to the prince of Dēr, recovered at Mari where it had been held up in transit.[2] In this message, Iarimlim reminds his 'brother' that he had saved his life fifteen years before, at the time when he was coming to the help of Babylon, and that he had also given his support to the king of the town of Diniktum, on the Tigris, to whom he supplied five hundred boats. Outraged by the prince of Dēr's ingratitude he threatens to come at the head of his troops and exterminate him. The campaign thus recalled by the king of Aleppo took place in the north of Babylonia and in the region beyond the Tigris, as far as Badrah, the modern site of Dēr. The only opponent it can have had seems to be Eshnunna, and it might have been a counter to Ibalpiel II's advance along the Euphrates. In that case, it would be as a consequence that Zimrilim returned to Mari. Whatever the circumstances of the expedition were, it says a great deal for the military power of Iarimlim, who led the soldiers of Aleppo as far as the borders of Elam.

The assistance which Iarimlim had given to Babylon explains the consideration Hammurabi showed to the ambassadors of Aleppo at his court.[3] The friendly understanding survived the decease of Iarimlim, for his son Hammurabi was persuaded to send a contingent of troops to his namesake in Babylon.[4] It is likely enough that the new king's reign was less brilliant than his father's, although Zimrilim's more relaxed demeanour is not proof of this. The consolidation of his authority and the prevailing prosperity he had brought about may have given Zimrilim more assurance, besides the fact that he was now dealing with a younger prince. The king of Mari went to Aleppo again in the time of Hammurabi, but perhaps his veneration for Adad, the great god of Aleppo, had something to do with his journey.[5] There was never a break in the friendly relations between Aleppo and Mari: letters and accounts reveal messengers making frequent journeys in both directions and numerous 'presents' exchanged by the two courts.[6]

The kingdom of Iamkhad occupied a privileged position for trading relations. To the east it bordered on the Euphrates; to the west it stretched as far as the Mediterranean coast, if not

[1] §III, 4, 235 f.; §III, 8, 56.   [2] §III, 3.
[3] §III, 4, 232.   [4] §III, 8, 62.
[5] §III, 2, 49; §III, 4, 233.   [6] §III, 4, 236 f.; §III, 8, 58, 64 f.

directly, at least through the intermediary of a vassal state. It was through Aleppo that merchandise imported by sea, bound for either the upper Tigris or for Babylonia and the Persian Gulf, entered Mesopotamia. Caravans and travellers going from Babylonia to Syria or Palestine were obliged to pass through territory belonging to Aleppo, if they wished to avoid the dangers of the desert route through Palmyra. In exchange for tin Aleppo sent much the same commodities as Carchemish—clothes, vases and local products.[1] The city must also have served as a staging-post for copper from Cyprus and luxury goods from the Aegean.[2] It is known from other evidence that there were herds of elephants in northern Syria, and tusks have been found in the palace of Alalakh, a town on the lower Orontes, on the way from Aleppo to the coast.[3] It is therefore likely that the profitable ivory trade was controlled by the kings of Aleppo, whose power was based at once on the economic prosperity of their country and on its pivotal strategic position between the Mediterranean world and Mesopotamia.

The few names of persons at Aleppo so far recovered can be assigned to the 'West Semitic' category.[4] Nevertheless, the tablets discovered at Alalakh have established that there must have been Hurrians in Upper Syria at this time. Indeed, the oldest group of tablets, which is about half a century later than the Mari documents, gives us a glimpse of a society in which the Hurrian element occupied an important position and revealed its presence in various fields.[5] This presupposes that the Hurrian penetration was already of relatively long standing. A further indication is to be found in the Hurrian names of several of the princes of Upper Mesopotamia. None the less at Aleppo, as at Babylon and Mari, the royal power was in the hands of Amorites.

An Amorite dynasty also ruled over the neighbouring kingdom of Qatna. The city of Qatna stood at the centre of a district rich in cereals, the plain of Homs, where the vine and olive-tree also flourished. It was at one extremity of the caravan-route running from the Euphrates through Palmyra, and its communications with the sea were secured by the Tripoli pass, which cleaves its way between the Lebanon and the Ansāriyyah mountains. Numerous ancient *tells* survive in this area to bear witness to the importance of Qatna. To the east a belt of pasture-land, fre-quented even today by sheep-rearing tribes, forms the transition

---

[1] G, 1, vol. VII, 337 f.; vol. IX, 346; §III, 2, 48.
[2] See above, p. 13.   [3] §VII, 10, 102; §VII, 11, 74 f.
[4] §III, 4, 237 f.; G, 6, 232 f.   [5] See below, p. 23.

between the lands under cultivation and the desert steppe, stretching as far as the Euphrates valley; the Mari letters refer to the rich pastures of the land of Qatna.[1] How far the kingdom extended to west and south is not known.

The two states of Aleppo and Qatna appear to have developed almost simultaneously. We are better informed about the history of the second during the reign of Shamshi-Adad because he was the ally of Ishkhi-Adad, who occupied the throne of Qatna at that time. The agreement between the two monarchs had been sealed by a marriage, Iasmakh-Adad, the viceroy of Mari, having married Ishkhi-Adad's daughter.[2] Co-operation was political and military as well as economic. There were frequent movements of troops between Mari and Qatna, and it seems likely that a detachment from Mari was stationed in the Syrian town.[3] The presence of these foreign soldiers at Qatna does not seem to indicate a relation of dependence, for Ishkhi-Adad himself insists on their being sent, and invites his son-in-law to take part in an expedition which seems likely to yield some spoils.[4] It was Shamshi-Adad who had taken the first steps towards the marriage, stressing to his son that the house of Qatna had a 'name'. He also dealt on level terms with Ishkhi-Adad, whom he called his brother.[5]

The end of Ishkhi-Adad's reign is still obscure. Committed as he was to the 'Assyrian' alliance his position must have been considerably weakened by the crumbling of Shamshi-Adad's empire. From then onwards he could rely only on his own forces to defend himself against his powerful northern neighbour, the king of Aleppo, who, for his part, helped Zimrilim to evict Iasmakh-Adad from Mari. It is possible that another faction then gained power in Qatna. At all events a new name appears in Zimrilim's correspondence, that of Amutpiel, who had therefore succeeded to Ishkhi-Adad in the interval. Owing to a change of political trend, or merely to its very favourable geographical situation, Qatna seems to have been able to recover its position quickly. The city maintained constant relations with Mari, from which it obtained tin, and a succession of messengers journeyed in both directions.[6] With its prosperity founded on trade, Mari had every interest in being on good terms with the important city of the middle Orontes on the other side of the Syrian desert. It was no doubt Zimrilim in person who worked for a reconciliation between the former enemies, Qatna and Aleppo, and the

[1] G, 6, 179; §III, 5, 422.   [2] §III, 4, 231; §III, 5, 417.
[3] §III, 8, 76 f.   [4] §III, 5, 420 f.
[5] §III, 8, 80.   [6] G, 1, vol. VII, 337 f.; §III, 8, 83.

treaty restoring peace was concluded in Aleppo.[1] This step need not be interpreted as a gesture of submission on the part of the king of Qatna. His multifarious diplomatic relations with Mari, Babylon, Larsa, Eshnunna, Arrapkha and even Susa[2] fully establish his independence. Iarimlim of Aleppo no doubt had a greater number of vassals at his disposal, but in this respect Amutpiel could rival Hammurabi, Rim-Sin or Ibalpiel.[3] Qatna was looked upon during his reign as one of the great capitals of the Fertile Crescent.

Immediately to the south of Qatna, it seems, began the country of Amurru, which was divided up between several petty kings.[4] The name of Damascus has not yet appeared in the Mari documents. The town of Apum, in which some have proposed to find Damascus under the name known from the Amarna letters,[5] also figures in the Cappadocian tablets; it must have been in Upper Mesopotamia.[6] Syria really occupied a peripheral position in relation to Mari, and since the Mari documents are the only source for this period at our disposal, information is spasmodic and fragmentary. It naturally becomes more scarce the farther one gets from the Euphrates. Of the coastal towns, only two are mentioned in the Mari texts, Ugarit and Byblos. The first does not seem to have had any direct relations with Mari, for it is through the king of Aleppo, whose ally or vassal he was, that the king of Ugarit expresses his wish to visit Zimrilim's palace.[7] Byblos, which had contacts with Mesopotamia from the time of the Third Dynasty of Ur,[8] is often encountered, especially in financial documents.[9] Its messengers accompanied those of Aleppo and Qatna, and the king of the city gave Zimrilim a golden vase. The name of this king, Iantin-Khamu, is 'West Semitic', as are also those of his predecessors, known to us from objects discovered in their tombs.[10] A dynastic seal, still used by the kings of Ugarit in the fourteenth and thirteenth centuries, proves that 'West Semitic' kings ruled over the city at about the beginning of the First Dynasty of Babylon.[11] Adding these facts to the information supplied by the Egyptian execration texts, we may conclude that the Amorites had succeeded in imposing themselves everywhere, even in Palestine, to the west of the Syrian

[1] §III, 5, 423.   [2] §III, 8, 83.   [3] See above, p. 10.
[4] G, 6, 179. See now G. Dossin in *R.S.O.* 32 (1957), 37.
[5] Cf. G, 7, 115 n. 234.
[6] See M. Falkner in *Arch. f. Or.* 18 (1957), 2.
[7] §III, 4, 236; §III, 8, 69.
[8] See E. Sollberger in *Arch. f. Or.* 19 (1959–60), 120 ff.
[9] G, 2, 111.   [10] §III, 8, 88.   [11] G, 6, 235.

desert.[1] This conquest is not merely of political significance. It must have helped to make Syria look towards Mesopotamia and play a more intimate part in the common civilization which had developed there in this period.

IV. THE HURRIANS c. 1800 B.C.

The Hurrians had already penetrated into northern Mesopotamia in the Sargonic period. However, under the Third Dynasty of Ur, their main centres of population were still to the east of the Tigris. The situation does not appear to have changed during the period of the Mari documents. A tablet from the Chagar Bazar excavations contains a list of workers in the palace of Ekallatum, where more than half of the names are Hurrian.[2] At Shusharra, on the lower Zab, to the south-east of Rania, the majority of the population was Hurrian.[3] Probably on Shamshi-Adad's death the town had to be abandoned under pressure from the Turukkians.[4] One of the chiefs of the latter, Zaziya, has a name which appears to be Hurrian; two other Turukkians mentioned in a letter from Mari answer to names which certainly are such.[5] It is conceivable, therefore, that the whole warlike race of Turukkians, which lived on the slopes of the Zagros and entered into conflict with Hammurabi himself, belonged to the Hurrian family.

For Upper Mesopotamia the Mari documents yield the names of a score of princes, the majority of them 'West Semitic'. Four or five of them, however, are Hurrian, like Adalshenni of Burundum and Shukru-Teshub of Elakhut.[6] In some cases, therefore, the advance of the Hurrian population achieved political ascendency. This did not necessarily mean that the country had to be densely occupied. At Chagar Bazar, the only place where we can take a test of the personal names, the Hurrians must have constituted a little less than a third of the population, the Akkadian section supplying the biggest contingent.[7] Apart from Harran, where the king was an Amorite, none of the towns in which the princes in question reigned has been definitely located. For this reason it is not known where in Upper Mesopotamia the Hurrian principalities lay, whether grouped together or scattered across the whole region.

In Syria power was generally in the hands of the Amorites, but Hurrians had nevertheless crossed the Euphrates and conquered

[1] Cf. §v, 5, 38 f.   [2] G, 6, 227 f.   [3] §1, 6, 75.
[4] G, 1, vol. iv, 44, no. 25. Cf. §1, 6, 31.   [5] §1, 6, 73; G, 6, 232 n. 1.
[6] G, 6, 230 n. 1. See now A. Finet, R.A. 60 (1966), 17 ff.   [7] G, 6, 229.

some territories on the right bank. The principalities they occupied, like Khashshum and Urshu[1] were situated to the north of Aleppo, between the river and the foot-hills which prolong Mount Casius and the Amanus. Here the division between the Hurrian and the Amorite zones may have been fairly close to the limit which today separates the Kurdish from the Arabic-speaking inhabitants.

This geographical division holds good only on the political plane, for it is probable that the Hurrian population had already swarmed farther southwards. Our evidence on this point is very poor, only a few names of royal messengers from Aleppo and Qatna, all 'West Semitic'.[2] On the other hand, we have in the Alalakh tablets a more recent source which nevertheless allows us to make an instructive comparison. These tablets divide up into two main groups, the older (level VII) going back to the time of the First Dynasty of Babylon. In the society there described the Hurrians appear to be firmly established. Leaving aside the throne, on which there are Amorites, they occupy high civil and religious offices, while the religious practices bear traces of their presence. The texts contain a number of Hurrian terms, particularly in technical matters, and certain indications suggest that possibly Hurrian was the language of the scribes.[3] Such a state of affairs makes it necessary to push the beginnings of Hurrian penetration back to a more remote date. Between these texts, however, and the Mari documents, there is a gap which we shall see reason to estimate as at least fifty years.[4] The second group of Alalakh tablets (level IV), which belongs to the fifteenth century, reveals a society Hurrianized in every respect; the 'West Semitic' element represents no more than a tiny minority.[5] The Hurrian advance had therefore persisted and gathered force in the interval between the two groups, but it must already have been in progress at the time the tablets of level VII were written. The deed by which king Abbael of Aleppo cedes the town of Alalakh to his vassal Iarimlim shows that the great Hurrian goddess Khepat had been accepted into the official religion at this time.[6] The existence, during Zimrilim's reign, of Hurrian kingdoms in the north of Syria is another pointer tending to prove that the Hurrian expansion in Upper Syria had begun at the time of the Mari documents.

It is now possible for us to appreciate the scope of the Hurrian

[1] G, 2, 109. See also A, 5, 258 ff.
[2] G, 6, 232 f., 236.
[3] G, 6, 234 f.; §v, 5, 39.
[4] See below, p. 31.
[5] G, 8, 9. See also below, p. 35.
[6] See below, p. 41.

movement as a whole about 1800 B.C. The heaviest concentrations can be observed to the east of the Tigris, but there are also Hurrians in Upper Mesopotamia, where they control several small states, and they have gained a foothold on the western bank of the Euphrates. It looks as if, coming from a generally north-easterly direction, the Hurrians moved down in ever-increasing numbers from the mountainous border of the Fertile Crescent, and advanced to meet the Amorites, who for their part had come out of the Syrian steppe. At Chagar Bazar, in the heart of Upper Mesopotamia where the two streams meet, it is the Hurrians who come off best. On the other hand, to the south, at Mari, on the edge of the desert, the Amorites are completely triumphant. There the Hurrians play hardly any part, although a few religious texts written in Hurrian have been discovered in the palace,[1] and a fragment of a letter indicates that the language was understood in Zimrilim's chancellery.[2] On the other side of the desert, at Qatna, the situation must have been roughly the same as at Mari, while at Aleppo and Alalakh the Hurrians made their presence felt more markedly.

V. THE BENJAMINITES AND OTHER NOMADS, AND THE HABIRU

The steppe occupies a great part of the territories now under consideration. The valley of the Euphrates, which separates Syria from Mesopotamia, is but a fertile ribbon unrolling along a desert landscape. Between the land under cultivation and the desert proper, the limits of which are determined by the annual rainfall, stretches a belt of steppe on which the flocks of nomads find enough to support them. To the west of the Euphrates, this belt goes down as far as the region of Palmyra; to the east, it takes in the region traversed by the Balīkh and the Khabur.

In fact, the people in question were semi-nomads. Nomadic life in the full meaning of the word depends on the use of the camel. At the period now reached, the camel was still unknown.[3] The herdsmen were sheep-rearers, who move slowly from one place to another, and cannot go too far away from the rivers or watering-places. They generally have more or less precarious settlements in the valleys, to which they have to return to work at seed-time and harvest. Living on the edge of the desert in this way, close to the cultivated lands, these were in permanent contact

---

[1] See below, p. 40.   [2] Cf. E. Laroche in *R.A.* 51 (1957), 104 ff.
[3] G, 6, x; §v, 5, 27.

with the settled population, and gradually many of them allowed themselves to become rooted to the soil and ended by joining the ranks of the peasants, while, unremittingly, other groups formed behind them.

As has been established by study of the names, all the tribes at this time were closely related. They belong to the great complex of 'West Semitic' peoples commonly called 'Amorites', who had originally come out of the Syrian desert. After the fall of the Third Dynasty of Ur they had spread into Babylonia and as far as the other side of the Tigris, leaving traces of their settlement in the place-names and founding new dynasties. Advance guards had broken into the old Babylonian cities in earlier years, and had peopled the towns along the desert which bordered the rivers, but the mass of nomads, constantly recruited, nevertheless continued to wander across the steppes of Syria and Upper Mesopotamia, keeping up unremitting pressure on the fixed population. The most vivid evidence of this is to be found in the Mari documents.

Pre-eminent among this turbulent population, which the texts have made known to us, are the Benjaminites.[1] They were scattered over a wide expanse of territory, their encampments spread out along the Euphrates, but they were continually on the move between the river banks and the pasture-lands of Upper Mesopotamia, and were especially active in the region of Harran. Their grazing-routes also led them over to the right bank of the Euphrates, and sometimes they took their flocks to feed on the western fringe of the Syrian desert, in the lands of Aleppo, Qatna and Amurru. The Benjaminites in fact formed a vast confederation, made up of a number of tribes. Four of them are known to us; two of them gave their names to the localities of Sippar-Amnanu and Sippar-Iakhruru, while Sin-kashid, founder of a dynasty at Uruk, came of the Amnanu tribe.

At the head of the Benjaminites were shaikhs and, occasionally, 'kings', that is, war-chiefs, a distinction which also exists among the Bedouin.[2] Their relations with the settlers were most frequently strained, if not openly hostile, especially during Zimrilim's reign. The reports which that king received about them talk of surprise attacks, assaults on towns, suspicious gatherings which might degenerate into general insurrection. The Benjaminites were continually making raids which sometimes took on

---

[1] §v, 4; G, 6, 47 ff.; G, 1, vol. VII, 224. This name has been retained as quasi-traditional, but it would be more exact to call them 'Iaminites'; cf. §v, 3, 49, and §v, 5, 37 f.

[2] G, 6, 59; §v, 6, 120.

considerable proportions. Moreover, the petty kings of northern Mesopotamia and even the king of Eshnunna himself did not hesitate to take sides with them. There were times when the only places of safety were inside the towns. In this struggle, naturally, setbacks alternated with successes. In one of his date-formulae Zimrilim commemorated the severe defeat he inflicted on the Benjaminites at Sagaratim, in the Khabur valley, massacring their leaders. But, by its very nature, the conflict was unending, and faced with opponents like this, who were as tenacious as they were elusive, the established authority could never relax its vigilance.

The Benjaminites, moreover, were not the only ones threatening the peace. To the west of the Euphrates the danger came from the Sutians,[1] who dominated the Syrian desert. The Sutians have long been identified as scattered intruders into Babylonia at the time of the First Babylonian Dynasty, but we now learn where the main body of this people, which also included several tribes,[2] was to be found. According to the Mari correspondence, the Sutians were bold and inveterate plunderers. Their activities extended over the whole Syrian steppe and along the edge of the desert beside the Euphrates, as far as the approaches to Babylonia. Like the Benjaminites, they were not afraid to attack towns—now a locality situated on the Euphrates, downstream from 'Anah, now a staging-post on the route from Palmyra to Damascus, now they would take it into their heads to raid the great caravan city of Palmyra itself. They sometimes operated in strength, for Iasmakh-Adad was warned that a body of 2000 Sutians was on the march towards the Qatna region. It is rare for the texts to record peaceful relations.

There is less to be told about other similar peoples. Some of them were perhaps related to the Benjaminites, like the Rabbians,[3] who lived in the Iamkhad region and were called brothers of the Benjaminites. From their name, the Benē-sim'āl,[4] that is to say 'sons of the north', seem to be a group analogous to the Benjaminites, 'sons of the south'. Until now, they have been seldom encountered, and only in the 'High Country'. Their disposition appears to have been more friendly. About the Numkha and Iamutbal tribes[5] we know hardly anything, but it is interesting to note that there were still groups of these peoples moving about the middle Euphrates in this period, at a time when other groups had long ago given their names to localities on the left bank of the Tigris.

[1] G, 6, 83 ff.; G, 1, vol. vii, 224. [2] §v, 7, 198.

[3] G, 6, 53. [4] G, 6, 54 f.; A, 5, 258 ff. [5] G, 6, 216 f.

About the Khanaeans, on the other hand, whose history is intimately bound up with that of the kingdom of Mari, there is a great deal of information.[1] They were established in strength in the Euphrates and Khabur valleys, for the district of Terqa alone, between Mari and the mouth of the Khabur, could muster several thousands. They were found in Upper Mesopotamia, particularly in the grassy steppes extending between the Balīkh and the upper Khabur. They too were semi-nomadic, but already on the way to fixed habitation, transferring from their encampments on the steppe to their settlements on the banks of the Euphrates, where they occupied land granted by 'the Palace' in reward for their services. The Khanaeans were in fact soldiers by profession, for they had taken armed service with the kings of Mari ever since Iakhdunlim had succeeded in subduing them. They are found mounting guard in the palace, manning local garrisons, keeping order in the desert, and serving in all campaigns. A few minor incidents apart, they seem to have done their duty loyally. They were completely under the control of the central power, and their shaikhs were unobtrusive, though their tribal organization was respected; in their quarters, the Khanaean troops were grouped by their clans, of which about ten are known. The important part played by the Khanaeans at Mari earned their name the privilege of being used occasionally, by extension, for all the 'Western Semites' in the kingdom. The possibility that it sometimes had the general meaning of 'nomads' is not excluded.[2]

A final group was formed by the Habiru.[3] Gathered in battle formations, the Habiru plundered towns, or else fought intermittently for the petty kings of the 'High Country'. Their field of operations was chiefly in the west of Upper Mesopotamia, that is, in the territory bounded by the Euphrates and the upper Khabur. Later on, during the reign of King Irkabtum of Aleppo, we find them making their appearance in Syria as well.

As regards the name Habiru, despite numerous studies devoted to it, a lively controversy still subsists, but the idea that it bore an ethnic signification is more and more abandoned. The Mari tablets have accentuated this by showing that Habiru could be recruited among 'West Semitic' nomads, for a Sutian and men belonging to the tribe of Iamutbal are designated as Habiru. Consequently it seems that the Habiru do not form a distinct group within the great nomad family. Their name has a descriptive sense, but its origin and significance are unknown. Its

[1] G, 6, 1 ff.; A, 6, 107.   [2] §v, 5, 37.
[3] G, 6, 249 ff.; §v, 2, 18 ff., 26; §v, 7.

applications certainly varied according to time and place,[1] but at
the time of the Mari documents it denoted bands of 'free companions' who devoted themselves to brigandage and spread disorder in Upper Mesopotamia.

VI. HAMMURABI'S CONQUESTS IN THE NORTH AND THE DECLINE OF THE EASTERN AMORITE STATES

The diplomatic archives discovered at Mari say nothing about
the circumstances of the sudden rupture between Hammurabi
and Zimrilim. Even with an inkling of the underlying reason,[2]
we still do not know the train of events which was to bring about
the ruin of Mari. Only the list of regnal years of the Babylonian
monarch has preserved the memory of a victory over Mari (date-
formula for the 33rd year), then, two years later, of the dis-
mantling of the city (date-formula for the 35th year). It is
probable that in the intervening time Zimrilim had sought a re-
trial of his lost cause either by resort to arms or in the diplomatic
field. The first defeat, however, had been severe. It had been
followed by an occupation which left its mark in the form of
military registers and labels of tablet-baskets, dated in the 32nd
year of Hammurabi.[3] While the conqueror's soldiers were
quartered in the city, therefore, the officials who had come with
them were rearranging the palace archives.

The Babylonian conquest cannot have finished its course at
Mari. The 33rd year of Samsuiluna is dated from works which
Hammurabi's successor had carried out at Sagaratim, an important locality on the Khabur, which had previously been the principal town of a province dependent on Mari.[4] From this it will be
deduced that Hammurabi had annexed all the territory of Zimrilim's former kingdom to his empire. But did he advance any
farther in the direction of the 'High Country'? To the north-
west he ran the risk of coming into conflict with the land of
Iamkhad, because the disappearance of Mari certainly prompted
the kings of Aleppo to extend their influence on the left bank of
the Euphrates. In the north it is sometimes allowed that Hammurabi got as far as Diyārbakr, but this statement is unfounded.[5]
If he seized Assyria, while Ishme-Dagan took refuge somewhere,
it was by going up the Tigris valley.

---

[1] See §v, 1, 131.   [2] See above, p. 10.   [3] G, 6, 40 n. 1.
[4] §vi, 3, 22.   [5] G, 6, 176 n. 2.

A thick veil now falls over Upper Mesopotamia. For the Amorite principalities which dominated the greater part of the country in Zimrilim's time, that silence was to be final; one after the other they were to be engulfed in the Hurrian tide. When the darkness disperses, nearly three centuries later, it is the Hurrian state of Mitanni which emerges in full power.[1] As for Mari, the town survived, but went into a complete decline. The land of Khana which was subsequently born out of the ruins of its kingdom adopted Terqa, about forty-five miles north of Mari, as its centre.[2] Terqa, formerly the chief town of a district during Zimrilim's reign, housed the principal sanctuary of Dagan, the supreme god of the middle Euphrates. The official title of the sovereigns of Mari comprised a threefold designation: 'King of Mari, Tuttul, and the land of Khana.'[3] The town of Mari, abandoned as the capital, could no longer count, while Tuttul was certainly not under the new princes' control. Of the old title, all that was left was the land of Khana, which was identified with the Mari region and took its name from the Khanaeans established there.

The history of this kingdom of Khana, which might help to clear up some greater problems of chronology, is still very confused. It is known only from a small group of documents which have preserved the names of six sovereigns,[4] and there is uncertainty about the exact period to which they should be assigned. To judge from the script they are scarcely different from the Mari tablets, though they do reveal certain divergences in the utilization of signs, and they employ values of signs attested only at a more recent date. The most reliable criterion seems to be provided by the seals imprinted upon them. The collection of seal cylinders and cylinder imprints recovered at Mari now offers a sound basis for comparison. The glyptic art of Mari follows the Babylonian classical tradition fairly closely, but tends to diverge towards the so-called Syrian style.[5] The seals on the tablets from Khana display different characteristics, either the style peculiar to the end of the First Babylonian Dynasty or the style heralding the Kassite period.[6] Clearly, therefore, there is a break in the glyptic tradition. It can be explained both by a new impulse, due no doubt to a lengthy Babylonian occupation, and by a certain separation in time.

The order of succession of the six princes of Khana is itself

---

[1] See below, p. 37.
[2] §II, 4, 154 ff.
[3] G, 6, 30.
[4] See G, 5, 63 f.; §VI, 2, 205.
[5] §II, 8, part 3, 248 ff.
[6] G, 5, 63 f.

uncertain. It is probable that they followed one another fairly rapidly on the throne, like the kings of the first 'West Semitic' dynasties in Babylonia. In any case, the documents belong to the same period, and from the names preserved, the population seems stable. With one exception, the royal names are 'West Semitic'— Ammimadar, Hammurapi', Isikh-Dagan, Isharlim, Shunukh-rammu. In the population as a whole the Akkadian element predominates. There are no Hurrian names and no Kassite names apart from that of a king Kashtiliash.[1] The latter followed the same traditions as the other kings of Khana. According to the Babylonian custom he named one of his regnal years after an act of social justice (*mīšarum*), and he took oath by the gods Shamash, Dagan and Iturmer.[2] Nothing in these documents lends support to the hypothesis of a real Kassite kingdom established in the middle Euphrates valley. From his name Kashtiliash must have been connected with the family which seized power in Babylonia, and thus, in spite of certain difficulties, he may be taken as the last known king of the dynasty of Khana.[3]

Born out of Babylonia's weakness, the land of Khana was doomed to a proportionate mediocrity as the decadence of Babylonia itself became more pronounced, bringing with it the closing up of the roads. At the other end of the great river-way, the Hittites were shortly to intervene in Upper Syria. The small kingdom of the middle Euphrates was fated to disappear in the upheaval caused by the encroachments of the Hittites and the advance of the Hurrians whose empire progressively extended over the whole of Northern Mesopotamia.

VII. THE 'GREAT KINGSHIP' OF ALEPPO

Until the discovery of the Alalakh tablets, the history of Syria at the time of Hammurabi's successors in Babylon was unknown. It was clear, however, that the city of Aleppo had continued to play the same dominant role as in the days of Zimrilim. The famous treaty, known as the Treaty of Aleppo, concluded between Murshilish II and Talmi-Sharruma of Aleppo in the fourteenth century B.C., gives the history of relations between Aleppo and the Hittites. It recalls, in particular, that in former years the kings of the land of Aleppo had a 'great kingship', to which Khattushilish, the great king of the land of Khatti, had put

---

[1] Cf. G, 7, 64. [2] Texts quoted in G, 5, 64.
[3] Cf. G, 5, 65. In this detail we suggest an order differing from the scheme of this *History*.

an end; after him, his grandson Murshilish had ruined the kingship and country of Aleppo.[1] The term 'great kingship' is
significant, for it tells us that the Hittites considered the kings of
Aleppo as their equals.

The chronology of the Alalakh texts is not yet definitely
established. Most of the tablets of the earlier group (level VII)
were found in a chamber adjoining the central court of the palace,[2]
so it is certainly a collection of archives. They cover the reigns of
two princes of Alalakh, Iarimlim and his son Ammitaqum. This
is a normal span for administrative archives and it fits the
archaeological observations, which assign only a fairly short life
to level VII.[3] But for the same length of time the documents
name six kings of Aleppo, who succeed each other mostly, if not
all, in a direct line. It is likely that the first of these, Abbael, was
nearing the end of his reign when he handed over Alalakh to
Iarimlim. On the other hand Hammurabi II, the last but one of
his successors, must have had but a short reign, for he is known
only by a few tablets dated in his accession-year.[4] But the pair
Hammurabi and Samsuiluna alone occupied the throne of Babylon for eighty-one years. By assigning the maximum to the
reigns of Iarimlim and Ammitaqum one might probably allow
them seventy-five years, so it is not impossible to include within
the same span the end of Abbael, the four kings who succeeded
him, and the first years of Iarimlim III, in whose time the records
of Alalakh come to an end. The texts make it certain that Ammitaqum was contemporary with four kings at Aleppo.[5]

To set in time the period which we have thus defined is
another problem. It is generally assumed that Abbael's father,
named Hammurabi, was identical with the king Hammurabi
who ruled Aleppo in the time of Zimrilim. It is now known from
the *res gestae* of Khattushilish I, discovered at Boğazköy in 1957,
that the Hittite king sacked Alalakh in the first years of his reign.[6]
To this event must be ascribed the radical destruction which
closes level VII at Alalakh.[7] Taking our earlier conclusions into
account, we are able to date Iarimlim's accession and the oldest
Alalakh tablets from the end of the eighteenth century B.C., that
is to say, probably during the reign of Abieshu' at Babylon.
Roughly fifty years, therefore, separate the disappearance of
Zimrilim from the foundation at Alalakh of a vassal dynasty of

[1] G, 7, 52 n. 89.
[2] G, 8, 121 f.; §vii, 10, 102.
[3] §vii, 10, 91.
[4] §vii, 4, 111.
[5] G, 5, 70 n. 181 *a*; §vii, 4, 110 f.
[6] §vii, 5, 78.
[7] §vii, 11, 83 f.

Aleppo. There is still, however, one difficulty: Iarimlim certainly seems to be the brother of Abbael,[1] that is to say the son of Hammurabi of Aleppo, Zimrilim's contemporary, and this prevents us from bringing the date of his installation in Alalakh too far forward.

The Alalakh tablets throw only an indirect and most incomplete light on the history of Aleppo. The principality of Alalakh was created after a rebellion by Abbael's brothers. In particular the town of Irrid, which belonged to Iarimlim already or was destined for him, rose against the king of Aleppo. The latter captured and destroyed the rebel city, but he decided to give Iarimlim, who had remained loyal to him, the city of Alalakh in exchange for it—in return for an act of vassalage drawn up in due form.[2] The episode demonstrates that at this time the king of Aleppo had brought territories beyond the Euphrates under his domination, because the town of Irrid was to the east of Carchemish. After Abbael the dynasty carries on from father to son, with Iarimlim II (Iarimlim I being the father-in-law of Zimrilim), Niqmiepuʻ and Irkabtum. That the two last sovereigns, Hammurabi II and Iarimlim III, were father and son cannot be proved but it is probable.[3] Hammurabi II has been seen as but a transitory figure on the throne of Aleppo, and Iarimlim III had occupied it only a few years when Khattushilish came and destroyed Alalakh. Several year-names commemorate important events: they inform us that Niqmiepuʻ seized Aranzik on the Euphrates, almost on a level with Aleppo, and that Iarimlim III gained a victory over Qatna.[4]

The *res gestae* of Khattushilish, for their part, carry on from the Alalakh tablets and give glimpses of the history of the last years of Aleppo, before it fell under the blows of the Hittites.[5] After his action against Alalakh, Khattushilish turned against Urshu and laid the country waste. From the well-known account of the siege of Urshu, of which there is no mention in the Khattushilish text, it is known that the town had the support of Aleppo and Carchemish.[6] After this, Northern Syria had a brief respite. While Khattushilish was engaged in operations against the land of Arzawa he was taken in the rear by the Hurrians, who dealt him some hard blows before he was able to break out of their grip. The attack he launched on Khashshum marks his return

[1] Cf. §vii, 8, 129; *C.A.H.* I³, pt. i, p. 213.   [2] §vii, 1, 27 f.; §vii, 8, 129.
[3] For their order of succession see *C.A.H.* I³, pt. i, pp. 213 ff.
[4] §vii, 4, 110 f.   [5] §vii, 5, 78 ff.; see below, pp. 14 ff.
[6] G, 7, 64 n. 157; A, 5, 261 f.

to the offensive to the south-east of the Anatolian plateau. In spite of reinforcements of troops sent by Aleppo, the Hittites triumphed; they seized Khashshum and plundered the town, carrying off a rich booty.

With the aid of this Boğazköy document, we can now follow the manœuvres directed against Aleppo. The Hittite king, reaching Syria via the passes through the Amanus mountains, struck first at Alalakh, in order to interrupt direct communications between Aleppo and the sea. Then, in a sort of enveloping movement, he attacked the neighbouring states of Urshu and Khashshum, to the north-east of Aleppo. It was in the course of a campaign against Khahhum that he crossed the Euphrates for the first time in pursuit of the opposing army.[1] The *res gestae* make no reference to the ill-fated operations against Aleppo itself. It fell to the successor of Khattushilish, Murshilish I, to avenge the defeat and destroy the city before launching an expedition against Babylon.[2] But the protocol of the Treaty of Aleppo was not at fault in asserting that it was Khattushilish who had begun the weakening of the 'great kingship' of Aleppo. It will be noted that the sovereigns of Aleppo, faithful to ancient custom, kept to the title of 'king of Iamkhad'. The Alalakh texts sometimes give them that of 'great king', but only after Ammitaqum had designated himself as king.[3]

The status of Alalakh before it was ceded to Iarimlim is not known; perhaps the city was directly dependent on Aleppo, unless it had been confiscated from one of the king's rebellious brothers. It had an excellent situation near the Orontes, bordering on a plain, which was then fertile and well populated, whereas its central depression is today occupied by the marshy lake of the 'Amuq.[4] It dominated the road linking Aleppo with the Mediterranean, and being near to the Amanus mountains, it must also have benefited from the timber trade. The resources afforded by this favourable situation enabled the princes of Alalakh to build themselves an imposing palace, the state rooms of which were decorated with frescoes.[5] They were also able to raise strong fortifications,[6] which bore witness at once to their power and their virtual independence. But it is quite possible that the territory under their sway was confined to the plain mentioned above.

Iarimlim lived on into the reign of Niqmiepu'. His son Ammitaqum, who succeeded him, soon began to assume the title

---

[1] §VII, 5, 83.

[2] G, 7, 53 n. 89; 64.

[3] G, 7, 53 n. 90; §VII, 4, 109.

[4] §VII, 11, 17 ff.

[5] See Plate 67(*a*).

[6] See Plate 67(*b*).

of 'king', no longer satisfied to be called 'man of Alalakh', and he occasionally made use of his own date-formulae.[1] He had married a Hurrian princess, who had given him a son named Hammurabi, and the deed ratified in the presence of Iarimlim, by which Ammitaqum appointed Hammurabi as his heir, has been discovered.[2] The latter does not seem to have come to the throne; at all events, the archives leave off before his accession. Ammitaqum's reign was very long, for it began under Niqmiepu' and ended only in the time of Iarimlim III, third successor to him.

The land of Iamkhad must have had more than one vassal state. The Alalakh archives mention the names of a number of important towns, such as Carchemish, Qatna, Ugarit, Ibla, Emar and Tunip, without giving any details of their political status.[3] The first two were capitals of independent kingdoms. It is impossible at present to form an opinion regarding Ugarit, but Ibla does appear to have been a vassal city. As for the last two towns, they may have been directly under the rule of Aleppo. But caution is in place here for we find 'kings' at the head of places less prominent than these, such as Nashtarbi and Tuba.[4] The case of Nashtarbi, the site of which is unknown, makes an interesting study. Towards the end of Iarimlim's reign the town was still a dependency of Alalakh, and after some dispute, sanctions were prescribed against anybody who disputed his possession of it,[5] but under Ammitaqum the town had a 'king' of its own.[6] Should we see in this fact a sign of a tendency for the territory to split up? Here is the same phenomenon of a decline in the central power which might have led Ammitaqum to take the title of king. The title 'great king' with which the sovereigns of Aleppo were graced would do no more than mask an increasing weakness, which, in the long run, would have suited Hittite designs very well. This enfeeblement might be traced to Hurrian penetration, the newcomers gradually attaining power and remoulding the governing classes.

The Hurrians did, in fact, leave a deep impression on the Alalakh archives.[7] Hurrians figure among those occupying high positions, their language was widely used, even in the cultured sections of society, they had introduced names of months into the calendar, and king Abbael recalls the help he received from their goddess Khepat in reconquering Irrid. In the aggregate, however, to judge from the personal names, Hurrians were in the

[1] §vii, 4, 111.   [2] G, 8, 33, no. 6.   [3] G, 8, 154 ff.
[4] G, 8, 101, no. 367.   [5] G, 8, 38, no. 11.
[6] G, 8, 86, no. 269.   [7] G, 6, 233 ff.; §v, 5, 39.

minority, the Semites being almost twice as numerous. Attention has also been drawn to a series of names belonging to a people not yet identified. This people, which must have been established in the country for a long time, reveals its presence also in the place-names, where Semitic and Hurrian names are the exception.[1] This ancient layer had been followed by the 'West Semitic' element, and the period covered by the archives had, in its turn, experienced an intensive penetration by Hurrians. The trend increased; towards the middle of the millennium the Hurrian element was predominant at Alalakh (level IV), and the organization of society itself bore the Hurrian stamp.[2]

Practically nothing is known of the rest of Syria. The Alalakh tablets mention only the names of Qatna[3] and Ugarit,[4] together with the land of Amurru,[5] already known to the Mari documents, which was situated to the south of Qatna. Later documents inform us that in about the fifteenth century B.C. Hurrians were numerous at Qatna, where their influence made itself strongly felt.[6] The Ugarit texts, on the other hand, bear witness to a much higher proportion of Semites, and there too are found many more Semitic place-names than at Alalakh.[7] It seems that during the period under consideration the surge of Hurrians had spread southwards, but with varying results from region to region.

So far we have not had occasion to speak of the Hyksos. Some historians have, in fact, turned their eyes upon Syria, seeking far away from Egypt the starting-point of the Hyksos invasion.[8] The different opinions expressed upon this still-debatable subject are largely dependent upon the view which is taken of chronology. It is generally allowed that the Hyksos period opened in Egypt towards the end of the eighteenth century, the invaders having occupied Avaris in the Delta about 1720 B.C.[9] Regarding Syria and Mesopotamia we are not on such firm ground. According to the system adopted in the present work, the date of the occupation of Avaris falls in about the middle of the reign of Samsuiluna at Babylon. In view of the conclusions we have reached, it would be placed in the interval between the Mari documents and those of Alalakh; the latter would all be included within the Hyksos period. Neither in the Mari tablets, where one surely ought to perceive some anticipatory signs, nor in those of Alalakh, is there any trace of a new political power which could be connected with

[1] §v, 5, 39 f.   [2] G, 7, 56 ff.; §vii, 7, 19 f.
[3] §vii, 9, 25, no. 259; see also above, p. 32.
[4] G, 8, 99, no. 358.   [5] G, 6, 179.   [6] §vii, 2, 13 n. 1.
[7] G, 4, 69; §v, 5, 40.   [8] §vii, 2, 8 f.   [9] See below, p. 52 (Ed.).

the Hyksos. It is true that certain movements of peoples may have escaped attention, but there are some facts already known which bear upon the origin of the Hyksos. At the time when these were moving into the Delta the Hurrians were just beginning to spread into Northern Syria, the only route they could have followed to Egypt. This being so, it is impossible, without pushing Hammurabi's date considerably farther back,[1] to connect the Hyksos with the Hurrian migration. In the same way there can be no influence of the Indo-Aryans, who appeared distinctly later, certainly after the period of level VII at Alalakh.[2] To sum up, the local evidence leads one to believe that Syria played no part in the Hyksos invasion. This result is not simply negative; it gives the direction in which a solution to the Hyksos problem as a whole will be found.

VIII. DEVELOPMENT OF THE HURRIAN STATES

Urshu and Khashshum, the northern neighbours of Aleppo, were under Hurrian rule at the time of Zimrilim, and there is no doubt that their Hurrian transformation was of long standing. Several figures of deities appear among the spoils which Khattushilish brought back from Khashshum, and these belonged to the Hurrian pantheon.[3] On the other side of the Euphrates the Hurrian states of Upper Mesopotamia must have continued to spread, but this region is plunged into almost total obscurity. After the disappearance of Mari our sources fall silent. Towards the beginning of the fifteenth century, when the silence is finally broken, we are suddenly confronted with an important state, Mitanni, which has united the whole of Northern Mesopotamia and already extended its influence beyond the two rivers.[4] Nothing is known about the phases of its development.

At the time of the Mari documents the Hurrians already dominated several principalities in the north of Mesopotamia, where conditions favoured their expansion. The unification of the country by Shamshi-Adad had been ephemeral, and his territory was divided up among numerous small states.[5] Some of them had submitted more or less completely to the authority of Zimrilim, but the fall of Mari freed them from any kind of tutelage, because Hammurabi does not appear to have extended his conquests as far as the 'High Country'. With the break-up of the Babylonian

[1] Cf. §vii, 4, 113.   [2] See below, p. 38.   [3] See below, p. 41.
[4] G, 4, 75 f.   [5] See above, p. 15 f.

empire under Abieshu' there was not even any prospect of intervention from the south. To the east, Assyria too had ceased to be a great power. Even when freed from Babylonian occupation it remained absorbed in its internal difficulties, and efforts to bring about a revival, later on, came to very little. At the beginning of the fifteenth century Assyria was annexed by Saustatar and attached to the Mitannian empire as a vassal principality.[1] In the west of Upper Mesopotamia only one state capable of playing a significant part survived, the kingdom of Iamkhad. It has been seen that the sovereigns of Aleppo had taken advantage of the eclipse of Mari to gain a foothold on the left bank of the Euphrates (above, p. 32), but they do not seem to have pushed on very far in this direction.

For the Hurrians who had spread into the fertile country of Upper Mesopotamia the way was open for seizing power to the detriment of the Amorite invaders who had preceded them. Settlement and conquest no doubt went hand in hand, and the division of the country into small units made conquest easier than in Syria. This first phase, which is one of progressive Hurrian domination, was to be followed by a second, which would witness the regrouping of the petty states before their final unification within the kingdom of Mitanni. About the progress of this unification, which must have been completed in the second half of the sixteenth century, there is no information.

The existence of Hurrian principalities in Upper Mesopotamia towards the end of the First Babylonian Dynasty is confirmed by the Hittite evidence relating to Khattushilish and Murshilish.[2] While he was making war in the land of Arzawa, Khattushilish was attacked in the rear by the Hurrians. The Hittite campaign against Urshu had taken place during the previous year. Conscious of the danger menacing them, the Hurrians had perhaps decided to grasp the initiative by carrying the war into the enemy's camp. It is certainly from Mesopotamia that they came: instead of naming the Hurrians, as in the Hittite version, the Akkadian version of the *res gestae* makes the aggressor come from the land of Khanigalbat.[3] The blow was severe and it brought Khattushilish to the verge of disaster: the greater part of his territory revolted, and the town of Khattusha alone, he says, remained loyal, but in the end he was able to survive the ordeal. The effort put forth by the Hurrians seems to have exhausted them, for Khattushilish seized Khashshum a few years later, and

[1] §1, 5, 32 ff.   [2] G, 7, 64; §VII, 5, 78 ff.; §IX, 1, 384.
[3] §VII, 5, 79 n. 16; see below, p. 242.

even crossed the Euphrates. When Murshilish returned from his expedition against Babylon, he had to repulse a final assault by the Hurrians from Mesopotamia. Those from the kingdoms to the west of the Euphrates had certainly been put out of the fight before the capture of Aleppo. It has been observed that the Khana tablets contain no Hurrian names (above, p. 30). The Hurrians therefore seem to have settled especially in the northern regions.

The formation of the Mitannian empire is linked with the onset of a new immigration, that of the Indo-Aryans, coming from the north-east. There is proof enough of their intervention in several fields, although there is sometimes a tendency to overvalue their contribution to the so-called Mitannian civilization. Basically, Mitanni was a Hurrian state, in which the language was Hurrian; names of Indo-Aryan origin never represented more than a minute percentage. It is usually believed that the Indo-Aryans formed a military aristocracy imposed upon the local peasantry. In spite of numerical weakness, therefore, their political influence may have been dominant. However, the Hurrians did not wait for the stimulus of an Indo-Aryan ruling class before spreading into Mesopotamia and Syria, nor even before seizing power. There were already Hurrian kings in the days of Zimrilim. The Hurrians occupy an increasingly important position at Alalakh, but the Indo-Aryans do not figure in the tablets of level VII,[1] and appear only at level IV: it is in the time between that they must have penetrated into Syria, that is to say, in the course of the sixteenth century. Moreover, it has not so far been possible to establish for certain the existence of Indo-Aryan elements before the end of the First Babylonian Dynasty.[2]

Mysterious invaders known by the name of Umman-Manda, *i.e.* 'Manda-host' or 'Host (of the) Manda', have sometimes been connected with the irruption of the Indo-Aryans.[3] The first mention of these Umman-Manda in an historical context goes back to the reign of Khattushilish I.[4] In a passage dealing with the Hittite king's campaigns in North Syria the leader of the Umman-Manda figures among his adversaries, in company with the general commanding the troops of Aleppo. At about the same time, according to an account preserved in the great collection of observations of the planet Venus, Ammiṣaduqa of Babylon won a victory over the Umman-Manda.[5] But at this date the Umman-Manda had long been known in Babylonia. They al-

---

[1] G, 7, 56 f.; §VII, 7, 19.

[2] G, 7, 53, 58; §VII, 2, 13 ff.

[3] Cf. §VII, 1, 31.

[4] §VII, 5, 78 n. 14.

[5] §VII, 1, 31 n. 16.

ready appear in omen-texts of the Hammurabi period,[1] which do no more than record a more ancient tradition. Umman-Manda were spoken of long before the arrival of the Indo-Aryans; so that the one must not be confused with the other. If, as is most frequently believed, the term Umman-Manda has in fact a descriptive sense, designating particularly noxious bands of warriors, it may have been applied in certain circumstances to the Indo-Aryan invaders. But in any case, further evidence is needed to attest the presence of the latter; the mention of the Umman-Manda alone is not enough. In the existing state of our knowledge the Indo-Aryan invasion does not appear to have touched Mesopotamia or Syria before the end of the First Babylonian Dynasty and the break-up of the old Hittite empire, following the assassination of Murshilish I. Until this period, the Indo-Aryans could not have had any influence upon the destiny of the Hurrian states.

IX. HURRIAN ELEMENTS IN ART AND RELIGION

The search for Hurrian elements in art encounters two major difficulties: the rarity of the available monuments and the uncertainties which persist even as to the definition of Hurrian art. The problem of knowing what properly belongs to the Hurrians is far from having been resolved, and some authors have gone so far as to deny them the slightest originality in the artistic field. The Hurrians, it is true, showed a marked capacity for assimilating the cultural values of the more advanced peoples with whom they came into contact. To the Mesopotamian civilization, above all, they were vastly indebted. However, the exchanges did not in every case flow one way only: there is to be considered, for example, the extent of Hurrian influence on the Hittite world.[2]

The most objective method is to survey the monuments and works of art throughout the Mitannian kingdom as a whole at the time of its greatest extension. This comparative study has for its object to define the characteristics of a 'Mitannian' art, the inspiration of which must have been mainly Hurrian. The survey has been made; it has yielded positive results, notably for the glyptic and ceramic arts.[3] But all certainty vanishes once a search begins for the direct antecedents of this art. There is nothing to justify adherence to any view without reservation: the problem

[1] See J. Nougayrol in *R.A.* 44 (1950), 12 ff. On the possibility of the Umman-Manda being at Mari, see J. Bottéro in G, 1, vol. VII, 224 f.

[2] §IX, 1.   [3] §IX, 2.

remains unresolved. Sometimes the Hurrians had been preceded by peoples of whom we know very little, which makes the task of giving the Hurrians their due even more complicated. This is the case in Syria, where the most ancient layer of the population is composed of an unknown ethnic element.[1] The Hurrians arrived late in the country, and only after the Amorites. They cannot therefore be allowed any part in the development of the so-called Syrian glyptic art,[2] the characteristics of which were settled at the beginning of the period considered in this chapter.[3]

In the religious field the traces of Hurrian influence are more easily discernible. At Mari six texts have been recovered among the archives which are composed wholly or partly in Hurrian, and are extracts from rituals.[4] In order to preserve their full efficacity great care was taken to pronounce the rituals in their original form. At Boğazköy, too, Hurrian was to occupy an important position in the religious ceremonies. Such tablets are proof of the value attached to the religious practices of the Hurrians. Apart from them there is nothing to justify us in assuming that other aspects of religious life at Mari were affected. No Hurrian deity was worshipped there. Attention has been drawn, however, to three names of women, each composed of an Akkadian element and the sacred name Khubat,[5] which must be a special form of the name of the Hurrian goddess Khepat, and this would be her earliest appearance.[6] In the absence of other information, these hybrid names would seem to come from mixed Akkadian–Hurrian families rather than to be a sign of Hurrian religious penetration. The women who bear them were weavers in the royal workshops. They were not necessarily natives of Mari, since the palace also recruited the numerous female workers it needed from outside. In Babylonia, during the reign of Ammiditana, a Subarian slave-woman had a name formed in a similar way, Ummi-Khepet.[7]

On the other hand a Hurrian god certainly makes his appearance under the kingdom of Khana, when the king Shunukh-rammu dates one of his years from a sacrifice made to 'Dagan of the Hurrians' (*ša Ḫurri*).[8] This was evidently an exceptional occasion, for the pious acts commemorated in date-formulae are normally the building of a temple or the dedication of a statue, a

[1] See above, p. 35.
[2] See Plate 68.
[3] §VII, 4, 119 ff.; §II, 8, part 3, 248 ff.
[4] §IX, 4.
[5] G, 1, vol. IX, 350.
[6] The name of *Ḥé-ba-at* has now appeared in a letter sent to King Zimrilim (*T.C.L.* 31, no. 92, 23).   [7] G, 4, 106.   [8] G, 4, 63.

throne, or an emblem. Perhaps the sacrifice in this case had a political significance, for the god so honoured could not have been the ordinary object of worship in the land of Khana. The god Dagan had long been considered the supreme master of the middle Euphrates, and it is possible that under the designation 'Dagan of the Hurrians', it was in fact Teshub, the great god of the Hurrians, that was intended.

In Syria, Hurrian influence in the religious field was naturally more marked. In one of the most ancient documents discovered at Alalakh, which concerns the cession of this town, the king of Aleppo, Abbael, makes a point of recalling the support given him by the goddess Khepat.[1] Worship of the goddess had therefore been officially introduced to Aleppo by this date. Khepat was the titular wife of Teshub, and in this instance she is associated with the god Adad, written with the ideogram IM; it is a question whether the reading should not be Teshub rather than Adad. But perhaps the question is superfluous, for in the Hurrian personal names yielded by the Alalakh tablets ideograms concealing names of Hurrian deities are encountered. The practice is especially common during the late period (tablets of level IV), but it is not unknown during the earlier.[2] Teshub being identified with Adad, each ethnic community could express the name of the Weather God in its own language. In the Boğazköy texts, the great god Adad of Aleppo, to whom Zimrilim had dedicated his statue in former years, was to become Teshub of Aleppo.[3] The change was beginning to take place in the time of Abbael since Khepat had already taken her place beside the god of Aleppo. The mark left by the Hurrians is revealed, too, by other references in the Alalakh documents. Certain religious festivals have Hurrian names,[4] and several names of months are also Hurrian, one of them containing the name of the god Ashtapi.[5]

In addition to this, the influence of neighbouring countries reinforced the influence exerted by the Hurrians installed in Syria itself. Among the northern allies of Aleppo, religion was dominated entirely by Hurrians. When Khattushilish I sacked Khashshum, some years after the destruction of Alalakh, he returned with a batch of statues he had removed from the temples in the city.[6] Among them were effigies of the god of Aleppo and his wife Khepat, as well as a pair of silver bulls, which must have represented Sherri and Khurri, the two great bulls which were attributes of Teshub.

[1] G, 8, 25.
[2] G, 7, 57 n. 111; §IX, 1, 384 n. 6.
[3] §IX, 1, 390.
[4] G, 8, 86, no. 269; §VII, 9, 27, no. 264.
[5] G, 8, 85, no. 263.
[6] §VII, 5, 82.

CHAPTER II

EGYPT: FROM THE DEATH OF AMMENEMES III TO SEQENENRE II

I. THE LAST YEARS OF THE TWELFTH DYNASTY

WHEN, in 1798 B.C., King Makherure Ammenemes IV ascended the throne of Egypt his father and grandfather before him had ruled the land for the greater part of a century. It is inevitable that he himself should have been well advanced in age at the time of his accession and it is hardly surprising that his reign, including a period of co-regency with his father, did not exceed ten years.[1] In spite of its brevity, an understandable absence of brilliant achievement, and a slight falling off in the quality of the works of art produced, the reign shows little evidence of a serious decline in Egyptian prosperity and prestige. The monuments of Ammenemes IV are fairly numerous and frequently of excellent workmanship.[2] They include a small, but handsome, temple at Medīnet Ma'ādi in the Faiyūm which he and his father together dedicated to the harvest-goddess Renenutet.[3] At Semna in the northern Sudan the height of the Nile was recorded in the king's fifth regnal year,[4] and at Sinai working parties of Years 4, 6, 8, and 9 have left testimonials of continued activity in the turquoise mines.[5]

Syria evidently acknowledged Egypt's ascendancy as of old. Beirut has yielded a gold pectoral and a small diorite sphinx of

---

[1] G, 5, pl. 3, col. vi, 1; G, 7, 43, 86, pl. 15; §1, 7, no. 122; §1, 6, 312; §1, 18, 68. Newberry (§1, 17) has suggested that Ammenemes IV had no independent reign, but ruled only as his father's co-regent and was succeeded before the latter's death by Queen Sobkneferu. The inclusion of his name in the kings' lists of later times (G, 5, pl. 3, col. vi, 1; G, 16, pl. 1, left, 19; G, 11, pl. 1, Abydos 65, Saqqara 45) and the number of inscribed monuments which bear no other name but his (footnote 2, below) tend, however, to make such a supposition extremely unlikely. See also §1, 8, 464–7; G, 9, 62.

[2] G, 6, vol. 1, 338–41; §1, 1, 177–81; G, 8, part 1, 200–2, 246, fig. 157; G, 22, vol. iii, 215, pl. 71, 2. See also, below, nn. 3–5 and p. 43, nn. 1, 2.

[3] §1, 22, 2, 10–11, 17–36, pls. 6–15, 31–5, and plan; §1, 3; §1, 15; G, 22, vol. ii, 619–20.

[4] §1, 5, 135, pl. 95A (R.I.S. 16).

[5] §1, 7, nos. 33, 57, 118–22; G, 15, vol. vii, 349, 355, 356, 359.

Ammenemes IV[1] and in the tomb of Prince Ypshomuibi of Byblos were found a gold-mounted obsidian casket and a fine grey stone vase with his cartouches.[2] As under Ammenemes III and his predecessors, the native rulers of Byblos continued to write their names in Egyptian hieroglyphs and to use the purely Egyptian title, ḥꜣty-ꜥ, 'Count', 'Mayor', borne from time immemorial by the governing officials of the provinces of Egypt itself.[3]

The remains of two small pyramids at Mazghūna, between Dahshūr and El-Lisht, were once thought to have been the tombs of Ammenemes IV and his successor, Queen Sobkneferu;[4] but their close similarity to the pyramid of King Khendjer at Saqqara (§11) makes it more likely that they are to be dated to the middle of the Thirteenth Dynasty.[5]

The last ruler of the Twelfth Dynasty, the Female Horus, Meryetre, the King of Upper and Lower Egypt, Sobkkare, the Daughter of Re, Sobkneferu, was probably a daughter of Ammenemes III and a sister or half-sister of Ammenemes IV.[6] She survived her predecessor on the throne by less than four years, but is known to us from the Karnak, Saqqara, and Turin lists[7] and from a number of inscribed monuments—among them a Nile mark at the Second Cataract, dated to Regnal Year 3.[8] A sphinx and three statues of Sobkneferu were found at Khatā'na in the Delta,[9] and a fragmentary architrave from Kōm el-'Aqārib, near Heracleopolis, bears her praenomen as 'king' and her personal name.[10] On a fragment of column in the Cairo Museum[11] and on a plaque from Hawāra the name of the queen appears with that of Ammenemes III, a fact which has been interpreted—probably erroneously—as indicating that she had ruled as a co-regent with her father.[12] Like that of Queen Nitocris of the Sixth Dynasty,[13] her reign, occasioned presumably by the absence of a male heir to the throne, marks the virtual end of a great epoch in Egyptian history.

[1] G, 15, vol. vii, 384–5, 391. See §1, 14; §1, 9; §1, 4, 302; G, 22, vol. ii, 214–15; G, 28, 171.

[2] §1, 13, 157–61, nos. 611, 614, pls. 88, 90, 91, fig. 70; G, 15, vol. vii, 386.

[3] §1, 13, 277 ff.; G, 3, 256; §1, 23, 234.

[4] §1, 20, 49, 54; G, 15, vol. iv, 76; G, 3, 260; G, 22, vol. ii, 197–200.

[5] §1, 11, 12, 33, 55 n. 1, 63, 65 n. 1; §1, 12, 142 n. 4; §1, 10, 34.

[6] §1, 8, 458–67, pls. 6–9, 11–15; §1, 17; G, 3, 251, 268–9, 283.

[7] G, 16, pl. 1, left, 18; G, 11, pl. 1 (Saqqara 46); G, 5, pl. 3 (col. vi, 2).

[8] §1, 5, 141, pl. 96f (R.I.K. 11).

[9] §1, 16, 21, pl. 9c; §1, 8, 458–60, pls. 6–9; G, 22, vol. ii, 597.

[10] §1, 2, 34.   [11] §1, 8, 464–5, pls. 14, 15.

[12] §1, 17. See, however, §1, 8, 464–6.

[13] See *C.A.H.* i³, pt. 2, ch. xiv, sects. ii and iv.

II. THE DECLINE AND FALL OF THE MIDDLE KINGDOM: THE THIRTEENTH AND FOURTEENTH DYNASTIES

In the light of the discoveries of recent years the old conception of the century which followed the end of the Twelfth Dynasty as an era of political chaos and cultural collapse has had to be extensively revised. From their number, the brevity of their reigns, and the evident lack of any continuous dynastic succession it would appear that the kings of the Thirteenth Dynasty, dominated by a powerful line of viziers, were for the most part puppet rulers, holding their offices, perhaps by appointment or 'election', for limited periods of time.[1] It is certainly true that the weakness and instability of the crown had an increasingly detrimental effect on the internal prosperity of the country and on its relationships with neighbouring foreign states. On the other hand, it is evident that for more than a hundred years, in spite of frequent changes in the persons of the rulers, the power of a single central government continued to be respected throughout most of Egypt itself; royal building activities were carried on in both the south and the north, and, until late in the eighteenth century B.C., Egyptian prestige in Nubia and western Asia remained largely unshaken.[2]

The extant versions of Manetho's history describe the Thirteenth Dynasty as consisting of '60 kings of Diospolis' (Thebes) 'who reigned for 453 years'.[3] If we substitute '153 years' (1786–1633 B.C.) for the obviously erroneous '453 years',[4] we shall find this statement to be essentially correct. The Turin Canon appears to have listed between fifty and sixty kings for the dynasty[5] and to have omitted a number of names known to us from other sources.[6]

---

[1] §II, 16, 104–5; §II, 15, 146–8; §I, 10, 38–9; §II, 5, 263–8.
[2] See below, pp. 45–9.   [3] G, 23, 72–5 (Fr. 38, 39a, b).
[4] The ease with which this particular scribal error (ΥΝΓ, 453, for ΡΝΓ, 153) could be made by Greek copyists of the early centuries of the Christian Era is illustrated in the case of the year figure given by Manetho for the Fourteenth Dynasty (G, 23, 74–5). In two manuscripts this figure was copied correctly as 184 and in two others as 484. The discrepancy occurs also in two copies of the same version of Manetho (that of Eusebius). Cf. also the figures 100 and 409 given by Manetho for the Ninth Dynasty (G, 23, 61).
[5] Cols. VI–VIII (G, 5, 16–17, pl. 3).
[6] Notably, in the table of kings from the temple of Amun at Karnak (G, 16, pl. 1; G, 19, 608–10). Among the rulers whose names were not included or are now missing in the Turin Canon are: Seneferibre Sesostris (G, 3, 314 [8]), Mersekhemre Neferhotep (*ibid.* 316 [21]), Sewahenre Senebmiu (*ibid.* 316 [28]), Djedankhre Mentuemsaf (*ibid.* 317 [29]), Menkhaure Senaayeb (*ibid.* 317 [30: 'Seshib']),

Like their predecessors of the Eleventh and Twelfth Dynasties, most of these kings do, in fact, seem to have been Thebans. Their works at Deir el-Bahri, Karnak, El-Madāmūd, and Tōd[1] show a continued devotion to the Thebaid and its gods (especially Mont), and many of their personal names—Ammenemes, Inyotef, Sesostris, Neferhotep—are of pure Theban type. Until about 1674 B.C., however, the seat of the government evidently remained, as before, in the region of Memphis and the palace and fortified city of Itj-towy, near El-Lisht, continued in use as a residence of the kings.[2]

It is probable that the transition from the Twelfth to the Thirteenth Dynasty had little or no immediate effect on the condition of Egypt and its dependencies. Sekhemre Khutowy Ammenemes Sobkhotpe, the first pharaoh of the new dynasty, may, indeed, have been a legitimate heir to the throne, related by blood or marriage to the rulers whom he succeeded.[3] During the first four years of his brief reign the height of the annual Nile flood was duly recorded at the Second Cataract,[4] census-lists were drawn up at El-Lāhūn, as under the last kings of the Twelfth Dynasty,[5] and additions were made to the temples at Deir el-Bahri and El-Madāmūd.[6] The next king, Sekhemkare Ammenemes Senbuef, is named on monuments from both Upper and Lower Egypt;[7] and, although under him the Nile-marks at Semna come to an abrupt end, it would appear that a peaceful control over Lower Nubia and the region of the Second Cataract continued to be maintained throughout the greater part of the dynasty.[8] In Asia, also, Egyptian influence was still strong, and on a cylinder seal of Sekhemkare's second successor, King Sehetepibre II, the prince of Byblos, Yakin-ilum, acknowledges himself to be the servant of the king of Egypt.[9] Sankhibre Ameny Inyotef Ammenemes, the sixth ruler listed for the dynasty in the Turin Canon (VI, 10), is

Djedhetepre Dudimose (*ibid.* 317 [33]), Sekhemre Wadjkhau Sobkemsaf (§II, 15, 113, 145), Sekhemre Sankhtowy Neferhotep (§II, 38, 219–20; Stela Cairo 20799 [J. 59635], unpublished, etc.). See G, 21, 158.

[1] G, 15, vol. II, 35, 41, 50, 52–5, 59, 74, 133–4; vol. V, 143–9, 169–70.

[2] §I, 10, 33–8.

[3] G, 13, sect. 299; G, 20, 48–9; G, 3, 283, 313, 322–3; G, 7, 26. Cf. A, 2.

[4] G, 15, vol. VII, 150, 156; §II, 12, 130–1, pl. 93 B (R.I.S. 2 and 3). See also §II, 31, 36, 53.

[5] G, 7, 25–9, pls. 10, 11.

[6] §II, 25, vol. II, 11, pl. 10 B; §II, 37, 147–56; G, 26, 9–10; G, 15, vol. V, 143, 145–6; G, 3, 313 (1); §II, 10, 7 ff., pls. 5 ff.

[7] G, 3, 313 (2); §II, 39, 188–90.

[8] G, 18, 118 ff.; §II, 31, 26–9.

[9] §II, 1, 11 n. 15; G, 8, part 1, 342, fig. 226.

perhaps to be identified with 'King Ameny, the Asiatic', the remains of whose small pyramid were uncovered at Dahshūr in the spring of 1957.[1] A place early in the list of Queen Sobkneferu's successors must be reserved for King Hetepibre Sihornedjheryotef, also called 'the Asiatic',[2] a statue and scarab of whom, found, respectively, near Khatā'na in the eastern Delta and at Jericho in Palestine, indicate that his domain was by no means confined to the neighbourhood of Asyūt, as was once believed.[3] As the eleventh king in the succession the Turin Canon lists a second Sobkhotpe, the son of a commoner named Nen(?)-...,[4] and, after him, an obscure ruler, Renseneb, who reigned for only four months and whose name is followed by a heading, probably only because it happened to fall at the beginning of a page or column in the Canon's source document, not because he was the first of a new 'group' of kings.[5]

Inscribed monuments from Tanis, El-Madāmūd, and Elephantine tend to show that Renseneb's four successors, Awibre Hor,[6] Sedjefakare Kay Ammenemes, Khutowyre Ugaf, and Seneferibre Sesostris (IV), followed one another in that order.[7] Khutowyre (or Re Khutowy), confused by the compiler of the Turin Canon with Sekhemre Khutowy, the first king of the dynasty, thus takes his proper place as the fifteenth ruler in the succession.[8] A statue of this pharaoh, found at Semna, suggests that under him the Egyptians were still maintaining their border defences at the Second Cataract.[9]

Userkare, with the un-Egyptian personal name, Khendjer, built for himself at South Saqqara a small brick pyramid, cased with limestone and provided below ground with a complicated system of stairways and passages leading to a quartzite burial chamber.[10] Nearby is a larger royal pyramid of the same type and obviously of the same period, but unfortunately without any indication of the name of its owner; and at Mazghūna are two other unidentified pyramids so like those of Khendjer and his companion

---

[1] §II, 21, 81–2; §II, 40. See *Orientalia*, 37 (1968), 325–38.

[2] Or 'the Asiatic's son', Hornedjheryotef.

[3] §I, 8, 458–61, 470. Cf. §II, 39, 194; G, 3, 288, 317 (31).

[4] See G, 5, pl. 3, col. 15 (p. 16).

[5] G, 9, 83–4. Cf. G, 13, sects. 299–301.

[6] Turin Canon VI, 17. §II, 24, 88–106, pls. 33–8. See Plate 70.

[7] §I, 10, 34 n. 19; G, 3, 284–5, 314 (6–8), 322–3. See also Turin Canon VI, 17–19.

[8] G, 3, 322–3; G, 20, 49, 52. Cf. A, 2.

[9] G, 18, 119.

[10] §I, 11.

that they must be assigned to the same general time.[1] Userkare Khendjer was probably also the owner of a much-discussed stela in the Louvre, on which his usual praenomen appears to have been replaced by that of his famous predecessor, King Nymare (Ammenemes III) of the Twelfth Dynasty.[2] This and a companion stela refer to restorations and other work carried out in the Twelfth Dynasty temple at Abydos by the phyle-leader, Amenyseneb, in one case under the direction of the Vizier Ankhu.[3] After a reign of probably not more than four years Khendjer was succeeded by a general of the army, who adopted the throne-name, Semenkhkare, and who is known chiefly from two colossal statues found at Tanis in the north-east Delta.[4]

The high point of the dynasty was reached during the reigns of Sobkemsaf I, Sobkhotpe III, and the brothers, Neferhotep and Sobkhotpe IV.

King Sekhemre Wadjkhau Sobkemsaf I is apparently not listed among the kings of the Thirteenth Dynasty in the Turin Canon;[5] but a number of architectural elements bearing his name, found at El-Madāmūd, associate him with Sekhemre Sewadjtowy Sobkhotpe III and tend to identify him as the latter's predecessor.[6] He is known from inscriptions in the quarries of the Wādi Hammāmāt, one dated to Year 7 of his reign,[7] from a graffito in the Shatt er-Rigāl, at the beginning of a caravan route to Nubia,[8] and from various monuments discovered at Abydos, Thebes, Karnak, Tōd, and Elephantine.[9] A papyrus in the Brooklyn Museum preserves, among other texts, two royal decrees addressed to the Vizier Ankhu and dated to Years [5?] and 6 of a reign which appears to have been his.[10] To his reign, also, is probably to be assigned the shorter of the

[1] See above, p. 43, nn. 4, 5.

[2] §ɪɪ, 5, 265–6. Cf. G, 3, 314 (11, 12), 325–8.

[3] §ɪɪ, 5, 263 n. 5, 265; G, 3, 314 (12).

[4] Turin Canon vɪ, 21. G, 3, 314 (13).

[5] For a partial list of similar omissions see above, p. 44 n. 6.

[6] G, 15, vol. v, 146 (also 144–5, 148); vol. vɪɪ, 332–3. See especially §ɪɪ, 37, 170 and nn. 1, 2. See also §ɪɪ, 10, 3–9; §ɪɪ, 39, 189. Formerly assigned by Winlock (§ɪɪ, 41, 268–9, 272) to the Seventeenth Dynasty, Sekhemre Wadjkhau was subsequently conceded by the same author (G, 27, viii, 132–3, 135–7) to have belonged to the Thirteenth Dynasty and to have been buried, not at Thebes (where there is no record of his ever having had a tomb), but in northern Egypt. Among those who adhere to Winlock's earlier view are Stock (G, 20, 57–8, 76–9), Drioton-Vandier (G, 3, 328–9), and Beckerath (§ɪɪ, 5, 266 n. 29).

[7] G, 15, vol. vɪɪ, 332–3.

[8] G, 27, 72, 132–3, pl. 38 ғ; G, 15, vol. v, 207 (no. 385).

[9] G, 15, vol. ɪɪ, 52, 133; vol. v, 46–7; §ɪɪ, 39, 189–90; §ɪɪ, 36, 76, pl. 7 (2, 5).

[10] §ɪɪ, 15, 71–85, 145–6.

two documents known as Papyrus Bulaq 18, a fragmentary account-papyrus dated to 'Regnal Year 5' and containing mention of a storehouse of the Vizier Ankhu.[1] A canopic chest, found at Thebes and at present in Leiden, is now believed to have belonged, not to this king, but to Sekhemre Shedtowy Sobkemsaf II of the Seventeenth Dynasty.[2]

Like many of his predecessors and successors, Sobkhotpe III made no attempt to conceal his humble birth, and the names of his untitled parents, Mentuhotpe and Yauheyebu are found with some frequency on his monuments.[3] These are both numerous and widely distributed.[4] At El-Madāmūd he re-inscribed a colonnade and several doorways in the temple of Mont[5] and at El-Lisht, near the Residence city of Itj-towy, he contributed offerings to the pyramid-temple of King Sesostris I of the Twelfth Dynasty.[6] His name occurs at El-Kāb both in the temple[7] and in the tomb of Sobknakhte, a provincial official, whose titles are reminiscent of those of the nomarchs of the earlier Middle Kingdom and whose autobiographical inscriptions suggest a local attempt to revive the past glories of the feudal nobility.[8] Members of the king's extensive family, including two of his wives, appear on three Upper Egyptian stelae and a sandstone altar from the island of Siheil, in the First Cataract.[9]

The longer manuscript of Papyrus Bulaq 18, a journal itemizing the revenues and expenses of the pharaonic court during a month's sojourn at Thebes, is probably to be assigned to the reign of Sobkhotpe III.[10] This document not only lists the numerous beneficiaries of the king's bounty—members of the royal family, high government officials (including, notably, the great vizier, Ankhu), and minor functionaries of the court—but also names three departments (*warut*) of the administration which, besides their other functions, handled various classes of royal revenue: 'the *waret* of

[1] *Op. cit.* 73, 145–6, footnotes 279, 505.
[2] G, 27, 139–40, pl. 20; §II, 41, 268.
[3] G, 24, 411–12, 416–17, 838; §II, 23, 20–8.
[4] G, 6, vol. II, 19–22; G, 3, 315 (16); G, 14, 234–5.
[5] G, 15, vol. V, 146–9; §II, 37, 163–71; §II, 10, 3–9, pls. 5 ff.
[6] §I, 10, 34 n. 20. [7] §II, 38, 218f.; §II, 8, 22–3, 87, pls. 30–2.
[8] §II, 35 (see especially pls. 7, 8). [9] §II, 23, 20–8.
[10] §I, 10, 38–9; §II, 15, 145–6. Cf. Beckerath (§II, 5, 266–8), who rightly points out that the members of the king's family listed in Pap. Bulaq 18 differ from those named on the extant monuments of Sobkhotpe III; but whose reading of the king's name in the papyrus as 'Amun[emḫē't]'-Sobkhotpe is almost certainly incorrect (see G, 3, 327) and whose creation of a second and earlier vizier, also named Ankhu, seems unjustified (see A, 2).

the Head of the South', 'the Treasury', and 'the Office of the Provider-of-People', or Labour Bureau.[1] Studied in conjunction with the El-Lāhūn papyri and other documents of the same general period, it is a most valuable source of information on the elaborate administrative organization of Egypt during the late Middle Kingdom.[2]

Among these other documents is a fragmentary papyrus in the Brooklyn Museum, the verso of which carries a long list of servants, dated to Sobkhotpe III's first and second regnal years and including forty-five Asiatic men, women, and children attached to the household of a single Upper Egyptian official.[3] If, as seems likely, similar groups of these outlanders were to be found in well-to-do households throughout the whole of Egypt, the Asiatic inhabitants of the country at this period must have been many times more numerous than has generally been supposed. Whether or not this largely slave population could have played a part in hastening, or in paving the way for, the impending Hyksos domination is difficult to say; but through intermarriage and the like it presumably would have had the effect of lessening appreciably the resistance of Egypt's population as a whole to an Asiatic overlordship.[4]

A careful estimate places the eleven-year reign of King Khasekhemre Neferhotep I at about 1740–1730 B.C.[5] The date is important, for a fragmentary relief found at Byblos shows that at this time the sovereignty of the Egyptian king was still acknowledged in Syria and makes it reasonably certain that the whole of the Delta, except for the district of Xoïs,[6] was still under his control. The relief apparently represented King Neferhotep I and, seated before him, his vassal, the Byblite Prince Yantin, tentatively identified as a son of that Yakin-ilum who governed Byblos in the days of Neferhotep's predecessor, King Sehetepibre II.[7] Southwards the king's authority extended at least to the First Cataract, as is indicated by a statue in the sanctuary of Hekayeb at Elephantine[8] and by graffiti on the island of Konosso and elsewhere in

---

[1] §II, 33, 51–68. See also §I, 10, 36 n. 33.

[2] G, 3, 302–8, 321–2; §II, 15, 134–44.

[3] §II, 15, 87–109, 133–4, 148–9; §II, 2; §II, 28.

[4] §II, 15, 149.

[5] Figuring from the end of the Twelfth Dynasty in 1786 B.C., but taking into consideration the reigns of such unlisted kings as Sesostris IV and Sobkemsaf I, we arrive at the same dating for Neferhotep I as that obtained by Albright in 1945 (§II, 1, 16–17).

[6] See below, pp. 53–4.   [7] G, 15, vol. VII, 389. See §II, 1, 11 ff.

[8] §II, 39, 189.

the neighbourhood of Aswān.[1] Two of these rock inscriptions record the names of the king's wife, Senebsen,[2] and four of the royal children. One of Neferhotep's most interesting monuments is a great sandstone stela which he caused to be set up at Abydos.[3] Here it is told how the pharaoh, seeking guidance for his projected works in the temple of Osiris, consulted the ancient writings in the library of the temple of Atum at Heliopolis before despatching an agent upstream to Abydos to carry out the work. Funerary figures of the king's son, Wahneferhotep, and a court official, named Bener, were found near the pyramid of Sesostris I at El-Lisht,[4] and it is highly probable that the king himself and the rest of his court were buried not far away.

Haankhef and Kemi, the parents of Neferhotep I, are also claimed as father and mother by Khaneferre Sobkhotpe IV, who, following the brief reign of a King Sihathor, occupied the throne, which his brother had recently vacated, for at least eight years.[5] It may have been during a later period—perhaps the Twenty-fifth Dynasty—that a statue of this pharaoh was transported to the island of Argo, above the Third Cataract.[6] Similarly, three other statues of Sobkhotpe IV, found at Tanis (modern Sān el-Hagar) in the north-eastern Delta,[7] appear to have been carried thither from Memphis or Avaris—Pi-Ramesse—in the Twenty-first or Twenty-second Dynasty, and a fourth may have been brought from Tōd or Asfūn el-Matā'na in southern Upper Egypt.[8] We know, in any event, that within a very few years after the accession of this king the ancient town of Avaris, twelve miles south of Tanis, was in the hands of the Hyksos,[9] and we must suppose that even during his reign Egyptian authority in the Delta was being gradually overshadowed by that of the Asiatic intruders. The existence of a king of the Fourteenth Dynasty at Xoïs,[10] and perhaps also of a Hyksos prince at Avaris, lends colour to the statement of Artapanus (first century B.C.) that King 'Chenefres'

---

[1] G, 15, vol. v, 246, 250, 254.

[2] Often confused with a later Queen Senebsen of the Seventeenth Dynasty, mentioned in the tomb of Rensenep (no. 9) at El-Kāb (G, 15, vol. v, 184). See G, 3, 329; G, 20, 57.

[3] G, 3, 315 (17); G, 15, vol. v, 44.

[4] G, 8, part 1, 349–50; §11, 22, 22.

[5] §11, 3, 32–3, pls. 16 (2), 17 (2). See also G, 6, vol. 11, 31–8; G, 3, 315 (18); §11, 11, 81–2.

[6] G, 3, 286–7; §11, 6, 41 ff., fig. 26; §11, 29, 363 n. 4.

[7] G, 3, 315 (18, 1); §11, 18, 160, 167.

[8] G, 15, vol. v, 167; §11, 18, 160, 167. See §1, 8, 558–9; G, 8, part 1, 339.

[9] See below, sect. III.   [10] See below, pp. 53–4.

(= Khaneferre?) was 'ruler of the regions above Memphis, for there were at that time several kings in Egypt'.[1] A great stela set up by Sobkhotpe IV at Karnak lets it be known that the pharaoh, though an infrequent visitor to Thebes, was a native of that city, and tells of his additions and donations to the temple of Amun, including four steers supplied, respectively, by the Department (*waret*) of the Head of the South, the Office of the Vizier, the Treasury, and the Office of the Provider-of-People.[2] The Vizier Iymeru, son of Iymeru, who held office in this reign, was probably a member of the extensive and powerful family of the great Vizier Ankhu, mentioned with such frequency in the preceding paragraphs.[3]

The monuments of Khaankhre Sobkhotpe V include several scarabs on which his praenomen and that of Sobkhotpe IV seem to be written together in the same cartouche.[4] The names of Sobkhotpe V, Mersekhemre Neferhotep II,[5] and, possibly, Sekhemre Sankhtowy Neferhotep III[6] may have occupied the three lines which appear to be missing at the bottom of column VI of the Turin Canon.[7] The last of these three kings is said on a stela from Karnak to have been 'one who entered' and nourished Thebes 'when it had fallen into need', 'one who lifted up his city when it was sinking and protected it and foreign peoples, one who [un]ited(?) for it foreign lands which had rebelled' and 'one who overthrew the enemies who had rebelled against him, inflicting slaughter on those who had attacked [him]'. In the same text the pharaoh is spoken of as being 'adorned with the *khepresh*-helmet', or Blue Crown, in what is apparently the earliest mention of this crown in existing Egyptian records.[8]

After Khahetepre Sobkhotpe VI[9] at the top of column VII the Turin Canon lists a King Wahibre Yayebi, who was perhaps identical with the Vizier Yayebi, named on a stela from western Thebes and on a statuette now in Bologna.[10] His relatively long

---

[1] G, 23, 73 n. 3.

[2] Stela Cairo J. 51911, unpublished, but referred to in §II, 9, 149; §II, 17, 87, 89; §II, 27, 8–9; §I, 10, 37; §II, 15, 54–6, 134; G, 3, 306–7, 322.

[3] §II, 29; §I, 10, 39; §II, 15, 73; §II, 5, 263 ff.

[4] G, 24, 848, 850. See G, 3, 287, 316, 630; G, 21, 162; G, 13, sect. 300A (13).

[5] G, 3, 288, 316 (21).   [6] §II, 38, 218–20; §II, 7, 625.

[7] G, 5, pl. 3 (cf. cols. VII and IX).

[8] Stela Cairo 20799 (J. 59635). See §II, 38. I am grateful to J. J. Clère for an annotated hand-copy of the text of this unpublished stela. On the Blue Crown see §II, 34. Naville's 'XIth Dynasty' relief from Deir el-Bahri with a king wearing the Blue Crown (§II, 25, vol. II, pl. I I E) is actually a fragmentary votive stela of the New Kingdom.

[9] G, 3, 287, 316 (20).   [10] G, 8, part I, 345, fig. 227; §II, 26, 130 n. 3.

reign of almost eleven years appears to have produced few monuments, and he is known to us chiefly from the stela of a Theban
official, named Sihathor, the small fragments of a faience bowl,
found at El-Lāhūn, and a number of seals.[1]

The principal existing monument of King Merneferre Iy,[2]
who came to the throne about 1700 B.C., is the diorite capstone of
his pyramid, found, with a second, uninscribed pyramidion, on or
near the site of Avaris in the eastern Delta.[3] This ruler would thus
appear to have been not only a native and perhaps a resident of
Avaris, but also a vassal of the Hyksos, whose occupation of the
town in about 1720 B.C. seems reasonably well established.[4]
Faced with the growing power of the Asiatics in Lower Egypt,
the dynasty now began more and more clearly to show its lack
of stability and other basic weaknesses, and the decline, which
heretofore had been slow and irregular, was greatly accelerated.
Although King Iy himself ruled for nearly twenty-four years[5]—
the longest recorded reign of the whole dynasty—few of his
successors have left monuments of a historical nature and most of
them exist for us only as names in later kings' lists. An interesting
exception is Merhetepre Ini (Turin Canon VII, 4), who is shown
by the so-called Juridical Stela of Karnak to have had as his
contemporary the grandfather of a subject of the pharaoh
Nebiryerawet I of the Seventeenth Dynasty.[6]

King Djedneferre Dudimose, part of whose name may be preserved in column VII of the Turin Canon, ten places after that of
Merhetepre, has been plausibly identified by a number of modern
scholars with the King 'Tutimaios', in whose reign, according to
Manetho, Egypt was subdued by the Hyksos.[7] Since the accession
of Dudimose cannot be placed before 1674 B.C. and we have seen
that the Hyksos were firmly established in the eastern Delta as
early as 1720 B.C., it is probable that the event which Manetho
had in mind was the occupation of Memphis (and the Residence
city of Itj-towy) by the Hyksos King Salitis, the founder of the
Fifteenth Dynasty.[8]

With the ancient capital in the hands of the Asiatics, the Middle
Kingdom fell to pieces. The last score or so of kings assigned to
the Thirteenth Dynasty[9] were clearly only local rulers—Lower
Egyptian vassals of the Hyksos or Upper Egyptian dynasts,

[1] G, 3, 316 (23).
[2] Ibid. 316 (24).
[3] §I, 8, 471–9, 558.
[4] See below, sect. IV.
[5] G, 5, 16, pl. 3 (col. VII, 3).
[6] §II, 20, 35 ff.; §II, 19, 893 ff.
[7] §II, 1, 15 n. 44; G, 20, 63; G, 27, 96; §II, 32, 62.
[8] See below, sect. III.
[9] Turin Canon VII, 14—VIII, 3.

reigning at the most over a few nomes and frequently over no more than a single town. Djedneferre Dudimose himself is known to us only from monuments found in the nome of Thebes, at Deir el-Bahri and Gebelein.[1] The titulary of his successor, Djedhetepre Dudimose II, occurs on a stela from Edfu.[2] One or the other of these two kings is named on another stela from Edfu, in a rock inscription at El-Kāb, and, perhaps, on a piece of an alabaster bowl from Kerma.[3] Like those of Dudimose I, the known monuments of King Sewahenre Senebmiu of the Karnak List and of King Djedankhre Mentuemsaf are limited to Deir el-Bahri and Gebelein in the Theban nome.[4] The king's son, Nehsy ('the Nubian'), on the other hand, seems to have resided at Avaris, the Hyksos capital, where, like his Asiatic overlords, he contributed monuments to the temple of the god Seth.[5] With the now meaningless title, 'King of Upper and Lower Egypt', he appears in the Turin Canon as one of the last rulers listed there for the Thirteenth Dynasty.[6] To this period may belong also an Upper Egyptian king, named Menkhaure Senaayeb, whose authority was apparently confined to the nome of This,[7] and a King Meryankhre Mentuhotpe, the owner of a headless figure from Karnak and a green schist statuette in the British Museum.[8]

Following the fall of Memphis in 1674 B.C., Thebes evidently became the principal rallying-point of the native rulers who, in the shadow of a foreign overlordship, attempted to carry on the traditions of the Middle Kingdom; it was here in about 1650 B.C. that the founders of a new native dynasty—the Seventeenth—arose to keep alive the embers of Egyptian independence and to prepare the way for their warlike successors, under whom the Hyksos were eventually defeated and driven from the country.[9] Technically, the Thirteenth Dynasty of Manetho and of the Turin Canon continued to exist until 1633 B.C.—probably in the persons of various Upper Egyptian princes, allied with or subordinate to the Seventeenth Dynasty of Thebes.

Throughout the regime of the Thirteenth Dynasty and for some thirty years after its fall the district of Xoïs in the swamplands of

---

[1] G, 3, 317 (32); G, 27, 94–5 ('The base of an alabaster statue' from Kerma, referred to there, evidently never existed).

[2] §II, 4; G, 27, 94–5; G, 3, 317 (33).

[3] §II, 14, 189–90; G, 26, 27–8; §II, 30, parts 1–3, 101, 391; parts 4–5, 517, 554; G, 18, 111; §II, 32, 62.

[4] G, 3, 316 (28), 317 (29).

[5] Op. cit. 288, 317 (34); §II, 18, 157.

[6] G, 5, pl. 3 (col. VIII, 1).

[7] G, 3, 317 (30, 'Seshib').

[8] §II, 13. See Plate 71(a).

[9] See below, sect. v.

the western Delta maintained at least a nominal independence and was ruled by a long line of local kings, or governors, known to us, through Manetho, as the Fourteenth Dynasty. In the fragments of Manetho's history preserved in Africanus and in one of the versions of Eusebius the dynasty is assigned seventy-six kings and a duration of 184 years.[1] Assuming Xoïs to have seceded from the rest of Egypt with the break-up of the Twelfth Dynasty in 1786 B.C., this would carry the independent government of the redoubtable little state through to 1603 B.C., three-quarters of a century after the greater part of the country had fallen prey to the Asiatic intruders and less than thirty years before the rise of the New Kingdom. Although scarcely any monuments of the rulers of the Fourteenth Dynasty are known, many of their names are preserved in columns VIII–X of the Turin Canon, and the total number of seventy-two kings indicated there agrees well with that derived by Manetho from evidently dependable historical sources. The fall of the dynasty is heralded, perhaps, by the appearance of the Asiatic (?) ruler Bebnem, or Beblem, at the end of column IX of the Turin Canon.[2]

III. THE HYKSOS INFILTRATION AND THE FOUNDING OF THE FIFTEENTH DYNASTY

It is now generally recognized that the Hyksos domination of Egypt was not the outcome of a sudden invasion of the country by the armies of a single Asiatic nation. It would seem, rather, to have resulted from the infiltration into the Delta during the declining years of the Middle Kingdom of groups of several different western Asiatic peoples, chiefly Semites, forced southward, perhaps, by widespread disturbances in the lands to the north and east of Egypt.[3] To the Egyptians the intruders appeared to be the same Asiatic folk ('Amu', 'Setjetiu', 'Mentjiu [of] Setjet', men of 'Retenu') as those who from time immemorial had harassed the north-east border and already, during the First Intermediate Period, had overrun the Delta.[4] Their tribal leaders, or sheikhs, were called *Hikau-khoswet*, 'Princes of the Desert

---

[1] G, 23, 74–5 (fr. 41); G, 27, 95–6.

[2] G, 5, pl. 3 (IX, 30); §II, 32, 55; G, 20, 64 f. According to Gardiner (A, 5, 442) the name of the preceding ruler is now to be read Nebennati.

[3] §II, 32, 54 ff.; §III, 21, 120; §III, 4.

[4] §III, 12, 8; §III, 6, 98–9, 102–5; §III, 7, 47–8, pl. 6 (col. 37); §III, 14, 14–33 *passim*; §III, 8, 45–6; §III, 9, 198 ff., pl. 1, lines 4, 11, 16. See also §III, 12, 7; §III, 22, 84–6.

Uplands', or 'Rulers of Foreign Countries', from which was probably derived the Manethonian term, 'Hyksos', now commonly used to describe the peoples as a whole.[1] The title had been applied by the Egyptians to the chieftains of Nubia as far back as the late Old Kingdom[2] and to the bedawin princes of Syria and Palestine at least as early as the first half of the Twelfth Dynasty; it occurs, for example, in the Story of Sinuhe and in a well-known scene, showing a group of Amu, in the tomb of the Nomarch Khnumhotpe at Beni Hasan.[3]

That the Hyksos rise to power met with some resistance on the part of the Egyptians goes without saying and in the course of the resulting conflict it was inevitable that towns should be burned, temples damaged, and segments of the native population subjected to hardships and cruelties.[4] Once the foreigners were in control they undoubtedly ruled the country with a firm hand, imposing heavy taxes upon the people of the occupied areas and collecting tribute from the vassal kingdoms to the south. Their administration, in which Egyptian officials apparently participated, seems, however, not to have been unduly harsh or oppressive and was probably accepted with complacency and even actively supported by many of their subjects.[5] However we may evaluate them, they were evidently not the ruthless barbarians conjured up by the Theban propagandists of the early New Kingdom and the Egyptian writers of later periods.[6] The Hyksos kings of the Fifteenth Dynasty sponsored the construction of temple buildings and the production of statues, reliefs, scarabs, and other works of art and craftsmanship; and, curiously enough, some of our best surviving copies of famous Egyptian literary and technical works date from the time of these kings.[7]

On the other hand, with the well-founded doubts which now exist regarding their association with the so-called 'Hyksos forts' the Tell el-Yahūdīya pottery, and other products formerly attributed to them,[8] there seems to be little ground left to support the view that they possessed a distinctive culture of their own. In Egypt they borrowed extensively from the ancient civilization in the midst of which they found themselves. Their rulers wrote their

[1] §II, 32, 56; §III, 12, 7.   [2] §III, 23, 109, 134.
[3] Sinuhe B.98, 176; G, 15, vol. IV, 145–6; §II, 32, 56 n. 3.
[4] G, 23, 78–9 (fr. 42); §III, 7, 47–8, pl. 6 (cols. 36–8); §III, 22, 84; §III, 12, 8, 34 ff.
[5] §II, 32, 65, 70; §III, 20, 56.   [6] See above, n. 4.
[7] See, for example, §III, 13, 17 ff.
[8] §III, 19, 88–90; §II, 32, 56–61; §III, 17, 107–11.

names in Egyptian hieroglyphs, adopted the traditional titles of the
kings of Egypt, used throne names compounded in the Egyptian
manner, and sometimes even assumed Egyptian personal names.[1]
Their admiration for Egyptian art is attested by the number of
statues, reliefs, and minor works which they either usurped or had
copied—probably by Egyptian craftsmen—from good Middle
Kingdom originals; and their production of that peculiarly
Egyptian type of seal-amulet, the scarab, was nothing short of
prodigious.

Like the native rulers, the Hyksos princes instituted an official
religion, modelled on that of the Egyptians, and adopted as their
state god an Egyptian divinity who happened to be especially
revered in the region where they established their first base of
operations. This was Seth of Avaris, originally an Upper Egyptian
god, whose cult seems to have been transplanted to the Sethroïte
nome in the north-east Delta sometime before the beginning of
the Fourth Dynasty.[2] It is not improbable that the Hyksos recognized in Seth of Avaris the counterpart of one of their Asiatic
deities, and his appearance, as preserved for us on one of their
scarabs,[3] is distinctly Asiatic in character; but his identification
with the Semitic Baal or Resheph or with the Hittite Teshub was a
subsequent development, resulting from, rather than leading to,
his appropriation by the Hyksos.[4] A nude female figure which
also appears on scarabs of the Hyksos Period has been thought
to represent the goddess Anat or Attar-Astarte, referred to in
later texts as the consort of Seth-Baal.[5] Contrary to a New Kingdom tradition,[6] other Egyptian divinities besides Seth seem to
have been accepted by the intruders, notably the sun god Re,
whom they honoured in their throne names.

For the Egyptians, in return, the Hyksos did two things. They
rid them once and for all of the old feeling of self-sufficiency and
false security, born of a misplaced confidence in Egypt's unassail-
able superiority over, and aloofness from, the other nations of the
world; and, because they themselves were Asiatics with a kingdom
which appears to have embraced northern Sinai and much of
Palestine, they brought Egypt into more intimate and continuous
contact with the peoples and cultures of western Asia than ever
before in her history. Over the bridge established by the Hyksos

---

[1] Three Hyksos rulers, for example, adopted the common Middle Kingdom
personal name, Apopy (Apophis).
[2] §III, 10, 77–84; §II, 32, 64; §III, 25, 149. Cf. §III, 11, 364.
[3] §II, 32, 64.   [4] §III, 25, 149. Cf. §III, 11, 23–4, 364.
[5] §II, 32, 64 nn. 6, 7.   [6] *Op. cit.* 64 n. 8.

and maintained by the pharaohs of the New Kingdom there flowed into the Nile Valley in unprecedented quantity new blood strains, new religious and philosophical concepts, and new artistic styles and media, as well as epoch-making innovations of a more practical nature. Though the horse and, probably, the horse-drawn chariot may indeed have been known in the valley of the Nile, as in Mesopotamia, before the time of the Hyksos,[1] our earliest references to their use in warfare are found in a text of the Theban king Kamose, late in the history of the Hyksos occupation.[2] Through their Hyksos adversaries the Egyptians probably first became acquainted with the composite bow, bronze daggers and swords of improved types, and other advances in the equipment and technique of war, as well as with some of the important western Asiatic innovations in the arts of peace which we encounter in Egypt for the first time under the Eighteenth Dynasty.[3] Represented as an unmitigated disaster by native historians of later times, the Hyksos domination appears actually to have provided the Egyptians with both the incentive and the means towards 'world' expansion and so laid the foundations and, to a great extent, determined the character of the New Kingdom, or, as it is often called, 'the Empire'.

In Egypt we can recognize two principal stages in the Hyksos rise to power, the first of which had its origin in the north-eastern Delta during the last quarter of the eighteenth century B.C. This was the time of the Asiatic occupation of the town of Hatwaret, or Avaris, and the elevation of its local divinity, Seth, to the status of chief god of the newly established principality, a move probably accompanied by an extensive rebuilding of the temple of the god. By great good fortune the 400th anniversary of this event, apparently celebrated about 1320 B.C. in the reign of the Eighteenth Dynasty pharaoh, Horemheb, is commemorated on a granite stela erected on the site of Avaris by King Ramesses II of the Nineteenth Dynasty.[4] From this monument, generally known as 'the Stela of Year 400', we gather that the 'accession' of 'King Seth Apehty, the Ombite'—evidently the god Seth himself— took place at Avaris around 1720 B.C., and we may infer that the installation there of his Hyksos worshippers occurred at the same time.

There followed a period of consolidation and expansion of the Hyksos power in Lower Egypt under a series of Asiatic princes, whose names are for the most part unknown to us. One of the

---

[1] §III, 3, 249–51. [2] §II, 32, 59; §III, 20, 56, 58.
[3] G, 27, 150–70. See, however, §III, 19, 88–90; §II, 32, 60–1; §III, 20, 58.
[4] G, 15, vol. IV, 23.

first of these chieftains, however, may have been the King Aqen, whose name—meaning 'The-Donkey(-God)-is-strong'—appears in the Berlin genealogy of Memphite priests early in the interval between the Middle and New Kingdoms.[1] To the latter part of this phase may perhaps be assigned such early Hyksos princes as Anather and Semqen,[2] listed in our chronological table as the founders of the Manethonian 'Sixteenth Dynasty'.

In 1674 B.C. began the succession of six important Hyksos rulers, whom Manetho calls the Fifteenth Dynasty[3] and who, according to the Turin Canon (column x, 15–21[4]), reigned for a total of 108 years.[5] Since this would bring us down to 1567 B.C., when the last Hyksos was driven from Egypt by the founder of the New Kingdom, it is probable that the numerous other Hyksos 'kings' of the same period were merely chiefs of the many different Asiatic tribes banded together under the leadership of the Great Hyksos. In this category would fall the seventy-five 'shepherd kings' assigned by Africanus to the Sixteenth and Seventeenth Dynasties,[6] the eight foreign (?) names listed at the end of column x of the Turin Canon[7] (= the Sixteenth Dynasty ?), and the quantity of unplaced Hyksos rulers mentioned on scarabs and other small monuments.

Since our present information on the first two kings of the Fifteenth Dynasty is drawn chiefly from a portion of Manetho's history, cited by Josephus in his *Contra Apionem*, we can do no better than to quote from a standard translation of this work.[8] After describing the ease with which the Hyksos gained their initial control of Egypt and the barbarities which they subsequently committed against its cities and their inhabitants, the account goes on to say: 'Finally, they appointed as king one of their number whose name was Salitis. He had his seat at Memphis, levying tribute from Upper and Lower Egypt, and always leaving garrisons behind in the most advantageous positions. Above all, he fortified the district to the east, foreseeing that the Assyrians,[9]

[1] §III, 2, 106, pl. 2 (3, 12); §III, 12, 12, 25. See also §III, 1, 171–2.

[2] G, 24, 473 n. 2, 492, 534 n. 3, 729–30, 825; G, 20, 64.

[3] See G, 9, 36–8.

[4] =G, 5, pl. 3, col. x, 14–21. In Gardiner's plate the three small fragments below fr. 152 evidently need to be moved down one line. See §III, 5, 56, pl. 10.

[5] The figure '108' read by Farina in his publication of the Turin Canon (§III, 5, 56), has been questioned by Parker (§III, 16). See, however, G, 5, 17 [x, 21]; §II, 1, 17 and n. 49.

[6] G, 23, 92–5; G, 9, 38.　　[7] G, 5, pl. 3, col. x, 22–29.　　[8] G, 23, 78–83.

[9] Manetho's anachronistic term for some warlike people of western Asia, whose real name is unknown to us.

as they grew stronger, would one day covet and attack his kingdom. In the Saïte [Sethroïte] nome he found a city very favourably situated on the east of the Bubastite branch of the Nile and
called Auaris after an ancient religious tradition. This place he
rebuilt and fortified with massive walls, planting there a garrison
of as many as 240,000 heavy-armed men to guard his frontier.
Here he would come in summertime, partly to serve out rations
and pay his troops, partly to train them carefully in manœuvres
and so strike terror into foreign tribes. After reigning for 19
years, Salitis died; and a second king, named Bnôn, succeeded
and reigned for 44 years.'

In the Manethonian 'Salitis' we may probably recognize the
King Sharek, or Shalek, who in the genealogical table of Memphite
priests is placed one generation before the well-known Hyksos
pharaoh, Apophis (I), and two generations before Nebpehtyre
(Amosis), the founder of the Eighteenth Dynasty.[1] It is not
unlikely that he is also to be equated with a King Mayebre Sheshi,
whose seals and seal impressions, of early Hyksos types, are both
numerous and widely distributed, examples of the latter having
been found as far south as the Middle Kingdom trading post at
Kerma, near the Third Cataract of the Nile.[2] This does not necessarily imply that the Hyksos rule had been extended to the
northern Sudan or even to Lower Nubia, where a line of native
princes may already have set up an independent government.[3]
There is, on the other hand, considerable likelihood that, as
Manetho suggests, Salitis, besides occupying the old capital city
of Memphis, overran the whole of Egypt and that his successors,
down to the time of Apophis I, controlled the country as far south
as Gebelein and probably all the way to the First Cataract.[4] In
the Turin Canon (column x, 15[5]) the first Hyksos ruler of the
Fifteenth Dynasty is ascribed a reign of [1]3 (or [2]3 ?) years,
which is at no great variance with the nineteen years assigned to
Salitis by Manetho.

Another early and evidently powerful Hyksos ruler, known to
us chiefly from scarabs, was Meruserre Yak-Baal or Yakeb-Baal,
whose Semitic personal name was transcribed into Egyptian as
'Yakubher'.[6] Like those of Mayebre Sheshi, sealings of Yakub-

---

[1] §III, 2, 99, 106–7, pl. 2 (3, 6); G, 9, 37.
[2] G, 8, part 2, 4–5; §II, 30, parts 4–5, 75–6, fig. 168; §III, 20, 59–61. Cf. G,
20, 43–5, 64–7; §III, 19, 88; §III, 18, 56; §II, 32, 62, 63 n. 1.
[3] §III, 18; §III, 20.   [4] §III, 20, 60–1; §II, 32, 63 n. 1; G, 20, 65.
[5] =G, 5, pl. 3, col. x, 14. See above, p. 58 n. 4.
[6] G, 24, 184–7, 790–1, 858–9; G, 20, 67; §II, 32, 62 (n. 5); see §III, 26.

her have been found at Kerma; and, in general, the two kings seem to have been closely associated in time and in the geographic areas which they controlled. Though it is difficult to equate him with the king whom Manetho calls Bnôn, or Beôn, there is some probability that Yakubher was Mayebre's immediate successor and, as such, the second of the Great Hyksos rulers. If so, he would have occupied the throne of Egypt, according to the Turin Canon, for more than 8 (or 18?) years.

Also associated stylistically and geographically with the scarabs of King Mayebre Sheshi are those of an important Hyksos official, who bore the well-known Semitic name Hur (written in Egyptian, 'Har') and the titles 'Treasurer of the King of Lower Egypt', 'Sole Companion (of the King)', and 'Overseer of the Treasury'. The scarabs of this man—charged, no doubt, with the receipt of taxes and tribute for King Sheshi and for an approximately contemporary Hyksos pharaoh—have been found all the way from the region of Gaza in Palestine to that of Kerma in the Sudan.[1] Another Hyksos Treasurer, whose titles are the same as those of Hur and whose scarabs are almost as numerous, bore the Egyptian name Peryemwah and may have been an Egyptian in the employ of the Asiatic rulers.[2]

IV. THE HYKSOS KHYAN AND HIS SUCCESSORS

King Khyan (or Khayana), the Iannas, or Staan, of the Manethonian lists,[3] was probably the third 'Ruler of Foreign Countries' named in column x of the Turin Canon, where a few illegible traces are all that now remain of the figure which gave the length of his undoubtedly fairly long reign.[4] In contrast with the first two rulers of the Fifteenth Dynasty, he is known to us from monuments widely distributed throughout the Near East: a piece of granite torus moulding from Gebelein in Upper Egypt,[5] a fragmentary granite statue from Bubastis in the Delta,[6] an alabaster jar-lid discovered in the foundations of the palace at Cnossus,[7] a scarab and a seal-impression in Palestine,[8] and a granite lion

[1] G, 20, 68; §II, 32, 65–6.
[2] G, 8, part 2, 8; §III, 15, 153, pl. 23 (24–6); §III, 24, 169 (59), 171 (71), pls. 2, 3; etc.
[3] G, 23, 82–3, 90–1 (frs. 42, 43). Cf. G, 9, 36–7.
[4] Col. x, 17 (=G, 5, pl. 3, col. x, 16). On Khyan in general see G, 3, 293–4, 318 (35); §III, 12, 31–2; G, 13, sects. 304A, 306; §II, 32, 58 n. 3, 62–3.
[5] §IV, 4, 42 (lxxxviii).   [6] G, 15, vol. IV, 29.
[7] G, 15, vol. VII, 405.
[8] A, 6.

built into a wall in Baghdad.[1] Besides assuming the Egyptian throne-name, Seuserenre, and the traditional kingly titles, 'the Good God' and 'the Son of Re', Khyan concocted for himself the Horus name, 'Embracer-of-Regions', suggestive of world-wide domination. Though we cannot conclude from this fact and from the few and, for the most part, insignificant monuments mentioned above that he was the head of a great Near Eastern empire,[2] it would appear that in his day trade relations existed between Egypt, Mesopotamia, and the Mediterranean islands. On the other hand, contact with the trading post at Kerma in the Sudan seems to have been lost[3] and no monuments of Khyan have been found in Nubia, now apparently an independent state governed by an Egyptianized native chieftain named Nedjeh, who was known as the Ruler of Kush and whose entourage included one or more Egyptian officials.[4]

According to the Turin Canon the fourth of the great Hyksos rulers reigned for forty or more years.[5] This is far and away the longest reign of the Fifteenth Dynasty and can be assigned only to King Auserre, the first of the Hyksos sovereigns to adopt the Egyptian personal name, Apophis. The thirty-third regnal year of this king is recorded on the title-page of the Rhind Mathematical Papyrus, a document apparently copied at Thebes from a Middle Kingdom original at a time when the Theban rulers still acknowledged the sovereignty of their Asiatic overlord.[6] Further evidence of the influence of Apophis I in Upper Egypt is a limestone door-lintel, found at Gebelein, which carries his throne-name, twice repeated, on either side of a winged sun's disk.[7] An alabaster vase inscribed for his daughter, Princess Herit, appears to have been handed down at Thebes from one generation to another, until at last it was placed in the tomb of King Amenophis I of the Eighteenth Dynasty.[8] It is possible that this daughter of a Hyksos king was actually married to a contemporary prince of Thebes and was thus an ancestress of the Theban pharaohs of the early New Kingdom.[9] However that may be, the presence of her vase, with its inscription intact, in a Theban royal tomb certainly bears out the evidence of the title page of the Rhind Papyrus and

[1] G, 15, vol. vii, 396.   [2] §ii, 32, 63 n. 2.
[3] No sealings or other objects of Khyan and his Hyksos successors have been found at Kerma.
[4] §iii, 18; §iii, 20, 54; G, 28, 172–3, 175.
[5] Col. x, 18 (=G, 5, pl. 3, col. x, 17).
[6] §iv, 3, 49, ph. 1, pl. 1. See Plate 69.   [7] G, 15, vol. v, 163.
[8] §iv, 2, 152, pl. 31 (1); G, 8, part 2, 7, fig. 2.   [9] G, 27, 147.

indicates clearly that during most of the long reign of Apophis I the Hyksos and Thebans were on good terms with one another and that the memory of the Asiatic rulers was not as hateful to the Egyptians of the early New Kingdom as some of our sources would have us believe.[1] In addition to the Rhind Papyrus, Auserre's patronage of the learned professions is attested by the appearance of his names and titles on a scribe's palette found somewhere in the Faiyūm and at one time in the Berlin Museum.[2] Here, as on his numerous scarabs,[3] he bears the ancient title, 'King of Upper and Lower Egypt', and, in spite of an alleged Hyksos disdain for all Egyptian gods save only Seth,[4] allows himself to be called 'the Son of Re, of his body, whom he loves'.

Towards the end of Apophis's reign the Egyptians, spear-headed, as at other times in their history, by the proud and war-like princes of Thebes, began to stand up against their Asiatic overlords. Echoes of the opening of hostilities are preserved for us at the beginning of a fragmentary New Kingdom legend describing an arrogantly provocative order sent by 'King Apophis' of Avaris to King Seqenenre (II ?) of Thebes and the summoning by the latter of 'his great officers and likewise all the chief soldiers that he had'.[5] In the fighting which evidently ensued Seqenenre may have lost his life,[6] but the Hyksos and their Egyptian allies were driven out of southern Upper Egypt and thrust back as far as Cusae, north of Asyūt.[7] The crushing reverses subsequently suffered by the 'wretched Asiatic', 'Auserre, the Son of Re, Apophis', at the hands of the embattled Thebans are recounted on two great stelae set up in the temple of Amun at Karnak by Seqenenre's son, Kamose, the last ruler of the Seventeenth Dynasty.[8] Before his death Apophis had been routed out of Middle Egypt, had apparently withdrawn his boundary to Atfih near the entrance of the Faiyūm, and the women of his harim had had the frightening experience of seeing a Theban fleet below

[1] §II, 32, 69.   [2] §III, 12, 27.

[3] G, 6, vol. II, 140–1; G, 20, 45–6, 65; G, 8, part 2, 7, figs. 1, 2.

[4] §III, 8, 40, 44–5; §II, 32, 64, 67.

[5] §III, 8, 42.

[6] §II, 41, 249–50; G, 3, 299; §IV, 1, 224. Cf. §III, 8, 43; §II, 32, 67.

[7] Cusae marking the southern boundary of 'the territory of the Asiatics' before the drive initiated by Seqenenre's successor, Kamose (§II, 32, 68–9), but probably not before the dating of the Rhind Papyrus in Apophis I's thirty-third year (cf. G, 28, 174).

[8] §IV, 8 (cf. §III, 6; §III, 8, 45 ff.; §II, 32, 67–70); §III, 9, 198–202; §IV, 7; §III, 20.

the walls of either Avaris itself or of an important city in the territory of Avaris.[1]

Since Auserre Apophis, though by then an aged man, was obviously still alive at the beginning of Kamose's reign[2] and since the Hyksos were driven from Egypt in the third or fourth year of Kamose's younger brother and successor, Amosis,[3] the reigns of the last two kings of the Fifteenth Dynasty[4] must have been relatively brief—as, indeed, we should expect in a dynasty tottering on the verge of ruin. The first of these rulers was probably Aqenenre Apophis II, whose name, except for its appearance on a dagger purchased in Luxor,[5] has not been found south of Bubastis in the eastern Delta. In the Delta, however, he is represented by a number of sculptured monuments usurped for the most part from earlier pharaohs—two granite sphinxes of King Ammenemes II of the Twelfth Dynasty, a pair of colossal statues of King Semenkhkare, 'the General', of the Thirteenth Dynasty, and a fine grey granite offering table.[6] In the temple at Bubastis a King Apophis 'erected numerous masts and doors of bronze for this god'. This, too, was presumably Aqenenre Apophis, whose Horus name, 'He-who-Contents-the-Two-Lands', occurs on a block found near the fragmentary door-jamb on which the king's benefactions are described.[7]

At the end of the dynasty belongs a ruler whom the redactors of Manetho call Aseth, Assis, or Arkhles,[8] and who is probably the King Asehre, named on a small obelisk from Sān el-Hagar, not far from the site of ancient Avaris.[9] This is the only monument preserved from the reign of Asehre, which was evidently extremely short—perhaps not more than a year or two. The obelisk does not bear Asehre's personal name, but we may logically suppose him to have been the 'Khamudy', who is listed as the last king of the Fifteenth Dynasty in the Turin Canon.[10]

The Sixteenth Dynasty, as we have seen (§ III), must have been

---

[1] Kamose Stela II, lines 5–10, 27–8. See §III, 9, 200–2; §III, 20, 54–5, 58.

[2] The text recounting Kamose's triumphs over Auserre is dated to Regnal Year 3 (§IV, 8, 249–50, pls. 37–8; §III, 6, 97).

[3] 1567 B.C. It is unlikely that the expulsion of the Hyksos was achieved by Amosis in his first year on the throne (1570 B.C.), the siege of Avaris alone having apparently been a long operation (G, 23, 86–9 [fr. 42]; G, 19, 3–4; §III, 8, 53; §IV, 1, 226–7. See §II, 1, 17 n. 50).

[4] Turin Canon, col. x, 19 and 20 (=G, 5, pl. 3, col. x, 18–20). See G, 9, 37.

[5] §IV, 6.   [6] G, 15, vol. IV, 16–17, 19, 69.

[7] *Ibid.* 28–9.   [8] G, 23, 82–3, 90–1, 240–1; G, 9, 36.

[9] G, 15, vol. IV, 25; G, 3, 318 (38).

[10] Col. x, 20 (G, 5, pl. 3).

contemporaneous with the Fifteenth and included, presumably, such minor Hyksos rulers as Anather, Semqen, Khauserre, Seket, Ahetepre, Sekhaenre, and Amu.[1] At or near the end of this dynasty is probably to be placed Nebkhepeshre Apophis III, for whom there is no place either in the Turin Canon or in any of the lists derived from Manetho. We possess, however, a number of small monuments bearing his names and kingly titles.[2] The most interesting of these is a bronze dagger found at Saqqara in the coffin of a man whose name, Abd, suggests that he was of Semitic race.[3] The handle of the weapon, carved in ebony and overlaid with electrum, bears on one side the figure and name of its owner, 'the Henchman of his Lord, Nehmen', probably also a Semite. On the other side is carved the titulary of the royal donor: 'The Good God, Lord of the Two Lands, Nebkhepeshre, the Son of Re, Apophis, given life.'

The fall of Avaris and the expulsion of the Asiatics from the soil of Egypt took place in or about 1567 B.C., and a few years later King Amosis, the Theban founder of the Eighteenth Dynasty, wiped out the remaining vestiges of Hyksos power in southern Palestine.

V. THE RECOVERY OF THE THEBAN KINGDOM: THE SEVENTEENTH DYNASTY TO THE DEATH OF SEQENENRE II

About 1650 B.C., in the reign of one of the earlier Hyksos pharaohs, the Theban branch of the Thirteenth Dynasty was succeeded by a new line of Theban rulers who are designated in the Africanus version of Manetho's history as belonging to the Seventeenth Dynasty.[4] Of the fifteen kings' names once listed for this dynasty in columns x–xi of the Turin Canon[5] nine occur also in the table of ancestors of Tuthmosis III from Karnak[6] and in several similar, but shorter, New Kingdom lists[7] and ten are known from monu-

---

[1] See G, 24, 929 (Ahotepre), 933 (Anther), 943 (Khaousirre), 957 (Semken); G, 20, 42–6, 64, 67–8, 70; G, 6, vol. I, 210–11; vol. II, 138, 145, 404; G, 8, part 2, 7; etc.

[2] G, 3, 318 (37).   [3] §IV, 5; §II, 32, 70–1. See Plate 71(b).

[4] G, 23, 94–5 (fr. 47).

[5] Col. x, 30—col. XI, 15 (G, 5, pls. 3–4).

[6] G, 16, pl. 1; G, 19, 608–10 (I, 8, III, 7, IV, 2–5, V, 7, VII, 1, 3).

[7] In the tombs of Khabekhenet and Anhurkhau at Deir el-Medîna (G, 15, vol. I, 54, 167), on an offering table of the Scribe Qen in the Marseilles Museum (G, 6, vol. II, 162), and on the base of a statuette of Harpocrates in Cairo (§V, 4, 55–6, no. 38189; G, 20, 78, 81).

ments found either at Thebes itself or on other sites in southern Upper Egypt.[1] The existence at Thebes of the tombs of seven of these rulers and of an eighth king who is not included in the Turin Canon has been established by the discovery either of the tombs themselves or of items of their equipment, or from the records of investigations conducted in the Theban necropolis during the Twentieth Dynasty.[2]

In the first of the two groups into which the Turin Canon divides the Seventeenth Dynasty[3] are five rulers who form a compact and fairly well documented series at the beginning of the list and who may have been the 'kings of Thebes, five in number', who, according to one Manethonian tradition, comprised 'the Sixteenth Dynasty'.[4] They are, in the probable order of their succession: Sekhemre Wahkhau Rehotpe, Sekhemre Wepmaat Inyotef (V), Sekhemre Heruhirmaat Inyotef (VI), Sekhemre Shedtowy Sobkemsaf (II), and Sekhemre Sementowy Thuty.[5] Following Sekhemre Se[mentowy Thuty], in the same group, the Turin Canon names six more kings, beginning with Sankhenre and ending with Sekhemre Shedwast.[6] Of these last six kings only three are known from sources other than the Canon itself and only one, Sewadjenre Nebiryerawet, has left us any record of his reign.[7] Altogether the group appears to have ruled at Thebes for, roughly, forty-five years, coming to an end about 1605 B.C., early in the reign of the Hyksos king, Auserre Apophis I.

It is probable that the territory claimed by the kings of the early Seventeenth Dynasty coincided closely with that ruled, five centuries earlier, by the Theban princes of the Heracleopolitan Period and comprised only the first eight nomes of Upper Egypt, from Elephantine on the south to Abydos on the north. Other local dynasts, including, as we have seen, remnants of the old Thirteenth Dynasty, apparently held sway in other nome capitals of Upper and Middle Egypt.[8] Nubia was now almost certainly an independent nation with its capital at Buhen,[9] and in the north the royal Hyksos sat enthroned at Memphis or Avaris, while his tax collectors scoured the whole land gathering tribute for their Asiatic master.

[1] §II, 41, 217–77; G, 3, 319–21. [2] §v, 13; §v, 2; §v, 3.
[3] Col. x, 30—col. xi, 10 (G, 5, pls. 3–4).
[4] G, 23, 92–3 (fr. 46). Cf. G, 27, 104–49; §III, 19, 87–8.
[5] G, 27, 104–49. Cf. §II, 41, 272; G, 20, 79–80.
[6] Col. xi, 4–9. Gardiner (G, 5, pl. 4) reads col. xi, 4 as 'Sewadj-...'; but see G, 5, 17, and §v, 7.
[7] §II, 20. [8] See above, sect. II.
[9] §III, 18; §III, 20; G, 28, 175.

Isolated and impoverished, the Thebans, while bending every effort to perpetuate the traditions and customs of the Middle Kingdom, began, as in the First Intermediate Period, to develop a provincial culture of their own. Cut off by the Hyksos and the rulers of Kush from the timber of Syria, the fine limestone of Tura, the gold of Nubia, and the ebony and ivory of the Sudan and unable to support expeditions to the quarries at Aswān and Wādi Hammāmāt, they were forced to make the best of the limited materials available locally. The pyramids of the kings, lined up along the southeastern slope of the Dirā Abu'n-Naga in western Thebes, were small, steep-sided structures of mud brick.[1] Anthropoid coffins, frequently 'dug out' of sycomore logs and adorned with a characteristic vulture-wing decoration (called *rishi*, 'feathered', by the modern fellahīn), took the place of the stone sarcophagi and great rectangular cases of cedar, typical of the Middle Kingdom.[2] Stelae, inscribed architectural elements, and small works of art continued to be produced in a provincial style which with time departed more and more from that of the Middle Kingdom models.[3] Learning, on the other hand, flourished, and it is to the Theban scribes of this general period that we owe our copies of several famous literary and technical works of earlier periods of Egyptian history.[4] Above all, we find in this small Upper Egyptian kingdom evidence of the indomitable spirit which had already in the Eleventh Dynasty lifted Egypt out of a state of depression and disorder and which was again destined, within the next hundred years, to bring her to new heights of prosperity and power.

Something of this spirit is reflected in the building repairs piously undertaken by King Sekhemre Wahkhau Rehotpe, the founder of the Seventeenth Dynasty, in the temple of Min at Koptos and the temple of Osiris at Abydos.[5] In his decree at Koptos the king, after describing how 'the gates and doors' of his 'father, Min', had fallen into decay, adds significantly: 'Never were things destroyed in my days...of the things that existed aforetime.' Rehotpe's name appears in the list of kings from Karnak;[6] but it is not apparently his tomb at Thebes which is mentioned in a well-known 'ghost story' of the late New Kingdom, the royal name there, formerly read as 'Rahotpe', being evidently only a faulty

[1] §II, 41, 217–77 *passim*; §v, 16, 30–2; A, 1; Edwards, *Pyramids*, 195–6.
[2] G, 8, part 2, 29–32; §II, 41, pls. 14, 16, 21.   [3] G, 8, part 2, 14–35.
[4] See above, p. 55 n. 7; and below, p. 67 n. 5.
[5] G, 15, vol. v, 129; §v, 10, vol. IV, no. 283, pl. 24. See also G, 20, 79–80; G, 27, 121–6.
[6] G, 19, 610 (VII, 1).

writing of the praenomen of Nebhepetre Mentuhotpe of the Eleventh Dynasty.[1]

Of the second king of the dynasty, Sekhemre Wepmaat Inyotef, 'the Elder', we know only that he was of royal birth and that he was buried, after a reign of three years, by his younger brother and successor, Sekhemre Heruhirmaat Inyotef VI.[2] His tomb on the Dirā Abu'n-Naga, however, was inspected during the Twentieth Dynasty and from the record of this inspection, preserved in the Abbott Papyrus,[3] it would appear to have been situated immediately to the south-west of that of King Nubkheperre Inyotef VII of the later Seventeenth Dynasty (see below). Although the tomb itself has not been found, the capstone of its pyramid has survived, as have also the king's canopic chest and anthropoid coffin, the latter bearing an inscription stating that it was made 'as a gift to him by his brother, King Inyotef'.[4] It was 'in all likelihood' in this coffin that natives of El-Qurna a century ago discovered one of the greatest of all Egyptian literary documents, the Papyrus Prisse, with copies of the Maxims of Ptahhotpe and the Instruction to Kagemni.[5] The brother, Sekhemre Heruhirmaat, has left us nothing but an extremely shoddy anthropoid coffin, now in the Louvre.[6] His reign, which probably lasted only a few months, was evidently not regarded by the author of the Turin Canon as worth recording.

This was far from being the case with Sekhemre Shedtowy Sobkemsaf II, who appears to have occupied the throne for sixteen years[7] and who is the most copiously documented ruler of the whole dynasty. His tomb, broken into and extensively plundered in the reign of Ramesses IX, figures prominently in the Abbott and Ambras Papyri[8] and in a fuller record of the statements of the tomb-robbers preserved in the combined Amherst-Leopold II Papyrus.[9] These accounts not only tell us that Sobkemsaf was recognized by posterity as 'a great ruler' whose 'monuments stand to this very day', but would have us believe that his burial and the burial of his queen, Nubkhas, were of a richness approaching magnificence. Although the last impression is not borne out by the mediocre quality of the king's canopic chest, in Leiden, a

---

[1] §v, 11, 170–1; G, 3, 319 (40).
[2] Turin Canon, col. XI, 1; §II, 41, 234–7; G, 27, 126–32.
[3] §v, 13, 38, pl. 1 (P. Abbott 2, 16–18).
[4] §II, 41, 234–7; G, 27, 126–32.
[5] G, 27, 129–30. [6] *Ibid.* 130–2, pl. 19. [7] Turin Canon, col. XI, 2.
[8] §v, 13, 38, pl. 2 (P. Abbott 3, 1–7); 181, pl. 38 (P. Ambras 2, 7).
[9] §v, 3, 171, 177–80, 183 ff. (2, 5—3, 2); §v, 2, pls. 2, 3.

number of other inscribed monuments, chiefly from Thebes, point
to a relatively long and prosperous reign, featured by building
activities and other public works at both Karnak and Abydos.[1]
The still strong influence of the Thirteenth Dynasty tradition is
evident in the king's own name, Sobkemsaf,[2] and in those of three
of his subjects—Sobkhotpe, Sobknakhte, and Yauheyebu—
inscribed on a small limestone obelisk from western Thebes.[3] The
fact that a green jasper heart scarab, made originally for 'King
Sobkemsaf', was found on the mummy of Nubkheperre Inyotef,
the first of the later group of Seventeenth Dynasty pharaohs,
clearly establishes the chronological sequence of these two kings.[4]

In the tomb of Renseneb (no. 9) at El-Kāb a Queen Nubkhas
and her daughter, Princess Khons—perhaps the wife and daughter
of Sobkemsaf II—are named, respectively, as the great-grand-
mother and grandmother of one of Renseneb's two wives.[5]
Another queen, Senebsen, is mentioned in the same tomb as a
contemporary of the mother of Renseneb's second wife and must
therefore have been two generations later in date than Queen
Nubkhas. Since we cannot equate the brief reigns of the Seventeenth Dynasty with the generations of the officials of El-Kāb, it
is not at present possible to identify Senebsen's royal husband.[6]

The next ruler listed for the dynasty in the Turin Canon was without much doubt Sekhemre Sementowy Thuty,[7] whose name occurs
in the table of kings from Karnak and on part of a limestone door-
jamb from Deir, north of El-Ballās.[8] For some reason the king's
canopic chest was re-inscribed and used as a cosmetic box by his
queen, the King's Great Wife, Mentuhotpe, and was found,
together with a handsome rectangular coffin, in the queen's tomb
at Thebes.[9] After a reign of only a year Thuty yielded the throne

[1] §II, 41, 237–43; G, 27, 132–41; G, 20, 77–9, 81. Yoyotte (G, 28, 174) has
suggested that it was Sobkemsaf II who drove the Hyksos back beyond Cusae, but
the title-page of the Rhind Papyrus indicates that Thebes itself acknowledged the
sovereignty of an Asiatic overlord as late as the thirty-third year of Auserre Apophis,
the Hyksos contemporary of Seqenenre II and Kamose.

[2] On King Sekhemre Wadjkhau Sobkemsaf I of the Thirteenth Dynasty see
above, §II.

[3] §II, 41, 242.

[4] Winlock (G, 27, 135–7) notwithstanding.

[5] G, 6, vol. II, 28 n. 1; G, 3, 328–9; G, 20, 57–8.

[6] The unwarranted assumption that the Queen Senebsen of the El-Kāb tomb
inscription was the wife of King Neferhotep I of the Thirteenth Dynasty has
contributed to some fantastic historical conclusions regarding the Second Intermediate
Period (see, for example, G, 24, 343–5; §V, 19).

[7] Turin Canon, col. XI, 3 (G, 5, pl. 4). See G, 20, 79, 80.

[8] §II, 41, 269–72.   [9] *Ibid.*

to Sankhenre Mentuhotpe (VI),[1] known from a pair of limestone sphinxes found at Edfu.[2] Before another year had passed Sankhenre was himself succeeded by the first of the two kings with the common Theban name, Nebiryerawet.[3]

The full, fivefold titulary of King Sewadjenre Nebiryerawet I is preserved on an exceptionally interesting stela erected during his reign in the temple precinct at Karnak.[4] The text of the stela cites a contract whereby the governorship of El-Kāb was transferred by deed by its holder to his brother to cancel a debt amounting to approximately twelve pounds in gold, and records the actions taken in connexion with this transaction by two bureaux of the pharaonic government, namely, the Office of the Reporter of the Northern *Waret* and the Office of the Vizier. In addition to its administrative and juridical interest, the stela is important in fixing the reign of Nebiryerawet as not more than three generations removed from that of King Merhetepre Ini of the late Thirteenth Dynasty.[5] Elsewhere the king's praenomen, Sewadjenre, appears in two New Kingdom lists[6] and on a bronze dagger of late Middle Kingdom type, found at Hū, seventy miles downstream from Thebes.[7]

The last four kings of the earlier Seventeenth Dynasty group are now little more than names in the Turin Canon.[8] The inscriptions on a statuette of the god Harpocrates in Cairo suggest that the throne-name of Nebiryerawet II was Neferkare.[9] 'Seuserenre', assigned a reign of twelve years, may be the King Userenre named in the Karnak list[10] and on a scarab in the Greg Collection,[11] but this identification is highly conjectural. His predecessor, Semenmedjat(?)re,[12] is unknown from any other source, as is also his successor, Sekhemre Shedwast,[13] whose reign closes the group.

In the Turin Canon the names of the five rulers who comprised the Seventeenth Dynasty's second and final group[14] are destroyed,

---

[1] Turin Canon, col. xi, 4. See above, p. 65 n. 6; G, 20, 79, 80.

[2] §v, 7.

[3] Turin Canon, col. xi, 5. The reign of '29(?) years' attributed by Gardiner (G, 5, pl. 4) to this obscure ruler is difficult to believe in.

[4] §11, 20; §v, 8; §v, 9, 58–9.   [5] §11, 19.

[6] G, 16, pl. 1 (right, 2 and 28); §v, 4, 55, no. 38189.

[7] G, 15, vol. v, 109 (Cairo 33702); G, 20, 78, 80–1.   [8] Col. xi, 6–9.

[9] §v, 4, 55, no. 38189. See G, 20, 78, 80–1.

[10] G, 16, pl. 1 (left, 28).   [11] §v, 5, 57.

[12] So read, apparently, by Gardiner (G, 5, pl. 4, col. xi, 7).

[13] There is no basis for identifying this king with Sekhemre Shedtowy (Sobkemsaf II), as is done by Stock (G, 20, 76).

[14] Col. xi, 10–15.

but there can be no doubt that the last three were the well-known Theban kings, Seqenenre Tao I, 'the Elder', Seqenenre Tao II, 'the Brave', and Wadjkheperre Kamose. In the first two places we may, without much hesitation, insert an equally well-known ruler, King Nubkheperre Inyotef (VII), and, as his successor, the King Senakhtenre of the Karnak and Marseilles lists.[1]

Nubkheperre Inyotef is for many reasons the logical choice as the founder of the new and vigorous succession of kings whose appearance at Thebes marked the first serious challenge to the power of the Hyksos. His re-use of a scarab of Sobkemsaf II has already established him as a successor of that king[2] and as probably belonging to another family. In the Karnak list his name appears in close proximity to those of Senakhtenre and Seqenenre.[3] His anthropoid coffin in the British Museum is closer in proportions and style to that of Seqenenre Tao II than to any other example now known,[4] and the similarity between his throne-name and that of King Wadjkheperre Kamose is obvious. The position of his tomb, apparently north of those of Inyotef V and Sobkemsaf II, indicates, not that he was earlier than these two kings,[5] but that with him a new row of royal tombs was commenced.

Though the 'enemies' referred to in a famous decree of Nubkheperre Inyotef in the temple of Min at Koptos are now recognized as having been not real enemies, but magical figures which had been stolen by one Teti, son of Minhotpe, the decree clearly reflects the growing power and autocratic tendencies of the Theban Dynasts.[6] Issued in the king's third regnal year, the violently worded edict is addressed to the Mayor of Koptos, the military Commander of Koptos, the Treasurer Menekhmin, the Scribe of the Temple, Neferhotep, 'the entire garrison of Koptos and the entire priesthood of the temple'. It not only deposes from office and vigorously anathematizes the erring Teti, but also calls down imprecations upon 'every king and every potentate' and threatens with severe penalties 'every commander and every mayor' who shall forgive him and his descendants.

Temple reliefs of Nubkheperre at Koptos, Abydos and El-Kāb, and stelae and other monuments bearing his name from Karnak and Edfu testify to his activities as a builder and occasionally hint at his prowess as a warrior.[7] Thus, a block of relief from

---

[1] See below, pp. 71–2.   [2] See above, p. 68 n. 4.   [3] G, 16, pl. 1 (left, 27).
[4] §11, 41, 229–30, 248–9, pls. 14, 16.
[5] So G, 27, 105–7; but see G, 20, 76–8, and cf. §11, 41, 224–5.
[6] G, 15, vol. v, 125. See §v, 17, 214 and n. 2; G, 28, 170–1.
[7] G, 15, vol. v, 44, 48, 125; G, 27, 108–12.

Koptos showed the king with upraised mace striking down a group of enemies in the presence of the god Min, and a small pedestal from Karnak displays his cartouches above bound figures of Nubian and Asiatic captives. Although too much significance should not be attached to such traditional representations, a warlike character for the reign is further attested by the high military title, Troop Commander, borne by a 'King's Son of the Ruler, Inyotef', named Nakhte,[1] and by the fact that the pharaoh himself was buried with two bows and six flint-tipped arrows beside him in his coffin.[2]

Before the king's pyramid on the Dirā Abu'n-Naga stood a pair of small sandstone obelisks and in his coffin was found a handsome silver diadem, now in Leiden.[3] The walls of the tomb chambers were decorated with paintings and on one of them may have been inscribed the famous Song of the Harper, described by later generations as 'the song which is in the house of King Inyotef, the deceased, before the singer with the harp'. This poem, the theme of which is 'Eat, drink, and be merry, for tomorrow we die', was apparently a Memphite composition, written during the years of uncertainty following the end of the Old or Middle Kingdom.[4]

Inyotef's queen, Sobkemsaf, was evidently born and buried at Edfu, whence come various monuments bearing her name—two stelae, a pair of gold bracelet bars, and a gold pendant.[5] On the stelae she is described as a king's sister, king's daughter, and king's granddaughter, and was undoubtedly related by blood either to the earlier rulers of the Seventeenth Dynasty or to a local dynasty at Edfu contemporary with them. The honour in which Queen Sobkemsaf was held as an immediate ancestress of the Eighteenth Dynasty is attested by a stela of that period whereon she is worshipped together with Queen Ahhotpe, the wife of Seqenenre Tao II and mother of King Amosis.[6]

The name of King Senakhtenre appears in the Karnak list between those of Nubkheperre (Inyotef) and Seqenenre (Tao).[7] In another listing of royal ancestors, preserved on an offering slab of the Nineteenth Dynasty in Marseilles, it occurs again, immedi-

[1] G, 15, vol. v, 45.   [2] §II, 41, 230–1.
[3] *Ibid.* 229, 231.
[4] G, 27, 120–1; §v, 12, 191–5, 211–12. The ruler referred to in the title of the song may indeed have been one of the Inyotef kings of the Eleventh Dynasty. See, for example, §v, 6, 41.
[5] G, 6, vol. I, 222; vol. II, 124–5; §II, 41, 233; G, 27, 112, cf. also 123–4.
[6] G, 19, 29.   [7] G, 16, pl. 1 (left, 29).

ately preceding the names of Seqenenre and Wadjkheperre (Kamose).[1] A third occurrence of the name, carelessly copied as 'Sekhentenre', is found in the tomb of Khabekhenet at Deir el-Medīna, where it accompanies the names of Seqenenre (in this case, Tao II, 'the Brave') and his successors.[2] Thus, although no contemporary monuments of Senakhtenre have yet been discovered, his existence and his position in the Seventeenth Dynasty seem reasonably well established.

The Abbott Papyrus records the inspection of the tombs of two kings named Seqenenre Tao and after the name of one of them adds the explanatory comment, 'making a second King Tao'.[3] Seqenenre Tao II is listed by both his names and his distinguishing epithet, 'the Brave', in the inscriptions in the tombs of Khabekhenet and Anhurkhau at Deir el-Medīna,[4] but the Karnak list,[5] the Nineteenth Dynasty offering table in Marseilles,[6] and a number of small monuments of the period[7] give only the noncommittal praenomen, 'Seqenenre'.

This shortened form of the name is also found in the tale of Papyrus Sallier I, cited above (§IV), which tells us that in the time of a Hyksos king Apophis 'King Seqenenre was ruler of the Southern City' (Thebes) and that he did not worship 'any god which is in [the entire land] except Amon-Re, King of the Gods'.[8] In his day the Thebans were apparently represented as having revived the ritual harpooning of hippopotami in their pool or canal at Thebes, 'a holy rite, which guaranteed amongst other things the safety of the Egyptian monarchy' and which was offensive to the Hyksos king not only because of its political implications, but even more so because the hippopotamus was a form of his chief god, Seth.[9] The rather peremptory order sent by Apophis to Seqenenre to 'come away from the pond of the hippopotami' presumably led to the outbreak of war between them, and most modern authorities are therefore inclined to identify the Theban ruler of the legend as King Tao II, 'the Brave'.[10]

This conclusion leaves us with little or nothing of a historical nature on Seqenenre Tao I. His queen, Tetisheri,[11] however,

---

[1] G, 9, vol. II, 162, 169.   [2] G, 15, vol. I, 54.
[3] §v, 13, 38, pl. 2 (3, 8–10); §II, 41, 243 ff. See G, 3, 330–1.
[4] G, 15, vol. I, 54, 167.   [5] G, 16, pl. I (left, 30).
[6] G, 6, vol. II, 162 (v).
[7] Including a small silver sphinx in the Museum at Mariemont (§v, 18, 34, no. E. 55 [136], pl. 9). See also §II, 41, 248 ff.
[8] §III, 8, 39–45; §v, 11, 131 ff.   [9] §v, 14, 43–5.
[10] G, 28, 175; G, 3, 298–9; §II, 32, 66–7; §II, 41, 250; §III, 20, 61.
[11] See Plate 86.

lived on into the early years of the Eighteenth Dynasty and, as the grandmother of Amosis, its founder, was held in high esteem by the Thebans of that period.[1] From the cache of royal mummies at Deir el-Bahri come some inscribed bandages giving the names of her parents—evidently commoners—and perhaps also her mummy, that of a white-haired little woman, well advanced in age at the time of her death.[2] Two statues, probably also from Thebes, show her as a slender and charming young girl clad in a long white dress and wearing the vulture head-dress of a queen.[3] Among the honours bestowed on her by King Amosis were the erection of a funerary chapel at Abydos and the donation of a series of farms recaptured from the Hyksos in Lower Egypt.[4]

King Seqenenre Tao II, 'the Brave', and his wife, Queen Ahhotpe, were apparently brother and sister, children of King Tao I and Queen Tetisheri.[5] Like Tetisheri, Ahhotpe had a long life, surviving the death of her husband and three of her six children and dying at last in the reign of her third son, King Amosis, by whom she was richly endowed with jewellery and buried with fitting honours.[6] King Tao II, on the other hand, met a violent end while still in his early thirties. His mummy, found with his anthropoid coffin in the royal cache at Deir el-Bahri,[7] shows a number of terrible head wounds which suggest that he was either assassinated by his attendants or—which seems much more likely[8]—was slain in battle against the Hyksos. However that may be, it was not until after his death that his son, Kamose, launched the offensive which was to lead to the expulsion of the Asiatics from Egyptian soil and the great expansion of Egyptian power under the New Kingdom.

[1] §II, 41, 246–8; §v, 20; G, 6, vol. II, 159–60; G, 8, part 2, 10–11, 44, 170.
[2] §v, 15, no. 61056; G, 6, vol. II, 160. See §II, 41, 246–8.
[3] G, 3, 309, 321; §II, 41, 247. See Plate 86.
[4] G, 15, vol. v, 91, 92; §v, 20, 14–15.
[5] §II, 41, 246, 250–1; G, 6, vol. II, 161–4.
[6] §v, 1. See §II, 41, 251–5.
[7] §v, 15, no. 61051. See §II, 41, 249–50.
[8] Although the principal wound, a dagger blow beneath the left ear, indicates that the king was struck down unexpectedly, from behind, it is hard to believe that the leader of the resurgent Thebans and champion of Egyptian liberty would have been murdered by his own followers. That the Thebans were at war at this time is suggested by the statement of Ahmose, son of Ibana, that his father served as 'a soldier of the King of Upper and Lower Egypt, Seqenenre, the deceased' (G, 19, 2; §III, 8, 49).

VI. THE PAN-GRAVE PEOPLE

Contemporary with the Hyksos occupation of Egypt we find in the southern part of the country, between Asyūt and Aswān, copious evidence of the immigration into this area of a people of mixed Hamitic and negro blood, whose homeland appears to have been the desert east of Lower Nubia.[1] Fifteen Upper Egyptian sites, from Deir Rīfa in the north to Daraw in the south, have yielded the characteristic circular or oval graves of these immigrants and at El-Mustagidda and Qāw are the scanty remains of small settlements occupied by them.[2] At Hū, near Abydos, where the presence of this people first became known to modern excavators,[3] their graves are shallow, pan-like cavities in the desert surface and, although this is not the case in the majority of their cemeteries, the name 'pan-grave' has been retained as a convenient term, applied both to the graves themselves and to the culture which they represent.

In common with other Nubian cultures of this period that of the pan-grave people still preserves features which had originated, millenniums earlier, in the predynastic civilization of southern Upper Egypt. It is closely related to, but not identical with, the latest phase of the so-called C-Group culture found in Lower Nubia during the Middle Kingdom and shows also less well-defined affinities with the approximately contemporaneous civilization of the Kerma people of the northern Sudan.[4]

The homogeneity of the pan-grave culture is accentuated rather than weakened by the occurrence at different sites of minor variations in the forms of the graves and their contents. The graves, ten to fifteen inches deep at Hū, range in depth at other sites to as much as six feet. The bodies, clad in leather garments and adorned with primitive jewellery, usually lie on their right sides in a contracted position with the heads to the north and the faces to the west. Among the more distinctive items of jewellery are bracelets made of rectangular strips of shell or mother-of-pearl threaded together side by side. Pan-grave pottery is confined almost entirely to small, deep bowls of red, black, or black-topped ware with or without incised decoration. Near the graves, in shallow deposit pits, were stacked more pottery bowls and the skulls of various horned animals crudely adorned with painted decoration.

---

[1] G, 18, 51, 130, 135–40; §II, 32, 70; §III, 20, 57; §VI, 13.
[2] §VI, 3, 114–33, pls. 69–76; §VI, 2, 3–7, pls. 5–11; §VI, 9, 108–9.
[3] §VI, 11, 20–1, pls. 13 E, 23–6.
[4] G, 18, 138. See §VI, 14, 63–4, 68; §III, 18, 57; §III, 20, 57; §VI, 9, 108–9; A, 8.

Egyptian objects found in the pan-graves include much worn stone and pottery vessels of late Middle Kingdom types and a few inscribed objects of the Hyksos Period. A grave at Mostagedda has yielded an axe-head bearing the name of the pharaoh Neb-maare, who was apparently a successor of the ill-fated King Dudimose of the late Thirteenth Dynasty;[1] and from other burials, at Deir Rîfa, come scarabs of the Hyksos King Sheshi and the Chancellor Hur.[2] The forepart of an ivory sphinx, found in a pan-grave at Abydos,[3] has been thought, from the strongly Semitic character of the face, to represent a Hyksos ruler,[4] though the captive which the sphinx holds between its paws can hardly be an Egyptian.

Numerous weapons—axes, daggers, arrows, bow-strings, and archers' wrist-guards—recovered from the relatively small number of unplundered graves, indicate clearly that the pan-grave people were a warrior race and suggest the conclusion that they were imported into Upper Egypt as professional soldiers. This conclusion is supported by the types of the weapons, which are all of Egyptian design and manufacture, and by the presence in the same graves of gold, jewellery and other objects of intrinsic value. It is furthermore made plausible by the evidently amicable relations which existed throughout most of the Hyksos Period between the independent Nubian tribes and their Upper Egyptian neighbours.[5] Most significant is the fact that the cemeteries and settlements of the pan-grave people, though widely distributed throughout southern Upper Egypt, do not extend northward into Hyksos territory, but are confined to the country south of Cusae—in other words, to the realm governed by the Theban rulers of the late Seventeenth Dynasty. They must, then, have been Nubian troops who served as auxiliaries in the armies of Thebes and are in all probability to be identified with the famed Medjay, used as scouts and light infantry by the Egyptians from the late Old Kingdom onwards and twice mentioned by King Kamose in the account of his campaign against the Hyksos.[6] If the identification is correct, we must abandon the old conception of the pan-grave people as casual, semi-nomadic settlers on the fringes of the Nile Valley and recognize them as active participants in Egypt's

---

[1] §vi, 3, 117, 127, 131, pl. 74 (9); §vi, 9, 108. See pp. 52–3.
[2] §vi, 12, 21, pl. 13 E (3, 4). See p. 60.   [3] §vi, 6.
[4] Ibid.; §ii, 32, 66.
[5] See G, 18, 135, 140; §iii, 20, 57.
[6] Carnarvon Tablet i, lines 11 and 12. For recent discussions of the Medjay see §vi, 13; §vi, 5, vol. i, 73*–89*; vol. ii, 269*–272*.

struggle for independence and in that phase of Egyptian history which led to the founding of the New Kingdom.

In addition to Egyptian weapons and stone vases the pan-grave people, as time progressed, adopted more and more of the products and customs of the country in which they had settled. The later burials contain increasing quantities of Egyptian pottery, scarabs, and jewellery, and among the circular and oval pits with contracted burials there begin to appear oblong, rectangular graves containing bodies extended in the contemporaneous Egyptian fashion and often encased in wooden coffins. In the settlements the circular Nubian hut gives way to the small Egyptian house with rectangular plan. By the end of the Hyksos Period the Nubian immigrants had apparently become completely Egyptianized and in the New Kingdom their presence in Egypt is no longer demonstrable on purely archaeological grounds. Men of Nubian race, however, have continued to serve in the Egyptian army and police force until the present day, and we may be sure that throughout the Dynastic Period many Nubian tribesmen, particularly the war-like Medjay, resided with their families within the boundaries of Egypt itself.

CHAPTER III

PALESTINE IN THE
MIDDLE BRONZE AGE

In a previous chapter[1] the nomadic way of life of the inhabitants of Palestine during the period roughly equivalent to the First Intermediate Period of Egypt was described. It was sharply differentiated from the Early Bronze Age, for instead of people living in walled towns there was a population quite uninterested in town life, bringing with them new pottery, new weapons and new burial practices, of types best explained as those of nomads. In Syria there is a similar break, and there are many links to show that the newcomers in the two areas were connected. In Syria, there is documentary evidence to suggest that these nomadic intruders were the Amorites, and it can thus be accepted that it was at this time that the Amorites, described in the Biblical record as part of the population of the country,[2] reached Palestine.

The break at the end of this period of nomadic occupation is as sharp as that at its beginning. Towns once more appear, and there are once more new burial practices, new pottery, new weapons, new ornaments. There is a most surprising lack of any objects or practices which, where the archaeological evidence is sound, can be shown to carry through from the earlier stage to the later. It is for this reason that it seems misleading to apply to the stage of nomadic occupation the term Middle Bronze I, as was done when the evidence of the period was first becoming apparent,[3] though this is still used by many archaeologists in the United States and Israel. Instead, the term Intermediate Early Bronze–Middle Bronze, first introduced by J. H. Iliffe in his arrangement of the Palestine Archaeological Museum, has been used, and the term Middle Bronze Age is confined to the new developments with which this chapter is concerned.[4]

---

[1] *C.A.H.* I³, pt. 2, ch. xxi, sects. v–vii.　　　　[2] Numbers xxi. 13.

[3] E.g. G, 1, ch. ii; G, 2, ch. iii; G, 9, 5.

[4] What is here called M.B.I is called M.B.IIa by those who adhere to the older terminology.

I. MIDDLE BRONZE AGE I:
CHARACTERISTICS, DISTRIBUTION, ORIGIN

The first salient point concerning Middle Bronze I is the appearance of a completely new repertory of pottery forms. In place of the monotonous range of E.B.-M.B. vessels, the overwhelmingly large proportion of which are jars, though varying in size and as to whether they have spouts or handles, accompanied by only a few bowls, there is now a wide variety of bowls, jugs, juglets, dippers and vases. The jars, proportionately much fewer in numbers, have pointed instead of flat bases and loop handles instead of ledge handles, and even such a utilitarian object as the lamp is now a circular bowl with a slight pinch to form a nozzle for the wick, instead of the four-nozzle form of the E.B.-M.B. period. The contrast may be seen by comparing material of the two periods from, for instance, Megiddo[1] and Tell Beit Mirsim.[2]

Difference in form is accompanied by difference in appearance and technique. The pottery of the E.B.-M.B. is almost uniformly drab in colour with a rough finish. It never has a coloured slip or any burnish, and only a very few vessels, in one only of the separate groups, have a simple painted decoration. The pottery technique is highly characteristic. The bases of the vessels are almost invariably flat, the walls thin and hand-made, with finger marks clearly visible on the inside, but the rims wheel-made on a fast wheel. In contrast, the Middle Bronze vessels are made of well-levigated clay, which often has a fine slip, most characteristically red, and this is often burnished to a high finish, suggesting an imitation of copper. The vessels (see Fig. 1), with the exception of such coarse types as cooking-pots, are entirely wheel-made. Even if only a sherd is found, there is almost never any difficulty in differentiating between the wares of the two periods.

The difference extends to all other classes of objects of which there is evidence, that is to say weapons and ornaments in metal. Such evidence as there is[3] suggests that the difference extends to the metal, and that copper was the metal employed during the E.B.-M.B. period and bronze during the Middle Bronze Age, but more work is required on this subject. The difference in forms is however clear. In the E.B.-M.B. period in Palestine, the only axes that can be securely dated to this period are of the fenestrated

[1] E.g. G, 4, Tomb 1101 B–1102 Lower, pls. 6–7 and *ibid.* Tomb 877 A 2, pls. 11–12 with *ibid.* Tomb 911 A 1, pls. 28–9.
[2] E.g. G, 2, pls. 2–3 with *ibid.* pls. 4–5.
[3] G, 4, 160 ff.

type,[1] though in Syria the simple flat celt found from Ghassulian times onwards apparently continued in use[2] as well as the fenestrated axes found there in quantity.[3] In Middle Bronze Age Palestine the characteristic type is a thin socketed blade.[4] The other main weapon found is the dagger. This is a very common weapon on many E.B.-M.B. sites, and is characterized by a thin

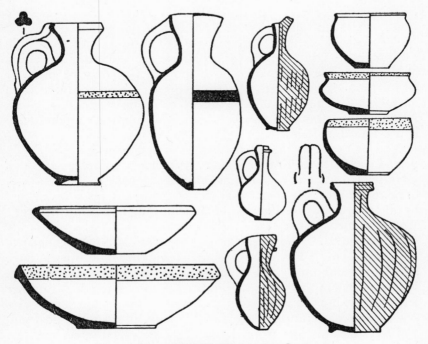

Fig. 1. Selected Middle Bronze Age I pottery.

lengthy blade, attached by rivets at the butt to a handle of which the only evidence is the survival of a number of metal (copper or bronze) rivets.[5] The Middle Bronze Age weapon is an entirely different affair, short, with a wide shoulder, giving a triangular appearance. The earliest are beautiful examples of craftsmanship, with a pronounced mid-rib outlined by further ribs.[6] The earliest

[1] E.g. G, 16, Abb. 105; G, 3, pl. 163.8.   [2] §1, 2, pl.LXVIII.
[3] E.g. §1, 3, pls. LX, CXIX; §1, 12, figs. 18.22, 19.13–14.
[4] E.g. G, 7, fig. 312.6; G, 8, fig. 111.15; G, 4, pl. 122.1–2, §1, 13, pl. XX.2.
[5] E.g. G, 12, pls. X–XIII; G, 17, pl. 21.8, 10, pl. 22.4–6; G, 7, fig. 70; G, 8, fig. 22.
[6] E.g. G, 12, pl. XIV.70; G, 4, pl. 122.9, pl. 149.6–7.

are probably also attached to the handle by rivets at the butt, but tangs soon develop. The only other E.B.-M.B. weapon, the javelin,[1] has no counterpart in the Middle Bronze Age.

The other item of equipment in which comparison can readily be made is that of the pins. In both periods there are toggle pins, the type of pin with a pierced shaft to which a thread or string was presumably attached, to be wound round the lower part after piercing the garment. In the E.B.-M.B. period there were two types, with a club-like or swollen head[2] or with a mushroom-head,[3] both relatively rare in Jordan, but common at this period in Syria.[4] In the Middle Bronze Age, there was no marked swelling at the head, but the shank above the piercing may be more or less elaborately decorated.[5] There can be no possibility of confusion in the types. They presumably have a common origin, possibly in Mesopotamia, but the development from one type to the other is not found in Palestine.

The evidence is therefore clear that between the E.B.-M.B. period and Middle Bronze I there was such a complete break in material equipment that it can only be interpreted as a cultural break introduced by the arrival of new groups. This is confirmed by all other evidence. Though finds belonging to Middle Bronze I are not numerous, they are sufficient to show that a new way of life was introduced. Most of the finds come from burials, for instance at Tell el-'Ajjūl,[6] Ras el-'Ain[7] and Megiddo.[8] The burials have nothing in common with the tombs of the E.B.-M.B. period. Most are in simple graves within the area of the town. A number are of single individuals, though some are multiple, but the bodies are disposed as complete skeletons, mainly in a supine position, and are quite distinct from the skeletalized, disordered, remains of most of the E.B.-M.B. burials, and equally from the crouched burials that are found in the other types of burials of that period.[9] Only two sites have so far yielded detailed evidence of the occupation of the period, though evidence from a third, Jericho, will be available when work on the material has been completed. To one of these sites, Megiddo, it will be necessary to return. The other site is Tell Beit Mirsim, where Strata G-F belong to this period.[10]

[1] G, 8, fig. 41.11, 13, 15; G, 11, pl. xix.48–9; G, 18, pl. 22.1–3.
[2] G, 4, pl. 86.2.   [3] G, 4, pl. 102.9–10.
[4] E.g. §1, 2, pl. lxix; §1, 8, pl. lxix; §1, 3, pl. lxxvi.
[5] E.g. G, 7, fig. 128; G, 8, fig. 114; G, 9, pl. 227; G, 11, pl. xx.
[6] G, 12, 5, sect. 26.   [7] §1, 9.
[8] G, 4, e.g. pls. 28–9, 31, 35.
[9] For a description of the different burial methods see G, 6, 139 ff.; G, 8, 33 ff.
[10] G, 1, 14 ff.; G, 2, 67 ff.; G, 3, 17 ff.

Here, there was evidence that the first stage of the flourishing Middle Bronze Age town belongs to this period, a town with closely built houses and, at least towards the end of the period, a town wall. For the other sites where remains of this period are found, for instance Tell el-'Ajjūl and Ras el-'Ain, there is no evidence at present of towns at this period. The uninterrupted development of this stage into M.B. II, described below, supports the conclusion that the new culture was essentially urban.

As already mentioned, the new material equipment also appears at Megiddo. For a contrast between the E.B.-M.B. period and the earliest Middle Bronze Age remains, it is only necessary to compare the finds from the two groups of E.B.-M.B., tombs 1101–2 B Lower[1] and the Shaft Tombs,[2] and those of their successors.[3] The clearest evidence here again comes from burials, some re-using E.B.-M.B. Shaft Tombs, others in graves within the town area. There certainly was a town of the period, but the mechanical method of recording so-called stratification,[4] in which no floor levels were established and in which the contents of graves are recorded as belonging to the level to which they happened to penetrate, has made it extremely difficult to establish the true chronology of the successive building levels. It is, however, probable that elements in the plan ascribed to Stratum XIV represent the first stage of the M.B. I town.

The Middle Bronze I of Megiddo is, however, not quite the same as Middle Bronze I in the rest of Palestine. The metal equipment is probably identical.[5] Similar pottery forms are found,[6] and some of the Megiddo forms have the same burnished red slip. But a number of the forms, particularly the dipper juglets, though the form is similar, have a different finish, with a drab slip decorated with coloured bands in red or red and black.[7] There is also a range of bowls with thickened rims, similarly decorated with bands in red,[8] which are not found elsewhere. Juglets, too, have individual neck forms.[9] These features, and

---

[1] G, 4, pl. 6.22–31, pl. 7.

[2] *Ibid.* pl. 10, pl. 11.19–35, pl. 12.1–9, pl. 21.4–21, pl. 22.

[3] E.g. *ibid.* pls. 28, 29, 31.8–21.   [4] See §1, 5, 51*–52*.

[5] Compare, for example, G, 4, pl. 149.6–7 and G, 9, pl. 178.3 with G, 11, pl. xiv.71, 74.

[6] Compare, for example, bowls: G, 4, pl. 28.24–30, 34–8 and G, 9, pl. 19.2–3 with G, 12, pl. xxviii.25 E^4, 25 G^5, 28 P^5 and §1, 9; juglets: G, 4, pl. 29.1 and G, 9, pl. 20.14, 16 with G, 12, pl. xxx.35 R, 35 R^2. See also G, 6, figs. 36 and 37.   [7] E.g. G, 4, pl. 29.2–3; G, 9, pl. 16.5.

[8] E.g. G, 4, pl. 28.1–18; G, 9, pl. 9.1–3.

[9] E.g. G, 9, pl. 11.2, pl. 16.2.

particularly the decoration in coloured bands, are important, and to them it will be necessary to return.

The break between the material remains of the Intermediate E.B.-M.B. period and Middle Bronze I has been emphasized in the preceding paragraphs. In Palestine there is no development from one to the other. There must have been an infiltration of new groups. That it was an infiltration rather than a large-scale invasion is suggested by the relatively few sites on which the evidence of M.B. I is found, though this impression may be modified as further sites are completely excavated and more evidence accumulates. The suggestion of small infiltrating groups is supported by the evidence[1] that there was a small group at Tell el-'Ajjūl at this period, but that there was then a gap before the Middle Bronze Age town was founded. The origin of the newcomers has therefore to be sought.

The cultural continuum of the northern part of Syria and of Palestine has been emphasized already.[2] The connexion between the coastal area of Syria and Palestine in the Middle Bronze Age is very clear from comparison of finds stretching from Ras Shamra in the north to Tell el-'Ajjūl in the south. The same culture, contrasting so markedly in character with that of the immediately succeeding period, appears from north to south of the Mediterranean littoral. But a new way of life cannot appear out of a vacuum. There is no evidence at all from the material equipment to suggest that the new influences came from further afield. On present evidence it must be concluded that it evolved within this area of the Mediterranean littoral.

The major claimant to be the originator of the new urban civilization that evolved from the amalgamation of the old Early Bronze Age civilization and the revitalizing influence of the E.B.-M.B. Amorite invasions is Byblos. The strength of the impact of newcomers on the civilization of this important port on the Mediterranean coast can be judged both from the architecture and the finds.[3] The finds, which can best be studied in the foundation deposits,[4] include a long range of objects that establish clearly their relationship to finds of the E.B.-M.B. period at other sites. But the impression of wealth given by this great mass of metal objects, and of the strong connexion of the people who made these offerings with an urban centre suggests that a more sophisticated way of life had developed than that of the semi-nomadic pastoralists who must be assumed to have left the evi-

---

[1] See below, pp. 103 f.   [2] *C.A.H.* 1³, pt. 2, ch. xxi, sect. vii; see also G, 5.
[3] *C.A.H.* 1³, pt. 2, ch. xxi, sect. vii.   [4] See G, 5.

dence on most other sites. The recorded stratification at Byblos is too unsatisfactory for it to be possible to conclude to what degree the town was built up at this period (though the observation[1] that the houses were planned haphazardly, without reference to one another does not suggest a truly urbanized community), nor is it possible to say whether there was a town wall. But whether or not Byblos was a true town at this stage, it was at least the regional and religious centre of a thriving artisan population, whose members made their offerings in its temples.

Byblos thus stands out in the whole western Syrian area as something more than a village centre or tribal headquarters of a population of semi-nomadic pastoralists who in the last centuries of the third millennium B.C. had destroyed the pre-existing urban civilization. At Byblos too are to be found a number of connecting links between the artifacts of the E.B.-M.B. period and those of Middle Bronze I that are completely missing in Palestine. In the first place, the daggers found in some of the foundation deposits are, with their broad shoulders and developed mid-ribs, perfectly good typological predecessors for the short, broad-shouldered Palestinian Middle Bronze daggers,[2] which the long narrow E.B.-M.B. daggers[3] could never have been. More important still, the possible ancestry of the Middle Bronze Age pottery is to be found. The influence of metal vessels upon it, both in the appearance of copper given by the red burnished slip, and in the addiction to sharp angles in the bowls, is evident, as was long ago pointed out by W. F. Albright,[4] who also pointed out[5] that a bronze bowl from Montet's foundation jar at Byblos[6] provided a very good metallic prototype for the Middle Bronze Age pottery vessels.[7] Similar metal vessels were found in other Byblos foundation deposits subsequently discovered.[8]

Thus it is reasonable to suppose that it was in Byblos that were made the first pottery imitations of the metal vessels that were the ancestors of the Middle Bronze Age pottery of the Syro-Palestinian coast. This assumption is strongly supported by the fact that close parallels to most of the Middle Bronze I pottery vessels are in fact found in Byblos. The list of royal tombs discovered in Byblos is headed by that of Abi-shemu and Ypshomuibi, probably

[1] §1, 1, 85f.
[2] Compare, for example, §1, 2, pl. LXX.2184 and §1, 3, pl. LXVI.9618, 9619 with G, 4, pl. 149.6–7 and G, 11, pl. XIV.71, 74.   [3] E.g. G, 6, fig. 24.
[4] G, 2, 69, sect. 17.   [5] *Ibid.*   [6] §1, 8, pl. LXXI.605.
[7] Compare the Byblos vessel with, for example, G, 6, fig. 36.5 (=G, 12, pl. XXVIII.25 S).   [8] §1, 2, pl. LXVI.

his son. The former is dated by Egyptian imports to the time of
Ammenemes III (1842–1797 B.C.) of the Twelfth Dynasty, and
the latter to the time of Ammenemes IV (1798–1790 B.C.). The
whole range of pottery from these tombs[1] is very close indeed to
that of the M.B. I deposits in Palestine.

There are, so far, many gaps in the evidence. The production
of pottery of this degree of sophistication must have been preceded by more tentative efforts. Of these objects, and the potters'
workshops, with efficient potters' wheels and kilns capable of
firing pottery of a much higher standard than anything that had
gone before, there is as yet no material evidence. It is probable
that with this increased skill in pot-making went an increased
skill in metallurgy, in which weapons, ornaments and vessels in
copper were succeeded by those in bronze. Of this there is even
less evidence, for the necessary analyses have not been made, and
there is only meagre analytical evidence in Palestine[2] that it was
at this stage that a major change occurred, though to the naked
eye of the layman the difference in the products seems clear.
Perhaps in the future the metal-workers' installations at Byblos,
where far more objects have been found than in the whole of the
rest of the Syro-Palestine area, will be located.[3]

With these technological developments must have gone a development of an urban way of life. As has been already said, the
excavation methods at Byblos make it difficult to trace the stages
in the development of the town, from a walled town of the Early
Bronze Age, maintaining active relationship with Egypt over
almost a millennium, through the E.B.-M.B. interruption to a
revived town whose kings (see above) were again in contact with
Egypt during the time of that country's Twelfth Dynasty. But
throughout the length of the Syro-Palestine littoral, from Ras
Shamra in the north to Tell el-'Ajjūl in the south, towns appear
again early in the Middle Bronze Age. It is not always easy to
assess the evidence of M.B. I on these sites (probably owing
simply to lack of excavation evidence), but, as will be seen, the
development of M.B. II from Middle Bronze I is direct and
incontrovertible, and the strong probability is that it was the
newcomers of M.B. I who reintroduced an urban way of life.

The connexion of M.B. I sites, particularly Tell el-'Ajjūl and
Ras el-'Ain, the classic sites for Middle Bronze I in Palestine,
with Byblos has already been emphasized. From Byblos or its
neighbourhood groups with the equipment developed, as has

[1] §1, 8, pls. cxvi, cxviii.
[2] G, 4, 160 ff.　　　　　　[3] On this subject, see §1, 12, 67 ff., sect. 33.

been suggested, in this area, came down into Palestine and settled at first in small numbers, and scattered settlements, usually on the sites of old towns that developed again into towns. One may presume that they settled amongst the E.B.-M.B. semi-nomadic pastoralists, for the latter cannot have vanished overnight, but so far there is no material evidence of interaction in the way of trade or cross-fertilization of cultures.

There is supporting evidence that it was a matter of infiltration of comparatively small groups rather than an organized invasion. This comes from the difference, already referred to, of the pottery at Megiddo and that from other sites. As far as present evidence goes, the practice of decorating pottery with coloured bands is not found at this stage at Byblos. It is on the other hand found further north on the coast, at Ras Shamra, and also on inland sites such as Qatna. It also occurs at Megiddo. At both Ras Shamra and Megiddo vessels are found, especially jugs and juglets, which are very close in form to similar vessels from 'Ajjūl, Ras el-'Ain and Byblos, but whereas in the latter case the vessels have a burnished red slip, in the former they have a drab slip and a decoration of painted bands.[1] There are many other parallels between the pottery of Ras Shamra and Megiddo at this stage which are variations on what is found elsewhere. The practice of decorating pottery with coloured bands would seem to be a north Syrian one, for it is found, for instance, at Qatna.[2] The forms here are different, and remain so throughout the Middle Bronze Age. From the pottery and other finds it is clear that in this period there were two well-defined cultural spheres, coastal Syria and inland Syria. It is possible that at this early stage some contacts between northern sites, Ras Shamra on the coast and others further inland, led to the adoption of the practice of decorating with bands vessels that in other respects were copied from those in use at Byblos and elsewhere to the south.

From this northern coastal area must have come the new groups at Megiddo. Other elements in the repertory of forms in Middle Bronze I at Megiddo cannot at present be exactly paralleled in published material, for instance the juglet with the upward-pointing rim,[3] and the bowls with thickened rims, but the former has a somewhat Anatolian look, and the latter has some resem-

[1] Compare for instance G, 12, pl. xxx.35R, from 'Ajjūl, §1, 9, from Ras el-'Ain and §1, 8, pl. cxviii.800 from Byblos with G, 4, pl. 29.3 from Megiddo and G, 12, fig. 100.12–14 from Ras Shamra.

[2] §1, 7, pls. xxxi–xxxii, Mishrifé, Tombe 1.

[3] G, 9, pls. 11.2, 16.2.

blance to bowls from Qatna,[1] so again a northern origin is indicated. It can therefore be concluded that groups both from the northern coastal area and from the neighbourhood of Byblos were penetrating into Palestine at this time.

The culture established at this stage, of which the pottery is the most widespread and easily recognizable evidence, is of great importance, for it is the culture that dominated the Syrian coast down to the time of disruption by the Peoples of the Sea *c.* 1200 B.C. For this continuity, pottery is again the best evidence. In the north, the succession can be seen at Ras Shamra,[2] in the south at sites such as Megiddo,[3] Tell el-ʿAjjūl,[4] Tell el-Fārʿah[5] and Tell Beit Mirsim.[6] The basic pottery repertory develops without break. To it is added, especially in the Late Bronze Age from the sixteenth century B.C. onwards, an increasing amount of foreign imports, especially Cypriot and, later, Mycenaean, which provide useful dating evidence. Not only is this basic continuity important, but it is equally necessary to stress the cultural continuum over the whole area. With minor variations, the groups of finds at Ras Shamra, for instance, can be closely compared at all periods with those from Megiddo, Tell el-Fārʿah and Jericho.[7]

This is the culture of the land of Canaan, known as Kinakhna to the Akkadians from the purple dye[8] for which it was famous. Its claim to fame in world history is that Canaan produced the alphabet that was to be the ancestor of all western alphabets, and a literature to which, through the Old Testament, all literature owes a great debt. It is generally agreed that Canaanite is not an ethnic term, but one that is more properly applied to a culture.[9] With this the archaeological evidence outlined above agrees. Out of the elements of the pre-existing Early Bronze Age civilization and the intruding Amorite semi-nomadic way of life of the E.B.-M.B. phase emerged the Middle Bronze Age Canaanite civilization, of which the evidence is to be found from north to

---

[1] §1, 7, pl. xxxiv, Mishrifé, Tombe 1.

[2] Material assembled in §1, 12; e.g. figs. 101, 105–8, published in more detail in, for example, §1, 10, fig. xiv; §1, 11, figs. 6, 31, 35, 36.

[3] G, 4; 9.   [4] G, 11; 12; 13; 14.

[5] G, 15; 10. This Tell el-Fārʿah is to be distinguished from the Tell el-Fārʿah near Nablus (see below p. 108), which is probably the site of Tirzah.

[6] G, 1; 2.

[7] E.g. for early M.B.II compare §1, 12, fig. 105 with G, 8, figs. 95–98; for sixteenth century B.C. compare G, 4, pls. 45–8 and §1, 11, fig. 19; for fourteenth century B.C. compare §1, 11, fig. 11 and G, 9, pls. 63–7.

[8] See E. A. Speiser in *Ann. A.S.O.R.* 16 (1936), 121 f.; *C.A.H.* ii³, pt. 2, ch. XXXIII, sect. II.   [9] See, for example, §1, 4.

south of the Syro-Palestinian littoral for the greater part of the
second millennium B.C.

Though this Canaanite culture played such an important part
in the development of written records, it is still possible, throughout the Middle and Late Bronze Ages, to establish absolute dates
only by reference to contacts with Egypt, for Canaan did not
advance to the stage of formulating a calendar. Dates in both
Syria and Palestine are therefore ultimately dependent on finds
of Egyptian objects in recognizable contexts, and in the first stage
Palestinian chronology must be dependent on that of Syria, since
the contacts there were better. The best evidence comes from the
comparison of the finds in the various foundation deposits in the
Byblos sacred area with those in the tombs of Abi-shemu and
Ypshomuibi, dated by finds to the reigns of Ammenemes III
(1842–1797 B.C.) and Ammenemes IV (1798–1790 B.C.). Most
of the foundation deposits have no Egyptian objects, but one,
Montet's jar,[1] has a large number of scarabs that are probably of
the First Intermediate Period.[2] The rest of the contents of this
jar were of the typical E.B.-M.B. range. In the deposits in the
Champs des Offrandes there is a change of emphasis. In groups
for which a late date can be suggested, on the grounds that
typical E.B.-M.B. weapons, particularly fenestrated axes, are in
gold with elaborately moulded decoration,[3] and are thus ceremonial and no longer functional, there is a considerable increase
in Egyptian objects.[4] These deposits could be contemporary with
the Eleventh Dynasty, when Egyptian power was beginning to
recover. In between that time and the end of the Twelfth
Dynasty, the type of pottery characteristic of M.B. I had evolved
for, as already stated, this is found in the royal tombs.

A date for the beginning of M.B. I in Palestine of the second
half of the nineteenth century B.C. is thus probable. It cannot be
put too late, for the transition to M.B. II had taken place by the
early eighteenth century,[5] but it is not necessary to allow more
than half a century for it in view of the small amount of material
to be ascribed to it. The presence in Palestine of a few Twelfth
Dynasty scarabs starting with Sesostris I (1971–1928 B.C.) suggests that there were some contacts as early as that. Unfortunately, the early scarabs have not been found in significant

---

[1] §1, 8, pls. LX–LXXI.
[2] They were dated by Albright to the Thirteenth Dynasty (G, 2, 24, sect. 24),
but a more recent study by Miss O. Tufnell makes an earlier date seem probable.
[3] E.g. §1, 3, pl. CXIX.   [4] E.g. §1, 3, pls. CXXIII–CXXVI.
[5] See below, p. 94.

contexts; for instance the scarabs of Sesostris I at Duweir come
from the fill of a quarry and from a Late Bronze Age context,
and at Megiddo from Stratum X, belonging to the end of the
Middle Bronze Age. They cannot therefore be used to date
M.B. I deposits. In any case, the paucity of Twelfth Dynasty
scarabs compared with later ones shows that contact between
Egypt and Palestine at this period was slight, which would fit
better with the state of affairs in E.B.-M.B. Palestine than in
M.B. I.

II. MIDDLE BRONZE AGE II

The small number of sites on which evidence for Middle Bronze I
is found suggests that the period was of short duration. The
general spread of the culture took place in M.B. II, when a large
number of the places that had been towns in the Early Bronze
Age once more attained that status. Exceptions are some towns
in the central hill country such as 'Ai and Shiloh, and this area
was perhaps less fully occupied than previously. The towns were
not large in size. For sites of which the size can be ascertained,
they range from some 7 acres at Jericho to 13 acres at Megiddo
and 182 acres at Hazor in its period of maximum expansion.
They were all enclosed by defensive walls, probably at all stages
in their existence. Within the defences the houses were close-
packed. There is little evidence of any regular town-planning,
and none of any architectural pretensions. Fine stone-working is
in fact alien to Palestine until comparatively modern times; when
it is found, as in ninth century B.C. Samaria, it is the result
of temporary foreign influence. There is also not much evidence
of public buildings even of a religious nature, though this may be
a result of the chances of excavation. In the material culture, the
pottery reaches a considerable degree of technical competence,
and some of it is pleasing in appearance (see Fig. 2). There is
evidence of competence also in other arts and crafts, for instance
in wood-working[1] and the manufacture of vessels in the local
equivalent of alabaster.[2] But of any true artistic achievement there
is no evidence at all; the carved bone strips applied to wooden
boxes are attractive but they are not art. There is also no evidence
of any high degree of wealth. Objects in precious materials are of
course liable to be looted, but this applies to all periods, and it
cannot only be chance that in the Late Bronze gold objects are
found in relative abundance, for instance at Tell el-'Ajjūl,[3] and

[1] G, 7, ch. 5 and Appendix B.   [2] §II, 1.
[3] G, 12, 6–8, sects. 32–5, pls. I–III.

also carved ivories, for instance at Megiddo,[1] while scarcely anything of the sort comes from Middle Bronze contexts.

There is also little evidence of foreign trade or connexions. Scarabs are of course found in enormous numbers. A few have Egyptian royal and other names, and are presumably imports, and the fineness of cutting of others also suggests they are imports,

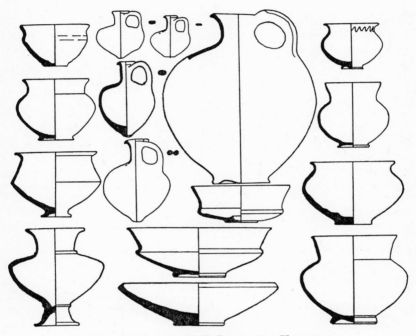

Fig. 2. Selected Middle Bronze Age II pottery.

but the great majority are probably locally produced. The alabaster-workers and the joiners, whose products have just been mentioned, based their work on Egyptian originals or perhaps the original craftsmen were trained by immigrant Egyptians, but objects actually imported from Egypt were very few. A very few imported Cypriot vessels are found, so few that it is almost possible to give an exhaustive list,[2] and infinitesimal in number

[1] §II, 2.

[2] Six tombs on the *tell* at Megiddo, Tombs 5134, 5068, 3111, 3065, 5050, 5243, 4109 and two in the cemetery (8 and 7) have one or occasionally two vessels: G, 9, pls. 26 and 34; G, 4, pls. 38, 41; from the southern Tell el-Fār'ah, tomb 551, §III, 5, 68 R².

compared with those found in Late Bronze Age deposits. It would seem that at this time Palestine had little in the way of surpluses available to exchange for luxury goods.

Within M.B. II falls the period of the Hyksos in Egypt. Such importance has been attached to this that the period in Palestine is sometimes given the overall name of Hyksos and the pottery and other objects typical of this stage designated specifically Hyksos. This is incorrect, for the cultural continuity from M.B. I to M.B. II has already been suggested and will be further emphasized below, and the cultural continuum at this period from north to south on the Syrian littoral has been emphasized. Unless this whole new culture is to be ascribed to the Hyksos none of it is Hyksos. The significance of the Hyksos will be discussed below.

In the following section, the evidence derived from the excavation of the most important sites is described, as providing the basis for these introductory remarks and for the conclusions on the course of Palestinian history and culture that follow. It is in fact only by assembling this evidence that the history of Palestine can be established.

III. MIDDLE BRONZE AGE II: SITES

It is convenient to begin with *Jericho* because, though this town was small and of this only a very small part has survived, an exceptionally large number of tombs has been excavated, and these, combined with evidence from the excavated part of the town, provide a framework for much of the finds from elsewhere.

The *tell* at Jericho has suffered exceptionally severe erosion; over most of the mound, the latest surviving levels within the town area are Early Bronze Age, though on the slopes there are E.B.-M.B. remains. This erosion took place before Iron Age II, since in places buildings of that period immediately overlie erosion wash and gulleys cutting into earlier levels. The only area in which anything of the Middle and Late Bronze Ages survives is on the east. The contours of the mound have a somewhat half-moon shape, with a dip towards the centre of the east side. This is the point at which to-day the spring, for millennia the reason for the existence of the town, emerges from the ground. It was this no doubt that was responsible for the slope of the mound in this direction since access to the spring had to be maintained. This area suffered less denudation than the higher part of the mound, and here therefore Middle Bronze houses survived, with also a very small patch of Late Bronze Age levels above.

Of the uppermost Middle Bronze Age houses an area of about 37 m. by 24 m. has been excavated in the campaigns of 1930–6 and 1952–8.[1] Of the lower levels only a much more restricted sounding has been made.[2] Of the plan of these lower buildings, not a great deal could be established. But one very important point was clear. A lower succession of levels was associated with a line of town wall on the extreme surviving edge of the mound, where it is cut into by the modern road. The town wall showed some three rebuilds, all of them of mud brick, in style resembling that of the Early Bronze Age. It was also almost certain that immediately to the south of the excavated area there was a gate, probably of the type with inturned passage-way divided by buttresses, which is normal in the period.[3] The area to the south had unfortunately been already disturbed by previous excavations, so could not be examined.

The upper succession of building levels passed over the top of this line of defences, and were associated with a line further to the east, but the continuation of the surfaces was cut by the modern road, and all traces of the defences at this point destroyed by modern reservoirs in connexion with the spring. It is, however, virtually certain that the new defences were those of which the great plaster-faced rampart[4] formed the most important element, which can be traced round a considerable part of the site. The surviving part of these defences is where they are backed against the mound built up by the earlier occupation. The rampart had the effect of steepening the slope to an angle of 35°, and raising its height by some 6 m. with a slope down inside of this amount. At the base of the bank was a stone revetment. From it a smooth plastered surface sloped up to a wall on the summit, of which only the foundations survived, and that only in one place. There were three successive stages in this composite system of defence, of which the final one had a very massive stone revetment at the foot, resting on bed-rock with all earlier deposits in front of it removed, and standing to the height of c. 4·50 m.[5] This revetment has been traced round a considerable part of the mound, and in particular was traced by the Austro-German expedition sweeping round to the east across the

[1] For 1930–6 see §III, 8, 118 ff.; for 1952–8 §III, 11, 229 ff.
[2] §III, 13, 81; §III, 14, 106 f. The full report will be published in *Jericho III*.
[3] G, 3, 30 ff., sect. 38.   [4] See Plate 72.
[5] §III, 12, pl. xxxix; G, 6, pl. 31.

modern road.[1] This indicates that the rampart defences are those
to which the upper series of building levels on the east side must
have run. On this east side, however, they must have had a
different character, for if one can judge from the line as traced,
they must have swung out into the plain to a distance of some
50 m. east of the pre-existing walls. Here they must have formed
a rampart free-standing on both sides, which is an important link
with similar fortifications to be discussed below.

The final stage of buildings belonging to these defences is that
already mentioned, of which an appreciable area was cleared in the
course of the two expeditions.[2] It shows a plan based on two roads,
separated from each other by a distance of 27 m., climbing the
slope of the mound with wide-cobbled steps. Flanking them were
houses of irregular plan and consisting of small, unpretentious
rooms. The buildings were in terraces, following the slope of the
mound, as indeed had been their Early Bronze Age predecessors.
In character, it is very probable that they resembled their modern
successors in many oriental towns, for instance the Old City of
Jerusalem, having on the ground floor single-roomed shops with
no direct connexion with the rest of the building and storerooms,
while on the upper floor there are living quarters and industrial
establishments. The storerooms[3] formed the most striking feature
of the excavated remains, for in a number of them were great
storage jars full of grain,[4] calcined, and thus preserved, in the
fire that destroyed the building. Evidence of an industrial
establishment on an upper floor came from the area excavated in
the 1952–8 campaigns, in which fifty-two saddle querns and
many rubbing stones, a number far in excess of domestic require-
ments, were recovered in the débris of collapse, suggesting that
there was a milling establishment in the upper floor.

This final stage of the Jericho Middle Bronze Age town was
destroyed by a violent fire. Walls and floors are hardened and
blackened, burnt débris and beams from the upper storeys fill the
rooms, and the whole is covered by a wash from burnt walls that
accumulated during a period of abandonment. Since, as will be
seen, the contents seem to go down to the end of the Middle
Bronze Age and not beyond, it is probable that this destruction

[1] G, 17, Tafel I.   [2] For combined plan, see G, 6, pl. 31.
[3] In the report of the 1930–6 excavations, §III, 7, 41, §III, 8, pl. xv, these are
erroneously described as 'Palace Storerooms'. This has proved to be incorrect, both
since the so-called Palace is certainly, on visual surviving evidence, later, and
since they extend north of the road into the next block.
[4] §III, 8, pls. xli–xlii; §III, 11, pl. 47.

is connected with the disturbances caused by the expulsion of the Hyksos from Egypt.[1]

Work on the finds from these Middle Bronze Age levels has not yet (1965) been completed. But enough has been done to enable the finds from the tombs[2] to be used to elucidate the sequence and to fill in details of the contemporary culture. Almost all the Jericho tombs so far discovered lie outside the town to the west and north. The exceptions are one tomb built of mud-bricks and two graves which were in the excavated area just described. They belong to an early phase in the Middle Bronze Age, perhaps late M.B. I, and presumably belong to a stage of tentative, small-scale occupation. Even in M.B. I, however, the practice of burying in rock-cut tombs outside the town had begun.[3]

The areas on the low slopes outside the town to the west and north had been used as burial grounds from the Proto-Urban period onwards.[4] In the area to the north there had been a tremendous expansion of tombs during the E.B.-M.B. period, owing to the practice of tombs being devoted to a single individual.[5] In both areas are also found tombs of the Middle Bronze Age. All are rock-cut chambers approached by a vertical shaft. In the northern area, at least, a large proportion are re-used E.B.-M.B. tombs of all types,[6] but some are newly excavated at this period.[7] But though many of the tombs are re-used, the complete change in burial methods is strong supporting evidence of the introduction of a new culture. With very few exceptions, the burials are multiple and successive. They can best be interpreted as family vaults. A burial would be made, with accompanying offerings. When a second was made, or at least when the available floor space was occupied, the earlier deposits, skeletons and offerings, were pushed unceremoniously to the rear, and the new burial placed in a cleared space in front. In some cases, if the tomb was small, long bones were thrown out, and only skulls preserved. Thus, as the use of the tomb continued, a mound of 'ancestral' remains accumulated round the wall of the chamber, with the latest burial placed low down in front.[8] The number of individuals

[1] See below, ch. VIII.   [2] G, 7, ch. 5; G, 8, ch. 4.
[3] G, 8, 203 ff.   [4] G, 7, ch. 2; G, 8, ch. 2.
[5] The evidence concerning the area to the west of the *tell* is less precise, since the E.B.–M.B. period had not been recognized at that time.
[6] See *C.A.H.* I³, pt. 2, ch. XXI, sect. VI.
[7] The proportions are 41 re-used to 11 new (uncertain 17). See G, 8, 547.
[8] Since this process was not comprehended during the 1930–6 excavations, and the tombs were excavated in rigidly horizontal layers, the conclusions made as to contemporaneity and succession are not valid.

buried in the tombs excavated in the 1952–8 campaigns ranges from one to forty-five, with only three (one an infant) single burials and only five others with under ten.[1]

In each tomb, therefore, there may be two or three generations buried. In some cases an earlier tomb was re-used after an interval. But a study of the finds, particularly of the pottery, shows that a classification can be made of finds characteristic of a succession of phases. One tomb only probably belongs to M.B. I.[2] From the stage when the initial characteristics of M.B. I begin to be altered down to the time before new imports usher in the Late Bronze Age, the tombs at Jericho suggest five main phases.[3]

The contents characteristic of these phases can be used as a yardstick for establishing contemporaneity of levels on the site at Jericho, and also for levels on other sites, for the great majority of the finds, pottery, toggle-pins, alabasters and so on, are found on every Palestinian site. They do not, of course, provide absolute dating. The only clue for this comes from the associated scarabs. A very thorough study of these with reference to the phases with which they can be associated[4] shows that most of the decorative designs have little chronological significance. On the basis of the few occurrences of royal names and official titles, and features that can reasonably be associated with the history of Egypt in the Second Intermediate Period, a date of late in the nineteenth century can be suggested for the beginning of phase i, of c. 1716 B.C. for the beginning of phase iii, and the end of phase v coinciding with the end of the Second Intermediate c. 1567 B.C.[5]

As far as the chronology of the successive building stages on the town site of Jericho is concerned, the evidence has not yet (1965) been fully worked out. It would, however, seem from the evidence so far assessed that the main event in which the rampart defences succeeded the free-standing brick walls occurred within phase iii of the tomb classification, and therefore about 1700 B.C.

Besides the evidence for the classification of pottery and other objects, the tombs provided invaluable evidence concerning the contemporary culture. The best evidence came from the latest tombs,[6] for in them were made multiple burials, presumably as a result of some epidemic, at a date so shortly preceding the

---

[1] G, 7, 264; G, 8, 169.   [2] G, 8, 203 ff.
[3] G, 7, ch. 5, esp. 266 ff.; G, 8, ch. 4, esp. 171 ff. For a summary, with selected pottery types, see G, 6, 170 ff., figs. 38–42.
[4] By Miss D. Kirkbride in G, 8, Appendix E.
[5] *Ibid.* pp. 592 f.   [6] G, 7, 264 ff., 443 ff.

destruction of the Middle Bronze Age town that they were not disturbed by subsequent burials. Moreover, conditions in the tombs at Jericho[1] allowed organic material such as wood and basketry to survive to an extent not hitherto found in Palestinian tombs. It is clear that the dead were buried with provisions and equipment for the after-life which must have been based on their needs and equipment during life. Drink was provided in great storage jars, often with a dipper juglet suspended in the mouth for ladling it out, food was usually in the form of joints of mutton (or goat), though there were as well some traces of what was probably bread. Pomegranates and grapes were also found. Goblets and platters were provided as table-ware. The chief personal possessions were toilet accessories, usually placed in baskets, juglets which probably held oil, alabaster juglets and bowls probably for scent and cosmetics, small wooden boxes to contain perhaps the pins and combs which were found on the bodies, and amorphous masses of hair that were probably wigs. Ornaments were few. The only common ones were toggle-pins. The dead person was apparently buried clothed, and a toggle-pin secured the garment; from the position of the pin it can be deduced[2] that the garment was secured on the shoulder or chest. Of the actual garment only fragments survived, but the material was apparently a loosely woven textile of vegetable origin.[3] Scarabs were very common. They seem more often to have been suspended from a pin, necklace or attached to a wrist, than worn on a ring.[4] Bead necklaces were not common. When a single individual was buried, his possessions were placed round him; when a whole family group was buried together[5] the food was ranged round the walls of the chamber and items of toilet equipment placed with individual bodies.

The most interesting evidence comes from the furniture. Many dead persons were provided with a table, and this was almost invariable when a number were buried simultaneously. It was a long narrow affair made of a single plank with a separate border attached by dowel pegs. Invariably there were three legs, two at one end and one at the other, presumably to stand better on uneven ground. This was apparently the only common object of household furniture. Only in tombs in which there was evidence to suggest the burial of an important person was there other furniture. In a few cases there were stools, some with legs which in the earlier tombs had zoomorphic mouldings, but which in

---

[1] G, 8, Appendix L.   [2] G, 8, 566 ff.   [3] G, 7, 519 ff.; G, 8, 662 f.
[4] G, 8, 571 ff.   [5] E.g. G, 7, 500 ff.

the later ones had become stylized. These stools have resemblances to those found in Egyptian tombs, and show the woodworkers must have learnt their art from imported originals or itinerant craftsmen. In one instance a bed was provided. Otherwise the dead person lay on the ground, usually on a reed mat, though there were three instances of a mud-brick platform being provided.[1]

From this evidence it can be deduced that the equipment in the average house of Middle Bronze Age Jericho was simple, a low table, mats to sit and sleep on, utensils for eating and drinking, and little else, and that the personal equipment and ornaments were also simple. Jericho may from its geographical position have been something of a backwater. It could well be that in towns such as Megiddo and Tell ed-Duweir there was greater luxury. The tombs in these places have not provided the wealth of evidence that those of Jericho have, but in fact there is little in their surviving contents to suggest much difference, and it may be that the deductions that can be made from the Jericho evidence concerning the way of life of the Middle Bronze Age townspeople are valid for Palestine as a whole.

One further point is very striking. Provision is made only for the purely material needs in the after-life. Not a single object suggests the necessity of helping the soul of the dead person by placating any deity. There are no images or representations of any deities (with the exception of those on scarabs, which are hardly relevant) and no cult objects. The contrast with contemporary Egypt is most striking, and is strong evidence that any contacts with Egypt, even at the time of Hyksos domination there, had only a superficial effect.

Finally, there is absolutely no evidence of any acquaintance with writing. Gaps in evidence concerning the development of the proto-Semitic script are rightly explained by the fact that, unlike cuneiform used on durable clay tablets, it was used on papyrus. But if there had been any papyri in the Jericho tombs, they could have survived just as well as the flesh and other organic material, and not a single trace was found.

The site that is most often quoted as providing evidence for successive periods is *Megiddo*, the magnificent *tell* that guards the pass over the neck of the Carmel ridge through which the coast road from Egypt passed to reach the Plain of Esdraelon and thence across the Jordan to Syria. But, as mentioned above, the evidence of Megiddo cannot be used without much sifting, since what is published as one stratum takes no account of

[1] G, 8, 576 f.

disturbances such as tombs penetrating to that level, or of the fact that, as is inevitable in a site which previous occupation had built up into a high mound, contemporary buildings are not at one absolute level, but climb the mound in a series of terraces.

As a result of this method of excavation, neither the plans assigned to the so-called strata nor the finds ascribed to these strata can be taken as the entities as which they are published. In the case of the plans, not only is there the failure to recognize the terraces, but it is in many instances obvious that what is published in the plan of one stratum is merely the foundations of the buildings of a succeeding one; evidence on two or even more successive plans must be used to build up the true plan of any one phase. In the case of the pottery and other finds, the contents of the tombs have to be abstracted, but even then what remains cannot safely be used to date the building phases, for the state of the structures shows that there were many disturbances from wall-robbing and the like, and also it is seldom that finds are related to floor or occupation levels.

In spite of these difficulties it is possible to work out the history of Megiddo in the Middle Bronze Age, though this history does not correspond with the publication of the two areas which were excavated to the levels of the period.[1] The evidence of the succession and dating for the structures must be taken from the tombs. It is a curious feature of Megiddo that most of the burials seem to have been made within the town. In the area on the slopes in which the E.B.-M.B. shaft tombs were cut,[2] there were a few burials from M.B. II onwards, either in re-used shaft tombs or rough pits in the rock, but only thirteen in an area of c. 14,000 sq. m.[2] In the two areas on the *tell* totalling c. 625 sq. m.[2], there were 123 burials. From the contents of the tombs, it is possible to work out a succession of nine phases with distinctive contents covering M.B. I and M.B. II. By comparing the position of the tombs with the structures, that is to say whether they are beneath walls or intact floors or break into them, the structures can be dated with reference to the tomb phases. Also, since there is no gap in the pottery sequence in the tombs, it can be proved that the tombs must have been made adjacent to existing buildings, and do not represent a series of periods when there was no occupation in the particular part of the town. The only exception is that in Area BB many of the M.B. I tombs may have preceded the earliest Middle Bronze Age buildings. This would agree with the

[1] G, 9, Area AA, 6–16, Area BB, 84–102.
[2] *C.A.H.* 1³, pt. 2, ch. XXI, sect. VI; G, 4, 135 ff.

evidence from other sites already mentioned that the earliest Middle Bronze groups in Palestine were small in numbers. The Megiddo evidence, however, suggests that there was heavier occupation here than anywhere else.

The successive Middle Bronze building phases worked out on this basis are five in number. It is possible that there was already a town wall in M.B. I. The fine gateway with an oblique stepped approach, and the adjacent section of the town wall, uncovered in the area excavated on the northern side of the mound,[1] is earlier than tombs belonging to the beginning of M.B. II. It may therefore belong to M.B. I, but since this was the lowest level excavated in this area, it cannot be proved that it was not Early Bronze Age. In the eastern area excavated, a town wall[2] appears only in the third of the building phases, the earlier walls being presumably further down the slope to the east.

The houses within the walls had for the most part smallish and irregularly planned rooms, though there is some suggestion in the fragmentary remains that some of the houses were of reasonable size. Only in the final M.B. II phase does a more regular layout with a defined and regular street plan appear, and in this there is clear evidence of houses of some size. At this stage, the town wall on the east had once more moved down the slope to the east of the area excavated; in the northern area it remained in approximately the same position throughout. There is, however, a curious feature in all the plans of the eastern area, in that there is a complete blank in the centre. This is the site occupied by the successive temples of the Early Bronze Age and the E.B.-M.B. period. In the levels ascribed in the publication to the Late Bronze Age, there was also a temple here.[3] It is too much of a coincidence that an area that was sacred for some twelve hundred years should be derelict for some four hundred years, and then once more become sacred for three hundred years. The interpretation is clear. From the one schematic and unsatisfactory section published,[4] it is obvious that the massive structures of the earlier periods had been built up a mound. Though published pottery evidence in the actual area of the temples is completely lacking, it can be asserted with confidence that the earliest temple[5] belongs to the Middle Bronze Age, and probably to such an early phase that the existence of the earlier temples was still remembered, and that the three stages of this temple covered the whole of the

---

[1] G, 9, fig. 378, stratum XIII.
[2] G, 9, fig. 397.
[3] G, 9, figs. 402–4.
[4] G, 9, fig. 416, BB.
[5] G, 9, fig. 402.

Middle and Late Bronze Ages. There is a close similarity in plan to that ascribed to the end of the Middle Bronze Age at Shechem.

In terms of absolute chronology, the contents of successive tomb phases correspond well with those at Jericho. In particular, those of the latest phase, to which the fifth of the building phases belongs, correspond well with the last of the phases at Jericho, dated as already described to the end of the Second Intermediate Period of Egypt. At the latter site the town was destroyed, presumably in connexion with the disturbances caused by the expulsion of the Hyksos from Egypt. At Megiddo, the break was not so complete, and the main layout of the town continued throughout the Late Bronze Age.

Hazor is situated in the Jordan valley, south-east of Lake Hūleh and 25 km. north of the Sea of Galilee. In the Middle and Late Bronze Ages, it was the largest town in Palestine, with an area of *c.* 182 acres. As such it justifies its description in Joshua xi. 10 as 'the head of all those kingdoms', and its international importance is shown by mentions in the Mari letters,[1] in the annals of a number of the pharaohs of the New Kingdom[2] and by its appearance in four of the Amarna letters.[3]

The remains of Hazor[4] consist of a mound at the southern end and a great plateau, approximately rectangular, defended by artificial and natural features, extending to the north. The original occupation in Early Bronze III was, like that of the Iron Age, confined to the *tell*. Above the Early Bronze Age remains, a level containing a considerable amount of pottery but without any structures shows that this town too was destroyed by the E.B.-M.B. invaders, and the pottery links the particular group with that found at Megiddo. Here too the newcomers of the Middle Bronze Age appear in small numbers. Of the finds published from the excavated areas, there is not much to suggest a M.B. I occupation, and the newcomers may have appeared only at the beginning of M.B. II, but admittedly only a small area of the *tell*, to which the first Middle Bronze settlement was confined, has been excavated to this level. In this first stage of occupation, down to the beginning of M.B. II, only burials are found in the plateau to the north.[5] The more important burials may have been grandiose in style, for the excavators believed that a complex of

[1] §III, 2, 39, 101. [2] Cited in §III, 20, 242 ff.
[3] §III, 15, nos. 148, 227, 228; *R.A.* 19 (1922), 95 f.
[4] See §III, 30; §III, 31. See Plate 73.
[5] §III, 30, Area D, 99–141, Area E, 146–158.

tunnels and underground chambers was designed for use as burial chambers for the princes and aristocracy.[1]

The second main stage in the history of Hazor in the Middle Bronze is marked by a dramatic development. The plateau to the north of the *tell*, partly bounded by natural wadis, was included in the city, and at those points at which there were no natural defences a great fosse was cut, and the materials from the excavation of the fosse were built up into a bank some 12 m. high. The analogy of this kind of defence with that of the second type of defence at Jericho is clear. A gateway, with two M.B. II stages was partly excavated;[2] in the second phase it had an entrance passage flanked by triple buttresses, which is a common plan at this time.[3]

This great expansion, adding some 178 acres to the area of the town, comes comparatively late in M.B. II. The excavators had difficulty in relating the rampart closely to the occupation levels, but it seems probable from the pottery and other evidence, that both the rampart and the first occupation of the area correspond with the third phase at Jericho, in the late eighteenth century B.C. The addition of this great area to the city represented a true city growth and not, as has been suggested, a mere camp enclosure, for within it, in all the areas that have been tested, were buildings of the Middle Bronze Age, some of them temples and sanctuaries of great interest. One building was on a scale suggesting a palace or public building.[4] Another building partly uncovered in a sounding on the *tell* was also palatial in character.[5]

The remains of the final Middle Bronze Age buildings were covered with a thick layer of burning. A comparison of the pottery suggests that this was contemporary with the destruction of Middle Bronze Age in Jericho. It is possible that at Hazor too there was some gap in occupation. There is not much material corresponding with that of Stratum IX at Megiddo, which probably covers the second half of the sixteenth century. Either Hazor was abandoned for part of this period, or occupation was on a much reduced scale. Any abandonment was not however sufficiently long for traces of preceding buildings to disappear; the temple at the north end of the site[6] and the gate on the eastern side of the plateau[7] were, for instance, rebuilt on approximately the same plan.

Tell ed-Duweir in southern Palestine, probably the site of the

[1] §III, 28, 11; §III, 27, 11 f.
[2] §III, 29, 84 ff. [3] G, 3, 31. [4] §III, 3, 127.
[5] §III, 29, 76 f. [6] *Ibid*. 84. [7] *Ibid*. 85 f.

Biblical Lachish, is comparable in size with the great northern sites of Megiddo and Beth-shan. Like them, it was an important town in the Middle Bronze Age, but it achieved importance certainly at a later stage than Megiddo. Its history may be comparable with that of Hazor, though as at Hazor the levels which could possibly provide evidence concerning the earlier stages of the Middle Bronze Age have been little examined.

Excavations at Tell ed-Duweir were tragically curtailed by the death of its excavator, J. L. Starkey, in 1938. As a result, soundings only were carried out on the town site. These revealed something of the defences of the Middle Bronze Age, but nothing of the town inside. The only other evidence is derived from tombs. Two cuts into the lower part of the defences, and some clearance along their base show that in the later part of M.B. II the site was defended by an earth rampart similar to that at Jericho, Hazor and elsewhere. The structure seems to be similar to that at Jericho, a rampart piled on the slope of the earlier city mound. In the only cut that penetrated far into the mound,[1] there were at the base occupation levels belonging to Early Bronze III. From a height of 6 ft. above bed-rock, these were overlaid by what was apparently a homogeneous fill containing much derived Early Bronze Age material but including throughout it a number of M.B. II sherds. In the highest surviving levels were some layers of plaster[2] which, from the evidence of the use of plaster in a second cut at Duweir, and from the methods employed at Jericho, probably represent plaster tongues or keys over successive layers of fill in the rampart. In this second cut at Duweir, at the north-west corner,[3] a stretch of the sloping plaster surface was well preserved, and compares closely with that at Jericho, though it is not quite so steep. From this north-west section came clear evidence that this rampart at Duweir does not belong to the beginning of the Middle Bronze Age, for it overlies one burial of the period and probably two others.[4] The pottery with the burial certainly sealed by the rampart would equate with the second phase at Jericho, and one of the two less certainly sealed would be of the same period and the other would equate with the third Jericho phase. The sherds in the fill agree in suggesting that the Duweir rampart belongs to about the same period as that at Jericho.

The excavators at Duweir were not certain that the rampart there was associated with a revetment at the foot,[5] but here again

[1] G, 18, 45 ff., pl. 96.   [2] Ibid. 46.
[3] Ibid. 46, pl. 5.1–2, pl. 90.   [4] Ibid. 47, 62, pl. 5.3–4.   [5] Ibid. 46.

the Jericho evidence can assist the interpretation. A comparison of the sections through the two[1] shows not only that the massive stone revetment leaning back against the fill at Duweir (for which there was no close dating evidence), is very closely similar to that at Jericho, but also that at Duweir too there had been an earlier revetment. This must be the explanation of the curious slot on the published section, for the stones at its base cannot possibly be explained as a collapse of a Late Bronze Age wall,[2] but rather as the remains of an original revetment, largely dismantled to construct the later one, precisely as was done at Jericho. In the north-west cut, no revetment survived; its disappearance would account for the erosion shown on the section of the lower part of the plaster facing. In this area there was found that other component of the Middle Bronze Age defences at Duweir known as the Fosse. As the section[3] shows, this is a rather grandiose name for a flat-bottomed ditch with a maximum depth of 0·75 m. This ditch was found only on the west side, where it was traced for 140 m.[4] It is probably in fact little more than a flattening of the external contours to increase the height of the retaining wall at the foot of the rampart, a flattening which elsewhere, as at Jericho, was provided by the clearance to rock of the pre-existing levels, as shown in the north-east section.[5] It may have served the incidental purpose of a quarry for the stones of the revetment.

The surviving defences of Duweir therefore come comparatively late in M.B. II, perhaps at the end of the eighteenth century B.C. The present evidence does not prove that there was a town here in the first stages of the Middle Bronze Age. As already stated, the town site was not excavated to this level and the only evidence comes from tombs. In addition to the three burials on the mound already mentioned, seventeen Middle Bronze Age tombs were excavated in the surrounding areas, being found in four of the six cemeteries. Three of these may be equated with Jericho phase ii (probably late in it), four with phase iii, six with phase iv and four with phase v. This would suggest that there was no town here in M.B. I or the beginning of M.B. II. The evidence is not however conclusive. The number of tombs is very small. For the very much smaller town of Jericho, sixty-nine tombs of the Middle Bronze Age were identified. It may well be that many burials, as at Megiddo and Tell el-'Ajjūl, were on the *tell* itself, and at both these sites M.B. I burials on the *tell* are a prominent feature.

[1] G, 18, pl. 96; §III, 11, fig. 4, pl. 44A.   [2] G, 18, 48.
[3] *Ibid.* pl. 90.   [4] *Ibid.* 46.   [5] *Ibid.* pl. 96.

The site of *Tell el-'Ajjūl* is on the Wādi Ghazzeh, some 4 miles from Gaza. With an area of 33 acres, it is one of the most important in the south of Palestine. It would appear that the earliest town on this site belongs to the Middle Bronze Age. There was an E.B.-M.B. population in the neighbourhood, for two separate cemeteries of this period adjoin the *tell*, but on the *tell* itself there is so far no evidence of occupation either at that period or in the Early Bronze Age.

The Middle Bronze Age town moreover probably dates only from the end of this period. It is true that 'Ajjūl is one of the sites which have produced evidence of M.B. I. This comes from burials on the *tell* in the Courtyard Cemetery, so-called because it was adjacent to the building which Petrie designates as a palace. The evidence is, however, clear that the burials are earlier than the building, and all the finds associated with the buildings are of a later period.

The published evidence from the *tell* is limited in extent, for comparatively small areas were excavated. The lowest buildings, founded on rock,[1] are, so far as can be judged from the published evidence, difficult as it is to interpret, associated with pottery of the very end of the Middle Bronze Age, and the building designated as Palace I certainly continued in use into the sixteenth century B.C., for associated with it is bichrome pottery and Cypriot White Slip I ware. The numerous burials discovered, both on the *tell* and in a cemetery area at its foot, may none of them be earlier than Jericho phase v, though in some cases the evidence is difficult to assess.

Petrie associated this Palace I with the great fosse which runs round three sides of the site (the fourth being defended by the Wādi Ghazzeh), for he considered that the blocks which formed a stone socle for the building were derived from the excavation of the fosse.[2] Since Palace I was based on rock and thus belongs to the first occupation, this seems probable, and the fosse thus belongs to the very end of M.B. II, late seventeenth to early sixteenth century B.C. A *terminus ante quem* is given by a Late Bronze Age tomb, probably fourteenth century, which is cut in it.[3] The fosse is said to be 19 ft. deep,[4] with a vertical outer edge[5] and an inner side sloping at an angle of 34°.[6] Presumably also associated therewith is a bank of sandstone grit with a stone revetment at its foot and a mud-brick wall on its summit.[7] The

---

[1] See, for example, G, 12, 3, sect. 11 and G, 15, 23, sect. 69.
[2] G, 12, 2 f., sect. 10.   [3] *Ibid.* 15, sect. 58.   [4] G, 15, 5, sect. 6.
[5] G, 12, 1, sect. 3.   [6] G, 11, 2, sect. 8.   [7] G, 12, 3, sects. 15, 16.

bank can be seen in photographs as upstanding towards the interior.[1]

It would thus seem that the defences at 'Ajjūl are of the same general type as those on the preceding sites, but that here there was a definite ditch, perhaps because here height could not be given to the slope at the rampart by truncating the slope of earlier occupation levels. The date is again towards the end of M.B. II, perhaps rather later than elsewhere.

The southern Tell el-Fār'ah,[2] like Tell el-'Ajjūl, is situated on the Wādi Ghazzeh, some 14 miles further upstream to the southeast. Its history seems to have been very similar to that of 'Ajjūl, except that there is no evidence of a preliminary settlement in M.B. I. The earliest buildings seem to date to the end of the Middle Bronze Age, to a period corresponding to Jericho phase v. Of the numerous Middle Bronze Age tombs excavated, sixty can be closely dated, and of these fifty-eight seem to equate with Jericho phase v, and the remaining two might be of phase iv.

As at 'Ajjūl, the M.B. II town was, where there were not natural defensive features, defended by a ditch, 80 ft. wide from lip to lip, with an inner slope at an angle of 33°.[3] On the north side a bank standing to a maximum of 24 ft. was traced, with a wall on its summit,[4] probably contemporary, though there is no evidence to this effect. At the south end there was a gateway, which the pottery shows to be dated to the end of M.B. II (Jericho phase v), and this had the familiar three-buttress entrance passage.[5] The only other buildings excavated, at the north end of the site,[6] belong, from the evidence of the register of pottery, also to the end of M.B. II.

A site in southern Palestine, almost due east of Tell el-'Ajjūl, but lying in the low hill-country, is Tell Beit Mirsim, which has in Palestinian archaeology an importance that is perhaps out of proportion with its original status. Its importance lies in the fact that it was the first to be excavated with an attempt to record the finds in significant archaeological strata. It was excavated between 1926 and 1932[7] and though the methods could nowadays be refined, the framework that the excavation provided for periods from the end of the Early Bronze Age to the time of the destruction of the kingdom of Judah has been the basis on which all subsequent work on these periods was founded.

---

[1] G, 15, pl. xxxvi, 2.   [2] See above, p. 86 n. 5.   [3] G, 16, 15 f., sect. 45.
[4] Ibid. 17, sect. 48.   [5] G, 10, 29 f., sect. 18, pl. lxxviii.
[6] G, 16, 17, sect, 48, pl. lii; G, 10, 27 f., sects. 12, 13, pl. lxvi.
[7] The Bronze Age material is published in G, 1, G, 2 and G, 3.

A first occupation at the very end of the Early Bronze Age was followed by the appearance of the E.B.-M.B. people. As elsewhere, there is a complete break between this period and the beginning of the Middle Bronze Age. As already described, Tell Beit Mirsim is one of the few sites from which there is evidence, in Strata G-F, of occupation in M.B. I. The M.B. II levels are Strata E and D.

The pottery of Strata G-F is said to be indistinguishable. There are, however, two different structural phases separated by a layer of ashes.[1] The published pottery[2] therefore indicates that there were two periods close to M.B. I, though the stratification was not sharply enough defined and there is not enough published pottery to indicate whether there was any extension into the beginning of M.B. II. Associated with the general phase is a very massive stone-built town wall c. 3·25 m. thick, surviving in one area to a height of 5·30 m.,[3] constructed of fairly regularly coursed smallish stones. This wall is ascribed to Stratum G, but the evidence is not entirely convincing, for the fragmentarily surviving G walls[4] have strikingly no relation to it in alignment or any other aspect. The better preserved Stratum F walls are, however, in many cases related to the town wall in alignment, and the fact that a thin wall is added against the back of the town wall is no evidence that the latter belonged to an earlier period, for the thin wall 0·30–0·50 m. wide is not a buttress to a 3 m. wall, but a wall of houses of period F built against it.

But though this fine wall may belong to Stratum F rather than G, it is nevertheless a town wall of an early stage in the Middle Bronze Age, late M.B. I or early M.B. II. The wall was cleared only in the south-east sector, but there was evidence of it elsewhere, and pottery finds and soundings suggested that the town of the period spread over the whole area of the later settlement. Of the plan of the interior, the surviving remains were fragmentary. They suggested that houses were on a reasonable scale, and one house ascribed to Stratum G,[5] had a large main room with a roof supported on central posts, and is considered to be of a *Breithaus* type.

The second stage in the defences of Tell Beit Mirsim was the addition against the outer face of the wall ascribed to Stratum G of a bank of *terre pisée*, described as a solid mass of hard clay,[6] or in one case as layers of gravel and red earth.[7] No sections or

[1] G, 3, 17, sect. 25.
[2] G, 1, pl. 41; G, 2, pls. 50–51.
[3] G, 3, 29, sect. 37.   [4] *Ibid.* pl. 49.   [5] *Ibid.* 22 f., sects. 29–30, pl. 56.
[6] *Ibid.* 27 ff., sect. 36.   [7] *Ibid.* 19, sect. 27.

clear photographs are published, so the extent and angle of the bank cannot be established. It would, however, appear to convert the free-standing wall of the earlier stage into a wall surmounting a sloping bank, for it is stated[1] that the wall survives to a height of 1·25 m. above the top of the bank. The inner side of the wall remained free-standing, for one of the schematic sections[2] shows a wall of Stratum E against its base. The rampart is ascribed to a late stage in the period of Stratum E, since beneath it were sherds of G-F and E types, while a pit containing sherds of D type was dug into it.[3] The pottery as published from Stratum E[4] would seem to equate with Jericho phase iii, late eighteenth century B.C. On the published evidence it is not possible to say whether Stratum F extended down to this period, without any diagnostic pottery of the first stage of M.B. II being published, or whether this period was included in Stratum E, though, again, types characteristic of the beginning of M.B. II are not published.

At a later stage, the *terre pisée* rampart was strengthened by a revetment of stones on a steep batter.[5] It is not clear to what extent this was a facing added to the existing rampart, or a base for a higher rampart, as at Jericho and Tell ed-Duweir. Associated with the stone revetment was a gateway of which a single pair of buttresses survived, and it may have had the triple buttresses found elsewhere.[6]

The second stage in the rampart defences may go with the town of Stratum D. The plan of the town is orientated similarly to that of E, the walls of the houses being radial to the successive stretches of the town wall. Most of the houses seem to be small, but there is at least one large house, the so-called palace[7] incorporating a large courtyard. Since, in two houses, courtyards in Stratum D seem to have succeeded large rooms in Stratum E, with ceilings supported on posts,[8] it would seem that the introduction of courtyards was a feature of the period.

The period of Stratum D would seem to cover phases iv and v of Jericho. Like Jericho, the site was probably destroyed in the disturbances connected with the expulsion of the Hyksos from Egypt. Like Jericho, too, this final Middle Bronze stage was followed by a period of abandonment.

At the time when excavations were carried out on the great site of *Gezer*, on the edge of the coastal plain west of Jerusalem,

[1] G, 3, 25, sect. 36.
[2] *Ibid*. pl. 53
[3] *Ibid*. 28, sect. 36.
[4] G, 1, pl. 41; G, 2, pls. 52–57.
[5] G, 3, 29, sect. 37.
[6] *Ibid*. 30 ff., sect. 38.
[7] *Ibid*. 35 ff., sects. 42–45.
[8] *Ibid*. 39 f., sect. 46.

excavation was too undeveloped to produce accurate evidence on a site in which the buildings were mainly of stone. Constant robbing of older walls for stones to be used in later building, added to the cutting of cisterns and other disturbances, produces intricate stratification that can be interpreted only by advanced techniques. The pottery and other finds were meticulously studied and classified, but without sound observed stratification the published material cannot be associated with published plans, and indeed it is clear that the groups assigned to the phases called First to Fourth Semitic cover long periods and contain many intrusions. Only an outline picture of the period of occupation can be deduced, assisted to some extent by the evidence of true groups from tombs or caves.

Pottery assigned to the First Semitic period ranges from the Chalcolithic (Ghassulian) to the Middle Bronze Age, so no safe conclusions can be drawn as to the date of the walls assigned to the period. If it can be assumed that the examples published are proportionately representative of those found, it would seem that there was strong occupation in the Ghassulian, Proto-Urban (Late Chalcolithic) and Early Bronze I and II periods, but possibly abandonment in Early Bronze III, for which no diagnostic finds are published. The Intermediate E.B.-M.B. period and M.B. I seem also to be missing. Middle Bronze II vessels are included in the First Semitic group,[1] but mainly come in the Second Semitic group. A good group belonging to an early stage of M.B. II is published from Tomb 1,[2] which is probably contemporary with Jericho phase ii, though there are at least two late Bronze Age intrusions.[3] Tomb 3[4] probably corresponds with Jericho phase iii, and the pottery and other finds from Cave 28 II[5] indicate that an Early Bronze occupation was followed by considerable Middle Bronze use at the time of Jericho phase iv.

All therefore that can be said about Gezer is that it was occupied, probably after an interval of abandonment, from a time early in M.B. II. Presumably the settlement of the period covered the whole built-up area, c. ½ mile long by 500 ft. wide, but there is no evidence concerning the defences of the period. Professor Macalister may be right in thinking that because the great water passage[6] became silted up in Late Bronze II, it must have been constructed at least 500 years previously,[7] which would

---

[1] E.g. §III, 17, pl. CXLII.6, 16, pl. CXLIII.15, pl. CXLVI.1.
[2] §III, 17, pls. LX–LXIII. [3] Ibid. pl. LXIII.56, 74.
[4] §III, 16, 303 f. [5] §III, 17, pls. XXXI–XLII.
[6] §III, 16, 256 ff. [7] Ibid. 262.

assign it to the Middle Bronze Age, but this is hypothesis only.

The site of the northern *Tell el-Fār'ah*, near Nablus, is important for its control of the route via the Wādi Fār'ah from the Jordan valley to the central ridge. It can be identified with great probability as Tirzah, the capital of the Northern Kingdom before the foundation of Samaria.[1] It was a town with very imposing defences during the Early Bronze Age. It was however abandoned before the end of that period, perhaps early in Early Bronze III, and it was not re-occupied until the Middle Bronze Age.

The history of Tell el-Fār'ah in the Middle Bronze Age is very similar to that of Jericho. It begins in M.B. I, and at that time and in the first stages of M.B. II, the occupation was sparse, and the only defences were the patched-up remains of the Early Bronze Age walls. Within this area houses were found in some places, but in others there were none. In the unbuilt-up areas there were a number of burials, mainly containing single bodies only, the most being four. A number of these burials belonged to M.B. I, the latest going down to the period of Jericho phase ii-iii.[2]

This first stage in the Middle Bronze Age of Tell el-Fār'ah was quite clearly prior to the first true Middle Bronze defences, for both buildings and burials were overlaid by the Middle Bronze wall.[3] The first stage in these defences was a stone wall 2–2·25 m. wide,[4] with, in part at least, shallow internal pilasters. On the west side, the wall followed the line of the Early Bronze defences, except that in the south-west corner it curved inside them to leave an area of the Early Bronze town outside. The limits on the north and south were approximately the same, but to the east an appreciable area of the Early Bronze town was excluded. The plan of the gate is one of the best preserved of the period in Palestine (see Fig. 3).[5] A gate tower of two chambers projected in front of the walls. The gate in the inner chamber was opposite that in the town wall, but that in the outer chamber was in the southern side wall, so that those entering had to make a right-angle turn to the right. A bastion projecting in front and to the rear of the wall, with interior rooms, was found *c.* 50 m. south of the gate; others may have existed in the unexcavated parts of the wall.

To these original defences was added[6] what is probably a divergent form of the rampart found on other Palestinian sites.

---

[1] §III, 22, 587 ff. See above p. 86 n. 5. [2] §III, 24, 237 ff.
[3] *Ibid.* 221, 236, 249. [4] §III, 21, 422; §III, 24, 328.
[5] §III, 21, pl. VI. [6] §III, 24, 239.

Outside the wall was a ditch or sunk area, of which the outer side was formed by the inner revetment wall of a flat-topped bank. Of this, the outer side was revetted with a facing of large boulders, preserved to a height of 2·50 m., and against this was a sloping bank of red earth. The top of the bank had a maximum width of 10 m., which diminished to about 2 m. where it met the gate at the inner side of the entrance through the outer gate chamber.

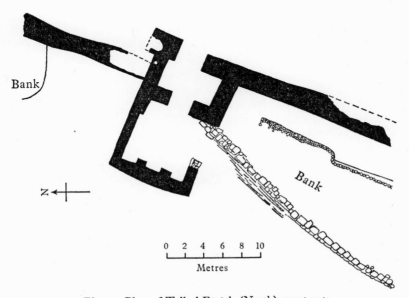

Fig. 3. Plan of Tell el-Fār'ah (North), west gate.

The greater part of the buildings contemporary with the defences was ill-preserved. The best preserved area excavated was in the south-west corner of the town, where a series of rooms were built against the inner side of the wall. This area gave the best evidence of the more closely built-up town of the later stage of the Middle Bronze Age, for beneath the rooms contemporary with the wall were only burials and an occasional installation such as an oven. The date of the burials, down to perhaps the beginning of the period of Jericho phase iii, shows that the wall cannot have been built till that time.

The most interesting structure was, however, immediately inside the gate. A rectangular building could be identified as a sanctuary from its bench for offerings, its semi-circular area serving as a *favissa*, and the remains of sacrificial offerings. The structure was entirely subterranean, and must have been approached by a ladder or wooden stairs, and it may have been associated with a cult centre above ground. Its subterranean character and the fact that young pigs were among the sacrificial offerings, suggests that it formed part of the sanctuary of a chthonic deity.[1]

The burials within the occupied area belong only to the period before the defences were constructed. Thereafter, burials were made in multiple tombs in the slopes of the valleys overlooking the site, many of them re-used from earlier periods.

The evidence from Tell el-Fārʻah, therefore, conforms very well with that of Jericho, and confirms that from less well-documented sites, namely that the first stage of Middle Bronze Age occupation was on a small scale, with full development reached only in the second half of the eighteenth century, and with the earth rampart coming out in a late phase of the Middle Bronze Age.

A site entirely different from the others described is that of *Nahariyah*, about 5 miles north of Acre, only 100 yards from the Mediterranean shore, for it consists of an isolated sanctuary, not directly associated with any settlement. The remains were covered by a mound only 3 m. high.

Three successive stages of the sanctuary were identified.[2] In the earliest a small square temple had immediately adjoining it to the south a *bāmāh* or high place built up of a conglomeration of stones. In the second stage, a new rectangular temple was built to the north, with a roof supported on a central line of uprights based on flat stones, and the original temple became the framework of an enlarged *bāmāh* of piled stones, forming a circle with a diameter of *c.* 14 m. with two steps leading to its summit. At the third stage, after some modifications in accessory structures, the walls of the temple were rebuilt and thickened and some side rooms were added.

Many finds indicated that the structure was a cult centre. The stones of the *bāmāh* and the soil between them were saturated with dark oily material, suggesting the pouring of offerings. Between the stones were found many pottery bowls containing seven small cups. Some seven-spouted lamps were also found. Innumerable fragments of cylindrical incense burners likewise have a cult significance. Very numerous model pottery vessels were found, set in groups in the successive floor levels. Clay figurines of doves were common. Fireplaces, smashed cooking pots and bones of animals were evidence of sacrifices. Most important were a

---

[1] §III, 23, 559 ff.   [2] §III, 3; 4.

number of figurines of bronze and silver, mostly of female deities, some being flat plaques, some in the round, and one mould for casting a figurine. It is suggested that the deity worshipped was Ashrath-Yam, Ashtoreth of the Sea.

The sanctuary lasted from the Middle Bronze Age into the beginning of the Late Bronze Age. Pottery published in the first report is clearly M.B. I.[1] Though the stratigraphical connexion is not shown in the publication, these vessels probably belong to the first stage. The second stage is dated to the second half of M.B. II by the occurrence in the temple of this period of the round-based cooking pots which appear only at this time.[2] In the uppermost levels were found Cypriot sherds[3] indicating a date at least as late as the second half of the sixteenth century B.C., at the beginning of the Late Bronze Age.

The site of *Shechem*, near the modern village of Balāṭa, is one of considerable strategic importance. It guards the entrance to the valley between Mount Gerizim and Mount Ebal, through which at all periods the north–south route along the central backbone of Palestine must have run, at that point, moreover, where the route up the Wādi Fārʿah from the Jordan valley joined the central route.

The present evidence,[4] however, rather surprisingly indicates that Shechem became a town only in the Middle Bronze Age. Above an original occupation of the Pre-Pottery Neolithic period,[5] the first structures belong to the Middle Bronze Age, perhaps M.B. I to early M.B. II.[6] The earliest buildings excavated may belong to a series of temples, though the evidence for this is slender.[7] Associated with the third of these levels was an infant burial which should correspond with Jericho M.B. II phase ii. The earliest of the five successive levels may precede the first stage in the defences of the town. The history of these defences follows the pattern of defences elsewhere, though with interesting additions. The first stage was a free-standing wall,[8] which could be dated to the eighteenth century B.C. In the next stage this wall was used as the rear retaining wall of an earth bank *c.* 32 m. wide at its base, retained on its outer side by a stone wall built on a batter.[9] The date suggested for this is late eighteenth century[10]

---

[1] §III, 3, figs. 24 *a–c*, 34, 35.

[2] §III, 3, figs. 32–33. It should be noted that, in this report, the earliest stage had not been identified, see §III, 4, 15.

[3] §III, 5, 22.   [4] §III, 25.

[5] *Ibid.* 109 f.   [6] The evidence has not yet been published in detail.

[7] §III, 25, ch. 7.   [8] *Ibid.* 62 ff.   [9] *Ibid.* fig. 22.   [10] *Ibid.* 66.

though the evidence has not yet been published in detail. So far, the succession is that found on other Palestinian sites, for instance at Jericho and Tell Beit Mirsim. The next stage, however, has no parallel. Outside the revetment wall forming the base of the bank was a very massive cyclopean wall, built free-standing, with the interval of about 8 m. between the two walls levelled up

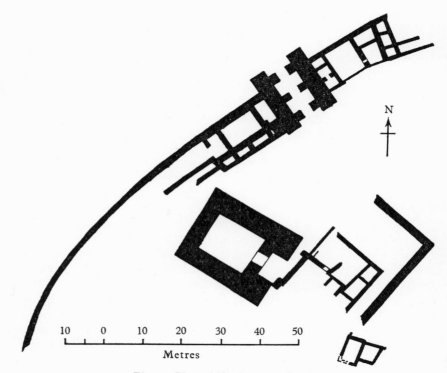

Fig. 4. Plan of Shechem, north gate.

with an imported fill.[1] This fill is with great probability to be derived from the summit of the preceding bank. Partially projecting from this wall was a fine gateway of triple-buttress plan (see Fig. 4).

The material of the bank was probably also used to raise the level to the rear, over the earlier Middle Bronze buildings,[2] to create a platform for the most imposing building uncovered, a temple with very massive walls, consisting of towers flanking an

[1] §III, 25, 58. [2] *Ibid.* fig. 22.

entrance into a cella with a roof supported on two rows of uprights. In the courtyard in front there were two *maṣṣēḇōṯ* and an altar.

A late component in the defences,[1] believed by the excavators also to belong to the Middle Bronze Age, was a wall on the crest of the mound which on the north-west side joined the rear of the gate in the cyclopean wall, and on the east had associated with it a two-buttress gateway in which pairs of remarkably fine ortho-stat slabs apparently formed recesses into which the gates were withdrawn or, alternatively, lowered as portcullises.

Shechem was one of the sites destroyed at the end of the Middle Bronze Age and then deserted. Succeeding structures which can be dated by pottery to the latest phase of the Middle Bronze Age was a stage not earlier than the mid-fifteenth century B.C. The whole of the period represented at Megiddo by Stratum IX is, as at Jericho and Tell Beit Mirsim, missing.

The earliest occupation of *Beth-shemesh* was late in the Early Bronze Age. The first town of any size belonged to the Middle Bronze Age. It was dated by the excavator[2] to *c.* 1700 B.C., and had a massive wall of stone. The published evidence does not make it possible to establish the connexion between structures and datable objects, so the validity of this dating cannot be assessed. Contents from a number of tombs,[3] mostly within the town area, suggest an initial occupation at least as early as the time of Jericho phase ii. It is possible that, as at the northern Tell el-Fār'ah, during the earlier part of M.B. II the built-up area did not cover the whole of the later town and that in parts there were tombs and no buildings, while the construction of the town wall came later.

On a number of other sites, excavations in progress or not yet published have given evidence of towns of the Middle Bronze Age, but so far only preliminary accounts or notes have been published. At *Tell Nagila*, north of Beersheba,[4] the defences consist of a thick wall, with, against its outer side, a bank *c.* 3 m. high of alternating layers of crushed limestone and soft sandstone conglomerate. Buildings of M.B. II date in the interior of the town are well-preserved and there are four layers of this period. No evidence of M.B. I or E.B.-M.B. have been found, and there was apparently a gap after an Early Bronze Age occupation. At *Achzib*,[5] the lowest stage in the wall system is said to be M.B. II, but it is not yet clear whether it is to this that the steeply-sloping revetment of stone coated with clay belongs. The earliest occupation of *Tell Mor*,[6] on the coast near Ashdod, was

---

[1] §iii, 25, 66 ff.   [2] §iii, 9, 27.   [3] §iii, 10, Tomb 3; §iii, 18.
[4] *I.E.J.* 13, 143 f., 333 f.   [5] *Ibid.* 337.   [6] *I.E.J.* 9, 271 f., 10, 123 ff.

late M.B. II. In the area cleared were remains of a sanctuary. At *Tell Poleg*,[1] about 6 km. south of Nathanya, on the Poleg river (Nahr el-Faliq), remains have been found of a fortified brick building with pottery apparently of M.B. I, and a large fortress of M.B. II, with a brick wall and a bank of layers of crushed sandstone conglomerate. At *Beth-Yerah* (Khirbet Karak),[2] at the south end of the Sea of Galilee, a length of *c.* 750 m. of the Middle Bronze Age town wall has been uncovered, consisting of a substructure of basalt boulders 4–5 m. wide, preserved to a height of 3·50 m., and a superstructure of mud-bricks preserved to a height of *c.* 2 m. Towers, alternately rectangular and curved, project from its outer side. In two places there was evidence of a stone-faced bank, apparently connected with these defences. In the interior, a portion of the town, with one broad street leading to the south gate and several narrow passages, has been excavated.

The conclusions to be drawn from this history of the individual sites produce an entirely coherent picture. The arrival of new groups at a date that can probably be placed in the second half of the nineteenth century B.C. marks the beginning of the M.B. I period. An entirely new culture is introduced, which can best be called Canaanite, of which the origins are probably to be sought in the coastal Syrian area centred on Byblos.

The newcomers came in small groups, and there is some evidence that they came from different districts in coastal Syria. Only at Megiddo is there evidence of a considerable population at this stage. Only at Megiddo and at Tell Beit Mirsim is there as yet evidence of walled towns at this stage, and in neither case is it conclusive. During the first half of the eighteenth century, the growth of the towns must have been rapid, for a considerable number of sites provide evidence of occupation by the period of Jericho phase ii. The earliest type of fortification, for which there is evidence at Jericho, Shechem, Megiddo and the northern Tell el-Fār'ah, is a free-standing wall of brick or stone. At the last place this may be no earlier than the last quarter of the eighteenth century, but on the other sites the walls are probably earlier.

The evidence of a major historical event comes with the introduction of a new type of defence, in which a bank or rampart is added to the wall, either backed against the pre-existing slope of the mound, or free-standing, or as a combination of the two. Not only must this indicate an important military innovation, but it goes with significant urban developments. In most of the sites

[1] *I.E.J.* 14, 109 ff. [2] *I.E.J.* 4, 128 f.

described, the new defences are an addition; at Jericho, Shechem, northern Tell el-Fār'ah, Tell Beit Mirsim and Megiddo, the new system is an addition to, or a substitute for, earlier defences. At Tell ed-Duweir it is later than a stage of occupation within M.B. II, but it is not known whether there was an earlier wall. At at least three other sites, its significance is different. In the north, at Hazor, with the new defences goes a vast extension to the size of the town, increasing its size seven times. In the south, the important sites of Tell el-'Ajjūl and southern Tell el-Fār'ah only come into existence at this time, and the rampart type of defences belongs to their earliest Middle Bronze Age occupation. These facts must have historical implications, though admittedly the number of sites in which the evidence is precise is limited. When there is fuller information concerning those other towns briefly listed above[1] the picture will be clearer.

The chronological evidence from the sites referred to in the last paragraph is unambiguous. The rampart type of defences appears only during the period covered by Jericho phase iii, at a round date of *c.* 1700 B.C. The two new sites in the south come slightly later, possibly not before mid-seventeenth century B.C.

This is the period of the Hyksos domination in Egypt. The exact interpretation of what is meant by Hyksos is still debated. But there is a general consensus of opinion that during the period the rulers of Egypt were Asiatic intruders. In such an intrusion, Palestine must be concerned. The distribution of the new type of defences shows that this is the material evidence of the Hyksos period in Palestine. Defences of this type can be traced from Carchemish in the north-east through inland Syria and Palestine to Tell el-Yahūdīya north of Cairo.[2] There is no uniformity in the culture of the towns so defended. Rather, the defences are the evidence of an alien aristocracy, superimposed on the pre-existing population. What military interpretation is to be placed on the new method of defence, which must be the response to a new method of attack, is still debated, but the probability is that the new (or improved) method of attack was the battering ram.[3]

As far as Palestine is concerned, the introduction of the new type of defence meant no break in culture. From the first beginnings of the Middle Bronze Age down to its end, and long past it, all the material evidence—pottery, weapons, ornaments, buildings, burial methods—is emphatic that there is no break in culture and basic population. As suggested above, this is the Canaanite culture of the Mediterranean littoral.

The rest of the evidence from the sites concerns this culture.

[1] Pp. 113 f.   [2] G, 5.   [3] §III, 26.

It suggests a way-of-life that is simple and lacking either luxuries or anything of importance in the development of civilization. In some places there are suggestions that the so-called palaces of local dynasts have been found. But for the most part the houses are simple, the layout of the towns the product of haphazard development. Temples or sanctuaries have been found, but there are many variations in form, and there is little certainty as to the deities worshipped. Foreign trade was at a minimum. There is some influence from Egypt and some imports, and this provides, as might be anticipated, the closest contact. A very few vessels from Cyprus, and the odd cylinder seal of North Syrian or Mesopotamian origin, cover the rest of the non-indigenous products. Palestine formed part of a larger Syro-Palestine group, but within it was a comparative backwater, receiving little except the overlordship of the Hyksos aristocracy, and itself offering no contributions to progress.

CHAPTER IV (a)

GREECE AND THE AEGEAN ISLANDS IN THE MIDDLE BRONZE AGE

I. INTRODUCTION

TRANSITION from the Early to the Middle Bronze Age in Aegean lands came about gradually at some places but suddenly and with violence at others. There can be no doubt that new people came into the land. The process of change, which is reflected by archaeological evidence from many parts of the region, cannot have been simple. Rather, as was generally the case when migrations took place, the newcomers arrived in groups of various sizes, probably over an appreciable period of time. The people whom they found in possession also varied in the size and prosperity of their communities, some ready to resist while others deemed it necessary or prudent to make terms with the foreigners. Unquestionably the immigrants in the present instance were strong and the pressure of the movement was unrelenting.

The culture which they brought and the period in which it flourished on the Greek mainland are called Middle Helladic (M.H.). In the islands of the central Aegean the corresponding term is Middle Cycladic (M.C.). Roughly parallel and contemporary was the age of the first great palaces in Crete, known by Sir Arthur Evans's designation as Middle Minoan (M.M.).[1] The limits of this period cannot be determined precisely, but it is known to have spanned the early centuries of the second millennium B.C., the time of the 12th Dynasty and of the Hyksos in Egypt, and in Mesopotamia the Isin–Larsa period and the 1st Dynasty of Babylon. The end of the Aegean Middle Bronze Age is most clearly observable on the mainland of Greece where certain characteristic elements of the M.H. culture were replaced in the sixteenth century by conspicuously different elements of the early Mycenaean civilization.

This early part of the second millennium is of special interest and importance in Greek history. On the one hand, the complex organization and astonishing elegance of Minoan life were new

---

[1] See below, p. 141.

phenomena in the Aegean, and on the other, we see in continental Greece the humble beginnings of a culture which was to produce still greater achievements in times to come. For it has been shown with little room for doubt that the Helladic people of this age were the ancestors in direct succession of those whom we call Mycenaeans, and that the same stock survived disaster and impoverishment in the Early Iron Age, to furnish a basic element in the formation of classical Hellas.[1]

If so much of the sequence is clear, however, the manner in which the changes came about is by no means obvious. Some of the evidence is missing and some of it is not yet capable of interpretation; certain elements are perhaps already visible but unrecognized. That which can be observed best, in the present stage of our knowledge, is the body of contemporary original documents that have come from archaeological excavation, the towns and houses and implements of daily life. Therefore the following account of the period will begin with a survey of these raw materials of the inquiry, and then proceed to a brief consideration of their historical setting.

II. THE ARCHAEOLOGICAL EVIDENCE

Remains of Middle Helladic habitations have been found abundantly in central and southern Greece. In Macedonia and Thrace the characteristics of contemporary settlements are somewhat different and one hesitates to apply the term Helladic to them, especially since most of the excavation has been by soundings only and the information obtained is incomplete. In the islands, material that can be defined as Middle Cycladic has come from a score of sites. Elsewhere the evidence, though not lacking altogether, is scanty.

POTTERY

Local pottery, as usual, is of basic importance in the archaeological analysis. It will be well to have the principal fabrics in mind before surveying the places where they have been found.

The foremost of these fabrics is Minyan ware,[2] so named by excavators because it was discovered first in large quantities at Boeotian Orchomenus. It has no ascertainable connexion with King Minyas or his people and may indeed have been out of

---

[1] *Pace* R. Carpenter, A, 2.

[2] G, 5, 140–3; G, 6, 80–3; G, 13, 1463–5; §ɪɪ, 6, 15–9; §ɪɪ, 11, 35–6; §ɪɪ, 19; §ɪɪ, 28; §ɪɪ, 32, 135–44; §ɪɪ, 60, 62–77; §ɪɪ, 62, 67–70; §ɪɪ, 87, 180–1.

fashion before they came upon the scene. The adjective is properly applied to the *ware* (in its narrower sense; that is, the biscuit and substance of the pots), rather than to the shapes in which they were fashioned, but by extension it is often used to designate the latter also. Normally this ware is of fine quality and well fired, grey or yellow in accordance with the amount of oxidation and the temperature in the kiln. The surface is generally smooth but not always even; only the best examples have the 'soapy texture' which has become a cliché. Two characteristic shapes are easily and frequently recognized: a big goblet with a ringed stem, somewhat ungainly, usually grey in colour; and a cup, suitably called a kantharos, with two opposed ribbon handles that swing high above the level of the rim.[1] These vessels, angular in profile and often marked by horizontal grooves and ridges, are easily turned on the potter's wheel. That the forms are deliberate imitations of metal prototypes, as has been declared again and again, is not necessarily the case; smoothly rounded forms are easier and more natural for a primitive metalworker to produce. There was indeed an interplay of influences, for on certain clay vases one sees small flat knobs set like metal rivet-heads at the places, for example, where handles are attached; but this feature may be a reciprocal borrowing. One should admit a possibility that the potter's work preceded that of the smith or was contemporary with it in the creation of M.H. shapes, answering a general preference of the age for forms that appear 'metallic' to us.

Pots of the same general period and of similar angular forms, but different in colour, have been classed sometimes as red[2] or brown or black 'Minyan'. If we hold to the strict usage these are misnomers, since the wares are substantially different from those which were made grey or yellow. Usually the clay was not well refined; hence the biscuit was rough and needed a coating of better quality. A type called Argive Minyan, after one region where it is found in abundance, is reddish-brown at the core and is covered with a thick slip, black or grey, sometimes with a brown tinge. In this ware almost the only shape is a broad bowl horizontally fluted below the rim and marked on the sides with festoons of incised lines.[3]

The second major class of M.H. pottery is called Matt-painted ware,[4] by a casual adaptation of the German word *Matt-malerei*. Its biscuit may be hard or soft, coarse or fine and smooth

---

[1] See Plate 74.
[2] E.g. §II, 32, pl. x; *Archaeology*, 6 (1953), 102, fig. 7.
[3] E.g. §II, 32, figs. 178–81; *Hesperia*, 23 (1954), pl. 7c.   [4] §II, 14, 240–1.

like the best of yellow Minyan, and its light surface provides a
good ground for decoration in dark 'paint' (a solution of fine
clay containing manganese,[1] applied with a brush); this is near-
black or purplish in colour and quite lacking in lustre. There is a
very wide variety of shapes in this ware: cups (including the
kantharos), bowls, jugs, small and large jars, some with narrow
necks, others open and barrel-like.[2] The patterns were at first
rectilinear but spirals and other curves appeared later, and with
them a few figures of men and animals. On certain of the most
elegant pots red paint was used in conjunction with the black.[3]

Minyan and Matt-painted fabrics are distinctive in themselves,
generally easy to recognize, and they are found widely distributed on the mainland. Hence these modest products of minor
craftsmen have played an important, perhaps exaggerated, role
in the reconstruction of the history of Greece in the Middle
Bronze Age.

There are other fabrics that were popular in the different
regions. Notable in the Argolid especially is a class of handmade
pots, chiefly jars and jugs, with hard, brittle, light-coloured
biscuit and decoration in dark lustrous paint.[4] Sometimes the
upper half of the vessel, or the whole surface, is coated with this
dark glaze and patterns are added in white or red, or both, in
imitation of the Minoan Kamares style. Coarse wares, made
rapidly and cheaply for ordinary domestic uses, are found everywhere in great quantities and are rarely distinctive. Some,
fashioned and finished with care, resemble Minyan ware; others,
much rougher, may be casually burnished or not at all. These
vessels range from tiny bowls to great storage jars. Knobs, too
small to grasp, often appear on the shoulders.

Pottery exported to and from the islands of the Aegean provides evidence of the trade that was carried on. Grey Minyan
ware is found at sites in the Cyclades but seems not to have been
made there. The corresponding local fabrics are coarse in biscuit,
smoothed on the surfaces and often burnished to a high lustre.
They are fired black, grey, brown, or deep red. Cups and bowls
with sharply angular profiles are characteristic.[5] In contrast, the
light-coloured wares with patterns drawn in dark paint tend to
have rounded contours. This paint begins as a shiny glaze in the
final stage of the E.C. period, in Melos if not elsewhere, but is
gradually replaced by a dull variety like the matt paint of the main-

[1] §II, 26.   [2] See Plate 75 (a).
[3] §II, 7, pl. IV.   [4] See Plate 75 (b).
[5] §II, 71, pl. 2c.

land.[1] Cycladic potters were imaginative, producing not only the necessary household containers but also vases of outlandish shapes and multiple vessels, possibly for ritual use but perhaps only to please their own tastes. Some had a humorous turn of mind and drew engaging cartoons of people and imps on their vases.[2] Fragments of pottery of the types described above are the first and most reliable means of recognizing the places that were inhabited in this period. A recent study of Matt-painted ware (1964)[3] includes a survey of nearly 140 sites on the mainland, 20 in the Cyclades, and a few elsewhere; very many more are known to individual explorers whose observations have not been recorded.

Northern and Central Greece

In central and western Macedonia Heurtley noted sixteen sites that were surely inhabited in the Middle Bronze Age and four others that may have been.[4] Since the local wares and shapes at this time are not sharply distinguished from certain of their precursors, imported pieces give the best evidence. True grey Minyan ware is found most often in Chalcidice, which is easily accessible by sea from the south. It abounds there at Molyvopyrgo, a town apparently of some importance since it was fortified by a wall and moat. However, the whole problem of Macedonian chronology and foreign relationships is fluid at present and further excavation is needed. Heurtley, though noting that some features of the pottery were seemingly anticipated in the Early Bronze Age by a 'proto-Minyan' ware, yet believed that there was a distinct break in cultural continuity. Others would say that these similarities were more than accidental and would argue that Macedonian pottery of the Middle Bronze Age with patterns drawn in dull paint owed more to the preceding local wares with incised decoration than to the Matt-painted class of central and southern Greece. In any case, proof of a real change of population has not yet been established.

The inland plains of Thessaly show a cultural sequence not unlike that of Macedonia, in so far as it can be analysed. Some few pieces of imported Minyan ware serve to fix the date in relative terms. As to the great mass of handmade local pottery and household implements, there are differences of opinion, some authorities inferring that a change of population took place at the beginning of the Middle Bronze Age while others see evidence of

[1] G, 19, no. 133 (earlier style), nos. 281–6 (later).
[2] G, 6, fig. 172; G, 19, nos. 172, 276; §III, 1, figs. 235–6.
[3] §II, 14.   [4] §II, 33.

continuity. Excavations at Argissa on the Peneus have shown that it was a long period of slow development.[1] A fire destroyed the town at the end of the Early Bronze Age, and over the burnt layer there are remains of at least seven successive rebuildings, the houses rather flimsy at first but later of solid construction. The coastal towns on the Gulf of Pagasae not surprisingly show closer relations with regions to the south; both Minyan and Matt-painted wares are relatively common. There were important settlements at Iolcus and Neleia, and probably at Pteleum in Phthiotis.[2]

At Lianokladhi on the Spercheus the third main layer yielded an abundance of grey Minyan pots, among them large ring-stemmed goblets. Other pots from this general level are light-coloured and decorated with rectilinear patterns and a few spirals in dark paint; some of these seem to reflect a Peloponnesian E.H. III style but the appearance may be deceptive.[3]

Phocis and Boeotia, rich in agricultural land by Greek standards, were closely dotted with settlements both large and small; the bordering districts of Locris and Euboea only a little less. This east-central region is better known through excavations than most other parts of the mainland. Here we find Orchomenus and Thebes, so situated as to be the chief centres; a remarkable burial tumulus at Drakhmani (Elatea); Eutresis, dominating the good plain of Leuctra; Cirrha, a port on the Corinthian gulf for shipment of produce from the Crisean valley below Delphi; a big site, probably Hyria, at the modern village of Dramesi on the Euripus and another, called Palaiochori, across the water near Amarynthus in Euboea. North of the latter is the big site of Lefkandi, recently excavated.[4] These are only a few of the dozens that exist.

The M.H. settlement of Orchomenus survived through a number of phases, which are attested by stratified building levels;[5] these follow the *Bothrosschicht*, which should probably be ascribed to the end of the E.H. period. The various deposits were disturbed by successive occupations, and M.H. objects found in the excavations of 1903–5 have not been fully reported. Investigation of Thebes is hindered by the clustered buildings of the modern town on the Cadmea.[6] Eutresis and Cirrha are well known, however, from reports of attentive excavators.[7] There are at least three major levels at each of these, and several subdivisions. Some of the houses of the earlier phases at Eutresis

[1] §II, 52; §II, 53.   [2] §II, 82.   [3] §II, 88, figs. 125–6.   [4] A, 13.
[5] §II, 15; §II, 88, 193–6.   [6] §II, 63; A, 17.   [7] §II, 32; §II, 24.

were apsidal in form, whereas those of Cirrha were generally rectangular from the first. Types and styles of pottery develop in the same order as elsewhere in this region and eastern Peloponnese: grey Minyan, Argive black Minyan and standard Matt-painted wares are present from the beginning, yellow Minyan and polychrome Matt-painted wares starting later and growing in popularity till the end of the period, when they are superseded by glaze-painted Mycenaean fabrics. This final transition is not clearly marked at either site, however, and Miss Goldman felt sure that the late M.H. wares continued to be made at Eutresis throughout the chronological period of L.H. I–II. In the problem of relative dating imported Cycladic pots and imitations of Minoan wares in the early stages at Eutresis and a small handmade flask of foreign (central European?) provenance at Cirrha are significant.[1]

Middle Helladic settlements in Attica were plentiful, though apparently less numerous than those of E.H. II. As noted in an earlier chapter, the painted pottery and other characteristics of E.H. III are scarce. A few sherds were found at Ayios Kosmas; rather more, though not in abundance, on the nearby island of Aegina. Some pieces from Eleusis, including a two-handled bowl with everted rim, are probably of this period. In general it appears that there was an interval between the abandonment of the old sites and the choosing of new ones by the M.H. settlers in Attica, but it is possible that the old culture survived longer in some of the towns. Athens itself has yielded many sporadic remains, but later occupation has disturbed most of the contexts. This is true to some extent also at the Eleusinian sanctuary, where there was an important settlement throughout the Middle Bronze Age. The cemetery, however, being in a separate area, was less subject to damage and gives a picture of the continuous development.[2] In the outlying districts, a thriving community existed at Brauron and apparently another at Aphidna, where a large tumulus with thirteen burials was discovered in 1894.[3] The character of these and a dozen other Attic sites that have been noted is clearly Helladic, influenced only slightly by contact with the Cyclades and Crete.

On the coast at Megara there was a Bronze Age village at one of the places called Minoa;[4] M.H. potsherds, as well as earlier and later wares, have been found there.

[1] §II, 24, pl. XLIV, no. 34.
[2] A, II, 29–31.
[3] §II, 92.   [4] §II, 78, 50–4; the name, R.E., s.v.

The Peloponnese

Nine or more sites on the Isthmus and in the region of Corinth have yielded evidence of habitation in the Middle Bronze Age. In the central area of the city itself the earlier settlements, which go back to the beginning of Neolithic times, seem to have ended abruptly with E.H. II, but other places in the immediate vicinity continued to be occupied. Graves in the North Cemetery contained Matt-painted pots and part of a gold diadem, a rare object on the mainland at this time.[1] At Korakou the sixth stratum of E.H. deposits was covered, as far as could be seen in the areas excavated, by ashes of a fire that had destroyed the houses. This was followed by three M.H. levels, in which were remains of houses and household goods.[2] The development of ceramic styles as observed there in the excavations of 1915–16 has proved to be canonical in north-eastern Peloponnese: grey Minyan, black Argive Minyan, and the coarser varieties of Matt-painted wares were dominant in the earlier deposits whereas yellow Minyan and fine Matt-painted pots bulked larger in the later phase. Blegen refrained from multiplying the subdivisions. He noted the appearance at the end of this period of pottery with patterns in glaze paint, derived probably from Cretan styles of M.M. III and leading without interruption to those seen in the Mycenaean shaft graves of L.H. I. At this stage there were no signs of a break in cultural development.

Great buildings of the Late Bronze Age at Mycenae obliterated most of the remains of those which had preceded. In M.H. times there may have been a circuit wall high on the citadel;[3] undoubtedly there were houses on the slopes, and a cemetery lay at the foot, in ground partly covered subsequently by the Lion Gate and adjoining fortifications. The royal shaft graves of Circle A were a special unit of this cemetery, and the oldest of them, No. vi, belongs to the very end of the M.H. period. Circle B, beginning earlier, contained a number of graves in which all the offerings were of M.H. character.[4]

Palatial structures of the Mycenaean period at Tiryns also prevented thorough investigation of the earlier levels, but a long sequence of occupations is attested.[5] A house with an oval plan, at least three architectural phases later than the great tholos of E.H. II, is among the first that can be assigned to the M.H. period.

[1] A, 1, 3–4.
[2] §II, 6, 3, 76–9, 113–16.
[3] §II, 86, 21, 84; cf. *B.C.H.* 86 (1962), 712.
[4] §II, 57, 103–75.
[5] §II, 55, 97–105.

Above it, parts of at least four other house walls were found superposed in succession, all preceding the Mycenaean installations. Cist graves were scattered, under and among the houses in characteristic fashion. Middle Helladic fortifications have not been discovered here, but a part of the rounded hill called Aspis, at Argos not far away, was surrounded by a wall of defence,[1] probably in this period. The rocky height is much eroded; on the lower ground where the modern town is situated there is evidence of widespread habitation, again with successive strata of debris, objects of familiar types, and intramural burials.[2]

Lerna, about five miles south of Argos, preserves a well-stratified record of habitations from early Neolithic times onward. This place was burned at the end of E.H. II, settled anew in E.H. III, and occupied continuously in the Middle Bronze Age.[3] Four or five principal M.H. phases, each with minor subdivisions, can be recognized, and other strata have undoubtedly been lost through denudation of the mound. Grey Minyan pottery, bored stone hammer-axes, and apsidal houses appear here in E.H. III.[4] In Lerna V, the settlement of the M.H. period, these types continue and Matt-painted, Argive Minyan, and lustrous-patterned wares are added. Along with these features, which are characteristic of the mainland, the first phase of this settlement saw the importation of a few M.M. Ia pots from Crete, 'duck vases' from the Cyclades, and handmade flasks possibly from central Europe.[5] Bones of a few horses (*equus caballus*) appear now for the first time.[6] Burials within the town also became frequent at this stage. A grave from one of the middle phases contained a significant group comprising a kantharos in grey Minyan ware, another in Matt-painted ware, and a spouted jar of Early Palatial style (M.M. Ib or M.M. IIa), certainly imported from Crete.[7] A number of fixed points in the relative chronology are established at Lerna by synchronisms of this kind, since Cretan and Melian wares were imported down to the time of M.M. III. Examples of the latest M.H. vases at Lerna, abundant but fragmentary, have been found in the shafts of two large royal graves which are contemporary with some of those in Circle B at Mycenae. Houses of this period have not been discovered.

Asea, a well-favoured site in Arcadia, was inhabited in the

[1] §ii, 83; §ii, 84; §ii, 85. [2] §ii, 67, 164, 167, 176–7.
[3] §ii, 17. [4] §ii, 16; §iii, 9. See Plate 76(*a*).
[5] *Hesperia*, 25 (1956), pl. 43*b*; 26 (1957), pl. 40*d,f*; cf. §ii, 24, pl. xliv, no. 34. See Plate 76 (*b*). [6] A, 5. Flora of Lerna: §ii, 40; §ii, 41.
[7] *Hesperia*, 26 (1957), pl. 43*c*; see Plate 76(*c*).

M.H. period, apparently by new settlers after the place had been destroyed by fire in a late phase of E.H.[1] It is on the top of a rocky hill, somewhat eroded, and the strata are not very thick. Black Minyan ware, chiefly of Argive type, is reported from the first M.H. deposits and even from those immediately preceding. Matt-painted ware is relatively scarce, and later. Incised coarse ware of the kind called 'Adriatic' at Malthi in Messenia (see below) is abundant. Thirty-one graves were found within the settlement. Asea may have been abandoned before the close of the M.H. period, or the latest remains may have been lost through erosion of the hilltop. Evidence of habitation has been noted elsewhere in Arcadia, for example at Orchomenus near the modern Levidion, but archaeological exploration of the province has not progressed far.

In Laconia extensive surveys show widespread occupation in the Middle Bronze Age.[2] Some of the sites had been inhabited in E.H. times also, but an appreciable number of the older were given up and new were chosen, frequently on high ground. There is as yet little stratigraphical information. The standard types of M.H. pottery are present and there are pieces with light patterns on dark surfaces, a reflexion of Minoan contacts. The island of Cythera on the route to Crete had at least one important Minoan outpost, at Kastri, looking south-eastward.[3] Relations with the Peloponnese were maintained there from M.M. II through L.M. I. Among the principal M.H. sites known in Laconia up to now are Ayios Stephanos near Skala and Karaousi near Asteri, both in the Helos plain at the mouth of the Eurotas; Amyclae up the river toward Sparta; and Yeraki in the hills toward Parnon. Settlements extended northward in Thyreatis to Astros near the border of the Argolid.

Messenia and Elis have also been surveyed with care.[4] In the former more than twenty sites give firm evidence of occupation during the Middle Bronze Age; scarcely half that many in the latter. Undoubtedly there are many others. In general it appears that the number of settlements increased after the E.H. period. Good farmland exists in these western provinces, and the inland sites are as numerous as the coastal.

Pottery of types that are standard along the Aegean shores is relatively scarce here and this makes comparisons somewhat uncertain, but Minyan ware and local varieties of it can be recognized.

---

[1] §II, 36, 12–20.   [2] §II, 89.
[3] *Arch. Reports, 1963–64*, 25–6; *1964–65*, 27; *1965–66*, 21.
[4] §II, 50; §II, 51; §II, 74; A, 10.

These help to provide a date for one of the principal towns, Malthi—thought to be the ancient Dorium—on the north-western edge of the Messenian plain, where a wall of defence surrounded a great number of buildings on a hilltop.[1] Two groups of houses are found in the central area and continuous rows of rooms, separated only by party walls, cling to the inner face of the fortifications. The excavator recognized two stages of construction, the earlier marked by a more open arrangement and houses with curving walls, quite possibly built before the great defensive circuit, while the later phase saw compact and orderly planning of rectangular rooms in larger numbers. Erosion of the site has made distinction of the strata difficult, particularly between the latest E.H. and the first M.H. remains, and undue emphasis was given in the report to a so-called 'Adriatic ware', coarse with incised patterns, which belongs clearly to M.H. settlements elsewhere but seems to crop up in all contexts at Malthi.[2] Transition to the early Mycenaean period came about gradually.

Graves at Malthi are of the usual M.H. types. Pithos burials are not uncommon in Messenia. The latter were sometimes grouped in tumuli, a practice that is rare in eastern Greece though noted once in Attica. The scheme is perhaps to be compared with that seen in the grave circles (both E.H. II and M.H.) in the Nidri plain of Leucas. The tumulus at Ayios Ioannis near Papoulia[3] is probably early (possibly E.H. III), whereas one further north near Samikon contained late M.H. and L.H. burials. Especially notable is a small tholos tomb near the village now called Koryphasion;[4] containing chiefly M.H. funeral gifts, it is the earliest yet known of the type which was to become wide-spread in L.H. II–III.

Among the western districts settled in the Middle Bronze Age are those of Pheia,[5] Pisa and Olympia. Within the Altis itself, at a low level near the Heraeum and Pelopium, houses with apsidal ends were excavated by Dörpfeld.[6] Some of the pottery is of familiar M.H. types, probably from an early phase; other vessels are altogether strange to the Aegean sphere and clearly have different antecedents. Recent investigations near the Altis have revealed further traces of M.H. habitations and of a preceding E.H. settlement.

[1] §II, 81.
[2] §II, 81, pl. I, 1; cf. §II, 36, figs. 105–7.
[3] §II, 47, 42–3.
[4] §II, 4.
[5] §II, 93.
[6] §II, 23, vol. I, 81–94; vol. II, *Beilage* 25.

North-western Greece

At the 'Wall of the Dymaeans' on the border between Elis and Achaea, another E.H. settlement, which ended in a fire, was succeeded by M.H. occupation.[1] From there eastwards in Achaea only a little M.H. material has been gathered; there are tumuli like those of Messenia, and much of the pottery shows local variations. Crossing the Gulf, one finds similar remains in Aetolia and Acarnania. The most famous are at Thermum where, in a striking parallel to the sequence at Olympia, apsidal houses of the Middle Bronze Age were discovered near and under an archaic Greek temple (seventh century).[2] One, House A, was 22 m. long, canonical in form with two rooms and a deep porch at the south; another was apparently composed of two apsidal structures joined at right angles; a third was oval. Associated with these houses was pottery of a crude variety, some pieces close in shape to normal Minyan ware but others having a pointed foot or spiky out-turned handles. Directly below the temple of Apollo there was an earlier megaron, B, oriented like House A and bordered by slabs of stone that once held wooden columns. This peristyle, if such it was, described a hairpin curve around the north end of the megaron. Rhomaios maintained persuasively that building B formed a link in an unbroken series from M.H. to archaic times, and many have followed him. Unhappily, the first excavations (1898–1908) were conducted without proper records and the stratigraphical evidence remains weak.

Epirus in the Bronze Age is not well known to us.[3] There are early potsherds at Dodona,[4] probably representing a settlement of M.H. times and perhaps showing distant connexions with Macedonia; but new excavations are needed throughout the province.

The Ionian islands have been more systematically surveyed. Grey Minyan ware appears at several places in Cephallenia and in Ithaca. Heurtley's observations at Pelikata support the conclusion that a phase of M.H. culture succeeded one of E.H. III without interruption. In Leucas Dörpfeld found important grave-plots of the Middle Bronze Age, his *Familiengräber* S and F, which are clearly later in date than the *Königsgräber* R (E.H. II).[5] Although quite mistaken about the chronology and significance of these discoveries, he provided his usual exemplary descriptions. Plot S was circular (12·10 m. in diameter), surrounded by a wall and covered probably by a low mound. It

[1] §II, 49.   [2] §II, 65; §II, 66.   [3] A, 6; A, 7.
[4] §II, 25.   [5] §II, 22, 206–50, 286–318.

contained at least thirteen graves of normal M.H. types, eleven stone cists and two pit-burials. Two further graves were built outside the wall. Plot F, rectangular (9·20 × 4·70 m.), held eight cists and two others were placed in an added enclosure. Gifts were not plentiful but included pots of recognizable Minyan shapes, some simple jewellery, and tools and weapons of bronze. The form of Plot S reminds one of the grave circles at Mycenae, though the Leucadians were obviously poorer; this cemetery probably represents a somewhat earlier phase, and may well follow a local tradition.

The Aegean Islands and the fringes

Sites of more than a dozen Middle Bronze Age settlements have been discovered in the Cyclades, disproving the old theory that these islands had been altogether depopulated after the flourishing E.C. period.[1] That there were fewer towns and not so many people does indeed appear probable. As stated in an earlier chapter, the distinctive culture of the third millennium seems to have been eclipsed suddenly at the end of the phase that one may call E.C. II, corresponding to E.H. II on the mainland. A separate E.C. III phase is scantily represented; but in the M.C. period old sites were resettled and new towns arose.

The first of three 'cities' at Phylakopi in Melos was destroyed, probably by an earthquake, but not annihilated, for certain characteristics are retained and carried on in the second.[2] Changes did occur: the houses were rebuilt in new positions, not merely repaired, and at some time in this period a fortification wall was constructed on the exposed flanks of the town. Classes of light-coloured pottery with rectilinear ('geometrical') patterns in dark paint began to be made in the First City, a shiny paint being used as early as the penultimate phase, and a dull variety, parallel to if not identical with the matt paint of the mainland, appearing soon afterwards as a rival.[3] Both styles survived in the Second City, but the dull paint gradually won preference. Grey Minyan pots, almost certainly imported from the Greek mainland, and Kamares ware from Crete are found in the middle phase of Phylakopi II. Here as elsewhere in the islands these fabrics inspired local imitations. Late in the period, Cretan influence became dominant; M.M. III styles are evident and, in testimony of the exchange, Melian (or possibly Theran) vases are found in the Temple Repositories at Cnossus.[4] Funerary practices in

---

[1] §II, 71.
[2] §II, 2; §II, 21; cf. §III, 1, 110–27.
[3] §II, 2, pl. VII. See Plate 77.
[4] Evans, *P. of M.* I, 557–61; G, 8, fig. 75.

Melos included the burial of children under or near the houses and the construction of chamber tombs, presumably for adults, outside the town. These tombs had been thoroughly plundered before the excavation of 1896.

Remains of a comparable settlement, which may well have been influenced by the people of Phylakopi, are known at Paroikia in Paros.[1] The modern town there hindered extensive investigation. More is accessible at Ayia Irini in Ceos, where excavations began in 1960.[2] This place, near the coast of Attica, was occupied in the era of the sauceboat, E.H. II, and had a thriving population in the Middle Bronze Age. There may or may not have been an interval between these periods of habitation; links with the third phase of the E.H. period, as seen for example in north-eastern Peloponnese, have not yet been observed in Ceos.[3] Grey Minyan and Matt-painted wares of mainland origin are found in the deposits next after those containing sauceboats, and M.H. pottery persists through many building levels. A few sherds of Kamares ware have been found, and there are cist graves and pithos burials of Cycladic types. Cretan influence increases very perceptibly toward the end of the Middle Bronze Age. At that stage the promontory of Ayia Irini was guarded, on the landward side at least, by a defensive wall. Clearly this was a prosperous era, which continued to flourish, in spite of severe earthquakes, into the time of L.M. Ib and L.H. II. There can be little doubt that the situation of the town, on a great landlocked natural harbour near principal east–west and north–south shipping lanes, led to its commercial activity. Trade was maintained with the mainland, with Crete, and with other islands of the archipelago.

A long narrow building, immediately to the left as one entered the main gateway of the town, has been recognized as a temple. It is a free-standing single structure unlike any previously known to us. One room was near the shore and has been partly lost through encroachment of the sea; the central section comprised a room with a corridor and a small cupboard on one side; the third section, at the inner end, had two narrow rooms side by side. All these chambers were partly below ground-level and one may guess that there was an upper storey over them. Details of the construction and stratified floors and debris inside make it evident that the building underwent frequent alterations and

[1] §II, 68; §III, 1, 104–10.   [2] §II, 18.
[3] New evidence (1969) suggests that people with customs different from those of Peloponnesian E.H. III may have settled at Lefkandi, in Ceos, and elsewhere in western Aegean regions at this time. See preliminary notes in A, 13, A, 3.

repairs from the time of its erection, not later than the Middle Bronze Age, down to the Hellenistic period. As early as the sixth century B.C. the shrine had become sacred to Dionysus.

Chief among the many objects found in the rooms are fragments of large terracotta statues, nineteen or more in number, made of local clay. Most of the pieces lay in one of the innermost chambers, a few in other parts of the building; many are missing. Like the temple itself, the statues are without close parallels, although certain Minoan features appear in them. They are standing female figures with hands on hips in a posture of dancing. All wear long skirts; above the waist some appear to be quite nude but for thick garlands which hang loosely around their necks, while others wear the short-sleeved open bodice of Minoan fashion. The latest datable pottery on the floor of the inner room was of L.M. I b style. Very few pieces of the sculpture, if any, can be later than this; and since the figures were not made all at once some may be appreciably earlier, going back quite possibly to the Middle Cycladic period. As to their significance, we can only guess; the largest single figure, of which few parts survive, may have been a cult image around 5 ft. tall, whereas the many others, 2 ft. to 4 ft. in height, might plausibly be taken to be attendants or worshippers.

On the sacred island of Delos there were settlers in the E.C. period and probably thereafter without interval, but material evidence of occupation in the Middle Bronze Age is scanty.[1] Minoan influence is attested. Nearby in Tenos there was at least one coastal town. At Ayios Loukas in Syros a grey Minyan kantharos was found in a grave with other pots that belong to an earlier tradition; its presence has been explained as intrusive but the group is more probably intact and ascribable to a phase of transition from E.C. III to M.C.[2] Graves in Amorgos may belong to that phase.[3] The houses found in Thera and Therasia under lava and volcanic ash from a great eruption must be assigned to a late stage, contemporary with M.M. III or L.M. I. The exact date of this seismic cataclysm, which opened the wide bay and separated Therasia from the rest of the island, is a subject of speculation which may be resolved by new excavations and purely scientific research.[4]

Turning from the centre to the borders of the Aegean area, one finds only a little evidence of expansion or direct contact. Traces of M.H. habitation have been noted in Scyros. The great citadel of the Early Bronze Age at Poliochni in Lemnos had a brief

[1] §II, 31.   [2] §II, 80, cols. 94–5.   [3] §II, 13.
[4] §II, 34, 37–47; §II, 48; §II, 64; §III, 1, 127–37; A, 8; A, 9; A, 12.

revival in the time of Troy V and then again some centuries later when pottery of the last M.H. and M.M. styles was imported, but the material is not plentiful.[1] A new era at Troy began with the arrival of a foreign population that founded the Sixth Settlement, a walled citadel.[2] They came with horses, which had not been seen there before, and their pottery was Minyan, grey as in Greece or a variant light red. After a time Matt-painted pots appear also, but these are rare. The Minyan types persisted and developed throughout the late Bronze Age in this conservative community. Pottery like that of early Troy VI is found southward along the coast at Larissa on the Hermus and at Old Smyrna (Bayraklı), settlements established on sites where much earlier towns had been abandoned.[3] At Emporio near the southern tip of Chios there are a few Matt-painted M.H. sherds above a burnt layer of Early Bronze Age habitations.[4] The sixth preclassical period at the site of the Heraeum in Samos is equated with early Troy VI.[5] At Miletus, near the later temple of Athena, there are stratified remains that lead back to the end of the Middle Bronze Age, when Cretans first settled there.[6] This is a little earlier than their first appearance at Ialysus in Rhodes (L.M. I a); up to now there have been very few indications of M.H. or M.M. penetration in the Dodecanese, but graves are reported from Cos and further discoveries may be expected.[7] In the west, Matt-painted pottery that came probably from Greece has been found at sites in Sicily and the Aeolian islands.[8]

ARCHITECTURE AND TOMBS

Generally in the Middle Bronze Age, as indeed in most other periods, the towns and villages were unwalled. The nearly complete circuit of fortifications at Malthi is an exception, as is that upon the Argive Aspis. The coastal sites of Phylakopi and Ayia Irini in the islands were fully protected on the landward side; inland in Siphnos there is a remarkable fortress on the hill of Ayios Andreas, quite possibly of the same date; and in Tenos also there may have been a walled town. Few of the places have been adequately excavated. The existence of fortifications is reasonably well attested at Molyvopyrgo in Chalcidice and in Aegina. Segments of enclosure walls are reported at Brauron, Yeraki and the site of the Palace of Nestor, but these and the largely inferential evidence at Mycenae and Tiryns may not be taken as final proof that all were fortresses. A structure running

[1] §II, 3.   [2] §II, 8; §II, II.   [3] §II, 12; §II, I.   [4] §II, 37.
[5] §II, 54.   [6] §II, 90.   [7] §II, 38.   [8] §II, 75.

along the south-eastern border of the inhabited area at Lerna might be restored in the mind's eye to a defensible height, but it may better be seen as a retaining wall, built to make a level terrace. All indications being taken together, fortified towns seem to have been relatively less common in the Middle Bronze Age than in E.H. II/E.C. II; certainly much less than in L.H. III. Presumably there was not so much wealth to attract marauders, and the people may have put trust in their weapons, like Spartans of a later age.

Houses within the settlements were not grand. Usually they stood as small single units, each probably sheltering a fairly numerous family and perhaps some animals.[1] Normal daily life was out of doors. The well-known apsidal and oval plans appear early in M.H. times, and at Lerna this curved form is very clearly an inheritance from E.H. III. Often the inner end is closed by a partition, forming a private room or place for storage. The main hall then is rectangular, entered from an open porch at the front. A circular hearth may be found on the earthen floor in the middle or at one side of the hall, and traces of benches or other solid furniture appear occasionally. The walls are rarely more than 0.45 m. thick. Their foundations and socles are of rough stone, a material plentiful in most regions of Greece, and the upper parts of the walls are of crude bricks or clay where that is at hand; in steep rocky country, for example in the islands, stone may have been used throughout. Roofs were undoubtedly gabled, curved or hooped when the apsidal scheme was first devised but later they may often have been flat, with extra support from wooden posts. Lumps of the clay that covered walls or roofs sometimes preserve impressions of the timbers and reeds against which it had been packed. Rectangular plans are found from the beginning and seemingly become more popular as the period progresses, but the fashion probably varied in different districts. The only temple—indeed the only public building—which has come to light in recognizable condition is the one in Ceos, and even there its form and function in the Middle Bronze Age are obscure.

Burial practices, some of which have been noted above, are illustrated by many hundreds of graves found on the mainland and by a smaller number in the islands.[2] The general custom was to bury the dead near or under the houses, within the settlement. Cemeteries outside the towns are known at Sesklo, Eleusis, Corinth, Mycenae and the Argive Heraeum. Single large tombs and tumuli with one or more burials are also recorded, especially

[1] See Plate 78 (a).   [2] §II, 10.

but not exclusively in the western provinces.[1] Bodies of children were not infrequently placed in jars before interment, and large pithoi were sometimes used for adults. Normally, however, a pit was dug vertically into the ground, pebbles were strewn to make a clean floor, and the dead person was placed upon this in a contracted position. The grave might be lined with clay or crude bricks or it might be walled with small stones or with large slabs set on edge.[2] Every combination of these elements is attested; there was no uniformity, the grave itself was usually covered with slabs and the pit above it, rarely more than 2 ft. deep, was filled with earth. A ring of small stones or a flat stone set upright might mark the place.

In most instances the graves each contained one burial, with little or no room to spare, but two skeletons side by side are found occasionally and a grave of an early M.H. phase at Lerna held four adults and a child.[3] There too graves were sometimes opened and used for a second burial. Only rarely were gifts placed with the dead, and then generally they consisted of a small pot or two, a pin, a spindle whorl, or a few beads. Thus most of the graves, though neat enough, were certainly unpretentious. Sometimes they appear very casual indeed, as in the case of a body thrown sprawled and face downward in one of the unlined pits at Lerna, but perhaps this was a deliberate sign of disrespect. One has the impression that the living were practical and unsentimental about corpses, in a way that Heraclitus would have applauded.

In contrast, however, there are notable exceptions. A gold diadem was found in one of the cists at Corinth; small offerings were sometimes placed piously on or near graves, rather than inside, and we may guess that many such offerings have been lost; the tumulus at Drakhmani in Phocis was large and elaborate, with numerous valuable gifts and what is thought to have been a sacrificial pit;[4] and clearly the great round plots in Attica, Messenia, and Leucas indicate serious regard for mortal remains. At Eleusis M.H. graves in the cemetery developed from the simple standard type to a larger size, in which bodies lay at full length, and doorways were provided at one corner of the chamber. In the Cyclades, where indeed the customs may have been different from those on the mainland, we know two graves with valuable jewellery in Ceos[5] and the careful cutting of the chamber tombs at Phylakopi reflects attentive consideration for the dead.

---

[1] A, 6; A, 7.   [2] See Plate 78 (b).   [3] *Hesperia*, 26 (1957), pl. 40a.
[4] §II, 10, 34–5; §II, 72, 254–6, 285; §II, 73, 94–6; §II, 88, 204–5.
[5] §II, 20.

Precise dating of graves by stratigraphy is usually difficult, often impossible, and the comparative method fails when distinctive objects are lacking. Pithos burials, we may feel sure, appear early in the sequence and decrease as time goes on. Whether dead children were kept near the houses for superstitious reasons, or merely because a small grave took little space, we can only guess. The question most often debated concerns the origin of the royal shaft graves at Mycenae, some of which belong quite certainly to the late phase of M.H. culture. In form they obviously resemble cist graves and thus logically constitute a development of the established type, illustrating continuity of customs from the Middle to the Late Bronze Age. Their size offers no problem; the sudden appearance of enormously rich gifts is the surprising feature. But this was more startling when only Schliemann's royal tombs were compared with the little graves of the preceding age. Grave Circle B, with its great array of both small and large, the modest and the spectacular, provides an ample picture of the transition.[1] The development was indeed quick. Wealth must have been acquired and concentrated in a short time, along with a desire to rival Egyptian and oriental manners, but the events were those of a transition, not of a break in the essential continuity of Helladic culture.

III. THE PEOPLE: QUESTIONS OF RACE, LANGUAGE AND CHRONOLOGY

The Middle Bronze Age in the regions here being examined has stubbornly resisted subdivision. A system of phases, tripartite or otherwise, may be devised at any one site for convenience in archaeological analysis but there is no certainty that it will be applicable at the next. This intractability is more evident in the M.H. than in the E.H. period, which has allowed at least a tentative division, and it probably indicates that progress and development were steadier, with fewer interruptions. There are sound reasons for believing that the whole period was long, that changes did take place within it, and that some characteristics of the early phases can be distinguished from those of the late.

Holding firmly to the archaeological framework for the moment, let us review certain facts known from Lerna, a site in a central area, recently excavated, with many strata intact. The fourth settlement there (E.H. III) was succeeded by the fifth (M.H.)

[1] §ii, 57, 128–75; §ii, 58.

without violence. Some features survived: apsidal house-plans, wheel-made grey Minyan ware and various types of implements. There were changes, however. In Lerna V *a* one finds new kinds of local pottery and tools, new imported goods and, most notable, intramural burials in large numbers. Bones of an equine animal, larger than an ass but not a true horse, appeared in strata of Lerna IV; the first bones of *equus caballus*, still rare, and of domesticated fowl came in those of Lerna V.[1]

These indications both of continuity and change are obviously significant. They have not been found everywhere. Some may have been lost by accident, or left unrecorded in the older excavations, but it is evident that the sequence was not identical in all places. Especially clear is the fact that certain features characteristic of Lerna IV, e.g. the patterned pottery of E.H. III, are scarce or lacking altogether in many other districts. We do not know why. Although sharp changes in the styles of pots and pans may and obviously do occur without major shifts in culture, one is yet reasonably certain in this instance that the Argolid was invaded with disastrous consequences for the inhabitants at the end of E.H. II, and almost equally sure that another wave of settlers, having similar customs, came later and established themselves without much opposition, inaugurating the M.H. period.[2] As an hypothetical explanation in the present stage of our ignorance, one may suppose that the former bands met determined resistance in most parts of the Argolid and therefore acted with greatest violence there, while sparing other communities that had been cowed by the example and had come to terms.[3] Perhaps not numerous, the redoubtable invaders in any case would have been unable to occupy all the older towns and villages immediately. Then after an appreciable interval—if we follow the same line of speculation—a kindred group arrived, landing again on the Argive coast, to find people with familiar customs and no great wealth, speaking perhaps an intelligible language. Here the newcomers would settle peaceably; but in other places, where there was more of the old hostile stock, conflict and destruction would ultimately ensue.

The second of these incursions, however it came, is that of the people whom we call Middle Helladic, the makers of grey Minyan ring-stemmed goblets and kantharoi and of Matt-painted pottery. Soon after their arrival they imported vases of M.M. I*a* style from Crete, probably to be dated in the twentieth or nineteenth century B.C. Carbon-14 analysis of vegetable matter from Lerna

[1] A, 5.   [2] §III, 9.   [3] Cf., however, Berbati, §II, 69, 158-9.

V *a* has yielded a date of 1948 ± 117 B.C.[1] Since Kamares ware of M.M. I b–II a is found in middle strata and M.M. III a pottery in late strata of a very long Lerna V sequence, there is no reason to question the accuracy of the chronological scheme in general. Minoan dates depend of course on synchronisms with Egypt and the Near East (over which there is room for debate),[2] and leeway must be allowed upward and downward in each single instance, but to seek all possible maxima or minima is a mistake.[3] Thus the M.H. period, for which in this respect Lerna provides an adequate index, may be taken to have begun very early in the second millennium and to have continued until the time of the Mycenaean shaft graves in the sixteenth century B.C. In the Cyclades less evidence is available altogether, and there is no indication at all of an invasion at the end of E.C. III, but one need not doubt that the period of M.C. culture spanned the same centuries as its counterpart on the Helladic mainland.

Who were the people who came and established the Middle Helladic way of life? Persuasive arguments have been advanced that they were the first who can properly be called Greeks, and this conclusion must almost certainly be accepted; but the terms need to be defined and the very uncertainties of the factors need to be recognized. By 'Greeks', whom do we mean? Assuredly they differed from those whom we know in Aeschylus, Thucydides and Isocrates. 'Race', if used here, is a vague word; it is best limited to the sense in which it is applied by physical anthropologists, and they report that Middle Helladic people were of thoroughly mixed stock.[4] Bodily characteristics may indeed have contributed to the success of these people in adapting themselves to their new surroundings, but of this there is no tangible proof. On the contrary, we know that they were painfully subject to mortal ills.[5] The modes of daily life and the few glimpses of religious thought that come to us from remains of the settlements comprise nothing that is necessarily Greek. Therefore we come to the final criterion, that of language.

It is permissible to recognize as Greeks those people who spoke an Indo-European language that had been sufficiently separated from its parent stem to be defined in modern linguistic terms as Greek. Many philologists, though not all, have long believed that this division occurred before the middle of the second millennium

---

[1] §III, 19, 365.

[2] E.g. concerning the 'Treasure of Tôd', §III, 6; §III, 18; §III, 21, particularly p. 119; §III, 36. Cf. also §III, 14; §III, 39; and p. 143 below.

[3] *Contra*, §III, 5.   [4] §III, 2; §III, 3.   [5] §III, 2; §III, 4.

and possibly as early as 2000 B.C.[1] At present the earliest documents known to be in Greek are texts in Linear Script B, which are dated between 1400 and 1200 B.C. That a few of them might be a little older, preserved exceptionally by accident or design, is not positively excluded but appears improbable.

Linear Script A, which is earlier than B, has been found chiefly in Crete but brief inscriptions, consisting of single signs or groups of a few consecutive signs at most, have appeared in the islands of Melos, Thera and Ceos, and in Argolis and Messenia.[2] This form of script, presumed to be the model upon which Linear B was patterned, may well have been derived by adaptation from the Cretan 'hieroglyphic' or pictographic writing that goes back at least to M.M. Ia. Texts in Linear A are securely dated by archaeological evidence to M.M. III and L.M. I; at Phaestus a few have been found in contexts with pottery of the Early Palatial period (M.M. I–II). All together, they make up only a small corpus, and hence do not furnish data for systematic attempts at decipherment. Although efforts to analyse and intrepret them have been renewed, especially in the decade since Linear B has become legible, up to now no generally acceptable solution has been presented. The consensus is that the language is not Greek, although a few would allow that it may contain Greek elements.[3] Some, led by C. Gordon, have thought it to be a western Semitic dialect; others identify it with Luwian; but it is not by any means certain that all the texts are in a single language. Obviously caution and patience are called for.

The existence in later times of distinct Greek dialects has led to speculation that several waves of early Greek-speaking people immigrated successively and branched into different parts of the peninsula. This theory, however, as is observed by J. Chadwick in the pertinent chapter,[4] would imply that the language had been formed still earlier, in another region—a supposition without firm evidence and hard to reconcile with either linguistic or archaeological data. The hypothesis that Greek was developed by people of I-E speech after they had reached Greece is more convincing, though admittedly not subject to final proof.

Remnants of a pre-Greek language, recognized long ago by Kretschmer and others,[5] furnish positive testimony to at least one fundamental change in the population of the Aegean world. The

---

[1] §III, 8; §III, 10; §III, 16; §III, 24.   See also *A Companion to Homer* (London, 1962), ch. 10.

[2] §III, 7; §III, 11; §III, 33; §III, 34.

[3] §III, 25.   [4] *C.A.H.*, II³, pt. 2, ch. xxxix, sect. III.   [5] §III, 13; §III, 20.

significance of this change, its general character, and relative date in terms of cultural development were expounded in 1928 by Blegen and Haley in a brief statement that scarcely brooks question.[1] They showed that un-Greek, and hence assuredly pre-Greek, place-names (notably those formed with –νθ– and -σσ-, e.g. *Korinthos, Tylissos*) must belong to the Early Bronze Age and not any other. From the beginning of the Middle Bronze Age onward there was no real break in the continuity of cultural development, in spite of the several spectacular advances and retreats that occurred, and therefore the people of Middle Helladic times must be looked upon as the first true Greeks in the land. Only a few minor adjustments in this conclusion are called for in consequence of recent discoveries. One must allow that people akin to those of the M.H. migration arrived in the Argolid and probably some other regions a bit earlier than had been supposed, introducing a new culture in E.H. III, and one must accept the possibility that certain of the foreign place-names, though evidently pre-Greek, may prove still to be of Indo-European origin.

The fact that these names appear in Asia Minor, as well as in mainland Greece, Crete and the Cyclades, makes it presumable that they came to the Aegean from the east, but up to now search for their origin has failed to produce verifiable results. Frequently mentioned in connexion with this problem are the Luwians, who are almost impossible to place and are indeed so named only because elements of their speech are identified as Luwian in later Hittite documents. It is probable that they occupied south-western Anatolia at some time, and one is tempted to think that a people of this sort may have carried to the Aegean the new ways of life that are seen in the middle phases of Phylakopi I and in Lerna IV. On the other hand, it has been suggested that Luwians came, slightly later, to Crete, or were in fact the bearers of Minyan ware who founded M.H. culture in central Greece.[2] But these theories are mutually exclusive and none of them can be substantiated at present.

Let us therefore turn back and summarize the more nearly established facts. A new people arrived in central Greece, probably in the twentieth century B.C., coming either from the north or the east or both. They spoke an Indo-European language, which either was Greek or was about to become Greek, and one of their

[1] §III, 15.
[2] For differing points of view see G. Huxley, *Crete and the Luwians* (Oxford, 1961); §III, 23; §III, 28; §III, 35.

technical accomplishments was the making of Minyan pottery, the knowledge of which probably came with them but was developed chiefly in their new home.[1] They soon established contact with the inhabitants of the Cyclades, to whom they may have had some degree of kinship, and they traded with the Cretans from M.M. I a onward, though at first only on a small scale. They were related in culture and probably in race to the people of Troy VI, who arrived at the Hellespont about the same time or a little later. In some parts of Greece they settled peacefully in the communities of those who had come before, while elsewhere they captured towns and killed or absorbed the older inhabitants. Before long they were spread through all the Peloponnese and established in the north-west and the north, but the interior parts of Thessaly and Macedonia were never deeply affected by them. This Middle Helladic folk was hardy and tenacious, made up largely of farmers, conservative in outlook, doubtless truculent in defence of their property but not quick to seek new fields of activity or to develop their latent artistic sense. The stage of consolidation and gradual adaptation lasted some three hundred years.

By the end of the seventeenth century this period of gestation was completing its term and foreign impulses, coming largely from or through the Minoans whose enterprise was potent now in the Aegean, helped to bring forth new interests and ambitions on the mainland. The change in outlook was rapid, although probably not quite so sudden as a comparison between Middle Helladic mud-brick villages and the splendour of the Shaft Graves used once to make us think. Princes arose at Mycenae, tall powerful men who could organize and lead soldiers and win booty, but there is no compelling reason to suppose that they had come recently from abroad. On the contrary, the mass of evidence suggests that this was a local flowering rather than an interruption—a phenomenon not wholly explicable but of a sort that was to be seen more than once again in the course of Hellenic life on Hellenic soil.

[1] *Contra*, J. Mellaart, *C.A.H.* I³, pt. 2, pp. 682 and 700 ff.; §III, 22, 15–18.

CHAPTER IV(b)

THE MATURITY OF MINOAN CIVILIZATION

IV. THE CHRONOLOGY OF THE EARLY
PALACE PERIOD (c. 2000–1700 B.C.)

T H E first palaces in Crete were built soon after the turn of the millennium. Could there be a more obvious mark than this for the beginning of an epoch? With them Minoan civilization rose from its prehistoric beginnings and attained the rank of an advanced civilization. But did it really even now enter the realm of history? Names, personalities and direct written sources are lacking. On the other hand the historical setting of this civilization cannot be disputed. It finds expression in its involvement in contemporary and subsequent events of Mediterranean history. Monuments consequently play a greater part than actions and people in providing a picture of this period, and the archaeological interpretation of these monuments is of cardinal importance. The Greeks later associated this period with the figure of Minos in their mythology. Any attempt to separate the historical and the mythical features of Minos is hopeless, but his name has rightly been given to this civilization which we can discern in the strange light of early history.

The palaces stood for about 600 years. After their destruction in about 1400 B.C. they were not rebuilt. The Palace Period can be split into an earlier and a later stage in terms of stratification and architectural developments. The present chapter is concerned only with the earlier stage of the Palace Period. Hitherto, however, there has been no real *consensus doctorum* to fix the points where the line of demarcation is to be drawn, or to establish the relative and absolute chronology of the stages. During the excavation of Cnossus Evans and Mackenzie worked out a system of three periods which was based on the stratigraphy of the site and was intended to establish the relative chronology in the first place. Each of the three periods—Early Minoan (= E.M.), Middle Minoan (= M.M.) and Late Minoan (= L.M.)—was divided into three subdivisions, designated by numbers which could, if necessary, be differentiated further by labelling sub-periods a, b and c.

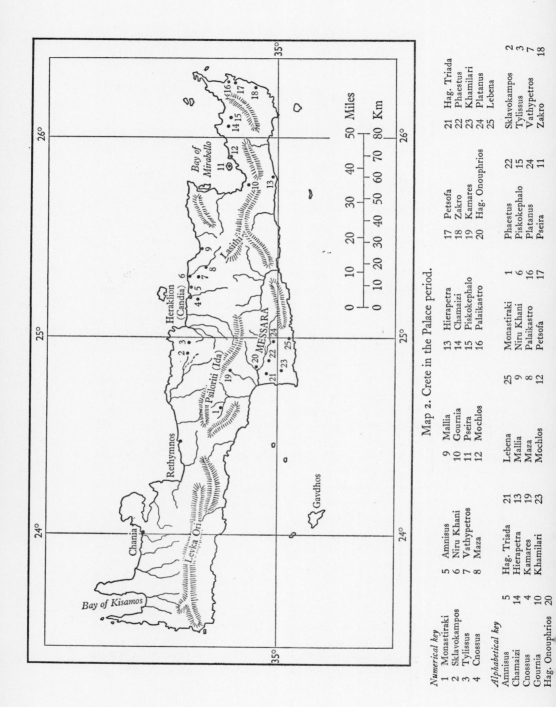

Map 2. Crete in the Palace period.

Numerical key

1	Monastiraki
2	Sklavokampos
3	Tylissus
4	Cnossus
5	Amnisus
6	Niru Khani
7	Vathypetros
8	Maza
9	Mallia
10	Gournia
11	Pseira
12	Mochlos
13	Hierapetra
14	Chamaizi
15	Piskokephalo
16	Palaikastro
17	Petsofa
18	Zakro
19	Kamares
20	Hag. Onouphrios
21	Hag. Triada
22	Phaestus
23	Khamilari
24	Platanus
25	Lebena

Alphabetical key

Amnisus	5
Chamaizi	14
Cnossus	4
Gournia	10
Hag. Onouphrios	20
Hag. Triada	21
Hierapetra	13
Kamares	19
Khamilari	23
Lebena	25
Mallia	9
Maza	8
Mochlos	12
Monastiraki	1
Niru Khani	6
Palaikastro	16
Petsofa	17
Phaestus	22
Piskokephalo	15
Platanus	24
Pseira	11
Sklavokampos	2
Tylissus	3
Vathypetros	7
Zakro	18

On the whole, the three periods correspond with the Early, Middle and Late Bronze Age periods. This correspondence has been essentially confirmed in the case of the first of the three periods. Between E.M. II and M.M. I there is a genuine break, whereas E.M. III overlaps already with the following period. The Early Palace Period[1] and the Middle Bronze Age both begin with M.M. I. It was soon pointed out, however, that the division between M.M. III and L.M. I was unimportant compared with that between M.M. II and M.M. III, when fundamental changes took place not only in architecture but also in the style of pottery and other objects. The naturalism which is characteristic of Minoan art began with M.M. III. Moreover, it was clear from the very beginning that the end of the Palace Period fell in the middle of the last of the three divisions, that is to say in the very short period L.M. IIIa. On the whole it was therefore agreed to let the Early Palace Period extend from M.M. I to M.M. II and the Late Palace Period from M.M. III to L.M. IIIa. The question whether the Late Palace Period should be divided into an initial and a final stage (M.M. III/L.M. I and L.M. II/IIIa) belongs properly to the next chapter. This system, however, has been called in question recently in view of the excavations at Phaestus.[2] The final destruction of the old palaces is said to have occurred at the end of M.M. III, that is in the early sixteenth century B.C. The rise of the new style then would have taken place during the Early Palace Period.

The absolute chronology[3] of the Minoan periods is fixed by relations with Egypt and the Near East. At three Egyptian sites (El-Haraga, El-Lāhūn, Abydos)[4] M.M. IIa and b pottery has been dated by objects of local origin to the period between 1850 and 1775 B.C. This date is supported by the fact that M.M. IIb sherds were associated at Cnossus with a diorite figure of the late Twelfth Dynasty, which places the beginnings of M.M. IIb pottery as early as the first half of the eighteenth century B.C. On the south coast of Crete at Lebena a later group of burials in a vaulted tomb was separated from an older one by a barren layer,[5] above which an ivory scarab of the Twelfth Dynasty was found associated with M.M. Ia vessels. The most important evidence for the end of the Early Palace Period is an alabaster lid with the cartouche of the Hyksos king Khyan (c. 1663–1625) which was found together with M.M. IIIa pottery at Cnossus in a level belonging to the first part of the Late Palace Period. That the Late Palace Period did not begin at the end of the seventeenth century B.C. must be deduced from the correspondence between Egyptian finds of the

[1] §IV, 9.   [2] §IV, 6, 81.   [3] §IV, 7, 3.   [4] See Plate 79.   [5] §IV, 1, 2.

early Eighteenth Dynasty (1567 B.C. onwards) and Minoan finds of the stage L.M. Ia. Thus the end of the Early Palace Period and the beginning of the Late Palace Period are brought nearer to 1700 B.C. Finally there comes from Tholos B at Platanus a Babylonian cylinder seal of haematite which is dated to the time of Hammurabi. It was therefore deposited at the earliest in the second quarter of the eighteenth century B.C. The latest finds in the same context consist of M.M. Ia/b pottery.

In this scheme of things the smallest possible weight is attached to the subdivisions of Evans' system. They are certainly not to be dispensed with, but their use is unfortunately still too arbitrary and will remain so until the requisite work on the classification of the pottery has been completed.

For the duration of M.M. II we get a clear picture. It began before rather than after 1850 B.C. and lasted until the end of the Early Palace Period, that is until about 1700 B.C. The stage M.M. I then began earlier than 1850 B.C. but included nearly the whole duration of M.M. II. Attempts have been made to explain this overlap of M.M. I and M.M. II by pointing to the Palace character of M.M. II pottery. The other groups of pottery are said to have continued to exist alongside it, especially outside the Palaces, and this means that they lasted for 200 years. It must be added that the group of Tholoi to which the Tholos at Platanus belongs began as early as the end of E.M. I. These Tholoi, then, would have lasted over 500 years. Neither the method of construction nor the material found in them admits of this interpretation. Consequently there has even been a demand for a radical shortening of the Early Minoan period and the early Middle Minoan period.[1] That, however, is quite impossible because these finds cannot be detached from their own chronological connexions with Egypt and the Orient. These connexions go back essentially before the turn of the millennium. Such a shortening would lead to far greater difficulties than the assumption that the Babylonian cylinder-seal from Platanus came belatedly and by chance into this complex of finds, which would then overlap only in its later part with the early period of M.M. II.

It has been established that there were three consecutive destructions of the older palace at Phaestus. Even the level of the first is characterized by M.M. II pottery, and so it may be assigned to the second half of the nineteenth century B.C. A lower dating could be considered only if the Early Palace Period did not end until early in the sixteenth century B.C. But that is impossible,

[1] §IV, 5.

because what we know for certain about the preceding phase has fixed the beginning of the Early Palace Period so early that the inclusion of M.M. III in it is ruled out. The first of the two subsequent destructions then took place in the course of the eighteenth century and the second in about 1700 B.C. This conclusion provides, at least for the destruction in about 1700 B.C., an agreement with the situation at Cnossus, where on stylistic grounds the new epoch began about 1700 B.C. and not as late as 1550 B.C.

On the strength of his observations at Phaestus, D. Levi has expressed doubts about the view of the finds at Cnossus which goes back to Evans and Mackenzie. These doubts are resolved if it is realized that the question cannot be decided by stratigraphy alone, but, as things are, by the combined contribution of stratigraphy and typology, as expressed in the following Table.

	ARCHITECTURE		Egypt	POTTERY						
	Cnossus	Phaestus		MM					LM	
				Ia	Ib	IIa	IIb	III	I	II
1975			1991							
1950										
1925										
1900										
1875		Ia	Twelfth Dynasty							
1850										
1825	I									
1800		Ib								
1775			1786							
1750		Ic								
1725										
1700			1720							
1675										
1650			Hyksos					a		
1625	IIA	IIA								
1600								b		
1575										
1550			1570						a	
1525	IIB	IIB								
1500			Eighteenth Dynasty							
1475									b	
1450	IIc	IIc								
1425										
1400										

TABLE 1. *Correspondence of stratigraphy and types of pottery*

In correlating architecture and chronology in the Table the older palaces are denoted by I, the later ones by II in the column 'Architecture'. The three destruction levels which have been identified for the older palace at Phaestus and for the later one at Cnossus have been given the letters A–C. L.M. IIIa containing the destruction level covers not more than the first quarter of the fourteenth century.

The pottery of the older palaces, which according to Evans consists of the four groups M.M. Ia–M.M. IIb, has been classified here in view of recent observations in three groups, M.M. Ib being combined with M.M. IIa.

V. THE EVIDENCE OF THE MONUMENTS

Of the three great palaces at Cnossus, Mallia and Phaestus, those at Cnossus and Phaestus rest on older settlements which reach back to the Neolithic Age, but the residences of the earlier rulers have disappeared through subsequent levelling of the sites. The general layout and the size of the palaces were already established by the time of the earliest buildings. The largest palace is that of Cnossus. Those at Mallia and Phaestus are only a little way behind. In each case the central court is a rectangle which runs from north to south and is almost a standard length (something over 50 m.). At Mallia and Phaestus the width is almost the same (23–4 m.) but at Cnossus it is a good 5 m. wider. The palaces at Mallia and Phaestus were obviously modelled on Cnossus. Moreover, all three palaces have a monumental façade on the west which faces on to a forecourt, and they include only a few features which may have been designed for purposes of fortification. The layout of the early phase in detail can be inferred only at a few points from the later alterations.

At Cnossus the western forecourt was terraced and supported by an outer retaining wall. On the south-west side a ramp led up to it, and there were at first a few houses in the court. Opposite the top of the ramp the façade of the palace was pierced by a passage, which was paved with slabs and led into the interior of the palace.[1] The central court was reached along an indirect route which led through a north–south corridor into passages running east. At the entrance to the west court the façade probably curved inwards. On the north-west side of the central court there are outer walls with curves instead of corners. This rules out the possibility of an overall roof. The inside corridors ran, at least partly, under the open sky. As Evans originally suggested, the

[1] I owe this information to N. Platon.

palace developed from a number of units (*insulae*) grouped round
the court. It has been established that there was on the northern
edge of the court an isolated building with strong foundations,
which go down more than 7 m. This building, known as the
Early Keep, rose like a tower above its surroundings, and it commanded the northern entrance to the court. Its foundations were
already filled in and it was built on in the course of the Early
Palace Period. It is clear that the roofs of the individual parts
of the palace varied even at the time when the tower was built.
The eastern wing of the palace, where the Domestic Quarter was
later situated, had at first a ground-floor on the same level as the
central court. The entrance leading through the west façade was
closed at an early date and a corridor with two bends now leads from
a doorway facing north to the southern edge of the central court.

At Phaestus the nature of the site caused the forecourt in the
west to be laid out in two parts, the northern one on a higher level
and the southern one a good 6 m. lower. Behind the lower part the
palace rose in several storeys up the slope.[1] On the ground floor,
which alone has been preserved, were living rooms and storerooms. The thick walls were built of undressed stone cemented
with earth, like the Early Keep at Cnossus. Even in the earliest
stage the outer wall had a foundation of orthostats or large stone
slabs set upright. Some entrances gave on to the forecourt.
Beside one of them a window has been recognized in a part of the
wall which has no orthostats. Renovations to this part of the
palace were carried out on several occasions before its final destruction at the end of M.M. II. The excavators identified three
levels which were due to earthquakes. On each occasion the
rooms were filled in and new floors were laid with a thick layer
of mortar (*astraki*) as a pavement. A ramp led to the upper part of
the forecourt from a point near the north end of the façade of the
lower court, which was about 20 m. long. To the west this ramp
made a sharp bend, at the end of a terrace wall about 10 m. long,
which was later strengthened to form a bastion. In the upper
part of the court the façade had already at the end of the Early
Palace Period the monumental feature which is observed later at
Cnossus: orthostats of Cretan alabaster (gypsum) set above a
foundation layer.[2] Flat projections seem to indicate the arrangement of the windows in the upper storey, while the storerooms
behind the façade of the basement had no windows. Above the
two foundation courses the wall consisted mainly of undressed
stone cemented with earth and bonded with timber. In the

[1] §v, 7.   [2] See Plate 80.

construction of the later palace this whole part was pulled down as far as the foundation course of orthostats; the rest was filled in and the outer wall of the new building was shifted to the east on the raised level. As the rubble was moved away in the course of the excavation, both buildings can be seen today side by side. In addition to storerooms this basement contained small cult-rooms. Three more were added later, being built outside against the façade. They were accessible from within by means of an opening in the basement. Moreover, they were directly connected with the court by doors. They thus had a part to play in the religious ceremonies which took place in the court. In this part of the palace little has been discovered about the oldest buildings of the early phase except that they existed.

In the southern part of this wing a gently rising passage, paved with alabaster slabs, led directly eastwards to the central court. The porch had a big central column. The diameter of its stone base measures 1·24 m. The distance to the walls was about 3·5 m. on either side. These features, the column and the possibilities for wide openings which it offered, thus go back to the Early Palace Period. There was also a room with columns and pillars forming interior supports in a group of buildings loosely joined to the palace in the north-east. In its oldest form, however, the whole structure seems to have had a more utilitarian character.

At Mallia[1] the west façade of the later palace again used pieces of the foundation layer of orthostats which had belonged to the older one. An uncovered passage leading eastwards gave access to the north–south corridor of the basement, along which storerooms were ranged. The main entrances were in the north and the south. In the north-west, where the royal living-rooms were situated later, a portico of the older building has been identified on a lower level. The foundations of this palace too suggest that as at Cnossus the original isolation of the *insulae* had been superseded. At Monastiraki on the west slope of Mount Ida some storerooms of a palace have been excavated. The method of construction and the shape of the rooms correspond to the south-west wing at Phaestus.[2]

There are precedents for many of the constituent parts of the Cretan palaces in the Aegean area, in the Near East and in Egypt. An examination of them, however, serves to demonstrate the extraordinary nature of the creative spirit which marks the Cretan palaces. The agglutinative kind of planning, which knows nothing of surrounding rows of outer walls, is already familiar in older

[1] §v, 3.   [2] §v, 6.

houses from East Crete (at Vasiliki). It has neolithic precedents on the island (at Cnossus) and is not unknown during the Early Bronze Age elsewhere in the Aegean area (at Poliochni and Thermi) and in the Near East. But the older examples are not organized around a central court. The early Aegean buildings which have courts place the ruler's mansion within a ring wall (at Troy, Dhimini, Lerna and Tiryns). Of the type which we find in the Minoan palaces, where the buildings are arranged along the outside of the court, only one older example is at present known in a model of a granary from Melos. The house with a court at Chamaizi in East Crete belongs to this phase. It already presupposes the existence of the palaces. Its oval ground-plan is due to its position on the top of a hill. It was probably not used as a dwelling, but it housed votive offerings dedicated at the shrine on the hill where it stood.

In the palaces and temples of the Ancient East a central court was also the rule. But its relationship to the surrounding rooms was a different one. The whole was held together by the outer walls, which were laid out as far as possible without openings, on straight lines and at right angles to one another. The shape of the inner rooms, which were rectangular, derived from the plan of the outer walls. The court in the centre corresponded with this plan as well. The layout of the Cretan palace, however, developed from within outwards. The groups of rooms were ranged round the outside of the court, which had been marked out first. The Cretan system may be called conjunctive rather than injunctive. The Cretan architects endeavoured not to present an unbroken external appearance but to keep the quality of openness both in the ground plan and in the superstructure. The specific character of their consciousness of space should be particularly noted. This is clear if a comparison is made with the somewhat older or approximately contemporary palaces of Tell Asmar, Açana or Beycesultan which are injunctively arranged. The striving for monumental effect is also differently achieved. In the palaces of the East this is found in the distinctly blocklike outlines of the whole. In the case of the Cretan palaces it finds expression in the west façade standing on the layer of orthostats. At Açana orthostats were used in a later renovation, which may reflect Aegean influence. This feature in Crete, like the use of curves in the building, is related to the ancient Mediterranean megalithic structures. It is enough to mention those of Malta. The rounded corners of Near Eastern buildings, for instance in the royal graves of the Third Dynasty at Ur, presuppose building with sun-dried brick and cannot be considered as prototypes. While many elements of the Cretan palaces derive from the local tradition, familiarity with the palaces of the East cannot be overlooked. The use of columns may go back to Egyptian models. The whole complex, however, has no precedents elsewhere; it is more extensive and more rich than anything which preceded it, except in the most ancient civilizations of the East. The history of the Early Palaces, so far as we can recapture it, indicates that they developed from an early form, which was itself determined by many characteristics peculiar to a utilitarian building and by the accumulation of unplanned accretions, until they achieved their own monumental character and their own structural unity—qualities which are best illustrated in the remains of the third phase of building at Phaestus.

What can be said about the historical events which lay behind this development? An answer is possible only if we take into account the other evidence which the excavations have brought to light. In the construction of the tombs and in the cult of the dead the old forms continued but with greater splendour. The offerings which were made testify to an increase in wealth. If we disregard plain single burials in clay pithoi or larnakes, three types of built tombs are known: the ossuaries, particularly in the east and the north of the island; the beehive-like vaulted tholoi, especially in the Messara with outliers in the northern Pedias at Krasi as far as Cnossus and Mirsini in East Crete; and the small house-tombs on the little island of Mochlos off North Crete. All were family vaults and they were often in use for centuries. Older buildings continued to be used in the Early Palace Period (at Platanus, Koumasa, Hagios Onuphrios and Lebena) and new tholoi were built during it (at Apesokari, Cnossus and Kamilari). Rectangular rooms which were added to the tholoi were employed as ossuaries or served the cult of the dead. The emergence of a monumental character in the construction of these tombs corresponds to the development in the living accommodation of the palaces. One example has survived at Mallia between the palace and the shore, at Khrysolakkos. The foundation layer of the rectangle, which measures 38 m. by 29 m., consisted of big blocks. The interior was divided into many chambers which were accessible from above; and a cultroom was adjacent to them. In front of the long side on the east there ran a portico which looked on to a paved court. This building is basically of the ossuary type. The character of the grave offerings in these tombs is similar to those found in the Cycladic tombs, but it was richer and more varied. Above all there were vessels of stone and clay which provided the dead with food and drink, daggers for the men and jewellery for the women. In the tholoi of the Messara the men were usually given their official seal, which was regarded as the outward symbol of the living person. During the sacrifices which were offered on the altar the dead man was conjured up, and he was believed to be there in person. Such a belief during the Late Palace Period has often been inferred from the sarcophagus at Hagia Triada. It has now been confirmed by a recently discovered terracotta model from one of the two tholoi at Kamilari which depicts four dead men, who are enthroned in a building which is open at the front, and in front of them two votaries and four altars. This model is probably not earlier than M.M. III.[1]

The sanctuaries in the palaces are small crypts, and their ceilings are frequently supported by pillars.[2] The cult objects and the votive offerings which have been found in them illustrate their function, which can be understood only in connexion with Minoan religion (p. 162). These rooms, like the open-air shrines, have no cult images. In the Kamares cave, high on the south slope of Mount Ida, the cult is attested by a large number of clay vessels, which together with their contents were set up as votive offerings. The products of the palace workshops at Phaestus show that this was not a feature of a rural cult only. Most of the sanctuaries on peaks which are known go back to this period: for instance on Mount Juktas near Cnossus, on Mount Hagios Elias south of Mallia, at Maza in the Pedias and in East Crete at Chamaizi, Petsofa and Piskokephalo.[3] In many of them the cult with its votive offerings continued into the following epoch. As a rule they were stone-walled enclosures with simple votive gifts of terracotta and with traces of burnt sacrifice inside. The great building at Chamaizi with its oval ground plan served as a repository for votive gifts (p. 149). In other places the chapel-like buildings do not go back beyond the beginning of the Late Palace Period.

Examples of large sculpture are still lacking. Small figures of man and animal at this time were predominantly of terracotta. Apart from a few finds from the palaces and tombs they came from the sanctuaries on peaks. Narrow-hipped men, standing on a plaque, are represented with short, often curly hair and rust-coloured skin, and they wear only a belt to which a codpiece and a dagger can be fastened. Their arms are raised, or bent with the hands in front of the body, in an attitude which identifies them as worshippers. The women, white skinned and tightly corseted,

[1] §v, 4.   [2] §v, 11.   [3] §v, 10.

wear a bell-shaped skirt and often a bodice as well which leaves the breasts exposed. The ends of the padded girdle which they wear wound twice round the body are usually tied at the front and hang down low. The head-dress is magnificent and strange. The gestures of the women correspond with those of the men. There are similar figures in stone or ivory in one of the Messara tholoi at Koumasa. One is in the form of a signet, which shows that the others too should not be interpreted as idols.

These statuettes bear no relationship to Egyptian or oriental prototypes, although the differentiation of the sexes by the colour of the skin betrays a familiarity with Egyptian works. Formally they are developments of the Cycladic idols, of which many have also been found in Crete in the earlier levels, but the naturalistic features are new and genuinely Minoan. In the development towards naturalism the increased use of three dimensions in sculpture is generally speaking more important than the animation of the stiff forms. These statuettes show features of the physical ideal which marked Minoan civilization at its height: the wasp waist and the court dress consisting of a kilt for the men and a bell-shaped skirt with a bodice for the women.

The modest offerings which come from the sanctuaries on peaks are of interest only for our understanding of the Minoan cult. The small animals, which are generally domestic animals, and the terracotta beetles were intended to bring blessings on the herds and to ward off plagues carried by vermin. Small parts of the body represented in terracotta, generally arms and legs, which are often fitted with holes for hanging up, can only have been thank-offerings for the healing of the sick. Inside one clay bowl a herdsman with a herd of at least 150 animals is represented in a most primitive manner. In other such bowls worshippers or birds are to be found. The popular and unsophisticated character of this clay modelling is also known from the tholoi of the Messara. There we find for example spouted vessels in the form of bulls on whose horns little men are performing their acrobatic tricks. They are the first representations of the bull-games which are so popular in the art of the Late Palace Period. The tendency towards naturalism is as remarkable in these cases as the subject. Rhytons in the form of bulls and painted in the style of the contemporary pottery were also used in the cults at the palace of Phaestus. They were the immediate forerunners of the later rhytons in the form of bulls' heads in terracotta.

In the minor arts there were further developments on the lines of the preceding period, but there is none of the richness and

wealth in material of the following period, nor the quantity of
work produced, nor the form or expression. The competition of
pottery with objects of gold, silver or bronze was not new, for
from the beginning of the Palace Period there had been silver
beakers with crinkled walls which resembled those made in
clay. The manufacture of vessels from precious, coloured stone
did not cease, but steatite was displacing the finer stones. The
long sword appeared beside the elongated dagger with curved
edge, flat medial rib and no tang, this form of dagger having
been developed earlier. The oldest example of the long sword in
the Aegean area is a ceremonial piece from Mallia. The hilt of
fine limestone, which is riveted to the upper end of the 0·80 m.
long blade, is covered with gold foil embellished with embossed
work and is crowned by a pommel of rock-crystal cut in facets.
A small ceremonial axe, which comes from the same find and is
made of brown slate (length 0·15 m.), is in the shape of a springing
panther. It is probably to be explained as the ornament of a
sceptre. There are precedents for the modelling and the decoration in Cycladic art. The wild animal, which is native to Anatolia,
may have been intended to guard a god or a goddess. A gold
pendant, probably from a necklace, which was found at Khrysolakkos near Mallia, portrays a queen bee, which is repeated
heraldically, and a honeycomb in the middle. The technique of
granulation which originated in Egypt was already known in the
Aegean area. The direct expression of natural form, in spite of the
stylized decoration, is Minoan. The predominance of the decorative scheme over the expression of natural form is characteristic
also of the palace pottery and of the seal carving.

The richest source of information for the period is provided by
the painted pottery.[1] Some of the work which was done in the
early period of the excavations has not been superseded in spite of
the very great increase in material.[2] The task which confronts
research with increasing urgency is a clearer understanding of the
differences between the various workshops in date and place and
of the relations between them. The multiplicity of techniques,
shapes and systems of ornamentation, and above all the expressive
artistic character and the high quality of a great part of the work
offer a broad basis for such an undertaking, which would be
beneficial to the study of stratigraphy and also of chronology.
If it is rightly used, this material can provide answers to questions
which concern the artistic and historical development of the
Minoans.

[1] See Plate 81.   [2] §v, 2, 7.

The classes of pottery which are decorated with white paint dominate the picture. The use of white paint was developed in East Crete some time before the foundation of the palaces, and it is accompanied by red and orange. It was in East Crete too that the potter's wheel first appeared on the island, and its use now predominates. The development of the wheel to the so-called 'fast wheel' was achieved in the later part of this period. The two classes of pottery, each with two subdivisions, which Evans established, are still valid for Cnossus and provide categories in relation to which the other finds may be classified. Of course the classes of pottery cannot be given strict chronological limits. Apart from isolated exports, the pottery attributed to M.M. II is found only at Cnossus and Phaestus and in the neighbourhood of these two palaces. These wares are products of the palace potteries. In East Crete, as far as and including Mallia, the types classed together under M.M. I were produced right up to the beginning of the new phase, M.M. III. Because the wares of M.M. II and their predecessors were found in the Kamares cave, the name 'Kamares pottery' has been adopted for them, but it is apt to obscure the lines of demarcation between the different groups, especially in East Crete.

One problem that can only be solved by further excavation is the chronological relationship between the groups of pottery. The Italian excavators of Phaestus have challenged the conclusions of Evans, Mackenzie and Pendlebury, which were derived from their observations of the stratigraphy at Cnossus. Since the Second World War the Italians have carried out extensive excavations, which have added a fund of new material. They have made important observations on the stratigraphy of the site and they have attempted to clarify the chronological problem.[1] They think that the M.M. I ware is contemporary with the later M.M. II wares in the palaces, and in general they allow a much shorter space of time for the whole period. The instances at Cnossus where a layer with M.M. II pottery lies above one with M.M. I pottery (in the Royal Pottery Stores and the Loom Weight Area) are not regarded by them as decisive because they argue that a fill of earth may have been brought in from elsewhere. At the moment it is only possible to form an opinion from the very detailed preliminary reports. The exclusion of the stratigraphical proofs is striking. The interpretation which the Italians give to their discoveries is not so compelling that we should accept as contemporary wares which are so different in

[1] §IV, 5, 5; §V, 7.

style. Indeed a reconciliation of stratigraphical conclusions with the stylistic considerations, which the system of Evans achieves, is essential to any convincing solution. Moreover at Cnossus those forms of M.M. I pottery which are closest to the latest E.M. wares are represented in closed deposits which are shown to be early by their stratigraphical position (in the Vat Room Deposit and in the earliest house under the west court). On the other hand the corresponding finds from Phaestus are rare (the Patrikies Ware). This can only mean that this group did not compete with the other at either place for long and that the palace at Cnossus was founded somewhat earlier than that at Phaestus. All the evidence falls into place more clearly and a parallelism emerges naturally from the developments at Cnossus and at Phaestus, if we bear in mind the conclusion of a distinguished authority 'that the distinctions between M.M. I a and b or M.M. II a and b are much clearer than the distinction between M.M. I b and M.M. II a'.[1] Thus three ceramic phases emerge: M.M. I a–M.M. I b/II a–M.M. II b. The first building at Phaestus was destroyed in the course of the middle phase, the second at the beginning of the third phase and the last at the end of it.

In the large repertoire of shapes, which in general are developments of those known in the preceding period, the 'Kamares Cup' may be singled out for its delicate outline and for the technical mastery which is expressed in its eggshell-thin wall. The ornamentation testifies to an incomparable wealth of decorative imagination. While earlier elements such as bands of angular hatching and semicircles lose ground, spirals of every shape and size and rosettes, accompanied by wavy lines and scales, now set the pace. The tendency towards unifying decoration of the surface and torsion is also not new, but it adopts more concentrated and more elegant forms. Great delight is taken in twirls and running tendril formations. The most striking development is that of the impulse towards naturalism. Mussels, fish, polypods, leaves, blossoms, branches and palms are portrayed. But the pictorial motif is always evolved from one of the earlier ornamental motifs. Thus the most mature and the most beautiful of these vases, those of the M.M. II a period, are distinguished by a balanced relationship between decoration and natural form. This matches the final architectural shape of the early palaces. The few examples where human figures are depicted on pottery do not maintain this high standard, because the subject did not lend itself to this kind of stylization.

[1] §IV, 4, 158.

At the same time there are skilful imitations of brightly coloured rock in the ceramic painting. In M.M. II b painting on a light ground became popular again, and there was now a vogue for the accompaniment of white lines. At this time too decoration in relief in a barbotine technique was executed in a masterly way. Simple ribs, preferably arranged obliquely to the perpendicular axis of the vase in the so-called motif of torsion, and jagged or prickly surfaces resembling coral and deep-sea crustacea were especially popular in an early group called Hagia Photini Ware. Knobs and moulded crustacea were also added to vases, and a stemmed *crater* from Phaestus is decorated with seven free-standing lily blossoms. The storage jars (*pithoi*) of the Early Palace Period have a squat, bulbous shape. They are often provided with horizontal rows of handles for cords to pass through, and they are embellished with knobs.

The art of seal cutting also developed from Minoan tradition. The change which it underwent in the Early Palace Period is just as important for our understanding of historical events as the changes in palace architecture. In the past it was possible only to differentiate between an early group and a most brilliant period. The line separating them ran between the two phases of palace culture.[1] Today, thanks mainly to some lucky finds, differences between the two classes in time and in place are beginning to be defined more clearly, but the clarification which is necessary and possible will not be achieved until all the material is collected systematically. The work is still in its early stages.

The changes which are obvious at the beginning of the period do not appear to express any new inspiration. The reverse is rather the case. In matters of pictorial and decorative imagination the same high standard was not achieved. The same is true of the technique.[2] In the town outside the palace of Mallia the workshop of a lapidary has been excavated which, to judge from its pottery, belonged to the beginning of the period. The steatite prisms from it are developments of a type which was native to the northern part of Central Crete. In any case they were amulets, and any use of them for sealing must have been secondary. The only innovations were an increase in the revival of ornamental motifs from M.M. I pottery and a clarification of the symbols for pictographic writing. In the tholoi of the Messara seals continued to be the real concern of the gem-cutter.[3] It has been possible to collect a number of conventional, less expressive, pieces from the tholoi which may be contemporary with the beginnings of the

[1] §v, 9.   [2] §v, 5, 32.   [3] §v, 12.

palaces. It is natural to see in this state of affairs a strengthening of the central authority.

During the time of the first palaces a change took place. Nearly 3,000 seal impressions on clay were found in 1955 at Phaestus under the floor of the later palace in room 25 on the west edge of the central court.[1] These had evidently belonged to an inventory, in which goods delivered to the palace had been registered after examination, and seal impressions had been kept. More than 400 small clay jugs were also found, and they shed some light on the manner in which impressions were taken. To judge from the surviving remains, the number of sealings must originally have been almost three times as great. About 280 types can be classified, most of them being represented by several specimens. The style in the oval impressions made by prisms is surer and more splendid. Rectangular prisms with rounded corners, previously unknown, are more popular. Circular impressions, which are in the majority, show the use of stones with a convex sealing-surface which predominated from the Late Palace Period onwards. The designs on more than two thirds of the types are ornamental and correspond with those of the pottery of M.M. I b/II b. The latest of the pieces are to be dated in M.M. III a.

The typological connexion with the preceding phase can be seen in the gems even more clearly than in the pottery. Although the representation of insects, birds, quadrupeds and men is not new, the seals are perceptibly different from the older seals and from contemporary pottery. There are a few examples of monsters, including griffins, and these are new. Above all the naturalistic quality of the style is new. It is as far removed from the previous primitive designs as it is from the decorative limitation of the natural forms on the vases. This however is true only of the animals; for the representation of human figures is schematic in a manner reminiscent of their portrayal on vases. The fact that the 'flying gallop', which has always passed for a Minoan invention, appears here for the first time deserves all the more attention as the tendency towards naturalism appears to be still stylized in a high degree, when we compare these seals with those of the following period.

The seal impressions from the Hieroglyphic Deposit[2] at Cnossus are on the border-line between the Early and the Late Palace Period.[3] Apart from seals with decorative designs and hieroglyphic characters, there are some with pictures which have no precedent in Crete, Egypt or the East for the directness of

[1] §IV, 5.   [2] See Plates 82 and 83.   [3] §V, 5, 37.

their reproduction of nature. The motifs are mainly animals and
the subjects are taken from the natural landscape. A hind is at
rest in a grotto; a fish stalks an octopus among coral-like reefs; a
deer is hunted by a dog in a wood; a horned animal stands at a
crib, and a human figure on the ground crouches beside it; even a
wild goat, alone, lying at rest, is made the subject of a picture.
We must also mention the portrait heads of a ruler and of a
young prince. The treatment of the animals is in the tradition of
earlier gem-cutting. Its place in that tradition can be recognized
by reference to seal-stones which lie stylistically between the two
groups. In these intermediate seal-stones the stylization is still
stronger than in the sealings from the Hieroglyphic Deposit but
no longer so strong as in the sealings from Phaestus. Moreover,
trees are represented in gems in the same way as in mature M.M. II
painted pottery, and this resemblance establishes a relative and
absolute chronology for the groups of seals. Unfortunately the
stratigraphy of the Hieroglyphic Deposit is not clear. The
ornamentation stands nearer to M.M. III than to the preceding
period, and this too makes only a border-line date possible for the
deposit. But since the tradition can be traced continuously
throughout all its stages, it is a matter of minor importance
whether the Hieroglyphic Deposit is to be dated immediately
before or shortly *after* the catastrophe which befell the old palace.
What is certain is that pictorial representation, in the sense of
that word in western art, developed first in Crete during the
Early Palace Period in the art of gem-cutting. It is uncertain
whether the last decisive step on this path was taken before or
after the catastrophe. The development of this form of pictorial
representation, which is distinct from anything earlier in Crete
and elsewhere in its degree of naturalism, must be regarded as
one of the two great achievements of the Early Palace Period, the
palace architecture being the other. It is typical of the Minoan
character that this step, which had even more important consequences than the building of the palaces, was taken in the
sphere of a miniature art. The new importance attached to seals is
expressed in an increasing use of semi-precious stones and rock-
crystal and in the development of some standardized forms of
signet.

The seal with hieroglyphs developed step by step with the
pictorial seal. The original masterpieces of this group belong to
the same transitional period as the impressions from the Hieroglyphic Deposit. Their importance as amulets must be considered,
because the seal and the amulet began to diverge from one

another.[1] The Minoan hieroglyphs, which continued in use during the Late Palace Period, emerged from a pictographic script under Egyptian influence in the course of this period. They are also known from clay labels and small tablets on which, however, they appear in cursive form. The solemn and decorative stylization of hieroglyphs on seals is as much an expression of Early Palace culture as the painted pottery of the period, and it reminds us of the religious and ceremonial uses of these stones. The other class of seals too, which are adorned with pictorial scenes or decorative designs, cannot be explained without reference to Egypt. The impulse to develop the pictorial imagination may have come from the East, but the spiral ornamentation points to intercourse with the Nile Valley too. This kind of ornamentation was evidently adopted from Crete. Minoan textiles may have introduced it into Egypt. In the spiral ornamentation of the Egyptian scarabs of the Middle Kingdom the decisive influence was Minoan.

VI. THE HISTORICAL CONCLUSIONS

We have described the most important material from which any insight into historical events of the period may be derived. They may reveal only a little of what the historian seeks, and they set their own limits to the questions he may ask. We are concerned with a highly developed civilization and no longer with a prehistoric way of life, and we find ourselves face to face with the first contacts between Europe and the ancient civilizations of the East. What light do the material remains of the Early Palace Period in Crete throw on the first interplay of these forces? The answer has historical as well as archaeological implications.

The peaceful character of Minoan civilization is astonishing even in the pre-Palace Period. The repeated destructions of the palaces were caused not by enemy hands but by earthquakes. Although the coasts of Crete are long and exposed, the Cretans showed surprisingly little interest in the art of fortification which was highly developed elsewhere, as we know from important remains in the Aegean islands, on the Anatolian coast and in Greece itself. The conclusion is inescapable that the Cretan ships, which were already carrying on a brisk trade with their Aegean neighbours, Egypt and the Levant, provided sufficient protection against piracy. What form of political constitution prevented the eruption of internal tensions into war we do not

[1] §v, 5, 44.

know. It is clear enough that the political links, which had certainly been loose hitherto, were tightened into a strongly centralized monarchy at the foundation of the palaces. The position of the three palaces in the centre of the island only makes sense if it is assumed that there was no political rivalry between them. The defensive features in them are of a very rudimentary kind. The fact that the residential area beside the palace of Mallia had a ring wall is sufficiently explained by its proximity to the shore. Previously the lead in civilization had been held by East Crete. The Messara culture was rural, though admittedly rich and prosperous. Penetration into the land west of the Ida massif began at this time when the palace of Monastiraki is probably to be regarded as an economic outpost (p. 148). Several features of the later period were included in the picture of 'Minoan thalassocracy' which the Greeks from the time of Herodotus painted for themselves. Nevertheless modern doubts[1] about the elementary fact on which this picture was founded, namely Minoan sea-power, do not do justice to the archaeological evidence. Pictures of Minoan ships[2] have survived mainly in glyptic miniatures. They must not be interpreted literally, and Minoan craft should not be regarded as small and scarcely seaworthy craft. There is evidence to show that Minoan ships may have been about 20 metres long.

The large number of storerooms and storage vessels in the palaces suggests the existence of a highly organized administrative service with many branches, even if we suppose that the supplies of grain, oil and wine were intended only to serve the needs of the royal household. These supplies, together with the valuables which lay in the treasuries, seem to have formed the wealth of the prince and not to have been destined ultimately for export.[3] The insight into the archive system of the period which has been afforded by the great find of sealings at Phaestus has shown us that even then the administration was carried out in accordance with a system which had been known previously only from the later palaces of Crete and from the citadels of the Mycenaean period. The first stage of Linear Script A was already being developed alongside the Minoan hieroglyphs in the Early Palace Period. As the finds at Phaestus show, it was devised for administrative purposes, and the prototype of this kind of administration is as likely to be found in Syria as in Egypt.

The seals provide an insight also into the structure of society. It can be seen from the archives at Phaestus that the administration

<hr>

[1] §vi, 8.   [2] §vi, 6.   [3] Cf. §vi, 2.

considered it important to control the suppliers and that they for
their part required documentary proof that they had fulfilled their
obligations. The general resemblance of the seals to those in the
tholoi of the Messara shows that the goods delivered to the
palace came from the landowners whose family vaults were the
tholoi. These relations, however, can be interpreted only in a
general sense, because the impressions from Phaestus represent
an advanced stage of gem-cutting and the seals in the tholoi are
mainly earlier in date. It is evident, that now, if not earlier, the
farmers had become vassals, as we may infer from the later seals
such as those from the Hieroglyphic Deposit. The magnificent
development in the art of seal-cutting, which had reached its
peak when the older palaces had already been destroyed, enables
us to arrive at some conclusions about the owners of the seals.
A nobility had arisen round the court of the rulers and drew its
members from the class of those who had probably been free
landowners. There is evidence of a pause in the development of
gem-cutting at the time when the palaces were founded, and this
pause may reflect the changing status of the landowners upon the
rise of the central power (p. 156). The find at Phaestus comes *after*
the crisis and marks the beginning of a rising curve of development.

   The material remains of religious cults also provide an
insight into the culture and life of the palaces. The open-air
shrines were still used with the conservatism which is always
characteristic of religious cults. If the court and the country landowners shared in services at these shrines, as evidence from the
Kamares grotto shows, then this suggests that the object of worship was common to the palace and the countryside. The mother
goddess was also worshipped in crypts, and this is probably connected with her worship in caves. As Minoan representational
art was developing during this period, the absence of cult
images is striking.[1] The small figures in the shrines are votive
offerings which represent the worshippers, and they portray
members of the nobility. Their costume has now become that
of the court (p. 152). There is no archaeological evidence which
proves the existence of a bull-cult, and such a cult would be
inconsistent with our knowledge of the sacrifice of bulls which is
derived from the monuments. Nor was there a pillar and tree
cult in the sense that worship was paid to them as embodiments
of divine power. The goddess, however, was probably believed
to appear by invocation of the worshippers, and a tree or pillar
may have been the sacred place where she appeared. That she

[1] §vi, 7.

revealed herself in the form of a bird or a snake is shown by a great deal of later evidence, and we may assume that it was already so in this period. A painted clay bowl from Phaestus indicates that already in this early period the goddess could reveal herself in human form in moments of ecstasy. Clay pipes, partially provided with moulded snakes, which have been found in the later palace chapels, are also to be connected with the epiphany of the goddess, and their use may go back to the Early Palace Period. The epiphany may have taken place in the crypts or even at this time in the open air where a large congregation could take part; at Phaestus, for instance, the flight of steps in the north of the upper west court would have provided room for several hundred people. Was the space reserved for the retainers or for the nobility which was attendant on the ruler? At any rate the cult in Crete differs from the cults in Egypt and the Near East just in this respect that provision is made for more active participation by the worshippers. On the other hand the area is too small for bull-sports, although sacrifices of bulls occurred at this period in preparation for the epiphany of the goddess.

Evidence of trade with the Aegean islands is provided by finds of Cycladic pottery in the early palaces and of imported Minoan vessels on the islands of Cythera, Melos, Thera and Aegina and on the mainland at Lerna. Local instances of decoration in white paint in Middle Helladic levels at Korakou, Asine and Aegina are best explained as due to Minoan influence. On the other hand Minyan ware of the Middle Helladic period is represented in Crete by only a single example from Cnossus. Thus the superiority of Crete is obvious, although it cannot be inferred that she exercised any kind of overlordship over the Aegean area. Her supremacy was based on wealth, protected by an impregnable position.

Cretan trade with the Levant[1] can be traced on the evidence of pottery by way of Cyprus to Ugarit and Qatna on the Upper Orontes valley. Of two silver vessels from Byblos one has the Minoan teapot shape, and the spiral pattern on the other shows that it was made at least under strong Minoan influence. The spirals on the frescoes of the Palace at Mari on the upper Euphrates in the eighteenth century B.C. were originally inspired by imported Minoan goods. Letters from the archives of this palace also mention the acquisition of valuables from Crete.[2] Conversely, some Babylonian cylinder seals reached Crete by this trade route.

The magnificent M.M. II clay vessels which have been found in Egypt have already been mentioned (p. 143). The silver vessels

[1] §VI, 5.   [2] §VI, 4.

in the treasure from Tōd in Upper Egypt, dated by the cartouche of Ammenemes II (*c.* 1929–1895 B.C.), are markedly Aegean in shape and ornaments.[1] Early M.M. II pots, decorated in relief (Hagia Photini Ware), provide such close parallels that here too we must assume at least indirect Minoan influence. Reference has already been made to the adoption of the spiral ornamentation by the Egyptians (p. 159). The close connexion between Egypt and Crete is also illustrated by the Egyptian scarabs or imitations of them which have been found in Crete. Through them the hippopotamus goddess of Egypt, Thoeris, entered the repertoire of the Minoan seal-cutter. A seated statuette, made in diorite, which was found with M.M. IIb pottery under the central court at Cnossus, represents an Egyptian of high rank according to the inscription on its base (p. 143), and is with good reason regarded as a personal present. That Egyptian ships visited Crete is mentioned in a text of the Middle Kingdom. The 'Admonitions of an Egyptian Sage' (handed down, it is true, only in a papyrus of the New Kingdom) contain one of the first references to the country of the Keftiu;[2] and it can now be accepted in conclusion to a once lively debate that this name, which is known from many documents of the New Kingdom, was originally the name of Crete.

It can be inferred from Egyptian sources that the Egyptians were particularly interested in timber. Pines are mentioned first and later cypresses, which were famous in Crete in later antiquity. Textiles, purple, wine and oil may be added as exports from Crete to Egypt. In exchange the Cretans acquired ivory, faience, ostrich eggs and the precious stones which were indispensable for their seals. These articles as well as gold and ivory will also have played a part in trade from the Levant, while copper and tin came to Crete from Asia Minor mainly by way of Cyprus but perhaps also across the Aegean. Connexions with the West are indicated by finds of liparite, a vitreous volcanic stone from the Aeolic Isles, which was used for the manufacture of vessels in Minoan workshops. We can only guess how the trade was carried on. We may imagine that the prince claimed a monopoly for himself, especially at the time when the central power was strengthened. As we can see from later Egyptian and oriental documents, trade was already carried on extensively by an exchange of presents between princes. A glance at the Assyrian merchants of the *karum* Kanesh (Kültepe) shows us that private trade as well was already organized.

[1] §VI, 3.   [2] §VI, 9, 40 ff., 407, 417.

The consolidation of the state, in terms of its society and economy, is the concern and the achievement of this period in Crete during which Minoan civilization, breaking away from its prehistoric beginnings, rose to the rank of a highly developed civilization. Inevitably the island was drawn into the political and economic field of rivalry which, during the first third of this millennium, extended from the Nile valley to Mesopotamia, Syria and Anatolia. This can be inferred rather than proved from the archaeological evidence, and we must also beware of applying modern ideas too readily. The only thing that is certain is that Crete had no rival of equal standing on the sea routes. The great and the medium-sized powers of the period were land-powers. Egypt was interested politically in the sea route to Syria alone, and this provided Crete with a good basis for economic and cultural exchange. The states of Asia Minor too looked away from the sea towards the interior and the East. The destruction of Troy II and the rise of Minoan Crete not long afterwards can hardly be entirely unrelated, even if there is no question of any direct connexion. The study of affairs in this area during the first half of the second millennium is still in its infancy, but there is some hope that the most recent discoveries, for example at the palace of Beycesultan, will contribute to the clarification of Anatolian–Aegean relations in the very near future. The Aegean area became Crete's sphere of interest at this time. She assumed a leading place in it as the cultural balance shifted in favour of the Minoans. This had consequences for both areas. The island grew in wealth and prosperity, and her Aegean partners entered into the civilized world. Those who attempt to wrest further details from the myth of Theseus and the Minotaur venture into the realm of fancy. But as we pass from this period to the following period we are faced with the question: how did it come about that, shortly after Minoan civilization reached its height, the leadership began to pass to the Mycenaean mainland? In the light of this development which was to ensue, we may regard the Early Palace Period, mature though it was in relation to the past, as an archaic phase leading to the high level of pre-Greek classicism.

CHAPTER IV (c)

CYPRUS IN THE MIDDLE BRONZE AGE

VII. THE NATURE OF THE MIDDLE
CYPRIOT PERIOD

THE transition from the Early to the Middle Bronze Age in Cyprus is a most difficult process to define, for the later period evolves from the earlier without cultural break or natural disaster to provide a landmark. Although very few settlement sites have been investigated, it seems clear from the evidence of cemeteries which were used both in E.C. and M.C. that the transition in material culture was gradual. Probably the least unsatisfactory way of drawing the distinction between the two periods is by recognizing the decorated pottery known as White Painted II ware as diagnostic of M.C. I.[1] Other material aspects of M.C. I are almost indistinguishable from those of E.C. III.

The Middle Cypriot period has been divided into three phases, I, II and III.[2] M.C. I appears to have lasted from c. 1850 B.C. until c. 1800, while M.C. II covers the period c. 1800–1700; estimates for the duration of M.C. III vary between c. 1700–1600 and c. 1700–1550 B.C.[3] The opening date is fairly closely tied to Minoan chronology in view of the imported Early Minoan III (Middle Minoan I a) bridge-spouted jar[4] from a tomb at Lapithos identified as transitional E.C. III A–B, and the Middle Minoan II Kamares cup from a late M.C. I tomb at Karmi.[5] The date of the end of the M.C. period is determined by the contexts in Palestine and Egypt in which the earliest L.C.[6] objects have been found; in Egypt, these are no earlier than the 17th Dynasty, and a date in the middle of the sixteenth century B.C. for the end of the M.C. period seems desirable. There are few, if any, fixed dates within the period itself.[7]

The earlier part of the M.C. period is no more than an extension of the Early Bronze Age. It shares its material culture, and continues to occupy many of the old-established sites. On the other hand, M.C. III acts as a prelude to L.C. I, so that

[1] §vii, 1, 172; §vii, 5, 272.   [2] §vii, 1.   [3] §vii, 1, 273; §vii, 6, 204.
[4] §vii, 4; §x, 1, 109–10.   [5] §vii, 6.
[6] §vii, 1, 257–73; §ix, 3, 52–6; *Bull. A.S.O.R.* 138, 47–9.
[7] §vii, 2; §vii, 6.

the cultural overlap between M.C. III and L.C. I is as ambivalent as that between E.C. III and M.C. I. When the M.C. period began, Cyprus was still very largely isolated from her neighbours, as she had been throughout the Early Bronze Age. By the end of the period, the record of imported goods found on Cypriot sites and of Cypriot goods found in the Levant and Egypt shows that this insularity had been overcome, and that Cyprus was playing an appreciable part in the economic life of the region. It was, in fact, somewhere in mid-course, and not at the beginning or the end of the M.C. period that the changes of greatest significance took place. Were it not for the confusion which would certainly result, a case could be argued for apportioning M.C. I and II to the Early Bronze Age, and reforming the M.C. period from a combination of M.C. III and L.C. I, so that the landmark for the onset of the Late Bronze Age in Cyprus would be the appearance of the Mycenaean III A I pottery imported from the Aegean.

Sources of evidence for the course and character of the M.C. period are restricted. M.C. I and II are known only from the evidence of cemeteries; M.C. III, in addition to information from tombs, has settlement evidence from Kalopsidha[1] and Nitovikla.[2] Field exploration has broadened the picture by locating many as yet unexcavated sites.[3]

VIII. MIDDLE CYPRIOT SETTLEMENT

Areas in which it has been possible to study M.C. settlement in detail offer strong hints of tribal organization.[4] There are hints, too, that much of the period was far from peaceful and that, at least in some areas, tribal units were sufficiently insecure to feel the need for fortified refuges in the vicinity of their open settlements. This situation may have reached its peak in M.C. III. It invites the question whether the island was ever unified during the Bronze Age.

The M.C. period saw the accomplishment of the preliminaries for a major reorientation of the chief centres of population. When the period began, the chief sites appear still to have been ranged[5] along both sides of the lower slopes of the Kyrenia mountains, or to have been located in key positions in the river valleys as they entered or crossed the central plain, well illustrated by the

[1] §vii, 3, 27–37; §viii, 6.   [2] G, 8(i), 371–407; G, 19, 61–97.
[3] §viii, 2, 154–60.   [4] §viii, 2, 139–41.
[5] See map in *C.A.H.* ii³, pt. 2; §viii, 2, 154–60, with map of M.C. settlement.

settlements at Dhenia,[1] Politiko,[2] Nicosia[3] and Alambra.[4] By the end of the M.C. period, however, a substantial withdrawal had taken place from the area of the Kyrenia hills, so that, for example, the former centres of power at *Vounous*[5] and at Lapithos[6] had passed from view. There was also a steady reduction in the importance of several of the valley 'capitals', so that Alambra was deserted and Dhenia and Politiko were greatly impoverished by the time the Late Bronze Age began.

These losses were probably more than offset by the expansion of settlement in other parts of the island. Occupation increased considerably on the north fringe of the Mesaoria, between Nicosia and Trikomo, which raises at least a suspicion that agriculturists were moving into the plain from the foothills, in search of new cornlands. As an eastward extension of this new line of settlement, the Karpass peninsula became thickly populated, with particularly important centres adjoining the modern villages of Galinoporni[7] and Rizokarpaso.[8] Further west, the extensive plateau land that lies between the western end of the Kyrenia Hills and the Aloupos river valley 15 miles to the south became densely occupied, though the adjoining area to the west in the Kormakiti peninsula seems not to have been taken up until the beginning of L.C. I.[9] Little interest was shown in west Cyprus, whose inaccessibility and mountainous character evidently deterred the M.C. pioneers as they had their predecessors. West of a north–south line from the Marathasa valley to the Kouris river near Episkopi no M.C. settlement has been recognized.

Before the end of the M.C. III period the first hesitant steps had also been taken towards settling the east and south-east coast, which, in the Late Bronze Age, was to come to exceptional prominence as a result of the dominant role that foreign trade came to play in the island's economy,[10] trade that was to be handled by the port-towns which Middle Cypriot foresight had established. The origins of Enkomi,[11] Hala Sultan Tekke,[12] Arpera,[13] Pyla[14] and Klavdhia[15] all belong to this phase of expansion. Unfortunately, the mechanism of these changes eludes us. Though

[1] §ix, 1.   [2] §viii, 5.

[3] §viii, 6, 134–8.   [4] §vii, 3, 19–27; §viii, 2, 154.

[5] §viii, 3; §viii, 8.   [6] G, 8(i), 33–162; §viii, 7.   [7] §viii, 1.

[8] G, 12 (1961), 276.   [9] §viii, 2, 142

[10] G, 6, 29–30; §ix, 4, 138–90.

[11] *C.A.H.* ii³, pt. 2, ch. xxii(*b*), sect. ix, 8.

[12] §viii, 2, 163.   [13] §viii, 2, 161.

[14] §viii, 2, 168.   [15] §viii, 2, 164.

Kalopsidha, the old capital of the east Mesaoria, may have founded Enkomi[1] to manage the trade streaming to and from the Levant more efficiently, this can be no more than a hypothesis, though it is strengthened by the virtual close-down at Kalopsidha once Enkomi was firmly established.

Acquaintance with M.C. settlement soon calls attention to the large number of fortifications. The most striking standing monument of the Bronze Age in Cyprus is the Middle Cypriot promontory fort at Krini,[2] on the south side of the Kyrenia hills, 3 or 4 miles west of the Kyrenia pass. It was built above the modern village on a high spur, the south edge of which is a vertical rock-face where no man-made protection was required. On the accessible north side, however, the promontory is entirely sealed off by a great curtain wall built of undressed limestone blocks eroded from the mountain behind. The wall is reinforced at regular intervals by a number of solid bastions. Wall and bastions still stand to a height of 2 m. There is an inner defence consisting of a smaller wall parallel to the main fortification. The complex is a little reminiscent of Chalandriani in Syros.[3] Between 5 and 6 miles east of Krini, on the other side of the Kyrenia pass, not far from Dhikomo, is another M.C. fortified hill-site.[4] Other forts have been found in the Karpasha Forest area, north of the Aloupos river valley;[5] these immediately adjoin contemporary open settlements, and it seems probable that they were intended to serve as fortified compounds, into which in time of danger people and their flocks could be gathered from the villages below. A precisely similar arrangement exists at Ayios Sozomenos in the Yalias valley,[6] where two large open settlements little more than a couple of miles apart are situated at the edge of the plain under the shadow of the bluff of a high plateau on which are the remains of at least two M.C. fortified compounds.

Were these fortified sites in coastal districts, it would be reasonable to explain them as a precaution against the raids of seaborne marauders. Though Krini is near the sea on the map, the Kyrenia hills intervene. Ayios Sozomenos is 15 miles from the sea, and again the mountains intervene. It seems clear that these fortresses were built to guard against danger from within the island itself; they suggest a period of serious internal unrest.

---

[1] §VII, 1, 277 n. 4; §VII, 5, 299.
[2] G, 12 (1960), 298; §VIII, 2, 158.
[3] A. W. Lawrence, *Greek Architecture* (London, 1957), p. 13, fig. 8.
[4] §VIII, 2, 140.   [5] §VIII, 2, 154, no. 9 and 157, no. 85.
[6] §VIII, 2, 155, nos. 26 and 32.

Corroboration may be found in the large number of weapons buried with the dead in M.C. graves, nowhere better seen than in the *Vrysis tou Barba* cemetery at Lapithos.[1]

IX. MIDDLE CYPRIOT DEVELOPMENTS IN MATERIAL CULTURE

Little is known of domestic architecture apart from the plan of a house of M.C. III date at Kalopsidha.[2] The building evidently formed part of a well-planned urban unit; another house (unexcavated) lay to the east, and there was a street to the south. The north and west boundaries were formed by courtyards. The house, consisting of some ten rooms and a central courtyard, measured 15 × 12 m. Its construction was rough, with small unwrought limestone blocks forming the lower part of the walls, the upper courses being completed in mud-brick. The inner wall faces were rendered with mud-plaster, while the floors were of trodden earth or clay laid over gravel. The roof, which was probably flat, was made by covering the joists with brushwood or straw and water-proofing with clay; the same method is still widely employed in the island at the present time. The plan of this house was based on a simple alignment of rooms arranged round three sides of a rectangle, at the heart of which was the small open court used for domestic purposes, on to which a *liwan*-type room fronted. Domestic installations in certain rooms suggest that functions varied from room to room. The building was probably single-storied.

The fortress of Nitovikla,[3] built in M.C. III on the south coast of the Karpass, offers a contrast to the Kalopsidha house. The building acted as the keep within a large fortified plateau, to which no doubt the local population could resort in time of trouble. The keep was designed as a quadrangle with massive curtain walls,[4] against whose inside faces a series of chambers was constructed. The flat roofs of these chambers, reached by wooden ladders, were on a level with the parapets of the ramparts, and could have been used as fighting platforms. The entrance was on the north-east side; it was flanked by two square towers. At the gateway itself were two large monolithic ashlar conglomerate slabs resting on bossed foundation blocks; other ashlar blocks were used in the corner structures and the gate. Many features of the plan and

[1] G, 8(i), 33–162.   [2] §VII, 1, 1–3; §VII, 3, 27–37.
[3] G, 8(i), 371–407; G, 19, 61–97; §VII, 1, 3–5.
[4] §VII, 1, 4–5.

construction of Nitovikla find parallels[1] in Anatolia, particularly at Boğazköy, and in the Syro-Palestinian area. The construction and use of the fortress have been connected with the Hyksos.[2] While it is sufficiently unlike the fortified sites in the centre of Cyprus to suggest that the engineer responsible for its design may have been a foreigner, there is no need to suppose that this part of the Karpass was a foreign enclave, and that Nitovikla was garrisoned by foreigners.[3] From the beginning of M.C. III onwards for centuries to come Cyprus can be divided into two cultural zones, east and west. This division is too imprecise to define any frontiers, as it is too subtle to permit historical interpretation. But the divergencies between the two are insufficient to suggest an intrusion of foreigners in east Cyprus during the Middle Bronze Age.

Treatment of the dead during the M.C. period[4] continued a general tradition hallowed by generations of Early Bronze Age practice. Cemeteries like those at *Vounous*, Lapithos, Dhenia and Politiko continued in uninterrupted use from E.C. well into M.C. There is as much evidence for contemporary variations in tomb-plans as between one cemetery and the next as there is for changes in design that have a chronological significance. The idiosyncrasies of tomb-makers in the *Mali* and *Kafkalla* cemeteries at Dhenia[5] emphasize the individual character of that site; their remarkable tomb-plans are not of general chronological significance. North-coast cemeteries, particularly Lapithos[6] and Karmi,[7] specialized in a type of tomb in which several separate burial-chambers radiate from a common entrance pit or passage. Individual chambers were enlarged at need by additional niches and recesses cut in their walls. A Karmi tomb has the unique feature of a human figure sculptured on its *dromos* wall.[8] Throughout the period it was customary to treat a grave as a family sepulchre, so that its use might span several generations. The bodies were sometimes placed in a sitting position, sometimes were extended. During M.C. I and II the dead were accompanied by abundant gifts of food and drink in pottery vessels; at some sites, bronze or copper tools, weapons and ornaments were also given in profusion.[9]

Tombs rather different from those so far considered occur in some M.C. III cemeteries.[10] Here, in place of the rectangular or squarish rock-cut pits which form the *dromoi* of normal Cypriot

[1] §IX, 5, 138–43. [2] §IX, 5, 198–9. [3] §VII, 1, 277–9.
[4] §VII, 3, 78–81. [5] §IX, 1. [6] G, 8(i), 33–162.
[7] §VII, 6. [8] G, 11, 510; §VII, 6, 197. [9] G, 8(i), 33–162.
[10] §VII, 1, 6–10.

Bronze Age tombs, a long wedge-shaped passage has steps cut in it leading to a kidney-shaped chamber; alternatively there may be a projecting rectangular buttress of rock left unquarried in the back wall, dividing the chamber into two parts.[1] This type of tomb evokes comparison with the so-called Hyksos tombs of Tell el-Fār'ah.[2] In Cyprus, the best-known group of tombs of this class belongs to the cemetery of Paleoskoutella,[3] a mile or so north of the Nitovikla fortress and contemporary with it. This cemetery has many unusual features, including the choice of the flat top of a prominent hill for its location. The least normal feature, however, was the use of large tumuli of earth and rubble both to protect the graves and to act as markers. While some of the tumuli were thus heaped over tombs, others concealed elaborate complexes of pits, cuttings and holes in the roughly levelled bedrock, which may have featured in the conduct of a funerary cult.[4] In addition, two of the graves under their respective tumuli were found emptied of their contents; they had been entered by means of small pits dug accurately through the superincumbent mounds to reach the entrances, and so suggested to their excavator that this 'robbing' must have been the work of those within whose active memories the tombs had last been used.

It has been suggested[5] that those to whom this burial ground belonged took alarm, possibly in face of the same threat of danger which culminated before the end of M.C. III in the violent destruction of the Nitovikla fortress.[6] Before taking flight from the region, however, piety demanded that they exhume their dead from the smaller and more vulnerable graves and rebury them in a single large chamber-tomb, which was then covered by the largest tumulus in the cemetery, 22·0 × 17·5 m., still standing more than 3·0 m. high at the time of excavation. In addition, extra tumuli were raised over the areas which had been used for funeral ceremonies to prevent their profanation. It is at least certain that the cemetery was abandoned before the end of M.C. III.

The artistry and technological achievements of the M.C. period are both disappointing.[7] Great quantities of material objects have been recovered from M.C. tombs, whose general implications cannot be mistaken. The period opens before the creative qualities of the Early Bronze Age had been utterly exhausted; it ends before new ideas brought from overseas had had time to exercise the influence from abroad that is felt in the Late

---

[1] G, 8(i), 427, fig. 166; *Q.D.A.P.* viii (1939), 1–20.
[2] §vii, 1, 205–6; §ix, 4, 146–7.   [3] G, 8(i), 416–38.   [4] §vii, 1, 10.
[5] §ix, 5, 198.   [6] §vii, 1, 278–9.   [7] §vii, 1.

Bronze Age. The *Leitmotiv* throughout the history of Cyprus is its dependence on foreign sources for the reinfusion of vitality; by the end of the Middle Bronze Age the island had been too long without outside interference. The lesson is clear in the M.C. pottery sequence, where the charm and vigour of the E.C. potters is missing. The only positive contribution was the M.C. revival of painted pottery, a form of expression which had lain dormant and forgotten since the Philia stage.[1] Even here, however, the initiative had been taken in E.C. III, when the very rare fabric, White Painted I,[2] was evolved. White Painted II,[3] the early painted pottery of M.C. I, may be admired for its technical quality, if not for its decorative originality. Its ornament, in common with the whole M.C. ceramic decoration, is strictly linear, making much use of hatched and cross-hatched panels or groupings of triangles, lozenges and the like.[4] These ornamental schemes were executed in a dark-coloured paint on a light-coloured surface; this tradition, which was most especially at home in north and central Cyprus, spans the whole of the M.C. period, even lingering on, long past its usefulness, into L.C. I.[5] It is questionable whether the potter's wheel was employed in M.C. times. Not surprisingly, the deterioration in ceramic ornament corresponds to a deterioration in shape. Where much E.C. pottery had exhibited a sound sense of form, this characteristic steadily deserted the M.C. potters, so that much of their work can only be contemplated with regret. They exhibited certain extravagant tendencies in the employment of plastic embellishments (particularly well exemplified by Åström's 'string-hole style')[6] which really deserve to be described as baroque. The development of Red Polished ware, whose origins belong to the beginnings of the E.C. period, continued during the Middle Bronze Age, where the end of this once-splendid fabric is to be seen in the Red Slip and Black Slip wares[7] that sprang from it. The somewhat rustic Red-on-Black ware[8] that is especially characteristic of M.C. III had no E.C. predecessor. This fabric belongs to east Cyprus in general, the Karpass in particular. It has been found further west in small amounts.[9]

Though there was a prolific output of metal objects, the Middle Bronze Age saw no significant progress in the development of the

---

[1] §vii, 5, 224–5.
[2] §vii, 3, 148–51; §vii, 5, 229–30.
[3] §vii, 1, 12–17; §vii, 3, 151–5.
[4] §vii, 1, figs. iii–viii. See Plate 84.
[5] §vii, 1, 163–4.
[6] §vii, 1, fig. xi.
[7] §vii, 1, 84–108.
[8] §vii, 1, 108–18; §ix, 2. See Plate 85.
[9] §vii, 1, 117; §ix, 2, 68–79.

metal industry;[1] there was probably an improvement in the types of mould used by the end of M.C. III. With hardly an exception, the types of object in production can be traced to the E.C. period. The few foreign metal objects found, including Minoan daggers[2] and Asiatic shaft-hole axes,[3] merely serve to expose the archaic designs and retarded techniques of the Cypriot smiths. But it is quite certain from the constant availability of metal goods that mining and smelting activities continued unabated throughout the period. It is possible that increased production of the raw material enabled Cyprus to gain her economic foothold in the Levant before the end of M.C. III. Nevertheless, there were fewer M.C. sites located in juxtaposition with the mining areas than there had been in E.C. or there were to be in L.C.[4]

After the splendours of E.C. plastic work, M.C. modelling comes as an anti-climax.[5] A few uninspired copies of the old plank-shaped figures were made in both Red Polished and White Painted techniques, and there is a somewhat jejune series of female figures breaking away from this degree of stylization. A lively ship model, a full crew perched on its gunwales, shows that a creative spirit was not wholly dead.[6]

Seal usage was unknown in Cyprus before the L.C. period, a revealing symptom of her undeveloped and isolated state.

X. CYPRUS AND HER NEIGHBOURS IN THE MIDDLE BRONZE AGE

The foreign contacts of the earliest part of the M.C. period were a continuation of the sporadic links between Cyprus and her neighbours which can be observed in the Early Bronze Age.[7] Trade with Crete persisted. In addition to a small number of Minoan bronze weapons from Lapithos,[8] a M.M. II Kamares cup was found in a late M.C. I tomb at Karmi;[9] its decoration is suggestive of an origin near Phaestus rather than Cnossus. There are no contemporary finds of Cypriot objects in Crete, but later, in M.C. III, a White Painted IV–V jug reached Zakro,[10] and there is a rather doubtful case of a Red-on-Black import at Mallia.[11] There is no positive evidence for exchanges between

---

[1] *C.A.H.* II³, pt. 2, ch. XXII(*b*); §IV, 6, 76–7.
[2] §X, 1, 110–12.
[3] §VII, 1, 139, 244–5.
[4] §VIII, 2, 138–44.
[5] §VII, 1, 152–5.
[6] G, 1, pl. 39:111; §VII, 1, 153, fig. 16:13.
[7] §VII, 5, 274–80.
[8] §X, 1.
[9] §VII, 6.
[10] §X, 3.
[11] §IX, 2, 79.

Cyprus and the mainland of Greece, or between Cyprus and the Cyclades in the M.C. period. During M.C. I there was little or no sign of contact with Egypt or the Levant; it is significant that no White Painted II pottery has been found abroad.[1] Specific contacts with Syria, Palestine and Egypt start during M.C. II. Cypriot pottery of this period has been found at Ras Shamra, Megiddo and El-Lāhūn.[2] Contemporary references in the Mari texts[3] to the receipt of copper from 'Alashiya' would be of outstanding interest if the constantly urged identification of Cyprus with Alashiya could be established beyond dispute (see ch. xxii b, §ix).

What in M.C. II had been a mere trickle of exports to the eastern markets became a flood in M.C. III; at the same time there was a reciprocal flow of foreign goods into Cyprus. Painted pottery that represents a wide variety of M.C. III wares has been found in Palestine, at Tell el-'Ajjūl, Megiddo, Askalon, Ṭanṭurah, Tell el-Fār'ah, Gezer and Lachish.[4] Return traffic from Palestine to Cyprus included Tell el-Yahūdīya juglets[5] ('Black Punctured Ware') and whatever unguent, scented oil or drug they contained. Cypriot trade with Syria has left traces at Ras Shamra (including a bronze dirk, as well as abundant pottery),[6] Qal'at er-Rus, Tell Sukas and Tell Açana.[7] Trade from north Syria to Cyprus included some Khabur ware, found as far inland as Nicosia, *Ayia Paraskevi*.[8] The trading range extended as far north as Cilicia, where Cypriot objects occur at Tarsus, Kabarsa and Domuz Tepe.[9] Though trade goods from abroad have been found well distributed in Cyprus in M.C. III, from the Galinoporni cemeteries in the Karpass[10] to *Aloupotrypes* at Dhiorios at the west end of the Kyrenia hills,[11] they occur in greatest profusion at Kalopsidha, both in the settlement[12] and the cemeteries.[13] If this was indeed the parent town of Enkomi, this preponderance of foreign trade was an appropriate augury for the mercantile future of the daughter foundation. The commitment of Cyprus to the markets of western Asia in the M.C. III period, a commitment which continued into the first phase of the Late Bronze Age, makes all the more remarkable her eventual change of allegiance to the merchants of the Aegean late in the fifteenth century B.C.

[1] §vii, 1, 206.   [2] §vii, 1, 277.   [3] §x, 2, 111.
[4] §vii, 1, 278.   [5] §vii, 1, 130–2 and 233–9.
[6] §vii, 1, 242. *Syria*, xix (1938), 219 ff., figs. 18, 23A and pl. xxii.1.
[7] §vii, 1, 278.   [8] §x, 4, 64.   [9] §vii, 1, 278; §x, 5, 154.
[10] §viii, 2, 156.   [11] *Ibid.*   [12] §vii, 3, 36 and 306.
[13] §viii, 6, 138–47.

XI. MIDDLE CYPRIOT ORIENTATIONS

While it is clear that the M.C. period effectively involved Cyprus in the affairs of the world around her, bringing about a radical change in settlement pattern and the development of urbanization in the process, the factors which precipitated this revolution remain obscure. The inspiration doubtless came from east Cyprus, and perhaps originally stemmed from the federation of which Kalopsidha was the capital. Such moves perhaps took place without the co-operation of the north and centre of the island, whose embattled condition may have been organized in defiance of the eastern group. Yet Kalopsidha remained an open settlement throughout its history, and Gjerstad[1] found no level of violent destruction within its stratification; it was evidently not involved in the trouble further east when Nitovikla[2] was burnt; unless perhaps Kalopsidha was responsible for this. Could the changes that took place in the M.C. period have come about without foreign interference? It has been suggested that some of the peoples of the Syro-Palestinian area who were involved in the turbulent conditions contemporary with the Second Intermediary period in Egypt may have left the mainland and established themselves within the Karpass. They would then have formed the catalyst by which Cypriot insularity was finally broken down, and have taken the lead in promoting economic relations with the area from which they had come. Attractive though this proposal undoubtedly is, the archaeological evidence is as yet insufficient to sustain it. But, in any event, it is clear that the Aegean leanings which the north coast towns had evinced in E.C. III and M.C. I were in abeyance,[3] and that for the time those regions that actively pursued an eastern policy were dominant.

[1] §VII, 3, 36. But Åström has recently reported a burnt stratum in a M.C. III house in an adjoining area.

[2] §IX, 5, 198. [3] §VII, 6; §X, 1.

CHAPTER V

HAMMURABI AND THE END OF HIS DYNASTY

I. EVENTS OF HAMMURABI'S REIGN

T H E sixth of his line, Hammurabi was the inheritor of a kingdom established by a century of peaceful succession, unimpaired by major calamities, but hardly grown beyond the pale which his ancestor Sumuabum had reserved for himself amid the tide of Amorite invaders. In the general equilibrium of weakness Babylon had lost its upstart character, but had gained little else than recognition as an abiding feature in a world of close horizons. Even the fall of Isin, to which the predecessor of Hammurabi had contributed, did not result in any apparent increase of Babylon's territory or importance, all the fruits being gathered by Rim-Sin of Larsa. The first five kings of Babylon ventured seldom abroad, and their date-formulae,[1] which are virtually the sole authority for their reigns, show them occupied mainly in religious and defensive building, and the clearing of canals.

What extent of territory was controlled by the predecessors of Hammurabi is defined only by the places where tablets dated in the reigns of these kings happen to have been found. Most prominent among these is Sippar represented under all the early kings of Babylon; then Dilbat and Kutha, sometimes Kish, which however at other times was independent.[2] In the date-formulae occur as conquests some more distant towns such as Kazallu, Akuz, Kar-Shamash, Marad, and Isin, after its fall. It was never, before Hammurabi himself, more than a diocese of about fifty miles radius about the capital city, and even this by no means tightly compacted, but subject to invasions and erosions on all its bounds. At the height of his power this one king had indeed enlarged it, if not, as formerly supposed, to a 'world-empire', at least to the normal extent of a Mesopotamian unity, but this combination of ability and fortune made only a fleeting impression upon the unstable conditions of the age, and his creation crumbled in his son's grasp even more quickly than it had sprung up under the father's hands. Thereafter the kingdom dwindled to

[1] G, 9, II, 178 ff.   [2] G, 10, 130 ff.

its former stature and lingered for above another century under four kings within still narrower bounds than the founder had defended.

The materials left by the king himself, or derived from any source directly connected with him, which can be of use in writing the history of his reign are scanty in the extreme. His official inscriptions are few and formal, almost wholly devoted to his buildings. Much more productive are the date-formulae of his reign, the only immediate authority for his political and warlike acts deserving of note. Later ages, which knew his name and preserved at least a literary regard for his laws, remembered only one episode, transmitted in a chronicle.[1]

According to his date-formulae the warlike passages fell in two groups, one near the beginning and the greater towards the end of his forty-three years' reign. It is possible that the first group refers to operations not conducted by Hammurabi in pursuance of his own policy but at the behest of a superior.[2] No doubt the capture of Uruk and Isin, named in his seventh year, may be viewed as a local reaction against Larsa, but the capture of Malgium, Rapiqum, and Shalibi in his tenth and eleventh years were perhaps no more than partially his own work, achieved as a member of a coalition. A contract written in Babylon itself, in the tenth year of Hammurabi, associates with him in the oath Shamshi-Adad,[3] and this has been generally admitted to prove that he was, at the end of his first decade, under the dominance of that formidable Assyrian. The same influence may lie behind the attacks upon Rapiqum, for this opponent figures in the date-lists both of Hammurabi and of Ibalpiel II of Eshnunna. The latter captured it in his ninth year, four years after the death of Shamshi-Adad,[4] whereas Hammurabi's victory was achieved in his eleventh, and Shamshi-Adad is known to have been alive in the year before. The chronological link is missing, but there must have been two separate assaults upon Rapiqum, and both might be traced to policies pursued under, or in reaction against, Assyrian leadership.[5] If it is correct that Hammurabi in his early years of rule acted by this impulse, the break between his early and later wars may be explained in that he was soon freed from the necessity of marching at the command of another, and afterwards preferred to consolidate his strength before setting out upon his conquests.

For whatever cause, his years between the eleventh and the thirtieth were, according to their 'names', given up to defensive

[1] G, 19, 11, 17.　　[2] §1, 6, 130; §1, 12, 451.　　[3] §1, 17, no. 284.
[4] §1, 1, 37 f. and 42 f.　　　　　　　　　　[5] §1, 12, 453.

and religious building and to digging canals. Both of these activities may be regarded as a recruitment of strength for his land, but the latter in a more material fashion, which is pictured in one of the king's own year-dates[1] referring to the canal called 'Hammurabi is the abundance of the people'. The digging of this canal is significantly coupled with a fortress erected at the same time. These intervening years were for history almost a blank until recent times, when the letters found at Mari have provided many an interesting glimpse of the future conqueror in his own court, and, still more objectively, as seen by the eyes of foreign envoys, eager to note and transmit in the most candid terms their impressions of an actual or suspected rival.

After the death of Shamshi-Adad (assuming this to have occurred soon after the tenth year of Hammurabi) the connexion between Babylon and Assyria seems to have remained unbroken for some time, though it is clear that the balance of power was swaying. At least once Hammurabi was in a position to order or request a military reinforcement from Ishme-Dagan, the new king of Assyria; the response was grudging, and the recipient complained of this poor support.[2] Ishme-Dagan, despite the lavish praises which his father had heaped upon him (though chiefly to point a moral to his degenerate brother),[3] and despite his forty years of rule, does not seem to have been a very forceful character, for he maintained tolerable relations with all three of the greater powers, Babylon, Eshnunna and Mari (notwithstanding Zimrilim's expulsion of his brother from that city), seeming thereby to proclaim himself no more than one of the petty rulers held in the equilibrium of bitter but timorous rivals. With the Assyrian king the relations of Hammurabi were distant, until the latter period of his military activity, when Ishme-Dagan was probably the king under whom Hammurabi was destined to vanquish and occupy Assyria.[4] It must be assumed that his defeat was not so complete as to cause his abdication.

The middle years of Hammurabi's reign display the same condition of uneasy truce between Babylon and its other eventual enemies. With Eshnunna there were various exchanges, generally hostile, but sometimes of a kind which caused uneasiness to the envoys of Mari, who jealously watched the political scene;[5] through one of these envoys Hammurabi sent a message[6] asking

[1] The 33rd, §1, 11, 33; G, 10, 115. [2] G, 3, 11, no. 49; §1, 9, 51.
[3] See above, pp. 3 f.
[4] See above p. 28; §1, 10, 17; G, 3, 11, no. 49; §1, 9, 52.
[5] §1, 16, 99 ff. [6] G, 3, 11, no. 33.

for aid when he was on the point of attacking Rim-Sin, with the co-operation of Eshnunna. So long as the relations between Hammurabi and Assyria remained unbroken, his policy towards Eshnunna was hardly different, for throughout these years, and especially towards their end, a close alliance subsisted between Eshnunna and Assyria with mutual military support, and the two finally shared the same overthrow. From the days after this decisive battle dates a letter[1] referring to advice given to Hammurabi by Zimrilim (almost upon the brink of his own ruin) urging him to assume in person the throne of Eshnunna or to instal a nominee.

The most important matters upon which the Mari letters throw light are the dealings of Hammurabi with Mari itself, and with Rim-Sin of Larsa, in the early and middle periods of his reign. He was not always, as the letters reveal, a bitter opponent of Rim-Sin, for indeed they were such near neighbours that a bare co-existence for thirty years upon their respective thrones must have necessitated a multitude of contacts which could not be altogether unfriendly. So far from this, the two are found, before their collision, upon excellent terms, and standing in a posture of mutual defence.[2] One of the envoys of Zimrilim at the court of Babylon writes to inform his master about his zeal and success in his mission. He begins with a calculated detail aimed to show the intimacy of his acquaintance with all that goes on at Babylon. Two agents of Hammurabi, he writes,[3] who have long been residing in Mashkan-shapir[4] have now arrived back in Babylon. 'Four men of Larsa, riding on asses, came with them; I learned their business, and this is the message they were sent with.' Rim-Sin had formerly written to Hammurabi[5] proposing that each should go to the other's aid with his army and river-boats in case of attack upon either. But it was now revealed that Rim-Sin was a shifty associate—'as touching the soldiers you are always writing to me about, I have heard [a report] that the enemy has set his face towards a different land, and that is why I did not send my soldiers'—nevertheless, he went on, if the enemy turns again upon either of us let us give each other aid. Strangely, the Mari letters have not yielded any evidence of direct contact between Mari and Larsa.

Whereas there are no letters from Mari to Hammurabi while that city was under the rule of Iasmakh-Adad, or rather of his masterful father through him, it was not long before Zimrilim

[1] §1, 2, 120; §1, 6, 244.   [2] §1, 2, 118.   [3] G, 3, 11, no. 72; §1, 16, 104.
[4] §1, 4, 159 ff.   [5] §1, 2, 118.

when he came into his own, was in frequent correspondence with the Babylonian king. It is not possible to fix with accuracy the beginning of this interchange of letters and embassies; the tenth year of Hammurabi's reign is the earlier limit, for Shamshi-Adad was then alive, and it was an unknown number of years before his death and the subsequent expulsion of his son from the usurped throne of Mari. The later limit is, of course, the thirty-third year of Hammurabi, the year of his defeat and occupation of Mari.[1] All of the references in the letters, to Subartu, Esh-nunna, to Rim-Sin, and to Mankisum,[2] which are datable by reference to the year-formulae of Hammurabi, suggest the four or five years previous to that, and indeed it is not likely that, in the rapidly shifting politics of the time, there would have long subsisted the close relations which the letters reflect so vividly. At this period Zimrilim had several correspondents, not to call them spies, at the Babylonian court,[3] just as Hammurabi had his at Mari,[4] where they enjoyed the standing of known representatives, charged with negotiations between their masters. They used their position, like modern ambassadors, to report freely upon the military and political situation which they observed there, making use of their own personal relations with the king, of which they complacently boast.

Most prominent of these ambassadors were two men with the confusingly similar names Ibalpiel and Ibalel, the former of whom is unending in his claims to inside knowledge, mostly derived, he says, from Hammurabi himself; whenever any business is in the king's mind he sends to Ibalpiel, 'then I go to him, wherever he may be, and whatever matter is engaging the king he tells me'.[5] When messengers were sent to Hammurabi by his namesake the king of Kurda, the artful ambassador drew them aside in the palace gate before they were admitted to audience, and thus he became possessed of their inmost designs.[6] Another time he had picked up intelligence of strategic movements which Hammurabi did not see fit to impart.[7] Ibalel reports the coming conflict between Babylon and Larsa,[8] and divulges his seeming duplicity with Hammurabi over a matter of reinforcement, when claiming military aid for his lord.[9] The regular theme of these exchanges was mutual assistance by contingents of troops and barges. These operated in both directions; sometimes it is Zimrilim who

[1] See above, p. 28; §1, 13.   [2] G, 23, 215 f.
[3] §1, 16, 104; G, 4, 354.   [4] §1, 9, 40.   [5] G, 3, 11, no. 31.
[6] G, 3, 11, no. 23.   [7] G, 3, 11, no. 26.   [8] G, 3, 11, no. 33.
[9] G, 3, 11, no. 34.

requests as many as 10,000 men from Babylon,[1] and even further reinforcement is spoken of as possible. On the other side Hammurabi claimed and received similar help from Mari, and a letter of his[2] reveals him in alliance with Zimrilim striving to raise the siege of a place named Razama, against the forces of Elam and of Eshnunna. Once, when the resources of Mari were inadequate, he obtained through the good offices of Zimrilim a large contingent from the distant Iamkhad, the region of Aleppo, the advent of which caused Hammurabi to express lively satisfaction with his 'brother',[3] whether the king of Iamkhad (another Hammurabi) or the king of Mari to whose influence the benefit was owed. The number of troops mentioned in the letters is surprising, and reaches its height in the possibly exaggerated reference of Zimrilim to 30,000 in a letter concerning military affairs.[4]

The general view of the political and warlike situation in Babylonia and the neighbouring lands, which is so brightly illuminated by these letters, is that of a general weakness. Shamshi-Adad is dead, and although Hammurabi is in the ascendant he is still fighting for supremacy; sometimes he is hard-pressed, and occasionally in mortal danger, as when three desperadoes were gathering forces at a place called Andarik with the intention of making a *coup-de-main* upon Babylon itself.[5] Meanwhile all of the 'powers' are reduced to diplomacy, demonstrations, and makeshift alliances, not so much to win supremacy as to stave off disaster at the hands of neighbours only momentarily more potent than themselves. Hammurabi, even upon the threshold of his victories, did not impress his contemporaries as a world-conqueror, not even as *primus inter pares*. The decisive evidence for this is the now celebrated letter of a certain Itur-Asdu,[6] another emissary of Zimrilim, this time among the half-nomad tribes of the Euphrates, whose blunt candour explodes so much flattery and self-praise heaped upon his contemporaries by their own inscriptions and the servile panegyrics of their citizens. This man informed his lord that he had conveyed to the local shaikhs an invitation to assemble at a regale offered by Zimrilim, where a sacrifice was to be made to the goddess Ishtar. When they had come together at a place called Sharmanekh, Itur-Asdu advised them as follows: 'There is no king who is mighty by himself. Ten or fifteen kings follow Hammurabi, the man of Babylon, a like number Rim-Sin of Larsa, a like number Ibalpiel of Eshnunna, a like number

[1] G, 3, II, no. 34.   [2] G, 3, VI, no. 51; §1, 9, 35 f.   [3] G, 3, II, no. 71.
[4] G, 3, II, no. 67.   [5] G, 3, II, no. 43; G, 3, XV, 121.
[6] §1, 2, 117 f. See above, p. 10.

Amutpiel of Qatana, and twenty follow Yarimlim of Yamkhad.'
The object of this exposure was no doubt to bid for the allegiance
of the head-men by convincing them that Zimrilim was better
situated than others to achieve the mastery, but however much
discount must be allowed for bias, the fact that such an estimate
could be given without evident absurdity is sufficient proof of its
substantial accuracy. None of the proud rivals in Babylonia is
rated even as high as a distant ruler of Aleppo, unknown to
history until scarcely more than a decade ago, thanks to the
excavations at Mari and Alalakh.[1] Too remote, perhaps, to bid
decisively, since the centre of influence was still in the south, he
was yet a barrier against expansion from thence beyond a certain
point; there could be no empire of a Sargon again in the days of
Hammurabi.

Nevertheless, this delicately poised scale was destined to tip
eventually in favour of the king of Babylon. In his thirty-first
year was recorded the defeat of that old rival Rim-Sin of Larsa,
or rather, as he is called in the proclamation of victory, king of
Emutbal,[2] the Elamite district in which centred the power of
Kudur-Mabuk and his two sons whom he made successively kings
of Larsa.[3] Of the hostile passages which led to this final clash
hardly anything is known, only a glimpse is caught of Hammurabi
upon the eve of his enterprise when he sent to Mari for help,
revealing that he was about to attack Rim-Sin with the co-
operation of Eshnunna.[4] As the fruit of this victory there came
into the hands of Hammurabi all the old southern cities which had
hitherto obeyed his rival, and these are included in the prologue
to the law-code, with Hammurabi figuring as the benefactor of
the god who presided over each of them.

It is apparent from the date-formulae of these years, no less
than from the said prologue, that Hammurabi was now fully
conscious of having succeeded to the traditional 'kingship' of
Sumer and Akkad, last held by Isin, to which Larsa had never
been recognized as a legitimate successor, though the local
scribes had retaliated for this neglect by foisting a king of theirs
among the antediluvians.[5] Extant copies of the Sumerian king-
list cease with Isin, but if it found continuators under Hammurabi they would not fail to adduce Babylon as the last heir of
that ancient glory. The thirty-third year-date, besides recording
victories over Mari and Subartum displays the king organizing

---

[1] §1, 18; §1, 19, 2 ff.; G, 28. See above, pp. 30 ff.
[2] G, 10, 182.   [3] C.A.H. i[3], pt. 2, pp. 640 ff.
[4] G, 3, 11, no. 33.   [5] §1, 7, 71 f.; §1, 5, 46.

his now-complete empire in the south, where a great canal named 'Hammurabi is the abundance of the people' furnished water to Nippur, Eridu, Ur, Larsa, Uruk, and Isin. It is clearly implied that these old centres were in a state of decline and depopulation. No doubt the two centuries of the Amorite invasions had in fact seriously impaired the resources of the ancient 'land'.

The fatal quarrel with Rim-Sin must have arisen suddenly, for the struggle was preceded by more distant campaigns in the north and east upon which the Babylonian king would never have ventured had he believed an enemy was left in his rear. His twenty-ninth year witnessed a great victory over a coalition of enemies along the Tigris. The defeated powers were Elam,[1] Assyria (Subartum), Gutium, Eshnunna, and Malgium, and the triumphant formula reveals, what the sequel was to establish, that the victory was as yet only defensive, for it boasts that Hammurabi 'made havoc of [the adversaries] who had raised up their might, and [thereby] secured the foundation of Sumer and Akkad'. Almost the same list of enemies occurs again in the formula for the thirty-second year, when another victory made the Babylonian king master of the banks of the Tigris up to the bounds of Assyria. Two stubborn enemies, Assyria itself with Eshnunna, continued the struggle through still later years, and Assyria, at least, was never subdued, though the thirty-third year-date and the prologue of the Code claim rule in its cities, but the end of Eshnunna was recorded in the thirty-eighth year—it was laid waste by a vast artificial inundation, cunningly engineered by Hammurabi, who prided himself upon the ingenious operation.

With this exception the Babylonian successes in the east and north were hard-won and probably ephemeral. They were celebrated not only in the date-formulae but upon a stele which Hammurabi set up at Ur[2] after capturing that city from Rim-Sin. In its now fragmentary lines the king proclaimed his victory over Elam, Gutium, Subartum, and Tukrish 'whose mountains are distant, whose languages are crabbed'. These 'barbarian' districts do not appear in the prologue to the Code, for they had no gods and no temples which a Babylonian ruler could recognize as worthy of his patronage. The last echo of these distant campaigns resounds from the thirty-ninth year, when 'he smote upon the head the whole mass of the enemies up to the land of Subartum'. By these unremitted efforts the king of Babylon was able to advance and even to hold for a few years the shores of the Tigris up to and including the Assyrian cities. In northern Mesopotamia

[1] See below, pp. 264 f.   [2] G, 16, no. 146.

a monument of his was perhaps discovered near Diyārbakr;[1] as to the Euphrates, the Mari letters show that his conquest of that city must have carried his sway up to the limit of its territory, perhaps about the confluence of the River Balīkh.[2] Wider dominion than this he can never have achieved.

II. PERSONAL RULE OF HAMMURABI

It has to be admitted that the discoveries of recent years have been damaging to the reputation of Hammurabi as a dynast, in the sense of a conqueror and the founder of a far-flung empire. It is now apparent that he was for the greater part of his reign no more than a struggling aspirant, and that even his brief supremacy was much more narrowly circumscribed than once assumed by estimates for which there was, indeed, never any evidence. His other fame was that of an able and assiduous manager of his kingdom, and, above all, a lawgiver. More of these glories subsist, yet even they are dimmed. Zimrilim of Mari was doubtless a more indolent and less capable man, but his correspondence appears more extensive, his 'foreign office' better organized, and his attention to detail, especially in his supervision of his dependency of Terqa[3], no less careful than his eventual conqueror's. An elder contemporary, Shamshi-Adad of Assyria, governed a wider empire with a stream of dispatches to his sons in their provinces displaying a strength of mind and a comprehensiveness of interest which surpass anything attested by the letters of Hammurabi. Nevertheless, the number and scope of these is sufficiently remarkable; hitherto there have been discovered about 150 letters bearing his name as writer; none of these proceed from regular excavation like the Mari letters but are all the chance survivors of haphazard finds. It may be expected that the future will reveal others and perhaps better attested in context.

Those already known belong to two archives distinguished by the names of the recipients, Sin-iddinam[4] and Shamash-khazir.[5] Both of these royal officials resided at Larsa, and this fact alone, apart from the evidence of other places named in the letters, proves that both collections date from the closing years of the reign, after the defeat of Rim-Sin in the twenty-ninth year. The two recipients were not successors in office, for there is internal

---

[1] But see G, 23, 176 n. 2.
[2] See above, p. 9; G, 4, 351.
[3] §II, 12; G, 3, III.   [4] G, 18, nos. 1–46; §II, 19, nos. 2–58.
[5] §II, 18; §II, 3; §II, 1, Introd. 3; §II, 7.

proof of their contemporaneity,[1] but holders of different functions. Shamash-khazir's is the easier to define, for the majority of the commands to him concern the assignment of land to various servants of the king either as rent-paying tenants or as feudal holders on a liability to military or civil service. Most of the letters consist of directions to the agent that he should assign land on one or other of these terms to specified persons, or that he should remedy causes of complaint which have been brought to the king regarding his administration. Of the two classes of holders the chief interest of the rent-paying tenants is their designation of *iššakkum*, or 'lieutenant', the ancient title borne by the city-governors of Sumerian times, who were 'lieutenants' of their city-gods—the decline in the status of this rank is none the less instructive as to the position held by the old governors, who are thus seen to have been regarded as 'farmers' of the divine possessions,[2] of the cities which the gods owned and leased for improvement to human managers.

The more numerous class of landholders were those who occupied their fields solely in consideration of service rendered, or rent paid,[3] to the king, the service going along with the field indissolubly, so that any other coming into enjoyment of that piece of land automatically assumed the same duty. The holders of these fiefs were not only military personnel, but a multitude of sundry callings, craftsmen and rural labourers,[4] and sometimes a group of workers at the same trade shared a larger estate in common. All who were to be given a field were furnished with a certificate[5] and upon production of this their possession was delimited, and their assumption of it symbolized by the act of 'knocking in the pegs' which marked out their boundaries. Once in possession the holder enjoyed a large measure of security, subject to the regular discharge of his duties, and customarily, at least, the field was regarded as hereditary and might be taken over by a son, upon whom the duty then devolved. But the holder was not free to dispose of his lot,[6] since thus the essential service attached to it might be in danger of neglect by the new possessor not having the ability to discharge it; this reservation in freedom to dispose of a feudal holding is found in force in a later age in the land of Arrapkha where it led to an ingenious legal fiction[7] designed to overcome this disability.

[1] §II, 18, no. 74; §II, 3, no. 1.　[2] G, 25, 45 f.　[3] §II, 18, 2; G, 7, I, 116.
[4] §II, 18, 3; G, 7, I, 112.　　[5] §II, 18, 9 n. 2; G, 5, Vol. 7, 73 ff.
[6] This was forbidden by the Code, art. 37–41; G, 7, II, 24 f.
[7] §II, 9, 59 ff.; §II, 16, 14 f.

The situation of Sin-iddinam, recipient of the other collection of letters from Hammurabi, is not so clear, for the contents of the missives addressed to him are much more various. They cover, in fact, almost every department of administration, including the appointment of officers, military affairs, legal business, finance, public works, trade, and agriculture. A representative entrusted with such multifarious functions could be no less than a provincial governor, yet there is little in the letters to him which indicates that he employed responsible subordinates or enjoyed much freedom of decision. The highest subordinate to be mentioned is a *rabiānum*,[1] the rest being mere servants such as the *girseqūm*[2] or the class of minor officials called *šatammū*,[3] and for the rest labourers and herdsmen. Sin-iddinam was, at least the superior of a *šāpir mātim* (perhaps no more than a superior foreman)[4] whose workmen he is directed[5] to unite with his own. But nothing is more striking in the letters, whether to Sin-iddinam or to Shamash-khazir, than the constant denial to them of all effective initiative or even authority. Sin-iddinam is ordered to make a requisition of clothing for the army,[6] and yet an auditor is sent to check his herds and flocks,[7] he is continually countermanded over details of recruitment,[8] and we even hear of a 'strike' against his orders, the participants in which are not to be conscripted.[9]

Shamash-khazir seems to have occupied a still more subordinate station. Not only is he addressed as a mere executive of arrangements and leases emanating from the court, and no more than a referee in cases of disputed possession (where he may go no farther than presiding over a tribunal to administer the oath),[10] but the letters to him are full of complaints detailed at second hand against his measures, and generally he is given curt orders to do what the complainants desire. So frequent is this that it must be supposed the subjects in dispute had been already settled judicially in Babylon, for not all of such complaints could be justifiable. But the purport of all these official letters is curiously complaisant towards the unknowns who are so free with criticism against the actions of the royal agents, and these latter seem to receive oddly ungracious treatment, as though the king were concerned chiefly to avoid blame or trouble; the keynote is in such phrases as 'content him immediately',[11] 'let him not come back here and

---

[1] G, 7, 1, 110. [2] G, 5, Vol. 5, 96. [3] §11,18, 5. [4] §IV, 43, 135 ff.
[5] G, 18, no. 27; §11, 19, no. 48; §IV, 27, 74 ff.
[6] G18, no. 44; §11, 19, no. 34. [7] G, 18, no. 15; §11, 19, no. 55.
[8] §11, 19, nos. 35–39. [9] §11, 19, no. 47. [10] §11, 3, no. 1.
[11] §11, 18, no. 31.

appear before me again',[1] 'know you not he is not a man to be slighted?',[2] 'let him have no complaint',[3] or such a spiritless avowal as 'let him not take the palace to task'.[4] There are even menaces to the agent if he does not give satisfaction—'I shall have this as a grudge against you'[5] and 'because you have gone beyond the limit you will not be forgiven'.[6] A superior, and some other ministers, write also to Shamash-khazir, in terms which scarcely differ from those used by the king himself, even if a slightly more collegial tone is allowed to pervade them.

In general it may be thought that the letters of Hammurabi and his ministers hardly give the impression of a strong administration; what appears is a system too much absorbed in day-to-day detail, sadly lacking in proper support of its officers, and rather unworthily timid of criticism, even from interested parties. Such excessive complaisance is most probably due to a conscious insecurity of the régime; the officers addressed were newly installed in a conquered territory, and appeasement of the subjects at any cost is doubtless the policy which prompts these uneasy phrases. Although it is true that direct dependence upon the royal pleasure is hardly less marked in the position of Kibri-Dagan, governor of Terqa, *vis-à-vis* his sovereign Zimrilim of Mari, there is certainly in the correspondence[7] of these less of the harsh tone of subordination than in the Babylonian letters.

It has been observed above that the second abiding pillar of Hammurabi's fame is that celebrated 'code' of laws, the revelation of which placed him among the greatest figures of ancient history. His achievement is still without peer, but no longer without comparison and challenge. The existence of Sumerian laws had long been known by survival of examples—these were attributed to Lipit-Ishtar of Isin, and a part of his actual text has now been recovered,[8] having prologue, corpus, and epilogue in the complete form of Hammurabi's 'code'. Still more closely comparable, not merely in form but in content, and perhaps even earlier are the laws of Eshnunna.[9] These were written in Akkadian scarcely distinguishable from the phraseology of Hammurabi, and they were issued with a short preamble, and probably an epilogue, if the text were preserved. In the portion now extant they deal with prices and tariffs, are much concerned with valuation especially of damage sustained, have something to do with family

---

[1] §II, 18, no. 49.   [2] *Ibid*. nos. 53 and 55.   [3] §II, 19, no. 13.
[4] §II, 18, no. 64.   [5] *Ibid*. no. 68.   [6] *Ibid*. no. 11.
[7] G, 3, III; §II, 12.   [8] §II, 17; G, 10, 95; *C.A.H.* I³, pt. 2, pp. 634 f.
[9] §II, 8, 4 ff. and 21 f.

affairs, marriage and divorce, and touch upon sales and deposit, slavery and theft. They even include usage of the same three terms 'man', 'subject', and 'slave', as are held to indicate a threefold division of society in the Babylonian code. At about the same time as these various bodies of law were being promulgated, there was reigning in the more distant and supposedly more backward land of Elam a prince named Attakhushu, and he too is now known to have set up in the market of his capital a 'stele of righteousness',[1] evidently surmounted by an image of the sun-god, under which was inscribed a (possibly adjustable) list of 'fair' prices for the guidance of all who resorted there to buy and sell. Nor is this all, for not only is there a legislative act of a special kind issued by Ammiṣaduqa,[2] the fourth successor of Hammurabi, but it is now clear that similar measures were put in action by a whole succession of kings who reigned not only in Isin, Larsa, and Babylon, but in other cities as well during the period which has been called the 'heptarchy'.[3] These measures, customarily taken at the outset of a reign, were mainly concerned with remission of debts and other burdens. Later in the reign, certainly of Hammurabi, probably of Lipit-Ishtar, came the issue of 'codes', enactments of a more general but still limited scope. Since it has long been observed that no evidence exists for the actual application of Hammurabi's laws in the documents of the period, and no appeal is made to them[4] (not to mention their omission of so many topics which a real law-code would have to include)[5] it has been difficult to define what was the precise standing and function of those collections[6] among which Hammurabi's is the classic. In his case, at least, something must be allowed for unity of practice over a freshly conquered realm hitherto governed under local dispensations. The epilogue pictures the joy of a litigant going to the temple of his city and reading the article governing his rights[7] inscribed upon a public monument. A like purpose of forwarding good administration might explain why that department of public law regulated in most detail is the condition upon which officials and soldiers held their fields, which has been observed above as so important a subject in the letters from the royal chancellery. On the other hand, the slight treatment, or total omission, of the criminal law[8]

---

[1] See below, p. 262.   [2] §II, 10; see below, pp. 195 f., 224.
[3] *C.A.H.* I³, pt. 2, p. 632; G, 4, 343.
[4] G, 7, 1, 53; §II, 11, 284.   [5] G, 7, 1, 46 f.; §II, 5, 7 n. 1.
[6] §II, 5; §II, 14; G, 7, 1, 45 f.; §II, 11; §II, 6, 101 ff.; §II, 20.
[7] §II, 11, 285.   [8] G, 7, 1, 490 ff.

and certain topics in civil law such as the regulation of sales and partnerships might be explained by supposing that these were already ruled by a more uniform custom.

Before quitting the actions and government of Hammurabi himself for a survey of Babylonia under his rule, it will not be without interest to see what is now to be gathered concerning the personality of a king who left so marked an impression upon the development of his country and even upon its native tradition. Ancient oriental history is notoriously weak in the display of individuality, and if there were no documents other than those which bear his name Hammurabi would be hardly more distinct than even greater figures of his past such as Sargon and Naram-Sin. In this particular, as in others of perhaps greater moment, the letters of Mari have proved illuminating. There we find the king under the observation of outsiders, by no means always favourably disposed, and perfectly exempt from the adulation which rulers lavished upon themselves and required from their subjects. The irreverent candour of Itur-Asdu's speech to the tribes has already been noticed,[1] and there is nothing else which approaches this in frankness; but the dispatches of Zimrilim's agents at Babylon afford at least several glimpses of the busy and capable administrator immersed in affairs of war, diplomacy, and even society. He is ever prominent and in personal control— no ministers seem to be mentioned. He confers with Rim-Sin,[2] dictates dispatches to neighbouring[3] and distant[4] states, personally inspects reinforcements,[5] decides the strength in which he will send his own soldiers abroad,[6] writes to a secretary of Zimrilim when he fails to get an answer from the principal,[7] keeps in touch with the policy of Mari through two local confidants of his own,[8] and even writes a letter of introduction for a visitor.[9] He is represented as being generally of easy access, at least to those with whom he was prepared to discuss business, and to these he expressed himself so freely that they perhaps unduly flattered themselves upon holding his confidence.[10] But he could keep his own counsel,[11] and his indulgence was not to be abused; a certain ambassador impudently demanded of a high officer why the envoys of Iamkhad had been used with invidious honour and given garments of ceremony, whereas he and his companions had been 'treated like little pigs'. Hearing of this Hammurabi

---

[1] See above, pp. 181 f.   [2] G, 3, II, nos. 33, 72.   [3] Ibid. no. 72.

[4] G, 3, II, no. 49, and VI, nos. 33 and 51–54.   [5] G, 3, II, no. 71.

[6] Ibid. no. 25.   [7] §1, 2, 119.   [8] §1, 9, 40.   [9] §v, 31, 74 n. 1.

[10] G, 3, II, no. 31.   [11] Ibid. nos. 20, 26.

rebuked the petulant complainant—'you do nought but make trouble; I shall bestow garments upon whomsoever I please'.[1] If he has a fault in this picture it could be only the want of those interesting touches which enliven the public labours of his ally at Mari, who so visibly indulged himself in the luxuries of architecture[2] and good cheer,[3] and so ardently collected lions[4] to sustain the royal chase.

III. ECONOMIC CONDITIONS

The preceding pages have attempted to relate the achievement of Hammurabi, to estimate his contemporary and historical importance, and to discern something of his character. It is now time to consider the state of the land and people under his rule, and first place may be given to the economic conditions as they are reflected in the laws and in the private documents which survive from this period in such extent and variety. A certain number of the sections in the Code is devoted to regulating the cost of labour and transport by fixed tariffs,[5] and this element is much more prominent in the laws of Eshnunna,[6] which fix also the prices of some principal commodities. Even more significant though less explicit is the inscription already noticed of the Elamite prince Attakhushu, upon bricks originally supporting (it may be supposed) a stele adorned with a figure of the sun-god[7] and inscribed with a list of prices which were to be paid in that market; 'whosoever understands not the just price, the Sun-god will instruct him'. The practice of price-fixing by royal decree was not, indeed, a novelty in this Old Babylonian period. Much earlier than this the reforms of Urukagina included a compulsory revision of wages and fees.[8] With the stele of Attakhushu and the laws of Eshnunna these measures seem to take on the aspect of regular state policy. The latter document begins (after a preamble) with a list of prices, so much of grain, fats, wool, salt, and copper for one shekel of silver, followed by a special entry for certain fats in terms of grain. There follow tariffs of hire for carts, boats, asses, and labourers, which are specially instructive as these

---

[1] G, 3, 11, no. 76; §1, 16, 105.
[2] See above, pp. 11 f.; G, 3, 11, no. 127, and 111, nos. 22–6.
[3] G, 3, 11, no. 15, and 111, nos. 28, 62; §1, 16, 97; and see below, p. 219.
[4] See below, p. 219.   [5] §11, 5, 8; G, 7, 1, 469 ff.
[6] §11, 8, 32 ff.
[7] See below, p. 262; §111, 10, 296 f.
[8] *C.A.H.* 1³, pt. 2, pp. 140 f.

have attracted to themselves laws concerning negligence and compensation. In general it may be observed that the element of valuation is particularly strong in this newly-revealed code. Again, it is from one of the prominent figures of this age that emanates what was until recently the earliest of the set price-lists, which is found in a building-inscription of Shamshi-Adad I.[1] In the light of what is now seen to be a frequent contemporary practice,[2] Shamshi-Adad's cheap rates, usually dismissed as false propaganda, must be taken seriously, and their lowness otherwise explained.

A general conclusion seems to arise, or at least a conjecture is derived, from all this price-fixing coupled with legislation, that the latter may have been a gradual outgrowth of the former. From the posting in a market of an official schedule of prices there developed both disputes about the application of these and demands for valuation of goods and services not included in the lists, as well as questions of a more general kind, until the subject, who had first approached the just god to learn from him the due price of his sales and purchases, came more and more frequently to ascertain his rights in all the perplexities of life—'let the injured citizen who falls into a lawsuit come before my figure [as] king of righteousness: and then let him have read out to him the writing on my monument, let him hear my precious words, and let my monument expound to him the article governing his rights'.[3] Such was the intention of Hammurabi as announced in the epilogue to his laws.

Within the limits covered by the issue of the above-mentioned tariffs, in different places and in a variety of circumstances, the level of prices shows great variations. A tablet from Ur may be dismissed as untypical, being written under siege,[4] for it indicates a price vastly higher than the average of the period, but it proves, for example, that in the basic commodity of grain the purchasing-value of a shekel of silver could range between 10 *sila*-measures (about $8\frac{1}{2}$ litres) in besieged Ur and 2 *gur* (60 times as much) under Shamshi-Adad. In Eshnunna at about the same time a shekel would buy only 1 *gur*,[5] and, although no price for grain is fixed by Hammurabi the contemporary equivalent, according to the contracts, was about two-thirds of a *gur*. Whatever may have been the cause of these divergences they were obviously such as to provide another reason for kings who extended their boundaries to attempt the imposition of uniformity in their domains. On the

[1] G, 8, 24 f.   [2] §III, 3, 33; G, 10, 154.   [3] G, 7, II, 96 f.; §II, II, 285.
[4] *C.A.H.* I³, pt. 2, p. 616.   [5] §II, 8, 29 f.

economic side, as on the administrative, the motive of law-giving at this period seems not to be reform but the need of forging a single government out of differing elements. That such diversity corresponded in any way with the assumed distinction of Sumerians and Akkadians is very unlikely, for, as it has already been observed, this distinction was now unreal, the true contrast having long been between the settled, urban population of south Babylonia and the more primitive immigrants from the north-west.

The prerequisite for the existence of that multitude of business documents and letters, so characteristic of this time, is the wide distribution of private property. In this regard an extreme contrast is generally painted with the former ages of Sumerian dominance, when the city-god, or the ruler as his agent, might appear as the actual possessor of most of the material resources of the community, whether land or chattels. More exactly, in the Early Dynastic period these resources were, according to our evidence, largely the property of the temples, which employed in their service and maintained out of their production much of the population. Under the Third Dynasty of Ur the emphasis shifted to the king who, as he assumed the god, had tended to assume also his temporalities, and now administered the whole through a laborious bureaucracy. It has been noted in preceding chapters[1] that it is possible to overdraw the contrast, to minimize unduly the extent of private property under the Sumerians, and of temple property under the Amorites. But when all reserves have been made it is still evident that the great influx of Euphratean tribesmen which transformed the whole population of south Babylonia had altered considerably the social and economic conditions; the less completely, indeed, because the immense strength and prestige of the Sumerian tradition had so largely taken the captors captive.

Under the Amorite dynasties there is found, in any case, a universal and vigorous upgrowth of private trading. The laws include, perhaps spring out of, economic regulations,[2] and the economy of private life is superabundantly demonstrated in action by the 'Old Babylonian contracts', which are a characteristic written legacy of this period.[3] They include sales of all kinds of possessions, from offices of profit to slaves, and a great variety of other transactions, exchange and gifts, loans, deposits, leases, hire of persons and things, sureties, partnerships, and family affairs such as marriage, divorce and adoption. Others record

---

[1] *C.A.H.* I³, pt. 2, pp. 130 and p. 622. [2] §II, 6, 101 f.

[3] The principal collections of translated documents are §III, 11 and §I, 17.

legal proceedings and decisions of courts, some regulated by the surviving laws, some apparently ruled only by custom, some even managed otherwise than the law directs. Amid all this freedom, however, not a little of the old corporate property and right subsisted. The temples were still great landowners and capitalist organs, not merely exploiting their own domains with their own labourers and slaves,[1] but lending out large values in money, seed-corn, and cattle to traders and private farmers at rates of interest which the importance of their operations enabled them to regulate.[2] A characteristic development of this age was the private possession of temple-benefices, i.e. of priesthoods and their emoluments, by individuals, who freely traded in these and bequeathed them to heirs[3]—the mercantile gods were not offended by this commercialism in their service, the house of prayer became a mart of traders without reproach.

Moreover, the state itself retained a large share in trade. According to the language of the time this authority is called 'the palace', and the evidence relates partly to its control over the caravan-traffic, conducted by merchants as state agents, but especially to the trade in fish,[4] an ancient prerogative of the gods as certain historical traditions indicate.[5] It seems that all fishing was done by crews of Amorite (i.e. immigrant) labourers under their own foremen, the latter being charged with the duty of selling the surplus catch to middlemen, through whom it reached the public. A tax was levied on behalf of the palace in other staple commodities such as wool, dates, and vegetables.[6] Beyond doubt dealings, perhaps monopolies, such as these made up a share of the state revenues, which were supplemented by the produce of the royal domains, and the valuable proportion of the date-harvest (as much as one-half or two-thirds) which the exploiters of palm-gardens belonging to the Crown had to pay in to the Treasury.[7] Cattlemen and shepherds were subject to the same dues, and the animals they kept were property of the State, the guardians enjoying only a share of the increase.[8] This was by no means the end of the king's emoluments, for there was certainly some taxation of private business;[9] the laws of Eshnunna allow the palace to intervene in family concerns,[10] and in later Assyria, at least, it was entitled to a share of inheritances.[11] Hammurabi may be seen in his letters keeping a careful watch on the collection of his rents

---

[1] §III, 14, 536; §III, 7.   [2] §III, 14, 540.   [3] *Ibid.* 537; §III, 21.
[4] §III, 13; §III, 16, 79 ff.   [5] §VII, 9, 54 ff.   [6] §III, 8.
[7] §II, 18, 2; §IV, 30, 150.   [8] §III, 9, 110 ff.   [9] §III, 22; §II, 19, no. 164.
[10] §II, 8, 91.   [11] §II, 9, 44.

and dues, and when obliged to decree an intercalary month he hastened to add that for revenue purposes the coming month shall be deemed to occur in the normal order[1]—the debtors were not to benefit by a month's moratorium.

By far the most of all the transactions regulated by the Old Babylonian contracts are of a purely local character, dealings between people living in the same town or at no great distance apart. Yet Babylonia was poor in natural resources and constantly in need of imports to sustain her civilized life, silver[2] and copper[3] from Asia Minor, tin[4] which came in through Assyria, timber from the Syrian mountains and other forested regions,[5] and slaves from up the Euphrates, who were called Subarians and were especially valued for the quality of being 'bright', which is doubtfully supposed to indicate a fair complexion.[6] These imports were paid for by exchange of Babylonian farm produce and articles of industry, though the slave-trade operated in one direction only since the law forbade the selling of native Babylonians into foreign slavery.[7] Such exchanges were carried on by travelling traders, who conducted caravans into distant lands.

From the laws, contracts, and letters alike much is to be learned about the business arrangements for this traffic, and something of its organization. Its basis was the relation between a merchant and a 'commercial traveller',[8] not in the modern sense of one going out to seek orders for his principal, but the actual trader who conducted capital or goods abroad in order to employ the former or sell the latter at a profit. Thus the merchant entrusted to his representative either a sum in silver or a quantity of grain, wool, or oil,[9] and the latter went out with this and, in addition, a small amount of money or necessaries to ensure his maintenance and the expenses of his journey; this subsidy was not liable to interest, though it had to be repaid upon the traveller's return. As for the capital with which the venture was made, the traveller had to keep exact accounts of his dealing with this. His first obligation was to refund to the merchant the original capital lent to him and the journey allowance in addition.[10] If the venture had been a success and there was a profit it had to be divided

---

[1] G, 18, no. 14; §II, 19, no. 14.
[2] §III, 2, 935 ff.; §III, 6, 78 f.; §III, 4, 267; §III, 17, 130 ff.
[3] §III, 2, 925 ff.; §III, 6, 78; §III, 4, 294 f.
[4] §III, 2, 915 ff.; §III, 6, 78; §III, 18, 95 ff.; §III, 4, 282 ff.; §III, 17, 123 ff.
[5] §III, 17, 125 f.   [6] §III, 5, 43; §III, 23; G, 7, II, 272 n. 1.
[7] G, 7, I, 482 ff.; §III, 20.
[8] §III, 16, 22 ff.; §III, 15, II Teil, no. 1; §II, 2, 285 ff.
[9] §III, 16, 26.   [10] §III, 16, 24 f.

between traveller and merchant, but the law did not fix the proportion, which was no doubt regulated by individual bargains. The traveller had every incentive to diligence over and above the hope of gain, for if he failed to make a profit he had nevertheless to reimburse the merchant with double the value borrowed. But the luckless agent was excused this if his failure was due to accident, when he need make only simple reparation, and if he had lost the goods in an attack by enemies abroad he was free of all liability on condition of swearing an oath to this effect. Other provisions of the law punished attempts at fraud between the parties, an abuse which was also hindered by the necessity of settling accounts before an auditor. The caravans were certainly made up, on land, of asses, mules, or even ox-waggons, but larger freights were sent up the river by boat, and tariffs for the hire of all these kinds of transport and their conductors, as well as rules of navigation, with penalties, are prominent in the laws both of Babylon[1] and of Eshnunna.[2] The cost of such expeditions was consequently high, and it was greatly swelled by local and foreign dues, both official and those exacted, then as always, by potentates or bandits through whose territory the merchants had to pass. In the somewhat later Amarna letters a king of Assyria is found complaining that the cost of an official mission to distant Egypt was so great that the modest gold subsidy thereby obtained did not cover the return expenses of the envoys.[3] In spite of this, it must be supposed that private enterprise was more productive, for the rule in Hammurabi's law[4] that the agent who returned unsuccessful must pay back double what he received gives a hint of the level of gain normally expected.

Significant of the broader social effect of a change from a centralized economy to a looser system of private trading and individual property is a recurrent act which came to be automatically the first in each new reign—the issue of a decree of 'righteousness' (*mīšarum*), as it was called. Although not a novelty, for its use goes back to the kingdoms of Isin and Larsa,[5] and can already be traced in the 'reforms' of Urukagina,[6] it was not until Hammurabi that it became regular. By good fortune, large parts have been preserved of this edict as issued by Ammi-ṣaduqa,[7] the fourth successor of Hammurabi. From this it is made clear that the main purpose of these recurring measures

[1] G, 7, 1, 470   [2] §11, 8, 33 ff.   [3] G, 21, no. 16, 26 ff.
[4] Clause 101.
[5] §11, 10, 194 ff.; §vii, 3, 146 f.
[6] *C.A.H.* 1[3], pt. 2, pp. 140 ff.   [7] §11, 10; §11, 6.

was to ease the burden of indebtedness, both to the state and to individuals, accumulated during the preceding reign. The beneficiaries were not slaves but free men, although the 'freedom' restored may have included debtors in bondage for default.[1] All the population shared in these reliefs, both 'Akkadians and Amorites', the original inhabitants and the later immigrants from the west.[2] More particularly consideration was given to certain classes or to certain districts which, perhaps for temporary reasons, were seen as suffering especial hardship. Those kings who, later in their reigns, issued 'codes' of law seem to have been inspired by the ideal of extending to wider fields the reform of taxation and private debt which they undertook at the beginning of their reigns.[3] But whereas the debt-remissions were effective it is far from clear that the 'laws' were implemented by the courts or much observed in communal life. That the outset of each reign should thus (as it appears) be confronted by widespread impoverishment suggests that a continuing economic maladjustment haunted the whole age of relaxation which followed the tight bureaucracy of the Third Dynasty of Ur.

IV. SOCIAL CONDITIONS

In the society of southern Babylonia under Hammurabi the most salient feature is without doubt the celebrated distinction drawn by the Code between three classes of inhabitants, the 'man' (*awīlum*), the 'subject' (*muškēnum*), and the 'slave' (*wardum*). These literal meanings of the first and third terms are undisputed, but the legal and social sense in which 'man' is to be understood depends much upon the meaning of *muškēnum*, a word which has survived the centuries and still lives, by descent through the later Semitic languages, in modern Italian and French[4] with the sense of 'mean, paltry'. This sense certainly existed when the word was used by Darius[5] as a correlative to *kabtu*, the powerful, important man, and thus denoted the poor and needy, the traditional object of royal justice, to be protected from the oppressor. It is evident that the same general contrast already inspires the distinction in the Old Babylonian period,[6] despite the great difficulty which has been found, throughout a long and still inconclusive discussion,[7] in fixing degrees of social esteem or of wealth upon the two classes

---

[1] §11, 6, 104. [2] §11, 10, 188. [3] §11, 6, 100 ff.; see above, p. 188.
[4] §1V, 45, 47. [5] §1V, 38, 119 and 121, lines 28 f.
[6] §1V, 34, 67; §11, 10, 155.
[7] Most recently, G, 7, 1, 90 ff.; §11, 8, 51 f.; §11, 10, 150 ff.; §11, 6, 96 ff.

of free men. How strictly were these classes distinguished in contemporary society, and upon what basis? If the qualification was by property, what kind or what amount of this made an *awīlum*? To these questions neither the laws nor the private documents furnish any answer, nor is there the slightest evidence that birth played any part in the distinction. It seems possible, therefore, that the Code in this matter as in others which have been observed purports to make rules which were not applied in ordinary practice; the difference of the *awīlum* and the *muškēnum* was one of social estimation[1] rather than of strictly factual ascertainment, though doubtless resting ultimately upon wealth. This tripartite organization of society is, nevertheless, so far from artificial that it seems to have a noticeable persistence throughout history. The example nearest in time and place is yielded by Assyria and the north-western regions about the middle of the second millennium, when various documents reveal the existence of a middling class of men called *hupšu* who occupied a station perhaps not fully free, certainly subject to imposts such as compulsory service, and dedicated to mechanical trades.[2] At a greater remove it is possible to observe something like the same organization in classes dependent upon wealth among the Romans, and afterwards under Merovingian[3] and Anglo-Saxon kings[4] in the early Middle Age of Europe.

If the Code presents a somewhat artificial picture of life in the days of Hammurabi the same objection cannot be urged against the multitude of official and private letters which are characteristic of this period.[5] Whatever their source, these are, as they would be in any age, unrivalled evidence for the social conditions of the land, being for the most part unstudied effusions of the national mind, concerned with the everyday interests of very ordinary persons and expressed in language not, indeed, markedly differing from the formal compositions, but free from literary constraint, although subject to a few conventions of form. Most prominent of these are the introductory phrases which scarcely differ, beginning 'to X say, thus Y . . .'; the assumption is of a society in which literacy was confined to a professional class of scribes who 'said', that is, read out to the recipient the tablet addressed to him. So old-fashioned was this exordium that the

---

[1] Perhaps best illustrated by the negative phrase *la awīlum* 'no gentleman', G, 26, 90.
[2] §ɪv, 32; §ɪv, 20.   [3] §ɪv, 36, 67; Gibbon, ch. 38 (Vol. ɪv, 134 ff.).
[4] F. M. Stenton, *Anglo-Saxon England* (ed. 2), 300.
[5] G, 9, ɪɪ, 63 ff.; §ɪɪɪ, 15, 1 Teil, 1 f.

Sumerians had called a letter a 'say-to-them',[1] and letters were commonly inscribed to several or read out in a council.[2] This formula is generally followed by a conventional greeting 'may Shamash and Marduk (or some other gods) keep you well', a phrase hardly less perfunctory than our 'dear Sir', and no more exclusive of a less agreeable sequel. Kings, however, did not honour their inferiors even with this, but went immediately to the commands which they had to transmit. Nobody else felt justified in omitting the salutation, unless it was done deliberately, as occasionally happened, by very irate correspondents,[3] and sometimes this blessing was expanded, either in genuine affection, as when a lover writes solicitously to his mistress,[4] or for beguilement as when a certain Marduk-naṣir addresses a woman as his 'sister' and showers her with eight lines of blessings and fair words—but the rogue owed her the balance of a debt, and his long epistle is filled with lame excuses and pleas of ill-luck.[5] Unlike our letters, there was no concluding formula. It was probably the general custom to enclose letters in clay envelopes; most are found open, but so they would naturally remain after perusal. A few envelopes have been found, bearing only the name of the recipient, but a cover and seal were used for official letters, and the receiver was often bidden to act immediately 'as soon as you see (or, hear) this tablet'.

Military affairs bulk large in the letters as they do in the laws. There are not a few references to the fortunes of private men in service, or in dealings with the army. One man writes to a business friend an appeal for five shekels to make up a fine imposed upon the writer by a military tribunal,[6] and another sends news of a deserter.[7] Elsewhere there is a reminder that the property of a serving soldier must be held free from all private claims,[8] as the law directed.[9] Moreover, it has been related above[10] that one of the most important branches of administration, to which a whole archive of letters is devoted, was the assignment of land to men capable of holding it under a kind of feudal tenure in consideration of army service. Apart from these standing resources it is clear that soldiers were recruited, as labourers were gathered for public works,[11] by a levy based upon a census of the man-power[12] of a whole district, as many being taken as were

---

[1] §iv, 8, 9 f.　　　[2] §iv, 7, 64 and 67.　　　[3] §iii, 15, 2 Teil, 97.
[4] §ii, 19, no. 160.　[5] §iii, 15, 1 Teil, 49 ff.　[6] §iii, 15, 1 Teil, 29.
[7] *Ibid.* 27 f.　　　[8] *Ibid.* 32 f.　　　　[9] G, 7, 1, 123 ff.
[10] P. 185.　　　　[11] §ii, 19, no. 135.
[12] G, 23, 24 ff. and 194; §ii, 12, 161 f.; see above, p. 4.

needed. This oppressive measure was hated and evaded by the population then as in every other age, and was enforced with like severities; in one of the Mari letters a levy-officer who had brought in few recruits was bidden to cut off the head of one recalcitrant and parade it round the villages, with appropriate threats.[1] Not much is known about the organization of the armies thus raised;[2] they were, necessarily, divided into companies, and something is heard of officers in various grades. A list belonging to the Third Dynasty of Ur[3] distinguishes three ranks in the garrison of the city, and it seems that the superior soldiers were accompanied by servants. Similarly, in the letters[4] are found as constituents of the army 'gentlemen's sons' and 'poor men' or 'stout knaves', but the former were not *ipso facto* officers, since a force is found to be constituted from equal numbers of each, though they were promised superior accommodation in the palace, while the baser sort were to be billeted out in the town.[5] Among the latter was, naturally, to be found even a criminal element.[6] Perhaps in the cities and villages of Babylonia there was not so much difficulty in recruiting as among the less settled peoples, whether it was for military or for civil operations, but always the levies were pressed and reluctant soldiers,[7] ready abettors of any malcontent,[8] unless the contrary fit possessed[9] them, when they were all zeal and high spirits, with no thought but of victory.

It has already been observed that the forces assembled were of very considerable strength. Even if we regard Zimrilim's 30,000 as an exaggeration[10] we still find Shamshi-Adad, a sober and capable organizer, reckons up 20,000 as a force which his son could rely upon having under his command—this was to be composed of several contingents.[11] There is no information as to the manner in which such forces engaged upon the open field, but much is heard, in the letters and elsewhere, about the capture of cities. Sieges were conducted by approach-works, of which this was the classic age. These included the battering of breaches through the walls,[12] and the building of towers[13] to command the defences; but the principal effort went into the heaping up of a

---

[1] G, 3, II, no. 48; G, 23, 13 and 29.

[2] §IV, 15, 136 f.; G, 3, XV, 289; G, 23, 20.

[3] §IV, 29, no. 1499.   [4] G, 3, II, no. 1; G, 23, 22.   [5] G, 3, II, no. 1.

[6] G, 3, V, no. 81.   [7] G, 3, II, no. 20.   [8] G, 3, II, no. 31.

[9] G, 3, II, no. 118.

[10] G, 3, II, no. 67; a story about Sargon of Agade credits him with an army of 40,000, §IV, 35, 173.

[11] G, 3, I, no. 62.   [12] §IV, 19; G, 3, I, nos. 131, 135; §IV, 34, 77; §IV, 44.

[13] G, 3, I, nos. 131, 135; G, 2, 304 n. 8.

great inclined ramp of earth, which was gradually carried forwards and upwards until it touched and equalled the height of
the city wall, when the grand assault stormed up its slope and
encountered the defenders at the level of their own battlements.
The besiegers could usually depend upon success, as it is recorded
in letters of Shamshi-Adad and of his elder son,[1] whose confidence
was to be echoed by a Hebrew prophet—'they shall deride every
strong hold, for they shall heap dust and take it'.[2] But the toil
and perils of construction were preceded by the exact calculations
of engineers, specimens of which are preserved in a collection of
mathematical problems for the use of schools. 'With a volume of
3 *bur* of earth', begins one,[3] 'I shall capture the city hostile to
Marduk'. Then follow the data and the question: 'from the base
of the earth I paced 32, the height of the earth was 36. What
distance in length must I cover so as to capture the city?' Other
problems, after supplying various data, put the questions 'what
is the height of the wall?'[4] or 'what is the volume of the soil?' and
'how much of the length can each man construct?'.[5]

This authentic and completely factual science provides a strong
contrast with another method of calculation which had outstanding importance in Babylonian warfare, and was certainly looked
upon as even more reliable, namely, the consultation of omens,
especially in the entrails of sacrificed victims.[6] There is repeated
allusion in the letters of Mari[7] to the taking of omens by kings
and generals, to plans and marches being directed in obedience
to them, and to the high position or even command entrusted to
the 'seer' of the army. The Babylonian military academies may
be imagined, without extravagance, as divided into the faculties
of applied mathematics and of divination, and the general in the
field might hesitate whether to time his operation by computing
the mass of his ramp and the number of his hands or by meticulously scrutinizing the blemishes upon a sheep's liver. And many
centuries later, in a neighbouring land, the march of the Ten
Thousand was still determined, in successive moments of danger,
by this persistent and powerful superstition.

Agriculture, at once the mainstay and the dependent of military
power, was conducted at this time by individual farmers working
either their own land[8] or lots of the royal domain portioned out
to them as soldiers or servants in consideration of their duties,

[1] G, 3, 1, nos. 4, 131.   [2] Habakkuk i, 10.   [3] §iv, 40, 109; §iv, 41, 35.
[4] §iv, 40, 110; §iv, 41, 49.   [5] §iv, 41, 21; §iv, 33, 165.
[6] See below, pp. 214 f.   [7] References in G, 3, xv, 302.
[8] G, 10, 4 f.; § iii, 9, 86 ff.; §iv, 25, 128 ff.

as already described. These men were assisted by their families or
their own slaves, but also by hired labour.[1] Such aid was especially required at the harvest, and many private deeds are concerned
with the provision of extra hands for this transient need. The
workers might be slave or free, debtors, or prisoners of war. If
bondsmen they were hired from their masters, but free men disposed of themselves, the formula in that case being '*A.* has hired
B. from himself'. There is a form of document also in which one
party appears as the receiver from another of a specified sum for
the harvesters whom he contracts to furnish.[2] These labourers
worked in gangs under a foreman who made arrangements for
them and probably drew all their pay, but the foremen themselves
were often subject to a high official of military rank called the
wakil Amurrī,[3] 'overseer of the Amorites', and this points to the
general composition of the gangs, as being mainly composed of
immigrants. The most important element in farming the soil of
a dry country was irrigation; the great arteries of water were
provided and maintained by the pious care of kings, and this
principal function had by no means been neglected by the predecessors of Hammurabi, the kings of Isin and Larsa, whose date-
formulae abound in commemorations of such works.[4] Yet there
is some evidence that many of the ancient cities over whom the
rule of Larsa then extended were in a state of decay[5] at the time of
Hammurabi's conquest, and only two years after this was achieved
the victor, in his thirty-third year, undertook a vast work, the
canal called 'Hammurabi is the abundance of the people' in
order to supply water to Nippur, Eridu, Ur, Larsa, Uruk, and
Isin. From such main waterways branched off a multitude of
veins decreasing in width until they were reduced to the ditches
and channels which supplied the fields of individuals. Water
rights, though carefully specified in contracts, were a perpetual
source of complaint and dispute among the farmers, and these
were adjudged on the spot by subordinate governors such as
Sin-iddinam and Shamash-khazir, the correspondents of Hammurabi; but, as observed before, their decisions were far from
carrying decisive weight, and discontented subjects were for ever
writing or informing the king and he ordering his representative
to take cognizance of their grievances. The same governors had
the duty of undertaking the repair and maintenance of subsidiary
waterways, and received orders to this effect from their masters.

[1] §IV, 27, 1; §III, 9, 16.   [2] §IV, 27, 146 f.
[3] *Ibid.* 203; §IV, 25, 122; G, 23, 185 ff.; G, 10, 37.   [4] G, 10, 112 ff.
[5] G, 7, 1, 37.

For public works of this kind a general levy of local labour was enforced, unless they were of a small enough kind to be carried out by the riverain proprietors and population. Sin-iddinam is ordered[1] to turn out his workmen and join with them the men of a subordinate commander, and to take care that they do not include any old and unfit men but only strong workers. More is revealed upon this subject by the letters of Kibri-Dagan, the governor of Terqa under Zimrilim, which form part of the archives of Mari.[2] These give a striking picture of the ills which affected the canals when they were for a time neglected, and of the public works of various kinds which were required for their proper functioning. Not only the digging out of water-courses which had become silted up, but repairs to weirs and dams and reservoirs, and measures to restrain the effects of a flood when the canal had broken its banks, were all tasks incumbent upon the local authority, and performed by the governor with a staff of skilled personnel, and such labour as could be impressed in each emergency. The operatives were sometimes moved about in the same way as soldiers, as need dictated; and indeed the language of the time made no distinction, in speaking of 'workers', whether their duties were to be military or civilian.

A very interesting view of the actual methods of agriculture at this time is given by a Sumerian treatise on the operations of farming[3] which, although in a religious dress (as the instructions of a god), and although probably the work of a scribal 'expert' rather than of an actual countryman, follows in considerable detail the 'works and days' of the farmer's year. Combined with information preserved in another and better known grammatical work,[4] and with side-lights from the contracts, this remarkable specimen of scientific literature (so characteristic of the period)[5] gives not only by far the earliest but the most factual description of the raising of food-crops in antiquity. If all of its contents were fully intelligible, its adherence to sound practice would no doubt be more manifest.

The private documents and, more surprisingly, the law-codes having little to say of criminal offences,[6] the evidence for judicial procedure relates almost entirely to civil actions. It may be observed that penalties laid down for transgressions against fellow-

---

[1] G, 18, no. 27; §II, 19, no. 48.   [2] §II, 12, 175 ff.; G, 3, III.
[3] G, 22, 105 ff. and 340 ff.; §IV, 24, 150 ff.; §V, 25, suite 84.
[4] §IV, 24, 150 ff.
[5] See below, p. 212.
[6] G, 7, I, 45 ff. and 499; §II, 8, 121 f.; §II, 2, 394 f.

citizens were inflicted by a public authority, as necessitated by the severity of these, which itself appears to mark the intrusion of the 'state' into the retribution of wrongs which had formerly been adjusted by private compensation.[1] Since the laws both of Hammurabi and of Eshnunna indicate the capital punishment even for slighter offences it may be assumed that death was the doom of the murderer, although this is nowhere expressly stated, and may still have been left, for inflicting or compounding, to the victim's family. The exaction of an eye for an eye and a tooth for a tooth was prescribed by Hammurabi both as equivalent and symbolic punishment; not only if a man had broken the bone of another was his own broken in requital, but the hand was hewn off from an impious son who had struck his father. The executioner was kept busy with more grisly work; for he had to wreak savage deaths on others by drowning, burning alive, and even impalement, not always to avenge the inflicting or compassing of death, but for such breaches as thefts, wrongful sales, or even careless building. Of penalties less severe, or reputed such, were reduction to slavery and scourging, the latter inflicted with an ox-hide lash in the public assembly for assault upon a superior.[2] A son who disowned his mother,[3] a lout who made disrespectful allusions to honourable women,[4] and a concubine who saucily presumed to put herself on the level of a wife[5] had one side of their heads shaved as a badge of ignominy, or another mark set on them of servile condition, into which they were afterwards sold.[6]

As Hammurabi was the new lawgiver to his composite and lately won kingdom, so he was the inspirer of a new order in the custom of the courts. Under his predecessors[7] disputes between citizens were tried before benches of judges who sat at the gate or in the courtyard of temples. The members were not priests but generally local officials, the mayor of the town presiding over a council of elders, other functionaries whose duties are not well distinguished, or bodies bearing such names as assembly, senate, the city, wardsmen, and merchantry. The procedure of these courts was circumstantial, and is so faithfully reflected by the 'contracts' that it can be studied in detail. The actions of the parties to a civil suit before they went into court were formal and partly symbolic. One party raised a claim or complaint against the other; before witnesses he then proceeded to 'lay hands

---

[1] §IV, 5; G, 7, 1, 497.   [2] Clause 202.   [3] §IV, 24, 101 f.
[4] Clause 127.   [5] Clause 146.
[6] G, 7, 1, 495 ff.; §IV, 31, 441 f.; §III, 12, 207 ff.
[7] §IV, 43, 184 ff.; G, 7, 1, 490 ff.; §IV, 26, 68 ff.; §IV, 13.

upon' his opponent, and apparently could exercise physical restraint upon him.[1] Unless the parties then came to an agreement,
the person arrested could escape only by proposing, or at least
consenting, to go before a court. A possible preliminary to this
was the agreement to submit the dispute to a single arbitrator,[2]
who, if he could not obtain or impose an agreed settlement, sent
them on to the court, perhaps stating their case. The tribunal
thereupon permitted them to plead, and the cause was elucidated
by the production of documents and the evidence of witnesses.
The course of these proceedings might be so dubious that the
parties would prefer to compromise rather than risk the costs
entailed by continuing.[3] The normal outcome of the court's
decision was to dictate a settlement to the contestants and oblige
them to enter into an agreement called a 'tablet of not-claiming'[4]
any other issue than that decided by the court, or any property
subject to this disposition. When the dispute was sustained and
the ordinary evidence was indecisive on either side the last resort
was to an oath[5] in the presence of the god, taken by the parties
as they grasped the divine emblem or submitted to an ordeal[6]
by which the god revealed the truth. It generally happened that
one of the parties weakened at this supreme moment, and declined
the oath, yielding the victory to his opponent.[7] In preparation
for this ultimate test, and with the purpose of holding all the
proceedings under the god's eye, courts had formerly sat in the
temples, and this was the custom under all the predecessors of
Hammurabi, as noted above. But a tendency to secularization
had already shown itself, and this was accelerated and confirmed
under the reformer of his country's laws. His official letters
reveal him as hearing many pleadings from suitors, and afterwards sending directions to his local officers bidding them make
arrangements on the basis of his decisions.[8] From this it was but
a step to appointing district judges in the various regions, who
now bore the name of 'king's judges'[9] and kept in their own hands
the administration of justice, leaving to the older temple officials
only the subsidiary function of administering the oaths, when
that final criterion had to be applied.

The abundant material furnished by the contracts and letters
gives a vivid impression of the social and family life which in this
period, as always at the heights of civilization, was so much under

---

[1] §iv, 26, 16. [2] Ibid. 22 f. [3] Ibid. 34 f.
[4] Ibid. 39 ff. [5] Ibid. 38. [6] G, 7, 1, 63 ff.; §iv, 42, 263.
[7] Even the oath did not always satisfy, §iv, 12, 177 ff.
[8] See above, p. 186. [9] §iv, 26, 73 ff.; G, 7, 1, 491; §iv, 13.

the influence of women that the position of these may be considered as a most significant factor. Very prominent alike in the Code of Hammurabi and in the private documents are certain classes of priestesses and other women[1] attached to the temples, among whom the supreme in rank was the *ēntum*,[2] high-priestess and reputed bride of the god who ruled over the city. In some places, especially at Ur,[3] these ladies were of the most exalted rank, being daughters or sisters of kings, and a succession of princesses from the days of the ancient Sargon until the last native king of Babylon were honoured by holding this office, for which they were supposed to be demanded by the god himself. The custom extended as far as Mari, where Zimrilim is found busied in consecrating an unnamed female relative and preparing her residence;[4] his contemporary, Rim-Sin, endowed his sister under the sacral name of Enanedu in this office at Ur, where her commemorative inscription was found by Nabonidus as he set about doing the same thing more than twelve hundred years later,[5] and has been re-discovered once more in recent years.[6] Similar priestesses were found in various Babylonian cities, as at Isin, Larsa, Uruk, and Babylon, as well as at Ashur[7] and Nuzi[8] in subsequent times. It is probable there was only one *ēntum* in each city, although a stringent paragraph of the Code,[9] which combines them with the *nadītum*, might suggest they were more numerous. This law forbids such women, under penalty of being burnt alive, to keep or even to enter a tippling-house, thereby demeaning their character, which was protected by another clause[10] from false aspersion. The second class of priestesses, the *nadītum* (Sumerian *lukur*),[11] seems to have been larger, and certainly played a more prominent part in civil life. These were also of good birth, and like the *ēntum* were regarded as wives of the god (though of lower rank), yet there is some indication that they belonged at the same time to the class of temple-prostitutes, a situation which doubtless seems more paradoxical to us than to contemporary ideas.

Unhindered by either character, the *nadītum* could be a wife and also, at least in name, a mother, but when a child is mentioned it is never given a father's name, and when a *nadītum* married

---

[1] §IV, 22; §IV, 23, 146 ff.
[2] §IV, 22, 71 ff.; G, 7, 1, 361 ff.; G, 5, Vol. 4, 172 f.; G, 26, 220a.
[3] §IV, 39, 23 ff.; *C.A.H.* 1³, pt. 2, pp. 435 and 633 f.
[4] G, 3, III, nos. 42 and 84; §II, 12, 174.   [5] §IV, 1, 162 f.
[6] §IV, 11.   [7] G, 8, 108 f., no. 30.
[8] §IV, 21, 52; G, 5, Vol. 4, 172.   [9] Clause 110.
[10] Clause 127.   [11] G, 7, 1, 364 ff.; §III, 7, 124 ff.

she did not bear children to her husband but supplied him with a substitute (*šugītum*)[1] or a handmaid for this necessity, or sometimes adopted a child. The explanation of these apparent inconsistencies may lie in the existence of two orders of these priestesses, those who lived in a cloister (*gagūm*),[2] especially at Sippar, and could be formally married but childless, while a second order of 'lay' votaresses[3] (the *šugītum*) lived outside this community and were commonly married; both were regarded as in some sense wives of the god, and when they were dedicated to this status they took with them a dowry as if for a mortal marriage. The *nadītum* are often encountered in the contract-literature, where some at least of them are owners of houses and lands, and buy or sell these both to outsiders and to their companions in the cloister. In addition to these women of the higher orders several other classes of votaresses are mentioned in the Code under such names as *sikirtum*, *qadištum*, and *kulmašītum*;[4] their distinctions are uncertain as their functions, but they served in the temples and may probably be regarded as making up the general company of the hierodules, whose sacred standing undoubtedly conferred a reputation superior to that which commonly attends their manner of life.

In secular society the wife of a citizen enjoyed a position of honour and privilege, guarded with jealous care from usurpation by mere concubines.[5] Her status was guaranteed by the possession of a 'bond', that is, a deed of marriage, and she attained the esteem of a married wife immediately upon the acceptance by her father of a bride-price.[6] From her father and the bridegroom[7] she herself received marriage-gifts, and was entitled to keep this property even in the case of divorce.[8] As a wife she possessed all legal and business capacities, and married women are found in the contracts engaged in the transaction of sales, exchanges, loans, debts, leases, gifts, and legacies; they are plaintiffs or defendants in court, where they figure also as witnesses in the suits of others.[9] Though not the property of her husband, the wife was liable to share his financial misfortunes,[10] and he could engage her services in discharge of debt, but not for a term exceeding three years.[11] The greatest affliction she had to fear was failure to bear children,[12]

---

[1] §IV, 23, 145 ff.; G, 7, 1, 366. [2] G, 5, Vol. 5, 10; G, 7, 1, 359 f.; §III, 7.
[3] G, 7, 1, 371 ff. [4] §IV, 22, 73; §IV, 23, 146 f.
[5] Clauses 128 and 146 f. of the Code; §II, 8, clause 27; G, 7, 1, 247; §IV, 37, 62 and 84 f.; §III, 12, 189 f. [6] G, 7, 1, 249 ff.; §II, 8, 80 ff.
[7] G, 7, 1, 257 and 265 ff.; §IV, 37, 160 f. and 173 f.
[8] G, 7, 1, 272; §III, 12, 198. [9] §III, 11, Bd. III, 224 f.; §I, 17, 4 f.
[10] G, 7, 1, 230 ff. [11] Clause 117.
[12] Clause 138.

and especially sons.[1] In presence of this disability she could not
refuse to tolerate, and sometimes was fain to supply, a concubine
to remedy her defect, as a preferable alternative to divorce, which
was looked upon as the normal consequence of barrenness. But
in respect of divorce the wife in Hammurabi's Babylonia was not
so well protected. Childlessness might be an all-sufficient reason
for repudiation, but it was hardly necessary for the man to have
this or any other excuse if he wished to put away his wife. At
least she was entitled by law to a monetary compensation,[2] and
it argues a low estimate of the constancy of wedlock that provisions for the event of divorce are found incorporated in the
marriage deeds themselves, and occasionally include a stipulation
that the husband shall not afterwards raise objection to re-marriage
of his divorced wife.[3] Whereas the man was, at the most, liable
to a fine for an especially unjustified divorce,[4] the woman who
presumed wrongfully to renounce her husband might be hurled
from a tower[5] or into the river to perish. But the law, which disgraced itself with these barbarous enactments, at least permitted
an ill-used wife to separate herself from a cruel husband.[6] A
more humane remedy for the evil of childless marriage was the
practice of adoption,[7] which was used not only to supply heirs
in marriages with temple-women who could have no offspring
of their own, but by other couples who feared the like inability,
and it was sometimes laid down in deeds of adoption that the
child should keep the right of an eldest son even if the parents
afterwards had children of their own.[8] One of the duties of an
adopting father was to teach the boy his own trade; if he did this,
he was protected against the greed of the natural parents who
might covet a youth with so valuable an acquisition, but when
the adopter neglected this the boy might go back, if he wished.[9]
Both the laws and the contracts regulated with care the rights
and duties of adoptive parents and children alike.

Apart from these laws and institutions affecting the life of
women in families the private letters of the time afford many
glimpses of female influence and character, revealing them as
much more than the petted and despised inhabitants of harims.
There are, indeed, a few letters which show women in adversity
and cast off by men. A former favourite writes to Zimrilim with

[1] §iv, 16, 179 n. 140.   [2] G, 7, 1, 291, 296.   [3] §i, 17, no. 7.
[4] Clauses 139, 140 of the Code.   [5] §i, 17, nos. 2, 4; Code, clause 143.
[6] §iv, 6, 119 f.; §iv, 9, ii Teil, 268 f.
[7] Code, clauses 185–193; G, 7, 1, 383 ff.; §iv, 4.
[8] §iii, 11, Bd. iii, 17; §iv, 4, 46 f.   [9] Code, clauses 188, 189; G, 7, 1, 387.

mingled indignation and pathos 'how much longer am I to stay at Nakhur? Peace has been established and the road is free. Let my lord only send, let them bring me back to see my lord's face again.'[1] Another writes piteously in the same letter addressed to one and two men together, pleading for a little relief by a gift of corn and oil: 'I am starving because of your neglect.'[2] These suffering frailties are in sharp contrast with an Amazonian character in the news passing at the time, a 'woman of Nawar' who commanded 10,000 Gutian kernes in a reported raid—'their faces are set towards Larsa'.[3] On the other side are letters from men expressing a deep solicitude for the welfare of their loved ones at home; one has gone upon a journey and finds threatening circumstances endangering both himself and the woman he has left behind.[4] He sends news of the enemy's ominous movements and promises if he can to dispatch servants and a carriage to remove her from danger. If this is not possible he counsels resignation[5] and assures her of his constant thoughts: 'whatever you do my dreams will always tell me'. There is even a love-letter sent from Babylon to a girl in Sippar, with fervent wishes for her health and counting the days until she will rejoin the writer.[6] More numerous than these personal notes are letters which reflect the activity of women in business,[7] sometimes from wives to husbands concerning their mutual interests,[8] sometimes from subordinates to women of influence—two men write as 'your servants' to their colonel's lady[9] telling her they have been imprisoned in a town of the enemy. They beg her to induce their fathers to commission a merchant, so that he may redeem their captivity.[10] Even so great a king and so busy an administrator as Shamshi-Adad of Assyria found time to occupy himself with the musical education of some young women in his charge.[11] On the other hand an officer of Zimrilim writes[12] about a company of girls, not of lowly condition or of mean attainment, rather too much in terms of negotiable commodities.

---

[1] G, 3, II, no. 112, *cf.* no. 113.   [2] §II, 19, no. 180; G, 5, Vol. 3, 149*a*.
[3] G, 3, VI, no. 27; §I, 9, 50.   [4] §II, 19, no. 222.
[5] G, 5, Vol. 7, 16*b*.   [6] §II, 19, no. 160.
[7] G, 3, II, nos. 66, 114, 117; §IV, 31, 441.   [8] §II, 3, A. 67.
[9] §II, 19, no. 134; §III, 16, 8; G, 23, 191.
[10] Code, clause 32; G, 7, 1, 119 f.; §III, 16, 6 ff.
[11] G, 3, I, no. 64; §V, 9, 185 f.   [12] §IV, 14, 62 ff.

V. CULTURAL CONDITIONS

There is little to suggest that the establishment of the Amorite invaders in Babylonia and the complete supersession of the Sumerians as the dominant race in the country brought about any fundamental change in the religion. The ancient land was in possession of so strong a cultural tradition, and so used to absorbing newcomers, that a contrary result was not to be expected. It is true that certain gods seem to come more to the fore, especially the westerners Adad (the Storm-God) and the deity of 'the west' himself, the god Amurru, not unknown already to the Babylonians,[1] but especially identified with the invaders and their desert home. At this time he becomes ubiquitous upon the cylinder-seals, both as a leading figure in the designs, and as an element in names of the owners. This god's fortunes mirrored curiously those of his people; in Sumerian times both were despised foreigners, the god being derided in even more odious terms than the people.[2] But this powerful interloper could not be denied marriage into the aristocracy of heaven,[3] just as his worshippers were forcing themselves into supremacy on earth. Yet the god, at least, was far from dispossessing the ancient lords, secure in their seats as patrons, or owners, of the great cities of the south. How strong this metropolitan tradition was can be observed in the adjacent region of the middle Euphrates, now so clearly illuminated by the Mari documents. There too the specifically Babylonian gods make an impressive appearance[4] as equalling, at least in priestly esteem, the regional divinity Dagan and even Itur-Mer, the city-god of Mari. For personal names the favourites are Adad and El, followed by the obscurer but doubtless more homely deities Lim and 'Ammu, leaving room still for adherents of Shamash and Sin as well as the great goddesses Ishtar, Mama, Nin-khursag, and Anunitum, and several patronesses of individual cities. On the other side it is striking to notice how the strangers among these figures were decisively eliminated at the boundary of the ancient 'land'.

Within Babylonia itself the most notable evolution in the pantheon was the emergence of Marduk, the patron god of Babylon, who appears almost dramatically in the first words of Hammurabi's prologue to the Code[5] as the appointee of the two highest gods to exercise lordship over the land and its people. Despite this proclamation, it has been ascertained that, even at the court,

---

[1] §v, 23, 55 and 84. [2] *Ibid.* 75. [3] G, 15, 6.
[4] §v, 7, 46 ff. [5] G, 7, ii, 6 f.

no less than in common usage, the upstart deity was far from
taking the first rank, which remained with three or four of the
old-established gods.[1] Not until after the end of the First Dynasty
came the true exaltation of Marduk, god of the predominant city,
as himself sovereign among his compeers in heaven. There was
nothing new in this to Sumerian ideas, which had always viewed
the situations in earth and in heaven as parallel and corresponding.
But Marduk was the last of these divine overlords; with him the
old order by which one god had succeeded another, as their cities
rose or fell, came to a standstill.[2] There were no more vicissitudes
of city-states, and under Marduk grew up a tradition, which fixed
him finally in his position of the supreme god, so that henceforth
Babylon on earth and Marduk in heaven remained unchallenged.
A measure of his prestige is that whereas for all his might Ashur,
a younger rival, made only the slightest impression upon the
southern kingdom, Marduk early began to establish his fame in
the north,[3] merely grew in honour[4] through his captivity in
Assyria under Tukulti-Ninurta I,[5] and was finally admitted to the
Assyrian royal pantheon[6] at the beginning of the ninth century.

The religion of the Old Babylonian period is intimately connected with a far-reaching change then making its first appearance, and beyond question the most important contemporary
development. This was the rise of an extensive written literature.
Study of the various classes of written material which have come
down to us in cuneiform reveals that most of these have their
origin, and often their first copies, in this period, the particular
glory of which is this literary outburst, in virtue of which it may
vie confidently with the materially more brilliant age of the
Sumerians. But the very character of this manifestation is such
as to throw light upon its cause and to suggest that it was not a
spontaneous blossoming of national genius. For first, the greater
part is written in Sumerian, which thereby attains for the first
time a wider range of literary expression than it had found in all
the formal, if sometimes comprehensive, inscriptions of the preceding centuries. Secondly, the subjects as well as the language
belong to the past. A wealth of legends[7] relates the history of
the Sumerian gods since the first creation and their dealings with
men, or of ancient kings and heroes of Sumer, among whom
Gilgamesh is the pre-eminent figure. Even characters of the
comparatively recent past, kings of the Third Dynasty of Ur,

---

[1] §v, 34, 202 ff.   [2] G, 15, 1 f.   [3] §v, 12, 108 f.   [4] §v, 40, 119 ff.
[5] §v, 41, no. 37.   [6] §v, 35, 320 f.; §v, 36, 115 n. 8.
[7] The latest general account in G, 22, 112 ff.

and still later of the Isin-Larsa[1] and even of the First Babylonian[2] dynasties were the subjects of hymns and panegyrics. Thirdly, the literary forms, so far from being primitive and artless, are highly finished, and couched in elaborate language which, fortified by the existence of much grammatical material, indicates very plainly an old and strong scholastic tradition. There are writing exercises, lists of words and things, verbal paradigms, and some translations from Sumerian into Akkadian; above all large parts are preserved of several highly curious compositions[3] in Sumerian which profess to describe not only what the pupils were taught in school, and the drastic methods by which it was inculcated, but the life of these pupils themselves, at school and at home, with their enthusiasm for learning marred by childish jealousy, their occasional revolts against authority, and their adolescent quarrels about superiority. These have a strong satirical, rather unedifying, bent—it is as though the writers, indulging frankly their delight in schooldays' memories, did not realize how dubious a recommendation they were giving to the scribal education which they wished to praise. But, without seeking further motive, they evidently enjoyed for its own sake the mere fun of these stories about testy dominies, officious ushers, bullied but conceited scholars, and worried parents. For it is now clear that Babylonian literature was by no means deficient in a humorous element,[4] which included laughable stories, mock-serious dialogues, and even acted scenes of comedy.[5] Despite these rallies the scribe was in supreme honour, and he alone had access to the most influential and most lucrative[6] positions. Even kings (Shulgi,[7] Lipit-Ishtar,[8] or Hammurabi[9]) condescended to value themselves as bright ornaments of the scribal art and as lords of language.

Nevertheless, what was studied in the schools was a 'classical' literature, of which the abundant remains, from Nippur and from Ur (the only centres at present fully represented), suggest that it was substantially the same everywhere. The scribes did not, in general, compose but only committed to writing. This Old Babylonian period witnessed some change which necessitated fixing and making available to wider circles an oral tradition which had already passed through many generations. With this movement goes the beginning of translations from Sumerian into

---

[1] §v, 25, and §v, 19 provide lists of this literature.
[2] §v, 10, 213 f.   [3] G, 22, 229 ff.; §v, 25, suite 83 f.
[4] §v, 22, 117.   [5] §iv, 12, 181 ff.   [6] §v, 17, 37 f.
[7] *C.A.H.* i³, pt. 2, p. 607; §v, 18. Description 8 f., nos. 80–83.
[8] G, 11, 124 f.   [9] G, 7, ii, 97.

Akkadian, which became so frequent in the late Assyrian texts, and herein is doubtless a clue to the main cause which underlay the whole development.[1] The Semitic tongue had at this moment decisively established itself in the land with the western invaders, and Sumerian was henceforth more and more a dead language like the Latin of the European middle age, with which it has been so often compared. In both cases the prestige of the old language was absolutely supreme, and though gradually undermined by the new vernaculars, it lasted for some centuries as the only medium in which it was thought fit to cast works of literature and learning. In this process, moreover, Sumerian did not escape the degeneration which overtook its later counterpart. To the end of Babylonian history kings sometimes felt obliged to couch formal dedications in the old and sacred tongue, less and less understood until it ended in such a travesty as the 'bilingual' inscription[2] of Shamash-shum-ukin, the brother of Ashurbanipal.

Under the Amorite kingdoms the learned sort, assiduously as they studied the Sumerian, clearly felt themselves unequal to maintaining its literature in the traditional form which had preserved it through so many ages before. Its words were strange upon their tongues, its significance now had to be studied, and this was impossible without books. It is, of course, not to be assumed that the whole of the literature which appears in the Old Babylonian period was ancient and hereditary, and indeed there is sufficient evidence to prove that actual composition was going on at the time. This is found in the before-mentioned hymns to recent and contemporary rulers,[3] and perhaps even more in the scientific literature which is so clearly founded at this time. The mathematical and geometrical[4] problems, which in their application to practical matters of mensuration and surveying disclose a knowledge of many purely mathematical processes aided by an ingenious and difficult number-notation,[5] have at least one trace of their origin in Babylon itself. When the military engineer sets himself the questions how much earth or what height of structure he will require to 'capture the city hostile to Marduk'[6] he sufficiently discloses the origin and date of his problems.

Literature of the Old-Babylonian period is employed principally in these twin services of religion and science. The Sumerian myths so abundantly exemplified, if often so imperfectly preserved, and generally difficult to interpret, appear as large fragments of

[1] §v, 17, 7 ff.   [2] §v, 38, Einleitung cclxi.
[3] §v, 21, 260 n. 3; §v, 19, 114 f.   [4] General description in §v, 27, 166 ff.
[5] Ibid. 93 ff.   [6] §iv, 40; see above, p. 200.

a remarkably complete theological system. They are concerned principally with the proceedings of gods in ages regarded as remote, when either the earth and its creatures were newly made and their forms or functions in process of settlement, or the gods were in active contact with earthly heroes directing these to the fulfilment of their wills. According as the stories are more concerned with the gods themselves or with 'human' characters it it usual to divide them into 'myths' and 'epics';[1] but in fact gods and men (or rather creatures not altogether divine) are so intermingled that the distinction has little reality. By a particular quality of Sumerian thought, these stories of primeval days were evolved with the apparent object of explaining not only how the world came to be arranged and governed as it was, but how all sorts of things came to possess the qualities which distinguished them in the use of men. In its complete form it seems to have been more than a cosmogony; rather an ambitious system of theology and philosophy which aspired to account for the conditions of life and the properties of everyday things as well as the higher causes.

The second leading division of this Sumerian literature is the hymns and psalms[2] addressed not only to the praise of gods and of temples, but to the honour and indeed flattery of kings, to whom divine attributes are given, as they were by them often openly assumed. Among the hymns may be reckoned too, as an important subdivision, elaborate poetical laments[3] over cities and sanctuaries destroyed by the inroads of national enemies. These uninspiring compositions are curiously prominent among the surviving texts, and their recitation had evidently an attraction, perhaps a purpose, which is not now apparent. Indeed, this question of purpose haunts all the 'higher' literature which may be described as religious. We know nothing of the occasions and the reasons for which these works were recited, and yet we may be confident that they were not intended merely for perusal, although they seem to have been copied almost exclusively in schools. The hymns, of whatever kind, may be assumed to have accompanied rituals, but what could be the religious use of the so-called epics, such as Gilgamesh, whose exploits already were famed in the tablets of this period?

More obvious is the use of another class of religious letters which also makes its appearance at this time, the incantations and prayers[4] used by private persons, or at least by priests on

---

[1] G, 22, 144 ff. and 37 ff.; §v, 25, 179 ff.
[2] G, 22, 205 ff.; §v, 25, 195 ff. and suite 81; §v, 19.
[3] §v, 25, 190 f.; §v, 22, 125 f.   [4] G, 11, Einführung 23 ff.; §v, 8, 8 ff.

behalf of these, at moments of sickness or affliction. Accompanied by an elaborate mummery which is much more fully outlined in later texts and illustrated by later monuments[1] these solemn conjurations were recited by or over the sufferer to expel the demons to whose maleficent possession all ills were ascribed. The banishment of these demons was assisted by administration of medicines for which the prescriptions, so abundant in the Assyrian tablets, also begin to appear in the Old Babylonian period.[2] These again betray by a similar feature the probability of their composition having actually taken place at this time, for here also it is the god Marduk who continually appears in a stereotyped incident where he, having heard the complaint of the patient, goes to his father Ea and begs of him the magic and the substances which will be efficacious against the devils now in possession; his father answers with a set protestation that his son has no need of teaching, for he knows already—nevertheless, Ea gives the prescription. Such a relation of the two gods, as well as the name of the young successor, suits very exactly the circumstances of the rise of Babylon under the ascendancy established by Hammurabi.

The most important of all the classes of literature, according to native ideas, which in this case we are very far from sharing, was the strange medley of superstitious practices and learned accomplishments comprised under the general name of divination. The religious character of this is apparent enough; what is altogether curious to us is that for the Babylonians it was the supreme science, and this because it seemed to them, what is falsest of all to us, the most practical and necessary guide in all human affairs, and most so in the most important.[3] Though nearly all of the kinds of divination attested in such detail by later texts have already appeared in specimens from the Old Babylonian period,[4] the most in honour at this time, as it indeed remained for ever, though later challenged by astrology,[5] was the practice of haruspicy, the ceremonial examination of the entrails of sacrificed victims as a guide to the conduct of political and above all military action. As a method of divine consultation upon this subject of opportunity in war we see in the letters from Mari the rival kings of the day depending implicitly upon the omens for their moves against the enemy, their prognostications of victory or risk, and their giving or withholding of alliance. No army moves without

---

[1] §v, 15; G, 1, nos. 657 ff.   [2] §v, 25, suite 85; §v, 5; 6; 13.
[3] §v, 14, 463 ff.   [4] §v, 2; 20.
[5] The most notable evidence for the Old Babylonian period is found in the 'Venus Tablets' of Ammiṣaduqa; see below, p. 224.

the consent, or often without the actual leadership of the all-important 'seer',[1] who is found marching before its ranks,[2] leading it even in battle,[3] and winning glory[4] or sometimes disgrace[5] from the issue of a project counselled by him. In this capacity of a trusted guide to the whole conduct of politics and warfare the 'science' of the haruspices provides us with many an interesting glimpse into the public affairs of the period, and the sentiments of those who carried them on.[6] Concerning the affairs of a council of statesmen or a council of war certain signs revealed that 'thy words will be carried to the enemy'[7] or that 'a town on my frontier is for ever reporting the very words to the enemy'.[8] Treason of this kind is a constant menace, and the omen-texts reveal the range of confidants of whose fidelity the king was anxiously in doubt. 'The word of the palace' or 'thy secret' was always in danger of 'getting out',[9] there was always a bird of the air to carry the voice, when disclosure to an enemy or to a friend might be equally dangerous. A ruler must be on his guard against the intimates of his court, a barber, a woman, a counsellor, a secretary, a chamberlain, a janitor, a noble, his own son,[10] or even the court-diviner himself, whom the omens do not blush to include.[11] Spies are found coming and going between the armies upon their nefarious errands—if caught, they will be put to death.[12] These precautions are not without a measure of cynicism, proper to a time of brittle alliances and insecure faith: one omen foresees what will happen if they 'are harbouring hostility against an ally, but the matter gets out',[13] and another has a word of warning for the subjects against the ruler, 'the king will take with him the best things in the palace and make his escape'.[14] In a general sense the omen-texts bear eloquent testimony to the politics and intrigues of their day, which it is not surprising to find little different from those of any other age, and it would need only some more contemporary allusions (which they prudently avoid) to make them as valuable for history as they are for ideas.[15]

Finally it may be asked whether the use and prestige of this superstition which makes its appearance so suddenly at this time must be considered a new invention, and something unknown or unesteemed by the Sumerians? Probably not, although the

---

[1] G, 3, II, no. 15.   [2] G, 3, I, no. 85 and II, no. 22.   [3] §IV, 34, 87.
[4] *Ibid.*   [5] §V, 29, 218.   [6] §V, 3, 6 f.
[7] §V, 29, 205.   [8] §IV, 34, 68.   [9] *Ibid.*
[10] *Ibid.* and §V, 29, 204.
[11] §IV, 34, 69 and 80; §V, 29, 204 f.; *cf.* Xenophon, *Anab.* v, ch. 6, §17.
[12] §IV, 34, 73.   [13] *Ibid.* 69.   [14] *Ibid.* 70.   [15] §V, 14, 462 f.

omen-texts differ from the other religious literature in the significant exception of being written from the first only in the Akkadian language, for the wealth of 'ideograms' which they later
abused is now known to be simply a device of shortening and
mystification. But their appearance is no more sudden than all
the other kinds of texts which the Old Babylonian period spawned,
and their contents do not differ in kind from these, in the respect
that their historical allusions, which are fairly frequent, concern
mainly such figures of the past, sometimes the remote past, as are
found in the legends and 'epics'; though this must be said with
the reservation that the most celebrated of all omens concerned
the Semitic heroes Sargon and Naram-Sin. If the Sumerians used
divination (and there is no reason at present to deny it)[1] we may
at last believe that it came into far higher account with the
establishment of the Semites as the masters and leaders of culture
in Babylonia. The scientific bent is not usually associated with the
Semitic mind, and so it is curious to observe that the two kinds of
literature revealed in the Old Babylonian period which have the
best claim to be considered original are the mathematical texts
and the books of divination.

In the arts there is hardly sufficient evidence for a proper
estimate of the achievement of the age,[2] but what we have is not
altogether impressive, and since survival is not wholly a matter
of chance, but governed necessarily in some degree by the original
abundance or poverty of examples, we cannot but conclude that
works of art were neither very plentiful nor very original, and the
remaining specimens certainly bear out the latter judgment. There
are some supposed portraits of Hammurabi himself, in which
nothing is of any particular novelty or mastery, and the same is
true of a few roughly contemporary figures of local rulers found
at Mari and Eshnunna.[3] The style of these works is generally
that of the Gudea statuettes, but they are distinctly feebler and
lack the life of their predecessors. The date-formulae of the Larsa
period and of the First Dynasty kings often record the setting
up in temples of divine figures and emblems of gold (doubtless
most often merely overlaid with the precious metal); these have
perished, but their level of accomplishment may perhaps be
judged from the pair of doorway-lions which were found at
Mari,[4] executed in the old style, metal hammered over a wooden
core, with inlaid eyes, which was centuries before employed by

<hr>

[1] §v, 28, 31 ff.; §v, 14, 464 n. 13.　　　[2] G, 14, 59 ff.
[3] *Ibid.* 58; §v, 11, 167; §v, 39, 72 ff.; G, 24, 256 ff.
[4] §v, 31, pl. x; G, 24, 286.

A'annipada at Al-'Ubaid,[1] but apparently more crude in appearance than those ancient prototypes. There are a few good smaller bronzes,[2] found here and there, but nothing which can be called remarkable in any of the art-forms so long familiar to the history of Babylonia. In two directions the age possesses some distinction: in wall-painting and in a certain characteristic development of the cylinder-seals. For the former we are again indebted to the finds at Mari.[3] From several fragments removed from the walls of the palace there, two scenes have been reconstructed. One shows the leading of a bull to sacrifice by a very elaborately dressed person followed by attendants; the other, more interesting, is a ritual scene of the king's investiture by the goddess of the city, the principal figures being accompanied by others of inferior gods and two trees, one of which is the date-palm up which climb two men to gather the fruit. This scene is completed by a bull and two winged sphinxes. The drawing of these groups does not lack vitality, and the use of colour is bold though the tints are few and simple. These pictures are, of course, not highly studied works of art, but simply the few chance survivals of the handiwork which once covered great areas in the principal apartments of the vast palace. Its quality attests the respectable level attained by the members of what must have been the large school of local decorators, as well as the antiquity of the tradition in which they worked.

If these paintings seem to us a comparative novelty, it is different with the cylinder-seals, which are a familiar study, although the Old Babylonian period could boast its own development of the traditional styles.[4] But here its achievement was modest, being no more than a further restriction of the already plain and stereotyped fashion of the Third Dynasty of Ur; the characteristic of this period is still the 'introduction-scene', but instead of the owner of the seal being led into the presence of a greater god by a personal attendant deity, the worshipper approaches the god face to face, and his personal deities, now generally goddesses, stand behind him with arms upraised in intercession. Often the owner himself disappears and only the goddesses are left interceding on his behalf, he being represented only by the inscription bearing his name.[5] Thus the style tends to become very bare and jejune. The principal deity represented is now often found to be standing in an aggressive-looking pose, this being representative of his character, for he is now generally one of the western

---

[1] *C.A.H.* I³, pt. 2, p. 136. [2] G, 24, 285.
[3] §v, 1; G, 24, 275 ff. [4] G, 13, 156 ff. [5] *Ibid.* 150.

Weather-gods, Adad or Amurru.[1] The other feature of the style, doubtless developed to mitigate the bareness of the main figures, is the addition of a medley of little subordinate, or filling, devices, such as monkeys, dwarfs, fish, lions, and divine emblems, not apparently disposed in any order designed to tell a story or illustrate a ritual, but simply of general amuletic value.[2] Neither of these manners, the over-plain or the aimlessly crowded, can be described as among the finer achievements of the Babylonian glyptic tradition. After the reign of Hammurabi this style not only fails to make progress, but shares in the general decline of power and civilization and even the workmanship, often highly finished if uninspired in the greater days, becomes careless, and neglects to work over the surface and conceal the technical process by which the seals were carved.

While it may be true that the revelations of more recent years have somewhat dimmed earlier conceptions of the 'golden age' of Hammurabi it remains clear that his reign and time were marked by much higher material prosperity than its troublous political circumstances might seem to promise. Kings, at any rate (and it is of these that we necessarily hear most), lived with no small luxury, the abundance of the deeds of business may suggest that well-being extended lower in the social scale, and the multitude of slaves, continually recruited from the spoils of foreign wars, provided a source of wealth and amenity even to the middle ranges of society. Whatever be the correct meaning to be attached to the *muškēnum* it is at least certain that he was not necessarily a poor man—too much is heard of his property. If prices in silver had risen compared with preceding ages,[3] this perhaps indicates no more than an increased supply of the metal. In this direction as in several others the discoveries at Mari have produced much illustrative material. The immense palace of Zimrilim, in which more than 260 chambers of different usage have been counted,[4] was perhaps only adapted from that inhabited by his predecessor, the usurping Iasmakh-Adad, whom his energetic father reproached for not giving due attention to its upkeep,[5] but it was almost a wonder of the contemporary world, and a prince of distant Ugarit sought an introduction[6] so as to observe this Neronian conception of living like a human being. Other palaces are mentioned at Sagaratim[7] and Dūr-Iakhdunlim,[8] and

---

[1] §v, 23, 18 ff.   [2] G, 13, 171 ff.
[3] §II, 8, 30; §v, 26, 436 n. 86; G, 10, 154; §III, 3, 33.
[4] §v, 33, 5; see above, pp. 11 f.   [5] G, 3, 1, no. 73, *cf.* no. 113.
[6] §v, 31, 74 f.   [7] G, 23, 2.   [8] §II, 12, 161.

for the life which was led in them we have but to recall the reproaches of Shamshi-Adad to his son, who was accused of spending his time in delights among the women while his sterner brother commanded armies and subdued cities.[1]

Despite all the ravages of plunder, fire and time, some traces of the luxury which reigned within the palace of Mari still remained to surprise the modern explorers. The walls were richly adorned, pastries were baked in fancifully shaped moulds,[2] and an inscription, illustrated by several letters, seems to prove even the use of ice[3] for imparting freshness and agreeable flavour to food and wines; this in a torrid region, where the ice had to be fetched from many miles away by gangs of bearers, after which it was carefully prepared and stored in a special cellar.[4] Many glimpses are caught of the good cheer regularly enjoyed by the princes, to whom the keeping of a table befitting their rank was a matter of prestige[5] as well as pleasure. Game,[6] fish,[7] honey,[8] truffles[9] and (no less relished) locusts[10] are found gracing the royal entertainments, and kings by no means disdain to concern themselves about cooks.[11] Wine was imported from Syria,[12] choice vintages being bestowed as kingly gifts, and once a convoy of servants engaged in its transport was suddenly requisitioned for urgent public work.[13] Upon arrival the wine was stored and before service was brought out from the refrigeration-chamber.

The 'sport of kings' then, as in many ages afterwards, was hunting the king of beasts, not over the open plains but in arenas near the royal residences. Zimrilim of Mari was strongly attached to this exercise, and letters of his officers show that lions were trapped in his provinces by the inhabitants, preserved and fed by them until they could be forwarded, enclosed in a wooden cage, by river boat to the capital.[14] Their lives were protected in the king's interest by game-laws, the headman of a town being obliged to make excuses for the killing of a lioness in his district without authority.[15] Horses were kept for the royal cars both by Iasmakh-Adad[16] and by Zimrilim, although a fashion of the time forbade the latter to use these as mounts—the dignity of an Akkadian king could be preserved only by riding in his chariot

---

[1] G, 3, I, no. 69. [2] §v, 31, 75 ff. [3] §v, 30, 145.
[4] G, 3, IV, no. 29. [5] G, 3, I, no. 52. [6] G, 3, IV, no. 9.
[7] G, 3, I, no. 89 and III, no. 9. [8] §v, 4.
[9] G, 3, III, no. 28. [10] G, 3, III, no. 62. [11] G, 3, I, nos. 14; 28; 89.
[12] G, 3, v, nos. 5; 6; 31. [13] G, 3, II, no. 3. [14] G, 3, II, no. 106.
[15] §I, 2, 125.
[16] §v, 16, 31; G, 23, 35 f.; a characteristic example of 'horse-dealing' in G, 3, v, no. 20.

or (strangely) by sitting upon a mule,[1] a very unexpected reversal of the esteem generally accorded to the *caballero*. None of these picturesque details has yet been learned about southern Babylonian kings or about Hammurabi himself, but no doubt the old and wealthy cities of the 'land' were still able to provide their rulers, and doubtless wider circles, with indulgences as great as the half-settled realm of the middle Euphrates.

VI. THE SUCCESSORS OF HAMMURABI

Hammurabi had conquered all opponents and reigned supreme during his last four years; but it is ominous that two of these were named after defensive works upon the Tigris and Euphrates, designed to protect his realm. To this throne, already insecure, his son Samsuiluna succeeded, and began a reign not much shorter but less distinguished than his father's. It was not, however, as a measure of mere conciliation that he issued, on his accession, a decree establishing 'the freedom of Sumer and Akkad', for this had been done by Hammurabi and became a routine followed by his successors.[2] Nevertheless, it is clear that after the first few years of Samsuiluna's reign the kingdom of Babylon was in ever-worsening straits, with enemies springing up both at home and on the frontiers. As might be expected in these circumstances the evidence becomes scantier, while the connexions of events are hidden and the chronology is undefined. No more than occasional glimpses are revealed by the date-formulae, themselves not always completely reliable,[3] reinforced by the few royal building-inscriptions and by inferences of various kinds based upon the dates of private contracts and the names of persons figuring in them. King-lists and chronicles, written at a later period, afford valuable secondary information.

Much is heard of battles in the reign of Samsuiluna, both on his frontiers and even in the homeland, but very little of the event most important in historical perspective, that commemorated in the ninth year-date, when 'Samsuiluna the king . . . the Kassite host', i.e. no doubt 'defeated' them, but this barest of mentions is all that marks the first appearance of the power[4] destined to supplant the First Dynasty of Babylon. This menace remained in the background, at least during the reign of Samsuiluna, but its pressure was behind a revolt of subjects on the north-eastern

---

[1] G, 3, vi, no. 76; §v, 24, 191.
[2] See above, pp. 188, 195 f.
[3] §vii, 3, 146 ff.   [4] See below, sect. vii.

border. The next (tenth) was the 'year (when) Samsuiluna the king (defeated) the host of Idamaraz, Iamutbal, Uruk, and Isin'. The two opposite situations of these enemies (to the north-east and to the south) is explained by a long inscription of Samsuiluna recording his fortification of Kish.[1] This attributes the hostile leadership to 'Rim-Sin, instigator of the revolt of Iamutbal, who had been raised to the kingship of Larsa'. The inscription relates his defeat, together with 'twenty-six usurping kings' and especially 'Iluni, king of Eshnunna', who was taken prisoner—his neck was set in a yoke[2] and he was put to death.[3]

Rim-Sin, known also from dates upon business-documents,[4] was an ephemeral figure, whose threat was soon extinguished by defeat and (violent) death in his palace, as a broken chronicle related.[5] His interest resides in his name and what is related about him—that he instigated revolt in Iamutbal, and had been made king of Larsa. Both of these circumstances relate so nearly to the actual history of Rim-Sin, the last king of the Larsa Dynasty, that it has long been a question whether this was not the same person, seeking revenge upon Babylon in his latest days. But Rim-Sin of Larsa is credited with an exceptionally long reign of over sixty years before his overthrow by Hammurabi, so that only by unlikely assumptions[6] can his life be extended to the reign of Samsuiluna—moreover, a nephew of the old Rim-Sin, bearing the same name, is attested.[7] The rising of this Rim-Sin broke out in about the ninth year of Samsuiluna,[8] for one of his extant year-dates is applied to the same year as Samsuiluna's tenth, when the latter defeated Idamaraz and its allies. But the victory was not decisive, for both the southern allies remained unsubdued, and so did Eshnunna, centre of disaffection in the north-east. In the thirteenth year two smaller cities in the south, Kisurra and Sabum, were won back; in the fourteenth came the final victory over Rim-Sin at Kish, and the rebel disappeared, perhaps in a flood[9] created by the military engineers of Samsuiluna. Thus was the revolt extinguished in Sumer, the hostile strongholds in the land of Warum (centred upon Eshnunna)[10] were demolished, but trouble broke out there again in the twentieth year, necessitating another campaign and the building of a fortress (Dūr-Samsuiluna,

[1] §vi, 18, no. 35; §vi, 19, 10 ff.   [2] G, 17, 266 (*šigārum*).
[3] G, 26, 63*b*.   [4] G, 9, 11, 164; §vi, 9, 215 ff.; G, 10, 168 n. 910.
[5] G, 19, 11, 18.   [6] G, 20, 97 ff.
[7] G, 10, 167.   [8] §vi, 19, 14.
[9] The interpretation as 'sea' is not admitted by the dictionaries, G, 5; G, 17; G, 26, all under *damtum*.   [10] §vi, 16; §vi, 19, 15 ff.; §vi, 2, 43 f.; §1, 6, 140.

on the site of the modern Khafājī) to hold down the country.
Thereafter the Babylonian king was able to pursue a policy of
forgiveness and restoration in that quarter, re-building towns and
maintaining the waterways.

In the latter years of his reign, after his triumph over Rim-Sin,
the king of Babylon was faced with a more persistent if hardly
stronger rival in the south, Iluma-ilum,[1] who established a
regular dynasty 'of the Sealand', which found its place in subsequent lists of kings.[2] Little was known then, and less now, of the
eleven or more obscure figures who made up this line, but their
fanciful royal names,[3] doubtless assumed, suggest that they
vainly aspired to lead a Sumerian revival. The founder, who is
credited with a suspiciously long reign of sixty years, has left no
record of his own, and all that is known about him comes from a
later chronicle,[4] which records that he sustained with success
three attacks from successive kings of Babylon. Samsuiluna
twice marched against him, the first time fighting a costly but
indecisive battle, the second time suffering a defeat. In his
fifteenth year Samsuiluna had broken down the wall of Isin, and
in his eighteenth had strengthened himself by building up the
temple and wall of Sippar,[5] after the neighbourhood of Nippur
had also been secured by a line of six fortresses,[6] to hold his
southern border. Even in this he did not succeed, for he lost
control of Nippur before the end of his reign, and Iluma-ilum
replaced him there in the datings of tablets.[7] Samsuiluna now
paid more attention to the Euphrates front—not only did he
transport hewn stones for the basin of a canal from 'a great mountain of the Westland', but in his twenty-eighth year he records
how his terrible mace crushed the hostile kings Iadikhabum and
Muti-khurshana, about whom nothing more is known, but their
names bespeak them as westerners. Five years later he was still
able to build at Sagaratim, a place some sixty miles upstream from
Mari, on the Khabur.[8] Whatever losses had been sustained nearer
home, the Babylonian rule subsisted longest among the peoples
of the Euphrates from whom it had first sprung. The last days
of that rule are possibly announced by a laconic reference to the
'host of the Westland' in the thirty-sixth year of Samsuiluna.

[1] Or Ili-mān, §vi, 6, 69 n. 176; §vii, 12, 189.
[2] *C.A.H.* I³, pt. 1, pp. 198 f.; G, 2, 271 f.
[3] §vi, 6, 69 n. 175.   [4] G, 19, ii, 20 f.
[5] §vi, 19.
[6] G, 18, iii, 199 ff.; G, 20, 148 and 204.
[7] G, 27, 242; otherwise §vi, 6, 68 n. 174.   [8] G, 23, 2.

A third expedition against the southern rebel was sent by
Abieshu', son and successor of Samsuiluna, whose long reign of
twenty-eight years was marked by no known external event other
than this spectacular failure, which is related only by the chronicle; he attempted to trap Iluma-ilum by damming the Tigris, but
although his earthwork was successful, the rival leader escaped.[1]
The remaining acts of Abieshu' as recorded in his date-formulae
were not much more than dedications of statues, with some building and canal-digging in his restricted bounds. Two dates which
refer to setting up statues in the temple of the Moon-god have
been thought to attest his control of Ur, but it seems rather that
he had a shrine in Babylon to which the ancient name of the
Moon-temple at Ur had been appropriated,[2] and this was the
recipient of his dedications. Upon this question the tablets found
at Ur are decisive in the negative, for not one bears a date of this
king.[3] Thus unsuccessful in the south, Abieshu' fared worse in
the north, for it seems to have been in his reign that the middle
Euphrates was lost to Babylon, and a new kingdom was founded
in the district of Khana.[4]

The three successors who were still to maintain through long
if inglorious reigns the royal line at Babylon followed the pattern
which had been traced by so many kings since the downfall of the
Third Dynasty of Ur—they remained for the most part at home
in a narrow realm, attending to their religious functions and
neither giving nor receiving much trouble among their neighbours. Ammiditana indeed, the next king, bestirred himself in
the south at the end of his reign, for he then destroyed a fortification[5] 'which the people of Damiq-ilishu had built'—this must
have been an attempted encroachment of the Sealand kings, for
Damiq-ilishu was doubtless the third-named in the lists of these,[6]
and in this synchronism resides the chief interest of the incident,
for the chronology of this period is far from certain.[7] Some
letters sent by these last kings of Babylon still remain;[8] their
contents are not of much importance and they give no indication
of the extent of the realm, for they are mostly addressed to Sippar.
Under Samsuiluna many directions were issued to the judges of
that city about cases which had been pleaded and settled before

[1] G, 19, II, 21. [2] G, 20, 206; §VI, 4, 101.
[3] Nor of his successor, §VI, 8, 115 n. 22. The same is true of Nippur, §VI, 15,
119; §VI, 1, 67. [4] See below, sect. VII.
[5] §VI, 11, 52; §VI, 6, 68 n. 174(c). [6] G, 2, 271 f.; §VI, 6, 69 f.
[7] C.A.H. I³, pt. 1, p. 211 and see below, p. 225.
[8] §II, 19, nos. 59 ff.

the king's bench. Abieshu' and Ammiditana were concerned chiefly with exacting dues said to be in arrear, and Ammiṣaduqa's letters are almost all devoted to ordering sheepmasters to come in with their flocks to the wool-gathering which was held at the House of the New Year Feast in Babylon. Of far more interest than any of the minor events recorded in this king's reign are two surviving documents with which his name is connected almost incidentally—the 'Venus tablets', which have provided important (if inconclusive and much-discussed) evidence to modern chronologers,[1] and the 'edict' which has revealed in large part the actual terms of an official enactment[2] which it had become a necessity at this time for every king to promulgate upon his accession.

VII. BEGINNINGS OF THE KASSITE DYNASTY

In the ninth year of Samsuiluna, and again in the third (?)[3] of his son, occurs a mention, tantalizing in its bareness, of 'the Kassite host'. These encounters were more than thirty years apart, an appropriately slow beginning to the movement which introduced an era of no less than 576 years,[4] the Kassite Dynasty, centuries which witnessed a lingering stagnation of Babylon and the south, with the transfer of power and interest to Assyria and the north. The Kassites were as alien as the Gutians in a former generation, but the old 'land' had lost its force of reaction and recovery—another Utu-khegal never arose.

These earliest glimpses of the future rulers are as fleeting and insubstantial as the first recorded kings themselves, who have scarcely any existence outside the later historical tradition found in king-lists and chronicles. Of necessity, therefore, their interest to modern historians is limited to a mere question of chronology, for three principal figures together occupy the foreground in these years, the dynasties of Babylon, of the Sealand, and of the Kassites, in the back-stage presence of mightier powers, the Assyrians and the Hittites; all of these have to be brought into one act, and the light of available evidence is too scanty and dim to discern their interplay.

This chapter is not concerned with the question of chronology: according to the system adopted in this *History*, the first Kassite king Gandash or Gaddash is taken to be contemporary with

---

[1] §vɪ, 7; *C.A.H.* ɪ[3], pt. ɪ, pp. 231 f., with references.
[2] See above, pp. 188, 195 f.
[3] §vɪ, 6, 66 n. 162. 　　　　　[4] G, 2, 272.

Samsuiluna,[1] and his reign of sixteen years to have begun with his assumed invasion in the ninth year of that king. This has, indeed, been strongly disputed[2] on the ground that practically no trace of Kassite rule or population has been found in any of the evidence relating to the long period between Samsuiluna and the end of his dynasty. To this the most notable exception is a king named Kashtiliash who has been discovered reigning, with other local kings, in the land of Khana,[3] about the confluence of the Khabur and the Euphrates. None of the other members of this group nor of the persons concerned in the documents bear Kassite names, though there is one more Kassite element in the name of a canal[4] dug by another of this line. Feeble as these indications are it is not possible to dispute their significance nor to deny the presence of Kassite influence and even supremacy, although in a quarter strangely remote[5] from the presumed origin of the Kassites, as a people of the Zagros, where they were often harried by Assyrian kings[6] in later generations. Nothing more is known about this small kingdom of Khana, and even any contact in time, or relations with the kings of Babylon is not attested; only from its names may the inference be drawn that it was a short-lived successor in a vacuum left by the withdrawal of these from their last hold on the Euphrates.

No direct evidence, in the form of contemporary inscriptions, relates to the first Kassite kings—they have no history. Only half an exception to this is a late copy of a short text[7] ascribed to Gandash, the first of all Kassite kings (and calling him 'king of Babylon'). This does no more than record his repair of a temple E-kur, 'which had been desecrated at the capture of Babylon'. The genuineness of this has been variously asserted or denied, but the only available arguments are indirect, and where these can be adduced on both sides we may be content with the mere unlikelihood of a downright forgery for some purpose which can only be hypothetical. If then Gandash did leave in Babylon such a memorial, the 'capture of Babylon' to which it refers could, again, be understood of a conquest by himself or of the attested conquest by the Hittites, soon to be related. In either case we should be obliged, it appears, to place the reign of Gandash after the end of Samsuditana and the First Dynasty of Babylon.

---

[1] See also §vii, 12, 191 and 197. [2] §vi, 6, 66 ff.

[3] §vii, 18, 266 ff.; §vii, 15, 205 ff.; G, 23, 39 ff.; see above, pp. 29 f. and below, pp. 250 f. [4] §vii, 2, no. 52, line 32.

[5] §vii, 12, 204. [6] G, 25, 215 and 271.

[7] §vii, 12, 226 f.; §vii, 16, 69 f.; §vi, 6, 67 f.

Last of his dynasty, Samsuditana reigned for thirty-one years[1] unillumined by any notable achievement, and faintly outlined by year-dates partly unrecovered, partly unplaced, and partly unreliable.[2] It is remarkable how uniformly long and undisturbed seem the reigns of these last four members of the First Dynasty, an age sinking slowly into decline and spinning itself out only because there was no neighbour with force enough to cut even so thin a thread. A destroyer came at last, with a speed and from a distance as of lightning—'in the time of Shamash-ditana', says, a late chronicle,[3] 'the Hittite came to the land of Akkad'. This laconic note, all that records the event from the Babylonian side, is phrased with an obvious reserve which has cast doubt[4] upon the natural interpretation, that a Hittite attack at length put an end to the lingering Dynasty of Babylon. From the Hittite side there is fortunately a clearer, though still a very summary account.[5] That the 'prisoners and possessions' carried away to Khattusha do in fact indicate a capture and sack of Babylon is best established by a preserved inscription[6] of the ninth Kassite king Agum (II, called kakrime),[7] which relates that he brought back to their temple the god Marduk and his consort Ṣarpanitum, the gods of Babylon, from 'a distant land, the land of Khani'. This is most naturally to be understood as the ransom of these gods from their Hittite captors and their reception by the Babylonian king at a half-way point on their journey home. The information[8] (allegedly from the god himself) that he had passed twenty-four years 'in the Hittite land', promoting the export-trade of Babylonia, is almost certainly making a virtue of necessity, a handsome explanation of his actual captivity; but it has provided an authentic piece of evidence for the much-disputed chronology of this period.

Material testimony to the civilization of these final reigns is uncommonly scanty, and the quality of the remaining objects evinces clearly an age of decline. No major works of sculpture or metallurgy have survived, only the frequent allusions in the date-formulae to divine or human statues or emblems of the gods adorned with precious metal and stones—such were probably made in the old technique of a thin metal overlay upon a core of wood. Small figures are equally lacking, and we have not even

---

[1] G, 2, 271.   [2] §vii, 3; §vii, 4.   [3] G, 19, ii, 22.
[4] §vi, 6, 71.   [5] See below, pp. 249 f.
[6] In a later copy, §vii, 12, 207; §vi, 6, 65 n. 160.
[7] 'The second', §vii, 1, 157.
[8] §vii, 9, 79 ff.; §vii, 6, 70 f.; ibid. 101 f.; §vii, 12, 208; §vii, 8, 8.

those minor offerings with royal or private inscriptions which are seldom wanting from other generations. Only the cylinder-seals remain in fair number, and it has already been said[1] that their style and workmanship become retrograde at this time, poverty of design going hand-in-hand with growing neglect of finish. One singular piece of evidence attests, however, a flourishing art, which seems to have arisen rapidly about this time. In the first year of Gulkishar, sixth king of the Sealand Dynasty, is dated a very curious tablet inscribed with secret recipes for the making of various kinds of glass,[2] each bearing a trade-name. So advanced was the technique of this art that it had already become a cherished mystery among the craftsmen, and consequently this tablet, wherein the secrets are enshrined, was written in a style of scribal ingenuity, probably meant to be intelligible only to those in possession of certain vocabularies restricted to adepts of this trade. Whether the ascription (which is original and explicit) of these recipes to the time of Gulkishar is accepted or disbelieved[3] must depend partly upon the date which is assigned to his reign, but in general it would seem to be about a century earlier than the earliest glass vessels in Egypt, which appear under the rule of Tuthmosis III (1504–1450).[4] Glass working evidently came into a rather sudden perfection about this time, its development being the work of a school of inventors and technicians, perhaps of Syrian origin (for tradition placed the beginning of glass in that country) but of international activity.

The glass reflects a last gleam in the 'dark age' which settled over all the lands of western Asia, as new peoples came in to inherit but to transform the legacy of Sumer and Akkad. In the centre, our chapter fitly closes at the withdrawal of Marduk from his city, leaving it to strife and affliction, a void to be filled gradually by wondering strangers.

---

[1] See above, p. 218.   [2] §VII, 7; §VII, 17, 197.   [3] §VI, 6, 68 f., n. 174(c).
[4] §VII, 13, 183; §VII, 5, 5 ff.; §VII, 11, 194; §VII, 10, 311 ff.

CHAPTER VI

ANATOLIA *c*. 1750–1600 B.C.

I. SOURCES

HISTORY begins in Anatolia with the records of the Assyrian trading colonies, described in the first volume (ch. XXIV) of this work. The period covered by these documents, hardly more than two centuries in all, closes with the disappearance of the colonies not long after 1780 B.C. The art of writing appears to have been temporarily lost, for it was an entirely different form of cuneiform script that was introduced by the Hittites about a century later. Of the many thousands of baked clay tablets unearthed by the German excavators on the site of the Hittite capital at Boğazköy since work started in 1906, and constituting the Hittite royal archives, only a handful can be dated by their script as early as the seventeenth century B.C.[1] However, many historical texts of this date have come to light in the form of later copies, inscribed like the greater part of the archives during the fourteenth and thirteenth centuries B.C.,[2] and such copies can be used confidently as a first-class source for much of the earlier period. Statements contained in them about events already past at the time of the original inscription are of course of less certain value, but in default of other relevant evidence they cannot be ignored.

Archaeology has comparatively little to contribute for this period. Few sites on the plateau of Asia Minor survived the widespread destruction at the end of the Early Bronze Age: fewer still have as yet been excavated. The key sites are Kültepe (ancient Kanesh) and Boğazköy (ancient Khattusha),[3] with Alişar (possibly ancient Ankuwa) of secondary importance.[4] Throughout the Middle Bronze Age at these sites there is a fairly stable culture. The occasional strata of destruction should be capable of a historical interpretation; but no major change can be detected until the appearance of 'Phrygian' pottery which marks the downfall of the Hittite empire at the end of the Late Bronze Age in the twelfth century.

[1] H. Otten in G, 9, 12–13.
[2] For the nature and contents of these archives see §1, 1 and 2.
[3] Interim reports on both sites are published annually in *A.J.A.*, *A.St.*, *Belleten*, and *M.D.O.G.*   [4] See below, sect. III.

External evidence bearing on the history of Anatolia during these centuries is virtually non-existent. Following the great age of Hammurabi in Babylon and of the Middle Kingdom in Egypt, the frontiers again contracted and contacts between the nations were few. Thus it is upon the tablets from Boğazköy that we must mainly rely for such information as can be gleaned about the history of Asia Minor in this period.

II. LANGUAGES AND PEOPLES

As a background to this history, something must be said about the linguistic and ethnic divisions of the Anatolian population in the second millennium B.C. A remarkable feature of the Hittite archives, which was very early observed, is the number of distinct languages represented in them.[1] The language in which the great majority of the texts are written has been given the name of 'Hittite' because it was the official language of the 'Land of Khatti'. Beside Hittite, however, we find not only Akkadian, the international language of the time, but also four other languages which were evidently spoken in parts of Asia Minor. The names commonly given to these tongues are derived from the adverbs in *-ili* or *-umnili* which are used to introduce them in the Hittite texts. Thus from the adverbs *ḫattili*, *luwili*, *ḫurlili* and *palaumnili*, the corresponding languages are known as Khattian, Luwian, Hurrian and Palaic; Akkadian would more properly be termed 'Babylonian', from the adverb *pabilili*.[2] For the Hittite language itself the term used has been identified in three forms, namely *našili*, *nišili*, and *nešumnili*, that is 'in the language of (the town) Nesha'. A more strict terminology would therefore use 'Neshian' rather than 'Hittite' as a name for the official language.

The language in which the 'singer of Kanesh' recites, once called *kanešumnili*, seems on the evidence to be a language at least very closely related to Hittite, perhaps even Hittite itself in an earlier form.[3] But if Kanesh and Nesha, as has been proposed,[4] are merely the Akkadian and Hittite forms respectively of one and the same name—that of the well-known centre of the Assyrian commercial organization already described[5]—this 'Kaneshite' language would not be a distinct language at all, but identical

[1] §II, 1, 2 and 10; best recent accounts in §II, 17, 1–9 and G, 7, 45 ff.
[2] §I, 3, no. 468.
[3] §II, 2, 191–8; §II, 5, 263; A, 16, 151.
[4] §II, 12, 46–50; §II, 10, 235; A, 14, 192 n. 4.
[5] *C.A.H.* I³, pt. 2, pp. 707 ff.

with 'Neshian'. The theory is attractive, but has not yet been generally accepted.[1]

Of these five languages, three, namely Hittite, Luwian and Palaic, are closely related to the Indo-European family. Archaeological and toponymic evidence have suggested that the first Indo-European elements, the Luwians, may have arrived in Anatolia from the west at the beginning of the Early Bronze Age, moving up on to the plateau towards the end of that period and putting an end to an earlier culture, the bearers of which are nameless.[2] In the period with which we are here concerned the Luwians constituted the predominant population of the southern and western portions of the peninsula. In Hittite documents the geographical term Luwiya includes the state of Arzawa which played an important part in the history of the second millennium as a rival of the Hittite kingdom and is certainly to be located either in the west or the south-west.[3] Kizzuwadna, in Cilicia, appears also to have had in early times a largely Luwian population.[4] Luwians cannot be identified in any numbers among the native Anatolians mentioned in the archives of the Assyrian traders,[5] and we can infer that they had not yet penetrated into the more northern areas at that time. It is clear, however, that Luwians and their language played an increasingly important role in the Hittite kingdom. Not only do Luwian names appear more frequently in the Hittite texts as time goes on, but the Luwian dialect written with hieroglyphic characters, commonly known as 'Hieroglyphic Hittite', was used by the later Hittite kings for monumental inscriptions and perhaps also for other purposes.[6] It is uncertain whether this implies a large Luwian-speaking element in the population or merely the employment of Luwian scribes.[7]

The north-central area, roughly within the basins of the Çekerek (classical Scylax) and Delice (classical Cappadox) rivers,[8] must have been inhabited from prehistoric times by the non-Indo-European race whose language appears in the texts as *ḫattili*. This adverb, evidently derived directly from the geographical or ethnic term *Ḫatti*, is properly the philological counterpart of the English 'Hittite'; but because the latter has become inseparably linked by usage with the better known but secondary use of the

---

[1] Cf. §II, 8, 51 n. 7; A, 38, 103–4; A, 37, 59–60; A, 13, 10 ff.; A, 47, 108 f.

[2] §II, 14, 15–33; §II, 15, 76 ff.

[3] For the west: G, 4, ch. VII, and A, 9, 10. For the south-west: G, 7, map, and A, 22, 47. Cf. A, 10, 395 ff. See Map 6.

[4] G, 6, 8. 　　　　　　　　　　[5] §II, 7, 80.

[6] A, 5 and 6; also G, 7, 53; §II, 10, 236 ff.

[7] §II, 9, 138 ff. 　　　　　　　　[8] §II, 13, 341.

name for the kingdom and empire of Khattusha and with the Indo-European language in which most of the texts are written, it has been necessary to devise another name for the non-Indo-European substratum, and the terms 'Khattian' or 'Khattic' have been widely adopted, though some prefer the rather misleading expression 'Proto-Hittite'. The Khattian language bears no recognizable relation to any known linguistic group.

Hittite, like Luwian, is a language of Indo-European structure but with a strong admixture of non-Indo-European vocabulary. An analysis of the personal names of native Anatolians found in documents of the Assyrian traders has shown that 'Kaneshites' (that is, Hittites) were already present in the country during the most flourishing period of the Assyrian colonies;[1] their arrival can therefore hardly be associated with the destruction of the second level of the *karum* at Kanesh and of many other sites *c.* 1900 B.C. (a view which depended on the distinction drawn between Kaneshite and Hittite)[2] but must be regarded as a much earlier movement, possibly to be connected with the introduction of the polychrome 'Cappadocian' (Ališar III) pottery at the end of the Early Bronze Age.[3] As their name implies, they must have settled in the central area, mainly to the south of the Khattians, especially around Kanesh; but the two populations evidently mingled freely, and the more flexible Neshian language gradually replaced Khattic as the language of the country. By the second millennium there is little evidence that the Hittites had any consciousness of ethnic differences within their homeland. It has been suggested that the historical conditions for this mingling of populations were first created when the whole region was unified *c.* 1750 B.C. by the conquests of the (Khattian) kings of Kushshar;[4] it could, however, have been a natural development in the preceding centuries, and there is nothing to show that the two populations were still consciously distinct even at the time of the Assyrian colonies.[5]

Of the third Indo-European language, Palaic, much less can be said. It was obviously the language of the district called Palā, later an outlying province of the Hittite kingdom. Prevailing opinion places Palā in classical Paphlagonia (modern Kastamonu) where there was a district called Blaene;[6] though arguments have been adduced for locating it rather in the vicinity of Sebasteia

---

[1] §II, 6; A, 16, 141–52.   [2] §II, 14, 9 ff.
[3] G, 7, 43 f., 60 f.; §II, 4, 220; cf. *C.A.H.* I³, pt. 2, ch. XXIV, sects. III and VI; A, 43, 51.
[4] §II, 13, 341–3.   [5] §II, 4, 215 n. 6.
[6] A, 7, 178; G, 7, map; A, 22, 45; A, 51, 95; A, 24, 216. See Map 6.

(modern Sivas)[1] or even far to the north-east in Armenia Minor (near modern Bayburt).[2]

The Hurrian language, which was later the vehicle for an extensive literature (at present known mainly through Hittite versions), is a much later intruder into Asia Minor. In the early years of the rising kingdom of Khattusha the Hurrians were still a distant little-known nation beyond the eastern mountains, and it was not till after 1550 B.C. that their political consolidation caused them to exert a substantial influence on the Hittites. They seem then to have infiltrated into southern parts of the peninsula which were previously inhabited by Luwians.[3]

III. ORIGIN OF THE KINGDOM OF KHATTUSHA

The political history of Anatolia begins with the rise of Anitta, son of Pitkhana, king of Kushshar, mentioned in a previous chapter of this *History*.[4] The conquests of this king are recorded in detail in a Hittite text from Boğazköy, one manuscript of which is known to be ancient.[5] We learn from it how Anitta transferred his residence to Nesha, which had been conquered by his father, and proceeded to capture successively the cities of Ullamma, Harkiuna, Zalpuwa and Khattusha itself, destroying the latter utterly and declaring it accursed; and how finally he defeated the king of Shalatiwara in a battle, and the king of Purushkhanda submitted to him, bearing a throne and a sceptre of iron as gifts. As already mentioned, three Old Assyrian documents and a bronze 'dagger'— properly a spearhead[6]—inscribed with his name prove that this first Anatolian empire-builder was contemporary with the Assyrian trading colonies and confirm his assumption of the title 'great king'. But whether he belongs to the most flourishing period of the colonies (level II at Kültepe) as maintained above,[7] or to the very end of the later period of partial revival (level I*b*), as most authorities believe,[8] there remains a gap between his reign and the subsequent history of Anatolia which the Hittite archives have failed to bridge, and an attempt must therefore be made to assess the inarticulate data of archaeology.

---

[1] G, 4, 30; A, 17, 58. [2] A, 10, 244.

[3] See above, pp. 22 ff.; G, 6, 4 ff.; A, 28, 7; but cf. A, 39, 402–15; A, 47, 344 n. 25.

[4] *C.A.H.* I[3], pt. 2, pp. 714 f.

[5] H. Otten in G, 9, 12–13; §III, 2, 47; §III, 7, 38 ff.; A, 45, 334–6.

[6] §III, 10, 33–4; A, 45, 334. [7] So also A, 16, 63–79.

[8] §III, 1 and 2; A, 13, 15; A, 45, 336–7; A, 47, 111.

At Kültepe (Kanesh) the spearhead of Anitta 'the king' was found in a large building which was destroyed in a violent conflagration.[1] The natural assumption that this building must have been the palace of Anitta has been challenged:[2] it has been suggested that the dagger might have been left there by one of the soldiers of Anitta when his army sacked the city. But if we accept the identification of Kanesh with Nesha, we must reject this suggestion, for Nesha was conquered not by Anitta but by a predecessor, perhaps his father Pitkhana, apparently with the minimum of violence. Anitta was able to reside at Nesha without further military action. The building where the spearhead was found should then be the palace of Anitta, and the conquest by Pitkhana will have left no trace on the mound (unless it be in the destruction of the palace of Warshama near by).[3] On the ruins of the palace of Anitta there arose a Hittite building in *megaron* form which survived in its essentials till the end of the Hittite Empire.[4]

At Boğazköy (Khattusha), level IV*d* on the acropolis (Büyükkale) and the contemporary Assyrian trading colony or *karum* (level IV) in the lower city both show evidence of violent destruction, followed by a period of desertion.[5] These facts agree well with the literary tradition, according to which Khattusha was destroyed and declared accursed by Anitta of Kushshar.[6] Level IV*c* which follows on the citadel must be identified with the prosperous period of the Hittite Old Kingdom. Thus neither the destruction of IV*d* nor that of IV*c* can be connected with the destruction of the palace of Anitta at Kültepe.

At Alişar the stratification is far from clear. The Assyrian tablets were found in the third (lowest) phase of level 10*T*, now called 10*Tc*. Only a few fragments were found in the second phase 10*Tb*, which succeeds the third without intermission and contained at least one monumental building, the so-called 'mansion'.[7] Level 10*Tb* ended in a conflagration and after a final phase of occupation by squatters the site was deserted.[8] Level 10*Tb* with its 'mansion' was at one time identified with the Hittite Old Kingdom.[9] On this assumption, we should have here a site at which the *karum* gave way peacefully to a Hittite regime.

[1] §III 1, 78; §III, 2, 3; §III, 10, 33–4.
[2] §III, 5, 60. Cf. also A, 16, 67 ff.
[3] §III, 2, 3; §III, 11, xxi; *A.St.* 6 (1956), 25–6, and 7 (1957), 20.
[4] *A.St.* 4 (1954), 19 and 5 (1955), 19; also §III, 10, 33–4.
[5] *A.St.* 10 (1960), 20–1; A, 12, 14 ff.
[6] A, 3, 13; §III, 3, 60; A, 13, 2.   [7] §III, 6, vol. II, 15 ff.
[8] §III, 5, 63.   [9] A, 20, 512.

One could infer that an internal revolution at 'Alişar' brought a change of dynasty there and that subsequently the new rulers conquered and destroyed Kanesh and reoccupied the deserted Khattusha. Furthermore, if Alişar could be equated with Kushshar, as has been suggested,[1] this would agree with the Hittite tradition that their earliest kings had been kings of Kushshar. A change of dynasty at Kushshar would explain the flouting of the curse of Anitta by the reoccupation of Khattusha, an action unlikely to have been committed by one of his own descendants.[2] The destruction of level 10 *Tb* at Alişar would present the same difficulty as that of level IV *c* at Boğazköy[3] and would enhance the probability that some disaster occurred which the Hittites failed to record.[4]

However, the Hittite character of level 10 *Tb* at Alişar has been rejected by the excavator of Kültepe, who has stated that he has found similar buildings at his site in pre-Hittite levels.[5] This would mean that Alişar was destroyed and ceased to exist as a city at the end of the colony-period. It could not then be the site of Kushshar, and indeed the place is rather small to be the site of a city of such historical importance.[6] The stratification of Alişar is therefore better left aside in reconstructing the history of this dark period. We have to look elsewhere for evidence of the emergence of Hittite power; in fact it now seems probable Kushshar was not in this area at all, but far to the south-east, in the vicinity of Şar (Comana Cappadociae).[7] Nevertheless, that it was the Hittites who destroyed the palace of Anitta at Kanesh-Nesha remains virtually certain in view of the character of the succeeding levels, and it is therefore unlikely that the Hittite kingdom was a direct continuation of the kingdom of Pitkhana and Anitta.[8] A change of dynasty at Kushshar remains the most likely hypothesis.[9] It is the history of this new dynasty that is told by the Hittite archives, beginning *c.* 1650 B.C.

[1] §III, 5, 60; 12, vol. I, 142 n. I.   [2] §IV, 4, 185–6.

[3] See below, ch. xv.   [4] §III, 3, 60.

[5] §III, 9, 215–16 n. 407.

[6] So A, 1, 31. The new reading of an Alişar tablet quoted in §III, 2, 39 n. 56, which would prove the identification of Alişar with the ancient Ankuwa, has been checked by the present writer against the tablet in Ankara and found to be incorrect.

[7] A, 42, 45 ff.; A, 16, 14–20.

[8] G, 5, 15; §III, 2, 48.   [9] So apparently §III, 4, 144–5.

IV. THE OLD HITTITE KINGDOM

Hittite history, as revealed by the archives, falls into two distinct periods, usually termed the Old Kingdom and the Empire. The texts relating to the Old Kingdom are few in number and for the most part badly mutilated,[1] and historians of this period have always taken as basis the well-preserved constitutional decree of Telepinush, one of the last kings of the Old Kingdom, which contains a long historical preamble contrasting the firm and orderly government of former kings with the anarchy into which the kingdom had subsequently sunk,[2] and thus giving in effect the outline of Hittite history down to the author's time. This document begins as follows:

Formerly Labarnash was Great King; and then his sons, his brothers, his connexions by marriage, his blood-relations and his soldiers were united. And the country was small; but wherever he marched to battle, he subdued the countries of his enemies with might. He destroyed the countries and made them powerless(?) and he made the sea their frontier.[3] And when he returned from battle, his sons went each to every part of the country, to Khupishna, to Tuwanuwa, to Nenashsha, to Landa, to Zallara, to Parshukhanda and to Lushna, and governed the country, and the great cities were firmly in his possession(?).[4]

Afterwards Khattushilish became king. And his sons, brothers, connexions by marriage, blood-relations and soldiers were likewise united. And wherever he marched to battle, he subdued the countries of his enemies with might. He destroyed the countries and made them powerless(?) and he made the sea their frontier. And when he returned from battle, his sons went each to every part of the country. And the great cities were again firmly in his hands(?).[5]

Such, apparently, was the tradition. For the Hittites of later generations their history had begun with King Labarnash. When offering sacrifices to the spirits of former kings and queens, deified by death, they placed him, with his queen Tawannannash, at the head of the list.[6] Indeed, this pair, it seems, were invested with a special sanctity. Their names were assumed, almost as titles, by every reigning king and queen from Telepinush onwards and held by each for life, in a way which suggests that the spirits of the ancestors were believed to live on in each successive

---

[1] §1, 2, nos. 1–28.   [2] *Ibid.* no. 21; translation §IV, 14, 183 ff.
[3] Literally 'he made them frontiers of the sea'.
[4] Meaning uncertain; literally 'were assigned, associated'.
[5] Literally 'were assigned, associated, to his hand also'.
[6] §IV, 10.

royal pair.[1] When used in this way, the name Labarnash commonly appears (especially in Akkadian and Luwian contexts) in the variant form Tabarna(sh), possibly because the name was originally Khattic and began with a peculiar consonant which was rendered differently in the different languages.

Yet Labarnash is an elusive figure. Telepinush does not state explicitly that he was the father or even the immediate predecessor of Khattushilish I. For information on this point and for further details of this king's reign we naturally turn to the old Hittite documents, and here we find a strange situation. The earliest texts can be dated to the reigns of Khattushilish and his son Murshilish I. None can be assigned to Labarnash, and indeed we may search in vain for a single reference to the events of his reign. The name Labarnash occurs fairly frequently; but it appears to be used mainly for King Khattushilish himself, though also for a nephew whom he had adopted as his successor but disinherited, and in one passage only for the 'son of his grandfather', who is usually assumed to be identical with Labarnash I, though the reference is to an incident before he became king.[2] We have to conclude either that Khattushilish ascended the throne as Labarnash (II) but later adopted the surname of Khattushilish, or alternatively that his personal name was Khattushilish and that he took the 'throne-name' of Labarnash. Only in one of the contemporary texts does this king give his own name as Khattushilish, namely in the record of military exploits, in annalistic form, of which parallel Hittite and Akkadian versions were found in 1957.[3] This text is also the only one in which Khattushilish refers to his lineage, but his choice of words has served only to make the position more obscure. The two parallel versions run as follows:

Hittite	*Akkadian*
[Thus Tabar]na Khattushilish, Great [King, King of Khattu]sha, man of Kushshar: in the Land of Khattusha [he ruled as king,] the brother's son of Tawannannash.[4]	Great King Tabarna exercised kingship in Khattusha, the [brother's son] of Taw[annannash].

Here again, where we should most expect to find it, the name of Labarnash (I) is omitted.

[1] §IV, 13, 20 ff.
[2] §IV, 13, 12 ff., and see below.
[3] §IV, 11; A, 11; A, 29 and 49; A, 45, 339 ff.; A, 47, 113 ff.
[4] In both versions 'Khattusha' is written with the Akkadogram *Ḫatti*, on which see §II, 13, 340 n. 59 (but cf. A, 39 and A, 40, 6 n. 26).

The other passage just mentioned remains the only contemporary reference to an older Labarnash and may be quoted in full:

My grandfather had proclaimed his son Labarnash (as heir to the throne)[1] in Shanakhuitta, [but afterwards] his servants and the leading citizens spurned (?) his words and set Papakhdilmakh on the throne. Now how many years have elapsed and [how many of them] have escaped their fate?

From these two passages it is at least certain that in the generation before Khattushilish there lived a Labarnash and a Tawannannash and that the father of this Labarnash was king before him, though we do not learn his name (it is doubtful whether he is to be identified with the PU-Sharruma, son of Tudkhaliash who is mentioned among former kings and princes in a sacrificial list).[2] The whole of Hittite usage demands that we should recognize Labarnash and Tawannannash as wedded king and queen. But marriage between brother and sister was abhorrent to the Hittites and even punishable by death,[3] and we cannot therefore identify this Labarnash with the brother of Tawannannash who was the father of Khattushilish. It must be assumed that Labarnash had a sister who was married to the brother of Tawannannash and became the mother of Khattushilish.

The failure of the contemporary texts to provide any further information about the reign of this Labarnash or to suggest that he was in any way outstanding casts some doubt on the validity of the tradition and on the theory that he and his queen were the immortal pair whose spirits lived on in the persons of later rulers. This usage is indeed likely to be far older in origin.[4] It must also be recognized that Telepinush, by his own account, lived some five generations after Labarnash, and it may be that he was not in fact recording a living tradition but rather attempting to construct history out of the documents in his state archives, as later kings undoubtedly did.[5] Such a supposition would explain why it was that this and later Hittite documents know nothing of any predecessor of 'Labarnash' and make him the first of his line; for the written archives actually seem to have begun with Labarnash-Khattushilish.

According to Telepinush it was Labarnash, the predecessor of

---

[1] The translation of the phrase 'his/my son Labarnash' as 'his/my young-Labarnash', that is, successor, suggested by J. G. Macqueen in §v, 3, 184, is unlikely to be correct in view of the variable order of the words and the attachment of the enclitic pronoun to the word for 'son' in each instance.

[2] §iv, 4, 21 ff.; §iv, 8, 187 n. 27; §iii, 3, 54; G, 8, 216.   [3] G, 7, 94.
[4] Cf. §v, 3, 180 ff.   [5] §iii, 4, 96.

Khattushilish, who started the Hittite kingdom on its road of conquest and extended its frontiers to the sea; but it is perhaps suspicious that almost the same words are used to describe the reigns of Labarnash and Khattushilish in this decree. Can it be that his historians were misled by the rather confusing use of the name Labarnash by king Khattushilish in the ancient texts?[1]

None the less, the decree of Telepinush remains good evidence for the historian that the expansion of the Hittite kingdom began with the incorporation of the territory south of the Kızıl Irmak (Halys), where Tuwanuwa (classical Tyana), Khupishna (classical Cybistra), Lushna (classical Lystra), Parshukhanda (classical Soandus?), and probably also Nenashsha and Zallara, are to be located.[2] Evidently this first stage had already been accomplished before the time of 'Labarnash', whose sons administered these territories peacefully on their return from their father's campaigns. Indeed there is reason, as we shall see, to believe that the first penetration of the Taurus passes by a Hittite army took place some time during this dark period of history. To assume, however, that this occurred as early as the reign of Pitkhana, on the basis of a single place-name in a later treaty,[3] seems rather speculative.

It is unquestionably with Labarnash II Khattushilish, rather than with Labarnash I, that we re-enter the full light of history after the dark period following Anitta of Kushshar. His reign is documented by several authentic inscriptions, the foremost of which is the bilingual annalistic text mentioned above. Here, as we have seen, he is entitled (in the Hittite version) 'King of Khattusha, man of Kushshar', and centuries later his connexion with the city of Kushshar was still remembered by his namesake and successor, Khattushilish III.[4] The expression 'man of Kushshar', used at a time when he was already 'king' of Khattusha, can only mean that Kushshar was his place of origin and therefore the original seat of his dynasty, though the place does not happen to be mentioned in connexion with his immediate predecessors. That these rulers were the direct descendants of Pitkhana and Anitta has already been shown to be unlikely.

If the capital of the kingdom was transferred, as it seems, by this king from Kushshar to the deserted site of Khattusha, the event provides a ready explanation for his change of name.

---

[1] In the sacrificial lists for the spirits of former kings the first name preserved is Tawannannash, followed by Labarnash; see A, 48.

[2] G, 4, 63 f., with earlier references. For Parshukhanda cf. Purushkhanda, above, p. 232, and *C.A.H.* I³, pt. 2, p. 707.

[3] §IV, I, 33 n. I.   [4] §IV, 13, 105.

Khattushilish 'man of Khattusha' would be a surname which he
adopted to commemorate the move and which he used henceforward in conjunction with his dynastic name Labarnash.[1]

Khattusha was a mountain stronghold dominating the northern
sector of the plateau within the bend of the Halys river. The earliest
settlement on the site was on the huge rocky eminence now called
Büyükkale, which towers high above the modern Turkish village
of Boğazköy. To the east, Büyükkale is protected from assault
by the precipitous gorge of the torrent Budak Özü, but the more
gentle slopes on the opposite side of the hill necessitated a certain
degree of fortification. Later, when Büyükkale could no longer
contain the expanding city, the settlement was extended west and
north down the mountain slope as far as the deep gorge of another
torrent which unites with the Budak Özü at the foot of the hill;
and later still the rising ground to the south was also taken in and
defended by the cyclopean walls, much of which can still be seen
today.[2]

As the administrative capital of a kingdom which embraced
most of the central Anatolian plateau the city was badly situated
on account of its peripheral position in the far north, and this
defect was further accentuated when the empire was extended
southwards beyond the Taurus. If it was none the less deliberately
chosen as a capital by the Hittite king, he was doubtless impelled
mainly by strategical considerations. History can show many
examples of the siting of a capital city at the point of danger, and
in later centuries the hills to the north of Khattusha were the
home of turbulent tribes, the so-called Kaska or Gasga folk, who
formed a constant menace to the security of the kingdom.[3] We
do not know when these tribesmen first appeared on the northern
borders or whence they came; they are first mentioned in the time
of Khantilish,[4] but it may well be that it was their appearance
which induced Khattushilish to adopt this northern stronghold as
his capital.

The events of six years of this reign are concisely described in
the bilingual document already quoted. Whether these are
actually the first six years is not made completely clear. Valuable
though this document is, our full understanding of it—and
indeed of all Hittite historical texts—is severely limited by our
ignorance of the location of the many places mentioned in them.
For in spite of the considerable amount of research which has

[1] So §iv, 13, 20.   [2] See A, 2 and 26.
[3] G, 6, 178; G, 7, 33.
[4] §iii, 3, 60; but cf. A, 50, 19 n. 1. See below, ch. xv.

been done on the subject, very little agreement has yet been achieved.[1]

The first of these years was devoted to campaigns against 'Shakhuitta' (var. Shanawitta) and 'Zalpar', presumably the cities better known in the forms Shanakhuitta and Zalpa. Shanakhuitta, as we have already seen, is the location of the earliest event in Hittite history, the attempt by the nobles to replace 'Labarnash I' by their own nominee, one Papakhdilmakh. It was undoubtedly in the central Hittite area and in the vicinity of the important garrison centres Khakpish and Ishtakhara,[2] whether the group as a whole is to be placed round Amasya,[3] in the Kanak Su valley,[4] or on the upper Halys above Sivas.[5] A personal connexion of Shanakhuitta with the king is suggested by its appearance in a tablet of instructions for palace servants.[6] Perhaps the place contained an ancient royal residence. Nothing is known to explain its hostility at the beginning of the reign of Khattushilish.

Of Zalpa, the site of an important Assyrian colony in the preceding age, somewhat more is known.[7] It seems to have been one of the most tenacious rivals of the Hittite kingdom in its rise to power. Already before the time of Anitta the king of Zalpa had raided the city of Nesha (Kanesh) and carried off the statue of the local god. Anitta, as king of Nesha, recaptured it and restored it to its home. The wars of the kings of Khatti against Zalpa are related in a much damaged text of the legendary type.[8] The raid in the first year of Khattushilish, in which it is not stated that Zalpa was captured, would seem to have been a minor episode in a conflict extending over many years. The localization of Zalpa is bound up with that of Tawiniya, which was evidently near it and also one of the nearest towns to the capital. If Tawiniya is classical Tavium, Zalpa must have been situated to the south or southeast of Khattusha.[9] However, the more satisfactory equation of Tawiniya with classical Tonea would compel us to place this and a large group of other cities, including Zalpa, to the north of Khattusha,[10] and the location of Zalpa at Alaca Hüyük,[11] with Tawiniya at Eskiyapar,[12] has much to recommend it. Thus the campaigns of this year are merely local operations.

[1] Cf. G, 4, especially 109, and critical comments in A, 10; A, 22; and A, 24.
[2] G, 4, 8 ff.; A, 19, 21.   [3] A, 21, 98.
[4] G, 4, 14 ff.   [5] A, 8, 51.
[6] §1, 2, no. 167.   [7] §iii, 2, 58 f.; A, 19, 27.
[8] §1, 2, no. 26; §iii, 4, 101 ff.   [9] G, 4, 11 ff.
[10] So A, 19, 27, and A, 24, 87. See Map 6.
[11] A, 8, 50; A, 10, 377.   [12] A, 24.

All the more surprising, therefore, is the record for the second year:

In the next year I marched against Alkhalkha (var. Alalkha) and destroyed it. Afterwards I marched against Urshu (var. Warshuwa); from Urshu I marched against Igakalish; from Igakalish I marched against Tashkhinya (var. Tishkhiniya). On my way back I destroyed the land of Urshu and filled my house with treasures.

Alalkha (Alkhalkha) can hardly be anything but the city of Alalakh in the plain of Antioch, well known from the excavations of Sir Leonard Woolley from 1937 to 1949. We thus find Khattu-shilish at the beginning of his reign conducting a campaign in the Syrian plains. The absence of any preliminary operations is most striking and we must conclude that a road through the Taurus mountains was already under Hittite control. The area demar-cated by the seven cities of Labarnash in the decree of Telepinush suggests that this road may have been the Cilician Gates, and since the land of Adaniya (that is, modern Adana) is mentioned by Telepinush among territories lost to the Hittites in a succeeding reign,[1] it would seem that Cilicia also must have been already in their hands. The appearance of a central Anatolian ware at Tarsus has already been taken as a sign of Hittite expansion at approximately this time,[2] and the Hittite fortress at Mersin, which belongs to the same period,[3] lends further support to this con-clusion. An approach by way of Cilicia would indeed explain how Alalakh came to be the first town in Syria to succumb to the Hittites, while Aleppo remained undefeated.

Khattushilish claims to have destroyed Alalakh on this cam-paign. This, then, should be the destruction which marked the end of level VII on the site—an important chronological datum, for the destruction of Alalakh VII has been dated by a combination of archaeological and historical reasoning to c. 1650–1630 B.C.[4]

After capturing Alalakh, Khattushilish proceeded to attack Urshu, Igakalish and Tashkhiniya. The situation of the last two places is unknown; but Urshu is now located with reasonable certainty on the right bank of the Euphrates to the north of

[1] G, 6, 57. See below, chapter xv.
[2] §iii, 5, 68.   [3] Ibid. 68–9.
[4] §iv, 1, 26 ff.; 6, 25. See above, chapter i. It is necessary to place Hammurabi II of Iamkhad, the contemporary of Ammitaqum of Alalakh (§iv, 15, nos. 21, 22, 39; cf. the table in §iv, 6, 23) before Iarim-lim III, the opponent of Khattushilish; the Hammurabi son of Iarim-lim of K.U.B. xxxi, 5 (§iii, 3, 70, and §iv, 9, 52) could be a Hammurabi III, not attested in the Alalakh archives. See C.A.H. i³, pt. 1, pp. 211 ff. and cf. A, 32, 161.

Carchemish;[1] its role in Syrian history is treated in chapter I of this volume. The country of Urshu was destroyed on the return journey and booty taken. It is not stated whether the king returned home by the same route. In this account the remarkable thing is the absence of any reference to Aleppo (Khalap), the king of which might have been expected to come to the aid of his vassal, the king of Alalakh, or at least to interfere with the free passage of the Hittite army through his territories. It may be that Khattu-shilish had seized the opportunity provided by a dynastic dispute at Aleppo, as a result of which Ammitaqum of Alalakh had assumed his independence and was therefore unable to call on the assistance of his more powerful neighbour in the hour of danger.[2]

The following year Khattushilish set out from his capital for a campaign against Arzawa. This is the earliest reference to the kingdom which was to become in later centuries the strongest rival of the Hittite kings in their struggle for the domination of the Anatolian peninsula—it lay to the west or south-west of Khattusha with a royal residence on the sea coast.[3] Thus there can be no doubt that this was a major operation for the Hittite king; but his absence in the West was taken as an open invitation by his enemies in the East. The kingdom was invaded in his rear by a power called in the Akkadian version 'Khanikalbat' and in the Hittite 'the Hurrians', and the whole country fell to them with the exception of Khattusha itself. Here again we have the earliest reference in Hittite history to a nation later to exercise a powerful influence on the civilization of Anatolia.[4] Khanigalbat always denotes a Hurrian power situated to the east of the Euphrates, whatever its exact limits may have been at any given time;[5] and there are already other grounds for believing that northern Meso-potamia was invaded and settled by Hurrians at this time, when Assyria was in decline.[6] But the population of North Syria had also for some time been predominantly Hurrian,[7] and the sequel suggests that the North Syrian kingdoms had a part in the invasion. Khattushilish, faced by this menacing situation, aban-doned the Arzawa campaign and turned against the eastern enemy. Three cities are mentioned as the object of his vengeance Nenashsha, Ullumma (Ulma), and Shallakhshuwa. The account is laconic, but evidently the situation was temporarily saved and the king was able to return to Khattusha for the winter.

[1] G. 4, 55–6; §IV, 3, 11 and 34; A, 32, 258 f. [2] §IV, 2, 21 f.
[3] See above, p. 230. [4] See above, p. 233.
[5] §IV, 5, 64 with n. 7; §IV, 11, 79 n. 16; A, 18, 72–3. [6] A, 18, 66.
[7] §II, 14, 23; §IV, 7, 384; §IV, 9, 64; §IV, 15, 9.

The next two years seem to have been occupied in local operations. 'Shanakhut', the objective of the fourth campaign, may or may not be another variant of Shanakhuitta, which the king had failed to capture in the first year. The place was taken after a six months' siege. Alahha, which was captured in the fifth year, is difficult to locate.

In the sixth year, however, the king embarked on another major campaign through the Taurus Mountains. His objective was the city of Khashshu (or Khashshuwa), a Hurrian kingdom probably situated just east of the Euphrates,[1] which may have lent its support to the invasion of Hittite territory three years earlier and thus invited retribution. Zaruna, which lay on his route, was first destroyed. Khashshu then offered resistance and was supported by Khalba (Aleppo), which here appears for the first time. Battle was joined at Mount Adalur, elsewhere associated with the Amanus Mountains,[2] and the Syrian forces were routed, after which Khattushilish crossed the Euphrates and destroyed Khashshu. He then returned to the west bank to attack the city of Khahhu (Hittite Khahha).[3] Capturing *en route* the town of Zippashna, he defeated the troops of Khahhu, destroyed and plundered the city and led its king into captivity. Summarizing the campaign, he compares his exploit in leading his troops across the Euphrates on foot with a previous crossing in the opposite direction by Sargon of Akkad. This exploit, which had never before been accomplished by a Hittite king (but was later repeated by Cyrus the younger)[4] forms the climax of the king's narrative, and with it the text ends abruptly.

For further details of the reign of Khattushilish we have to depend on brief allusions in the contemporary Hittite documents some of which seem to refer to the campaigns just described, and on the Hittite traditional literature, in which historical material is often mixed with anecdotes of a trivial nature and—for older events—with supernatural elements.[5]

In the recollection of succeeding generations it is clear that the reign of Khattushilish was dominated by his Syrian wars, and that the kingdom of Iamkhad (Aleppo, Khalba) was his real opponent and rival. We are told in a later treaty that 'in former days the kings of Aleppo possessed a great kingdom; Khattushilish caused (the days of) their kingdom to be full, but Murshilish destroyed

[1] A, 25, 4; above, ch. I, sect. IV.   [2] §III, 2, 34 ff,
[3] On the location of Khahhu see §IV, 3, 10–11, with earlier literature and A, 25, 4.
[4] Xenophon, *Anabasis*, I, 4, 17.   [5] §III, 4, *passim*.

it'.[1] It is generally agreed that the second clause implies that Khattushilish began to attack and diminish the territories of this 'great kingdom' (a status not yet claimed by the Hittites themselves).[2] He must, however, have met with a reverse, perhaps even received a mortal injury. For in a fragmentary inscription summarizing Hittite dealings with Aleppo it is stated that 'Murshilish (adopted son and successor of Khattushilish) set out [against Aleppo] to avenge his father's [blood]; and whereas Khattushilish passed on Aleppo [to his son] to deal with, he (Murshilish) punished the king of Aleppo'.[3] An edict of Khattushilish threatens destruction on Aleppo: 'The man of the city Zalpa rejected the father's word: behold that city Zalpa! The man of the city Khashshuwa rejected the father's word: behold that city Khashshuwa! Now even the man of the city Aleppo has rejected the father's word: Aleppo also shall be destroyed.'[4] The long-lasting feud with Zalpa and the destruction of Khashshuwa in the sixth year have already been mentioned. We may infer that further campaigns in the Syrian arena occupied the rest of the reign of Khattushilish without achieving a decisive result, perhaps even ending in disaster.

Fragments of a Hittite legend about these Syrian wars, which have recently come to light, have provided a welcome link with the history of Alalakh and Aleppo in the personality of one Zukrashi, a general of the king of Aleppo,[5] for this individual is recorded as a witness on a document from Alalakh by which Ammitaqum of Alalakh declared his will before his suzerain, Iarimlim (III) of Aleppo. In the Hittite text this general, together with a leader of the Umman Manda, brings troops to the aid of the king of Khashshu in his resistance to the Hittite king. In another fragment, probably of the same text, the kings of Aleppo, Iarimlim and his son Hammurabi, are mentioned. The text, as far as preserved, is free of mythological elements and is likely to refer to a campaign of Khattushilish rather than to events of a remote past, as has been claimed.[6] On the other hand, it cannot be too far removed in time from the downfall of Ammitaqum of Alalakh, since Zukrashi still holds the same appointment which he held in the reign of Ammitaqum. We may

---

[1] §IV, 5, 60 f. Text: §I, 2, no. 49.

[2] §IV, 9, 52 f., n. 89; §IV, 12, 12. But cf. A, 46, 122 n. 26.

[3] §IV, 9, 52 f., n. 89. Text: §IV, 4, no. 20.   [4] §IV, 4, no. 10, 30 ff.

[5] §III, 3, 70; §IV, 1, 30; §IV, 2, 22; §IV, 6, 22, 26; §IV, 9, 52; §IV, 11, 78 n. 14.

[6] §IV, 1, 30 ff.; A, 46, 118 ff.

therefore conclude that this composition described events in the campaign against Khashshu which took place in the 'sixth' year, four years after the destruction of Alalakh. The precise meaning of Umman Manda in this context is uncertain. Whatever the original significance of the term, its use in the Hittite laws shows that it had a special connotation for the Hittites, though this cannot at present be determined.[1]

A particularly well-preserved text, in the Akkadian language, describes in literary form a siege of the city of Urshu which, as is generally agreed, must have been an episode in these wars of Khattushilish I.[2] The composition takes the form of a series of anecdotes about the incompetence of the Hittite officers but contains much valuable historical material. The king directs the operations from the city of Lukhuzzantiya (elsewhere Lawazantiya) in the Taurus foothills of eastern Cilicia[3] (it has been conjecturally identified with the mound Karahüyük near Elbistan[4]). Urshu is in contact with, perhaps allied with, the state of the Hurri, the city of Aleppo, and the city of Aruar or Zaruar,[5] perhaps also with the city of Carchemish, the forces of which are ensconced on a mountain overlooking the city and keeping watch. All these powers maintain ambassadors within the city and the Hittites are unable to prevent their free passage in and out. At one point a messenger reports that the Hurrians are preoccupied with a dynastic dispute and the moment is considered opportune for a decisive attack by the Hittites, but the general in command fails to act in time and the opportunity is lost. At another point the king gives orders for a battering-ram to be hewn out from the trees in the mountains of Khashshu, which presumably indicates that the town of Khashshu was already in Hittite hands.[6] This narrative is historically of great interest; for the 'destruction' of the land of Urshu is placed by the bilingual 'Annals' in the 'second' year, that of Khashshu not until the 'sixth'. The episode of the siege can hardly, therefore, have been part of the campaign of the 'second' year. It must in fact have occurred later in the reign, and it appears to follow, either that the 'destruction' of Urshu in the second year amounted to no more than a raid on the city's territories, or that the Hurrian invasion of the

---

[1] Cf. above, ch. I, sect. VIII; §II, 2, 247 f.; §IV, I, 31.
[2] G, 8, 178–9; §I, 2, no. 29; §III, 4, 133 ff.; A, 32, 261 f.
[3] G, 4, 52–3; G, 6, 71–3; §IV, 3, 10–11.
[4] A, 4, 320; cf. A, 36, *s.v.* no. 346.
[5] §III, 3, 72 n. 208; §IV, 9, 64 n. 157; A, 32, 168 n. 83.
[6] But cf. A, 25, 4; A, 34, 459.

'third' year reconstituted the kingdom of Urshu under Hurrian tutelage and necessitated its reconquest.

Khattushilish, like Labarnash, is said to have made the sea his frontier, and in view of the facts just described, it is clear that the Mediterranean Sea is intended. In the north, we are told in a later treaty, 'Labarnash-Khattushilish'[1] established a defended frontier on the River Kummeshmakhash.[2] This river was in a remote area not often visited by the Hittite kings and has been tentatively identified with either the Devrez,[3] the Yeşilirmak (Iris),[4] or the Çekerek (Scylax);[4] the region beyond it remained till the end of the empire more or less *terra incognita*. In another late treaty it is stated that 'Labarnash' had conquered Arzawa and Wilusa.[5] Whether this refers to Khattushilish I or a predecessor it is difficult to say. We have seen that early in his reign Khattushilish was obliged to abandon a campaign against Arzawa when danger threatened in his rear; but a collection of anecdotes relating to a later part of his reign records the land of 'Arzawiya' as already the seat of a resident governor.[6] If Arzawa was indeed in the possession of either Khattushilish I or his predecessor, it would mean that these early kings controlled, for a time, a territory which in a south-westerly direction at least represented the farthest limit of expansion attained by the most powerful emperors of the fourteenth and thirteenth centuries.

The internal harmony of the realm, by which Telepinush sought to explain the successes of these early monarchs, seems to have been largely a figment of his imagination. We have seen how already the accession of Labarnash was disputed by the nobles and a rival pretender named Papakhdilmakh was set on the throne.[7] In this young kingdom each successive ruler had to establish his own authority and Labarnash was no exception. Once secure on the throne, he dealt mercilessly with the offenders. However, the latent rivalries and factions within the royal family broke out again during the reign of his successor, Khattushilish, as we learn from the records of pronouncements made by him at the end of his reign, when apparently on his death-bed. One son named Khuzziyash, who had been appointed ruler of a city Tapashshanda (otherwise unknown), listened to the seditious

---

[1] Usually translated 'Labarnash (and) Khattushilish' but the conjunction is not in the text and has to be supplied. (See, however, A, 50, 19 n. 1.)

[2] §1, 2, no. 62 (ii, 5); G, 4, 119.   [3] G, 4, 24.

[4] A, 24, 96; A, 50, 19 n. 2.

[5] *Alakšanduš* treaty, §1, 2, no. 50; G, 4, 102.

[6] §IV, 4, no. 12A (i, 11); §IV, 8, 189 ff.   [7] See above, p. 237.

advice of the citizens and was apparently punished for his disloyalty. Simultaneously the people of Khattusha itself approached a person described as 'the daughter' (presumably the king's daughter) and persuaded her to lead a revolt which caused grave loss and destruction. Another son, Khakkarpilish, who had been sent to govern Zalpa at the request of its elders, himself initiated a rebellion, the result of which is unknown.[1] Well might Khattushilish lament bitterly that no member of his family had obeyed his will. It appears that he had no more sons to succeed him and was obliged to adopt a nephew, also named Labarnash, a son of his sister. But this young man too proved disloyal. We possess the text of a speech in which the king, lying sick at Kushshar, still apparently his residential, though no longer his administrative capital, announced the disinheritance of Labarnash and the final adoption of a boy named Murshilish, probably his grandson.[2] The following passages from this remarkable text (one of the earliest in the whole archive, though preserved only on later copies) bring vividly to mind the stern embittered personality of this ancient king.

Behold, I have fallen sick. The young Labarnash I had proclaimed to you, saying 'He shall sit upon the throne'; I called him my son, embraced (?) him, and cared for him continually. But he showed himself a youth not fit to be seen; he shed no tears, he showed no pity, he was cold and heartless.... The word of the king he has not laid to heart, but the word of his mother, the serpent, he has laid to heart.... Enough! He is my son no more.... Then his mother bellowed like an ox: 'They have torn asunder the womb in my living body! They have ruined him and you will kill him!' Have I, the king, done him any evil?... Now he shall never again go down (from the city) freely [wherever he will]. Behold, I have given my son Labarnash a house, I have given him [arable land] in plenty, [sheep in] plenty I have given him. Let him now eat and drink. [So long as he is good] he may come up to the city. [But] if he stand forward (?) as [a trouble-maker (?)]... then he shall not come up, but shall remain [in his house].

Behold, Murshilish is now my son.... In place of the lion [the god will set up another] lion (?). [And in the] hour [when] a call to arms goes [forth] ...you, my servants and leading citizens, must be [at hand to help my son]. [When] three years have elapsed, he shall go on a campaign.... If you take him [while still a child] with you on a campaign, bring [him] back [safely]!

Let your kindred be [one] like that of the wolf. There shall be [strife] no more....

[The daughter has disgraced my person] and my name.... A father's word she has cast aside, [the life-]blood [of the sons of Khatti] she has sucked. Now she [is banished from the city].... In the country [a house has been assig]ned to her; she may eat and drink, [but you] must not do [her

---

[1] §IV, 4, no. 13.   [2] So given in the Aleppo treaty, §IV, 5, 60 ff.

harm]. *She* has done wrong; *I* will not do [wrong in return]. *She* [has not called] me father, *I* will not call her my daughter.

Till now none [of my family] has obeyed my will. [But you, my son] Murshilish, *you* must obey it. Keep [your father's] word. If you keep your father's word, you will [eat bread] and drink water. When maturity [is within] you, then eat two or three times a day and do yourself well! (And when) old age is within you, then drink to satiety! And then you may set aside your father's word.

[Now] you are my chief servants, and you must keep my words. You shall only eat bread and drink water. [So Khattu]sha will stand high and my land will be [at pea]ce. But if you do not keep the king's word,...you will not remain alive, you will perish.

And you, (Murshilish), shall not delay nor relax. If you delay, (it will mean) the same old mischief.... What, my son, has been laid in (your) heart, act thereupon always.[1]

This text is unique in cuneiform literature; the nearest parallel to it is to be found in the didactic literature of the Egyptians, in the 'Instructions' to Merykare and of Ammenemes I. Whether this comparison is of any significance, however, is doubtful. Contact between Anatolia and Egypt, first attested in the time of the Fifth Dynasty, is shown by sporadic finds of Egyptian statues in Syria and Asia Minor to have been maintained, or perhaps re-established, during the Middle Kingdom.[2] But it is difficult to believe that a literary tradition deriving from the Egypt of the Middle Kingdom should have been fostered in Khatti for a century and a half without leaving any trace. The Hittite document differs in fact so widely from the Egyptian as to constitute an essentially new form of literature.

What is of greater historical importance than this speculative Egyptian parallel is the sudden appearance of Hittite cuneiform writing at this time. For the Anittash text, the only document of the archive which belongs to an earlier age, was probably not composed in its present form and cannot be used as evidence that the Hittite language was written down in cuneiform in the nineteenth century. The earliest texts composed in Old Hittite seem to belong to the later years of the reign of Khattushilish, and the natural inference is that it was shortly before this time that scribes of cuneiform were transported from one of the ancient cultural provinces of Babylonia to the Hittite capital and taught to write the Hittite language. The particular form of the script which

---

[1] §1, 2, no. 6 (= §IV, 4, no. 8); ed. and trans. §IV, 13.

[2] Cartouche of Sahure, found at Dorak, see *C.A.H.* I³, pt. 2, p. 391. Middle Kingdom statues, see A, 52, 139 n. 4; *C.A.H.* I³, pt. 2, p. 503.

they introduced cannot be derived immediately from any known school of the period and its immediate antecedents present a problem for the future. Doubtless it stems from one of the cities of northern Syria, such as Aleppo, with which the Hittites first came into contact in their southward expansion, but the early history of which is still largely unknown to us except through external sources. It is very similar to the script of level VII at Alalakh.[1]

It has been held that Khattushilish I died while his adopted son, Murshilish, was still a minor, and that a brother of the late king named Pimpirash (or Bimbirash) became regent for the boy until he should reach maturity.[2] If this were so, however, it would be strange that no reference should be made to the appointment of Pimpirash in any of the extant decrees of Khattushilish or in the edict of Telepinush, and in fact this view rests on an interpretation of a fragmentary document which cannot be sustained.[3] The evidence is insufficient to determine the role played by Pimpirash in the early Hittite kingdom.

The reign of Murshilish was critical in the history of the Hittite kingdom. If we may believe the brief accounts of it that have survived, the king's attention was entirely devoted to a military adventure far to the south. His first care was to 'avenge his father's blood' by settling accounts with Aleppo. No details are known, but more than one document records the fact that Aleppo was destroyed by Murshilish.[4] Presumably this meant the end of the powerful kingdom of Iamkhad which had governed northern Syria since the time of Hammurabi of Babylon.

For the sequel we have nothing but the statement of Telepinush that Murshilish destroyed Babylon and defeated all the lands of the Hurrians. The destruction of Babylon was remembered with pride by later generations as a feat of arms never again equalled by the Hittite kings. It is also the one event in early Hittite history which is confirmed by external sources; for the Babylonian Chronicle, recording the end of the First Dynasty of Babylon, states: 'In the time of Samsuditana the men of Khatti marched against the land of Akkad.' It thus links Hittite chronology with that of Babylonia, for if the death of Samsuditana occurred in 1595 B.C., the Hittite raid must be placed either at or shortly after that date.[5] None the less it raises questions which can as yet be only partially answered. For the result of this Hittite victory

---

[1] See A, 15, 406 ff.   [2] §IV, 4, 6*; §IV, 13, 211.
[3] The statement 'I, Pimpirash, have protected the king' may be translated 'I, Pimpirash, have been loyal to the king'.
[4] See above, p. 243.   [5] §IV, 9, 71 f.; *C.A.H.* I³, pt. 1, pp. 212 f.

was the establishment not of a Hittite, but of a Kassite dynasty in Babylonia. Why then did the Hittite king undertake this ambitious campaign if only to yield the fruit of victory to others? Why was the Hittite army allowed to march apparently unopposed for a distance of roughly five hundred miles down the Euphrates and to capture at a blow a city which only a few generations earlier had been the capital of a powerful empire? And at what point in the campaign did Murshilish encounter the Hurrians and defeat them?

The clue to these problems must lie in the history of the district of Khana on the Middle Euphrates, around the mouth of the River Khabur. This region, once part of the kingdom of Mari, had been captured by Hammurabi of Babylon in the year 1761 B.C. and remained firmly in Babylonian hands till at least the end of the reign of Samsuiluna. Under Abieshu' or Ammiditana it seems to have regained its independence. At least six kings are known to have ruled at Khana contemporaneously with the last four kings of the First Dynasty of Babylon,[1] and it is in their records that the first traces of Kassite influence in Mesopotamia have been detected;[2] one of these kings of Khana even bore a Kassite name. Now there is reason to believe that the early kings of the Kassite dynasty which later ruled Babylon as its Third Dynasty, belong to this same period. There would then have existed at that time a Kassite kingdom somewhere in central Mesopotamia and in close contact with the kingdom of Khana at the mouth of the Khabur.[3] The matter is highly controversial and can at present only be treated as a hypothesis. It is clear, however, that in 1595 B.C. Murshilish could not have attacked Babylon without passing through this region, and, if indeed it was part of the Kassite sphere of influence, since he clearly did not defeat the Kassites, he must have become their ally. Thus the initiative for the attack on Babylon might have come from the Kassites. We might suppose that the Hittites were invited to assist on the understanding that they were to receive a share of the booty, and it is precisely the rich booty brought back to Khattusha that is emphasized in the Hittite accounts. Alternatively, it has been suggested that Murshilish sought the alliance with the Kassites as a bulwark against the rising power of the Hurrians.[4] In either case the permanent conquest of Babylon could never have been con-

---

[1] §III, 3, 63 ff.; §IV, 9 62 ff.; above, ch. I, sect. VI.

[2] This is disputed, §III, 3, 64 f.; above, ch. I, sect. VI.

[3] See again above, ch. I, sect. VI.

[4] §IV, 9, 65. For a different explanation see A, 46, 121 ff. and A, 47, 119 ff.

templated by Murshilish and his abandonment of the city to his Kassite allies would need no further explanation.

The reference to the Hurrians is less obscure. It would be natural to assume that their defeat was connected with the destruction of Aleppo, for we have seen that Khattushilish had frequently encountered the Hurrians in that area; and indeed one text clearly associates the two events.[1] In view of this, Telepinush, in recording the defeat of the Hurrians after the destruction of Babylon, would seem to have placed the two events in the wrong order. Otherwise we must infer that the Hurrians attacked Murshilish on his way home.

Laden with booty, the young king returned to Khattusha; but he was not to enjoy the fruits of his victory. After an unstated period, probably only a year or two, Khantilish, the husband of his own sister, Kharapshilish, was prevailed on by his son-in-law, Zidantash, to take part in a conspiracy. Murshilish was struck down by the hand of an assassin and Khantilish assumed the throne.

Thus ended the first period of Hittite expansion. Murshilish had apparently taken no steps to consolidate his successes or to provide for a firm government at home, and his assassination marked the beginning of a period of disasters which brought the Hittite kingdom itself to the verge of extinction.

V. EARLY HITTITE SOCIETY

Central Anatolia, now a bleak and desiccated plateau crossed by fertile but isolated valleys, seems to have enjoyed in antiquity a much more copious rainfall than today, with consequent effects upon its vegetation and easier living conditions for its inhabitants.[2] None the less, the nature of the country would foster the growth of largely self-contained communities, and it is clear that throughout the Hittite period these local communities preserved their individuality, though in consequence of the unification of the country under the dynasty of Khattusha the many local kings (Assyrian *rubaum*) attested during the period of the Assyrian merchants had been eliminated. Local government was apparently in the hands of 'Elders'.[3] Whether there were holy cities, as in Strabo's time, governed by the priesthood of the local temple, cannot be stated with any certainty owing to insufficient evidence.[4]

Scarcely anything is known of the general social structure of these communities. The majority of the population would be

---

[1] §IV, 4, no. 20. On this episode see §IV, 7, 384 f.
[2] §V, 4.   [3] A, 33, 223 ff.   [4] §V, 2, 18.

engaged directly in the tilling of the land, but there was apparently a well-defined class of artisans,[1] and travelling merchants are also mentioned;[2] it is impossible to estimate the proportion of the population engaged in these pursuits. Slavery is attested in the later centuries of the Hittite empire; but in the law code, which reflects conditions obtaining under the Old Kingdom, the position of the slave (or servant) resembles rather that of the Babylonian *muškēnum*, for he apparently pays and receives compensation for injury, may own land and other property, and is thus a legal 'person', with rights and duties of his own. This is not slavery in the usual sense of the term.[3]

Since kings and palaces had once existed in many Anatolian cities, there is no reason to suppose that the eventual supremacy of Kushshar and Khattusha was the result of special conditions in those two places. Hence the apparent absence of any authority higher than the council of Elders in other cities during the Hittite period is presumably the result of the Hittite conquest. For at Khattusha there was a sharp cleavage between the government and the governed, and the 'Elders' together with the common people belong to the latter. This is clear from the words of King Khattushilish addressing his son Murshilish: 'The Elders of Khatti shall not speak to you, neither shall a man of. . . nor of Khemmuwa nor of Tamalkiya, nor a man of. . .nor indeed any of the people of the country speak to you.' This probably implies merely that the king was always to be approached through his ministers. But this speech was delivered to an assembly specially convened to take cognizance of the king's decision in the matter of the royal succession; the assembly consisted of the 'fighting men of the whole body (of citizens) and the dignitaries', that is, all those concerned in affairs of state, and it is evident that the 'elders and the people of the country' were not among them.[4] We may contrast the institutions of the ancient Sumerians, as when Gilgamesh consulted the assembly of townspeople and the elders of the city of Uruk on a question of peace or war.[5] Clearly the Hittite state was the creation of an exclusive aristocracy, but there is no textual support for the view that this class division had a racial basis and that the ruling caste is to be identified with the Indo-European element in the nation.

Within the aristocracy there were certain distinctions of class and function. The kinsmen of the king apparently formed a

---

[1] G, 7, 104; G, 8, 70; §v, 1, 97.
[2] §v, 1, 16 and 50, Laws 5 and III (cf. *ibid.* 91); G, 7, 120.
[3] A, 35; A. Goetze in G, 9, 28–9.   [4] §v, 2, 19–21.   [5] A, 30, 159 ff.

privileged group, known as the 'great family', but it is not clear
in what their privileges consisted. They frequently, if not always,
hold the chief offices of state, such as Chief of the *meśedi* (a kind
of body-guard), Chief Wine Pourer, Chief of the Palace Servants,
Chief of the Golden Grooms, etc., and the holding of one or other
of these appointments seems often to have carried with it a high
military command. It is doubtless these 'heads of departments'
who are referred to, as a body, under the titles *kabtuti* 'dignitaries',
rabuti 'great ones, noblemen', and *ḫantezziyaś* 'men of the first
rank'.[1] Each department had its own personnel under the command of its respective officer, and it is probably they who are
alluded to collectively as the 'fighting men and servants of the
king'.[2] Thus if the titles of the functionaries are any guide, the
historical structure of Hittite society would seem to have developed
out of what was originally nothing but the staff of the king's palace.

What was the position of the king in this society? It has been
maintained that the assembly convened by Khattushilish and
Telepinush was a constitutional body possessing rights which
limited the power of the king, hence by implication that the
monarchy was originally elective (as we know it to have been
among the Anglo-Saxons and other Indo-European peoples),
and that during the period we are considering we may detect a
constitutional struggle between the nobles with their ancient
rights and the king who was endeavouring to establish the principle of hereditary succession.[3] However, the first part of this
theory can hardly be maintained. Whether or not the citizens had
ever claimed certain rights, it is clear from the great speech of
Khattushilish that the king did not recognize them. In the matter
of the succession the king's will is made known to his citizens and
they are ordered to comply. But it is significant that the earliest
recorded event in the history of this kingdom is the nomination
by the noblemen of a rival king in opposition to Labarnash, who
had been officially designated as heir by his father and predecessor. The king relates this incident as an offence, not as an assertion
of ancient rights; yet it shows the great power possessed by the
nobles in the early Hittite state. The danger of a conflict of will
between the nobility and the king is implicit in the constant insistence by the king on 'unity' in the realm, in the inculcation of
obedience by means of admonitory examples which is such a
typical feature of the texts of this period, even in the very fact that
a public act of designation of the heir to the throne was felt to be

[1] §IV, 13, 153 f.; § V, 5.   [2] §IV, 13, 4 f., line 22.
[3] G, 7, 86; A. Goetze in G, 9, 25 ff. Cf. §IV, 13, 209; §V, 2, 19.

necessary at all. The edict of Telepinush finally established a legal basis for the succession, but only after a century of blood-shed had taught the nobles by bitter experience the consequences of a lack of civic discipline.

Though we thus accept the existence of a political struggle between the nobles and the king during the Old Kingdom, it is now clear that the evidence on which this view rests is not neces-sarily connected with the term *pankuš*, which, though primarily an adjective meaning 'entire', is used in the edict of Telepinush as if it were the name of the popular assembly and has been ren-dered above as 'whole body of citizens'. In this assembly the emphasis is on the rank and file, the 'fighting men and servants of the king', indeed it seems probable that they and they only constitute the *pankuš*, and that the 'dignitaries', who appear among the audience in the address of Khattushilish but not in the edict of Telepinush, were strictly speaking not included in that body. The assemblies convened by these two kings play a purely passive role as the audience before which they made known their will in important affairs of state.

But at the same time it seems clear from the proclamation of Telepinush that in the judicial sphere the *pankuš* possessed a posi-tive function in the state, namely as a court of law for the punish-ment of malefactors. It is somewhat difficult owing to our lack of knowledge to disentangle the reforms instituted by Telepinush from the system which he was reforming. For the latter the most useful passage is that in which Telepinush describes how three minor officials, who had carried out the murder of two former kings at the instigation of certain high-ranking dignitaries, came up before the *pankuš* and were condemned to death, and how as soon as the king heard of it he ordered their reprieve and the con-version of their sentence into one of degradation and banishment. In the sequel Telepinush twice reminds his audience of this case as an illustration of his purpose, which was to ensure that the instigator of a crime, however high his rank, should suffer punish-ment in his own person and should not in future expect to escape scot-free by employing a 'man of straw' to commit the deed. He accordingly orders the *pankuš* to execute stern judgement not only on the dignitaries (who are actually their own officers in a functional capacity) but also on the king himself and the royal princes if the occasion should arise. To what extent this was an innovation it is difficult to say, but it is at least certain that Telepinush did not create, though he may have extended, the judicial functions of the *pankuš*.

The undeniably Indo-European character of early Hittite institutions such as the *pankuš*, which are no longer found in the later Empire, suggests that the Indo-European aristocracy had not yet merged, as it did later, with the native Khattian population. This inference may, however, be only partially true; for in other respects this aristocracy must even at this early stage have totally assimilated the customs and beliefs of their subjects. Their royal names—Labarnash, Tudkhaliash, Khattushilish— are purely Khattian. So too is their religion. Khattushilish the 'man of Kushshar', brings booty to the temple of the 'Sun-goddess of Arinna' exactly as do the emperors of the fourteenth century. Anitta acknowledges allegiance to the 'Weather-god of Heaven' and Khalmashuitta. These are Khattian deities. It has indeed been suggested that the Weather-god of Heaven, whose name (concealed behind an ideogram) ends in -*unna*, was the Indo-European Zeus, who had been married to the local matri-arch;[1] but until sound philological support can be adduced for this theory it remains a mere hypothesis. The one deity whose name is genuinely Hittite, the god Shiushmish (literally 'their god'), is of secondary importance; he appears as the local god of the conquered city of Nesha, the very home of the *našili* language, and it is only after his conquest of Nesha that Anitta acknow-ledges allegiance to him.[2] The Khattian deities are in a full sense the national patrons of the Hittite rulers; there is no suggestion that in paying respect to them they are placating the local popula-tion. In the political sphere, moreover, the prominent position accorded to the queen has a strongly Anatolian appearance.[3] If this was an Indo-European aristocracy, such a thoroughgoing adoption of native customs implies a considerable lapse of time and does not favour the view that at the beginning of the Hittite Old Kingdom, or even at the time of Anitta, they were recent arrivals in the country. Whether, conversely, the native popula-tion had already adopted the Hittite language is difficult to say. The tablets in which Khattian passages are furnished with trans-lations into Hittite appear to be all comparatively late. On the other hand, since the texts contain no ethnic designation for the subject population, such as, for instance, the term *Kaška* of later centuries,[4] we may be justified in assuming that they in their turn had become, or were fast becoming, linguistically assimilated to their rulers and were therefore no longer felt by them to be racially distinct.

[1] §v, 3, 179 f.
[2] §ii, 13, 343 n. 69.
[3] G, 7, 92; §v, 3, 181.
[4] G, 7, 178 f.; A, 50, 14–15 and 88.

CHAPTER VII

PERSIA *c.* 1800–1550 B.C.

I. THE DYNASTY OF THE 'GRAND REGENT' RULERS IN ELAM

To posterity the history of Persia at the time when the First Dynasty of Babylon held sway in Mesopotamia seems to narrow itself down to the history of Elam, and indeed almost down to the history of Susiana, the Elamite plain which bordered on Mesopotamia. Whatever took place in the mountainous parts of the country at this time remains shrouded in impenetrable obscurity. From the whole of Persia not a single archaeological monument has come down to us for this period, not even from Susiana. From only one Elamite ruler during the Early Babylonian period has a record in the Elamite language survived. Apart from this our sources from the country itself (leaving aside certain indications in Elamite inscriptions of the later, 'classical' period of the thirteenth to the twelfth centuries) consist of 837 clay tablets, written in Akkadian and in many cases damaged. Of these, somewhat more than half are legal documents, the remainder commercial texts; nearly all come from Susa, only a few from Mālamīr (possibly the ancient Khukhnur).

In view of this state of affairs with regard to the sources, the main task of the next section in this chapter must be to trace a picture of the legal system in ancient Elam. However, the records in question also provide important information about its political history, in so far as the Elamites often took oath by invoking the reigning princes. By careful assessment of all the documents, not only is it possible to sketch an outline of the history of the 'Grand Regents' (*sukkal-maḥ*), but light can be thrown on the internal structure of the Elamite state. Before passing on to the history of the rulers, it seems useful to make clear what this structure was, a matter already touched upon more than once by anticipation.[1]

As far back into the past as the historian's gaze can penetrate the constitution of Elam appears to have been federal.[2] Only as a federation was it possible for an empire to hold together which

---

[1] *C.A.H.* I³, pt. 2, ch. XXIII.   [2] G, 3, 38.

was made up of utterly different components, namely the plain of Susiana on the one hand, and the mountain ranges and high valleys of Anshan—the modern Bakhtyari district—on the other. However, it was not only in the interest of the ruler, but also of the people of Elam to live in an empire uniting the fruitful agricultural plains of the lowlands with the mountainous regions of the north and east, which were rich in timber, stone and metal. It was precisely in this union that Elam had the advantage over Mesopotamia.

From earliest times we find at the head of the Elamite confederation an overlord ruling over a body of vassal princes. With him—and this is the peculiar feature of Elam—ruled, as viceroy and heir presumptive, the brother next in age to the overlord. Thus the Elamite constitution was based on a fratriarchy; the successor to the throne was not the ruler's son, but his brother. Only in the Middle Elamite period was this system altered in favour of succession by the son.

The overlord of Elam bore different titles at different times. During the Old Babylonian period, now under consideration, his title was, as a rule, *sukkal-maḫ* in Sumerian, or 'Grand Regent'. The grand regent's town of residence was the federal capital Susa. The viceroy, on the other hand, who bore the title of 'Regent (*sukkal*) of Elam and Simashki', did not live in Susa like his elder brother, but probably in the town which was the ancestral seat of the dynasty at that time. During the period of the *sukkal* this was presumably Simashki (possibly Khurramābād in modern Luristān). In this respect the grand regents appear as a continuation of the Dynasty of Simashki.[1] The Elamite ruling house before that, on the other hand, had its ancestral seat in Awan (possibly Shustar).

The third important factor in the structure of the Elamite state was the 'Regent' (*sukkal* in Sumerian) or 'King' (*šarrum* in Akkadian) of Susa.[2] By Susa, in this title, is meant not the town itself, but the province of the same name. The basic principle was that the prince of Susiana should be the overlord's eldest son. Father, father's brother and son thus formed the ruling triumvirate in Old Elam.[3] G. G. Cameron was the first to deduce from the ancient Elamite law of inheritance the division of power between these three which follows.[4]

---

[1] See *C.A.H.* I³, pt. 2, ch. XXIII, sect. II.

[2] To avoid confusion, the local ruler, although bearing the title *sukkal* 'Regent', will hereafter be called the 'Prince' of Susa.

[3] §I, 5, 2. [4] G, I, 71 f.

Father and son, as overlord and prince of Susa, both lived in the federal capital. A partnership of this sort in the same town might well have led to continual tension, both human and political; but no sign of this can be detected in Elam. The overlord seems to have allowed his son (or, in the event of his not having one, his nephew) a high degree of freedom of action within the borders of Susiana. Thus, for example, the overlord's measures relating to Susiana had to be specially ratified by the prince of Susa.[1] Moreover, inscriptions from a later period show that in building operations in the federal capital, father and son worked harmoniously together. From the days of the Dynasty of Simashki, the father Indattu-In-Shushinak and his son Tan-Rukhuratir provide an example of praiseworthy co-operation of this kind. We shall encounter proof of a similar state of affairs for the period of the *sukkal*. For all their aridity our legal sources nevertheless allow the fact to emerge that in Elam family ties were extremely strong— not only in the ruling house, but also among the people.

On the death of the overlord, by law, the viceroy succeeded him. Even in the legal system of the Elamite people there are traces of a right of inheritance of this sort for brothers during the period of the grand regents, although by then it already appears to have been superseded by inheritance of the sons.[2] It was not the existing prince of Susa, therefore, in his capacity as son of the dead overlord, who became viceroy, but the brother nearest in age to the former viceroy. So the prince of Susa stayed in office under his two uncles.[3] In the period between 1850 and 1550 it happened no less than five times that a prince of Susa held office under two grand regents. This again is a demonstration of the strength of family ties in the ruling house of Elam. For on the death of an overlord his sons must have felt an urge to enter into their father's inheritance. Yet from the sources relating to Ancient Elam there nowhere emerges a shadow of a revolt on the part of the sons against the ancestral law of succession by the father's brothers.

The former viceroy, now become overlord, forbore to drive his nephew out of Susiana and put his own son in his place as prince of Susa. It is true that in three cases a grand regent reigned in conjunction with two princes of Susa, one after the other, and in one case even with three; the reason for this is not to be sought in family quarrels, but in the high rate of mortality in the ruling family.

[1] *Mém. D.P.* 23, no. 282, 9 f.
[2] See below, pp. 282 f.   [3] §1, 16, 33.

It was just this high mortality-rate which manifestly hampered the free working of the rule of succession in the majority of cases. For instance, it never happened that three brothers were overlords one after the other. Two brothers were the most there ever were, and often enough a cousin had to step into the place of a missing brother. If the generation to which the brothers and their cousins belonged was exhausted, then—and only then—the existing prince of Susa was promoted viceroy, and only then could the ruling overlord name a son of his own to be prince of Susa. If he had no sons then he chose a nephew, unless he preferred to delay acting, in which case he reigned for the time being in Susa alone. It must however be emphasized that the clarity with which the rule of succession can be inferred from the sources is matched by the rarity of its working out perfectly in practice. Only three times in three centuries occurred the theoretical situation[1]—upon the overlord's death his brother the viceroy inherited the throne, while the prince of Susa, in the absence of other uncles, was promoted to viceroy, and the new overlord's eldest son became prince of Susa.

The high rate of mortality in the ruling house was presumably the consequence of incest. It resulted from two further special features of the rule of succession in the royal houses of Ancient Elam: levirate and the marriage of brothers and sisters.[2] It seems that, as a rule, on the overlord's death the viceroy brother who succeeded him married his widow. She again was customarily the sister of both of them.

Until now marriage of brothers and sisters has been deduced only from the sources indirectly; but there is direct evidence of it in a document from the Late Elamite period. In about 710 B.C. the prince Khanni at Mālamīr referred to the princess Khukhin as his 'beloved wife-sister'.[3] As already mentioned there were continually breaks in the line of succession as a result of incest of this sort, so that not infrequently the son succeeded to the father simply because on the grand regent's death none of his brothers or sisters was still living. From as early as the third generation of the Eparti family onwards there would be in one generation of rulers two brothers or cousins, of whom one generally ruled for a longer time, the other for a correspondingly shorter time. After them the next generation, that is the princes of Susa, the generation of sons and nephews, already came into play. In this way marriage between brothers and sisters, levirate, and the division

---

[1] G, 1, 72. [2] §1, 9, *passim*; §1, 10, 72 f.
[3] §1, 4, 112.

of power between three rulers, determined the structure of the ancient Elamite state. Nowhere can there ever have been anything like it.

In the second half of the nineteenth century B.C. the manifestly effete Dynasty of Simash was superseded by a new and vigorous ruling family. Its founder was named Eparti. The sources are significantly reticent about his origin. This inclines one to conclude that he was an upstart, who had not inherited power, but had won it by force, possibly as the successful general of the last of the kings of Simashki.[1] The scanty records have little to report about Eparti. The most important item is his title: 'King of Anshan and of Susa'.[2] This is new and sounds like a flourish of national trumpets. Geographically the title embraces the whole of Elam: the mountainous region of Anshan as well as the plain of Susiana.

Eparti's road to royal power some time after 1850 B.C. must have been long and difficult. For only records from the first two years of his reign as ruler of the united empire were found at Susa.[3] It would appear that he died only a few years after coming to the throne, presumably in about 1830. Eparti bore the title 'King', throughout, on all his tablets, never 'Grand Regent'; he was therefore nobody's vassal. But even more significantly, the only tablet surviving from his first year of rule[4] contains, in the Sumerian date-formula 'year in which Eparti became king', the 'god' sign in front of his name. This is the first and only time that an Eparti ruler was deified in a document,[5] a procedure familiar among the Sumerians and not infrequent among the Akkadians. The inconspicuous 'god' sign on an inconspicuous tablet, serving as a receipt for the delivery of sacrificial animals from the royal flocks of sheep in Susa, make us suppose, thousands of years later, that Eparti's usurpation of power in the federal capital must have been a quite exceptional occurrence. This is borne out by the survival in Babylonia of an omen referring to him.[6] However, the deification of Eparti was straightway abandoned: the kings of Elam certainly felt themselves to be the instruments of the gods, but not their equals.

In conformity with the established rule Eparti installed his son

---

[1] §1, 10, 51.   [2] §1, 17, 1.

[3] *Mém. D.P.* 23, nos. 291, 292, 295–302, 305.

[4] *Ibid.* no. 292, 6 f.

[5] In the proper name Tan-(d)Temti-agun (*Mém. D.P.* 10, no. 104, rev. 10) the 'god' sign refers solely to Temti, the divine element in the name.

[6] §1, 23, 239.

Shilkhakha as prince in Susa. This is apparent from a cylinder-seal which Shilkhakha's chancellor Kuktanra dedicated to his two masters.[1] At all events Shilkhakha, who also ruled as over-lord probably for quite a long time, so completely eclipsed the fame of his father in the memory of later generations that he—and not Eparti—went down to history as founder of the dynasty. Even after more than 500 years an Elamite king included Shilkhakha in his inscription as a powerful invocation for warding off spells.[2]

A third figure stands out at the beginning of the dynasty of Eparti kings: his daughter. We do not know her name, but as 'Shilkhakha's sister' she attained the status of an ancestral mother to the dynasty. Of the later Eparti kings only those were con-sidered truly entitled to the throne who were descended from Shilkhakha's sister, who also appears in the sources as 'gracious mother' (*amma ḥaštuk*). It is clear that there was in ancient Elam, embedded in the fratriarchal succession to the throne, a legiti-mating right in the female line.

As Eparti's successor Shilkhakha named himself 'Grand Regent, King-Father of Anshan and Susa'.[3] Pompous though this sounds, here for the first time in Elam appears the title 'Grand Regent' (*sukkal-maḥ* in Sumerian), which nevertheless gives a suggestion of dependence on Babylonia. In those days Apil-Sin was probably ruling as king in Babylon. Clearly Shilkhakha had not been able, in the long run, to maintain the national independence which his father had wrested from Sabium of Babylon. At all events, after Shilkhakha the proud title 'King of Anshan and Susa' disappears from the records of the rulers of Elam. The title was assumed once again by the national regene-rators of the 'classical' period; from Untash-Khumban[4] (*c.* 1250 B.C.) onwards it became definitely the Elamite royal title.

On his succession to the throne about 1830 B.C. Shilkhakha installed his 'sister's son' Attakhushu as prince of Susa, doubtless because he had no son of his own. The sources do not say who Attakhushu's father was: whether he was Shilkhakha's brother or someone else who had married the sister. The deciding factor in Attakhushu's nomination was that he was the son—presumably the eldest—of Shilkhakha's sister, the renowned 'gracious mother' herself.

Attakhushu at once gave a most vigorous display of industry

---

[1] §1, 14, 159 f.
[2] *Mém. D.P.* 11, 72. [3] *Mém. D.P.* 29, 7.
[4] Written Untash-(*d*)*GAL*; see *C.A.H.* II³, pt. 2, ch. xxix, sect. II.

in Susa. Like his grandfather Eparti and his uncle Shilkhakha he built a temple for the god of the town, In-Shushinak, whose 'beloved servant' he called himself.[1] He completed the temple to the moon-god which Eparti and Shilkhakha had started.[2] An Akkadian inscription states that as 'Shepherd of the people of Susa' he had, for the welfare of his life, founded a temple for the 'Great Mistress Nin-egal', who, we may suspect, conceals the Elamite goddess Pinikir.[3] The Elamite goddess of victory Narunde, as well as her Akkadian counterpart, the goddess Anunitum, was also honoured with a temple by Attakhushu.[4]

Besides these the sources record other buildings of a secular nature. Thus, on the far side of the river Attakhushu constructed a 'tower', that is doubtless a fortified palace.[5] He linked this bastion to the town of Susa by means of a bridge over the Ulai (Karkhah).[6] A final testimony to his multifarious administrative activities as prince of Susa is to be found in the 'Stele of Righteousness', which Attakhushu had set up in the market-place of the capital and which probably laid down an official tariff for basic commodities.[7] In the inscription on the stele the sun-god Nahhunte is called upon to help everyone to get a fair price. Attakhushu's example clearly served as a model, for in later documents mention is made, in connexion with transactions in cereals, of the 'Great Table', on which no doubt the prices were laid down.[8]

But when Shilkhakha died in about 1800 B.C., Attakhushu was no longer alive. For his younger brother Shirukdukh[9] succeeded to the throne, and he again named his younger brother, Shimut-wartash, as viceroy. Both of them (like Attakhushu) called themselves Shilkhakha's sister's sons. Evidently Shirukdukh I had no son, because at first, after succeeding to the throne, he ruled without a prince of Susa. In the end he found an astonishing way out of the difficulty: he named his own mother, Shilkhakha's famous sister, as ruler of Susa. It is the only occasion on which we hear of an Elamite princess ruling in an official capacity. Unofficially no doubt princesses ruled to an appreciable extent in association with their husbands; but for a 'gracious mother' in person to form part of the ruling triumvirate was unprecedented.

---

[1] §1, 6, 60; *Mém. D.P.* 4, 10.　　　[2] *Mém. D.P.* 28, 7.
[3] *Ibid.* 8.　　　[4] *Mém. D.P.* 5, 26; 28, 9.
[5] *Mém. D.P.* 10, nos. 75 and 76.　　　[6] *Mém. D.P.* 4, 10.
[7] See *Mém. D.P.* 28, p. 5.
[8] *Mém, D.P.* 22, no. 197: 5; no. 242: 18; §11, 9, 227 n. 3.
[9] §1, 19, 152.

Only after the death of the ancestral mother of the Eparti kings did Shirukdukh I appoint his nephew Siwe-palar-khuppak as prince of Susa.[1]

With the triumvirate Shirukdukh I, his brother Shimut-wartash and his nephew Siwe-palar-khuppak we are already within the period of the expansion of the First Dynasty under Hammurabi of Babylon (1792–1750). Certainly the second half of Shirukdukh's reign lay under the shadow of Hammurabi's increasing power; but the scanty sources make no more precise reference to this. Only one single tablet throws a shaft of light on Shirukdukh's foreign policy. It comes from the ancient Shusharra, near modern Rania in the Kurdish district of Iraq; it dates roughly from the period around 1790 B.C., and it states that Shirukdukh, king of Elam, had written to a certain Tabitu asking: 'Why does the land of Itabalkhim not send an emissary to me?' The Elamite army was standing ready to strike, and he, Shirukdukh, was directing his attention towards the ruler of Gutium (that is the land between modern Hamadān and Lake Urmia). He also had placed twelve thousand men under the command of a certain Nabili.[2]

This tablet, first discovered in 1957, the details of which cannot yet be placed within a wider context, makes two things clear: first that Shirukdukh I was still ruling as 'King' of Elam in about 1790, and was therefore independent of Babylonia; secondly, that he evidently pursued an aggressive foreign policy. This would fit in with certain statements in letters from Mari (on the Middle Euphrates) dating from the time of king Zimrilim (1782–59)—if they refer to Shirukdukh. In one such letter it says that an emissary of the 'Regent' (*sukkal*) of Elam to the prince of Qatna (near the modern Homs in Syria) had come to Mari on his way there.[3] It is clear, however, that the prince of Qatna had first sent an emissary to Susa, which gives some idea of the powerful position Shirukdukh occupied at that time. Yet the title 'King' is nowhere encountered in the Mari Letters: it is always, so far as Elam is concerned, the *sukkal*.

Other documents from Mari prove that a grand regent of Elam had allied himself with the king of Eshnunna (not far from Baghdad), and had gone himself to Eshnunna with his army;[4] this grand regent might again be Shirukdukh I. The allies had marched together into the district of the Idamaraz beduin, and a certain Khali-sumu[5] wrote at that time: 'none can save the country

[1] §1, 5, 3.   [2] §1, 11, 74 and 97.   [3] §1, 1, vi, no. 19.
[4] §1, 1, ii, no. 73.   [5] §1, 1, ii, no. 66.

of the Idamaraz'. The allied troops laid siege to the town of Razama.[1] Upon receiving a call for help from Zimrilim of Mari, Hammurabi sent a force to the relief of Razama, and the troops of Elam and Eshnunna had to withdraw.[2] Before this happened the grand regent had already returned to Susa, and he sent no more forces to Eshnunna in support of his allies. It is likely that Shirukdukh died about this time.

His successor (about 1770) was his younger brother Shimut-wartash, until then viceroy, of whom, as the only direct piece of evidence, there has survived an alabaster cylinder from the temple of the goddess Kiririsha at Liyan (now Bushire on the Persian Gulf).[3] Shimut-wartash named his nephew Siwe-palar-khuppak viceroy, and his nephew Kuduzulush, prince of Susa. But he reigned for only a short time, perhaps until 1768 B.C. It may be that it is with reference to Shimut-wartash that a tablet from Mari states that according to letters captured in a skirmish, the 'Sukkal of Susa, of Elam' had been killed.[4]

The grand regent was then succeeded by his nephew Siwe-palar-khuppak, the former viceroy, who at first retained his brother as prince of Susa, but afterwards, it appears, promoted him viceroy. To join these two 'sister's sons of Shirukdukh' as the new prince of Susa came a certain Shullim-kutur (known only from Mari), who was probably a nephew.[5]

In the first quarter of the eighteenth century the ever-shifting balance of power among a round dozen states in the Near East had moved more and more in Babylonia's favour.[6] Under pressure from this rising power Zimrilim of Mari also changed sides at this time,[7] and a coalition of extremely dissimilar partners was formed against Hammurabi. Siwe-palar-khuppak must have played an important part in its formation. The king of Eshnunna stood alongside Elam as an old ally. Newcomers to the alliance were a queen of Nawar, in the Irano-Kurdish mountain district of Gutium, who is said to have raised ten thousand men, and the king of Malgium (on the Tigris, south of the mouth of the Diyālā), as well as the king of the Subaraeans at Ashur.

But in the course of several great campaigns Hammurabi mastered all his opponents. He struck first (and for Elam it was an annihilating blow) in the year 1764, even before Zimrilim of Mari had joined the alliance. With justifiable pride Hammurabi

---

[1] §1, 1, vi, nos. 52, 54.   [2] §1, 12, 69 f; §1, 21, 55.

[3] *Mém. D.P.* 15, 91.   [4] §1, 1, vol. II, no. 121.

[5] §1, 2, 109.   [6] G, 12, 582.

[7] §1, 21, 56.

reports that he had 'inflicted a defeat on the army of Elam—which has invaded from the border near Warakhshe—as well as on the Subaraeans, Gutians, Eshnunna and Malgium, who had collected their forces'.[1] After this Elam withdrew from the political scene of Mesopotamia.

We find this defeat reflected in an inscription of Siwe-palar-khuppak, the only surviving Elamite document, incidentally, from the millennium 2250–1250. In it the grand regent calls himself quite modestly 'Governor of Elam'. The title of 'King' has disappeared; even the title 'Grand Regent' is avoided by Siwe-palar-khuppak. This Elamite clay tablet is also illuminating because locutions appear in it which are not attested again until six hundred years later—significantly, without any linguistic change. Again and again the historian is amazed by the Elamites' gift for doggedly holding on to things and for handing them down to later generations. For its value in relation to cultural history I reproduce the document below in so far as lacunae and linguistic difficulties make translation possible. It reads:[2]

'O God In-Shushinak, lord of the citadel [of Susa]! I am Siwe-palar-khuppak, enlarger of the empire, Governor of Elam, Shirukdukh's sister's son. For the welfare of my life, for the life of my gracious mother, of my older relatives and their children, I have....' In the lacuna presumably stood: 'founded a temple'. Then it goes on: 'O God In-Shushinak, great master! I, Siwe-palar-khuppak, have prayed as I sacrificed—hear my prayer! To obtain your favour I have dedicated the people of Anshan and Susa to you as a pledge so long as night and day endure....' After another unclear and partly mutilated section the document ends: 'The fire shall destroy the enemies, [their] allies shall hang from the stake! Burnt, flayed, fettered at my feet shall they lie!'

If this inscription was composed only after the humiliation of 1764, as we surmise, the title 'Enlarger of the Empire', which Siwe-palar-khuppak assumes, might appear strange. But it is conceivable that the grand regent tried to offset the reverse in Mesopotamia by making conquests in the mountainous region of Iran. This is borne out by a document of the twelfth century, which for all its obscurity makes it clear that by later generations in Elam Siwe-palar-khuppak was counted as one of the country's great men.[3]

He was succeeded, presumably in about 1745, by his brother

[1] G, 4, 181.   [2] Mém. D.P. 31, 162 ff.
[3] §1, 8, 28A: 23–4.

Kuduzulush I, who evidently likewise had no son, because he reigned at first without a prince of Susa. Shullim-kutur had doubtless died in the meantime. Later on, Kuduzulush I appointed Kutir-Nahhunte prince of Susa, probably one of his nephews.[1] This Kutir-Nahhunte, first of the name, himself became grand regent in about 1730 and at once appointed his brother Lila-ir-tash as viceroy, while he made his eldest son, Temti-agun, prince of Susa.

Kutir-Nahhunte I impressed himself not only on the minds of Elamite kings, but even on the minds of later Assyrian rulers. The power of Babylonia had evidently sunk so far under Hammurabi's successor Samsuiluna (1749–1712) that Kutir-Nahhunte could finally dare to launch a counterstroke. Perhaps he seized the favourable moment for this when Samsuiluna succeeded his father on the throne of Babylon. More than a thousand years later this terrifying onslaught of the Elamites is commemorated in a building-inscription of Ashurbanipal[2] who writes: 'Kutir-Nahhunte the Elamite, not fearing the oath by the great gods, and blindly trusting in his own might, had laid hands upon the sanctuaries of Akkad and brought Akkad to the ground.' At that time Kutir-Nahhunte had also carried off to Susa the statue of the Mesopotamian goddess of fertility and victory, Nanai. Of this the Assyrian king writes: 'Nanai, who for 1635 years had been angry' (here, it is true, Ashurbanipal's chroniclers were mistaken: at that time, about 640 B.C., something like 1080 years at the most had elapsed since Kutir-Nahhunte's attack) 'who had gone away and settled in Elam, a place not befitting her, entrusted me with the task of bringing her home.'[3] And so Ashurbanipal brought the statue back to Uruk.

In the eyes of Shilkhak-In-Shushinak (*c.* 1165–1151), on the other hand, Elam's victory over Babylon appeared bathed in radiant light. On an aragonite stele this most brilliant of Elamite kings proclaims that he wished to do honour to Kutir-Nahhunte and his [prince of Susa] Temti-agun,[4] because he had conquered thirty cities. Kutir-Nahhunte had seized the land of Akkad as 'owner and ruler' and had consigned the native ruler to oblivion. In so doing he had taught the Babylonians 'respect and fear of the Elamite people' once more. Since the inscription also expressly mentions Temti-agun, the prince of Susa—as was to be expected —must have accompanied his father on the campaigns against Mesopotamia. The remembrance of Kutir-Nahhunte I's great

[1] §1, 5, 4 f.   [2] §1, 20, II. Teil, 178 f.
[3] *Ibid.* 58 f.   [4] §1, 18, 73.

victory must also have been the reason for king Shutruk-Nah-hunte (c. 1200) giving his eldest son the name of his famous ancestor, and as conqueror of the Kassites this crown prince Kutir-Nahhunte (III) lived up to the hopes which had been placed in him.

This Shilkhak-In-Shushinak mentioned above, who was so historically minded, has also preserved for posterity a dedicatory inscription of Kutir-Nahhunte I found on the rebuilding of the upper town in Susa and set in place there after being restored. This Akkadian inscription says that Kutir-Nahhunte I and his son Temti-agun had venerated the god In-Shushinak's statue and for the welfare of their lives had founded a temple for the image, with paved processional walk.[1] Finally, from the time of Kutir-Nahhunte I we have an Akkadian tablet indicating that the prince of Susa Temti-agun (I) had erected a temple there to the goddess Ishme-karab.[2] This document is at the same time an eloquent testimony to the family feeling of the rulers of Ancient Elam, because Temti-agun built the temple expressly for the benefit of his father, the grand regent Kutir-Nahhunte I; his uncle Lila-ir-tash; himself; his younger brother Temti-khisha-khanesh, and for the benefit of his 'gracious mother' Welkisha.

When Kutir-Nahhunte died after a long and successful reign he was succeeded by his brother Lila-ir-tash, while his son Temti-agun remained prince of Susa. But Lila-ir-tash, who was already old, ruled only for quite a short space. Then finally, about 1698 B.C., Temti-agun I could himself mount the throne as grand regent. Having apparently no son of his own, he installed his sister's son Kuk-nashur as prince of Susa, while his own cousin Tan-Uli became viceroy.[3]

During his reign as grand regent, which did not last very much longer, Temti-agun founded a citadel and temple for In-Shushinak. It is Shilkhak-In-Shushinak again, full of piety, who passes on this information. Temti-agun I's building, the king records, had fallen into disrepair in his time (that is, in the twelfth century); 'he had cast his eye upon the bricks, had made a vow and had used them for the reconstruction'. Then Shilkhak-In-Shushinak added: 'The name and title of Temti-agun, which he had set up there, I did not remove, but rather set it up again after restoration and set up my own name also.'[4]

About the year 1685, perhaps even a little earlier, Temti-agun I was succeeded by his cousin Tan-Uli. After reigning at first

---

[1] §1, 18, 69.   [2] *Mém. D.P.* 5, p. x, note.
[3] §1, 5, 8.   [4] §1, 18, 70.

without a prince of Susa—Kuk-nashur I was evidently already dead—he put Temti-khalki, probably a nephew, on the throne of Susa. The ruling partners grand regent Tan-Uli and Temti-khalki prince of Susa are mentioned in numerous legal documents, from which it is to be inferred that they both enjoyed long and probably undisturbed reigns.

When Temti-khalki was eventually promoted viceroy, the grand regent Tan-Uli appointed another of his nephews, Kuk-nashur II, to be prince of Susa. Soon afterwards, however, probably about 1655, Tan-Uli must have died, and in conformity with the rule of succession Temti-khalki came to the throne. He kept his cousin Kuk-nashur II as prince of Susa. Although the titles 'Grand Regent, Regent of Elam and Simashki' and 'Grand Regent of Elam and Simashki' have been handed down to us with reference to Temti-khalki, in the same breath the inscriptions name his 'beloved brother Kurigugu', which implies that Kurigugu had been appointed viceroy.[1] Even though Temti-khalki cannot have had much longer to reign—he had been prince of Susa under his uncle Tan-Uli for many years—he nevertheless showed himself extremely active in constructional work upon In-Shushinak's temple in Susa, to which many brick-inscriptions bear witness.

About 1650 he had already been succeeded by his cousin, the former prince of Susa, Kuk-nashur II, from which it must be concluded that the viceroy Kurigugu had not survived his brother Temti-khalki. For a considerable time Kuk-nashur II exercised exclusive power over Elam, without viceroy and without princes of Susa. This is shown not only by several legal documents but also by his title 'Grand Regent of Elam, Governor of Simashki and Susa'.[2] But the document on which the title appropriate to a sole ruler appears is dated—and this is significant—by the year of the succession to the throne of Ammiṣaduqa in Babylon,[3] that is, c. 1646 B.C. The date-formula shows that Elam had long ago come under the suzerainty of Babylonia once again, and that Kutir-Nahhunte's triumph over Mesopotamia had therefore been only transitory.

Eventually Kuk-nashur II appointed his brother or cousin Kutir-Shilkhakha (I) as viceroy, and his nephew Kuduzulush (II) as prince of Susa. The latter died after a relatively short time, and was replaced by Shirukdukh (II), son of a sister of Kuk-nashur II.[4] The latter, like his cousin and predecessor Temti-khalki, extended

---

[1] *Mém. D.P.* 2, 77 and *Mém. D.P.* 6, 27.   [2] §1, 22, 3.
[3] See *C.A.H.* 1³, pt. 1, pp. 234 ff.   [4] §1, 5, 8.

the High Temple of the god In-Shushinak; he had the building constructed of burnt bricks 'for the welfare of his life'.[1]

Kuk-nashur II was succeeded about the year 1635 by his brother or cousin Kutir-Shilkhakha I. His nephew, Shirukdukh II, until then prince of Susa, probably became viceroy, and his place was taken by another nephew, Kuk-nashur III. But the latter does not seem to have had a long life, for he was replaced at Susa by Temti-raptash, doubtless yet another nephew of the grand regent. Temti-raptash, by contrast, ruled under his uncle Kutir-Shilkhakha I for a considerable time, until in about 1625 or later be became grand regent himself.[2]

With Temti-raptash begins the eighth generation of the Eparti kings. Our most important sources, the legal records from Susa, now become increasingly sparse. They nevertheless make it possible to follow the dynasty down to its twelfth generation, that is, until approximately 1520 B.C.[3] Only two figures stand out from the obscurity which shrouds its close: Pala-ishshan and his nephew Kuk-kirwash, who belonged to the tenth and eleventh generations, as may be seen from the chronological table. Temti-raptash had reigned at first without a prince of Susa, but had finally appointed Kuduzulush III. How, in the next generation, about 1570, Pala-ishshan came to power can no longer be established. An inscription of Shutruk-Nahhunte in the Middle Elamite period mentions out of the whole Eparti line of kings only Siwe-palar-khuppak (of the fourth generation) and Pala-ishshan (presumably of the tenth). Both these grand regents, it seems, captured spoils in the mountainous regions of Eastern Iran and brought them back to their capital.[4] Obscure though the age of Pala-ishshan appears to us today, by the contemporary Elamite world and by later generations this grand regent was reckoned among the most important rulers of Elam.

A cylinder-seal belonging to his chancellor Ibni-...., son of a certain Khashtuk, has survived, on which, in a delightful sketch, Pala-ishshan is depicted sitting on his throne, while the chancellor stands respectfully in front of the grand regent.[5] Kuku-sanit, supposed to be a son of Pala-ishshan, died while still prince of Susa, and was succeeded by Kuk-kirwash, son of Lankuku, who was one of Pala-ishshan's brothers. Regarding this new pair we are informed by the year formula of a commercial agreement from

---

[1] *Mém. D.P.* 6, 28.   [2] §1, 5, 9.

[3] See below, p. 272. For the order of the *sukkal* from the ninth generation onward I have followed Professor G. G. Cameron.

[4] §1, 6, 54f.   [5] §1, 15, 36.

Susa that Pala-ishshan and Kuk-kirwash had 'restored justice and righteousness'.[1] It may be presumed that this was said with reference to, among other things, a general remission of taxes and debts.

Pala-ishshan's successor, about 1545, was in fact his nephew, the prince of Susa Kuk-kirwash. He is the last of the grand regents who is reported as being active in the constructional field. Not only is this activity expressly mentioned by Shilkhak-In-Shushinak in the twelfth century, but several Akkadian brick-inscriptions have been found in Susa in which Kuk-kirwash emphasizes that he has not repaired the old asphalt walls of the High Temple of In-Shushinak, but rather replaced them with new brick walls.[2] Kuk-kirwash's constructional activity seems to have taken place in the period immediately after his assumption of power, when— following known precedents—he at first ruled by himself, for on the bricks in question his titles run: 'Grand Regent, Regent of Elam, Simash and Susa'. Only later on did he select Temti-sanit and—on his death—Kuk-Nahhunte as prince of Susa, both of them probably nephews. It may be mentioned in passing that a seal impression of Kuk-kirwash's chancellor has also survived.[3]

The last of the grand regents, constituting the twelfth generation of their line, Kuk-Nahhunte and lastly Kutir-Nahhunte II, remain mere names to us.

Since the beginning of history the pendulum of supremacy had swung backwards and forwards continually between the hostile neighbours Mesopotamia and Elam, bringing now one power to the fore, now the other. During the Old Babylonian period, on the whole, Mesopotamia had kept the upper hand. This is made clear by the Akkadization of Susiana, as it is reflected in the almost exclusive use of Akkadian as the official language. Gradually, however, a new power had forced its way on to the scene of world affairs: the Kassites. When the Kassite king Agum II marched into Babylon about 1593 (after the departure of the Hittites), the renowned First Dynasty of Babylon came to an end, and with it ended Babylonian suzerainty over Elam. The great question is whether it was superseded there by a Kassite supremacy.

Certain tablets from Susa—which unfortunately cannot be dated—lead us to understand that Kassites were present in Elam. For names like Ani-kilandi in Khukhnur (Mālamīr) or Rushupi-

---

[1] *Mém. D.P.* 24, no. 348: 13–16.
[2] *Mém. D.P.* 2, 74.
[3] §1, 15, 35.

ash, Birgalzu, and [. . .]ur-bugash in Susa are Kassite.[1] More-over, even today the river name Kashgan commemorates the Kashshu (Kassites).[2] It is true that no document states explicitly that the Kassites had put an end to the rule of the Eparti kings. In about 1520 all sources simply give out.

The obscurity surrounding Elam clears again only with the conquest of Susa by the Kassite king Kurigalzu II (1345–24).[3] We do not know what was happening in Elam during the two preceding centuries. The end of the Eparti dynasty remains shrouded in the same obscurity as the exit of the Dynasty of Simashki before it. However, one cannot escape the impression that a 'Kassite darkness' had fallen over Elam, shrouding all forms of expression of the national life. Only the new Dynasty of Pakhir-ishshan about 1300 B.C. helped these to come through once more, ushering in the great 'classical' period of Elamite history.

II. LEGAL LIFE IN OLD ELAM

Since the sources for the history of Persia in the Old Babylonian period consist, as we have seen, above all of legal texts, our knowledge of the political development of Elam under the grand regents undoubtedly remains fragmentary; on the other hand, however, these very texts make it possible to give a relatively detailed picture of the Elamite legal system, especially with regard to Civil Law. For the round 450 documents in Akkadian from Susa and the twenty documents from Khukhnur (Mālamīr) deal, to all intents and purposes, only with transactions relating to the law of property. We learn about Elamite penal law, inci-dentally, from the sanctions with which those breaking agree-ments are threatened.

Outside the period of the *sukkal* rulers, only seven legal tablets in all (and these from the late period of Elam) are known.[4] The element of chance in the discoveries which have been made can hardly be held entirely to blame for this state of affairs. On the contrary, the records from the period of the grand regents make it appear probable that in those days, owing to the prevalence of Akkadian ideas in Susiana, Elamites had first started to commit legal processes to writing. The indigenous legal system of Elam had originally been purely oral,[5] and this system held its ground

---

[1] *Mém. D.P.* 22, no. 132: 2; no. 77, rev. 6; no. 115: 2; *Mém. D.P.* 28, no. 504: 13.

[2] V. Minorsky in *B.S.O.A.S.* 1945, 660.

[3] §1, 7, 216.

[4] *Mém. D.P.* 11, nos. 301–7.

[5] §11, 13, 252.

Gener-ation	Accession year (approxi-mate)	Grand Regent (*sukkal-maḫ*)	Viceroy (*sukkal* of Elam and Simashki)	Prince of Susa (*sukkal* of Susa)
1	1850	Eparti		
2	1830	Shilkhakha	Shirukdukh (?)	Attakhushu
3	1800	Shirukdukh I		Shilkhakha's sister
	"		Shimut-wartash	Siwe-palar-khuppak
	1772	Shimut-wartash	Siwe-palar-khuppak	Kuduzulush I
4	1770	Siwe-palar-khuppak		
	"		Kuduzulush I	Shullim-kutur
	1745	Kuduzulush I		
	"			Kutir-Nahhunte I
5	1730	Kutir-Nahhunte I	Lila-ir-tash	Temti-agun I
	1700	Lila-ir-tash		"
6	1698	Temti-agun I	Tan-Uli	Kuk-nashur I
	1685	Tan-Uli		
	"			Temti-khalki
	"		Temti-khalki	Kuk-nashur II
7	1655	Temti-khalki	Kurigugu (?)	"
	1650	Kuk-nashur II		
	"		Kutir-Shilkhakha I	Kuduzulush II
	"		"	Shirukdukh II
	1635	Kutir-Shilkhakha I	Shirukdukh II (?)	Kuk-nashur III
	"		"	Temti-raptash
8	1625	Temti-raptash		
	"			Kuduzulush III
9	1605	Kuduzulush III		
	1600	Tata	Atta-merra-khalki	Temti-agun II
	1580	Atta-merra-khalki		Temti-agun II
10	1570	Pala-ishshan	Lankuku	Kuku-sanit
	"		"	Kuk-kirwash
11	1545	Kuk-kirwash		
	"			Kuk-Nahhunte
	"		Kuk-Nahhunte	Tem-sanit
12	1520	Kuk-Nahhunte		Kuk-nashur IV
		Kutir-Nahhunte II		Kutir-Shilkhakha II

TABLE 2. *Chronology of the Eparti dynasty*

alongside the written one imported from Babylon. The mutual influencing and interpenetration of the two forms make for the special character of the Elamite legal system in ancient times.

A case report[1] from the declining days of the Eparti dynasty provides a graphic picture of this system.

[1] *Mém. D.P.* 23, nos. 321–2.

Two brothers are claiming the surrender of a piece of land from a certain Bēli, son of their deceased uncle by adoption. They appear before Atar the chancellor and the judge Khabil-kinu. But Bēli defends himself, saying 'the father of the two plaintiffs, Damqia, had adopted my father as his brother. The "legal path" in virtue of which adoption as a brother creates a brother-relationship, and adoption as a son creates a son-relationship, which "legal path" the god In-Shushinak and the goddess Ishme-karab laid down—this has been followed, and thus I inherited the estate which my father had obtained' (from Damqia who had adopted him).

The case seems to have created a considerable stir in the minds of people in Susa. For in addition to the chancellor and judge, the governor, the provost, as well as numerous inhabitants of the city took part in the judicial proceedings. An inventory was drawn up of what Damqia and a brother of his own kin had inherited from their father, and had shared between them, taking oath by the grand regent Tata and the prince of Susa Temti-agun II. 'Atar the chancellor and the judge brought the tablets relating to this division of the inheritance, and examined them along with numerous inhabitants of Susa, and they gave judgement in the case of the litigants.' Bēli was allowed to keep the particular estate which his father had obtained as adopted brother of Damqia; the claim of the two plaintiffs was therefore dismissed. The judgement is followed by a list of witnesses, twenty-three altogether, headed by Atkalshu the governor and by the provost In-Shushinak-kashid, ending with the god In-Shushinak, the goddess Ishme-karab and the clerk to the court. The document closes with an injunction to the two plaintiffs that they should return to the house of their parents in peace.

The clay tablet bears a large seal-impression representing a god wearing a horned crown, standing on a ceremonial stool and raising his arms in prayer. The accompanying note states that the holder of the seal had left his seat of office in the centre of Susa in order to ratify this sealed tablet. Anyone disputing the decision, be he plaintiff or defendant, would come under the sentence of the gods Khumban and In-Shushinak. 'Let the goddess Ishme-karab's sceptre, at the bidding of the gods In-Shushinak and [Nahhunte], strike upon the head anyone who destroys this document.'

Here, then, reference is made to so-called 'legal paths' of the gods In-Shushinak and Ishme-karab. In other tablets In-Shushinak alone is named as originator of such 'legal paths' or 'guide routes' (*kubussûm* in Akkadian). Other deities do not figure as law-givers. That in fact the *kubussûm* of the deity was taken to mean a law established by the priesthood is made clear by the expression used on several occasions: 'legal path which the Temple of In-Shushinak laid down.'[1]

Alongside the 'sacred' law of the temple, however, there was in Old Elam a 'secular law', likewise referred to as *kubussûm*. For in a number of documents the rulers in office at the time (the grand regent and his prince of Susa) appear as originators of 'legal paths' of this kind. Often it is simply a question of the *kubussûm* without any mention of its originator. The meaning of the word extends from 'universal legal norm', through 'law', to 'decree' by a ruler in individual cases. Depending on the matter in hand, the expression 'legal path' in our sources refers to adoption, division of inheritances, the purchasing of estates, the reaping of fields,[2] loans, payment of fines on failure to fulfil contracts, and guarantees for possession of a piece of land after sale.[3]

In the Elamites' estimation, then, certain legal norms were divinely established, stemming in particular from In-Shushinak, occasionally working in conjunction with his close associate Ishme-karab. But it was in no sense a matter of purely sacred law; as the fields of law enumerated above indicate, the *kubussûm* of the deity also concerned itself with completely secular matters.[4] All other statutes and customary laws were ascribed to the ruling diarchy of the time, as if the then grand regent together with his prince of Susa was their originator.[5] Naturally the Elamite rulers not only preserved existing laws, but also added new ones to those which had been handed down. This is attested both for the prince of Susa Attakhushu (*c.* 1810), and for the grand regent Pala-ishshan and his prince of Susa Kuk-kirwash (*c.* 1560). How far Elamite law had been codified, we cannot tell. But a fragmentary tablet discovered in Susa may relate to codified land law.[6]

It may be presumed that the 'legal paths' for which divine authorship is claimed belong to the most ancient body of laws, to which legal decisions handed down by rulers in the past, as well as the former customary law, were added. Customary law of the kind in question is laid down for the 'citizens of Susa', for instance, and even for particular professional groups, such as

---

[1] *Mém. D.P.* 22, no. 44: 30–1; also nos. 45, 50, 51, 53; see §11, 20, 6.
[2] Transactions characterized by the formula *esip-tabal*.
[3] Further details in §1, 10, 39 ff.   [4] §1, 10, 64.
[5] §1, 10, 66.   [6] *Mém. D.P.* 24, no. 395.

couriers.[1] But it is not possible to draw a dividing line between divine and secular law, nor would it be possible even to make out an opposition between the two established forms of law. On the contrary, everything points to the fact that for the Elamites all law, even secular law, was rooted in the numinous. To such a view of things the ruler-legislator appears completely united with the deity. This is illustrated by a late Elamite inscription, which says: 'The law which the God In-Shushinak and King Shutruk-Nahhunte (II) have graciously given....'[2] In Elam divine and secular law always form one whole.

Yet another author of 'legal paths' appears in our documents, however, who has not so far been noticed. In one tablet we read in fact of legal paths, 'which the Kingdom of Babylon,[3] as well as Tan-Uli the [Grand-] Regent and Kuk-nashur [II, as prince of Susa], laid down for runners and couriers'. In two further tablets[4] mention is made of the 'legal paths' which the *Kingdom* as well as Temti-khalki the [Grand-] regent and Kuk-nashur [II, as prince of Susa] laid down. It is highly probable that all three of the documents (from *c.* 1670–1650) refer to Babylonian law current in Susa, even though only one of them expressly links the word 'kingdom' with Babylon. From this it may be concluded that the Code of Hammurabi was also to some extent valid in Elam, if only as a supplement to the customary law of the land. So, for instance, it would appear in the case of the law of tillage by partners as if Hammurabi had even incorporated legal provisions from Susa in his Code in order that he might extend its validity into Elam.[5] The reference to 'legal paths of the Kingdom of Babel' at the same time confirms the suzerainty exercised by Babylonia over Susiana, which we had inferred during the period of the *sukkal*-rulers.

In Elamite law, however, it is not only the activity of In-Shushinak and Ishme-karab, respectively, as law-giver which belongs to the divine sphere, but also that manifestation of the numinous which the Elamites conveyed with the expression *kiten*. *Kiten* denotes that shielding power radiating from the deity, the magical protective charm, without which, it appears, human

---

[1] *Mém. D.P.* 23, no. 181; 12 f.; no. 206: 26 f.

[2] *Mém. D.P.* 5, 71 (lines 11 f.).

[3] *Mém. D.P.* 23, no. 206: 28: *zu-uk-ki-zu-uk-ki ba-bi-il*(KI). The Elamite expression *zunki-zunki* has the known root *zunk-*, 'to be king'; the abstract noun 'kingship' is formed by reduplication (cf. §1, 4, 113, n. 2, where *ḫu-ut-ḫu-ut* [from *ḫutt-*, 'to make'] = 'handiwork, building').

[4] *Ibid.* nos. 208 and 209.   [5] §11, 17, 134.

life is unthinkable. Thus we learn from an inscription of the
prince Khanni of Mālamīr, from about 710 B.C., that a ruler was
under the particular *kiten* of the god Khumban; he stresses too
that over his image he had spread 'the mighty protective charm
of the gods'.[1] All gods in fact are endowed with *kiten*, but in
legal matters the *kiten* of In-Shushinak plays the biggest part—at
all events in Susa itself; in Khukhnur (Mālamīr) its place was
taken by the *kiten* of Rukhuratir the local god there.[2] In numerous
legal texts from Susa anyone breaking an agreement is threatened
that he will forfeit the protective charm of In-Shushinak. At the
same time it is made clear that anyone losing the *kiten*, the magical
protection of the deity, will be 'outlawed'[3]—and not infrequently
the text adds laconically: 'he dies!' On one occasion too it says:
'He will be delivered up to the god In-Shushinak'—meaning that
he will be executed.

The threat of outlawry is frequently clothed in the expression:
'he is driven out of the realm where deity and ruler have power!'
This is most explicit in a document contemporary with Hammurabi, which indeed refers to two members of the Eparti
family already dead; even dead rulers therefore had a *numen* which
was still powerful as a spell. The text reads: '[He who breaks the
agreement] will truly be driven out of the realm in which Shilkhakha, Shirukdukh, Siwe-palar-khuppak [as the grand regent at the
time] and Kuduzulush [as prince of Susa] hold sway; the God
In-Shushinak, Susa's king, [will annihilate him!]'.[4] Frequently
Khumban and Nahhunte appear along with In-Shushinak as
punishing gods, as can be seen again from the seal impression on
our 'case report'.[5] In all these threats the indivisibility of divine
and profane legal conceptions makes itself evident.

But it is clear that the Elamite word *kiten* (it penetrated into
Akkadian as the loan-word *kidinnu*) not only had the abstract
value of 'magical protective charm of the deity', but also a
concrete value as a 'taboo emblem'.[6] For the sanction: 'he has
forfeited the protective charm of the god In-Shushinak' literally
translated reads: 'he has set his hand on the *kiten* of In-Shushinak',
and this could well be taken to mean that anyone breaking the
agreement was brought into contact with the god's taboo sign and
as a consequence of this was killed (if, at all events, this was still
necessary). In this context we must perhaps also consider the

---

[1] §I, 4, 110 f.   [2] *Mém. D.P.* 23, no. 273: 10.
[3] §I, 10, 43; *Mem. D.P.* 22, no. 14.   [4] *Mém. D.P.* 23, no. 242
[5] See above, p. 273; also *Mém. D.P.* 23, no. 282, and *Mém. D.P.* 24, no. 338.
[6] §II, 10, 43 f.

sanction:[1] 'he shall pass by the graven image of the god'. To which might well be added—'and this he does not survive'. In-Shushinak's emblem was probably an eagle with outstretched wings.[2]

Proceeding from the concrete meaning as taboo emblem, by extension, *kiten* also signified the area in which it was effective. For it is said in a contract that the parties concerned had reached an amicable agreement 'in Susa, under the *kiten* of the god In-Shushinak',[3] and clearly a particular locality is meant. But where should we look for these places? Where were the cases heard?

Our sources are extremely laconic upon this matter; the following case report is most relevant:[4] several plaintiffs alleged against the defendant that their father had not sold his house during his life time: 'your tablet is forged'. 'Many witnesses were present at the hearing', it continues, 'and fulfilled their legal functions by making the defendant take oath by the deity. Then [the defendant] swore in the temple of the goddess Ishtar: "O goddess Ishtar, you know it to be true that I have not forged any tablet, but that this deed was left me by my father." Thus did Iqishuni swear, and the house was declared his. In the presence of thirty-four witnesses did Iqishuni swear in the temple of Ishtar.'

By the Akkadian Ishtar may have been meant the Elamite goddess Narundi, in whose temple the defendant made his oath. But this is not to say that the judicial proceedings had also taken place there. Perhaps the defendant had to go into the goddess's temple only in order to take oath, because she was in fact 'his' deity. For in another case[5] it is explicitly stated that the defendants took oath 'by their god'; and as the scene of the oath-taking the document names the byre where cattle were fattened.

We get more help from two other tablets which expressly name the 'garden' of the sun-god Nahhunte as the scene of the judicial proceedings.[6] We have already made acquaintance with Nahhunte[7] as god of justice, a position he occupied throughout Elam. His special domain, however, was trade; he fixed the rate of interest, standardized weights and did business in commercial partnership with human businessmen as a large-scale capitalist. It is very probable then that in Old Elam civil cases were heard in a courtyard of Nahhunte's temple planted with trees. This

[1] *Mém. D.P.* 22, no. 130, 17 f.
[2] See F. Thureau-Dangin in *R.A.* 24 (1927), 200.
[3] *Mém. D.P.* 22, no. 160; 36 f.   [4] *Mém. D.P.* 24, no. 393.
[5] *Mém. D.P.* 28, no. 399.
[6] *Mém. D.P.* 23, no. 320: 13, and no. 325: 5.
[7] See *C.A.H.* 1³, pt. 2, pp. 667 f.

temple grove was situated in the sacred 'Upper City' on the artificially constructed hill in the north-west corner of Susa, not far from the river Karkhah. One tablet indeed mentions that the plaintiff had made the woman he was prosecuting in the case 'come up' to the court; after her acquittal she was permitted to go down from it again.[1]

Since reference is very frequently made to the fact that the proceedings had taken place 'in the *kiten* of In-Shushinak' it may be surmised that the emblem or taboo sign of the god had been brought into the temple grove of Nahhunte, or else was permanently erected there. The possibility is not ruled out that a statue of the ruler on the throne at that time stood in the courtyard of the sun-god's temple, because it is stated on one occasion that the person breaking the agreement shall 'go past the graven image of the god and of the king' (in order to be executed).[2] One may remark in passing on the trouble it must have been to look after a grove of this kind, water for the purpose having to be brought up daily from the river. Yet it is stated on one occasion that in the protected precinct of the temple of Shimut alone ten trees had been felled,[3] which gives some idea of the size of the sacred groves.

In the case we quoted at the beginning, it was not the judge, Khabil-kinu, who had precedence in court, but Atar the chancellor (*teppir* in Elamite). Presumably Atar was chancellor to the then prince of Susa, Temti-agun II; he is hardly likely to have been chancellor to the grand regent Atta-merra-khalki, brother and successor to Tata. For in a document from Khukhnur (Mālamīr) again, a *teppir* is named as the person presiding over the court;[4] in this case it can only have been the chancellor to the prince of Khukhnur. In Old Elam, then, the chancellors to the individual rulers of the various parts of the empire presided in civil cases, and the judges merely assisted them.[5] However, since there are isolated case reports in which only judges appear, and no chancellor,[6] it may be assumed that the chancellor functioned only as a superior court—perhaps in appeal cases. Wherever possible such appeal proceedings (*ḫaslut* in Elamite) took place at specially appointed times. The 21st of Lanlupe (middle of October) and the month of Kizir-zun-kalik (December?) appear in the sources as specially appointed times of this sort.[7]

[1] *Mém. D.P.* 22, no. 160.   [2] *Ibid.* no. 131: 17 and 28.
[3] *Mém. D.P.* 24, no. 390.   [4] *Mém. D.P.* 23, no. 327, rev. 3.
[5] Cf. *Mém. D.P.* 22, no. 161; *Mém. D.P.* 23, nos. 320 and 323.
[6] E.g. *Mém. D.P.* 23, no. 325.
[7] *Mem. D.P.* 22, no. 165: 23–4; *Mém. D.P.* 23, no. 318: 12.

It is clear, however, that lawsuits could be taken direct to the rulers of the various parts of the empire, over the heads of judge and chancellor. In one document,[1] indeed, it says: '[Such and such men] have appealed to Temti-raptash about the garment they had given me as security, and he has sent the governor and imprisoned me within the [. . .] gate.'[2] The ruler in question was no doubt Temti-raptash, prince of Susa under the grand regent Kutir-Shilkhakha I (therefore about 1630 B.C.).

It remains a significant fact that civil cases in Elam were entrusted to secular judges only; priests appeared in court mainly as witnesses.[3] In the case quoted above it was exceptional for the governor and provost, that is the police authorities of Susa, to share with the chancellor and judge in the session held within the temple-grove of the sun-god. It was likewise unusual for these two officers to head the list of witnesses, for according to all Elamite legal protocol, the gods Nahhunte and In-Shushinak (usually in that order) appeared first among the whole group of witnesses. This fact fits in with the theory that the legal proceedings took place in front of the taboo-emblem of In-Shushinak in the forecourt of the temple of Nahhunte. The two gods were counted as real witnesses, for in the total at the end of the list of witnesses, they were always included. In Khukhnur (Mālamīr) the local Rukhuratir appeared, logically, in the place of the witness In-Shushinak.[4]

Witnesses played a dominant part in Elamite law. Even their number, in most cases, was considerable, as many as forty-two.[5] Only one tablet names Nahhunte and In-Shushinak as sole witnesses;[6] apart from this two human witnesses (in addition) seem to have been the lowest number required; most tablets name between five and twenty. It was in fact a business essential in Elam, not only that a written contract should be drawn up, but that at the same time identical verbal declarations be made before witnesses, and expressly noted at the end of the document.[7] It seems likely that, originally, such oral declarations were made by both parties; the legal practice was therefore decidedly dualistic. This was superseded by unilateral declaration only under Babylonian influence. The same witness who took part in the verbal settlement of a business transaction often had to vouch for the authenticity of a document in court.[8]

[1] *Mem. D.P.* 23, no. 315.   [2] §II, 9, 230.
[3] *Mém. D.P.* 22, nos. 10, 27.
[4] *Ibid.* nos. 52, 71, 72, 73, 76, 81, etc.   [5] *Ibid.* no. 14.
[6] *Ibid.* no. 39.   [7] §II, 13, 248.   [8] §II, 13, 249 f.

In contrast with the commercial documents juridical texts are practically never dated. This too reflects the prevailing influence of the oral business-practice of Elam. People accustomed to verbal legal transactions naturally do not attach so much importance to the precise dating of agreements as under a legal system of a characteristically written stamp. So it was logical too that witnesses never thought of ratifying the tablets with a seal-impression or nail-mark, as was the rule in Mesopotamia.[1] The verbal declaration sworn before witnesses was conclusive in itself. In consequence practically all documents contain sworn statements. The oath before witnesses appears to be the mainstay of all Elamite legal thinking.

The attempt has been made to simplify the confusing picture of forms of oath encountered in Susa by assigning to an earlier date the oath sworn by the ruler—as the original form—which would then give way gradually to the oath sworn by the deity.[2] But now that the grand regents have been arranged in chronological order with a fair degree of certainty, this assumption can no longer be made. During the whole of the Old Babylonian period oath was taken in Susa *either* by the ruler (the grand regent and the prince of Susa), *or* by the deity. Two exceptions, in which oath was taken by the deity *and* by the two rulers, prove the rule.[3]

However, a certain pattern can be seen in the forms of oath in Susa, in so far as the oath made in a lawsuit, which is by its nature declaratory, was made only by the deity. All others, and therefore those which were mainly promissory, could apparently be sworn either by the deity or by the two rulers at choice. Preference was given to the oath by the deity, possibly, in leasehold and harvesting (*esip-tabal*) agreements, oath by the rulers was preferred in loan and partition agreements; in cases relating to purchase and exchange both kinds of oath occur with roughly the same frequency.[4] Another principle underlying the system is that in documents which refer to 'legal paths' of the rulers, the oath is made only by them, while in documents which cite In-Shushinak as author of the law oath is taken only by him and Ishme-karab,[5] rarely by In-Shushinak alone. Exceptions to this are: a tablet which records an oath sworn by In-Shushinak and the Sumerian god of the underworld Nergal,[6] and a second one which mentions that oath was taken by In-Shushinak, Nahhunte, the Sumerian goddess Nin-shubur and yet another (obscure) deity.[7]

[1] §II, 13, 252.
[2] §I, 10, 55.
[3] *Mém. D.P.* 22, nos. 8 and 11.
[4] §I, 10, 55.
[5] §I, 10, 46 f. [6] *Mém. D.P.* 23, no. 334.
[7] *Ibid.* no. 331.

In Khukhnur (Mālamīr) we observed a variant treatment of
the oath in that it was taken either by ruler and deity or by the
ruler alone; oath by the deity alone, however, did not occur. But
we do not know to which period our texts belong, since the local
rulers named in them (Salla and Temtiakhar) are not attested
elsewhere. The oath formula in Khukhnur ran: 'May [the god]
In-Shushinak live for ever, may [the prince] Salla be saved!'[1]
In Susa the oath formula referring to In-Shushinak read the same
as in Khukhnur, but the astonishing thing is that there (in Susa)
the oath by the ruler took the same form as that by the deity. The
form of oath is in fact attested as: 'May Kuk-nashur [II the
grand regent] live for ever!'[2] In places in the Susa documents
where we encounter the ancient Sumerian note 'he took oath by
the life of the king', it refers to the grand regent reigning at the
time, not to the king of Babylon.[3]

It is possible that in the grove of the temple of Nahhunte there
was a special little hill on which oath was taken; in one document,
indeed, it says that the persons involved had taken oath on the so-
called 'Hill of my God'.[4] It is not easy to discern what lay behind
the statement that on swearing the persons concerned 'had been
touched by the head of the god'.[5] This may be connected in some
way with the taboo-emblem of the god In-Shushinak.

The documents from Susa and Khukhnur (Mālamīr) regularly
contain a penalty-clause, variously worded, which affords us a
glimpse of Elamite penal law. Truly Elamite—and therefore
un-Babylonian—are the threats of severe mutilation in the
punishments attached to the agreements, and the evil threatened
in curses upon anyone breaking the agreement.[6] The perjurer has
'hand and tongue cut off', those organs, that is, which are needed
to conclude an agreement: the tongue to testify, the hand to
touch the taboo-emblem.[7] To this was frequently added the
payment of a considerable sum of money, from a half *mina* of
silver plus one *gur* of grain to a talent (60 *minas*) of silver.[8]
Reference to both punishments together in the same document
in no way implies that the threatened mutilation could be
averted by making a payment in money; it meant that both were
to be inflicted.[9] Nor was this all, for, as already indicated, the

---

[1] *Mém. D.P.* 22, no. 162   [2] *Mém. D.P.* 23, no. 317, 15.
[3] This is made clear by *Mém. D.P.* 24, no. 328; cf. §1, 10, 49.
[4] *Mém. D.P.* 22, no. 159, 10 f.   [5] §1, 10, 57, no. 1.
[6] §11, 7, col. 320.   [7] §11, 10, 47.
[8] *Mém. D.P.* 24, nos. 329, 330, 334.
[9] §11, 12, 162, no. 4, and §11, 6, 15, against §11, 2, 152 f. and §11, 10, 47.

perjurer who had taken oath by the ruler also forfeited the magical protection of In-Shushinak; he had violated the *kiten* of the god and was an outlaw, and this was in practice synonymous with the death sentence. Violation of an engagement secured by an oath invoking the ruler thus brought on not only earthly punishment, but had results of a definitely religious nature as well; 'a closer unity between the profane and the divine systems of justice can hardly be expressed'.[1]

In the case of adoptions, inheritances and donations the punishment of drowning was often threatened, and with it was linked a malediction by deity and ruler. One such clause runs 'he who breaks the agreement shall go into the water; may the (river)-god Shazi shatter his skull in the raging whirlpool, may the sceptre of god and king smite his head, let him be driven out of the realm where god and king hold sway'.[2] Of interest also is a document containing the record of a proof by trial, with an oath and ordeal by water.[3] Ten witnesses confirm on behalf of a woman-plaintiff a gift which the alleged donor contests. The court requires the plaintiff to submit to an ordeal by water—if she sinks in the river the defendant has won, if she survives he must hand over the gift, but in that case he still incurs no penalty for having denied making it. Thus the ordeal by water, used both in Mesopotamia and on the Middle Euphrates,[4] was practised also in Elam.

From the multitude of other facts revealed to us by the documents from the period of the grand regents a few more may be noted here, above all the peculiar law of inheritance. As observed above,[5] in the ruling family there was a fratriarchal system giving a brother preference to inherit before a son.[6] Even among the ordinary people it is probable that similar arrangements originally existed. The basic principle was that brothers held their fortunes in common. This is shown by a document whereby two Elamites entered into a brother-relationship with one another.[7] They confirm that their fortune belongs to them jointly; what the one obtains by his labours, whether in money or kind, is the property of the other. Whichever of the two is first to die charges his 'brother' with the burial. 'If one should say to the other: "you are not my brother"—then he pays ten *minas* of gold and gets hand and tongue cut off.'

---

[1] Quoted from §1, 10, 64.
[2] *Mém. D.P.* 22, no. 1.
[3] *Ibid*. no. 162.
[4] §11, 3, 112.
[5] See above, p. 257.
[6] §11, 8, 47 ff.
[7] §11, 16, 106 f.

It is true that this brotherhood agreement comes—and this is important—from the days of the early Eparti rulers: it was sworn by invoking the grand regent Shirukdukh I, soon after 1800 B.C. But it is clear that during the period of the grand regents the right of the brother in the fratriarchal system lost ground continually in favour of a patriarchal system with reversion of inheritance to the children alone. Only in this way is it possible to explain the case discussed at the beginning of this section. It will be recalled that this was occasioned by the adoption of Bēli's father as 'brother' of Damqia, whose sons were claiming that the fortune Bēli had inherited, through his dead father from his adoptive uncle, should be handed over to them. Although Bēli received judgement in his favour, it was only because his adoptive uncle Damqia had once made over the fortune to his adopted 'brother' by a deed of gift. According to the law of inheritance at this late period Bēli would have gone away empty-handed; only Damqia's own children, the two plaintiffs, would have inherited.

In Elam during the period of the grand regents, and probably later too, the brother's right of inheritance continued to survive without restriction only when the deceased was childless. A similar right of inheritance was possessed by an adopted brother too. This is why a woman with neither parents nor children, who wanted to make her father's sister her heir, adopted her aunt as 'brother'.[1] That the aunt was not adopted as a sister proves that in the pure fratriarchy of former years women were excluded from the right of inheritance. But, again, for this very reason the woman adopting was obliged to donate her fortune to the inheriting aunt explicitly by a legal covenant. In other words: the brother's right of inheritance was no longer sufficient by itself even in the case of the testator being childless; the fortune had to be made over to the adopted 'brother' in the form of a gift while the testator was still alive. In the case against Bêli mentioned above the latter had emphasized that in the matter of the inheritance things had been transacted in accordance with the 'legal path' which the gods In-Shushinak and Ishme-karab had established regarding 'brotherhood'. This vouches for the antiquity of the rule of inheritance through the brother, and shows, therefore, that fratriarchy was the original form in Elam. In the sixteenth century at the latest, however, it had been displaced by inheritance of the children.

In the Elamite legal system attention may be drawn to certain

[1] *Mém. D.P.* 22, no. 3.

other practices not attested in Babylonia. To this category belong
the stressing that the party in question was acting 'of his [own]
free will', an expression attested especially in connexion with
adoptions, partitions, donations and settlements.[1] In this way it
was intended to guard against anyone contesting the agreement
by asserting that there was influence by a third party.[2] In the case
of donations *mortis causa* there is as well the notice that the
testator is making his dispositions 'with sound mouth, sound lip';[3]
it stresses the fact of the testator being capable of coherent
speech, failing which no testatory dispositions were valid in law.
Finally, one may count among the characteristic features of the
Elamite legal system the nailmarks of parties concerned which
appear on nearly all the documents from Susa, and in particular
intersecting impressions in the form of a cross. The fact that these
occur also in Mesopotamia (there, as a rule, three parallel nailmarks) might be due to Elamite influence.[4]

The Elamite credit system was based on three kinds of security.
The first, making a deposit of something as surety, was confined
to movable objects. The second was the mortgage, in which a
piece of land was offered as surety for the repayment of a debt
(whether in money or grain). If the debtor was not able to pay at
the appointed time, he had to sell the piece of land and pay off the
creditor with the proceeds. The third kind was the so-called
antichresis, in which the creditor received the right to use the
mortgaged piece of land, that is, he could gather the harvest from
the field or garden in question and use it to pay off the capital loan
and the interest.[5] The piece of land itself remained in possession
of the debtor and reverted to his ownership when the debt had
been paid.[6]

If a piece of land had been pledged as security for a debt, the
creditor could drive a stake in it, so that everyone knew that it was
mortgaged. If payment was delayed, in some way which is still
not clear, the land passed into the hands of the creditor to dispose
of it. Cattle could also be pledged as security.[7] It is stated in one
document that so long as some barley which had been loaned had
not been paid back, the bolt [on the stall] of the debtor's cows and
sheep should remain broken. Where cattle were pledged 'breaking of the lock on the stall' corresponded with the driving of a
stake into the field. It seems likely that in the event of payment

[1] §II, 7, col. 320.   [2] §I, 1, 50.
[3] §II, 7, col. 321.   [4] §II, 12, 171.
[5] Transactions characterized by the formula *esip-tabal* in Babylonia.
[6] §II, 20, 1 f.   [7] *Mém. D.P.* 22, no. 187.

being delayed the debtor had to pay off the creditor with these very cattle.[1] But although the pledging of land and cattle as security was widespread in Old Elam, nowhere in the documents—in contrast with other ancient eastern countries—do we come across the pledging of human beings, of a slave, for instance, or some other member of the debtor's household, as security.[2]

The documents from Susa recording debts are drawn up according to a simple formula. They contain the origin of the debt, the creditor, the debtor, the object which has been pledged, or any other security, the witnesses and debtor's nailmarks. As a rule the time and place at which the debt was acknowledged, the time allowed for paying it off, and the place where payment was to be made were indicated. In the case of money debts the rate of interest as well was never omitted. It varied between 0·6 and 40 per cent per annum. In contrast with Hammurabi's Babylonia, therefore, there was no uniform rate of interest in Elam. In the case of debts in kind the tablet contains no reference to the interest. In fact there was an annual yield of between 10 and 20 per cent, arranged in such a way that it was not the amount of cereal on loan which had to be repaid, but cereal at the same level of value as at the time the debt was acknowledged; at a higher rate, consequently. Since the price was much lower when repayment was made at harvest time, in the month of the 'Great Goddess' (August), well known as the month for the payment of debts, the debtor had appreciably more cereal to give back.[3]

The impression is gained from the documents that extensive communally cultivated properties certainly still survived in Old Elam—belonging to the rulers, the temples and even to Elamite families—but that communal husbandry, in the case of the families, was already in full process of disintegrating. Numerous deeds of purchase bear witness to a splitting up of this kind and to an individualization of land-tenure.[4] If children inherited their father's fortune on his death they could divide it up by casting lots for it, and dispose of it individually. There is evidence of this in the case of seven brothers who shared out their whole inheritance —property inside and outside Susa, cattle, gold, silver and all other possessions—amongst themselves.[5] One of them was then able to increase his share by further purchases and became a prosperous landowner.[6] However, land purchases for which there is documentary evidence constitute, all told, only a relatively

---

[1] §11, 18, 50 f., against §11, 9, 229.   [2] §11, 18, 53 f.
[3] §11, 18, 46 ff.   [4] §11, 19, 21.
[5] *Mém. D.P.* 22, no. 14.   [6] §11, 20, 7.

small part of the total area of the country, and so one may surmise that large areas of Elam remained under communal cultivation. But the possibility of breaking up the family estate and disposing of it in separate parts was always there.

On the evidence of our sources Elamite women in the period of the grand regents had won a large measure of equal rights for themselves, in contrast with the fratriarchy of earliest times, when the right of the brother alone to inherit was prejudicial to the sisters. The more that patriarchal forms of law, with reversion of the estate to the children, gained ground, the more the position of Elamite women improved. From then onwards sons and daughters had equal rights of inheritance.[1] In partition settlements women appear along with the men, indeed there were partitions among women only.[2] Women could appear as witnesses without special formality; we have come across them already both as plaintiffs and as defendants. In making agreements they left their nailmarks in the clay tablet along with their male counterparts.[3]

The following case throws light on the legal position of Elamite women.[4] On a father's death his married daughter inherited from him in her capacity as only child. Her husband made an objection because this money did not form part of the dowry, and consequently he had no control over the way it was used. The woman conciliated him by making a documentary affirmation under oath in these words: 'You are my husband, you are my son, you are my heir, and Atta-khubitir [no doubt her daughter, and therefore possessing a right to the inheritance after her mother] will love you and cherish you.' With this the husband declared himself satisfied, and wisely did not contest his dead father-in-law's will in a lawsuit. By his wife's declaration he received power to dispose of the money which would hardly have been granted to him by the court.[5]

A tablet which records that a father had given a field to his daughter may be considered in the same context;[6] she left this land to her own daughter, and the latter again to her daughter, who finally sold it.[7] This case shows that a right of inheritance in the female line naturally adhered mostly to personal property. There is a parallel in this to the right of legitimacy in the Elamite ruling house; as observed above, this legitimacy among the grand

---

[1] §II, 4, 131.
[2] *Mém. D.P.* 24, nos. 335–7.
[3] *Mém. D.P.* 22, no. 21 or no. 168.
[4] *Mém. D.P.* 28, no. 399.
[5] §II, 6, 49.
[6] *Mém. D.P.* 23, no. 200.
[7] §II, 20, 8.

regents was based upon descent from Shilkhakha's sister, and was therefore handed down in the female line.

Further evidence is to be found in the will of a mother who made over her whole fortune to her daughter.[1] In forceful phraseology, with a highly personal ring about it, she sought to make her dispositions secure. 'If after my death', the testator declared, 'anyone rises against [my daughter] and spits his spittle on the arrangements I have made, let him go forth and into the water.' Although the mother had two sons as well, who would have had equal rights as heirs, she made her fortune over to her daughter, because she had cared for her and cherished her. The sons had to guarantee, taking oath by the ruler, that they would not contest the will which their mother had sworn by In-Shushinak and Ishme-karab.

In many respects, as the tablets make clear, Elamite men, too, were considerate towards women, not infrequently allowing them privileges. In one tablet the dying father leaves his fortune equally divided among his children, but names his daughter before the son.[2] In another a man gives his wife a garden, adding the explicit direction that she may keep the garden even if he should ever part from her and marry another woman.[3] A similar thoughtfulness was shown by an Elamite who made over the usufruct of his fortune to his wife during her lifetime;[4] the sons were to inherit after that, but none would do so who had failed to show consideration for the mother.

Favouring of the daughter by the father is to be seen in one document,[5] by which the testator left all his fortune to his daughter, and at the same time broke 'the clods of earlier or later'. This meant that no one, neither his two wives nor his sons, might keep any of his fortune which he had given them previously, and that he prevented himself from giving them or anyone else anything in the future. 'So long as I am still living, she [the daughter] will look after me, and when I die she shall offer up sacrifices for the dead'—this was otherwise the duty of the sons, so it may be that the father had quarrelled with them, or perhaps they were absent, or did not live in Susa at all. But it is clear that the interests of his two wives were also prejudiced in favour of the daughter. If one of the sons contests the will, the document ends, he shall be destroyed by the river-god Shazi, he shall lose hand and tongue, pay four *minas* of silver by way of fine, and incur the

---

[1] *Mém. D.P.* 28, no. 405.
[2] *Mém. D.P.* 22, no. 16.
[3] *Mém. D.P.* 24, no. 380.
[4] *Mém. D.P.* 28, no. 402.
[5] *Ibid.* no. 285.

anathema of In-Shushinak. Among the sixteen witnesses to this tablet are four women.

The last document to be quoted here has a special appeal.[1] In it the husband leaves his whole fortune to his wife, giving as reason, 'because she has cared for him and worked for him'. And the dying man makes still further provision for his trusty companion in life: the sons shall one day be allowed to inherit the fortune only on condition that they remain with the mother and care for her. The daughter, on the other hand, need not fulfil this condition; she will inherit in any case on the mother's death—a further indication of the favoured position given to the female sex by Elamite men. Only the sons have pressure applied to them by the father; mother and daughter remain privileged.

All these testimonies throw a great deal of light on the position of Elamite women.[2] It fits in with this unusual picture that an Elamite woman once even rose to be ruler of Susiana—Shil-khakha's sister, the renowned ancestral mother of the dynasty of the grand regents.

[1] Mém. D.P. 24, no. 379.   [2] §II, 6, 39.

CHAPTER VIII

EGYPT: FROM THE EXPULSION OF THE HYKSOS TO AMENOPHIS I

I. THE CAMPAIGNS OF KAMOSE

THE literary tradition of the New Kingdom, represented by the *Story of Apophis and Seqenenre*,[1] suggests that the clash between the Hyksos and the native Egyptian kings of the Seventeenth Dynasty occurred in the reign of Seqenenre (II ?), as the result of deliberate provocation on the part of the Hyksos ruler.[2] The first sentences of the story tell the condition of Egypt at the time: Seqenenre rules in the Southern City (Thebes), while Apophis rules in Avaris; the whole of Egypt pays tribute to the Hyksos. Egypt is described as a divided land, and there is no suggestion that the whole of Egypt is occupied by the Asiatics. The evidence in support of a total occupation is slender and inconclusive;[3] even the famous description of Hyksos devastation in the inscription of Hatshepsut in the Speos Artemidos specifies only that 'the Asiatics were in Avaris in the Northland, roving foreigners being in the midst of them'.[4]

It is generally assumed that the lost portion of this story described a struggle between the Hyksos and the Egyptians, the outcome of which may have been a limited victory for the Egyptians. It is also assumed that Seqenenre was killed in the course of this struggle, the evidence in support of this assumption being the shattered skull of the king's mummy.[5] The fragmentary beginning of a New Kingdom romance is, however, an uncertain foundation on which to build an historical edifice. Probably the most that can safely be extracted from the story is a general indication of the state of affairs in Egypt during the last years of the Hyksos domination. To this extent it may be legitimate to accept the description of the division of the country and the assertion that the whole of Egypt was tributary to the Hyksos. Confirmation for both of these points is obtained from another source.

[1] §1, 4, 40–2.
[2] §1, 12, 44–5 explains its ritual significance without suggesting that the charges of Apophis were less than trumped up.
[3] See above, pp. 58 ff.; §1, 7, 113.
[4] §1, 2, 47–8 (l. 37 of the text).
[5] See above, p. 73 n. 8. See also §1, 4, 43; G, 3, 164.

The historical documents which recount the campaigns of Ka-mose, the son and successor of Seqenenre II, against the Hyksos, comprise two stelae set up in the Temple of Karnak. Of the first only fragments have survived,[1] but the beginning of its text has fortunately been preserved on a writing-board known as the Car-narvon Tablet.[2] The second, known specifically as the Kamose Stela, continues, apparently without a break, the account given on the first.[3] In the beginning of the text of the first stela, pre-facing the account of Kamose's first sortie, is a description of the condition of Egypt which closely resembles that contained in the *Story of Apophis and Seqenenre*. The date is the third year of Kamose's reign (about 1575 B.C.): the Asiatics are ensconced in Avaris, and their influence extends as far south as Cusae in Middle Egypt; from Cusae to Elephantine the land is controlled by Kamose; south of Elephantine is the princedom of Kush. Kamose's desire to lead a campaign of liberation against the Hyksos receives little support from his courtiers. The latter see no reason to disturb the *status quo*; Egypt is at peace, agriculture can be carried on without the fear of raids and spoliation; they are able to pasture their cattle in the papyrus-marshes. From this last claim it has been concluded that grazing rights in the Delta were held by the Egyptians dwelling in the Theban kingdom, and consequently that a settled state of affairs existed with little friction between north and south.[4] It is hardly possible that this situation could have obtained if the Theban kingdom under Seqenenre had been in combat with the Hyksos only a few years before. A possible alternative explanation is that the result of the hypothetical struggle between Apophis and Seqenenre was so indecisive that an uneasy peace was concluded, under which the Thebans were allowed to pasture their cattle in the Delta (the only satisfactory grazing area in Egypt) according to ancient practice.[5]

Pride was undoubtedly the principal motive which prompted Kamose to launch his attack on the Hyksos, who were at that time ruled by Auserre Apophis I. The traditional boast of the Egyptian king was to call himself 'King of Upper and Lower Egypt', and the claim to this title had to be justified—by conquest if necessary.[6] There is no reason to suppose that Apophis was terrorizing the south, or behaving in such a way as to deserve the strong language used about him by Kamose. His presence in Avaris was sufficient excuse for the opening of hostilities. The first object of Kamose's

[1] §I, 1, 111; §I, 8.   [2] §I, 3.
[3] §I, 5; §I, 6.   [4] §I, 11, 69; A, 2, 166–7.
[5] G, 4, 30, 88.   [6] §I, 11, 67–70.

campaign was Nefrusy, a town which lay north of Cusae, and north also of Khmunu (El-Ashmunein), both of which places are mentioned as the limit of Hyksos power in the southerly direction.[1] In Nefrusy was garrisoned a pro-Hyksos force under the command of Teti, son of Pepi, who was probably a local Egyptian adherent to the Hyksos, not an Asiatic.[2] Before reaching Nefrusy, Kamose's forces had apparently to engage in no operations more serious than plundering and skirmishing. The Nefrusy garrison seems therefore to have been the most southerly in the territory nominally held by the Hyksos. Consequently it may be concluded that no attack had been expected, and that the relations between south and north were superficially peaceful early in Kamose's reign. The successful attack on Nefrusy was executed by a detachment of Medjay troops, who were of Nubian origin, employed by the Egyptian kings as auxiliaries since the late Old Kingdom.[3]

A gap exists in the record of Kamose's campaign between the attack on Nefrusy and the events recorded on the second stela. Much of the text on this monument consists of grandiloquent claims by Kamose. An obscurity of language hinders a precise determination of whether much that is said refers to actual events in the past, or to the king's boastful intentions.[4] A description is given of a raid by Kamose's forces as far north as the Hyksos stronghold of Avaris in the course of which the neighbourhood of that city is devastated. It has, however, been doubted whether Kamose ever succeeded in achieving more than a partial penetration into the heart of Hyksos-held territories.[5] The lack of mention of Memphis and other important towns on the northward route to Avaris, certainly supports this opinion. In a passage of good historical narrative, the text of the stela recounts the capture by Kamose's forces of a messenger on his way between Apophis and the Prince of Kush; he bears a letter requesting immediate aid for the Hyksos. From it the name of the Hyksos king is established as Auserre; from it also emerges the fact that Kamose had previously made some move against Kush. The capture of this messenger took place while Kamose was campaigning in the neighbourhood of Sako (El-Qēs). Apophis had reacted to the Theban's success in Middle Egypt by seeking aid from his southern ally. With tactical skill

---

[1] For Cusae, §1, 3, 103 (l. 5 of the text); §1, 2, 46 (l. 15 of the text); for Khmunu, §1, 3, 89 (l. 4 of the text); §1, 6, 206 (l. 16 of the text).
[2] §1, 11, 70; G, 3, 166–7; A, 2, 169.
[3] Probably to be identified with the 'pan-grave' people, see above, pp. 74–6.
[4] §III, 13, 54.
[5] §1, 9, 116.

Kamose anticipated a conjunction between the forces of the Prince of Kush and those of Apophis by sending a detachment to occupy the Bahrīya oasis, and therefrom to control the desert route to the south.[1] Operations were then curtailed by the approach of the season of the inundation, and Kamose withdrew his forces to Asyūt. This withdrawal was effected apparently not without rear-guard actions. The text of the stela ends with a description of the joy with which the victory over the Hyksos was welcomed in Thebes.

Kamose's success, the extent of which remains doubtful, was achieved, it would seem, without great difficulty, and should be attributed probably as much to the element of surprise in the attack as to the superiority of the Theban forces. Hyksos rule did not involve close armed surveillance of the subject territories; it was exercised through local nobles, like Teti of Nefrusy. A determined attack would therefore achieve considerable initial success, if it were unexpected; but success would continue only as long as the forces of the principal object of the attack, the Hyksos ruler, remained unmarshalled. It has been suggested that Kamose probably resumed his operations northwards after the end of the season of inundation which had brought his first sortie to a close. There is no evidence to support this view.[2]

This attack, which represented the first historically attested attempt to oust the Hyksos from the Delta, took place in Kamose's third year. No higher regnal year than the third is recorded for Kamose, and opinion is divided over the length of his reign.[3] There exists a difference of opinion also on whether there was more than one king named Kamose. Three different Horus-names have been found on monuments bearing the royal *nomen* Kamose, and it has been suggested that there were certainly two and possibly three kings of this name. The most generally accepted view is that there was one Kamose only, who changed his Horus-name once after the defeat of Apophis and again after some other important event in his reign.[4] The problem cannot, however, be solved without further evidence. Apart from the changes in name, there is no evidence for the existence of two or three kings Kamose; equally there is no evidence in support of a long reign. The nature of his burial, moreover, suggests that he died suddenly, before adequate preparations had been made for his interment. In the report con-

---

[1] §III, 13, 58; G, 2, 652.   [2] §I, 9, 119.

[3] *C.A.H.* I[3], pt. I, ch. VI, sect. I; §I, 13, 149; G, 3, 173.

[4] For a good summary of the problem see G, 2, 331; also A, 1, 35 ff.; §I, 9, 119–20. The existence of several variant forms of the *nomen* occurring with the *praenomen* Wadjkheperre has not been used as evidence in this debate; see §I, 14, 264–5.

tained in the Abbott Papyrus, his tomb is listed as being still intact during the reign of Ramesses IX;[1] at some later date, probably to preserve the body from desecration, the coffin was removed from the tomb and buried in rubble nearby. It was discovered in 1857, undamaged and unviolated, but in a poor condition. The coffin, of the *rishi*-type common during the Seventeenth Dynasty, was not gilded, and it lacked the royal uraeus; a few items of jewellery and other articles of personal equipment were found inside with the body.[2] One piece of jewellery bears the name of Amosis, Kamose's brother, who may therefore be considered responsible for the burial, and consequently as Kamose's successor. Inasmuch as Kamose was the initiator of the movement to liberate Egypt from the Hyksos, the simplicity of his burial equipment is surprising; it does, however, provide some indication of the modest character of Theban civilization at the end of the Second Intermediate Period.

II. THE EXPULSION OF THE HYKSOS BY AMOSIS

No immediate sequel to Kamose's campaign is found in surviving records. On the part of the Thebans it is possible that the results achieved in the first attack were not sufficiently encouraging to inspire a quick renewal of hostilities. Alternatively, Kamose may have died unexpectedly, to be succeeded by his younger brother Amosis. On the part of the Hyksos, the apparent failure to seek revenge for the attack may have been due to the death of Apophis after a reign of possibly forty years or more.[3] It may have been about this time that Ahhotpe, the wife of Seqenenre II and mother of Kamose and Amosis, played an important part in re-establishing stability in the Theban state after some serious troubles, later referred to in a stela set up by Amosis in Karnak.[4]

When Amosis eventually resumed the war against the Hyksos, he may already have been the Prince of Thebes for some time. The only contemporary account of the final campaigns against the Hyksos is included in the inscription of Ahmose, a soldier, and native of El-Kāb in southern Upper Egypt, whose father, Baba, had served under Seqenenre (presumably the second of that name).[5] Ahmose explains that he first served under Amosis while he was young and unmarried. No mention is made of service by his father in the campaign of Kamose, from which it may be

[1] §1, 10, vol. 1, 38. [2] §1, 14, 259 ff. [3] See above, pp. 61–3.
[4] See below, p. 306. On the family of Amosis, see A, 1, 28 ff.
[5] G, 7, 1 ff.; §1, 4, 48 ff.

deduced that his father had died or retired from active service before Kamose's third year. After some time had passed, and he had married, Ahmose was old enough to go north with Amosis and participate in a series of attacks on Avaris, and in other encounters in the neighbourhood of Avaris. On one occasion he was appointed to serve in a ship named 'Appearing-in-Memphis'; from this name it can safely be concluded that the old Lower Egyptian capital had been occupied by Amosis,[1] and consequently that one or more campaigns had been fought before Ahmose joined the victorious army. The task of driving the Hyksos from Egypt undoubtedly gave Amosis more trouble than might be thought from the proud boasts made on the great Kamose stela. It probably lasted several years;[2] it has even been suggested that it was not until his fifteenth year the Amosis reduced Avaris and drove the Hyksos from their Delta strongholds. A late date is defended by some on grounds of general plausibility, by others in order to accommodate the reigns of the supposed successors of Auserre Apophis;[3] but so little is known of these rulers that no reliable estimate of the lengths of their reigns can be given.[4] No indications are given in Ahmose's simple and laconic biography; he specifies the successive operations in which he took part, details his particular acts of bravery, and enumerates the rewards and promotions he received. Of the fall of Avaris—that great moment of fulfilled ambition for the Theban king—all he has to say is: 'They sacked Avaris; I brought plunder from there: one man and three women—total, four heads. His Majesty gave them to me to be slaves.'[5] This brief account is the only surviving record of the final defeat of the Hyksos on Egyptian soil.

Ahmose next recounts the siege of Sharuhen, a town in southwest Palestine, which was reduced after three years. Sharuhen is usually described as a Hyksos stronghold,[6] and it is indeed probable that the town was occupied by people ethnically related to the Hyksos ruling in Avaris. There is, however, no evidence to support the view that Sharuhen was the bridgehead of a Hyksos empire which extended considerably further north, and the base from which the attacks on Egypt were launched earlier in the Second Intermediate Period.[7] After the capture of Avaris, the logical next move for Amosis was to secure the safety of Egypt's eastern frontier from the threat of retaliatory incursions by the Asiatics. By the capture of Sharuhen he achieved this end, and at the same time

[1] §I, 7, 115.   [2] See above, pp. 62 f.   [3] §I, 7, 115; A, I, 49.
[4] See above, pp. 63 f.   [5] G, 7, 4, 10–13.
[6] G, I, 227; G, 2, 301.   [7] §I, 7, 115.

demonstrated to the Asiatics that Egypt was again ruled by an active king. What cannot be decided, however, is whether the Sharuhen siege followed closely on the capture of Avaris. If it was the result of a quick campaign of exploitation, it is probable that Amosis found his immediate tasks in the north-east accomplished by his sixth or seventh year. He was then able to devote his attention to the reconquest of Nubia, and did not resume activities in Asia until late in his reign. Ahmose, son of Ibana and Baba, recounts no more exploits in Asia during the reign of Amosis, but his fellow townsman Ahmose-Pennekheb describes[1] how he campaigned with Amosis in Djahy, a geographical term used in the New Kingdom to refer to Palestine and Syria.[2] On the basis of this report, certain historians have claimed that Amosis followed up his capture of Sharuhen with a drive deep into Palestine,[3] but there are good reasons for believing that the Djahy campaign took place late in his reign. Ahmose-Pennekheb, who mentions the campaign, lived on to serve under successive kings, until he died in the reign of Hatshepsut; he must have been quite young at the end of Amosis's reign, and could scarcely have served in campaigns in the first half of that reign.[4] Further support for a late campaign in Asia is provided by the reference in a text of Year 22 of Amosis to the use of oxen in the quarries of El-Ma'sara which came from the land of the *Fnḥw*.[5] Unfortunately an uncertainty in the reading of this text makes it doubtful whether the oxen were captured in a campaign or supplied as tribute by the Asiatics.[6]

The end of the Hyksos domination of Egypt, so little recorded in surviving texts, could scarcely have been secured without considerable campaigning. Ahmose's inscription makes it clear that many assaults were needed before Avaris fell; but nothing is known of the clearance of the rest of the Delta. Possibly no large-scale military operations were needed to secure the allegiance of the whole area to the new Egyptian king. The capture of Avaris and the expulsion therefrom of the Hyksos probably involved the removal of the threat which had determined the local Delta dynasts to support the Hyksos. For Apophis, Amosis was now substituted.

According to Manetho, in the words of Josephus,[7] 240,000 Hyksos left Egypt peaceably as the result of a treaty signed after

---

[1] G, 7, 35, 16–17.   [2] §II, 3, vol. I, 145*; §II, 2, 52.

[3] E.g. G, 1, 227; cf. §II, 4, 82.   [4] G, 2, 396; §I, 7, 115.

[5] G, 7, 25, 12. The identification of the *Fnḥw* remains uncertain, cf. §II, 4, 97; §I, 7, 115.

[6] Thus compare §II, 1, §27 with §II, 5, 14. The latter is unconvincing, and the parallel quoted in support is uncertain.   [7] §II, 6, 89.

Amosis had repeatedly failed to take Avaris. This account, unsupported by contemporary records, must be explained in terms of
the exaggeration and misrepresentation concerning the Hyksos
occupation and defeat which formed such a strong element in
Egyptian historical tradition during the New Kingdom and later.
Concerning the extent to which the Hyksos domination was a
disaster for Egypt, there must be considerable doubt;[1] but it cannot be denied that as a result of this episode Egypt became more
conscious of the outside world and more expansionist.

III. THE PRINCE OF KUSH AND THE REOCCUPATION OF NUBIA

In the text on the Carnarvon Tablet, Kamose is quoted as saying:
'I wonder what the point of my strength is, that there should be
one chief in Avaris and another in Kush, and I sit joined with an
Asiatic and a Nubian, each man holding his portion of this Egypt.'[2]
The Nubian chief is elsewhere called the Prince of Kush (*ḥḳꜣ n Kꜣš*);[3]
he ruled over a territory which extended from Elephantine in the
north,[4] southwards into the region of the Second Cataract. From
information derived from the stela of Ha'ankhef, who may have
served the Prince of Kush, it seems possible that his dominion
extended as far south as Kerma.[5]

It is thought that the princedom of Kush came into being as an
independent state during the late Second Intermediate Period. At
the time when Egypt ceased to be a unified kingdom, the forces of
the Theban king were no doubt withdrawn from the south, and
control there passed into the hands of a powerful local chief or a
high official engaged in the administration of Lower Nubia.[6]
Kamose calls his southern rival a Nubian (*Nḥsy*), a general term used
to describe natives of the several different tribes living in Nubia.[7]
The name Kush, used in his title, places his origin in Lower
Nubia, but his dominion extended far to the south of the limits of
Kush as it was known in earlier times.[8] The Prince of Kush may
have been a Nubian, but he did not apparently lack a veneer of
Egyptian civilization. The process of egyptianization which had
started during the period of intensive occupation of Nubia in the

---

[1] See above, pp. 54 ff.
[2] Line 3, see §1, 3, 98.
[3] E.g. §III, 12, 50, 54.
[4] Carnarvon Tablet, l. 5, see §1, 3, 103.
[5] §III, 6, 8–10; §III, 12, 57–8; but cf. §III, 8, 56.
[6] §III, 11, 126 f.
[7] §II, 3, vol. I, 74*.
[8] §III, 8, especially p. 60.

Middle Kingdom, was continued, and perhaps deliberately fostered by the Prince of Kush.[1] Officials who served the prince had Egyptian names, and were probably expatriate Egyptians left behind after the withdrawal or expulsion of the main Egyptian forces.[2] One ruler bore apparently the name Nedjeh, which is not un-Egyptian in form, although not attested elsewhere; he too may have been Egyptian in origin. Even Egyptian gods were worshipped in Kush. The official Sopdhor, who calls himself 'Governor of Buhen' (*tsw n Bhn*) built a temple at Buhen dedicated to Horus, Lord of Buhen 'to the satisfaction of the Prince of Kush'. No trace now remains of this building, but it may have been on the site of the northern temple at Buhen built at a later date by Amenophis II.[3]

Friendly relations existed between the Prince of Kush and the Hyksos ruler in Avaris, but there is scant evidence to support the view that the relationship of the former to the latter was that of a tributary.[4] Typical Hyksos scarabs found in Lower Nubian graves testify to some communication between Kush and Avaris,[5] but the clearest evidence that this communication was more than a simple trade connexion is offered by the letter sent by Auserre Apophis to the Prince of Kush, the text of which is reproduced in the Kamose stela.[6] In this letter, which was intercepted by Kamose's forces, Apophis greets the Prince of Kush as 'my son', and chides him for having failed to inform him of his accession to the princedom. He tells him of Kamose's attack, reminds him of some earlier foray by the Thebans into Kush, and urges him to attack Egypt while Kamose is in the north. From this letter a number of interesting historical points emerge. In the first place, the reference to the recent installation of the prince confirms the opinion that the native princes ruled Kush for at least two generations.[7] Secondly, it reveals that there existed at this time a standard of diplomatic etiquette which required that rulers on accession should inform their allies of their enthronement.[8] Thirdly, it suggests that Kamose had made some attack on Kush. A vestige of this attack may be found in the rock-inscription containing Kamose's name once seen near Tōshka.[9] The king's name is, however, here associated

---

[1] §III, 11, 129 f.; §III, 12, 57; §III, 1, 21. On the continuing process of egyptianization in the Early New Kingdom, see §III, 14, 44; §III, 15, 96; §III, 16, 59.
[2] §III, 12, 51, 55; §III, 1, 20.   [3] §III, 12, 55.
[4] §III, 11, 125 ff.; modified in §III, 13, 59–60. See also A, 2, 169.
[5] §III, 11, 121–2; §III, 15, 90; §III, 16, 54.
[6] Lines 20–4, cf. §III, 13, 54 ff.; A, 2, 68–9.
[7] §III, 1, 21–2.
[8] §III, 13, 56.   [9] §III, 18, pl. 65, 4, and p. 127.

with that of Amosis I, and it is generally thought that both names were inscribed during Amosis's drive into Nubia at a later date.[1] The discovery at Faras of scarabs bearing Kamose's name equally does not prove that the Thebans invaded Nubia in his reign.[2] Trouble between the two realms probably amounted to no more than border skirmishes during Kamose's reign.

The elimination of the hostile princedom of Kush was effected by Amosis I after he had secured the north-eastern frontier of the newly reunified Egypt by the reduction of Sharuhen. Three campaigns into Nubia in his reign are recorded in the inscription of Ahmose, son of Ibana.[3] The initial campaign, which achieved considerable success, was followed by two expeditions aimed at suppressing insurrections. Opposition to the change in overlordship from the Prince of Kush to the King of Egypt was probably slight from the egyptianized inhabitants of Lower Nubia, the reassertion of Egyptian rule being in the nature more of a political adjustment than the outcome of a bloody conquest. The leader of the second insurrection was Tetian, and from the evidence of his name he may well have been an Egyptian, possibly the successor of Nedjeh, the earlier Prince of Kush; he may equally have been an official who had served under the prince. No further opposition is reported by Ahmose. It is probable that after putting down Tetian's revolt, Amosis was able to proceed peaceably to consolidate his Nubian conquests. The extent to which he succeeded in penetrating Nubia is not known. A statue bearing his name and a block with the name of his wife Ahmose-Nefertiry have been found on the island of Sai, over 100 miles to the south of Buhen, and it has been suggested that Amosis built the first New Kingdom temple on that site.[4] These pieces may, however, belong to a temple of later date, built by one of Amosis's successors. Better evidence exists for a temple of Amosis at Buhen; a doorway has survived bearing his name and that of his mother Ahhotpe, and also an ex-voto text added by the Governor of Buhen, Tjuroy.[5] It is unlikely that Amosis was able to extend his conquest of Nubia far to the south of Buhen; possibly he instituted the rehabilitation of the fortress of Buhen which had been sacked and had fallen into disrepair during the Second Intermediate Period; but no objects have been found in the fortress area which can with certainty be dated to his reign.[6] Buhen undoubtedly became the principal

---

[1] §III, 11, 141–2; §III, 13, 57; §III, 7, 56.
[2] §III, 5, pl. 18; cf. §III, 13, 57 n. 14.
[3] G, 7, 5, 4–6, 15.   [4] §III, 17, 77–8.   [5] §III, 9, Plate Vol., 35.
[6] §III, 2, 9; for well-dated early Eighteenth Dynasty finds, §III, 3, 10.

town of the reconquered Nubian territories; it was provided with a governor whose title (_tsw n Bhn_) was the same as that held by his predecessor Sopdhor under the sovereignty of the Prince of Kush. Tjuroy, the governor whose name is preserved on Amosis's temple doorway, was probably the official who later became Viceroy of Kush under Amenophis I. The office of viceroy originated possibly during the reign of Amosis, its first known holder being Ahmose Si-Tayit, the father of Tjuroy.[1] Early viceroys were called 'king's son' and 'overseer of the southern lands', and it has been thought that the first holder of the office was in reality not Ahmose Si-Tayit but a son of Amosis. The evidence of the title, however, is not conclusive, and it remains unsupported by other facts.[2] Necessity obliged Amosis to place the administration of Nubia under an official of high standing with power backed by royal authority. In the absence of the king from Nubia, his representative occupied the position so recently held by the Prince of Kush. As royal representative or viceroy, he earned the title 'king's son', later to become 'king's son of Kush'.[3] Before the first king's son was appointed, authority in Nubia was held apparently by Hormeni, mayor of Hierakonpolis, who claims that he annually brought tribute to the king from Nubia (Wawat).[4] By the careful organization of royal power through officials like Hormeni, Ahmose Si-Tayit and Tjuroy, Amosis laid the foundations for the successful administration and exploitation of Lower Nubia which, later in the Eighteenth Dynasty, were to prove so important for the economy of Egypt as an imperial power.

IV. REUNION AND REORGANIZATION UNDER AMOSIS I

Amosis I, the son of Seqenenre II and Ahhotpe, succeeded his elder brother Kamose in about 1570 B.C. The first years of his reign were probably taken up wholly with the campaign which drove the Hyksos from Egypt. Their expulsion in about 1567 B.C. may be taken as marking the moment from which Egypt could again be considered a unified country with one king. Amosis was faced with formidable tasks of reconstruction and rehabilitation after the years of division and neglect. With the Asiatic boundary secure, and the land of Kush quickly restored to a state of subjugation, he was in a position to concentrate on domestic matters.

[1] §III, 7, 47 ff.; §III, 4, 183–5; §III, 11, 178.
[2] §III, 4, 185; §III, 10, 28 ff., 73 ff.; G, 2, 463; §III, 7, 56.
[3] See below, p. 348.   [4] G, 7, 76–7; §III, 11, 177–8.

It is commonly stated that, as a result of the campaign of liberation, Egypt at the beginning of the Eighteenth Dynasty was a land
destined inevitably to achieve great things. The Egyptians had
tasted the joys of military success; they had shown that they were
not naturally servile, and that they were capable of great feats of
arms. Amosis was backed, it is claimed, by a strong and efficient
army which demanded further use.[1] The remarkable military
triumphs of Amosis's successors may indeed be ascribed to a new
and unusual confidence inspiring the traditionally peaceable Egyptians, but there is no evidence to show that this confidence already
existed during Amosis's reign. That the country should be restored
to settled economy as soon as possible was, no doubt, the desire
which inspired Egyptians more effectively than that their country's
power should be extended in an imperial manner. Warlike activities
were, apparently, rare during Amosis's reign after the reconquest
of Nubia. According to Manetho, Amosis reigned for 25–26
years, a length of reign supported by the highest regnal year recorded—Year 22 in the quarry inscription at El-Maʿsara.[2] In this
inscription there is a passing reference to a possible campaign in
Syria,[3] but no other campaigns distinguished the last years of this
relatively long reign. By the standards set by his successors,
Amosis had a peaceful reign which in the field of foreign conquest
exhibited little activity.

In domestic affairs, however, much activity can be discerned.
Administration, agriculture, trade and religion, all needed careful
attention once reunification had been achieved. A primary task
was to establish throughout the country an administration which
would properly maintain the king's authority, and effectively carry
out his orders. During the Second Intermediate Period local administration had continued along the lines established during the
late Middle Kingdom, in so far as the scanty evidence permits a
judgement to be made.[4] The ancient nome-structure of the country,
which involved a high degree of local administration, rendered less
disastrous the fragmentation of the land when central control
lapsed. Individual nomes could operate as independent states.
Consequently the task facing Amosis was to secure the allegiance
of nome administrations either by blandishment, or by replacing
hostile officials by loyal followers. The paucity of important tombs
from the Second Intermediate Period in the provincial centres
suggests that there had been no revival of the old nomarchic system
which had been suppressed during the Twelfth Dynasty.[5] In

[1] G, 1, 233; G, 2, 391.   [2] G, 7, 24–5.   [3] See p. 295.
[4] See above, pp. 44 ff.   [5] *C.A.H.* 1³, pt. 2, ch. xx, sect. xiii.

Thebes the vestiges of true Egyptian monarchy had been preserved; in El-Kāb there were, it seems, influential families;[1] elsewhere in Upper Egypt, in the sphere of the humble kings of the Seventeenth Dynasty, control was no doubt exercised by royal officials of modest standing. In those parts of Egypt controlled by the Hyksos, the provincial centres were probably in the hands of the Hyksos sympathizers like Teti, son of Pepi, at Nefrusy. There is no evidence to suggest that local control was in hands other than those of Egyptian officials, except possibly in parts of the Delta.

After the reunification Amosis in all probability re-established administration throughout Egypt by confirming the authority of local officials where loyalty to the new regime was unquestioned, and by installing loyal followers where allegiance was doubtful. The career of Ahmose, son of Ibana, shows that faithful service was rewarded by grants of land, slaves and gold.[2] Ahmose, however, was a man of modest origin, and his early rewards were small. The two parcels of land he received from Amosis were both in the neighbourhood of his home-city, and were insignificant in size.[3] Such grants may not be considered good evidence for a policy of settling trustworthy supporters in districts formerly hostile. Additional evidence for such a policy is thought to be provided by the inscription of Mesesia, which records a lawsuit brought during the reign of Ramesses II concerning the ownership of land said to have been granted by Amosis in the neighbourhood of Memphis to an overseer of boats named Neshi.[4] This late reference to an act of settlement by Amosis is the only known fragment of evidence relating to activities of that king in the northern part of the land, apart from the campaigns at the beginning of his reign. Its significance is unfortunately very uncertain: Neshi, like Ahmose, may have been given land in the neighbourhood of his native city, and he may have received it for good service in Nubia rather than for fighting against the Hyksos. Remains of an account on the back of a copy of the *Book of the Dead* in Cairo contain references to estates called 'the House of Tetisheri' and 'the House of Sitkamose'.[5] The papyrus was found at Abusīr, and it has been suggested that land in the region of Memphis was settled on Kamose's grandmother and daughter after the defeat of the Hyksos.[6] Again, unfortunately, this evidence is far from con-

---

[1] G, 2, 308.

[2] The 'gold of valour' received by Ahmose may not have been simply a military decoration (cf. G, 3, 169), but an actual grant of gold (cf. §IV, 4).

[3] In each case, 5 *arouras*, G, 7, 6, 8, 15. Subsequently he did rather better; see *Chron. d'Ég.* 41 (1966), 110.   [4] §IV, 5, 25.   [5] §V, 4, 150.   [6] §V, 10, 14–16.

clusive in establishing the existence of a deliberate policy of resettlement during Amosis's reign. Nevertheless, in spite of the
lack of evidence on this and other aspects of Amosis's reorganization of administration, it cannot be doubted that the success of
Egyptian administration later in the Eighteenth Dynasty must
very greatly have been due to the sound foundation laid by the
early kings of the dynasty. The speedy settlement of Nubia and
the setting-up of an efficient administration there testify to
Amosis's ability in this direction.

It is easy to overestimate the damage which may have been
caused in agricultural matters by the lack of overall control of the
irrigation system of Egypt during the Second Intermediate
Period. The Theban courtiers of Kamose apparently were able to
pasture their herds in the Delta,[1] and it is probable that agricultural activities were not affected by the political division of the
land. Inevitably, however, a period of political disunity weakens
operations which depend for their success on comprehensive
control. Hence Amosis was surely faced with the problem of
rehabilitating neglected canal- and dyke-systems, and with restoring order after the war of liberation. Similarly, the administration of agricultural matters, including the assessment and
collection of taxes on crops, needed reorganization. It is perhaps
not surprising that two of the three tombs in the Theban Necropolis belonging to officials who served under Amosis were
made for overseers of granaries, whose duties were widely agricultural.[2]

The Hyksos supremacy is said to have opened Egypt to outside
influences as never before. In the fields of art, trade and warfare,
great strides were made which may be placed to the credit of this
alien occupation.[3] What happened in these fields can, on the contrary, be considered the results of the continuance of a process
already well started in the Middle Kingdom. The Egyptians had
become acquainted with many peoples in Asia during the Twelfth
Dynasty,[4] and the resumption of contacts during the Eighteenth
Dynasty was a natural development following the contraction of
the economy suffered by the Theban state during the Second
Intermediate Period. The Hyksos accelerated this process since,
in expelling them, the Egyptians were obliged to direct their
attention to the east. Yet no dramatic changes in Egyptian life and
culture can be discerned in the early years of the Eighteenth

---

[1] §1, 3, 103.
[2] Tombs of Hray and Nakhte, see G, 6, vol. 1², pt. 1, nos. 12 and A20.
[3] §1, 13, 150 ff.   [4] C.A.H. 1³, pt. 2, ch. xx, sect. XIII.

Dynasty. Under Amosis the recovery of the economy was necessarily slow, but there exists some evidence to show that much was done to repair the weaknesses which had developed during the years of restriction. Raw materials obtained from sources outside Egypt began to be available. A great stela set up in Karnak, commemorating Amosis and his mother Ahhotpe, enumerates the vessels and other objects presented to Amon-Re. Silver and gold are the materials most used for the objects listed; lapis-lazuli and turquoise are mentioned as forming decorative elements in various pieces.[1] The metals in quantity probably came from Asia and Nubia, the lapis from Central Asia, by way of Near-Eastern trade-routes;[2] turquoise, the characteristic product of Sinai, was obtained by expeditions organized under royal monopoly.[3] Fragments of votive objects inscribed with the name of Amosis's queen, Ahmose-Nefertiry, have been found in the Temple of Hathor at Serābīt el-Khādim in Sinai,[4] and turquoise was used in the jewellery found buried with Queen Ahhotpe, much of which is inscribed with Amosis's name.[5] Ahhotpe's jewellery also contained silver objects,[6] incorporated lapis-lazuli,[7] and exhibited decorative motifs and techniques which have been linked with contemporary Minoan work.[8] Trade contacts with Crete are not directly attested at this time, but it is not inconceivable that Amosis resumed the enterprises of his Middle Kingdom predecessors in this direction also. In the Karnak stela the Hau-nebu[9] are claimed as followers of Amosis, while Ahhotpe is called 'mistress of the regions of the Mediterranean islands'. These references may be purely bombastic, but it is noteworthy that the only other foreign countries mentioned on this stela are Nubia ($\underline{H}nt$-$\underline{h}n$-nfr) and Fenkhu (see p. 295), against both of which Amosis mounted undoubted expeditions. It is possible, however, that the so-called Minoan influences arrived in Egypt by way of Syria, through Byblos. The same stela records the gift of a bark to Amon-Re 'of new cedar (?) from the best of the Terraces (i.e. the Lebanon)'; trade with Byblos was clearly resumed by Amosis.

Economic recovery during the reign of Amosis is further confirmed by the increase in temple-building, the development of funerary practices, and the remarkable improvement in standards of artistic design and execution. This last improvement is especially noticeable in the funerary equipment of Queen Ahhotpe, in those

---

[1] G, 7, 22–3.   [2] G, 5, 399 f.   [3] §IV, 6, vol. II, 16.
[4] Ibid. vol. II, 149.   [5] G, 5, 405.   [6] §IV, 11, nos. 52666, 52667.
[7] The identification of this stone is uncertain; §IV, 11, 205–7; G, 5, 250.
[8] G, 5, 250–1; §IV, 10, 126.   [9] See C.A.H. I³, pt. 2, ch. xx, sect. XII.

pieces made for her by Amosis as compared with those made by Kamose.[1] The royal stelae of Amosis found at Abydos and Karnak exhibit, in the form of the hieroglyphs and in the execution and arrangement of the scenes, a very considerable advance over the simply inscribed stela of Kamose from Karnak. Inspiration for this revival was found apparently in the art of the early Middle Kingdom as expressed in the works of Theban artists and craftsmen. The absence of works of the period from Lower Egypt suggests that there may have been a deliberate suppression of the artistic tradition of the north.[2]

Little remains of the temples built by Amosis, probably because mud-brick was the material chiefly used with architectural elements only in stone, such as the inscribed doorway found at Buhen (p. 298). At Karnak some building was erected, forming part of the Temple of Amon-Re, of which the columns, roof and floor were made of cedar-wood;[3] the walls of this building may have been of stone.[4] A temple of Mont was also restored or rebuilt at Thebes or Armant, according to a fragmentary inscription now in University College, London.[5] The most substantial traces of Amosis's building works have survived at Abydos. In the southern part of the necropolis, far from the Osiris Temple and the Middle Kingdom cemeteries, he constructed a series of buildings, mostly out of mud-brick, which included cenotaphs for himself and for his grandmother Tetisheri, a chapel dedicated to the memory of Tetisheri, a small temple, a strange terraced building, and a small settlement.[6] The reopening of the Ma'sara quarries in his twenty-second year foreshadowed undoubtedly a more ambitious building programme. Under the direction of the high official Neferperet, fine white limestone was to be extracted for all the building subsequently to be undertaken by Amosis.[7] A temple of Ptah is specified (probably to be in Memphis), and a temple of Amun in Luxor (*'Ipt-rst*). Of these buildings no trace has survived, and it is possible that they were never started. An alabaster quarry at Bīsra, on the east bank of the Nile upstream from Asyūt, contains an inscription which includes the name of Ahmose-Nefertiry;[8] it too was probably opened by Amosis, who seems to have revived interest in alabaster as a building stone; it was

---

[1] §I, 14, 254; §IV, 10, 125.   [2] §IV, 1, 7 ff.
[3] G, 7, 23, 14–15.   [4] §IV, 3, 137, and pl. 2, 1.
[5] §V, 10, 15; §V, 8, 67–8. Fragments inscribed with Amosis's name have been found at Armant in the temple area and elsewhere, §IV, 7, vol. III, pl. 54, 1; §IV, 8, vol. II, pl. 100, 6.   [6] §IV, 2, 29–38; §IV, 9, 75–6; G, 8, vol. II, 218–23.
[7] G, 7, 24–5.   [8] G, 6, vol. IV, 247

much used by his successors.[1] Of domestic building the only traces surviving which can be associated with Amosis, apart from the vestiges of simple houses in the settlement at Abydos, are the remains of two palaces and some houses at El-Ballās, on the western side of the Nile opposite Koptos. A jar-sealing of Amosis has been found in the northern palace, and scarabs with his name in burials in the vicinity. The settlement here was clearly import-ant in the early Eighteenth Dynasty, but it remains unstudied and its significance undetermined.[2]

In religious matters Amosis, in addition to building new tem-ples, and restoring old temples, made costly gifts to the great national sanctuary at Thebes, and fostered the reputation of Amon-Re. The extent to which he succeeded in restoring the forms and equipment of religion throughout Egypt is not known,[3] but it is probable that he concentrated his attention on the southern part of the country, and did little for Middle and Lower Egypt. When Hatshepsut claimed that she had rebuilt the temples of Middle Egypt which had fallen into ruin during the Hyksos period, she may indeed have been speaking the truth.[4]

Amosis was buried in a tomb in Dirā Abu'n-Naga in the Theban Necropolis, near those of his predecessors of the Seven-teenth Dynasty. He also built for himself the cenotaph at Abydos (p. 304). A special piety seems to have drawn him to that holy place, and after his death his memory was revered there, and a local cult was established.[5] This cult, however, never flourished to the same extent as that of Amenophis I and Ahmose-Nefertiry in the Theban Necropolis.[6]

V. THREE ROYAL LADIES

From the scanty records surviving from the beginning of the Eighteenth Dynasty, it emerges that a remarkable part was played in the history of the newly unified state by three ladies, Tetisheri and Ahhotpe, the grandmother and mother of Kamose and Amosis, and Ahmose-Nefertiry, the wife of Amosis. There can be little doubt that their behaviour served as an inspiration to the leading women of the country (of whom Hatshepsut is the out-standing example) throughout the Eighteenth Dynasty.[7]

[1] G, 5, 59.   [2] §iv, 10, 156 ff., and n. 1 on p. 273.
[3] His care for monuments of the past is demonstrated by the measures he took to repair damage caused by natural disaster, A, 5, 145.   [4] §i, 2, 47–8.   [5] G, 4, 244.
[6] An interesting stela from Abydos shows Amosis, Ahmose-Nefertiry and Ameno-phis I with Amon-Re, §iv, 9, pl. 32 (now in Manchester Museum, no. 2938).
[7] §i, 14, 246; G, 3, 172.

TETISHERI

Tetisheri, born of non-royal parents, was the wife probably of Seqenenre Tao I and the mother of Seqenenre Tao II and of his wife Ahhotpe. She lived through the stirring times of the late Seventeenth Dynasty, survived her husband, her son and her grandson Kamose, and died during the reign of her other ruling grandson, Amosis.[1] She was specially honoured during the early Eighteenth Dynasty, probably because she was regarded as the founder, on the male and female sides, of the conquering royal line. She was shown on a monument now in University College, London associated with Amosis,[2] as on later monuments were, first, Ahhotpe, and then Ahmose-Nefertiry. Amosis was assiduous in perpetuating her memory. A fine stela found in the chapel which he erected for her at Abydos tells, in the literary language employed in some royal inscriptions of the period, how Amosis desired further to honour her;[3] in addition to her tomb and her cenotaph she was to receive a pyramid and a chapel at Abydos, with a pool and trees, equipped with land and staff, both priestly and secular (pp. 304, 307). An estate for her (or in her name) may also have been established in the region of Memphis.[4] The impression of a determined, influential woman, derived from the documents, contrasts strongly with her appearance when young as represented in a surviving statuette in the British Museum.[5]

AHHOTPE

In the early part of Amosis's reign, probably after the death of Tetisheri, and possibly before Ahmose-Nefertiry became his wife, the position of principal lady of Egypt was occupied by his mother Ahhotpe. Amosis's great Karnak stela which, from its similarity in design to the Kamose stela (also from Karnak), is surely to be dated early in his reign,[6] includes in its text a striking passage in which Ahhotpe is praised. She is described as 'one who cares for Egypt. She has looked after her (i.e. Egypt's) soldiers; she has guarded her; she has brought back her fugitives, and collected together her deserters; she has pacified Upper Egypt, and expelled her rebels.'[7] These words suggest that Ahhotpe had at some critical moment seized the initiative in restoring order in Egypt when control had been lost, possibly on the death of

[1] See above, pp. 72–3; A, 1, 30.   [2] §v, 10, 15; §v, 8, 67.   [3] G, 7, 28–9.
[4] §v, 10, 14; §v, 4, 150; A, 1, 40.   [5] §iv, 1, pl. 3. See Plate 86.
[6] Compare §v, 7, pl. 1 with §1, 5, pl. 1 (after p. 219).
[7] G, 7, 21, 10–16.

Seqenenre or of Kamose.[1] The terms of her praise are unusually precise and they may well signify that her behaviour had been crucial to the establishment of the unified kingdom at the time of the expulsion of the Hyksos; she may even have acted as co-regent with Amosis early in his reign, which would explain why her name is associated with his on the doorway found at Buhen.[2] When she died her burial equipment was lavishly provided with precious objects, many of which carried Amosis's name.[3] An official named Kares, who described himself as the 'chief steward of Ahhotpe', set up an inscription in the tenth year of Amenophis I, enumerating the honours paid him by Ahhotpe.[4] This text has been used to prove that Queen Ahhotpe survived until at least the tenth year of Amosis's successor. In view, however, of the strong evidence that Amosis arranged her burial, and also of the clear ascendancy of Ahmose-Nefertiry towards the end of Amosis's reign, it is likely that the Ahhotpe whom Kares served was the wife of Amenophis I.[5]

AHMOSE-NEFERTIRY

The third outstanding royal lady was Ahmose-Nefertiry, the wife of Amosis. She was herself of royal blood, being perhaps the daughter of Kamose,[6] or even a sister or half-sister of Amosis himself.[7] In the inscription of Year 22 at El-Ma'sara, she is associated prominently with Amosis;[8] in the Abydos inscription in which Amosis records his intention to honour the memory of Tetisheri, Ahmose-Nefertiry participates in the planning of the chapel and pyramid.[9] Her name is found at Sinai,[10] and as far south as the island of Sai in Nubia.[11] An unusual stela found at Karnak depicts Amosis, accompanied by Ahmose-Nefertiry and their son Ahmoseankh, presenting bread to Amon-Re. The text recounts the transfer of the office of second-prophet of Amon-Re in return for a substantial payment in the form of goods, valued in terms of gold. Unfortunately the part of the text describing the character of the transfer is lost, and it is by no means clear whether the office is being given or sold to the queen or to another.[12] In the scene accompanying the text the queen is shown at the same scale

[1] G, 3, 173; §II, 4, 55.   [2] §v, 10, 16.
[3] §v, 1, pls. I, II, V–VIII; §IV, 11, nos. 52004, 52069–72, 52642, 52645, 52658.
[4] G, 7, 45–9.
[5] §I, 14, 251, with n. 3; G, 3, 173, with n. 3.
[6] §v, 5, 159 n. 2, 183 n. 2.   [7] §I, 14, 257.
[8] G, 7, 25.   [9] G, 7, 26–7.
[10] §IV, 6, vol. II, 149 (no. 171).   [11] §III, 17, 77; but see above, p. 298.
[12] §v, 6, 57–63; §v, 3, 10–19. Words in this text suggesting that the Queen was of humble birth should probably not be taken at their face value; see A, 1, 30 f.

as the king and the god—a further indication of the special dignity of her position. It may be the case that her influence during the reign of her husband was no greater than that of Tetisheri and Ahhotpe, but subsequently her fame far surpassed that of her two predecessors. Living on into the reign of her son Amenophis I, she remained the most important lady in Egypt, and finally she shared a mortuary temple and perhaps a tomb with him. In later times she was linked with him in a cult which received particular devotion in the Theban Necropolis, especially in the artisans' quarter at Deir el-Medîna.[1]

Born of royal blood and possessing perhaps as much royal power as their husbands, these outstanding women established a pattern of female authority within the framework of Egyptian kingship which was to have a considerable effect on Egyptian history in the following centuries. In addition to their hereditary rights, they acquired religious power by closely associating themselves with Amon-Re, the god of the new Egyptian state. The office of 'God's Wife of Amun' was established early in the Eighteenth Dynasty, and the first two recorded holders were Ahhotpe and Ahmose-Nefertiry.[2] It was in late times usually held by a princess, not a queen, and it eventually became an instrument of great political importance.[3]

VI. CONSOLIDATION UNDER AMENOPHIS I

By astronomical calculation from a date in a calendar in the Ebers Medical Papyrus, the ninth year of Amenophis I has been fixed at 1537 B.C.,[4] and consequently the first year of the reign at 1546 B.C. A Theban official, Amenemhet, declares in an inscription in his tomb, that he served twenty-one years in the same office under Amenophis I.[5] The figures given by Manetho's epitomists confirm a length of twenty-one years, or a little more.[6] Scarcely anything of the happenings of this reign has been preserved in surviving records, and yet there can be no doubt that during this time Egypt's ruler proceeded steadily to consolidate the gains of the equally long and shadowy reign of Amosis I. In matters of foreign policy alone, some idea of the scale of success, only tenuously suggested by contemporary records, can be obtained

---

[1] On the tomb and the cult see below, p. 312.
[2] §v, 9, 5–6; A, 1, 71 ff.   [3] §v, 2, 132; G, 3, 318, 343.
[4] C.A.H. I³, pt. 1, ch. vi, sect. 1.   [5] §vi, 3, 60–3 and pl. 18.
[6] §ii, 6, 101, 111, 115.

from the claim made by Tuthmosis I, the successor of Amenophis I, in a stela set up in his second year at Tumbos in the region of the Third Cataract in Nubia, that his southern boundary was as far as 'this land' (probably the region of Tumbos) and his northern on the Euphrates.[1] It cannot be believed that Tuthmosis had reached these limits as early as his second year without very considerable territorial gains on the part of Amenophis I.[2]

In Nubia campaigns are reported by Ahmose, son of Ibana, and by Ahmose-Pennekheb. The former, declaring that Amenophis campaigned to 'broaden the boundaries of Egypt',[3] describes an expedition against the Nubian *iwntyw*, who may have been desert-dwellers to the east or west of the Nile valley, accustomed to raid the settled inhabitants of Egyptian Nubia.[4] The latter mentions only a campaign in Kush in which he captured a prisoner.[5] It seems probable that conditions in Nubia remained fairly peaceful throughout the reign, the emphasis of policy being concentrated on administration and building. Tjuroy, the commandant of Buhen under Amosis I, became viceroy under Amenophis I, and graffiti giving his name have been found at Semna, dated to Year 7, and on the island of Uronarti, dated to Year 8. Records of his presence and activities occur elsewhere in Nubia, but as dates are lacking they may refer to the years when he served under Tuthmosis I.[6] On the island of Sai there has been found good evidence of temple-building by Amenophis I, and it is possible that fragments from the site bearing the names of Amosis I and his wife are also part of the work of Amenophis.[7] Sai probably marked the limit of the Egyptian advance into Nubia during this reign, and the association of Amenophis I with Karoy (a more southerly region of Nubia) in the stela of an official named Pentaweret, is probably an anachronism.[8]

Evidence for aggressive activity in Asia is minimal. A mention of Qedmi (a part of Palestine or Transjordan)[9] on a fragment from the tomb often identified as that of Amenophis I,[10] and a hostile mention of Mitanni in the inscription in the tomb of Amenemhet,[11] are the only hints that Amenophis did follow up the campaigns of Amosis in Asia. This evidence, which incorporates no mention of

[1] G, 7, 85, 13–14.

[2] G, 2, 397.

[3] G, 7, 7, 2.

[4] §III, 11, 145–6.

[5] G, 7, 36, 1–2.

[6] §III, 7, 57 ff.; §VI, 10, 211.

[7] G, 6, vol. VII, 165; §III, 17, 75, 77, 79.

[8] G, 7, 50, 12, with n. *a*; §III, 11, 146.

[9] §VI, 9, vol. V, 181.

[10] §VI, 5, pl. 21, 4; cf. §VI, 18, 182 (which wrongly states that the fragment comes from the funerary temple of the king). On the owner of this tomb, see later.

[11] §VI, 3, pl. 18, l. 1.

military operations, is of small value. It is possible that the part
of the text referring to Mitanni may belong to the reign not of
Amenophis I, but of one of his successors.[1] In the early Eighteenth Dynasty, Mitanni and Naharina were apparently synonymous geographical terms, being applied to the area to the east of
the Euphrates; it is inconceivable that Amenophis crossed that
river in campaign.[2] Mitanni influence probably extended far to
the west of the Euphrates, and formed the principal threat to
Egypt in Asia.[3] During the early Eighteenth Dynasty, after the
Egyptian triumph over the Hyksos, Asia as far as the Euphrates
may have been considered properly an Egyptian sphere of influence.[4] There may have been no organized warfare during this
period, but a clash with Mitanni was ultimately inevitable. It can
hardly be claimed that the equivocal mention of Mitanni in the
text of Amenemhet exemplifies the fiercely aggressive attitude of
Amenophis I.[5]

On the basis of one sentence in the record of Ahmose-Pennekheb, it has sometimes been stated that Amenophis I undertook a campaign against the Libyans to avert an invasion of the
Delta.[6] Ahmose says that he captured three hands 'on the north
of Iamu in the land of Kehek (or Iamu-Kehek)'. Kehek is otherwise unknown; it is to be distinguished from Qeheq, a tribe of
Libyans encountered by the Egyptians in later times;[7] it may have
been in Nubia, or even in one of the oases in the Libyan desert.[8]
That the Egyptians remained on relatively peaceful terms with
the Libyans throughout the greater part of the Eighteenth
Dynasty is more probably true than that the two countries were
involved in continuous warfare during this time.[9] Undoubtedly
the positive policy adopted by the early kings of the dynasty towards their foreign neighbours, exemplified in Nubia and Asia,
restrained the Libyans from attempting to follow their ancient
practice of infiltrating the Delta.[10] Yet it is difficult to believe that
this peaceful relationship between Egypt and Libya was not
reached without some demonstration of strength on the part of
Amosis or Amenophis.

The oases in the Libyan desert which had been within the
administrative sphere of Egypt since the Old Kingdom,[11] may

[1] §vi, 4, 327.
[2] §ii, 3, vol. i, 180*.
[3] G, 3, 197–8.
[4] §i, 7, 116.
[5] *Ibid.* 117.
[6] G, 7, 36, 3–4; cf. G. i, 254.
[7] §vi, 12, 59 n. 3.
[8] §ii, 3, vol. i, 123*; §ii, 5, 19 nn. 7, 8.
[9] §ii, 4, 81; §vi, 2, 212; cf. §vi, 12, 59–60.
[10] §vi, 12, 70.
[11] §vi, 8, 226–7.

have been occupied by Hyksos sympathizers during the Second Intermediate Period. Kamose found it necessary to send a force to the Northern Oasis during his campaign against Auserre Apophis, and it is probable that early in the Eighteenth Dynasty central control was reasserted over all the oases. By the reign of Amenophis I there already existed a high official described as 'mayor of the oases'.[1] In Sinai, too, Amenophis was active. Small votive offerings in the temple-area at Serābīt el-Khādim testify to the presence of his agents in the peninsula; he also instituted new building in the temple there, and undertook some reconstruction of the Middle Kingdom structure.[2]

Records of the domestic activities of Amenophis I are even scantier than those of Amosis. Nevertheless, the flourishing condition of the country, which enabled his successors to achieve so much, must have owed a great deal to the diligence with which Amenophis continued and amplified the policies of Amosis. Traces show that in building he was active in many parts of Egypt, but as his buildings were mostly dismantled by his successors, very little remains standing. At Karnak much has been recovered from the foundations of later buildings and from the inside of the third pylon.[3] One whole alabaster shrine has been retrieved from the third pylon of the great temple. This shrine may be the very building mentioned by Ineny, who subsequently became mayor of Thebes.[4] On the west bank of the Nile at Thebes a mud-brick temple or shrine to Hathor was built at Deir el-Bahri, which was later removed to make way for Hatshepsut's great temple;[5] along its avenue of approach were erected sandstone statues of Amenophis I.[6] Elsewhere in Upper Egypt, many remains of temple buildings erected by Amenophis have been found. A few blocks on Elephantine Island and at Kōm Ombo give no indication of the scale of operations at these places.[7] In the temple of Nekhbet at El-Kāb very considerable works were carried out, as might be expected in a locality which at this period seems to have been particularly devoted to the Theban royal house.[8] Like his father Amosis, Amenophis built at Abydos. He did not, however, erect separate funerary monuments like Amosis, but he added a chapel to the Osiris Temple in which he honoured Amosis

---

[1] G, 7, 50–1.   [2] §iv, 6, vol. ii, 37, 149.

[3] G, 8, vol. ii, 868; §vi, 1, 85, 88, 269, 276, 280.

[4] §vi, 13, pls. 123–5; G, 7, 53, 14–17; cf. below, p. 391.

[5] G, 6, vol. ii, 113; §vi, 16, 208–9.

[6] G, 6, vol. ii, 131; §vi, 16, 209.

[7] G, 6, vol. ii, 226; vol. vi, 201.   [8] §vi, 15, 99–102; §vi, 7, 37.

in particular.[1] No trace of his work has been found in Lower Egypt.

In making the arrangements for his burial, Amenophis I, it is thought, departed from the long-established custom of having a funerary complex of tomb with mortuary temple adjoining it. He separated the temple from the tomb. The tomb usually identified as his, cut into the rock of Dirā Abu'n-Naga, was probably the precursor of the tombs prepared in the Valley of the Kings for all the New Kingdom pharaohs who followed him. Considerable doubt exists, however, about the identification of the owner of this tomb, and it is possible that it was made for Ahmose-Nefertiry.[2] Nevertheless, the existence of an independent mortuary temple shared by Amenophis and Ahmose-Nefertiry, built on the edge of the cultivated area in western Thebes, renders valid the claim that Amenophis I separated temple from tomb.[3] The innovations introduced by Amenophis into royal funerary practice, and the establishment of a special corps of trained necropolis-workers installed in an exclusive workmen's village, account for the particular devotion paid to the memory of this king in subsequent times. The centre of this cult was in the workers' village at Deir el-Medīna, but there were other shrines to the king in the Theban Necropolis and elsewhere in Egypt.[4] In this cult Amenophis was closely associated with his mother, Ahmose-Nefertiry.

A fragment of an alabaster vessel found in the tomb of doubtful ownership, bears the name of Auserre Apophis and of a princess named Herit. Its discovery has prompted the suggestion that the royal house of the Eighteenth Dynasty was linked by marriage to the Hyksos house.[5] No other evidence supports this suggestion of what to later generations certainly would have been thought a monstrous alliance. Unfortunately too little is known of the early rulers of the dynasty for any conclusion to be drawn about their attitude to the Asiatics who had so recently been expelled. A political marriage might well have been effected either before or after the expulsion; but as for so much else at this time, satisfactory answers cannot be provided.

[1] §vi, 14, frontispiece and pls. 62–4.
[2] G, 6, vol. i², pt. ii, 599; §i, 10, vol. i, 43.
[3] §vi, 5, 153–4; §vi, 17, 11–15.
[4] §vi, 6, 159–203; §v, 2, 73–4; C.A.H. ii³, pt. 2, ch. xxxv, sect. iii.
[5] §vi, 5, 152; §vi, 11, vol. ii, fig. 2; §i, 13, 147; G, 2, 332; §i, 7, 116.

CHAPTER IX

EGYPT: INTERNAL AFFAIRS FROM TUTHMOSIS I TO THE DEATH OF AMENOPHIS III

I. THE RULE OF THE MILITARY KING

Out of the struggles to regain her independence and her ascendancy over the warlike nations of Western Asia, Egypt during the Eighteenth Dynasty emerged, for the first time in her history, as a predominantly military state under the rule of a king dedicated from early youth to the leadership of his army and navy and to the expansion and consolidation of his empire by force of arms.

Elevated while scarcely more than a boy to the rank of commander-in-chief of the armed forces, the heir apparent to the Egyptian throne under Tuthmosis I and his successors devoted a considerable portion of his early years to training himself in the arts of war.[1] Proficiency as an archer, a charioteer, and a ship-handler, achieved under the supervision of his father's veterans, ranked high among the qualifications demanded of the future king and were the accomplishments in which throughout his life he took his greatest pride.[2] Experience in actual combat followed shortly after the young ruler's accession to the throne, an occasion almost invariably seized upon by the princes of Nubia and Asia to revolt against their Egyptian overlord. Following the conquests of Tuthmosis III one or two campaigns usually sufficed to restore order throughout the empire and eliminated the need for further show of force on the part of the pharaoh. Nevertheless, the military point of view remained with the king throughout his reign and profoundly affected the nature of his government and the internal conditions of the land which he governed.

At home the pharaoh ruled his country with the same absolute power, the same taut efficiency, and the same meticulous attention to detail as had characterized his command of the army in the field. Although theoretically a god, as in the Old and Middle Kingdoms,[3] his power no longer rested on any such fictional

---

[1] §1, 7, 30–1; §1, 3, 454–5.
[2] See below, p. 333.　　　　[3] §1, 11, 192; §1, 9, 72.

basis, but rather on 'his control of the machinery of government, including the army and police', the legislative and judiciary branches of the state, and apparently also the priesthood.[1] The host of crown officials whom he appointed to assist him in the administration of Egypt itself constituted a tightly organized chain of command through which the will of the ruler was imposed upon every department and activity of the kingdom and was transmitted ultimately to each of its subjects. The unique power centred in the pharaoh was further emphasized by the division (or re-division[2]) of the country into two administrative units, the South and the North, each with its own vizier and its own treasurer,[3] and by the appointment of still another royal official to the viceregency of the crown provinces of Nubia.[4] From this arrangement it resulted that, apart from the king himself, there was no single person or group of persons whose jurisdiction extended, even in a subordinate capacity, over the whole of the kingdom, let alone the whole of the empire. To maintain a government so organized at peak efficiency and free from corruption required the king's personal supervision to an extent never before demanded of an Egyptian ruler; and it was because the great pharaohs of the Eighteenth Dynasty devoted the same care to the administration of their kingdom as they did to the training and leadership of their armed forces that Egypt under them rose to new heights of prosperity and cultural achievement.

It must be confessed that this picture of the military king is based chiefly on the career of Tuthmosis III, the years of whose independent reign were divided equally between his conquests abroad and his administrative tours of inspection at home and whose amazing versatility and vigorous personality made themselves felt in every branch of the government and every phase of the national life. On the other hand, it is clear that the pattern of kingship followed by Tuthmosis III had already been established by his grandfather, Tuthmosis I, and was maintained, in so far as their abilities permitted, by his father, Tuthmosis II, by his son and grandson, Amenophis II and Tuthmosis IV, and, in the early years of his reign, by his great-grandson, Amenophis III.[5] Although during the period dominated by Hatshepsut and her satellites no major military operations were undertaken[6] and some of the Asiatic garrisons may even have been withdrawn, both the army and the navy appear to have been maintained at

---

[1] §1, 4, 154–6. See also §1, 9, 59–71 *passim*; §1, 2, 235.
[2] §1, 8, 19–21.   [3] See below, pp. 354 ff.   [4] See below, p. 348.
[5] See below, pp. 315, 334, 338.   [6] See, however, §1, 6, 102–4.

full strength and in a reasonable condition of readiness.[1] In any case, this period, fortunately for Egypt's position as a great power of the ancient world, was only a brief interlude in the vigorous rule of the succession of soldier-statesmen who formed the backbone of the Eighteenth Dynasty.

II. THE TUTHMOSIDE SUCCESSION[2]

At his death in 1526/5 B.C. Amenophis I was succeeded by a middle-aged soldier named Tuthmosis, who may have been his co-regent during the last years of his reign,[3] but who appears to have been his brother-in-law rather than his son.[4] It would seem, in any case, that the new king acquired the throne chiefly through his wife, Ahmose, a princess of the blood royal, who is probably to be identified as a younger sister of Amenophis I and a daughter of King Amosis and Queen Ahmose Nefertiry.[5] On the other hand, though his mother, Seniseneb, was neither a king's wife nor a king's daughter, it is not unlikely that Tuthmosis himself belonged to a collateral branch of the royal line or was descended from an earlier family of Theban kings.[6] Certainly in spirit, if not in blood, he was a true successor of the warlike founders of the Eighteenth Dynasty and the agent by whom their plans for the aggrandizement of Egypt, held in abeyance during the period of reconstruction, were effectively carried forward.

The beginning of the reign of Tuthmosis I was announced in a circular letter dated to Regnal Year 1, Month 3 of Proyet, Day 21, the day of his accession to the throne, and issued apparently to all the key officials of the realm. Two copies of this letter, addressed in both instances to Tjuroy, the Viceroy of Nubia, are preserved for us on stelae from Wādi Halfa and Qūbān.[7] In it the new ruler proclaims his kingship, prescribes the oath to be taken in his name, and publishes his royal titulary, including his praenomen

---

[1] This is evident from the promptness with which Tuthmosis III, following Hatshepsut's disappearance, was able to launch a full-scale and highly successful campaign in Asia. See also §1, 5, 46 (pl. 6, line 15); §1, 10, 13–19.

[2] Scholars have generally abandoned the elaborate and unconvincing reconstruction of this succession presented by Kurt Sethe in §11, 40, and restated in §11, 41. Both of these publications, however, are extremely useful for the collected source material which they contain and are therefore listed in the bibliography and cited in the footnotes accompanying this section.

[3] The names and figures of both kings appear on an alabaster chapel of Amenophis I at Karnak (§11, 7, vol. XLVII, 167, pls. 24, 25).

[4] §11, 12, 41; §1, 9, 75–6; §11, 40, 1 ff.; §11, 41, 8–9.

[5] §11, 41, §11, 7, 112; §11, 12, 41; §1, 3, 336–7.

[6] §11, 41, 9.   [7] §11, 34, vol. VII, 84, 141; §11, 42, 79–81.

and cult-name, Akheperkare. Though he may have celebrated a *Sed*-festival,[1] his reign, characterized by brilliant campaigns in Nubia and Syria[2] and by extensive building activities at Karnak and elsewhere,[3] probably did not exceed the thirteen years assigned him by Manetho, coming to an end in 1512 B.C., when the elderly pharaoh 'rested in life and went up to heaven, having completed his years in gladness of heart'.[4]

Prince Wadjmose and Prince Amenmose, the two eldest sons of Tuthmosis I,[5] having died during their father's reign, the crown passed at the king's death to his third son, Tuthmosis, the child of a royal princess named Mutnefert, who was perhaps a younger sister of the queen.[6] To strengthen his right to the throne Tuthmosis II had been married to his half-sister, Hatshepsut, the elder of two daughters born to Tuthmosis I and Queen Ahmose.[7] Together the young couple buried their royal father in his tomb in the Valley of the Tombs of the Kings[8] and together, as king and queen, ruled Egypt for perhaps eight years, their reign ending in 1504 B.C.[9] when Tuthmosis II, still in his early thirties, died suddenly—presumably of an illness.[10]

Though hampered by a frail constitution which restricted his activities and shortened his life, the king seems to have had, on the whole, a successful and productive reign, his armies crushing a revolt in Nubia in his first regnal year[11] and later quelling an uprising among the bedawin of southern Palestine;[12] his architects contributed buildings to the temple of the state-god Amun at Karnak.[13] Knowing the temper of his ambitious consort, he contrived before his death to have his only son, Tuthmosis (III), born to him by an obscure harim-girl named Isis,[14] appointed as his successor; and when he 'went up to heaven and joined the

---

[1] §II, 41, 73–4, 97. See §II, 12, 33, 39, 41 n. 3.

[2] See below, p. 347, and ch. x.   [3] See below, p. 391.

[4] §II, 42, 58 (11–13). See §II, 26, 64–5.

[5] §II, 17, 209–11 (here listed as sons of Amenophis I); §II, 41, 19.

[6] §II, 17, 234; §II, 41, 11–12.

[7] §II, 17, 226; §II, 41, 10. The other daughter, Neferubity, died while still a child (§II, 17, 227; §II, 40, 9–10, 125).

[8] §II, 51, 60, 66 (B); §II, 19, 13–14, 140, 143–4.

[9] §II, 29, 41 (possibility 4). Astronomically 1504 B.C. for the accession of Tuthmosis III is just as plausible as the date 1490 B.C. favoured by Parker and from the general chronological point of view is decidedly preferable. A very doubtful 'Year 18' (='Year 8'?) of Tuthmosis II (§II, 8, 99) is discussed by Edgerton (§II, 12, 33).

[10] §II, 12, 42; §I, 9, 112; §II, 19, 15, 50, 144. Cf. §II, 44, no. 61066; §II, 41, sect. 110.   [11] See below, p. 347.   [12] §I, 3, 397–8, 443; §I, 11, 182–3.

[13] See below, p. 391.   [14] §II, 17, 235; §II, 41, 12.

gods' this son, a mere child at the time, 'stood in his place as king of the Two Lands and ruled on the throne of him who begat him'.[1] In texts composed many years later Tuthmosis III recalls how as a youthful acolyte in the temple of Amun he was singled out by the god as Egypt's future king and how he was 'promised the rulership of the Two Lands...at the side of' his father, Tuthmosis II.[2] This assertion would seem to imply that a co-regency was established between the two kings, a state of affairs which, however, is unattested elsewhere. The legitimacy of the young king's claim to the throne may have been reinforced by his marriage to his little half-sister, Neferure, apparently the only child of Hatshepsut and Tuthmosis II,[3] but this, too, is far from certain.[4]

Since at the time of his accession Tuthmosis III was apparently still a child,[5] it was only natural that the dowager queen, Hatshepsut, should have acted as regent and, in the words of the mayor of Thebes, Ineny, should have 'conducted the affairs of the country, the Two Lands being in her control'.[6] For a brief while nothing untoward occurred. At the beginning of the reign Hatshepsut allowed herself to be represented on public monuments standing behind her stepson and bearing only the titles of queen which she had acquired as the wife of Tuthmosis II.[7] It was not long, however, before this shrewd, ambitious, and unscrupulous woman showed herself in her true colours. Stressing the purity of her royal ancestry and evidently relying on the backing of a group of powerful officials, she contrived, late in the second regnal year of Tuthmosis III (1503 B.C.), to have herself crowned king with full pharaonic powers, regalia, and titulary,[8] calling herself the Female Horus Wosretkau, the King of Upper and Lower Egypt Makare, the Daughter of Re, Khnemetamun Hatshepsut.[9] A few years later work was started on her temple at Deir el-Bahri, in the reliefs and inscriptions of which attempts were made to justify her seizure of the throne by scenes purporting to represent her divine birth and by equally fictitious accounts of her appointment and coronation as king under Tuthmosis I.[10] As a key

[1] §II, 42, 59.
[2] §II, 42, 157–9, 180–91; §I, 1, sects. 131–66. See §II, 12, 37–8.
[3] §II, 17, 250–2. Meryetre Hatshepsut (II) was evidently not a daughter of Hatshepsut. See §II, 41, 17; §II, 21, part 2, 106.
[4] See §II, 41, 16; §II, 21, part 2, 105–6. Cf. §II, 39, 198.
[5] §I, 3, 338; §II, 39, 199 n. 15.   [6] §II, 42, 60 (1–2).
[7] §II, 41, 19 n. 2; §II, 39, 203.   [8] §II, 39, 212ff.
[9] §II, 17, 236ff.; §II, 41, 22.
[10] §IV, 15, vol. II, pls. 46–55; §II, 42, 216–34. See §II, 39, 199–201; §II, 12, 31.

figure in his daughter's propaganda the long-dead Tuthmosis I was subjected to a series of highly publicized attentions, including reburial in Hatshepsut's own tomb in the Valley of the Tombs of the Kings and a share in the mortuary services conducted in her Deir el-Bahri temple.[1]

The person who probably contributed most to Hatshepsut's success was her Chief Steward, Senenmut, a canny politician and brilliant administrator who, having entered the royal household during the reign of Tuthmosis II, rose to be the queen's most favoured official, adding one important office to another until he had become, in his own words, 'the greatest of the great in the entire land'.[2] Other influential members of her following were the High Priest of Amun Hapuseneb, the Chancellor Nehesi, the Viceroy of Nubia(?) Inebny, the Treasurer Thuty, the Chief Stewards Amenhotpe, Wadjrenpowet, and Thuthotpe, and Senenmut's brother, the Steward Senmen.[3]

It took Tuthmosis III almost twenty years to break up this powerful coalition and rid Egypt of his now detested stepmother. Still a stripling at the time of her *coup d'état*, he had been allowed to remain on the throne as Hatshepsut's co-regent; and, though during this period his position as a ruler seems to have been more nominal than actual, events continued, as before, to be dated to the years of his reign. It is probable that the young Tuthmosis spent most of his time, as co-regent, with the army, training himself as a soldier, and that it was with the aid of the army that he finally succeeded, in his twenty-second regnal year (1482 B.C.), in making himself sole master of Egypt.[4] Our evidence does not tell us what became of Hatshepsut. It is quite possible that she died a natural death. We know, however, of several incidents which could have contributed to her downfall, such as the premature death of Neferure some time after the eleventh year of the reign,[5] the fall of Senenmut in or before the nineteenth year,[6] and the revolt of the Asiatic principalities in the twenty-first or twenty-second year.[7] We know, too, that in 1482 B.C. Tuthmosis III was no longer a child, but a fiercely energetic and extremely capable leader of men, whose impatience with Hatshepsut's weak foreign policy[8] and whose long-cherished desire

---

[1] §II, 51, 56–7; §II, 19, 146–9, 158–60.

[2] §I, 8, 356–63. See §II, 42, 410 (11).

[3] §I, 8, 286–9, 346–8, 362–5, 397–400, 434–5, 467, 478–9; §II, 38, 176, 208.

[4] §II, 26, 66; §II, 39, 215–16 n. 68. See §II, 50, 175.

[5] §I, 8, 363.   [6] §II, 52, 141, 152; §I, 8, 363.

[7] §II, 42, 647 ff.; §I, 3, 398; §II, 50, 177.

[8] §II, 50, 174–7; §I, 9, 117, 121; §I, 3, 339.

to see her out of the way cannot for a moment be doubted. It is unlikely that 'the Female Horus' was buried in her tomb in the Valley of the Kings[1] and it is certain that, following her death, her statues were destroyed, her obelisks walled around, and her name and figure erased from temples and other public structures throughout Egypt and Nubia.[2] Though some officials survived their service with Hatshepsut to serve again under Tuthmosis III,[3] many of the queen's partisans suffered a fate similar to that of their royal mistress.[4] In later kings' lists of the dynastic period Hatshepsut's existence is ignored,[5] and in the Manethonian lists she is only with difficulty to be recognized under the alias 'Amensis', or 'Amessis'.[6]

During the thirty-two years of his independent reign (1482–1450 B.C.) Tuthmosis III proved himself to be, incontestably, the greatest pharaoh ever to occupy the throne of Egypt. The successive stages in his conquest of south-western Asia will be described shortly.[7] In the present chapter we shall have occasion to follow his expansion and consolidation of Egyptian control over Nubia and the northern Sudan,[8] his vigorous exploitation of the resources of the empire, his very considerable augmentation of the national wealth of Egypt, his efficient organization of the internal administration of the country,[9] his vast programme of building,[10] and the notable advances in Egyptian art and culture achieved under his sponsorship.[11] Thus we may gain some insight into the many-sidedness, the diverse abilities and talents of this Napoleonic little man[12] who appears to have excelled not only as a general, a statesman, and an administrator, but also as one of the most accomplished horsemen, archers, and all-round athletes of his time.[13] He is even credited with having designed furnishings for the temple of Amun[14] and, though the evidence for this achievement is somewhat questionable, there can be no doubt that he was an ardent and discriminating patron of the arts. A

[1] §II, 19, 149–51; §II, 12, 34.

[2] §II, 41, 28–54; §II, 52, 153, 158–9, 189; §II, 19, 138 n. 2; §II, 39, 219; §II, 50, 176–7. See, however, A, 4 (Ed.).

[3] §II, 24, 116; §I, 8, 292–3, 348–52, 365, 385, 401.

[4] §I, 8, 347, 363, 364, 400; §II, 52, 152–3; §II, 22, 82–4.

[5] See, for example, §II, 37, 46–9.

[6] §II, 48, 100–1, 108–15; §II, 26, 40; §II, 41, 6. Cf. §II, 40, 5, 20; §II, 28, 89.

[7] See below, ch. x. [8] See below, p. 347.

[9] See below, p. 353. [10] See below, pp. 392 ff. [11] See below, pp. 407 ff.

[12] On the evidence of his mummy Tuthmosis III was less than 5 feet 4 inches in height (§II, 44, 34). [13] See below, p. 333.

[14] §II, 42, 173 (12 ff.), 637 (12); §II, 9, 11, pl. 10. See §I, 1, sects. 164 (43), 545, 775; §I, 2, 310, 319–20.

serious, methodical, and industrious ruler, his reign—with the exception of one childish outburst of rage directed against the memory of Hatshepsut[1]—was singularly free from acts of brutality, bad taste, and vainglorious bombast, and his records, for their period, are for the most part moderately phrased and sincere in tone.

The next four generations witnessed no major irregularities in the royal succession, the throne in each case passing from the king to his eldest surviving son—though not always, as we shall see, to the original heir apparent.

The death of Tuthmosis III was announced on the last day of the third month of Proyet in the fifty-fourth year of his reign (17 March 1450 B.C.), and on the following day, 'when the morning brightened', his son Amenophis II ascended the throne[2] and plunged energetically into the difficult task of re-placing his great father as the ruler of the Egyptian empire. Born to Tuthmosis III by the King's Great Wife Meryetre Hatshep-sut, the new pharaoh was possessed of great physical strength[3] and had inherited, presumably through his mother, a stature exceeding that of the other Tuthmoside pharaohs.[4] As a soldier he distinguished himself in three or four eminently successful, if somewhat ruthless, campaigns in Syria,[5] and in the Sudan he formally established his frontier at Napata, near the Fourth Cataract of the Nile.[6] The rise to prominence of the solar deity Aten has been traced back to his time,[7] as has also the establish-ment in Egypt of the cult of the Syrian storm god Resheph.[8] As a builder and patron of the arts Amenophis II has left us many handsome monuments at Karnak and elsewhere throughout Egypt and Nubia,[9] and it is under him that marked changes in Egyptian sculpture and painting begin to be apparent.[10] His reign was long and prosperous, exceeding twenty-five years and including at least one celebration of the *Sed*-festival.[11]

Of Amenophis II's queen, the King's Daughter and King's Great Wife, Tio, we know little except that she was the mother of his son and successor, Tuthmosis IV,[12] who came to the throne

---

[1] See, however, A, 4 (Ed.).

[2] §II, 42, 895–6. He appears to have been associated with Tuthmosis III as co-regent for four months preceding the latter's death. See §II, 15, 27; A, 6; A, 5.

[3] §I, 3, 340, 372. See below, p. 335.   [4] §II, 44, no. 61069 (p. 36).

[5] §II, 11, 97–176.   [6] §II, 38, 155–6.

[7] §II, 18, 53–61; §II, 10, 185 ff.   [8] §II, 43, 63 ff.

[9] See below, pp. 391 ff.   [10] See below, pp. 407 ff.

[11] §II, 33, pl. 5 (3). See §II, 26, 64, 66; §II, 25, 25.

[12] §II, 17, 287–8, 300–1; §II, 42, 1561 (497), 1564 (505), 1581.

about 1425 B.C. and died while still a fairly young man after a reign of probably not more than nine years.[1] A granite stela which Tuthmosis IV caused to be erected between the paws of the Great Sphinx at Giza describes how, as a young prince, he used to rest from hunting and target practice in the shadow of the huge figure and how on one occasion the god Harmakhis, with whom the sphinx was then identified, had spoken to him in a dream, promising him the kingship as a reward for freeing the god's image from the encumbering sands of the desert.[2] This fanciful tale, which must have prefaced a record of restorations actually effected at Giza by the king, suggests that Tuthmosis IV was not his father's heir apparent, but had obtained the throne through an unforeseen turn of fate, such as the premature death of an elder brother.[3]

The military career of the youthful pharaoh, though not comparable with those of his father and grandfather, included an armed tour of the Asiatic provinces which carried him over the boundaries of Naharina,[4] and a Nubian expedition which he sent upstream in the eighth year of his reign to check an incursion of desert tribesmen in the region of the province of Wawat.[5] As a builder he was active at Karnak, where, among other projects, he was responsible for the erection (or re-erection) of an obelisk of his grandfather, Tuthmosis III.[6] A pillared hall in the temple at Amada in Lower Nubia appears to have been built to commemorate the second of his two *Sed*-festivals.[7]

In the field of foreign relations Tuthmosis IV's most noteworthy achievement was the marriage which, with some difficulty, he arranged between himself and a daughter of Artatama, ruler of the influential Asiatic state of Mitanni and, potentially at least, Egypt's most valuable ally against the rising power of the Hittites.[8] It was, perhaps, at the time of this marriage that Egypt ceded to Mitanni the important north Syrian town of Alalakh (modern Açana).[9] Unhappily, we do not know the name of the Mitanni princess, and her identification with Queen Mutemweya, one of Tuthmosis IV's chief wives and the mother of his successor, King Amenophis III,[10] rests on no very substantial basis.

[1] §II, 26, 64, 67.   [2] §II, 42, 1539–44; §II, 49, 449.
[3] §I, 3, 341.
[4] §II, 42, 1556, 1560, 1597–8, 1617 (17–18), 1620 (7–9); §I, 3, 409, 446.
[5] §II, 42, 1545–8; §II, 38, 156–8.
[6] §II, 42, 583–5, 1548–52; §53, 81–91; §II, 5, 1–4, §II, 4, 269–80.
[7] §II, 34, vol. VII, 67–9; §II, 42, 1566–8.
[8] §II, 27, vol. I, 247, 1067, no. 29, lines 16–18; §I, 3, 309–10.
[9] See §II, 25, 27.   [10] §II, 17, 310–12, 329–31.

An analysis of the long and peaceful reign of Amenophis III (1417–1379 B.C.) shows it to have consisted of two distinct phases. During his first ten years as king the new ruler exhibited his prowess as a sportsman in a series of widely publicized big-game hunts[1] and led a military expedition into Upper Nubia.[2] This period of youthful activity was followed for the pharaoh by almost three decades of luxurious ease, enhanced by an unparalleled production of magnificent works of architecture, sculpture, and fine craftsmanship and punctuated by the entry into his harim of a succession of Asiatic princesses.[3] From the middle of the reign onwards it is probable that Amenophis III spent much of his life amid the beauty and luxury of his great rambling palace in western Thebes; and it was here in Years 30, 34, and 37, respectively, that he celebrated his first, second, and third jubilees.[4] Through it all Queen Tiy, the daughter of a commoner,[5] remained the dominant influence in the king's life and when he died, probably early in the thirty-ninth year of his reign,[6] Tiy's son, Amenophis IV, later known as Akhenaten, succeeded to the throne[7] and plunged Egypt into that brief, but significant, phase of her history generally referred to today as the Amarna Period.

The final stage in the Tuthmoside succession was inaugurated when Amenophis III, sometime before his thirty-first regnal year, married a woman named Sitamun, believed to have been his own eldest daughter;[8] for among the children of this union was, apparently, Akhenaten's successor, Smenkhkare,[9] the last ruler of Egypt whose ancestry we can trace in a direct line back to Tuthmosis I.[10]

---

[1] §II, 42, 1738–40. See below, p. 338.   [2] §II, 42, 1659–66. See §II, 158–62.
[3] See below, p. 338.
[4] §II, 20, 82–6. A re-examination of the date of the third *ḥb-sd* given in the tomb of Kheruef at Thebes (cf. §II, 14, 475; §II, 23, 193) has shown that it is to be read 'Year 37'—not 'Year 36' (letter from Professor Charles F. Nims of the Oriental Institute's Epigraphic Survey).
[5] §II, 42, 1741; §II, 17, 331–5; §II, 1, 30 ff. See also §I, 9, 323–4.
[6] §II, 20, 87–8.
[7] Apparently without having served previously as his father's co-regent (§II, 23, 189–207; §II, 16, 13–14; §I, 3, 384–6, 631; §II, 45, 173, 184–5; §II, 6, 7–10). See, however, §II, 31, 198; §II, 30, 12; §II, 32, 152–7; §II, 2, 114–17; §VI, 2, 19–33; §II, 3, 113–20; §II, 13, 134–5, 137; §II, 46, 80, 81, 275.
[8] §I, 7, 11 n. 5; §I, 3, 385; §II, 47, 651–7.
[9] §I, 3, 384; §II, 13, 153–60; §II, 36, 44–5.
[10] Tutankhamun, who was less than ten years old when Akhenaten died after a reign of at least seventeen years, obviously cannot have been a son of Amenophis III unless we envisage a long co-regency between the two last-named kings (§II, 13, 153–60; §II, 47, 651–7). See, however, *C.A.H.* II,³ pt. 2, ch. XIX (Ed.).

III. THE POWER OF AMUN

Among the more significant developments of the early New Kingdom were the domination of the national religion by the state-god, Amon-Re, and the important role played by his Karnak temple and its priesthood in the economic and political life of the period.[1]

The ascendancy gained by the once obscure deity of Karnak over the ancient leaders of the Egyptian pantheon—Re of Heliopolis and Ptah of Memphis—was due primarily to the intense and unswerving devotion accorded him since the beginning of the Twelfth Dynasty by the royal house of Thebes, the varying fortunes of which he shared to the full.[2] During the troubled times of the Second Intermediate Period it was Amun of Thebes who became the divine champion of Egyptian independence, and during the Hyksos wars and the subsequent expansion of Egyptian power in Asia and Nubia it was to the favour of Amun more than to any other single factor that the kings piously attributed their victories in the field and their political and administrative successes at home.[3] Furthermore, it was as the son of 'his father, Amun', that the Pharaoh now claimed divine right to the throne, and in at least two Eighteenth Dynasty temples—that of Hatshepsut at Deir el-Bahri and that of Amenophis III at Luxor—considerable space was devoted to scenes purporting to represent the theogamous union of Amun with the queen-mother and the subsequent birth, as a result of this union, of the future king.[4]

Aided and abetted by the Tuthmoside pharaohs, the priesthood of Karnak during the middle years of the Eighteenth Dynasty succeeded in consolidating Amun's supremacy over his fellow divinities and in raising him to a status approximating to that of a 'national god', as we now understand the term. The process, greatly facilitated by the fact that Thebes, the ancient home of his cult, was also the royal Residence and the capital of the empire, is discernible to us in a number of ways. All along the Nile from the Delta to the northern Sudan new cult places of the god were established and new temples erected in his honour, frequently

---

[1] §III, 23, 344 ff.; §III, 34, 150–1; §II, 50, 170–1, 185–6; §I, 11, 194–5; §I, 9, 72–4.

[2] See *C.A.H.* I³, pt. 2, ch. xx and above, ch. II.

[3] §III, 23, 362–5; §III, 19, 41, 44.

[4] §II, 34, vol. II, 106–8, 118–19; §III, 36, 48–65; §I, 4, 154; §III, 4 (reviewed *J.E.A.* I [1914], 230–1).

replacing or overshadowing the shrines of the old local deities.[1] At Karnak the subordination to 'Amon-Re, King of the Gods', of other prominent divinities of the Egyptian pantheon was emphasized by the construction of small temples to these deities within the precincts of Amun's own vast shrine.[2] We find priests of Amun including in their protocols the titles of the High Priest of Re and the High Priest of Ptah[3] and, already under Hatshepsut and Tuthmosis III, claiming jurisdiction, not only over all the priesthoods of Thebes, but also over all the temples and priesthoods of 'Upper and Lower Egypt' and, later, over the priesthoods 'of all the gods'.[4] With the change of Egypt's foreign policy following the reign of Amenophis II from one of military aggression to one of relatively peaceful relations with the rest of the known world, Amun began to subordinate his role as a god of war and bringer of victory and to absorb more completely than ever before the identities of the solar divinity and world-ruler, Re, and the primaeval god Tatenen of Memphis.[5] He was now represented to his worshippers throughout the empire as a cosmic creator-god, and his cult-centre at Thebes was identified as the birthplace of the universe.[6] Long before the end of the Eighteenth Dynasty the dominating influence exerted by the priesthood of Amun on the national religion had become oppressive to minds stimulated by contacts with the outside world and Egypt was ripe for a religious revolution—a revolution which, as we shall see,[7] was presently forthcoming.

Even more oppressive to the nation as a whole and, in the centuries to come, far more undermining to its general welfare were the vast and constantly growing endowments of property and personnel granted by the kings to the temples of Amun and, above all, to his principal temple at Karnak. These endowments, which included the construction and repair of the temple buildings and the huge estates necessary to their maintenance and operation, surpassed by far those accorded to the other divinities of Egypt and were exceeded in their magnitude and richness only by the properties and incomes of the kings themselves.[8] To the temple of

---

[1] §III, 11, 105; §II, 38, 154, 210; §III, 13, vol. II, 127, 128, 140, 147, 148, 155, 156; vol. IV, 100–1; §III, 33, 88–9.

[2] §III, 23, 360–2; §III, 21, 427–2; §II, 34, vol. II, 3 ff., 66–8; §III, 35.

[3] §III, 23, 361; §III, 22, 26–7; §III, 20, 253–4; §III, 21, 431; §I, 11, 195.

[4] §III, 14, vol. I, 30–1 (A100); §III, 23, 366; §III, 22, 12, 17, 80, 81.

[5] §III, 23, 345 ff.; §III, 34, 150–1.   [6] §III, 23, 346–7, 349.

[7] See *C.A.H.* II³, pt. 2, ch. XIX.

[8] §I, 4, 156. The classic references are Papyrus Harris I, drawn up under Ramesses IV of the Twentieth Dynasty (§III, 10; §III, 31; §III, 30, 53), and the

Amun at Karnak fell a major share of the spoils of Egypt's foreign conquests in the form of raw materials, prisoners of war, and slaves taken from the subjugated lands.[1] Hundreds of thousands of acres of the country's best farmland were owned by the temple and cultivated on its behalf by a veritable army of serfs, and on the estates of Amun were to be found vineyards and truck gardens as well as vast herds of livestock of all kinds.[2] Grain and other commodities, collected as rents up and down the land,[3] were transported to the granaries and warehouses of Amun by the god's own fleets of ships, which included sea-going vessels for traffic with the Syrian and Red Sea coasts.[4] In numerous workshops artisans employed by the temple converted gold from Amun's own mines[5] and other valuable materials from his holdings at home and abroad into the lavish furnishings and equipment of his shrines.[6] Although the statement, frequently made by modern scholars,[7] that all temple property was exempt from taxation, is probably incorrect,[8] there can be little doubt that the possessions of the temples of Amun and the other gods were often protected by special royal decrees from seizure and other high-handed acts commonly perpetrated by agents of the Crown on less sacrosanct institutions.[9]

During the Eighteenth Dynasty the various departments of Amun's temporal domain and the numerous trained lay personnel attached thereto were usually entrusted to the charge of high-ranking officials of the pharaonic government. In the reign of Hatshepsut, for example, it was the queen's great administrator, Senenmut, who managed the estates of Amun, and the offices

great Wilbour Papyrus of the time of Ramesses V (§III, 13); but the crushing economic superiority of Amun reflected in these documents had evidently already been established under the Tuthmoside pharaohs.

[1] See, for example, §II, 42, 625–763; §I, 1, §§391–573 (see especially §394); §III, 16, 6–23; §III, 8, 47; §III, 7, vol. I, 79–92; §II, 50, 184–5; §III, 23, 365; §III, 20, 131; §III, 33, 88; §I, 11, 194.

[2] §III, 20, 44–5, 51; §I, 3, 469–70, 505. See §III, 8, 39–42, 47–8; Pap. Harris I, 11, 4–11 (§III, 10, 14; §III, 31, 51 ff.; §III, 30, 53); §III, 13, vol. II, 11, 20 ff., 73 f., 86, 127–56; vol. III, §§23, 24, 30, 31, 52, 96–8, 103, 117, 129, 131, 161, 170, 173, 174, 208, 223, 253, 270.

[3] §III, 12, 20 n. 4, 37–56 (see also §III, 15); §III, 31, 59.

[4] §I, 10, 90–3; §III, 12, 20 n. 4, 37, 41, 47, 62; §III, 20, 255. See Pap. Harris I 11, 8 (§III, 10, 14).

[5] §III, 27, 33–4, 41, 47, 73, 77, 80; §II, 38, 180, 221; §II, 50, 184; §III, 20, 131.

[6] §III, 8, 36–9, 48–59; §III, 7, vol. I, 66–76.

[7] See §I, 4, 156 n. 11; §III, 13, vol. II, 202.

[8] §I, 4, 156–7; §x, 17, 230; §III 17, 32–3; §III, 13, vol. II, 201–10.

[9] §III, 18, 193–208; §I, 4, 157; §x, 17, 219–30; §III, 17, 24–33.

which he held in the temple administration throw considerable light on its size and complexity. Included among his titles were those of Chief Steward of Amun, Steward of the barque 'Amen-Userhet', Overseer of the Granaries of Amun, Overseer of the Fields of Amun, Overseer of the Cattle of Amun, Overseer of the Gardens of Amun, Chief of the Weavers of Amun, and Overseer of Works, or supervisor of building construction, of the god.[1] Scenes and inscriptions in the tomb of Rekhmire at Thebes show that—at least in the reign of Tuthmosis III—the whole economic organization of the temple of Amun at Karnak was under the supervision of the southern vizier (see below, §VIII). It was, on the other hand, by no means rare for members of the priesthood of Amun, especially the high priest, to take active part in the administration of the temple property.[2] Hapuseneb, who under Hatshepsut was First Prophet, or High Priest, of Amun, and Menkheperreseneb, who held the same exalted post in the reign of Tuthmosis III, call themselves Overseer(s) of All Offices of the Estate of Amun;[3] and the High Priest, Mery, under Amenophis II, exercised the function of Steward of Amun, Overseer of the Treasuries of Amun, Overseer of the Fields of Amun, and Overseer of the Cattle of Amun.[4] The last two titles were borne also during the reign of Hatshepsut and Tuthmosis III, by the Second Prophet of Amun, Ipuyemre, who in his tomb at Thebes is shown inspecting the workshops and other activities of the estate of the god at Karnak, including a pair of large gold and silver obelisks dedicated by Tuthmosis III in the sanctuary (?) of the temple.[5]

Although the estates of Amun, like those of Egypt's many other divinities, had been established primarily as a 'God's Offering', to provide the supplies and equipment necessary for the maintenance of the cult of the god,[6] there can be no doubt that a sizeable portion of the income from these estates reverted to the priesthood, which became thereby one of the country's wealthiest and most envied classes, attracting more and more of the nation's youth into its already numerous ranks.

The priesthood of Amun, headed by the First Prophet, or High Priest,[7] was composed of an upper clergy often referred to

[1] §I, 8, 359, 476. [2] §III, 22, 10ff., 25; §III, 30, 55–8.
[3] §III, 25, 55–6, 228–31, 233–5, §III, 22, 10–15; §I, 8, 286–9, 434.
[4] §III, 25, 56, 235–7; §III, 22, 16–17.
[5] §III, 7, vol. I, 59–76, 96–102, pls. 8, 12–19, 23–7, 37–9. See §III, 9, 47–61.
[6] §II, 20, 160 (zz), n. 302.
[7] §III, 25; §III, 22, 10–18; §III, 30, 59–60; §I, 3, 467–72. On the priesthood in general see §III, 2, 596–608; §III, 26, 56–8.

as the 'Fathers of the God'[1] and included the Second, Third, and Fourth Prophets of Amun;[2] ordinary priests called simply 'Purified Ones' or, perhaps better, 'Purifiers' (w⁽bw);[3] and various 'specialists', such as lector-priests (ḥryw-ḥbt), hierogrammats (sšw mḏ3t-nṯr), horologers (wnwtyw), carrier-priests (w⁽bw nw f3yt), and musicians (šm⁽w).[4] Except for its highest ranks the temple personnel was divided into four phyles, or shifts, each of which served for a month at a time and at the end of its period of service turned over an inventory of temple property to the phyle relieving it.[5] Ladies of rank frequently served as musicians (šm⁽ywt) in the temples of Amun[6] and as members of companies of priestesses described collectively as the 'harim of the god'.[7] Participating—normally through a representative, or substitute—in the cult of Amun was the so-called 'Wife of the God', a title assigned, primarily for political reasons, to the queen (or crown princess) in token of her mythical union with the deity, referred to above.[8]

After what has already been said it seems hardly necessary to add that from the Eighteenth Dynasty on the High Priest of Amun was one of Egypt's richest and most influential dignitaries. In addition to the control which he exercised over the properties of his god both he and the Second Prophet of Amun possessed great houses and estates of their own, staffed by impressive retinues of minor officials, secretaries, and servants of all kinds.[9] In the period with which we are now dealing only a few of the appointees to the office of high priest seem to have been men of ecclesiastical background and training, most of them having been, rather, favoured courtiers of the reigning pharaohs[10] and having held, in addition, key positions in the national government, including in the case of Ptahmose, under Amenophis III, the all-important office of vizier.[11]

Researches of recent years have shown that the political power wielded by the priesthood of Amun was more limited than was

---

[1] §iii, 14, vol. i, 47*–53* (A 127); §iii, 2, 256.
[2] §iii, 22, 10–29, 317–22; §iii, 30, 58–9.
[3] §iii, 14, vol. i, 53*–55* (A 128); §iii, 30, 54, 69–70; §iii, 26, 58; §iii, 3, 21, 53, 336.
[4] §iii, 30, 60–7; §iii, 26, 58; §iii, 14, vol. i, 55*–63* (A 129–36), 95* (A 214); §iii, 16, 19 n. 5; §iii, 2, 300–1, 307, 490–1, 766–8; §iii, 24, 45–6.
[5] §iii, 22, 300–8; §iii, 30, 68; §iii, 2, 602–3.
[6] §iii, 30, 65–7; §iii, 14, vol. i, 95* (A 215); §iii, 3, 21, 333.
[7] §iii, 2, 578–80, 607–8; §iii, 1, 8–30; §iii, 25, 33–5; §iii, 23, 350.
[8] §iii, 28; §iii, 2, 256–7.   [9] §iii, 25, 23, 32–3; §i, 3, 469.
[10] §iii, 22, 10–8.   [11] §i, 8, 299–302; §iii, 25, 99–102, 241–3.

previously supposed.[1] The temple of the god at Karnak, like those of the other divinities of Egypt, appears to have functioned in the strictest sense as a department of the royal administration. It was as representatives of the king that the priests performed the daily ritual in the temple and it was by him that all of them, from the high priest downwards, could on occasion be appointed to or removed from their offices.[2] In spite of the fact that such appointments were sometimes made to appear to come from the god himself[3] and that a priest might also, and frequently did, acquire his office through inheritance, election, or even purchase,[4] it is certainly true that during the New Kingdom 'a strong pharaoh normally controlled the priesthoods as completely, and by essentially the same methods, as he controlled his household or his army'.[5]

There were, however, occasions of doubt or contention regarding the royal succession when aspirants to the throne courted the loyalty of the High Priest of Amun, who, as the principal interpreter of the will of the god, could add divine sanction to the claims of the ruler of his choice. Such an occasion arose towards the end of the reign of Tuthmosis II, when, according to his own later account of the incident, young Tuthmosis III, at that time an acolyte in the temple of Amun at Karnak, was publicly chosen by the god to succeed his father on the throne.[6] In this case the high priest—in the presence of Tuthmosis II and undoubtedly with his approval—caused the image of Amun, which was being borne around the temple in festival procession, to 'seek out' the young prince and stop before him, thereby designating him as the future king.[7] The fickleness of the god—or, rather, the agility with which his priesthood adjusted itself to changing circumstances—is shown by the manner in which a few years later another (or just possibly the same) High Priest of Amun, Hapuseneb, vigorously supported the rival claims of Tuthmosis III's stepmother, Hatshepsut.[8]

Finally, mention should be made of a much damaged passage

---

[1] See §1, 4, 153, 156.

[2] §III, 30, 43–6. See §III, 22, 12–18 *passim*, 79–81, 83.

[3] §1, 4, 157–8; §III, 32, 30–5.   [4] §III, 30, 41–6.

[5] §1, 4, 156.   [6] See above, p. 317 n. 2.

[7] Similar manifestations of the will of the god are said to have inspired Hatshepsut's expedition to Punt (§II, 42, 342, 11–12) and Tuthmosis III's building activities in the temple at Karnak (§II, 42, 833, 16). Later in the New Kingdom 'oracles' were obtained by having the statue of a god move forward or backward to indicate, respectively, an affirmative or negative answer to a question posed (§III, 5, 56–8).

[8] §III, 25, 76–81, 228–31; §1, 8, 286–9, 434–5.

on several of the boundary stelae of King Akhenaten at El-Amarna which has often been cited as evidence that Tuthmosis IV and Amenophis III had trouble with the priesthood of Amun;[1] but which does not, in point of fact, mention the priesthood at all and is susceptible of an entirely different interpretation.[2]

IV. HATSHEPSUT'S EXPEDITIONS

In the absence of any extensive military activity[3] Hatshepsut's trading expedition to Punt and the quarrying and transport of her two pairs of Karnak obelisks stand out among the major achievements of her régime. The voyage to Punt and the first of the obelisk expeditions were, in any case, the two episodes which, together with her allegedly divine origin as the daughter of Amun, she chose to commemorate in the superb reliefs of her temple at Deir el-Bahri;[4] and the vivid manner in which they are there represented more than makes up for the queen's exaggerated estimate of their importance.

Although maritime traffic with the 'incense-land' of Punt, on the east coast of Africa near the southern end of the Red Sea, had been maintained by the Egyptians intermittently since the Old Kingdom,[5] Hatshepsut's temple inscriptions hail her expedition as the first of its kind and attribute its initiation to an oracle of the god Amun.[6] As was usually the case, the principal purpose of the expedition was, in fact, to procure an aromatic tree-gum (myrrh or frankincense), much prized as an incense in the temple rites of Egypt and apparently not obtainable in quantity north of Punt,[7] and to bring back a cargo of living 'myrrh'-trees for replanting in the temple groves of Amun.

It was in the sixth or seventh year after her assumption of the pharaonic titles (Year 8 or 9 of the reign of Tuthmosis III) that Hatshepsut's fleet of five fast sea-going ships, dispatched by the Chancellor Nehesi,[8] set sail for the long voyage southward— probably from a port on the Red Sea coast in the neighbourhood

---

[1] §III, 22, 79–81; §III, 23, 367 (see, however, 495); §III, 6, vol. v, 30–1, pls. 30 (20–1), 32 (22–3). See §III, 29, 116 (7–14).

[2] §I, 8, 300 n. 7.

[3] See, however, §I, 1, sects. 137, 213; §I, 6, 102–4; §I, 5, 46 (line 15); §I, 10, 17 n.1.

[4] §IV, 15, pls. 46–64, 69–86, 153–6; §III, 36, 39–81, pls. 10–17. See §I, 10, 8–18, 29.

[5] §I, 1, sect. 247; §I, 10, 10–13.

[6] §II, 42, 342–3; §I, 1, sect. 285; §II, 50, 169–70.

[7] §IV, 14, 111–14; §IV, 13, 41–53; §IV, 23, 279 ff.

[8] §II, 42, 354 (15–17); §I, 10, 93. On the ships see §IV, 7, 7–9, and §I, 10, 15–16.

of modern Wādi el-Gāsūs. It is now believed that in Hatshepsut's day no navigable waterway existed between the Nile and the Red Sea and that, as in the Old and Middle Kingdoms, a part of the journey, both going and coming, was made overland along the ancient road leading eastward from Koptos across the desert to the sea coast.[1]

In the temple reliefs at Deir el-Bahri we see the expedition, which included detachments of soldiers or marines, arriving at its destination and being hospitably received by the Puntites—a long-haired Hamitic people, similar in physical type to the Egyptians themselves. Perehu, the elderly chief of Punt, and Eti, his corpulent, sway-backed wife,[2] are portrayed with lively interest by Hatshepsut's artists, as is also the characteristic scenery of the tropical land: the domical pile-dwellings of the inhabitants and the groves of palms and incense-trees, with cattle, dogs, apes, giraffes, hippopotami, and other local fauna wandering among them.

In return for weapons and jewellery of Egyptian manufacture the visitors were allowed to load their ships with incense-trees, their roots packed in baskets(?), sacks of aromatic gum, gold, ivory, ebony and other valuable woods, leopard skins, live apes, and 'with natives and their children'. Chiefs of Punt and of several Nubian countries, further to the north, apparently accompanied the fleet on its return journey to Egypt to do homage to Hatshepsut, and a statue of the queen with the god Amun was set up in the remote land which she had 'rediscovered'.[3]

The greater part of the Punt reliefs is taken up with scenes showing the weighing and measuring of the cargoes and with formal announcements of the success of the expedition in the presence of Amun and the court at Thebes. It is interesting to note that in all these scenes Tuthmosis III, Hatshepsut's co-regent, appears only once and then only in a minor capacity, offering incense to the barque of Amun.[4]

Some eight years earlier, while still bearing only the titles of queen, but in obvious anticipation of her impending coronation as 'king', Hatshepsut dispatched a very much larger expedition to the quarries of red granite near Aswān to procure the first of her two pairs of obelisks in the temple of Karnak.[5] Her steward, Senenmut, has left an inscription on the rocks at Aswān stating

---

[1] §iv, 17, 270, 273; §i, 10, 13–15; §iv, 16, 64.
[2] §ii, 34, vol. ii, 115–16. See §iv, 18, 44–6, pl. 9; §iv, 4, 307–11; §iv, 9, 303–16; §iv, 26, 149–51.
[3] §iv, 20, 91–9.   [4] §iv, 15, vol. iii, pl. 82.   [5] §i, 6, 92–6.

that it was he who initiated the work on 'the two great obelisks' of 'the God's Wife and King's Great Wife, ...Hatshepsut', for the festival of 'Millions(-of-Years)';[1] and her treasurer, Thuty, tells us that these obelisks were (together?) 108 cubits (185 feet) in height and were 'sheathed in their entirety in gold'.[2] By the time the two towering monuments were set up at the eastern end of the Amun temple[3] Hatshepsut had been crowned 'king', and it is her titles as a 'pharaoh' which appear on the tip of the southern obelisk, now in Cairo,[4] and on relief representations of the two obelisks preserved at Deir el-Bahri[5] and on a block from her quartzite sanctuary at Karnak.[6]

A famous relief in Hatshepsut's temple at Deir el-Bahri[7] provides a detailed representation of the transport by river of what is now recognized as the first pair of the queen's obelisks.[8] Lashed between transverse baulks of timber and mounted on long sledges, the great shafts lie butt to butt on an enormous barge, built of sycomore wood, heavily braced athwartships, and fitted with four oversize steering oars. An estimate based on the stated dimensions of a similar barge used in the transport of the somewhat smaller obelisks of Tuthmosis I[9] has placed the length of this vessel at over 300 feet and its beam at over 100 feet.[10] The barge is towed by twenty-seven ships, deployed in three columns, and propelled by 864 oarsmen.[11] Each column of tow-boats is led by a pilot vessel and there are, in addition, three escort ships on which religious ceremonies seem to be in progress. At Thebes, the fleet was welcomed by troops of marines and recruits, mustered to unload the obelisks, and by priests and dignitaries of the court, all rejoicing and acclaiming Hatshepsut and, after her, Tuthmosis III. In a final scene we see the obelisks, now standing in the temple, being dedicated to Amon-Re, Lord of Karnak.

Late in Regnal Year 15 of Tuthmosis III, seven years after the return of the trading fleet from Punt, the quarrying of Hatshepsut's second pair of Karnak obelisks was begun under

---

[1] §1, 6, 92–5, fig. 3.   [2] §11, 42, 425–6. See §1, 6, 99; §1v, 11, 247.
[3] §1v, 25, 140–2, pls. 4–6; §1, 6, 92–6.
[4] §1v, 10, no. 17012. See also §1v, 25, 140–2; §1, 6, 95–6.
[5] §1v, 15, vol. v1, pl. 156.
[6] §1v, 12, pl. 12A; §11, 42, 374–5. See §1, 6, 95–6. See Plate 89.
[7] §1v, 15, vol. v1, pls. 153–6.   [8] §1, 6, 95.
[9] §11, 42, 56 (13–15).
[10] §1v, 3, 109. Cf. §1v, 1, 290–306; §1v, 2, 158–64; §1v, 21, 237–56; §1v, 22, 39–43.
[11] §1v, 15, vol. v1, pls. 153–4; §1, 1, sect. 323ff.

the direction of Senenmut's colleague, the Steward Amenhotpe, who has left records of his achievement both in his tomb at Thebes[1] and in a graffito on the rocky island of Siheil, near Aswān.[2] One obelisk of this pair, ninety-seven and a half feet high, still stands where it was set up, in the hall of Tuthmosis I between the fourth and fifth pylons of the temple;[3] and on its shaft is the statement that the queen made it for her father, Amun '(on) the first occasion of the *Sed*-festival', or royal jubilee.[4] An admirably worded inscription on the base-block of the huge monolith describes how it and its fallen mate were freed from the quarry in seven months, being ready for loading and transport downstream to Thebes in Year 16, on the last day of the fourth month of Shomu.[5] The work was evidently carefully timed, for the latter date fell late in the summer when, thanks to the yearly inundation, the Nile was beginning to reach its maximum width and depth. Unlike those of the earlier pair, only the upper halves of the shafts of the jubilee obelisks were overlaid with gold, the metal in this case, however, being applied in a thick layer to the surface of the stone.[6]

Although none of these obelisks was as large as two of Tuthmosis III's,[7] their quarrying, transport, and erection represent remarkable achievements in engineering and reflect the absolute control exercised by the queen over Egypt's vast and efficiently organized resources of manpower, equipment, and materials.

The activity of Hatshepsut's mining expeditions in the turquoise mines of Sinai is attested by a rock-tablet in the Wādi Maghāra and ten inscriptions in the temple at Serābīt el-Khādim.[8] Dates in Regnal Years 11 and 16 (counted from the accession of Tuthmosis III) occur among these inscriptions;[9] and a stela of Year 20 erected at Serābīt on behalf of Hatshepsut and Tuthmosis III is the latest dated monument of the queen which we now[10] possess, antedating by only a short time her disappearance in Year 22.

In a desert valley near Beni Hasan Hatshepsut dedicated two rock-cut shrines to the lioness-goddess, Pakhet,[11] and on the

---

[1] §IV, 19, 2, pl. 2.   [2] §I, 6, 89–91, pl. 16 B, fig. 1.
[3] §II, 34, vol. II, 28–9, §IV, 24, vol. II, 880f., fig. 420. See also §II, 7, vol. XLVI, 30.   [4] §II, 42, 358–9. See §II, 39, 204–6; §II, 15, 26.
[5] §II, 42, 361–9 (see especially 367 [3–5]).   [6] §IV, 11, 246; §I, 6, 98–9.
[7] The Lateran obelisk (height 105–6 feet) and the Constantinople obelisk (height 94–105 feet). See below, p. 391.
[8] §IV, 8, nos. 44, 174 A, 177–9, 181, 182, 184, 186, 187, 340(?).
[9] Nos. 179 and 44.   [10] No. 181.
[11] §II, 34, vol. IV, 163–4; §IV, 6, 709–23; §IV, 5, 12–20.

façade of the larger shrine, generally known as the Speos Artemidos, caused to be carved a long inscription in which she records her restoration of a number of temples of Middle Egypt, damaged or destroyed during the Hyksos occupation of the region. 'I have raised up what was dismembered,' says the queen, '(even) from the first time when the Asiatics were in Avaris of the North Land, (with) roving hordes in the midst of them overthrowing what had been made.' At the end of the text she adds: 'My command stands firm like the mountains, and the sun's disk shines and spreads rays over the titulary of my august person, and my falcon rises high above the kingly banner unto all eternity.'[1]

V. THE SPORTING TRADITION

Wholly consistent with the vigorous spirit which brought them success on the field of battle was the enthusiasm displayed by the rulers and other prominent Egyptians of the New Kingdom for such activities as target shooting with the bow and arrow, ship handling, and, above all, the training and driving of teams of chariot horses.[2] There can be no doubt that, apart from their value as military exercises, these occupations, like the hunting of big game, were entered into, as sports, for the pleasure and excitement which they provided. This was as true of the young prince, whose education as a matter of course included training as a bowman and charioteer, as it was of his father, the king, seeking relaxation from the rigours of war or the cares of state. We have no reason to question the caption in a private tomb at Thebes which describes the boy-prince Amenophis (the future King Amenophis II) as 'enjoying' a lesson in archery being given him by the elderly mayor of This,[3] or the statement of Tuthmosis IV on his famous Sphinx Stela that in his youth 'he did a thing which gave him pleasure' when, all alone except for two attendants, he indulged in target practice, lion hunting, and 'coursing in his chariot' in the wastelands west of Memphis.[4] Moreover, pride in their undoubted ability as sportsmen and athletes led kings like Tuthmosis III and Amenophis II to publicize their accomplishments along these lines with the same insistence that they advertised their prowess as warriors and their wisdom as statesmen. So there grew up the tradition that, as in all other fields of

---

[1] §1, 5, 43–56.
[2] §v, 1, 9–14; §v, 3, 49–53; §v, 17, 234–57; §11, 50, 195–200.
[3] §v, 3, 52–3, fig. 7; §11, 35, 227 (5, IV, 1).
[4] §11, 42, 1541 (8–15); §11, 49, 449.

endeavour, the king must excel his contemporaries in the field of sport and must strive to surpass the sporting achievements of his royal predecessors. By the latter part of the Eighteenth Dynasty this tradition had grown so strong that even a naturally indolent ruler like Amenophis III laid great store, during the first decade of his reign, on building up an enviable reputation as a big-game hunter.[1]

The introduction of the horse and chariot into Egypt during the Hyksos Period[2] not only revolutionized the science of war, but provided a sport more dashing than any previously known and added both verve and a quality of knightly dignity to such ancient pastimes as archery and hunting. The equestrian spirit which during the first century of the Eighteenth Dynasty developed in the pharaohs and their followers found full expression in the person of King Amenophis II, whose youthful activities are described in vivid fashion on a great limestone stela which he caused to be set up near the Sphinx at Giza.[3] 'Now when he was (still) a lad', says the inscription on this stela, 'he loved horses and rejoiced in them. It was strengthening of the heart to work them, to learn their natures, to be skilled in training them, and to enter into their ways. When (it) was heard in the palace by his father, ...[Tuthmosis III]..., the heart of his majesty was glad when he heard it, rejoicing at what was said about his eldest son....' 'Then his majesty said to those who were at his side: "Let there be given to him the very best horses in my majesty's stable which is in Memphis, and tell him: 'Take care of them, instil fear into them, make them gallop, and handle them if there be resistance to thee!'"' Now after it had been entrusted to the King's Son to take care of horses of the king's stable, well then, he did that which had been entrusted to him....He trained horses without their equal: they would never grow tired when he took the reins, nor would they sweat (even) at a high gallop.'[4]

The horses owned by the kings and other well-to-do Egyptians of the Eighteenth Dynasty were primarily harness animals, driven in pairs, or spans, from chariots of light construction.[5] They were, however, also occasionally ridden, and not, as was once supposed, only by grooms and stable-boys.[6] In type they resembled the present-day Arabian and the Barb of North Africa,

---

[1] See below, p. 337 nn. 8 and 9.
[2] §v, 19, 152–8; §v, 13, 59–60; §v, 14, 56, 58; §v, 6, 250, fig. 8.
[3] §v, 7, 129–34; §v, 16, 31–8.
[4] Translation by Wilson in §ii, 49, 244. See also §ii, 46, 67–9; §v, 17, 256–7.
[5] §v, 19, 155–7. [6] §v, 15, 263–71.

but were smaller than the average modern horse, being, in fact, scarcely more than ponies—fast and high spirited, but obviously incapable of heavy work.[1] A small mare, not more than twelve and a half hands high, was found buried with full honours near the tomb of Senenmut at Thebes, its back protected by a leather-covered saddle-cloth, or blanket, its short mane tied up in tufts with strips of leather.[2] Probably of somewhat earlier date is a horse whose body was found lying on the Middle Kingdom rampart of the fortress of Buhen in the northern Sudan.[3] In general, the horse appears to have been a costly, highly prized, and much pampered animal and to have been treated by its owner with consideration often exceeding that which he accorded his fellow men.[4]

To perfect themselves in firing rapidly and accurately from a fast-moving chariot and in obtaining the maximum penetration from the recently imported composite bow and its heavy, bronze-tipped arrows, the royal bowmen of the Eighteenth Dynasty frequently indulged in a spectacular type of mounted archery practice, in which the usual target of wood or reed was replaced by a thick plate of copper fastened to a tall, sturdy pole. 'In the presence of the whole army' Tuthmosis III drove an arrow deeply into such a target, which he subsequently set up in the temple of Amun as a sample of his prowess.[5] He was, however, outdone by his son, Amenophis II, one of the greatest archers of ancient times, who, riding in his chariot at full speed past a row of four copper plates, 'a palm (three inches) in their thickness' and spaced about thirty-five feet apart, shot an arrow clean through each of them, so that it 'came out of it and dropped to the ground'.[6] A fine granite relief from Karnak shows Amenophis II on another occasion shooting from his chariot into a copper ingot, which he has 'pierced with many shafts, three hand-breadths of them standing out at the back of the plate'; the accompanying inscription states that 'His Majesty performed this act of sportsmanship in the sight of all the land'.[7] Or again, we are told how this famous athlete and sportsman 'drew three hundred stiff bows, comparing the workmanship of the artisans who made them in order to distinguish the ignorant from the

---

[1] §v, 19, 153–4.
[2] §v, 9, 8, figs. 14, 15, 17; §v, 2, 317–19.   [3] §v, 6, 249–51.
[4] §v, 19, 154; §II, 52, 34, 77, pls. 44, 80.
[5] §II, 42, 1245 (3–11); §II, 49, 243.
[6] §II, 1280 (12)–1281(7); §II, 49, 244.
[7] §II, 42, 1321–2 (see also 1322–3); §v, 3, 51, fig. 4; §v, 17, 246–7, fig. 2.
See Plate 95 (a).

wise'[1] and how there was no one who could draw the pharaoh's own bow either in the Egyptian army or among the hardy hill-chieftains of Syria, 'because his strength is so much greater than (that of) any other king who ever existed'.[2] Mention has already been made of the target practices held by Tuthmosis IV in the vicinity of Memphis,[3] and in a great inscription on the third pylon at Karnak Amenophis III is described as 'a star of fine gold when he circles upon his horse, a mighty archer, shooting the target'.[4]

Although the ability to row and steer a boat and handle a ship under sail must have been almost inbred in a river people like the Egyptians, during the Eighteenth Dynasty these accomplishments too were elevated to the status of sports, in the mastery of which men of high rank exhibited a self-conscious pride. In the reign of Amenophis II a prominent army officer, Amenemheb, relates how he attracted the attention of the king while 'rowing under him in [his ship of state]' on the occasion of the Feast of Southern Opet;[5] and on his limestone stela from Giza the pharaoh himself devotes considerable space to extolling his own youthful prowess with the oar.[6] In the instance cited, the 'oar of twenty cubits (thirty-four feet)' wielded by Amenophis II 'at the stern of his falcon-ship' may have been, not a pulling oar, but the rudder of the vessel, which would account for the king's ability to outlast by far the other two hundred oarsmen of the ship's complement. Nevertheless, those who witnessed the exploits of the royal mariner are represented as being fittingly impressed, the inscription telling us in conventional terms that their 'faces were joyful at watching him'.

In the New Kingdom Egypt's most ancient sport, the hunting of wild game, was transformed from a more or less static pastime, wherein the royal or noble hunstman stood on foot and fired into a group of animals penned up in an enclosure or driven toward him by his beaters, into a free-running, mounted chase across the deserts, wastelands, and veldts of Africa and western Asia.[7] Thanks to the mobility of the chariot and the range and power of the composite bow the hunter was now able to run down and kill

---

[1] §11, 42, 1280 (9–10); §11, 49, 244.   [2] §11, 42, 1290 (3–6); §11, 49, 247.
[3] See above, p. 333 n. 4.
[4] §11, 42, 1723 (13–15); §1, 1, sect. 900.
[5] §11, 42, 897 (1–5); §1, 1, sect. 809.
[6] §11, 42, 1279 (17); §11, 49, 244; §v, 17, 256.
[7] Amenemheb's account of Tuthmosis III's elephant hunt in Neya (§11, 42, 893–4) suggests, however, that at the time of the episode described both he and the king had dismounted from their chariots and were hunting on foot.

with relative ease the largest and most dangerous of beasts—the lion, the wild bull, and the elephant—and it was game of this type which became the quarry most avidly sought after by the sporting pharaohs of the Eighteenth Dynasty.

It was Tuthmosis I who, during his Asiatic campaign, appears to have inaugurated the first great elephant hunt in the north Syrian country of Neya;[1] and it was here some fifty years later that Tuthmosis III claims to have laid low one hundred and twenty of the huge beasts, aided, among others, by that redoubtable soldier, Amenemheb, whose courageous action in cutting off the trunk ('hand') of the largest elephant perhaps saved his royal master from death or serious injury.[2] A rhinoceros which Tuthmosis III bagged during his first campaign in Nubia is represented on the temple pylon at Armant, the figure of the animal accompanied by detailed measurements.[3] A granite stela from the same temple not only mentions the taking of the rhinoceros and describes the elephant hunt in Neya, but also tells us that the great pharaoh on one occasion 'killed seven lions by shooting in the completion of a moment' and on another 'secured a herd of twelve wild cattle' in the hour after breakfast;[4] while a scarab, now in New York, refers to Tuthmosis III as the 'harpooner of the hippopotamus, powerful of arm when he takes the spear'.[5] A number of monuments, both royal and private, record the hunting exploits of Amenophis II[6] and Tuthmosis IV;[7] and two well-known series of large commemorative scarabs issued by Amenophis III publicize that king's bag 'with his own arrows' of 'one hundred and two fierce lions' during his first ten years on the throne[8] and of ninety-six wild cattle on a single great hunting expedition in the second year of his reign.[9]

Although the hunting of big game from the chariot was a pastime in which only kings, princes, high-ranking army officers, and great officials had the opportunity to indulge, the pursuit of river animals like the hippopotamus and the crocodile, of the

[1] §II, 42, 103–4; §V, 11, 75 n. 1. On the location of Neya see §III, 14, vol. I, 158*–168*.

[2] §II, 42, 893–4, 1233–4, 1245 (18–19); §I, 1, sect. 588; §II, 49, 243; §V, 12, 30–31 (lines 16–18); §V, 10, 183, pls. 88, 103.

[3] §V, 10, 26–7, 159–60, 204, pls. 9, 93 (6); §II, 42, 1247–8.

[4] §II, 42, 1245 (14–17); §V, 10, 183.

[5] §II, 21, part 2, 127, fig. 66 (bottom row); §V, 20, 35, pl. 19 (bottom row).

[6] §V, 4, 37–46; §V, 3, 49–51; §II, 42, 1304 (5–7); §II, 49, 246; §II, 11, 130, 143–4.

[7] E.g. §II, 42, 1541 (11); §II, 49, 449.   [8] §II, 42, 1740 (D); §I, 1, sect. 865.

[9] §II, 42, 1738–9 (C);   §V, 5, 85–92.

smaller land animals, and of birds and fish continued, as before, to be enjoyed by all classes of Egyptians, as witnessed by many lively scenes in the private tombs of the period.[1]

There can be little doubt that during the Eighteenth Dynasty, as later in the New Kingdom,[2] competitive sports, such as wrestling and fencing with single-sticks, were popular with the people of Egypt and were regarded as an appropriate part of the fêtes held in honour of the kings. Indeed, it has been stated as highly probable that 'the ancient Egyptians, like the modern, seized the occasion of any festival for athletic contests'.[3]

VI. AMENOPHIS III'S DISPLAY

The accession to the throne of King Nebmare, Amenophis III, came at a moment in Egyptian history when, thanks to almost two centuries of unparalleled achievement both at home and abroad, the country was at the pinnacle of its political power, economic prosperity, and cultural development. The conquests of Tuthmosis I and III, zealously consolidated by their successors, had established Egypt as a dominant power in the Near East and endowed her with a sphere of influence which stretched from the Fourth Cataract of the Nile to the shores of the Euphrates.[4] In addition to the incalculable wealth in slaves, raw materials, and manufactured goods which poured into the Nile Valley from the Lands to the north, the prolonged and vigorous exploitation of such natural resources as the mines of Nubia and the Eastern Desert made Egypt in gold alone the richest nation on earth.[5] Years of prosperity, royal patronage, and the demands of an increasingly sophisticated and discriminating clientele had developed a veritable army of highly trained architects, artists, and craftsmen, whose technical skill and sense of design, stimulated by close and frequent contacts with the other great civilizations of the Near East, have rarely been surpassed.[6] Above all, diplomacy had largely replaced warfare in Egypt's dealings with her neighbours and there was leisure for her king and her people to enjoy the many pleasures and luxuries which life now had to offer them and to indulge to the full a truly oriental penchant for opulence and display.

Typical in every respect of the brilliant setting over which he presided, Amenophis III contrived throughout his long reign to

---

[1] §v, 8, 75–89.   [2] §v, 18, 211–20.   [3] §v, 18, 211; §v, 8, 223–6.
[4] See below, p. 431–2.
[5] See below, p. 346.   [6] See below, p. 407.

combine the unwavering pursuit of all manner of worldly pleasures with a programme of self-glorification more elaborate and on a far grander scale than any previously undertaken.

The king's desire that his every action be made known to the world is attested by the extraordinary series of large commemorative scarabs which he caused to be issued during his first twelve years on the throne and which, like modern news-letters, were distributed throughout the country and even dispatched to the more distant outposts of the empire.[1] The first series of these scarabs, carved at the very beginning of the reign, announces the pharaoh's marriage to Tiy, a woman of non-royal birth; and with engaging frankness, which is repeated on many of the king's later monuments, gives the names of her untitled parents, Yuya and Tjuyu,[2] adding, however, that 'she is (now) the wife of a mighty king' whose dominion extends from Karoy in the northern Sudan to Naharina in western Asia. The great wild cattle hunt of Year 2, held in the neighbourhood of the Wādi Qena and attended by army officers, soldiers, and cadets from a military colony nearby,[3] is described in detail on a second series of scarabs; and a third issue, of which more than forty examples have survived to the present day, records, as we have already noted,[4] the number of lions shot by Amenophis III during the first ten years of his reign. After the tenth year there is no further mention of hunting expeditions or, indeed, of any activity involving physical exertion on the part of the king, who thenceforward appears to have given himself over to the pleasures of the harim and the banquet hall and to have devoted his attention chiefly to the rebuilding and beautification of Thebes and other favoured sites in Egypt and Nubia.

In Year 10 itself Amenophis III, following a lengthy correspondence with King Shuttarna of Mitanni,[5] arranged a marriage between himself and the king's daughter, Gilukhepa, whose arrival in Egypt with a retinue of three hundred and seventeen ladies and attendants was regarded as a 'marvel' worthy of being recorded on a fourth set of commemorative scarabs. Even on these scarabs Tiy and her parents occupy the place of honour after the king himself. A fifth series of similar 'bulletins' tells how at the end of the following year (Year 11) water was admitted

---

[1] §II, 42, 1737–41. See §V, 5, 85–92; §VI, 13, 12–14; §VI, 11, 221–6; §VI, 3, 82; etc.

[2] See §VI, 5; §VI, 18; §II, 1, 30–41 *passim*.

[3] §VI, 16, 174 n. 1; §I, 7, 18.   [4] P. 333.

[5] §II, 27, no. 29 (18–20), see also no. 23 (7–8); §VI, 6, 659–61.

to an irrigation basin, 1200 feet wide and over a mile in length, which had been prepared 'for the King's Great Wife, Tiy (may she live!), in her town of Djarukha', near Akhmīm.¹ Fifteen days later, early in Regnal Year 12, the 'festival of the opening of the basin' was celebrated and the king was rowed into it in the royal ship, 'Splendour-of-Aten'.

Although the entire military career of the easy-going, luxury-loving pharaoh seems to have consisted of one relatively unimportant expedition into Nubia and possibly the sending of a few troops into Syria some years later,² Amenophis III lost no opportunity in his reliefs and inscriptions of representing himself as a mighty warrior and world-conqueror. Florid accounts of the Nubian campaign of Year 5 are preserved for us in seven different inscriptions—at Thebes, Aswān, and Semna³—and in these records the king is described as a 'fierce-eyed lion', a 'lord of strength', and a 'fire' which 'rages' against his enemies. His southward advance probably did not carry him beyond the region of the Fourth Cataract, already subjugated by Tuthmosis III and Amenophis II;⁴ but he characteristically claims on his Konosso stela that 'there was no king of Egypt who did the like except his Majesty'. His Golden-Horus name, 'Great of Strength who Smites the Asiatics',⁵ seems peculiarly inappropriate to a ruler whose indolent neglect of the Asiatic provinces paved the way for the decline of Egypt's control over Syria; and the epithets 'Crusher of Naharina' and 'Plunderer of Shinar' certainly present an inaccurate picture of the peaceful relations which the king was at pains to maintain with his powerful allies.⁶ Long rows of bound figures, personifying conquered foreign states, on temple walls and statue bases of Amenophis III give the impression of continuing foreign conquests;⁷ and in the great dedicatory inscription of the temple of Amen-Re-Mont at Karnak we are asked to believe that the building was constructed from 'the tribute of the chiefs of all foreign lands which His Majesty had taken in his victories as trophies of his strong arm'.⁸

It was as a builder and patron of the arts that Amenophis III most truly earned the reputation for magnificence which to the present day is associated with his name. Superlatives fall thick and

¹ §VI, 34, 23–33.   ² §II, 27, no. 55 (10–13); §VI, 14, 237; §I, 10, 64.
³ §II, 42, 1654, 1658–66, 1793; §II, 38, 158 n. 5.
⁴ See below, p. 347.   ⁵ §II, 17, 306 ff.
⁶ §II, 42, 1658 (16); §II, 17, 325 (LXXIX).
⁷ §VI, 29, 161–71; §VI, 30, 173–9; §VI, 31, 205–14. See also §I, 9, 150, 319.
⁸ §II, 42, 1667 (19–20).

fast when one attempts to describe the vast size, the elegance
of design, and the breath-taking richness which characterized his
palace south of Medīnet Habu, his mortuary temple a mile and a
half to the north, his great temple of Amun at Luxor, the impressive additions which he made to the principal shrine and precinct
of the god at Karnak, and the huge, rock-cut tomb which he
prepared for himself in the western branch of the Valley of the
Tombs of the Kings.[1] 'The House of Rejoicing', as the pharaoh's
palace was called, and the complex of royal buildings adjoining it
formed a sizeable town covering an area of over eighty acres.[2]
The king's mortuary temple, demolished in the Nineteenth
Dynasty, appears to have been the largest of its class ever constructed, and the two fifty-foot statues of Amenophis III which
stood before it (long famous as the 'Colossi of Memnon')[3] still
dominate the western plain at Thebes.[4] In the field behind the
Colossi lies the gigantic stela, once 'wrought with gold and many
costly stones', which marked the 'Station of the King',[5] and
another stela from the same temple tells us that the whole
building was 'wrought with gold throughout, its floors adorned
with silver and all its portals with fine gold'.[6] In size the great
central colonnade of the Luxor temple surpasses any previously
attempted and in their proportions and spacing the towering
shafts with their huge calyx-capitals are as noble and impressive
as anything which Egyptian architecture produced.[7] In the
construction of these magnificent buildings, dedicated to his own
glory and well-being no less than to the service of the state-god,
Amon-Re, Amenophis III not only taxed the resources of his
empire to their utmost limit, but dismantled the monuments of his
predecessors in his search for materials. Thus, the foundations of
the mighty pylon which he erected in the temple of Amun at
Karnak have been found to be composed of hundreds of sculptured
blocks taken from a chapel of Sesostris I of the Twelfth Dynasty,
from structures of all the preceding kings of the Eighteenth

[1] §II, 34, vol. I, 28 (no. 22); §II, 19, 27–30, 57–60, 123–31, 170–1; §II, 21,
part 2, 240–4.

[2] §II, 34, vol. I, 200; §II, 20, 35–56, 82–111, 156–83, 231–42; §II, 21, part 2,
244–55; §II, 45, 159–72.

[3] Actually only the northern colossus was so called. See §VI, 4, 345–6; §VI, 32,
246–8.   [4] §II, 34, vol. II, 160–1.

[5] §II, 42, 1671–7, see 1649 (1–2); §II, 34, vol. II, 161. In August 1956 fragments
of a companion stela were found by the Service des Antiquités (letter from Dr
Labib Habachi, dated 6 September 1956).

[6] §II, 42, 1646–57 (see 1648, lines 9–11).

[7] §II, 34, vol. II, 102–3; §VI, 17, 138, figs. 109–12.

Dynasty, including Amenophis III's own father, Tuthmosis IV, and even from an earlier building of Amenophis III himself.[1]

Whereas every king of Egypt was in theory a god, there were few who interpreted this tradition so literally or emphasized their divinity with such insistence as did Amenophis III. In the temple at Luxor a series of reliefs, similar to those of Hatshepsut at Deir el-Bahri, portray in detail the divine birth of the king;[2] and in his mortuary temple across the river the cult of the deified pharaoh ('Nebmare, Ruler of Rulers') was maintained side by side with that of 'his father, Amun'.[3] At Sulb, fifty-five miles below the Third Cataract of the Nile, Amenophis III dedicated a handsome fortified temple to the worship of himself and of Amun, several inscriptions from this building stating plainly that 'He made (it) as his monument for "His living Image upon Earth, Nebmare, Lord of Nubia in the Fortress Khaemmat"'.[4] Nearby, at Sedeinga, the king erected a temple to his queen, Tiy, who, in spite of her humble birth, appears also to have been deified and to have been worshipped, together with her husband, as a patron divinity of the region.[5] In texts of the later New Kingdom Amenophis III is named with Ptah as one of the gods of Memphis and there is evidence that his 'living Image' was worshipped there in a great temple of his own building called 'The House of Nebmare'.[6]

Side by side with the fanfare and magnificence for which the reign of Amenophis III is famous we find in the sculpture and painting of the period, in the house furnishings and personal possessions of the court, and in the graceful and elaborate costumes which came into fashion at this time the sophistication and refinement, the impeccable taste and lively imagination, and the aristocratic standards of beauty demanded by a people accustomed to the utmost in luxury and gracious living. Nowhere do these qualities appear with greater clarity than in the superb reliefs preserved in the tombs of the great officials of the reign at Thebes and Memphis—notably, in those of the Vizier Ramose, the Granary Overseer Khaemhet, the King's Scribe Kheruef, and the Chief Steward Surere.[7]

[1] §II, 34, vol. II, 25; sect. II, 7, *passim* (see especially vol. XXXVIII, 597, 601).

[2] §II, 42, 1713–21; §II, 34, vol. II, 106–7. See above, p. 323 n. 4.

[3] §VI, 28.

[4] §II, 34, vol. VII, 168–72; §VI, 7, vol. VII, 154–20. See §II, 42, 1748 (8–9); §II, 38, 203–4.   [5] §II, 34, vol. VII, 166–7; §II, 38, 203. Cf. §II, 35, 354 (7).

[6] §I, 1, sect. 880 n. *a*; §II, 20, 98–9.

[7] §II, 35, 105–11 (no. 55), 113–19 (no. 57), 298–300 (no. 192), 87–91 (no. 48); see Plate 97.

Thanks largely to the close relations maintained with the Mediterranean and Asiatic nations to the north and east, to the steady influx of foreigners into the Valley of the Nile itself, and to the inevitable intermarriages which had taken place between these foreigners and the native Egyptians we find also under Amenophis III a highly cosmopolitan society, acutely conscious of its place in world civilization and endowed with both the desire and the ability to think in terms of the universal and to cope with problems of world-wide significance. In the religion this new point of view resulted in a return to the universal principles inherent in the worship of the sun as personified especially in the god Re-Harakhte of Heliopolis and in a related form of the solar deity recently risen to prominence and called quite simply (*pa*) *Aten*, 'the Disk'.[1] It also led, as we have seen (§III), to the intensified 'solarization' of the state-god, Amun, whose functions as a bringer of victory in war and as the special patron of the Theban dynasts had already begun to be over-shadowed by his new role as a cosmic creator-god and ruler of the universe. Precisely this concept of the god is expressed in a hymn composed in the reign of Amenophis III for the king's architects, Suti and Hor, and here also we meet with ideas and phraseology closely similar to those found in the famous hymns to the Aten compiled under the 'heretic', Akhenaten.[2]

The emergence of the Aten as a recognized member of the Egyptian pantheon probably occurred during the period of imperial expansion under Tuthmosis III and Amenophis II.[3] A royal commemorative scarab carved a few years later has been interpreted as providing 'definite proof, not only that the Aten was already regarded as a separate and distinct form of the sun-god by Tuthmosis IV, but that he was actually worshipped as a god of battles who gave victory to Pharaoh and ensured his pre-eminence over the rest of the world, making all mankind the subjects of the Disk'.[4] It is not, however, until the reign of Amenophis III that we find the new god officially honoured in the nomenclature of such important items as the king's flagship, 'Splendour-of-Aten', and a royal palace of the same name.[5] Whether Amenophis III himself actively promoted or merely tolerated the rapidly expanding cult of the Disk is a moot question. The king's devotion to Amun and the munificence with

---

[1] §III, 2, 59ff.   [2] §II, 42, 1943–9; §II, 49, 367–8.
[3] §VI, 33, 109–19; §II, 10, 181–99; §III, 23, 366ff.; §VI, 10, 414–15; §II, 18, 53–61.
[4] §VI, 26, 24.   [5] §II, 20, 178–9.

which throughout his life he supported the temples and priest-hoods of the state-god suggest, however, that the growth of the Aten worship was sponsored by other and more restless minds than his.

Prominent among those who moulded the character of the reign was Queen Tiy, whose portraits—especially a small head of green schist in the Cairo Museum[1]—preserve her arresting appearance and reflect something of her shrewd mind and energetic nature. The king is frequently represented with her slender, erect figure by his side[2] and it is clear that throughout his life she enjoyed, not only his deep affection, but also his confidence in matters of state. Her detailed knowledge of his foreign policy and his relations with the rulers of neighbouring lands is referred to in two letters written after the death of Amenophis III by King Tushratta of Mitanni, requesting that these relations be maintained during the reign of her son, Amenophis IV.[3] Although, as queen-mother, she seems to have supported Amenophis IV with the utmost devotion and to have constituted a great influence in his life, there is no evidence that she encouraged or even shared his radical religious views. Indeed, the maintenance of her cult after the collapse of the 'Aten heresy' and the wholesale anathematization of its adherents indicates that, in the eyes of posterity at least, she was not associated with it.[4]

Second only to Tiy in Amenophis III's favour was their eldest daughter, Sitamun, whom her father seems to have married sometime before the thirty-first year of his reign and by whom he had several children, including apparently the future king, Smenkhkare.[5] We have almost no material on which to base a character study of Sitamun, but if, as some think, she was the subject of a wonderful ebony portrait head in the Berlin Museum[6] she was a person of very pronounced character, not all of it pleasant. Her name appears frequently in inscriptions both at Thebes and at El-Amarna; and the stewardship of her evidently large estates was entrusted to a man who was not only the outstanding official of her father's reign, but one of the truly great figures in New Kingdom history.

This official was Amenophis, son of Hapu, a native of Athribis

[1] §II, 34, vol. VII, 361–2; §VI, 1, 66, figs. 78–9.

[2] §II, 35, 87, 89, 234, 298, 299; §II, 34, vol. II, 192; §VI, 9.

[3] §II, 27, nos. 26, 28 (42 ff.). See §I, 9, 324.

[4] §VI, 21, 42; §VI, 22, 624; §II, 35, 338, 354. See also §I, 3, 346.

[5] §II, 13, 160; §II, 36, 45.

[6] §II, 34, vol. IV, 113; §VI, 23, 81–6; §II, 45, 155, pl. 117. See §VI, 1, 67 (no. 81).

in the Delta, whose family included also the Vizier Ramose and another Amenophis who was Chief Steward in Memphis.[1] Following a brilliant career as King's Scribe, Scribe of Recruits, and Overseer of All Works of the King, Hapu's famous son was honoured by his sovereign with a mortuary temple in western Thebes, comparable in magnificence with the temples of the kings nearby and endowed in perpetuity by special royal decree.[2] By succeeding generations the King's Scribe Amenophis (frequently also called Huy) was revered as one of Egypt's great sages and proverbs attributed to him were translated into Greek twelve centuries after his death. Under Ramesses IV his mortuary cult was maintained together with those of the deified kings, and early in the Ptolemaic period he himself was worshipped as a god.[3]

During the last decade of his reign Amenophis III, then flabby, diseased, and prematurely senile,[4] probably spent the greater part of his time in his palace at Thebes. There was, however, no apparent reduction in his building activities or in the luxurious splendour of his existence. His three jubilees, or *Sed*-festivals, in Years, 30, 34, and 37, respectively, were celebrated with elaborate ceremonies and lavish exchanges of gifts between the king and his court[5] and were accompanied by the construction of such magnificent buildings as the temple at Sulb[6] and a great festival Hall adjoining the Theban palace.[7] In addition to Queens Tiy and Sitamun, the crown prince Amenophis (IV), and the younger royal children, a host of courtiers attended the king at Thebes and on jars of food and drink contributed to his *Sed*-festivals we find the names of the King's Scribe, 'Huy', the Vizier, Ramose, the Chief Steward, Surere, and many others.[8] The procession of Asiatic princesses into the royal harim continued as before. Having earlier in his reign married the sister of King Tushratta of Mitanni and the sister of Kadashman-Enlil, the Kassite ruler of Babylon, Amenophis III now requested and received as wives the daughters of these same kings, as well as the daughter of King Tarkhundaradu of Arzawa.[9] That the ageing

---

[1] §I, 7, 2–13.

[2] §VI, 20. The decree regarding this temple is preserved for us only in a 'forgery' of the Twenty-first Dynasty (§VI, 20, 1–17, pl. 1. See also §VI, 15, 932; §VI, 24, 21; §I, 7, 11–12).

[3] §I, 7, 2–3; §VI, 25, 111–16.

[4] §VI, 9, 1–2, pl. 1. See below, p. 346 n. 6.

[5] §II, 20, 83–6.   [6] See above, p. 342 n. 4.

[7] §VI, 12, 10; §II, 20, 36, 41, 85, 240.

[8] §II, 20, 100–1, 242.

[9] §II, 27, nos. 1, 3, 4, 11, 17, 19–22, 24, 31, 32(?).

pharaoh actually married Tushratta's daughter, Tadukhepa, is doubtful, since when we next hear of her it is as the wife of Amenophis IV.[1]

In his thirty-sixth year[2] on the throne the pharaoh's infirmities, which included painful abscesses in his teeth, had become so acute that his 'brother', King Tushratta, was prevailed upon to send him an image of the goddess Ishtar of Nineveh famous for its healing powers.[3] The goddess's magic was apparently effective, for Amenophis III was still alive two years later, as witnessed by a number of dated jar labels from his Theban palace.[4] So far as is now known, he died at the age of about fifty-five in his thirty-eighth or thirty-ninth regnal year and was buried with characteristic magnificence in his great tomb in the western branch of the Valley of the Tombs of the Kings.[5] The identity of his mummy, found cached in the tomb of Amenophis II, has been questioned, but convincingly reaffirmed.[6]

VII. THE NUBIAN GOLD TRADE

Since, in the course of her dynastic history, Egypt's national economy and position in world commerce had come to depend more and more on her access to the raw materials of Nubia and the lands further to the south, the resumption of control over the sources and thoroughfares of these imports was, to the founders of the New Kingdom, a matter of immediate and primary importance. Shortly after his capture of the Hyksos bases in Palestine Amosis turned his attention to Nubia and before his death had regained possession of the region between the First and Second Cataracts including the town of Buhen[7] where he appears to have built a temple and repaired or remodelled the Middle Kingdom fortifications.[8] The reconquest of Nubia proper (Wawat) was consolidated by Amenophis I, and we find inscriptions of his viceroy, Tjuroy, dated to the king's seventh and eighth regnal years, at Semna and Uronarti, near the old southern boundary

---

[1] §II, 27, nos. 27–9. See §I, 3, 384, 411.

[2] §II, 27, 181, 1050. The pertinent date has recently been read—somewhat doubtfully, it would seem—as Year 39.

[3] §II, 27, no. 23; §VI, 19, 412–18. See also, below, n. 6.

[4] §II, 20, 87–8.   [5] See above, p. 341 n. 1.

[6] §II, 44, no. 61074; §VI, 27, 94–5. See §VI, 8, 116 n. 1; §IV, 18, 168, 170, 177, 178.

[7] The capital of the independent Nubian kingdom of Hyksos times. See §VII, 13, 56–8; §V, 14, 54–61.

[8] §II, 38, 143–5; §VII, 3, 1048–51; §V, 6, 232–3, 249–51; §VII, 4, 7–14.

line established by the pharaohs of the Twelfth Dynasty.[1] The names of both kings have been found still further to the south, on monuments from the fort and temple which Amosis seems to have founded on the island of Sai.[2]

To Tuthmosis I belongs the credit for extending Egyptian control deep into the Sudan ('Kush'[3]), 'casting out violence' southward to the island of Argo above the Third Cataract and apparently inaugurating the final thrust to the region of the Fourth Cataract.[4] One of the fortresses which he built in the newly subjugated territory is referred to by his son, Tuthmosis II, who in his first year on the throne strengthened Egyptian prestige in the southern provinces by crushing with great savagery a rebellion 'on the north of the wretched Kush'.[5] Tuthmosis III's granite stela at Gebel Barkal shows that before the forty-seventh year of his reign the Egyptians had occupied the district of Karoy, immediately below the Fourth Cataract, and had founded there the important fortified town of Napata.[6] Beyond this point Egyptian political control was never extended, and all subsequent royal campaigns in Nubia and the Sudan, including that of Tuthmosis III's own fiftieth year,[7] were clearly no more than disciplinary expeditions directed, not against the peaceful and largely Egyptianized inhabitants of the river valley, but against the wild and predatory tribesman of the adjoining deserts.[8]

In the Eighteenth Dynasty temples at Amada and Elephantine, Amenophis II casually mentions hanging the body of an Asiatic prince 'on the wall at Napata',[9] and we may be sure that in his day the southern boundary of the Egyptian empire was firmly established there. The expedition of Tuthmosis IV's eighth year smashed a coalition of desert nomads far to the north, in the valleys east of Wawat;[10] and Amenophis III's single military enterprise accomplished similar results in the desert *wādis* of Ibhet—probably to the south-east of the Second Cataract.[11] For the latter operation, in which 312 of the miserable bedawin were slaughtered and 740 carried off as prisoners, the viceroy Merymose recruited an army of Nubians from the villages lying between the

[1] §II, 38, 145–6.   [2] §VII, 14, 75–9. Cf. §II, 38, 145.
[3] On the use of the name 'Kush' during the New Kingdom see §VII, 11, 67.
[4] §II, 38, 146–51; §VII, 14, 68; §VII, 1, 36–9.
[5] §II, 42, 138–41. See §II, 38, 150ff.
[6] §V, 12, 24–39; §II, 38, 153–5.   [7] §II, 42, 814–15; §II, 38, 153.
[8] See, for example, §VII, 12, 41–2.   [9] §II, 42, 1297–8; §II, 38, 155–6.
[10] §II, 42, 1545–8, 1555–6, 1560; §II, 38, 156–8.
[11] §II, 42, 1654, 1658–66, 1793; §II, 38, 158–62. See also §VII, 14, 79–81 (nos. 27, 28).

fortress of Baki (Qūbān) and the fortress of Taroy, some eighty miles to the south. Following the skirmishing, Amenophis III proceeded southward on a triumphal tour of inspection as far as Karoy, bringing thence gold for the adornment of his pylon in the temple of Amun at Karnak. 'The Pool of Horus', where the king erected a tablet of victory, is probably to be placed in the First Cataract near the island of Konosso, where a victory stela mentioning this locality was found.[1]

During the New Kingdom the whole area south of the First Cataract was administered on behalf of the pharaoh by an important official, best described as a viceroy, whose jurisdiction some time between the reigns of Tuthmosis III and Amenophis III was extended to include also the three southernmost nomes of Upper Egypt, northward to El-Kāb.[2] The office and the titles, 'King's Son and Overseer of Southern Countries', which went with it originated under Amosis or possibly Kamose, the first appointee to the viceroyalty of Nubia having been a Theban(?) named Ahmose Si-Tayit.[3] Early in the reign of Amenophis I this man was succeeded in office by his son, Ahmose called Tjuroy,[4] but the viceroyalty was not normally hereditary and there is no evidence that the viceroys were ever of the blood royal,[5] being, rather, members of any of the various government services (civil or military), selected by the king because of their known loyalty and outstanding ability as administrators.[6] Under Tuthmosis IV the viceregal title was changed to 'King's Son of Kush'—perhaps to differentiate at that time between the governor of Nubia and the Sudan, whose name happened to be Amenophis, and the real King's Son, Amenophis, the future King Amenophis III.[7] It was also under Tuthmosis IV that the viceroy was first given the honorary office of 'Fan-bearer on the King's Right Hand'[8]—a title reflecting the close personal relations which existed between the pharaoh and his representative in the south countries.

From his Residence at Mi'am (modern Anība[9]), 140 miles south of the First Cataract, the viceroy governed his extensive

---

[1] On a fragmentary inscription from Bubastis, which Breasted (§1, 1, sect. 846 ff.) assigns to Amenophis III and from which he draws some rather sweeping conclusions concerning the king's Nubian campaign, see §11, 38, 160–2.

[2] §111, 27, 28–55, 73–88; §vii, 7, 179–238; §11, 38, 175–81; §vii, 8, 13–25.

[3] §vii, 9, 45–7, 54, 56.   [4] §vii, 9, 45–62.

[5] §vii, 7, 184, notwithstanding. See §vii, 9, 56; §111, 27, 84.

[6] §11, 38, 181; §1, 3, 464; §111, 27, 83–4; §11, 25, 28–31.

[7] §111, 27, 32 (no. 5); §vii, 7, 192 (no. 5); §1, 3, 464–6.

[8] §vii, 16, 157–8; §1, 8, 281–4.   [9] §11, 34, vol. vii, 75–81.

domain through an administrative organization modelled on that of Egypt itself.[1] Corresponding in a general way to the viziers of Upper and Lower Egypt were two deputy-governors (*idnw*), one in charge of the old Nubian province of Wawat, the other, stationed at Amāra in the northern Sudan,[2] administering the affairs of more recently subjugated territory of 'Kush'. Like Upper and Lower Egypt the provinces of Kush and Wawat appear to have been subdivided into administrative districts or townships, each with its local count or mayor (*ḥȝty-ꜥ*). The armed forces of the viceroy, including the commanders (*ṯsw*) and garrisons of the numerous fortresses, were under the over-all command of a high-ranking Egyptian officer called the Battalion Commander of Kush.[3] Later in the New Kingdom we hear also in inscriptions from Nubia and the Sudan of Chief Treasurers, Overseers of Cattle, Overseers of Granaries, Chief Priests of All the Gods, and of manifold scribes, accountants, and attendants attached to the courts of the viceroy or his deputies. In addition to hundreds of resident Egyptian officials the viceroy's government seems to have depended to a great extent on the loyalty and co-operation of Egyptianized native princes, some of whom had undoubtedly been brought up as children at the court of the pharaoh.[4]

With the extension of the frontier region southward to Napata the Middle Kingdom fortresses between Aswān and Semna lost much of their military significance and some of them were abandoned or transformed into open settlements with houses and cemeteries outside the ancient walls.[5] Others, located in key positions at the ends of caravan routes or valley-roads to the gold mining areas, were repaired and enlarged. Among the latter were the forts at Elephantine and Bīga at the First Cataract, at Ikkur and Qūbān by the mouth of the Wādi el-Allāqi, at Anība, Faras, and Serra, and at Buhen and Semna at either end of the Second Cataract.[6] More important strategically were the new fortresses or fortified settlements founded by the kings of the Eighteenth Dynasty in the northern Sudan—at Amāra West, Sai, Sedeinga, Sesebi, Sulb, Kawa, and Napata.[7] In nearly all these places, as well as at other well-known sites in Nubia—

[1] §II, 38, 181 ff.; §I, 3, 464–6; §III, 27, 83–6; §VII, 7, 229–38.
[2] §II, 34, vol. VII, 157–64.   [3] §I, 7, 38.
[4] §II, 38, 184–6.   [5] §II, 38, 193, 198; §III, 20, 347.
[6] §II, 34, vol. VII, 80–2, 126, 128, 129, 144–56; §II, 38, 189, 192. See also, above, p. 346 n. 8.
[7] §II, 34, vol. VII, 157–74, 180–92, 203–23 *passim*; §II, 38, 193–4.

Kalābsha, El-Dakka, Amada[1]—we find temples dedicated to such local divinities as Khnum, Satis, and Anukis of the cataract region, to the ancient Nubian god, Dedwen, and the various Horus-gods of Nubia, to Amun of Karnak, Re-Harakhte of Heliopolis, Ptah of Memphis, to the deified rulers Tuthmosis III, Amenophis III, and Queen Tiy, and frequently to Nubia's great patron deity, King Sesostris III of the Twelfth Dynasty.[2]

As access to the rich natural resources of the lands of the Upper Nile was the primary goal of the Egyptian occupation of Nubia and the Sudan, so also were the exploitation of these resources and the punctual delivery of a huge yearly tribute in gold and other valuable materials the principal functions of the viceregal administration.

Although gold occurs in veins of quartz rocks throughout almost the entire north–south length of the Eastern Desert and in alluvial sands and gravels along the course of the Nile between Buhen and Kerma, far and away the richest sources of the precious metal and the ones most vigorously worked by the Egyptians of the Middle and New Kingdoms were the mines east and south-east of the Nubian province of Wawat, especially those at Umm Qareiyāt, Darahib, Seiga, and Umm Nabardi, reached from the Nile Valley at Qūbān through the Wādis el-Allāqi and Cabgaba.[3] Records show that in the late New Kingdom the income from the Nubian workings was almost five times that of the ancient mines east of Koptos in Upper Egypt,[4] and we may suppose that a similar ratio existed in the Eighteenth Dynasty. The annals of Tuthmosis III further indicate that over a period of years the amount of gold extracted under Egyptian supervision from the mines of Wawat (including apparently those of Umm Nabardi, south-east of the Second Cataract) was seventeen times as great as that obtained from Kush and, through raids or peaceful trade, from the negro lands to the south of Kush.[5] The total imports of gold from Nubia and the Sudan, as listed for the later years of the reign of Tuthmosis III, averaged around 10,000 ounces per year;[6] and under Amenophis II 150 men were required to carry a single shipment of Nubian gold.[7] We have no basis on which to compare the gold imports from Nubia with the output of the Barrāmīya-Sukari mines, east of Edfu, which in the time of

[1] §II, 34, vol. VII, 10f., 20, 40f., 65–73. See §II, 18, 195–7.
[2] §II, 38, 200–4; §III, 20, 349–50.
[3] §II, 38, 86–7; §VII, 15, 128 ff., maps, 1, 2.
[4] §II, 38, 211; §VII, 15, 135.   [5] §II, 38, 210–11; §VII, 15, 129–30, 135.
[6] See n. 5.   [7] §II, 38, 207; §VII, 15, 135.

Tuthmosis I were under the jurisdiction of the Count of El-Kāb.[1] In, or shortly before, the reign of Amenophis III, however, these mines were added to the 'gold lands' controlled by the King's Son of Kush and their produce thenceforth was classed as part of the Nubian tribute.[2] 'The Gold Lands of Amun', which are mentioned as early as the reign of Tuthmosis III and which under Amenophis III came under the control of the viceroy of Nubia, may have been specific mining areas presented by the king to the temples of the state-god. On the other hand, the expression may have been simply a poetic term piously applied to all the gold regions of Upper Egypt and Nubia.[3]

During the Tuthmoside period gold was imported from Nubia and the Sudan chiefly in unworked form—as dust in bags and in lumps, bars, or ring-shaped ingots.[4] Placer mining seems to have been confined largely to the stretch of river between the Second and Third Cataracts and to the gold regions of the remote south (Karoy, Amu, Punt).[5] The method employed by the Egyptians in, for example, the mines of the Wādi el-Allāqi was evidently similar to that described about 130 B.C. by Agatharchides of Cnidus.[6] In this process the gold-bearing quartz was laboriously extracted in chunks from the mines, reduced by stages to a fine powder, and then 'washed' in special basins equipped with sloping stone benches, the last operation normally being carried out in the vicinity of the river.[7] The mineral gold so obtained was fused into ingots, probably at the fort or fortified settlement which invariably guarded the mouth of every important gold *wādi*.[7] In the New Kingdom the mine-gangs, whose lot was a hard one, were composed mainly of prisoners of war, slaves, and convicted criminals; and consignment to the mines of 'Kush' was evidently regarded by the Egyptians as a very severe form of punishment.[8] Inscriptions in the Wādi el-Allāqi and elsewhere contain the names and titles of Treasury Scribes, Gold Accountants, and other Egyptian officials charged with the operation and inspection of the mines[9] and we hear also of the 'miners', 'gold-washers', 'smelters', and 'goldsmiths' who worked under these officials.[10]

---

[1] §II, 38, 179.   [2] §II, 38, 180; §III, 20, 130.
[3] See above, p. 325 n. 5.
[4] §II, 38, 213–14. See, however, §VII, 15, 135.
[5] §II, 38, 212; §VII, 15, 149–51.
[6] Diodorus, III, 12–14. See §II, 38, 87; §IV, 14, 261–2; §VII, 15, 139–41.
[7] §VII, 15, 120–7, 139–44, 151–3. See also §VII, 5, 439.
[8] §VII, 15, 140, 145; §II, 38, 87–8, 188; §III, 20, 224.
[9] §VII, 2, 52–7; §VII, 15, 146–9.
[10] §VII, 15, 142–6.

It is perfectly clear that the mining of gold in Nubia was a government monopoly, not open to private individuals and therefore not an incentive to wholesale colonization.[1]

In addition to gold, the principal imports which reached Egypt from or by way of Nubia were elephant ivory, Sudanese ebony and other fine African woods, fragrant gum resins for use in perfumes and incense, ostrich plumes and ostrich eggs, and leopard skins.[2] Some copper appears to have been mined in the desert valleys east of Wawat,[3] and semi-precious stones like amethyst, carnelian, and feldspar formed part of the yearly tribute.[4] Many of the ships which bore the tribute to Egypt were certainly built in Nubia, but otherwise manufactured goods were rare during the early centuries of the New Kingdom.[5] Animals, including three breeds of cattle, hunting dogs, leopards, giraffes, and apes, were imported in some quantity;[6] and each military expedition brought back fresh batches of male and female captives destined to serve as slaves in Egypt or in Nubia itself.[7]

Although numerically these captives were surpassed many times over by the hordes of Asiatic prisoners taken in the great campaigns in Palestine and Syria, both they and other classes of immigrants from the southern provinces played an important role in the economic and military organization of the New Kingdom. In the Eighteenth Dynasty we find Nubians and Sudanese in Egypt not only as workers, house servants, and personal attendants, but, above all, as soldiers and police.[8] Many appear to have enjoyed the status of free citizens and a few, like Tuthmosis III's fan-bearer, Maiherpri, attained positions of wealth and influence.[9]

An important result of the expansion of the Egyptian empire southward to Napata was that for the first time in world history direct contact was established with the negro peoples of central Africa, whose natural habitat then, as now, was confined to the regions south of the Fourth Cataract of the Nile.[10] Groups of true negroes as well as Hamitic half-breeds were met with by Hatshepsut's trading expedition to the Somali coast;[11] but it is from the independent reign of Tuthmosis III onwards that we begin to find numerous representations of authentic negro types in

[1] §II, 38, 188.   [2] §II, 38, 206–22.   [3] §II, 38, 87; §IV, 14, 236.
[4] §II, 38, 216–17; §IV, 14, 445, 451; §VII, 6.
[5] §II, 38, 214–16, 220.   [6] §II, 38, 223–5.
[7] §II, 38, 226–9.
[8] §II, 38, 230–4; §III, 20, 237. See also, below, pp. 361 and 370.
[9] §II, 38, 238–40; §I, 8, 281.
[10] §VII, 10, 121–32; §III, 20, 350; §VII, 15, 149–51.
[11] §VII, 10, 129. See above, p. 329.

Egyptian art and we may assume that men of the black race were employed in the mines and quarries and attached to the fortresses and temples of Nubia.[1]

VIII. THE CIVIL SERVICE

The suppression of the political power of the hereditary nobility in the late Twelfth Dynasty had led to the organization of a complex and highly centralized administrative system which, with the return of Egyptian autonomy in the early New Kingdom, was re-established in a somewhat altered and simplified form, dominated by the pharaoh and his entourage and characterized by a sharp reduction in the number of the officials of subordinate rank who had comprised the old 'middle class'.[2] To a great extent membership in the civil service was based upon education, ability, and devotion to the interests of the state and was open to any Egyptian possessed of these qualifications, regardless of birth. It was the boast of more than one great official of the Eighteenth Dynasty that at the start of his career he was 'without (influential) kindred' or that he 'was humble of family, one of small account in his town'.[3] Some of the highest offices in the land seem indeed to have been filled by men whose parents were little better than peasants.[4] Frequently, however—especially under the later Tuthmoside rulers—the more important posts were awarded to intimates of the king, including boyhood friends who had grown up with him at court, former companions-in-arms who had accompanied him on his campaigns, and husbands or sons of ladies of the inner palace group.[5] Since, moreover, the candidates best qualified by nature, training, and experience for certain government positions were often the sons or nephews of their predecessors, we occasionally find an office monopolized by one family for several generations in succession. An outstanding example was the southern viziership during the reigns of Hatshepsut and Tuthmosis III which passed successively from Ahmose, called Amotju, to his son, Amenwosre, and then to the latter's nephew, Rekhmire, the post of northern vizier being assigned to a man named Neferweben who may have been Amenwosre's brother.[6] Under Amenophis III three key positions in the administration were occupied by the members of

---

[1] §vii, 10, 130.   [2] §i, 11, 192 ff.; §i, 8, 537 ff.
[3] Leiden Stela V, 1 (§viii, 1, 1, pl. 1 [line 5]); §i, 2, 245.
[4] §v, 9, 16.   [5] §i, 8, 538; §ii, 25, 30.
[6] §i, 8, 289–96. See also §viii, 6, 164–6; §iii, 20, 211; §ii, 35, 210.

a single provincial family of Athribis in the Delta: the King's Scribe, Amenophis, son of Hapu, the Chief Steward, Amenophis son of Heby, and the Vizier, Ramose.[1]

Thus, from the ranks of the civil service, as also from those of the army and the priesthood,[2] there sprang up a new aristocracy composed chiefly of men whom devoted service had established in the favour of one or more of the individual kings. Kingly patronage, however hard-earned, being at best an uncertain factor, membership in the new nobility was more fluctuating than that in the hereditary aristocracy of old; and the tombs of the New Kingdom at Thebes provide not a few instances of prominent dignitaries demoted and relegated by their royal masters to the obscurity from which they or their parents had arisen.[3] Furthermore, a man's official rank as reflected in his titles was not always an index of the influence which he exerted in the land. Under Hatshepsut and Amenophis III, for example, there can be little doubt that the vizier wielded less real power than the royal favourite—in one case, the Chief Steward, Senenmut, in the other, the King's Scribe, Amenophis, son of Hapu.[4]

Normally, however, as in the Old and Middle Kingdoms, the co-ordinator and mainspring of the pharaoh's government was his vizier, an exceedingly busy official who seems to have exercised at least supervisory control over every branch of the national administration. By the middle of the Eighteenth Dynasty—as, apparently, previously, in the late Middle Kingdom[5]—the office had become too exacting for one man to handle and too powerful to be entrusted to any one individual. It was therefore divided, on a geographical basis between two great functionaries: a vizier of the South, who had his headquarters in the capital city and administered the ancient realm of the Theban kings northward to Cusae(?);[6] and a vizier of the North resident at Memphis (or Heliopolis?),[7] whose jurisdiction extended over Middle and Lower Egypt—that is, over the whole of the territory recently recovered from the Hyksos. Accidents of time have left us little information concerning the northern viziers. The part of the country which they administered, however, was by far the larger and more productive of the two vizierates and there seems

<hr>

[1] §I, 8, 302–4, 368–70; §I, 3–4, 47, 53–4.
[2] See below, p. 363, and above, p. 323.
[3] §I, 8, 221, 289, 347, 363–4, 366–7, 400; §II, 25, 31.
[4] §I, 8, 356–63, 473–8; §I, 7, 2–13.   [5] §I, 8, 13, 19–20, 536.
[6] §I, 8, 14–15.
[7] *Ibid.* 26–7; §VIII, 15, 35.

to be no basis for the belief that they were subordinate in rank to their colleagues in the south.[1]

A group of extremely important texts preserved at Thebes in the tomb-chapels of four Upper Egyptian viziers of the mid-Eighteenth Dynasty—Amenwosre, Rekhmire, Amenemopet, and Hepu—include a copy of the king's instructions to his vizier on the occasion of the latter's installation in office, a treatise on the duties of the vizier and the procedures to be followed by him, a more or less standardized autobiography of the great dignitary with an account of his installation, and a list of officials of the eighty districts of Upper Egypt from which taxes were received by the office of the southern vizier.[2] Though all of these texts appear to have been composed during the late Middle Kingdom or even earlier and some of the titles, conditions, and procedures recorded in them were, doubtless, obsolete in the days of Amenwosre and Rekhmire,[3] the prominence accorded them in the tombs of the Eighteenth Dynasty viziers indicates that much of their content was still valid, and if used with discretion, can be helpful in filling out our picture of the viziership of the early New Kingdom.

The primary function of the two viziers was to govern Egypt in conformity with the wishes of the king and to keep him informed of conditions within their respective domains. The daily routine of the Eighteenth Dynasty vizier probably differed little from that of his Middle Kingdom predecessor, as described in the so-called Duties of the Vizier, one of the texts to which we have just referred.[4] According to this source the vizier, whenever possible, started his official day by reporting to and receiving instructions from the pharaoh in person and by exchanging reports with the royal chancellor who stood waiting to meet him at the entrance of the inner palace. Thereafter he caused the doors of all the administrative offices to be opened for the business of the day and himself proceeded to the Hall of the Vizier, which appears to have been located in western Thebes.[5] Here, in formal session surrounded by his staff, he co-ordinated the reports of his local administrators, issued instructions to the various departments of the central government, made and rescinded appointments of

---

[1] See, for example, §VIII, 32, 105 ff.; §I, 8, 28, 294, 296–9, 304–5, 438–40, 443–4.

[2] §II, 35, 246, 206, 209, 46, 132 (Tombs, 131, 100, 29, and 66); §I, 8, 2 n. 1, 29–43, 212–20.

[3] §I, 8, 2 n. 1, 11, 29 ff., 51 ff., 280; §I, 11, 192. Cf. §VI, 24, 20–1; §VIII, 29, 404; §VIII, 30, 55.

[4] §III, 8, 88–93, pls. 26–8; §I, 8, 2 (n. 1), 29–43.   [5] §I, 8, 25–6.

judges, subordinate officials, and priests,[1] received taxes, and attended to the pleas of a steady stream of petitioners. Here also, in his capacity of Chief Justice, he presided over the so-called Great Council, or superior court,[2] and passed judgement on important civil cases,[3] referred to him for the most part by the numerous local courts, or District Councils, up and down the land. Among the seemingly endless duties and prerogatives of the vizier were the sealing of legal documents;[4] the maintenance in his office of government records, both legal and administrative; the opening and closing of the palace workshops (*pr-nbw*) in company with the king's chancellor;[5] the reception of foreign embassies and foreign tribute;[6] the supervision of the workshops, storehouses, and estates of the temple of Amun;[7] the leading of expeditions and the direction of building construction both at Thebes and, in the case of the northern vizier, at Memphis;[8] the levying and inspection of troops, especially those concerned with the security of the king;[9] and, on occasion, the inspection of the Theban necropolis.[10] Like his Thirteenth Dynasty model, the Eighteenth Dynasty vizier was probably also responsible for the re-establishment of district and estate boundaries erased by the annual inundation; the issuing of orders to fell trees, dig irriga-tion canals, and corvée labour for the summer tillage; the security of Egypt's borders; and the making of all arrangements for the king's journeys, including the fitting out of ships and the mobi-lization of military escorts.[11] Reports seem to have been made regularly to the vizier on the material resources of the country, the periodic census of cattle, the condition of the palace fortifications,[12] incipient rebellions and disturbances, the rise and fall of the Nile, the heliacal rising of the dog-star Sirius (for purposes of calen-drical correction), and the occurrence of rainfall in any part of Egypt. Occasionally the great official left the Residence-city, of which he himself was, traditionally at least, the mayor, and made a personal tour of inspection through the provinces.[13] Ordinarily, however, he relied on the Scribes of the Vizier, the 'Heralds', or

---

[1] §I, 8, 48.   [2] §I, 8, 28, 61 ff.

[3] The vizier's court did not apparently handle criminal cases. See §VIII, 13, 29. Cf. §VIII, 21, 141–3.

[4] §I, 8, 61, see also 35 (§11), 57–9; §VIII, 23, 33.

[5] §I, 8, 78.   [6] §II, 35, 207 ff.; §I, 8, 186.

[7] §II, 35, 209 ff.   [8] §I, 8, 45; §VIII, 22, 44–6, 51–2.

[9] §I, 8, 49, see also 36 (§16).

[10] §I, 8, 28 (the example cited is of Ramesside date).

[11] §III, 8, 91–3, pls. 27–8, 120–1; §I, 8, 36–7; §II, 35, 206.

[12] §I, 8, 31.   [13] §I, 3, 460; §I, 8, 28.

spokesmen (*wḥmw*), of the Vizier, and the Henchmen (*šmsw*) of the Vizier[1] to represent him afield—to deliver his orders, investigate disputes, furnish information on local problems, and, in general, to maintain liaison between his office and the provincial officials.

In the New Kingdom the provincial officials consisted chiefly of the mayors (*ḥȝty-ꜥ*) of the principal towns of Upper and Lower Egypt. The jurisdiction of these local dignitaries extended not only over the towns themselves and their harbours on the Nile, but probably also over the rural districts (*kꜥḥt*), including the culti- vated fields (*ȝḥt*), adjoining the towns.[2] Their primary function was the collection and transport of the taxes in grain and other com- modities levied upon their districts,[3] and for these, as in the Middle Kingdom, they were directly answerable to the office of the vizier. The mayors (notably the mayor of Thebes) were also responsible for the support of the local temples[4] and a few of them, like the hereditary nomarchs of bygone eras, bore the title, Overseer of Prophets.[5] In the late Eighteenth Dynasty we find the mayors of towns serving with 'the priests of the temple' and 'the *wꜥb*-priests of the gods' on the local courts of law (*ḳnbt*).[6] Other local administrators mentioned in the Middle Kingdom tax-list in the tomb of the vizier Rekhmire—the Rulers of Do- mains, the District Councillors, and the district scribes—are still referred to occasionally in inscriptions of the New Kingdom, but only the last-named and the once-common *waꜥrtu*-officers appear to have survived as functioning officials in the new provincial administration.[7] We hear, too, in the Eighteenth Dynasty, of a deputy mayor and his personal scribe.[8]

In the government of the New Kingdom legislation appears to have been a function of the king alone and the laws of the country to have been simply the expressions of his will, published as occasion arose in the form of royal edicts and either superseding or augmenting the laws already laid down by his predecessors.[9] It is probable, however, that an actual code of law existed at least as early as the Twelfth Dynasty[10] and that forty leather objects, shown laid out before the vizier in his hall, are, in fact, the rolls of the pharaonic law in codified form.[11]

[1] §I, 8, 54–6.
[2] §I, 8, 223–6, 235–6, 240; §III, 14, vol. I, 31* (A 101).
[3] §I, 8, 235.   [4] §I, 8, 236.   [5] §I, 8, 221.
[6] §I, 8, 237–8.   [7] §I, 8, 238–40, 243–5.   [8] §I, 8, 245.
[9] §I, 4, 154; §VI, 24, 19–21; §VIII, 24, 150–9.
[10] §VIII, 21, 47–52; §VI, 24, 19.
[11] §III, 8, 31–4, 50 n. 24, notwithstanding. See §VI, 24, 19; §VIII, 11, 114–15; §I, 4, 154 n. 5; §I, 8, 30; §VIII, 31, 8–9; §I, 9, 64.

Judicial functions, on the other hand, were performed under the king, as supreme judge, by a great variety of office holders, from the viziers downwards;[1] and in the Eighteenth Dynasty both the high court of the vizier at Thebes (and Heliopolis?) and the local, or district, courts seem to have varied in composition from one occasion to another and to have included not only high-ranking administrative officials, but also army officers and priests.[2] In an important civil lawsuit tried during the reign of Tuthmosis IV we find the court, or 'Council of Examiners', at Thebes headed by both viziers and made up of five other members who apparently served only in an advisory capacity, one or the other of the viziers making the decision and taking full responsibility for it.[3] The records of this and another lawsuit, instigated during the late Eighteenth Dynasty by a herdsman named Mesesia,[4] give us an insight into court procedure at this period. Each of these documents contains the following entries: an introductory paragraph with the date of the session and the name of the ruling pharaoh; the speech of the plaintiff; the speech of the defendant or his counsel; the verdict of the court; and a list of the judges and other persons present, including the name of the court recorder. Testimony presented in court was usually given under an oath taken in the name of a god or of the king and often accompanied by a statement of the penalties to be inflicted in case of perjury.[5] Complete impartiality, strict adherence to law, precedent, and rules of procedure, and an earnest endeavour to arrive at the truth from a careful assessment of the evidence were the ideals around which the trial system current in the Middle and New Kingdoms were constructed.[6] Unfortunately, it would seem that these ideals, so vigorously stressed in precept, were often neglected in practice and that the courts of Egypt were no more impartial or incorruptible than those of any other nation of the ancient Near East.[7]

Apart from the departments of the government which operated directly under the vizier there were others which, though subject to his general supervision, had their own heads and their own extensive internal organizations. The most important was the

---

[1] §I, 4, 155 f.; §VIII, 31, 56–9, 63; §III, 20, 219; §VIII, 21, 140–1.

[2] §I, 8, 28, 47, 61–4, 240; §VIII, 14, 22–32; §VIII, 31, 57–9, see also 13–63 *passim*; §VI, 24, 32–40; §VIII, 26, 268.

[3] §VIII, 32, 105–15; §VI, 24, 25–6, 32; §I, 8, 28.

[4] P. Berlin 9785 (§VIII, 16, 38–45, pl. 3; §VIII, 15, 23–4; §VI, 24, 64, no. 47).

[5] §VIII, 35, 129–56; §VI, 24, 16, 18, 25, 26, 37; §VIII, 31, 70–8.

[6] §VIII, 13, 22–3, 28–9; §VI, 24, 33; §I, 3, 459.

[7] §VIII, 31, 48–9, 57, 67; §VI, 24, 17–18, 20, 38; §VIII, 13, 29.

treasury which, as in the Old and Middle Kingdoms, was both the repository and the accounting and disbursing centre of the national wealth.[1] Over this department there were apparently two Overseers of the Treasury, corresponding with the two viziers and co-operating with them in the handling of the vast income in raw materials and manufactured goods received as taxes and foreign tribute, produced by the numerous government industries, and obtained in trade with other lands. Closely associated with the treasury was the national granary and its branches, administered from a central office by the Overseer of the Granaries of Upper and Lower Egypt, whose duty it was to supervise the harvesting, recording, and storage of the yearly crops of cereal grains.[2] A central bureau under the direction of the Overseer of Cattle administered the state's herds of beef-cattle and other farm animals, with the assistance of the mayors of the provincial town-ships, the Overseers and Herdsmen of individual herds, the Overseers and Scribes of the Cattle Stables, and the Accountants of Cattle charged with taking the annual census of the herds.[3] On the other hand, there is no trace during the earlier New Kingdom of a centralized administration of cultivated lands, the function of Overseer of Fields being taken over by the Overseer of Gran-aries or being left entirely in the hands of the mayors and other local officials (see above).[4] In the Eighteenth Dynasty we find the measurement and assessment of the fields for purposes of taxation being carried out under the direction of an official called the Scribe of the Fields of the Lord of the Two Lands.[5] A special group of government officials devoted themselves to the manning, equipping, and provisioning of the army and navy;[6] and we have seen how the temples of the gods functioned to all intents and purposes as departments of the pharaonic administration (§111). There was apparently no single division of the government corresponding with our Ministry of Works. Building and the allied arts and crafts came under the jurisdiction of a variety of departments and officials—viziers, treasurers, stewards, mayors, scribes, and priests—whose duties associated them in one way or another with the construction of the royal buildings or the operation of the quarries, and who, in recognition of these activities, were awarded the title Overseer of Works or—more

[1] §1, 8, 180–91, 396–405, 508–12; §III, 14, vol. I, 26* (A 90).
[2] §1, 8, 103, 153–62, 384–90, 495–500; §III, 14, vol. I, 42* (A 121).
[3] §1, 8, 172–9   [4] §1, 8, 112–14, 235.
[5] §1, 8, 114–15, 139.
[6] See below, p. 363.

expansively—Overseer of all the Works of the King.[1] The perhaps excessive centralization of the whole administrative system required such close and constant co-operation between the various departments that there was inevitably considerable overlapping both in their functions and personnel and in the titles borne by their respective heads.

As administrators of the vast personal estates of the pharaoh and his family the Chief Steward of the King and the other royal stewards occupied positions somewhat apart from the hierarchy of officials who staffed the bureaux of the national government.[2] The office of Chief Steward was usually bestowed as a mark of special royal favour and often as a reward for distinguished service with the armed forces. It brought its holder into close contact with the king and frequently during the Eighteenth Dynasty encouraged him to allocate to himself executive powers as the pharaoh's personal representative in excess of, and inconsistent with, the purely administrative functions of the office proper. This tendency on the part of the Chief Steward constituted a menace, not only to the national administration as organized under the vizier, but also to the authority of the king himself, and on more than one occasion forced the latter to remove his erstwhile favourite from office.[3] In the reign of Amenophis II, and again under Amenophis III, the situation was alleviated by dividing the administration of the king's properties between two chief Stewards, one resident at Thebes, near the court and the centre of government, the other at Memphis, nearer the geographical centre of the royal estates, the greater part of which lay in the Delta.[4]

Under the earlier Tuthmoside rulers the most important of the numerous functionaries charged with the administration and provisioning of the royal palace was the king's chancellor, whose activities included not only supervision of the royal exchequer and the palace granaries, but also the tutoring of the royal princes and the organization of mining and trading expeditions calculated to enrich the treasuries of both the pharaoh and the state.[5] In the course of the Eighteenth Dynasty the functions of the chancellor were gradually taken over, especially at Memphis, by the king's Chief Steward and early in the Ramesside Period we find the former reduced to the status of Overseer of the Harim.[6] Entry

---

[1] §1, 8, 45, 80, 104–5, 185–6, 272, 287–8, 295, 361–2, 396–9, 421–2, 434–524 *passim*.
[2] §III, 14, vol. I, 45*–47* (A 124); §1, 8, 81–2, 92–108, 172; §1, 7, 43–54.
[3] §1, 8, 363, 364, 366–7, 547.
[4] §1, 8, 98, 99, 104, 157, 164; §1, 7, 49.   [5] §1, 8, 80–2.   [6] §1, 8, 82.

to the palace and approach to the persons of the pharaoh and the vizier were achieved by way of the Gate-house, or Guardhouse (ʿrryt), the Overseer or First Herald of which, often a retired soldier, was in general charge of the palace programme and ceremonial, and seems also to have registered and guarded incoming taxes and to have conducted hearings of a judiciary nature.[1] The ancient title, Chamberlain (imy-r ʿẖnwty), was now borne by a courtier, usually a former Page of the Court (ẖrd n kȝp), who served as general manager of the living quarters of the palace (the king's suite and the harim) as well as of the areas in which food and drink were prepared and stored—the kitchens, wine-cellars, breweries, and slaughter-houses.[2] Among his host of underlings we find the Scribe of the Table, the king's personal wine-steward or cupbearer (a functionary destined shortly to achieve considerable influence in the kingdom[3]), shop and department heads, their deputies and their staffs, and an untold number of minor servants, including youthful apprentices. The Overseer of the Harim seems to have been concerned not only with the great royal harims at Thebes, Memphis, and the entrance to the Faiyūm,[4] but also with the travelling harim which accompanied the king on his journeys.[5] From records of the later New Kingdom we know that the staffs of these extensive institutions contributed to the economy of the palace by the production of cloth and the milling of flour. Other members of the pharaoh's entourage, both at home and afield, were his herald, or spokesman (wḥmw),[6] his letter-writer, or private secretary, his court attendants (imy-ẖnt) and 'Familiars' (rḫ-nsw), the holder of his sunshade (ḥbs bḥt), and his fan-bearer—the two last-named offices being normally performed by Nubian or Syrian servants, but being also claimed, as high honorary positions (especially 'Fan-Bearer on the King's Right'), by such top-ranking officials as the royal chancellor, the king's Chief Steward, and the Viceroy of Nubia.[7]

Lists of the principal New Kingdom officials with indications of their relative importance are preserved in a decree issued in favour of the temple and funerary cult of Amenophis, son of Hapu,[8] and in a somewhat later relief from the tomb of a high

---

[1] §II, 42, 968–9, 975 (11). See §I, 8, 65–70; §VIII, 20, 12.

[2] §I, 8, 161–2, 252–61; §III, 14, vol. I, 44*–45* (A 123).

[3] §I, 8, 269–76.

[4] §I, 8, 236, 263–4; §VIII, 18, 145–9.

[5] §I, 8, 161, 253, 260, 262–8.

[6] §I, 8, 67–70, 154–5; §III, 14, vol. I, 22* (A 80), 91*–92* (A 197); §VIII, 12, 46; §VIII, 20, 11–14.

[7] §I, 8, 281–2.   [8] See above, p. 345 n. 2.

priest of Memphis.[1] The first of these two lists is headed by the vizier, followed in order by the Overseer of the Treasury, the Chief Steward of the (Royal) Domain, the Overseer of the Granaries, the High Priests, the God's Fathers, and the *Wēʿb*-Priests of Amun. The second list begins with the figure and titles of 'the Hereditary Prince and General'. Then come the two Viziers, the King's Scribe and Steward, the Chancellor, the Overseer of the Guardhouse, the Commander of Soldiers, the Chamberlain, the Overseer of the Treasury, two High Priests (of Heliopolis and Memphis), a *Setem*-Priest, and, finally, the Mayor (of the district of Memphis).

As heretofore, a primary prerequisite for entry into the civil service was a sound education, and it was from the schools of scribes, especially those at Thebes and Memphis, that most of the young career officials were drawn.[2] Through long and arduous years of study, punctuated by many beatings from his exacting instructors,[3] the embryonic civil servant learned to read, spell, and write in three different scripts—the formal hieroglyphic characters reserved for monumental inscriptions, the elegant hieratic script used for literary, technical, and religious compositions, and the more cursive hand employed in taking dictation, making rapid notes, and drawing up business and legal documents.[4] While at school he also developed the ability to express himself correctly and gracefully by prolonged study of the classic works of Egyptian literature and acquainted himself thoroughly with the proper forms to be used in letters, petitions, reports, and the like.[5] Other subjects of which he was expected to acquire a working knowledge were arithmetic, book-keeping, practical geometry, drawing, surveying, geography, and simple engineering.[6] Even after his graduation from school and his admission as a junior official into one of the bureaux of the national administration he continued his studies, usually under the guidance of his immediate superior in office. Now, however, his exercises were of more

---

[1] Berlin 12411 (§VIII, 28, 180). See §VIII, 7, 18, pl. 1; §I, 8, 22; §II, 34, vol. III, 197.

[2] §VIII, 9, 185–9, see also xxvii ff., 68, 71–2, 196–7, 215, 223–4; §I, 9, 67–8; §VIII, 34, 16 ff.; §VIII, 10, 376 ff. See also §VIII, 2; §VIII, 3; §VIII, 25.

[3] Pap. Anastasi III, 3, 13; V, 8, 5–6 (§VIII, 17, 24, 59; §III, 3, 83, 85, 231). See §VIII, 31, 68–9; §VIII, 33, 176.

[4] §VIII, 19, §§5–8. Under Amenophis III and IV some Egyptian scribes must also have been familiar with cuneiform and the Asiatic languages written in it (§I, 9, 67).

[5] §VIII, 8. See also §VIII, 17; §III, 3; §VIII, 27.

[6] See, for example, Pap. Anastasi I (§VIII, 9, 214–15, 223–33; §II, 49, 475–9).

advanced type and instead of scribbling them, as formerly, on pot-sherds and bits of limestone, he wrote them out in rolls of papyrus, which he sometimes carried with him to the tomb as examples of his skill.[1] Above all, he was now established as a fully-fledged 'Scribe' and as a member of the highly privileged and much envied official class and could look down on the uneducated masses of the people who performed the menial tasks from which he himself was normally exempt.[2] If capable, ambitious, and diligent in the performance of his duties he was assured of steady promotion up through the ranks of the pharaonic government and of growing favour with the king, and no office in the land, including that of the vizier himself, was beyond his grasp.

In spite of the military character of the kings and the strong military spirit which pervaded the nation as a whole, the internal administration of Egypt remained thoughout the greater part of the New Kingdom almost entirely in the hands of trained civilian officials and the official class continued to be the most influential of the several recognized categories of Egyptian society.[3] The other divisions of this society, as defined by an Eighteenth Dynasty census-taker, comprised the 'soldiers', or what we should call the military class, the 'priests', the 'king's servants', and 'all the craftsmen'.[4] The priesthood we have already dis-cussed (§III) and the compositions of and roles played by the other three classes will form the themes around which the sections to follow are constructed.

IX. THE ARMY, NAVY, AND POLICE FORCE

The Egyptian army as re-organized under the pharaohs of the early New Kingdom was the direct outgrowth of the lessons learned by the rulers of Thebes in their war against the Hyksos and owed much to the evidently efficient and well equipped fighting machine of the Asiatic invaders.[5] The small body of regular combat troops, maintained during the Old and Middle Kingdoms,[6] was expanded into a standing national army of con-siderable size, composed in large part of professional soldiers (regulars and reserves) and led by professional officers uniformly

[1] §1, 9, 68. On the use of ostraca in general see §VIII, 4.
[2] See, for example, Pap. Anastasi II, 6, 7–8, 5; Pap Sallier I, 6, 9–7, 9(§ VIII, 17, 16–17, 84–5; §III, 3, 50–6, 317–19).
[3] §1, 7, 1.
[4] §II, 42, 1006 (15–17); §II, 35, 146; §1, 1, 165 n. a; §1, 2, 246.
[5] §III, 20, 235; §1, 9, 68–9; §1, 3, 455 ff.; §1, 7, 59; §V, 19, 152–63; §IX, 5.
[6] §VIII, 12, 33, 37; §1, 7, 17.

trained in their duties and functioning as links in a co-ordinated chain of command.[1] Squadrons of the now indispensable war-chariot were added to the existing infantry arm and operated in conjunction with it or as independent striking forces of great mobility and effectiveness.[2] The fire-power of the Egyptian archer was increased enormously by the adoption of the composite bow; and heavy bronze axes, swords, and spearheads replaced the light copper weapons of former times.[3] Military standards of numerous, readily distinguishable forms enabled commanders in battle to keep constant track of the disposition and fortunes of the units under their command and served as rallying points for the individual companies;[4] and a light but raucous war-trumpet was used extensively as a signalling device.[5] Strategy began to play an important part in the conduct of campaigns and indi-vidual battles, and the latter were transformed from simple encounters of bodies of armed men into carefully planned engagements often involving a succession of precisely executed tactical manœuvres.[6]

Like its successors of the late Eighteenth and early Nine-teenth Dynasties, the army which participated in the foreign campaigns of the Tuthmoside pharaohs probably comprised several divisions of infantry named in honour of Egypt's principal gods (Amun, Re, Ptah, etc.) and carrying the standards of these deities before them into battle.[7] Each division was commanded by a general (*imy-r mšʿ* or *imy-r mnfȝt*), assisted, especially in the area of service and supply, by an adjutant (*idnw n mšʿ*), by high-ranking combat officers known as 'battalion commanders' (*ḥry pḏt*), often assigned to fortresses and other posts along the border or in the provinces (§vii), and by some twenty-five 'standard-bearers' (*tȝy sryt*), each in charge of a company (*sȝ*) of 200 soldiers (*wʿw*).[8] Like the divisions, the companies had names of their own which were sometimes reflected in the forms of their standards.[9] Thus, under Amenophis II we hear of a company of Nubian auxiliaries called 'Bull-in-Nubia' and under Amenophis III of two companies named, respectively, 'Manifest-in-Justice'

[1] §III, 20, 233; §VIII, 12, 41 ff.; §IX, 20, 1 ff.; §I, 7, *passim*. See also §IX, 4.
[2] §VIII, 12, 43; §IX, 20, 22–6, 47–51; §I, 7, 59–66.
[3] §IX, 24, 60–99; §IX, 1, *passim*; §V, 19, 158–66.
[4] §IX, 11, 12–18; §IX, 20, 92–3.   [5] §IX, 15; §IX, 16; §IX, 20, 94.
[6] §I, 3, 456–7; §IX, 20, 62–9; §IX, 12; §IX, 13.
[7] §IX, 20, 11–15, 92–3; §IX, 11, 17; §VIII, 12, 42; §III, 20, 234.
[8] §IX, 20, 11–22, 32–7, 42–3, 98–9; §VIII, 12, 42–6; §I, 7, 27–8, 36–9, 54–6; §III, 14, vol. I, 25*–26*, 29*, 113*.
[9] §IX, 11, 15.

and 'Splendour-of-Aten'. A unit of unknown size which served under Tuthmosis IV bore the name 'Menkheprure, Destroyer of Syria', and Tuthmosis III's *corps d'élite* was honoured with the title, 'Braves of the King'.[1]

The relatively small squadron of chariotry attached to each division of the army was led by a Battalion Commander of Chariotry (*ḥry pḏt nt-ḥtrі*) and was under the over-all charge of a senior service officer called the Master of the Horse (*imy-r ssmt*), assisted by remount and training officers known as Stablemasters (*ḥry iḥw*).[2] In battle each chariot was manned by a driver (*kḏn*) and a fighter (*snn*), the leading chariot, frequently that of the pharaoh, being driven by the Charioteer of the King, later also known as the First Charioteer of His Majesty.[3]

Corresponding with the administrative partition of the country into two vizierates there were two main sections, or corps, of the Home Forces of the army, one based in northern Egypt with its principal garrison and headquarters at Memphis, the other in the south with its headquarters at Thebes.[4] Each section was under the command of a senior adjutant of the army (*idnw n mšʿ*) and in the later Eighteenth Dynasty we hear of a Commander-in-Chief, or generalissimo (*imy-r mšʿ wr*), of the Home Troops. The duties of these troops were to supply trained replacements for the foreign-service armies, garrison frontier stations, furnish royal escorts and parade groups for pageants and the like, suppress riots and other disturbances, and provide labour companies for work in the quarries and on the royal monuments.[5]

Recruiting, supply, the keeping of battle records, and other administrative functions associated with the army, both in the field and at home, were attended to by a host of military scribes (*sš mšʿ*), presided over by the Chief Scribes of the Army and the King's Scribe of Recruits, an official whose numerous responsibilities included jurisdiction over the northern border forts and coastal stations.[6] General administrative supervision of the army was in the hands of the general officers (*imy-r mšʿ*) and their adjutants, referred to above. The post of Minister of War appears to have been exercised by the vizier.[7] We have seen, in any case,

[1] §IX, 20, 18–21; §IX, 11, 17–18.
[2] §I, 7, 59–66; §IX, 20, 22–6, 47–52, 100–1 (also letter dated 16 August 1960); §VIII, 12, 43.
[3] §I, 7, 64; §IX, 20, 49; §VIII, 12, 43.
[4] §VIII, 12, 43; §I, 7, 19–20; §IX, 20, 53–4; §III, 20, 233.
[5] §VIII, 12, 43.   [6] §I, 7, 14–27; §IX, 20, 37–43; §VIII, 12, 46.
[7] §VIII, 12, 42; §IX, 20, 79; §I, 3, 461–2; §I, 2, 243. See §I, 8, 36 (sect. 16), 37 (sects. 19, 21), 39 (sects. 24, 25), 49.

that in the late Middle Kingdom, and probably also in the early
New Kingdom, the vizier presided over the General Staff of the
Army,[1] mustered the military escort which was to accompany the
king on his journeys, saw to the garrisoning of Thebes and other
Egyptian towns, and assumed responsibility for the upkeep of
fortifications.

Throughout the Eighteenth Dynasty the armed forces appear
to have been made up principally of freeborn native Egyptians,
augmented by troops of Nubian auxiliaries and, from the time of
Amenophis III onwards, by foreign prisoners of war, among them
the famed Sherden.[2] Replacements for the rank and file of the
regular army were recruited chiefly from the families of former
soldiers and other 'reserves' quartered in military colonies up and
down the land.[3] Officers were selected from the ranks of the
regular soldiers (w^cw)[4] from the civil service,[5] and from the
so-called 'pages of the (royal) court' ($hrdw$ n k^3p).[6] During their
training period new recruits ($nfrw$) were organized into drill
companies ($shprw$), garrisoned at Memphis or Thebes.[7]

In times of peace units of the regular army were sometimes
detailed to the transport of the royal obelisks and other operations
which required the concerted effort of large bodies of trained men
and which might lead the workers involved into regions not
altogether immune from attacks by hostile tribesmen.[8] For the
most part, however, tasks of this type were performed by levies of
'militia', or conscripts (d^3mw), raised as the occasion required
among the young manhood of Egypt and organized into companies according to the towns or districts from which they were
drawn.[9] Lists were kept by the Scribe of Recruits and his assist-
ants of all able-bodied men available for service as conscripts,
and these were carefully revised from time to time to avoid
imposing too heavy a burden on sparsely populated or poverty-
stricken districts. Furthermore, although the ratio of one con-
script out of every hundred candidates, current during the
Middle Kingdom, probably did not still prevail in the Eighteenth
Dynasty, the men taken by each draft certainly constituted a very
small percentage of the total male population.[10] Nevertheless,

---

[1] §VIII, 12, 42; §IX, 20, 79.

[2] §I, 4, 152; §VIII, 12, 44–5; §IX, 20, 26–9, 72–4; §I, 7, 17 ff.; §III, 14, vol. I,
194* (A 268). Cf. §IX, 3; §IX, 4.

[3] §I, 7, 17–20; §IX, 20, 54–5, 72, 74, 77.

[4] §VIII, 12, 45.   [5] §I, 7, 14 ff.

[6] §I, 7, 34–6.

[7] §I, 7, 19; §IX, 20, 72–3.   [8] §IX, 20, 18 n. 67.

[9] §I, 7, 18–21; §IX, 20, 5–6, 81.   [10] §I, 7, 20. Cf. §IX, 10, 43–5.

force was often required to separate the victims of a draft from their pleading relatives, and squads of police nearly always assisted at the inductions.[1] In scenes on tomb and temple walls conscripted recruits appear armed and accoutred in much the same manner as members of the regular army; it is evident that they not only served as escorts and labour battalions, but were also sent into combat side by side with the young volunteers (*nfrw*) and the seasoned soldiery (*mnf3t*).[2] More often than not the squads of conscripts assigned to a quarrying or transport job, though commanded by their own officers, were under the over-all supervision of one of the royal architects or some other civilian official.

Naval warfare in the sense of engagements between armed ships being as yet undeveloped, the Egyptian 'navy' of the early New Kingdom continued to function primarily as a transport, communications, and freight service for the army, as a mobile base of operations for military expeditions up the Nile and along the Syrian coast, and as an exploratory and trading fleet in the service of the pharaoh.[3] Except for the splendid royal flagships— the so-called 'falcon-ships'—the vessels used in military operations appear to have been ordinary merchantmen (transports and freighters) such as were employed by the temples, the treasury, and similar non-military institutions, but carrying, besides their regular crews, armed companies of specially trained amphibious troops.[4] There were, moreover, notable differences in the sizes and forms of the ships themselves depending on whether they were destined for service on the Nile, the Mediterranean, or the Red Sea.

The ships designed to operate on the Nile were for the most part light, shallow-draft vessels capable of threading their way through the numerous sandbanks of the river and of being hauled by force up through its turbulent, rock-strewn cataracts.[5] Regular features of these ships were their lofty cabins, from the tops of which lookouts were able to command a view of the river banks for miles ahead.[6] The seagoing ships of the two other fleets were larger vessels without cabins or other flimsy superstructure, their sturdy hulls, decked over and braced fore-and-aft with the clumsy but effective hogging truss, displaying considerably more freeboard than the river boats.[7] Since drinking water and other supplies were not obtainable on the long voyage

[1] §I, 7, 20. [2] §IX, 20, 6–7; §VIII, 12, 45. [3] See §I, 10.
[4] §I, 10, 3, 42, 72 ff. See §IX, 20, 9, 45, 68–9; §IX, 14, vol. LXVIII, 109; §IX, 14, vol. LXVIII, 16, 22, 28.
[5] §I, 10, 1–7. [6] §I, 10, 2 n. 2; §IX, 14, vol. LXVIII, 21–2. [7] §IV, 7.

down the barren Red Sea coast speed was a primary requisite, and the ships built for the journey to Punt (§ IV) had huge, wide-spreading sails and the long clean hulls of racing craft.[1] For the shorter runs between the Delta coast and the islands of the eastern Mediterranean or between the numerous harbours of Palestine and Syria speed could be sacrificed to carrying capacity; and the troop and cargo ships of the Mediterranean fleet appear to have been broad craft of moderate rig, offering stowage space for chariots and other bulky equipment and even provided at times with stalls for horses.[2] Among the several classes of seagoing vessels in service during the Eighteenth Dynasty the so-called 'Byblites' (*Kpnwt*) and 'Cretans' (*Kftiw*) are now generally conceded to have been ships designed and built by the Egyptians for journeys *to* Byblos and Crete—and for voyages of similar type and duration.[3] Furthermore, it is evident that in ship design and construction and in seafaring knowledge in general the Egyptians of the New Kingdom owed little or nothing to their Minoan and Phoenician neighbours, but were, in fact, the originators of at least one type of ship adopted and used by the latter.[4]

The fighting complement of a ship on naval service consisted, as has been said, of a crew of amphibious troops (*ḥnyt*), composed on the larger vessels of as many as 200 soldiers (*wꜥw*) trained for duty as marines and led by a 'standard-bearer' (*ṯꜣy sryt*) and by an officer of comparable rank called a 'crew-commander' (*ḥry ḥnyt*).[5] The ships themselves were commanded and handled when under way by their own 'skippers', or 'navigators' (*nfww*), a title apparently also applied to the mates of a vessel as well as to its captain.[6] The names of the ships to which men and officers were attached are often included in their titles (for example, 'standard-bearer of the king's ship, "Beloved-of-Amun"') and, conversely, ships were not infrequently identified by the names of their skippers (for example, 'the ship of Amenophis, son of Neferhotep').[7] Transfer to a more important vessel was a common form of promotion, and during the reign of Amenophis III we hear of a standard-bearer who served successively in the royal ships 'Star-in-Memphis', 'Manifest-in-Justice', 'The-Ruler-is-

---

[1] § IV, 7, 7–9; § I, 10, 16.   [2] § I, 10, 16, 43 f.; § IX, 8, 41.

[3] § I, 10, 47–50; § IV, 7, 3 ff.

[4] § I, 10, 15, 16 n. 1, 43–58; § IV, 7, 3 ff.; § IX, 8, 41–3. See also § IX, 17, 21–34; § IX, 23, 430–69.

[5] § I, 10, 71–85; § I, 7, 36–7; § IX, 20, 5, 8–10, 35, 37, 45, 68, 69, 95.

[6] § I, 10, 85–7. Cf. § IX, 20, 10, 69; § III, 14, vol. I, 94*.

[7] § I, 10, 85 n. 4; § IX, 14, vol. LXVI, 111, 112, 115; vol. LXVIII, 8, 20, 35.

Strong', and 'Splendour-of-Aten', the last-named being the king's flagship.[1] Among the higher officers (or officials?) of the navy the 'Overseers of Ships' were probably only division or squadron commanders; but the rare title, 'Overseer of All Ships of the King', almost certainly designated its holder as the Admiral of the Fleet, or, perhaps better, as the First Lord of the Admiralty.[2] Neither of these offices, to judge from the previous careers of their incumbents, required any naval experience, but were rather of a purely administrative nature. At least two important naval expeditions, sent out, respectively, by Hatshepsut (§IV) and Tuthmosis III,[3] were commanded by treasury officials; and all units of the fleet stationed in Egypt itself appear to have come under the more or less direct jurisdiction of the vizier (§VIII). The common practice of assigning the same men and officers to duty with the armed forces both ashore and afloat is well illustrated by the case of Suemnut who, having served as standard-bearer of an infantry company and as chief stablemaster of the army's chariotry division, was appointed by Amenophis II to be Admiral of the Fleet.[4]

The principal base and dockyard of the Egyptian navy was located on the Nile near Memphis in the approximate geographic centre of the empire and not far above the junction point of the channels from the harbours of the Delta coast. It was called Peru-nefer, 'Good departure' ('Bon Voyage'?), and appears to have been developed during the reign of Tuthmosis III from the ways and shed for a single royal barque into an extensive harbour installation with shipyards, temples, and resthouses for the reception of foreign envoys. A record of intensive shipbuilding activity carried on at Peru-nefer during the thirtieth regnal year of Tuthmosis III is preserved in a papyrus in the British Museum, which lists in detail the kinds and amounts of wood issued to the master shipwrights over a period of eight months and specifies the types of ships and boats under construction.[5] It is from this source also that we learn that the senior official in charge of the dockyard was none other than the 'King's Son, Amenophis', the future King Amenophis II, who seems to have maintained extensive estates in the vicinity and to have resided at or near Peru-nefer for considerable periods of time.[6]

[1] §I, 10, 83.
[2] §I, 10, 88–90.
[3] §II, 42, 531–5; §IX, 21, 356–63.
[4] §I, 7, 42 n. 4; §I, 10, 90.
[5] §IX, 14, vol. LXVI, 105–21; vol. LXVIII, 7–41; §I, 10, 37 ff.
[6] §IX, 14, vol. LXVI, 106, 108; vol. LXVIII, 29–30; §I, 10, 37; §IX, 7, vol. I, 10, 12, 18, 20, 33.

The commander-in-chief of the armed forces was the king himself. In time of war most of the Tuthmoside rulers not only planned and directed their campaigns, but actually led their chariot divisions in battle and commanded their flagships during important movements of the fleet.[1] Apart from his bodyguard and the high-ranking officers who formed his board of strategy, the pharaoh was attended in the field by a large personal staff, including one or more heralds, or 'repeaters' (*wḥmw*), whose duty it was to relay all reports to him and to repeat his orders and decisions to the persons most concerned.[2] The title, 'Commander-in-Chief of the Army' (*imy-r mšꜥ wr*), was borne during the Tuthmoside period by at least two princes of the blood royal: Amenmose, the eldest son of Tuthmosis I,[3] and Nakhtmin, a son of Amenophis III;[4] and it was almost certainly in this capacity that Amenophis II and Tuthmosis IV were assigned, while still young princes, to the headquarters of the northern army corps at Memphis.[5] Although we have no evidence that, as in the Twelfth Dynasty, the crown prince during his father's lifetime ever led the armed forces in war, it is not unlikely that this also was sometimes the case.

By the Eighteenth Dynasty the name 'Medjay', once confined to certain desert tribesmen of Nubia who served as scouts and light-armed auxiliaries with the Egyptian armies,[6] had come to be the regular term for 'policeman', or 'ranger', and was used to describe the companies of constabulary which patrolled the deserts, guarded the cemeteries, and in general maintained order within the boundaries of Egypt itself.[7] Although the police force of Egypt has always included in its ranks a large number of Nubians and Sudanese, it is certain that during the New Kingdom many of the so-called Medjay and nearly all of their officers were native Egyptians. In deference, however, to the ancient tribal origin of the organization the senior police officer was called the 'Chief of Medjay' (*wr n Mḏꜣy*) and as such appears to have exercised authority over the entire force, assisted by one or more deputy chiefs, or adjutants (*idnw n Mḏꜣy*). Each large town or district had its own company of police, commanded by a 'Captain of Medjay' (*ḥry Mḏꜣy*) who, though subordinate to the chief and his deputies, was a person of importance in his community and in

---

[1] §I, 7, 30; §I, 10, 89; §IX, 20, 32, 79; §VIII, 12, 42; §I, 3, 454.
[2] §I, 8, 67–70; §III, 14, vol. I, 91*–92* (A 197; see also A 80); §VIII, 12, 46.
[3] §II, 42, 91. See §I, 7, 30.
[4] §II, 42, 1908. See §I, 7, 31. See also §III, 14, vol. I, 21*.
[5] §I, 7, 30–1.
[6] §III, 14, vol. I, 73*–89* (A 188); §VII, 12, 38–43; §II, 38, 232–3.
[7] §III, 14, vol. I, 82* ff.; §I, 7, 57–9; §IX, 20, 29.

western Thebes bore the rank of an army troop-commander (*ḥry pdt*).[1] Troops of Medjay represented in the tomb of the police-captain Nebamun at Thebes (reign of Tuthmosis IV) carry military standards and are armed for the most part with bows, though some bear spears and shields.[2] The use of Medjay as frontier guards and desert patrols is indicated by their frequent association in New Kingdom records with the parties of huntsmen (*nww*) and other groups active in both the eastern and western deserts.[3]

The growth during the Eighteenth Dynasty of a large and increasingly influential military class was stimulated chiefly by the rich rewards and high honours which the career of a professional soldier or marine now had to offer and by the handsome provisions which the kings made for the support and well-being of their veterans between wars and following retirement from active duty. The 'Gold of Valour' (or 'of Praise')—gold ornaments, weapons, and orders of various forms—was lavishly and repeatedly bestowed on officers and men for deeds of bravery and devotion in time of war;[4] and all members of the armed forces shared in one way or another in the rich booty in slaves, cattle, weapons, jewellery, clothing, and household effects captured from an often prosperous and luxuriously equipped enemy.[5] At home the troops and their families were established in comfortable settlements of their own, set aside for the purpose of maintaining ready sources of reserves for the armed forces.[6] Frequently a veteran was provided out of the royal holdings with fields, servants, and cattle on which he was normally required to pay taxes, but which remained in the possession of his family so long as one of its male members in the direct line of succession continued to be available for service with the army or navy.[7] So it was that the military profession was passed down from father to son for generation after generation and became in time the principal means of support of an increasingly large proportion of the population. The growing appeal which a military career made to the young manhood of the country and the growing importance of the military class as a whole are reflected in the frequent and bitter diatribes against the soldier's profession which we find in the school writings of the New Kingdom—writings

---

[1] §I, 7, 57–8.   [2] §IX, 6, 35–7, pl. 27; §IX, 11, 16.
[3] §II, 38, 232–3; §III, 14, vol. I, 85*–86*, 89*.
[4] §IX, 9, 83–6; §IX, 19, 10–13; §IX, 20, 81; §IX, 22, 143–5; §I, 9, 71.
[5] §I, 4, 152; §I, 3, 438; §I, 9, 68; §IX, 2, 41–2; §IX, 18, 298–302.
[6] §IX, 20, 2, 54–5, 72; §I, 7, 17–18; §I, 8, 123.
[7] §I, 7, 17–18; §I, 8, 125; §IX, 20, 55, 81; §I, 10, 84–5; §I, 438.

intended to fortify the embryonic civil servant in his pursuit of learning.[1]

More far-reaching in its effect on Egypt's future history than the type of pensioning just discussed was the practice adopted by the kings of appointing their old comrades-in-arms to positions of intimacy and trust in the royal household and to important administrative offices, not only in connexion with the armed forces themselves, but also in the management of the vast royal domains. During the Eighteenth Dynasty we find retired army officers serving as the pharaoh's personal attendants (honorary butlers, fan-bearers, and the like), as the tutors of the king's children, and, above all, as stewards of the royal estates.[2] Without attempting to insert themselves into the structure of the national administration, which remained, as has been said, largely in the hands of the civil service, these men formed at court a party of their own which, since it enjoyed on the one hand the closest relationship with the king and, on the other hand, the backing of the armed forces, both active and retired, was exceedingly powerful. Later we shall see how, when the opportunity presented itself, this military group was able to oppose successfully the combined power of officialdom and the priesthood and to take the reins of government into its own hands.[3]

X. THE EMPLOYMENT AND SOURCES OF LABOUR

During the New Kingdom, as in all periods of Egypt's history, the greater part of the country's population was employed throughout the year as field hands and herdsmen on the agricultural estates which provided the nation's livelihood and were the principal source of its wealth. A large proportion of the scenes of daily life preserved in the private tombs of the Eighteenth Dynasty at Thebes and elsewhere show farm labourers engaged in the sowing, cultivating, reaping, threshing, winnowing, transportation, and storage of the two principal cereal grains, barley and emmer, in the sowing, cultivating, and harvesting of flax, employed extensively in the production of cloth, and in the gathering of the wild-growing papyrus plant, among the many uses of which may be cited the manufacture of writing paper.[4]

---

[1] §VIII, 9, 194–7. See §III, 20, 239–40; §IX, 20, 72; §IX, 2, 41–2.
[2] §I, 7, 43–54; §I, 8, 108; §II, 25, 28 ff.; §III, 20, 233; §I, 2, 246–7.
[3] §I, 7, 1, 86 ff. See also §I, 4, 153.
[4] §V, 8, 1–6, 8–22, 42–4, 191; §X, 22, 90–156; §X, 8, 4–11; §X, 21, 22–8; §X, 26, 36 ff.; §IV, 14, 162–5.

Numerous workers were required to cultivate the vegetable and flower gardens which formed important parts of the estates, and gangs of pickers were periodically assembled to harvest the yield of the vineyards, the groves of date and dōm-palms, and the orchards of fig, olive, pomegranate, and other fruit trees.[1] Trees like the sycomore, tamarisk, and acacia provided, besides firewood, wood which could be used in rough carpentry and construction work and were felled in quantity by bands of wood-cutters.[2] Bee-keeping was a well-established farm industry and, in addition, wild honey and beeswax were systematically gathered by roving collectors.[3] Stock farming included the maintenance not only of large herds of beef cattle, sheep, goats, and donkeys, but also of droves of antelopes and other ruminants brought in from the wastelands on either side of the Nile Valley.[4] Horse breeding had probably been instituted, though during the early New Kingdom most of the horses used by the Egyptians appear to have been imported from western Asia.[5] Poultry raising was, as always, a major activity of every Egyptian farm, and in addition to the personnel needed to tend the flocks of ducks, geese, and pigeons, a staff of fowlers was maintained to keep the runs and lofts constantly stocked with birds of all kinds.[6] Hunting and fishing, carried on day in and day out by professionals, served to augment the supply of food grown on the farm and were among the recognized occupations of the rural classes.[7] Considerable numbers of men and women attached to the great estates were employed in converting the raw produce into usable form. Among the more common types of workers so employed were the millers, butchers, and brewers, the treaders of wine and pressers of oil, the basket and rope makers, and the spinners and weavers of cloth, the last-named being usually women.[8]

Since all of Egypt's agricultural activity, and indeed its very

[1] §v, 8, 22–42, 49–53; §x, 22, 111–12, 156–75; §x, 26, 40–1; §x, 21, 32–3; §1, 8, 162–70.

[2] §III, 8, 92, pl. 27 (24); §VIII, 10, figs. 192, 203, 226; §IV, 14, 501–8; §v, 8, 191–2. 'Tree-fellers', or 'woodcutters' ($\check{s}^c d$ $\underline{h}t$) are mentioned with great frequency in administrative documents of the New Kingdom (e.g. §x, 18, 423 [1]; §x, 7, nos. 36 r. 12 and v. 2, 39 r. 15, and *passim*).

[3] §x, 27, 84–93; §II, 20, 94 nn. 145–8; §x, 22, 204–6.

[4] §v, 8, 62–75; §x, 22, 196 ff., 243–72; §x, 21, 31–2.

[5] §x, 15, 3–13; §x, 16, 97–103; §1, 7, 59; §x, 22, 209–12; §VIII, 10, 583 ff., 615 ff.; §v, 19, 152–5.

[6] §v, 8, 70–1, 78–86. See also §x, 25, 85–9.

[7] §v, 8, 75–8, 86–9; §x, 22, 229–43; §x, 21, 28–30.

[8] §v, 8, 51–6, 171–91.

existence as a habitable land, depended upon the control and distribution of the waters of the Nile, the construction and repair of
dykes and revetments and the excavation and clearance of
irrigation basins and canals ranked first on the list of public
works carried out under the pharaonic government and absorbed
at times a very large percentage of the country's available supply
of labour.[1] Each year the wreckage of embankments and river
walls and the clogging of waterways brought about by the
inundation had to be set right; and, with a rapidly growing
population to be supported, new tracts of arable land had to be
reclaimed, new basins created, and new networks of canals,
ditches, and runnels laid out. Even when all this had been
accomplished the water during the spring and summer months
had to be raised to the level of the fields; and although this
operation was facilitated by the introduction (from Asia?) of the
shadūf, or counterpoised well-sweep,[2] it was still a long and arduous
task, involving thousands of man-hours of back-breaking toil.

Mention has already been made of the companies of miners and
gold-washers attached more or less permanently to the gold mines
of Nubia and Upper Egypt (§vii). To these must be added the
equally numerous crews of pitmen, shorers, and porters employed
in the turquoise mines of Sinai,[3] and the very much larger gangs
of stonecutters and handlers assigned to the six or seven principal
quarries, the operation of which during the Eighteenth Dynasty
must have been almost as continuous as that of the mines (§xii).
The number of masons, bricklayers, plasterers, and the like
employed in the construction of the gigantic New Kingdom
temples certainly ran into the thousands[4] and, in addition to
these, sizeable troops of workmen of many different types are
known to have found steady employment in the preparation of the
royal and private tombs of the Theban necropolis.[5] Even more
numerous than the builders, miners, and quarrymen was the
auxiliary personnel required for each great project: the trans-
porters of stone and other materials and equipment, the porters and
drovers of the pack trains, the ship and barge crews, the provi-
sioners, and the water-carriers.[6] Every atelier of craftsmen was

[1] §iii, 20, 38; §iii, 8, 92, pl. 27 (24–5); §iii, 26, 139–40; §x, 22, 113–22.
See also §vi, 34, 23–33.
[2] §v, 19, 164–6; §x, 24, 314; §x, 22, 117–18.
[3] §iv, 8, vol. ii, 17 ff.; §x, 6, 384–9; §x, 14, 281–5; §ii, 50, 191.
[4] §iii, 26, 208–9; §i, 9, 65, 71, 320; §x, 30, 130 ff.; §iii, 20, 169; §i, 7, 20–21.
[5] §x, 5, 200–9; §x, 3, vol. xvi, 13 ff.; §iii, 20, 168; §i, 8, 46, 186, 242.
[6] §x, 3, vol. xvi, 13, 17; §ix, 3, 21–31; §x, 30, 146; §iii, 14, vol. i, 59*, 72*,
94*, 97*; §iii, 20, 168.

provided with common labourers and semi-skilled workmen to sharpen tools, grind paint and glue, pump forges, fetch supplies, and perform all the other onerous and tedious jobs associated with the various manufacturing industries;[1] and every royal palace and great house throughout the land maintained a huge staff of domestic servants—cooks, butlers, valets, nurses, washerwomen, bath attendants, janitors, and quantities of others.[2]

Inasmuch as ownership of all landed property and control over all the institutions and activities in which the various types of workers described above were employed rested ultimately with the pharaoh, we find members of the labouring class referred to collectively as 'king's servants' (ḥmw nsw).[3] Actually, only certain specified groups were attached to the personal estates of the ruler and his family, while others were assigned to the temple administrations, the national treasury, the national granary, the national administration of cattle, the various local administrative organizations, and the estates and households of the great officials.[4] Carefully revised lists of the different companies of labourers were apparently kept by the office of the King's Scribe of Recruits and were referred to in settling disputes which arose between the departments regarding jurisdiction over the persons and products of individual workers or groups of workers.[5]

Almost all common labourers in ancient Egypt seem to have worked under compulsion, received no payment for their labours other than the bare necessities of life, and enjoyed few of the rights of free citizens as we now understand the term. It is, however, possible to distinguish among them several different categories.

Lowest on the social scale were the slaves, whose existence in Egypt during the New Kingdom is well established and whose numbers during that period increased steadily with each succeeding reign.[6] They were usually foreigners (Syrians or Nubians) either captured in war or brought into the country by itinerant merchants.[7] The distinguishing characteristics of the slaves, as compared with other classes of labourers, were that they could be bought and sold like any other form of merchandise, could be

---

[1] §x, 3, vol. xvi, 13; §viii, 10, 139.

[2] §i, 8, 253–76 passim; §iii, 20, 63–76; §viii, 10, 218–19.

[3] See above, p. 363 n. 4. Cf. §x, 2, 30; §viii, 21, 90–1.

[4] §i, 8, 103, 127, 150, 154, 159–70, 174, 185–6, 189, 255–61, 267. See also above, p. 324 n. 8, and p. 325 nn. 1, 2 and 6.

[5] §i, 7, 21.

[6] §x, 2, 31 ff., 69–82, 124; §vi, 24, 42 ff.; §x, 24, 338–9. Cf. §viii, 21, 133–4.

[7] §x, 2, 70–2, 109–16; §x, 13, 37 ff.; §x, 24, 339; §iii, 8, 47.

hired out by their owners for indefinite periods of time, and could
be owned not only by the state, but by private individuals, even
by persons themselves of very low social standing.[1] A group of
contracts drawn up during the Eighteenth Dynasty shows that
the fee for four days' service by a female slave was equal to the
value of an ox;[2] and later in the New Kingdom we find a Syrian
slave-girl fetching a price equivalent to 41 *ḳidet* (13 ounces) of
silver.[3] In the lists of labourers mentioned above the name of
each foreign slave is accompanied by the names of his parents, his
place of origin, the name of the person who brought him to
Egypt, and the name of the official to whom he was assigned
upon arrival.[4] Although slaves were frequently branded, like
cattle, as a further ready means of identification,[5] they appear on
the whole to have been reasonably well treated and to have had
some legal rights.[6] In addition to their food and lodging they
received a yearly allowance of 'linen, ointment, and clothes',[7]
and there are instances from the later New Kingdom not only of
the emancipation of slaves, but also of marriages arranged
between slaves and members of their owner's families, though
the children of such unions did not necessarily inherit their
parent's state of freedom.[8]

Scarcely better than the lot of the slaves was that of the
Egyptian peasants who, though technically free men and women
capable of owning property, more often than not laboured as
serfs on the royal, government, or temple estates and received as a
reward only a small portion of the products of their toil.[9] In the
case of farm labourers this appears to have consisted of one day's
reaping out of every so many days of the harvest,[10] and we may
suppose that other types of workers were paid, or maintained, on a
similar basis. Although in theory he had the same recourse to the
laws of the land as men of higher station, in practice the peasant
seems to have been as completely subject to the dictates of the
owner or manager of the estates on which he worked as the slaves
who laboured at his side and who performed tasks in no way

---

[1] §x, 2, 7, 31, 53 ff., 69–74; §viii, 16, 44; §i, 4, 159; §viii, 23, 24, 31 (lines
9–10).

[2] §viii, 16, 27–45.

[3] §x, 19, 140–6; §v, 3, 54–7; §x, 9, 907.

[4] §i, 7, 21; §x, 35, 90 ff. See also §x, 29, 183–97; §x, 33, 15–18.

[5] Pap. Anastasi V, 7, 6; Pap. Harris I, 77, 56. See §iii, 20, 169; §viii, 10, 144;
§x, 2, 110.

[6] §x, 2, 84–90; §vi, 24, 42–3; §iii, 26, 107.   [7] §i, 7, 22.

[8] §x, 2, 82–4; §x, 24, 339.   [9] §iii, 20, 38; §viii, 10, 138.

[10] §x, 21, 27.

dissimilar to his own.[1] Even in the rare instances when he rose from the ranks of the common field-labourers and achieved the status of a tenant-farmer, he received little or no consideration from his superiors and could be cruelly maltreated when for any reason he failed to deliver the full amount of the oppressive taxes imposed upon him.[2] By and large these men and women who formed the bulk of Egypt's population and the source of most of its unskilled labour have left behind no traces to dispel the anonymity in which, for us at least, they will probably always remain enshrouded. When they are mentioned at all in texts of the New Kingdom it is usually collectively—as groups of workers belonging to such and such an organization or under the supervision of such and such an official.[3]

An ancient and very common method of raising large gangs of labourers for the carrying out of specific work projects—the harvesting of crops, the upkeep of the irrigation system, the construction of public buildings—was by corvée, an institution which survived in Egypt until the closing years of the last century.[4] During the New Kingdom only the official class seems to have been exempt from statute labour, even priests being forced, upon occasion, to serve as field hands and to toil in the mud and dampness of the irrigation canals.[5] Funerary scenes and texts show that all Egyptians expected to be conscripted for labour in the Hereafter;[6] and the spells written on the *shawabty*-figures buried with the dead—including those inscribed for the king himself—make it clear that these little facsimiles of the deceased person were to serve as substitutes for him when he was 'registered for work which is to be done in the Underworld as a man under obligation, to cultivate the fields, to irrigate the banks, to transport sand of the east and of the west'.[7] In real life substitutes were undoubtedly hired by well-to-do Egyptians to take their places in the labour gangs and exemptions could probably be obtained by paying sums equivalent in value to the amounts of labour required. Thus, as in later periods of world history, the burden imposed by the corvée system fell chiefly on the poorer

[1] §I, 9, 65; §III, 12, 21; §X, 35, 92 ff.; §III, 20, 48; §X, 30, 125.

[2] §III, 12, 19–22, 56–8 (Pap. Louvre 3171, Eighteenth Dynasty), 58–60. See also Pap. Sallier I, 5, 11 ff. (§VIII, 9, 193).

[3] §VIII, 10, 139.

[4] §VIII, 21, 130–1; §X, 23, 34; §III, 20, 38; §I, 4, 160; §VI, 24, 53.

[5] Pap. Sallier I, 6, 9; Pap. Anastasi II, 6, 7 ff. (§VIII, 9, 197 n. 1). See §III, 20, 38; §I, 8, 125.

[6] §III, 20, 38; §II, 35, 3 (9).

[7] §X, 32, 78–171; §X, 1, 72–7. See also §II, 21, part I, 350.

classes.[1] Abuses of the system were evidently common and in
consequence royal decrees were occasionally issued forbidding
crown officials from arbitrarily seizing and transporting to other
districts the personnel attached to an institution such as a temple.[2]
The procedure normally used in calling out the corvées was
similar to that employed in raising bodies of military conscripts
(§ix) and was based on lists, or 'numberings', drawn up by duly
authorized government commissioners.[3] Indicative of the magnitude of the gangs sometimes assembled in this manner is the
order, issued under Amenophis IV, to muster all workmen 'from
Elephantine to Sambehdet' (that is, from one end of Egypt to the
other) to provide stone for the great solar obelisk of the Aten
at Karnak.[4] Smaller gangs were apparently not uncommonly
conscripted for semi-private enterprises, as, for example, the excavation of the tomb of the Steward Senenmut, for which there
was employed, among other groups of workers, a 'corvée (*bḥ*) of
(temple) servants who came' to the tomb under the supervision
of a priest.[5] Under the general heading of 'corvée' we should
perhaps also include the not infrequent commandeering by
government representatives of boats and other equipment owned
by institutions and private individuals.[6]

Generally superior to the status of the common labourer was
that of the skilled artisans who staffed the royal, government, and
temple workshops and who included in their number sculptors,
painters, jewellers, lapidaries, metal-smiths, glass-workers, leather-
workers, potters, carpenters, cabinet-makers, and ship-builders.[7]
Designated by the Eighteenth Dynasty census-taker as 'all the
craftsmen', these men formed, as a whole, a relatively well-to-do,
and respected class, membership in which was to a great extent
hereditary, for the skills which were its essential characteristic
were ordinarily passed down from father to son for generation
after generation.[8] Although many of the sculptors, painters, and
goldsmiths would rank today as artists, it is doubtful whether
they ever regarded themselves in so self-conscious a manner, but
strove only to satisfy their patrons and to maintain the same high

[1] §x, 11, 210.
[2] §1, 4, 157; §x, 17, 219–30. Cf. §iii, 17, 24–33. See also §vi, 24, 21.
[3] §1, 7, 20–1.
[4] §x, 28, 263. See §1, 7, 20–1; §x, 20, 40–1.
[5] §x, 23, 22, 34, pl. 14 (no. 69).
[6] See §viii, 26, 261 ff.; §x, 17, 221 ff., 228–9.
[7] §v, 8, 92–171; §iii, 20, 163–8; §x, 36, 595 ff.; §1, 9, 320. Cf. §x, 31, 351–65;
§x, 34, 231–49.
[8] §iii, 20, 163 ff.; §viii, 10, 139–40; §x, 21, 33–4. Cf. §iii, 8, 57.

standards of fine workmanship as those achieved by their fellow-craftsmen, the armourer, the cobbler, the furniture-maker, and the boatbuilder. In addition to their salaries, which were paid in naturalia, craftsmen often received special recognition, such as mention in the tombs of their noble patrons, and rewards in the form of landed property and funerary endowments;[1] and their overseers, or guild masters, sometimes attained high honours and positions at court. Early in the Eighteenth Dynasty an Overseer of Sculptors, named Tehuty, achieved fame and fortune under Tuthmosis I;[2] and later, in the reign of Amenophis III, two sculptors, Ipuky and Nebamun, prepared for themselves at Thebes a decorated tomb-chapel comparable in quality and interest with those of the great officials buried nearby.[3] Not all craftsmen, to be sure, were so prosperous. Some certainly started and perhaps ended their careers as bondmen, while others were evidently foreign slaves.[4] The popularity of the so-called Satire on the Trades in the schools of the New Kingdom tends, however, to indicate that the craftsman's profession was at this time still sufficiently attractive to divert the youth of Egypt from the pursuit of learning.[5]

Our knowledge of the New Kingdom craftsmen, derived chiefly from tomb paintings and inscriptions,[6] has been greatly augmented by the clearance in western Thebes of a walled settlement established in the reign of Tuthmosis I for the artisans and other workmen attached permanently to the royal necropolis—the so-called Servitors in the Place-of-Truth.[7] Laid out in a small natural amphitheatre at Deir el-Medina, the village and its adjoining cemetery are within easy walking distance of the Valley of the Tombs of the Kings, to the north, the Valley of the Queens, to the west, and the line of royal funerary temples along the edge of the cultivation, to the east and south-east. During its 450 years of continuous occupation its inhabitants, comprising from the first a mixed population of Egyptians, Nubians, and Asiatics, ranged from ordinary labourers—stone-cutters, plasterers, water-carriers—to such important functionaries as royal building superintendents (Overseers of Works) and

[1] §x, 34, 243–4; §x, 12, 36–7; §iii, 13, vol. ii, 82; §x, 21, 33–4; §viii, 10, 503–6.
[2] §ii, 42, 131–3. See §iii, 20, 166. [3] Tomb no. 181. See §ii, 35, 286–9.
[4] §x, 3, vol. xvi, 15; §x, 13, 37 ff.; §iii, 20, 168–9; §viii, 10, 139; §i, 9, 65, 73. See also §i, 11, 193.
[5] §viii, 9, 67 ff.; §ii, 49, 432 ff.; §iii, 26, 29. [6] See above, p. 378 n. 7.
[7] §x, 3, vols. i–viii, x, xiv–xvi, xx, xxi and xxvi (see especially, vol. xvi, pp. 3–18).

included every type of technician, artist, and artisan required for the cutting and decoration of the royal tombs and for the construction and adornment of the royal mortuary temples.[1]   In addition to the small, but comfortable houses for the workers and their families the settlement was provided with a post for a company of police (Medjay) and contained a shrine to the deified King Amenophis I, the recently established patron divinity of the Theban necropolis.[2]   Nowhere else may we study to greater advantage the organization and development, the living and working conditions, the social and professional standings, and the merging family relationships of a corporation of workers of so many different races, classes, and types.

At a period when nearly all of the country's activities and resources were controlled by the crown, the state, and the temples it is not surprising to find few records of agricultural, industrial, and commercial enterprises undertaken by private citizens on their own initiative and in their own behalf.   Apart from the estates bestowed by the king on his favoured officials, small, privately owned plots of land and herds of cattle certainly existed and were exploited for personal profit by their owners.[3] There were apparently merchants, or 'traders', who carried on small businesses of their own[4] and there must have been craftsmen whose products were made to be sold in the shops and market places.   These men, however, formed only a small percentage of Egypt's total working population, most of whom, as we have seen, were either compelled or found it to their advantage to seek employment with one or another of the branches of the pharaonic government.

The times, then, were not favourable to the development of private enterprise and it is undoubtedly true that 'the common man...had scarcely begun to emerge as an element whose wishes required serious consideration in political or economic life'.[5] On the other hand, the barriers of class were not nearly so impregnable as the foregoing discussion might lead one to suppose, and personal ability, as already stated (§VIII), was certainly a prime factor in determining a man's station in life. A peasant or a freed slave could, if he were intelligent, indus-

---

[1] §x, 5, 200–9; §x, 10; §11, 35, 16–18 (Tomb no. 8).

[2] §x, 4.

[3] §1, 4, 159–60; §1, 8, 118, 122–3, 149–50, 162, 178.

[4] §1, 4, 159; §v, 8, 230–3. See also §111, 14, vol. 1, 94*–95* (A 210), and below, p. 381.

[5] §1, 4, 160.

trious, and ambitious, elevate himself to the status of a skilled craftsman and even to that of a government official; and from the school writings of both the Middle and New Kingdoms we gain the clear impression that the choice of a profession—and with it a standing in society—lay to a very great extent with the individual himself.

XI. TAXATION, COMMERCE, AND EXCHANGE

As in other periods, the government of Egypt during the New Kingdom depended for the major portion of its revenues on a highly developed and extremely efficient system of taxation. The huge annual taxes collected in the name of the pharaoh were levied chiefly on the activities and products of the working classes —the fieldhand, the herdsmen, and the craftsman—and the word *bȝk.t*, 'labour', continued, as before, to be used also as a general expression for 'taxes'.[1] These were paid, however, not by the workers themselves who, as we have seen, received for their toil little more than their bare maintenance, but by the individuals and institutions who, frequently through the king's own bounty were the owners, tenants, or managers of the lands, herds, factories and other taxable assets. The taxpayers, to be sure, ranged all the way from administrators of large estates and officials in charge of whole districts down to small 'cultivators' of modest plots of land;[2] but shared in common the opportunity of extracting from their holdings profits in excess of the revenues required by the crown. Although tax exemptions may have been granted in certain individual cases, no institution or class of society, including the priesthood, seems to have enjoyed general immunity from taxation.[3] The taxes themselves, known to us largely from documents of the Ramesside period, were many and various and were for the most part paid in kind out of the commodities on which they were imposed.

Among the more important were the taxes on cattle and the corn- or harvest-tax. The former were based on a periodic national census of farm animals carried out in the New Kingdom by scribes, accountants, and herdsmen of cattle under the supervision of the chief Overseer of Cattle and included not only a direct tax paid in animals out of the yearly increase of the herds, but also a fee paid in produce on draught beasts rented by the state

[1] §x, 18, vol. I, 429; §I, 2, 238.
[2] §I, 4, 159–60; §I, 8, 123 ff.; §III, 12, 19–22.
[3] §I, 4, 157; §III, 13, vol. II, 202–3, 207.

to individual farmers and farming institutions.[1] At the beginning
of the Eighteenth Dynasty the mayor Renny of El-Kāb paid out
of the state herds pastured in his district a cattle tax of 2922
animals (122 steers, 100 sheep, 1200 goats, and 1500 pigs)[2]—a
sharp contrast with the very small number of beasts shown being
delivered by the officials of the same district in the evidently
archaic and incomplete 'tax-list' reproduced during the reign of
Tuthmosis III in the tomb of his vizier, Rekhmire.[3] Later in the
New Kingdom the rental fee on draught animals seems to have
been estimated in copper.[4] It would appear that the branded
hides of animals which had died in the interim between the
taking of the census and the collection of the tax were offered
either in lieu of the animals themselves or as evidence of the fact
that they were dead.[5]

The harvest-tax (*šmw*), the bulk of which was collected in
emmer and barley, was assessed in the case of the larger farms at a
rate of 5 *khar*-sacks (10 bushels) per *aroura* ($\frac{2}{3}$ acre) of ordinary
arable land—approximately one-half of the total estimated produce of this class of land.[6] The rate, however, varied in proportion
to the area and productivity of the land involved, and for very
small holdings amounted to as little as $1\frac{1}{2}$ sacks per *aroura*.[7] The
cornlands appear to have been surveyed anew each year to keep
track of changes in area or condition brought about by the
inundation and other factors.[8] On these occasions the positions of
the stone boundary-markers were verified or re-established, the
dimensions of the fields were taken with measuring cords and
their areas re-computed on the basis of the new measurements by
the Scribes of the Fields.[9] Disputes which inevitably arose concerning boundary lines obliterated by the annual flood were
apparently still handled by the office of the vizier.[10] Part of an
Eighteenth Dynasty tax register (Pap. Louvre 3171) records how
out of an assessed harvest-tax of 1000 *khar*-sacks of emmer 'the
cultivator Maḥu...of the village of Meḥ' paid 714 sacks, which
were delivered by ship 'to the granary at Memphis', had another

---

[1] §III, 20, 22–5, 207; §I, 8, 173, 177–9; §II, 42, 2149; §VIII, 26, 263. See
also §III, 12, 21 n. I.

[2] §II, 42, 75 (14–15). See §III, 20, 24; §I, 8, 172 (for 'P₃-ḥrj' read 'Rn-nj').

[3] §III, 8, 32–6, 105, pl. 32. See §I, 8, 2 n. I, 113, 212–14, 216; §I, 2, 238.

[4] §III, 20, 22. See also §III, 12, 20–1.

[5] §II, 42, 2149 (3); §VIII, 26, 263.

[6] §III, 13, vol. II, 197–8; §I, 8, 141.   [7] §III, 13, vol. II, 91, 100, 209.

[8] §I, 8, 139–40, 143. Cf. §III, 20, 35. See also § XI, 10, 196, 204, 214–15, 22.

[9] §XI, 1, 54–6; §XI, 2, 70–2. See §I, 8, 139.

[10] §II, 42, 1110, 1111, 1113. See §I, 1, 8, 138–9.

200 sacks requisitioned by an army quartermaster, and was left with a deficit of 86 sacks charged against him.[1] Another cultivator, Amenmose, appears to have delivered only 821¾ sacks out of an assessed 1421, and out of his payment was loaned by the government 80 sacks to be used as seed the following year.[2] The leniency and consideration reflected in these records suggest that the treatment of delinquent taxpayers by government scribes and bailiffs was not always so harsh as the school writings would have us believe.[3]

A scene in the tomb of the king's steward, Ḳenamun, at Thebes shows the annual presentation to the pharaoh (Amenophis II) of objects produced during the year in the workshops of the royal estates: 'chariots of silver and gold, statues of ivory and ebony, collars of various hard stones of value, and weapons'.[4] It has been pointed out that these objects, referred to in the accompanying inscriptions as 'New Year's gifts' and as 'the yield of the various crafts', 'more nearly partake of the character of dues, though not, perhaps, of a regulated value; being the condition on which the schools and workshops retained the patronage of the king'.[5] Similar scenes are preserved in at least two other Theban tombs of the Eighteenth Dynasty. In that of Hatshepsut's chief steward, Amenophis, the so-called New Year's 'gift' is described as 'the best productions of the workshop and the main departments of *His* Majesty' and include a pair of the queen's obelisks![6] Although we might hesitate to class as 'taxes' products delivered to the kings from their own personal estates, such products are nevertheless so referred to by Ḳenamun, who appears elsewhere in his tomb 'making the tax-assessments on the cattle and fowl, receiving all the excellent dues of the Delta', and 'giving heed to his opportune visits for computing the taxes (*b3k.w*) of the Two Lands'.[7]

In addition to the revenues derived from the herds, the corn-lands, and the workshops, taxes appear to have been paid to the crown out of practically everything else which the country produced—flax, wine, oil, honey, incense, textiles, hides, eggs, vegetables, fruits, timber, and all metals not obtained directly from the government mines.[8] There was even a tax paid in game, wild

---

[1] §III, 12, 56–8.   [2] §III, 12, 57.   [3] See §III, 12, 19–21.
[4] §IX, 7, 24 ff., pls. 13 ff.; §II, 35, 191; §I, 7, 48.
[5] §IX, 7, 24. See also §I, 7, 48.
[6] §IV, 19, 2–8, pls. 2–6; §I, 6, 91–3; §IX, 7, 24 n. 3.
[7] §IX, 7, 16 (no. 69), 33.
[8] §I, 8, 150–2 (Pap. Louvre 3326), 182–9; §III, 20, 45–67, 72–4, 104 n. 1, 132
164, 190, 207, 213; §I, 9, 70; §I, 2, 237.

birds, and fish, on the yearly catch of the hunter, the fowler, and the fisherman.[1] A huge annual tribute in manpower, materials, and manufactured articles was levied on foreign lands;[2] and customs dues were collected on all merchandise imported into Egypt by non-government agencies, and perhaps also on certain types of exports.[3] For this purpose, and for the collection of tolls on foreign and privately owned ships using the state's waterways, stations were maintained at the mouths of the Nile and at key points along the river itself.[4] Statute labour, prevalent throughout Egypt and the empire (§x), is certainly to be classed as a form of tax or duty exacted from the population as a whole in return for the use of the irrigation canals and other public facilities. One of the more oppressive of the various types of taxation was the requirement imposed upon communities everywhere to lodge, feed, and otherwise support not only all messengers and other individuals travelling on government business, but also the often large bodies of troops and officials who accompanied the king on his military expeditions and tours of inspection.[5] It would seem, too, that units of the army, navy, and police force were permitted to requisition supplies from the districts in which they were stationed, such supplies, however, being deductible from the general taxes paid by the inhabitants of these districts to the government.[6]

In the Eighteenth Dynasty the assessment and collection of taxes due to the state were carried out under the general supervision of the two viziers, functioning, however, through the local administrative organizations and in close co-operation with the heads of the appropriate departments of the national government (see above, §viii). As in the late Middle Kingdom, tax payments in gold, silver, cattle, and textiles may still have been brought directly to the offices of the viziers;[7] and it is clear that an important function of the viziers was the reception of foreign tribute earmarked for government use.[8] The harvest-tax, on the other hand, appears to have been collected by the mayors of the townships with the assistance of the overseers and scribes of the central bureau of granaries;[9] while the collection of the tax in cattle and

[1] §iii, 20, 27, 45.
[2] §ii, 42, 668–734 *passim*; §ii, 38, 206–30; §i, 10, 46; §i, 11, 183–4, 189–90; §i, 9, 70 ff.
[3] §iii, 20, 104–5, 107.
[4] §iii, 20, 105–6; §i, 7, 22–3.
[5] §iii, 20, 46.
[6] §iii, 12, 57 (2, 6). Cf. §i, 7, 56; §i, 8, 149; §ii, 42, 2147–8; §viii, 26, 262–3.
[7] §iii, 8, 32–6, 103–6, pls. 29–35, 40; §i, 3, 461. Cf. §i, 8, 47, 185–6.
[8] §ii, 35, 207 (4), 245 (4), 246 (11); §i, 2, 239.
[9] §i, 8, 146–55; §iii, 20, 30, 35–7, 46–7.

hides 'in the entire land' is stated to have been the responsibility of the 'Overseer of the Cattle of Pharaoh'.[1] Taxes in raw materials, commodities other than grain and animals, and manufactured articles were handled by the officials of the dual treasuries of Upper and Lower Egypt,[2] the items which were received and administered by this department including, it would seem, honey, incense, oils, wine, fruit, sandals, baskets, papyrus mats, cloth, wood, and charcoal, as well as foreign products such as hides, elephant tusks, bows, shields, and, finally, precious metals of all kinds.[3] Tax-goods delivered to the Residence of the pharaoh were, under Tuthmosis III, received and registered by the King's First Herald in his capacity as head of the palace gate-house, or guardhouse.[4] It is probable that, between them, the viziers and the heads of the principal departments of the government were able to furnish the king with accurate monthly statements, not only of current national assets and expenditures, but also of prospective income from taxation and other sources.[5]

The existing evidence does not permit an estimate of the over-all rate of taxation or of the total annual revenues accruing therefrom. An oft-cited passage from the Book of Genesis (xlvii. 23–7) tells us that 'Joseph made it a law over the land of Egypt...that Pharaoh should have the fifth (part)' of the produce of the land; and, while this late Hebrew tradition cannot be accepted as definitive, it is probably not far wide of the mark.[6] No conclusion regarding the total amount of the yearly taxes can be arrived at from the figures given in the tomb of the vizier Rekhmire, since these figures appear to have been derived from a Middle Kingdom prototype, are not completely preserved, and covered, when complete, only certain categories of taxes collected in the southern vizierate.[7]

Although tomb and temple inscriptions of the New Kingdom persist in classing as 'tribute' the whole of the now very great wealth in raw materials and manufactured goods imported into the country from abroad, it is clear that a large percentage of these imports was actually obtained through trade.[8] We have no reason to believe that Egypt was ever in a position to levy tribute on, for

[1] §II, 42, 2149 (1–2); §VIII, 26, 263 (for 'cattle-census' read 'cattle-tax' [§x, 18, vol. I, 114 (v)]). See §I, 8, 173, 177–9.

[2] §I, 8, 182ff.; §III, 20, 213.   [3] §I, 8, 184 (see also 186, 189).

[4] See above, p. 361 n. 1.   [5] §I, 3, 461; §I, 2, 239. Cf. §I, 8, 39.

[6] §III, 20, 46; §I, 9, 70; §I, 2, 238. See also §III, 13, vol. II, 202.

[7] §I, 8, 2 n. 1, 113, 212–20, 239; §I, 2, 238–9; §III, 8, 34.

[8] §III, 20, 117–18. See also §x, 18, vol. I, 91 (13–17); §III, 8, 17–30; §xi, 19, 55 ff., 68 ff., 73–4; §xi, 9, 21–2.

example, the islands of Crete and Cyprus, the nations of Mesopotamia and Asia Minor, or the African lands to the south of the Fourth Cataract; we must assume that, as in the case of Punt (§ IV), the products of these localities were normally acquired on a purely commercial basis in exchange for Egyptian wares and commodities.[1] Even the vassal princes of Byblos seem to have been paid in gold and silver for their deliveries of timber wood to the pharaohs of the New Kingdom;[2] the ostensibly diplomatic exchanges of 'gifts' between Amenophis III and the rulers of Babylonia and Mitanni smack strongly at times of commercial transactions, characterized by some decidedly undiplomatic haggling over the quantity and quality of the objects exchanged.[3]

Throughout the early centuries of the New Kingdom Egypt's foreign trade appears to have been practically a royal, or government, monopoly, heavily protected by tolls and tariffs and carried out largely by caravans and ships owned or controlled by the crown or by one of the departments of the pharaonic administration.[4] The few commercial expeditions of which we have direct accounts were led by chancellery officials,[5] and the so-called 'traders for foreign lands', mentioned occasionally in inscriptions, were probably government agents, rather than independent merchants.[6] Moreover, apart from a tomb painting showing some primitive Puntite sailing rafts bringing goods to a port on the Red Sea coast,[7] there is only one Eighteenth Dynasty representation of foreign merchant ships in an Egyptian harbour, and even here the vessels, though manned and probably owned by Syrians, are of Egyptian type.[8] In the scene referred to a little informal bartering is taking place between the Syrian sailors and three Egyptian pedlars who have set up their booths on the waterfront; but the bulk of the ships' cargoes is being offered for sale to the mayor of Thebes, Ḳenamun, probably in his capacity as granary overseer and purchasing agent for the temple of the state-god, Amun.

---

[1] § III, 20, 115–25; § X, 26, 77; § XI, 16, 75–92; § XI, 11, 56 ff., 79 ff.; § VII, 15, 149–51; § II, 50, 83, 190–1. In the case, however, of a ruler like Tuthmosis III the nations referred to undoubtedly regarded it as advisable to court the favour of the conquering pharaoh with gifts. See, for example, § XI, 19, 62–3.

[2] § VIII, 9, 179, 181.

[3] § II, 27, nos. 1, 9, 10, 24, 26, etc.; § VI, 14, 11–153 *passim*; § I, 9, 71, 152; § III, 20, 118; § X, 26, 76.   [4] § III, 20, 104; § X, 26, 76; § XI, 19, xvii.

[5] § I, 8, 80.   [6] § III, 20, 104 n. 1; § I, 4, 159.

[7] § V, 3, 46–8, figs. 1–3; § I, 10, 22–5, fig. 6.

[8] § IX, 8, 40–6; § XI, 9, 25–6; § I, 8, 235–6; § II, 35, 275–6. A badly damaged painting of a Syrian ship under sail occurs in Tomb 17 at Thebes (reign of Amenophis II). See § IV, 19, 26–7, pl. 23; § I, 11, 55–6, fig. 10; § II, 35, 31.

Elsewhere, when delegations of Hittite, Keftiu, Puntite, and other foreign traders are represented in Egyptian tomb paintings, they are invariably shown delivering their merchandise (nearly always called 'tribute' or 'gifts') to a crown official—the vizier, the treasurer, the king's steward, the king's herald, or some other representative of the central government or of the royal or temple estates.[1]

In Africa, in addition to the extension southward of the important river traffic with the regions of the Upper Nile (§vii) and the resumption and intensification of the ancient maritime commerce via the Red Sea with the land of Punt (§iv), the New Kingdom brought with it a marked increase in the caravan trade with and through the oases of the Libyan Desert (Sīwa, Bahrīya, Farāfra, El-Khārga, El-Dākhla, and probably also Kurkur, Dunqul, Nakhlai, and Selima).[2] In the north, pack-trains streamed back and forth between Africa and Asia across the Isthmus of Suez, and in the eastern Mediterranean Egyptian shipping held the dominant position assumed in later times, after the collapse of the New Kingdom, by the Phoenicians.[3] Although Egypt's famed Keftiu-ships appear to have ranged northward to Cyprus, Cilicia, Crete, Ionia, the Aegean islands, and perhaps even to the mainland of Greece,[4] the great bulk of her Mediterranean trade was concentrated along the coast of Syria, the numerous harbours of which had in the course of Tuthmosis III's campaigns come fully under Egyptian control.[5] Through these harbours passed not only the cargoes of timber and other products of Syria itself, but also goods brought overland from Mesopotamia and the region of the Persian Gulf, with which Egypt at this time seems to have had no direct contact by sea.[6]

In conformity with a policy already evident in their African trade (§§iv, vii) the pharaohs of the New Kingdom limited their imports from Asia and the Mediterranean islands chiefly to essential raw materials and commodities of a nature or variety not available or not produced in sufficient quantity in Egypt itself.[7]

---

[1] §ii, 35, 72 (11), 140 (3), 177 (8), 207 (4), 246 (11), 263 (3). See §i, 8, 182, 185–6, 189; §i, 2, 239; §i, 11, 22–7; §xi, 19, 185–368 *passim*.

[2] §x, 26, 69–73; §iii, 20, 107; §ii, 20, 89 nn. 96, 97; §iv, 19, 15, pls. 12, 13; §i, 8, 163; §xi, 5, 633–5; §xi, 6, 14–16, 41; §xi, 7, 24–5. Cf. also §ii, 38, 9, 15, 20, 28, 84, 145.

[3] §i, 10, 42–70; §xi, 12, 131–2.

[4] §xi, 19, 54–5 121–2, 399ff., 417–22; §i, 10, 49–50; §xi, 12, 131; §xi, 15; §xi, 16; §xi, 11, 73–6, 83–4. See also §x, 26, 74, 77.

[5] §i, 10, 33 ff., 42, 44.   [6] §iii, 20, 125.

[7] §iii, 20, 105; §x, 26, 73 f.; §xi, 19, 120–1.

High up on the list were coniferous woods from the Lebanon, oak from Asia Minor, Syrian wines, oils, and resins, silver from the Aegean area, 'Asiatic copper', and a breed of humped cattle unknown in the Nile Valley before the Eighteenth Dynasty.[1] Some manufactured articles were imported; especially notable were the wonderfully worked vases, ornaments, and weapons of metal from the ateliers of Crete and the cities of the Syrian coast.[2] There seems also to have been an import trade in Asiatic slaves, though during the Eighteenth Dynasty it is probable that most of them were prisoners of war or part of the yearly tribute rather than items of merchandise.[3] Besides gold, which she possessed far in excess of any other country of the ancient world, Egypt's most avidly sought-after exports were her linen cloth, papyrus paper, leather goods, and cereal grains.[4] Thanks to these exports, to her incomparably favourable position midway, as it were, between the continents of Africa and Asia, and to the size and efficiency of her navy and merchant marine, she dominated the trade of the eastern Mediterranean world until the Amarna Period, when 'the political impassiveness of Amenophis III and Akhenaten' resulted in 'the gradual weakening of Egyptian authority in Asia' and 'the decline of Egyptian supremacy at sea'.[5]

With the great bulk of the nation's goods owned or controlled by the government the internal commerce of Egypt under the pharaohs of the New Kingdom was of necessity confined to relatively unimportant transactions between private individuals and to the type of small-scale retail trading carried on in village market-places of the present day. The already cited waterfront scene in Tomb 162 at Thebes shows us the unpretentious booths of three Eighteenth Dynasty pedlars (two men and a woman), each booth stocked with one or two pairs of sandals, a few bolts of cloth, and some foodstuffs, and equipped with a small balance, probably for weighing the precious metals used as media of exchange.[6] A fragmentary papyrus in Cairo (Pap. Bulaq 11) lists deliveries of meat, wine, and cakes to two 'traders' (*šwtyw*) named Minnakhte and Sherybin, whose inventories, as recorded over a period of fourteen days, were so modest as to make it probable that they were small, independent merchants trading for

---

[1] §III, 20, 104, 115 ff., 120; §x, 26, 74–5; §I, 8, 164; §xI, 19, 364–6, 423–4, pls. 64–5; §v, 19, 167.

[2] §xI, 19, 55 ff., 192–5, 305–68, pls. 35–62; §xI, 4, 42 ff., figs. 1–3, 6.

[3] See above, p. 375 n. 7.   [4] §III, 20, 104, 118.

[5] §I, 10, 62.

[6] §IX, 8, 45–6; §II, 35, 275–6.

their own account.[1] Records of several lawsuits conducted during the latter part of the Eighteenth and the early Nineteenth Dynasty tell of purchases, sales, and rentals of various types of property (slaves, cattle, land) by sundry private individuals—the herdsman Mesesia, the woman Iritnefert, and others.[2] From these documents, studied in conjunction with numerous business records of Ramesside date, we obtain a clear picture of the system of exchange current in Egypt during the New Kingdom and of the relative values, or 'prices', of various raw materials, goods, and commodities in use at that time.

Although money, in the sense of coinage, had not yet been developed,[3] the system of barter had been simplified by the adoption of certain fixed and generally recognized media of exchange—gold, silver, copper, and grain—in terms of which other trade goods could be priced with a fair degree of accuracy and consistency.[4] Values in metal were usually expressed by weight, the units employed being the *deben*, a weight of about 91 grammes, its tenth part, the *kitĕ* (9·1 grammes), and a weight equal to $\frac{1}{12}$ *deben* (7·6 grammes) which modern scholars have agreed to call a 'piece'.[5] Since the last-named appears to have been 'a flat, round, piece of metal... possibly with an inscription to indicate' its 'weight or the name of the issuing authority', it 'was practically a coin'.[6] The ratio of 2 : 1 for the values of gold and silver seems to have remained fairly stable throughout the New Kingdom, dipping momentarily to $1\frac{2}{3}$: 1 at the beginning of the reign of Amenophis II because of 'the influx of large quantities of gold as booty and tribute from Palestine and Syria, then recently conquered'.[7] Copper, with only $\frac{1}{100}$ the value of silver,[8] is always quoted by the *deben*, 2 *deben* of copper being generally equivalent in value to 1 *khar*-sack (2 bushels), of corn which itself was used as a form of currency.[9] In the Eighteenth Dynasty 8 'pieces' ($\frac{2}{3}$ *deben*) of silver or their equivalent in other commodities would

---

[1] §xi, 14, 185–99; §xi, 21, 45–87, 243–4, pls. 3, 4; §i, 4, 159. See also Pap. Lansing, 4, 8 – 5, 1 (§viii, 17, 103; §iii, 3, 384, 386 [also 17, 26–7]; §xi, 18, 65–119); §xi, 22, 97; §iii, 20, 103–4.

[2] §viii, 16, 27–47; §viii, 15, 23–4; §x, 19, 140–6; §vi, 24, 10, 64 (no. 47); §v, 3, 54–7.

[3] See, however, below, n. 6.

[4] §x, 9, 903–21; §xi, 13, 122–7.

[5] §viii, 19, §266, 4 (nn. 9–13); §x, 9, 906 ff., 910 ff.; §xi, 14, 188 ff.

[6] §x, 9, 912, 913. See also §xi, 9, 26–7.

[7] §x, 9, 904–6. Cf. §xi, 21, 80–2.

[8] §x, 9, 905 ff.

[9] §x, 9, 914–16; §xi, 8, 44.

buy a bull[1] or a cow or the service of a female slave for four days;[2] 6 'pieces', a heifer or 3 arouras (2 acres) of (poor) land;[3] and $3\frac{1}{2}$ 'pieces', a linen garment (*dꜣiw*) of good quality.[4] Later in the New Kingdom the same garment was priced at $13\frac{3}{4}$–20 *deben* of copper, a tunic at 5 *deben* of copper, a calf at 30 *deben*, a prime bull at 130 *deben*, and so on.[5]

Silver was so commonly employed as an exchange-metal that in business documents the word for 'silver' (*ḥd*) is often used with the general meaning of 'payment' or perhaps even of 'money'.[6] Any illusion regarding the existence of a true monetary system, however, is shattered when we find the dynastic Egyptian not only using silver (or gold) to 'buy' (*int*) corn, but also using corn to 'buy' silver.[7] Furthermore, although the quality of a metal was sometimes guaranteed by official stamp, or hallmark,[8] the amounts of metals used for exchange were almost always weighed, or otherwise measured out, like any other material or commodity.[9] Finally, it is clear that, although an item of merchandise was as a rule priced in gold, silver, or some other accepted medium of exchange, it did not have to be paid for in that medium, but could be acquired in return for whatever goods the 'buyer' happened to possess, so long as the total value of these goods was the equivalent of the price stipulated. By way of example there may be cited the purchase by an early Nineteenth Dynasty house-wife of a Syrian slave-girl, valued at 4 *deben* and 1 *kitĕ* of silver, but paid for with 6 bronze vessels, 10 *deben* of copper, 15 linen garments, a shroud, a blanket, and a pot of honey.[10] On the other hand, from the records preserved in the tomb of the vizier Rekhmirē it would seem that as early as the Thirteenth Dynasty payment of taxes in gold and silver had begun to replace the older and clumsier method of payment in kind.[11]

---

[1] §VIII, 19, sect. 266, 4 (n. 16). A weight in the form of an ox (*iḥ*) (§XI, 3, 89–90, figs. 2 (B), 7; §XI, 20, xiv–xv) perhaps represented the value in gold or silver of a real ox (see, for example, §III, 35, part I, 12 n. 6).

[2] Pap. Berlin 9784, 7–8 (§VIII, 16, 28, 31); Pap. Berlin 9785 (§VIII, 16, 39, 40).

[3] Pap. Berlin 9784, 16–17 (§VIII, 16, 29, 31, 45; §X, 9, 912).

[4] Pap. Berlin 9784, 5–6 (§VIII, 16, 28, 31).

[5] §XI, 8, 43–4, pl. 27; §X, 9, 908–10.

[6] §XI, 13, 124–5; §X, 9, 914; §III, 3, 386–7.

[7] §XI, 13, 123–4. See also §VI, 24, 52–3.

[8] §III, 20, 103; §XI, 21, 84 n. 1; §X, 24, 408.

[9] §XI, 17, 71; §III, 20, 102–3.

[10] §X, 19, 140–6; §X, 9, 907.

[11] See above, p. 384 n. 7.

XII. BUILDING AND THE STATE
MONOPOLY OF STONE

The building activities of the Tuthmoside pharaohs and the new architectural trends developed under them may be studied to greatest advantage in the additions which they made to the temple and temple precinct of the state-god Amun at Karnak. The first major enlargement of the temple proper was carried out on behalf of Tuthmosis I under the inspired direction of the mayor of Thebes, Ineny.[1] The brick and limestone shrine of the Middle Kingdom and an extensive area to the west of it was enclosed within a girdle wall of sandstone, once believed to have been adorned on all four of its inner surfaces with columned porticos and with statues of the king wearing the sheathlike *Sed*-festival costume.[2] Across the front, or western end, of the great oblong court, so formed, was built the present fifth pylon of the temple— a monumental gateway, flanked by broad rectangular towers of masonry crowned with brilliantly painted cavetto cornices and provided with two tall wooden flag-masts mounted in slots in their sloping-forward walls. The tips of the masts were sheathed 'in fine gold' and the portal between the massive towers was fitted with 'a great door of Asiatic copper whereon was the "shadow" of the god wrought in gold'.[3] Later in the reign of Tuthmosis I the now firmly established east–west axis of the temple and the processional way leading along it were extended by the construction, fourteen yards to the west of Pylon V, of a second and much larger pylon (IV). The space between the pylons was converted into a hall by the addition of side walls of stone and a wooden roof supported on five slender papyriform columns, perhaps also originally of wood, but replaced under Tuthmosis I himself by columns of sandstone. Before the outer pylon, in commemoration of the king's *Sed*-festival, were erected two 64-foot obelisks of red Aswān granite, their sides inscribed with the names and titles of Tuthmosis I, their pinnacles encased in burnished sheet gold to catch the rays of the sun.[4] Here, then, at the very outset of the

[1] §II, 42, 55–6. See §IV, 24, vol. II, 868–71, 879–80, fig. 420 (light blue areas); §II, 34, vol. II, 27–30; §XII, 3, 145 ff.

[2] §XII, 5, 8 ff. See, however, §IV, 24, vol. II, 870. See also §XII, 27, pls. 5, 6; §II, 34, vol. II, 28 ff.; §II, 7, vol. LIII, 13–14.

[3] §II, 42, 56 (6–10).

[4] §II, 42, 56 (11–12), 93 (6–7); §II, 34, vol. II, 27. The erection of Tuthmosis I's obelisks appears actually to have been carried out under Hatshepsut and Tuthmosis III. See §II, 39, 206 and n. 33.

Tuthmoside period we have the essence of the great processional temple of the New Kingdom and later times and all of its component parts: the ancient sanctuary enclosed within screening walls, the deep, colonnaded courtyard, the hypostyle reception-hall of the god, and the monumental entrance feature, the pylon, repeated with each new re-establishment of the temple façade. Here, too, we find the already extensive use in temple construction of brown Nubian sandstone, usually overlaid with white stucco and adorned with brightly coloured relief sculpture.

The successors of Tuthmosis I concentrated a large part of their building activities on those portions of the temple already delimited by his constructions. Hatshepsut, as we have seen (§ IV), erected her first pair of obelisks at the eastern end of the temple and her second pair in the narrow hall between Pylons IV and V,[1] which was dismantled for the purpose, only to be later rebuilt by Tuthmosis III and Amenophis II around a sandstone massif designed to conceal the lower portions of the intrusive shafts.[2] To Hatshepsut we owe also a fine quartzite chapel for the barque of the god built originally on a raised platform immediately against the front of the Middle Kingdom temple and flanked by two groups of small sandstone cult chambers.[3] After the queen's death Tuthmosis III first defaced and later removed this chapel, converting the space so gained into a Hall of Annals, in the midst of which, during or after his forty-sixth regnal year, he constructed a red granite chapel of his own.[4] Earlier in his reign the great pharaoh had built or rebuilt a series of little chapels along the sides of Tuthmosis I's court and near the western end of the enclosure had inserted a shallow, colonnaded courtyard and a small pylon (VI). Between Pylons V and VI he installed two rooms containing lists of feasts and offerings and, behind Pylon VI, the so-called First Hall of Records, its roof supported by two handsome granite piers with the heraldic plants of Upper and Lower Egypt carved in high relief on their sides. Across the eastern end of the temple, behind the enclosure wall of Tuthmosis I, was built Tuthmosis III's great Festival Hall with its complex of adjoining chambers; and this, together with the rest of the temple as far west as the fourth pylon, was

---

[1] §I, 6, 92 ff.; §IV, 25, 140–1; §II, 34, vol. II, 28–9.

[2] §IV, 24, vol. II, 880–1; §XII, 27, pl. 5; §II, 34, vol. II, 29.

[3] §IV, 24, vol. II, 799–800, 871 ff.; §II, 34, vol. II, 28, 38–9; §II, 7, vol. LIII, 37–9, pls. 23–6; §XII, 20, 79–81, 99–102; §XII, 27, pl. 6. See Plate 89.

[4] §XII, 5, 29–32; §II, 42, 625; §II, 7, vol. LI, 561; §II, 34, vol. II, 36–7. It has been suggested that Tuthmosis III had previously replaced Hatshepsut's chapel by one built of sandstone (§XII, 6, 85–6, pl. 18; §IV, 24, vol. II, 799–801, 875).

surrounded by a massive girdle wall of sandstone.[1] On the occasions of his first and second *Sed*-festivals (Years 30 and 33) Tuthmosis III embellished Karnak with a pair of granite obelisks, the first pair (now in fragments) having been set up before the fourth pylon, in front of those of Tuthmosis I.[2] The Lateran obelisk in Rome (height 105·6 feet) appears to have been prepared by Tuthmosis III primarily as a symbol of the sun-god and to have been erected (or re-erected[3]) by his grandson, Tuthmosis IV, in a chapel of its own at the extreme eastern end of the temple.[4] Amenophis II apparently also contributed a pair of obelisks, of which only the foundations of the pedestals now remain to the west of the fourth pylon.[5] Finally, in the reign of Amenophis III, the temple received a new western façade in the form of the gigantic third pylon, a magnificent structure provided in front with an ornate vestibule and eight towering flag-masts.[6] The double row of huge campaniform columns which leads westward from the front of this pylon and forms the central aisle of the temple's famous hypostyle hall is now also thought to have been planned and erected by Amenophis III.[7]

Meanwhile, the Tuthmoside pharaohs had developed a second processional way leading southward towards the temple precinct of Amun's consort, the goddess Mut, and composed of three (or four?) great pylons, spaced 40–90 yards apart, each fronted by an imposing group of colossal royal statues.[8] The first of these two pylons (VII and VIII) we owe, respectively, to Tuthmosis III and Hatshepsut. The southernmost pylon (X), though rebuilt by Horemheb, appears to have been founded by Amenophis III or perhaps even by Amenophis II, and this must have been true also of the intermediate pylon (IX), though the latter structure in its present form dates in its entirety from the time of Horemheb.[9] Of the two obelisks of Tuthmosis III which stood before Pylon VII one is represented by fragments found on the site and the

[1] §IV, 24, vol. II, 874–901, fig. 420 (dark blue areas); §XII, 27, pls. 5–7; §II, 34, vol. II, 31–7, 41–7. See also §II, 7, vol. LIII, 13–14; §XII, 3, 146–55; §XII, 21, 191.
[2] §XII, 22, 22–3; §II, 42, 588, 641–2; §II, 7, vol. XXVII, 135–7. On the pair of obelisks represented in the tomb of Ipuyemre see §III, 9, 47–61.
[3] §II, 42, 584 (10). See §II, 5, 4 n. 2.
[4] §II, 42, 1549–50. See §IV, 24, vol. II, 930–1; §II, 53, 81–91.
[5] §XII, 3, 146 n. 5.
[6] §II, 34, vol. II, 25–7; §IV, 24, vol. II, 910; §XII, 27, pls. 3–4.
[7] §IV, 24, vol. II, 910–12; §II, 7, vol. LIV, 35 ff.
[8] §II, 34, vol. II, 54–63; §IV, 24, vol. II, 894, 902, 913–14; §XII, 27, pl. 8.
[9] §IV, 24, vol. II, 913–14; §II, 7, vol. XLVII, 177–8; vol. L, 434–6; §XII, 23, 27; §II, 46, 161.

other is probably the huge shaft now in Istanbul, erected in honour of the king's second jubilee in Year 33 and originally about 115 feet in height.[1] In the area east of the line of pylons and south of the temple proper lies the sacred lake, a large rectangular basin with a quay and revetments of sandstone.[2]

Except for a small shrine to the Memphite god, Ptah, rebuilt by Tuthmosis III to the north of the great temple of Amun,[3] all the other Tuthmoside temples of the standard processional type at Karnak owe their existence or their present forms to Amenophis III. Among them special interest attaches to the temple of Mut in the southern lake-precinct, called Ishru, and the temple of the ancient Theban god Mont (Amen-Re-Mont) in an enclosure of its own on the north of the precinct of Amun. The Mut temple, half surrounded by its horseshoe-shaped sacred lake, contains over 500 diorite statues of the lioness-headed goddess (Mut)-Sakhmet, lined up in rows around its ample courts.[4] The temple of Mont once fronted by two tall granite obelisks of Amenophis III, is remarkable for a great dedicatory inscription around the base of its walls, in which is described the almost incredible richness of its adornment and furnishings.[5]

Karnak also offers the opportunity to study two other types of ceremonial buildings: the basilica-like halls, constructed for the royal *Sed*-festivals and the small peripteral shrines designed as resting places, or 'stations', for the portable barque in which during certain feasts the image of the god was carried around Thebes in solemn procession.[6] In the limestone *Heb-Sed* temple founded by Amenophis II and rebuilt by Sethos I beside the southern processional way to the temple of Amun the roof of the five-aisled main hall is supported on square piers as are also those of the smaller, flanking halls and that of the open portico which runs across the whole front of the building.[7] In Tuthmosis III's Festival Hall the massive sandstone columns of the central aisle have the bell-shaped tops and inverted taper of the tent-poles

---

[1] §II, 34, vol. II, 55; vol. VII, 400.

[2] §II, 7, vol. XXXIII, 182; vol. XXXIV, 171; vol. XXXVI, 82, pl. 1; vol. XXXVII, 179–82, pl. 1; vol. XXXIX, 565–6, pls. 107–8; §XII, 27, pl. 11; etc.

[3] §IV, 24, vol. II, 903–6; §II, 34, vol. II, 66–8; §II, 7, vol. LIII, 18, pls. 9–11; §II, 42, 765, 878–9; §XII, 27, pl. 10.

[4] §IV, 24, vol. II, 914–17; §II, 34, vol. II, 89–93; §III, 20, 160; §XII, 27, pls. 18, 19.

[5] §IV, 24, vol. II, 917–18, fig. 427; §II, 34, vol. II, 3 ff.; §XII, 27, pl. 20. See §III, 35, vol. I, 10 ff., pls. 16–34.

[6] §IV, 24, vol. II, 793 ff., 805 ff., 890 ff.; §XII, 6, *passim*; §III, 20, 159–60; §XII, 24, 26 ff. [7] §IV, 24, vol. II, 805–8; §XII, 27, pl. 8; §II, 34, vol. II, 61.

used in the light pavilions in which the *Sed*-festival was traditionally celebrated.[1] Thanks to the height of these columns, the roof of the three central aisles is raised well above those of the side aisles, thus providing an ample clerestory through which the hall is lighted. A hall of similar type and purpose was constructed by Tuthmosis IV in the Eighteenth Dynasty temple at Amada in Lower Nubia[2] and another by Amenophis III in the northern quarter of his palace in western Thebes.[3]

Of the 'stations of the barque' at least seven examples of Tuthmoside date have been found at Karnak, either *in situ* along the processional way between the sanctuaries of Amun and Mut[4] or broken up and incorporated in the foundations of Amenophis III's pylon (III).[5] Each consisted of a small cella of alabaster or other fine stone, open at both ends and surrounded by a roofed and balustraded peristyle of square piers, the whole mounted on a raised platform provided at either end with a gently sloping stairway. Following the example of Sesostris I of the Twelfth Dynasty every ruler of the early New Kingdom from Amenophis I to Tuthmosis IV contributed to the celebration of his *Sed*-festivals by embellishing the route of the barque with one or more of these handsome little structures. In western Thebes a similar shrine was erected by Hatshepsut and Tuthmosis III at Medīnet Habu[6] and the remains of two others have been found on the approaches to the Eighteenth Dynasty temples at Deir el-Bahri.[7] To the same class belongs the small peripteral chapel built by Amenophis III on the island of Elephantine, destroyed in 1822, but well known to us from the drawings of early travellers.[8]

The gigantic sandstone temple of Amun, Mut, and Khons at Luxor, a mile and a half south of Karnak, has the distinction of having been planned as a unit and three-quarters constructed by a single king.[9] The first pylon and forecourt were added by Ramesses II, but the rest of the present temple, with the exception of a

---

[1] §iv, 24, vol. ii, 890–901; §xii, 27, pl. 7; §ii, 34, vol. ii, 41–6.

[2] §ii, 34, vol. vii, 67–9; §iv, 24, vol. ii, 960–1.

[3] §vi, 12, 8–14; §ii, 20, 36, 85.

[4] §iv, 24, vol. ii, 801–5; §xii, 34; §xii, 31; §xii, 32; §xii, 6, 79–83, 90–3; §xii, 27, pl. 8; §ii, 34, vol. ii, 56, 95, 97.

[5] §ii, 34, vol. ii, 25; §ii, 7, *passim*; §iv, 24, vol. ii, 910.

[6] §xii, 18, 16–20, pls. 1, 2, 4, 10–21; §ii, 34, vol. ii, 166–70; §iv, 24, vol. ii, 749–50; §xii, 27, pl. 27.

[7] §ii, 52, 213 n. 17; §xii, 41, 31, fig. 24; §xii, 6, 58–61, pl. 14; §viii, 22, 50–2.   [8] §xii, 6, 95–8, pl. 21; §xii, 26, 59–60, pl. 7.

[9] §ii, 34, vol. ii, 98–9, 102–8; §iv, 24, vol. ii, 843–50; §ii, 45, 152–3; §xii, 27, pls. 21–3; §xii, 4, 122–38.

small shrine built by Tuthmosis III and some minor constructions of Tutankhamun and his successors, is the work of Amenophis III. From the two sanctuaries and their complex of surrounding chambers at the southern end of the temple the processional way leads northward through two halls, a monumental pronaos and courtyard adorned with ninety-six magnificently proportioned papyriform columns of the clustered 'bud' type, and, thence, between two rows of seven huge columns with spreading calyx capitals once enclosed within walls to form a long entrance corridor jutting out from the front of the temple.[1] Known as 'the Southern Sanctuary'—a name already current in the Middle Kingdom— the vast shrine was linked with the main temple of Amun at Karnak by a paved avenue flanked on either side by a long row of ram-headed sphinxes, each having before it a small figure of Amenophis III.[2]

The mortuary temples of the Tuthmoside kings, far removed from their tombs, are lined up in a row along the desert's edge in western Thebes, extending in more or less chronological order between the Dirā Abu'n-Naga on the north and Medīnet Habu on the south.[3] Of these only the remarkable limestone temple of Hatshepsut at Deir el-Bahri is preserved in anything like its original condition.[4] Built by the queen's steward, Senenmut, in accordance with a design evidently inspired by the adjoining Eleventh Dynasty shrine of Nebhepetre Mentuhotpe, this temple is composed of two broad, retreating terraces fronted by well proportioned double colonnades and preceded, on the east, by a deep, walled forecourt. The central sanctuary, rock-cut in the towering cliffs against which the temple is built, was dedicated to the god Amun and there are, in addition, shrines to Anubis and Hathor, the divinities of the necropolis, an open altar court for the worship of the sun-god, Re-Harakhte, and vaulted funerary chapels for Hatshepsut and her father, Tuthmosis I. In the north-east corner of the Mentuhotpe temple platform Tuthmosis III rebuilt a shrine to Hathor and Amun which was preceded by a peripteral chapel for the barque of the latter and, like the larger temples on either side of it, was provided with a long avenue leading eastward, down to a small 'Valley Temple' on the edge

---

[1] See §XII, 36, 52–7. Cf. p. 393 n. 7, above.

[2] §XII, 35, pl. 74. Cf. §II, 46, 160; §XII, 8, 66, fig. 44.

[3] §II, 34, vol. II, 112ff., 147–9, 159–61; §IV, 24, vol. II, 664–90; §XII, 28, 60–72, 108–10, pl 4; §XII, 33.

[4] §II, 34, vol. II, 113–28; §IV, 24, vol. II, 669–80; §II, 52, *passim*, figs. 9, 12–14, and end-papers; §XII, 42, 176–8; §XII, 27, pls. 33–6.

of the cultivated land.[1] Rivalling the royal mortuary temples in size and quality was that of the King's Scribe, Amenophis, son of Hapu (§vi), a structure of brick and sandstone, 115 yards in length, situated immediately behind the huge funerary enclosure of Amenophis III.[2] Like the royal temples it was of modified processional type, its forecourt, however, being treated like a walled garden, with a broad central pool surrounded by trees.

Outside Thebes the long line of temples founded, rebuilt, or enlarged by the pharaohs of the Eighteenth Dynasty stretches northward into Syria[3] and southward to Gebel Barkal, below the Fourth Cataract of the Nile,[4] and includes not only monuments of considerable size and splendour, like the Nubian temple of Amenophis III at Sulb,[5] but also smaller buildings of great charm, like the same king's chapel to the goddess Nekhbet at El-Kāb.[6] Some time prior to the reign of Akhenaten (Amenophis IV) the ancient shrine of Re at Heliopolis appears to have been converted into a full-fledged processional temple with three big courts, each preceded by a pylon;[7] and before one of these pylons Tuthmosis III in the thirty-sixth year of his reign (third *Heb-Sed*) is known to have erected the obelisk which now stands on the Thames embankment in London and its mate, the Central Park obelisk in New York.[8] Although there are interesting accounts of building construction undertaken during the Tuthmoside period in the great temples of Ptah at Memphis and Osiris at Abydos, only traces of these once magnificent structures have survived to the present day.[9]

The domestic architecture of this period is represented, at one end of the social scale, by the palace of Amenophis III south of Medīnet Habu (§vi) and, at the other, by the artisans' village at Deir el-Medīna (§x). In both instances we have to do with one-storeyed, flat-roofed structures of sun-dried brick, faced inside

---

[1] §II, 34, vol. II, 129; §XII, 6, 58–61, pl. 14; §XII, 28, 61; §VIII, 22, 43–52; §II, 52, 75–6, 201–3.

[2] §VI, 20; §IV, 24, vol. II, 688–90.

[3] §II, 34, vol. VII, 376–8, 387–9, 393–5.

[4] §II, 34, vol. VII, 215–23 *passim*; §IV, 24, vol. II, 970.

[5] §II, 34, vol. VII, 168–72; §IV, 24, vol. 2, 968; §VI, 7, vol. VI, 82–6; pls. 1–7; vol. VII, 154–70.

[6] §II, 34, vol. V, 188–9; §IV, 24, vol. II, 840.

[7] §XII, 30, 123–33; §III, 20, 158.

[8] §XII, 16; §II, 42, 589–94. See also §II, 34, vol. IV, 60.

[9] §II, 42, 1346–7, 1494, 1540, 1558, 1561, 1795, 2109; §XII, 29, 127, 128, 189; §II, 34, vol. III, 217, 218, 220, 221, 225; vol. V, 41–4, 47, 49, 51.

and out with mud-plaster and provided with ceiling beams, columns, and window-grills of wood and often with door-frames, column bases, and wall-foundations of stone. The palace is composed of groups of big, rambling buildings spread over an area more than 700 yards in length and 500 yards in width and containing in various combinations all the elements of the large Egyptian dwelling house—the courtyards, porticos, vestibules, columned reception-halls, bed chambers, dressing rooms, bathrooms, harim suites, servants' quarters, offices, kitchens, workshops, and storerooms.[1] In the artisans' houses, crowded together along the narrow village streets, we find much the same elements, with the exception of the courtyards and servants' quarters, condensed into suites of four or five small rooms.[2] Most of these houses have stairways leading to the roof, and in contemporary tomb paintings are preserved representations of larger townhouses, two and even three storeys high.[3] Enough of the painted and gilded plaster and tile decoration of Amenophis III's palace has been recovered from its ruins to give an idea of the elegance and charm of this great royal pleasure-city. For the interesting New Kingdom developments in the field of military architecture our best sources are the well-designed brick fortresses of Nubia and the Sudan, built or remodelled by the kings of the Eighteenth and Nineteenth Dynasties in conformity with recent advances in the science of attack and defence.[4]

Since the carrying out of the vast programme of building inaugurated by the pharaohs of the New Kingdom depended directly upon a continuous and practically unlimited supply of good structural and ornamental stone, it is not surprising to find the quarrying and use of this material included among the royal, or government monopolies.[5] Indeed, the quarrying and transportation to Thebes and other centres of population of any of the five principal stones employed by the Eighteenth Dynasty architects and sculptors required resources of manpower and equipment which only the state was in a position to command (§§VIII, IX, X).

Even limestone, of which the greater part of the Egyptian

---

[1] §II, 34, vol. I, 200; §II, 20, 35–6, 41 (fig. I), 85, 162–4, 177–81, 236–41; §II, 45, 159–72. Cf. §IV, 24, vol. II, 1004–22.

[2] §X, 3, vol. XVI, 13–78; §IV, 24, vol. II, 991–4, cf. 984–90; §XII, 1, 8–44. See also §XII, 2.

[3] §XII, 11; §XII, 12.

[4] §II, 34, vol. VII, 81, 82, 129, 142ff., 152ff., 164–5, 233; §IV, 24, vol. II, 995–1004; §VII, 14, 71–81; §XII, 39, 153–64; §VII, 3; §V, 6; §VII, 4.

[5] §III, 20, 137ff.; §VIII, 10, 559ff.

Nile Valley is formed, was obtainable in a quality suited to fine
building and carving in a limited number of localities and then
only by cutting back or tunnelling into selected strata.[1] The best
limestone ('the fine white stone of 'Ainu') came, as always, from
the quarries at Tura and El-Ma'sara, on the east side of the Nile
between Cairo and Helwān, where the ancient cuttings are in
the form of huge, pillared galleries, twenty feet high and running
back hundreds of yards into the cliffs.[2] Here, in addition to the
well-known stela of Amosis, we find others of Amenophis II and
III, stating in each case that 'His Majesty commanded the
quarry-chambers to be opened anew' after he had found them
'beginning to go to ruin'.[3] Another great limestone quarry, used
by Tuthmosis III and Amenophis III, is located in the Wādi
Deir en-Nakhla, near Deir el-Bersha in Middle Egypt,[4] and
extensive cuttings occur also at Beni Hasan, Qāw, and to the
north-east of El-Amarna, where the cartouche of Queen Tiy is
still preserved on the face of the cliff.[5]

The sandstone region begins at Es-Sibā'īya, forty-five miles
upstream from Thebes;[6] but the quarry from which the New
Kingdom pharaohs extracted the bulk of the stone used in the
construction of their great temples lies some fifty miles further
south where, at Gebel es-Silsila, the steep brown cliffs come down
to the river's edge on either side.[7] The quarrying here is in huge
bays, the sheer walls of which rise in places to a height of forty
feet above the present floor of the quarry. Sixteen small shrines,
rock-cut in the western cliffs by royal architects and other great
officials of the Tuthmoside period, owe their existence in part to
the fact that the gorge at Gebel es-Silsila was hallowed as one of
the traditional 'sources' of the Egyptian Nile.[8] Among the
owners of these shrines were the viziers Amotju and (Amen)-
wosre, the High Priest of Amun Hapuseneb, the Chancellors
Nehesy and Sennefer, and the Chief Steward Senenmut—all of
whom, as we have seen, held office during the reigns of Tuthmosis
II, Hatshepsut, and Tuthmosis III.[9]

[1] §iv, 14, 66–70; §xii, 37, 5–12.
[2] §xii, 9, 12–22 *passim*, figs. 9–11, 18; §xii, 37, 6 ff.; §iv, 14, 66–7; §iii, 14, vol. ii, 126*–130* (A 395); §xii, 40, 90–100.
[3] §ii, 34, vol. iv, 74; §xii, 10, 257–9, 262–5; §ii, 42, 24–5, 1448, 1680–1; §xii, 9, 21.   [4] §ii, 34, vol. iv, 185.
[5] §ii, 34, vol. iv, 237; §iv, 14, 67–8; §xii, 9, 12 ff., 18, figs. 8, 15–16.
[6] §iv, 14, 70–2.
[7] §xii, 9, 13–16, 19–21; §xii, 19, 337–8, pl. 21; §xii, 7, 51–5, pls. 12, 13.
[8] §xii, 37, 13; §iii, 2, 716; §iii, 23, 218. See also the references cited in §iii, 14, vol. ii, 6 (A 317).   [9] §ii, 34, vol. v, 214–15.

Red granite (syenite) and black, or dark grey, diorite were quarried chiefly in the region of the First Cataract,[1] which abounds in inscriptions of the Tuthmoside kings and their architects (§VII). The two main quarries of red granite lie, respectively, a mile and three miles south by east of the modern town of Aswān (the Greek Syene). In the northern quarry a 137-foot royal obelisk, partially trenched out of the surrounding rock mass, has provided invaluable information on ancient Egyptian methods of quarrying hard stone;[2] and an unfinished colossal statue of Amenophis III (?) in the south quarry shows the very considerable amount of work done on such monuments before transportation.[3] Although quartzite, an intensely hard, silicified sandstone used for the royal sarcophagi and other fine monuments of the Eighteenth Dynasty,[4] occurs in various localities in Egypt, the only quarry known to have been used by the kings of this period is the one north-east of Cairo, called in antiquity, as at the present day, the Red Mountain (*dw dšr*; Gebel el-Ahmar).[5] It was here that Amenophis, son of Hapu, quarried the gigantic blocks for the 'Colossi of Memnon' (§VI) and for another huge monolithic statue of Amenophis III set up at Karnak and stated to have been 40 cubits, or almost 70 feet, in height.[6] There are no inscriptions of Tuthmoside date in the ancient greywacke quarries at Wādi Hammāmāt or in the well-known 'alabaster' quarry at Het-nub, south-east of El-Amarna. It is probable that at this period the latter stone, which is actually calcite,[7] was quarried elsewhere in the eastern desert, though it was still customary to describe it as 'the pure šs-stone of Het-nub'.[8] One likely source is a quarry at Gauata, twenty miles east of Asyūt, which contains royal inscriptions of the early Eighteenth Dynasty[9] and which is perhaps to be identified with 'the mountain of pure šs-stone', mentioned on an alabaster stela of the reign of Amenophis III.[10]

Numerous statues of granite, diorite, quartzite, and other hard

[1] §IV, 14, 72–4, 465–6; §XII, 37, 15–21. Most of the Egyptian stone commonly referred to as 'black (or grey) granite' is (porphyritic) diorite.

[2] §XII, 13; §XII, 14, 20–51; §XII, 9, 27–30, figs. 25–9.

[3] §XII, 38, 173–6; §II, 34, vol. v, 224; §VI, 32, 409; §VIII, 10, 563.

[4] §IV, 14, 79–80, 87, 477; §XII, 37, 28–33; §II, 19, 31–2; See Plate 88.

[5] §XII, 15, vol. VI, 126; §III, 14, vol. II, 130*, 138*; §XII, 9, 23, 30–2, figs. 30–3; §II, 34, vol. IV, 65. At Gebel el-Ahmar, as elsewhere, the dark red quartzite, much admired by the ancients, is actually far less common than the ordinary light brown variety, of which most of the extant monuments are made.

[6] §II, 42, 1822–3, 1833. See §I, 7, 5; §VI, 28, 86–93.

[7] §IV, 14, 75–7; §XII, 9, 20.

[8] §II, 42, 424 (2), 1890 (1). See §XII, 37, 22–3.

[9] §XII, 25, 157–8; §XII, 37, 24.   [10] §II, 42, 1888 (11). See §XII, 37, 24.

stones, belonging to private persons, were presented to their owners 'as favour(s) of the king's bounty'.[1] The same seems to have been true of the blocks of sandstone and limestone used by Senenmut, Ipuyemre, Amenophis, son of Hapu, and the Treasurer Sobkmose in the construction or adornment of their funerary monuments.[2] The fact that all these men were without exception kings' architects in direct charge of the royal quarrying operations would, in any event, explain their access to a supply of good building stone—an opportunity which we cannot assume was open to the average Egyptian.

XIII. TOMB DEVELOPMENT

Faced with the plundering of the royal pyramids of the Old and Middle Kingdoms, which during the Hyksos period must have reached wholesale proportions, the founders of the Eighteenth Dynasty adopted the policy of separating their mortuary temples from the underground complexes of their tombs and concealing the latter in the desert hills behind the Theban necropolis, where, unmarked by superstructures of any kind, it was hoped that they might escape detection.[3] The tomb of Amenophis I, its entrance-pit half hidden under an overhanging boulder, was excavated high up on the rocky slope overlooking the Dirā Abu'n-Naga and more than 850 yards north-north-west of the king's mortuary chapel in the plain below.[4] The site selected for his burial by Tuthmosis I lies some 2300 yards further west, on the far side of the lofty cliffs behind Deir el-Bahri, at the inner end of a long and tortuous valley famous today as the Wādi el-Bibān el-Mulūk, the Valley of the Tombs (literally 'Doors') of the Kings.[5] Here, 'in solitude, without being seen or heard', the mayor of Thebes, Ineny, supervised the excavation of the tomb of his royal master[6] and here in the course of the next four centuries were hewn the tombs of almost all the pharaohs of the Eighteenth, Nineteenth, and Twentieth Dynasties.

The tombs of the Tuthmoside kings, from Tuthmosis I to

[1] §II, 42, 404 (7), 407 (9), 464 (7), 471 (10), 1376 (4), 1437 (6), 1494 (7), 1793 (16), 1829 (9), 1832 (16), 1834 (6); §x, 18, vol. III, 158 (7).

[2] The sandstone used in the tomb of Ipuyemre, for example, was evidently part of that quarried primarily for Tuthmosis III's avenue at Deir el-Bahri (§III, 7, vol. I, 13; vol. II, 56–7; §II, 52, 202–3). See also §VI, 20, 27–8; §XII, 17, 23 n. 172, 27; §II, 21, vol. II, 129, fig. 67.

[3] §XIII, 23, 73, 75, 79; §XIII, 11, 22–3; §VI, 1, 5. Cf. §XIII, 7, 109–10.

[4] §XIII, 2, 147–54; §XIII, 22, 320–1.

[5] §XII, 23, 73 ff.   [6] §II, 42, 57 (3–5).

Amenophis III, conform with a basic type and contain in every case the following essential elements: an entrance stair-well cut down into the rock, usually at the base of a cliff (described in a royal tomb plan of the Twentieth Dynasty[1] as 'the Corridor of the Sun's Path'); a long, sloping tunnel ('the Passage of the God') leading downward to a rectangular antechamber ('the Hall of Waiting'); a second stairway and corridor descending to the pillared sepulchral hall, a big oval or rectangular room called 'the House of Gold' and containing, at its inner end, the king's quartzite sarcophagus mounted on a base of alabaster; and, finally, one to four small storerooms, or 'Treasuries', opening off the sepulchral hall.[2] The five later tombs (Hatshepsut–Amenophis III) have also a deep protective well or corresponding feature, situated just before the antechamber, and a flight of steps or stair-chamber located between the protective well and the entrance; and the tombs of Tuthmosis IV and Amenophis III insert a small additional room between the sepulchral hall and the antechamber.[3] Nearly all the royal tombs of this period have a right-angle bend in the plan at the antechamber and those of Tuthmosis IV and Amenophis III have a second bend at or just before the entrance of the sepulchral hall. The irregular curve followed by the extraordinarily long corridors of Hatshepsut's tomb appears to have been unpremeditated, for it was clearly the original intention of its architect (Hapuseneb) to extend the tomb in a long straight line eastwards towards the queen's mortuary temple at Deir el-Bahri.[4] In each tomb the walls of the sepulchral hall were, or were to have been, adorned with scenes and texts from the so-called Book of What-is-in-the-Underworld (ʾImy-Dēt)—here entitled 'the Text of the Hidden Chamber'—drawn and written in cursive fashion on a yellowish brown background in obvious imitation of an unrolled papyrus version of the book.[5] The ʾImy-Dēt, an illustrated record of the subterranean journey of the sun-god through the demon-infested regions of the twelve hours of the night, was evidently intended as a sort of guide book for the deceased king in his own journeyings through the underworld.[6] The tomb of Tuthmosis III has, in addition,

[1] §XIII, 4, 134–56; §XII, 23, 88–9.

[2] §II, 19, 5–30, figs. 1–8; §XII, 23, 79–83; §XIII, 12, 12–39.

[3] §IV, 24, vol. II, 232–6.

[4] §II, 19, 17–19; §XIII, 22, 323; §II, 34, vol. I, 28 (20).

[5] §XIII, 1, 1–77, 117–95, pls. 1–12, 27–40; §XIII, 22; §II, 34, vol. I, 30; §XIII, 23, 90–1.

[6] See §XIII, 20, 227–318; §XIII, 21, 7–14; §XIII, 19, 284; §XIII, 12, 30–9; §XIII, 13, 134.

an abridged version of the book together with excerpts from the Litany to the Sun on the pillars of the sepulchral hall and the names of the gods of the regions of the underworld arranged in tabular fashion on the walls of the antechamber.[1] In the tombs of Amenophis II, Tuthmosis IV, and Amenophis III we find large-scale figures of the king accompanied by various gods and goddesses painted or drawn on the walls of the upper part of the protective well, the walls of the antechamber (Tuthmosis IV), and the pillars of the sepulchral hall (Amenophis II).[2] The series of royal sarcophagi—beginning with that made for Hatshepsut as the queen of Tuthmosis II and ending with that of Amenophis III, now represented only by its granite lid—shows a type development which is similar to that of the royal tombs and which consists of a gradual increase in the size of the monuments and a gradual rationalization and elaboration of their forms, decorations, and texts.[3]

During the greater part of the Eighteenth Dynasty there seems to have been no special cemetery for the kings' wives and children, whose tombs are found widely scattered throughout the desert valleys to the south and west of Deir el-Bahri.[4] The cliff-tomb which, as the wife of Tuthmosis II, Hatshepsut prepared for herself in the Wādi Sikkat Taka ez-Zeida, a mile west of Deir el-Bahri, is similar in plan to that of the king and contained, when found, the quartzite sarcophagus referred to in the preceding paragraph.[5] Hatshepsut's daughter, Neferure, appears to have been buried a thousand yards further to the west;[6] and in a still more distant valley was found a rock-cut chamber containing the jewel-bedecked bodies of three lesser wives of Tuthmosis III.[7] It was in the same general vicinity that native diggers also discovered a group of tombs belonging to the women of the harims of Tuthmosis IV and Amenophis III.[8] Queen Tiy, on the other hand, appears to have been buried with Amenophis III in his tomb in the western branch of the Valley of the Kings;[9] and her

---

[1] §xii, 1, 84–115, pls. 14–26; §xiii, 22, 318–19, pls. 2, 3, 11; §xiii, 23, 90–1.

[2] §xiii, 1, 213–17, pls. 41–2; §ii, 34, vol. i, 28; §xiii, 6, xxx–xxxiii, fig. 6.

[3] §ii, 19. The inscriptions on the sarcophagi are drawn chiefly from the Pyramid Texts and the Book of the Dead.

[4] §xiii, 25, 109–10; §xiii, 26, 3; §v, 20, 4; §xiii, 3, 107.

[5] §ii, 19, 16–17, 155 (Bibliography).   [6] §xii, 3, 109.

[7] §v, 20, 4 ff. Queen Ahmose Meryetamūn, whose tomb at Deir el-Bahri is dated by Winlock (§xiii, 26, 57–65) to the reign of Tuthmosis III, would seem, rather, to have been a contemporary of Amenophis I (§ii, 21, part ii, 53–4. Cf. §xiii, 18, 123).   [8] §xiii, 16; §xiii, 3, 111–12; §xiii, 25, 110.

[9] §xiii, 5, 79; §xiii, 23, 78 n. 2, 92 n. 1; §ii, 19, 29.

parents, Yuya and Tjuiu, were provided with a tomb of their own in the royal valley.[1]

The typical private tomb of the Eighteenth Dynasty at Thebes consists of a rectangular courtyard and an inverted T-shaped chapel, rock-cut in the side of a hill and containing, at the rear of the chapel or in a corner of the court, a hidden burial shaft descending to one or more subterranean chambers.[2] In a few instances the walls of the burial chambers are inscribed with excerpts from the Pyramid Texts, the Book of the Dead, or the Book of ʾImy-Dēt,[3] and in one tomb (that of Sennefer, mayor of Thebes under Amenophis II) the underground rooms are adorned with painted scenes of a funerary nature.[4] Normally, however, only the chapels are decorated—either with paintings executed in gouache on a coating of stucco and mud-plaster or with reliefs carved in the native limestone—and it is these which claim the major share of our attention (see below and §xiv).

A direct descendant of the rock-cut corridor and portico tombs of the Middle Kingdom,[5] this type of tomb-chapel comprises, in addition to the *courtyard*: a transverse *forehall*, sometimes treated as an open portico; a longitudinal *passage*, running back into the hill from the centre of the hall; and, at the inner end of the passage, a small *sanctuary*, or cult-place, having in its rear wall a niche with statues of the deceased and his wife, less frequently a painted, carved, or monolithic false-door stela, and, in a few of the larger tombs, both a false-door and a statue niche.[6] Secondary cult-places, each marked by a false-door or round-topped stela, were established at the ends of the forehall and before the façade of the tomb on either side of the entrance doorway.[7] The pyramidal superstructure, abandoned by the kings, had been taken over by private individuals, and a small pyramid of whitewashed brick with a capping of limestone appears to have been a regular feature of the New Kingdom tomb-chapel.[8] Pottery cones, stamped on the base with the name and titles of the tomb-owner and imbedded point first in the masonry, were frequently used in rows to form friezes across the top of the chapel façade and around the upper part of the pyramid.[9] The tombs of Hatshepsut's great officials (Senenmut, Senmen, Amenophis, Ipuyemre) tend to imitate the terraced arrangement and colonnaded porticos

---

[1] §ii, 34, vol. i, 30–1.   [2] §xiii, 23, 44 ff.; §xiii, 9, 30–1.
[3] E.g. Tombs 61, 82, 87 (§ii, 35, 125, 166–7, 179).   [4] §ii, 35, 200–3.
[5] §xiii, 15, 13–15. Cf. §xiii, 23, 44.   [6] §xiii, 15, 13–22.
[7] §xiii, 15, 23–6.   [8] §xiii, 23, 45–6; §xiii, 8, 25–40.
[9] §xiii, 23, 45 n. 2; §xiii, 8, 27 (figs. 1–3); §xiii, 10.

seen in the queen's temple at Deir el-Bahri.[1] In a number of the smaller chapels the transverse forehall and longitudinal passage are replaced by a single rectangular chamber.[2] Although numerous variations and exceptions are found, the inverted T-shaped chapel remained the basic form throughout the Tuthmoside period and is still recognizable in the elaborate private tomb-temples which came into fashion in the reign of Amenophis III and which are best exemplified by those of the Vizier Ramose and the Chief Steward Amenemhet-Surere.[3] In these great rock-cut complexes the forehall and the passage are treated as monumental columned halls and in the tomb of Surere a five-aisled festival hall, similar to those of the kings (§xii), is inserted between the passage and the sanctuary.[4] Sixty-five yards in length from forehall to sanctuary, the tomb of Surere has been justly described as 'one of the proudest works of Egyptian rock architecture'.[5]

Turning to the decoration of the Theban tomb-chapels we find that the painted or sculptured scenes are distributed on their walls according to a logically conceived plan, from which during the greater part of the Tuthmoside period there are relatively few important variations.[6] As a general rule the forehall is given over to scenes taken from the daily life of the tomb owner. Those on the rear wall are devoted to his professional career, with special emphasis on his services to the king; those on the front wall, to the various aspects of his private life—his devotion to the gods, his family relationships and social activities, his sports and recreations, and his tours of inspection through the fields and workshops of his personal estates. In the passage and sanctuary, on the other hand, the subject matter is almost exclusively funerary in nature. Concerned mainly with the burial of the deceased and his existence in and beyond the tomb, it included such episodes as the pilgrimage to Abydos, the funeral procession and burial rites, the consecration of offerings, the funerary banquet, and the appearance of the dead before the gods of the Hereafter. In the reign of Amenophis III we find a marked tendency to expand the principal funerary cult and the scenes associated with it into the forward portions of the tomb-chapel —the forehall and even the courtyard—at the expense of the

[1] §xiii, 15, 15; §xiii, 23, 48, 54. See §ii, 35, 71–5, 139–42, 143–4, 337 (Tombs, 39, 71, 73, 252).   [2] §xiii, 15, 16–17.
[3] Tombs 55 and 48 (§ii, 35, 87–91, 105–11). See also §xiii, 23, 49–51; §xiii, 15, 153.
[4] §iv, 19, 33 n. 5, pls. 60, 62, 63; §xii, 23, 51.
[5] §xiii, 23, 51. See also §xiii, 24, 44.
[6] §xiii, 24, 53–5; §xiii, 15, 26; §xiii, 23, 61–4; §xiii, 9, 30–1.

secondary cult-places, the biographical inscriptions, and the scenes of daily life with which these spaces were formerly occupied.[1]

Most of the decorated tomb-chapels of the Eighteenth Dynasty are excavated in the easterly slopes of a series of rocky prominences which extend along the front of the Theban necropolis from the Dirā Abu'n-Naga on the north to the Qurnet Mur'ai on the south, the greatest concentration of chapels being found in the hills of the Sheikh Abd el-Qurna and El-Khōkha, southeast of Deir el-Bahri.[2] In the artisan's cemetery at Deir el-Medīna (§x) we encounter a somewhat different form of tomb, in which the chapel, often constructed of masonry, is regularly surmounted by a hollow brick pyramid and preceded by a portico, a walled courtyard, and a small brick pylon.[3] The burial chambers of these tombs, cut in the rock immediately below or slightly to the rear of the chapels, are vaulted and their walls are adorned with painted scenes taken from the Book of the Dead and other funerary works.[4] One of the most remarkable private tombs in the Theban necropolis is that which Senenmut toward the end of his career excavated for himself under the forecourt of Hatshepsut's temple at Deir el-Bahri.[5] Like the queen's own tomb in the Valley of the Kings it is without a superstructure and consists of a succession of long sloping passages leading downward through two rock-cut chambers to an unfinished crypt 140 feet below the surface of the ground. In addition to its well-known astronomical ceiling the first chamber, or antechamber, of this tomb is inscribed with 224 columns of funerary texts and contains a handsome false-door stela carved in the rock at the centre of its west wall.

West of the great city of Memphis there grew up during the second half of the Eighteenth Dynasty an important upper-class cemetery which extends along the desert's edge for a distance of almost a mile and includes the tombs of such well-known dignitaries of the reign of Amenophis III as the Chief Steward Amenophis and the High Priest Ptahmose.[6] Since the desert here is flat and open the burial shafts are deep vertical pits and the tomb-chapels were freestanding structures of brick and limestone surmounted by small pyramids with pinnacles of limestone or granite. Many of these chapels were adorned with painted reliefs of great interest and beauty and were provided with one or more fine stelae of limestone or quartzite.

---

[1] §xiii, 15, 153.
[2] §xiii, 23, 32–40; §ii, 35, 495 ff.
[3] §xiii, 23, 40–3, 54–9.
[4] §x, 3; §ii, 35, 16–18 (Tomb 8).
[5] §ii, 35, 417–18.
[6] §xiii, 14, 16–18, 24.

Among the provincial cemeteries of Tuthmoside date[1] those at Abydos and El-Kāb are particularly deserving of our attention. The typical tomb of this period at Abydos is in the form of a miniature temple, built of brick and composed of a series of small, open courts leading to a little brick sanctuary.[2] The sanctuary, containing a statue of the tomb owner, is usually preceded, at the centre of the innermost court, by a massif of brick surrounding the mouth of the burial shaft. The vaulted rock-tombs of El-Kāb, though of little architectural significance, preserve interesting scenes from the daily lives of their owners and biographical inscriptions of considerable historical importance.[3]

XIV. ART

In sculpture and painting, as in architecture, the era of imperial expansion under Tuthmosis I and his successors witnessed the transition from the somewhat austere artistic traditions of the Middle Kingdom to the elegant and vivacious style characteristic of the late Eighteenth Dynasty.[4]

The royal temple statues of this period display a new slenderness in the proportions of the figures and an increased care and delicacy in the treatment of the hands, feet, and other details. The poses, costumes, and accessories are for the most part traditional; but the representation of the king as a kneeling figure holding in each hand an offering jar is used with far greater frequency than heretofore. The faces, though retaining the quality of portraits, tend to be softened and idealized and the modelling of the torsos and limbs is smooth and restrained as becomes figures designed primarily as elements in grandiose architectural lay-outs. Typical is a series of big red granite statues from Hatshepsut's temple at Deir el-Bahri, in which the female ruler is represented as a king with the full pharaonic regalia including the customary artificial chin-beard.[5] Smaller in scale and more sensitive in treatment are a beautiful seated figure of the queen in hard white limestone, also from Deir el-Bahri,[6] and a superb standing statue of Tuthmosis III in fine-grained schist, found at Karnak in 1904 in a great cache of

---

[1] §IV, 24, vol. II, 373–86.

[2] §XIII, 17, 64, pls. 24 (2), 25 (4).   [3] §II, 34, vol. V, 176–84 *passim*.

[4] §VI, 1, 7–21; §II, 45, 128–55; §XIV, 31, 39–114; §I, 9, 76.

[5] §XIV, 53; §XIV, 54, 159–60; §II, 21, part II, 92–101, figs. 51–3, 55; §VI, 1, 11, nos. 20, 22, 24; §IV, 24, vol. III, 299–302, pls. 98–9.

[6] §XIV, 53, vol. XXIV, Nov., sect. II, 8–9, figs. 4–6; vol. XXV, Dec., sect. II, 8–9, figs. 3–4, §II, 21, part II, 97–9, fig. 54; §II, 45, 135, pl. 95. See Plate 87.

royal and private statues.[1] From the same cache comes a charming little seated statue in black diorite of Tuthmosis III's mother, Isis, and a green schist statuette of Amenophis II, notable for the youthful freshness of the king's face and figure.[2] In a black diorite group from the great temple of Amun Tuthmosis IV appears seated side by side with his mother, Queen Tiʿo, the unusual heaviness of the figures contrasting strangely with the delicate modelling of the heads and faces.[3] The British Museum possesses a splendid series of over-lifesize statues and statue heads of Amenophis III from his mortuary temple in western Thebes, including a pair of strikingly handsome portrait heads of the king in brown breccia.[4] Before the seventh, eighth, and tenth pylons at Karnak stand the remains of pairs of gigantic royal statues, of limestone, granite, or quartzite erected by the pharaohs of the early and middle Eighteenth Dynasty, from Amenophis I to Amenophis III.[5] In addition to the so-called Colossi of Memnon (§vi) the colossal statues of the last-named king include a number of huge figures in the temples at Karnak and Luxor (usurped by Ramesses II and Merneptah)[6] and a 24-foot lime-stone group from Medīnet Habu showing Amenophis III and Queen Tiy seated together and attended by smaller figures of three of their daughters.[7] In spite of their vast size most of the Eighteenth Dynasty colossi are as well proportioned as their smaller counterparts—a quality which contributes enormously to their beauty and effectiveness and distinguishes them sharply from the ponderous monstrosities of the Ramesside period. Vying in interest with the big, temple sculptures are numerous small and exquisitely executed royal statuettes of stone, wood, faience, and other materials, coming for the most part from the tombs and palaces of the kings. Among these special mention is merited by a little ebony portrait head of Queen Tiy (or Sitamun?)[8] and a small serpentine statuette depicting Amen-ophis III as a corpulent, foppishly dressed old man,[9] both of which

---

[1] Cairo 42.053 (§xiv, 30, 32, pls. 29–30); §ii, 45, 135, pl. 96; §vi, 1, 52–3, no. 37; §xiv, 4, no. 40 A. See also §ii, 34, vol. ii, 50–3; see Plate 94 (a).

[2] Cairo 42.072 and 42.077 (§xiv, 30, 41–2, 44–5, pls. 42, 47).

[3] Cairo 42.080 (§xiv, 30, 46–7, pl. 49); §xiv, 29, pls. 148–9.

[4] §xiv, 9, pl. 21; §ii, 45, 154, pl. 114c; §vi, 1, 65, no. 75; see Plate 94 (b).

[5] §ii, 34, vol. ii, 53–5, 58, 62–3; §xii, 8, figs. 14, 15, 151; §ii, 46, 161–2.

[6] §ii, 34, vol. ii, 62–3, 100, 102 (also 156, 159); §iv, 24, vol. ii, 914. See §xii, 8, 229–30, figs. 16, 150; §xiv, 1, 114. See also §xiv, 29, pls. 162–3.

[7] §xiv, 25, pl. 77; §ii, 45, 154 n. 39.

[8] §xiv, 5; §vi, 23. See §vi, 1, 67, no. 81; §iv, 24, vol. iii, 330.

[9] §xiv, 12; §ii, 21, part ii, 236–7, fig. 142.

display the nervous sensibility and exaggerated naturalism of the art of the Amarna period.

The relatively few statues of divinities which have survived from the Tuthmoside period conform with three more or less well-established types: the anthropomorphic figures in which the god is normally represented with the facial features of the ruling pharaoh or the king himself is portrayed in the guise of a god; the composite, or hybrid, type of divine figure with an animal head and a human body; and the straight animal form, often accompanied by a small figure of the king. Examples of the first type include a lifesize statue in limestone of Amenophis II wearing the plumes and other attributes of the god Ptah-Tanen;[1] a life-size diorite statue of the god Ptah with the features of Amenophis III;[2] and the colossal 'Osiride' figures so frequently employed in royal temple decoration, as in the courtyard and hall of Tuthmosis I at Karnak and on the pillars of the uppermost colonnade and elsewhere in Hatshepsut's temple at Deir el-Bahri.[3] Almost every large Egyptian collection contains one or more of the black diorite statues of the lioness-headed goddess Sakhmet contributed by Amenophis III to the temple of Mut at Karnak;[4] and the Ny Carlsberg Glyptothek in Copenhagen possesses a fine diorite statue, also made under Amenophis III, representing the god Anubis with human body and canine head.[5] A great sandstone figure of the cow of Hathor carved by Amenophis II's sculptors for a shrine of the goddess at Deir el-Bahri must be counted among the finest examples of animal sculpture produced by any ancient people,[6] as must also the stone rams and the magnificent recumbent lions from the temple of Amenophis III at Sulb.[7] To Amenophis III we owe long avenues of ram-headed sphinxes leading to the temple of Amun at Karnak[8] and the remarkable granite scarab-beetle of the sun-god Atum-Khepre which stands on its cylindrical base near the north-west corner of the sacred lake.[9] The same genius in the handling of

---

[1] Cairo 38069 (§xiv, 14, 25, pl. 6).

[2] Turin, Cat. no. 86 (§vi, 1, 20, 66, no. 77).

[3] §iv, 24, vol. iii, 297–8, 300; §ii, 52, 141, 161–3, 214–17, figs. 9. 12, 13, pls. 54–6; §vi, 1, 10–11, 44–5, nos. 13–14; §ii, 21, part ii, 89–91, figs. 49, 50; see Plates 90 and 91.

[4] §ii, 34, vol. ii, 93; §ii, 21, part ii, 237–9, fig. 143.

[5] §xiv, 32, 25 (A 89), pl. 21.

[6] §ii, 34, vol. ii, 129; §xiv, 29, pls. 142–3.

[7] §ii, 34, vol. vii, 169, 212, 216, 219; §ii, 46, 192, fig. 25; §xiv, 10, vol. ii, pls. 48–9.

[8] See above, p. 396 n. 2.   [9] §ii, 34, vol. ii, 73 (R); §xiv, 48.

animal forms appears in the couched lion bodies of the majestic royal androsphinxes of granite and sandstone with which Hatshepsut, Tuthmosis III, and other kings of this period lined the processional ways of their temples.[1]

The temple reliefs of the Tuthmoside kings exhibit the same slender proportions and clean profiles, the same delicacy of detail, and the same quality of suppressed energy seen in the statues. In the painted limestone reliefs of Hatshepsut's mortuary temple we find an essentially Middle Kingdom style of relief sculpture imbued with new vitality and adapted, in the colonnaded porticos of the temple, to the representation of a host of new subjects: the queen's conception and birth, the transport of her obelisks, the tropical scenery and exotic inhabitants of the land of Punt.[2] In the great processional temples of sandstone the subject matter is largely of a traditional and symbolic nature— the king offering to the gods, celebrating the *Sed*-festival, ceremonially slaying his enemies—and the compositions here tend, as in the Old and Middle Kingdoms, to be simple, formal, and static.[3] This is true even of scenes for which no Middle Kingdom precedent exists, such as the presentation to Amun of the booty of the Asiatic conquests and the pictorial cataloguing by Tuthmosis III's artists of the animals and plants brought back from Syria in the king's twenty-fifth year.[4] A fine relief preserved on a block of red granite from Karnak shows Amenophis II shooting at a target from a rapidly moving chariot;[5] but the earliest representation of the king in battle occurs on a chariot-body found in the tomb of Tuthmosis IV.[6] Here for the first time we see the pharaoh charging in his chariot into a confused mass of stricken foreign enemies, whose bodies, horses, and chariots are distributed pell-mell over the field with no regard for ground lines or division into registers. This naturalistic and highly dramatic type of composition, thought to have been inspired by contemporaneous Helladic art,[7] we shall find extensively employed in

[1] §xiv, 46, 58–61, pls. 10, 15; §xiv, 17, 98–115; §ii, 52, 141, 160, 170, 172, 189, 212–14, pls. 48–50; §xiv, 42, 28–32; §xiv, 6, part ii, 125–6 (nos. 576–7), pl. 98; §vi, 1, 47–8 (nos. 22–3); §iv, 24, vol. iii, 300 ff., pls. 98 ff.; §xiv, 4, nos. 37, 38A.

[2] §ii, 34, vol. ii, 113–28; §iii, 36; §vi, 1, 10, 46 (nos. 17–19); §ii, 45, 135–8, pls. 92–3; §xii, 8, figs. 95–8, 140–6, 158, 160, 191.

[3] §ii, 34, vol. ii, 25–46, 54–8; §xii, 8, figs. 25, 26, 121; §xiv, 29, pl. 136.

[4] §xiv, 55, pls. 26–33; §xii, 8, figs. 25, 100–3.

[5] §ii, 7, vol. xxviii, 126, fig. 5; §v, 3, 51 n. 5; §xi, 22, 89, pl. 72; see Plate 95 (*a*).

[6] §xiii, 6, 24–33; §ii, 34, vol. i, 30; §x, 36, 489–91, figs. 463–4; see Plate 95 (*b*).

[7] §i, 9, 310–11; §ii, 50, 191. See below, p. 416 nn. 1 and 3.

Egyptian relief sculpture and painting from the end of the Eighteenth Dynasty onwards. It does not, however, occur in the known temple reliefs of Amenophis III at Luxor, Karnak, El-Kāb, and Sulb, which, in spite of the great sophistication and elegance of their style, are conservative in their subject matter and mode of representation.[1] The formal figures of kings and gods prominent in these reliefs find their counterparts in the paintings of the tombs of Tuthmosis IV and Amenophis III and in the big outline drawings in the sepulchral hall of Amenophis II.[2] Much freer in style and lighter in colour are the charming paintings of harim ladies, dancing dwarf-gods, running animals, flying birds, and flowering marsh plants which once adorned the plaster walls, ceilings, and pavements of Amenophis III's palace in western Thebes.[3]

From the private statues, reliefs, and paintings, less dominated by traditional forms than those of the kings, we obtain a clearer picture of the evolution of the art of the early New Kingdom and can distinguish within the Tuthmoside period itself two successive stages of development, the first of which may be said to have reached its climax in the reign of Tuthmosis III, the second in the reign of Amenophis III.[4]

While exhibiting a considerable variety of types and poses the tomb-statues of private persons carved under the earlier Tuthmoside pharaohs are characterized by a quality of unadorned simplicity, which is particularly noticeable in their clothing and headdresses and in the almost complete absence of jewellery and other distracting accessories.[5] As in the Old and Middle Kingdoms the sculptor concentrated his attention on the modelling of the strong, healthy faces, handling the figures in a generalized and often cursory manner. A favourite type is the so-called 'block-statue', in which the owner is represented as seated on the ground with his knees drawn up before his chest and his arms crossed over his knees, the whole cubical form being thought of as enveloped within a long mantle, so that only the head projects above the mass of the 'block'.[6] Almost equally popular is the kneeling figure holding a votive offering in the form of a small

---

[1] §ii, 34, vol. ii, 27, 103–8; vol. vii, 169–72; §iii, 35, vol. i, 8 ff., pls. 12, 14, 36, 63; §xiv, 45, *passim*; §xii, 8, fig. 54; §xiv, 4, no. 80.

[2] See above, p. 403 n. 2.

[3] §ii, 34, vol. i, 200; §ii, 45, 164–71, pls. 120–2.

[4] §iv, 24, vol. 3, 434–517; §vi, 1, 11–21; §x, 36, 432–50; §ii, 46, 188–93; §xiv, 43, 551.

[5] §xiv, 26; §vi, 1, nos. 30–3, 38, 40–3; §viii, 20, 6 ff., plate.

[6] §iv, 24, vol. iii, 450–2, pl. 151. Cf. §xiv, 7; see Plate 92.

shrine or other sacred object[1] or having before it a stela bearing
the words of a hymn which the owner is presumed to be in the
act of reciting.[2] These and other types are admirably represented
in a fine series of black diorite statues and statuettes carved for
Hatshepsut's great steward, Senenmut, who in several instances
is shown accompanied by his ward, the infant princess, Neferure.[3]
Nowhere does the calm strength and dignified simplicity of these
earlier statues appear to greater advantage than in the slender
figures of the vizier Amenwosre and his wife, preserved for us in a
black diorite group from Karnak, datable to the middle years of
the reign of Tuthmosis III.[4] Before the death of Amenophis II,
fifty years later, all this had been changed and in the well-known
group statue of the Theban mayor Sennefer and his family we
find a new set of values coming to the fore.[5] Here the sculptor
was obviously preoccupied with producing in the figure of this
fashionably dressed official an image of the wealth and luxury to
which the people of Egypt had recently fallen heir. Sennefer's
face is fat and soft and his midriff is covered with rolls of loose
flesh, indicative of a life of ease unmarred by physical exertion.
His intricate wig is carved with meticulous care, as are also the
four heavy gold(?) necklaces which encircle his thick neck, the
massive amulet which he wears suspended over his chest, and the
armlets which adorn his upper arms. Even more elaborate and
more sophisticated are the private statues and statuettes produced during the reigns of Tuthmosis IV and Amenophis III,
which, though lacking the sturdier qualities of the early figures,
are often works of great beauty, sensitivity, and human appeal.
Outstanding are a black diorite portrait statue of Amenophis,
son of Hapu, in Cairo,[6] and the upper part of a limestone statue
of a woman, in Florence.[7] In these and other works of the time,
including a series of charming wooden statuettes of court ladies
and gentlemen,[8] a striking contrast is visible between the
luxurious and somewhat frivolous intricacy of the costumes and
the grave, even melancholy, expressions of the faces which seem to

---

[1] §iv, 24, vol. iii, 464ff., pls. 155, 164, 166; §xiv, 6, part ii, 127–30, pl. 99
(no. 579); §vi, 1, 13, 54 (no. 41).

[2] §vi, 1, 54 (nos. 42, 43); §iv, 24, vol. iii, 471–4, pls. 159–60.

[3] §vi, 1, 12–13, 50–2 (nos. 30–3); §xiv, 22; see Plate 93.

[4] §xiv, 30, no. 42.118; §vi, 1, 13, 53 (no. 38).

[5] §xiv, 30, no. 42.126; §vi, 1, 61 (no. 62).

[6] §iv, 24, vol. iii, 515, pl. 171 (3); §vi, 1, 21, 69–70 (no. 91); §xiv, 29, pl. 156.

[7] §xiv, 4, no. 43; §xiv, 20, 28, 41, pl. 64; §ii, 46, 189–90, fig. 63.

[8] §xiv, 20, 41, pls. 63–7, 70–6; §xiv, 19, 31ff., pls. 61ff.; §iv, 24, vol. iii,
524–5, pls. 170, 172–3; §xiv, 23.

reflect an inner consciousness of the transitory nature of worldly splendour.[1]

Far and away the richest source of material for a study of both the art and life of the New Kingdom is the painted or sculptured decoration of the private tomb chapels of the Theban necropolis (§XIII). Of the ninety chapels datable to the period with which we are dealing more than half were executed during the lifetimes of Hatshepsut and Tuthmosis III, the remainder belonging to the reigns of Amenophis II, Tuthmosis IV, and Amenophis III.[2] In style, composition, and colouring the decoration of the chapels of the earlier group shows a general similarity to the royal temple reliefs, especially those in the temple of Hatshepsut at Deir el-Bahri. The figures, drawn with firm, clean outlines, are widely spaced in quiet, rather stiff compositions which are not closely interrelated, but arranged serially like the parts of a long, continuous narrative. The backgrounds are a pale bluish grey and the colours, including blue, canary yellow, pink, and brick red, are fresh, clear, and light in tone.[3] The diversity of content which is characteristic of these earlier tomb paintings is particularly well exemplified in the great chapel of Tuthmosis III's vizier, Rekhmire, long recognized as the masterpiece of its type and period.[4] The tomb of Kenamun, executed a few years later, in the reign of Amenophis II, is distinguished by a new richness in design and colouring;[5] and in the succeeding tomb-chapels we find a growing tendency towards livelier, more rhythmic, and more integrated compositions and towards figures in which grace and suppleness are combined with a new feeling of depth and plasticity. Individual incidents intimately connected with the life and career of the tomb owner tend to replace the broader and more diversified representations of the world at large seen in the earlier tombs. The backgrounds are now a chalky white and the colours bright and harmonious, changing, however, to duller tones as the end of the dynasty is approached.[6] Relief sculpture, fairly common in private tombs during the reigns of Hatshepsut and Tuthmosis III,[7] disappears entirely under Amenophis II and Tuthmosis IV; but is revived on a grand scale in the great rock-cut

[1] Cf. §VI, 1, 21, 70; §II, 46, 189–91; §I, 3, 488.

[2] §XIII, 24, 141–5; see Plate 96.

[3] §XIII, 24, 100–14, 153–4; §XIII, 23, 67; §XIV, 15, xxiv-xlvi, 28–61, pls. 12–28; §XIV, 31, 36, 40–52.

[4] §II, 35, 206–14. See above, p. 405 n. 6.

[5] §II, 35, 190–4. See §XIV, 47, 115–16; §XIV, 15, 62–9, pls. 29–34.

[6] §XIII, 24, 114–46, 153–4; §XIII, 23, 67–8; §XIV, 15, 74–139, pls. 36–73; §XIV, 31, 36–7, 52–114.   [7] §XIII, 24, 46; §XIII, 23, 66.

chapels of the reign of Amenophis III (§xiii), where it is characterized by the utmost delicacy both in the draughtsmanship and
the modelling.[1] Numerous stelae of the period, both royal and
private, carry small-scale reliefs often of great beauty;[2] and no
study of Egyptian painting is complete which does not take into
consideration the fine, coloured vignettes of the funerary papyri[3]
and the hundreds of lively sketches preserved for us on potsherds
and flakes of limestone.[4]

During the reigns of Amenophis III and his predecessors the
minor arts and crafts of Egypt flourished as never before in the
country's history. Especially notable advances were made in the
production of vases, inlay plaques, and other objects of coloured
glass and faience, often adorned with polychrome patterns and
designs of astonishing brilliance and intricacy.[5] A treasure of
jewellery belonging to three minor wives of Tuthmosis III, though
lacking the technical perfection and purity of design of the best
Middle Kingdom jewellery, shows a great variety of charming and
effective combinations (headdresses, broad collars, girdles, and
bracelets) worked in gold and semi-precious stones;[6] and five
carved bracelet plaques of carnelian and sard, coming from the
tomb of Amenophis III, are marvels of the gem-cutter's art.[7]
Taste, fantasy, and skill are admirably combined in a series of
exquisitely carved small objects of wood, alabaster, and tinted
ivory—cosmetic boxes and spoons adorned with human, animal,
and plant forms, and little figures of girls, dwarfs, and animals
clearly intended for no more serious purpose than to delight and
amuse their owners.[8] The intact tombs of the architect, Kha, and
of Yuya and Tjuiu, the parents of Queen Tiy, have yielded many
pieces of elaborately carved and inlaid furniture—beds, chairs,
stools, and chests[9]—and fragments of equally fine examples of the
cabinet-maker's craft have been recovered from the plundered

---

[1] Tombs 47, 48, 55, 57, 107, 192 (§ii, 35, 87–91, 105–11, 113–19, 224–5, 298–300). See §xiii, 24, 46, 132–6; §xiv, 47, 128. See Plate 97.

[2] §xiv, 28; §xiii, 15, 21–2, 32–42; §xiv, 4, nos. 76, 78, 79.

[3] §xiv, 35, vol. i; §xiv, 36; §xiv, 10, vol. i, pl. 75; §xiv, 13, no. 24095; §xiv, 44, 32–63. See the references to Eighteenth Dynasty illustrated papyri listed in §x, i, xviii–xxxiii. See also §i, 3, 489–90.

[4] §xiv, 3; §xiv, 8; §xiv, 49; §xiv, 40; §xiv, 16.

[5] §xiv, 51; §xiv, 52; §xiv, 13, nos. 24753–853; §xiii, 6, 58–142; §ii, 21, part ii, 148–51, 193–5; §xiv, 37; §ii, 46, 196–7; §xiv, 10, vol. ii, pls. 80–1.

[6] §v, 20. See also §ii, 21, part ii, 130–7, 179–87.

[7] §xiv, 21; §xiv, 24.

[8] §xiv, 19, 128–54; §i, 3, 493; §ii, 21, part ii, 190ff., 266–9; §xiv, 38; §xiv, 50; §xiv, 27; etc.

[9] §xiv, 44, 112–45; §vi, 5, 37–47, pls. 33–42; §vi, 18, nos. 51108–19.

royal tombs.[1] From the same tombs and from that of the king's fan-bearer, Maiherpri, come numerous objects of leather, including two delicately fashioned network loincloths of gazelle skin,[2] quivers, bow-cases, and archers' bracers with embossed floral designs, and quantities of richly ornamented elements from the harness and trappings of horses.[3] The newly developed craft of the chariot-maker is represented by a complete chariot of wood, leather, and gilded plaster from the burial of Yuya and by the lavishly adorned body of one of Tuthmosis IV's chariots of state.[4] The carved and gilded coffins of Yuya and Tjuiu are superb examples of the funerary art of the Eighteenth Dynasty; and the kings' sarcophagi, hewn with remarkable precision from single great blocks of quartzite, are eloquent testimonials to the skill of the New Kingdom stone-cutters.[5] Apart from the jewellery, the gold funerary trappings, the mirrors, and the handsome gold and silver table services of the three wives of Tuthmosis III referred to above, few metal objects of Tuthmoside times have survived to the present day; but from the tomb paintings, temple reliefs, and temple inventories we know that intricately decorated bowls, weapons, and ornaments of metal were turned out in enormous quantity by the craftsmen of the period.[6] Gracefully shaped and highly polished vessels of alabaster and other ornate stones, on the other hand, are copiously represented in our museums,[7] as are also jars of red or buff pottery adorned with floral and animal designs in light blue, red, purplish brown, and black.[8] The weaving of coloured grass baskets reached during the Eighteenth Dynasty a very high level of excellence;[9] and the production of fine linen cloth, either plain or decorated with woven or embroidered patterns in several different colours, continued to rank high among the country's leading industries.[10] By and large, it is from the applied arts, rather than from the

[1] §xiv, 13, nos. 24669ff.; §xiii, 6, 20–3.

[2] §xiv, 47, 124–6; §i, 10, 75–8.

[3] §xiv, 13, nos. 24071–6, 24144–55; §xiii, 6, nos. 46098–118.

[4] §vi, 18, no. 51188; §vi, 5, 35–6, frontispiece, pl. 32. See Plate 95(b). See above, p. 410 n. 6.

[5] §ii, 19. See Plate 88.

[6] §ix, 7, vol. i, 23, 24, 28ff., pls. 13–24; vol. ii, pl. 22A; §ix, 6, 10–15, pls. 7, 8, 12; §iv, 19, 4–5, 50–1, pls. 2–4, 72. See also §xiv, 44, 134–6, 143–4.

[7] E.g. §ii, 21, part ii, 80, 85, 138–40, 190, 207, 276, figs. 43, 47, 76, 106, 122, 169; §vi, 18, nos. 51102–6; §xiv, 10, vol. ii, pl. 79; §xiv, 41, 78, 409.

[8] E.g. §ii, 21, part ii, 207–8, 247–8, figs. 123, 150; §xiv, 34, passim; §xiv, 41, 78–9, 408–9; §xiv, 44, 140–2, 157–9.

[9] §x, 3, vol. xv, 13–14, 52–6, figs. 3, 26; §v, 9, 8, 26–8, figs. 12, 28, 38, 40.

[10] §xiv, 39, 20ff.; §xiii, 6, nos. 46526–9. See also §xiv, 44, 91–100, figs. 62–71.

major works of architecture, sculpture, and painting that we obtain our most vivid impression of the incomparable technical ability of the Eighteenth Dynasty craftsmen and of the life, the spirit, and the tastes of the Egyptian people of the early New Kingdom.

The extent to which the new trends seen at this period in Egyptian art are to be attributed to contacts with the other great civilizations of the eastern Mediterranean world is difficult to gauge. Certain vase forms, both in metal and in pottery, and certain decorative motifs, such as the contiguous S-spiral, the interlocked cross, the palmette, the griffin, and the pairs of heraldically grouped animals, can with some assurance be traced back to Helladic or Syrian originals.[1] The same is probably also true of the representation of animals in a lively pose known as the flying gallop,[2] the use of a 'rocky-landscape' border to frame out-of-door subjects, and the adoption in hunting and battle scenes of a free, naturalistic type of composition—all of which are characteristic of the approximately contemporaneous pre-Greek art of the Aegean area.[3] These, however, are superficialities. The major changes in Egyptian art during the Tuthmoside period are not importations from abroad, but reflect, rather, developments in the character, outlook, and tastes of the Egyptians themselves—attributable in part to an intensified participation in world affairs, but following lines which we still recognize as fundamentally 'Egyptian'.

[1] §xi, 11, 74–6; §xiv, 33; §i, 3, 491; §ii, 50, 180, 191.
[2] See, however, §xiv, 18.   [3] §xi, 11, 74–6; §i, 9, 310–11.

CHAPTER X

SYRIA *c.* 1550-1400 B.C.

I. SYRIA IN THE SIXTEENTH CENTURY B.C.

THE march of Murshilish I and his Hittite army down the Euphrates, and pillage and destruction of Babylon, in the early years of the sixteenth century,[1] marked the end of an epoch, and ushered in an era of great political change. Governments were overthrown and dynasties ended, and in the confusion which ensued, new peoples moved into the area which at one time used to be known as the Fertile Crescent.[2] During the seventeenth century, a time when archaeology shows a decline in civilization[3] and almost no written evidence has survived, the ethnic map of the Ancient Near East was redrawn, new city states were founded, and old ones declined and were abandoned, or grew prosperous and increased their territory. Though the changes appear sudden, they must have happened gradually, and had begun much earlier. Chief and most vigorous of the newcomers were the Hurrians, whose appearances in the Near East as early as the third millennium have already been mentioned.[4]

From their homeland in the southern Caucasus and the mountains of Armenia[5] these vigorous warriors had spread gradually south and west during the course of the third millennium and the first centuries of the second; they are found as the ruling class at Urkish in the time of the Akkadian kings,[6] and this hilly region somewhere south of Diyārbakr[7] remained a stronghold of Hurrian civilization throughout their history. In the mythological text known as the Song of Ullikummi, Urkish is named as the seat of Kumarbi, one of the great deities of the Hurrian pantheon.[8] Hurrian names appear thereafter with increasing frequency in the texts of the period of the third dynasty of Ur, when their presence as a minority group in the south of Iraq is attested[9] and

---

[1] See above, ch. VI, sect. IV.   [2] §I, 11, 186 ff.

[3] §I, 68, 390; §I, 69, 86 ff.; §I, 49, 550 ff.

[4] *C.A.H.* I³, pt. 2, ch. XXII, sect. IV; see above, ch. I, sects. IV and IX.

[5] G, 12, 102 ff.; G, 29, 212; §I, 57, 312; G, 21, 46 ff. Otherwise §I, 8, 102 ff.; G, 11, 79.   [6] *C.A.H.* I³, pt. 2, ch. XXII, sect. IV; §I, 19, 380 f.

[7] §I, 57, 313 f.; §I, 26, 62 f. The city Urkish has now been identified with Tell 'Amuda (§I, 64, 91 ff.).

[8] §I, 29, 138 ff.; G, 21, 48.   [9] G, 11, 58 ff.; 109 ff.; §I, 40, 147 ff.

in the archives of Mari,[1] Chagar Bazar,[2] and Shemshāra, in Kurdistān,[3] where they appear as a significant but not very numerous element in the population of northern Mesopotamia.[4] Names of individuals which occur in the tablets of the earlier palace level at Alalakh, in the kingdom of Yamkhad, show that here in North Syria, in the eighteenth and seventeenth centuries, during the two generations after the end of the Mari archive, Hurrians already formed a considerable proportion of the citizen body, though not yet a majority,[5] and Hurrian names used for the months at Alalakh show that the Hurrian calendar was in use.[6]

The earliest known text in the Hurrian language is the inscription of 'Tishari (or Tishatal), King of Urkish and Nawar', dated to the late Akkadian period.[7] Among the Mari archives are a handful of texts written in the same language.[8] The Hittites called it the language of the Khurri.[9] It was usually written in the Babylonian cuneiform script, but the language is quite different from Akkadian or any of the other languages of the Semitic group, nor is it related to Hittite or to Kassite; its nearest relative appears to be Urarṭian,[10] the tongue spoken during the first millennium B.C. in Armenia, in the area between Lake Vān and Lake Urmia, where the Hurrian homeland must perhaps be sought.[11] The language was first encountered in modern times in a large tablet found among the correspondence unearthed at El-Amarna.[12] The short introduction, which is in Akkadian, made it clear that the letter was written to Amenophis III, king of Egypt, by Tushratta, king of Mitanni, and the language was consequently at first called Mitannian.[13] A considerable body of Hurrian texts is now available for study and the main features of the language can be discerned,[14] though a comprehensive study of grammar and morphology awaits further material, perhaps from fresh discoveries on the sites of Hurrian cities. The language is agglutinative; suffixes and associative particles are added to the word-root in order to express attribution, case and tense.[15]

[1] §I, 33, 232.

[2] §I, 17, 34 ff.

[3] §I, 34, 56, 75; §I, 35, 131 ff.

[4] G, 10, 39; G, 21, 44.

[5] §I, 67, 9; G, 10, 39, in disagreement with §I, 33, 233.

[6] §I, 67, 5; §I, 57, 319 f.

[7] §IX, 38; §I, 32, 4 ff. and pl. I; §I, 48, 1511.

[8] §I, 60, I ff.

[9] §IV, 12, 123 ff.; §I, 52.

[10] §I, 58, 10; §I, 57, 325; §I, 16, 211 ff.; §II, 20, 128; §I, 24, 194.

[11] §I, 25, 168; §I, 32, 19 f.; §I, 57, 312; G, 12, 106. Otherwise §I, 8, 103 f.

[12] EA 24 (the Amarna letters, as numbered in G, 16); *C.A.H.* II³, pt. 2, ch. xx.

[13] G, 16, 1051; §I, 10, 79.

[14] §I, 58; §I, 52.

[15] §I, 58, 198 ff.

Wherever texts written in this language, or Hurrian personal names, appear, the presence of this people must be assumed. The names, however, are of two distinct kinds. By far the most are linguistically Hurrian and consist in many cases of two elements, one being the name of a Hurrian deity such as Teshub or his consort Kheba(t); longer names are sometimes abbreviated so that Akia appears to be a shortened form of Aki-Teshub, or Tadua of Tadu-Kheba.[1] The other and much smaller group is composed of names which are indubitably Indo-Aryan and therefore unrelated linguistically to those of the first category. Considerably more than a hundred of these names have survived, and almost all of them belong to kings, princes or officials of high rank.[2] They are composed of elements which are probably Indian rather than Iranian,[3] and in the theophorous names, it is the Vedic deities Indar, Soma, Vaya the god of the wind, the Devas and Svar (Heaven), as well as Rta, the divine Law, which have been most generally identified.[4] Many of the names recall the Indo-Aryan proper names of a later age; references to horses and chariots are frequent—Tushratta, for example, may mean 'owner of terrible chariots', and Biridashwa 'possessing great horses'.[5] Here, then, we have evidence of the presence among the Hurrians of a small ruling class of Indo-Aryans worshipping gods different from those of the Hurrian pantheon. Further proof of the Indo-Aryan character of the Mitannian aristocracy is afforded by the presence of proto-Indian or Vedic deities, Mitra, Indra, Varuna and the Nāsatyās, as witnesses in a treaty between the Hittite king Shuppiluliumash and Kurtiwaza of Mitanni, in the fourteenth century.[6] A treatise on horse-training attributed to a Hurrian named Kikkuli, to which reference will be made later,[7] contains a number of technical words which are explicable by comparison with Vedic terms, and the numerals used in describing the number of turns to be taken around a course are likewise Indo-Aryan.[8] Moreover, the chariot-owning nobility or chivalry who formed the aristocratic class among the Hurrians were called *mariyanna*,

---

[1] §vi, 25, 65 n. 46; G, 21, 53; §ix, 44, 306; A, 30, 349.

[2] §i, 20, 194; G, 21, 56 ff.; §i, 14; §ix, 44, 306; A, 24; A, 33, 29 f.; *C.A.H.* ii³, pt. 2, ch. xx, sect. iii.

[3] §i, 41, 140 ff.; G, 8, vol. i, 144 ff.; G, 29, 385 n. 6; P. E. Dumont in G, 21, 149 ff., and §i, 14, 252.

[4] G, 29, 213, 385 n. 6. Dumont in §i, 14, disagrees with many of the identifications of Mironov (§i, 41).   [5] §i, 14, 253; G, 21, 149, 151.

[6] *K. Bo.* i, no. 3 = §i, 66, 2 ff.; G, 24, 205 f.; §ix, 11, 9 ff.; § ix, 44, 315.

[7] See below, p. 493.

[8] §i, 32, 50 f.; G, 21, 64; §vii, 31, 20 f.; §vii, 16, 125.

almost certainly to be equated with *márya*, an Indo-European word meaning 'young man or young warrior'.[1]

There is so far no evidence for the presence of *mariyanna* or of Indo-Aryan names among the Hurrians of the eighteenth-century or earlier texts,[2] a fact which might tempt us to suppose that during an early phase of their southward migration into Meso-potamia and North Syria the Hurrians were their own masters, and that only after they had become established in this area were they joined by a small, vigorous tribe of horse-breeders from far to the north or east, who, perhaps by reason of their superior armament, especially in the novel use of the light war-chariot,[3] were able by force of arms to impose their leadership upon the Hurrian-speaking majority.[4] That the ruling class in the fifteenth and fourteenth centuries was quite small is suggested by the com-parative paucity of Indo-Aryan names, by the small number of individuals bearing them, and by the fact that the same names appear in widely separated areas, a fact which has prompted the suggestion that the Aryan royal families intermarried;[5] this is in any event a probability since, as will be seen, marriage between ruling houses was a feature of diplomacy in the centuries to come and, as the seal set upon a pact of friendship between states, was considered virtually essential.[6]

In the age of confusion following the fall of the Amorite dynasties, the Hurrians moved in. A vacuum had been created: the Hittites had returned to their homeland,[7] where internal matters occupied their rulers and were to keep them from further enterprise in the direction of Syria for more than a century. They may even themselves have been hard pressed by the Hurrians to the east, for the text known as the Deeds of Khattushilish relates that, even earlier than 1600, Hurrians had taken advantage of the absence of the Hittite king to move into the eastern part of the Hittite realm.[8] The failure of the Assyrian record after the reign of Ishme-Dagan, early in the eighteenth century B.C., may in part be due to their inroads. At first the Hurrian chieftains may have obtained a foothold as vassals of the Amorite princes. A curious mythological text of the seventeenth century B.C., found at Boğazköy, and known as the Legend of the Cannibals,[9] which

---

[1] §1, 44, 309 ff.; §vii, 56, 19 f.; §1, 32, 46.   [2] §1, 67, 11.
[3] §vii, 72, 74 f., 86 ff., 186 ff.; §vii, 52, 273 ff.; G, 12, 85.
[4] G, 26, 160; §1, 32, 51.   [5] G, 21, 64.
[6] See below, pp. 487 ff.
[7] See above, ch. v, sect. vii; ch. vi, sect iv.
[8] *K.Bo.* 10, §5; §iv, 12, 178 f.; §vii, 28, 113 f.; §1, 28, 384 f.
[9] *K.Bo.* iii, 60B; *K.U.B.* 21, iii, 14 f.

probably contains an element of history,[1] relates how 'kings of the Khurri', with the (possibly Indo-European[2]) names Uwanta, Urutitta and Uwagazzana, together with a fourth whose name is lost, brought golden gifts to a king of Ilanṣura. A phase of the Hurrian struggle for mastery in North Syria may be reflected in another Hittite text of about the same period: 'The sons of the the Son of the Storm-God are fighting amongst themselves for the kingship.'[3]

When the curtain rises again after the dark period, in the sixteenth century, there are great changes: Hurrian names abound in North Syria, and in many cities Hurrians were in control.[4] The leading citizens at Alalakh were now *mariyanna*, and most of them bore Hurrian names and worshipped Hurrian gods.[5] Glosses on an Akkadian letter from the king of Tunip to the king of Egypt were written in Hurrian, showing this to have been the language officially spoken in Tunip in the fourteenth century,[6] and the people of Qatna appear to have used it too, at least for administrative purposes.[7] Even on the coast, at Ugarit, there was a considerable Hurrian element in the population during the fourteenth century and probably earlier; Hurrian texts were written in the local alphabetic script,[8] bilingual texts are found written in Akkadian and Hurrian, and there are glossaries compiled for the use of scribes.[9] The pharaohs who marched north into Palestine and Syria in the fifteenth century make it clear in their inscriptions that they encountered Hurrians in number, and among the prisoners taken in their campaigns it was the *mariyanna* with their chariot teams who were the most highly prized;[10] it was they who, as rulers in their cities, were persuaded or coerced into sending their children to Egypt for education. The presence at court of these alien aristocrats must have left a mark on Egyptian life and thought,[11] and conversely, Egyptian manners and tastes must have been brought back by these young princes to influence their own kingdoms when they succeeded to power.

Hurrian names abound among the rulers of vassal states mentioned in the Amarna letters.[12] The ruler of Jerusalem in the

---

[1] §ii, 22, 104 ff.   [2] §i, 3, 30 f.; §ii, 22, 109 ff.
[3] *K. Bo.* i, 11, rev. l. 7; §ii, 22, 114 ff.; §vii, 28, 114 ff.
[4] G, 21, 54; A, 17, 146 f.
[5] §i, 67, 11; G, 21, 66; G, 11, 69, 72 ff.; §i, 53, 40 ff.
[6] EA 59, ll. 8, 9, 11; G, 16, vol. i, 41; §vi, 25, 245.
[7] EA 52–5; G, 16, vol. ii, 1108.   [8] §i, 50, vol. iv, 51, 83 ff.
[9] §i, 50, vol. iv, 85 ff.; §viii, 79; A, 38, 230 ff.
[10] G, i, vol. ii, sect. 590; G, 14, 360 f.; cf. §i, 18, vol. i, 145*.
[11] See below, p. 481 f.   [12] G, 21, 54, 65.

fourteenth century was 'Abdi-Kheba,[1] who bears a Semitic name but was a devotee of the Hurrian goddess whose worship must have been well established in the Judaean hills. The very name used by the Egyptians for Syria-Palestine was the Land of Khor, or Khurri-Land,[2] a word which at first probably had a purely ethnic connotation but was later used geographically, Khor and Kush being synonymous in the Nineteenth Dynasty with Asia and Nubia or, more vaguely, North and South;[3] the appellation persisted long after the identity of the Hurrians had melted into anonymity among the heterogeneous peoples who made up the population of Iron Age Palestine, but may survive in the 'Horites' of the Old Testament,[4] formerly interpreted wrongly as 'troglodytes'.[5]

The Hurrians also moved eastwards and crossed the Tigris; Tepe Gawra and Tell Billa felt their influence[6] and they settled in force in the district around Kirkuk, the ancient Arrapkha.[7] This large and always important city has not been excavated, but a nearby mound, Yorgan Tepe, eight miles to the south-west, proved on excavation to have been a prosperous small town called in the Akkadian period Gasur;[8] some time after 1600 B.C., when the population became predominantly Hurrian, the newcomers changed the name of the town to Nuzi and, while adopting the language and many of the customs of the earlier inhabitants, introduced certain social and legal practices of their own, some of which are discussed later in this chapter,[9] and enriched the language with a large technical vocabulary of Hurrian words.[10] During the early part of the sixteenth century Nuzi and Arrapkha were already part of the kingdom of Mitanni, for Parattarna the king is mentioned in one of the tablets from Nuzi, in a context which shows that he was the overlord of the region.[11]

The Hurrian kingdom of Mitanni (early 'Maitani'[12]) appears to have had its focal point in the steppe land of northern Mesopotamia, the area which was known to the Assyrians as Khanigalbat.[13] Its capital, Washshuganni, was somewhere in the region of the headwaters of the Khabur river, perhaps at Tell Fakhāriyyah

[1] EA 280, 285–90.   [2] §I, 32, 33; G, 14, 275; G, 11, 50 f.; §I, 21, 228.
[3] §I, 18, vol. I, 180* f.
[4] G, 11, 69 n. 163; §III, 4, vol. III, 33; § I, 55, 26 f.; otherwise §III, 39, 44.
[5] G, 21, 54 n. 8; §I, 55, 26 ff.; §I, 21, 228; §I, 43, 156; §I, 10, 80 f.
[6] G, 21, 72; G, 11, 67; §I, 56, 61, 186.   [7] §VII, 61, vol. I, 42 ff.; §I, 20.
[8] §VII, 61, vol. I, xxxvi.   [9] See below, sect. VII.
[10] §VII, 61, vol. I, 528 ff.   [11] §I, 5, 17 n. 27.
[12] §I, 32, 35 ff.; §I, 59, 274; §I, 53, 43.
[13] §I, 59, 274; G, 29, 210, 247 ff.; §I, 32, 35 f.; §I, 10, 78 n. 13.

near Ras el-'Ain, a very large mound which appears to cover an important city of the mid second millennium B.C.;[1] preliminary investigations have not, however, established the identity of this site with the Mitannian capital. King Saustatar, the first Mitannian king to leave records, and his successors refer to their kingdom in Akkadian as 'the land Mitanni'[2] or as 'Khanigalbat',[3] and in Hurrian documents, to 'the Hurrian land' (*Ḫurruḫe*).[4] Parattarna is referred to by his vassal in Alalakh as 'King of the warriors of the Khurri-Land',[5] an indication that he presided over a confederacy of feudal princes; but, in its narrower sense, the Khurri-Land appears to denote the northern region, the Hurrian homeland, which later became separated from the rest of Mitanni.[6] The term Mitanni must in fact be regarded first and foremost as a political term, denoting the state or kingdom ruled over by the paramount king of the Hurrian confederacy;[7] its boundaries were always changing as one kingdom or another succumbed to Mitannian rule or was drawn into alliance or vassaldom elsewhere. Besides Khanigalbat, which is more particularly definable as the area around Nisibis, an early centre of Hurrian activity,[8] Ashtata, the land on the Euphrates junction below Carchemish,[9] and Alshe or Alzia, the region of the upper Tigris north of the Murad Çay,[10] were at one time or another within the confines of the kingdom of Mitanni. It is probable that the Hurrian rulers of kingdoms outside the Mitannian confederacy may at times have tended to feel an affinity with their kin in Mitanni, and that the stubborn opposition which Tuthmosis III encountered during his bid to subjugate Palestine and Syria can be explained in part by the encouragement and even active support given to cities like Qadesh and Tunip by the king of Mitanni.

Not all the city states were ruled by Hurrians, and the names encountered in documents of the fifteenth century and later show that the basic population of Syria and Palestine was of the older Semitic stock.[11] In Alalakh, the Khanaeans, whom we have met earlier as nomads at the time of the Mari letters,[12] are mentioned

---

[1] §VII, 42; §I, 31, 26 f.; G, 8, vol. III, 31 f.   [2] §I, 32, 32 ff.; G, 11, 70 n. 167.
[3] EA 20, l. 17, 29, ll. 48 ff.; G, 11, 72 n. 184.
[4] §I, 32, 32; EA 24, *passim*.   [5] §I, 54, 17, 25 f.
[6] G, 11, 79 f.; G, 12, 101; §I, 25, 167; G, 13, 67 f. argues that the two kingdoms coexisted from the beginning.
[7] G, 26, 159 n. 8; §I, 18, vol. I, 178*; §I, 32, 34 ff.   [8] G, 28, 35.
[9] G, 8, vol. I, 304 f.; §I, 23, 117 and n. 40; G, 28, 39.
[10] G, 8, vol. I, 88 ff.; G, 28, 35; §I, 32, 75.
[11] *C.A.H.* I³, pt. 2, pp. 320 f.; §III, 4, vol. III, 25 ff.; G, 10, 41.
[12] See above, ch. I, sect. v; §I, 33, 44 ff., 249 ff.; G, 10, 46 f.

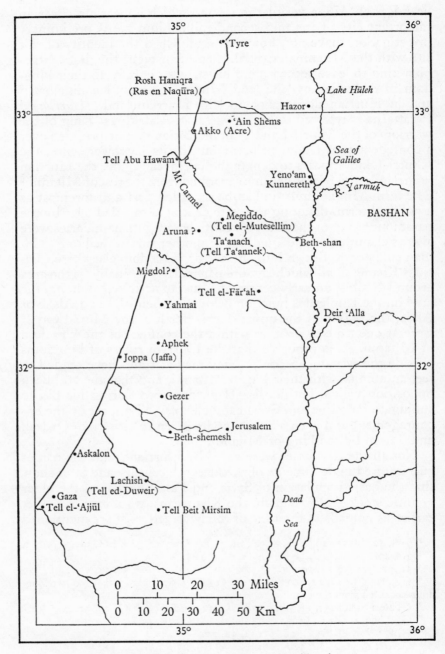

Map 4. Palestine in the mid-second millennium.

as forming a numerically large middle class including tradesmen, herdsmen and grooms.[1] In some of the coastal cities, in particular Ugarit, there was a further admixture of foreigners from the Aegean, small minority groups of Cypriots, Rhodians and Cretans living abroad for commercial reasons.[2] In the countryside and on the desert steppe beyond, and between the cultivated zones around cities, a large semi-nomadic population roamed at will, threatening the security of those who travelled on the highways, and sometimes raiding towns and villages, stripping the vines, and carrying off livestock.[3] Those of whom we hear most during the period of the Alalakh tablets and the Amarna letters were the Sutu[4] and the *Ḥapiru* ('Apiru),[5] both of whom had troubled the world of the Mari letters. These tribes were large and powerful; punitive expeditions had to be mounted against them from time to time[6] and attempts were made to settle them,[7] but the problem of the bedawin remained insoluble and is not today entirely solved. The depredations of the *Ḥapiru* were a source of constant complaint from Egypt's vassals during the fourteenth century in Palestine.[8]

No single word is used in the ancient texts to define Syria-Palestine as a political or geographical entity; the concept is a more modern one. The nearest approach to an all-embracing term is the Egyptian name Retenu, or Lōtān, used in the New Kingdom, as in the Middle Kingdom, as a general designation for territories north of Egypt;[9] sometimes the particular reference is to Upper Retenu, or rather perhaps 'the highlands of Retenu,' for the term is normally used of the hillier parts of the country.[10] The coastal plain, later called Phoenicia by the Greeks, was Djahy,[11] a word not used before the Eighteenth Dynasty and not always clearly distinguished from Retenu. 'The Lands of the Fenkhu', the old term for the Lebanese coast, was still occasionally revived in Egyptian texts.[12] Canaan (*Kinaḥni*) a name which occurs frequently in the Amarna letters, appears to denote the

[1] §I, 67, 11; §I, 39, 633 f.

[2] §I, 50, vol. I, 53 ff., vol. III, 227 ff.; *C.A.H.* II³, pt. 2, ch. XVII, sect. IV.

[3] §I, 33, 240 ff.; §I, 39, 634.   [4] G, 29, 221 ff.; §I, 5, 16 n. 18; A, 4, 168 f.

[5] §VII, 10, 215; §VII, 8, 129, 293; §VII, 6; §VII, 27; § V, 8, 64, ff. See *C.A.H.* II³, pt. 2, ch. XX sect. IV on the 'Apiru.   [6] §I, 34, 83 ff., 252 ff.; §I, 39.

[7] §I, 54, 20 f.; §III, 30, vol. III, 189 = *RS*, II, 790; §VI, 27, 113 f.

[8] *C.A.H.* II³, pt. 2, ch. XX, sect. III.

[9] §I, 18, vol. I, 142*; §III, 34, 201; G, 14, 272 ff.; otherwise *C.A.H.* I³, pt. 2, ch. XXI, sect. III; A, 2, 60.   [10] G, 14, 273.

[11] §I, 18, vol. I, 145*; G, 14, 274 f.; §I, 43, 176 ff.

[12] *E.g.* G, 27, 1560, l. 4; G, 14, 277 f.; G, 20, vol. II (1) 97 n. 1.

coast of Palestine from Gaza to somewhere near Ras en-Nāqūra, the modern frontier between Israel and Lebanon, though the term could be extended to include the coastal plain further north.[1] The word Canaan[2] appears to have neither an ethnic nor a political connotation, except in so far as it denotes an administrative area under Egyptian control in the fourteenth century,[3] but it is used occasionally in the Amarna letters as a more general term for the predominantly Semitic population of Syria-Palestine in general,[4] the sense in which the word is used in the Old Testament,[5] and Amenophis II classified the prisoners taken in Palestine and Syria as *mariyanna* and Canaanites.[6] We may therefore be justified in employing the latter as a convenient general term for the population of Syria-Palestine during the second millennium B.C., in particular for the inhabitants of the coastal plain, later called Phoenicia.

During the period preceding the sixteenth century, a number of powerful walled cities with formidable defences were built in Syria and Palestine;[7] each formed the centre or nucleus of a city state with its satellite villages and its surrounding acres of arable land and pasture.[8] Confined within natural boundaries, in enclaves of fertile territory bounded by sea and mountain and desert, these urban communities maintained their existence by trade and warfare against their neighbours. Some were ancient cities with a long tradition; others are not mentioned in the records of the third millennium and may have been of more recent foundation. A number of them commanded wider allegiance; their territories were loose-knit confederacies, and to their kings the rulers of the towns that were their vassals paid tribute and labour-service. One of these was Ugarit,[9] the modern Ras Shamra, on the Lebanese coast north of Latakia. A natural harbour and a commanding position, and above all the nearness of Cyprus, gave this city a great commercial advantage, and excavation of the city with its palaces and temples and prosperous merchant houses has shown its importance at this time, though the peak of Ugarit's prosperity lasted through the fourteenth and thirteenth centuries, the period covered by the archives found in the palace.[10] Its neighbour to

---

[1] §I, 38, 11 f.; G, 14, 279 f.; §III, 39, 15 f.; §IV, 1, vol. I, 318 f.

[2] §VIII, 6, 348; §I, 38; §VII, 25, 15 f.; G, 20, vol. II(1), 88 f.; §I, 27, 230.

[3] G, 14, 188 f., 258 ff., 279 ff. See below, pp. 471 f.

[4] E.g. EA 9, l. 19; 30, l. 1; 151, l. 50 ff.; §I, 43, 205 ff.   [5] §I, 21, 217 ff.

[6] G, 27, 1305; §III, 28, 38; *C.A.H.* II³, pt. 2, ch. xx, sect. III.

[7] §V, 2, 86; §VIII, 3, 403 ff.; §VII, 72, 90 ff.; §I, 15, 20 ff.; §VII, 66, 118 f.; A, 34, 91 ff.; A, 41.   [8] A, 9, 34 ff.   [9] A, 28, vol. II, 326 ff.; §I, 50.

[10] *C.A.H.* II³, pt. 2, ch. XVII, sect. IV; ch. XXI (*a*).

the north, in the fourteenth century if not before, was the small kingdom of Danuna,[1] perhaps the modern Hatay around the Gulf of Alexandretta.[2]

Mukish, with its capital Alalakh, lay to the north-east and bordered on Unqi, or Umqi, the 'Amūq plain north of the Orontes.[3] The name is not known from earlier records, for Alalakh in the eighteenth century belonged to Yamkhad, the kingdom of Aleppo.[4] In the fifteenth century, Mukish extended as far as the sea-coast on the west, to the north of Ugarit,[5] and bordered on the kingdom of Ama'u, the location of which will be discussed later.[6] The geographical position of Neya, the other component state of Idrimi's kingdom, has long been a matter of controversy;[7] rather than the salty lake of Jabbūl,[8] or the banks of the Euphrates,[9] a location in the area east of the Orontes around Apamea (Qala'at el-Madhīq)[10] is here preferred. This was elephant country; herds of the great beasts (not so big perhaps as the Indian elephant of today, but formidable enough, judging by tusks found in the palace of Alalakh[11]) roamed the marshy valley of the Ghāb, where successive Egyptian kings, Nimrods of the chase, were to hunt them for sport and for their prized ivory.[12]

The site of Tunip, whose kingdom lay inland, south of Mukish,[13] has not been identified; it was not very far from Nukhashshe and Amurru,[14] and west of the River Orontes. This city withstood repeated efforts of the Egyptians to take it; and, like Qadesh, was a focal point in the defence of Syria against the invader from the south. Its territory extended along the coast to include Ullaza.[15] Amurru lay to the south, also on the narrow coastal plain and in the mountains behind. Originally a rather indeterminate name for the west,[16] it was applied, in the fourteenth century, and perhaps earlier, more particularly to a kingdom situated to the north of Byblos.[17] The Amarna letters indicate that it was subject neither to Neya nor to Tunip but bordered on both, and it may have had

---

[1] EA 151, l. 52; §vi, 1, 190 f.; §i, 18, vol. i, 125* f.; §ix, 2, 108 ff.

[2] §i, 22, 50. [3] §i, 69, 17 ff.

[4] §i, 67, 2 ff. [5] §i, 27, 230.

[6] See below, p. 435. [7] §i, 18, vol. i, 158* ff.; G, 14, 307.

[8] §i, 54, 57; §iii, 6, 223. [9] §iii, 45, 218 ff.; §viii, 9, 5.

[10] §i, 18, vol. i, 158* ff.; §i, 5, 15 n. 12; §i, 27, 230; §iii, 45, 222 n. 148.

[11] §i, 68, 102, pl. xvi; §vii, 75, 277; §i, 5, 15.

[12] G, 14, 307; §i, 54, 48 ff.; see below, pp. 458, 482.

[13] G, 14, 142, 304 ff.; G, 6, 108 ff.; G, 28, 32 n. 91; A, 28, vol. ii, 75 ff.

[14] EA 161; §i, 18, vol. i, 179*; §iii, 6, 223; G, 16, 1123 ff. See below, p. 430 n. 3.

[15] §v, 23, 4. [16] C.A.H. i³, pt. 2, ch. xvii, sect. i.

[17] G, 8, vol. i, 99 ff.; G, 10, 41 f.; G, 14, 258, 293 f.; §ii, 26, 92 f.; §iv, 1, 236 f.; A, 28, vol. ii, 178 ff.

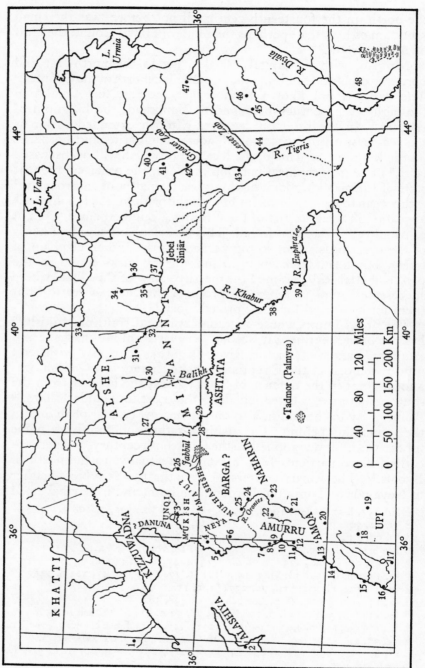

Map 5. The Lebanon, Syria, Mesopotamia and Assyria in the mid-second millennium.

Numerical key		Alphabetical key	
1	Ura	Alalakh (Açana)	3
2	Enkomi	Ardata	12
3	Alalakh (Açana)	Arrapkha (Kirkuk)	46
4	Zalkhi	Arwada	7
5	Ugarit (Ras Shamra)	Ashur	43
6	Siyannu	Ba'albek	20
7	Arwada	Beruta	14
8	Ṣumura	Chagar Bazar	35
9	Ullaza	Dimashq (Damascus)	19
10	Irqata	Diyārbakr	33
11	Tripoli	Ekallate	44
12	Ardata	Emar ?	28
13	Gubla (Byblos)	Enkomi	2
14	Beruta	Eshnunna	48
15	Sidon	Gubla (Byblos)	13
16	Ṣur (Tyre)	Hamath (Hama)	24
17	Hazor	Harrān	30
18	Kumidu	Hazor	17
19	Dimashq (Damascus)	Irqata	10
20	Ba'albek	Kargamish (Carchemish)	27
21	Qadesh (Kinza)	Khalba (Aleppo)	26
22	? Tunip	Kumidu	18
23	Qatna	Mari	39
24	Hamath (Hama)	Meskineh	29
25	Zinzar	Nineveh	42
26	Khalba (Aleppo)	Nisibis	36
27	Kargamish (Carchemish)	Nuzi	45
28	Emar ?	Qadesh (Kinza)	21
29	Meskineh	Qatna	23
30	Harrān	Shusharra	47
31	? Washshuganni	Sidon	15
32	Tell Halaf	Siyannu	6
33	Diyārbakr	Ṣumura	8
34	Urkish ?	Ṣur (Tyre)	16
35	Chagar Bazar	Tell Billa	40
36	Nisibis	Tell Brak	37
37	Tell Brak	Tell Halaf	32
38	Tirqa	Tepe Gawra	41
39	Mari	Tirqa	38
40	Tell Billa	Tripoli	11
41	Tepe Gawra	? Tunip	22
42	Nineveh	Ugarit (Ras Shamra)	5
43	Ashur	Ullaza	9
44	Ekallate	Ura	1
45	Nuzi	Urkish ?	34
46	Arrapkha (Kirkuk)	? Washshuganni	31
47	Shusharra	Zalkhi	4
48	Eshnunna	Zinzar	25

a common frontier with Ugarit at the time of her greatest expansion.[1] Simyra and Irqata were its ports; its capital is unknown. Nukhashshe, whose territory bordered on Neya and Qatna, is almost certainly the later La'ash which, with Hamath, made up the kingdom of king ZKR in the eighth century B.C.[2] There was a city Nukhashshe, but its site has not been found. The kingdom of Barga, or Parga, lay between Hamath and Aleppo[3] and bordered on Nukhashshe;[4] in a fragment of a letter from the Amarna files it is mentioned with Qatna.[5] Qatna itself, the modern El-Mishrifeh north of Homs,[6] was an imposing city of great size, whose fortifications withstood Egyptian attack until Tuthmosis III's thirty-third year. Its commercial importance during the Mari period has been discussed elsewhere;[7] its rock-cut silos were able to store large quantities of grain in time of siege.[8] Tablets found on the site, dating perhaps to the sixteenth century, preserve the names of several rulers of Qatna, one of whom, Adad-nirari, enjoyed a long reign of forty-five years.[9] Zinzar and Tunanab were important city states in the neighbourhood, the former probably to be identified with Qala'at Seijar on the Orontes.[10] Although Hamath was a flourishing town in the eighteenth century[11] and again in the thirteenth,[12] it is not mentioned by name in the period between, either in the lists and annals of the Egyptian kings or in the Amarna letters; the archaeological record confronts us with the puzzling fact that during the fifteenth and fourteenth centuries, when it might have been expected to play an important political role, the site appears to have been virtually unoccupied.[13]

Qadesh, also called Qizza and Kinza,[14] the most southerly of the great Syrian city states, lay athwart the north–south highway commanding the Biqā', the valley of the Litani river between Lebanon and Anti-Lebanon.[15] Excavations at Tell Nebi Mend, the site of the city, revealed the formidable size of its fortifications.[16] At the beginning of the sole reign of Tuthmosis III, its kingdom

---

[1] *C.A.H.* II[3], pt. 2, ch. xxi, sect. iv.

[2] §1, 37, 403 ff.; G, 14, 291 ff.; §1, 18, vol. i, 168* ff.; A, 5, 386 n. 1.

[3] G, 6, 243; G, 24, 278; A, 15, 5.

[4] G, 14, 302; G, 8, vol. i, 401; *K.Bo.* iii, 3.   [5] EA 57, l. 3.

[6] §1, 13, 277 ff.; G, 6, 108 ff.; §1, 61, 73 ff.; G, 14, 307 ff.; A, 28, vol. ii, 96 ff.

[7] See above, ch. i, sect. iii.   [8] §1, 12, 176 ff.   [9] §1, 65, 94 f.; A, 16, 243 ff.

[10] G, 6, 109 f.; G, 14, 308 f.   [11] §1, 61, 93.   [12] G, 14, 308.

[13] §1, 61, 93; §1, 49, 112 ff. disagrees. Astour (in A, 5, 394 f.) suggests that at this period Hamath was called Tunip; this however is in disregard of the archaeological evidence.   [14] G, 16, vol. ii, 1118 ff.

[15] §1, 18, vol. i, 137* ff., no. 252; G, 14, 309 ff.; §1, 43, 213 ff.; A, 28, vol. ii, 139 ff.   [16] §1, 46, 15.

reached south to Galilee and the plain of Esdraelon, and the resistance of the city to the Egyptian advance proved so formidable that it, too, was not captured till the eighth campaign.[1] This kingdom at its greatest extent included Amqi, the region of the southern Biqā',[2] situated to the south of Qadesh and containing the town of Khashabu, perhaps south-west of Ba'albek.[3] Over the mountains to the east at a meeting-place of trade routes lay Upi or Ube, the oasis-kingdom in which Damascus was situated.[4] This city had a predominantly Hurrian population in the second millennium B.C.;[5] it is mentioned both in the Mari letters[6] and in the 'Execration Texts' from Egypt.[7]

The caprice of discovery plays a large part in writing the history of man's early past. The turn of a spade, the chance finding of a broken crock or a torn fragment of papyrus may add another chapter to knowledge. The hazards which beset the historian are nowhere better illustrated than in the record of the Egyptian conquest of Asia in the Eighteenth Dynasty. Some phases of this achievement are known to us in detail, year by year and even day by day, by the chance survival of the official record, whereas the stirring story of the early exploits of the dynasty, in the sixteenth century when the foundations of the Egyptian empire were laid, can only be guessed at from scraps of evidence—the mere crumbs of history.

Amosis I must have begun the conquest of Palestine and Syria early in his reign, perhaps about 1565 B.C.; his capture of Sharuhen has been related in another chapter.[8] His subsequent campaign in Djahy took the Egyptian army up the coast of Phoenicia into *Fnḫw* territory[9] but we are given no indication of the whereabouts or extent of the operation. Of the campaigns of Amenophis I, who must surely have prepared the way in Syria for the spectacular achievement of his son, no record remains;[10] if he did not campaign in the north, the coronation decree, dated to his second year, in which Tuthmosis claims the Euphrates as his boundary,[11] must have been erected, not in his second year, but later in his reign. The statement might indeed be dismissed as a

---

[1] See below, p. 457. [2] §IV, 1, 153 ff.; G, 14, 276.
[3] §IV, 7, 155 n. 61(*a*); G, 14, 128, 158.
[4] §I, 62, 6; G, 14, 276; §I, 2, 35 ff.; §VII, 66, 110.
[5] §I, 55, 33 n. 70. [6] §I, 62, 7. [7] §I, 2, 33 n. 6.
[8] See above, ch. VIII, sect. II. The absolute dating of reigns and events in the early part of the dynasty may have to be reduced by a few years in view of recent chronological studies (A, 23, 15 ff.; A, 22, 14 ff.; A, 26, 78 ff.).
[9] G, 27, 25, l. 12; *ibid.* 35, l. 17. [10] See above, ch. VIII, sect. IV.
[11] G, 27, 85, l. 14; G, 1, vol. II, pp. 69 ff.

formal declaration of the limits of Egypt's sphere of interest or as a definition of the boundaries of the civilized world at the time, seen from an Egyptian viewpoint,[1] were it not for the fact that Tuthmosis III, some sixty years later, claimed to have erected his frontier stela on the banks of the Euphrates next to the one which his grandfather, Tuthmosis I, had set up.[2] If the date on the Tumbos stela is to be taken seriously, then it must be supposed that this remarkable achievement was accomplished at the very beginning of his reign, and that his march through enemy territory met with very little resistance, perhaps because the way had already been prepared by his predecessor.[3] No official record survives, but the autobiographical inscriptions of two army officers from El-Kāb in Upper Egypt recount their own exploits while in the king's following. One of these, by name Ahmose, traversed Retenu with the king and reached the land Naharin, which in texts of the subsequent period denotes Mitannian territory,[4] and there fought in a battle in which Tuthmosis took prisoners 'without number';[5] his colleague and namesake, who bore the sobriquet Pennekheb,[6] also fought in Naharin and claimed twenty-one foes slain, enumerating their severed hands, by the grisly accountancy of the age.[7] Each of the two makes especial mention of a chariot and horse captured,[8] a rare prize since chariots were not yet in common use in the Egyptian army. In the Tumbos stela, the Euphrates is described as 'that Topsy Turvy River upon which one travels downstream when putting up sail'[9] (in contrast with the Nile, on which the prevailing wind is from the north, and sail is therefore hoisted when travelling upstream).[10] The campaign may have taken the king to the banks of the river somewhere south of Carchemish; his stela was carved 'in the mountain',[11] perhaps the cliffs near Eski Meskineh. On the return journey through Syria, he hunted elephant in Neya, setting the trend for his descendants, the sporting pharaohs of the mid Eighteenth Dynasty.[12]

Of the route taken by Tuthmosis I on his march to the Euphrates we are wholly in the dark; nor do we know who the opponent

---

[1] Cf. the definition of the boundaries of Egypt as 'the horns of the earth and the marshes of Qebeḥ' (G, 27, 270, ll. 8 f.); the former must be Nubia, the latter perhaps equivalent to 'the marshes of Satet', the land of the Sutu (§1, 54, 44; G, 29, 221 ff.; G, 14, 268; §1, 18, vol. 1, 177*).   [2] G, 27, 697, l. 5.   [3] G, 14, 116.
[4] G, 16, 1040, 1065; §1, 18, vol. 1, 171 ff.; §vi, 25, vol. 11, 825. Cf. G, 21, 131 ff. See above ch. viii, sect. 11. The name Mitanni occurs in an Egyptian text of about this period (§1, 9).   [5] G, 27, 9, l. 14.   [6] See above, ch. viii, sect. 11.
[7] G, 27, 36, ll. 9 ff.   [8] G, 24, 234; G, 27, 9, l. 17—10, l. 1; ibid. 36, l. 11.
[9] G, 27, 85, l. 14; G, 1, vol. 11, 31, n. d; §1, 18, vol. 1, 160* f.
[10] §1, 54, 45 f.   [11] G, 27, 697, l. 5.   [12] Ibid. 103 f.; see above, ch. ix, sect. v.

may have been who barred his way. Perhaps the dynasty of rulers who later called themselves Kings of Mitanni and Kings of the Khurri-warriors were already established at Washshuganni, the city which was their capital in the fifteenth and fourteenth centuries. The first ruler of Mitanni whose name has survived is Kirta, of whom we know nothing but that he was the father of King Shuttarna; both names occur on a seal of Saustatar naming his dynastic forebears, perhaps the founders of the line.[1] Was it perhaps Shuttarna I who, after the Egyptian army had retired from its spectacular raid, extended his rule westwards into North Syria? The next king of Mitanni, Parattarna, is known from documents found at Açana, the ancient Alalakh, over which he maintained control for at least part of his reign;[2] he also controlled Kizzuwadna, the eastern part of Cilicia,[3] as will be shown.

The Alalakh tablets were written in a western dialect of Akkadian,[4] and their contents are varied: some are letters, one or two are treaties, others are lists, records of legal proceedings, a few lexicographical texts and literary tablets; many of them mention the king or concern him. The tablets are dated in the reigns of three kings of Mukish and Alalakh, and it was the first of these, Idrimi, who was a vassal of King Parattarna of Mitanni.[5] The story of his adventurous career is told in a remarkable inscription[6] carved over much of the surface of a white stone statue of the ruler himself, found in the ruins of the final destruction of Alalakh, when it was hurled from its pedestal and smashed. Clearly it was an heirloom; for some reason it had been held in especial honour, for not only had it been preserved and set up in successive rebuildings of the temple throughout three centuries, but, in the final wreck, some devoted hands must have buried it to preserve it from further desecration.[7] The Akkadian inscription, again in a local dialect,[8] tells the story, in the first person, of Idrimi's accession and subsequent adventures till he was confirmed in the throne of Alalakh. His father, it seems, had been king of Aleppo, Ilim-ilimma by name; after his death— perhaps in a rebellion—Idrimi and his brothers were forced to flee eastwards to Emar, a town on the Euphrates bend east of Aleppo, perhaps near the modern Meskineh,[9] where their mother's

[1] §1, 67, 7, 39, no. 13, pl. 7, no. 14, pl. 8; G, 13, 67; §v, 8, 103. See Plate 102 (b).
[2] §1, 67, 5, 31 f. He is called 'King of the warriors of Khurri-land'.
[3] G, 13, 71 f.; §1, 23, 34 ff.; see below, ch. xv, sect. 1.
[4] §1, 67, 18 f.   [5] Ibid.   [6] §1, 54; §1, 5, 11 ff.
[7] §viii, 1, 122 f.; §1, 54, 2; §1, 68, 393.   [8] §1, 54, 12.
[9] §iii, 23, 26; §iii, 25, 77, 81; otherwise §1, 54, 73 f. and map.

family lived. Finding his brothers unwilling to fight for their
inheritance, he again fled, this time alone but for his groom, and
crossed the desert westwards, sleeping in encampments of the
Sutu bedawin in his covered wagon. Reaching Canaan, the
coastal plain of Phoenicia, he took refuge in Ammia, perhaps in
the Tripoli region,[1] where he encountered and was recognized
by compatriots, and forced to flee once more. For seven years
he lived in exile with the *Ḥapiru*. When at last the omens
appeared favourable for a return, he gathered troops, built ships
and sailed northwards, landing in Mukish, beyond Mount Casius,
perhaps at a spot a little to the north of the mouth of the River
Orontes;[2] Neya, Mukish, Ama'u[3] and Alalakh immediately accepted him as their king, and he was reconciled with his brothers.
He then had to negotiate for a treaty with Parattarna, whereby he
was confirmed in the kingship and his vassals paid homage. One
of the Alalakh tablets, an agreement concluded with Pillia, probably the king of Kizzuwadna,[4] concerning the obligation to return
runaway slaves and the payment of rewards to their captors, implies that now that both countries were under the same aegis, as
vassals of Parattarna, their former enmity must change to friendship. A fragmentary text of a treaty between Pillia of Kizzuwadna
and Zidantash the Hittite king,[5] however, suggests that at the
time when it was made—perhaps earlier than the treaty with
Alalakh—Kizzuwadna was independent of Mitannian control.

The rest of the inscription recounts, more briefly, Idrimi's subsequent exploits in war and peace. An expedition northwards
against the Hittites is briefly described, in the course of which
seven Hittite towns, all perhaps Cilician ports, were captured.[6]
Since there was apparently no retaliation on the part of the Hittite
king, it must be supposed that the raid took place at a time when
the Hittite monarchy was pre-occupied with internal affairs and
ineffective.[7] The booty was divided between the troops, and the
king and his friends took their portion. Idrimi then returned in
triumph to Mukish, and entered Alalakh, which he embellished
with the spoils of war as befitted a successful ruler; he appears
to have been inspired by what he had seen in Uluzi, the local
capital of the Hittites which had fallen into his hands, for he says
'I made my throne exactly like the thrones of the kings (of the

---

[1] G, 6, 117 n. 1; §1, 54, 73.   [2] §1, 5, 17 n. 24; §1, 54, 75.
[3] See below, p. 435.   [4] §1, 67, 5, 31 f., no. 3.
[5] §1, 45, 129 ff.; G, 13, 72 f. = *K.U.B.* xxxvi, 108.
[6] §1, 54, 18 f., ll. 64 ff., 76 ff.; otherwise §iv, 13, 28.
[7] See below, ch. xv, sect. 1.

land Khatti)',[1] a statement verified by the discovery of the basalt throne-base of the king's statue, which was flanked by lions in the Hittite manner.[2] The fortresses which he built to guard his kingdom, on the other hand, were built in the traditional local style.[3]

Acts of piety and wise administrative measures occupied Idrimi, it would seem, for the rest of his reign. In gratitude no doubt for their kindness to him when he was an exile and a fugitive, he took particular care for the welfare of the Sutu in his realm, and 'those who had no settled abode, I made to abide in one'.[4] It may have been for these achievements that Idrimi was remembered as one of the founders of the city's prosperity. Ama'u, which may perhaps be located in the Jebel Anṣāriyyah, rather than north[5] or east[6] of Alalakh, is later mentioned as a source of timber.[7] One of the tablets bearing the impression of his seal contains a list[8] of large amounts of silver from the land Mukish, and also from Zalkhi (a town in the Jebel Aqra' not far from Ugarit)[9] and Zela'e, perhaps received as tribute. Yet Idrimi was not able to recover all his father's kingdom; Aleppo probably passed into the control of Parrattarna.

Idrimi reigned for thirty years, and then handed over the management of his affairs to his son Adad-nirari, as he himself relates.[10] Whether this means that he abdicated in favour of his son, a practice seldom encountered in the ancient Near East,[11] or whether it should rather be understood that the responsibility for pious upkeep of mortuary service for the family ancestors was entrusted to Adad-nirari, it is difficult to say; the latter's name does not appear among the texts from Alalakh, and it was apparently Niqmepa who succeeded Idrimi.[12] In pursuance of the custom whereby a king used the seal of his predecessor, both to ensure the continuity of royal authority and to emphasize the legitimacy of his claim to the throne,[13] Niqmepa used the seal of Idrimi, surcharged with his own name;[14] the probability is then

---

[1] §I, 54, 20 f., l. 81.
[2] Ibid. 6 f. and fig. 2. See Plate 98 (a).　　[3] §I, 54, 20 f., l. 87.
[4] Ibid. ll. 84–6.　　　　　　　　　　　　[5] G, 14, 280.
[6] §I, 54, 57 and map; §I, 5, 15, 16 n. 13; §I, 27, 230; A, 5, 384 f.
[7] G, 27, 1393, l. 9; G, 14, 280.　　　[8] §I, 67, 104, no. 395, pl. 38.
[9] G, 14, 171 n. 113; §I, 54, 53.　　　[10] §I, 54, 20 f., l. 91.
[11] Ibid. 87; §I, 27, 229.　　　　　　　[12] §I, 67, 7.
[13] §I, 53, 43.
[14] §I, 67, 40, no. 17; §I, 5, 19; §II, 54, 58 ff. places the King Idrimi of the statue in the late fifteenth or early fourteenth century B.C. and makes him the grandson of Niqmepa. See also §III, 6, 239; C.A.H. I³, pt. I, ch. VI, sect. II.

that he was Idrimi's son and successor; perhaps Adad-nirari was an elder son who died before his father.

Meanwhile, Parattarna had died and Saustatar, king of Mitanni, son of Parsatatar, ruled in his stead.[1] He, too, was overlord of the rulers of Mukish; his seal appears on legal documents from Alalakh dealing with lawsuits in which he had acted as adjudicator.[2] Neya may also have been a vassal;[3] a treaty between Niqmepa of Alalakh and Ir-Adad, king of Tunip, provides for the extradition of fugitives from one kingdom to the other,[4] so that the territories of the two kings must have been contiguous. Saustatar must also have concluded a treaty with Shunashshura of Kizzuwadna, perhaps Pillia's successor:[5] continued Mitannian control over this kingdom is proved by the fact that he acted as arbiter in a boundary dispute between Shunashshura and Niqmepa.[6] A letter from Saustatar found at Nuzi, near Kirkuk, and sealed with his seal,[7] conveyed peremptory orders about the assignment of territories and adjustment of boundaries in the district around Kirkuk, clear proof that he held undisputed sway east of the Tigris. The sum of this evidence, slight though it is, indicates that under Saustatar, the Mitannian empire reached its greatest extent and included territory from the Taurus to the Zagros, from the Amanus to the Biqā'. The kings who were his vassals were held on a loose rein; they could, it would seem, enter into treaty relations with their neighbours, and even, if we understand aright, make war on their own behalf, as Idrimi did against the Hittites; they could collect tribute from the smaller states that made up their own confederacies. Yet the documents from Alalakh leave no doubt as to the relationship of a vassal to his lord: Idrimi is not the legitimate king of his realm until Parattarna has confirmed his appointment by a treaty ratified by solemn oath and sacrifice,[8] and Niqmepa, in a case involving a dispute with a man who claimed to be a citizen not of Alalakh but of Khanigalbat (Mitanni) and therefore out of his jurisdiction, was obliged to appeal to the Great King, Saustatar himself, to decide the case.[9]

---

[1] §vii, 61, pl. 118; §i, 32, 58 f. discusses the possible identification of Parattarna with Parsatatar.

[2] E.g. §i, 53, 39, no. 13, pl. 7, and no. 14, pl. 8; G, 28, 40.

[3] §i, 67, 6 n. 10.　　　　　　　　　[4] §i, 67, 7, and 26 ff., no. 2.

[5] G, 13, 72.　　　　　　　　　　　[6] §i, 67, 39, no. 14, pl. 8.

[7] §i, 59; §viii, 51, pl. 1.　　　　　[8] §i, 54, 17 f., ll. 45–58 and p. 76.

[9] §i, 67, 39, no. 13, pl. 7; §i, 53, 41 ff., pl. 18, 4 and 6.

II. THE KASSITES AND THEIR NEIGHBOURS

In a previous chapter of this history,[1] the arrival in Mesopotamia of an alien people, the Kassites, is traced from the reign of the first king, Gandash, to that of Agum II, who occupies the ninth place in the king-list. Their homeland is presumed to have lain to the north-east of Babylonia, somewhere in the Zagros mountains, perhaps in the Pusht-i-Kuh, where a thousand years later a people called Kashshu were still living, harried from time to time by the Assyrians and a source of fighting men for the Babylonians of the late empire.[2] The Greeks knew the descendants of these people as Κοσσαῖοι,[3] and they were therefore at one time known among scholars as Kossaeans. The Achaemenid kings of Persia, forced to pass through their territory on the annual migrations of the court between Susa and Ecbatana, were constrained to buy their safe passage by making presents to their chieftains by way of blackmail.[4] Little is known of their origins and less of their early history. Unlike their neighbours, the Lullubu and the Guti, they receive no mention in the records of the third millennium B.C., and they do not appear in the Mari correspondence. It is to be presumed that they were newcomers at the time when Samsuiluna of Babylon encountered a Kassite army and presumably defeated it, since the event was regarded as of sufficient importance to date the year.[5] It was not, however, until the reign of the ninth Kassite king of the dynasty of Gandash, Agum II (*kakrime*), that a Kassite king is found ruling in Babylon itself.[6] His reinstallation of the gods of Babylon in their ancient shrine was an act of great significance: nobody could legitimately claim to be king in Babylonia without first 'grasping the hand of Marduk'; by doing so, King Agum hoped to command the loyalty of his newly conquered subjects and the support of the priesthood.[7]

The Kassites did not commit their language to writing, and it is known to us only from a few dozen words and a few hundred names.[8] Among the tablets from Nippur, for instance, are some which contain lists of horses, written in Akkadian but containing certain technical terms for parts of chariots, and for various colours and types of horses, which are not Akkadian but Kassite.[9] Some

[1] See above, ch. v, sect. vii.
[2] §II, 9, 91 ff.; *C.A.H.* III, 14 f. K. Jaritz (§II, 24, 78 ff., and map, p. 19) derives them from south-east Anatolia. See also *XVᵉ Rencontre assyriol.* (ed. J. R. Kupper, 1967), 123 ff.   [3] §II, 48, 1499 f.
[4] *Ibid.* 1500.   [5] G, 28, 24; §II, 33, 245.
[6] §II, 2, 111 ff.; §II, 25, 207.   [7] §II, 33, 256 ff.; §II, 25, 208.
[8] §II, 23, 860 ff.; §I, 20, 195 f.   [9] §II, 2, 11 ff. and 127 ff.; §II, 24, 65 f.

of the horses have Kassite names, often resembling personal names in that they are compounded with the name of a deity, usually Minizir, who appears to have been the goddess who exercised special protection over horses.[1] We owe our knowledge, such as it is, of the Kassite pantheon to the painstaking lexicographical work of Babylonian scribes; a tablet from the library of Ashurbanipal contains a list of the kings of Babylon in which the Akkadian equivalents of the names of Kassite kings are given:[2] Kurigalzu, for instance, was said to mean 'Shepherd of the Kassites', and Meli-Shikhu, 'the man of Marduk', while Nazi-Maruttash meant 'the shadow of Ninurta'. Perhaps this tradition is not entirely trustworthy, for a school text gives a list of gods with their Akkadian counterparts, and here Shikhu is equated not with Marduk but with Sin, while Kharbe, whose name is translated 'Enlil' in the list, is equated with Anu in the vocabulary.[3] The latter goes on to list Akkadian translations for common words such as 'star', 'king', 'slave', 'head', 'foot' and the like.[4] From such scant material, and from an analysis of names of non-Akkadian appearance in the texts of the period,[5] attempts have been made to find affinities between Kassite and other languages, but so far with little success; it appears to be one of those agglutinative languages, sometimes termed 'Asianic', which defy classification.[6] Similarities between the Kassites and the Hittites and Hurrians, however, have not escaped notice. All three peoples appeared in the Near East during the early second millennium B.C. at a time of political upheaval, and all had at their head a chariot-owning, horse-breeding aristocracy. The Hittites spoke an Indo-European tongue, and the rulers of the Hurrians, judging by their names, were Aryans; many scholars are inclined to discern an Indo-Iranian element in the Kassite pantheon also, and have equated the god Suriash with the Hindu Surya, Maruttash with the Indian Marut, and Buriash very tentatively with Boreas, the Greek god of the north wind.[7] These identifications are not, however, universally accepted,[8] and in the absence of further evidence it would be rash to base upon them a firm assumption that the ruling class among the Kassites was Aryan. Other deities of the Kassite pantheon appear to have come from

[1] §II, 2, 111 ff.   [2] *Ibid.* 2 f.; cf. G, 19, vol. II, 360.
[3] §II, 2, 3, 142 f.; §II, 12, 25 ff.; G, 19, vol. II, 359.
[4] §II, 2, 4, 142 ff.
[5] §II, 11, 41 ff.; §II, 2, 45 ff.; §II, 10, 3 ff.
[6] §II, 23, 896.
[7] §II, 2, 191 ff.; §II, 20, 128; §II, 9, 91; G, 26, 172; §I, 41, 142 f.
[8] §II, 2, 104 ff.; 193, n. 19; §II, 39, 1197.

the Zagros region, and perhaps ultimately from the Caucasus.[1] Among them were Sakh, identified in the lists with Shamash; Dur and Shugab, both equated with Nergal, the plague god; Kharbe and Kamulla, corresponding with Enlil and Ea,[2] and the king's personal deities, Shuqamuna and Shumalia, perhaps the high god and his consort, in whose temple in Babylon the later Kassite kings were crowned.[3]

The Kassites have left few royal inscriptions, and most of them are short, uninformative statements concerning buildings which they erected or repaired, with little historical content.[4] Of some of the early kings not even these sources are preserved, and there is at least one Kassite ruler whose name we do not know, since the king-list on which it was preserved is broken at this point.[5] A few royal and private letters have survived[6] and some legal, administrative and economic texts,[7] but it is probably true to say that more information is to be obtained about political happenings in Babylonia from sources outside the country than from within. The so-called Synchronous History, which was compiled in Assyria and preserved among the documents from the library of Ashurbanipal at Nineveh,[8] gives a brief history of the relations between the two countries and the vicissitudes of the boundary which divided them, while the correspondence found at El-Amarna in Egypt, between successive Kassite kings of the fourteenth century B.C. and their brother monarchs in Egypt, illuminates yet another aspect of their relations with other powers.[9] For more than four hundred years, under Kassite rule, the history of Babylonia is almost unknown; the silence of the records and the absence of evidence of aggressive wars and spectacular conquests is often attributed to the mediocrity and inactivity of the rulers; yet they appear to have restored peace and prosperity to the country and maintained a stable government;[10] art and literature flourished, canals were maintained and temples and palaces built; the country was protected by fortifications against possible attack, and diplomacy, skilfully employed as a defensive weapon, usually contrived to ward off the threat of strong and predatory neighbours. Under the Kassite régime, Babylonia took her place among the great emergent nations in that era of power politics

[1] §II, 2, 114 ff.; §II, 9, 90.　　[2] §II, 2, 3 ff.
[3] §II, 2, 116 ff.; G, 19, vol. II, 10; §VI, 12, vol. II, 530 ff.
[4] §II, 18; §II, 25.　　[5] §II, 25, 187 f.; §II, 21, 97 ff.
[6] §II, 38; §II, 45.　　[7] §IV, 12, 131 ff.; §II, 10.
[8] G, 4, 38 ff.; G, 29, 349 ff.; G, 24, 272 f.; §II, 40, 24 ff., 84 ff.; §II, 46, 70 f. See also *C.A.H.* II³, pt. 2, ch. XVIII, sect. III.
[9] See below, sect. VI.　　[10] §II, 36, 273; §II, 10.

which is often called the Amarna Age, not, it is true, the foremost
of them, but with dignity among her peers.

The Kassite kings appear to have come to power as leaders of
a powerful, but perhaps quite small, aristocracy who wrote elegant
letters full of compliments to each other[1] and were expert and
enthusiastic horsebreeders.[2] Among the most significant relics of
the Kassite rule in Babylonia are the conical boulders or stelae
known as *kudurrū*, which are usually sculptured at the top or on
one side with symbols of the gods, and are inscribed below, or
on the other face, with a long text in Akkadian cuneiform.[3] The
word *kudurru* itself is Akkadian and means a boundary or limit,
and the monuments are often described as boundary stones; they
may well have originated in the stones which the Kassites planted
in the fields of their Persian homeland to mark the boundary
between field and field.[4] Those found in Babylonia, however,
appear to have had a rather different purpose, for they were deposited in temples, and were designed to record or confirm a
charter whereby the king, perhaps in gratitude or recognition of
some service, made a grant of land to a private individual. The
text of the decree defined in some detail the limits of the estate
in question; a list of witnesses sometimes followed, and the inscription closed with a comprehensive list of curses upon anyone
who should hide or deface or destroy the stela or deprive the
owner of his land.[5] Both the sculptured emblems[6] and the male-
dictions thus invoked divine protection upon the property and
rights of private individuals, not altogether an innovation, though
it has significance for the social history of the period.[7] Private
persons now become the hereditary owners of large landed estates,
and are given exemptions and special privileges which are defined
in the decrees. The texts are, in fact, our principal source of information concerning land tenure during the period, and also
throw light on legal procedure in cases where reference is made
to former disputes about the property, in which the king appears
as chief arbiter. Many of the names of the grantees, though not
by any means all, are Kassite, and one may surmise that most of
the feudal aristocracy surrounding the court of the Kassite king
of Babylon were his compatriots.[8]

[1] §II, 30, 13 f.; §II, 38, 76 ff., see also *C.A.H.* II³, pt. 2, ch. xviii, sect. v.
[2] §II, 2, 11 ff.; §vii, 28, 473 f.; §II, 24, 62 ff.
[3] §II, 27; §II, 42; G, 19, vol. I, 127 f.   [4] §II, 27, vii f.; G, 22, 719 f.
[5] §II, 27, x.   [6] §II, 24, 59 ff.
[7] See, further, *C.A.H.* II³, pt. 2, ch. xviii, sect. v.
[8] §II, 30, 14 f.; G, 26, 173.

The language of the boundary stones is Akkadian, and most of the building inscriptions of the early Kassite kings are in Sumerian, the archaic tongue of ritual. Although they kept their foreign names till the end, and perhaps still spoke Kassite among themselves, they corresponded in Akkadian and appear to have been quick to absorb the whole civilization of the ancient people whose home they had adopted as their own. Their kings still called themselves 'King of the Kassites' and 'King of Karduniash (or Karanduniash)',[1] using the old Kassite name for Babylonia, whose meaning has not been satisfactorily explained,[2] but they claimed also the old titles 'King of Sumer and Akkad' and 'King of the Whole World'; and, in building temples to the gods of Sumer and Akkad, in Babylon and in the sacred cities of the south, Ur and Uruk, Eridu and Nippur and Sippar, and endowing them with land,[3] they showed the same assiduous piety as the rulers of an earlier age whom they were eager to emulate. The shattered fragments of a statue of Kurigalzu I,[4] found in the ruins of the new capital which he filled with temples, preserve a small part of a once lengthy inscription in which the king defines the duties and functions of the Sumerian gods and describes the measures he took to revive the old rituals and cult practices and restore their accustomed offerings to a number of ancient deities whose worship had long since been discontinued.[5]

Agum-kakrime, to whom we now return, is described, in the long inscription recording the restoration of Marduk to Babylon, as King of the Kassites and Akkadians, King of the Wide Land of Babylon, King of Padan and Arman, and King of the Land of Gutium. The inscription is preserved only in a late copy[6] but the titles, if genuine, show that the links with his highland homeland were not yet broken, for the land of Gutium was in the Zagros, and Padan and Arman may be the Ḥulwan region.[7] How long a period elapsed between the Hittite raid and his occupation of the capital is not known; it is unlikely that, once the city walls were destroyed and it lay defenceless, he would long have delayed his descent upon it. However, a *kudurru* inscription refers to a grant of land in the region of Dēr, east of the Tigris, by a king of the Sealand, Gulkishar,[8] so that it is possible that during the

[1] §II, 2, 95 ff.; G, 26, 173; §II, 21, 97 n. 1, 98.

[2] §II, 13, 133 ff.; G, 16, 1013 f.; §II, 14, 122 ff.

[3] §II, 18, 44 ff.   [4] §II, 4, 15, pl. 17.

[5] G, 24, 57 ff.; §II, 44, 9 f.; §II, 34, 1 ff.

[6] §II, 18, 207, 228 f.; §II, 12, 56 ff.

[7] §II, 9, 92, 98; §II, 3, 737; §II, 7, 151; §II, 41, 69 f.

[8] §II, 14, 11 ff., 19.

interregnum this king of the still independent kingdom of the southern marshland may have seized the opportunity to come north, and perhaps even occupy Babylon for a short time, an achievement which would explain the inclusion of the Sealand dynasty in the list of the kings of Babylon.[1] In that case the first task of Agum II would have been to drive out the Sealanders and occupy the territory east of the Tigris, his second to restore order and obtain the sanction of Marduk on his assumption of the Babylonian throne.

His successor, Burnaburiash I, must have come into conflict with the Assyrians, for the Synchronous History records that 'Puzur-Ashur king of Assyria and Burnaburiash king of Karduniash swore an oath, and set fast the boundaries of this region'.[2] The Assyrian in question was Puzur-Ashur III, a descendant of Adasi and the sixty-first in the line of kings recorded in the great king-list of Khorsabad.[3] We know little of him except that he was the son of Ashur-nirari I and grandson of Shamshi-Adad III, and that he rebuilt part of the temple of Ishtar in his capital, Ashur, and the southern part of the city wall.[4] The adjustment of a boundary implies a peace treaty following previous aggression, but whether it was the Assyrians, nervous of the growing power of their southern neighbours, or the Kassites themselves who made the first move, cannot be determined. The kingdom of the Sealand is a problem still awaiting solution. Burnaburiash was succeeded by an unnamed king, perhaps a brother,[5] and then by his own son Kashtiliash, the third Kassite king of this name; he entrusted to his younger brother Ulamburiash the task of crushing the south. Taking advantage of the absence of Ea-gamil on a campaign in Elamite territory, Ulamburiash 'conquered the Sealand and exercised dominion over the region'.[6] An inscription on a macehead found at Babylon[7] shows that he ruled in the south, presumably as his brother's vassal or as vicegerent,[8] with the title 'King of the Sealand'.[9]

---

[1] §ii, 21, 99; G, 13, 66; §ii, 9, 94; §ii, 29, 105 f., 292.

[2] G, 4, 34, pl. 38; Goetze, in §ii, 21, 98 ff., following a different chronological scheme, attributes the pact to a second Burnaburiash, who, he suggests, was the successor to Agum III.

[3] §ii, 37, vol. ii, 86; §ii, 40, 54; §ii, 46, 74 ff.

[4] §ii, 17, xix, 30 ff.; §ii, 8, 20; G, 29, 228 f.

[5] §ii, 25, 208; §ii, 31, 68 f.; §ii, 7, 330 ff.

[6] §ii, 46, 68 f.; §ii, 28, vol, ii, 22 f., ll. 11 ff.; §ii, 25, 209, 230.

[7] §ii, 18, 44; §ii, 47, 3, 7 and pl. i, no. 3.

[8] It is doubtful whether he succeeded Kashtiliash in Babylon; see §ii, 21, 99; §ii, 25, 187 ff., and *C.A.H.* i³, pt. i, ch. vi, sect. ii (*b*).   [9] §ii, 18, 44.

After more than two hundred years, the whole of Babylonia was again under one rule. Ea-gamil, however, was still at large and the same late chronicle which preserves the tradition of the triumph of Ulamburiash, relates thereafter that 'Agum, the son of Kashtiliash' marched against the country of the Sea and conquered the city Dūr-Ea, ruthlessly destroying the temple of Ea.[1] Dūr-Ea must have lain somewhere near Eridu,[2] and have been the chief stronghold of a rebellion raised perhaps by the old king from his Elamite refuge. The revolt was successfully crushed, for the list of Sea Kings ends with Ea-gamil.[3]

Agum III was now undisputed ruler of all Babylonia. He has left no inscription and we know nothing of his reign. He must have been a contemporary of one or more of the kings of Assyria whose inscriptions, on bricks and clay nails from the excavated city of Ashur, record their building activities of construction or restoration.[4] Puzur-Ashur III had been succeeded by his son Enlil-naṣir I, who embellished the Anu-Adad temple with glazed bricks;[5] his son and successor Nur-ili, no. 63 in the king-list,[6] has left no monuments though he reigned for twelve years;[7] the son who succeeded him, Ashur-shaduni, was king for only a month before he was deposed by his uncle Ashur-rabi I.[8] The records now fail us completely: not even the length of the reign of Ashur-rabi and his son Ashur-nadin-ahhē has been preserved in any of the king-lists;[9] the former may have been a contemporary of Tuthmosis III and Agum III, the latter perhaps of Amenophis II and Agum's successor. Bricks from his palace were found at Ashur.[10] The identity of that successor has been much disputed;[11] the Kassite king-list gives Karaindash, followed by Kadashman-kharbe,[12] but on chronological grounds it is possible that the order of these two kings should be reversed, and that Kadashman-kharbe, who left no monuments and presumably had only a brief reign, was the father or the elder brother of Karaindash,[13]

---

[1] §II, 28, vol. I, 154 ff., vol. II, 24, ll. 14 ff., 154; §II, 25, 209; §II, 14, 26, 175 ff.

[2] §II, 14, 150 n. 475, 175 f. [3] §II, 40, 81; G, 24, 271.

[4] §II, 17, 32 ff.; §II, 8, 20 ff. [5] §II, 17, xix, 32 f., 89 n. 13.

[6] §II, 37, vol. I, 479. [7] §II, 37, vol. II, 86; §II, 40, 54; §II, 31, 44.

[8] §II, 37, vol. I, 479 and n. 202.

[9] *Ibid.* n. 204; §II, 40, 55. [10] G, 18, vol. I, 19.

[11] For a more detailed discussion of the chronological problem, see *C.A.H.* I³, pt. I, ch. VI, sect. II(*b*).

[12] §II, 18, 44; §II, 25, 209; §II, 40, 48; G, 26, 174.

[13] Chronicle P calls Kadashman-kharbe the *son* of Karaindash (§II, 47, 4 f.; §II, 21, 97 n. 5). Schmökel in G, 26, 174 assumes identification with Kadashman-Enlil, but see §II, 27, 3 ff.

the first Kassite king to make diplomatic overtures to Egypt.[1]
A late chronicle records of Kadashman-kharbe that he led an
expedition into the Syrian desert west of his realm against the
Sutu nomads, and slaughtered many of them, building a fortress
and a well in a place called Khi-khi, and leaving a garrison to
guard them,[2] but the tradition is chronologically unacceptable in
that it makes Kadashman-kharbe the grandson of Ashur-uballit,
who came to the Assyrian throne more than fifty years later.

III. THE EGYPTIAN CHALLENGE

Throughout the twenty-odd years of Hatshepsut's reign, little or
no interest was taken by the Egyptians in their erstwhile vassals
in Asia, in spite of her grandiose claims in the temple of Deir el-
Bahri, where the queen appears as a sphinx trampling on Asiatic
and Nubian foes alike.[3] The news of her death or fall from power
must have travelled quickly; it must have been common knowledge among the kings of Syria and Palestine that her nephew
and stepson, Tuthmosis III, a soldier by training and now a young
man in his late twenties or early thirties, had long been chafing
at the restraint imposed upon him by his aunt's unwelcome
usurpation of the reins of government.[4] The leader of a well-
organized resistance was the powerful city of Qadesh, on the
River Orontes;[5] a large army was mobilized, every city of the
region supplying a contingent of foot and many sending their
mariyanna warriors to swell the chariot force. The area controlled
by the king of Qadesh at this time appears to have been wide:
330 princes, according to an Egyptian estimate,[6] were in his
following. While this may be an exaggeration, it is clear that
he controlled Qatna[7] (inventory tablets from this city indicate
that his name was Durusha[8]); his western border was contiguous
with that of the kingdom of Tunip, his southern domains included the Galilee district and Megiddo in the Plain of Esdraelon.
In opposing Egypt, it is possible that both he and the king of
Tunip were acting as loyal vassals of Mitanni;[9] if so, then the
ultimate confrontation of the two great powers, eleven years later,
was inevitable from the start.

[1] EA 10, 8 ff. See below, p. 465.
[2] G, 4, no. 34; G, 29, 263 ff., 389 n. 14; §II, 25, 210.
[3] §III, 31, vol. VI, pl. CLX. But see A, 44, 57 ff. for arguments that at least one
Syrian campaign had been undertaken during her reign, and possibly two.
[4] See above, pp. 317 ff.   [5] See above, p. 430.
[6] G, 27, 1234.   [7] And perhaps Nukhashshe also (A, 21, 28).
[8] A, 16, 242 ff.   [9] A, 28, 157; A, 21, 29.

Tuthmosis introduces one of his triumphal inscriptions[1] with the date 'tenth day, second month of winter, of the twenty-second year', probably the day when he simultaneously took over the reins of government[2] and proclaimed a general mobilization.[3] Eager though he was to be off, preparations for a large-scale campaign into Asia took some time and it was two and a half months before the army, assembled in Memphis, had moved up to the frontier ready for the long and waterless crossing of the Sinai road, the Ways of Horus, as it was called.[4] They set out from Tjel,[5] the frontier fortress on the Pelusiac branch of the Nile near modern El-Qantara[6] on the twenty-fifth of the fourth month,[7] and, averaging between twelve and fifteen miles a day, reached Gaza ten days later on the anniversary of the king's childhood coronation.[8] These dates, and the narrative that follows, are based chiefly on a long text inscribed on the walls of the 'Hall of Annals' erected by Tuthmosis III in the Temple of Amun at Karnak.[9] This important inscription is clearly based on the day-by-day journal kept during the campaign; its compiler, Tjaneni, was a military scribe who accompanied the king and was charged with the task of keeping the diary.[10] The document, transcribed onto a parchment scroll, was deposited permanently in the temple,[11] and it was presumably in the course of transcription that the bald narrative of events and dates was given literary shape and embellished with picturesque detail emphasizing the heroic role played by the king personally in the campaigns: he is depicted as a superman, endowed by the gods with more than mortal skill and bravery, and miraculously aided by them in moments of danger.[12] Wiser than his counsellors, he takes the bold decision and is proved right; more daring than they, he goes ahead of his army and 'alone, none being with him', performs prodigies of valour; terrible like Mont or Resheph, the gods of battle of Egypt and Canaan, he strikes terror into his enemies.[13] Extracts from this edited narrative, in which some of the original terse, factual entries can still be discerned,[14] were inscribed on the walls of two

---

[1] G, 27, 1244 l. 14; G, 24, 234; §III, 28, 12 ff.
[2] §III, 12, 183 n. *b*; G, 14, 168 n. 54.
[3] §III, 5, 35 ff.
[4] §III, 20, 103 ff.; §III, 29, 116, 191; G, 14, 323 ff.
[5] Sile (Tell Abu Seifi).
[6] §III, 29, 117, 190 ff.; *C.A.H.* II³, pt. 2, ch. XXIII, sect. II.
[7] G, 27, 647, l. 12.
[8] §III, 16, 2; §III, 32, 6 n. 12, 33 n. 66.
[9] G, 27, 645 ff.; §III, 24, 6 ff., plan on p. 16.
[10] G, 27, 1004, l. 9 f.
[11] *Ibid.* 662, ll. 4 f.
[12] G, 14, 121; §III, 34, 167. Cf. §III, 8, 65 f.
[13] E.g. G, 27, 657, l. 8, 1302, l. 7, 1311, ll. 2, 7, 14. Cf. §III, 8, 66.
[14] §III, 34, 167 ff.

chambers in the temple of Karnak some time after his last campaign in his forty-second year. For the most part the narrative style is confined to the first and, for the king perhaps, the most memorable campaign; other extracts were inscribed on stelae set up in temples in various parts of his realm.[1] Further information is provided by the lists of captured places on the sixth and seventh pylons of the Karnak temple.[2] A number of the towns or villages enumerated in these lists can be identified, either by mention made of them elsewhere, where their location in relation to other places is made clear, or, more tentatively, by the similarity of the name to modern place-names in the region;[3] a combination of the two types of evidence, taken together, makes identification fairly certain, but this is rare. Recent study of the lists has established beyond probable doubt that they are based on itineraries,[4] that is to say that they are extracted from the narrative of campaigns or from the day-books kept in the field;[5] but it is also clear that the order has been tampered with by the copyists.[6] The reconstruction of events and marches given here must therefore be regarded as tentative only.

Remaining only one night in Gaza, the army moved on the next day, and eleven days later, following the coastal road,[7] arrived at *Yḥm* or Yahmai, the modern Yemma, south of the ridge of Mount Carmel.[8] The route taken by the king on his march through the Shephēlah is perhaps indicated by the fifty-seventh to sixty-seventh names in the list of places 'of Upper Retenu, captured by His Majesty in the wretched town of Megiddo...on his first victorious expedition',[9] for they include places such as Yurza (Tell el-Fūl),[10] Joppa, Lydda, Aphek and Sucho, all of them possible stopping-places on the way to Yahmai, which is number 68 on the list.[11] The distance between Gaza and Yahmai is about eighty miles, and one must suppose that in the well-watered plain the army, weary with forced marching, proceeded by easier stages, making perhaps seven or eight miles a day.[12] Only the city of Joppa (Jaffa), it seems, offered resistance and

1 §III, 36; G, 27, 1227 ff.; §III, 28, 5 ff.; G, 24, 238, 240.
2 G, 27, 779 ff.; §III, 40, 27 ff. and 109 ff.; §III, 33, 26 ff.; §III, 24, 16, 22; G, 23, 102, fig. 313. See Plate 98 (*b*).   3 A, 2, 105 ff.
4 Otherwise §III, 6; §III, 40, 37.
5 G, 27, 693, ll. 11 ff.; §IV, 4, 154; G, 14, 122; §III, 33.
6 G, 14, 122 f.; §IV, 7, 154.   7 §IV, 20, 78 ff.; A, 2, map p. 40.
8 §III, 16, 2 f.; §III, 32, 7; G, 24, 235 n. 18; G, 14, 168 n. 55.
9 §III, 33, 26 ff.
10 G, 14, 122; §III, 40, 218, identifies Yurza with Tell Jemmeh; cf. EA 314, 315.
11 §IV, 20, 79; G, 14, 122.   12 But see §III, 16, 2 n. 8.

shut its gates against the Egyptians, so that General Djehuty had to be left in charge of siege operations. The story of how Joppa was taken by a trick is known from a late legend[1] which has in it elements of the tale of the Trojan horse, or might equally well be regarded as the prototype of the story of Ali Baba and the Forty Thieves. Yet, although the details of the story, the capture of the garrison by Egyptian soldiers introduced into the city concealed in baskets or sacks, may be of the stuff of folklore rather than history, the central fact that the city was besieged and taken may well be true and the chief actor in the drama, General Djehuty himself, was a historical personality, a soldier of high rank who accompanied King Tuthmosis III on his campaigns, as the inscription in his tomb tells us, and who was left to administer the conquered territory as Resident.[2] A number of objects have survived from his tomb, among them a handsome cup, now in the Louvre,[3] which he received from his sovereign as a reward for his services abroad, and for filling the treasury with 'lapis lazuli, silver and gold'. So the army moved forward 'in valour and might, in strength and in justification'[4] through territory still held by Egypt since the days of Amosis I. It may have been in Yahmai that the news was received that the enemy was lying in wait for them on the other side of the Carmel ridge and that they had made the city of Megiddo in the valley of Esdraelon their headquarters.[5]

Here, we are told, the king held a council of war. Though the historicity of the council itself is doubtful (it bears a suspicious resemblance to those other councils called by Seqenenre and Kamose[6] in which the king disregards the cautious advice of his courtiers and is proved both more courageous and wiser than they),[7] the situation which the leaders discuss is almost certainly historical. Evidently they were well acquainted with the terrain. Three practicable routes lay ahead: a narrow, direct path over the ridge from Aruna, emerging on the plain less than a mile from Megiddo; a more westerly route by a better road which reached the plain at Djefty,[8] where it joined the road from Megiddo to Acre; and, thirdly, the most obvious route, along the main road skirting the south-east slopes of the Carmel range to Taanach, five miles from Megiddo, where part of the enemy host was

---

[1] §III, 21, 82 ff.; §III, 15, 216 ff.; §III, 41, 57 f.; G, 24, 22 f.
[2] G, 27, 999; §III, 35, vol. I (ed. 2), 21 ff.
[3] §III, 7, 341 ff., pl. 45.   [4] G, 27, 648, l. 13.
[5] *Ibid.* 649, ll. 5–12. For Megiddo (Tell el-Mutesellim) see §V, 32.
[6] See above, ch. VIII, sect. I.   [7] G, 14, 123.
[8] §III, 32, 24, 28, 48 f.; §III, 2, 110 ff.; G, 14, 125.

waiting.[1] The opinion was expressed by his generals that the nearest but most hazardous route should be rejected, since it led through a narrow pass in which 'horse must march after horse, and man after man';[2] the dangers of thus exposing the army to piecemeal destruction were obvious. Tuthmosis, however, is credited with a bold choice: he will take the shortest route and take the enemy by surprise. His decision is couched in characteristic terms: 'Let him among you who so desires go on those roads of which you speak, and let him among you who so wishes come in the train of my Majesty, for behold they will say (those foes whom Re detests): "Has His Majesty gone upon another road because he is afraid of us?"—thus they will say.'[3] The sentiment is in keeping with all that we know of the character of this small but lion-hearted pharaoh; here, perhaps, history speaks, and not court convention.

The thirteen-mile climb from Yahmai to Aruna, by way of El-Mejdel,[4] occupied two days;[5] Aruna, perhaps Tell 'Arā on the southern slope of the Carmel Range,[6] was reached towards the evening of the second day. Ahead lay the dangerous pass. The army camped for the night, and early next morning, led by the standard of the god Amun,[7] began the defile. The pass at its narrowest point is barely thirty feet wide and there are points along its rocky course where indeed there can have been scarcely room for two chariots abreast.[8] The whole traverse took about twelve hours;[9] when the vanguard reached the valley on the other side, it was noon, and it was seven hours more before the last troops emerged; the king himself waited at the head of the pass till the last of his men was safely through. By the time the whole army had reached the plain, and encamped by the brook Qina, it must have been late in the evening. Meanwhile the main enemy forces must have been recalled from their position near Taanach, only four or five miles away, and have pitched camp for the night between the Egyptian army and the city of Megiddo. Both sides settled down to wait for the morning. 'A tent was set up there for His Majesty, and the order was given to the whole army, "Prepare ye, sharpen your weapons, for One will engage battle

---

[1] §III, 32, 27 n. 54; §VII, 74, 103 n. 13.

[2] G, 27, 649, l. 15, 650, l. 4; G, 14, 124.

[3] G, 27, 651, ll. 9–13; G, 24, 235 f.

[4] §IV, 20, 79; G, 14, 123; §III, 2, 110 ff., and map, p. 117, fig. 4.

[5] G, 14, 124; III, 32, 33; §III, 16, 11 n. *h*, assumes an error in the annalist's dates.

[6] G, 24, 235 n. 20; §III, 16, 11; §III, 32, 10 f., 31; §IV, 1, vol. II, 24.

[7] §III, 32, 33 ff.   [8] *Ibid.* 11 ff., 28.   [9] §III, 16, 10; §III, 32, 41 and n. 76.

with that miserable foe in the morning. . .".'[1] The king went to his rest, having seen to it that his officers were briefed, rations had been distributed, and sentries posted with the instruction 'Be very steadfast and very vigilant!'[2] The nearness of the enemy camp must have given cause for anxiety to those of his officers who were less confident of success than the king.

The next morning—the date was that of the festival of the New Moon, no doubt a fortunate omen for the king, whose family regarded the moon as their especial patron—the order was given to form the battle-line. The king himself, resplendent in his chariot overlaid with gold and silver, led the centre; the wings spread out southwards towards a hill south of the Qina brook, and on the north-west towards the walls of Megiddo.[3] The enemy force, we are told, was immense: three hundred and thirty kings, each with his own army, were there 'with millions of men, and hundreds of thousands of the chiefest of all the lands, standing in their chariots'.[4] When they caught sight of the Egyptian battle array, however, 'they felt faint and flew headlong'[5], seeking the shelter of the city walls.[6] Some of the fugitives, including the king[7] of Qadesh and his vassal the king of Megiddo, found the city gates shut against them by the inhabitants, and had to be hauled up the walls by their clothing, an incident which, like a later episode of the battle of Qadesh in the time of Ramesses II, when the half-drowned king of Aleppo received rough and ready first aid from his men, implied the sorry plight of authority in a ridiculous situation, and so appealed to the Egyptian sense of humour.

Meanwhile the confederates' camp lay in confusion and their abandoned equipment proved too great a temptation for the Egyptian troops; greed prevailed over discipline and, in spite of the entreaties of the king, they fell to plunder.[8] The opportunity was lost; there was nothing for it but to lay siege to the city. The richly decorated chariots of the enemy princes, their horses and their equipment were presented to Amun by the king, and the hands severed from the slain were counted; there were but eighty-three of these, and the prisoners numbered only three

[1] G, 27, 656, l. 3 f. [2] §III, 16, 11 n. ff.
[3] G, 27, 657, ll. 10–12. [4] G, 27, 1234, ll. 9 ff.; §III, 28, 6.
[5] G, 27, 658, l. 1; §III, 10, 103 ff.; §III, 16, 15.
[6] §III, 32, 53 f.; §VII, 72, 103, and §VII, 74, 106 f., envisage a battle in which the Canaanites were worsted.
[7] The Egyptians had no word for 'king', since pharaoh was unique. Rulers of enemy kingdoms were each referred to officially as 'that miserable Fallen One of (the city) X'. [8] G, 27, 658, ll. 8 ff.

hundred and forty. The army was ordered to take the city at all costs, 'for the ruler of every northern country is in Megiddo, and its capture is the capture of a thousand cities'.[1] The method of investiture strongly recalls the method by which the Spartans laid siege to Plataea.[2] A moat was dug around the city walls, and the circumvallation was completed by a strong palisade, for the construction of which the surrounding neighbourhood was stripped of trees.[3] The king's headquarters were set up in a fortress east of the town and sentries were posted around with strict instructions to let nobody through except those who signalled at the gate that they wished to give themselves up.[4]

In spite of these precautions the siege lasted throughout the summer and it was not until the following December, seven months after the Battle of the Qina Valley,[5] that Megiddo surrendered. The vanquished kings sent out their sons and daughters to sue for peace, laden with gifts: 'All those things with which they had come to fight against my Majesty, now they brought them as tribute to my Majesty, while they themselves stood upon their walls giving praise to my Majesty, and begging that the Breath of Life be given to their nostrils.'[6] There is a discrepancy in the account of Tuthmosis' treatment of his prisoners; one source implies that some of them were taken to Egypt with their tribute, while new rulers were appointed in their stead,[7] but another says that before they were sent back ignominiously to their own cities on donkeys, an oath of allegiance was imposed on them: 'We will not again do evil against Menkheperre our good Lord, in our lifetime, for we have seen his might, and he has deigned to give us breath.'[8]

The booty taken at the end of the battle was paltry compared with what now became the property of the pharaoh and his soldiers. Most valuable of all were the horses—2041 of them, as well as 191 foals, 6 stallions and a number of colts.[9] Horses cannot yet have been common in Egypt, and this considerable addition to their breeding-stock would have been welcomed by the Egyptians, whose nobles, like the Hurrian aristocracy, now regarded the possession of a chariot as a mark of rank and prestige.[10] Some

---

[1] G, 27, 660, ll. 6–8.   [2] Thucydides, bk. ii, ch. 75–8.
[3] G, 27, 660, l. 16, 1231, l. 16.   [4] *Ibid.* 661, ll. 13 f.
[5] *Ibid.* 1234, l. 18. There seems no reason to suppose, with Klengel that 'seven months' here only means 'a long time' (A, 28, vol. ii, 157).
[6] *Ibid.* 662, ll. 7 ff.
[7] *Ibid.* 663, ll. 1 ff.
[8] *Ibid.* 1235, ll. 16 ff. to 1236, l. 5.
[9] *Ibid.* 663, ll. 8 ff.   [10] §iii, 27, 59 ff.

of the livestock, cows, goats and sheep, listed among the booty must have gone to feed the army.

The list of captured towns mentioned above contains in all a hundred and nineteen names; those between Gaza and Aruna number only fourteen.[1] It is possible that the rest may be just the names of the towns whose rulers joined the confederacy and were caught at Megiddo, though they do not amount to three hundred and thirty. Examination of them, however, reveals a certain order, as if not one but several expeditions were undertaken, after the siege had been raised or perhaps even during the course of it. That one such raid was undertaken by the king himself is expressly stated in the annals;[2] it took Tuthmosis to the region of Lake Galilee, where the king of Qadesh had an estate, an indication of the wide extent of his realm at the time. Three towns were taken, one at least by siege, since among the captives were a hundred and three 'pardoned persons, who had come out from that enemy because of hunger'.[3] Yenoam, called Yanuammu in the Amarna letters,[4] is to be identified with Tell en-Na'am on the shore of the lake,[5] and Halkuru is in the same district;[6] the third place, Nuges, cannot be the same as the city and district of Nukhashshe, similarly written in the Egyptian syllabic transcription,[7] but must be near the other two places. The booty from this foray was rich and included, as well as large numbers of male and female slaves, no less than eighty-four children belonging to the King of Qadesh and his confederates; it may be that the women and children of the allies had been sent here for safety from Qadesh before the battle.[8] The slaves, and large numbers of valuable pieces of furniture and vessels of metal and stone, and clothing, the princes' household goods, are listed apart from the main booty, since the captured towns, with their revenues, were dedicated in perpetuity to the temple of Amun in Karnak.[9] One of the items which receive special mention is 'walking sticks with human heads', doubtless similar to those found in the tomb of Tutankhamun, one of which strikingly depicts a bearded Syrian.[10]

The annals appear to relate only those campaigns in which the king himself took part, but a hint of the activities of groups under

[1] G, 14, 127 f.   [2] G, 27, 664, l. 16.
[3] G, 27, 665, l. 11.   [4] EA 197, l. 8.
[5] §1, 18, vol. 1, 146*; §1, 43, 204; §111, 4, vol. 1, 253 n. 4; G, 14, 137.
[6] G, 14, 132.
[7] G, 27, 716, l. 15, cf. 1309, l. 3; G, 14, 291 f.; §111, 4, vol. 11, 138 f.
[8] G, 14, 137.   [9] G, 27, 185, ll. 3 ff.   [10] *Ibid.* 666 l. 15; see Plate 107(*b*).

other subordinate officers is to be obtained from the lists of towns. One such reconstruction, based on those place-names which can be identified with reasonable certainty, suggests that no less than five other raids were made by contingents of the Egyptian army, perhaps during the course of the seven months' siege of Megiddo;[1] one, it is suggested, crossed the Lebanon through the Tripoli gap, then traversed the Biqā', the plain of Coele-Syria, by-passing Qadesh and many of the large towns,[2] but taking Damascus, then striking south through Bashan to Hazor, the modern Tell Qedah,[3] one of the greatest cities of northern Palestine, and finally passing west of Lake Galilee through Kinnereth (where a broken stela was found which may have been set up by this king),[4] to rejoin the main force besieging Megiddo. On another foray the district south of Lake Galilee was ravaged, together with the Yarmuk area east of Jordan, while others had the aim of cutting Megiddo off from any possible relieving force from the direction of Acre.[5]

The capture of Megiddo was a great triumph for Tuthmosis and his army, and it was celebrated as such; in one of the scenes accompanying the lists of conquered cities at Karnak the pharaoh is depicted as conqueror of Asia, holding by the topknot a bunch of kneeling prisoners whom he is about to slaughter with his mace,[6] while the goddess Mut, the consort of the god Amun of Thebes, leads on a rope the captured cities, each name surrounded by an oval fortified wall and surmounted by the bust of a Syrian with prominent hooked nose and a pointed beard, his arms tied behind his back.[7] In the following year the king met with no resistance; the chiefs of Retenu, as Syria-Palestine is very generally called, brought their tribute; and, though Tuthmosis probably found it necessary to march through the countryside making a demonstration of strength, it does not appear that this 'Second Campaign', and the 'Third' and 'Fourth' which followed in his twenty-fifth to twenty-eighth years, were much more than tours of inspection productive of welcome revenue in the shape of cedar and other precious woods.[8] One event of particular importance, however, is recorded for the twenty-fourth year: the king of Assyria sent as a present to the Egyptian court a large and

---

[1] G, 14, 127 ff., 134 f. For the strategic position of Megiddo, see A, 2, 49.
[2] §IV, 7, 147; G, 14, 127.
[3] §V, 27, 312; §V, 50; G, 16, 1300; G, 14, 129.
[4] See below, p. 476.   [5] G, 14, 131 f., 134 f.
[6] C.A.H. I³, pt. 2, ch. XVII, sect. VI. See Plate 98(b).
[7] G, 23, 102, fig. 313; §III, 40, 5 ff.   [8] G, 27, 675 ff.

valuable lump of lapis lazuli,[1] a blue stone brought from distant Afghanistān[2] to decorate the palaces of kings and the tresses of their court ladies.

The twenty-fifth year saw the king again in the land of Retenu; a mutilated block now in the Cairo Museum, perhaps a survivor from a part of the wall of the eastern Annals Room which is now missing,[3] refers to hunting and has an interesting and unique mention of fire-arrows shot into beleaguered towns.[4] During the course of his campaign the king made a collection of 'all rare plants and beautiful flowers' which he found in the Lebanon 'in order to let them be set before my father Amun in this great temple of Amun, for ever and ever'.[5] In small rooms at the back of the Festival Hall which Tuthmosis built in the Karnak temple, artists have carved representations of these alien plants and seedlings, as well as the foreign birds and beasts which the royal naturalist brought back from his travels.[6]

For the next three years Tuthmosis undertook no campaigns abroad. Palestine and southern Syria, and probably the Damascus area, paid tribute to Egypt; and though Qadesh still kept her independence, her territories had been greatly reduced. Perhaps the time was spent by the Egyptians in building a fleet in readiness for the next great task. Another great city lay between Tuthmosis and his ultimate goal: Tunip,[7] the powerful fortress-city on the slopes of Lebanon west of the Orontes, and north-west of Qadesh and Qatna, which was an ally and perhaps a vassal of Saustatar of Mitanni,[8] and an ally on terms of parity with Niqmepa, king of Alalakh.[9] This time, part of the army was to be transported by sea to a port on the Lebanon coast whence a march through the Eleutheros valley (Nahr el-Kebīr), which forms a gap in the chain of mountains between the Lebanon and the Jebel Anṣāriyyah, would bring them to the Orontes valley; the king would thus be spared the exhausting and time-wasting march through Palestine and Coele-Syria. The troopships were built in the dockyards of Perunefer, close to Memphis; a papyrus in the British Museum[10] records the issue of supplies of Syrian timber, both pine and cedar, to shipwrights. The work was so important that it was under the personal direction of the crown prince Amenhotpe,

---

[1] G, 27, 671, ll. 8–9.
[2] See below, p. 482.
[3] G, 27, 675 ff.; §III, 24, 15 f.
[4] G, 27, 676, l. 12.
[5] G, 27, 776, ll. 14–16.
[6] §III, 44, vol. II, 30; A, 35, 156.
[7] See above, p. 427.
[8] G, 14, 304 ff.; A, 28, vol. II, 94 n. 8.
[9] §I, 67, 26 ff.; A, 28, vol. I, 233 f.
[10] §III, 22. Dated by Glanville to the reign of Tuthmosis III; but Redford in *J.E.A.* 61 (1965), 110, suggests rather that of Amenophis II.

the commander in chief of the Memphite garrison.[1] It may well have been by ship that the 'fifth campaign of victory' began, for the king at once appeared, according to the annalist, in Djahy, 'to lay waste the foreign lands which were rebelling against him'.[2] The important city of Ullaza, perhaps the classical Orthosia at the mouth of the Nahr el-Bārid, north of Tripoli,[3] was captured. Among the defenders, it is interesting to note, were three hundred and twenty-nine infantry belonging to the king of Tunip. If Tunip was somewhere in the latitude of Tripoli, as has been suggested,[4] the defence of Ullaza, only about a score of miles away, is understandable. Ullaza was a wealthy city, judging by the quantity of gold and silver, precious stones and vessels enumerated among the booty.[5] No direct attack upon Tunip is recorded, but we may suspect that this city was the real object of the expedition, and that the Egyptian army met with a reverse, which is not of course admitted in the royal annals. The returning expedition had the good fortune to encounter, somewhere off the coast, two vessels laden with merchandise.[6] The nationality of these boats is not stated; perhaps they were carrying Cypriot wares, since the cargo consisted of copper and lead as well as slaves. This flagrant act of piracy has been thought by some to have been the means whereby the Egyptians for the first time acquired sea transport[7] and that Syrian vessels therefore formed the nucleus of the Egyptian fleet and provided prototypes for the vessels used thenceforward in war. It seems probable, however, that the Egyptian army had been using sea transport to a limited extent since the first of Tuthmosis III's campaigns, if not earlier, and it would not be surprising to learn that Tuthmosis I also went part of the way by water to his Euphrates destination. Cargo vessels must have been in use for the later campaigns of the pharaohs,[8] to carry troops and supplies and to bring back the very considerable quantity of booty, and also Syrian timber, both fir and pine,[9] which was used in the manufacture of sea-going vessels.[10]

On the homeward journey the countryside around Ardata, probably the modern Ardat, a little inland from Tripoli,[11] was laid

---

[1] Redford, *loc. cit.*, 108; §iii, 37, 37 ff.; §iii, 29, 197.

[2] G, 27, 685, l. 5.　　　　　　　　　[3] G, 6, 79 f.; G, 14, 139, 314 f.

[4] G, 14, 304 f. See above, p. 427.　　[5] G, 27, 686, ll. 6–10.

[6] G, 27, ll. 11–16.　　　　　　　　[7] G, 1, vol. ii, 196 n. *c*; §iii, 37, 34 f.

[8] §v, 28, 77; §iii, 37, 55 ff.

[9] §iii, 22, 8 f.; *C.A.H.* i³, pt. 2, ch. xvii, sect. v.

[10] §iii, 37, 45; §viii, 31, 100 ff.

[11] G, 6, 85; G, 14, 177, 315; §vi, 27, 119 and n. 56; §iii, 13, 4 n. 3.

waste and the city plundered.[1] Accustomed as they were to the barren hills of Palestine, the soldiers here found a land of milk and honey. In poetic phrases the annals describe the riches of Djahy, where the gardens were filled with fruit and the wine overflowed in the presses 'as water flows downstream' and grain brimmed over in the granaries 'more numerous than the sand on the seashore'.[2] The list of spoil includes huge quantities of food and wine: 'Lo, the army of His Majesty was drunk, anointed with oil every day, as if at a festival in Egypt!'[3]

The campaign of the following, the thirtieth, year was directed not against Tunip but against Qadesh, the arch-enemy among the Syrian city states. The countryside was devastated but the city itself seems to have resisted capture;[4] on the return journey Simyra and Ardata on the coast were ravaged.[5] Ṣumura or Simyra, the Zimyra of Strabo,[6] which makes its first appearance during this campaign, was to play an important role in Egyptian affairs henceforward; its exact location is uncertain[7] but it lay on the coast not far from Ullaza, with which it is frequently mentioned, and south of Arvad, and in the time of the Amarna letters it was hotly disputed between the Egyptians and the princes of Amurru.[8]

The next two years were taken up with preparations for the great offensive against 'that wretched Mitannian foe'. No campaign is recorded for the thirty-first year but work must have gone ahead at Memphis and in the following year a rising in Ullaza was suppressed; one of the prisoners turned out to be a royal retainer from Tunip, no doubt the instigator of the revolt.[9] Rich tribute was sent by the vassal kings of the neighbourhood and the order was given to them that in future all the supply bases suitable for use by the Egyptian fleet were to be kept supplied from year to year with bread, oil, incense, wine, honey and 'every good fruit of this country'.[10] There must have been a chain of these harbours, for the seafaring ships of the day, though large in comparison with Nile craft, were forced to hug the coast and be ready to put into port whenever a storm threatened.[11]

All was now prepared and a large army was brought up by sea, ready to launch an attack against Naharin,[12] the summit of

[1] G, 27, 687, l. 5. [2] Ibid. l. 16.
[3] Ibid. 688, ll. 15–16. [4] G, 14, 140; A, 28, vol. II, 158.
[5] G, 27, 689, ll. 11–15. [6] G, 6, 117 ff.; C.A.H. II³, pt. 2, ch. XVII, sect. I.
[7] G, 16, 1141; §III, 14, 13 f.; G, 14, 313 f.; §III, 4, vol. III, 116, 131; §III, 9, 218 ff.
[8] EA passim; G, 16, 1135 f., 1138. [9] G, 27, 691, ll. 3–4; G, 14, 140.
[10] G, 27, 692, l. 15, 693, l. 2; §III, 4, vol. III, 108 ff.
[11] See below, §VIII. [12] G, 27, 1231 ff.

Tuthmosis' ambition. Timber had been hewn in the forests on the mountain slope, 'the precinct of the Lady of Byblos', who was the presiding deity of the timber forests,[1] and pontoons had been built, probably in sections, for transport on ox-waggons in advance of the army 'in order to cross that great stream which flows between this foreign-land and Naharin'.[2] The river in question may be the Orontes, but is more likely to have been the Euphrates itself, the natural western boundary of the Mitannian homeland. A route for this campaign has been reconstructed[3] on the basis of a long list of place-names, apparently in reverse order, preserved on the seventh pylon of the temple of Karnak,[4] but only a small number of the places can be located and the route followed by Tuthmosis and his army is doubtful. Certain episodes of the campaign are seen through the eyes of an officer of bravery and resource, Amenemheb by name;[5] the sequence of events in his narrative is not, however, to be taken seriously.[6] The deeds of which he was most proud, and which are set at the end of his narrative, probably relate to incidents on the homeward march: in Neya, where he accompanied the king on an elephant hunt, he saw his royal master in danger from the biggest elephant in a herd of a hundred and twenty and, rushing into the water, cut off its trunk ('hand');[7] while, during an attack launched on the defence of Qadesh, he darted out with great presence of mind and killed a decoy mare sent out by the enemy to spread confusion among the stallions of the Egyptian chariotry; he was then first into the breach, and took two *mariyanna* prisoner. For all of these exploits the king, we are told, rewarded him liberally with gold. Before this, however, on the march to the Euphrates, he had fought in the engagement at Juniper Hill, to the west of Aleppo, where Tuthmosis encountered Mitannian troops for the first time. At or near Carchemish[8] the army crossed the Euphrates, and Tuthmosis there erected his stela by the side of that which had been put up by his grandfather Tuthmosis I,[9] thus perhaps fulfilling a boyhood ambition. Without encountering serious opposition, the army marched downstream, plundering towns and villages along the Euphrates bank, till they reached Emar, near Meskineh,[10] where the Euphates bends away to the east—a likely

1 *C.A.H.* I³, pt. 2, ch. xvii, sect. v.　　2 G, 27, 1232, ll. 4–6; §I, 54, 44.
3 G, 14, 142 ff.　　4 G, 27, 786 ff.
5 G, 27, 889 ff.; §I, 18, vol. I, 153* ff.; G, 5, 444 f.
6 §III, 17, 39 ff.; G, 14, 141 f.
7 G, 27, 893, l. 14, to 894, l. 2.　　8 G, 27, 891, l. 9.
9 *Ibid.* 697, l. 5, 1232, ll. 11 f.; §III, 24, 37, 57 f.
10 §III, 23; §III, 25, 81; G, 14, 144, 160 (map); see *C.A.H.* I³, pt. 2, ch. xvii, sect. III.

place for the decision to be made to abandon further march along the river and to turn for home. The return journey must have entailed a long desert crossing to Ara in the Orontes valley, which may be the Assyrian Ara near Hama, or perhaps Tell Ar, north-east of Apamea.[1] The homeward march, interrupted while the pharaoh took his pleasure in hunting elephant in Neya,[2] then brought him through Zinzar[3] and Takhsy,[4] in the valley of the Biqā', to the siege and capture of stubborn Qadesh.[5]

This campaign, the eighth, was the climax of Tuthmosis' military career. For the first time an Egyptian army had entered Mitannian territory and met and defeated a Mitannian army. Yet the number of prisoner taken—three prisoners, thirty women and six hundred-odd slaves—shows that the expedition was little more than a raid and that the main force of the enemy cannot have been engaged. Though the Jebel Barkal stela taunts the king of Mitanni with running away,[6] no further attempt was made to challenge Saustatar, if it was he,[7] in his own territory, and it would appear that the Egyptian army, so far from being successful against the Mitannians, had suffered a reverse on the Euphrates. Nevertheless, it was after this campaign that Babylonia,[8] Assyria and 'Kheta the Great', the Hittite king himself, sent gifts to the pharaoh with congratulatory messages.[9] Not a little apprehensive, perhaps, of the extent of the dominion of Mitanni, her neighbours joined in congratulating, in oriental fashion, the new power who could successfully challenge her. One other of the independent nations, whose name is unfortunately lost, sent a present of various sorts of birds, perhaps to swell the zoological collection at Karnak; they included 'four birds of this land, that lay every day',[10] surely a reference to the domestic fowl, which makes rare appearances in Egyptian art but does not seem to have become acclimatized in Egypt,[11] though it was known in Mesopotamia from Sumerian times.[12]

The psychological effect of this campaign must have been considerable, but the Egyptians could not yet be sure of the

---

[1] G, 14, 143; §VIII, 2, 33.   [2] See above, p. 427.

[3] G, 14, 309; §I, 18, vol. I, 157*.

[4] §IV, 7, 158 n. 69; G, 14, 275 f.; §I, 18, vol. I, 150*.

[5] G, 27, 894 f.; A, 28, vol. II, 158 f.   [6] G, 27, 1232, l. 10.

[7] As, e.g., G, 21, 77. W. Helck in §III, 28, 7 n. 1 suggests it was Parsashatar.

[8] Called Sangara in Egyptian inscriptions (§I, 18, vol. I, 209* ff.; G, 14, 286); in Akkadian, Shankhara (§I, 50, vol. III, 103 and n. 3). Perhaps specifically the Sinjār area, but at this period applied to the whole Kassite realm.

[9] G, 27, 700 f.   [10] Ibid. ll. 13 f.

[11] §VII, 75, 444, and fig. 22, 2.   [12] G, 19, vol. I, 222 f., vol. II, 308.

submission of all the city states of central Syria, some of whom were still defiant, while north Syria was still unconquered and probably still under Mitannian overlordship. The ninth campaign, in the following year, took the army to Nukhashshe,[1] in the middle Orontes region east of the territory of Ugarit;[2] the booty taken included large quantities of silver and gold, and tribute was brought to the victorious pharaoh by the princes of Retenu.[2] Prince Taku was installed by Tuthmosis as regent on the throne of Nukhashshe.[3] It was a prosperous year for the Egyptians, for in addition to timber for shipbuilding, they received a great amount of copper, as well as ivory, lapis lazuli and other of the luxury products which were wont to be exchanged between princes of the time, from Asy (Isy, Isia).[4] In the thirty-fifth year a rebellion broke out in the north, and Tuthmosis, marching to deal with it, encountered and defeated a Mitannian army at a place called Ara'na, perhaps Erin, north-west of Aleppo,[5] and sent them fleeing headlong toward the 'river-land of Naharin';[6] in spite of the chronicler's insistence on the great size of the Mitannian forces, only ten prisoners were taken; the chief prize was 60 chariots and 180 horses—a team and a spare for each chariot. Two subsequent campaigns in the years 36 and 37 are lost;[7] the thirteenth found the Egyptian army again in Nukhashshe, and as a result, perhaps, of the complete subjection of her neighbour, Alalakh to the north for the first time sent an embassy with conciliatory gifts.[8]

Several years passed. In the thirty-ninth year of Tuthmosis' reign, a campaign against the bedawin, perhaps in south Palestine, was followed by the collection of tribute.[9] The achievements of the fortieth year are lost, and in the forty-first year no information is provided save a list of the tribute of Retenu and the usual statement that the harbours were provisioned for the year from the harvest of the coastal plain.[10] The last and seventeenth campaign was undertaken in the pharaoh's forty-second year, when he was already an elderly man for whom the strenuous life of a soldier on the march must have been burdensome. Irqata, a

[1] G, 27, 716, l. 12 ff., 717; G, 14, 291. [2] See above, p. 430.
[3] EA 51, l. 13. [4] See below, p. 491.
[5] G, 6, 468 n. 5; G, 14, 152; otherwise §III, 6, 235, 238.
[6] G, 27, 710, ll. 3, 15. [7] §III, 24, 11; G, 27, 714 f.
[8] *Ibid.* 719, l. 16, to 720, l. 4; otherwise G, 28, 38. Astour (§III, 6) identifies many of the names in the lists and annals of Tuthmosis III with towns and villages in the kingdom of Mukish, and thinks that this region, too, was subjugated (see §III, 6, map, p. 240).
[9] G, 27, 721 f. [10] *Ibid.* 726 f.

harbour town between Simyra and Ardata, almost certainly the modern 'Arqa near Tripoli,[1] was taken over in preparation for an expedition against Tunip. This latter place is mentioned in the list associated with the eighth campaign but the city itself may have been by-passed on that occasion. Now the proud city was reduced, its harvest taken and its orchards cut down.[2] On the return march, three cities in the Qadesh region were captured and their Mitannian garrisons taken prisoner; the presence of these troops in the heart of what was now Egyptian territory leaves no doubt of the formidable opposition which the Egyptians were still to encounter in their attempts to dominate Syria.[3]

IV. THE BALANCE OF POWER

For the last twelve years of Tuthmosis III's reign, no Egyptian army was seen in Syria and the old king, too old for campaigning, remained at home, content to receive embassies from his vassals who came every year with their tribute and kissed the ground before him. Little by little, it may be surmised, they came less frequently, and when the news came that the pharaoh was dead, the cities of the Biqā' revolted and expelled their garrisons. The first campaign of Amenophis II[4] took him in 1448, the third year of his reign, to Takhsy,[5] the region around Qadesh where Tuthmosis III had campaigned in his thirty-third year, on his way back through Zinzar, Tunip and Qadesh.[6] Takhsy must have been of considerable extent, for the architect Minmose, in Tuthmosis' reign, speaks of plundering thirty towns here.[7] Seven local dynasts were now involved in an uprising, and they were treated with a savagery intended to demonstrate that Amenophis would brook no rebellion: they were executed by the king's own hand, and the bodies of six were exposed at Thebes, while the seventh was hung on the walls of Napata as a grisly warning to would-be rebels.[8] The deed is recorded on a stela in the sanctuary of the small temple at Amada which may have been built with the spoils of the campaign.[9]

---

[1] G, 27, 729, ll. 7–9; G, 6, 80 ff.; §III, 4, vol. III, 130; G, 14, 153, 177; A, 28, vol. II, 232, no. 13.

[2] G, 27, 729, l. 15, to 730, l. 1. The conquest is referred to in EA 59, 5 ff. and the ruler of Tunip himself is depicted in a Theban tomb bringing tribute (§III, 11, pl. 4; see below, p. 470).

[3] A, 17, 153.   [4] G, 27, 1296 ff.; §III, 28, 28 ff.

[5] §I, 18, vol. I, 150* f.; §IV, 1, vol. II, 6. The biblical Thakhash (Gen. xxii. 24).

[6] G, 27, 893, l. 6; G, 14, 275 f.; §IV, 7, 158 n 69.

[7] G, 27, 1442, l. 17.   [8] Ibid. 1297, ll. 3–15.   [9] Ibid. 1287 ff.

On a badly damaged stela from Karnak, and another, much better preserved from Mīt Rahīna (Memphis),[1] two further campaigns are described; the details differ in the two accounts but the main narrative is the same and argues a basic annalistic source for both.[2] In the seventh year of his reign, Amenophis led his army through Takhsy northwards, engaging a new rebel force at Shamshatam,[3] probably on the west bank of the Orontes not far from Qatna. The countryside was laid waste 'in the twinkling of an eye, like a lion ranging the deserts',[4] and on the next day the king crossed the river on a bridge of boats, over which the noise of his chariot-wheels was like that of his patron the thunder-god.[5] Near Qatna, perhaps the next day, a skirmish took place in which the king had a further opportunity of displaying the personal bravery which is the theme of these inscriptions.[6] Six Hurrian nobles with their chariots, and some Sutaean warriors, were captured. In the phrase of the court scribe, 'they retreated when His Majesty even looked at them... His Majesty laid them low with his battle-axe.'[7] The next event recounted is a success in Neya a fortnight later[8] and we are left to speculate whether in that interval the king reached the Euphrates, as he no doubt hoped to do, to range his stela alongside those of his father and great-grandfather, or whether he met with some reverse in conflict with the Mitannian army. The statement of the Royal Overseer of Works, Minmose, that he erected boundary stelae at the frontiers of empire in the land of Karoy (Napata) and the land of Naharin, though dated to year 4 of Amenophis II,[9] may refer to an earlier episode of his career, in the reign of Tuthmosis III, under whom he had already held office.[10] Official inscriptions in antiquity were not concerned with recording failure and defeat, and it appears highly probable that the Egyptian army met with a serious setback at this point, about which the chronicler would naturally remain silent.

However this may be, the king and his troops appear to have been well received in Neya, where the populace came out upon their walls to applaud the king; but on the way back, word was brought of a revolt which had broken out at a place _Ikt_, where a plot had been discovered to throw out the Egyptian garrison.[11]

[1] G, 27, 1299 ff.; §III, 28, 32 ff.; §IV, 7; §IV, 14, 129 ff.

[2] §IV, 7, 97 ff.; §III, 5, 39 ff.

[3] G, 27, 1302, l. 1, 1310, l. 11; §IV, 7, 147; G, 14, 156; §IV, 2, 177 ff.; §V, 21, 25.   [4] G, 27, 1302, l. 2, 1310, l. 13.

[5] §I, 54, 51; §IV, 26, 252.   [6] See above, ch. IX, sect. V.

[7] G, 27, 1302, ll. 9 f., 1310, ll. 13 f., cf. _C.A.H._ II³, pt. 2, ch. XX, sect. III.

[8] G, 27, 1312, ll. 1 ff.   [9] _Ibid._ 1448, l. 13.

[10] _Ibid._ 1441, ll. 15 f.   [11] _Ibid._ 1303, ll. 9 ff.

The suggestion that this was Ugarit[1] cannot be accepted; not only is the vocalization defective, but the assumption that Ugarit had been occupied, either by Amenophis II earlier in his reign or by Tuthmosis III before him, is not warranted by the evidence.[2] Moreover, the name of this seaport, which was to play so important a part in Egyptian affairs during the reign of Amenophis III and his successor,[3] does not appear in the (admittedly incomplete) lists of towns captured by kings during the fifteenth century B.C. Wherever *Ikt* was, Amenophis acted swiftly, besieged and took it, and crushed the rebellion;[4] five other places in the neighbourhood were plundered or yielded voluntary tribute. In approximately twelve days from his reception in Neya, he was back in the neighbourhood of Qadesh; the city opened its gates to him, an oath of fealty was administered to the grandees,[5] and Amenophis gratified his vanity by putting on one of his target-shooting displays[6] for their benefit, and hunting hares, gazelle and wild asses in the forest of Lebwe south of the city.[7] The town of Khashabu, in the Biqā',[8] was taken by the king, apparently singlehanded if the narrative is to be trusted; he returned from the fight, we are told, with sixteen *mariyanna* chained to his chariot and sixty bulls driven before him.[9] This is the stuff of legend, but the capture of a messenger from the Mitannian king, intercepted in the plain of Sharon with a letter hung around his neck which must have been intended for one of Egypt's Palestinian vassals, no doubt inciting to rebellion, is probably a true incident.[10] The homeward journey completed, the army arrived at Memphis and counted the booty, which included Hurrians and their wives, Canaanites and their young sons and daughters, and a large orchestra of two hundred and seventy female musicians, together with their musical instruments of silver and gold.[11]

The last campaign of Amenophis II, only two years later, was restricted to a comparatively small area of Palestine, surprisingly near home; it appears to have centred round the Plain of Esdraelon and the hills to the west of Galilee. Yahmai, south of the Carmel range, the scene of Tuthmosis III's council of war some forty

[1] A, 35, 199 ff.; A, 51, 122.

[2] §III, 28, 36; G, 5, 407; G, 14, 163, 171 n. 111; §IV, 7, 149 f., 164 f.; A, 28, vol. II, 336.

[3] *C.A.H.* II³, pt. 2, ch. XVII, sect. IV.   [4] G, 27, 1303, ll. 9 ff., 1312, ll. 13 ff.

[5] *Ibid.* 1304, l. 2, 1313, l. 4.   [6] See above, ch. IX, sect. V.

[7] G, 27, 1304, ll. 5 ff.; G, 14, 58, 131; §IV, 7, 154; §IV, 19, 127 f.; §V, 51, 53.

[8] §IV, 7, 155 n. 61 a; §III, 28, 34 n. 2; G, 14, 128, 158; §IV, 4, 15.

[9] G, 27, 1304, ll. 10 ff.   [10] G, 14, 158, 172 n. 117.

[11] G, 27, 1305, ll. 4 ff.; see below, p. 482.

years before,[1] was the first objective; other villages were plundered, and the king's chariot thundered across the plain: 'his horses flew like comets across the sky'.[2] The epic-heroic tone of the narrative of the Memphis stela, in which the king is again depicted as performing prodigies of valour single-handed, cannot disguise the fact that Amenophis was faced with a serious rebellion; five months and five days after the start of the campaign he was still fighting in the same area at Anukharta, perhaps Anaharath, north of the Jezreel valley,[3] and the capture of a few hundred head of cattle and the deposition of a local ruler at Geba-sumin[4] seem poor results for so lengthy a campaign, and indicate that Egypt may have suffered a serious reverse about which the records are silent. Moreover, no further campaigns were undertaken by a pharaoh who, though perhaps already in his mid forties, was physically in the prime of life and of unusual stamina. After the third campaign, we are told, embassies came from the Hittites, from Shanhar or Sangara, which is almost certainly another name for Babylonia,[5] and from Naharin,[6] and their felicitations on his success doubtless gratified Amenophis. Mitanni's embassy may have been an overture for peace, since at about this time Tudkhaliash, the Hittite king, marched on North Syria and captured Aleppo.[7] This city had been in the hands of the Mitannians ('Khanigalbat') since the time of Saustatar.[8] The Hittite advance must have alarmed both Egypt and her old enemy, and brought about a *rapprochement* between them. 'The chiefs of Mitanni came to him,' says another inscription of Amenophis II,[9] 'their gifts upon their backs, to beseech His Majesty for the sweet breath of life. [This was] an occurrence that nobody had heard of since the time of the gods: that this country, which knew not Egypt, besought the Good God.'

It is perhaps in this period that we must set a treaty agreement between the Egyptians and the Hittites to which reference is made both by Shuppiluliumash I and by Murshilish II.[10] The reason for the treaty is obscure; it appears to have concerned some people from the north Anatolian city of Kurushtama who for some unstated reason came south to Syria and settled on Egyptian

[1] See above, p. 447.   [2] G, 27, 1306, l. 4.
[3] *Ibid.* 1308, l. 5; G, 14, 161; §III, 39, 184; Joshua xix. 19. The site Tell el-Mukharkhash is suggested in A, 1.
[4] G, 27, 1308, l. 12; §v, 51, 57; §IV, 4, 21.
[5] See above, p. 457 n. 8.   [6] G, 27, 1309, l. 13; G, 24, 247.
[7] See below, ch. xv, sect II.   [8] G, 28, 39.
[9] G, 27, 1326, ll. 1 ff.; §III, 28, 45.
[10] *K.U.B.* xiv, 8; G, 24, 395; §IV, 11, 208 ff.; *C.A.H.* II³, pt. 2, ch. xVII, sect. II.

territory, in the land of Amqi between Lebanon and Anti-Lebanon, the southern Biqā'.[1] This must have been at a time when the power of Mitanni was not sufficiently widespread to bar the way.

But the Hittites could not maintain their hold on Aleppo. A passage, unfortunately badly damaged and incomplete, in the preamble of a later treaty between the Hittite king Murshilish II and Talmi-Sharruma king of Aleppo[2] relates that an unnamed earlier ruler of Aleppo 'sinned against Khattushilish, King of Khatti' (who must be Tudkhaliash's successor, Khattushilish II) and returned to his Mitannian allegiance.[3] The occasion appears to have been an invasion of the territory of both Aleppo and Nukhashshe by Ashtata, another of Mitanni's vassal kingdoms; Aleppo thereupon appealed to the Mitannian king, who gave back to both kingdoms their former dependencies, the Hittites being now powerless to intervene.[4] Thus by about 1430 B.C. the central part of North Syria was again firmly under Mitannian control.

In a fragmentary inscription Tuthmosis IV, who succeeded his father fifteen years later, mentions booty from his 'first victorious campaign against the miserable Naharin',[5] but almost at once negotiations began in earnest and a peace treaty ended the long hostility of the two powers. According to Tushratta, it was Tuthmosis who made the first overtures; his offer of marriage to the daughter of Artatama, now ruling in Mitanni, was at first refused, and Tuthmosis, in his anxiety for an alliance, pressed his suit repeatedly.[6] 'He repeated the message five times, six times, but he did not deliver her. He repeated the message a seventh time to my grandfather; then in reply he delivered her, perforce.' Since Tuthmosis reigned for only eight years, and the prolonged negotiations, entailing perhaps fourteen journeys to and fro on the long road between Memphis and Washshuganni and a suitable interval between each,[7] must have occupied at least four of them, we may suspect that the 'first campaign' was not of great moment, and that it met with little success.

Tuthmosis IV is depicted on the panels of the chariot found in his tomb[8] mowing down bearded Asiatics beneath his chariot-wheels and pouring arrows into a disordered mass of dead and dying foes. The legendary or symbolic character of this scene is

---

[1] §v, 1, 153 ff.; §iv, 8, 100 ff., 190 ff.; §iv, 12, 60 f.; G, 14, 276, 283 n. 70.
[2] §i, 66, 80 ff.　　　　[3] K.Bo. 1, 6, ll. 21 ff.
[4] A, 28, vol. i, 183, vol. ii, 35 ff.; A, 17, 154.
[5] G, 27, 1554, ll. 17 f.; §iii, 28, 147; G, 5, 409.
[6] EA 29, ll. 16 ff.; G, 16, 246 ff., 1065 ff.
[7] §i, 54, 60 f.　　　　[8] §iv, 6, 24 ff., pls. 9–12, figs. 1–14. See Plate 95 (b).

manifest in the figure of the hawk-headed warrior god, Mont, who stands at the king's elbow clad in coat of mail, and steadies his aim.[1] Tuthmosis may nevertheless have seen action in Palestine, for he is said to have settled Hurrians from Gezer as temple slaves in Egypt,[2] and it was perhaps on this occasion that he travelled farther north to visit Sidon[3]—an event which, if Rib-Adda, the later ruler of Byblos, is to be believed, marked the last occasion on which a demonstration of might was made in that area by an Egyptian army.

Artatama had succeeded to the throne of Mitanni some time during the reign of Amenophis II or perhaps late in that of Tuthmosis III. The empire which his father, the great Saustatar, had won in his youth had diminished but was still of great extent. Saustatar had conquered Assyria, carrying off in triumph from Ashur a door of silver and gold to adorn his palace at Wash-shuganni;[4] a letter from Nuzi shows that he governed territory in Gutium, in the Zagros mountains east of the Tigris valley, and that the region around Kirkuk was under his control.[5] Mitannian rule over Assyria is reflected in the Hurrian names of officials in legal texts of the fifteenth century found at Ashur;[6] and among the remarkable series of stelae erected in that city,[7] two are of officers of a later generation whose father and grandfather had been officials in Ashur of the 'king of Khanigalbat'. The dynasty of Adasi remained in the capital, but as vassals of their Hurrian overlords, and the absence of building records is eloquent of their impoverishment.

Ashur-bēl-nisheshu, however, the son of Ashur-nirari II and nephew[8] of Ashur-nadin-ahhē, rebuilt the fortification walls of Ashur,[9] built by Puzur-Ashur III before Saustatar's conquest,[10] a thing he would never have been permitted to do by a suzerain, and it may therefore have been he who was able to throw off the yoke of Mitannian rule.[11] He did not, however, feel himself strong enough to carry the war into the enemy's territory, and Shuttarna, the son of Artatama, still remained in possession of a

[1] §iv, 6, pl. 10.   [2] G, 27, 1556, ll. 10–11; §iii, 28, 148; A, 19, 55.
[3] EA 85, ll. 69–73; G, 16, 411, 1174. See further A, 19.
[4] §i, 66, 38 f. = *K.Bo.* i, 3, ll. 8–10.
[5] §i, 59, 273 f.; §vii, 61, pl. 118, 1; §iv, 21, 136 f., 151 f.
[6] §ii, 1, 103 ff.; §ii, 33, 262.
[7] §iv, 3, 61, pl. 10, fig. 103, 85, pl. 23, fig. 189; §ii, 1, 103 ff., pl. 25; §ii, 17, xix, 32 ff.
[8] §ii, 31, 44.
[9] §ii, 17, xx, 32 ff.; §ii, 35, vol. i, pl. 58.
[10] See above, p. 442.   [11] §ii, 33, 266 f.; but see §ii, 8, 21.

statue of Ishtar of Nineveh[1] earlier looted from Assyria, probably by Saustatar. Ashur-bēl-nisheshu strengthened his position by an alliance with Karaindash, the Kassite king of Babylonia.[2] The Assyrian's reign is well fixed by the king-list to approximately 1419–1410 B.C.,[3] and he must therefore have come to the throne within a year or so of Amenophis III.

Karaindash himself was the first Kassite king to enter into direct diplomatic contact with Egypt,[4] and to seal his friendship he gave to the Egyptian pharaoh, perhaps Tuthmosis IV,[5] his daughter in marriage. The Kassites were now entering the arena of power politics for the first time; long deprived of access to the sources of metal and timber, they were now able to acquire not only these essential raw materials but also luxury goods by trade. The increasing prosperity of Babylonia is reflected in the amount of building undertaken by Karaindash.[6] In a short inscription in Sumerian found at Uruk, where he built a remarkable temple,[7] he calls himself 'King of Babylon, King of Sumer and Akkad, King of the Kashshu-people' and also 'King of Karduniash', the first instance of the use of this title.[8] His successor Kurigalzu, son of Kadashman-kharbe, carried out an even more ambitious building programme—perhaps with the aid of Egyptian gold, for he is probably to be identified with the father of Kadashman-Enlil who talked 'friendship' with Amenophis III and sent him a daughter to wife;[9] on this occasion, at least, the two kings exchanged lavish presents.[10] Among the many building inscriptions in which the name Kurigalzu occurs it is difficult to determine whether the first bearer of the name[11] is to be understood, the son of Kadashman-kharbe,[12] or the second, the son of Burnaburiash II, who also did much building at Uruk, Ur and elsewhere;[13] it is generally agreed that it was Kurigalzu I who was responsible for the foundation of the greatest of the dynasty's monuments, the

[1] EA 23, 13–19; G, 18, 1051; but see below, p. 489.
[2] C.T. 34, 38 ff.; §II, 40, 84.
[3] §II, 37, 87 suggests 1416–1408.
[4] EA 10, ll. 8 f.; G, 16, 35, 1029.
[5] Otherwise A. Goetze in §II, 21, 101 n. 46.
[6] §II, 18, 44.
[7] §IV, 17; G, 25, 333; C.A.H. II³, pt. 2, ch. XVIII, sect. VI.
[8] §II, 18, 44; G, 8, vol. I, 372 f.
[9] EA 1, l. 12 ff.; 2, l. 8 f.   [10] EA 3, l. 9 ff.
[11] §II, 21, 99, suggests the existence of an earlier Kurigalzu in the sixteenth century, who would then be the first of three kings of the name. See A, 8.
[12] §II, 27, 3 n. 1.
[13] §II, 18, 44 f.; §IV, 9, 196; §IV, 10, 47 ff., nos. 152–64; §II, 49, 2 ff., 13 ff., 44 ff., 58 ff.

fortress-city of Dūr-Kurigalzu (the modern 'Aqarqūf),[1] which was designed both as a new residence city and as a bulwark against possible attack from the ever-menacing armies of Mitanni. The building of the city wall and the foundation of the great *zikkurrat* whose impressive remains, now being restored, are a landmark in the desert thirty miles west of modern Baghdad,[2] together with the erection of some of the chief temples in the city, is probably to be ascribed to this king.[3]

Kurigalzu's conquest of Elam is commemorated on an agate tablet found at Nippur, which had been originally dedicated to the goddess Inanna at Susa[4] for the life of Shulgi, of the Third Dynasty of Ur, and on a fragment found at Susa itself the defeat of Susa and Elam by Kurigalzu and his devastation of Markhashe are recounted.[5] 'All the kings of the Land', says a late chronicle, 'brought him tribute.'[6] The long, obscure and very fragmentary inscription on a broken statue found at 'Aqarqūf[7] claims that he took pains to 'set up the old days unto future days', restoring to the ancient Sumerian gods their due offerings, and reviving cults long discontinued.[8] A deed of gift describes his pious care for the holy cities, Ur, Uruk, Eridu, and his building of temples to Anu and Ishtar.[9] Another inscription, preserved only in a late copy, records large gifts of land by Kurigalzu to the temple of Ishtar at Uruk.[10]

Shuttarna II of Mitanni, who may also have come to the throne within a year or so of Amenophis III, or perhaps a little earlier, has left no memorial of his reign. The marriage of his daughter Gilu-Kheba to the pharaoh, in the tenth year of Amenophis, and her arrival at the Egyptian court with three hundred and seventeen Mitannian girls in her retinue, was commemorated by the issue of a large scarab,[11] of which copies have been found in Palestine, at Gezer and 'Ain Shems,[12] for so important an event was widely publicized in the territories under Egyptian control.

At the turn of the century, the five great powers of western Asia were in balance. Egypt and Mitanni had an agreed frontier and a close alliance. On the scarab which commemorated his

---

[1] G, 25, 334; §II, 4, 11 f.; §II, 5; §II, 6; G, 8, vol. II, 246 f.; otherwise §IV, 16, 322. See *C.A.H.* II³, pt. 2, ch. XVIII, sect. VI.   [2] §IV, 5, 17.

[3] §II, 4, 1 ff. Goetze (§II, 21) prefers the earlier Kurigalzu (see above, p. 465 n. 11), on the evidence of pottery from the lowest level.   [4] §II, 9, 96 f.

[5] §IV, 22, 7.   [6] Chronicle P.

[7] §II, 4, 15, pl. 7; G, 24, 58 f.   [8] See above, p. 441.

[9] §IV, 23, 19 ff.   [10] *C.T.* 36, pls. 6, 7; G, 19, vol. II, 61; §IV, 9, 96.

[11] G, 27, 1738; §III, 28, 234; cf. EA 29, l. 18.

[12] §V, 39, 19 f., no. 539, 128 no. 538.

marriage to Queen Tiy, in his second year, Amenophis III claimed that his northern frontier reached Naharin.[1] This boundary is nowhere defined, but the early Amarna letters give some indication of its whereabouts: the coast as far as Ugarit was now under Egyptian control, thanks to the continued activities of the Egyptian fleet;[2] the Damascus region, Amqi, Qadesh, Tunip and Amurru were held,[3] but the kingdoms of Qatna, Neya and Nukhashshe had thrown in their lot with Mitanni.[4] Geographical lists from Karnak include among the pharaoh's captives Nukhashshe, Carchemish and Aleppo,[5] and the lands of Khatti, Naharin and Sangara,[6] but these had by now become conventional boasts, divorced from reality.[7] The Hittites, after their initial success in North Syria, had been forced to withdraw and were held in check by their preoccupation with events in Anatolia;[8] Assyria was independent and had the Kassite king as an ally. Babylonia and Egypt, too, were allies. Early in his reign Kurigalzu had refused to entertain the proposals of would-be Canaanite rebels who sent an embassy to Babylonia asking for help against their Egyptian overlords. His reply,[9] couched in no uncertain terms, demonstrated the firmness of his loyalty to the treaty:

> If you cherish hostility against the king of Egypt, my brother,
> and wish to ally yourself with another,
> Shall I not come and shall I not plunder you?
> For he is in alliance with me.

The stage was set. The Amarna letters illuminate the scene with a brief flood of light during the years that followed, and a later chapter will tell how, with the advent of a young and vigorous king at Khattusha who was to prove a military genius, the drama unfolded.[10]

V. THE EGYPTIANS IN RETENU

The conquest of wide territories in Syria-Palestine, with its heterogeneous population, complex political structure and diversified regions, presented the Egyptians with a problem very different

[1] G, 27, 1741, l. 15, cf. 1841, l. 14; §III, 28, 235; §IV, 24, 208.
[2] §VII, 39, 23 f.; §V, 7 (EA 46–9); C.A.H. II³, pt. 2, ch. XVII, sect. IV.
[3] §VI, 17, 13; G, 14, 162 f.; A, 28, vol. II, 160. For the allegiance of Tunip at this time, see ibid. 91 f.   [4] §V, 23, 3 n. 17; A, 28, vol. II, 35 ff., 70 f., 133.
[5] §IV, 18, 4.   [6] Ibid., and §III, 40, 133; A, 15, 2 ff.
[7] The lists also name cities of the Aegean islands, Crete and perhaps the Greek mainland, 'all difficult-to-reach lands of the ends of the earth' (G, 27, 780; §IV, 18; A, 15).   [8] See below, ch. XV, sect. II.   [9] EA 9, ll. 19 ff.; G, 16, 1028.
[10] C.A.H. II³, pt. 2, ch. XVII, sect. I.

from that of administering their Nubian possessions. In the south they had spread gradually into the territory of peoples with little culture of their own, whose organization was tribal and primitive, and who therefore accepted the more readily the order imposed upon them and the civilization which accompanied it.[1] In the New Kingdom, the people of Nubia became in fact Egyptians and their country was regarded as part of Egypt; the viceroy and his staff were Egyptian officials, a branch of the bureaucracy which governed the Beloved Land.[2] In Syria, on the other hand, the Egyptians found themselves among people whose civilization, though in many ways different, was as ancient as their own and whose city states possessed an evolved constitution, an organized religion, and a complex social and legal system. In the Middle Kingdom, with the possible exception of Byblos,[3] little attempt had been made to interfere with the princes of Retenu; now for the first time the Egyptians found themselves in possession of an Asiatic empire. The campaigns of the Eighteenth Dynasty had as their express aim 'to extend the boundaries of Egypt'[4] and the newly won territories became in theory part of the realm of the pharaoh, with all that this implied in terms of administration. Nevertheless, to introduce into Syria the whole machinery of Egyptian government would have put too great a strain on manpower, even had it been wise. Each kingdom of Hither Asia was accordingly taken over as a going concern, and in general allowed to retain its ruler, albeit as a vassal of Egypt and under military supervision.[5]

Some insight into the workings of the administration in Asia can be obtained by piecing together the meagre information to be culled from the inscriptions of Tuthmosis III and Amenophis II, and the greater volume of evidence to be found in the foreign correspondence of Amenophis III and his successors, in the first half of the fourteenth century B.C., found at the modern El-Amarna, the site of Akhenaten's capital, and often referred to as the Amarna Letters.[6] A handful of tablets of a similar nature, found in the Canaanite citadel of Tell Ta'annek (ancient Taanach)[7] bridges the gap in time between the two sources, and the tombs of Egyptian officials who served in Asia or were responsible for

---

[1] §v, 41.   [2] See above, ch. IX, sect. VII.
[3] *C.A.H.* I³, pt. 2, ch. XXI, sect. II.   [4] G, 27, 1296, l. 15, and *passim*.
[5] §v, 23, 1 ff.; §v, 35, 106 ff.; G, 20, vol. II(1), 134 ff.
[6] EA refers to these, as numbered in G, 16; §VI, 25; *C.A.H.* II³, pt. 2, ch. XX.
[7] §1, 6, 30 ff. These letters, from their style and content, may well be royal documents; if so, the writer must be Amenophis II. A similar letter from Gezer is attributed to Tuthmosis IV (A, 31).

the reception of foreign envoys and their tribute provide a little autobiographical detail and a wealth of pictorial illustration.[1]

Wherever possible, the existing régime seems to have been allowed to continue; after a rebellion, the hereditary ruler might be deposed but another member of the same ruling family, perhaps a brother or a son, would usually be appointed in his stead.[2] The Egyptians referred in their inscriptions to a vassal ruler as 'the Great One' (wr) of such-and-such a city, a title which may be translated 'prince', 'regent' or in some cases 'king', since the same word is applied to the heads of state of Babylonia, Assyria and Mitanni and the Hittite king. In the Amarna letters rulers sometimes refer to each other as the 'headman' (ḫazan(n)u)[3] of the city X', and to themselves, humbly, as 'the man (awēlu) of X', the form of address invariably used by the pharaoh in addressing them by letter. The allegiance of these vassals was initially secured by the imposition upon them of a binding oath, renewed from time to time and always at the accession of a new pharaoh.[4] At the coronation of Tuthmosis III 'all the Great Ones of all foreign countries' came to do him homage[5] and advantage would be taken of the presence of the king in a certain district of Asia to hold a kind of durbar at which all the vassal princes in the locality would come to renew their oaths of allegiance. It was at such ceremonies, no doubt, that the humiliating proskynesis, 'seven times on the belly and seven times on the back', often mentioned when vassals write to the king, must have been performed.[6] A relief from the Memphite tomb of Horemheb derisively depicts the corpulent elderly Syrian vassals grovelling on the ground in both these undignified and inconvenient postures.[7]

A vassal ruler was obliged to carry out the command of the pharaoh and his deputies in all respects and to protect his kingdom and administer it aright, as part of the Egyptian realm.[8] It was his duty to ensure that the annual tribute which had been imposed upon his city was collected annually and forwarded to Egypt;[9] he was expected to keep the Egyptian troops in his territory supplied and must maintain and provision the supply ports and garrisons.[10] He had to summon his subjects for corvée duty if

---

[1] E.g. §v, 11; §v, 13; §v, 14; §III, 11. [2] §v, 35, 130.
[3] E.g. EA 107, ll. 24 f.; EA 125, l. 32; §v, 35, 107; G, 2, vol. VI, 164.
[4] G, 27, 1235, l. 16, 1304, l. 2; G, 14, 256 f.; §v, 23, 5.
[5] G, 27, 161, l. 14; cf. §v, 12, vol. II, pl. 37; §III, 11, pl. IV; §v, 14, pl. XXVIII.
[6] EA 64 and passim. [7] G, 23, 2, fig. 5. See Plate 99(b).
[8] §v, 35, 111 ff.; G, 14, 515 ff.
[9] E.g. G, 27, 1236 l. 17–1237 l. 10; §v, 23, 10.
[10] G, 27, 692 ff.; G, 1, vol. II, para. 472 and n. on 473.

required to do so.[1] It was his duty to keep the pharaoh informed of local events, especially of the movement of enemy troops[2] and he was forbidden to make contact with foreign powers or even to receive their embassies.[3] No copy has survived of a treaty between the pharaoh and any of his vassals, but it is likely that the terms of the agreement drawn up between conqueror and conquered were similar to those imposed by the Hittite kings on their vassals.[4] Many of the letters written by the regents to their 'lord' the king of Egypt are couched in obsequious terms: the writer professes himself 'thy slave, the dirt under thy feet', and declares himself ready to die if need be in his master's service.[5] The pharaoh, for his part, writes to his vassals curtly and to the point: 'To X say, Thus saith the king', and the same opening phrase, often without mention of the name of the addressee, is found in correspondence from the Hittite kings to their subjects at Ugarit.[6]

To ensure the good behaviour of a vassal, members of his family might be carried off as hostages to Egypt, his daughters to enter the royal harim,[7] his sons to be reared as pages at the Egyptian court.[8] Three princesses with Syrian names, identified as members of the king's harim by the gazelle heads on the diadem on the brow of one of them, were buried together in a rocky cleft at Thebes with their jewellery and cosmetics; each was called 'the king's wife'.[9] The young princes were housed in a 'castle' or closely guarded palace where they appear to have been well treated and given an education befitting their rank and future responsibilities.[10] The training of these young men, like the erstwhile schooling of the sons of rajahs at Harrow and Sandhurst, was an essential part of the imperial plan: 'Behold, the children and brothers of the regents [in this case, of Ṣumura and Ullaza] were brought to live in strongholds in Egypt. Now whosoever died among these princes, His Majesty would cause his son to stand in his place.'[11] Envoys of the rulers of Syria are shown in Theban tomb paintings bringing young children to Egypt with their tribute[12] and in one tomb the ruler of Tunip himself is shown carrying his little son on his arm.[13] The faithful allegiance of

---

[1] EA 248 a, 14; §1, 6, 20 f.; G, 24, 485 n. 7; §vi, 25, vol. ii, 648 f.; §vii, 46, 32.
[2] §v, 35, 113.   [3] EA 161, ll. 47; 162, ll. 9 ff.
[4] §vi, 21.   [5] G, 24, 483, cf. §vi, 30, vol. iii, xix, 4 = *RŠ*, 16, 112.
[6] §vi, 30, vol. iv, *passim.*   [7] EA 187, ll. 22–5; 99, ll. 10 ff.
[8] §v, 23, 34 f.   [9] §v, 48.
[10] G, 14, 366; §iii, 41, 105; EA 296, 25 ff.
[11] G, 27, 690, ll. 2–5; G, 1, vol. ii, para. 467.
[12] §iii, 11, pl. v, xx; §v, 13, vol. 2, pls. xxi–xxiii; G, 23, 15 f.; §viii, 22, fig. 42.
[13] §iii, 11, pl. iv; see Plate 99(*a*).

Rib-Adda, the regent of Byblos, sorely tried by Egyptian in-difference, yet always protesting his loyalty, perhaps reflects the successful side of this policy, but it was not wholly wise: the estrangement of Rib-Adda from his own people, the enmity of his brother, and his ultimate enforced flight from Byblos and de-position may show the other side of the coin. A young ruler returned to his native land after years of absence, imbued with Egyptian ideas and alien manners, his head 'anointed with oil' by the pharaoh,[1] must have been received with distrust and some-times with hostility; in several cases the rejection of their nominee had to be punished by the Egyptians as insurrection.

Flagrant disobedience on the part of a city ruler, the with-drawal of allegiance by flouting the authority of the overlord, withholding tribute, violating the territory of another vassal,[2] or treating with an enemy was not merely an act of rebellion but also of impiety: by the breaking of the oath of allegiance, the gods who had sponsored the treaty had been held in contempt. In exacting retribution for the crime, the Egyptian king became the instrument of divine justice.[3] Rebellion was punished by military action, the capture and sack of the rebel city, the devasta-tion of orchards and fields, and the enslavement of part of the population. The fate of the princes of Takhsy[4] for some par-ticularly flagrant act of defiance is an extreme, and unusual, in-stance of punishment; such grisly acts were not as a rule resorted to. Usually the mere threat of reprisal was enough: 'If for any reason you plot to exercise hostility, or harbour any thought of enmity or hatred in your heart, then you and your family are con-demned to death; therefore submit to the king, your lord, and you shall live.'[5] The mild treatment of the confederates at the surrender of Megiddo is an indication that conciliation was as a rule judged to be a wiser policy than frightfulness.[6]

Placed in general control of the vassals and responsible for the co-ordination of the administration of the province as a whole were the viceroys or commissars, the governors appointed by the pharaoh and invested by him with a ring in the presence of the assembled princes.[7] These important officials had the title 'Over-seer of Foreign Countries', or more precisely, 'Overseer of all Northern Countries',[8] in parallel with the title of the Nubian viceroy, who was 'Overseer of all Southern Countries', to whom in

[1] EA 51, ll. 5–6.   [2] §vi, 23, 72 f.   [3] §v, 34, 89.
[4] G, 27, 1297, ll. 3 ff.; G, 1, vol. ii, para. 797; see above, p. 459.
[5] EA 162, ll. 35–9; §iii, 41, 104.   [6] G, 14, 256 ff.; §v, 23, 4 ff.
[7] EA 107, ll. 21–4; §v, 35, 118; §v, 23, 5.   [8] §v, 35, 114 f.; G, 14, 260.

rank they were probably equal, though they do not bear the rank of 'King's Son'.[1] In Akkadian this officer was called *rābiṣu*,[2] 'overseer', or occasionally *šākinu*, 'resident' (*šakin māti*), in the Canaanite vernacular *sōkinu*.[3] The first known bearer of the title was General Djehuty, the conqueror of Joppa,[4] in the time of Tuthmosis III; it is probable that from the beginning there was more than one viceroy responsible for the northern possessions of the crown, the task exceeding the capacities of one man. Amenmose also held the office under Tuthmosis III and Amenophis II;[5] in the early part of the reign of Amenophis III there were certainly at least two, Penḥuwt[6] and Khaemwese,[7] and by the Amarna period Retenu seems to have been divided into three administrative districts, each under an Egyptian governor.[8] Amurru, the most northerly province, comprised most of what is today Lebanon, from Ugarit to Byblos, the capital in which the viceroy resided being at one time the port of Ṣumura.[9] Upi, the central province, included Qadesh and the Biqā' valley, Damascus and Anti-Lebanon, the Ḥaurān, and the northern part of Transjordania;[10] the residence was at Kumidu,[11] the modern village of Kāmid el-Lōz, strategically well sited in the valley of the Līṭāni river twelve kilometres north of Rasheya.[12] Canaan, the third and southernmost province, comprised the whole of Palestine from the Egyptian frontier to Tyre, and later to Byblos,[13] and was governed from Gaza,[14] which town appears later to have been called Pa-Kana'an.[15]

In each of these provinces there was a series of governors during the period covered by the Amarna letters.[16] Most of them bore Egyptian names: Pakhamnate and Kha'ip in Amurru,[17] Khamashsha in Upi,[18] and Pauru, Maya, Rianapa and Amenhotpe in Canaan;[19] but the name of Pakhura, the second governor of

---

[1] §I, 18, vol. I, 33*; §v, 41, 176.
[2] G, 16, vol. I, 1495; §v, 35, 116 f.; A, 26, 81.
[3] *C.A.H.* II³, pt. 2, ch. xvii, sect. I, and ch. xx, sect. II.
[4] G, 27, 999 ff.; see above, pp. 446 f. [5] §III, 11, 27 ff., pls. 32–39.
[6] G, 14, 260. [7] §III, 35, vol. I, no. 239.
[8] G, 14, 258 ff.; §v, 51, 51 ff.; §III, 34, 183 f.; A, 2, 146 ff.
[9] EA 106, 118, ll. 50–53; ll. 8 ff.; 155, ll. 66–7; G, 14, 258, 313 f.; §IV, I, vol. I, 326, vol. II, 3 ff. [10] G, 14, 258, 276; §I, 2, 35 ff.; §I, 62.
[11] EA 116, l. 75, 129, l. 85, 132, l. 49; G, 14, 258; §v, 23, 7.
[12] G, 6, 408; G, 16, 1241; A, 20. [13] G, 14, 258 f., 279 f.
[14] EA 289, l. 33; §v, 5, 139 f.; §v, 3, 352; G, 14, 259; §I, 18, vol. I, 191*.
[15] §III, 20, 104; §III, 44, vol. II, 34–39. [16] G, 14, 258 ff.; §v, 35, 114 ff.
[17] EA 60, l. 10; *ibid.* 68, ll. 19 ff.; *ibid.* 131, l. 35; §vi, 25, 249 n.; G, 14, 258.
[18] EA 198, l. 15; §v, 4, 10; G, 14, 258.
[19] EA 287, l. 45; *ibid.* 216, ll. 13 f., 300, l. 26; *ibid.* 315, ll. 13 f., 326, l. 17; §I, 6, 21 ff.; G, 14, 259 f.

Upi, means in Egyptian 'the Hurrian', and the first governor of Canaan at this period, Iankhamu,[1] had a Syrian name, as did his successor Addayu.[2] According to Egyptian practice the office appears to have passed at times from father to son.[3] A few letters of the Amarna collection are addressed not to the Egyptian king but to his viceroy; the tone is one of great respect.[4] Occasionally, however, a complaint is laid against one of these officers: Rib-Adda more than once expostulated to the pharaoh about a grave error of judgement on the part of Pakhura in sending bedawin irregulars (Sutu) to Byblos, where they had misbehaved; he alleged also that Pakhura had acted beyond his authority.[5]

Other officials are mentioned in the Amarna letters and it must be supposed that each governor had a staff of subordinates; few had Egyptian names, an indication that the imperial administration was seriously understaffed. Under the pharaoh, and within the limits of their jurisdiction, the authority of the governors was paramount, their responsibilities wide. They had to ensure that vassals under their charge performed what was required of them; they must act as liaison between them and the king, come to their aid with troops, negotiate with them, and on occasion escort them to Egypt.[6] Disputes between regents were dealt with by a court of arbitration consisting of the three commissars.[7] Contact with the central administration was maintained by the royal messengers, the king's personal envoys,[8] who carried diplomatic correspondence back and forth and conveyed decrees and proclamations such as that broadcast throughout the empire at the accession of a new pharaoh. These trusted couriers will be referred to later.[9] The headquarters in Egypt which dealt with the activities of the royal messengers and sent out directives to the viceroys and commands to the vassals was a building known as the Bureau for the Correspondence of Pharaoh;[10] it was the department for foreign and colonial affairs alike and was probably at Thebes for the greater part of the Eighteenth Dynasty, though it was moved to Akhetaten for the duration of Akhenaten's sojourn there.[11] This

[1] EA 83, l. 31; G, 18, 1169 f.; § vi, 41, 98 f.; §vi, 5, 90 ff.; G, 14, 265 n. 30; see, further, *C.A.H.* ii³, pt. 2, ch. xx, sect. 1.

[2] EA 254, l. 37, 285, l. 24; G, 18, 1316 f.

[3] G, 14, 258; G, 16, vol. ii, 1234.

[4] E.g. EA 73, 256.   [5] EA 122, ll. 31–44; 123, ll. 9–18.

[6] §v, 35, 119; EA 102, ll. 14–16, 29–34.   [7] EA 105, ll. 31–7; §vi, 23, 73.

[8] §i, 18, vol. i, 91* f.; G, 14, 260; §v, 35, 119 ff.; the Akkadian equivalent was *mār šipri* (§v, 35, 99 ff.).   [9] See below, pp. 485 ff.

[10] §vi, 29, vol. iii, 114, 150, pls. 48, nos. 5 and 6, 49, nos. 1 and 2, 83, no. 5; §v, 35, 123 f.   [11] §v, 37, 34; §vi, 5, 37.

department included among its staff Akkadian and Egyptian scribes[1] and, for a time at least, an Arzawan.[2] Egyptian–Akkadian glossaries, fragments of which were found at El-Amarna,[3] and copies of Akkadian mythological texts[4] were used to instruct the scribes in cuneiform.

To maintain the security of their possessions in Palestine and Syria, the pharaohs built fortresses[5] and installed garrisons in them.[6] Occupation troops were left in some cities to guard port installations at the naval bases[7] and to protect the vassals and governors. There were Egyptian garrisons at Ullaza[8] and Sharu-hen[9] in the time of Tuthmosis III, and in the Amarna period they are sometimes mentioned in cities further north, at Ṣumura[10] and Irqata.[11] The size of these garrisons, where numbers are given,[12] is surprisingly small, and in many cases a token force of a few hundred Egyptian or Nubian troops and fifty chariots[13] was considered enough to hold the city against hostile attack. Some towns or districts were made into royal domains: Gaza appears to have been one of these,[14] and later Kumidu.[15] Whole towns with their revenues were made over to the temple of Amun at Thebes.[16]

The Egyptians seem to have been perfunctory conquerors. An examination of the names of captured towns and districts reveals that there can have been no question of the complete subjugation of Syria and Palestine, or even of part of the area. About half the conquered places which can be identified lie along the great high road which links Palestine with North Syria, from the Shephēlāh, the coastal plain of what was later to be called Philistia, through the Taanach gap, crossing the Jordan south of Lake Ḥūleh to Damascus and the Ḥaurān, or continuing northwards through the Biqāʿ, past Qadesh and Qatna, towards Aleppo and Carchemish. The coastal cities of Phoenicia were held as far as the Tripoli region,[17] the northernmost as disembarkation ports for the interior; and Tunip probably guarded the route from the coast[18]

[1] G, 16, vol. I, 24. [2] EA 31 and 32; §VI, 5, 39 ff.
[3] §V, 44, 230 ff.; §VI, 25, vol. II, 796, no. 355*a*; §V, 37, 34 ff.
[4] EA 356–9.
[5] G, 27, 739 f.; G, 14, 262; §III, 4, vol. III, 134 f.; §V, 3, 352 f.; §V, 35, 128 f.
[6] §III, 4, vol. III, 107 ff.; G, 14, 262 f.; §V, 42, 17 f.
[7] G, 14, 264; §V, 29, 77. [8] G, 27, 1237, l. 15.
[9] *Ibid.* 656. [10] EA 104, 107.
[11] EA 100, 103. [12] G, 14, 263.
[13] EA 71, ll. 23–5. [14] G, 27, 648, l. 10.
[15] G, 14, 261; EA 116, l. 75, 129, l. 85, 132, l. 49, 198, l. 5.
[16] G, 27, 667, l. 10, 744, ll. 3 ff.
[17] §V, 23, 3. [18] §III, 4, vol. III, 136.

by way of the Eleutheros plain and the Nahr el-Kebīr to the Orontes valley, there linking up with the Aleppo road.[1] It is significant that Arvad and Ugarit are not mentioned among the conquests of Tuthmosis III and Amenophis II,[2] and would appear to have played no role in Egyptian history until the reign of Amenophis III; both cities appear to have enjoyed a special treaty relationship with Egypt during the early part of the fourteenth century, for the benefit of their mutual maritime trade. Aleppo and Carchemish, though they appear in the topographical lists of Amenophis III among his 'conquests',[3] probably remained at all times beyond Egypt's grasp.

A survey of the sites in Palestine and Syria where material evidence of Egyptian occupation during the Eighteenth Dynasty has been found confirms this impression.[4] Objects bearing the names of Egyptian pharaohs of this period are most thickly distributed in the Shephēlāh and the Plain of Esdraelon, and in the Biqā', that is to say, along the highway and its branches. In the hills, and in Jericho and Transjordanian sites, no such evidence is found, although the attractive products of Egyptian craftsmanship, vessels and amulets of faience,[5] scarabs and small stone vessels, spread to some extent over the country by trade, facilitated by Egyptian conquest; some were copied by local craftsmen.[6] Scarabs bearing the names of Hatshepsut, Tuthmosis IV, Amenophis II and Amenophis III are found sporadically, and a larger number bear the prenomen of Tuthmosis III,[7] but these little seal-amulets were always popular, travelled easily, and are not a reliable criterion for dating, since they could be inherited as heirlooms; moreover, great names likely to confer good fortune on their possessors appear to have retained their popularity long after the death of those who had borne them.[8] Several sites in Palestine show signs of destruction which may be attributable to the passage of the armies of Tuthmosis I, Tuthmosis III and Amenophis II,[9] but the towns were usually rebuilt on the same general plan as before and no great change, or sign of increased Egyptian influence, is found in the levels of the late fifteenth and fourteenth centuries.

[1] §III, 13, plan opp. p. 10; §III, 4, vol. III, 128 ff.; G, 14, 332.
[2] See above, pp. 460 f.   [3] §IV, 18, 4.
[4] §III, 35, vol. VII, 369 ff., 383 ff.; §V, 39, xiii ff.
[5] E.g. §V, 32, pls. 205–6.
[6] G, 23, figs. 69–71; §V, 46, 97, pls. 34–39; §V, 2, 106.
[7] E.g. §V, 38 fig. 70–71; §V, 25, 12 f., pl. I, no. 35; §V, 38, fig. 70; §V, 46, 35, 97; §VIII, 10, vol. II, 163; §VIII, 3, 424; §III, 35, vol. 7, 369 ff.; §V, 36, vol. III, pl. IV; §V, 6, 70 ff.   [8] §V, 25, 2.
[9] §V, 46, 34 f.; §VII, 65, 26; §VI, 47, 92; §V, 3, 352 f.

Part of a stela of one of the two latter pharaohs, commemorating a victory over Mitanni, was found at Tell el-'Oreima, the ancient Kinnereth, in Galilee,[1] and this appears to be the sole tangible relic of the triumphal passage of Egyptian arms. The city of Byblos, which was still delivering timber to 'her beloved lord',[2] continued to receive Egyptian goods, but most of the other harbour cities, which might also be expected to yield evidence of the Egyptian occupation, are unidentified or unexplored.

Egyptian objects dating to the reign of Amenophis III are rather more numerous in Palestine, and the conclusion might be drawn that though Egyptian civilization did not 'follow the flag', contact between Egyptians and Syrians increased as time went on. Temples were built to Egyptian gods in the royal domains:[3] there was a Ramesside temple at Gaza dedicated to Amun, and perhaps another sacred to Ptah at Askalon,[4] but these sanctuaries were for Egyptian officials; there appears to have been no attempt to impose Egyptian cults upon the subject population,[5] and no cult building of the period yet excavated in Syria or Palestine shows features which appear to be Egyptian rather than Canaanite[6] —again with the notable exception of Byblos,[7] where a fragment of relief bearing the name of Tuthmosis III is all that remains of a temple built by Minmose the architect and dedicated to Hathor, Lady of Byblos.[8] The gods of Egypt are occasionally mentioned by Syrians when writing to their overlord, but only when divine protection is invoked on behalf of the pharaoh and his envoy.[9] Egyptians in Palestine and Syria, on the other hand, dedicated stelae in reverence to the local gods, Mekal of Beth-shan and Ba'al Ṣephōn of Ugarit.[10]

The impact of Egypt upon the civilization of Syria and Palestine was nevertheless considerable. Captive princes educated in Egypt and returning to rule in their own countries must have imposed upon their court and subjects some of the ideas and manners they had learned during their upbringing. The influence of Egyptian religion upon Canaanite iconography is particularly noticeable in reliefs upon stelae which depict Canaanite deities[11]

[1] §v, 9; G, 27, 1347; A, 2, 148.   [2] §iii, 38, 362.

[3] G, 14, 480.   [4] §iii, 4, vol. i, 216 ff.; A, 26, 90.

[5] §iii, 4, vol. i, 217 ff.; §iv, 8, 128.   [6] §iii, 4, vol. i, 218 ff.; G, 14, 480.

[7] §v, 49, 200 f.; §v, 33, vol. i, 249, vol. ii, pl. 152; A, 26, 91.

[8] G, 27, 1443, l. 19; G, 14, 480.

[9] *E.g.* EA 71 ll. 4 f.; 86 ll. 3 ff.; §vi, 30, vol. ii, 33 f. = *RS*, 16, 117; §iii, 4, vol. i, 217 n. 3; G, 14, 480 f.

[10] §v, 40, 24 ff.; §1, 50, vol. i, 39 ff., fig. 30. See Plate 101.

[11] §viii, 12, 134 f., nos. 431–3; G, 23, 167 f. See Plate 100.

and in the current repertory of motifs employed by the ivory-carvers: Anubis, Bes, the *djed*-pillar, the papyrus and lotus plants are among the themes repeatedly employed;[1] and the ʿankh, the symbol of life which Egyptian deities hold in their hand and proffer to their worshippers, appears upon Syrian cylinder seals.[2] Such motifs were frequently distorted, misunderstood and misused: the sphinx, for instance, in Egypt a male figure symbolic of the pharaoh as the incarnation of the god Harmakhis,[3] became at Megiddo a female monster,[4] and the figures carved on the ivory panels of a bed-head from the palace at Ugarit,[5] though they adopt attitudes familiar from Egyptian art, and are dressed in the traditional loincloth of gods and kings in the valley of the Nile, yet differ from these in so many respects that it is beyond doubt that the craftsmen who carved them were natives of Syria deriving their inspiration at second hand from imported models.[6]

In other respects, too, life in western Asia benefited from increased contact with the ancient civilization of Egypt. The fame of Egyptian medicine had spread abroad: when he was sick, King Niqmaddu of Ugarit sent for an Egyptian doctor;[7] and the 'eagle-diviner' requested from Amenophis by the king of Alashiya at a time when his court was smitten with plague[8] was no doubt a priest skilled in exorcism. Egyptian scribes staffed the bureaux of the Egyptian governors, and, like the Byblites,[9] the people of Ugarit occasionally used the hieroglyphic script for their own purposes.[10] Although the influence of hieroglyphic writing upon the scripts of Syro-Palestine is not directly demonstrable, it is not surprising that great strides were made in the art just at this period, in the sixteenth, fifteenth and fourteenth centuries B.C.[11]

The aim of the Egyptian administration was twofold: to keep the vassal countries from rebellion, and to extract from them the maximum possible revenue. Each campaign produced wealth in the shape of booty and tribute. Campaigns went out in the late

---

[1] §IX, 10; §V, 32, pl. 4, no. 2*a*, *b*; §VI, 12, vol. III, 89 ff.; §VIII, 55, pls. 36–7.

[2] *E.g.* §IX, 15, 256 and pl. XLI; §V, 32, 25 f., 169 ff.

[3] G, 25, 98; §III, 29, 175.

[4] §IX, 25, 160 ff.; G, 30, 105; §VIII, 55, pls. 2, 7; see below, sect. IX.

[5] §IX, 41, 51 ff., pls. VIII–X.

[6] It is tempting to identify *Ḥkpt*, the land whence the people of Ugarit believed their craftsman god, Kathir-and-Khasis, to have come, with HikuPtaḥ, that is to say, Egypt (§VII, 12, 138; but see *ibid.* 169), but the equation is philologically improbable (§IX, 20, 263). *Ḥkpt* is regularly coupled with *Kptr* (Caphtor) and may therefore be in or near Crete (G, 30, 263).   [7] EA 49, ll. 22 ff.

[8] EA 35, ll. 13 ff., 26; G, 16, 1102.   [9] *C.A.H.* II³, pt. 2, ch. XVII, sect. IV.

[10] §I, 50, vol. 80 ff., 85, fig. 106; §VII, 39, 138 f.   [11] See below, sect. VIII.

spring, when the rainy season was at an end and when the grain
harvest in Egypt had been gathered in; the troops were in time
to collect a second crop in Palestine.[1] Part of the harvest, of grain,
vegetables and fruit, went to the garrison towns and ports;[2] much
of the rest was sent back to Egypt, when the wants of the army
in the field had been satisfied. Jars of oil of the moringa tree,
commonly used for cooking and for cosmetic purposes,[3] and olive
oil and sesame oil were sent in jars;[4] honey also came in jars, and
also Syrian wine, which was much prized in Egypt. Incense,[5]
which is mentioned in the Kamose stele as a Syrian import, and
fir resin were sent from the 'terraces' or hillsides of Lebanon.[6]
At the end of a campaign the soldiers would come home driving
herds of livestock and slaves. The chroniclers of Tuthmosis III
list large flocks of sheep and goats, mostly perhaps for the immediate consumption of the army; Syrian cattle, on the other hand,
were valued, and milch cows and prize bulls were sent to Egypt
as part of the annual tribute of Syrian princes forced to deplete
their stud.[7]

With the exception of large quantities of looted gold and silver
treasure obtained in the sack of cities, which is reckoned by
weight,[8] horses and chariots were perhaps the most valuable booty
taken in these wars. Egypt was not yet a horse-rearing country
and had only recently learned the use of chariotry in warfare,[9] so
that the army relied on Syrian campaigns to replenish their
stables. To begin with, the capture of even a few was worthy of
mention, but as time went on, a major campaign might produce
an average of some two hundred horses and a hundred chariots;
together with horses bred in Egypt, and chariots now manufactured locally,[10] the chariot force which could be mustered towards the end of the reign of Tuthmosis III must have been
considerable, perhaps even a match for Mitanni's formidable
array. Enumerated with the horses, but second in importance,
were the prisoners of war, male and female, who were driven
back to slavery in Egypt.[11] In the early part of the dynasty, a
soldier who took prisoners was allowed to keep them for himself.[12]

[1] §III, 42, 182.
[2] G, 14, 391; G, 27, 707, ll. 10 ff., 713, ll. 4 ff., 717, ll. 7 ff.
[3] G, 14, 415, 459 n. 197.   [4] G, 27, 1101, ll. 8–9.
[5] G, 14, 415.   [6] G, 27, 706, 11; §III, 30, 319 f.
[7] EA 242, l. 11, 301, l. 19; §IV, 6, pls. 34–6; G, 27, 743, ll. 11 ff., 664, l. 11,
1442, l. 6; §V, 20, 15 ff.
[8] G, 27, 717, ll. 11–13, 699, ll. 7 f.   [9] See above, ch. IX, sect. IX.
[10] G, 14, 439 ff.; §V, 28, 163 ff.   [11] G, 14, 359 ff.; §III, 42, 187.
[12] G, 27, 11, ll. 4 ff.; 36, l. 13.

Ahmose the ship's captain enumerates by name the nine slaves and ten slave-girls he had acquired in this manner; most of them were given Egyptian names, though Ishtar-ummi was allowed to keep her Canaanite identity.[1] By the time of Tuthmosis III the system had become unworkable. As larger numbers of prisoners were taken, they were sent to work on the crown and temple estates,[2] and only occasionally, as a special mark of royal favour, was an officer of outstanding bravery awarded his prisoners instead of the usual decoration, the Gold of Valour.[3] The number of prisoners captured in these campaigns is usually comparatively small, being reckoned in scores and hundreds rather than in thousands; the very high total of approximately a hundred thousand[4] on the Memphite stela of Amenophis II after a minor expedition is the more perplexing, and probably includes the prisoners taken in all that king's engagements,[5] possibly even those of his father as well.[6] In Egypt, prisoners of war were housed in camps,[7] and were set to work in the fields or in building and brickmaking;[8] the women were employed in domestic tasks such as weaving and cooking;[9] others as musicians and dancers.[10]

An annual delivery of tribute was expected from every conquered state; its collection was the responsibility of the regent. Each state was assessed; Minmose, who was constantly in Asia for his master, says that one of his duties was 'to make known to the princes of Retenu their tribute of every year'.[11] The word normally used for tribute, *inw*, means literally 'things brought', and is therefore employed not only for goods brought or sent under duress from vassals, but also for the gifts sent to the Egyptian king by the heads of independent kingdoms; doubtless not too much was made of this distinction by the Egyptians themselves, and official propaganda, which claimed the whole world as the pharaoh's realm, would have interpreted as tribute the gifts brought by envoys from the courts of distant powers. The word could also, by extension, be applied to commodities brought by way of international commerce, since the exchange of royal gifts was usually made on a strictly *quid pro quo* basis, as has always

---

[1] G, 27, 11, l. 11.
[2] *Ibid.* 172, ll. 6 ff., 185, l. 10, 742, ll. 10 ff.; G, 14, 362.
[3] G, 27, 890 f.
[4] The exact figure is uncertain: not 89,600 as on the stela !, §v, 26, 142 f.
[5] §iv, 7, 167; §iii, 5, 57 ff.
[6] G, 14, 361. Janssen in v, 26, 147 suggests it may be a census list of the occupied territory.   [7] G, 27, 1556, l. 10, 1649, l. 12.
[8] G, 27, 1153, l. 10.   [9] §v, 14, pls. 48–51.
[10] §v, 17, 263 f.; G, 14, 540 ff.   [11] G, 27, 1442, l. 7.

been the oriental custom: the sender of a present expected in return a consignment of approximately equal value, and did not hesitate to complain if dissatisfied.[1] It is frequently difficult to decide whether the articles depicted as 'tribute' in the hands of foreigners in the tomb paintings are part of the annual impost, or royal gifts, or even in some cases merchandise brought by traders. The well-known picture of Syrian traders arriving at an Egyptian port[2] may indicate that foreign trade in the Eighteenth Dynasty was no longer a royal monopoly, but the matter remains extremely obscure.

Foremost among the tribute of Asia was the timber of the Lebanese forests, hewn by Egyptian soldiery or by local labour under the supervision of Egyptian foremen.[3] The old arrangement with Byblos had produced enough for Egypt's needs during the Old and Middle Kingdoms; now the demand for coniferous woods was immeasurably greater and the forests were ransacked for timber of all kinds.[4] Cedar and fir were still the trees most in demand, but a number of other woods were sent from Syria, Mitanni and Alashiya, among them juniper and boxwood.[5] Elm, maple, ash, plum and willow were all used in the manufacture of chariots;[6] some of these may have come ultimately from further north, perhaps Anatolia or the Hurrian highland. Copper and lead came in ingots, some as tribute from Retenu, the rest, a much greater quantity, by trade from Alashiya on the island of Cyprus and also from Asy (Isy, Isia), which may be another name for the same island or part of it.[7] Silver was brought from Retenu and Naharin, as well as from Babylonia and Assyria: its ultimate source must have been the mines of Anatolia.[8] The handsome stone, lapis lazuli, greatly prized in every country of the Near East on account of its magical qualities,[9] was sometimes sent as tribute from Syria but most of it was obtained by Egypt from Babylonia and Assyria in return for gold.[10] Its ultimate source appears to have been the mines of Badakhshān, in Afghanistān.[11] 'Real lapis' is distinguished in the annals of Tuthmosis III from the 'fine lapis' of Babylonia,

[1] See below, pp. 486 ff.
[2] §v, 18, pl. viii.   [3] *C.A.H.* i³, pt. 2, ch. xvii, sect. v.
[4] §iii, 38; G, 24, 243; G, 14, 395 ff.; G, 27, 1237, 9 ff., 1241 f.
[5] G, 27, 670, l. 11, 672, l. 3; §iii, 30, 431 ff.
[6] §vii, 72, 87; G, 14, 398 f.   [7] See below, p. 491.
[8] §iii, 30, 249.   [9] G, 19, vol. i, 269, vol. ii, 131.
[10] G, 27, 668, l. 13; *ibid.* 671, l. 9; *ibid.* 701, ll. 1 ff.; EA *passim*; G, 14, 407 ff.
[11] §iii, 30, 399; §iii, 26, 124; see G. Herrmann in *Iraq*, 30 (1968), 21 ff. There remains the possibility that there may have been an Anatolian source of lapis lazuli, since lost (A, 45, 167 n. 3).

which may be an imitation of the stone in blue paste or frit.[1] Elephant ivory was obtained from Syria in small quantities as tribute;[2] there were probably game reserves in the valley of the river Orontes from which the tusks could be obtained,[3] though Egypt had a better source of supply in Africa and probably exported to Asia more than she received from this quarter.

As well as raw materials, manufactured articles of all kinds were included in the tribute of the Syrian princes, particularly luxury articles such as vessels of silver, gold and bronze.[4] Sometimes they were sent as containers of oil, incense, wine[5] or some other substance, and sometimes, no doubt, for their intrinsic value and the beauty and richness of their design.[6] Envoys are also shown bringing exotic animals and plants from Syria to add to the royal collection[7]—a young elephant and a bear,[8] a humped bull[9] and a lion.[10]

The influx of foreigners into Egypt, whether as prisoners of war, or slaves, or visitors, had a great and lasting effect upon Egyptian civilization. The further the Egyptians became embroiled in the affairs of Retenu, the more deeply they became involved in the life and thought of western Asia. For a highly individualistic people, insular in their traditions and hitherto hostile to the point of xenophobia to foreigners in general and Asiatics in particular, this change of attitude was revolutionary, and there was no escaping its effects. After years of campaigning, Egyptian soldiers came home with their horizons widened and their heads full of new ideas. For the first time it began to be generally realized that beyond the narrow bounds of the Nile valley there were people whose way of life, though very different from their own, was yet in some respects to be admired, whose standard of living was high and whose technical skill, especially in military matters, and craftsmanship in some respects surpassed their own. Re, the sungod, they found, shone also in Retenu and made the vines of Djahy burgeon.[11] Though they might deplore the barbarity of some Canaanite religious practices[12] and ridicule the fat, bearded nobles, and though they might shudder at the

[1] G, 29, 232 ff.; §vi, 30, vol. iv, 221 ff.=RS, 17, 383.
[2] G, 27, 718, ll. 14 f., 670, l. 11, 727, l. 3, etc.; §iii, 11, pl. 20; §v, 13, vol. ii, pl. 23; §iii, 30, 33; EA 40, 7 ff.; G, 14, 412.   [3] See above, p. 427.
[4] G, 14, 417 ff.; §ix, 31, 51 ff., figs. 46–86.   [5] G, 14, 414 ff.
[6] E.g. §v, 11, pls. xxiii, xxiv; G, 23, 16 f., figs. 47, 48, 52.
[7] C.A.H. I³, pt. 2, ch. xvii, sect. vi.
[8] §v, 13, pl. 12; §iii, 35, vol. i, 234.
[9] §iii, 44, vol. i, 340.   [10] §vii, 11, pl. 19.
[11] G, 24, 370 ff.; §v, 47, 140 f.   [12] §vii, 2, 347.

rigours of the climate, the rugged nature of the landscape[1] and the insecurity of roads infested by robbers and by lions, panthers and bears,[2] the Egyptians envied and admired certain aspects of Canaanite civilization and imported and imitated them.

The Egyptian army of the New Kingdom was augmented by foreign units: from the time of Amenophis III, if not earlier, they included both Sherden and Canaanite prisoners of war.[3] One of these, a black-bearded Syrian spearman, is depicted on a stele from Amarna seated at his ease with his wife, who from her appearance is an Egyptian, and drinking from a large wine-jar.[4] It was no doubt owing to the presence of these aliens, as well as the large number of foreign ladies and their attendants at the court,[5] that Babylonian, Canaanite and Hurrian words found their way into Egyptian speech and the vocabulary was enriched by numerous loanwords,[6] especially technical terms pertaining to horses and chariots, the names of weapons and musical instruments and of raw materials, animals and plants introduced from abroad. The influence of Asiatic on Egyptian music was profound: new instruments included the long-necked lute, the lyre (kinnōr), the angled harp and the double flute,[7] and the Syrian musicians who introduced them must have popularized new melodies and new dances.[8] Syrian motifs depicted on garments worn by Egyptians[9] remind us that Syrians were frequently employed as weavers. Several Asiatic deities were introduced into Egypt at the time of Tuthmosis III and Amenophis II, and their cults became increasingly popular as the dynasty drew to its close:[10] Ba'āl Ṣᵉphōn, the Canaanite god of seafarers, had his temple at Perunefer, the naval station near Memphis where Syrians were employed,[11] and here there was also a temple to Astarte, the goddess who, as protectress of the pharaoh's horses and chariot, had an important role in the official cult;[12] her popularity with the officers and men of the chariotry is evident. The hitherto discreetly clothed Egyptian pantheon was now enlivened by the more voluptuous goddesses of Canaan;[13] Astarte herself is depicted naked on horseback,

[1] G, 14, 328 ff., 334 f.   [2] Ibid. 336.
[3] See above, ch. IX, sect. IX.   [4] §v, 45; see Plate 102 (a).
[5] §vi, 13, 661.   [6] §v, 10; G, 14, 551 ff.
[7] §v, 22, vol. II, 23 ff., 197 ff.; §IV, 15, 35; §v, 24, 23; §III, 43, 158 ff.
[8] G, 14, 540 ff.; §v, 17, 263 ff.   [9] See below, pp. 511 f.
[10] §v, 47, 206 f.; §vi, 8, 125 ff.; G, 14, 482 ff.; §vi, 41.
[11] §III, 22, 26 ff.; vIII, 66, 128 n. 13.
[12] G, 27, 1282, l. 15; §v, 21, 39 ff.; §III, 28, 27 n. 5; §v, 30; A, 19, 59; C.A.H. II³, pt. 2, ch. XVII, sect. v.
[13] §III, 42, 192 f.

swinging her weapon and brandishing a shield,[1] and Qodshu, the Holy One, who stands on the back of a lion, also figures naked on votive stelae.[2] Resheph, the Syrian god of war, was identified with Mont as the king's protector in battle.[3] Egyptian personal names of the theophorous kind incorporate the names of these deities.[4] It may have been due to the healing reputation gained by the statue of Ishtar of Nineveh, twice sent from Mitanni to the Egyptian court in time of illness,[5] that a stele of the period represents a cripple and his wife making offerings to 'Astarte of Khor'.[6]

VI. THE AMARNA AGE

The discovery of the Amarna letters, as the tablets written in cuneiform script found at El-Amarna, the site of Akhenaten's capital, are usually called today, is described in a later chapter.[7] The documents had been buried in a room of the palace, presumably on the day when the court removed from Akhetaten back to Thebes, not long after the death of Akhenaten.[8] They appear to have been in fact the 'closed files' of the Egyptian Foreign Office, discarded because they were out of date; the more important ones, correspondence dealing with current Egypto-Hittite affairs in particular, would presumably have been taken away, just as some of the letters found may have been taken to Akhetaten when the court moved thither.[9]

The majority of the letters are addressed to the king of Egypt, some to Nimmuria, Amenophis III Nebmare, some to Napkhuria or Napkhururia, Amenophis IV, whose prenomen was *Nefer-kheprure<*, and one at least to Nipkhururiya (*Nebkheprure<*, Tut-ankhamun).[10] One at least is written to Tiy, the wife of Amenophis III and mother of Akhenaten,[11] and a number to Egyptian officials; in two cases the recipients were Egyptian ladies.[12] Among the documents are a few letters from the pharaoh, presumably draft replies or 'carbon copies' of letters sent. Thirty-six of the letters came from foreign potentates, the independent sovereigns of

---

[1] §v, 30, 23 ff. G, 14, 493 ff. identifies this figure rather with the goddess Ishtar.
[2] §v, 16, 49 ff. and pls. iii, iv; G, 14, 497 f.
[3] G, 27, 1282, l. 15, 1302, l. 7; §v, 21; G, 14, 485 ff.; §vi, 41, 54 ff.; §v, 43.
[4] EA 23, ll. 13 ff.; §iii, 42, 192.
[5] See below, pp. 488 ff.   [6] §vi, 33, 413 and pl. 66; §vi, 41, 107 n.2.
[7] *C.A.H.* ii³, pt. 2, ch. xx, sect. i.
[8] §vi, 5, 34; §vi, 18, 47; §vi, 37; §vi, 42, 76 ff.; §vi, 35.
[9] This hypothesis has a bearing on the vexed question of the co-regency between Amenophis III and his son and successor (*C.A.H.* ii³, pt. 2, ch. xix, sect. i).
[10] §vi, 5, 38 f., 49, 53 ff.   [11] EA 26.   [12] EA 48, 50.

Babylonia and Assyria, Mitanni, Arzawa, Alashiya and the land of the Hittites; several were inventories of presents sent from court to court.[1] The rest, with few exceptions, were from Egyptian vassals in Syria and Palestine, the regents of Byblos and Beirut, of Gaza and Askalon, Lachish and Jerusalem, and of Qatna and Qadesh and many other cities, some of which seem to have been of great importance in this period, while others were clearly of minor significance. This vassal correspondence will be dealt with in subsequent chapters.[2]

The word 'brotherhood' in the Amarna letters implies an alliance between rulers of equal rank and status; it is coupled with 'friendship', and was established by the conclusion of a treaty between the two powers. Strict rules of behaviour were laid down for intercourse between the states of western Asia, and rulers adhered to an international code of behaviour very similar to that of the Mari letters in the eighteenth century B.C.[3] The making of a treaty, with its concomitant ritual performed on behalf of the gods who were parties to the pact,[4] is not specifically referred to in the Amarna letters, though Teshub and Amun are said to bring about and maintain friendship between Mitanni and Egypt.[5] No parity treaties involving Egypt previous to the Ramesside treaty with the Hittites have survived;[6] those concluded with Mitanni, Babylonia and the other powers must have contained clauses similar to those of similar agreements found at Alalakh, Ugarit and Boğazköy.[7] Implementation of such clauses can be discerned in the Amarna letters: the state of brotherhood, for instance, precluded either party from entering into negotiations with the other's enemies,[8] and fugitives were to be returned to their country and not given asylum.[9]

Alliances formed between the powers were often cemented by dynastic marriages, and these were the subject of long negotiations and a suitable show of reluctance on the part of the prospective bride's father: 'After Nimmuria your father had written to Shuttarna my father, and when he had asked for the daughter of my father, my own sister, he repeated the message three times, four times, and he did not send her; he repeated the message five times, six times—then, perforce, he sent her.'[10] Marriage

---

[1] EA 13, 14, 22, 25, 120.

[2] *C.A.H.* II³, pt. 2, ch. xvII and ch. xx.   [3] §v, 34, 76.

[4] Perhaps pictured on a stela from Ugarit (§1, 50, vol. III, 92 f., pl. vI): this interpretation, however, is doubtful (§1x, 30, 76).

[5] EA 19, ll. 14–16, 75–6; EA 24, II, l. 65.

[6] *C.A.H.* II³, pt. 2, ch. xxIV, sect. III.   [7] §vI, 21; §vI, 30, vol. IV.

[8] EA 9, ll. 19–35.   [9] EA 29, ll. 173 ff.   [10] EA 29, ll. 16–20.

negotiations were accompanied by a good deal of hard bargaining about the bride-price. Both the king of Mitanni[1] and the king of Babylonia[2] imply that they will not send their daughters to Egypt until a sufficiently lavish bride-price has been sent, and when it is decided upon, although composed of manufactured articles such as inlaid furniture and luxury goods, it is reckoned in hard cash, that is to say, in terms of the weight of the gold, silver and bronze.

The relationship of 'brother and son-in-law'[3] involved both parties in the close ties of a family relationship, and the death of one king or a member of his family was mourned by his allies,[4] and messages of condolence were expected by the widow and son, together with messages of congratulation to the new king on his accession, and requests that the former alliance be tenfold renewed.[5] Protocol demanded an elaborate form of epistolary address: 'To X the King of A, my brother, say: Thus saith Y, the King of B: "With your house, your wives, your sons, your chief men, your soldiers, your horses and chariots, and with everything in your land, may it be very well!"' The omission of the formula was a sign that relations were becoming strained: 'Since on your side there is no salutation [, I also have none for you].'[6] When a king fell ill, his allies were expected to send inquiries after his health. A regular exchange of messages and gifts was expected, and there are a number of complaints in the letters that envoys have been detained at their destination and not sent back speedily enough.[7] These were men of high standing who occupied a position of great trust. In the Amarna letters they are often mentioned by name: Gilia, the Mitannian envoy, and Mane, his Egyptian counterpart, served their masters throughout the years covered by the Mitannian letters and must have known each other well and often travelled in company.

Envoys, called 'royal messengers' in Egyptian, were of ambassadorial status[8] and might be entrusted with important and delicate missions, and with the conduct of caravans conveying great riches. They were conversant with Akkadian, and must also have spoken the language of the country to which they were sent, or else taken an interpreter with them.[9] They carried the message

---

[1] EA 19; EA 24.   [2] EA 3; EA 11.
[3] EA 21, ll. 1–4; 27, ll. 1–3.
[4] EA 29, l. 55 ff.; 11, l. 5; §VI, 5, 46 n. 44.
[5] EA 6; 7; 8; 27. Cf. §VII, 68, 1ff.=RS, 10064.
[6] §VI, 30, vol. III, xx, 6=RS, 13, 7.
[7] EA 3, ll. 13 f.; 7, ll. 49 f.; 28, ll. 20–2; 35, ll. 35–9.
[8] §V, 34, 99 f.   [9] EA 21, ll. 25 f.

they were to deliver, together with their credentials and letters of introduction,[1] in some sort of despatch-bag slung round their neck for safe-keeping.[2] On arrival at their destination they were treated with the honour befitting their rank, and given robes and presents.[3] They then handed over the gifts they had brought with them, and attended as witnesses while the value of the consignment of gold was tested in the furnace.[4] Takhulu, the Ugaritian envoy to the Hittite court, incurred the wrath of one of the Hittite kings when, instead of lapis lazuli, he was found to have brought an imitation of less value;[5] he was obliged to send two letters to Ugarit urging his master to send the real stone if it could possibly be obtained, 'for the king is particularly fond of lapis lazuli'.[6] On the way home, envoys were provided by their host with the means of travel and given an escort; travel was a hazardous business and the caravan, laden with precious merchandise, was in constant danger of attack. Assyrian envoys were attacked by a band of Sutu,[7] and a Babylonian baggage train was set upon in Canaan, a piece of lawlessness for which the Egyptian king, on whose territory it was committed, was held responsible by Burnaburiash II and required to pay compensation.[8]

The exchange of gifts, which plays a large part in the Amarna correspondence, was made on the basis of value for goods, each king stating his needs, and offering in return what he and his envoy deemed to be the equivalent in value. If the amount sent fell short of expectations, the recipient would complain in no uncertain terms. Egypt's wealth was in gold from the Nubian mines, now being exploited to their utmost.[9] 'Lo, in my brother's land gold is as common as dust' was the refrain of the kings of western Asia, and they asked for ever larger quantities, each vying with his neighbours in the adornment of his palace, as a matter of national and personal prestige. 'Send me, therefore, very much gold, in great quantity' is the repeated request[10] and there are many complaints that the last consignment has not been of the expected amount or quality. In the fourteenth century, and probably since the time of Tuthmosis III, when the international exchange began, the Kassites and neighbouring countries had been 'on the gold standard', that is to say, gold had largely

---

[1] EA 30 is such a letter. Cf. §vi, 30, vol. iii, 12 and pl. v, 5 = *RS*, 11, 730.

[2] G, 27, 1314, l. 3.   [3] EA 21, ll. 24 ff.

[4] EA 10, ll. 21 f.; §vi, 45, 431.   [5] §vi, 30 vol. iv, 221 ff. = *RS*, 17, 383.

[6] *Ibid.* 223 ff. = *RS*, 17, 422, l. 23.   [7] *C.A.H.* ii³, pt. 2, ch. xviii, sect. iii.

[8] EA 8, ll. 16 ff.   [9] §v, 41, 210 ff.

[10] *C.A.H.* ii³, pt. 2, ch. xviii, sect. i.

replaced silver as a medium of exchange, and this put Egypt in an economically advantageous position. Only she could supply what everyone wanted. The kings of Babylonia and Mitanni were thus forced to keep a precarious balance between their desire to maintain their dignity and their prestige as independent and equal powers, and their greed for gold.[1]

The dilemma is well illustrated by the correspondence of Tushratta of Mitanni.[2] These letters date from the last few years of Amenophis III's reign and the first year or so of his son and successor Amenophis IV's. Relations between Thebes and Wash-shuganni had now been cordial for almost forty years, and both Amenophis III and his father had married Mitannian princesses. Tushratta's first surviving letter appears to have been written not long after his accession, since in it he recounts how his brother Artashuwara has been murdered by one UD-ḫi (perhaps Utkhi), who may have acted as regent while the two boys were still minors. Tushratta hints that there had been coolness, if not a rupture in diplomatic relations, between Mitanni and Egypt during the time when the usurper was in power, but declares that now that he, Tushratta, has taken his rightful place on the throne and has put to death the murderer and his accomplices, the good relations which had formerly existed between Shuttarna and Amenophis shall be re-established. The same letter announces that Tushratta has inflicted a heavy defeat on the land of Khatti and is sending part of the booty to the Egyptian king,[3] a custom between allies in the ancient Near East. This victory, which checked for a time the ambitions of the young Shuppululiumash, will be further discussed in a subsequent chapter.[4] To Gilu-Kheba his sister, now living among the other foreign wives in the royal harim at Thebes, he sends a present of jewellery.[5]

Not long afterwards, Amenophis sent Mane his envoy to request the hand in marriage of yet another Mitannian princess, Tushratta's daughter, Tadu-Kheba; in his letter of acceptance[6] Tushratta already called the pharaoh his son-in-law, and sent a handsome present of chariots and horses, saying very cordially, 'Whatever my brother desires for his palace, let him send and take it, for I will give tenfold what my brother asks. This land is my brother's land, and this house is the house of my brother!'[7]— a phrase which, like the hospitable 'My house is yours' to a guest in the Arab world today, was not to be taken too seriously. A

---

[1] §vi, 10.   [2] EA 17–29.   [3] EA 17, ll. 30 ff.
[4] C.A.H. ii³, pt. 2, ch. xvii, sect. i.   [5] EA 17, ll. 41–51.
[6] EA 19.   [7] Ibid. ll. 68–70.

condition, however, is implied in his acceptance: he wanted gold in large quantities, both for the bride-price and for the adornment of a funerary monument (the word is Hurrian) which he was building for his grandfather.[1] He withheld Tadu-Kheba until he was satisfied with the amount ultimately sent from Egypt;[2] the inventory which accompanied the princess is long, and contains many Hurrian words for the items of dress, jewellery and furniture she brought with her; in Mitanni, as in Babylonia and Egypt, there was a large technical vocabulary in court usage devoted to luxury objects with special shapes and functions.[3] Costly *objets d'art*, fluted golden bowls, and goblets chased and decorated around the rim with imitation flowers are carried in the hands of envoys depicted in the tombs of Egyptian officials who were charged with the duty of their reception,[4] and the exchange of styles and motifs resulting from this interchange of luxury articles between the rulers of the Near East led to the development of a kind of international court style in which Egyptian, Aegean and Mesopotamian motifs mingled and blended.[5] Envoys from Keftiu (Crete),[6] Menūs (a country whose whereabouts is unknown, but whose ambassadors resemble the Keftians and bring similar gifts[7]), and from 'the Isles in the midst of the Ocean', a designation for the Aegean world in the Mycenaean age,[8] carry similar vessels as 'tribute' to the pharaoh, together with such treasures as lapis lazuli, ingots of silver and copper, and elephants' tusks,[9] none of which are likely to have originated in the area from which they are said to come; these, too, were part of the currency of international diplomacy.[10]

The negotiations for Tadu-Kheba's marriage must have been completed in or before Tushratta's third year, for the reception of a letter to Amenophis III bearing greetings to her as 'my daughter, thy wife, whom thou lovest'[11] is dated by a hieratic docket to that year or the next.[12] The letter is of exceptional

---

[1] EA 19, ll. 44 ff.; EA 29, l. 146.   [2] EA 21.

[3] EA 22 and 25; G, 14, 423 ff., 445 ff.

[4] §VIII, 81, 201 ff., 305 ff.; §IX, 31. See Plate 103(*b*).

[5] G, 30, 32 f., figs. 51–3.   [6] §VIII, 81, 331 ff., against §VIII, 82.

[7] *Ibid.* 159 ff., on the temptation to identify with Minos of Crete. A large alabaster jar bearing the names of Tuthmosis III, found at Katsamta, the port for Cnossus (§VIII, 84, 349 and fig. 19), was evidently a royal gift.

[8] *Ibid.* 369 ff.   [9] *Ibid.* 362 ff., pls. 63–66.

[10] Compare the hoard of oriental treasure discovered in the palace of Boeotian Thebes (§VIII, 61) and some of the objects listed in §V, 31, 398 ff.

[11] EA 23, ll. 7 ff. See, however, above, pp. 345 f., where the doubt is expressed whether Amenophis III in fact married her.   [12] §VI, 25, 95 n. *e*; §VI, 5, 38.

interest since in it Tushratta informs the pharaoh that he is sending
him Ishtar of Nineveh, that is to say, a statue of the goddess
which he asks Amenophis to look after carefully and send back
promptly: on a previous visit, the image had been kept too long.
'Ishtar is my goddess,' he adds a little sharply, 'she is not my
brother's goddess.'[1] The sending on loan of deities with a reputation for healing has parallels in the ancient Near East[2] and it may
be that Amenophis, who was old and sick and had not long to
live,[3] had sent for the statue for himself. Ishtar of Nineveh had
a particular reputation in this respect; a Hittite invocation to the
goddess summons her from whatever town she may be visiting
on her route through Mitannian territory on her way from
Nineveh to Qadesh.[4] The significance of the fact that Ishtar
of Nineveh was in the possession of Tushratta has already been
commented upon,[5] though it is of course possible that this was
not the original statue of Ishtar, from her sanctuary at Nineveh,
but a Mitannian image of this popular deity.

Another letter from Tushratta[6] contains a second list of bridal
gifts, different from the first and even longer; these treasures may
have been sent to Amenophis IV when he succeeded to the
throne and in his turn[7] married Tadu-Kheba (Gilu-Kheba being
past marriageable age, if indeed she was still alive). One of the
items in the list, a steel dagger with a chased golden sheath and
a pommel of rock-crystal,[8] may perhaps be the very one preserved
to our day among the funerary furniture of King Tutankhamun.[9]
In a letter written to Tiy, the widow of Amenophis III, Tushratta
seeks assurance that her son's relations with Mitanni will be as
cordial as those of her husband. In fact, the friendship was clouded
by an incident[10] which so angered Tushratta that he refers to it
in subsequent correspondence:[11] Amenophis III had intended to
send him some statues of solid gold, and these had in fact
been cast shortly before the pharaoh's death, in the presence of
the watchful Mitannian envoys. On his accession Amenophis IV
had not sent these statues, but wooden ones overlaid with sheet
gold, which had been substituted, with or without his knowledge,
for the real ones.

Seven Amarna letters[12] are addressed to Egypt from the king

[1] EA 23, ll. 31 f.   [2] §vi, 33, 415 ff.
[3] See above, ch. ix, sect. vi.   [4] K.Bo. ii, 36, obv. 4 ff.; K.U.B. xv, 35, 1, 23.
[5] See above, p. 465. Cf. §ix, 6, 280 n. 1.   [6] EA 25.
[7] See above, p. 488 n. 11.   [8] EA 22, col. 1, ll. 32–4.
[9] J.E.A. 28, pl. 1; §vi, 31, 54 ff.   [10] EA 27, ll. 19 ff.
[11] EA 29.   [12] EA 33–9.

of Alashiya, whose name is not given, and one from his chief
minister to the minister (vizier?) of Egypt.[1] The letters are
cordial in tone and contain references to an exchange of gifts,
which come by sea.[2] The nature of the gifts is significant, for
Alashiya sends large quantities of copper, and receives in return
a variety of merchandise including silver, ebony and vessels of
oil. There are a number of references to this kingdom in Hittite
and Ugaritic texts of the late second millennium B.C.;[3] it was
evidently an important maritime power, for ships of Alashiya are
mentioned in texts from Ras Shamra,[4] and a Hittite text from the
reign of Shuppiluliumash II reports a victory of the Hittite navy
over the Alashiyan fleet.[5] The name, Yaduba'al, of a fugitive
from Alashiya at the Hittite court[6] indicates that there were
Semites among the inhabitants, a conclusion which is confirmed
by other evidence.[7] An Ugaritic tablet apparently listing Alashiyan families at Ugarit[8] has been thought to provide further evidence of a Canaanite element, perhaps a ruling class, in the
population of Alashiya;[9] the presence of this list in the archives of
Ugarit, however, suggests that it should rather be understood as
a muster of unnamed Alashiyan prisoners of war in the service of
Ugaritic masters who are named.[10]

Hittite texts make mention of copper 'from the mountain of
Taggata in Alashiya',[11] and the tribute lists and the enumeration
of royal gifts in the Amarna letters, taken together, make it plain
that copper was the country's chief product. The usual identification of Alashiya is therefore with the island of Cyprus, the
'copper land' *par excellence*,[12] where Apollo Alasiotas was later
worshipped.[13] Former doubts as to whether copper was mined on
the island so early have been dispelled by the discovery of ingots
inscribed with letters of the Cypro-Mycenaean script,[14] by evidence of Bronze Age mining at a number of sites,[15] and by the
discovery of ore and slag in excavations on the site of a city of

[1] EA 40.   [2] EA 39 and 40.
[3] G, 8, vol. I, 67 f.; §VI, 44; §VII, 39, 91 ff.; §VI, 12, vol. III, 218ff.; §VI, 28.
[4] §VII, 39, 91 f.; §VIII, 72, 41 f.; §VI, 12, vol. III, 218.
[5] *C.A.H.* II³, pt. 2, ch. XXIV, sect. IV.
[6] §VI, 30, vol. IV, 108 = *RS*, 18, 114.   [7] §VI, 2.
[8] §VI, 44, 267 ff. = *RS*, 11, 857; §VII, 39, 92 ff.
[9] §VIII, 22, 154; §VIII, 5, 255.   [10] §VI, 11, 372; §VII, 4, 15 ff.
[11] *K.Bo.* IV, 1, 40; G, 24, 356; §VI, 38, 238.
[12] G, 14, 289 f.; §VI, 7, 120 ff.; §VI, 30, vol. II, XXXIV f.; §VI, 11, vol. III, 218;
§VI, 16, vol. I, 48 f.; otherwise §VI, 46; §VI, 12, 152; §VI, 3, 77 f.
[13] §IV, 7, 111; §VI, 26, 380. Otherwise, A, 36, 66 f.
[14] §VI, 7, 122 ff.; §VI, 4, 92 ff.
[15] See above, ch. IV, sect. IX; and *C.A.H.* II³, pt. 2, ch. XXII, sect. III.

the Late Bronze Age thought by the excavator and others to be
Alashiya itself, at Enkomi near Salamis, on the east coast of the
island opposite Ugarit.[1] A Bronze Age wreck found during
underwater exploration off Cape Gelidonya on the south coast
of Turkey was carrying in its cargo a quantity of copper ingots
of characteristic ox-hide shape,[2] which may well have come from
Cyprus; some bore a Cypro-Mycenaean smelter's mark. Numerous imports, including tablets incised with the Cypro-
Mycenaean script, betray the presence of Cypriots in Ugarit
during the fourteenth and thirteenth centuries.[3]

Alashiya and Asy (Isy, Isia), are mentioned together in a list
of 'conquered' places dating to the reign of Amenophis III.[4] Isy,
too, sent large quantities of copper to Egypt in the reign of Tuthmosis III,[5] and is mentioned in his Hymn of Victory together
with Keftiu (Crete) as the two representatives of the West.[6] Any
attempt to locate either, or both, on the northern coast of Syria[7]
presents great difficulties not only for the reasons mentioned
above but also because the political map of that area is already
well filled with prosperous city states, and one would be hard put
to it to find room along the coast for another important kingdom.
In the first millennium B.C. the island of Cyprus was not united
under one rule but was divided into a number of separate principalities; we may therefore perhaps see in Alashiya and Asy two
Cypriot kingdoms of the Bronze Age, each deriving its wealth
from the exploitation of its copper resources and maintaining
contact with the powers of the mainland, with whom they traded
the raw material for manufactured goods.[8]

There are no letters from Asy in the Amarna files. Among the
seven letters, which come from the unnamed king of Alashiya,
is a missive[9] of congratulation on the accession of Amenophis IV;
the Alashiyan takes the opportunity to propose an annual exchange of correspondence.[10] But—alas for good resolutions—
in another letter[11] he apologizes for detaining the Egyptian envoy
for three years in his country, which, he explains, has been

[1] See in more detail *C.A.H.* II³, pt. 2, ch. XXII, sect. IX.
[2] §VI, 3, 52 ff.; cf. §VI, 7, 128 f., pl. 8; §VIII, 22, 61 f.
[3] §I, 50, vol. III, 27 ff.; *ibid.* vol. IV, 131 ff.
[4] §VI, 16, vol. I, 37.
[5] G, 27, 707, l. 16–708, l. 2, 719, ll. 13 f., 724, l. 12.
[6] G, 27, 616, ll. 1 f.; §VI, 16, vol. I, 38 n. 2.
[7] §VI, 46; §VI, 15, 47; §VIII, 82.
[8] E.g. EA 34, ll. 16 ff.; EA 35, 17 ff. See below and *C.A.H.* II³, pt. 2, ch. XXII,
sect. VI.
[9] EA 33.   [10] §VI, 5, 41 f.   [11] EA 35.

devastated by plague—even his own son had died of it.[1] In the same letter he urges the pharaoh not to make a treaty with either the Hittites or the king of Shankhar, by which we should probably understand Sangara, Babylonia.[2] This request may perhaps be prompted by the anxiety of Alashiya to keep her advantageous position in a world of political and commercial rivals in which it was impossible to remain an uncommitted neutral. The freedom of the seas was threatened not only by enemies but also by piracy, for in another letter[3] the Alashiyan denies responsibility for losses which Egyptian ships have sustained: he declares that it is the Lukki, freebooters from the Lukka-lands along the Lycian shore,[4] who yearly raid his shores, and not his own sailors, who are responsible.[5] Scarabs of Amenophis III and Queen Tiy were found at Enkomi.[6]

Two letters only have survived from the volume of correspondence, no doubt considerable, between Egypt and 'Great Khatti', the court of the Hittite king at Khattusha.[7] One is certainly from Shuppiluliumash, who came to the throne about 1380 B.C.; the other is in a similar hand, though very broken.[8] The addressee of the first is 'Khuria, King of Egypt'; reference to 'thy father', who has recently died, again suggests Akhenaten as the recipient.[9] While offering condolences to the pharaoh, the Hittite king expresses the hope that future relations between their two countries will continue to be cordial. It will be seen to what extent that intention was fulfilled in the subsequent actions of Shuppiluliumash. His neighbour in Asia Minor, Tarkhundaradu, king of Arzawa[10] (a region at that time free of Hittite control), wrote in Luwian, the local Hittite dialect,[11] and the reply sent from the Egyptian court in reply to this or another letter—the tablet may be a copy, or else an unsent original—is in the same language,[12] presumably because there was nobody at the Arzawan court who could read or write Akkadian.[13] Both letters, though imperfectly understood, appear to discuss a proposed match be-

---

[1] EA 35, ll. 13 f. and 35–9.   [2] See above, p. 457 n. 8.   [3] EA 38.
[4] §1, 18, vol. 1, 127*, no. 247; G, 14, 290.   [5] EA 38, ll. 7 ff.
[6] §vi, 15, 49 f. If, as seems possible, an important group of Hittite texts (including the Indictment of Maduwattas, see A, 12) once thought to be late, are to be dated on philological grounds to the late fifteenth or early fourteenth century B.C. (A, 10; A, 40 and below, ch. xv, sect. ii) then intermittent Hittite control of Alashiya must be assumed (but see A, 25). The tone of the Alashiyan letter from Amarna however is certainly that of an independent ruler writing to an equal.
[7] EA 41, 42; §vi, 36; §vi, 19, 330 ff.   [8] G, 16, vol. ii, 1093 f.
[9] §vi, 5, 39.   [10] §1, 18, vol. 1, 129*; see below, ch. xv, sect. ii.
[11] EA 32.   [12] EA 31.   [13] §vi, 5, 39; §vi, 36, 328 ff.; §vi, 20.

tween that much-married man Amenophis III and Tarkhundaradu's daughter; arrangements are being made through the
agency of a North Canaanite named Kalbaya,[1] and the bride-
price has been fixed. That so high an honour as an offer of marriage
from the pharaoh himself (called 'The Sun' in the Egyptian
letter[2]) should have been made to this princess of a far-off land
is a measure of the high political standing and commercial importance of Arzawa in the world of the eastern Mediterranean at
that period.

VII. WARFARE AND SOCIETY

It has already been said[3] that one of the most characteristic and
striking features of the civilization of western Asia in the Middle
and Late Bronze Ages was the widespread use of the horse and
the light two-wheeled chariot.[4] Perhaps originating on the Iranian
plateau or the steppes of central or south Russia,[5] this new weapon
spread rapidly through the countries of the Near East, and the
tactical superiority which it gave to its possessors ensured its
success. The Hurrians in particular appear to have been expert
in the art of horse-breeding, and active in the dissemination of
its techniques. Manuals of horse-training have survived from
this epoch. A Hittite text, which purports to be the translation
of a treatise by a Hurrian trainer named Kikkuli,[6] specifies the
number of laps or turns around the course (*wartanna*, an Indo-
Aryan word) to be run by horses in training, enumerating them
in numerals which resemble the Sanskrit.[7] Meticulous instructions concerning the amount of fodder the animals should be
given, the length of time and the distance they were to be walked,
trotted and galloped, and when they must be rested at grass, are
all laid down in this business-like manual.[8] An Assyrian text of
the fifteenth century contains similar directions for the use of
grooms and trainers and stresses the importance of rubbing-down
after exercise.[9] Two hippiatric texts from Ugarit[10] deal with
remedies to be applied *per nasum* to sick horses, a veterinary
practice still followed.[11] In the royal stables at Ugarit[12] a paved
and pillared hall some ninety feet long is thought to have served
the purpose of an indoor riding school; adjacent rooms had

---

[1] §VI, 5, 40 f. [2] EA 31, l. 13. [3] See above, p. 420.
[4] §VII, 52, 266 f., 274 ff.; G, 30, 22 ff.; G, 12, 110 f.; §VII, 57, 11 ff.
[5] §VIII, 3, 395. [6] §VII, 31.
[7] §I, 30, 23; §I, 32, 50 f. and 147 ff. [8] §VII, 28, 478 ff.; §VII, 32, 202 ff.
[9] §II, 15. [10] §VII, 69, 75 ff.; §IX, 21, 128 f.
[11] §VII, 24. [12] §VIII, 68, 314.

mangers and tethering-posts, and there was a large stone watering-trough.

Judging by the dimensions of the stalls, the horses of Ugarit were little larger than ponies,[1] and this impression is borne out by the mummy of a small horse found in an Egyptian tomb of the mid Eighteenth Dynasty,[2] and by the skeletons of equids found buried at Tell el-'Ajjūl in tombs of the Middle Bronze Age.[3] The horse found at Buhen in a level above the pavement of the Middle Kingdom fort was also quite small. The Hittites appear to have bred a larger animal, capable of pulling a heavier, three-manned chariot;[4] a horse buried near Boğazköy measured fourteen and a half hands, about the size of a modern Arab horse.[5] At Alalakh[6] and Nuzi[7] they were listed according to age and sex, colour and place of origin, and whether broken or unbroken. Though the price of horses in the fifteenth century was considerably less than it had been in the time of the Mari letters,[8] a good horse was still very valuable: at Nuzi a man would pay almost as much for a horse as for a wife,[9] and the price of a thoroughbred from the royal stables at Carchemish was two hundred shekels of silver.[10]

The light chariot, pulled by a pair of horses,[11] was used for hunting: on the wide Syrian steppe kings and nobles coursed after lion, wild cattle,[12] gazelle and oryx. Its chief role, however, was military. It provided a mobile platform from which a quantity of missiles could be discharged at the enemy,[13] and as long as the terrain was not too rocky, a small force of chariotry could harry the enemy's flank and rear, and form into a flying column to pursue detachments of infantry in flight.[14] As in Egypt, so in the city states and kingdoms of the Levant generally the introduction of new and improved techniques of warfare led to specialization, and the national militia, rallying in emergency for temporary service under arms, gave place to an army of professional soldiers with special status and privileges. The chariotry, the *mariyanna*,[15]

---

[1] §I, 50, vol. II, 13.

[2] §V, 22, vol. II, III.

[3] §V, 36, vol. I, 3 ff., pls. 8, 9, vol. II, 5. Add now the five equids, probably horses, found in an early Hyksos tomb at Tell ed-Dab'a in the eastern Delta of Egypt (A, 7, 90 ff. and fig. 3).

[4] §IV, 12, 105 f.

[5] §VII, 7, 62 f.

[6] §I, 67, 94, nos. 329–31.

[7] §VIII, 20, 22 ff.; §I, 47, 129 f.

[8] §VII, 5, vol. V, 20, ll. 7 ff.

[9] §VII, 20, 23.

[10] §VI, 30, vol. III, 41 = *RS*, 16, 180.

[11] §VII, 72, 86 ff.; §VII, 58, 60 ff.; A, 3.

[12] §I, 50, vol. II, 17, pls. I, VII.

[13] §V, 42, 75; §VII, 72, 109 ff.

[14] §VII, 74, 106 f.; §VII, 16, 125.

[15] §I, 44; §I, 32, 45 ff.

occupied a leading place in society as a *corps d'élite* around the king and his family.[1] But though ownership of chariots and horses may originally have been confined to a small, exclusive Indo-Aryan aristocracy,[2] the names of *mariyanna* of the fifteenth century and later are those of the mixed Hurrian and West Semitic population of Canaan, indicating that the term no longer conveyed a caste distinction;[3] this is borne out by the fact that although *mariyanna*-ship was hereditary, it could also be conferred by the king as a mark of especial favour, and a man so honoured could transmit the rank to his heirs.[4] The upkeep of a chariot and its equipment was costly and to some extent these men formed an aristocracy of wealth;[5] not every *mariyanna*, however, owned a chariot[6] and the occasional mention of substitutes (*bdl mrynm*) at Ugarit[7] suggests that military service might be avoided if a replacement could be provided.

The *mariyanna* were landowners and held their land in fief from the crown;[8] it is, however, uncertain to what extent the tenure of land in Ugarit, in Alalakh and in Nuzi was linked with a feudal or semi-feudal system.[9] In Nuzi, where under Mitannian rule Hurrian influence was strong, the word *mariyanna* is not found, though here also chariotry and horses are frequently mentioned and appear to have formed an important element in the conduct of war.[10]

The owner of a chariot probably drove it himself, but archers also rode in the chariots, and grooms and stable-boys formed part of a *mariyanna's* staff.[11] Spearmen and bowmen, who made up the rank and file of the infantry, were drawn from the ranks of the *ḫupšu*, free-born citizens who could own land but might be called upon to serve both in the *corvée* and in the army.[12] In the census lists at Alalakh, they were classed with the rural population (*ṣābu namē*[13]) and were less in social standing than both the knights and the *eḫele*, the class of craftsmen and professional people.[14] The employment of mercenaries at Ugarit and Byblos is suggested

[1] §VII, 48, 18; §VII, 56, 19f.
[2] G, 26, 160 f.; §I, 32, 51. See above, p. 420.
[3] §VII, 56, 20; §I, 44, 321.
[4] §I, 67, 54, no. 91; §VI, 30, vol. III, 140 f.=*RS*, 16, 132.
[5] §VI, 27, 117 n. 47.
[6] §I, 67, 11; §VII, 56, 21; §VII, 2, 346.   [7] §VII, 56, 21; §I, 44, 320.
[8] G, 21, 67; §VII, 48, 18; §VII, 26, 51.
[9] G, 12, 111 f.; §VII, 38; §VII, 26, 50 ff.; §VII, 9, 21 ff.; §VII, 4, 10 ff., 224 ff.
[10] §VII, 61, vol. I, 538; §VIII, 20, 22 ff., 56 ff.   [11] §VII, 56, 22 ff.
[12] §VII, 45, 10 ff.; A, 4, 91.   [13] §I, 67, 10.
[14] *Ibid.* 11. In A, 14, 93, 'freedmen'.

by references to the *šerdanu*,[1] the warlike Sherden who were to prove both friend and foe to the Egyptians.[2]

The Canaanite chariot, a favourite subject in the art of both Syria-Palestine and Egypt,[3] had a light frame of bent wood covered with leather or basketwork, and a wooden floor. The long pole, furnished with a double yoke at the farther end, ran under the body of the chariot and was attached to the axle; the latter was wide, and set far back to give stability to the vehicle and ease in turning.[4] Wheels were large and had four spokes; in the fifteenth century, Egyptian wheelwrights began to make six-spoked and occasionally eight-spoked wheels;[5] but Syrian chariots continued to have four spokes until the thirteenth century, and so did those of Mycenae and Crete.[6] The whole chariot, though strongly built, was very light and could be carried by one man; it was an altogether different affair from the heavy, lumbering, solid-wheeled carriage of an earlier age. One actual example, preserved in Florence, is thought to be a Canaanite chariot taken to Egypt as booty.[7]

A quiver fastened to the side of the vehicle held arrows, and another the bow; when the charioteer reined the horses to a halt he would loop the reins round his waist in order to shoot.[8] Warriors are often shown wearing coats of mail, long shirts of leather or cloth covered with overlapping scales of leather or bronze, such as are listed at Nuzi and Ugarit, where horses and chariots as well as men were thus protected.[9] They formed part of the booty taken after Megiddo.[10] In the ruins of this city,[11] as well as in the arsenal at Ugarit, scales from armour were found in quantity, together with arrows and other weapons.[12] Helmets of various shapes are worn by the warriors in the reliefs, the most usual being a pointed helmet with a horsehair plume or tassel.[13] Canaanite soldiers are usually depicted with small square shields worn on the forearm, whereas Egyptians carry oblong parrying shields with a rounded top.[14]

---

[1] §vi, 30, vol. iii, 131 = *RS*, 15, 118, l. 5; vol. iv, 234 = *RS*, 17, 112, l. 16; §vii, 39, 143; EA 122, l. 25; EA 123, l. 15.

[2] §i, 18, vol. i, 194*, no. 268.

[3] E.g. §vii, 72, 86 f.; §v, 11, pl. xxiv.   [4] §vii, 52, 276 ff.

[5] E.g. §iv, 6, pls. 10, 11. Cf. §vi, 6 vol. ii, 57 f.

[6] §vii, 59, 714 ff., figs. 1, 2; §vii, 40, 309 ff.

[7] §vii, 72, 190 f.; §vii, 40, 317 and 318 n. 1.   [8] §i, 50, vol. ii, 14.

[9] §vii, 61, vol. i, 475 ff.; *ibid.* vol. ii, pl. 126a–k: §vii, 57, 140 ff.; §ix, 41, 25.

[10] G, 27, 664, l. 3; cf. 732, l. 1.   [11] §v, 32, pl. 177, 2–8.

[12] §vi, 30, vol. ii, xxxiii; §viii, 68, 316.

[13] §vii, 72, 85 f.; §iv, 6, pls. 10, 11.   [14] §vii, 72, 192 f., 217.

The introduction of the composite bow of laminated wood, horn and sinew[1] greatly increased the range and power of the archer. This, too, may have been a Hurrian introduction. The bow made by the craftsman god for the hero Aqhat of Ugaritic legend was fashioned from these materials;[2] the goddess 'Anath is described as coveting the wonderful bow, which may have been a novelty at the time when the poem was composed. Such bows were costly and difficult to make, and are usually seen in the hands of nobles and princes, while the rank and file carry the simple bow of the Middle Kingdom type. Considerable strength was needed to string and draw a composite bow, and the proud challenge of Penelope on behalf of Odysseus[3] echoes the boast of Amenophis II that no man in the whole of his army, and none among the whole of the Syrian chivalry, could bend his bow.[4] Arrows were tipped with bronze, more deadly than the earlier wooden- or flint-tipped shafts; leather quivers held as many as thirty arrows.[5]

Other weapons of the Canaanite infantry in the Late Bronze Age were the hand-axe, the sling, the spear and the short sword. Hafted battle-axes of elaborate and often beautiful workmanship have been found on Syrian sites,[6] and it was upon these, rather than upon the narrow-bladed sword used as a thrusting weapon,[7] that the metal-workers lavished their skill; the slim inlaid rapiers of the Minoan world[8] have no parallel in the Orient. The weapon *par excellence*, however, of the princes of Syria and their body-guard was the short scimitar or sickle-sword, known to the Egyptians as *khepesh*; this weapon, too, was probably introduced from Syria-Palestine into Egypt;[9] early examples were found in one of the royal tombs of the eighteenth century at Byblos,[10] and on the reliefs it is usually brandished by gods and rulers.[11] The Nuzian armament included heavy bronze spears.[12]

The fortress-cities of Syria and Palestine were built for defence against such formidable weapons of attack.[13] The public buildings and main residential areas were usually set on a high natural

[1] §VII, 72, 80 f., 199 ff.; §VII, 30, 252 n. 3; §VII, 40, 289, fig. 37; §III, 43, 158 f.; A, 43, 91 ff., 145 ff.

[2] §VII, 63, 11 ff.; §VII, 12, 90 = 2 Aqhat VI, ll. 21 ff.

[3] *Odyssey*, XXI, 73 ff.

[4] G, 27, 1290, ll. 3–6; G, 24, 244. See above, ch. IX, sect V.

[5] §VII, 61, 542.   [6] §I, 50, vol. I, pl. 22; §VII, 72, 222.

[7] §III, 43, 159 f.; §VII, 23, 71 f.; §VIII, 18, 183 f.

[8] §VII, 40, 262.   [9] §III, 43, 161; §VII, 72, 79.

[10] §V, 33, 174 ff., pls. 99–101.   [11] §VII, 72, 204, 232.

[12] §VII, 61, vol. I, 542.   [13] §VII, 72, 90 ff.; G, 14, 338 ff.

eminence or on an artificial mound, the *tell* which accumulated
over the ruins of mud-brick buildings constantly demolished and
rebuilt. A double or triple wall with fortified gates surrounded the
city, and the citadel was frequently defended by an inner wall
built on the summit of a long sloping bank of beaten earth faced
with smooth clay, plaster or stone[1] and surrounded by a moat.
This slope afforded protection to the walls from sappers and
scaling-ladders, and also prevented the use of assault devices
such as siege-towers and battering-rams[2] which had been a feature
of Near Eastern warfare since at least the eighteenth century B.C.[3]
The Hittites appear to have learnt the use of siege engines in
North Syria, and regarded them as a Hurrian speciality.[4] Citadel
gateways were approached by a ramp, and though wide enough
to admit horses and chariots, the entrance was flanked by battle-
mented towers from which the defenders could rain down arrows
on an approaching enemy.[5] The construction of the corbelled
postern gate and tunnelled stairway in the glacis of the city wall
at Ras Shamra[6] is strongly reminiscent of Hittite defensive architecture[7] and suggests that the king of Ugarit may have benefited
by the advice of a military mission from Khattusha.

Houses within these fortified towns were built of mud-brick,
usually on a stone foundation.[8] In North Syria, as in Anatolia,
where heavy rain may wash away entire buildings, the walls were
often reinforced with half-timbering:[9] they were plastered and
whitewashed, and stairs led up to the flat roof,[10] on which the
family might sleep in hot weather, as they do today. The larger
houses had an upper storey and most were built round an interior
courtyard.[11] Large houses in the more prosperous quarters of
Ugarit had each a bathroom and latrine, with drainage leading
to enclosed sewers below the levels of the paved streets;[12] many
houses had a well in the courtyard.[13] Few cities of Canaan can have
rivalled the spacious plan of Ugarit with its wide intersecting

---

[1] §vii, 72, 67; §v, 2, 88 ff.; §iv, 25, 80 ff.; §i, 4, 224; §i, 68,133 ff.; §vii, 71, vol. ii, 73 ff. and fig. 14.   [2] §vii, 73, 23 ff.

[3] §vii, 72, 70 f.; §vii, 5, vol. i = *A.R.M.T.* i, 135, ll. 5–13; *ibid.* vol. ii, 15, l. 30; §iv, 12, 178 f.; §vii, 16, 128. For the development of the 'glacis' from earlier types of fortification, see A, 49, 27 ff.; A, 41.

[4] *K.Bo.* i, 11, obv. l. 15, ll. 29 ff.; §ii, 22, 113 ff.; §vii, 16, 128.

[5] §vii, 72, 97; §i, 13, pls. 60, 62; §v, 32, fig. 42; §v, 2, 89 f. and fig. 15.

[6] §viii, 69, 288 ff., pls. 42, 43. See Plate 104.   [7] §vii, 72, 92 ff.; G, 9, 148.

[8] §i, 69, 114 f.; §vii, 25, 56 f.; §viii, 34, 131.

[9] §i, 69, 108; §i, 50, vol. iv, 9, vol. i, pl. xix.

[10] §i, 50, vol. i, 30 ff., pl. vi, no. 3; §i, 68, 176 ff.

[11] §i, 50, vol. i, 23, fig. 14.   [12] *Ibid.* vol. iv, 22, fig. 17.

[13] *Ibid.* vol. i, pl. vi, 1 and 2; vol. iv, 31, 48 f., figs. 32–4.

streets and rows of imposing houses. At Tell Açana, the ancient Alalakh, excavation was concentrated upon the public buildings[1] and no plan could be made of the town as a whole, but at Nuzi (Yorgan Tepe), one of the eastern outposts of the Mitannian empire, a more complete picture was obtained.[2] Nuzi was a small but flourishing township, with a regular layout of intersecting streets. Here, too, most of the dwellings were built around a courtyard: they must have been very like houses of the region today, with mud-brick walls, and floors, door-sills and hearths of baked brick.[3] The wooden doors had pivots shod with copper, rotating in a stone socket. Some rooms, perhaps storerooms, had no doors but were reached by an opening high up in the wall; this unusual feature is not found elsewhere.[4] Some of the houses had a second storey, and many of the larger ones were furnished with bathrooms and privies and possessed an elaborate drainage system designed to carry away rainwater and household waste as well as sewage.[5] On the outskirts of the town were the large suburban houses of four prominent citizens: the largest, that of 'Shilwi-Teshub, son of the king', had no less than fifty-five rooms, some of which must have served for the management of his considerable estate.[6] Many of the tablets were found in these houses, where they had been stored on shelves or in boxes. Tekhip-Tilla's house contained the business records of five generations.[7]

In the centre of the town was the governor's house, by far the largest building, with rooms of impressive size built around a series of paved courtyards.[8] A large number of people appear to have lived in this building, but there was no mistaking the central audience chamber with its red-painted dais and heavy door studded with silver and copper nails.[9] The private living quarters lay behind: a fine marble bathroom and toilet revealed the high standard of living of the occupants, and in a neighbouring room[10] the remains of striking mural paintings gave some hint of the original decoration of the palace: a design of *guilloche* alternating with bucrania and human heads somewhat reminiscent of Egyptian wall-painting, and suggesting influence from the Syrian coast.[11]

In the cities of Canaan, too, a commanding position was occupied by the royal palace, the largest and most impressive

[1] §1, 69, 66 ff.   [2] §vii, 61.
[3] *Ibid.* vol. 1, 42 ff., 530 f.; vol. 11, pls. 12 ff.
[4] §vii, 61, vol. 1, 47 f.   [5] *Ibid.* 59 ff. and vol. 11, pls. 11–14.
[6] *Ibid.* vol. 1, 337 ff.   [7] *Ibid.* 334; §1, 10, 86 ff.
[8] §vii, 61, vol. 1, 123 ff. and vol. 11, plan 13.
[9] *Ibid.* vol. 1, 138, 141–3, 154 f.   [10] *Ibid.* 144, and vol. 11, pl. 15 A.
[11] *Ibid.* 491 f., and vol. 11, pls. 128 E, G, H, and 129 D.

building and far exceeding the temples of the gods in size. Tablets found in the archive rooms of the palaces of Ugarit[1] and Alalakh make it abundantly clear that besides housing the king and his family, his harim and his household of slaves, the palace was also the economic and administrative centre of the kingdom. For although the actions and policies of the city states of North Syria were governed in external matters by the will of their overlords, the kings of Mitanni, of Egypt or of the Khatti-land, the internal government was in the hands of rulers endowed with supreme power, whose authority regulated the daily lives of their subjects. The kingship was hereditary, and the fiction that the king was of divine nature was fostered by legend, by artistic convention which portrayed him suckled by a goddess,[2] and by the reverence paid to deified kings who had been the ancestors of the dynasty.[3] Something of this aura of godhead may still have clung to the petty kings of western Asia, familiar as they must have been with the attitude of the Egyptians towards their pharaohs.[4] Yet they appear in the business records as practical business men, owners of tracts of land and of flocks and herds, buying and selling property, and lending money at interest.[5] They acted as witnesses in legal transactions between private individuals, thus bestowing the guarantee of the state upon acts of adoption, wills, or marriage contracts and the like.[6] They made grants of land and property to members of their own families and to officials and nobles of their court, sealing the documents with their own seal and giving it the added guarantee of the ancient dynastic seal preserved from generation to generation,[7] which presumably placed the donation under the protection of both past and future rulers.[8] The rulers presided over courts of justice in their cities, either in the palace itself or by the city gate,[9] and delivered judgement in cases of litigation between their subjects, the records of which were preserved in the palace archives.

The basis of the social organization was the family unit, though traces of a tribal organization have been discerned at Ugarit.[10] Census records list landowners together with their wives, children

---

[1] §i, 50, vol. iv, xiv ff.
[2] §ix, 41, 51 ff., pl. viii.
[3] *C.A.H.* ii³, pt. 2, ch. xvii, sect. iv.
[4] G, 25, 62 ff., 138 f.
[5] §i, 67, 40, no. 18, 46, no. 49; §vi, 30, vol. iii, 102 = *RS*, 15, 109, 89 = *RS*, 16, 135, etc. See A, 38, 261 ff. for tablets from Ugarit recording real estate transactions by the queen.
[6] G. Boyer in §vi, 30, vol. iii, 283 ff.
[7] §vi, 30, vol. iii, xl ff., pl. xvi; §vii, 39, 137; §i, 53, 38 ff.
[8] G. Boyer in §vi, 30, vol. iii, 285.
[9] §vii, 15, 9 ff.; §vii, 25, 60.
[10] §vii, 67, 91; §vii, 25, 106.

and livestock, and estates passed from father to son in a strict rule of family inheritance.[1] In rare instances a son could be disinherited[2] but in the case of grants of land made by the king to individuals a clause is usually inserted to ensure that the descendants of the recipient shall inherit the property in perpetuity.[3] For fiscal purposes and for the allotment of terms of service on public works and in the army, a regional assessment was made on the basis of towns and villages,[4] and townspeople were grouped in their professional guilds or corporations.[5] Several classes of soldiers including *mariyanna* are among these guilds, and so also are a number of priestly categories, craftsmen such as tanners, weavers, potters, masons and silverworkers, merchants, and shepherds and field-labourers.[6] Exemption from *corvée* service could be granted by the king to favoured nobles in his train.[7]

Numerous Hurrian names found in the texts, and tablets in the Hurrian language, testify to the presence of a considerable Hurrian element in the population of Ugarit,[8] but no administrative or economic documents in that tongue have as yet been found, and it may be deduced that the Hurrians composed the poorer, less influential and less literate section of the community, while the rich merchants and officials were either Canaanites themselves or had become assimilated.[9] At Alalakh, on the other hand, many of the *mariyanna* class bore Hurrian names;[10] the Khanaeans constituted a separate ethnic element;[11] and there were a number of Sutu and other bedawin groups.[12]

In all countries of the ancient Near East, state slavery played an important role in the economy.[13] Male and female slaves, children as well as adults, were sent in droves by the kings of Syria and Palestine to their Egyptian overlords[14] and no doubt also to Mitannian and Hittite kings who were their masters; these must have been state slaves at the disposal of their owners. Slaves were usually acquired by conquest, however,[15] or by

---

[1] §VII, 34; §VII, 67, 137 ff. [2] §VI, 30, vol. III, 32 f. = *RS*, 16, 129.
[3] *Ibid.* 122 f. = *RS*, 15, 145; §VII, 34, 359 ff.
[4] §VI, 30, vol. III, 188 ff.; §VII, 70, 123 ff.
[5] §VII, 70, 137 ff.; §VI, 30, vol. II, xxiii; §VII, 39, 84 n. 90; §VI, 12, vol. III, 276 ff.
[6] §VIII, 79; §VI, 30, vol. II, xxv, 47 ff.
[7] §VII, 48, 22; §VI, 30, vol. III, 68 = *RS*, 16, 269, 162 = *RS*, 16, 348.
[8] §I, 50, vol. IV, 51, 83 f. [9] §I, 50, vol. IV, 89.
[10] §I, 67, 11. [11] G, 10, 46 f.; §I, 33, 1 ff.
[12] §I, 67, 12; §VII, 10; §I, 33, 83 ff. [13] §VII, 49, 94 ff.
[14] E.g. EA 120, ll. 20 ff.; EA 173, ll. 13 ff.; EA 268, ll. 15 ff.; EA 288, ll. 20 ff.; G, 14, 363 ff. [15] G, 14, 359 ff.

purchase;[1] since trade between countries was virtually a state monopoly, exchange might be made between a consignment of slaves
and the equivalent value in material goods.[2] At times when a
greater number of prisoners were captured than could be employed by the palace and the temples,[3] gifts of slaves were made
by rulers to private persons;[4] the king of Carchemish captured
so many that he sold some of them to slave-dealers in his realm.[5]
The activities of these persons are often referred to: Nuzian merchants imported slaves from Babylonia and the Lullu-country[6] (the
price of the latter, who were in especial demand, was fixed at 30
shekels a head). The presence of an Egyptian slave-dealer in
Ugarit is attested by a letter from the palace archive,[7] and
Tuthmosis III captured two shiploads of slaves off Ullaza.[8] Slaves
were sold and resold and might ultimately find themselves far
from home in an alien land. Amenophis II's viceroy in Nubia
had in his domestic establishment a Babylonian woman, a young
girl from Alalakh, and an old woman from Arrapkha (Kirkuk),
as well as a Byblite slave.[9] Defaulting debtors in temporary servitude to their creditors,[10] and privately owned slaves, bore the burden of the *corvée* called out in times of emergency,[11] for, though
in theory all citizens were subject to conscription for labour
service, in practice many exemptions were granted and the provision of substitutes was generally accepted practice. Registers
of slaves were kept for purposes of the *corvée*.[12]

Some four thousand texts were found in Yorgan Tepe, the
majority of them from the Nuzi period.[13] They are written in a
provincial dialect of Babylonian, with an unusual orthography and
some ungrammatical constructions which prove the authors to
have been writing in an unfamiliar tongue;[14] Hurrian proper names
predominate, and many Hurrian words appear in the tablets: the
titles of officials, certain technical terms,[15] and the names of trees,
cereals and crops,[16] of furniture, stuffs and raw materials and of
armour and chariot gear.[17] Hurrian and Semitic names for the
months are employed side by side, and the latter are not Baby-

---

[1] §vii, 49, 3 ff.; §vii, 47, 68.　　　　[2] EA 44, ll. 23–6; §vi, 9, 125 ff.
[3] §vii, 49, 101, 148 n. 23.　　　　[4] G, 14, 359 f.
[5] §vii, 3, 434 f.　　　　[6] §vii, 49, 4.
[7] §vi, 30, vol. iii, 19 = *RS*, 15, 11, ll. 8 ff.　　　　[8] See above, p. 454.
[9] G, 27, 1344, ll. 4–7; §iii, 28, 50.　　　　[10] §vii, 47, 66.
[11] §vii, 46, 32 ff.; §vii, 48, 21 f.; §v, 29.
[12] §vii, 49, 98 f., 149 n. 41. Cf. §vi, 30, vol. iii, xiv f.　　　　[13] §vii, 35, 164 f.
[14] §vii, 17; §vii, 35, 166; §vii, 9, 4.
[15] §vii, 61, vol. i, 528 ff.; §vii, 62, 20 ff.　　　　[16] *Ibid.* 533 ff.
[17] *Ibid.* 536 ff.; §viii, 20, 63 ff.; §i, 58, 8 f.

lonian but have affinities with calendars employed at various times in the west.[1] Above all, certain institutions and legal concepts appear in the Nuzi texts which are foreign to both Babylonia and Assyria and must therefore reflect a social organization which is Hurrian. Perhaps the most remarkable among these are the legal practices associated with the tenure of land, in which the ancient Babylonian custom of adoption plays a prominent part.

Some adoptions seem to have been genuine, in the sense that the motive for the adoption was the desire for an heir who should care for his adoptive parents in their old age, look after their estate for them and eventually, when they died, perform the rites of burial. In return for these filial services the adopted son would inherit the property and also, at the time of adoption, have certain specified property made over to him by his new parent. The arrangement was mutually beneficial and widely practised by those who were childless; the contract of adoption often stipulates that the prospective parent shall adopt no other son,[2] and that if an adoptive son fail in his duty he shall be disinherited.[3]

Another kind of 'sonship' is frequently encountered in the tablets, namely that acquired by a deed of false adoption or 'sale-adoption'.[4] Landed property was in theory, it seems, inalienable, perhaps because formally it belonged to the king, who granted it in feoff to individuals in exchange for their feudal service.[5] It passed by inheritance from father to son and could not be sold or given away. In order to circumvent this difficulty and enable real estate to be transferred to new ownership, a system was devised whereby the owner of land who was in financial straits could adopt as his son the would-be purchaser, in consideration for a gift; at his death, the adopted son would inherit the property. It is often stipulated that the seller retain his obligation to forced labour-service on the land.[6] These fictitious adoptions do not have any clause stipulating that the son shall honour and tend his new parent, and in fact they had all the force and effect of a commercial transaction. One instance of the same practice is known from Ugarit.[7] A similar ingenuity in adapting existing legislation to fit the circumstances is seen in the custom of temporary exchange in case of debt: the debtor, forbidden by law to sell himself

[1] §VII, 22.   [2] §VII, 60, 7 ff.; §VII, 9, 38 ff., 285 f.; §VII, 35, 173.
[3] §VII, 60, 12 f.
[4] *Ibid.* 13 ff.; §VII, 37, 55 ff.; §VII, 9, 42 ff.; §VII, 35, 167 ff.
[5] G, 12, 111 f.; §VII, 37, 60 f.; §VII, 38; §VII, 62, 14 ff.; otherwise §VII, 9, 22 ff.; §VII, 54.
[6] §VII, 60, 51 f.   [7] §VI, 30, vol. III, 64 = *RS*, 16, 200.

into slavery, might barter his services for a stated amount of wool, livestock or silver.[1] Similarly, a debtor could give his daughter to be 'daughter and daughter-in-law' to a householder who agreed to marry her to one of his family or to a slave of his household; he obtained thereby the services of a slave-girl, and her father received the bride-price in advance.[2] In order to keep her perpetually in his household, the prospective father-in-law might stipulate that if one slave to whom he married her died, the girl was to marry another, then a third, and so on—'even if ten of her husbands have died, in that case to an eleventh she may be given into wifehood'.[3] The owner of the slave in this case was Tulpunnaya, a wealthy woman in her own right, who appears to have lived in the 'governor's palace', the administrative centre at Nuzi; her acquisition of slave and real estate forms the subject of many transactions recorded on tablets found in a room of the building.[4]

The business affairs of Tulpunnaya are an illustration of the remarkably high status of women in contemporary society.[5] Though married, her husband hardly receives mention in the documents; she acquired property by means of pseudo-adoptions, and conducted lawsuits in her own name for breach of contract. Divorce of a wife seems to have been rare,[6] though women occasionally deserted their husbands. A father who gave his daughter in marriage, or a brother who, as head of the family, married off his sister,[7] received from the bridegroom a bride-price, usually forty shekels of silver;[8] the whole or a portion of this was sewn into the hem of the bride's outer garment and served as her dowry.[9] A marriage contract sometimes stipulates that the bridegroom shall not take another wife, though if the wife proved to be barren, her husband might take a concubine, called at Ugarit 'she who completes (the family)';[10] the wife in that case might not drive out the children of the union—a stipulation which recalls the story of Sarah and Hagar.[11] When devising property to his children, a man might insert a clause to the effect that his widow was to inherit a life interest in the property; one will from Nuzi provides that the son who best looks after his mother shall inherit

[1] §vii, 35, 169; §i, 47, 60 ff.
[2] §vii, 60, 21 ff.; §i, 47, 77 ff.; §vii, 9, 42 ff.; §vii, 49, 53 f.
[3] §i, 47, 84, no. 23, ll. 12 f.; §vii, 21, 152.　　　[4] §vii, 61, vol. i, 131 ff.
[5] §i, 47, 20 ff., 75 ff., nos. 15–45; cf. §vi, 30, vol. iii, 179 f.
[6] §vii, 33, 323 ff.; §vii, 21, 161.
[7] §vii, 21, 153 f.; §i, 47, 104 f., no. 54; A, 48.
[8] §vii, 60, 31 f., 59 f.; §vii, 21, 156 f.; §viii, 20, 41.
[9] G, 2, vol. 6, 136; §vii, 60, 24 f.; §vii, 9, 47 f.; §vii, 33, 323 ff.
[10] §vii, 55, 16.　　　[11] §vii, 21, 159 f.; §vii, 20, 35; A, 37, 106.

after her death.[1] Other testatory documents decree that the widow shall exercise the authority of parenthood over the property and the children; this power may even be conferred upon a daughter.[2] If a son failed in obedience to the mother or sister thus set in authority over him, he was to be punished by fetters or imprisonment, or even expelled from the house and disinherited.[3] Even a slave had the right to appeal in law against the decision of her owner; Tulpunnaya attempted to force one of her girls, Kisaya, into marriage with a man she disliked, whereas she wanted to marry Artaya whom she loved; the court decided in favour of Artaya.[4]

Justice was administered in Nuzi by a court presided over by a Hurrian official, the *ḫalzuḫlu*,[5] who appears to have been the highest civil authority in the town, though the king of Arrapkha, himself a vassal of the king of Mitanni, seems to have exercised authority and governed by decree.[6] The composition of the court of justice apparently changed frequently. A number of depositions have survived pertaining to a long-drawn-out series of criminal actions brought against a mayor of Nuzi[7] whose name, Kushshi-kharbe, proclaims him to have been a Kassite and perhaps suggests a reason for his unpopularity.[8] He was accused of accepting bribes, of abusing his position by making use of public materials and public labour for his private ends,[9] and of theft of the property of his fellow citizens; several of his henchmen were accused at the same time of a number of acts of violence including assault and kidnapping for ransom.[10] Proceedings in this sensational case were heard by a number of different judges and must have taken a considerable time; that a prominent official could be brought to justice is significant comment on the healthy condition of Hurrian society.

Both witnesses and litigants in court cases could be subjected to the ordeal by water;[11] or the severe test of 'the oath of the gods' might be employed to decide a case.[12] Theft was punished by enforcing the restitution of the amount stolen up to twelvefold; in the case of burglary, as well as the penalty for larceny there was a separate fine for trespass. Theft aggravated by a breach of trust was especially heavily punished. When a thief could not be

[1] §vii, 60, 49 ff., nos. 19, 20.
[2] §viii, 15, 115.
[3] *Ibid.* 116 ff.; §vii, 64, 249 f.
[4] §i, 47, 27 ff., 88 ff., nos. 30–3.
[5] §vii, 36, 171; §vii, 38, 5 ff., 12 n. 1.
[6] §vii, 36, 166 f.
[7] §i, 47, 13 ff., 59 ff.; §vii, 37, 61.
[8] §i, 47, 62.   [9] *Ibid.* 63 ff.
[10] *Ibid.* 64 ff.
[11] §vii, 18, 308.
[12] *Ibid.* 305; §vii, 36, 172.

found, the whole community was fined.[1] No trace is found in the law of Nuzi of the savagery which prescribed, in Babylonia and Assyria, death or mutilation for certain offences. The death penalty is found only once in the archives of Ugarit, and this was for the crime of treason.[2]

VIII. COMMERCE AND INDUSTRY

The prosperity of the city states and kingdoms of Syria depended largely upon trade. During the second millennium B.C. they were seldom, if ever, entirely independent of the control of one or other of the greater powers, who strove to gain access to the sources of raw materials and to command the routes by which those materials travelled. In a situation which their geographical position and lack of cohesion made inevitable, the kings of North Syria and Phoenicia paid tribute to their current overlord until the burden became intolerable or the pressure was removed, and meanwhile enjoyed the advantages of vassalage: a secure seat on the throne, military support in case of aggression by their neighbours, and preferential facilities for commerce with the controlling power and brother vassals. The archives of Ugarit clearly demonstrate the advantages enjoyed by that city as a result of almost two centuries of Hittite suzerainty.[3]

During the travelling season, donkey caravans[4] traversed a network of tracks across the steppe and over the mountain passes, and their safe passage was the concern of the state under whose aegis they journeyed. All caravan trade seems to have been under the direct control of the state, and merchants were government agents travelling on the king's business.[5] They were protected by treaty agreements made between their own master and the rulers of the lands through which they must pass. If harm came to them, the king in whose territory the incident had occurred was held responsible, and had to see to it that restitution was made to the relatives of the dead man, and the malefactors punished.[6] A merchant was a valuable asset and his price was high: an indemnity of a hundred and eighty silver shekels was imposed by their mutual overlord, Ini-Teshub of Carchemish, upon those Ugaritians responsible for the death of a merchant of the king of

---

[1] §vii, 18, 306 ff. [2] §vi, 30, vol. iii, 32, 68 = *RS*, 16, 269.

[3] §vi, 30, vol. iii, 32; §vii, 39, 158; §viii, 5, 253; §viii, 64, 54 f. See *C.A.H.* ii³, pt. 2, ch. xxi, sect. iv. [4] §vii, 1, 40 ff.; §v, 8, 62 ff.; A, 9, 85.

[5] §viii, 53, 78 ff.; §viii, 40, 375 f.; §vii, 5, vol. vii, 338.

[6] EA 7, ll. 73 ff.; §vii, 39, 115 ff.; §viii, 52, 106 n. 251 = *K.Bo.* i, 10, 98 ff.

Tarkhundasshi,[1] and a Hittite merchant was valued at the enormous sum of a hundred minas.[2] In spite of this, highway robbery was frequent; marauding bands of bedawin roamed the countryside[3] and it was no doubt for mutual safety, as well as for the regulation of their affairs, that merchants banded together in a guild or corporation.[4]

In return for safe conduct, merchants on their part were expected to fulfil their obligations to the governments of the kingdoms in which they found themselves. King Bente-shina of Amurru protested to Babylon because certain Akkadians had failed to pay a sum due while they were passing through his land,[5] probably some kind of toll levied on goods in transit; and when the king of Ugarit complained of the oppressive behaviour of certain Hittite merchants from the town of Ura in western Cilicia,[6] the Hittite king himself adjudicated the case and decreed a compromise solution, fair to both sides, whereby the Hittites were not banned from residence in Ugarit, but were permitted to stay there only during the summer months, and might not acquire houses or land in settlement of a debt.[7]

For the kingdoms of the Lebanese coast, with its numerous bays and small natural harbours, the sea was the best means of communication, for they were cut off from each other and from the interior by rugged mountains and torrential streams flowing down through deep ravines: the whole of this coastline has no navigable river. Ships hugged the coast, for the vessels of the time could make no headway against strong winds; moreover, sudden storms can blow up in the Mediterranean making it advisable to gain port with all speed,[8] and the danger from pirates was ever present.[9] Most sea-trading was done in the summer months, and during the stormy season, from October to April, cargo boats would stay in harbour or be drawn up on the beaches.[10] Blocks of masonry now under water, by reason of the sinking of the coatline, and traces of rock-cutting on the reefs betray the presence of ancient port installations from Ruad (Arwad) to Tell Abu Hawām in the Bay of Acre and even to Jaffa.[11] Though it

---

[1] §vi, 30, vol. iv, 22 and 170 ff. = RS, 17, 158 and 17, 42; cf. ibid. 172 ff. = RS, 17, 145 and 17, 234.   [2] K.Bo. vi, 1, 10 ff.; but see §1, 24, 115 n. 5.

[3] §vii, 66, 109; EA 7, ll. 74 ff.; G, 16, 1026.

[4] §vi, 30, vol. ii, xxiii and 53 ff., vol. iii, 204 = RS, 15, 172 and 232 ff.; §vii, 70, 147; §viii, 63, 315.   [5] §vi, 21, 88 f.; K. Bo. i, 10 rs. 26 ff.

[6] §vii, 39, 80 f.; §1, 22, 48 f.; §viii, 63, 319 f.

[7] §vi, 30, vol. iv, 102 ff. = RS, 17, 130; §vi, 22, 70; §vii, 39, 82 f.

[8] §viii, 17, 226; §viii, 62, 63.   [9] §viii, 74, 98.   [10] §viii, 62, 63.

[11] §viii, 35; §viii, 54; §iii, 1, 578 ff., figs. 8, 9.

is impossible to date these quays and moles, many of them may well have been constructed as early as the second millennium B.C.[1] Phoenician cities such as Byblos,[2] Sidon[3] and Tyre[4] were equipped with two anchorages, one facing north and the other, the 'Egyptian harbour', orientated towards the south-west. Smaller ships must have made frequent calls for watering, and for the unloading and loading of short-distance freight carried between city and city.

One of the main industries of the Phoenician coastal towns must have been shipbuilding. The forests of Lebanon provided an unlimited supply of suitable timber, and the shipyards of Byblos, and perhaps of Sigata, survived the attempt of Tuthmosis III to secure a monopoly.[5] This was an age of heavy freighters capable of transporting bulky cargoes.[6] They carried timber, livestock and agricultural produce, salt,[7] wine and oil in large jars.[8] Ugarit had grain-ships capable of carrying a hundred and fifty tons of grain.[9] No adequate picture of a Canaanite ship of the period has survived from Syrian sources, but an Egyptian representation of Asiatics unloading their cargo of amphorae and humped cattle from the decks of vessels with a high deck-rail[10] is instructive, for if the artist is to be believed, they are different in design from the swift 'Byblos-boats' built by the Egyptians for long sea voyages.[11] The Eighteenth Dynasty version of the latter shows several improvements on its Old Kingdom prototype: the hogging truss and canoe-shaped, keelless hull remain,[12] but the mast, heavily stayed, is set amidships[13] and the sail is very wide in order to catch all available wind. Such vessels ran before the wind and could only tack with difficulty, and this is probably true of all contemporary shipping.[14] Besides Byblos-boats, other types known as Keftiu-boats (for the Cretan run?) and *skt*-boats were built in the Memphite dockyards.[15] Ocean-going ships appear at first to have been used for transport only,[16] but by the thirteenth century B.C., if not earlier, they were used in warfare. The equipment of a hundred and fifty ships, presumably to reinforce an already existent fleet, was urged on the king of Ugarit by one of his

[1] §VIII, 35, 74; §VIII, 62, 67 ff.   [2] §VIII, 36, 96 ff.
[3] *Ibid.* 69 ff. and fig. 17.
[4] *Ibid.* 88 ff. and figs. 18–23; §VIII, 62.   [5] G, 27, 1237, ll. 9 ff.; G, 14, 395.
[6] §VIII, 5, 253; §VIII, 66, 132.   [7] §VI, 30, vol. V, 118 f.=*RS*, 18, 27.
[8] §VIII, 33, 222, fig. 753; §I, 50, vol. I, 30 f. pl. IX; vol. IV, 143=*RS*, 19, 26.
[9] §VIII, 59, 165. *RS*, 20, 212 and *RS*, 26, 158 (A, 38, 105 ff., 323 ff.).
[10] §V, 18, 40 ff. and pl. VIII.
[11] §III, 18, 119; §VIII, 66, 129; *C.A.H.* I³, pt. 2, pp. 348, 351.
[12] §VIII, 30, 7 ff.; §VI, 40, 735.   [13] §VIII, 33, 223 f.; §VIII, 30, pl. IV.
[14] §VIII, 8, 223; §VI, 40, 734 ff.   [15] §III, 22, 14 f.; §III, 37, 47 ff.   [16] *Ibid.* 42.

officers.[1] This is a navy larger than any single Greek state could muster for the siege of Troy.[2] The Hittite fleet which defeated the Alashiyans in the time of Shuppiluliumash II[3] must have been largely composed of Ugaritian ships. These may, like the ships used by the Sea Peoples,[4] have been warships especially designed and equipped with a beaked prow;[5] the crow's nest shown at the mast-head of vessels which attacked the Egyptian fleet in the reign of Ramesses III seems to have been a usual feature of Syrian ships.[6]

The basis of the Syrian economy was agricultural. Land was cheap[7] and the climate favourable. Barley and wheat were the staple crops, but flax, sesame, poppy and millet are also mentioned in the texts.[8] Vetches were grown as horse-fodder.[9] In Alalakh and Ugarit viticulture played an important part in rural life and wines were exported; Syrian wines were especially prized in Egypt and vine stocks brought in to improve the strain.[10] Kizzuwadnan beer had a more than local reputation.[11] The moringa tree[12] and, above all, the olive yielded edible oil,[13] and various oils and fats were used as bases in the cosmetic industry.[14]

Sheep and goats figure largely in the texts from Alalakh and Nuzi, where pastoralism was as important to the economy as agriculture.[15] The Euphrates region around Carchemish was a sheep-breeding centre, and in North Syria sheep were grazed on common land around the villages; on the steppe, the nomads pastured their flocks.[16] In summer, when the grass burned brown, sheep were fattened on corn,[17] while the bedawin moved northwards to better grazing-grounds. There were heavy penalties for sheep-stealing.[18] Sheep were kept primarily for their wool, which was plucked, not shorn.[19] The coarser hair of goats was woven by the nomads into cloth for cloaks and tents, but goats were also bred for their leather and for milk and cheese.[20] Goats were native to Syria, and the hunting of wild goats is depicted on a golden

[1] §vi, 30, vol. v, 88 f. = RS, 18, 148; §viii, 5, 256.
[2] Iliad, ii, 576.   [3] §viii, 60, 20 f. = K.Bo. xii, rev. iii.
[4] C.A.H. ii³, pt. 2, ch. xxiii, sect. xii.   [5] §iii, 44, vol. ii, pls. 115–17.
[6] §v, 18, 43.   [7] §vii, 66, 112 ff.
[8] §viii, 20, 32 ff.; §vii, 61, vol. i, 533; §i, 67, 15.
[9] §i, 67, 82 ff.   [10] G, 14, 414 f.
[11] Ibid. 414; §i, 18, vol. i, 136*.
[12] G, 14, 415.   [13] §vi, 30, vol. ii, xxix.
[14] EA 22, iii, l. 29 ff.; EA 25, iv, 51 ff.; G, 14, 417.
[15] §viii, 20, 28; §i, 67, 346 ff.   [16] §i, 67, 16.
[17] §viii, 20, 26 f.; §i, 17, 32 and 51.   [18] §viii, 20, 30; §vii, 18, 306 f.
[19] §i, 67, 98, no. 351, 100, no. 361; §viii, 20, 27 f.   [20] §viii, 20, 31.

patera from Ras Shamra.[1] Wild cattle, too, roamed the steppe and were hunted;[2] domesticated cattle were pastured in small herds and grain-fed in winter.[3] The draught-ox was yoked to a four-wheeled farm-cart,[4] and oxen and cows were both used for ploughing.[5] Then, as now, the donkey was the chief beast of burden;[6] grain was sometimes measured by the *imēru* (*homer*), the donkey-load, and the standard measure of land was also a *homer*, probably originally reckoned as the area of ground which could be sown by a donkey-load of grain.[7] The large wild ass, or onager, which had been domesticated and used as a draught animal in the third millennium, had by this time given way to a smaller breed.[8] Asses are classified at Nuzi according to age and sex[9] and figure prominently in the texts from Alalakh, where, as in Egypt, they brought in the harvest.[10] The horse was sometimes ridden,[11] but its chief role was as a draught-animal for the light chariot used in war and in the chase.[12] Pigs, which are not mentioned in the Alalakh tablets or at Ugarit, were fattened for the table in Nuzi[13] and in the Khabur area.[14] Flocks of geese were kept at Ugarit.[15]

Woollen rather than linen garments were worn in Syria and furniture was upholstered in wool.[16] Bolts of woollen cloth are listed by weight and by dimensions[17] and both dyed cloth and sewn garments were important commodities in commerce and figure prominently in the dowry lists and in inventories of tribute.[18] The production of purple-dyed cloth was among the foremost industries of the coastal cities of Phoenicia;[19] some scholars indeed derive the name of the country Canaan (*Kinaḫni*) from that of its most characteristic product, the dye *kinaḫḫu*.[20] This was obtained from several kinds of sea snails commonly found in the eastern Mediterranean, the most common being *Purpura haemostoma*, which Pliny calls *buccinum*, and *Murex brandaris*. The colour-bearing secretion, found in a cyst near the head of the creature, was boiled in a salt solution; cloth dipped in the dye and then

[1] §1, 50, vol. II, 6 ff., pls. I, VII.

[2] *Ibid.* 5 ff., pls. I, VII. [3] §VIII, 20, 19.

[4] §VII, 61, vol. I, 538. [5] §VI, 40, 539, figs. 351, 365.

[6] §VII, 75, 378; §VI, 40, 543, fig. 359; see *C.A.H.* I³, pt. 2, ch. XXIV, sect. IX.

[7] §VII, 61, vol. I, 532; G, 2, vol. 7, 114. [8] §VII, 75, 367 ff.

[9] §VIII, 20, 20 f. [10] §1, 67, 95 ff., nos. 332, 341 ff., 345.

[11] §VII, 29, 243 ff.; §VIII, 73. [12] See above, p. 494.

[13] §VIII, 20, 32. [14] §1, 17, 39.

[15] §VI, 30, vol. II, xxxviii f. [16] §VII, 61, vol. I, 536 f.; §VIII, 20, 48.

[17] §VIII, 20, 51; §VI, 30, vol. II, xxxi f.; *ibid.* vol. IV, 42 ff.

[18] §VI, 32; §VI, 30, vol. IV, 37 ff. [19] §VII, 41, 507; §III, 1, 575 ff.; §VIII, 50.

[20] §VIII, 20, 49; *C.A.H.* II³, pt. 2, ch. XXXIII, sect. II.

spread in the sun goes through a series of colour changes, becoming first yellow, then blue, and finally dark red or purple.[1] Two shades were particularly prized, red-purple (*argamannu*, Ugaritic *phm*) and violet (*takiltu*).[2] Tell-tale heaps of the crushed mollusc shells are found near the seashore at Ugarit,[3] Sidon and elsewhere; the factory at Mīnet el-Beidha, the harbour quarter of Ugarit, flourished from the middle of the fifteenth century till the fall of the city,[4] and a tablet from Ugarit lists merchants, some with Canaanite and some with Hurrian names, dealing in bulk consignments of purple-dyed wool.[5] Purple was the colour of royal raiment,[6] the robes of nobles and the hangings of palaces.[7] Garments of purple stuff and purple shoes were among the items of clothing sent by King Tushratta for the trousseau of his daughter[8] and purple cloth and robes were sent as tribute by the king of Ugarit to the king and dignitaries of the Hittite court.[9] So high was the prestige of this cloth, and so great was the demand for it in court circles that *argaman* became the usual word for 'tribute' in Syria and among the Hittites.[10] A cheap vegetable substitute for red-purple dye was obtained from madder.[11]

Egyptian paintings depict visiting envoys wearing robes patterned in red and blue,[12] and it has been thought that the art of weaving in patterns may have been brought to Egypt from Syria.[13] Coloured embroideries were applied to garments and hangings, and thousands of tiny beads found at Ras Shamra were probably sewn onto garments.[14] Tomb paintings of the time of Tuthmosis III and Amenophis II show nobles from Retenu wearing a tasselled kilt adorned with coloured braid;[15] others, like the king of Tunip, are depicted wearing a long-sleeved garment from neck to ankle, girdleless and adorned at the seams with tassels.[16] In the time of Tuthmosis IV a more elaborate style was in fashion, an overskirt being wound diagonally upwards from the hem and tucked into

[1] R. J. Forbes in §vi, 40, 247 f.; §vii, 14, vol. x, 335 f.
[2] G, 19, vol. i, 255; §vi, 12, vol. iii, 75 n. 5; §i, 47, 121 f.; §vii, 19, 128.
[3] *C.A.H.* ii³, pt. 2, ch. xxi(*b*), sect. iv. [4] §viii, 71.
[5] §viii, 78; §viii, 71. [6] Judges viii. 26; Esther viii. 15.
[7] Prov. xxxi. 22; Exod. xxxv–xxxviii; 2 Chron. iii. 14.
[8] EA 22, ii, ll. 36, 42; *ibid.* iii, l. 24 f.
[9] §vi, 30, vol. iv, 37 ff. = *RS*, 17, 227; *RS*, 11, 772 + 780 + 782 + 802; *RS*, 11, 732.
[10] §vi, 12, vol. iii, 75 f. and 76 n. 3; §vi, 30, vol. iv, 45; §vi, 24, 67.
[11] §viii, 6, 349 n. 29; §viii, 33, vol. iv, 106 ff.; §viii, 50, 111. The Hurrians may also have used the woad plant as a dye (A, 39, 242 f.).
[12] E.g. §ix, 31, 39 ff.; §vii, 11, pl. xix.
[13] §viii, 65, 31 ff. Perhaps ultimately from Crete (§viii, 51, 21).
[14] §vi, 30, vol. ii, xxxi f. [15] §vii, 53, 39 f.
[16] G, 23, 15, fig. 45; §vii, 53, 39, fig. B. See Plate 99(*a*).

the waist,[1] sometimes with the addition of a cape which covered the shoulders but left the forearms bare.[2] Women prisoners of war from Palestine and Syria wear a tiered skirt composed of three or four flounces, falling to the ankles;[3] a similar skirt is depicted on the carved lid of an ivory box from Mīnet el-Beidha depicting a goddess with animals,[4] and is familiar from the figurines of bare-breasted women or goddesses in the Minoan–Mycenaean world, whence the fashion may have come. Men as well as women wore bright colours and bold patterns,[5] and both sexes wore golden earrings, nose-rings and anklets.[6] Cylinder seals, often mounted in gold, were worn by men of rank, suspended round the neck,[7] and scarabs were mounted as rings;[8] both served as seals and amulets.[9] The figures and symbols of deities engraved on small plaques of gold and worn as pendants no doubt also had amuletic properties.[10]

Most of the tributaries depicted in the tomb paintings wear pointed beards and hair almost to their shoulders, bound with a fillet;[11] sometimes a headcloth and cord, like the *'iqāl* and *keffiyyeh* of the modern bedawin, appear to be depicted. Occasionally persons with short-cropped red hair are shown.[12] Egyptian artists were not infallible and were frequently mistaken in their ascription of racial types and attributes, so that it would be rash to attempt to identify the different nationals of Syria and Palestine by their appearance in the tomb-paintings. Moreover, current fashions, then as now, crossed political frontiers and were widely imitated. With these reservations in mind, it may only tentatively be suggested that the heavily bearded, thick-lipped racial type depicted in the late Eighteenth Dynasty, notably on the handle of one of Tutankhamun's walking-sticks[13] and in the Memphite tomb of General Horemheb,[14] may represent a typical *mariyanna*, perhaps a Hurrian; the physiognomy is quite different from the aquiline features and pointed beards of the Canaanite rulers

---

[1] §vii, 53, 40 f. See Plate 103(*b*).
[2] G, 14, 344. See Plate 107(*b*).   [3] §iii, 11, pl. 36.
[4] §i, 50, vol. i, frontispiece and pl. ii; §viii, 51, 86 ff. See Plate 106(*b*).
[5] §ix, 31, 42 f.; §v, 11, pl. xxiii.
[6] §viii, 10, vol. i, 398 ff.; §viii, 12, 342.   [7] §ix, 15, 7.
[8] E.g. §v, 15, pl. cxxxv, no. 2500, pl. cxxxvi, no. 1171.
[9] §ix, 15, 293.
[10] §viii, 10, vol. i, 398 ff. and fig. 149; G, 23, 165, fig. 478; §ix, 31, 47, fig. 36.
[11] *C.A.H.* i³, pt. 2, p. 358; G, 23, 2, fig. 4; *ibid.* 3, fig. 6; *ibid.* 17, fig. 52.
[12] §vii, 53, 39.
[13] G, 23, 14, fig. 43; §iii, 19, pl. 14. See Plate 107 (*b*).
[14] G, 23, 2, fig. 5, 4, fig. 8, 17, figs. 49–51. See Plate 99(*b*).

carved on a Megiddo ivory[1] or the portrait of a later ruler found at Ramat Raḥel.[2] The corpulence and bald heads of some of the figures[3] should indicate that they were important and venerable personages. A Babylonian envoy[4] wears the spiral skirt of Syria but has long ringlets hanging to his shoulders, a feature seen in Kassite portraiture.[5]

Ivory-carving was a craft at which the inhabitants of Syria-Palestine excelled. Ras Shamra, Byblos, Megiddo and Açana have yielded remarkable examples;[6] ivory panels were carved as a decoration for furniture, and small toilet articles were made of the same material.[7] Elephants were hunted in the royal game reserve in Neya—Tuthmosis III here killed a hundred and twenty of the beasts 'for their tusks'[8]—and tusks have been found in Megiddo,[9] and in a storeroom of the earlier palace at Alalakh,[10] as if awaiting the palace craftsmen. The fine timbers of Lebanon and Amanus provided the raw materials for a flourishing industry in wood-carving and cabinet-making,[11] a specialized branch of which was the building and adornment of the delicate and costly chariots owned by the *mariyanna*.[12]

The Syrians were skilled metallurgists. One of the most remarkable pieces unearthed at Ras Shamra is a bronze axe-head[13] inlaid with gold, and with a steel blade, modelled in the form of two couchant lions surmounted by the forepart of a boar. It finds a close parallel in the dagger carved on the rock in the open-air sanctuary of Yazilikaya near Boğazköy, where the Hurrian pantheon is depicted in procession,[14] and weapons of similar design, in which the blade or point appears to issue from the mouth of a lion, are found from Luristān to Anatolia, in the area of Hurrian domination.[15] Ugarit itself must have had large metal foundries, judging by the quantity of objects of copper and bronze which have been found on the site[16] and the large amount of copper and bronze which is listed in the accounts and notes of delivery.[17] Iron, on the other hand, obtained by trade from Anatolia, was

[1] G, 23, 111, fig. 332.   [2] §VII, 50, 59, fig. 11.
[3] Above, p. 512 nn. 13 and 14; cf. §III, 19, pl. 6.
[4] §III, 44, vol. II, pl. 3.   [5] E.g. G, 9, pl. 70 B.
[6] §VIII, 7, 164 ff.; §IX, 12, 83 ff.; §IX, 10; §IX, 25. See Plate 106(a) and (c).
[7] See below, pp. 524 f.   [8] G, 27, 893, l. 15; §VIII, 13, 14 ff.
[9] §VIII, 7, 165 n. 3.   [10] §I, 68, 102 and 288, pl. XVIa and b.
[11] §VIII, 9, 5.   [12] §VII, 72, 86 ff., pls. 190 and 191.
[13] §I, 50, vol. I, 107 ff., figs. 100–3, pl. 22; §VII, 25, figs. 42–3. See Plate 105(a).
[14] §I, 50, vol. I, 122 f., figs. 110–11.
[15] *Ibid.* 120, fig. 107.   [16] §VI, 30, vol. II; §VII, 13, 26.
[17] §VI, 30, vol. II, xxxiv ff.

still a precious commodity in the Near East.[1] At Ugarit it cost
double the price of silver and sixty times that of copper, and
objects of iron are scarcer than those of gold.[2] A few iron pieces
were found in the tomb of Tutankhamun[3] and these are likely
also to have been a royal gift from one of the northern kingdoms
—perhaps again Mitanni, since Tushratta sent iron rings[4] and
a steel dagger to Amenophis III.[5]

The uniformity of shapes and techniques in metal-working
over a wide area of the eastern Mediterranean suggests that the
industry was partly in the hands of itinerant craftsmen who
travelled from place to place by donkey caravan or by ship. The
Bronze Age ship which was wrecked among the Beş Adalar islands
off Cape Gelidonya in about 1200 B.C.[6] was carrying not only a
stock of ingots of copper and tin, but also an assortment of tools,
agricultural implements and household utensils, which may have
been part of the stock-in-trade of itinerant tinkers.[7] The weights
they were using were of the Egyptian *qedet* standard,[8] which was
probably current throughout the Levant, since it was in use in
Ugarit,[9] Crete and Cyprus, and on the Palestinian coast.[10]

Glass-making was another flourishing industry and glass an
object of trade. The art of manufacturing articles in a glazed quartz
paste had been known to the Egyptians since the predynastic age[11]
and the technique of making this so-called 'faience' was now
known throughout the Levant; objects of polychrome faience
which do not appear to have been made in Egypt are found on
sites in Palestine and Syria,[12] and a curious type of goblet in the
shape of a woman's head was so popular that examples have been
found in Ashur,[13] in Ugarit,[14] at Enkomi in Cyprus,[15] and at Tell
Abu Hawām near Haifa.[16] The first large glazed objects of earth-
enware are those found at Nuzi from the Mitannian period.[17] In
a previous chapter, a text revealing the early development in Babylonia of the art of glass-making has been discussed.[18] The glaze

---

[1] §III, 30, 235 ff.; §III, 26, 50 ff.; §I, 23, 33; §VII, 5, vol. VII, 301; §IX, 13, 162.
[2] §VI, 30, vol. II, xxxvi.　　　　　　　[3] §III, 30, 240.
[4] EA 22, col. II, ll. 1–3; §VI, 31, 54 f.
[5] EA 22, col. III, l. 7; §VI, 31, 54 f.; §III, 30, 240; §I, 50, vol. I, 116 f.
[6] See above, p. 491.　　　　　　　　　[7] §VI, 3, 84 ff.
[8] *Ibid.* 135 ff.　　　　　　　　　　　[9] §VIII, 67, 147 ff.
[10] §VI, 3, 139; A, 47, 135.　　　　　　[11] §III, 30, 155 ff.
[12] G, 30, 38 ff.　　　　　　　　　　　[13] §VIII, 4, pl. 33, 7.
[14] §I, 50, vol. I, pl. x. See Plate 107 (*a*).　[15] G, 30, 45.
[16] §VIII, 44, 65, pls. xxvi–xxix; G, 30, 45.
[17] §VII, 61, vol. I, 430 ff.; vol. II, pls. 110–12.
[18] See above, p. 227.

made at Nuzi and Alalakh is a soda and lime silicate, in composition and colour very like that used in Egypt for the making of faience,[1] but the technique of glazing pottery was a separate development which reached perfection in Babylonia and Assyria at a later age.[2] Glass itself appears in Egypt in quantity first in the Eighteenth Dynasty, at a time when Egypt and western Asia were in close contact, though there is no warrant for the tradition that the invention of glass (as distinct from glaze) was accidentally made in Syria.[3] Colourless or transparent glass is rare at this time, though it is found in the tomb of Tutankhamun.[4] Rare and costly stones such as turquoise, jasper and lapis lazuli were imitated in opaque glass for the purposes of mass production.[5] Small glass perfume-bottles with a scalloped decoration produced by dragging parallel lines of colour with a rod are commonly found, from Assyria to Egypt.[6] At Nuzi they have a blue-green body and chevron stripes in white, yellow, orange or black.[7] So many fragments were found there that the glass was probably made locally.

The luxury trade in precious or, as they would now be rated, semi-precious stones was of great importance to the rulers of the ancient Near East, who vied with each other in the magnificence of their personal adornment and the ornamentation of their courts. The trade in lapis lazuli has already been mentioned; it was said by the Egyptians to come from Tefrer, an unidentified locality which was probably known throughout the Orient as the market to which the caravans bringing the precious blue stone from Badakhshān would come; it may therefore be somewhere in Babylonia, or Persia.[8] Amber was prized not only for its unusual colour but probably also for the magical reputation derived from its property of acquiring an electrical charge by friction. Ornaments of amber combined with gold or lapis lazuli, scarabs, and a necklace of fifty-five beads of this material found in the tomb of Tutankhamun were perhaps a gift from Mitanni.[9] The ultimate source of the amber lavishly used in the Mycenaean world during the fourteenth and thirteenth centuries[10] was the Samland coast of the Baltic;[11] a branch of the trade route which passed thence through Central Europe to the Balkans may ultimately have reached Syria by way

---

[1] §III, 30, 160. [2] G, 3, vol. III, 1322 ff.; §VIII, 4, 84.
[3] Pliny, xxxvi, 65. [4] §III, 30, 190.
[5] G, 25, 344; G, 29, 232 f.; §III, 30, 171 n. 1; 187 f., 343.
[6] §III, 30, 160; §1, 69, 298 ff., fig. 74(b), no. 6; §II, 49, 101 and 105.
[7] §VII, 61, vol. I, 445 ff.; vol. II, pls. 128 B–F, 129 A, B, 130 A, C, D, N.
[8] G, 14, 407 ff.; §III, 30, 400; §III, 26, 126, 134 f. Perhaps Tabrīz?
[9] §VI, 31, 53 f. [10] §VII, 40, 16, 25.
[11] §VIII, 75; §VIII, 29, vol. II, 174 ff.; A, 18, 47 ff., 88 ff.

of Anatolia, and amber beads found at Ugarit are thought to be of Baltic origin.[1] Alternatively, the Mycenaeans may have been the middlemen in this small but important commerce.

The role of Ugarit as an entrepôt of Mycenaean trade will be discussed in another chapter.[2] Elsewhere, too, the expansion of that trade in the Levant has been discussed, and the particular part played by Cypriot wares destined for North Syria, Palestine and Egypt.[3] One of the exports from that island was probably opium, which came in small juglets of a distinctive type, in shape resembling opium-poppy capsules.[4] Drugs and aromatic essences used for both cosmetic and pharmaceutical purposes[5] were the object of another important luxury trade. Some of the characteristic pottery found on North Syrian sites with its handsome painted decoration[6] may have been containers for some such commodities, but the 'Nuzi ware',[7] tall slender goblets with a small foot, may have been traded for its own sake, as a fine ware for domestic purposes. The elegant variant of it found at Alalakh,[8] and called 'Açana ware', shows Cretan influence in the elaborate decoration and appears to be a local development of the late fourteenth century which is not found elsewhere.[9] A handsome bichrome ware having affinities with painted pottery of similar date in North Syria,[10] but so distinctive in its decoration as to be thought to be the work of a single artist living at Tell el-'Ajjūl,[11] is found dispersed throughout Palestine, on the Syrian coast, and on the east coast of Cyprus.[12]

As in the time of the Mari letters, correspondence between the rulers and officials of the cities and kingdoms of western Asia was conducted through the medium of the Akkadian language, or a western dialect of Akkadian,[13] written on clay tablets in the Babylonian script. In the courts of the kings of Canaan, local scribes were trained in this language and script.[14] A version of the epic of Gilgamesh found at Megiddo[15] probably served as a textbook

---

[1] §1, 50, vol. 1, 100, and fig. 95; *ibid.* vol. IV, 97. Alternative sources of amber in Romania and the Ukraine are considered by C. Beck *et al.* in *Archaeometry*, 8 (1965), 96 ff., but recent analyses of amber from Mycenae and Tiryns by infra-red spectrography (A, 6) confirm the Baltic origin of the specimens. (Cf. §VI, 31, 50 ff.)

[2] *C.A.H.* II³, pt. 2, ch. XXI, sect. IV.

[3] *C.A.H.* II³, pt. 2, ch. XXII, sects. V and VII. See §VIII, 77.

[4] §VIII, 58; A, 35, 154 ff.   [5] §VIII, 19.

[6] §VIII, 49, 53 ff.   [7] §VIII, 57; §1, 68, 347 ff.; A, 11.

[8] §1, 68, 350, pls. 102–7. See Plate 105 (*b*)–(*c*).

[9] §VIII, 49, 39; A, 11, 40 ff., 102 ff., figs. 231–98.

[10] §V, 27, 199 f.; §VI, 44.   [11] §VIII, 47.

[12] §VIII, 3, 418; *C.A.H.* II³, pt. 2, ch. XXII (*b*), sect. VII.

[13] *C.A.H.* II³, pt. 2, ch. XX, sect. I.   [14] See above, p. 485.   [15] §VIII, 42.

for teaching purposes, as did certain Sumerian and Akkadian glossaries found at Ras Shamra,[1] where the scribes of Ugarit employed Babylonian cuneiform not only for their international correspondence but even for business and administrative documents.[2] The practical Syrians, however, were at the time engaged in seeking for some simpler method of writing which should replace the difficult and cumbersome cuneiform script with its hundreds of signs[3] and the no less complicated Egyptian hieroglyphic writing known and used at Byblos since the Middle Kingdom if not earlier.[4] The scribes of Byblos, who knew both systems, appear to have been pioneers in experiment. Excavations at Gebal, the site of ancient Byblos, have brought to light several attempts to develop other systems of writing.[5] A number of fragments dated to the second millennium (the precise date is in dispute[6]) are written in a linear script containing a repertory of a little more than one hundred pictographic signs—too many for an alphabet and too few for a true syllabary, and probably therefore, like the linear writing of Mycenaean Greece,[7] a simple monosyllabic script in which every consonant is compounded with each of three or four vowels in turn.[8]

This was a step in the direction of simplification, but during the Late Bronze Age other scripts were in use which appear to have been based on the principle of 'one sound, one sign'—a principle which had already been applied by the Egyptians to the writing of Semitic names in hieroglyphs, by means of the so-called 'syllabic orthography'.[9] By the choice of a cursive linear character to represent each consonant[10] the number of necessary signs could be reduced to a minimum of about thirty. Thus the alphabet was born, the ancestor of the later Phoenician alphabet from which, through Greek, our own is derived.[11] More than a dozen small objects found on sites in Palestine and Syria, including Byblos,[12] are incised with characters which appear to many to be in the direct line

---

[1] §VIII, 59, 165; §IV, 30, vol. III, 211 ff. *RS*, 17, 10 with 17, 80 (A, 38, 23 ff.) is a school text in the form of a model letter, with Sumerian and Akkadian versions.

[2] §VI, 30, vol. III, IV.   [3] §VIII, 25, 67.

[4] §V, 33, vol. I, 165, 174, 196, 203. See *C.A.H.* I³, pt. 2, ch. XVII, sect. V.

[5] §VIII, 26, 71 ff., 139 ff. See Plate 103 (*a*).   [6] §VIII, 25, 92; §VIII, 26, 134.

[7] §VII, 30, 76 ff.; *C.A.H.* II³, pt. 2, ch. XXXIX, sect. I.

[8] §VIII, 25, 93 f.; §VIII, 23; §VIII, 32, 119 ff.

[9] §VIII, 2; §VIII, 27; §VIII, 28; §III, 40, 16 ff.; A, 15, 61 ff.; A, 27, 198 ff.

[10] §VIII, 41, 176.   [11] §VIII, 25, 171 ff.; §VIII, 24, 210 ff.

[12] §VIII, 25, 98 ff., figs. 44–51; §VIII, 41, 123 ff. A spatula from Byblos has the 'pseudo-hieroglyphic' on one side and the alphabetic linear script on the other, proving them to be contemporary (§VIII, 26, pl. XIII).

of ancestry to the proto-Phoenician script, as it appears on monuments of the Iron Age,[1] and perhaps as early as the inscription on the sarcophagus of King Ahiram of Byblos, of the tenth century B.C.[2]

Brief inscriptions in a linear script akin to this 'proto-Canaanite' writing and probably earlier, since they have recently been assigned a date in the nineteenth or eighteenth century B.C.,[3] have been found on crudely carved statues and stelae erected by Asiatics from Retenu (Palestine) who accompanied the Egyptian expeditions to the turquoise and copper mines of Serābīt el-Khādim in Sinai[4] as guides and interpreters.[5] One or two examples of this script, the letters of which are thought by some scholars to be carelessly formed hieroglyphs derived perhaps from Egyptian hieratic[6] have been found in Palestine itself.[7] The belief held by a number of would-be decipherers[8] that the acrophonic principle was used to determine the choice of these signs (that is to say, that each character of the Semitic alphabet was originally a picture of an object beginning with that letter, so that for *b* the shape of a house (*bayt*) was drawn, for *l* an ox-goad, *lāmed*, and so on[9]) led them to only limited success in the interpretation of the 'proto-Sinaitic' inscriptions:[10] nevertheless the word *Ba‘alat* 'Mistress', read by the application of this principle, was a likely interpretation since the monuments were found in the region sacred to the local deity whom the Egyptians called 'Hathor, Mistress of the Turquoise'.[11] The acrophonic theory is, however, denied by others, who would prefer to derive the later Phoenician alphabet from a prototype evolved in Phoenicia itself not much before the end of the Bronze Age.[12]

Other attempts to develop an alphabetic or simple syllable script[13] did not achieve permanence. The curious linear writing employed at Tell Deir ‘Alla has as yet no parallel elsewhere,[14] and the ingenious adaptation of thirty cuneiform signs developed as an alphabet by the local scribal school at Ugarit for writing on clay tablets[15] seems to have been largely confined to the North Syrian coast, though one or two variants of it have been found in

---

[1] §VIII, 76, 55; §VIII, 25, 192, fig. 96. Bibliography in §VIII, 45, 158.
[2] *C.A.H.* II³, pt. 2, ch. XXXIII, sect. II.
[3] §VIII, 38. Albright, in §VIII, 1, 10 ff., assigns to them a somewhat later date.
[4] §VIII, 39.   [5] §VIII, 16, 385.   [6] §VIII, 56.
[7] §VIII, 25, 98, figs. 41–3.   [8] §VIII, 25, 161 ff.; §VIII, 76, 1 ff.
[9] §VIII, 37; §VIII, 76, 49; §VIII, 24, 218 ff.; §VIII, 1, 7, and fig. 1; §VIII, 80, 313 ff.
[10] §VIII, 25, 96; §VIII, 76, 25 ff.; §VIII, 1.   [11] §VIII, 37, 15 f.
[12] §VIII, 11, 43 f.; §VIII, 41, 141 f.; A, 26, 85 ff.
[13] §VIII, 26, 135 ff.; §VIII, 41, 147 ff.
[14] *C.A.H.* II³, pt. 2, ch. XXXIII, sect. I.   [15] §VII, 13, 63 ff.; §VIII, 41, 129 f.

Palestine.[1] Its absence from nearby Alalakh, where the latest tablets are from the reign of Ilim-ilimma, may be explained by supposing that the script was not invented till after his time. Tablets on which all, or part, of the Ugaritic alphabet is written out for learners reveal the significant fact that the order of signs is the same as that of the later Semitic alphabets.[2] Another fragment[3] gives Babylonian transcriptions of the names of the Ugaritic signs, indicating that the acrophonic method of naming the signs goes back at least as early as the fourteenth century; the names may have been given to the letters for mnemonic purposes, as our nursery alphabet books give A for Apple, B for Ball and C for Cat.

It is possible, indeed probable, that during the Middle and Late Bronze Ages a number of other experimental scripts, written on a diversity of perishable materials such as papyrus, parchment and wood which have not survived,[4] were being employed simultaneously in different parts of Syria and Palestine, stimulated by the desire of the intelligent Canaanites, unencumbered by the tradition which rendered Babylonian and Egyptian scribes conservative in such matters,[5] to find an easier means of inscribing their names on their possessions and corresponding with each other. Writing was thus liberated from the role of a mystery which only initiates could master after years of study, and became accessible to the layman. One of the great revolutions in human progress had taken place.

IX. RELIGION, ART AND LITERATURE

During the second half of the second millennium B.C. the heterogeneous peoples of Syria and Anatolia achieved a remarkable symbiosis. The composite nature of the civilization which resulted from the interchange of populations and the flow of ideas in the wake of armies and merchants is seen alike in the spheres of religion, art and literature. It was an age of eclecticism; elements from different cultures were borrowed, blended and transformed. The pantheon of each city received with hospitality the gods of the strangers who settled within its walls; deities with similar attributes tended to be identified, their personalities fused, and their ritual and regalia adopted.[6] Thus Teshub, the head of the

---

[1] *E.g.* at Beth-shemesh (§VIII, 46), and Taanach (§VIII, 48).
[2] §VI, 30, vol. II, 199 ff.=*RS*, 12, 63; 10, 087; 15, 71; 187; §VIII, 43.
[3] §VIII, 21.   [4] §VIII, 25, 80 ff.; A, 32, 179.
[5] §VIII, 25, 62.   [6] §I, 1, 159 ff.

Hurrian pantheon and god of the thunderstorms and rainclouds, found his counterparts in the storm-gods of the Anatolian plateau, in Ba'al the Canaanite thunder-god and his older Mesopotamian equivalent, Adad or Hadad.[1] Cosmic divinities such as the Sun and Moon were worshipped under different names in their various cult centres, but the identity of these manifestations was realized. Members of the various priestly schools set to work to bring order and clarity from confusion, to arrange and to canonize. Theogonies and myths of origins attempted to bring the gods of the pantheon into an ordered hierarchy, to determine their relationships and their relative standing in terms of human society. Ancient gods gave birth to younger, divine marriages were arranged, struggles for leadership rent their ranks and were resolved; the powers and functions of each were defined and henchmen or satellites allotted to the most important.

Literary compositions, embodying ancient mythological beliefs, travelled from one country to another and enjoyed popularity. Legends of Adapa and Nergal, used as textbooks for Egyptian scribes for learning cuneiform, were found at El-Amarna;[2] a Canaanite story of Astarte and the Sea, known from Ugaritic, was translated into Egyptian;[3] Hittite and Hurrian translations of Akkadian divinatory texts have been found; fragments of the epic of Gilgamesh turned up at Ugarit and Megiddo,[4] and a Hittite copy of the Akkadian 'King of Battle' legend at El-Amarna.[5] Figurines of a goddess in Hittite style were found at Alalakh[6] and Nuzi.[7] Peripatetic deities crossed the frontiers, as captives or on loan from one ruler to another; we have already noted the travels of Ishtar of Nineveh and the spread of her cult from Assyria to North Syria, Anatolia and Egypt.[8]

In this process of diffusion throughout western Asia, the role of the Hurrians as intermediaries cannot be overestimated. Their early contacts with Babylonia and Assyria at a formative stage of their history had had a deep and lasting effect upon their own culture.[9] Besides cuneiform writing, many of their laws and institutions and the use of cylinder seals, they assimilated much of Mesopotamian religious beliefs; a number of Sumero-Akkadian deities appear in their epic literature, in particular the sky-god

---

[1] §IX, 29; §IX, 18, 247 ff.; §IX, 13, 44; §IX, 35, 75 ff.
[2] EA 356, 357; G, 16, 965 ff.   [3] §IX, 19, 74 ff.
[4] §VIII, 59, 170; §VIII, 42; A, 38, 300 ff.
[5] EA 359; §VI, 25, 809 ff.; G, 29, 83 f.
[6] §I, 68, 81, pl. LXIX(j).   [7] §VII, 44, pl. 20.
[8] See above, pp. 489 f. Cf. §IX, 9.   [9] §I, 57, 313 ff.; §IX, 33, 154 ff.

Anu, and Ea, while Enlil the high god shared many characteristics with the Hurrian god Kumarbi, who was said to have had a temple at Nippur.[1] A Hurrian legend includes among the list of early world-rulers the names of the great kings of Agade,[2] and there was a Hurrian version of the Gilgamesh epic.[3] At least as early as 1800 B.C. Hurrians, Amorites and Canaanites were intermingling in North Syria, and Hurrians and Hittites on the eastern fringe of Anatolia; by 1600, Hurrians and Luwians were living side by side in Kizzuwadna, the kingdom of eastern Cilicia.[4] In a subsequent chapter it will be shown that Hurrian influence in the Hittite imperial court itself was so strong that many suppose the dynasty to have had a Hurrian origin; the infiltration of the Hittite pantheon by Hurrian deities is therefore not surprising.[5] The tendency was carried even further in the thirteenth century when, perhaps under the dominating influence of Pudu-Kheba, daughter of a Hurrian priest from Kumanni in Kizzuwadna[6] who became the chief queen of Khattushilish III,[7] Hurrian cults and Hurrian mythology proliferated in Asia Minor, and the chief deities of the Hurrian pantheon—Teshub and his consort the earth-goddess Khebat,[8] their son Sharruma, Shimika the sun-god, Shaushga the goddess of love and of warfare, Kushukh of the sickle moon, the ancient god Lama, Kheshui and the rest[9]—were depicted in double procession on the rock walls of the open-air sanctuary at Yazilikaya, two miles from the Hittite capital.[10] That the fusion of Hurrian and Hittite deities was official recognition of a process of conscious syncretism[11] is indicated by the prayer of the queen (a devotee, as her name shows, of Khebat): 'O Sun-goddess of Arinna, my lady, queen of all the countries! in the Khatti-country thou bearest the name of the Sun-goddess of Arinna, but in the land which thou madest, the Cedar Land, thou bearest the name of Khebat.'[12] We may speculate whether the Land of Cedars is Kizzuwadna or whether the reference is to the Amanus or to the mountainous northern home of the Hurrian peoples. In Assyria, too, the Hurrian Teshub gradually gained popularity in the guise of his counterpart Adad.[13]

---

[1] §IX, 22; §IX, 23.
[2] §I, 32, 118.
[3] *K.U.B.* VIII, 61; §IX, 45.
[4] §I, 23, 48 ff.; §I, 24, 5 ff.; §I, 29.
[5] See below, ch. XV, sect. II; §IX, 28, 7 ff.; §IX, 8.
[6] §I, 24, 80 f.
[7] *C.A.H.* II³, pt. 2, ch. XXIV, sect. III.
[8] §IX, 29, 121 ff.
[9] §IX, 27; §I, 32, 102 ff.; §IX, 18, 250 ff.
[10] §IV, 12, 141 ff., pls. 12–15, and fig. 8; §I, 32, 116 f.
[11] §I, 1, 212 ff.; §I, 28, 389 ff.
[12] G, 24, 393; §I, 63, 167.
[13] §II, 19, 99 ff.; A, 46, 480.

In matters of magic and ritual the Hurrians acted as intermediaries and disseminators. Incantation texts for magical purposes, such as driving away plague and averting the ill effects of poison, found among the archives of Boğazköy[1] contain Hurrian passages, and the 'incantation of the worms' against toothache was found at Mari together with Hurrian versions of Akkadian magico-religious texts.[2] Haruspicy too was learnt from the Babylonians: models of a lung found at Alalakh[3] and of liver and lungs at Ras Shamra[4] show that the priests of North Syria were skilled in hepatoscopy, and Hurrian technical terms used in Hittite liver-omen texts indicate that the art was brought to Anatolia also by people speaking a Hurrian dialect.[5]

Fragments of a number of Hurrian myths have been found among the literary archives of Boğazköy.[6] Most important is the cycle of myths relating to Kumarbi or Kumarwi, father of the gods,[7] the centre of whose cult appears to have been at Tedi in Mitanni. It has been pointed out that there are striking similarities between episodes in this epic of the birth of the gods and their struggles for supremacy, and those of the Greek gods in the *Theogonia* of Hesiod;[8] in particular the story's sequel, the so-called 'Song of Ullikummi', which tells how the storm-god Teshub successfully rebelled against Kumarbi and strove in his turn against the monstrous 'man of stone', Ullikummi,[9] has a parallel in the episode of the war between Zeus, Cronus and the Titans.[10] Such myths may have been transmitted to Greece either through Greek colonial activity on the Anatolian mainland or else through commercial contact with Phoenicia through North Syrian ports.[11]

The remarkable iconographical consequences of syncretism can be seen in many of the artistic products of the period. On cylinder seals from North Syria and the Mitannian homeland, Babylonian, Egyptian and even Aegean elements can be distinguished[12] and some motives, elsewhere unfamiliar, may stem from the Hurrian homeland. Strange dragons and composite animals frequently appear on these seals, sometimes as central figures in what appears to be a mythological scene, and often as

---

[1] G, 24, 347.   [2] §1, 60, 1 ff.
[3] §1, 68, 250 ff., pl. LIXa–c.   [4] §VIII, 70, 210, 215, figs. 29, 34.
[5] §IX, 26, 19 ff.; cf. G, 3, vol. IV, 1906 ff. The language of the fifteenth-century liver models found at Hazor, on the other hand, suggests direct influence from Babylonia, perhaps *via* Mari (A, 29).   [6] §IX, 16; §IX, 17; §IX, 23; §1, 32, 120 ff.
[7] §IX, 22; §IX, 23.   [8] §1, 32, 124 f.   [9] §1, 29; G, 24, 121 ff.
[10] §IX, 3; §IX, 22, 130 ff.; *C.A.H.* II³, pt. 2, ch. XXX, sect. VI.
[11] §IX, 22, 133.   [12] §IX, 15, 263 ff.

decorative elements whose function seems to have been merely that of filling spaces in the design.[1] Winged lions, sphinxes with the body of a lion and a human head, male or female, and griffins with the lean body of a greyhound, a whiplash tail, and the crested head of a bird of prey[2] are frequent in the glyptic art of the period; on a golden bowl from Ugarit[3] these fantastic monsters are combined with conventional animal figures. On this piece, and on many of the Mitannian seals, the formalized sacred tree,[4] usually a stylized palmette, is flanked by animals or human beings; another favourite theme is the symbol known as the winged disc, a motif derived ultimately from Egypt, but given an un-Egyptian character by being supported on a pole between two genii.[5]

Several of the foregoing themes can be discerned on the sealing of King Saustatar of Mitanni, impressed on one of the tablets from Nuzi[6] which, as the official royal seal, may legitimately be supposed to represent Mitannian glyptic at its best and most characteristic. The central figure in this remarkable composition adopts the pose familiar from Early Dynastic, Akkadian and Old Babylonian cylinder seals of the hero vanquishing animals, for he grasps a lion in each hand and holds them upside down; the figures on either side each hold a lion in a similar position of subjugation. But here the similarity ceases. The central figure itself is that of a composite deity, part man, part lion, and part eagle; and the smaller figures which fill the field, and the winged disc above, stem from a different tradition; the arrangement of the motives, moreover, strewn lavishly over the field, is in marked contrast with the zonal treatment of Mesopotamian seal-designs, which have one or more horizontal bands, each figure standing on a ground-line and filling the whole height of the register.[7] Familiar scenes and motifs, such as the *guilloche*, banqueting scenes, presentation of the worshipper to a seated deity, and figures of deities with symbols and attributes familiar from earlier Babylonian glyptic are frequent in the repertory of the Syrian seal-cutter, but these are usually treated in a different style, and may be combined with typically Egyptian elements such as the vulture or the symbol of life (ᶜnḫ),[8] and also occasionally with the

---

[1] G, 9, 141, fig. 63; §IX, 34, 54; §IX, 15, 256; §IX, 5, 250 f.
[2] §IX, 5, 89 ff.; §IX, 47, 69.
[3] §I, 50, vol. II, 23 ff., pls. II, III, IV, V, VIII, figs. 4, 7; G, 9, 150, fig. 68.
[4] §IX, 36, 14; §VII, 43, 136 f.; §IX, 47, 64 f.; §IX, 39, 108 ff.
[5] §IX, 15, 264, and pl. 42 k, o; §IX, 39, 114 ff.
[6] §VII, 61, pl. 118(1); §IX, 15, 262 ff., pl. 42a. See Plate 102(b).
[7] §IX, 15, 263, 273.
[8] *Ibid.* pl. 42g, j, l, m; §IX, 42, 257 f., pl. XXI, no. 6; §IX, 37, pls. III, IV.

familiar Minoan group of the athlete leaping over a bull's back,[1] or wasp-waisted figures wearing a typically Minoan loincloth, belt and curls.[2] The exuberance and vitality of the designs on these cylinder seals of the west[3] are in marked contrast with the formality and restraint of the earlier Kassite seals,[4] on which one or two figures only are the rule, with the sparse addition of divine symbols such as the dog, the locust, the cross and the rhomboid as subordinate elements to the main design.[5]

A measure of restraint characterizes also the art of the Assyrian seal-cutters at this period, though they, too, used Mitannian motives such as composite monsters, griffins and two-headed eagles, and the winged disc on a pole.[6] This latter motif has been thought to symbolise the pillar supporting heaven, an Indo-Iranian concept found in the Rig Veda; as such, it might have been adopted and adapted by the peoples of Syria and northern Mesopotamia, who were already familiar with the winged disc as a sun symbol.[7]

Comparatively little sculpture in the round has come down to us from the Hurrian *milieu*, and what has survived is not of remarkable quality. The square-cut lions which flanked the entrance to the temple at Alalakh,[8] and the lion and the figure of a seated god from the sanctuary at Hazor,[9] are poor attempts to master the intractability of basalt, and the sculptor of the clumsy little statue of Idrimi[10] has had little better success with limestone: as the portrait of a ruler, the latter work was presumably the best that local resources could provide; yet, with its staring eyes, gauche modelling and stiff posture, it contrasts sadly with the fine head, assumed to be that of the Amorite ruler Yarimlim, found at an earlier level of the palace of Alalakh.[11] But if the Canaanites and Hurrians failed at this period to achieve mastery of stone-carving in the round, they were rather more successful in relief sculpture,[12] and entirely at home in the kindred craft of ivory-carving,[13] in which the rich variety of themes used by the seal-cutters and embroiderers could also be employed.

Many of the best examples of ivory-working which have survived come from Ras Shamra and are of late fourteenth- or even

[1] §IX, 43, 253 f., pl. XXI, no. 1; §IX, 43, 173 fig. 7; §IX, 2, 330 f.
[2] §IX, 13, 32 ff., figs. 1, 5*a*; §IX, 42, 254 f., pl. XXI, no.2; §IX, 43, 173, fig. 6.
[3] §IX, 20, 263. [4] §IX, 15, 180 ff.; §IX, 4, 261 ff., figs. 1–8; §IX 34, 56 ff.
[5] §IX, 48; §II, 24, 53 ff. [6] §IX, 15, 186 ff. [7] *Ibid.* 275 ff.
[8] §I, 68, 242 ff., pls. XLIX–LI.
[9] §V, 50, vol. I, pl. XXX, no. 2, pl. XXXI, no. 1.
[10] §I, 54, frontispiece and 3 ff. See Plate 98 (*a*). [11] G, 9, 140, pls. 137, 138.
[12] E.g. G, 9, pls. 141, 147; G, I, 50, vol. I.
[13] §IX, 10; §IX, 25; §VIII, 7; §VII, 42, 57 ff.; §VIII, 55.

thirteenth-century date, since little survived the fire which destroyed the palace in the early fourteenth century;[1] but a cache of ivories, piled outside to escape destruction, was found near a room in the palace identified by the excavators as a workshop.[2] Among the splendid pieces of this collection were a carved tusk used as a horn,[3] a series of seven panels carved on either side with mythological scenes,[4] a circular table-top more than a yard in diameter, carved in openwork,[5] and a large ivory head, perhaps from the chryselephantine statue of a goddess.[6] The eyebrows may have been inlaid with lapis lazuli or a similar stone, the eyes of crystal rimmed with copper, the locks worked in gold and silver *niello*.[7] Composite cult statues had a long history in Mesopotamia going back to the 'proto-literate' period in Sumer,[8] but the lavish use of ivory, which was obtained from Neya and perhaps also from Egypt, and is close-grained, easy to carve and takes a fine polish, enabled the image-makers of Syria and Palestine to achieve new richness.

The artistic tradition, formed of many elements but welded into a new and characteristic whole, which developed during the centuries of Mitannian supremacy and was disseminated in the zone of Hurrian expansion,[9] was not lost altogether when the main centres in which it had flowered had perished. It survived in the decorated orthostats of the Iron Age palaces of North Syria and south-eastern Anatolia and particularly in the old Mitannian kingdom not far from the capital Washshuganni, at Guzana, the modern Tell Halaf, where a fantastic repertory of sphinxes, griffins and winged demons,[10] as well as the stylized sacred tree and the winged disc flanked by bull-men,[11] recalls the glyptic of an earlier age.[12] The Canaanite tradition of carving plaques of ivory in low relief, as an inlay decoration for furniture, continued into the Iron Age, and examples of the craft found in the house of King Ahab at Samaria[13] and in the palaces of the late Assyrian kings at Nimrud, Khorsabad and Arslan Tash[14] preserve many of the old motives and reflect the same remarkable hotch-potch of ideas and influences which had inspired their forerunners in the Late Bronze Age.

[1] *C.A.H.* II³, pt. 2, ch. XVII, sect. IV.   [2] §I, 50, vol. IV, 17 ff.
[3] §IX, 41, 62 f., fig. 9.   [4] §IX, 41, pls. VII–X.
[5] §IX, 41, 51, pls. 71–2; §VII, 25, 169 f.; §IX, 41, 59 ff., pl. VII 3, 4 and fig. 8.
[6] §IX, 40, argues in favour of a male deity.   [7] §I, 50, vol. IV, 25 f., figs. 24–6.
[8] G, 9, 12 ff.   [9] §IX, 18, 247; G, 30, 97; §IX, 24.
[10] §IX, 50, passim.   [11] *Ibid.* pls. 70 ff., 98, 104.
[12] §I, 32, 114, 133, pls. 6, 7; §IX, 32, 44 ff.; §IX, 25, 171 ff.; §IX, 6, 263.
[13] §IX, 7.   [14] §VIII, 7; §IX, 45; G, 3, vol. III, 1333 ff.

CHAPTER XI

PALESTINE IN THE TIME OF THE EIGHTEENTH DYNASTY

I. HISTORICAL BACKGROUND

WITH the establishment of the Eighteenth Dynasty, written evidence for events in Palestine becomes available to a far greater extent than ever before. The Egyptian rulers extended their power up the Mediterranean coast and into Syria, and the records of their campaigns contain many mentions of identifiable sites. There is therefore the possibility of interpreting events suggested by the archaeological evidence in the light of the written evidence, and in this way providing a historical framework. Another effect of the restoration of Egyptian power was a considerable development of trade in the eastern Mediterranean, and the appearance of foreign pottery and other objects is often of chronological assistance.

The first event that is likely to have affected Palestine was the expulsion of the Hyksos by Amosis (1570–1546 B.C.).[1] The capture of the Hyksos capital Avaris came early in his reign. According to Manetho, this was followed by the exodus of a great number of the Asiatic Hyksos. Amosis's next step was to reinforce his position by a campaign in southern Palestine, in which the major event was the capture of Sharuhen after a siege of three years. It is suggested that Tell el-Fārʿah (South) is to be identified as Sharuhen. Such a length of siege does not suggest that Amosis's expedition was on a large scale. These events may have taken place in the first seven to ten years of the reign. It is probable that Amosis did not penetrate into northern Palestine until late in his reign. Immediate Egyptian interference in Palestine was therefore apparently slight. If an inference may be drawn from the considerable number of site destructions that, as will be seen, are to be ascribed to the end of the Middle Bronze Age, it is likely that they were due to attacks by the groups of Asiatics displaced from Egypt at this stage.

The next pharaoh Amenophis I (1546–1526 B.C.) seems to have consolidated the advance made at the end of the reign of Amosis,

---

[1] See above, ch. VIII.

and it is probable that Egyptian control was extended a considerable way into Asia. The records are however scanty, and no links can be established with archaeological evidence. Succeeding Egyptian rulers were active in maintaining control in Palestine, and in their campaigns it is highly probable that some towns were captured and possibly destroyed. The archaeological and historical evidence is not, however, sufficiently exact to establish any correlation.

The major events affecting Palestine were undoubtedly the campaigns of Tuthmosis III (1504–1450 B.C.). Early in his reign he had to face an organized revolt from a number of Palestinian and Syrian states, and for his campaign of 1482 B.C.[1] there are detailed records in an inscription at Karnak, in which the capture and destruction of Megiddo figure prominently. With this, archaeological evidence can be equated with some assurance.

Egyptian power was maintained throughout the rest of the fifteenth century, though not without further campaigns necessitated by fairly frequent revolts. Early in the fourteenth century, however, comes the episode known as the Amarna period,[2] in which Hittite pressure and the revolt of Amorite towns in the north fatally weakened Egyptian power, to be followed by incursions into Palestine of the warlike bands known as the Khabiru. The Amarna letters record the intrigues of the towns of Palestine with each other and the Khabiru. Some of the archaeological evidence can be linked with this episode, which is certainly reflected in reduced material prosperity. Egyptian control was not re-established until early in the reign of Sethos I, the first important king of the Nineteenth Dynasty, who, soon after his accession in 1318 B.C., marched up the coast, across the plain of Esdraelon and across the Jordan.

II. DATING EVIDENCE

The dating of the stages of occupation in the Palestinian towns of the Late Bronze Age is almost entirely dependent on pottery. Datable objects such as royal scarabs are regrettably unreliable. Often their find-spot is uncertain. Even when the evidence on this is reasonably precise, it is often clear that either the scarab was an heirloom, or was a later copy of a scarab of a powerful king; scarabs of Tuthmosis III must very often be interpreted in this way. The dangers of the use of scarabs are especially illustrated in the excavations of Beth-shan, carried out at a time when

---

[1] See above, p. 316 n. 9. [2] See *C.A.H.* II[3], ch. xx.

there was little precision in pottery dating, with the result that Level IX was ascribed to the time of Tuthmosis III, whereas in fact it was a century later. Scarabs and other inscribed Egyptian objects can be used as a *terminus post quem*, but not for exact dating.

It is therefore necessary to build up a corpus of pottery groups that form recognizable assemblages, to which a chronological framework can be given by historical evidence or external contacts.

The starting point is provided by a number of sites that show a recognizable break at the end of the Middle Bronze Age, a break which can be ascribed either to Egyptian campaigns at the beginning of the Eighteenth Dynasty or to the Asiatics expelled from Egypt after the fall of Avaris and pushed back into Palestine. The outstanding examples of this are Tell Beit Mirsim and Jericho. The first phase of the Late Bronze Age is marked by the appearance of pottery types not found in these groups, notably Bichrome Ware with elaborate patterns, Cypriot Black Lustrous Wheel-made and Monochrome vessels, and truncated dipper juglets,[1] and the continuance of Middle Bronze Age forms such as cylindrical juglets. The assemblage is taken as Group A, with Megiddo Tomb 1100 as the type group.[2] In Group B, most of the same forms are found, but though vessels with linear bichrome decoration continue, there is a marked decrease in vessels with elaborate patterns in bichrome, and in cylindrical juglets, while Cypriot Basering I ware is common and White Slip I ware appears. The type groups are Megiddo Tombs 77, 1145,[3] 3015, 3018, 3005,[4] and Hazor Cistern 7021 and Cistern 9024 Stratum 3.[5] The importance of the Megiddo tombs is that there can be shown to be a break at Megiddo following the period of these tombs, covering most of the fifteenth century B.C.[6] The long siege and destruction of Megiddo by Tuthmosis III in 1482 is one of the best documented links of a Palestinian site with fixed chronology, and it seems a very reasonable assumption that the break can be fixed at this date. A most valuable point in the dating of pottery groups can thus be suggested.

Group C is taken as the pottery associated with Lachish Temple I.[7] In considering this, only the deposits undoubtedly associated with the earliest temple have been used, the deposit found on the earliest altar[8] and the pits definitely beneath Temple

---

[1] G, 20, 50 f.   [2] G, 8, pls. 45–8.   [3] G, 8, pls. 41 and 49–52.
[4] G, 25, all published as Area BB, Stratum VIII; see also G, 20, figs. 22–4.
[5] G, 40, 1, pls. cxxv–cxlii and cxxii–cxxiv.
[6] G, 20, 59 f.   [7] G, 36.   [8] G, 36, 39.

II, and therefore belonging to the lifetime of Temple I. These groups cover a period not long after that of Group B, for many of the same forms continue. There is however a complete absence of bowls with elaborate bichrome decoration.[1] New types that appear are White Slip II milk bowls and the Late Bronze type of dipper juglets with pointed base. A terminal date for the group is given by the find of a plaque of Amenophis III (1417–1379 B.C.) above the ruins of a wall of Temple I and beneath a wall of Temple II. The date of Group C is therefore likely to be 1475 or 1450 B.C. to c. 1400 B.C.

There is a very distinct break between Group C and Group D, and it is likely that there should be an intervening phase for which there are no satisfactory groups. The representatives of Group D are Hazor Tomb 8144-5[2] and Lachish Tomb 216.[3] In these groups, almost all the forms characteristic of Groups A to C have disappeared, with the exception of Basering I, which is still common in Lachish Tomb 216, which may in fact begin rather earlier than the Hazor group. The Late Bronze Age dipper juglets are exclusively found, with a more round-based type also appearing in Tomb 216. White Slip II milk bowls and Basering II vessels are very common, and also some imitation Basering jugs. Pilgrim flasks appear. The importance of Hazor Tomb 8144-5 is that a considerable number of Mycenaean vessels are found, all Mycenaean IIIa, and the majority late IIIa2.[4] The date of transition between Mycenaean IIIa and IIIb is placed c. 1300 B.C. according to Furumark and the Hazor tomb, and with it Stratum I B of the lower town is therefore to be placed in the second half of the fourteenth century. Yadin suggests[5] that the destruction of the town of Stratum I B is the work of Sethos I (1318–1304 B.C.) in his Palestinian campaign at the beginning of his reign.[6] A general date for Group D could be c. 1350–1320 B.C.

This group brings us to the end of the period of the Eighteenth Dynasty. Brief mention only is made of subsequent groups to cover the rest of the Late Bronze Age, to indicate the grounds for assigning phases in the history of sites to a later period, and to justify the dates suggested for the groups already described. Group E consists of Lachish Tomb 1003, Megiddo Tomb 911

---

[1] A single elaborate bichrome vessel is published as associated with the temple, G, 36, pl. XLIX 256, but Miss Tufnell has stated that it really came from under debris beneath the temple.

[2] G, 40, II, pls. CXXVIII–CXXXVIII.

[4] G, 10, 123.

[6] See *C.A.H.* II³, pt. 2, ch. XXIII.

[3] G, 37, 232 ff.

[5] G, 40, II, 159.

and the latest material associated with Lachish Temple II. It may cover the period 1325–1275 B.C. Group F consists of Hazor Cistern 9024, stratum 1, Megiddo Tombs 912 and 877 (in both of which were Mycenaean IIIb vessels), and 989, Tell el-Fār'ah (South) Tombs 902, 936 (both containing scarabs of Ramesses II), 905, 914 (both containing scarabs of Merneptah), 949 and 939. The date range should therefore be c. 1275–1230 B.C. Lachish Temple III probably comes within this period. A group that on pottery is distinctively later consists of Tell el-Fār'ah (South) tombs 934 and 960, both of which have scarabs of Ramesses IV (1166–1160 B.C.). It presumably covers the first half of the twelfth century, and includes types of vessels also found in the Tell el-Fār'ah tombs that have Philistine pottery, so the date is not far from the appearance of that ware.

It is on the basis of the pottery chronology illustrated by this succession of groups that periods of occupation are assigned to the sites described in the next section. A firm ascription is of course possible only if a reasonable number of vessels are assigned to phases in the history of a site and are adequately illustrated.

III. THE SITES

The problems of interpreting the evidence from *Megiddo* have been described in connexion with the Middle Bronze Age remains.[1] The same problems affect the interpretation of those of the Late Bronze Age. The so-called strata cannot be accepted as entities. The plans have to be analysed in great detail to establish, as best the evidence allows, which structures are really associated; and the contents of tombs have to be separated from the contents of the levels in which they are cut. The strata as published that have to be considered in connexion with the period of the Eighteenth Dynasty are IX, VIII and VII B. Only two areas of the mound were to any extent excavated to these levels, area AA on the northern edge and area BB in the south-east sector.

Area BB has in its centre in the published plans a temple area in the Early Bronze, which has been shown to continue into the Intermediate Early–Middle Bronze period.[2] After a succession of plans in which the central area is shown as a blank, a temple again appears in the plans of strata VIII (see Fig. 5) and VII. It can be taken as certain that the sacred area continued in existence throughout, and it is in fact possible to work out evidence to this effect.[3]

[1] See above, ch. III.   [2] G, 21, 58*.   [3] G, 20, 25 ff.

There are no certain criteria for connecting the stratigraphical sequence in most sites with the reconquest of Palestine by the Egyptian rulers of the Eighteenth Dynasty. It is reasonable to

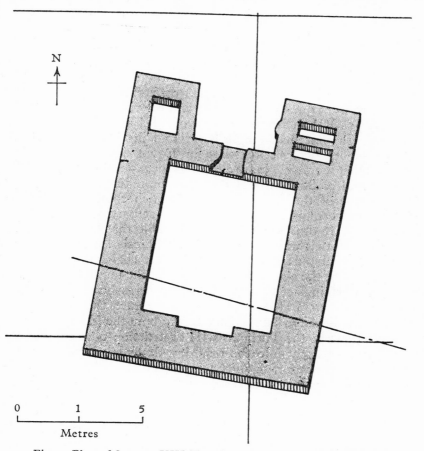

N

0   1   5
Metres

Fig. 5. Plan of Stratum VIII Temple at Megiddo. (After G. Loud, *Megiddo*, vol. II, fig. 402.)

suppose that the destruction of Jericho, Tell Beit Mirsim and Shechem[1] is associated with that event, and that the pottery of the final stages at Jericho and Tell Beit Mirsim can be used as a yardstick for dating levels elsewhere, with the reservation that new forms may begin to appear slightly earlier at important sites such as Megiddo and Tell el-'Ajjūl than at these sites. On this

[1] See above, ch. III, sect. III.

assumption, the plan, which is basically that of Megiddo stratum X,[1] though with the addition of an almost completely destroyed cult area in the centre, probably belongs to the town destroyed at the beginning of the Eighteenth Dynasty. The evidence for this is that a tomb[2] containing a few forms not found at the key sites is beneath one of the floors, whereas the bulk of the new pottery, especially Bichrome Ware, comes only in the next stage.

The destruction at this stage was not radical; there was no interruption in occupation and the buildings were reconstructed with only slight changes. In the next three-quarters of a century or so there were three further structural phases, down to the plan published as VII B. An intact floor of VIII appears to overlie a tomb[3] which contains a single Basering I juglet. An analysis of the find-spots of Basering ware in Egypt and Syro-Palestine suggests that it only begins to appear at the time of Tuthmosis III. But the end of Stratum VII B cannot be much later, since cut through one of the walls is a tomb[4] which could be sixteenth century and cannot be later than the first part of the fifteenth century B.C. It thus seems highly probable that Stratum VII B was the town that was destroyed by Tuthmosis III in 1482 B.C., for it is here claimed that there was thereafter a break in occupation.

In Area BB, the evidence for this is that the temple ascribed to Stratum VIII in fact cuts through structures belonging to the plan of Stratum VII B. It would seem[5] that the earlier cult structures believed to have existed throughout the Middle Bronze Age and down to the Tuthmosis III destruction were completely rooted out, and that into the resulting destruction mound were dug the foundations of the new temple. The foundation trenches of the temple were carried to a depth of 2 metres into this made-ground, the lower part consisting of a packing of small stones shown on the plan of IX, and the upper of the rubble walls shown on the plan of VIII. Ashlar masonry appears only on the VII B plan, and on the floor associated with this, which is the sole floor belonging to the temple, was pottery of the fourteenth century B.C., comparable with that of Lachish Temple II, c. 1400–1300 B.C. It is completely clear that there is an absolute gap here, between the dating evidence for the so-called Stratum VII B and for the earliest use of the new temple. A very significant point suggesting that Stratum VII A represents a real break is that for the first time since the beginning of the Middle Bronze Age

---

[1] G, 25, fig. 400.　　　　　　　　　　[2] G, 25, tomb 3033.
[3] G, 25, tomb 3005.　　　　　　　　　[4] G, 25, tomb 2006.
[5] G, 20, 50.

there were apparently no burials on the town site. As has already been said, graves or tombs are marked on the plans at the level to which they penetrated. They therefore belong at the earliest to the overlying level. With the exception of tomb 5106, already mentioned, which could be a burial immediately after the destruction, no burials at all are shown on the VII B plan (i.e. belonging to Stratum VII A), contrasting with all plans back to that of Stratum XV.

It is therefore claimed that Area BB provides evidence of a complete break between the destruction of Megiddo by Tuthmosis III in 1482 B.C. and some time in the fourteenth century B.C. At the time of the rebuilding, enough remained in the ruins to re-establish the same general alignment of the houses, and a tradition survived which caused the erection of a temple in the central area.

The evidence from Area AA[1] leads to the same conclusion. This area impinged on the northern defences, and in the earliest level exposed, called XIII, Late Middle Bronze I or Early Middle Bronze II, included a gateway. Subsequently, the gateway was moved east, and excavation was not carried to the requisite depth until what is called Stratum IX, and there is no evidence at all to associate it with the rest of the IX plan.

All the evidence in fact points to a break between the buildings shown on Stratum IX and the Stratum VIII plan. There are some similarities in lay-out, but detailed examination shows that almost every wall is rebuilt. The Stratum IX houses are closely connected with those of the full Middle Bronze Age levels. The dating evidence for this phase is non-existent. That of the preceding phase, basically the plan of Stratum X, is dated by pottery groups to the same period as that of the final Middle Bronze Age period at Jericho.[2] It seems very likely that the structures (not the gate) shown on the plan of IX last down to the break, postulated in Area BB, following the Tuthmosis III destruction in 1482 B.C. There are two grounds for this conclusion. There are virtually no burials shown on the plan of IX; there are none at all within the area of the intact structures, and the only exceptions are two in an area in which all the IX structures have disappeared, so the attribution of the level to IX must be quite hypothetical. Stratum IX in Area AA must therefore be compared with Stratum VII A in Area BB, as preceding a period in which burials were no longer made within the city boundaries.

The second reason for this conclusion is based on the finds. A

[1] G, 25, figs. 378–82. [2] G, 20, 36.

number of vessels are recorded from the areas on the plan of VIII in which there are intact floors, a regrettably rare piece of evidence. The complete forms can best be compared as a group with tomb 63 F,[1] which is developed Late Bronze Age and which includes a Basering II jug; another chamber, 63 E, in the same tomb included late IIIa2 or early IIIb Mycenaean vessels in its contents. The sherds published are equally important. On the gateway approach were two Mycenaean sherds and a sherd of a White Slip II milk bowl.[2] Still more important, a Mycenaean sherd[3] is recorded as coming from the wall of one of the VIII rooms. The structures of this period must therefore date to the fourteenth century B.C.

The conclusion is therefore that at Megiddo there was a gap covering most of the fifteenth century. This is entirely supported by the absence at Megiddo of typical fifteenth-century finds. This absence had already been noted by Miss Tufnell in connexion with the Tell ed-Duweir material.[4] The destruction by Tuthmosis III must have been extremely severe. Some time, presumably in the first half of the fourteenth century, for Megiddo appears in the Amarna letters, the town took shape again, and the structures shown as Area AA Stratum VIII and Area BB Stratum VII A must represent the town of the later part of the time of the Eighteenth Dynasty. The Area AA plan with its excellent gateway, triple-buttressed with an oblique, sloping, approach, and the large building that may have been a palace, shows the impressive scale of the town of this period. To it may belong a treasure hoard containing gold-mounted objects buried beneath its floor, but the stratigraphical evidence is inadequate.

A near neighbour to Megiddo is *Ta'anach*, likewise on the southern edge of the Plain of Esdraelon, and of almost equal size. The history of the two towns in the middle of the second millennium B.C. seems to have been very similar. The Middle Bronze Age town, defended by the typical rampart of earth and plaster, was destroyed at the same time as Megiddo, but there was no break in occupation. Though the finds of the most recent excavations have not yet been published in detail,[5] it would seem that these were substantial structures contemporary with the periods of Groups A and B. A victory at Ta'anach is included in the records of the campaign of Tuthmosis III, and the pottery evidence agrees very well with that of Megiddo in placing the end of the period of Group B at the time of Tuthmosis's campaign.

[1] G, 8, pls. 62 f.   [2] G, 25, pl. 137, 3, 9, 10.
[3] G, 25, pl. 137, 5.   [4] G, 37, 66.   [5] G, 24.

There may have been some slight occupation in the next half-century, but it would seem that there was then a complete gap in occupation until the late fourteenth century B.C. The abandonment of Ta'anach, therefore, lasted longer than that of Megiddo, suggested above. It would appear that a proposed reading of Ta'anach on the incomplete Tell el-Amarna tablet 248 is improbable.[1]

The great site of *Hazor* in the Jordan Valley, between Lake Hūleh and the Sea of Galilee has been described in connexion with Middle Bronze Age Palestine.[2] Its importance lay in its control of one of the main routes from the coast towards Damascus. Literary evidence of this importance in the Late Bronze Age is provided by its description in Joshua xi. 10, as 'the head of all those kingdoms', and its appearance in the annals of a number of the pharaohs of the New Kingdom[3] and in four of the Amarna letters.[4]

During the Middle Bronze Age, to the original tell dating back to the Early Bronze Age was added a great enclosure to the north.[5] Excavations between 1955 and 1958[6] carried out some soundings that reached Late Bronze Age levels on the tell and the clearance of a number of widely spaced areas in the lower city.[7] These excavations made it clear that occupation of the site continued not only on the tell but all over the lower city to a late stage in the Late Bronze Age.

It does, however, appear that at the beginning of the Late Bronze Age, that is to say at the time of the restoration of Egyptian power over Palestine, c. 1570–1560 B.C., there was a period of recession at Hazor. If there was not a drastic reduction in occupation at Hazor, there was at least an interruption of contacts with the coastal area. Virtually the only deposit that can be placed in Group A is tomb 8130 in Area F,[8] an area well away from the tell. The contemporary levels on the tell have hardly been touched in the published material. It might be reasonable to conclude that there was a serious reduction in population at this stage, and that occupation was restricted to the tell, with burials taking place in the area of the lower city.

---

[1] In a verbal communication Mrs Hankey states that in the sherds from the site she has identified at least four examples of Mycenaean IIIa2 vessels with clear parallels at El-Amarna. The break may therefore not be so complete as the excavators believed.

[2] See above, pp. 99 f. [3] Cited in G, 30, 242 ff.

[4] G, 23, nos. 148, 227, 228; *R.A.* 19 (1922), 95 f.

[5] See above, p. 100. [6] G, 40.

[7] G, 41, 88, fig. 1. [8] G, 40, III–IV, pl. CCXLII.

In the succeeding period, that of Group B, for which a terminal date of *c.* 1480 B.C. is suggested, sufficient deposits are
found to suggest that occupation on a relatively large scale was
once more established. On the tell, the limited areas excavated
suggest levels of this period.[1] In Area A, a portion of a building
on a palatial scale was excavated. In Area K, the Middle Bronze
Age east gate into the lower city was rebuilt with large ashlar
blocks.[2] In Area D Stratum 3 of cistern 9024 and in Area E
cistern 7021 belong to this period. In Area C appears the first stage
of a shrine, cut back into the inner edge of the Middle Bronze
Age rampart. The finds associated with this structure[3] are too
few to be closely diagnostic, but they seem to belong to this stage.

The most important sanctuary in the lower city of Hazor, in
Area H, at the extreme north-west end of the site, seems to belong
to a slightly later period. Its plan in Stratum 2 was similar to that
of an underlying temple of the Middle Bronze Age, and consisted
of a single room approached by a porch between two towers. In
front of the entrance was a cobbled courtyard with a fairly large
rectangular *bāmāh* and several small altars. Most of the ritual
equipment found in the temple came from the later levels, though
items could well have been derived from the earlier structures.
Two ceremonial objects only could be ascribed to this stage, an
excellent bronze plaque, 9·4 cm. high, of a man in ceremonial
garb, a worshipper or a deity, and a clay model of an animal's
liver inscribed with omens in cuneiform script.

Deposits of the later fifteenth—early fourteenth century do not
seem to have been isolated. This may be accidental, but there
does in fact seem to be a very noticeable break between the occupation of the period of Group B and that associated with pottery of
Group D. It will not be possible to assess whether there could have
been a stage of much reduced occupation until the stratigraphical
evidence is published.

The main deposit of pottery of Group D comes from Tomb
8144-5 in Area F, situated in the lower city some 250 m. north
of the tell. The burial chamber was very large, and was approached
by a stepped entrance. Most of the bones were completely
disarranged, and the probability is that the tomb was used for
multiple successive burials over a comparatively long period.[4] Its

---

[1] G, 40, III–IV, pls. CLVII, CXCIX.   [2] G, 41, 86.   [3] G, 40, II, pl. CXVI.
[4] The published description (G, 40, II, 140 f.) does not, in fact, give any evidence of the intact final burials that should be found in such a tomb, and on this
evidence one cannot rule out the possibility that it was a repository of bones and
offerings, in which case long use is not necessarily implied.

final use is firmly dated to the period of Stratum I B, as its mouth
was blocked by a wall of Stratum I A. The pottery in it can be
sharply differentiated from that in, for instance, Cistern 7021, and
is certainly later than that from Lachish Temple I, for which the
terminal date is *c.* 1400 B.C. The contents include vessels which
very satisfactorily confirm this evidence. There was a rich deposit
of Mycenaean pottery, one to be classified as Mycenaean IIIa1,[1]
and the rest all as Mycenaean IIIa2 (later) (1375–1300 B.C.), and
some at least, late in this period.[2] Stratum I B therefore comes to
an end in the last quarter of the fourteenth century.

Most of the areas excavated have material of this period. Some,
however, notably the sanctuaries in Area H and Area C and the
palatial building of Stratum XIV–XIII on the tell, seem to go a
little later, with finds approaching that of Lachish Temple II in
date. It could be, therefore, that there were no deposits in Tomb
8144-5 during the last part of the period of Stratum I B. But it
does not appear that there was any Mycenaean IIIb associated
with this stratum, which must therefore end by *c.* 1300 B.C. It
can thus be taken that there was full occupation at Hazor from
the Amarna period, when its king was accused of aiding the
Khabiru, down to the end of the fourteenth century.

The palatial building of Stratum XIV on the tell was only
partially excavated. A striking entrance constructed of basalt
orthostats is a link with the architecture of the Area H sanctuary.
Most of the area cleared consisted of courtyards, one of which had
a well-laid cobbled floor that served as a catchment area for a
great underground reservoir approached by a vaulted stairway.

The sanctuary in Area H[3] was reconstructed and enlarged at
this period. In its new form, it was tripartite with a porch, a central
chamber and a holy-of-holies, which followed the earlier one in
plan. The wall of the holy-of-holies incorporated a band of
orthostat slabs though curiously enough not at ground level.
Most of the cult objects were probably removed to the subsequent structure, but a fine lion-orthostat and a basalt figure of a
seated man could be ascribed to this stage.

In Area C, a considerable extent of buildings of this period was
recovered. At the west was the sanctuary,[4] a rectangular structure
recessed into the inner slope of the Middle Bronze Age rampart.
The entrance was on the east side, and facing it on the west side
was a semi-circular niche. Along the rest of the walls was a low
bench. In the succeeding Stratum I A were found a number of
miniature stelae, some with cult symbols, and a seated stone

[1] G, 10, 123.　[2] G, 40, II, 150 f.　[3] See Plate 108 (*b*).　[4] See Plate 108 (*a*).

figure, mostly about 45 cm. high, and a lion orthostat. There is reason to suppose that these were derived from the Stratum 1 B temple. The rest of the area cleared was closely built up with houses, which in their irregular plan and unimpressive architecture may be taken as a good example of Palestinian architecture of the period.

Everywhere, the buildings of Stratum 1 B were found seriously destroyed, possibly *c.* 1300 or *c.* 1318 B.C. by Sethos I. They were succeeded without interval by the buildings of Stratum 1 A, mostly inferior reconstructions of their predecessors. They are mentioned here only as a postscript, since they fall outside the chronological limit of this chapter, as does indeed the end of Stratum 1 B. They may extend into the thirteenth century, since a little very late Mycenaean IIIa2 or very early IIIb pottery was found.[1] They need not extend beyond the first quarter of the century, for the excavators make it clear that the town of this period was short lived, and the pottery found certainly is not as late as that of Lachish Temple III.

The evidence concerning the important site of *Beth-shan*, excavated in the 1920s, has not been completely published. The excavation was concerned mainly with the summit of the mound, which visual evidence suggests was a citadel or royal quarter area. In addition there was one sounding on the slopes to the lowest levels of Chalcolithic–Early Bronze Age date and an extensive clearance of tombs in the vicinity. Excavation on the main area of this tell did not reach Middle Bronze Age levels, and it so happens that there is no evidence of Middle Bronze Age tombs.[2] There is every reason to suppose that this is the chance result of incomplete excavation, for it is difficult to believe that this strategic site, the counterpart of Megiddo at the western end of the Plain of Esdraelon route towards the Jordan crossing and Syria, was not occupied at this time. At any rate, there is the evidence of a tomb of the period of Group A for occupation at the beginning of the Late Bronze Age, and Beth-shan is included in the list of cities conquered by Tuthmosis III, its capture presumably following shortly after that of Megiddo in 1482 B.C.

The interpretation of the results of the Beth-shan excavations, even to the extent that they have been published, has been a major complication in Palestinian archaeology for the past forty

[1] Verbal information from Mrs Hankey.

[2] My information concerning the tombs is based on the studies made by Mr C. Oren of material in the University Museum at Philadelphia, which will shortly be published.

years. In the 1920s no reliable corpus of dated pottery existed, and there were also the limitations of primitive stratigraphical observations. The excavators relied exclusively on datable objects of Egyptian provenance, stelae, dedicatory inscriptions and scarabs, for which Beth-shan provided exceptional riches. Lacking the yardstick of an established corpus of indigenous material, the excavators placed exclusive reliance in their interpretation on this imported material. A combination of the failure to consider chance or intentional survival of older objects, and of the then current excavation technique resulted in the firm ascription of the excavated levels to periods that present knowledge shows to be completely wrong.

The excavated levels (excluding those in the sounding to the earliest occupation) are designated level IX onwards. The finds from level IX have not in fact been published, but their ascription to the period of Tuthmosis III (from his conquests in Palestine in 1482 B.C.) has caused major confusion, especially with relation to the finds from the Late Bronze Age levels at Jericho. In the absence of published finds from level IX, it is only possible to establish a terminal date for it by the finds from level VIII (so-called Pre-Amenophis III).[1] The published material is not large. It includes vessels dated to late Mycenaean IIIa2,[2] and the general appearance suggests a slightly later date than that of Hazor Tomb 8144-5. The terminal date may therefore be c. 1300 B.C., and the material beneath the foundations of the level VII temple includes Mycenaean IIIb sherds.[3] As a completion of the picture, the material ascribed to the levels above the floor of the level VII temple covers the period of Group F, and the most recent authoritative work on the Late Bronze Age–Early Iron Age temples at Beth-shan[4] gives very strong reasons for placing the beginning of level VI at c. 1150 B.C.

It can therefore be broadly established that level VII belongs to the thirteenth century B.C.

The preceding level VIII (so-called Pre-Amenophis III) is structurally amorphous. All that can be said about it is that it carries back the terminal date of the preceding level IX (so-called Tuthmosis III), to about the middle of the fourteenth century B.C.

For level IX, we have a published plan and discussion,[5] but not the evidence of associated finds. On the published evidence of level VIII, the structures should continue in use until the middle of the fourteenth century B.C. Only further

---

[1] G, 5, pls. XLI–XLIII. [2] G, 5, pl. XLIII, 14, 21; G, 35, 62 f.
[3] G, 5, pl. XLIII, 10; G, 35, 82 f. [4] G, 12. [5] G, 33.

excavations will show whether it can be traced back to the six-teenth-century date for which the pottery evidence for occupation on the site has already been mentioned, or beyond, as historical and topographical probability would suggest. What is however clear is that at least from the fourteenth century B.C. onwards there was a holy site on the summit of the mound of Beth-shan that lasted even into the Christian period.

The structures of the level IX stage at Beth-shan are compli-cated, and this may be significant to an understanding of con-temporary religion. It is not a temple in the sense of a single coherent building but, rather, a maze of courtyards and rooms with various features of cult significance. The excavators describe the complex as a temple dedicated to Mikal and a second possibly for his female counterpart; the evidence for this is not obvious. Cult installations include a stepped altar, near which a *baetyl* was found, a sacrificial altar with a channel for the blood of sacrifices, a *maṣṣēbāh*, a great circular fireplace and a well. The *maṣṣēbāh* is likely to be a Canaanite emblem of the local deity. Another find in the temple, displaced but near a socket on which it could have stood, is a representation of a deity in a very different tradition. It is an Egyptian-type stela dedicated to 'Mikal, the (great) god, the lord of Beth-shan'. In the same building, therefore, there are cult objects of the non-representational Canaanite type, the 'stocks and stones' of the Bible, and the evidence of Egyptian influence translating these representations into human form. It is likely that we here have evidence of the many influences inter-mingled in the culture and religion of Late Bronze Age Palestine.

As has been said, the terminal date for level IX at Beth-shan is somewhere about the middle of the fourteenth century B.C. There is no evidence as to its initial date. It remains the only evidence available for Beth-shan during the period of the Eighteenth Dynasty. Tomb evidence suggests that there was occupation from the very beginning of the Late Bronze Age, probably in direct continuation of that of the Middle Bronze Age.

Shechem is situated at the point at which the main north–south route along the hilly crest of Palestine enters the valley between Mount Ebal and Mount Gerizim, and at the point at which debouches the route down the Wādi Fār'ah to the Jordan Valley. Its position is therefore of considerable strategic importance. This importance in the Late Bronze Age is vouched for by references to the town and its prince Labaya in the Amarna letters, two of this type being actually found at Shechem. Labaya's power was such that he was concerned with events all over

Palestine.[1] The town also appears in the biblical account of the early stages of the Israelite settlement in Palestine. Its foundation in the Middle Bronze Age is described elsewhere.[2]

Excavation has not however so far revealed much concerning this Late Bronze Age town. In most of the area excavated, it would appear that the recent excavations, as so far published,[3] did not penetrate below the Israelite levels of the tenth century B.C. The exceptions are two areas on the defences, on the north-west and east sides, and the area of the Temple.

The original massive temple had two building phases on approximately the same plan, both ascribed to the Middle Bronze Age. Above the second was another building on a different orientation and different plan. It was a very much slighter and simpler affair, a plain rectangle, slightly longer in one direction than the other. There is only the basis for an assumption that this was a temple in that it was built on top of the earlier one, though there are parallels for simple rectangles of this sort.[4] There were believed to be two phases for this temple, the later of the second half of the thirteenth century B.C., the first earlier in the Late Bronze Age, perhaps fifteenth century B.C., though the evidence is slight.

The interpretation of the evidence concerning the fortifications is not easy. The interpretation suggested here differs from that suggested in the publication[5] (admittedly only a popular account; one hopes that it will be followed by a full account from which the evidence can be more adequately assessed). In the excavation in the north-west sector, the succession common elsewhere of two different types of fortification is found, with a free-standing wall followed by an earth rampart. The rampart had a later, outer, cyclopean revetment, built against the levelling-over of the rampart, a feature not paralleled elsewhere,[6] since the rampart is usually the final Middle Bronze Age stage; it must however presumably belong to the Middle Bronze Age, since the first temple is constructed on top of the levelled-down rampart. There are therefore three very different stages of defensive systems all within Middle Bronze II, between late eighteenth century and early sixteenth century B.C., or if the excavator's dating is to be accepted, c. 1750–1625 B.C.

In the excavation at the east gate, there is said to be a yet later defensive system, a town wall and gate built on top of, but later

[1] See *C.A.H.* II[3], ch. xx.   [2] See above, pp. 111 ff.
[3] G, 39.   [4] G, 39, 99.
[5] G, 39, ch. 5   [6] See above, ch. III.

than, a wall said to be the cyclopean wall of the other sector (though here 1 m. thick compared with 5 m. thick on the north-west). This wall and gate are claimed to be still Middle Bronze Age, and dated to *c.* 1625 B.C., and there is said to be a yet further Middle Bronze Age stage in a rebuilding *c.* 1575 B.C.

Five such complete rebuildings, including four utterly different styles of defence within Middle Bronze II are difficult to accept. Moreover, a study of the details, stratigraphical and architectural, as far as they are published, seems to suggest it is based on a complete misreading of the evidence.[1] The original east gateway is said to be approached by a cobbled road, several times resurfaced. This is 1 m. wide, quite incredible as access to such a magnificent gate. Because the level of the cobbles outside the gate is 2 m. below the threshold, this last is interpreted as an addition, and the original internal level is assumed to be deep within the tower structure. Such architectural evidence as can be deduced from the plan all suggests that the threshold and a corresponding wall at the rear are in fact sleeper walls, which, with the beautiful double orthostats, in which the door or portcullis was fitted, standing on them, are integral with the original structure.[2] The 'cobbled approach' is almost certainly the filling of a foundation trench, and a photograph[3] strongly suggests that this cuts through a filling over an earlier room, a filling which is probably part of the earth rampart of which the revetment wall lay further down the slope.

The conclusion here suggested, therefore, is that the gate and wall are erroneously dated to Middle Bronze II by a mistaken identification of the associated surfaces. Into this Middle Bronze Age material the foundations of the gate were almost certainly cut; no foundation trenches were in fact observed in any of the areas excavated, on the evidence of the published records. It is therefore suggested that this represents the Late Bronze Age defences of Shechem. This would be certainly worthy of the powerful city of Labaya. A Late Bronze use of the gateway is in fact attested, with later a reconstruction at the rear.

Whether or not this is the correct interpretation, the evidence at Shechem shows clearly that there was a gap in occupation at the end of the Middle Bronze Age, for pottery of groups A and B is missing. Shechem was probably destroyed in the mid-sixteenth century B.C. in the Egyptian conquest of Palestine, and not rebuilt until early in the fifteenth century.

[1] G, 39, figs. 24 and 108. [2] See Plate 109(*a*). [3] G, 39, fig. 98.

The site of the northern *Tell el-Fār'ah*, in the Wādi Fār'ah north-east of Shechem, was an important town in the Middle Bronze Age,[1] but may have been unoccupied for most of the period dealt with in this chapter. The levels of the Late Bronze Age were for the most part badly denuded. The only structure of any importance identified[2] was possibly a temple, consisting of a shallow rear room raised 0·70 m. above a main room divided into three parts by two rows of columns and approached through a porch in one corner. The plan is comparable with the Beth-shan temples (*q.v.*). The only cult object found was a female figurine in silver-coated bronze with Hathor-type head-dress and probably of Syrian workmanship. The tell pottery has not yet been published, but that from the tombs[3] is late, probably of the period of Group F. In each case, the tombs published had a long history, with use in the Proto-Urban (or Late Chalcolithic) period, early in Middle Bronze II, and in the Late Bronze Age, the break between each period of use being absolute. There is no evidence at all of occupation in the sixteenth and fifteenth centuries, though Tell el-Fār'ah Tomb 6 has one Late Minoan IIIa pot with a pattern similar to those in use at Cnossus when it was destroyed c. 1380 B.C. Tell el-Fār'ah may not have been reoccupied until the time of the Nineteenth Dynasty.

The small town of *Tell Abu Hawām* is situated at the foot of Mount Carmel now on the silted estuary of a small river. It was first occupied in the Late Bronze Age, and the structural remains show at least two building phases during this period. The finds could not in most cases be clearly differentiated between the various building and occupation phases, and in general only an overall dating can be given.

It would appear that the site was first occupied early in the fourteenth century B.C. One pottery group[4] has links with the pottery of Group D, with perhaps some contacts with Group C, for instance a single bowl with linear bichrome decoration. This group was found on a layer just above the natural sand, and may antedate the first buildings. It must be noted that the group does not contain the Mycenaean IIIa2 pottery of the Group D Hazor tomb 8144-5. In fact, the total finds include only half-a-dozen sherds of late IIIa pottery,[5] in contrast with a very considerable amount of Mycenaean IIIb pottery.[6] In the thirteenth century, therefore, Tell Abu Hawām may have served as a port of entry

[1] See above, pp. 108 ff.
[3] G, 38, vols. 58 and 62.
[5] G, 35, 63.
[2] G, 38, vol. 64.
[4] G, 9, 47 ff., nos. 286–305.
[6] G, 35, 78 ff.

for Aegean and east Mediterranean trade. It would seem that during the period of the Eighteenth Dynasty the settlement was of relatively minor importance.

A cult centre at *Nahariyah*, on the coast 5 miles north of Acre, existed in the Middle Bronze Age,[1] consisting of a rectangular temple and a *bāmāh*, or high place, of piled stones. The final stage must last at least as late as the period of Group B, from finds of Basering ware, and the incense burners are certainly close to those found at Beth-shan from the fourteenth century B.C. onwards; the chronology of these vessels is however not well established. The site can nevertheless be taken as an illustration of the continuation of cult practices of the Middle Bronze Age into the Late Bronze Age.

The stratigraphical evidence from *Jericho* makes it quite clear that there was a major destruction at the end of the Middle Bronze Age, followed by a period of abandonment. Overlying the burnt Middle Bronze houses was a thick layer of wash, mainly of burnt material from houses higher up the mound.[2] The great majority of the tombs excavated were not used after the end of the Middle Bronze Age.[3] Three of the Middle Bronze Age tombs excavated between 1930 and 1936 contained also Late Bronze Age material,[4] but it has been shown[5] that the interpretation that there was continuous use between the two periods was erroneous. These tombs and a certain amount of material from the tell, mainly derived from the 1930–6 excavations, prove that there was occupation in the Late Bronze Age, but also prove quite conclusively that there was a gap after the end of the Middle Bronze Age. Absolutely nothing attributable to the period of Group A has been found. Tomb 5 has a few vessels that could possibly be attributed to the period of Group B, and might therefore date to the beginning of the fifteenth century B.C., but if reoccupation began at that stage, it was very slight.

The only buildings to succeed those of the burnt Middle Bronze Age town are the so-called 'palace' and Middle Building excavated by the 1930–6 expedition[6] and the building in Area H excavated in 1954.[7] Only the decorated pottery from the wash under the Middle Building has been published. An analysis of this[8] suggests links with Beth-shan level IX, of which the terminal date is *c.* 1350 B.C., Lachish Temple II and tombs at Megiddo

[1] See above, pp. 110 f.
[2] G, 18, 259 f.
[3] G, 17, 1, ch. 5; 11, ch. 4.
[4] G, 6, tombs 4, 5 and 13.
[5] G, 16, 114 ff.
[6] G, 6, 105 ff.
[7] G, 19, 47. See Plate 109(*b*).
[8] G, 16, 120 f., 130 ff.

that are to be ascribed to the time of Groups E and F. The terminal date for the construction of the Middle Building is therefore likely to be late fourteenth century.[1] It should be noted that the existence of a considerable amount of Late Bronze pottery in the wash beneath these buildings shows that there must have been appreciable occupation elsewhere on the site before these buildings were constructed. Levels associated with these buildings only scantily survived succeeding erosion. In Area H, a complete juglet *in situ* on the floor[2] is probably slightly later than any found in Hazor tomb 8144-5,[3] for which a terminal date *c.* 1325 B.C. is suggested, but close to one in the nearly contemporary tomb 8065,[4] and probably earlier than those in the final use of the cisterns in Hazor Area D.[5] The latest material in the tombs suggests a similar date. Three Mycenaean vessels were found in tomb 13. From shape, they should be Mycenaean IIIa2.[6] Parallels in general are with material assigned to Group E and Group F, with nothing suggestive of the later thirteenth century. The terminal date is perhaps rather nearer that of Hazor Stratum I B than Stratum I A.

It would therefore appear that Jericho was reoccupied on a small scale perhaps as early as the second half of the fifteenth century, with a built-up area so restricted that it is not found on the lower slopes. In the first half of the fourteenth century there was certainly occupation, but still restricted to the summit of the mound. Later in the century, houses were extended down the eastern slope. The final destruction of Bronze Age Jericho is likely to come soon after 1300 B.C.

The evidence concerning *Jerusalem* in the Bronze Age is scanty. Excavations on the eastern slope have established[7] the fact that a town wall was built low on the slope, in a position to defend the water supply, relatively early in the Middle Bronze Age. Only the base of this wall survived, and most of the deposits on the slope behind have been eroded. The wall undoubtedly continued in use into the Iron Age, so there is no doubt that it had a Late Bronze Age phase. It can be taken as reasonably certain that the town of the period occupied the southern end of the eastern of the two ridges that were included in the later pre-

---

[1] This date is rather later than that suggested in G, 16, 133.
[2] G, 19, 61, pls. xv. 2, xvi. 1.   [3] G, 40, 11, pl. cxxxi.
[4] G, 40, 11, pl. cxxxix, 8.   [5] G, 40, 1, pl. cxxviii, 6–8.
[6] Stubbings, in G, 35, 65 f., assigned them to Mycenaean IIIa or IIIb, but Mrs Hankey (verbal communication) considers that they are IIIa2.
[7] G, 13, 82; G, 14, 9 f.

Roman stages of Jerusalem, and covered an area of *c.* 10·85 acres. At some stage in the Late Bronze Age there was a major town planning development, in which the steep slope on the eastern side was built up in a series of terraces,[1] but the exact date will be established only when the pottery has been examined in detail. On the summit of the ridge, all evidence of early occupation has been destroyed by quarrying.

The best evidence for the Bronze Age occupation comes from tombs. The most important group comes from the slopes of the Mount of Olives on the opposite side of the Kedron Valley from the town site. In the construction of the Franciscan Chapel of Dominus Flevit, a very large quantity of pottery and other objects was recovered.[2] The finds were all ascribed to a single tomb, but the photographs suggest that the rock cuttings may represent the much-denuded bases of two or more tombs. There was certainly a period of use in the last part of the Middle Bronze Age. The main concentration of the Late Bronze Age is in the period of Groups A and B, but many objects belonged also to the period of Groups C and D. The tomb or tombs were certainly in use to the end of the time of the Eighteenth Dynasty, and possibly rather later, though there is nothing that need be later than *c.* 1300 B.C. Other smaller groups of the same period have been found in the neighbourhood of Jerusalem.[3] They provide the evidence that is lacking on the town site, owing to erosion and quarrying, of occupation in this period.

The site nearest to the north of Jerusalem for which there is evidence of Bronze Age occupation is *Gibeon* (*El-Jib*).[4] There was extensive occupation on the site in the Early Bronze Age, on the evidence of sherds found in later debris on the tell, and in the Middle Bronze Age on the evidence of an appreciable number of tombs. No town wall for either period has been located, but it is unlikely that a site that was obviously of some importance was not fortified. The evidence for the Late Bronze Age is much more scanty. It comes from two relatively rich tombs and single vessels in three other tombs of which the main period is Middle Bronze Age. The existence of even this small amount of material makes it likely that there was a town there at this period, and that the Late Bronze Age cemetery was outside the comparatively small area excavated. The dating of the Late Bronze Age occupation is therefore not conclusive. All that can be said is that there is no evidence for the earlier stages of the Late Bronze Age, and since

---

[1] G, 14, 12 f.; G, 15, 12 ff. See Plate 110. [2] G, 34.
[3] G, 21; G, 9. [4] G, 32; G, 31.

the Middle Bronze Age tombs come to an abrupt end, Gibeon may have been one of the sites abandoned at the beginning of the period of the Eighteenth Dynasty. The tombs found belong to the period of Group D, possibly rather late in it, therefore to the end of the period of the Eighteenth Dynasty. The next evidence of occupation is the building of a town wall in the twelfth century B.C.

It seems probable that *Shiloh*, in the central hill zone some 25 miles north of Jerusalem, was another site that was abandoned at the end of the Middle Bronze Age. The excavation evidence is inadequate, owing to an unfortunate series of events. A recent attempt has been made[1] to interpret the records and finds. For the earlier periods, virtually all that can be done is to say that finds of various periods were present or absent. Evidence on this basis suggests a relatively full occupation in the Middle Bronze Age, with nothing that can certainly be ascribed to the beginning of the Late Bronze Age. The finds of this latter period are not closely diagnostic, and could represent a reoccupation at the same time as Gibeon was reoccupied, towards the end of the fourteenth century B.C.

The site of *Bethel* lies some 11 miles north of Jerusalem. The excavations have been rather briefly reported[2] and the evidence is difficult to assess. It seems to have been a fortified town at the end of the Middle Bronze Age. It may have continued in occupation at the beginning of the Late Bronze Age. The main Late Bronze Age town, in which the houses were well-built, seems however to have been rather later, perhaps fifteenth–fourteenth century B.C.

Beth-shemesh is an important site guarding the exit of the Wādi Sorek from the hill country to the Shephelah. It was a town during the Middle Bronze Age,[3] followed by an occupation covering most of the Late Bronze Age. The excavators ascribe Stratum V to the later stages of Middle Bronze Age, with a terminal date of *c.* 1500 B.C.[4] The published evidence is not very easy to interpret, but almost all the characteristic vessels of Groups A and B are missing. The exception is a certain amount of bichrome ware. On this published evidence there would seem to be grounds for suggesting that the site was abandoned for a period following the beginning of the Eighteenth Dynasty, and was reoccupied early in the fifteenth century, following the campaigns of Tuthmosis III. This suggestion assumes that finds belonging to the first stage of reoccupation were not separated from those of the Middle Bronze Age occupation, which is quite possible in view of the excavation technique of the period.

[1] G, 4.   [2] *Bull. A.S.O.R.* 56, 57.   [3] See above, p. 113.   [4] G, 7.

The succeeding Stratum IV is divided into an earlier IVa and a later IVb, separated by a destruction level. The somewhat limited amount of material ascribed to Stratum IVa is comparable with that from Lachish Temple I, and would therefore be Group C. In this stratum, no Mycenaean sherds were found. A number of Mycenaean vessels were, however, found in Stratum IVb. These are probably all Mycenaean IIIa2.[1] The destruction that forms the break between Stratum IVa and Stratum IVb is thus likely to be about 1400–1375 B.C. The fact that no clear examples of Mycenaean IIIb are found suggests that Stratum IV does not extend beyond the fourteenth century. This is borne out by the bulk of the rest of the finds. The most consistent comparisons are with the pottery of Groups D and E, and it would seem likely that the stratum covers the greater part of the fourteenth century. There are some instances of tombs in which there are Philistine vessels, and also vessels comparable with those found in the Tell el-Fār'ah (South) 900 cemetery, most of the tombs of which are late thirteenth–twelfth centuries B.C. The use of the tombs can, however, hardly have been continuous, for the forms characteristic of Group F are largely missing. It seems likely on the published evidence, that there was a break in occupation at Beth-shemesh roughly at the time of the beginning of the Nineteenth Dynasty, with reoccupation at the beginning of the twelfth century B.C., under Philistine influence.

Gezer, on the edge of the coastal plain, must have always been an important and large town. Its occupation goes back at least to the Chalcolithic and Proto-Urban periods, but no sound chronology can be traced on the evidence concerning the excavated structures.[2] On the evidence in the tombs[3] there may have been an interval of abandonment at the beginning of the Late Bronze Age, but the site was certainly occupied in the period of Group D, with finds comparable with those of Hazor tomb 8144-5 and Lachish tomb 216, including Mycenaean IIIa vessels.[4] No Mycenaean IIIb vessels are recorded, and there are no groups that appear to belong to the thirteenth century; the next groups include Philistine pottery.[5] On the published

---

[1] G, 35, 64. Mrs Hankey considers that they are all IIIa2.

[2] G, 26; see above, pp. 106 f.

[3] G, 26, III, tombs 7 (pls. LXIV–LXVIII), 9 (pls. LXX–LXXI), 30 (pls. LXXIV–LXXV), 252 (pls. CXXI–CXXII).

[4] G, 35, 63 f.

[5] The recent excavations of the Hebrew Union College at Gezer have produced sherds of Mycenaean IIIa1 and 2, and one possible sherd of early IIIb. Verbal communication from Mrs Hankey.

evidence, it could be that there was an abandonment of the site between *c.* 1300 B.C. and 1200 B.C.

Tell ed-Duweir has been identified as the site of Lachish; it was certainly one of the most important cities of southern Palestine. Excavation has not yet revealed its full early history, for remains earlier than the Iron Age have been uncovered only in a partial cut into defences on the north-east side[1] and in extra-mural features, including tombs.

The interpretation of the north-east section[2] is not very easy. The Middle Bronze Age defences consisted of a plastered bank with a stone revetment at its foot.[3] Into the upper part of the bank were cut two walls in succession. No exact stratigraphical evidence was provided, but these may be successive town walls belonging to the Late Bronze Age. The upper wall is not likely to be earlier than the thirteenth century; there is no evidence for the dating of the lower wall.

On the evidence so far available it would seem quite possible that there was a gap in occupation at Tell ed-Duweir after the end of the Middle Bronze Age. There is very little indeed in the tombs or elsewhere to correspond to the tombs ascribed to Megiddo Level X (but later than it), or to levels IX–VIII; that is to say the phases which it is suggested[4] should be designated Q, ending, as suggested above, at the time of the destruction of Megiddo by Tuthmosis III in 1482 B.C. The very small amount of bichrome ware,[5] so characteristic of the material published as Megiddo X–VIII (ascribed to Phase Q) and so very common at the much nearer site of Tell el-'Ajjūl, is particularly striking. More excavation is however required to prove the existence of this suggested gap.

The only structure excavated belonging to the period under consideration is that known as the Fosse Temple. This lay in the slight ditch cut in the rock at the foot of the Middle Bronze Age rampart at the north-west corner of the mound. Three successive stages in the structure could be identified, and there is no doubt from the fittings and the finds, especially in the third stage, that it is to be identified as a cult centre.

The earliest structure, Temple I (see Fig. 6), was small and simple, with a sanctuary 10 metres north–south and 5 metres east–west, with small adjacent rooms to the north and west. In the sanctuary against the south wall was a low altar of mud-bricks with three projections in front, either for offerings of different

[1] G, 37, 55 ff.   [2] G, 37, pl. 96.
[3] See above, pp. 101 f.   [4] G, 20, 50.   [5] G, 37, 65.

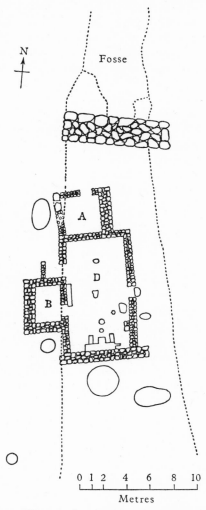

Fig. 6. Plan of Temple I at Lachish. (After O. Tufnell *et al.*,
Lachish, vol. II, pl. LXVI.)

sorts or indicating that a triad was worshipped. Along the west
wall was a narrow bench for offerings. In the debris overlying the
rock beneath the level belonging to the Temple were fragments of
a Bichrome crater, but no examples came from pits close to the
Temple and certainly associated with it. The earliest date for the
building is therefore likely to be about 1500 B.C. Dating evidence
for its use comes from associated pits, into which were thrown

vessels which had probably contained offerings, and which were then discarded. Some lay beneath the larger, later building, and therefore certainly belong to Temple I. The range of forms shows that the use of the Temple can be linked with the Megiddo phase Q which it is claimed comes to an end in 1482, but the Duweir material certainly goes later, particularly from the evidence of Basering ware. A group of pottery found beside the altar, presumably belonging to the last stage of the use of Temple I, shows the same characteristics, and included an early Mycenaean II kylix. It seems clear that the use of Temple I must have continued down to *c*. 1400 B.C., for a plaque of Amenophis III (1417–1379 B.C.) was found on the remains of a wall of the first temple, beneath a wall of the second temple. The subsequent suggestion[1] that Temple I was built *c*. 1600 B.C. and was succeeded by Temple II *c*. 1450 B.C. cannot possibly be right as regards the terminal date, if the evidence is correctly recorded, and is unlikely to be right for the initial date. The dates proposed in the original publication,[2] 1475–1400 B.C., are much more nearly correct. The pottery associated with this temple is taken as that typical of Group C.

Temple II, which immediately succeeded Temple I, was a considerably enlarged building. Only the altar remained in the same place. The sanctuary became approximately square, with the roof supported on four pillars, and offering benches on all sides except on that of the altar. Behind the altar was an additional room, but that on the west side was suppressed. As in the case of the earlier structure, there were associated pits for discarded vessels. The pottery shows a clear development from that of the first period, and belongs to Group F, but there is no precise dating evidence. It can only be said that the succeeding Temple III was in use in the thirteenth century, and is to be ascribed to Group F, the associated pottery having parallels with that from sites destroyed *c*. 1230 B.C. The end of Temple II could come *c*. 1300 B.C. Temples I and II therefore belong to the time of the Eighteenth Dynasty.

There is no certain evidence of the deity or deities worshipped. A small bronze statuette of Resheph, the Syrian storm god, was found in Temple I.[3] Some of the very varying interpretations of the inscription in Sinaitic script on a jar found in a pit ascribed to Temple III include the name of the goddess Elath.[4] The evidence of offerings and accessories, best preserved in Temple III, all suggest a fertility cult of Canaanite type. It is of course

[1] G, 37, 65.   [2] G, 36, 20 ff.   [3] G, 36, pl. xxvi.   [4] G, 36, 53.

remarkable that a sanctuary with a long life should be established outside the city. Perhaps the most probable explanation is that during the strong rule of the Eighteenth–Nineteenth Egyptian Dynasties, a place of the importance of Tell ed-Duweir was under direct Egyptian control, and the official centres of worship within the town had to be concerned with the Egyptian religion, with the Canaanite religion allowed only outside the defences. The destruction of Temple I could possibly belong to the troubles of the Amarna period.

The excavation of *Tell Beit Mirsim*,[1] in the low hill country south-west of Hebron, took place between 1926 and 1932. The site itself is not of major importance, but it was one of the first excavations in which a thorough attempt was made to assign the finds accurately to the successive stages of occupation, and the results for long provided the best evidence of pottery succession.

The destruction of the final Middle Bronze Age town, Stratum D, is to be placed, like that of Jericho, at the end of the Middle Bronze Age. As at Jericho, it was followed by a gap in occupation. The town of Stratum C was ill-preserved, but two phases are recorded, divided by a layer of burning. The C 2 town was walled, but no wall belonging to phase C 1 was found. The basic pottery forms did not differ greatly, but in Stratum C 1 no Mycenaean pottery was found. The Mycenaean sherds found in phase C 2 are probably all to be ascribed to Mycenaean IIIa.[2] Stratum C 1 is therefore probably to be dated to *c.* 1400 B.C. or a little earlier. The excavators claimed that the C 2 town lasted down to *c.* 1230 B.C. and was destroyed by the invading Israelites. On the evidence now available of comparative material, the pottery, however, does not seem to support such a late date. Basering ware and White Slip II ware were plentiful, and the Mycenaean ware would seem to be fourteenth rather than thirteenth century in date. The links in these respects and in the coarse pottery seem all to be with Groups D and E rather than with Group F and the Tell el-Fār'ah (South) tombs dated by scarabs to the thirteenth century.[3] The greater part of the life of the Stratum C town thus probably belongs to the time of the Eighteenth Dynasty.

The site of the southern *Tell el-Fār'ah*[4] was that of an important town late in the Middle Bronze Age, with the massive bank and ditch defences characteristic of the period.[5] There appears to be an abrupt end to the occupation at the end of the Middle Bronze

[1] G, 1; G, 2; G, 3. [2] G, 35, 66. [3] G, 27, tombs 905, 902, 939, 936, 914.
[4] G, 28; G, 27. [5] See above, p. 104.

Age. The excavation of the tell is by no means complete, but there is nothing published from the tell that suggests any occupation until the thirteenth century. It is clear from the finds in the tombs that there was no occupation here during the period of Group A, for if there had been a town here at this time it is improbable that there would have been none of the bichrome pottery so common at Tell el-'Ajjūl, only 14 miles away. It is quite probable that Tell el-Fār'ah is to be identified as Sharuhen, which was captured after a three-year siege by Ahmose in the reign of Amosis, in the first stage of the restoration of Egyptian rule in Palestine under the Eighteenth Dynasty.[1] Middle Bronze Age Fār'ah would have come to an end as a result of this capture.

A group of five tombs in the 600 cemetery[2] belong to the period of Group B, perhaps late in it. There could therefore have been some reoccupation early in the fifteenth century, but it was clearly slight. It also did not last long, for both tell and tombs have produced no other finds earlier than the thirteenth century, to which the tombs in the 900 cemetery[3] are to be dated.

Tell el-'Ajjūl[4] was one of the richest and most important sites in southern Palestine during the Late Bronze Age, on the evidence at present available from excavation. The first town dates from late in the Middle Bronze Age[5] to which period may be dated Petrie's 'Palace' I, a building clearly of official or public character. It would appear that the use of this building continued into the first stages of the Late Bronze Age, for in what were believed to be occupation levels were found some sherds of Cypriot White Slip I milk bowls and of vessels decorated in bichrome,[6] which are not elsewhere found in Middle Bronze Age levels. The fact that there was continuity into the period marked by pottery of Groups A and B is strongly emphasized by the large number of tombs that can be assigned to this period. To early in this period is probably to be assigned a distinctive group of tombs with burials in loculi, in one case associated with an equid that Petrie identified as a horse.

'Palace' I was destroyed by fire, leaving a layer of ash 6 in. thick. Above this was a layer of wash, presumably derived from decayed mud-brick, 3 ft. thick. In the wash was a considerable

---

[1] See above pp. 294 f.   [2] G, 28.   [3] G, 27.
[4] G, 29.   [5] See above, p. 103.
[6] This evidence comes from sherds at the University of London Institute of Archaeology, using only those sherds of which it seems possible to assess the stratigraphical position. The records are not, however, such that there can be absolute certainty.

number of fragments of Bichrome ware. Petrie deduced an interval of several centuries, but in fact no great length of time is needed to produce a considerable depth of deposit from a destroyed building of mud brick. It seems possible that this destruction could be ascribed to the campaign of Tuthmosis III.

Above the destruction level 'Palace' II was constructed, again a building public in character, though owing nothing in plan to its predecessor. Both this building and 'Palace' III, again distinct from its predecessor, should come within the period of Group C pottery, for a number of Bichrome fragments were found. There are also a number of tombs that may provide a link between the periods of Group C and D. Petrie ascribed to 'Palace' III a fine deposit of gold ornaments in what he believed to be a cenotaph.

On the evidence of the number of tombs, the fourteenth century B.C. was a period of great prosperity, for a very large number can be ascribed to the period of Group D. It seems possible that there was a considerable foreign immigration at this period, for Cypriot Basering II vessels constitute an enormous proportion of the finds, and very many tombs contain only vessels of this ware. There is also a fair quantity of Mycenaean IIIa vessels. Some tombs contained gold ornaments. 'Palace' IV is probably to be ascribed to this period. Subsequent occupation was apparently on a lesser scale, and the major prosperity of Tell el-'Ajjūl therefore falls within the period of the Eighteenth Dynasty.

One of the more surprising finds of Late Bronze Age materials in recent years has been in the area of the airport at '*Ammān*. In construction work for the runway, the remains were found of what was certainly a temple.[1] It was square in plan, with an ambulatory surrounding a square cella. In the make-up of the floor was a considerable number of fragmentary infant or child burials. The evidence points to a sun cult in connexion with which were child sacrifices. A further most interesting point is that there were a considerable number of Mycenaean vessels, ranging in date from Mycenaean II to IIIb.[2] Since Mycenaean IIIa2 sherds and one which may belong to Mycenaean IIIb1 were found associated with the original construction of the Temple, it must date to the very end of the fourteenth century B.C. or the beginning of the thirteenth century B.C. Its use continued into the thirteenth century B.C., with some modifications. None of the IIIb pottery is, however, late. It is unexpected evidence that trade contacts, direct or indirect, with the

---

[1] See Plate 111 (*a*).　　　　　　　　　　[2] G, 10, 135 ff.

Aegean extended thus far east during the period of the Eighteenth Dynasty. Rather later finds, dating to Mycenaean IIIb from *Madeba*, 35 km. south-west of 'Ammān, confirm these contacts.[1]

A tomb group from 'Ammān[2] is further evidence of occupation in Transjordan by people akin to those west of the Jordan during the period of the Eighteenth Dynasty. The bulk of the finds are Middle Bronze Age II in date, and some could be relatively early in it, about the period of Jericho phase iii.[3] Some vessels, especially the truncated juglets and the painted vessels, suggest a continuation into the period of Group A, implying occupation in the second half of the sixteenth century B.C.

Late Bronze Age settlements also existed in the Jordan Valley at the foot of the eastern hills. A site of especial interest was *Deir 'Allā*. The lowest levels have only been touched in excavation but it was apparent that early in the Late Bronze Age, probably in the sixteenth century B.C., a sanctuary was established on a massive artificial platform. It was finally destroyed by earthquake and fire early in the twelfth century B.C.

IV. HISTORY OF PALESTINE IN THE TIME OF THE EIGHTEENTH DYNASTY IN THE LIGHT OF THE EVIDENCE FROM THE SITES

The detailed analysis of the site evidence in the preceding section makes it clear that the events associated with the establishment of the Eighteenth Dynasty in Egypt and the expulsion of the Hyksos that must have thrown these Asiatics back into Palestine, must have had a tremendous effect on town life in that country. It has long been claimed that Tell Beit Mirsim and Jericho were destroyed at the end of the Middle Bronze Age and not reoccupied for a period. Analysis shows that, on present evidence, many other sites were unoccupied in the succeeding period. In the south, in addition to Tell Beit Mirsim, the important towns of Tell ed-Duweir (Lachish) and Tell el-Fār'ah were abandoned. The latter may be Sharuhen, captured by Amosis after a three-year siege. Further north on the edge of the coastal plain there is no evidence of occupation at Beth-shemesh or Gezer. In the central hill-country Gibeon, Bethel and Shiloh may have been abandoned, though in all cases the evidence is somewhat scanty. In the northern part of the hill country, Tell el-Fār'ah (North) and Shechem were both abandoned.

[1] G, 10, 143.   [2] G, 11.   [3] G, 22, 170 ff.

In the south, only one important town, Tell el-'Ajjūl, seems to have survived. In the centre it is probable that Jerusalem did, though the evidence is terribly scanty. In the north, it would seem that the great towns of the Esdraelon Plain survived, even though there may have been intervening destructions. This is reasonably certain for Megiddo and Ta'anach and probably for Beth-shan. At Hazor there was probably not a break but a period of considerably reduced prosperity and importance.

What archaeology cannot prove is the exact cause of the break. If Tell el-Fār'ah is to be identified with Sharuhen, the break is likely to be associated with the campaign of Amosis (1570–1546 B.C.) during the first years of his reign. He campaigned also into northern Palestine during the later years of his reign, and archaeological evidence is not yet so precise that some of the destruction could not be attributed to these campaigns. It is however possible that the Asiatics displaced from Egypt after the fall of Avaris became roving soldiers-of-fortune, and inflicted disasters upon their remote relatives in Palestine.

The campaigns of Tuthmosis III are the next major historical event, recorded in detail, to affect Palestine. The only two sites at which destructions and abandonments suggested by archaeological evidence seem to belong to this period are Megiddo and Ta'anach, both sites mentioned in the records of the campaigns of Tuthmosis. Hazor may have been affected, since the succeeding period seems to have been one of reduced prosperity.

After the campaigns of Tuthmosis III, the greater number of the ancient towns of Palestine began gradually to regain prosperity, presumably because restored Egyptian control meant more peaceable conditions. The period of the destruction associated with the Khabiru in the Amarna letters does not seem to be reflected in the history of towns, though there may be some indication of this in a low level of material culture, as shown by buildings, pottery and evidence of art.

By the last years of the Eighteenth Dynasty, it can in fact be said that almost every town for which there is evidence in the Middle Bronze Age was once more flourishing and some, such as Tell Abu Hawām, had been newly founded. There is little evidence to suggest direct contact with Egypt, but the restoration of a central power in Egypt at the beginning of the Eighteenth Dynasty certainly stimulated eastern Mediterranean and Aegean trade, from which Palestine clearly continued to benefit. Apart from this, Palestine seems to have continued on its own during the years of the decaying power of the Eighteenth Dynasty.

CHAPTER XII

THE ZENITH OF MINOAN CIVILIZATION

I. THE CHRONOLOGY OF THE LATE PALACE PERIOD (*c.* 1700–1380 B.C.)

THE palaces at Cnossus and at Phaestus were destroyed time and time again, but on each occasion they rose more splendid than before, bearing witness to the resilience and optimism of the inhabitants. Any traces of defensive building disappeared at an early date, which shows that the catastrophes were due not to enemy attacks but to natural causes. After an earthquake about 1700 B.C. the palaces were rebuilt, but this in itself is not an indication of the end of a period. Indeed a similar catastrophe occurred about 1575 B.C. at Cnossus, and it was at this point that Evans placed the division between Middle Minoan and Late Minoan, thereby coinciding with a general historical break which occurred with the expulsion of the Hyksos from Egypt, the beginning of the Eighteenth Dynasty and the New Kingdom in Egypt. It is tempting to assign the seventeenth century in Crete to the preceding phase, but this gives a distorted picture.

It is vital to understanding of the Early Palace Period to realize that during it the Minoans made their own decisive entry into the circle of the civilized world. Their rise had been based on their isolation and their ships, and they had become a seapower by contemporary standards. The eastern states had then no interest in disputing the position of Crete, and the Aegean world from which she had emerged was as yet no match for her. Danger could threaten her now only from the sea. Crete therefore had no reason to be afraid of Egypt, especially when there were Asiatic overlords in Egypt, but she was forced to turn her attention to her Aegean neighbours. In reality once Minoan civilization had become consolidated, its history depended less on relations with Egypt and the Near East than on those with the Aegean, and its situation became more complicated. For the rise of Crete brought about the first contacts between the highly developed civilizations of the East and the peoples of the Greek mainland, which in their turn led to one of the most important developments in the history of the ancient world. The beginning of the new era is therefore marked by a change in Crete and in her external relations. This came about not between M.M. III and L.M. I as Evans suggested but between M.M. II and M.M. III, when the zenith of Minoan civilization began about 1700 B.C. and lasted throughout the Late Palace Period.

The sub-divisions of the Late Palace Period are based on the considerations of the stratigraphy and the typology, especially of pottery, at Cnossus. The end of the M.M. III group is marked by a layer of destruction. Characteristic closed deposits which lay below it are the 'Temple Repositories' and the 'Magazine of Lily Vases'. As finds from the tomb of the Queen Mother Ahhotpe (1560–1550 B.C.) at Thebes in Upper Egypt show connexions with early L.M. I, the destruction layer is to be dated about 1570 B.C. A similar layer occurs in the later course of L.M. I, and it can be assigned to the years about 1500 B.C. mainly through affinities with representations of the Keftiu on the walls of Egyptian private tombs. The layer seems to be linked with an eruption of the volcano of Thera (Santorin).[1] The so-called Palace style of pottery was developed as a new form from L.M. I b pottery at Cnossus, and vases of this style were found in a tomb near the seaport of Cnossus (today Katsaba) in association with an Egyptian alabaster vessel which bore the name of Tuthmosis III (1504–1450 B.C.).[2] The Palace style which lasted until the final destruction of Cnossus probably began therefore about the middle of the century. The mainland pottery (L.H. IIIa2), which was found at El-Amarna and is to be dated about 1370 B.C., was already different from the mainland styles which had been associated with the Palace style of Cnossus and with contemporary parallels in Minoan pottery. Thus the catastrophe which befell the Minoan palaces is dated some time after 1400 B.C. The designation L.M. II can, strictly speaking, be valid only for one kind of pottery at Cnossus. As the change in ceramic style there is accompanied by other radical changes, it is still useful to consider the period between say 1475 B.C. and 1380 B.C. as the last phase in the history of the Palace period (see pp. 579 f.).

[1] §1, 2.   [2] §1, 1.

II. THE EVIDENCE OF THE MONUMENTS

Our knowledge of the period is based almost entirely upon evidence provided by the monuments, and among them the palaces give the most obvious indication of changes in the development of Crete and in her external relations. See Map 2 on p. 142 above.

At Cnossus the state rooms and the living rooms received their final form about 1700 B.C.[1] Only the general features of the state rooms are known, because being situated above the basement they were destroyed and left only a few remains. The royal apartments lay on the east side of the central court (Domestic Quarter). Here rubble from neolithic dwellings which had formed a slope was removed so that two storeys with the same ground plan could be constructed on the edge of the court but at a lower level. At least two more storeys were built on top of them, and a stairwell opened onto a pillared court with several storeys above ground level.[2] The main room below was a pillared hall, three of its walls opening through a row of pillars onto vestibules with colonnades, in front of which there are light-wells. A short, twisting corridor led into a similarly arranged, smaller and more intimate suite of rooms, grouped round a bedroom. It contained a latrine with a water flushing system, and it was linked with the upper storeys by two flights of backstairs.[3] Characteristic of the high technical level of the whole building is an ingenious drainage system, which is a further development of what had originated in the Early Palace Period. The rain water was brought down from the roof through clay pipes, and pipes and channels laid under the floor took care of its discharge. What is striking is not only the domestic luxury, with which the palaces of Egypt and the Near East have nothing comparable, but also the feeling for a generous and adventurous use of space, the charms of which are enhanced by a carefully planned alternation of light and shade.

There are similar groups of rooms at Phaestus, Mallia and Hagia Triada, where a dominant feature is the use of colonnades in the courts and the halls of entry.[4] At the small palace of Hagia Triada there are towering hills on the south and east and a magnificent panorama over land and sea on the north and west. Consequently the buildings were not arranged round a central court, but two wings, at right angles to one another, enclosed a court which lay behind them and faced the hillside.

The architects of the period endeavoured to relate the outside to the inside of the palace in such a way that space was used effectively

[1] See Fig. 7.   [2] See Plate 111(b).   [3] See Fig. 8.   [4] See Figs. 9–11.

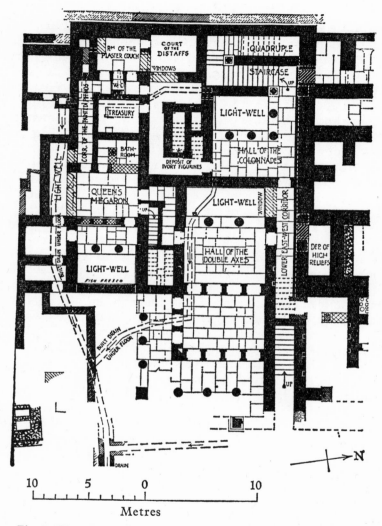

Fig. 8. Plan of the domestic quarter and adjoining halls at Cnossus.
(From *Annual of the British School at Athens* VIII (1901/2), 56, fig. 29.)

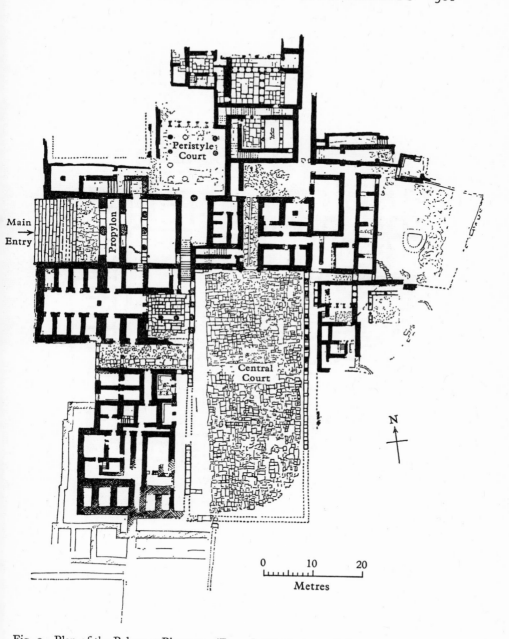

Fig. 9. Plan of the Palace at Phaestus. (From J. W. Graham, *Palaces of Crete*, fig. 4.)

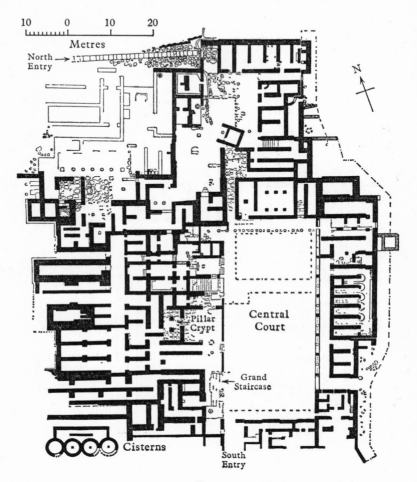

Fig. 10. Plan of the Palace at Mallia. (From S. Marinatos and M. Hirmer, *Kreta und das Mykenische Hellas*, p. 88, fig. 14.)

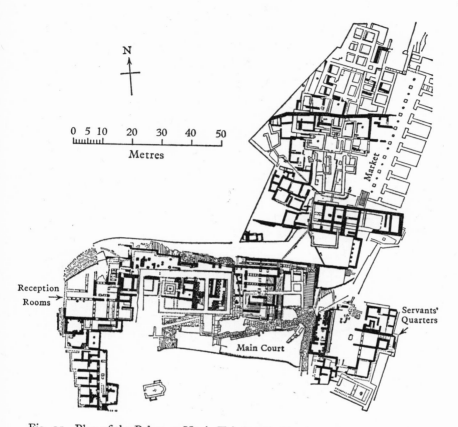

Fig. 11. Plan of the Palace at Hagia Triada. (L. Pernier, *Festos*, 1, 17, fig. 8.)

Fig. 12. Plan of the town of Gournia. (Harriet A. Boyd, *Gournia*, plan.)

and artistically.[1] Direct entrances to the court became rare. In the elevation the twisting flights of stairs corresponded with the twisting corridors which led within from outside. So visitors to the palace were led by a circuitous route to the reception room of the prince or to his living room, and they were conducted out again by a route of the same kind. As a group of rooms was held together by the pillared hall, so the whole palace was held together by the court.[2] In consequence the architects had an interest in the opening towards the outer world, and in this respect they differed from the contemporary architects of Egypt and the East. At Cnossus the main entrance from the south, which was used by visitors from the Messara or Egypt, lay at the southwest corner of the palace, whence a corridor ran east and then bent north, to lead into the central court. On the outside of the entrance there was the 'stepped portico' which extended down to the point where it met the road from the south.[3] The portico descended with two bends to a ravine over which it was carried on a massive viaduct, the arches being built on the system known as the 'false vault'.[4] On the other side of the ravine, opposite the centre of the south front of the palace, there stood a small building which the excavators called the caravanserai. It was arranged in such a way that it gave a vivid impression of the size and splendour of the palace before the visitor entered it. In the same way the architects were concerned with the view outwards, and they used the arrangement of colonnades and porticos for this purpose so that the eye could range over the landscape. There are examples at Phaestus and Hagia Triada (Figs. 9 and 11), but not at Cnossus and Mallia, where too little survives of the upper storeys. The downward-tapering columns of Minoan art are a very important feature of such openings in the walls of the palace. Sometimes architectural features were employed in the façade which were unrelated to what lay behind; for example the small tripartite shrine on the west side of the central court at Cnossus[5] and the so-called propylon in the west façade at Phaestus. The name propylon is misleading because there is nothing inside corresponding with the flight of steps and the wide opening with its mighty central column. Instead, narrow doors lead into rooms of humble character and to backstairs. Even the light shaft has no genuine function; for it served only to provide a light background to the porch and to people stepping forth from it. Religious

[1] See Figs. 7–11. [2] See Figs. 7, 9, 10.
[3] See Plate 113. [4] See Plate 112 (b).
[5] See Plate 114 (a).

ceremonies were therefore enacted on the landing above the flight of steps, and the spectators presumably stood in the west court.

There has been a deeply rooted belief that there was no real organization of space in Minoan architecture, but this does not do justice to the combination of refined and primitive features in the palaces. Above all it does not take into consideration the skilful composition and co-ordination, in which the outlying parts depend on the centre. This is a salient quality of other departments of Minoan art too. Therefore an understanding of Minoan architecture in this regard affects not only the history of art but also the historical picture. In this period the arrangement and connexion of the peripheral parts with the central court underwent a richer development, and achieved a more individual character than in the Early Palace Period. Thus finally Minoan art gained its full stature. There can be no doubt that it reflects a corresponding development in state and society.

The palaces were surrounded by aristocratic private houses. They are best known from excavations at Cnossus and Mallia. Most magnificent of all is the 'Little Palace', about 200 m. west of the great palace of Cnossus, which is supposed to have been the palace of the Crown Prince or something similar. The architectural features of the palaces are repeated in more modest proportions—pillared halls, porticos, peristyles, light shafts, pillared crypts, bathrooms, stairwells, etc. We know also a number of country mansions of the same type. At Tylissus there is a small group; others have been discovered at Achladia, Amnisus, Apodulu, Arkhanes, Korakies, Niru Khani, Sklavokampos, Vathypetros and Kato Zakro. The catastrophe in L.M. IIIa put an end to them all.

Small towns of this period have been excavated at Gournia[1] and Palaikastro and on the little island of Pseira in the Gulf of Mirabello. At Gournia small houses, sharing outer walls, were crowded together along narrow paved streets or stepped lanes.[2] The houses had a rather high foundation of undressed stone cemented with earth, and the upper parts of the walls were usually of sun-dried brick with a timber framework. The rooms were grouped in several storeys round a tiny inner court resembling a light-shaft. We can picture the outside appearance of the houses with the help of the little faience plaques from Cnossus, which are known as the 'Town Mosaic' and belong probably to the earlier period. We can see the lavish and decorative use of beams, the projections, the shapes of windows and doors and

[1] See Fig. 12. [2] See Plate 114(b).

a lantern-like superstructure above the light shaft. These little towns were peopled by agricultural workers, artisans, fishermen and sailors, and there is no reason to assume any considerable social differences among them. In Gournia there is an assembly place and on one side of it a small palace for the governor.

Only one royal grave has been discovered, the 'Temple Tomb' south of Cnossus, built in the sixteenth century B.C.[1] Its burial room is constructed with an antechamber in the slope of a hill. A paved forecourt with a small hall opposite the entrance and an upper storey with a terrace over the antechamber and the dromos were evidently used for the cult of the dead. The rock chambers of Mavro Spilio, which face the palace of Cnossus from the eastern slope of the Kairatos ravine, probably contained the burials of the aristocratic families who lived in the private houses. The chamber tomb at Isopata between Cnossus and the sea, where the keel vault was formed by projecting layers of stone, was built at the earliest about 1500 B.C. for a prince or a high official. The existence of an intermediate link between the beehive-shaped tholoi of the Messara and the later domed tombs of the mainland has been found at Cnossus (Kephala Hill). It is probably to be dated to the sixteenth century B.C.[2]

Cnossus is rich in frescoes. At Hagia Triada there is a small room painted in a masterly way, and frescoes have also been found at Amnisus and at Tylissus. There are practically none at Phaestus and Mallia. Contemporary Egyptian examples are not known, and the frescoes at Açana derive from Cretan models of the seventeenth century B.C. In general, however, Egypt and the Orient supplied the models for the art of painted frescoes. Even the earliest Minoan examples are not inferior in technique and form to the later ones. It is possible, however, to trace a stylistic development[3] from the stage of the Amnisus frescoes or of the Cnossian 'Saffron Gatherer' through the examples from the so-called fresco house at Cnossus and from Hagia Triada to the Cnossian 'Campstool Fresco'[4] and 'Toreador Fresco' which already form a transition to the stage of L.M. II.[5] The cult performances and the court ceremonial which were carried out in the palaces are illustrated on the walls. Thus the processions of life-sized bearers of gifts in the corridors are a Minoan version of an Egyptian theme.[6] The painted stucco relief of the 'Prince with the Feather Crown', the fragments of the 'Ladies in Blue', who are probably spectators at a public function, the 'Jewel Fresco', the

[1] See Plate 115 (a).   [2] §II, 3.   [3] §II, 6.
[4] §II, 5.   [5] See Plate 115 (b).   [6] See Plates 112 (a) and 116 (a).

'Campstool Fresco' and those with a Cretan officer leading a troop of black soldiers may be mentioned here. There are bull-games on a large scale and on a small scale. The miniature frescoes too show cult practices.[1] A keen effort is made to reproduce crowds of people, a subject which art does not attempt again until the Roman imperial period. The decorative rows of plants and flowers on the walls develop into prospects giving the illusion of a view over the park scenery which lies beyond the walls of the room. Birds, cats, apes and deer animate the scene. Human figures are rare. The painted alcove at Hagia Triada is of this kind.[2] Sea-scapes with dolphins, flying-fish and octopuses are similar in outlook. The most beautiful one, from the hand of a Cretan master, has been found at Phylakopi in Melos.

It is hardly a matter of chance that, except for one doubtful case, there are no remains of life-sized statues. The monumental character of the architecture too is restricted not so much by a preference for small rooms as by a desire for open spaces and freedom of movement in the whole. Modelled figures of men and animals are small, and Minoan cult still knows nothing of image worship. In this period too we mostly find votive offerings or utensils and their parts. Skill in portraying natural form and movement in this medium does not lag behind that shown in the frescoes. The faience figures from the Temple Repositories which are usually described as goddesses represent priestesses.[3] The Cretan prayer gesture with the right hand raised to the brow is often seen in bronze statuettes of men and women. Vaulting over the back of a charging bull is represented by groups of ivory and bronze figurines, in which the boldness of the modelling corresponds with that of the actual movement. Libation vessels of stone and terracotta appear in the form of bulls or heads of cattle and lions.

The figured relief which is used on a large scale in painted stucco for wall decoration is employed also for the embellishment of vessels of gold, silver, serpentine, steatite, ivory and faience. These supply us with innumerable pieces of information about the life of the Minoans. For instance, funnel-shaped libation vessels show us a procession of agricultural workers, bull-games, boxing matches and peak sanctuaries. A beaker found at Hagia Triada portrays foreigners, perhaps ambassadors, standing before a high-ranking Minoan.[4] Fragments from Cnossus represent a youth picking flowers in a shrine. The capture of wild bulls and the peaceful existence of a herd of cattle which are portrayed on two golden

[1] See Plate 117 (b).   [2] See Plate 116 (b).
[3] See Plate 117 (a).   [4] See Plate 118 (a).

cups from the domed tomb at Vaphio on the Greek mainland, are the work of a Cretan master, and they rank among the most significant achievements in the whole of Minoan art. All these vessels originated in the late sixteenth and early fifteenth century B.C. (L.M. I).

The painted vases of the first period of the later palaces are linked stylistically with the fresco-painting and with the gem-cutting of the period M.M. III b. The naturalistic achievement of the lilies and the crocuses on the finest examples reaches the same level. The use of white paint on a dark ground which was taken over from the preceding phase, and the subsequent addition of yellow or red paint ceased about the middle of the sixteenth century B.C. Late Minoan pottery was marked by the application of dark paint to a light ground, and it continued to use the glaze paint of the preceding epochs and supplementary white paint for details, a technique which lasted longer in East Crete than elsewhere. In the earlier stage which extended up to the destruction of the palaces about 1500 B.C., that is in L.M. Ia, floral patterns were most in use and the wavy tendril occurred for the first time—a decorative motif which came later to Greece probably through the exchange of tapestries and assumed an extraordinary importance in western art. The Doric capital too is due to Minoan art. We know for certain that it was modelled by Greek architects of the seventh century B.C. upon examples which survived from the Bronze Age. In the later stage of L.M. I the floral motifs were joined by motifs from the fauna and flora of the sea: octopus, nautilus, triton shell, star-fish, fish, seaweed, coral.[1] The shapes of the vessels are as expressive as the painting, and they help us to classify the plain utility ware. Slender forms were preferred with elegant rising curves and wide-spreading at the top. The first stirrup-jars were evolved at this time. They were more slender in their proportions and less standardized than they became later. Towards the end of L.M. Ib the representations became conventional and less vigorous, especially in painting. The latest wares of L.M. Ib were produced until the destruction of the palaces and perhaps even for some time afterwards. In Cnossus from about 1475 B.C. they are contemporary with the 'Palace Style', which is marked by a new hardening of the natural forms and a more positive emphasis upon the decorative aspect. The pottery of the Palace Style is directly derived from the class of L.M. Ib pottery which drew its decorative motifs from the sea.[2] But in it a more monumental effect was achieved,

[1] See Plate 118 (b). [2] See Plates 118 (c), 119 (a) and (b).

for instance in the large three-handled amphorae, and there was a remarkable agreement with the contemporary products of the mainland which adhered to the Minoan traditions (L.H. II).

The art of gem-cutting reached its classical phase in L.M. I. The gem-cutters of the Ancient East and of later Greek art fell far short of the Minoan artist in his combination of technical mastery, wealth of imagination, inventive genius, skill in composition and feeling for miniature. The invention of the picture in the sense of an artistic unit, which had been the great and truly European achievement of the Early Palace Period, now found its full development in an unequalled wealth and skill of representation. Gem-cutting is the most characteristic form of Minoan art, as sculpture is of Greek art.[1]

Three large finds of sealings enable us to classify the seals of this period. The 150 or so impressions from the Temple Repositories at Cnossus were deposited as early as about 1570 B.C.[2] The finds from Hagia Triada (about 290 impressions) and from Zakro (about 230)[3] belong to the following period (L.M. I) but include impressions closely connected with the preceding period.[4] We depend upon these finds for the dating of the original stones and for the relationship between Minoan products and mainland imitations and the independent products of the mainland which were now emerging.[5] The Shaft Graves of the citadel at Mycenae contained not only Minoan pieces but also pieces that were definitely mainland in origin and others that occupied a middle position and had probably been made by Cretan lapidaries on the mainland. The relationship was the same almost 100 years later in the seals from the domed tomb at Vaphio, where the buried prince wore a bracelet consisting of twenty-eight seal-stones strung together and twelve others were found. Clay impressions which are connected with finds of tablets of Linear Script B and which may themselves have characters of this script scratched on them were found at Cnossus and belonged to the last decades of the Palace's history. Stylistically they are of the same type as the original seals, and it is worth noting that this group of seals has the same hardening of style and monumental character as the Palace Style vases.[6] Features which are common to seals from the warrior graves at Cnossus and to those from Vaphio help us to establish a chronological basis; for the warrior graves belong to the L.M. II level.[7]

The evolution of the amulet as a special glyptic type has now been completed; for there is a class of stones which can be under-

---

[1] See Plates 120(*a*) and (*b*). [2] §II, 4, 41. [3] See Plate 120(*c*).
[4] §II, 4, 50. [5] §II, I. [6] §II, 4, 56. [7] §III, 9.

stood only as amulets, and impressions from them no longer occur. Among the forms of seal the signet disappears, and the lentoid is by far the most frequent. There are also masterpieces in the form of flat cylinders and amygdaloids. Steatite is only used for modest pieces. Agate, amethyst, chalcedony, cornelian, jasper, rock-crystal and similar stones are used. Their precious nature heightens the charm of the pictures. The highest level of achievement is marked by a group of golden rings, worn as pendants, each with a convex oval surface, and this group is often used with good reason to illustrate the best of Minoan production. Research has been concerned above all with the subject matter of the picture which represents cults, games and fighting, but many which portray demonic beings, animals or plants are in no way inferior to them. Study of the seals tends to raise questions which concern the history of art and religion. But it can also provide important information on the social and economic life of the times. We are, however, still handicapped by the large number of them and by their scattered publication.

III. THE HISTORICAL CONCLUSIONS

Our ideas about the Minoan state and especially the Minoan monarchy of this epoch are at the best vague. The only certain fact is that the development of a centralized system with a prince at its head continues. One may conjecture that the prince was also a priest, but the conjecture cannot be substantiated. This may seem surprising in view of the abundance of Minoan pictures, but the character of Minoan religion is such that portraits of the kings were not necessary, whereas they were in Egypt and the Near East. The ecstatic religion of the Minoans was not concerned to confer immortality on the king himself by means of his portrait, as was done in Egypt, nor to magnify his connexions with the gods, as was done in the Near East. The peculiarity of Minoan pictures lies in the ability to conjure up an appearance of life, a vision, and not in an attempt to recreate existence.[1] This quality marks a fundamental difference between the character of the Minoans and that of the Orient, so that it is possible to understand the absence or at least the unobtrusiveness of the king in monuments of art.

It has already been inferred from the sources of the Early Palace Period that the king exercised his government with the support of a nobility (p. 161). It is hardly fortuitous that clear

[1] §III, 17, 423 ff.

traces of this class have been found outside the palaces as well as within them during the Early Palace Period; for in the round tombs of the Messara we see the resting-place of the aristocratic landowning families. In the Late Palace Period they have largely changed into a court nobility. Their luxurious dwellings are grouped round the palace both at Cnossus and at Mallia. To them too belong the chamber tombs of Mavro Spilio and Hagios Elias on the east slope of the Kairatos ravine which faces the palace of Cnossus, and of Hagios Ioannes and Gipsades to the north and the south of it. We must imagine that the noble lords also resided in the villas scattered up and down the country, for example at Tylissus and Vathypetros (p. 566). We have, however, no means of judging whether they exercised their power in the name of the king or as free lords possessing free estates and owing only certain services to the court. The relationship between city and palace at Gournia may be taken as typical. In fact the lords of these small palaces can have discharged their duties only in the name of the king. A great deal about the forms in which they did so will probably be discovered if Linear Script A is deciphered.

The highly developed system of seals indicated, as we have seen, the existence of a noble class in the Early Palace Period. Its magnificence and the variety of shapes and motifs in the Late Palace Period not only bear witness generally to the creative spirit, imagination and enthusiastic nature of the Minoans, but they also convey an impression of the self-consciousness, the enjoyment of life and the passionate nature of the ruling class. Representatives of this nobility, within which there were no doubt wide differences, are to be seen in many pictures, for example in the 'Prince with the Feather Crown', the 'Cup-bearer', the figures of the Procession Fresco, the Keftiu of the Egyptian tomb paintings[1] and the long-haired youth with a staff on the serpentine beaker from Hagia Triada.[2] The 'Ladies in Blue', the ladies of the 'Campstool Fresco' with the famous 'Petite Parisienne', those on the miniature frescoes and the figures on a stucco relief from Pseira may be mentioned as representing their feminine counterparts. The fact that the ladies play an important role in the pictures is characteristic of Minoan life in general. In accordance with the pre-eminent position of the mother-goddess they appear in cult scenes, and we learn from the miniature frescoes that, when they were spectators at public functions, they were separate from the men and occupied privileged positions. The acrobatic feats which are performed by women as well as by men in the bull-games are

[1] See Plate 116(a). [2] See Plate 118(a).

most remarkable. It has even been suggested that Minoan society as a whole had a matriarchal basis, but there is no clear proof that this was so.

The small towns also yield some evidence for the existence of a middle class whose economic standards were modest. We cannot say how far members of this class participated in agriculture and seafaring, but they certainly carried on handicrafts, especially those of an artistic kind. The small clay tablets of a later period on the mainland indicate a wide variety of handicrafts, and this variety may have been taken over from Minoan Crete. Members of the middle classes may also figure in the crowds of spectators on the miniature frescoes. The procession on a steatite rhyton from Hagia Triada probably gives us an insight into the life of the serfs. They are going to the olive harvest. Agriculture and building in particular suggest that plentiful supplies of slave labour were available.

This outline of state and society has so far been based on the monuments. The documents in Linear Script B, which can be read since the decipherment by Michael Ventris in 1953, begin only in the course of the fifteenth century, and they show that the Greeks of the mainland had taken over the control of Cnossus, the only place in the island where the tablets have been found; for the tablets are in their language, an early form of Greek. The similarity of these tablets to the small mainland tablets which are dated to the late thirteenth century has given rise to doubts whether the excavators made a correct record of their stratigraphy,[1] and it has even been conjectured that the tablets originate from the period after the destruction of the palaces, that is from the so-called reoccupation phase. This conjecture and the far-reaching historical conclusions to be drawn from it have not stood up to further archaeological investigation. The connexions with the seal impressions which have been mentioned (p. 570) and the clarification of the stratigraphical findings make it certain that most of the small tablets belong to the destruction level. The fact that there are also some later ones, especially from the Little Palace, which are to be dated to L.M. III a, is important enough but does not fundamentally alter either the archaeological or the historical picture.[2] The information provided by these

---

[1] §III, 2. On the other hand §III, 21.

[2] §III, 11. L. R. Palmer, *Mycenaeans and Minoans* (London, 1961), a book which is intended for a wide circle of readers, has summarized his archaeological grounds for the late date to which he attributes the Linear B tablets. See now §III, 20 where he puts forward his reasons again and J. Boardman maintains the contrary view.

L.M. II and L.M. IIIa documents for the form of government and social relations cannot be projected backwards without some reservations, because they come after a clear historical break. The same is true of what they have to say about religious cult. But the highly developed forms of administration and economy were of course taken over substantially by the new lords. In this connexion the small clay tablets can supply welcome information as a supplement to the monuments.

A system of archives and government offices, which was necessary for any thorough organization of administration, had already been developed together with Linear Script A in the old palaces. This system was extended in the later palaces and remains of archives have been preserved in the finds of seal impressions from Hagia Triada and Zakro. The written documents themselves have perished, because they consisted of perishable material, papyrus or palm leaves.[1] Traces of the lacing have been preserved on the clay of the sealings. Inscriptions on some terracotta vases show that ink too was used for writing. The small clay tablets that have been preserved served administrative and economic ends only. Those with Linear Script A come from various sites. Those with Linear Script B are much more numerous, although they are found only at Cnossus. The excavators were able to see that the tablets had once been collected together and stored in chests or baskets. The records, and the tablets on which they were inscribed, were probably destroyed at intervals, when the matters with which they were concerned had been settled, and we may therefore say that the tablets which have been found refer fairly precisely to the time when the palaces were destroyed.

There are, for example, records of deliveries going into the palace and of goods redirected to an outside destination. It is essentially a primitive economy arranged to suit trade by barter. No standard of value such as money was used. Accounts were kept too for the domains of the palace, for their administrators and for the obligations of the latter. The herds—sheep, goats, cattle, pigs—were checked by people who are mentioned individually. At the same time the prescribed deliveries to the court and the losses discovered during the checking were also listed. One separate group was made up of entries concerning receipts of grain, oil or spices and their issue. Slave workers, men or women, the latter sometimes with children, are mentioned. There were also lists of vessels and textiles. Reasons why the contents of the

[1] §III, 15.

armouries played an important part—swords, lances, bows, arrows, cuirasses, chariots and chariot parts being listed—are to be found in the situation of the fifteenth century to which the documents belong (p. 580).

Among the workshops which functioned inside the palaces the excavations have revealed potteries and the workshops of lapidaries as well as weaving-rooms. There will have been many more besides. If we add to this what is known about Minoan foreign trade during the period (p. 577), then we can see how far the palaces, apart from their function as seats of government and administration and apart from their religious significance, were important as economic centres. Not only was the storing of agricultural and industrial products organized in them but also their commercial exploitation to a large extent.[1] The importance attached to commerce may indicate a fundamental difference of the Minoan palace in its organization from its Near Eastern and Egyptian counterparts. Even the size and the number of the storerooms in Crete are symptomatic, and so is the fact that they are grouped together in the basement. At Mari, Ugarit, Beycesultan and El-Amarna they are unobtrusive in comparison. A commercial purpose also was served by the highways with bridges and watch-houses which were constructed at the latest in the Late Palace Period.

There is a remarkable lack of interest in pictures of battles and of warriors generally. Finds of weapons are rare in Cretan tombs before the L.M.II level, whereas they are common on the Mycenaean mainland. The introduction of the horse into the island in the middle part of the Late Palace Period (L.M. Ia), when it also appeared on the mainland, brought with it new methods of warfare and new arms. The small shield, curved at the top but otherwise rectangular, which still occurred on seals of the Temple Repositories, was replaced by the figure-of-eight tower shield, which was a Minoan invention; it presupposes that the warrior carrying it was brought to the battlefield by chariot. At the same time the boar's tusk helmet with cheek protector and plume came into use, and the sword blade was refined and lengthened to form a rapier. The finest pieces from the Shaft Graves of Mycenae are rightly considered to be Cretan products. Cuirasses, consisting of buff-coats overlaid with bronze plates, are known from ideograms on the small clay tablets. A nearly complete specimen was recently found during the excavation of a mainland tomb of L.H. IIb/IIIa. All this formed a set of

[1] §III, 1.

equipment for aristocratic warriors, as was later the case in the *Iliad*. Clearly in the course of the sixteenth century B.C. the feeling of absolute security in the island was shaken, and the nobility drew the logical conclusions.

In the Late Palace Period Minoan religion, which originally had no cult images, underwent a change and became strongly influenced by the Oriental representations of gods.[1] Even so there were still no cult images, and there were no idols until after the destruction of the palaces. The belief in a divine epiphany which was induced by ecstatic rites—dancing, sacrifice, prayer—appeared in a richer form, as pictures on seals and frescoes bear witness. In this connexion the importance of the bull sacrifice is indicated by the double axe,[2] the most frequent cult symbol in this world of monuments. The 'Horns of Consecration' too are probably to be connected with the sacrificial victim. The mother goddess was differently represented. She appeared naked or clothed, with lions, griffins, birds or snakes accompanying her, and she sometimes carried a large shield. A male partner joined her. The inspiration and the prototypes of this are found in Syria and Asia Minor. The scene of the epiphany was usually a sacred tree or a shrine-façade, such as has been identified in the course of excavations at Cnossus and Vathypetros. The epiphany of course sheds light in a concentrated form on the religious nature of the whole palace and emphasizes its sacred character. In addition we learn from the pictures that the priestess too could appear in the costume and role of the goddess and that processions took place in which the goddess or the god was carried in a litter. Great fans of peacock feathers were used on these occasions. The assumption that in these cases priestess and queen were identical can hardly be avoided. The question may then also be raised whether something similar does not obtain for the king. For the cult of the dead we possess invaluable evidence in the set of pictures on the painted limestone sarcophagus from Hagia Triada, which was made about the time of the final destruction of the palaces.[3] If it is studied in conjunction with the other monuments of the cult of the dead, it gives us reason to believe that the dead were thought to depart to a happy world, an Elysium,[4] and that attempts were made to evoke them by means of cult practices and to secure their temporary reappearance.

All this was different from the religion of the Achaeans on the mainland which led on to Greek religion. Nevertheless if the deeper levels of Greek beliefs are examined, features can be found

[1] §III, 17.   [2] §III, 5.   [3] See Plate 121.   [4] §III, 14.

which may be incomprehensible without this Minoan background. They are of an ancient Aegean and pre-Greek kind but already in the Late Palace Period they represent the result of a rich development.

As we depend upon archaeological material for any view of foreign relations, we must look first for trading connexions. In the relationship with Egypt the change which took place during this period was made apparent. At first exchange between Crete and Egypt was at least as intensive as previously, as we see from the lid with the cartouche of the Hyksos king Khyan from about 1600 B.C., the objects found in the tomb of Queen Ahhotpe from the first half of the sixteenth century B.C., the large number of Egyptian motifs in Minoan art, especially in the fresco painting, and the representations of Keftiu which begin early in the fifteenth century B.C., as well as the Egyptian scarabs and alabaster vases of the fifteenth century B.C. found in Crete. It is therefore all the more surprising that only two L.M. I painted vases from Egypt are known (a jug in Marseilles, an alabastron from Sedment), whereas a long list could be compiled of L.H. I and II pottery from the mainland found in Egypt.[1] Indeed L.M. II ware has not been found in Egypt at all. Thus in this area the mainland Achaeans outstripped the Minoans in the competitive struggle even before the destruction of the palaces.

In Syria and Cyprus there are strikingly few Aegean imports during this period.[2] A stirrup-jar at Mīnet el-Beidha and a stone lamp at Açana are isolated cases. There is, however, evidence of an intensive exchange in other areas. Reference has already been made (p. 575) to the introduction of the horse into Crete, to Minoan influence in the fresco painting of Açana and to Anatolian and Syrian influences on Minoan religion. One Syrian piece imported into Crete is a steatite sphinx, found at Hagia Triada.[3] To this must be added the growth of so-called Mitannian art from the fifteenth century B.C. onwards, which was strongly influenced by Aegean forms.[4] The L.M. II motifs which occur in it cannot have come by the roundabout route via the Mycenaean main-land, and direct relations may be assumed. It should also be remembered that the form of keel-vaulted tomb which is known from Ras Shamra exerted an influence on Crete in the fifteenth century B.C. (Isopata). It came, however, to the mainland too, as is shown by grave Rho in grave circle B at Mycenae.

---

[1] §III, 22.
[2] Though the name 'Kuprios' is read on some Linear B tablets.
[3] §II, 2, 134 f. Nr. 300 (Hittite).   [4] §III, 16.

Connexions with the interior of Anatolia, where the Hittite empire arose at the end of the period, are hardly discernible. Some features of the Minoan cult may have come from here. The clay disk from Phaestus which was found with M.M. III b pottery and which is covered with an otherwise unknown hieroglyphic script probably had its origin in Asia Minor. The ships on it show that it came from a coastal region. In Crete from L.M. I onwards a relatively large number of copper ingots have been found in the form of plates with four concave sides.[1] A hoard of eighteen has been discovered at Hagia Triada.[2] The shape which is suitable for tying them together was no doubt determined by the needs of transport; it is not an imitation of an ox-hide as was at first thought. More than sixty such ingots are known from various sites. They mark the route taken in the Mediterranean area during the second half of the second millennium by the copper extracted in Cyprus. That Crete at least in the sixteenth century B.C. took part in this trade is a fact which emerges from the finds of ingots on the island and from their connexion with what the Minoans carry on the Egyptian pictures of Keftiu. As they differ in weight they cannot have served for payment. They represent only the form in which the unworked copper was transported. That western Mediterranean trade was dominated by the Mycenaean mainlanders at the end of the sixteenth century B.C. is demonstrated by the finds of L.H. I and II pottery in the Lipari Isles. Minoan imports went with them at first (in L.M. I) but they soon ceased.[3] Vessels of liparite stone (p. 163) were made in the Late Palace Period as well, and they confirm the existence of these connexions. For bringing copper and tin into the Aegean area this route seems to have been of only secondary importance. What later antiquity had to say about the connexions of King Minos with Sicily may contain a kernel of historical fact.[4] The tradition is, however, of a mythological character and has not yet been confirmed by archaeology. Aegean imports into Sicily are unknown before the fourteenth century B.C. (L.H. III a).

Within the Aegean area Minoan settlements on Thera and Melos (at Phylakopi) are attested as early as the beginning of the Late Palace Period, and at Miletus[5] and Rhodes (at Trianda)[6] for the second half of the sixteenth century B.C. This goes beyond anything in the Early Palace Period, but of course it can only be taken as an expression of a flourishing trade, not as proof of any political organization of this area under the leadership of Crete.

[1] §III, 4, 6.   [2] See Plate 122 (*b*).   [3] §III, 3.
[4] §III, 7.   [5] §III, 23.   [6] §III, 8, 17.

In Miletus, as in the Lipari Isles and Egypt, ceramic imports from the mainland replaced Cretan ones in the fifteenth century B.C.

The shift of forces is apparent in the developments which took place on the Greek mainland during this period. Minoan pottery was imported at various places and it was imitated locally. In general an increasing Minoanization in all branches of artistic handicraft showed itself more and more clearly. This has frequently been noticed, and it demands an explanation. Schliemann's finds in the Shaft Graves of the citadel of Mycenae, beginning within the level of M.M. III and ending in L.M. I a, made it necessary to draw a distinction between native and imported Minoan products. A third group should be added, namely objects made by Minoan craftsmen on the mainland (p. 570). The graves of grave circle B discovered in 1951, which begin earlier (probably as early as the seventeenth century B.C.) and overlap in time with the early parts of the later group, contain fewer Minoan imports. On the other hand even before the end of the sixteenth century B.C. the Minoan tholos, of which there had already been some older examples on the mainland, became the rule for the royal burials. To this may be added the similarity of L.M. II and L.H. II pottery. As the former develops from L.M. I b, the latter must be seen as the product of Cretan potters who went over to the mainland. That these influences were reciprocal can be seen from the so-called Ephyraean goblets. This mainland shape was taken over by the L.M. II workshops, but the decoration of goblets made on the mainland came from Crete.

Earlier scholars, following the lead of Evans, tended to see in this state of affairs the effects of Minoan overlordship on the mainland. Now the opposite opinion has triumphed: *Creta capta ferum victorem cepit*. For the discussion was settled by the decipherment of Linear Script B and by the discovery that the language of the script was an early form of Greek. But how are we to explain the change of control in Crete within the fifteenth century B.C.?

An important penultimate level of destruction has been observed round about the turn of the sixteenth to the fifteenth century B.C. (p. 558). It was caused by an earthquake and was followed by reconstruction. The new features which characterized the next phase were numerous at Cnossus, whereas there was a standstill elsewhere and even a decline in pottery. The palace style of the Cnossian vases was accompanied by a new, monumental and firm style in wall painting. The Griffin Fresco[1] in

---

[1] See Plate 122 (a).

the small throne room on the west edge of the central court is an example.[1] Later in date are some paintings from a house near the palace of Hagia Triada, and these come from the same work-shop as those of the famous limestone sarcophagus. A certain degree of stiffening is noticeable, and gem engraving undergoes the same change in style (p. 570). Some 'warrior graves' at Cnossus, which differ from the customary forms of Minoan burial, were abundantly provided with weapons: swords, daggers, lances, arrow-heads, helmets and cuirasses.[2] In the shaping of the hilt attachment, the sword form shows a characteristic change with important consequences. Further, weapons and war-chariots are mentioned very frequently on the small clay tablets, and even helmets occur on the painted vases of L.M. II. From this interest in weapons it has been inferred that people were beginning to prepare themselves for danger even before the turn of the century (p. 576). At the same time there is no evidence of such a change outside Cnossus, and the ruling position of mainland Greeks at Cnossus is shown above all by the tablets.

We must assume that peaceful relations between Crete and the mainland lasted throughout the seventeenth and sixteenth cen-turies B.C. (p. 164) in spite of the cultural advance and the grow-ing strength of the Helladic powers. The wealth in gold which is apparent in the Shaft Graves at Mycenae cannot be explained as the result of looting in Crete, unless there is a clear reflexion of such looting in the Minoan palaces. We have explained already (p. 579) that Minoan overlordship on the mainland cannot be assumed either. The silver rhyton from the fourth Shaft Grave of the citadel of Mycenae, which tells of an overseas enterprise and which is probably a Minoan work of art, must therefore be related to events which had nothing to do with a conflict between Minoans and mainlanders, but which resulted from collaboration between the two peoples in operations somewhere on the coasts of the Aegean Sea. We may then ask whether the Mycenaean lords acquired their gold in the course of such enterprises; we may prefer to suppose that subsidies were paid to them by the Minoans. The peaceful transfer of power in Crete from the Minoans to the Mycenaeans is difficult to explain. Since all other hypotheses do violence to the archaeological evidence in one way or another, we may be justified in suggesting that a passive renunciation of power was in accord with Minoan character, just as the skill of the Mycenaeans in usurping the position of

[1] §III, 21.
[2] §III, 9, 10.

their Minoan predecessors in the overseas markets was typical of their energy and thrust.

In the present state of our knowledge, any further step would be speculative and it is unwise to make any assertion on the reasons for the final catastrophe about 1380 B.C. It may be supposed that after the earthquake of about 1500 B.C. the Mycenaeans turned to account the confusion which must have followed, and it is possible to see in the catastrophe a century later some evidence for a revolt against the new lords or for a quarrel among them. But these are mere possibilities. The only certainty is that the palaces lay in ruins after 1380 B.C. Any political and administrative centres in Crete were thereafter of a very limited and subordinate kind (p. 573). The centre of historical activity in the Mediterranean area was no longer in Crete but in Hellas throughout the remaining centuries of the Late Bronze Age.

CHAPTER XIII

THE LINEAR SCRIPTS AND THE TABLETS AS HISTORICAL DOCUMENTS: (a) LITERACY IN MINOAN AND MYCENAEAN LANDS

I. ISOLATION OF MINOAN–MYCENAEAN LITERACY

IF some fairly high degree of literacy, and at least a modest production of literature, are to be expected in an original and in other respects notable culture, such as the Minoan in its great days, then the Minoan culture must be considered odd. As with all peoples before a certain measure of literacy is attained, doubtless there was 'oral literature', but about Minoan oral compositions nothing much can be inferred. When at length writing had been learned, at least writing for some purposes, the writing down of creative literature seems not to have been one of the purposes. Of written literature, indeed, not one scrap survives, nor is there any evidence pointing to the existence of any written literature. Oral compositions may well have been common right down to the end. Certainly there was no high degree of literacy.

For the understanding of this, many necessary facts are known only partially, and many more are lost. Theory too is weak. About literacy itself, generally, as a phenomenon, knowledge is rudimentary. There is no published study that has both scope and value. We know little of what to expect, how to understand. This is particularly true of the earlier stages. Until enough is known so that sharp delimitations are possible, it seems best to include a wide range of graphic expression and communication.

One comprehensive fact about Minoan literacy is clear, and is striking. This is its isolation. From an early period, and at various stages, the Minoans were in touch with literate peoples in Egypt, in the Levant, and in Asia Minor. The Minoans' opportunities, over the centuries, to observe writers and to learn writing may well have been equal to the opportunities which induced Greeks later to adopt the Phoenician alphabet. Along with the Phoenician alphabet, and from the East, the Greeks of the eighth and seventh centuries B.C. also adopted 'orientalizing' motifs in art. In Minoan art there is no oriental adoption that is quite parallel. The Minoans borrowed comparatively little from outside. They may have imitated others in making use of personal and business seals. They seem to have used as their standard heavy weight the Babylonian light talent; and, though perhaps by chance, their system of fractional measurements is Mesopotamian in method though not in significant details. A few of the 'Hieroglyphic' signs have been thought to have an Egyptian look. With respect to literacy, that is all. There is no reason to believe that it was the examples of other literate peoples which induced the Minoans to become literate. If it is true that much earlier in Babylonia writing on clay tablets developed through stages similar to the stages of Minoan writing later, still it seems unthinkable that the Babylonian development was in any real sense a model for the Minoan: the Minoans would never have looked back to find how, long since, the Babylonians had begun; then having mastered the beginning, to learn the next Babylonian steps, also long in the past, and so on. Rather, the two developments were similar because similar forces were at work. Nor was there any transmission of actual signs from Mesopotamia to Crete.

Moreover when the Minoans had developed a system of writing, they did not follow the Egyptian or any other example of using literacy prominently by setting up a wealth of public inscriptions. The extreme contrary is true. A few masons' marks and some single double-axe signs are the nearest the Minoans came to big public inscriptions. Like Minoan literacy itself, Minoan habits associated with literacy were home-grown; the Minoans were largely immune to the examples set by others.

In time literacy ceased to belong solely to Crete. The last form of Bronze Age literacy, called Linear Script B, is found on the Greek mainland as well as in Crete. When this script was being developed and propagated, there was a new opportunity for borrowing. As they came to see the advantages of literacy and became literate, the Mainlanders might perhaps have been expected to see advantages, if there were any, in borrowings. The system of fractional measures was in fact altered to resemble, consciously or not, the Egyptian. But that was all. Egyptian writing as a system was cumbersome and uninviting; and there was perhaps no obvious advantage in adopting any individual signs from it or from cuneiform. Like its predecessors, Linear B remained immune.

As we shall see at the end, Minoan literacy was isolated also in respect to its termination. Literacy later, in the Phoenician alphabet, once it started, spread far and wide, was modified for various languages, and has lived on continuously. Minoan–Mycenaean literacy, in contrast, came to an utter end. Except in remote Cyprus, with its other strange survivals, not a sign of Minoan writing, modified or unmodified, survived to be known in Archaic Greece.

II. SIGNS AND MARKS NOT SPOKEN

It will be convenient to begin with various signs and marks which evidently did not represent common nouns or other 'vocabulary' words; they were not a part of everyday speech. Many of them seem to have indicated persons.

POTTERS' MARKS

In Classical times, fine vases were often lettered with signatures, names, etc., but apart from a few prices and the like, special potters' symbols, i.e. marks for the trade, are comparatively rare. In the Bronze Age also, on the whole potters' marks are rare, though less so. Perhaps not significantly, more are recorded from some sites than from others.

For 'Greek' lands no collection has yet been made, but data will presently be available from the excavation of Lerna. Lerna yielded marked pots which not only are clear with respect to period but are also, after the Early Helladic period, fairly abundant. Although the earliest that can be claimed are few and somewhat dubious, their period is actually Late Neolithic: if any of a half-dozen candidates can qualify as intentional, they will be the oldest known writing in lands that later became Greek. The indications of intent seem to be present: not all are scratches made after firing, but one may have been painted, and one incised, before firing. As in Classical times, intent, i.e. the opposite of the casual incising of graffiti, is conclusively proved by painting or incising before firing. Applying this same test, we find indubitable instances, though not numerous, in Early Helladic. In Middle Helladic the number of marked pots from Lerna is well over 100, nearly all of them incised or painted before firing. The element of intent is now further emphasized by the variety of position of the marks; the handle, i.e. the prominent place, is favoured for the majority of marks. In Lerna VI (the Shaft Grave period), however, not so: in a total of 100, all but four are on the base, as commonly in the early period they had used to be; but they too were put there before firing.

Going further we may urge that most potters' marks are not meaningless whimsical scratches, but are lines drawn with full intent; they mean something. Whatever the purpose(s)—a form of signature (the potters' own mark?), certifying, or numbering, grading, pricing?—the impulse was common. Potters' marks are spread over a wide area, which includes Cyprus, Egypt and Palestine, and the West (Lipari Islands). In a sense, the marks are part of the potters' craft; they belong with it, more or less exclusively; they were not readily subject to use and development for other purposes. Potters' marks stand apart: it does not seem that they developed at all, nor can we trace any influence of them on any system of developed writing. This was perhaps natural, because whatever they meant, the message was meagre. Their only future was to be potters' marks. Nevertheless they have some remote bearing on literacy. A certain number of persons were accustomed to inscribing signs, and the signs were seen, though perhaps only occasionally, by everyone. Potters' marks were in the soil from which literacy grew.

MASONS' MARKS

Another class of artisans had occasion to use marks which may be personal. At some eighteen Cretan sites, Cnossus among them, as far back as Middle Minoan I, and continuing to the end of Middle Minoan III (M.M. III), building blocks are marked with signs. On the Mainland, masons' marks have been found at two, but only two, sites. Often more pictorial and distinctive than the simple linear marks on pots, typical masons' marks include double-axes, broad arrows, stylized trees and branches, crosses, stars, and tridents, as well as abstract and compound forms.[1] Sometimes two, or a few, are used together. Most important, as indicating a fairly advanced development, are small tokens of identification obviously added to qualify signs otherwise identical.

There is no inclusive collection or treatment of masons' marks, or even an accepted general doctrine. The meaning of one sign, however, is apparent. In at least one suite at Cnossus, the double-axe is used, not like other masons' marks, but evidently as a sign that the Pillar Crypts are sanctuaries. On the two (square) piers there are no fewer than twenty-nine double-axes.[2] These marks are of only moderate size. Many other masons' marks in M.M. I

[1] G, 5, I. 135, fig. 99.
[2] G, 5, I. 425 ff. and Suppl. Pl. x.

and M.M. II are fairly big and bold, but their position, often in the lower right-hand corners of blocks, is not conspicuous, and once the masonry was complete, they would be plastered over. At Cnossus, furthermore, the large masons' marks are usually on the upper or lower surfaces of the slabs. In this one respect, viz. in not being meant to be visible, they resemble masons' marks in the Classical period, which however were used largely for re-assembling buildings taken down and moved.

From the Cnossus palace of M.M. I, Evans collected thirty-three different designs.[1] They remind one of modern brand marks used on cattle, and it may well be that they are quarrymen's labels, or other builders' personal certifications, or the like. The only doubt about this interpretation arises from certain ones of them which are huge marks, up to 0·72 m. in width, large enough to extend across most of the area of the block, and deeply cut. These are the largest inscribed signs of any kind in the whole Minoan–Mycenaean period, and at first glance they suggest much more than mere personal labelling or certifying: so huge a sign, so much trouble for what was not to be visible, suggests some sort of magic, or consecration, or whatnot. It is probably wise to allow, however, for strong personal pride. Only a few blocks, after all, were thus marked. The labour may have been slave labour, and extra cost-less time may have been available. A childish desire for marks bigger than anyone's may have operated. The double-axe surely had cult significance, but the other thirty-two are too numerous to be magical.

In any case it is notable that the signs recur in identical form at many sites, both on palaces and (at Tylissus) private houses. Most impressive is the fact that of Evans's thirty-three M.M. I signs, some nineteen are identical with, or close to, signs on the earlier palace at Phaestus. This includes compound signs. Altogether it seems likely that the double-axes should be considered apart, and that the other marks are not magical at all, but designate quarries, contractors, guilds, or the like, several of which furnished blocks for many palaces.

Later, in M.M. III, masons' marks, at least in Cnossus, exhibit the opposite extreme in depth and size. They are so lightly incised as to be difficult to detect; all are smaller, and at least one is minute. Then, at or before the end of M.M. III, all the masons' marks come to an end.

Some masons' marks look like signs used in the various Minoan scripts, but the shapes are nearly all simple rectilinear

[1] G, 5, 1. 135, fig. 99.

shapes, and several are positively not related to the scripts. Considered as writing, masons' marks appear to be a class apart.

Comparable, however, to masons' marks, at least in proving an impulse to put personal marks of certification (?) on expensive products, are signs on bronze ingots. Objects of bone, ivory, and faïence also sometimes bear similar marks.

SEALS AND SIGNETS

There is yet a third group of personal signs, most of them pictures rather than writing. This group consists of seals and signets, together with sealings made from them.[1] The seals are fine stones, that is engraved gems. A great many are pierced, to be strung and worn on neck or wrist; others have small finger-grips to facilitate their use as stamps. The signets, so-called, are small gold or silver plaques mounted on rings. Large numbers of seals, signets, and sealings have been well published, but they are so abundant that adequate assimilation will take time. They offer a profusion of designs—abstract, natural, monstrous—many unpretentious, but many also of high quality. In contrast to the humble potters' and masons' marks, the seals and signets make up a corpus of symbolic communications almost unlimited in variability and expression. In a sense, this great series goes beyond anything which ordinary literacy might offer.

Cylinder seals, though comparatively rare, were also used in Crete, and in all three main periods. Their form, content, and in some instances provenience, bespeak foreign connexions, notably with Syria and Mesopotamia.[2] Rolled upon the clay, they may repeat a figure several times, producing a better impression than a single flat seal impressed several times. But the cylinder seal may also give an extended scene with several different figures, comparable to the largest (flat) signets. This was the direction their development took—toward pictures—rather than toward script.

From promising but limited beginnings in Early Minoan I all the way to the end of L.M. III, the series of seals and signets reaches throughout the Minoan periods. The story of literacy is involved with this history: in M.M. I a kind of 'Pictographic'; and then finally the Pictographic symbols turn into a Pictographic Script (the term 'Hieroglyphic', much used for this latter, has the wrong overtones). The Pictographic Script is used, or at least it survives, mainly on the seals. Early in M.M. III, however, the

[1] G, 6.
[2] G, 5, I. 197 f., II. 265 f., IV. 497 ff.

Pictographic Script is supplanted by, if it does not actually evolve into, Linear Script A. Linear A was evidently not felt to be suitable for the surfaces of seal-stones, which demand pictures or some other form of design. But more of this below: first it is in order to say a word about the seals which have no Pictographic writing but only designs, so to speak, of their own.

The distinction is of course not sharp. Any personal seal (or signet), whether the design is 'double sickles', or a dog baying at a mountain goat, does *mean* not just the design—the sickles or the goat—but the owner also. It is his mark, it symbolizes him, it speaks for him (or for her: women also used them). Unless the seal is a mere ornament or talisman, amulet, or the like, it usually has a fairly precise meaning, depending on the circumstances. Thus it might mean, 'N owns this'; or, 'The security of the contents is the object of this sealing, which is done under the aegis of N'; or, 'The quality of the contents is guaranteed by N'. In later, Linear B, times, a sign might be added by incision to qualify the meaning or to add a detail. Styles of design varied from period to period, so much so as to suggest that over long periods specific designs had no intrinsic meaning which made them significantly appropriate to their owners. Especially in the earlier periods, for century after century, a great many seals are indeed small and very humble—just two or three dotted circles, or the like—not much removed from an illiterate person 'making his mark'. It seems clear that many people of limited means used seals.

Once made, a seal, like a rubber-stamp, is easy to use and saves time. Eventually seals were developed with two, three, four, or even eight faces. Each face could, and probably did, have its own special meaning; and all of the faces, impressed in a row together, although they meant no more than a series of discrete co-ordinate entities, might rather make, in effect, a rudimentary sentence. This would be a considerable step toward literacy. The next stage would be to put more than one symbol on a given face of a seal (see Fig. 13). The seal then begins to speak, as it were, for itself, as sentences can, and with less, or with no, present thought of the owner. When two or more symbols are together, the range of meanings is of course enlarged. The individual pictures take on new significance through association with each other: for instance, the meaning of a given symbol is 'modified', adjective-wise, by juxtaposition. When this, or something like it, has begun to happen, literacy has begun to be attained.

The foregoing analysis is too brief and simple, and probably is otherwise faulty, but at least it can be said that in a world where potters' marks and masons' marks were often seen, and seals too were common, it is with seals that, in the record as it comes to us, the earliest literacy is associated. Seals not only had enormously greater variety of design and, no doubt, frequency of use; they also led easily to the conjunction of multiple symbols.

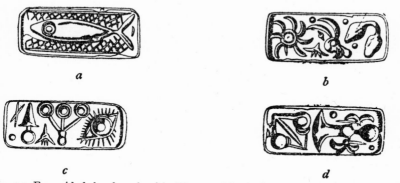

Fig. 13. Four-sided bead seal with Pictographic Script from Sitia. (A. J. Evans *Scripta Minoa* I, 155, no. P 28. By permission of Oxford University Press.)

III. SCRIPTS

PICTOGRAPHIC SCRIPT

The crucial stage was reached when pictograms ceased to be representations (usually conventional) of objects intended to signify those objects, and became symbols representing the sounds of speech, that is, began to have phonetic value. It is useful to call the body of such symbols a 'script';[1] when used, the symbols are 'written' (not 'drawn'); and the ability to write and to read them is developed, full, 'literacy'.

A Pictographic Script, scil. phonetic writing, has been recognized first in M.M. I. In Minoan and Mycenaean lands, writing eventually became one principal and distinctive feature of the palaces. Perhaps—but stronger proof is lacking—the fact that writing and the palaces originated in the same period is no accident. The development went on through the great days of M.M. I and II, and did not end until seal-like four-sided objects were made, still small but with room for enough writing to prove that writing had been attained. It was only a short final step to incising Pictographic Script on clay tablets, i.e. on temporary materials (see Fig. 14). When this had happened, though there are only a few tablets to prove it, Bronze Age literacy had reached its

[1] G, 3, 163 ff.

goal, its characteristic forms, both of signs and of material on which they were written. All that was left to do was refinements.

Seals themselves endure, and in our day a chance finder will usually sell his find, so that the generous number known to scholarship is no mystery. But it is a rare chance that we have any object on which they were impressed: there survives just one sealing which matches a known seal. The loss of nearly all the perishable matter which might have testified to the various stages in the development of literacy also makes it difficult to judge about the extent of that literacy. Again, with so few Pictographic texts as a basis, and with insufficient detailed study of the signs, development cannot be traced. As later in Linear A—but in sharp contrast with Linear B in Crete—there seem to have been local varieties.

Fig. 14. Clay label with Pictographic Script from Cnossus. The other side is plain. (A. J. Evans, *Scripta Minoa* I, 169, no. P 96 *a*. By permission of Oxford University Press.)

Only some general facts are plain. Pictographic literacy had over 300 years in which to develop, as long as or longer than the periods during which either Linear A or Linear B was in use. The number of Pictographic texts that survive is very limited, and as excavations go on year after year the number is not greatly increasing. Also very limited are the texts themselves: all of them are short. The contrast moreover with the extent and rapidity of the Greek adoption of the Phoenician alphabet later, and the fairly rapid development of it by the Greeks, is impressive.

Accounts, or at least lists with numbers, are the subject-matter of a few texts slightly longer than the rest. It is notable that although the total of signs is small enough to make it likely that they have phonetic value, an exception is certain signs—surviving pictograms doubtless—which function as complete words, like £ or $. As usually with us also, such ideograms are used only before numerals, a rule that holds also for Linear A and B.

Certain sign-groups in Pictographic Script appear to offer indications of inflexion, and since Crete had not been invaded, the language presumably is the same ('Minoan') as that of Linear A; but there is no hope of deciphering Pictographic writings until Linear A is read. A few ideograms, however, are clear, and so are the integral numerals.

NUMERALS

About numerals in nearly all stages there is some positive information helpful for understanding literacy. A recurrent primitive need, for instance, is the counting of flocks. Such counting can be done by laying out pebbles in rows of fixed lengths, or it can be done by finger-counting. Tallying however—e.g. one mark for each sheep, put down on a suitable surface—may be considered writing, or at least a primitive beginning of literacy. As distinct from finger-counting and also from rows of pebbles, tallying takes more trouble but produces some degree of fixity. It is writing which can be read later, although, if every sheep, whether ram, ewe, or lamb, counts alike as one, only one symbol need be used, and the meaning may be unknown to the later reader, who can only understand that n units are recorded. Whose they are, as well as what they are, he does not know from the writing alone.

This is one kind of primitive writing. We have no proper collection of such writings, but tallying went on for an indefinitely long time, and in due course there developed the Minoan Pictographic numerals:

$$) = 1 \quad \cdot = 10 \quad \backslash = 100 \quad \lozenge = 1,000$$
and fractions $\ell = ?\ 1/2 \quad \mathfrak{t} = ?\ 1/4 \quad \mathfrak{t} = ?\ 1/8$

These were all. Like the Indo-Europeans and other peoples, the Minoans used the decimal system of numerals, as opposed e.g. to the duodecimal system, in which the second distinct numeral would represent not 10 but 12, the third not 100 but 144, and so on; some elements of this were used in Mesopotamia, some are used by us for hours, etc. A separate numeral for five would have been a labour-saving device, to avoid repeating the symbol for 'one' as many as from five times up to nine. But whereas e.g. the Greeks later, and the Romans, had a separate symbol for five which saved writing the unit more than four times, the Minoans never did, either in the present period (that of Pictographs), or in the later Linear A and B; or for 50, 500, or 5,000. So here we have a simple illustration, partly of Minoan inertia when it came to writing, but also of the simplicity of their system itself.

LINEAR SCRIPT A

Linear A was developed out of Pictographic. Possibly a third of the signs are the same in form, and there are numerous less precise similarities. The Linear A numerals are at once closely related and an improvement:

$$| = 1 \quad - = 10 \quad O = 100 \quad \diamondsuit = 1,000$$

and fractions, capable of being combined in groups:

$$\lfloor 1 \wedge \dashv \quad \top + \ddagger \quad 2 \overset{?}{\leq} \overset{?}{\approx} \quad \maltese \overset{\mathbb{2}}{\Xi}$$

Whereas the Pictographic fractions are inadequate, the Linear A fractions, although not all are positively deciphered, surely are adequate. For integral 10 the dot is still sometimes used but eventually is lengthened; for 100 the small circle replaces a slant.

Fig. 15. Linear A tablet from Hagia Triada. (M. Ventris and J. Chadwick, *Documents in Mycenaean Greek*, fig. 8.)

The Pictographic writings have no uniformity of direction, and it is even hard sometimes to know which way they go. Linear A (and B) are uniformly orthograde. Another improvement in Linear A is the extensive use of ligatures, by which ideograms are given multiple differentiation.

These particulars suggest why Pictographic was replaced. Pictographic was probably crude; naturally so, if it had developed very slowly, never being much used. The development continued to be slow: at Mallia, Linear A and Pictographic were in use simultaneously, perhaps for decades. Evidently Linear A was not created suddenly, as if by decree. Nor is it uniform: there are definite local differences, reflecting local developments which are mostly lost to us.

Many of the Pictographic signs suggest incision in hard surfaces: a dot for a numeral is more likely to be definite if incised than if marked with ink, and the straight-edged diamond-shaped sign for 1,000 is natural for (straight) chisels, whereas the small circle is one of the most difficult characters to carve with any chisel, but is easy in ink. In general, the Pictographic Script does have a glyptic character, the Linear A signs a graphic. If then the impulse behind Linear A was not only to create a better vehicle for the language but also to create a set of forms more congenial for pens, we can only say that the impulse was not carried very far. A large number of the Linear A signs require a dozen strokes each, and are just about equally fussy for chisel, pen, or graver in soft clay. The pictogram originals should have been left farther behind.

Apparently in accord with the non-incised essence of Linear A is the fact that presently, in the course of M.M. III, the seals no longer have Pictographic writing; Linear A has supplanted it. The seals never have Linear A.

Even allowing for a slow adoption, the precise time of origin for Linear A is uncertain. Some inscriptions may be much earlier, but M.M. IIIb is the period of most of the inscriptions, apart from the only large group of texts, which is on 168 clay tablets from Hagia Triada (see Fig. 16); they are of L.M. Ia. The terminal date is also unknown, but at the least Linear A had a life of 200 years. Its distribution was wide but seemingly thin: Linear A has been found at no fewer than a score of sites in Crete, whereas outside Crete only one tablet is known at present (Kea) plus some individual signs on other objects, and of these signs many are potters' marks and the like, which may not be, properly, Linear A at all. From most of the Cretan sites, however, there are only one each, or possibly two, or a few, texts. Although there are no fewer than six (scattered) libation tables inscribed with Linear A, there are also single or few instances each of spoon-shaped mortars, a door jamb (but no other building inscription), a gold ring, a miniature gold axe, a bronze tablet; but a fair number of ingots of copper are inscribed with Linear A. All these inscriptions are short, but certainly the way was open to a wide use of literacy. Continuing from the use of the Pictographic Script for accounts, the palaces made use of Linear A. The only

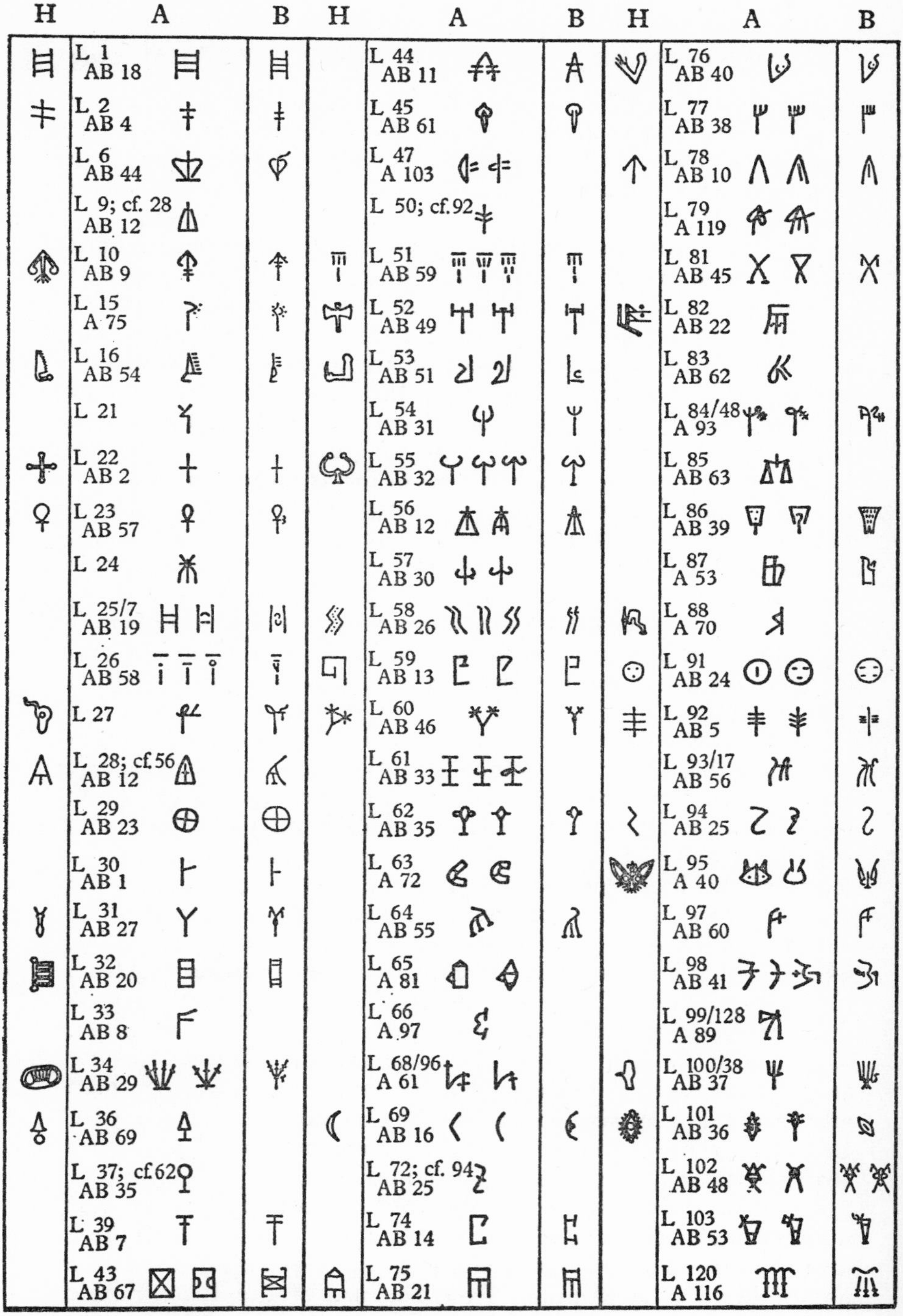

Fig. 16. The Linear A syllabary in use at Hagia Triada (after Carratelli), with possible cognates in the 'hieroglyphs' (H) and Linear B (B). (M. Ventris and J. Chadwick, *Documents in Mycenaean Greek*, fig. 6.)

surviving group large enough to be called 'archives' is that from Hagia Triada, but we should probably imagine, generously, that the smaller lots from Mallia and Kato Zakro, and even the few from Cnossus, are the meagre survivors of much use of Linear A over a long time. No doubt the losses of Linear A, and also of Pictographic, have been relatively enormous, so that it is only a minute fraction of the written matter which survives.

But even so, in view of the length of time available, and the large number of objects that *might* have been inscribed, we must again hesitate to believe that literacy was much more than a fringe activity: comparison with Classical times will enforce the point that it was not part and parcel of everyday life. The way was open but the Minoan world was little interested in writing. The Hagia Triada tablets were found with fragments of frescoes, the finest frescoes produced by the Minoan world; but the tablets themselves are uninspired and negligent. Again, although undoubtedly there was a certain amount of writing with ink on perishable materials, still the fact that ink and perishable materials were known and used may be a further illustration of the failure to write much with ink, because if there had been an abundance of writing, far more would surely have been put on imperishable objects.

The language of Linear A is definitely a different language from that of Linear B, and therefore is not Greek. Beset though they are with discouraging uncertainties, attempts to read Linear A have turned up interesting translations of single words, particularly Greek, but also others. History has perhaps one contribution to the problem. Linear A flourished in the period of the Minoan Thalassocracy, that is of the semi-piratical, tribute-collecting, crudely organized domination by Cnossus over various coastal areas, not inland; and in Crete itself not including any but a few distant ports. There was ample opportunity for loan-words to have been acquired, in Greece, in Asia Minor, in the Levant. Whatever words have been correctly translated are presumably just such loan-words. On the other hand, Linear A probably ought not to be conceived as an administrative tool specifically of the Thalassocracy, because the Thalassocracy is not to be thought of as that much organized.

THE PHAESTUS DISK[1]

An instance not merely of writing but an approximation to printing, immense in potentiality but null in effect—a freak—came to light in 1908, when L. Pernier stated that he discovered

[1] See Plate 123.

in the Palace at Phaestus a round clay disk covered on both sides with stamped signs. It was found in the north-west wing of the palace, which contained sunken stone treasure-chests ('Kaselles') like those at Cnossus; part at least of the wing was used for keeping valuables. The Disk was actually found, along with a Linear A tablet, in one of these Kaselles, but the excavator judged that the Disk and the tablet had come down from an upper floor. To this (limited) extent, the circumstances of finding suggest that the Disk was not a casual acquisition but a valued object. Moreover, as part of the process of manufacturing, it had been baked; it was intended to last, and it has lasted: nearly all the readings and details are clear. The context is of M.M. IIIb, perhaps about 1600 B.C.

Though not perfectly round (it is *c.* 0·17 m. in diameter) or quite evenly thick, the Disk is well designed. The clay, which is excellent, has an off-yellow colour; the expert verdict is that neither the clay itself nor the kind of firing are like anything known in Crete. An import, and possibly written in a foreign language, so that few persons could read it, still the existence of the Disk meant that a specimen of printing was physically present in the palace at Phaestus, so that conceivably its technique could have been inferred and followed.

The stamps themselves made such sharp impressions that they must have been metal, cast. All the indications show that the two sides of the Disk were both the work of one man, at one time. For each different sign he had one stamp; he used each stamp over and over, as often as the text demanded. On each side he ran the text in a spiral. Evidently he began, as is natural (the evidence is virtually compelling although disagreement persists), at the circumference, and wound in to the centre. To guide the reader's eye, a continuous line was incised, tracing the course of the spiral. On each side the beginning is marked; the other end, at the centre, is also unmistakable.

The signs are blocked off in groups, each group being delimited by a vertical line joined at either end to the spiral line. Thus each group is in its own box.

The clay had to be kept soft, presumably with a damp cloth, until all the signs had been imprinted. There is but little correction, and only one sign is crowded in as if late; yet the two surfaces are neatly filled. Not mere planning, but a fairly exact model, would have been needed. Indeed, the laying out of the model itself would have had to be so conditioned by the space available as to prompt the conjecture that the words themselves were chosen to fit; or that the text was composed in such a way that it would be adequately long, but could be cut off, or somehow adjusted, when the space was exhausted.

The groups, each in its own box, consist of from two to seven signs each, all but a few being three, four, or five signs: thus they are of the right length for words if each sign represents a syllable. Some, perhaps most, of the signs look like ideograms, but there are no numerals. Moreover the total number of different signs is forty-five, and linguistic studies show that this number, with the addition of some ten syllables not happening to occur here, is an adequate number for a syllabary.

On one side there are thirty-one words, on the other thirty. The text begins at the circumference (see above), and the words read clockwise, that is (since the signs regularly have their bases toward the circumference) from right to left. Obviously the signs themselves face the other way, i.e. toward the reader's right, so that the individual signs also must be read retrograde. This feature can be paralleled, however, in so many other early systems of writing that it is not an argument. Stamping, moreover, does not involve the same progressive one-direction movement as writing.

Strongly pictographic and vivid, so that the objects represented by all but a few signs can be identified, their general character ought to be ascertainable. Again there is dispute. Inscribed on a bronze axe of the same period from Arkalokhori is some incised writing in the form of a brief three-columned inscription, which makes use of ten different signs in all (different that is from each other). It is claimed that some of the ten resemble some of the signs on the Disk sufficiently to establish the Arkalokhori Axe as a link between other Pictographic writings and the Disk. In consequence, the Disk would be no import, but a development of Minoan writing on Cretan soil. Inspection will show, however, that although four of the Axe signs are not unlike four signs on the Disk, none of them, nor any others of the ten axe signs, definitely is the same as any of the Disk signs. Nothing strongly suggests, much less clinches, the hypothesis of a development from Axe signs to Disk signs. An inscribed block from Mallia has thirteen signs used for a total of only sixteen times. For this Mallia block similar claims have been made, but inspection of a photograph will show that it is even less related.

In not being Minoan, the character of the Disk signs would agree with the absence in Crete of any predecessor or successor either of the signs themselves as a group, or of the technique of

printing. The fount, as printers would call it, of the stamps themselves would have been made, not just for one document, but for
many. Highly advanced, bespeaking a long tradition, the technique would seem to have been developed elsewhere than in
Crete. Long ago certain particulars of the signs suggested Lycia
as the region of origin, and just recently an Early Bronze Age
graffito has been excavated which anticipates remarkably the
three principal characteristics of the Disk's house-sign (Evans's
no. 24). The preference for regarding the Disk as Lycian is
therefore strong. Lycia has been much less excavated than Crete,
but neither there or anywhere has an object like the Disk been
found.

For the content of the text, indications are scant. Acutely
finding some repetitions, like refrains, Evans conjectured that the
text is two 'chaunts', and this is a guess perhaps as good as any.
The possibility of translation into a modern language is of course
minimal. Beset with doubts, qualifications, and difficulties, the
Disk is almost unreal, and only the fact that it was found by an
excavator in an excavation compels its acceptance.

Scholars have always regarded the Disk as a distant and
amazing anticipation of printing, isolated in the millennia. Careful
thought will modify this opinion somewhat. Let it be recalled that
seal-stones had long been familiar in the older parts of the Aegean
world: in a sense the disk is only a series of 242 sealings. *Every*
seal is like type. Printing involves, of course, a whole group of
seals or stamps held in a frame and pressed together upon the
page. This device—the frame, the many stamps all the same for
each character, and the operation of printing the whole frame-load
simultaneously—was probably far from the imagination and the
capabilities of the makers of the Disk. Printing with ink on paper
(papyrus) would have been still another, and a very long, step.
The Ancient world undoubtedly produced wonderful carpenters
and metal-workers, but for machinery there was little inclination.

Even so, the potentialities of the Disk for literacy, though not
realized, were considerable. All at once consistency and fixity of
form in writing had been attained, along with perfect clarity in
the individual signs and in the ordering of them. Future records
could have been similar. It is true that many stamps would have
had to be cut, and in hard material. The scribes themselves,
doubtless, never gave a thought to such a project, and their
masters also saw no point in it. No sufficient need was felt for the
perfection which would result. Instead, rapid incising with a
point, even if the result were sometimes wretched, would serve.

LINEAR SCRIPT B

Sir Arthur Evans, excavating in 1900 at Cnossus, and C. W. Blegen, excavating in 1939 at Pylus on the Greek Mainland, came upon inscribed clay tablets in large numbers. At Cnossus eventually they mounted up to a total of nearly 4,000, at Pylus to over 1,200. No other city in Crete has yielded any tablets, but on the Mainland there are Linear B writings from Mycenae, Tiryns, Thebes—numbered, however, only in dozens—and a few from other places. Evans, who named the other styles, called this one Linear Script B, because like Linear A it is graphic, and it appeared to be subsequent to Linear A. The non-committal terms were good; Linear B has since been termed 'Mycenaean', against the principle that terms should never be prejudicial.

In 1952 M. Ventris proved that the language of the Linear B tablets—of all of them so far as is known, apart from loan-words—is Greek. Ventris lived to see the proofs of his own and J. Chadwick's *Documents* (1956), which will long be the incomparable work on the subject.

Classical Greek later, written in an alphabet (the one we still use), ran all the words together, but the Linear B texts had word-dividers. The words are short, much shorter than they would mostly be if written in an alphabet. Moreover the number of signs is much greater than any alphabet would need. Hence from the beginning of these studies it was clear that Linear B and also Linear A and Pictographic before it were each a syllabary. A syllabary is a system in the typical form of which each sign stands for a combination of a consonant plus a vowel. There are as many signs as there are combinations which the makers of the syllabary think are needed; there are also signs for vowels, at least five, when any of them is used by itself as a complete syllable. Thus the syllabary of Linear B has about ninety signs, of which fifty-nine are in regular and frequent use.

The decipherment itself was achieved by Ventris in two stages. The first stage, spread over many years, was the patient recording of signs (E. L. Bennett, Jr. did this for the Pylus tablets, and his determinations were vital), study of positions, and determination of frequencies. Ventris's work was carried on with rigid exclusion of influence by any known language (actually Ventris, following Evans and nearly all others, did not believe, despite historical considerations which might have made themselves felt, that the language was Greek). The second stage, swift and exciting, was when Ventris, with such clues as the frequencies and similar data

a		jo		nu		ra₂		ti		22	
a₂		ka		nwa		ra₃		to		34	
a₃		ke		o		re		tu		35	
au		ki		pa		ri		twe		47	
da		ko		pe		ro		two		49	
de		ku		pi		ro₂		u		56	
di		ma		po		ru		wa		63	
do		me		pte		sa		we		64	
du		mi		pu		se		wi		65	
dwe		mo		pu₂		si		wo		79	
dwo		mu		qa		so		za		82	
e		na		qe		su		ze		83	
i		ne		qi		ta		zo		84	
ja		ni		qo		ta₂		18		86	
je		no		ra		te		19		89	

Fig. 17. The Linear B syllabary. The signs with numerical values are still undeciphered.

had given him, boldly tried translating a certain group of words as place-names known in Greek, 'Knossos' among them (three signs: Ko-no-so). The boldness, and the long years of preparation, were rewarded, and the discovery was announced. Presently a Pylus tablet from the excavations of the previous summer, not examined before, was seen by Blegen to have actual pictures of tripods, and with it four signs which according to Ventris's table of equivalents should be the word ti-ri-po-de. This word, with others equally convincing, gave irrefutable proof. All that was left to do was to work out details: a legion of them, but details.

Wholly, apart from literacy, there was ample archaeological evidence for Greek rule in Cnossus. On the basis of this evidence, scholars had agreed, long before, that Late Minoan II was an exclusively Cnossian period. What made it exclusively Cnossian, though nearly all scholars failed to suspect it, was that Cnossus was in the hands of Greeks. The period began *c.* 1450; allow time for the development of Mainland features, and the Greek capture of Cnossus may be as early as *c.* 1480. It was a massive invasion: Cnossus itself had to endure at least fifty, probably a hundred, years of foreign control. During this period, or at least by the end of it, the palace accounts, to the extent of thousands of tablets each year, were being kept in Linear B. Hence the decipherment by Ventris confirmed—or, as many scholars would say, established positively—a major historical fact, viz. Greek rule in Cnossus. The use of Greek for the accounts is unimaginable otherwise.

In the early years after the decipherment, everything appeared to be simple. Where did Linear B come from? Answer: from Linear A, because some two-thirds of the signs of Linear B are similar to those of Linear A; and if the signs rarely used are omitted from consideration, the proportion is much larger. Where was Linear B developed? Answer: at Cnossus, in order that the Greeks, who had found the palace being administered in Minoan, could administer it in Greek. Why was Linear B developed? Answer: because Linear A, used for Minoan, was inadequate for Greek.

No positive alternative has been established, but closer study of the writings has convinced some linguists that an alteration of all these views must be considered. In their opinion, Linear B evidently cannot be derived from Linear A, but instead both must come from a common source, an earlier script totally lost. The time of creation may have been more than a century earlier than 1450 or 1480, say 1600; and if so, it was long before other evidence of Greeks in Crete. Since Linear B is for Greek, it would have had to be developed on the Mainland, and it would be imagined to be part of the Minoanizing process which reached its height in Late Helladic I. For such a view of the origin of Linear B, there are two difficulties. It has to assume that Linear B writing was used on the Mainland for perhaps three centuries (1600–1300) without leaving one trace. There is also the difficulty of imagining why illiterate Mainland rulers would go to the vast trouble of importing administrators and scribes to create a new system of writing, so as to use it for administrative procedures that they can hardly have known much about.

The linguistic evidence in question thus clashes with the historical evidence, and hesitation is indicated about acceptance of the difficult consequences to which the linguistic evidence leads.

In contrast, the Greek occupation of Cnossus is vividly real. The Linear B tablets from there have whole groups devoted to the very arms of the invaders, with many new ideograms for cuirasses, spears, swords, arrows, chariots. Once created—at Cnossus—and well learned, Linear B was carried back to Greece. It spread all over, not rapidly perhaps, but widely enough so that in many places many men who had to deal with administration, chiefly of the palaces but also perhaps in private business, learned and used it. The total number of different signs known to have been used in Linear B, when to the signs of the syllabary are added all the ideograms, is close to 199. To master them was not easy: models of the syllabary must have been constantly in front of the writers, and change could hardly be thought of. Learning to write was difficult enough.

Thus in the period after *c.* 1380, when Cnossus was burned and the Greek rulers probably scattered, most of them retiring to their former homes on the Mainland, Greece became literate, or at least literacy became a feature of the palaces. All of our tablets come from buildings which have been burned. For since the tablets were made of clay left to harden by drying but not by baking, they could only be preserved by a fire intense enough, as in the burning of a building, to bake them.

The palace at Pylus was destroyed by fire in a year not far from 1200 B.C.: the date of the tablets cannot be moved more than a few years, for they all or nearly all are definitely the ones of the last year. Another fact impossible to deny is that the Pylus tablets are very similar to the Cnossian. In the contents, of course, differences are not few, and merely by the look of them scholars familiar with the tablets from years of work can tell Cnossian and

Pylian tablets apart. The writing itself, however, scil. the shapes of the signs, is closely similar. The difficulty which this raises is acute. In the 200 years, or two or three decades less, since Cnossus was burned (that is, since the fire which baked the tablets there), changes in the shapes of the signs might perhaps be expected, despite the difficulty of change mentioned above. No one who has knowledge of the thousand years of inscriptions in later Greece could specify any stretch of two hundred or indeed of one hundred years which did not produce definite changes in the shapes of the letters.

It has been and is desirable, therefore, that scholars should re-examine thoroughly the bases for the date given by Evans to the Cnossus tablets. Linear B tablets were found in some fifty different places in the palace, and many years will be needed for a full understanding of all that is involved. The classes of evidence are: (1) the actual strata at Cnossus; (2) the evolution of pottery; (3) various data external to Cnossus. In all three classes, Evans's date is now upheld strongly enough to justify the summary account which has been given above.

The seemingly necessary hypothesis that Linear B, though exported to Greece and written for nearly two centuries, changed very little, can be confirmed to some extent by the evidence of the vase-inscriptions from Thebes. The signs there may be dated *c.* 1320 B.C., or at any rate hardly later than 1300; i.e. they are approximately in the middle of the two centuries. They too show no appreciable change.

Evidently the high degree of fixity in the signs over so many decades must be accepted. The fixity *can* be due to the aforesaid difficulty, and resulting conservatism—provincial at that—in handling 199 signs. The classical Greek alphabet is so simple in almost every one of its only twenty-four letters that variations would not easily cause misunderstandings. Such writing cannot be used as an analogue. At the other extreme from the flexible classical letters we have the signs in cuneiform, which sometimes are not datable by shapes in a span of five hundred years. With respect to fixity, Linear B may be somewhere in-between. Most relevant, perhaps, is the fact that even when they were free to do so—when they were creating a whole new way of writing (viz. Linear B)—the scribes altered very little those of the Linear A signs which they retained for Linear B. Similarly when Linear A was created out of Pictographic, and (it would seem to us) desirable simplification could have been attained, many of the new graphic signs, as we have seen, instead of being simplified, were elaborated. At that stage Minoan literacy was not practised enough to make the writers want efficiency; instead their prime desire was to make signs that would be recognized—they were timid, they did not dare to venture far from the old pictograms, they strove to copy exactly. And so a dominant trait was established for Minoan literacy which it never lost: whether executed by Minoans or Greeks, it remained far too largely pictographic throughout its history, and hence not simple; it tried to be faithful copying rather than to be efficient writing.

This does not mean necessarily that only a few people wrote, and little. At Mycenae six different hands have been identified, at Pylus thirty; at Cnossus up to seventy-five, although it was only a few scribes who wrote most of the surviving tablets. Records were kept in various parts of the palaces, but at Pylus there was also an archives room, with shelves, hinged wooden chests, and also wicker baskets for storing tablets. The tablets were filed and kept through the year. This seems cumbersome enough to imply that papyrus, with ink, was little used, though there may have been ledgers for monthly and annual entries. The tablets are not numbered, and presumably the whole was little organized. Some of the tablets however do bear check-marks; erasures and re-writings are not unknown.

Nearly all the surviving Linear B writing comes from the palaces. Short texts, one sign each or a few, are found on a few vases; sealings are often inscribed, and clay tags. But if writing is sought say among the belongings of upper-class families, as reflected in the extensive, carefully excavated, and carefully studied tombs of Prosymna, where perhaps, if it were a highly literate culture, *or* if there were only as much writing as in Linear A times, *some* writing would be expected, there is none whatever. Invented for continuing the Linear A administration of the palace at Cnossus, Linear B literacy may have had some use outside palaces, but not far outside and not much. The surviving writing suggests that Linear B literacy should not be thought of as being widespread and cheap, like ours, but rather as being one of the special skills fostered by the palaces. Its vitality was intimately bound to some of the very things it recorded, such as fine wood-working, metal-working, ivory-working.

With all this accords the fact that Linear B itself was a most imperfect syllabary for Greek. Distinctions of consonants vital for Greek are ambiguous in Linear B; other sounds are suppressed. Some short words in Linear B can have multiple different meanings in Greek. Verse such as the Homeric, but even much simpler verse, would be impossible in Linear B—even supposing that in this late, wintry, bureaucratic phase of the culture, epics were being composed.

But it might be an error to suppose that the inherent limitations of Linear B were really what limited its uses and ultimately its life. If there had been a strong will to *write* verse, or to *write* laws or history or hymns, the limitations would have been overcome. Presumably Linear B was created by fiat; by fiat also, no doubt, adequate improvements conceivably could have been effected.

IV. EVIDENCE ABOUT SURVIVAL

THE END OF LITERACY

The story of the first period of European literacy is not complete, nor even the evidence for the story, without a note about its end. Apart from Cyprus (below) which has its own peculiar circumstances, literacy did come to an end. The period of illiteracy in question begins at the destruction of Pylus and lasts all the way down to the Greek adoption of the Phoenician alphabet in the eighth century B.C. The interval is lengthy, at most ante-1200–c. 725 B.C.; at least 1100–post-800 B.C. From this interval, no writing whatever survives; careful excavation yearly has made the negative more compelling. The new Phoenician-derived literacy which followed has not a single character derived from the old.

The extinction of literacy, unimaginable for us without the mass extinction of literate persons, is now explicable. It was not due to massacres: World War II showed us that Greeks are virtually indestructible; they take off into the mountains. Literacy ended when older writers saw no reason to teach the young, and the young saw no reason to learn from the old. This time came when the palaces and all that went with them, particularly account-keeping, but also the whole series of activities involved with the palaces, were ended. Literacy had only a few and shallow other roots. It probably disappeared almost overnight.

CYPRUS

Potters' marks are found in Cyprus, together with numbers of one-sign or few-sign inscriptions on seals, clay balls, and copper ingots. As elsewhere, these are mere background. There are also at least five tablets with (seemingly) continuous prose—certainly not accounts consisting, as in Linear A and B, of items, amounts, and totals. Moreover they were baked: they were meant to be permanent. The earliest may be as early as *c.* 1500 B.C., thus ante-dating the Linear B tablets in Crete. On the four later tablets, *c.* 1225 B.C. or earlier, the signs are small, some very small, mere jabs with a point in the clay, clearly reflecting familiarity with writing and reading. One tablet preserves twenty-two lines but originally may have had 200. The script of these tablets, 'Cypriot Linear', is all in one tradition, but with marked changes over the centuries. If the script was derived from Minoan Linear A, it may have been not mere copying, but rather an adaptation with changes; but the material is much too scant to be sure.

What is sure is that some form of Cypriot Linear lasted on through invasions to emerge in the eighth/seventh centuries as the vehicle for inscriptions, chiefly sacred, to the number eventually (they extend down into the Hellenistic period) of well over 500. Of some of these, the language is an untranslated 'Eteo-cyprian', itself surviving or recently introduced (we do not know); but most are Greek, and can be read. The script, called the Classical Cypriot syllabary, has two principal variants, and although its relation to the few surviving specimens of the (Bronze Age) Cypriot Linear is far from established, still there cannot be any doubt that the Classical syllabary does descend from the Bronze Age, and that during the vast interval it was written either on solid materials now lost, or more likely on perishable materials.

On the face of it, therefore, Cyprus seems to prove that writing (presumably Linear B?) *could* have survived in Greece through the Dark Age without leaving a trace in the interval. This is impressive. Fuller consideration does, however, impose some hesitation. (1) The known uses of literacy, as shown by the few surviving Cypriot Linear tablets, were quite different from the uses known for any Cretan or Mainland writing. (2) Among the thousands of Greek inscriptions, some one, like the 500 on Cyprus, ought to reflect the transmission. (3) Despite invasions, other Bronze Age institutions survived, oddly, in Cyprus. Whether literacy there was as strongly linked to palaces as was Linear B is doubtful; but in Cyprus, monarchy of the old type survived: in Classical times the kings drove out homerically in chariots to battle. These considerations do at least suggest that as respects literacy, Cyprus may have been crucially different.

WRITING IN HOMER

The mere existence of oral epic poetry like Homer's, written down afterward but developed in the Dark Age, is itself evidence (if more were needed) that the Dark Age was illiterate. The technique of Homeric poetry, that is the tradition reaching far back beyond Homer, is oral through and through; in modern Jugoslavia, and doubtless anywhere, the acquisition of literacy naturally ruins the rhapsodic powers of a bard. Homeric poetry could never have been developed in a literate age.

But some trace of the possible duration of Bronze Age literacy into the Dark Age might come from chance survivals or from memories somehow preserved. The only possible survival is the ever-mysterious E at Delphi; but whatever the symbol really was, its origin was forgotten, its meaning was unknown, it gives no help with literacy.

In the *Iliad*, however, a memory of writing, and also a slight degree of literacy, can be alleged. The heroes can each inscribe on a token a symbol, which was clearly not a regular syllabic sign nor a letter, but rather was a sort of private personal signature, their individual mark, familiar only to themselves. The fact that it was not recognizable shows it was not thought of as a symbol from a syllabary or an alphabet: Ajax's token was not marked with an alpha. If Ajax's name had been written in characters intelligible to others, the token would not have had to be passed around. Thus the inscribing of the lots in the *Iliad*, like potters' or masons' marks (above), is merely a primitive, restricted kind of literacy, and proves nothing, though it may suggest that Homer thought of his heroes as unable to write their own names.

In the *Iliad* and the *Odyssey* there is only one occasion when the heroes are called upon to write or when there is need to mention writing, and that is the story of Bellerophon. Other epics, even including several which were *written* by their first authors and owe nothing to the (illiterate) oral technique, rarely have occasion to mention writing.

The Bellerophon story stands apart. The main events are drawn from the common store of folk-tales: the unjust exile of a handsome and able young prince; then, in the new land, trial, designed to kill the new arrival, but surmounted on his part by fabulous achievements. These are regular features. The essence of the story is that Bellerophon, going into exile, unsuspectingly carries on his own person the message bidding his new lord to kill him. The message is so essential to the plot that it can hardly be later and separable: it cannot have been added when literacy was reacquired. So here we have a definite graphic communication of some sort, certainly coming out of a period earlier than Homer. The message itself is described as 'baneful signs...many, life-destroying'; but there is an element of epic carelessness here, since the same message is presently referred to, in the singular, as 'an evil sign'.

Two interpretations are possible. The first is that the audience was to understand, dimly, perhaps, that the writer, Proetus, was literate and was employing mysterious written characters, which we should call Linear B. If this is correct the passage preserves a memory—the only such memory known to us—of the earlier literate time. The vague terms would suit with the vagueness and mystery, in the minds of illiterate persons, during the Dark Age, and in Homer's audience, of writing itself.

The other interpretation is that what the audience would naturally think of is one, or a few, or many, simple pictures. A modern equivalent would be the warning skull and cross-bones on bottles of which the contents, if swallowed, are lethal; or the Jolly Roger of pirates. The advantage of this interpretation is that the description of the signs does not have to be understood as especially vague and mysterious. On the contrary, in this interpretation literacy, unknown in the present (i.e. unknown to Homer's audience), is not even vaguely remembered from the past. Essentially the signs carried by Bellerophon would be like what Aias put on his token, or a potter might put on a pot: symbols without phonetic value, not intended to be uttered.

This is probably correct. If we adopt the second interpretation of the Bellerophon story, then the conclusion to which the evidence points is that outside Cyprus the Dark Age was illiterate —completely, for centuries—and that no memory whatever of the earlier period of literacy survived into the later.

THE LINEAR SCRIPTS AND THE TABLETS AS HISTORICAL DOCUMENTS: (b) THE LINEAR B TABLETS AS HISTORICAL DOCUMENTS

I. THE NATURE OF THE EVIDENCE

WHEREAS the Assyrian and Egyptian documents have long been readable and a general consensus of opinion is readily accessible, the Linear B tablets remain only partially understood, and there is much dispute about their interpretation. While the purely negative criticism which denies the decipherment is clearly unjustified, it remains true that excessive claims have sometimes been made by its supporters. The aim of this section is to present a brief account of the problems which beset the interpreter and the conclusions which, if not completely secure, look at present likely to withstand criticism.

Linear B tablets are so far known from four sites. Cnossus, the first site to yield them, has produced more than 3,000 tablets, but it must be emphasized that this figure includes many small fragments, and the number of complete and usable documents is much smaller. Tablets were found in all parts of the Palace, but the main archives were concentrated in certain areas: the area of the North Entrance Passage contained the remains of what must have been the principal office or archive room; the West Magazines and adjacent rooms contained large numbers of tablets, some at least of which must have fallen from offices on an upper storey, but in many cases relating to goods in the stores; the Domestic Quarter contained a very large archive dealing with sheep, and one or two smaller groups; the Arsenal contained tablets referring to weapons and military equipment. Strangest of all, the so-called 'Room of the Chariot Tablets' held a large and apparently self-contained archive with special features which have not yet been satisfactorily explained.[1]

The Palace of Pylus, by contrast, had almost all its 1,200 or more tablets concentrated in the area adjacent to the main entrance; clearly the main office was situated where messengers and officials arriving could report the facts to be recorded. Small

[1] G, 4.

groups have been found elsewhere in the Palace, notably in the store-rooms. At Mycenae the main archives were probably on the summit of the hill and have been destroyed by denudation, if not lost in the earliest excavations. A few badly preserved tablets have been found inside the citadel walls, but most have come from houses outside the walls. Their first excavator, A. J. B. Wace, regarded these as the houses of merchants;[1] but the evidence that Linear B is a tool of the royal administration suggests that they should rather be regarded as the residences of court officials, some of whom were in charge of productive departments and probably responsible for the manufacture of goods such as perfume.[2] The two small groups so far recovered from Thebes, though promising for the future exploration of the site, offer little evidence of value. All that can be said for certain is that all four sites show the same script, language and accounting procedures, a clear indication of the reality of the common culture inferred originally from pottery styles.

It is certain that the use of Linear B can be demonstrated for a short period only, but its limits are disputed. Traditionally the fall of Cnossus, which was accompanied by the violent fire necessary to bake the clay tablets, is dated to *c.* 1400–1375 B.C., and despite attempts to lower this date, it seems very unlikely that it can be far wrong.[3] All the Mainland tablets are confined to the L.H. IIIb period: those from Pylus belong to the very end of the period, those from the Houses outside the walls at Mycenae are perhaps half a century earlier, and those from Thebes may be earlier still. But the maximum chronological range seems to be 1400–1200 B.C., and all the inferences in what follows must be understood as relating to that period alone, and in Crete only to the beginning of it. It does not of course follow that Linear B was only devised around 1400 B.C.; it must have had an unrecorded pre-history.

The size of tablets varies from small flat bars with rounded ends to large roughly rectangular slabs similar in shape and size to the page of a modern book.[4] The great majority of tablets have a single heading to which are attached one or more book-keeping entries, each ending with a numeral. Thus a tablet may record the name of a man, a place name and a number of sheep; and these may be interpreted as the shepherd, the town or district to which he belongs, and the size of his flock. Another type may give a place name, a series of commodities either counted or weighed,

---

[1] G, 2, 3–14.
[3] G, 13.
[2] G, 9.
[4] G, 14, 110–12.

and notes of contribution or deficit. This must be understood as an assessment for tax and a record of how far this has been fulfilled. This is unpromising material for historical conclusions, but fortunately it is now becoming clear in what way many of the records are to be interpreted, and some documents can yield important information.

The typical tablet is a registration of a single fact or event, but there are also large, composite documents with numerous entries. In a few cases the same or parallel information is contained in two series of documents, and these allow us to estimate how well preserved the series is. Similar conclusions can be drawn from documents which give the total of figures listed in the relevant series of tablets. Generally speaking series appear to vary from about 60 per cent to 100 per cent complete.

All documents appear to refer only to the current year; there is no system of dating by years, though months are named. References to 'this year', 'last year', etc. also confirm that the tablets of previous years were not preserved.[1] Thus it is probably safe to assume that for each site we have a part of the year's records, immediately before the destruction which baked the tablets and rendered them durable. The presence at Cnossus of records of the wool-clip, but apparently not the grain harvest, suggests a date in spring or early summer; the five names of months recorded would confirm that date, if the year began at the winter solstice, but this is very uncertain. Similarly at Pylus, the evidence suggests a date early in the year; if the word *po-ro-wi-to* is the name of a month derived from πλέω 'sail',[2] since if correct it is likely to be the date of the destruction, then March–April would appear probable.

The majority of tablets contain no finite verbs, but where found they show a full range of tenses: both aorist and perfect are found, referring to past events, the present is used in a 'timeless' sense (in some cases implying annual repetition), and the future denotes expectations. It does not seem that the futures are to be construed as orders, and no imperatives have been certainly identified; thus the function of the tablets seems to be confined to recording and the script was not used to convey instructions, a risky business with so much ambiguity inherent in the writing system.

All tablets can theoretically be classified as relating to incomings, outgoings or stock; but owing to the nature of the record and its imperfect preservation, it is not always possible to

[1] G, 14, 113–14.
[2] G, 12, 254.

assign a tablet to the correct class. Incomings, large contributions imposed by the Palace on individuals or areas, are sometimes signalled by the word *a-pu-do-si* (*apudosis* = ἀπόδοσις) or appropriate forms of the verb δίδωμι.[1] Outgoings can often be recognized by the name of the recipient expressed in the dative or place names in the accusative with suffixed -*de*. A common type of this class is the ration document, assigning quantities of food to persons. Stock records are of various types, and include flocks of sheep, lists of furniture and textiles, and notes of men and women available as labour.

II. OBSTACLES TO INTERPRETATION

The difficulties in the way of interpreting these documents are such that archaeologists, inexpert in the epigraphic and linguistic techniques they demand, have been frightened of making much use of the information they can contribute, while other scholars have sometimes pursued an eclectic policy, picking at random among the numerous interpretations which they cannot evaluate. A brief review of the obstacles may also reveal how solid is the basis for some at least of the conclusions to be offered below.

The tablets are poorly preserved, often damaged and hard to read; in all too many cases they have been reduced to small fragments. The material from Cnossus has suffered most, mainly due to the inadequate care taken by the first excavators, who did not even seriously attempt to re-unite the fragments to make whole tablets, a task which has now been attempted with much labour by a new generation of Mycenaean epigraphists. But the other sites too, whose excavators deserve nothing but praise, have yielded their quota of tantalizing scraps and unintelligible fragments. We must continue to deplore the accident which has given us the name of Dionysus twice on fragments from Pylus so incomplete that we cannot even be certain it is the name of a god.[2] All too often vital information has to be qualified by a reservation arising from the incompleteness of the context.

When complete and well preserved, it is possible to transcribe the text: that is to say, we can replace the Linear B symbols by a phonetic transcription, which is then to be understood and filled out in accordance with certain well-defined rules which have been recovered empirically from the texts. Only a few very rare syllabic signs lack certain or probable identifications. Numerals

[1] G, 6.
[2] PY Xa 102, Xa 1419.

offer no problems, and the system of weights is well understood;[1] the system of dry and liquid measures is more difficult, since, although the relationship of the units to one another is known, there is as yet no agreement on the absolute values of the units. However, we can at least assign limits within which the values must fall. It seems likely that the size of the larger vessels in use in Mycenaean times will approximate to units of the measuring

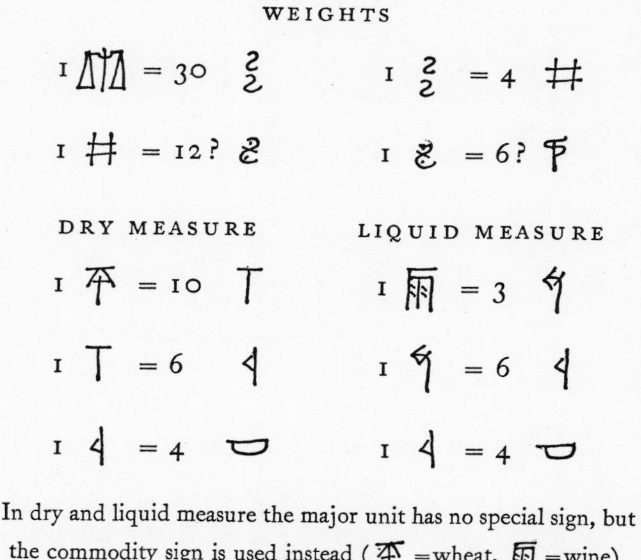

WEIGHTS

1 ⟨symbol⟩ = 30 ⟨symbol⟩   1 ⟨symbol⟩ = 4 ⟨symbol⟩

1 ⟨symbol⟩ = 12 ? ⟨symbol⟩   1 ⟨symbol⟩ = 6 ? ⟨symbol⟩

DRY MEASURE   LIQUID MEASURE

1 ⟨symbol⟩ = 10 ⟨symbol⟩   1 ⟨symbol⟩ = 3 ⟨symbol⟩

1 ⟨symbol⟩ = 6 ⟨symbol⟩   1 ⟨symbol⟩ = 6 ⟨symbol⟩

1 ⟨symbol⟩ = 4 ⟨symbol⟩   1 ⟨symbol⟩ = 4 ⟨symbol⟩

In dry and liquid measure the major unit has no special sign, but the commodity sign is used instead (⟨symbol⟩ =wheat, ⟨symbol⟩ =wine).

Fig. 18. The Mycenaean weights and measures.

system, and this has suggested that a value of 0·8 litre corresponds to an important step in the system; but it is impossible to deduce whether the smallest unit is around 0·4 or 0·2 litre. The higher figure seems to give the more plausible figures.

Some ideograms are self-evident, others have been identified from their context or equated with identifiable words in the text. But a number, especially the rarer ones, remain enigmatic. Syllabic signs are often used as a substitute for ideograms, or as abbreviated annotations to them. Here too some can be understood, others remain obscure pending further examples.

[1] G, 14, 53–60.

The words spelt with syllabic signs represent of course not only items of vocabulary but also proper names. It has been suggested that some tablets which do not apparently yield Greek words are in some other language; but in most such cases it can be shown, and it may be suspected in the rest, that the recalcitrant items are personal names. Many names are of the typical Greek compound pattern, such as *Ma-na-si-we-ko* = *Mnāsiwergos* or *Pi-ro-pa-ta-ra* = *Philopatrā*. But a much higher proportion than in classical Greece does not yield clear interpretations of this sort. Some may be hypocoristics of Greek origin, but, especially at Cnossus, we must clearly reckon with a large element in the population who retained a non-Greek tradition at least in their names. The place names, as in classical times, are largely without Greek etymologies, but can hardly be classed as foreign on that

Fig. 19. KN Ca 895: horses and asses.

account; Greek descriptive terms are also used as names (e.g. *Ka-ra-do-ro* = *Kharadros* 'the gully', *E-re-i* = (dative) *Heleï* 'the marsh').

The true vocabulary contains many of the familiar classical words, though their form is often unfamiliar and the syllabic spelling impedes recognition. Many words, however, can be regarded as certain because their meanings are confirmed by the context. This happens not only when the word is accompanied by a clear pictogram (as *i-qo* = *hiqquos* = ἵππος accompanied by a drawing of a horse's head),[1] but also when the context confirms the kind of word to be expected (as *ra-pte-re* preceding an entry of so many men must be a nominative plural of an agent noun in -τήρ,[2] and the interpretation *rhaptēres* 'sewing men' is thus highly probable).

But other interpretations depend upon little but the resemblance between the phonetic shape indicated by the syllabic spelling and a classical word, and here it must be admitted that some wild conjectures have been published. Judgment must depend upon the suitability of the meaning to all the contexts in which the word

[1] KN Ca 895; Fig. 7.   [2] PY An 207, An 424.

is used, the closeness of the form to that attested later, whether the differences are accounted for by known developments, whether the interpretation is in agreement with the empirically derived rules, and so forth. It is strange how many scholars have considered themselves competent to make such judgments, and how many more have ignored expert advice in pursuit of a cherished theory. Conjecture is a necessary first step, and verification may be impossible in the light of existing knowledge; but many interpretations can be firmly dismissed as contrary to the known facts.

The presence in the vocabulary of a number of words not to be identified in any classical source need occasion no surprise; chronologically the nearest source is Homer, and it is generally

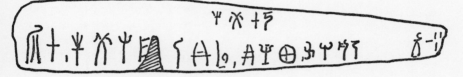

Fig. 20. PY Ae 303: the slaves of the priestess.

accepted that the Homeric text, whatever its antecedents, dates to about five centuries after the fall of Pylus. For many purposes we must use material eight or more centuries later than the tablets. Thus the disappearance from the later tradition of many Mycenaean words must be expected; and this is especially true of the technical vocabulary which is liable to replacement as techniques change. In some cases a word survives to classical times but proves to have had a different meaning in Mycenaean Greek (for instance, *harmota* 'wheels' must be equated with ἅρματα 'chariots'; *ophelos* 'deficit' recalls ὀφείλω rather than ὄφελος in later usage).

Despite these problems translation is often not difficult; but it is much harder to interpret aright the translated text. Since the tablets were not intended to be read by anyone but the writer or his colleagues in the administrative machine, they are notably laconic; their writers recorded only enough information to ensure that the figures could be referred to the correct headings. Fourteen women at Pylus are recorded as 'slaves of the priestess on account of sacred gold';[1] the words and syntax are familiar, the translation

[1] PY Ae 303; Fig. 20.

certain, yet the implications of the statement entirely escape us. The writer and his immediate circle knew which priestess was meant, why she had fourteen slaves, and what part the sacred gold played in the transaction; we can only speculate on a situation which would have led to the writing of that note, and it is unlikely that we shall ever achieve an agreed solution.

This is because the tablet in question is, to us, an isolated document. Fortunately many tablets belong to series dealing with the same subject, and progress is being made in some cases in restoring the original grouping of the tablets, as they were filed away in baskets or boxes. This is largely due to the fact that the handwriting of individual scribes can be identified, and since the Palaces employed a large number of clerks, separate sets of documents can sometimes be identified by the difference of hand.[1] If we were able to restore all the tablets to their original files, we should vastly increase our knowledge of the archive; but even the progress which has been made has led to significant results.

To quote one minor instance, we know that for administrative purposes the kingdom of Pylus was divided into two Provinces; a group of tablets recording women and children was written by two different officials, and it is now possible to demonstrate that the group, apparently homogeneous, falls into two sets, each dealing with a different province. Where it is possible to establish the grouping of tablets into sets, it follows that instead of a number of isolated statements we have a large document, containing in some cases as many as sixty or a hundred entries, all relating to the same subject. Thus the records of flax production at Pylus are contained in a series of about a hundred tablets, each of which conveys little information; but taken as a whole we can judge the way in which production was organized and draw conclusions about the economic system.

Although limited progress in this sense is now possible, it will probably never become possible to understand fully all the documents which have been recovered. We shall have to content ourselves with partial knowledge of part of the system; for not only are the surviving records incomplete, but even when intact they can hardly have covered more than some parts of the economy, and in the archives known to us much must have gone unrecorded, at least upon clay tablets. That other records existed on perishable materials is highly probable, and it is galling to realize that these would have contained the most interesting facts, for clay was a

[1] G, 3; 11.

second-class writing material in Greece, so that it was used for the collection of raw facts or the making of rough drafts, rather than the final digests which we may suppose the royal administration would have required of its staff.

III. CONCLUSIONS

The basic historical fact which emerges from the tablets is the presence of the Greek language in Mycenaean Greece; all doubts about the Greekness of the Late Helladic masters of Greece can be set aside. By Greek we mean here speakers of a language not merely ancestral to the dialects of classical Greece, but actually showing already many of the characteristic features of phonology, morphology and vocabulary which distinguish Greek from other languages. The presence of a non-Greek element is perhaps to be inferred from the personal names which are not of Greek type; and Greek names of the 'sobriquet' type (such as *Xanthos*, *Eruthros*, *Korudallos*, *Tripodiskos*) may perhaps have been given by Greek masters to their barbarian serfs.[1]

The presence of Greeks at Cnossus at the beginning of the fourteenth century B.C. is of course a fundamental blow to Evans's reconstruction of a Minoan civilization destroyed by Greek invaders; but the only correction necessary is to date the end of Minoan civilization to L.M. Ib, leaving the last phase as a continuation in modified form under Greek rule. It would seem that non-Greek names are more frequent at Cnossus than on the mainland, but it is hard to judge the extent of admixture even among the persons named on the tablets. It is perhaps significant that yokes of oxen were given Greek epithets as names, for this would be difficult to reconcile with a theory of a small Greek aristocracy dominating a non-Greek population.[2] The catastrophe which terminated the Minoan period must have brought about a very large influx of Greek blood into the island.

It is also worth noticing that all Linear B documents so far known employ a similar dialect, and that this cannot be ancestral to the West Greek (Doric) dialects of classical times. It therefore follows that a branch of the Greek-speaking people existed at this date outside southern and central Greece; and the suggestion that they were still located outside the south Balkans encounters severe difficulties. No positive statement beyond this can be proved; but any historical reconstruction should leave room for the Dorians, perhaps in the north-west of Greece.

[1] G, 7.   [2] G, 14, 105.

That the perusal of administrative archives should give the impression of a bureaucracy is perhaps inevitable; but the absence of literacy in any other context reinforces the picture which emerges of a society dominated by officials and clerks. Homer of course knows nothing of this side of Mycenaean life, r.or can archaeology demonstrate it. Apparently comparable states like contemporary Troy seem to have managed their affairs without committing anything to writing; but viewed in terms of administrative efficiency, the introduction of a system of written records must mark a great advance. Above a critical size of kingdom the need for written records is obvious, and this suggests that writing must have been introduced from Crete to the mainland long before it is attested by extant documents. The uniformity of the tablets from four scattered sites bespeaks a uniform system of accounting, and perhaps even centralized schools where the appropriate techniques were learnt.

On forms of government the tablets confirm the deduction from the existence of palaces that Cnossus and Pylus were monarchies, and add the information that the king was called *Wanax*. There was also a high-ranking officer called *Lawagetas*, but his functions are not to be securely deduced from his title. There was also an important class called *telestai*, possibly landholders, though this may not have been their prime function. We also hear of *heqᵘetai* 'followers', doubtless of the king; they possessed slaves and had distinctive garments and chariot-wheels. This suggests that they may have formed an élite corps of charioteers. At a local level there were officials whose title (*ko-re-te-re*) cannot be satisfactorily interpreted, each of whom seems to have been in charge of a small area and to have had a deputy. These men are, for instance, charged with making contributions of bronze or gold.

The existence of slavery is proved by mentions of *doeloi*, a form ancestral to δοῦλοι, but nothing can be deduced about their status. It is probably unwise to project back to Mycenaean times the classical dichotomy of the population into slave and free. A special category of people, both men and women, is described by the title *theoio doelos* 'servant of the deity', but they do not appear to be slaves, since they can hold land; the translation 'servant' may perhaps be more appropriate in all cases for *doelos*.

An elaborate series of records at Pylus,[1] apparently intended for the calculation or issue of rations, details a force of more than

[1] PY Aa, Ab.

750 women and a similar number of children.[1] Of these about three-quarters were located at Pylus itself, the remainder at various places in both provinces of the kingdom. A large number of these groups are described by terms which relate to textile production: spinners, weavers, carders, flax-workers, and so on. This indicates that the production of textiles was a major concern of royal establishments, and that the work-force was fed from the palace stores. A number of the groups of women are described by ethnic adjectives which are familiar to us as the names of places on the eastern side of the Aegean, and although any one of the identifications might be wrong (e.g. the *Milātiai* might come from *Milātos* in Crete rather than Miletus in Ionia), cumulatively they confirm one another. The places named appear to be: Miletus, Lemnos, Cnidus, possibly Asia (originally the name of Lydia) and Zephyrus, which is recorded as an old name in the region of Halicarnassus. The explanation of these names is not easy: they can hardly have been places raided by Greek slavers, since Miletus at least seems to have been under Greek rule, if it is the city named by the Hittites as Millawanda; and there is archaeological evidence of Mycenaean settlers there and in the Halicarnassus area. Perhaps these groups of women are named after the Greek trading posts through which they passed on their way from the interior of Asia Minor to mainland Greece.

A parallel set of documents at Cnossus confirms the interpretation of these groups as a labour force, primarily for the textile industry, and compels us to reject the theory that they were refugees in the troubled conditions preceding the fall of Pylus. The main difference in Crete is that the groups of women are named from Cretan towns, not places overseas, and there is some evidence that they performed their work in their native towns, though the organization of their work was astonishingly centralized. The issue of wool to the work groups and the return of finished cloth were meticulously recorded at Cnossus, even when the work was done at Phaestus or some other town.

Evidence of material wealth can be deduced from the mentions in the tablets of luxury goods.[2] Although these merely confirm the impressions of wealth gained from the architectural remains and the few unlooted tombs so far discovered, the richness of ornamentation described clearly demonstrates the existence of craftsmen and artists, and the means to support them. Not only are vessels of gold listed, but gold is used for decorative work on furniture. Another material mentioned in the same context is

[1] G, 5. [2] PY Ta.

kuanos, which can be securely identified as the blue glass paste which was used to counterfeit lapis lazuli; some fine specimens of jewellery of this material have recently been excavated at Arkhanes in Crete, and a mould found at Mycenae may well have been for this material, since tablets from nearby mention 'kuanos-workers'.[1] Silver was exceptionally used as a binding on chariot-wheels, where bronze is more common.[2] The ivory at least must have been imported, and probably also the gold.

There was of course no currency, and apparently precious metals were not in use as a medium of exchange. There are references to 'purchase' (a form ancestral to the verb πρίατο occurs), and in a few cases lists of goods appear to be the price of a transaction.[3]

The terms upon which land was held and cultivated are entirely unknown, despite ingenious speculation. The only evidence on this subject is a long series of documents from Pylus,[4] some preserved in a double recension; these are still not fully explained, though their translation does not offer much difficulty. The plots of land are never explicitly located; we have for one series the bare indication of the area, the location of the other two is not given in any way. The clerks were obviously concerned with the holders of the land, not the land itself. This suggests that these documents concern taxation or revenues, and to describe them as a cadastral survey is misleading. It is possible that the facts are here recorded only because these areas were abnormal, and that elsewhere a simpler system prevailed.

It is clear that in these areas at least there were two kinds of land: that in private ownership, and that belonging to the *dāmos*. It is dangerous to translate *dāmos* as we would its classical successor δῆμος, for the composition and limits of the community to which it refers are unknown. Land owned by the *dāmos* is described as *ke-ke-me-na*, another word of disputed form, but its effective meaning is agreed to be 'common'. Various persons are named as holding plots on land belonging to individual owners or the *dāmos*. Some land appears to be owned by collective groups (the swineherds, the oxherds, the bee-keepers), though the ambiguity of the script is such that it is not entirely sure that the words for these are in the plural rather than the singular.

The grains in use were wheat and barley, both collectively called *sītos*, but distinguished by their ideograms. Surprisingly

---

[1] MY Oi 703.
[2] PY Sa 287.
[3] E.g. PY An 35, Un 443.
[4] PY E.

wheat appears more often than barley, whereas in later times barley is the dominant crop in Greece and is only slowly overtaken by wheat. The rations of the Pylus slave-women are issued in wheat and figs, though there is an apparent conversion sum on one tablet which may suggest that these rations are nominal and might be issued as barley, which is the regular grain in other ration documents. The conversion factor appears to be about double the quantity of barley to wheat, as measured by volume.

Olive oil was in use, though it is hard to judge on what scale or for what purposes. We know that many of the issues of oil, both at Cnossus and at Pylus, were to religious shrines. Some of the oil was scented, and the so-called 'House of the Oil Merchant' at Mycenae has been convincingly explained as the royal perfumery.[1]

A variety of spices are mentioned, including coriander, cumin, cyperus, sesame, fennel and mint.[2] These seem to have been intended for flavouring food. Their interest lies in the possibility that some of them were imports from the East, and this is perhaps supported by the name of an unknown spice known simply as *po-ni-ki-jo* 'the Phoenician (spice)'. The presence of Semitic loan-words in Mycenaean Greek proves contact, whether direct or indirect, with the Semitic world; the same conclusion must be drawn from the system of weights and measures, both of which show the influence of the Babylonian sexagesimal system.[3] Although the words for the units of weight are not recorded, the ideograms strongly suggest that the terms 'talent' and 'mina' were already in use.

The vast series of tablets from Cnossus dealing with flocks of sheep and their wool demonstrates clearly the cardinal importance of this branch of agriculture for Mycenaean Crete. The total number of sheep on preserved tablets approaches 100,000, and there is no reason to suppose that sheep-rearing was exclusively a royal prerogative denied to other citizens, so the true sheep population may have been much higher. The labour force necessary to turn the wool into cloth has already been mentioned. If their production was in excess of local demand, the export of woollen goods may well have been one of the major sources of Cretan wealth.[4] Although our records date only to the Late Minoan II period, in the light of their information we may feel confident in assigning a flourishing textile industry to Crete in earlier times too; indeed the recent excavation at Myrtos strongly suggests a small-scale textile industry in Early Minoan times.

[1] G, 9. [2] G, 2, 107–8.
[3] G, 14, 55–6. [4] G, 5.

At Pylus, sheep, although important, do not occupy such a dominating position in the archive. But two other industries can be shown to have existed in Messenia. A very large number of villages in both provinces are assessed for contributions of flax.[1] It has been suggested that linseed is meant rather than flax-fibres, but this area is still today the principal centre in Greece for the cultivation of flax for fibre. Moreover a substantial number of the women workers mentioned above are called *lineiai* 'flax- (or linen-) workers'. It is thus probable that this commodity was a special product of Messenia, and may well have been exported. We have references in the Cnossus tablets to 'fine linen', but flax is rarely mentioned. An important use may have been for armour; heavy linen padding is very effective and was much used in medieval times for this purpose.

The second probable industry is metalwork. We have a long series of tablets recording the issue of bronze to smiths, and since it is here possible to obtain an estimate of the completeness of the record, it is evident that the total number of bronzesmiths in the kingdom was around 400.[2] This would work out at an average of about two per settlement, for archaeological search agrees with the tablets in putting the total number of settlements in the area around 200. But we know that these craftsmen were not, like the more recent village blacksmith, so distributed; they were grouped into small bands of up to twenty or more smiths, and were mostly not located in the major settlements. Probably their location was governed by the availability of timber for fuel, since this is more difficult to transport than raw material or finished products. If we assume the work force was normally kept fully occupied, its production must have far exceeded the needs of the kingdom, for bronze was always a relatively scarce and valuable commodity. This suggests an export trade in metal goods, and vessels appear along with textiles among the gifts brought by envoys from the Aegean to Egypt. It is almost certain that the raw materials would have had to be imported, so that this industry would have been doubly dependent upon overseas trade. Thus the fact that the tablets show that bronze was scarce and that local officials were being ordered to requisition metal from shrines for armaments may be a reflexion of the breakdown in foreign trade consequent upon the upheavals at the end of the thirteenth century, which led eventually to the destruction of the Mycenaean palaces, and may be identical with the movement recorded by the Egyptians as the attacks by the 'Peoples of the Sea'.

[1] PY Na.　　　　　　　[2] G, 8; Fig. 21.

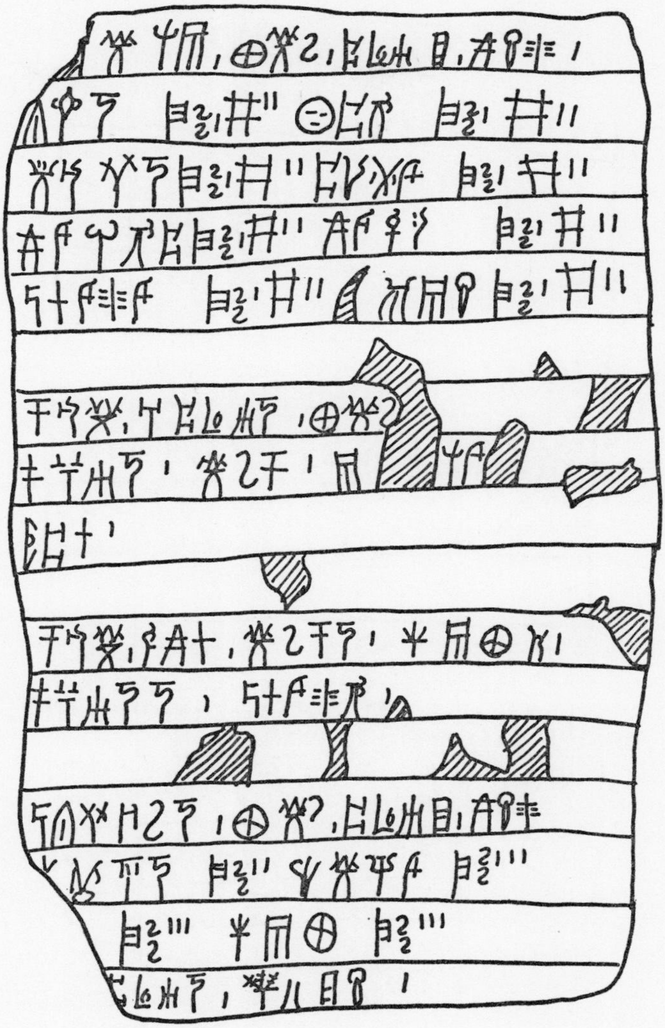

Fig. 21. PY Jn 310: bronzesmiths at Akerewa.

Since the Pylus tablets were written apparently within a few months of the sack of the Palace, it is justifiable to interpret the documents in the light of this event. While the majority of tablets are clearly concerned with the ordinary day-to-day functioning of the economy, there are two cases in which it seems legitimate to detect the pressing emergency.

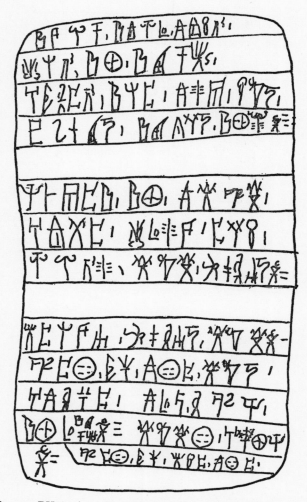

Fig. 22. PY An 657: the beginning of the series of 'coast-guard' tablets.

A set of five tablets records the organization and location of a force totalling around 800 men.[1] The introductory phrase is not seriously disputed, and reads: 'Thus the watchers are guarding the coastal regions.' The frontiers of the kingdom are probably bounded by the river Neda (in central Triphylia) to the north, and the river Nedon (on the east side of the Messenian gulf) to

[1] PY An 657, 519, 654, 656, 661; Fig. 22.

Fig. 23. PY Tn 316 showing evidence of hasty writing and scribbling.

the east. Thus the coastline to be guarded can hardly have been less than 150 km.; and with an average of little more than five men per kilometre this force is plainly too small to put up even a token defence. Its function must therefore have been to keep watch and give warning of the approach of enemy ships. At various points in the list occurs the note that one of the 'followers' is with them; these officers of the king must have served for liaison with the palace. It is clear that precautions were being taken against an attack coming by sea. This is of course no proof that this was how the final attack actually developed; but it matches the picture of large fleets of raiders operating in the Eastern Mediterranean which we gain from Egyptian and other sources.

The other possible indication of an emergency is much more doubtful, but is worth a mention. A single large tablet bears evidence of haste and changes of mind during its writing.[1] The retention of such an ill-written document in the archive might occasion surprise, unless it was in fact only written in the last day or two before the palace fell. The meaning of some key words is still uncertain, but there is no doubt that it records offerings to a long list of deities. The offerings are in each case a golden vessel, but the principal deities, if male, receive in addition a man, or, if female, a woman. It has been suggested that these human beings were being dedicated to the service of the deities, but the grisly possibility that they were human sacrifices cannot be lightly dismissed. At all events the offering of thirteen gold vessels and ten human beings to a whole pantheon of divinities must mark an important occasion; and what occasion more likely than a general supplication on the receipt of news of an imminent attack?

Further research will add to and amplify these conclusions, but we already know from the tablets a great deal which confirms and augments the deductions from purely archaeological evidence. That we have no political history, that we do not even know the name of the kings, that we know nothing of relations with foreign states, these are all things we must deplore. But a picture of the economic organization of a Mycenaean kingdom is beginning to emerge, and we may hope that fresh discoveries of archives will add to this picture of a world which seems increasingly more remote from the Homeric image.

[1] PY Tn 316; Fig. 23.

CHAPTER XIV

THE RISE OF MYCENAEAN CIVILIZATION

I. THE NATURE OF THE EVIDENCE

In attempting a history of the Mycenaean age we are still largely
confined to the history of material culture, to the generalized
story of the establishment of settlements, to their destructions and
rebuildings, which are often dated only in terms of the successive
styles of pottery used by the inhabitants. From the ruins of
houses and palaces we can reconstruct their appearance when
stone, brick, and timber were new; we can in patches see what
fresco pictures brightened their walls. Fragments of carved ivory
give hints of the adornment of wooden furniture long since
burned or rotted into ashes and dust; some weapons, tools and
vessels of metal survive, though most when outworn would have
gone for scrap to the melting pot, unless laid underground with
the dead; and though tombs may be robbed, we do sometimes, if
rarely, find in them vessels or ornaments of gold or the more
corruptible silver. We have, moreover, in various materials, these
peoples' own picture of themselves and their activities; we can,
from their precious objects, their houses and fortifications and
their monumental tombs, assess at least in degree their wealth and
power, their pride and their fears, in this world and the next;
we can trace from objects of commerce—or from such of them as
are less perishable—how far they travelled and traded, what other
cities of men they knew; to the extent that history is the account
of 'what it was like to be there then', we can write their history.
But in such an archaeological view we miss the individual events
and the individual persons. Kings conquer and rule and die and
are buried; but we do not know clearly where they came from, or
precisely when; still less their names. For the Mycenaean rulers
did not, like the Egyptians, record their names and exploits in
inscriptions on public monuments. Theirs was not, as the preceding chapter has shown, an illiterate civilization; but it seems
as though they were content to use writing merely for such facts
as it was tedious to remember, leaving the names and the acts
of the great to be willingly preserved in the thoughts and words
of their successors.

Fortunately, this did happen; imperfectly, no doubt; but the Greeks of later times inherited an immense body of legends and traditions, often confused or contaminated by myth and folk tale, but valid in their main sequences (at least where events are causally linked); valid too in their localizations, since each city had best reason to remember its own past, and so preserving in rough outline the history of the civilization which we call Mycenaean. That we do so call it is itself evidence of the validity of the tradition. Mycenae in legend was the city of Agamemnon, King of Men, commander-in-chief of the Greeks in that first united enterprise of Hellas (as Thucydides called it[1]), the Trojan War.

The Homeric epics crystallized this fact, as they did many other facts of the heroic age; but it is well to remember that Homer was not the only source or medium for classical Greek knowledge of the period. The existence of other tradition in plenty is implied by the manner of allusion to it in other Greek literature, notably in the epinician poems of Pindar and Bacchylides, who could rely on their audiences' familiarity with it. And certain kinds of legend cannot but be factually true: if Bacchylides describes how Minos conquered his own native isle of Ceos and shared out the territory among his comrades, this is surely valid evidence that such a conquest occurred, even without the archaeological corroboration that is now coming to light. Moreover, Greek memory of the Mycenaean period was associated with the surviving monuments around them: the walls of Tiryns and Mycenae, the great beehive tombs, still visible above ground when Schliemann began his work, must in the classical period have been yet more conspicuous. The 'Tomb of Aepytus' in Arcadia was a landmark in Homer's day (*Iliad* II, 604), and it was still of note for the tourist of Pausanias' time;[2] the 'Tomb of Minos' in Sicily was still well remembered when Diodorus[3] described it; and both these late descriptions seem to refer to genuine Late Bronze Age monuments. Other remains, especially burials, would come to light from time to time. The beehive tomb at Menidi in Attica was rediscovered in the Geometric period and for centuries revered as the tomb of a hero;[4] early Mycenaean graves at Eleusis were similarly 'identified' as those of the Seven who fought against Thebes.[5] We cannot feel confident that the bones of Minos, restored to Crete by Theron of Acragas in the early fifth century, or those of Theseus brought to Athens from

[1] Thuc. I, 3.   [2] Paus. VIII, 16, 3.   [3] Diod. IV, 79, 3–4.
[4] §1, 1, 5 ff.; §1, 2, 97; §1, 4, (*a*) 13, (*b*) 135; A, 5, 181 f.   [5] §1, 3.

Scyrus in 476,[1] were correctly labelled; yet in both cases the propagandist purpose shows that Bronze Age history was real to the fifth-century Greeks, and the other examples just quoted show that their archaeological understanding was broadly sound. Thus their traditions were not the nebulous and shifting mass that some modern historians would have us believe, but firmly anchored to places and objects.

It is thus important to note that it was the Homeric epics that led to the first excavations at Mycenae, in the 1870's, by Heinrich Schliemann. Other fields of archaeology may have been opened up in the desire to explain a monument; Mycenaean archaeology grew from the desire to explore sites—Troy and Mycenae first—associated with a remembered event in history. Schliemann's work has been followed by almost a century of further exploration, in the course of which Greek prehistory has become a more purely archaeological study, with only occasional glances at tradition. But for mainland Greece in the Late Bronze Age Mycenae is still the focus: archaeology confirms that this was in truth the metropolis of Greece in what we can now see clearly as the first major efflorescence of civilization in Hellas. This is the period which classical Greece recalled in epic verse with nostalgic pride as the age of the heroes, and drew upon in tragedy for great pathetic and monitory examples of human achievement and human frailty. It was an age of great development in all the material aspects of civilization, and as such it was, despite the recession after the end of the Bronze Age, a formative period for Greece. Equally it was the first age, as Thucydides rightly saw, to evince any panhellenic feeling. Its achievements were a heritage for all Greeks. But its passing was for all an unhappy memory, colouring the classical Greeks' view of history and human destiny, and ultimately responsible perhaps for that streak of pessimism so often noticed in Greek thought.

II. THE SHAFT GRAVES AT MYCENAE

If tradition and the epic led Schliemann to the centre of Mycenaean civilization, they also led him to its beginnings. For it is at Mycenae, in the famous Shaft Graves discovered by Schliemann in 1876[2] in the early years of his work on Greek soil, and in the further group excavated in 1952–4 by Papadimitriou and Mylonas,[3] and virtually in these alone, that we can observe those

[1] Diod. IV, 79, 4; Paus. III, 3, 7.
[2] §II, 5; §II, 3.   [3] G, 9, ch. VI; A, 5, 97 ff.

changes in material civilization which mark off Late Helladic or Mycenaean from Middle Helladic. Of Middle Helladic Mycenae as a settlement we know little enough.[1] Its position in a northerly corner of the Argive plain, controlling routes to north and north-east, its easily defensible rocky citadel, and its good water supply, made it from early times a desirable home. But it may be anachronistic to read much of military and strategic significance into the site in the simpler, smaller-scale, setting of Middle Helladic times. Inhabited it certainly was, for Middle Helladic potsherds turn up wherever you dig through to the rock; but later structures have obliterated most traces of buildings. The upper part of the hill may have been fortified with a rough stone wall,[2] but this is hardly certain.

The cemetery area for this settlement, at least in later Middle Helladic times, extended westward, from the base of the hard limestone outcrop forming the citadel, along a flattish ridge of lower ground. Within it lay the two groups of graves already referred to. That known as Grave Circle B, the recently discovered group lying to the west, is, taken as a whole, somewhat earlier than Grave Circle A—Schliemann's Grave Circle—which lies close to the rock-face, within the much later 'Cyclopean' fortifications of the citadel. There is however no gap of time between the latest graves of Circle B and the earliest ones of Circle A; and the two groups should be considered together. The respect shown to Circle A in later Mycenaean times (when the whole area was terraced up level and surrounded by a finely constructed double ring of stone slabs), and the way the city wall leaves the natural line of defence to include this monumental area,[3] show that this must have been the burial place of the rulers; and it was still pointed out as such to Pausanias, some 1700 years afterwards.[4] Circle B (the surviving wall of which is, according to the excavators, of Middle Helladic date), though presumably intended for the burial of persons of some distinction, did not meet with the same reverence in subsequent centuries.

The earliest of the graves in Circle B, such as Grave Eta, are of purely Middle Helladic character: in them was laid a single burial, in the contracted posture, with a few vessels of plain 'yellow Minyan' pottery. The Shaft Graves proper exhibit many departures from this single Middle Helladic type. The grave pits are larger, ranging up to 4·50 metres by 6·40 metres (Grave IV of Circle A), with a depth of anything from one metre to five; they were lined with rubble stone walling on which rested cross-

[1] G, 8, 155 ff.
[2] §II, 4.
[3] G, 13, fig. 22; see Plate Vol.
[4] Paus. II, 16, 6.

beams supporting a 'roof' of stone slabs or of reeds or twigs plastered with clay (a method familiar in Aegean Bronze Age houses). On the pebble-lined floor the dead lay at full length, apparently fully dressed, and in many cases with rich ornaments of gold on head, neck, and arms. Beside them lay weapons of bronze—spears, swords, and daggers—and vessels not only of pottery but of bronze, silver, gold, and in a few instances of alabaster or rock-crystal. Several of the dead had masks of gold foil over their faces.[1] The profusion of gold is startling, especially in contrast with the poverty of earlier Middle Helladic remains. Above the graves stood stone slabs, either plain or crudely carved in low relief, a panel of abstract spiral ornament often accompanying a pictorial scene of fighting, hunting, or chariot-driving.[2]

A number of these Shaft Graves had been used more than once; and it was noticeable that despite the elaboration of funeral care the earlier burials and their grave-goods were rudely shoved aside to make room for later arrivals in the tomb. Whether this collective use of a tomb is by itself a seriously significant departure from the Middle Helladic practice of single burial is debatable; the personal grave and the family vault can exist side by side in one period and culture. Again, the change from contracted to extended posture might be simply the result of using larger graves. But still the access of grandeur, the prodigal use of hitherto unparalleled riches, has to be explained; and in the grave-goods themselves there are numerous innovations of form and decoration that hardly allow us to regard these burials as a natural development and elaboration of Middle Helladic practice.

The spear-heads buried with the dead are of the 'split-socket' type, which was not known in Middle Helladic times and was presumably introduced from Crete, where it is found at least from Middle Minoan III. It has been suggested that the ultimate origin may be Near Eastern.[3] The swords have long narrow blades with a central rib, sometimes engraved or decorated in relief; their wooden hilts were covered with gold embossed with patterns of spirals;[4] they had pommels of stone or ivory, in a few instances carved or, like the hilt, covered with gold embossed in animal designs. The spiral and animal motifs might be of Middle Helladic inspiration, but the sword-type is in general Minoan, or at least cognate with the Minoan type, the earliest instance of which is a Middle Minoan II ceremonial sword from Mallia. The daggers are more varied; but some at least suggest a Minoan

---

[1] See Plate 124(a).   [2] See Plate 124(b).
[3] §11, 2, 32.   [4] See Plate 126(a).

origin in the form of blade. The most ornate have hilts and pommels like those of the swords, but the broad flat rib of the blade is adorned with pictorial scenes exquisitely inlaid in gold, silver, and niello. Later Mycenaean instances of this remarkable and already sophisticated technique occur, but its origins are still to seek.[1] One Egyptian parallel will be mentioned later, and the scene on one dagger, in which leopards or panthers chase wildfowl by a papyrus-lined river stocked with silver fish, seems laid in Egypt. Africa or hither Asia might again be the setting for the lion-hunt depicted on another, though some of the hunters carry great ox-hide shields of the Minoan figure-of-eight shape.[2] If such shields were used by the occupants of the graves, and buried with them, they have left no trace, being of perishable material; but of helmets there are remains, in the form of slices of boar's tusks pierced for sewing to a leather cap. Their purpose is identified by the representation of precisely such helmets in later Mycenaean art,[3] and the type was remembered through epic poetry (*Iliad* x, 260 ff.) for centuries later still.

The decoration of the gold diadems and many of the smaller gold ornaments from the Shaft Graves is largely based on circles, rosettes and spirals, and could stem from a native Helladic tradition; but octopus patterns strongly suggest Minoan influence; so does a small gold plaque with figures of swallows, and others depicting shrines of Minoan type. Again in the metal vessels we have mixed traditions; a gold *kantharos* is of 'Minyan' shape,[4] a beaked jug also is Helladic; but several gold cups of the 'Vaphio' shape, besides jug[5] and *phiale* forms, are as obviously due to Late Minoan I influence, perhaps even of Minoan workmanship. Again, there is a silver *rhyton* shaped like a bull's head, with golden horns, which has a perfect parallel from Cnossus, in serpentine. A gold lion's-head *rhyton*, however, is far more stylized and quite un-Minoan. A few vessels of faience are unmistakably Minoan in technique and decoration, probably imports in fact. Engraved gold signets are also thoroughly Minoan in style, but not so in their subjects, which include battle scenes.

The pottery too shows new departures. Besides the Minyan pieces there are matt-painted pots equally characteristic of Middle Helladic. But some few vessels of this latter ware have pattern-schemes obviously borrowed from the Late Minoan I style; and still more strikingly we find pots of what is really yellow Minyan decorated with Minoan patterns of this same phase in a glossy

---

[1] A, 2, 140 f.   [2] See Plate 125 (*a*).   [3] See Plate 124 (*c*).
[4] See Plate 126 (*b*).   [5] See Plate 127 (*a*).

black paint new to the mainland but already established in Crete.[1] It is this which the archaeologist calls Late Helladic (or Mycenaean) I; and its affinities with Late Minoan I date the Shaft Graves to about the same time (the early sixteenth century B.C.).

This fusion of Helladic and Minoan characteristics, which is the most obvious aspect of the new culture, was at one time interpreted as the result of an extension of Minoan rule to Mycenae; but the view is not really supportable. The manner of the burials is not Minoan; the tenants of the graves, to judge from the broad, bearded faces of the gold masks,[2] are quite unlike the elegant, smooth-chinned Minoans; their bones show a 'champion's physique', though the data are not sufficient to indicate racial difference;[3] and their prodigal ostentation in grave-gifts has something barbarous about it by comparison with anything known from Crete. Again, the emphasis in their *objets d'art* on scenes of fighting and hunting is alien to the spirit of Minoan art. The rulers of Mycenae at this time cannot be Minoan.

III. THE EGYPTIAN CONNEXION

If they are native Helladic princes, we must account for their new magnificence; if not, we must look for new rulers from some third region; and there are features about the Shaft Graves which at least show that, either way, the area of our inquiry is not to be confined to the Aegean. Several objects among their contents—a crystal bowl in the form of a duck,[4] a box of Egyptian sycamore with appliqué ivory figures of dogs—are imports from Egypt;[5] the influence of Egyptian mummy-casings has been suggested to account for the gold masks; the Nilotic scene on one of the daggers has already been mentioned. Further, the carved grave *stelai* have no precedents (or immediate successors) in Greece, and no parallels in Crete; but monuments of carved stone had long been usual in Egypt. The reliefs are our earliest evidence for the horse-drawn chariot in Greece; and it may have been introduced from Egypt, where it first appears under the Hyksos rulers. Syria or Asia Minor is another possible origin.[6] Yet another link with Egypt is provided by the metal-inlay technique. For, apart from Mycenaean examples, almost the only contemporary parallel is a copper battle-axe inlaid with a golden griffin of a type found also on one of the daggers from the Shaft Graves, and subsequently a persistent feature of the Mycenaean artists'

[1] See Plate 127(b)–(d).   [2] See Plate 124(a).   [3] §II, 1.
[4] G, 9, 146 and figs. 60, 61. See Plate 126(c).   [5] §III, 3, 179–181.   [6] §III, 4.

repertory.[1] This axe was found in the tomb of Queen Ahhotpe, and bears the name of her son Amosis, the first pharaoh of the Eighteenth Dynasty, who expelled from Egypt the foreign Hyksos kings.[2] The axe, like a dagger found with it, seems imitative of Mycenaean work, rather than the other way about; but even if we should look rather for a common origin, the implied contemporaneity gives welcome corroboration of the dating of the Mycenae graves to the early sixteenth century B.C.

It is clear that the rulers of Mycenae who were buried in these graves moved in a larger world than their predecessors, a world that stretched at least to Egypt; but what events caused this widening of horizons is still difficult to explain. Its contemporaneity with the expulsion of the Hyksos from Egypt is likely to be more than chronological coincidence, but the comparatively scanty Egyptian records of the period do not help us much. The queen Ahhotpe, it has been remarked, is described in one document as 'princess of the *Haunebt*', a word that in later times, and possibly here, refers to Greece and the Aegean; and the same document implies that the *Haunebt* were allies of Amosis. From this it has been suggested that forces from Greece may have served in Egypt, against the Hyksos, as mercenaries.[3] One scholar has even surmised[4] that the reliefs on the silver vessel from Shaft Grave IV known as the 'Siege Rhyton' actually depict a scene from some such campaign in the Egyptian Delta.[5] This is not implausible, though similarities with the well-known Middle Minoan III faience 'mosaic' from Cnossus[6] suggest the picture may be traditional rather than portraying a contemporary event. If Mycenaeans did campaign in Egypt, it could be there that they learned the use of chariots, there that they acquired the taste for the Egyptian luxury goods preserved in their graves. If it be objected that Minoan Crete would hardly have permitted such direct relations between Greece and Egypt, the answer has been given[7] that the Minoan power was temporarily disorganized by the devastating earthquake—possibly to be ascribed to the volcanic explosion of the island of Thera—which shattered the Minoan palaces towards the end of Middle Minoan III. The same cause would have given the opportunity for mainlanders to undertake large-scale raids on Crete, carrying off both treasure and captives. The looting would account for the sudden access of wealth we see in the Shaft Graves: the captives would include

1 See Plate 128(*a*).   2 G, 3, 203 ff. Cf. above, ch. II, sect. v.
3 §III, 5.   4 §III, 3, ch. VI.   5 See Plate 128(*b*).
6 G, 2, vol. I, 249, 301 ff.; vol. III, 87–106.   7 §III, 5.

Minoan craftsmen of various kinds, whose presence on the mainland at this time we must in any case assume (however they came) to account for the strong Minoan influences in pottery and other materials.

The weakness of this explanation is that it is hard to believe, from what we know of the Middle Helladic people, that they were by this stage sufficiently well organized to be acceptable and useful allies against the Hyksos. Compared to the Egyptians they were backward, even barbarous, apparently quite unacquainted with the Hyksos methods of warfare, such as the use of chariots, which we are asked to believe they only learned in the course of their campaign. The only other possible approach to the problem seems to be to assume that Mycenae, and other Helladic sites, came at this time under new leaders, conquerors from without, who brought new military strength and drive, a new desire for a more sophisticated and elaborate material civilization, and a new capacity to attain it. Such a conquest has more than once been postulated,[1] and the invaders have been alleged to come, vaguely, 'from the north'; but archaeology offers little or no evidence of northerly connexions at this date, apart from the objects of amber found in the Shaft Graves—a material which may indeed have come by indirect commerce from as far away as the Baltic, and in the reverse direction a horizontally fluted gold cup, technically comparable with two from Shaft Grave IV, found at Rillaton in Cornwall.[2] Rather, as we have seen, the foreign connexions are with Crete and the Eastern Mediterranean. Crete has already been dismissed, but the possibility of conquest by invaders from Egypt and the Levant deserves serious attention, not least because it is supported by Greek traditions.

IV. DANAUS AND THE HYKSOS

It seems to have been treated as common knowledge in classical times that in the earlier heroic age a leader named Danaus had come out of Egypt and landed in the Argolid, where he subsequently became king. The story is familiar to us through the *Supplices* of Aeschylus, in which Danaus arrives as a refugee; but other versions represented him as a conqueror. His name makes him the eponymous forefather of the *Danaoi*, a tribal name, seemingly (but not clearly) equivalent in Homer with *Greeks*; and

[1] G, 12, 71 and 248; G, 11, 71–82; §III, 1, ch. 1; §III, 2. For new evidence of possible northern influences in the Shaft Grave culture see A, 1.

[2] Cf. §III, 6, 52 and frontispiece; §II, 3, nos. 392–3, pl. CIV.

Aeschylus is at pains to demonstrate that though he came from Egypt he was not an Egyptian. Myth related that he was descended from the remote heroine Io who, beloved by Zeus, had been transformed by the jealous Hera into a cow and driven to wander over land and sea till she reached Egypt. There restored to human shape she gave birth to a son, Epaphus, who became at Memphis the father of a line of kings of whom Danaus was the latest. What vague recollections of the cow-goddess Hathor may be preserved in the myth of Io it seems now impossible to disentangle. There may be a trace of that cult in the Hera βοῶπις (cow-faced) who was worshipped at the Argive Heraeum. Nor is it clear how far the tale of Io's wanderings may have been invented, how far merely invoked, to give Danaus the respectability of an ultimately Greek pedigree. But the uncomfortable fact that he was a foreigner could not be forgotten. In a telling anecdote in the ancient life of Isocrates he is grouped as such with Cadmus and Pelops, from Syria and Asia Minor respectively, and with Philip of Macedon. Such a legend of foreign conquest cannot be pure fiction; even if we believe that the individual Danaus (who is never named by Homer) is merely the invention of some later logographer or genealogist, we must at least think of him as invented to personify an event of which there was an actual tradition. The literary sources[1] are in fact reasonably clear and consistent in their placing of the event. Danaus belongs to the earliest phase of the heroic age; he was the ancestor of Danaë, herself an eponymous figure, known to Homer as the mother of Perseus; and Perseus is in all tradition the founder of Mycenae, and an ancestor of Heracles and of Eurystheus, who was succeeded on the throne of Mycenae by the Pelopids, the dynasty in power at the time of the Trojan War. Danaus thus represents the beginning of the heroic age in the Argolid; and those who made it their business to co-ordinate and date the Greek traditions placed him in the sixteenth century B.C. (the *Marmor Parium* gives 1511). If the historian nowadays seeks a period in the Bronze Age history of Egypt when a king of that country, not being an Egyptian, could have crossed the seas to found a new kingdom in the Argolid, he will arrive at the first half of the sixteenth century, when the foreign Hyksos rulers were expelled by Ahhotpe's son Amosis.[2]

Thus the legendary conquest of Danaus, and the arrival of a new dynasty at Mycenae, which seems necessary to explain the efflorescence of material culture we observe in the Mycenae Shaft

[1] E.g. Hdt. II, 91; Paus. II, 16; Diod. I, 28, 2.   [2] §IV, I.

Graves, may be regarded as one and the same thing.[1] That is to say that, in tune with the tradition, we may postulate the conquest of the Argolid by some of the displaced Hyksos leaders from Egypt in the early sixteenth century B.C. By so doing we can readily account for the Egyptian imports or influences in the graves, and for the introduction of war-chariots. That their arrival is not accompanied by any more wholesale Egyptianizing is perfectly compatible with what we know of the Hyksos in Egypt. There they had introduced little but new military techniques and organization; they do not represent a mass movement of population; rather they were a warrior caste, taking over the highly developed Egyptian civilization as a going concern. They introduced no new language; for their few official inscriptions the native Egyptian served. Their organization was perhaps vaguely 'feudal': there seem to have been various more or less independent principalities in Hyksos Egypt, owing a general allegiance to a single king.[2] Useful analogies may be found, in more recent history, in the age of the Vikings and the Normans.[3] Individual leaders would be frequently on the watch for opportunities of self-aggrandisement at the expense of their fellows, even of their king. Against such a background we should not expect the arrival of 'Danaus' to be an isolated event, nor a large-scale national campaign. It is probably better, historically, to envisage it as one of a series of small-scale expeditions, perhaps spread over a considerable period of years. Perhaps we should regard him as a symbol rather than a historical personage. Though there is an intriguing similarity of name between his ancestor Epaphus and the Hyksos Apophis, the attempt to collate his genealogy with the sketchy records of the Hyksos dynasties[4] is not in detail encouraging.

In the legends, indeed, the story of Danaus is not wholly isolated.[5] At least in the later genealogies he is made the nephew of Agenor, a king in Syria, and so cousin to Europa, the mother of Minos of Crete, and to Cadmus. The latter is somewhat analogous to Danaus as a foreign invader and conqueror in Greece. From his home in Syria (Phoenicia) he is supposed to have come first to Samothrace and later to Boeotia, where he settled at Thebes;[6] that city in heroic legend is regularly *Cadmeia*, the city of Cadmus, its people *Cadmeans*. His eastern origin is at first sight as implausible as that of Danaus, and must equally

---

[1] Cf. §IV, 4. [2] Cf. above, ch. II, sect. III; also §IV, 2; 3; 5–7; A, 7.
[3] G, 10, 210; §III, 2, 6–8. [4] §IV, 1, cf. above, ch. II.
[5] Cf. §IV, 4, 80. [6] Diod. v, 48–9.

involve the memory of a historical reality, even though we cannot at present relate it to archaeological evidence. The story of the origin of Minos as son of Europa, who came from Syria, is not a tale of conquest, but here again we have the picture of a new dynasty with Near Eastern affiliations, such a new dynasty as the archaeologist deduces from the new drive and progress exhibited by the remains of the Middle Minoan III period. That, of course, was well before the age of the Shaft Graves at Mycenae; but the genealogical affiliations indicate that later Greece believed there was some connexion between all these movements; and it may well be that we ought ourselves to view the advances of Middle Minoan III and the rise of Mycenaean civilization as both phases in one big westward movement—the same movement, conceivably, that in a yet earlier phase had produced the Hyksos domination of Egypt.

None of this can be regarded as historically proved; but it is a working theory that will account for the observed archaeological facts of the beginnings of Mycenaean civilization. It helps us, moreover, to an explanation not only of the Egyptian features in the Shaft Graves, but also of the far more prominent Minoan influences. The postulated invaders, as in Egypt, did not introduce a culture characteristically their own. But neither, in Greece, did they find ready-made the luxuries and material conveniences that by their sojourn in Egypt they had learned to use and expect, and these had therefore to be imported from the nearest source— Crete. The older rulers of Mycenae may have been ignorant or afraid of the grandeurs of Cnossus; perhaps both. These new masters would be neither; they had the experience and background to approach the Minoans on an equality; they had alternatively, if they could not get what they desired by peaceable means, the military prowess to take it by force.

V. PELOPS

Whether the legend of Pelops, in its historical bearing, should be grouped with those of Danaus and Cadmus is not easy to decide. The later Greeks seem to have had no tradition or theory that directly connects them; but if we ourselves seek a historical context for Pelops, it must be found at any rate early in Mycenaean times, since his descendants are represented as in conflict with the Perseid descendants of Danaus. We can perhaps best place him at the beginning of the Mycenaean period.[1] That he was a

[1] Cf. §IV, 4, 80.

real figure of history was accepted even by so rational a historian
as Thucydides,[1] and there was general agreement that he came,
as an invader, from Asia Minor, though whether (as Pindar
implies) from Lydia, where in late antiquity visitors were still
shown the tomb of his father Tantalus, and a 'throne of Pelops'
on Mt Sipylus,[2] or from Phrygia or some other district, was not so
certain. The story of the chariot race with Oenomaus, as a result
of which he gained the kingdom of Elis in the north-west
Peloponnese, a story obviously very familiar to Pindar, is not told
by Thucydides, who is more concerned with the *successors* of
Pelops, who became rulers of Mycenae and so of all Greece.
Already in Homer Pelops is called πλήξιππος (*Iliad* 11, 104);
unless the race had been of venerable antiquity in the tale it
would hardly have been used, as it was, for the theme of the
sculptures in the pediment over the entrance to that most important of Panhellenic cult-places, the temple of Zeus at Olympia.
Pelops was indeed regarded as a grandson of Zeus; he had
received the sceptre of his sovereignty from the god Hermes; and
he was one of the most noted heroes of the Greek race.

In modern terms he appears to some to be the eponym of a
tribe called Pelopes, a tribe not otherwise known, but possibly
implied in the name of the Peloponnese, which could as well
mean 'Isle of the Pelopes', as 'Isle of Pelops'.[3] As an eponym he is,
like Danaus, not strictly a 'historical figure'; but in the same way
he does at least *represent* a dimly remembered event or period of
events—the conquest of part of the Peloponnese by invaders
from Asia Minor, perhaps indeed owing their success to the use
of war-chariots. Such an event we can hardly place very much
later than the era of the Mycenae Shaft Graves. As to his
Asiatic origin, the tradition is overwhelmingly strong, and the
establishment and gradual expansion of the Hittites[4] in central
Anatolia could easily by early Mycenaean times have resulted in a
displacement of peoples to the west of them, in Phrygia and Lydia.

Archaeologically, there is not much that can be collated with
the Pelops story. We cannot at present point to any clearly
Anatolian feature or influences in early Mycenaean civilization,
unless indeed we believe that chariots were introduced from that
quarter rather than from Egypt. That is not precluded, but the
story does not imply that chariots were a novelty at the time;
Oenomaus, king of horse-breeding Elis, was already familiar

[1] Thuc. i, 9.   [2] Paus. ii, 22, 3 and v, 13, 7.
[3] The latter interpretation is given by Thucydides, i, 9, 2.
[4] See above, ch. vi.

with them. Nor do we yet know much, either from settlement-sites or from tombs, about Elis at this time. Thus the only criterion for dating the conquest attached to the name of Pelops seems to be that it must come sufficiently far in time before the annexation of the Argolid by his descendants—an event for which there is, as we shall see later, a reasonable archaeological identification. In other words it must fall within Late Helladic I or Late Helladic II; and it could conceivably be contemporary with the invasion which at Mycenae we postulate to account for the rise of the Shaft Graves culture.

VI. THE PROGRESS OF MYCENAEAN SETTLEMENT

Mycenae is still the site at which we can best observe the transition from Middle Helladic to Late Helladic culture; it may indeed have been the first to feel the impact of the new influences. But it was not the only one, though nowhere else are the evidences so spectacular. 'Shaft Graves' of similar type, dated by pottery of the new Minoanizing Late Helladic I style, have been found at Lerna in the Argolid,[1] at Eleusis,[2] and on the island of Scopelos.[3] At least at Lerna the siting of the graves suggests a new régime: one is cut into an area which all through the Middle Helladic period had been *tabu*. Unfortunately most of the contents disappeared when at some date later in the Mycenaean period the graves were deliberately emptied. At Eleusis the actual graves differed from the classic shaft grave type in having a side-pit at right angles to the main grave, perhaps to serve as an approach to the burial place, to facilitate subsequent interments without disturbing the main roofing of the tomb. We have here a feature which is much more fully developed in the 'beehive' or 'tholos' tombs which at Mycenae soon succeed the shaft-grave type, and at several sites seem to be contemporary with it.[4] The tholos tomb[5] takes even further the monumental intentions of the shaft grave: it consists of a circular chamber, lined with masonry rising in corbelled horizontal courses to a point—the shape of an old-fashioned skep beehive—and is approached by a more or less horizontal open passage, this too being usually lined with masonry. Some of the earlier tholos tombs were built almost at ground level, and then covered with a great mound of earth; but the tendency was more and more to sink them well below ground

---

[1] §vi, 5. [2] §i, 3; A, 5, 89 f. [3] §vi, 25.
[4] G, 8, 161 ff., 170 f. [5] See Plate 129 (a).

in a sloping hillside, so that only the peak of the chamber needed covering with a mound, which incidentally served as a visible monument and landmark.

The origin of this kind of tomb has been much debated, and far too much emphasis has at times been laid on alleged Minoan affinities.[1] Very few of the circular burial places of the Cretan Messara can in fact ever have been stone-roofed, and scarcely any are late enough in date to suggest continuity of practice from Crete to Mycenaean Greece. The use of corbelling as a means of spanning a space with stone masonry was not new at this time, and may indeed have been borrowed from the Minoans (though it was not precisely confined to them). But in general we should probably think of the tholos tomb as the Mycenaean answer to the problem apparent also in the shaft graves—that of constructing a monumental tomb, both permanent and accessible for repeated use or tendance.

The earliest datable Mycenaean *tholoi* are not in the Argolid, but in unexpectedly outlying regions of Greece. One near Karditsa[2] in Thessaly is reported to have contained *Middle Helladic* pottery; and two in Messenia (at Koryphasion[3] near Pylus and at a site called Peristeria[4] near Kyparissia) are dated by that same mixture of Middle Helladic and Late Helladic I which characterizes the Mycenae Shaft Graves. At Peristeria below the floor of another such tomb were found rich grave gifts including gold vessels similar to those at Mycenae.[5] It is clear that these *tholoi* must belong to very early Mycenaean times. Such tombs, demanding much organized labour for their construction, can only be the tombs of the local rulers: nothing of comparable scale precedes them, and their appearance at this time implies the establishment of new centres of power, a new social and political situation, that is most readily explained on the assumption of invasion and conquest. Such conquest need not have involved large bodies of immigrants; Franks, Venetians, and Genoese have shown in the Middle Ages how the occupation of a limited number of harbours and commanding castles may be sufficient to ensure the control of large parts of Greece. Nor need we suppose that it all happened at once.

The course of events cannot indeed now be reconstructed; only the results of the new settlement are apparent. Of the actual habitation sites of the early Mycenaean period we know all too little, partly because the houses or palaces were so often damaged

[1] §vi, 12.   [2] §vi, 6; cf. A, 3, site no. 545.   [3] §iv, 2; A, 3, no. 207.
[4] §iv, 22 (1960), 152–8; §vi, 32; A, 3, no. 235.   [5] §vi, 22 (1965), 84–92; A, 4.

and rebuilt in later generations, as at Mycenae itself, or Tiryns, or Pylus, partly through lack of sufficient exploration. At Iolcus, for example (near the modern Volo), an important Mycenaean palace site, already inhabited at the transition from Middle Helladic to Late Helladic I, is known only from trial-trenches.[1] At Kako-vatos (Triphylian Pylus) the settlement implied by the three early tholos tombs has yet to be located.[2] Such tombs are in fact for the present far better evidence of the distribution of the new culture. By the Late Helladic II period (fifteenth century B.C.) they are scattered all over central and southern Greece. At least one in the Iolcus region (at Kapakli[3]) is of this period. Those in Messenia already mentioned are succeeded by others: it was obviously a forward area. There is one at Vaphio near Sparta,[4] famous for the two gold cups found in it. One of the most splendid, known in later antiquity as the Treasury of Minyas,[5] at Orchomenus in Boeotia, may also belong to Late Helladic II, for the carved stone ceiling of the side-chamber[6] closely resembles Late Minoan II designs. In Attica there is one in the plain of Marathon,[7] and others at Thoricus[8]—one of these on an unusual plan that suggests local experimentation in structural methods. Of the nine known at Mycenae itself, perhaps six belong to the first two centuries of the Mycenaean period; others of Late Helladic II date have been excavated at the Argive Heraeum and at Berbati.[9] This list is deliberately confined to examples that are known to date fairly early in the Mycenaean age, and even for that purpose it could probably be augmented; but it is enough to show their already wide distribution.

Under the new overlords Helladic Greece was taking on a different aspect; what had been a village civilization was replaced by a palace civilization, comparable soon in quality with that of Crete. Crete was indeed a continuing source of inspiration and innovation in all material things. We can see it most obviously in Late Helladic pottery. The Minoan decorative patterns which were first applied in the Shaft Graves period to the already technically excellent native ware (yellow Minyan) were at first haltingly drawn, and with incomplete mastery of the new glossy paint; but in the Late Helladic II style[10] of the next century they are under full control, gaining a restraint and refinement perhaps

---

[1] §vi, 22 (1957), 31 f.; (1960), 56–61.
[2] §vi, 8; 9; 21.
[3] §vi, 17.
[4] §vi, 31.
[5] Paus. ix, 36, 4; §vi, 27; G, 12, 126–9.
[6] See Plate 129(*b*).
[7] §vi, 22 (1958), 23–7.
[8] G, 12, 383–5; §vi, 28.
[9] §vi, 36, 387–96; §vi, 38; G, 13, 16 ff.
[10] See Plate 130.

deriving from an indigenous Helladic spirit, even somewhat in advance of the Minoan originals. The finest products of Late Helladic II are nearly indistinguishable from the Palace Style jars of Late Minoan II at Cnossus; and one peculiarly Mainland type, the so-called Ephyraean kylix (a Minyan goblet plus a Minoan flower-motif placed with subtle simplicity), actually finds inferior imitations in Crete.[1] Other forms common to both areas are so similar that they can be tied to their place of origin only by the closest stylistic analysis.

Much of the evidence again comes from tombs, for the Mycenaeans were lavish in the quantity of gifts deposited with the dead, even in the rock-cut chamber-tombs of the ordinary people. Cemeteries of such tombs, apparently family burial-places used for generations, have been explored in many parts of Greece. Both in the Argolid (as at Mycenae,[2] and at Prosymna[3] near the Argive Heraeum) and in less central areas (as Euboea[4] and Rhodes[5]) they date from Late Helladic II (occasionally Late Helladic I) onwards, and are the small-scale parallel to the tholos tombs, completely replacing the Middle Helladic type. In them we find, besides pottery, some vessels and tools of bronze, occasionally ornaments of gold or semi-precious stone or ivory, or perhaps a dagger with metal inlay. But these are nothing to the luxury objects used at a prince's funeral, as the very few unrifled tholos burials testify. The gold cups of Vaphio, with their repoussé designs of bull-hunting, represent the high-water mark of Minoan art—for Minoan they are, whether the artist worked in Crete or Laconia; others, from Dendra[6] in the Argolid, do suggest a more Helladic strain of design in their less pictorial composition; and one of these, with bulls' heads inlaid in the technique known from the Shaft Graves,[7] has no parallels in Crete.

The absorption of Minoan fashions was proceeding in architecture also, though it is not so precisely observable, because the main palace sites suffered damage and rebuilding in the course of their history, and the principal structures now surviving are of later Mycenaean date (Late Helladic III). But from fragmentary remains recovered from lower levels at Mycenae[8] and elsewhere, and from the only partially excavated palace that lies under the buildings of modern Thebes,[9] we can deduce that many Minoan

---

[1] §vi, 34; G, 2, vol. iv, 359–70. [2] §vi, 33, 121 ff. [3] §vi, 3, 231.

[4] §vi, 11. [5] §vi, 19; §vi, 29, 5–11; §vi, 10.

[6] §vi, 24, 31 f., frontispiece and pls. ix–xi.

[7] §vi, 24, 38, and pls. i, xii–xv.

[8] §vi, 35, 189–99; §vi, 36, 268 f.; G, 13, 22, 87. [9] §vi, 16.

features were early adopted: more finely-cut masonry, the decorative use of columns, the facing of thresholds and door-frames with gypsum, decorative carving in stone, and a full use of fresco painting on walls, in a style virtually indistinguishable from the Minoan.[1] The focus of the Mycenaean palace, however, was doubtless as in Late Helladic III the *megaron*, the big hall with a columned fore-porch and a central hearth, which appears to be traditional in Hellas from Middle Helladic times. Here again we find the new leaders accepting an established thing, but elaborating and improving on it with more luxurious adjuncts from abroad. The ready fusion of the new and the old implies that they had a considerable capacity for making themselves acceptable; but clearly Greece had much to gain by acceptance.

It is likely that the natural resources of Greece were being developed too in this period. We may be thought credulous if we believe literally the story that it was 'Danaus' who first introduced in the Argive plain a system of wells and irrigation[2] such as are still essential to its agricultural prosperity, but it is at least clear from settlements and tombs that in the Late Helladic period the area supported a far bigger population than ever before. Again, in Boeotia there is surviving evidence in the form of banked channels and rock-cut tunnels that at some time in the Mycenaean period the Copais basin was drained and made available for cultivation.[3] This must have been done at any rate within the first half of the Mycenaean period; it is a prerequisite of the prosperity that lies behind the magnificent 'treasury of Minyas', a prosperity remembered long after in Homer,[4] when Orchomenus and Egyptian Thebes could be mentioned in the same breath as cities possessed of extraordinary wealth. In Attica, moreover, the flourishing Mycenaean citadel and tombs of Thoricus may imply that mines of lead or silver were already being worked in that area.

That there was frequent intercourse with Crete is self-evident from the predominant Minoan influences in the remains, and among the Aegean islands the growing importation and influence of Mycenaean pottery in Melos[5] shows that this island had by Late Helladic II come to be culturally as well as geographically midway between Crete and the mainland. At Ialysus in Rhodes the tomb-contents show there must have been some Mycenaean settlement alongside the known Minoan one at Trianda.[6] On

---

[1] §vi, 26. [2] Strabo, I, 23; viii, 371. [3] §vi, 15. [4] *Iliad* ix, 381–2.
[5] §vi, 10, 192–201; §vi, 1, 159–65 and 263–72; §vi, 7, 16–21.
[6] §vi, 10, 180 f.; §vi, 20.

the mainland of Asia Minor, Mycenaean contacts are evident at Miletus[1] from the very beginning of the period, and at Troy[2] from Late Helladic II onwards.

Further afield exported Mycenaean pottery bears testimony to trade with Egypt, with southern Palestine, and with Syria.[3] The bulk of finds is not large, but in Egypt there seem to be more imports of Mycenaean pottery than of Minoan; and in all these areas it was the beginning of a trade destined to grow enormously in the next century. For the present, it is likely that the power of Crete hampered any free expansion in that direction, though the establishment of Mycenaeans in Rhodes would be a firm step forward in establishing the eastward trade routes. The Cretan obstacle may, too, have been responsible for a vigorous and questing Mycenaean activity in the central Mediterranean. Pottery as early as the transition from Middle Helladic to Late Helladic I has turned up in Lipari and adjacent islands, evidence perhaps of an attempt to exploit Lipari's obsidian and so avoid competition in Melos. (This explanation is supported by the fact that these contacts in the Aeolian Islands seem not to have been maintained after the fall of Crete.)[4]

To all these overseas areas the pottery itself was perhaps an export commodity, but there may have been others of a perishable kind. The same is true of imports, though some at least involve no guesswork. Gold must have come via Egypt or the Levant; so must ivory; so must exotics like the ostrich eggs which, mounted with gold and silver, have been found in royal tombs at Mycenae[5] and Dendra.[6] Troy was perhaps an entrepôt for various goods from beyond; perhaps, as the legend of Laomedon and Heracles implies, it also supplied Mycenaean Greece with horses.[7] And though there is but scanty evidence of contact with Cyprus until Late Helladic III,[8] it is difficult to believe that Greece was not already interested in the copper mines there.

VII. THE FIRST HEROIC AGE

If we are correct in believing that the events associated with the actual beginnings of Mycenaean civilization can be identified in legend, it will be proper to ask whether legend does not similarly remember some at least of the events of the first two centuries of

[1] §VI, 10, 201–3; §VI, 39.
[2] §VI, 4, vol. III, 16.
[3] §VI, 37; §VI, 29, 102–4; §VI, 10, 203–15.
[4] §VI, 30, 7–53.
[5] §II, 3, 146, no. 828 and pl. CXLI.
[6] §VI, 24, 37 and pl. III.
[7] §VI, 23, 70 and 252.
[8] §VI, 29, 25–31.

the Mycenaean age, the phases which we nowadays refer to as Late Helladic I and Late Helladic II. But before attempting to answer this question it may be well to consider further the general relationship between the happenings of history and the exploits of the heroic age. Greek tradition does from the earliest times look back to *two* heroic ages. This is already apparent in Homer, where we find that the heroes who fought at Troy are represented as having already a historic perspective of worthies of earlier generations. These *fortes ante Agamemnona* are sometimes directly referred to by older men, such as Phoenix and Nestor, who had known them and shared in their exploits in their youth; or there may be less direct reference, as when Odysseus recounts (in *Odyssey* xi, 235 ff.) the tale of fair women whom he had seen in Hades—Tyro, wife of Cretheus, who by Poseidon was mother of Pelias and Neleus; Antiope who by Zeus was made mother of Amphion and Zethus, who fortified Thebes; Leda, the mother of Castor and Polydeuces; Alcmena the wife of Amphitryon and mother (again by Zeus) of Heracles. Others too are listed who, though not so mated with gods, were wives or mothers of men already revered as heroes—Epicaste the mother and wife of Oedipus; Ariadne, whom Theseus brought from Cnossus; Procris the wife of Cephalus; Eriphyle who betrayed her husband Amphiaraus for a golden necklace, and so on. And in another passage (*Iliad* xiv, 313 ff.) Zeus, recalling his past amours, makes mention of Ixion's wife, the mother of Peirithous, of Danaë the mother of Perseus, of Europa the mother of Minos and Rhadamanthys, and of Alcmena and Semele. This last, as mother of the god Dionysus, should remind us that we have here to deal with religious myth as much as with legend of human heroes; but both these passages, as well as the more direct references to be discussed later, show that for the poet of the epics there was already a past beyond the era of the Trojan War; and for all their divine parentage these earlier heroes at least represent a historic period. Their stories are not always recounted; but even the passing mention of them suggests that for the audience of the epic the stories were known, even if not in the form in which later ages told them. Several of them—Perseus, Minos, Amphion and Zethus, Pelias and Neleus—are founders of cities or dynasties, and probably symbolize in their own way the beginnings of the Mycenaean period. Of the brothers Pelias and Neleus we are actually told that one dwelt at Iolcus and the other at sandy Pylus—both areas, as we have seen, of early Mycenaean settlement. The semi-divine pedigrees may well recall the coming of unknown strangers, with Zeus as their patron deity, who as conquerors took wives among the indigenous population.[1]

In Homer we are given no reason for Neleus' migration to Pylus; but later ages supposed the two brothers were rivals for power in the Iolcus region. Another hint of the kind of interrelation between the new principalities is preserved in the statement (*Odyssey* XI, 281–5) that Neleus married Chloris, the daughter of Amphion of Orchomenus, again a city whose greatness belongs to the early Mycenaean age. We cannot expect from such allusions to reconstruct the sequence of actual events in that age; but the legends do present a picture plausibly consistent with the general conditions of an age of resettlement, and generally consonant in their localization with what we know from archaeology of the distribution of the centres of power.[2] Thus we have in Homer from the lips of Nestor the reminiscence of local wars of the Pylians against the Arcadians (*Iliad* VII, 132 ff.), and against the Epeioi of Elis (*Iliad* XI, 670 ff.), besides a rather less specific reference to fighting against the forces of Heracles, who of course represents the Argolid (*Iliad* XI, 690). These references, together with the legend of Nestor's personal survival for several generations, are sufficient to suggest a kingdom of Pylus stretching from Messenia to Elis and Arcadia, and still maintaining its integrity (whatever may have happened to other parts of the Peloponnese) at the time of the Trojan War. Pylus, it seems, is as much the name of the kingdom as of its capital; and as this kingdom would include both the Messenian and the Triphylian city, the ancient question which was Nestor's seat is not here of much importance.

Another tale of earlier heroic warfare, the story of the siege of Calydon, is related (*Iliad* IX, 527 ff.) by the aged Phoenix—γέρων ἱππηλάτα Φοῖνιξ. It is a striking fact that this title of ἱππηλάτα or its parallel ἱππότα, with its curiously antique grammatical form, is only applied in the epics to heroes like Phoenix and Nestor who belong to this earlier age, ancestors of those who fought at Troy; moreover they almost all have names with the older termination -*eus*, as Tydeus and Oineus, father and grandfather of Diomede, Peleus the father of Achilles, and Phyleus, a son of Augeas (who himself belongs in the early chronological context).[3] This can hardly be fortuitous, and increases one's faith in the origin of these legends in historical events of the earlier Mycenaean age. The point is of special importance in relation to the siege of

---

[1] Cf. §VII, 1, 357 f.; §VII, 2, ch. VI *passim*; §X, 4, 233 f.
[2] §VII, 1, 374 f.; G, 10, ch. II.   [3] G, 10, 26 f.

Calydon, for here the legend gives us a piece of history not yet available from archaeological sources. The historian may not ignore the implication of the importance of Calydon in early Mycenaean times, an importance that had been lost by the time of the Trojan War, when, as the *Catalogue* tells us (*Iliad* II, 638 ff.), the dynasty of Oineus was extinct. Archaeologically, little is yet known of Mycenaean Calydon,[1] and more detailed investigation would provide an interesting test of the veracity of the tradition.

These tales are of interest too for the motivation of the wars of the time. The attack on Calydon resulted from a quarrel that arose in the hunting of the Calydonian boar; the war with Elis was caused by cattle-raiding, which was duly punished in kind. These are the activities—fighting, hunting, and raiding—that are regarded as typical of the heroic age; and there may be some truth in the picture at least for the earlier stages of the Mycenaean period, before the boundaries of the new princedoms were well defined. The subsequent more peaceful progress of Mycenaean civilization is no matter for epic, and Nestor or Phoenix has nothing to tell of trading voyages. Even so, there seems to be some tradition of the overseas activities of the early Mycenaeans. We find it, for example, in the story of Bellerophon, as related in Homer (*Iliad* VI, 155 ff.) by his grandson Glaucus of Lycia when he met Diomede in single combat. The chronological setting of the story is given by the fact that Bellerophon was a contemporary of Oineus of Calydon. The events are famous enough: how Anteia, consort of Proetus, the king of the Argolid, played Potiphar's wife to Bellerophon, and her husband therefore sent him off to Lycia with his own death-warrant in a sealed letter. Then the king of Lycia sends Bellerophon on various dangerous missions—to slay the Chimaera, to fight with the Solymi and the Amazons in the heart of Anatolia—missions from which Bellerophon unexpectedly returns successful and is rewarded with the hand of the king's daughter. The folk-tale form and the fantasy of the creatures involved should not blind us to the possible historical implications in the localization of this story. Perhaps there really was contact (and even written correspondence) between the Argolid of Late Helladic II and Lycia; perhaps Mycenaeans did fight, as allies or mercenaries, against the distant enemies of Lycia; perhaps they did really travel to the Aleian Plain in Cilicia, as the outcast Bellerophon did. We have seen that their merchandise reached as far as Syria and Egypt; there is nothing impossible in their warriors campaigning in Asia Minor.

[1] A, 3, no. 311.

Even more improbable, if we argue from the lack of archaeological evidence, is the story of the Argonauts, who sailed through
the straits and on to the far end of the Black Sea in quest of the
Golden Fleece. Yet this is as firmly planted in tradition as can be;
already in Homer their ship the Argo is πασιμέλουσα, the story
so well known that that one name is enough to evoke it. All
accounts, early or late, consistently place this adventure in the
first heroic age; it is already a theme of epic song by the time of
Odysseus; and Iolcus as the point of departure fits well with an
early Mycenaean setting for it. For later Greeks it was a panhellenic enterprise, the equivalent, along with the siege of
Calydon, of what the Trojan War was for the next heroic age.
The voyage through the Black Sea to Colchis may perhaps recall
real trading voyages; some have found in the Golden Fleece
itself an early technique of gold-washing practised in the rivers of
that Eldorado that later made Croesus so fabulously wealthy.
But we have to confess that there is no archaeological trace of such
trading; the Mycenaean potsherds reported from east of the Halys
seem to be an illusion.[1] Conceivably it was one particular voyage
to Colchis that was remembered, simply because it was so
exceptional an expedition; any normal direct trading through the
Hellespont may have been inhibited by the power of Troy. Thus
we can get no more than a grain of the pure metal of history out of
the Fleece; but we should be unwise to toss it aside as without
significance, since at least the localization of such tales, when all
fairy tale and religious myth have been sifted away, does in other
cases show a foundation of fact. Thus, for example, the scene even
of such a tale as that of Perseus and Andromeda was firmly set,
at Joppa on the south Palestinian coast;[2] and archaeology at least
shows that that coast was not unknown to Mycenaeans in the
Late Helladic II period[3] which Perseus represents. It would be
perverse of us to regard this as fortuitous coincidence.

VIII. PERSEUS: THE CONSOLIDATION OF THE MYCENAEAN ARGOLID

The mention of Perseus brings us back to the Argolid and to the
centre of Mycenaean civilization; for, to quote Pausanias (ii, 15,
4), 'that Perseus was the founder of Mycenae is known to any
Greek'. Much else Pausanias thereafter relates, as to how
Perseus came to found Mycenae, which he implies was not so

---

[1] §vi, 29, 24.   [2] Strabo i, 42 f.   [3] §vi, 29, 53–8.

well known, and which may involve the deliberate collation and conflation of several lines of tradition, though the account of Apollodorus (II. ii. I–II. iv. 4) differs but little from that of Pausanias. The essence of it all is that the kingdom of Argos, which was one under Danaus, was split up by his descendants, Acrisius ruling Argos, while Tiryns, Midea, and the Heraeum fell to his brother or nephew Proetus. So it remained until Perseus, the son of Danaë and Zeus, returned from the exile imposed by his grandfather Acrisius, took over Tiryns from Proetus' son Megapenthes (giving him Argos in exchange) and then annexed Midea and founded (or rather fortified?) Mycenae—which hence becomes the capital of a reunited Argolid.

How literally we are to believe this tradition archaeology cannot tell us: too little is known of the earlier history of Mycenaean occupation at all the sites concerned—at Mycenae and Tiryns because of the later buildings, at Midea through lack of evidence from excavation of the settlement. Argos seems never to have been a site of much importance in the period, and indeed once Mycenae was established it could hardly be so. But there are in the tradition strong inherent probabilities. The split-up of the kingdom, in the period before the new principalities were fully established, is consonant with the general picture of the age; it could be easily achieved by a strong leader at Tiryns, which powerfully controls the sea-approach to the rest of the area, and Tiryns plays the same important role in the reunification by Perseus. For him, coming by sea, it would be the first objective, and it is easy to imagine Megapenthes relinquishing it by 'strategic withdrawal' to Argos (though later Argives would prefer the story of exchange by consent). Then follows the annexation of Midea, the next line of defence, and the final consolidation of the conquest (for such, surely, it is) by the fortification of Mycenae, which controls the northern exits from the plain as Tiryns controls the sea approach. Henceforth the Mycenaean kingdom of the Argolid depends on these two cardinal points.

The only real difficulty in accepting all this as history is that archaeology shows us Mycenae as a place of wealth and importance from the very start of the Late Helladic period, while the tradition places its 'founder' Perseus a good deal later than that Danaus whom we have seen good reason to accept as representing the first Late Helladic invasions. The most likely explanation would seem to be a false collation of two traditions, that of Perseus preserved at Mycenae and that of Danaus preserved at Argos. Perseus, unlike Danaus, is already familiar in Homer

(*Iliad* XIV, 319 f.), and with *Danaë* (a woman of the *Danaoi*) for his mother and Zeus for his father he fits the pattern of invader-founder that we have already observed. His story should in its nature be parallel and contemporary with that of Danaus' invasion rather than subsequent to it; and it is odd that though Mycenae is represented as being established as Perseus' capital at the expense of Argos, yet Argos takes no effective part in the tale at all. What *seems* to have happened is that Argos preserved or developed a generalized tradition of the Late Helladic I conquest, under an eponymous Danaus, while Mycenae, the real centre, had the more particular tradition of an individual Perseus. In historical times, when Argos was the greater city, the early supremacy of Argos and the line of Danaus were given a respectably long innings by making Perseus only a later, secondary conqueror, descended from the Argive line. This is admittedly speculative; what emerges as fact, confirmed by archaeology, is that at an early stage in the Mycenaean settlement of Greece Mycenae assumed the supremacy in the Argolid, which thus became a major power in the north-east Peloponnese, matching the kingdom of Pylus in the south-west and that of Elis (which we meet in the Homeric account of Nestor's wars) in the north-west.

IX. HERACLES AND EARLY MYCENAEAN HISTORY

The expansion of the Mycenaean kingdom of the Argolid is further depicted, in a different and less historical form, in the stories of Heracles, who is commonly represented as a descendant of Perseus. Heracles is indeed in later times a figure of myth, who seems to bear on his shoulders the whole achievement of the early Mycenaean period, though largely transmogrified to the fairy-tale tasks of a Jack-the-Giant-Killer. But in Homer he is no more mythical or less human than other sons of Zeus by mortal mothers, though he was the mightiest and most famed of them, and few essentially fabulous deeds are related of him. His birth alone is remarkable: it was a famous tale how the jealous Hera dogged this favoured son of Zeus from the very first, when she colluded with Eileithyia to contrive that Eurystheus should be born before him and so obtain the power among men that Zeus had intended for Heracles (*Iliad* XIX, 96 ff.). As a result, Heracles spent much of his career as the vassal of Eurystheus, who imposed upon him the series of difficult tasks so familiar in later literature and art (though not specified in Homer) as the *Labours of Heracles*.

It is notable that he was born at Thebes (or at least brought up there as an exile); and we have here the picture of a political tension between Thebes and the Argolid, a struggle for supremacy, of which legend has indeed so much to say that we may well take it to be historical. Nor should we ignore the fact that while Heracles is the favourite son of Zeus, his opponent and master Eurystheus is patronized by Hera, who always had a specially strong cult in the Argolid.[1] There must be in this some reminiscence of a conflict of cults in the early Mycenaean period, before the immigrant rulers and their gods were fully accepted. Hints of similar conflicts are to be found in other areas: that of Athena and Poseidon, illustrated in the west pediment of the Parthenon, is perhaps the most familiar.[2]

Alongside the story of the twelve labours there seem always to have survived a number of other legends of Heracles, for which the later writers endeavoured to find a place either earlier or later in his career. Though some may simply represent forms of tradition alternative to the Twelve Labours, others are clearly separate, and in several cases they look more historical. Thus, for example, we cannot neglect the tradition that Heracles, in his youth, fought against Orchomenus on behalf of Thebes, and defeated it by flooding the land around.[3] What we know of Mycenaean Orchomenus shows that it may indeed have been a rival to Thebes in Late Helladic II; and the ascription to the Minyae (by Strabo) of the early drainage works of Copaïs which we have already noted shows sound historical tradition or insight.[4] Their destruction could really have sealed the economic fate of Orchomenus and left Thebes supreme in Boeotia.

As for the Labours themselves, their chief interest for the historian lies, as Nilsson long ago pointed out, in their localizations, which in the eventual forms of the list suggest an ordered programme of consolidation within the Argolid, followed by exploits in the neighbouring parts of the Peloponnese and then by expansion overseas.[5] Thus the killing of the Nemean lion is followed by the destruction of the Hydra at Lerna—a site of obvious eminence in Early and Middle Helladic, but eclipsed in Late Helladic:[6] we have already noted how the Late Helladic I Shaft Grave burials at that site were deliberately removed in Late Helladic II. Then come exploits in Arcadia—the Erymanthian boar, the Ceryneian stag, and the Stymphalian birds;

[1] §IX, 2, 71 f.
[2] Paus. I, 24, 3 and 5; Apollodorus 3, 14.
[3] Paus. IX, 38, 7.
[4] Strabo IX, 415; §VI, 15.
[5] G, 10, ch. III.
[6] §IX, 1, 143 f.

then the cleansing of the Augean stable. Augeas, we here recall, is already in Homer (*Iliad* xi, 670 ff.) renowned as king of the horse-breeding area of Elis; and indeed in Nestor's tale of fighting against him we learn that the Pylians had already suffered a defeat at the hands of Heracles. The epic thus recalls in more realistic form that same period of aggressive consolidation of the kingdom of Argos which is enshrined in the folk-tale of the Labours.

Of the overseas Labours, the capture of the Cretan bull must be reserved for a later section. The eighth labour, in which Heracles carries off from Thrace the horses of Diomede, is of interest in relation to a more historical-looking exploit, not in the canonical list, but referred to as early as Homer—the sack of Laomedon's Troy (*Iliad* v, 638 ff; xx, 144 ff.); for the occasion of the latter was also a dispute about horses. Cattle-raiding is of course regular material for heroic epic and ballads; but the two tales together suggest that in early Mycenaean as in classical times Greece depended on an imported supply of horses; moreover the Homeric epithets εὔπωλος and ἱππόδαμοι are peculiar to Troy and the Trojans, and may enshroud a historical fact.[1] Finds of Mycenaean pottery show that Greece was certainly in touch with Troy VI as early as Late Helladic II, but the destruction of that settlement does not come until early in Late Helladic III b. If we identify this destruction, which was caused by earthquake, with the sack by Heracles, accomplished with the aid of Poseidon the god of earthquakes, we must admit that the event is a good deal later than most of what is related of Heracles.

The ninth labour, the expedition against the Amazons, is interestingly parallel to that of Theseus, and to Bellerophon's campaigns in Anatolia; there is also a separate story of Heracles' servitude with Omphale, Queen of Lydia. Perhaps all four tales are independent traditions of some real mercenary activity of Mycenaeans in Asia Minor. Obviously the Amazons are not literally identifiable; but it may be that we should recognize in them, as Leonhard suggested, the Hittites, distorted and fabulized in a period when direct contact with them was a rarity.[2]

The voyage of Heracles to the western Mediterranean has many ramifications and deviosities; and for the most part there is no archaeological evidence which will justify our interpreting it as the memory of Mycenaean voyages in that direction. But the elaboration of his return journey in the area of Sicily and south Italy may be of some significance. It is easy to say that these

[1] §VI, 23, 70 and 252.　　　　[2] §IX, 3.

parts of the legend were invented by the later Dorian Greeks settled in those parts, who particularly revered Heracles. But those historical settlements were in fact in areas already known to Mycenaean enterprise; that is partly *why* they revered Heracles; and archaeological finds prove that some of these contacts go back to the very beginning of the Mycenaean period. This is particularly clear in the Aeolian Islands, where the earliest Greek wares are Middle Helladic and Late Helladic I;[1] and the same is probably implied for Sicily by a Middle Helladic cup from Monte Sallia.[2]

This section has by no means reviewed all the acts of Heracles as recorded in ancient literature, and it might not be profitable for the present History to do so. But his connexion with the southern Sporades seems significantly worth mention. In Homer (*Iliad* xv, 24 ff.) there is an allusion to his being storm-driven to Cos, and other sources tell us that this happened on his return from Troy, and that it resulted in the conquest of the island. We should probably link this with statements in the *Catalogue of Ships* (*Iliad* ii, 653 ff.), where we find a son of Heracles, Tlepolemus, ruling Rhodes, which he had colonized as an exile from mainland Greece. In the same context Nisyros, Carpathos, Casos, and Cos, are all ruled by sons of Thessalus, another Heraclid. Some at least of these islands came into the sphere of Mycenaean culture as early as Late Helladic II—this is particularly clear in Rhodes, where the contents of tombs imply that there was a settlement of Mycenaean character even before the destruction of the *Minoan* settlement at Trianda near by; and the general dating of Heracles to the earlier heroic age seems consistent with these facts. Yet Tlepolemus and the sons of Thessalus according to the *Catalogue* belong much later, in the generation of the Trojan War. Here as elsewhere there seems to have been some 'telescoping' of the chronology. We may ignore the view that these references to Heraclids in the southern Sporades indicate a post-Dorian date for this part of the *Catalogue*, since it apparently rests only on the unjustifiable assumption that all references to Heraclids must be made by Dorians.

X. THE MAINLAND AND CRETE

That intercourse between the Greek mainland and Crete was frequent throughout Late Helladic I and II has already been indicated (see pp. 642 ff.) in discussing the similarity of Mycenaean

---

[1] §vi, 30, 13 f., 16 ff.   [2] §vi, 30, 54 f.

pottery and other remains to Minoan objects; and by the mid-fifteenth century B.C. the pottery of Cnossus shows features which of themselves imply that the mainland has reached a degree of equality where it is exerting its own influences on the material culture of Crete. The possible political implications of such evidence were long ago suspected by Wace;[1] but since the decipherment of the clay tablets from the period of destruction of the Late Minoan II palace at Cnossus we need be in no doubt of the situation. The tablets are inscribed in an early form of Greek.[2] There is no reason to deduce the presence of Greeks in Crete *before* this Late Minoan II phase, though we are reasonably assured that they were already established in the mainland; and the conclusion is virtually inevitable that the rulers of Cnossus at this date were Greeks, and that Cnossus, if no more of Crete, had been conquered by Mycenaean Greeks some time within the fifteenth century B.C. The other evidence at once falls into place and becomes intelligible. The construction of the Cnossus throne-room at this period, a feature not found in other Cretan palaces, marks the new régime; the tablets themselves include lists of men with equipment of chariots and horses and armour[3] —evidence which was long ago commented on by Sir Arthur Evans as reflecting a military spirit which seemed quite new to the Minoan scene;[4] and excavation has revealed the tombs of some of the warriors concerned.[5] Several of these 'Warrior Graves' are of the mainland chamber-tomb type, and the pottery deposited in them is precisely of the class showing most Helladic influence, including 'Ephyraean' goblets and squat *alabastra*. The un-Minoan warlike profession of their occupants is plain from the swords and daggers and splendid spearheads which were buried with them. One tomb also contained a bronze helmet, of very much the same shape as the boar's-tusk helmets of the mainland. As the excavator comments, 'no doubt there was at Knossos in this period some kind of military aristocracy, which formed the core of the army, manning the chariots stored in the arsenals of the Palace...and such graves...may be supposed to belong to members of this body.'[6] We can say further that these warrior lords were Mycenaean Greeks.

Major questions still remain unanswered. One concerns the origins of the Linear B script.[7] Clearly this was based on Linear A,

[1] §x, 7, 229.
[2] §x, 1; 10.
[3] §x, 10, ch. XI.
[4] G, 2, vol. IV, 884 f.
[5] §x, 3.
[6] §x, 3, 245.
[7] See also above, pp. 601 ff.

which seems to have been devised for a language unlike Greek,
whatever it was, and needed both adaptation and supplementation
to be usable for Greek. But whether the adaptation took place in
Crete at the time when the Mycenaeans took over Cnossus, or had
been worked out already for use at the mainland sites, along with
so much else that was borrowed from Crete in Late Helladic I
and II, must remain uncertain; the fact that the Cnossus tablets
are at present the earliest known examples of this script perhaps
supports the former view.

No less difficult is the question of the political relationship
between the Mycenaean Greeks of the mainland and the Mycenaean rulers of Cnossus.[1] We do not know if the latter were
responsible to one of the mainland kingdoms—Mycenae, or
Pylus, perhaps—or independent of them. The title *wanax*, 'king',
in the Cnossus tablets suggests the latter;[2] and references to other
places in Crete seem to imply that he who was king of Cnossus was
king of the whole island. As such he would dispose of very great
resources and power, and we may well imagine Late Minoan II
Cnossus as a serious rival to the Mycenaean rulers of the mainland—a situation which may help to explain the end of the Cretan
palaces about 1400 B.C. What we know is that the palaces were
sacked and burnt; we do not know who did it. A nationalist
uprising intent on throwing off the Mycenaean yoke has been
suggested, but in that case it would be difficult to understand why
this resurgent Minoan Crete remained insignificant thereafter.
More readily acceptable is the view that the mainland Mycenaeans
were the destroyers; for the eclipse of Crete afforded opportunities
(duly exploited) for the expansion of Mycenaean activity from the
Aegean throughout the east Mediterranean. It is acceptable,
however, only if Cnossus was a rival rather than simply a subject
state.[3] Even so, the question is not proven. It is still possible
that the destruction from which the Mycenaeans profited was due
to some natural cataclysm.[4]

If we turn to legend, we find there no confirmation for the
theory of a Mycenaean *coup de main* on Crete, though traditions
of the Late Helladic II period when Cnossus and the mainland
flourished on an uneasy equality and rivalry are not lacking.[5]

[1] On this see also above, pp. 575 ff.
[2] G, 1, 16; §x, 10, 120.
[3] G, 1, 16 ff.; G, 14, 350; §x, 8, 114–20; §x, 9, 39.
[4] §x, 4, 300 ff.; A, 6.
[5] Plato, *Minos* 320e–321a; Diod. iv, 60–2; Apollodorus 3, 15 ff.; Plutarch,
Life of Theseus; etc.

Athens seems to have preserved the clearest tradition, perhaps because Attica had cause to remember an actual war with 'Minos', which resulted in her temporary subjection to Crete as a tributary state. The fact of such subjection there seems no possible reason to doubt: otherwise, Athenian sources would surely be found denying it; and there is therefore the more plausibility in legends of antecedent tension and rivalry between Athens and Cnossus. Thus we find Procris, the wife of Cephalus, King of Thoricus, taking refuge at Cnossus when a disagreement with her husband leads to exile; Daedalus, again, that Leonardo-like artist and engineer at the court of Minos, was a refugee from Attica; and the occasion given for Minos' campaign against Attica is an incident that occurred during a friendly state visit to Athens. Of the campaign itself we may note that Minos first seized Megara: in classical times the place-name Minoa survived there in a little offshore island—perhaps a reminiscence of a historical Minoan outpost or naval station, possibly the motivation of the story, which in either case has some strategic plausibility. We should note too that Minos did not occupy Attica; if he had, patriotic tradition might still have modified the fact to an exaction of tribute, but the tradition may well be true, since we find no greater trace of Minoan influence in Attica than in other parts of the mainland.

The tale of how Theseus freed his country from the Minoan yoke needs no re-telling. It is, however, important to observe that it is never represented as anything more; it is a raid, not a conquest of Crete, nor even of Cnossus; it is only modern theory that has taken this legend as evidence that the fall of Cnossus, about 1400 B.C., was due to Mycenaean arms. Mycenaean raids may, however, have helped to weaken the Minoan power, and there seems to be another memory of such raids in the story of Heracles, as one of his twelve labours, fetching home the Cretan bull.[1] But neither he nor Theseus is ever credited with a conquest of Cnossus; and in fact the classical Greeks had quite other traditions of the end of Minos and of his kingdom, which they attributed to his disastrous Sicilian expedition.[2] This is not the place to recapitulate the story, but some features of it should be noticed. That the expedition was ultimately caused by the presence in Sicily of Daedalus, a mainlander by origin, may hold a grain of history; for we have seen that the Mycenaeans early developed trade interests in the central Mediterranean, which might well

[1] Diod. IV, 13, 4.
[2] Hdt. VII, 169–71; Diod. IV, 77 ff. Cf. §x, 4, 113 ff.

cause Cnossus some anxiety. Alternatively, or perhaps at the same time, it could be that the *eastward* expansion of the mainland Mycenaeans was already forcing Cnossus to seek other outlets: we know that the Minoan settlement at Trianda in Rhodes came to an end about the same time as Cnossus. All that is really certain, however, is that the fall of Crete laid the way clear for a vastly increased Mycenaean activity.

CHAPTER XV

ANATOLIA *c.* 1600–1380 B.C.

I. THE OLD HITTITE KINGDOM (*continued*)

In this chapter we take up again the history of the Hittite Kingdom from the moment when an usurper first assumed the throne by violent means. Owing to the recovery in recent years of a well-preserved contemporary text we have been able to follow the events of at least part of the reign of Khattushilish I in considerable detail. The figure of this ancient ruler dominates the period of the Old Kingdom, down to the accession of Telepinush, principally on account of this much fuller documentation. For his successors we are dependent almost entirely on the Edict of Telepinush, described above;[1] but following the murder of Murshilish I, even this precious document becomes mutilated, and though no less than seven paragraphs were devoted to the reign of his successor, Khantilish I, as compared with only three to Khattushilish, little consecutive sense can be made from them.[2]

Khantilish had been a cup-bearer and was married to a sister of Murshilish named Kharapshilish.[3] It is likely, therefore, that Khantilish was a man of about the same age as his predecessor. The narrative of Telepinush is concerned to stress the impious and monstrous nature of the act of blood committed by Khantilish and his son-in-law, Zidantash, rather than to present the history of his reign in an objective manner. It even omits to mention that he became king, but this fact can hardly be doubted, since his wife is referred to as the queen.[4] The text states that after the assassination 'Khantilish was afraid', and goes on to describe how after an unspecified period, during which he was campaigning, possibly against the Hurrians, far to the south in the region of Carchemish, he came to Tegarama (probably modern Gürün, west of Malatya),[5] and then the gods sought vengeance for the

---

[1] See above, ch. vi, sect. iv. Text: G, 21, no. 21 (G, 7, no. 23).

[2] The broken sections are omitted in the translation, §1, 18, 183 ff.

[3] The text has 'wife' for 'sister'; but the emendation (a very slight one) is necessary because, even if it were possible that Khantilish could have been married in any sense to the wife of Murshilish, it clearly was not so, since the wife of Murshilish was named Kali (G, 23, 51, List 'A', 1, 5). See G, 12, 55.

[4] G, 12, 56 n. 36, etc.

[5] G, 8, 46 ff., with earlier literature.

blood of Murshilish. He returned to Khattusha, but apparently the Hurrians got the upper hand and 'the country was over-turned'. A fragmentary passage of the Akkadian version of the decree suggests that the Hurrians may even have captured the queen, Kharapshilish, and her sons, and brought them to Shug-ziya (not located, somewhere in the Taurus area). Here indeed they met their death, but hardly at the hands of the Hurrians, since Khantilish was able to punish those responsible.

Subsequently, we are told, Khantilish became old and was about to die. His reign must therefore have been a long one, but the decree of Telepinush, in its present state, gives no further details of events. Contemporary documents are few and contribute little. In one fragment Khantilish boasts that he was the first to build fortified cities in the country and that he 'built', i.e. forti-fied, Khattusha itself.[1] Another is concerned only with a ritual of purification.[2] In later texts, however, we learn from incidental references that on the northern frontier at two points the Hittites suffered reverses in his time. The holy city Nerik was captured by the Kaska (or Gasga) folk[3] and remained deserted for some 500 years; and the city of Tiliura was allowed to become 'an out-post' and eventually succumbed also to the invaders.[4] This is the earliest appearance of the Kaska folk in Hittite history, though we have surmised that their original occupation of the northern hills may have occurred in the reign of Khattushilish.[5] Their presence was a constant threat to the security of the Hittite homelands from this time on, and the combined pressure of these northern tribes, on the one hand, and the Hurrians on the other, fully accounts for the strengthening of the Hittite defences and for the decline in Hittite fortunes which occurred during the reign of Khantilish.

To return to the narrative of Telepinush: we are told that when the death of Khantilish seemed imminent, his son-in-law, Zidantash—the same who had instigated the murder of Murshi-lish, and therefore a man no longer young—now turned his hand against Kashshenish,[6] the son of Khantilish, and killed him to-gether with his sons and servants. He was thus able to claim the throne. But the gods avenged the blood of Kashshenish, and Zidantash was himself assassinated by his own son, Ammunash

---

[1] G, 7, no. 20 (=G, 21, no. 11), rev. 16.
[2] G, 7, no. 22 (= G, 21, nos. 15–16).   [3] G, 21, no. 504(4); G, 11, 24.
[4] G, 21, no. 62; G, 8, 119 f.; but cf. A, 27, 19.
[5] See above, ch. vi, sect. iv.
[6] Formerly read Pishenish; see G, 12, 56 n. 40.

(in his own inscription the latter, none the less, proclaimed that he had 'ascended the throne of his father', as if nothing unusual had occurred).[1] The reign of Zidantash was evidently short and he has left no inscriptions of his own. Some have ascribed to him the fragment of a treaty with Pelliya, a king of Kizzuwadna.[2] There are, however, strong arguments against this ascription of the fragment.[3] Above all, the 'Country of Adaniya' (= Adana), the central part of Kizzuwadna,[4] is named as a province lost to the Hittites in the following reign. Kizzuwadna cannot, then, have existed already as an established kingdom in the reign of Zidantash, and the fragment must be ascribed to Zidantash II (see below).

Under Ammunash the fortunes of the kingdom rapidly declined and his reign was remembered as a time of disaster. The army suffered constant reverses and many provinces of the kingdom were lost, among them the countries Adaniya and Arzawiya and the cities of Shallapa and Parduwata (the remainder are otherwise unknown).[5] This is an important piece of evidence for the extent of the kingdom in the preceding reigns and has already been used to show that the plain of Cilicia was probably in Hittite hands as early as the reign of Khattushilish I.[6] It is highly probable that in this terse statement we have an allusion to a momentous transformation in the political landscape—the conquest of Cilicia by a Hurrian or Indo-Aryan dynasty and the establishment of the kingdom of Kizzuwadna. This is the time, according to recent and (in our opinion) cogent arguments, when Idrimi became king of Alalakh in Syria and ruled for thirty years.[7] It is consistent with the abject condition of the Hittite state in the reign of Ammunash that this Syrian princeling is able to boast of having raided seven Hittite border towns with impunity, among them Zaruna, a place mentioned in the course of the campaign of the sixth year of Khattushilish I and so in the region of the Amanus.[8] Idrimi was a vassal of Parattarna, the king under whom the Hurrians first extended their influence over north

---

[1] G, 21, no. 19. But see below, p. 662 n. 8.

[2] G, 21, no. 17; §1, 16 (retracted in G, 24, 351); §1, 15, 108; §1, 19, 91; G, 28, 42 (von Schuler).

[3] G, 12, 72 f.; G, 15, 385 n. 17; cf. G, 19, 49.

[4] G, 10, 56 ff.

[5] G, 10, 57.

[6] See above, ch. VI, sect. IV. The Hittite land-deed found at Tarsus (§11, 25, 344) points to the same conclusion.

[7] C.A.H. I³, pt. I, ch. VI, sect. II. Cf. below, p. 670 n. 6.

[8] §1, 17, 18–19 (ll. 64 ff.).

Syria and Mesopotamia,[1] and he concluded a treaty with one Pelliya, concerned with the extradition of fugitives.[2] This Pelliya cannot, it is true, be identified with the king of Kizzuwadna who concluded a treaty with a Zidantash of Khatti, for the reasons just given, but the identity of name (and spelling) suggests that he was a predecessor in the same dynasty.[3] If he was the first king of Kizzuwadna, it is not unlikely that at the time of this treaty his country had not yet acquired a recognized name. The Hurrian conquests excluded the Hittites for about a century from the rich plains south of the Taurus mountains; indeed Kizzuwadna remained in control of Cilicia till about the end of the reign of Shuppiluliumash,[4] forcing later Hittite kings to take the more difficult route to Syria through the passes of the Antitaurus, even though from time to time kings of the two countries became sufficiently friendly to enter into a treaty relationship with one another.

Equally significant is the reference to the loss of Arzawiya, together with Shallapa and Parduwata. Since we know that the city of Shallapa lay on the road to Arzawa, and since Parduwata occurs in another document next to the River Shehiriya, which also lay on this road,[5] there can be no doubt that 'Arzawiya' is identical with the later 'Arzawa';[6] but unfortunately the location of this important country is one of the most controversial matters in Hittite political geography, and we are still unable to say more than that it lay to the west or south-west of the Hittite homeland with a capital city on the sea coast.[7] The loss of these areas must have thrown the Hittites back to the restricted territory formerly held by Labarnash.

The only existing text of Ammunash[8] is a mere fragment from which no consecutive sense can be extracted. A number of places are mentioned in it, among them Tipiya, Khashpina, Parduwata and Khahha. Of these, Parduwata, as we have just seen, was in the south or south-west, and Tipiya was in the north-east;[9] Khashpina is unknown, but Khahha—if identical with the Khahha attacked by Khattushilish I[10]—was by the Euphrates.

---

[1] §I, 17, 58; G, 12, 67 f.; §II, 15, 118 f. The question whether Parattarna 'King of the Hurrians' is to be understood as an early king of Mitanni is still undecided. See §I, 12, 253 ff.; §II, 15, 119 and 175 f.

[2] G, 29, no. 3.

[3] G, 27, 105 n. 46 (against G, 12, 67 f.).   [4] G, 10, 80 (cf. *ibid.* 70).

[5] G, 10, 57; G, 8, 76 and 124 (ll. 28–30). See Map 6.

[6] Cf. above, ch. VI, sect. IV.   [7] See above, ch. VI, sects. II and IV.

[8] G, 21, no. 19 (ascribed to a hypothetical earlier Ammunash in A, 21, 122 and 345 n. 28).   [9] G, 8, 32.

[10] See above, ch. VI, sect. IV; A, 8, 4; cf. G, 8, 25 f.; A, 3, 108; A, 4, 245.

The fragment thus at least confirms the widespread activities of this king and suggests a reign of considerable length.[1]

The death of Ammunash was followed by another outbreak of violence. Zurush, chief of the *mešedi*,[2] brought about the murder of Tittish and Khantilish (who are not otherwise identified), together with their sons, and thereupon a certain Khuzziyash 'became king'. We have now reached the events immediately preceding the accession of Telepinush, the author of the narrative, events which would have been so familiar to his audience that full details were unnecessary. Telepinush was married to Ishtapariyash, the elder sister of Khuzziyash; and when Khuzziyash was found to be plotting the death of his sister and brother-in-law, Telepinush acted promptly and 'drove them away', sending Khuzziyash with his five brothers into banishment. He concludes this outline of Hittite history with the formal statement that he 'seated himself on the throne of his father'.

It is not easy to fill in the background to these events satisfactorily. On the principle of *cui bono*, we may assume that Zurush acted at the instigation of Khuzziyash. The words suggest that, when once Tittish and Khantilish had been removed, Khuzziyash ascended the throne by right as the next in line. He would then have been a son of Ammunash, and Tittish and Khantilish his elder brothers.[3] His designs against his sister and brother-in-law are certainly to be accounted for by his desire to eliminate all remaining rivals. But it would not then be true that Telepinush 'ascended the throne of his father'. It has been suggested that this is an inaccurate way of referring to his father-in-law, Ammunash; or alternatively that it means no more than 'the throne belonging to the royal family'.[4] But neither explanation is entirely satisfactory. It would also be surprising, on this theory, to find that Khuzziyash had five brothers who, so far from being feared as rivals, were actually in collusion with him. This suggests rather a rivalry of families. Perhaps, then, Telepinush was telling the literal truth: he was a son of the previous king, Ammunash, and younger brother of Tittish and Khantilish. Khuzziyash, his brother-in-law, would then be an usurper who seized the throne by force with the help of the 'praetorian guard' and the support of

---

[1] G, 12, 56.   [2] See above, ch. VI, sect. V.
[3] So G, 5, 67; G, 12, 56.
[4] G, 12, 56; §1, 10, 208 n. 120. The theory that Telepinush means that he was a direct descendant of the line of Labarnash (§1, 14, 8 n. 20) would have required the plural *AB-BA-(A-)IA* (or AD.MEŠ–*IA*) '(throne) of my fathers', rather than *A-BI-IA*, which is in the text.

his brothers. His tenure of the throne evidently lasted a very short time.

Some idea of the extent of the kingdom at this time may be gleaned from a fragmentary list of storage depots which occurs towards the end of the decree of Telepinush. Many of these places are otherwise unknown and many are not located. Among them, however, are the following better-known cities: Shamukha, an important religious centre on a river, probably the upper Halys;[1] Marishta, in the zone inhabited by the Kaska folk, also to the north-east of the capital;[2] Khurma and Shugziya, in the Antitaurus;[3] Parshukhanda, near the central Salt Lake;[4] and the River Khulaya, south of Konya.[5] In this context the pair of names Damashkhunash and Khalippashshuwash can have no more than a chance resemblance to Damascus and Aleppo,[6] for none of these places is south of the Taurus. There is also a notable absence of any name connected with Arzawa and the west; but more than half the names in the list are broken away.

In foreign policy, the most notable event in the reign of Telepinush is his conclusion of a treaty with the king of Kizzuwadna, named Ishputakhshu. Fragments of the treaty are extant,[7] and it is mentioned in a catalogue of treaties;[8] moreover, a seal impression recovered from the mound at Tarsus bears the name 'Ishputakhshu, Great King, son of Pariyawatri', from which we learn the high standing of this ruler among his contemporaries, the name of his father, and (beyond any reasonable doubt) the location of his kingdom.[9] This is the first of the long series of treaties concluded by Hittite kings with rival powers, *protégés* and vassals,[10] and is also the earliest positive reference to the kingdom of Kizzuwadna; as recently as the reign of Ammunash we have heard only of the 'Land of Adaniya'. Ishputakhshu is a good 'Anatolian' name, perhaps belonging to the 'Kaneshite' dialect (if this is not identical with Hittite itself).[11] His father's name, however, has been claimed as Indo-Aryan, implying a connexion with the ruling clans associated with the expansion of

---

[1] G, 8, 32 ff.; G, 14, 47.
[2] G, 8, 13 (identified with Çorum).
[3] G, 8, 48.　　　　　　　　　[4] G, 8, 64.
[5] G, 8, 69 ff.　　　　　　　　[6] Suggested in G, 22.
[7] G, 21, no. 20.　　　　　　　[8] G, 21, no. 188(9).
[9] G, 10, 73.
[10] G, 18, *passim.*
[11] See above, ch. VI, sect. II. On the name Ishputakhshu see G, 19, 50; §1, 1, 15 ff. (criticized by H. G. Güterbock, in A, 7, 154); §1, 6, 354; §1, 7, 48 f.

Hurrian power at this time[1] (though there is an alternative analysis of the name as Luwian[2]); if so, it would conform with the names of his successors, Paddatishshu and Shunashshura,[3] whereas the name of Pelliya, who probably preceded him, is typically Hurrian. The name of Ishputakhshu himself is therefore anomalous in his country and cannot invalidate the otherwise natural inference that the kingdom of Kizzuwadna represents the conquest of Cilicia by a Hurrian or Indo-Aryan dynasty.[4]

Telepinush evidently consolidated his kingdom sufficiently to enable him to push forward once more towards Syria through the passes of the Antitaurus. He mentions that he destroyed Khashshuwa and put down the revolt of a certain Lahhash in Lawazantiya, two places which we have seen to be in this area,[5] and also that a battle occurred at Zazlippa, a place which is found later as a village in Kizzuwadna.[6] We may surmise that the treaty with Ishputakhshu represents an attempt to secure his flank while these operations were in train.

We may note in passing that the seal of Ishputakhshu is the oldest datable example of the Hittite 'hieroglyphic' script. The series of seals bearing this script begins at Boğazköy at about the same time; but there the earliest dated seal is that of Alluwamnash, the successor of Telepinush.[7] In the present state of our knowledge it would be premature to draw conclusions from these facts about the history of the script. Some of the signs themselves, used as isolated symbols, are attested on earlier seal-impressions which bear no royal name, and many centuries earlier again on pots and seals found at Kültepe (Kanesh).[8]

It is, however, the internal policy of Telepinush for which his reign is chiefly notable; though in this our judgement is undoubtedly influenced by the fact that the document which forms almost our sole evidence for the reign is a decree intended to restore order in the realm. Having shown by his outline of history how, as long as the aristocracy were united behind the king, the fortunes of the kingdom prospered, but as soon as dissension and sedition broke out, disaster ensued and the army was driven back, Telepinush goes on to draw the moral. In future the nobles must again stand united in loyalty to the throne, and if they are dissatisfied with the conduct of the king or of one

---

[1] G, 19, 50 ff. and 130. [2] §1, 5, 78.
[3] G, 19, 130. [4] G, 19, 50; G, 12, 73.
[5] See above, ch. VI, sect. IV. *K.Bo.* XII, no. 8 also refers to these events.
[6] G, 10, 44 f.; G, 8, 54. [7] G, 24, 349; A, 1, 67.
[8] H. Otten, in G, 28, 14, with earlier literature; A, 1, 59 ff.

of his sons, they must have recourse to legal means of redress and refrain from taking the law into their own hands by murder. The supreme court for the punishment of wrongdoers is the *pankuš* or 'whole body' of citizens, as described above.[1] 'Whoever hereafter becomes king and plans injury against brother or sister, you are his *pankuš*'—i.e. you are yourselves the authority charged with the duty of passing judgement on him. This was most probably a very ancient institution and no innovation.[2] History showed that it had not worked well in the past, and though the irresponsibility of the nobles seems to have been arrested for a time, we may surmise that this was due more to the strong personality of the reformer than to any reform, for in fact we hear no more of the *pankuš* from this time on.

Telepinush lays down a concise law of succession. 'Let a prince, a son, of the first rank, become king. If there is no prince of the first rank, let one who is a son of the second rank become king. If, however, there is no prince, (no) son, let them take a husband for her who is a daughter of the first rank, and let him become king.'[3] Here again we must attempt to determine to what extent this ordinance was an innovation or merely a formulation of what was in fact the established custom. We have described above[4] the bilingual text of an address delivered by Khattushilish I to the assembly of fighting men and dignitaries on the occasion of his public adoption of Murshilish as heir to the throne. It has been maintained[5] that this document represents a kind of 'contract', requiring for its full legality the active consent of the nobility and affording a close parallel to certain ancient Indo-European institutions. If this were so, the hereditary principle laid down by Telepinush would have been an entirely new dispensation and would represent a victory for the monarchy over the nobility, who were finally excluded by it from any further influence on the royal succession. We have pointed out above, that the address of Khattushilish does not appear to have this character, and that even though a case is on record in which the nobles attempted to set an usurper on the throne, this is recorded as an offence and not as a legitimate exercise of ancient rights. The most that can be said is that the king was recognized as having the right to choose his successor from among his sons and

---

[1] See above, ch. VI, sect. V.

[2] A. Goetze, in G, 28, 26; cf. G, 24, 348.

[3] G, 21, no. 21, sect. 28. The 'rank' of the child would depend on whether the mother was the queen or a secondary wife.

[4] See above, ch. VI, sect. IV.   [5] G, 13, 86 f.; §1, 11, 242 f.

the obligation to proclaim him publicly to the assembly.[1] If no son was available, an adoption was necessary. The effect of the law of Telepinush was to abolish this freedom of choice and to substitute a fixed order of succession.

More recently, the significance of the ordinance of Telepinush has been sought in another direction.[2] It is generally agreed that the peculiar position of the Hittite queen, whose title, *tawannan-naš*, was inherited only on the death of her predecessor and was retained for life, can only be explained as a survival of a system of matrilineal succession which must once have prevailed among the ancient Khattians.[3] It has been suggested that the king (*labarnaš*) was originally merely 'the queen's consort': the Indo-European immigrants would have achieved kingship by marrying the local 'matriarch', as did so many heroes of Greek legend who succeeded to thrones in Anatolia by marrying the daughter of the local king and, having done so, sought to establish their own patriarchal system. The recorded dynastic disturbances would then represent the struggle between two ways of life, a struggle which was resolved eventually in favour of the Indo-European aristocracy by the ordinance of Telepinush.

It is, however, characteristic of a matrilineal society that king-ship and authority in general are exercised, not by the husband, but by the brother of the 'matriarch'. Succession passes in the female line, and so in effect a ruler is succeeded by his sister's son: the husband is outside the family. Consequently, if Tawan-nannash represents the ancient 'matriarch', Labarnash should have been her brother and his successor should have been her son. Is it possible that some such ideas lie behind the enigmatical phrase 'brother's son of Tawannannash' used by Khattushilish I to describe his filiation?[4] As it stands, the phrase gives just the reverse of the sense required by this hypothesis. It has, however, been suggested most recently that in the most ancient texts the logogram DUMU ('son') conceals a Hittite word belonging to the matriarchal ideology, meaning 'heir' and therefore equivalent to 'sister's son'.[5] An example of this usage has been found in the expression used by Khattushilish I of his disinherited nephew, the young Labarnash, which on this view should be translated, not 'I called him my son', but 'him, my nephew-heir, I called (summoned)'.[6] This theory has not yet stood the test of criticism and is at first sight difficult to substantiate. It is worth noting,

[1] A. Goetze, in G, 28, 26; G, 24, 348.   [2] §1, 13, 180 ff.
[3] G, 13, 93, etc.   [4] See above, ch. vi, sect. iv.
[5] §1, 3, 75.   [6] See above, ch. vi, sect. iv.

however, that it would provide a possible explanation for the filiation of Khattushilish; for the phrase, in its original Hittite form, could then have meant 'heir of the brother of Tawannannash', i.e. of his predecessor, Labarnash.

On this theory it would have been Khattushilish who first flouted tradition by adopting as heir a descendant in the male line.[1] This provoked retaliation by Khantilish and Zidantash who, however, substituted the husband for the brother of the heiress as the possessor of authority and successor to the throne. With Ammunash and possibly Telepinush, both of whom proclaimed that they had 'ascended the throne of their father', the patriarchy would finally have gained the upper hand, Khuzziyash representing, perhaps, the last and unavailing effort of the ancient social system to assert itself against the newcomers. The hypothesis is attractive, but only if it can be established that the matrilineal tradition survived as an effective force as late as the reign of Khattushilish.

In the Hittite Laws, at least, the social background is entirely patriarchal.[2] This is implicit in the phraseology: a man 'takes' his wife and thereafter 'possesses' her. If she is taken in adultery, he has the right to decide her fate (and that of the adulterer). He may dispose of his children by sale. The language of the Laws is Old Hittite, and for this reason alone the text must date from some time in the Old Kingdom. On stylistic grounds the codification of the law was formerly ascribed to Telepinush, for his edict contains in its later parts certain ordinances couched in a style very similar to that of the Laws. It has now been recognized, however, that among the numerous manuscripts of the Laws (the majority of which are later copies) there are a few which can be judged from their script to be originals, contemporary with the drafting of the Laws;[3] and when these are isolated, they are seen to possess peculiarities of grammar and orthography which suggest that they are as old as the time of Murshilish I or Khattushilish I.[4] Moreover, these old manuscripts already record ancient laws which had been reformed by the legislator at the time of writing. These facts militate strongly against the survival of matrilineal institutions in historical times, even in the royal family.

---

[1] NUMUN ᴰUTU-*ŠI* (G, 7, no. 8, ii, 44).

[2] G, 13, 111 ff.; V. Korošec, in G, 6, vol. ii, 293 ff. Text of the Laws in §1, 4; translation by A. Goetze in G, 26, 188 ff.

[3] §1, 8, 64; §1, 9, 17 ff.; H. Otten, in G, 28, 13; A. Goetze, *ibid.* 27 f.

[4] §1, 2.

II. THE MIDDLE HITTITE KINGDOM

From the point in the reign of Telepinush when he promulgated his constitutional decree, with its elaborate historical preamble, the source which has been the basis for our reconstruction of Hittite history under the Old Kingdom ceases to flow and the paucity of other evidence becomes immediately apparent. As a guide to the succession of kings and queens we are dependent on the so-called 'King-Lists' which were compiled for the purpose of offering sacrifices to the spirits of former rulers and other members of the royal family.[1] We learn nothing from these lists about the persons listed except their names. It has been shown, however, that although here and there the name of a king (such as that of Zidantash I in List A) is unaccountably omitted, the order of the names is chronological and trustworthy.

Ishtapariyash, the wife of Telepinush, and his son, Ammunash, died before him in unknown circumstances.[2] Of the end of his reign nothing whatever is known. His successor was one Alluwamnash (a Luwian name),[3] whose queen was Kharapshekish (the name appears in error as Kharapshilish in the lists). Fragmentary documents give Alluwamnash the title 'King's Son' and Kharapshekish 'King's Daughter'. Obviously both titles cannot be taken literally, and since the former is common in the generalized sense 'Royal Prince' it is usually assumed that Kharapshekish was in fact the daughter of Telepinush.[4] The successors of Alluwamnash are given in the lists as Khantilish, Zidantash (with queen Iyayash), Khuzziyash (with queen Shummirish), Tudkhaliash (with queen Nikkal-mati) and Arnuwandash (with queen Ashmu-Nikkal). The last two are amply attested by contemporary documents as father and son[5] and impressions of the seals of Alluwamnash, Khuzziyash and Arnuwandash are found on land-deeds of a type which is characteristic of this period.[6] There is thus no adequate ground for questioning the existence of Khantilish, Zidantash and Khuzziyash, as was formerly done.[7] Since no queen is given as consort of Khantilish, it is reasonable to suppose that Queen Kharapshekish continued as *tawannannaš*

[1] G, 23, *passim*; §II, 16, 53 ff.; A, 24, 122 ff.
[2] G, 21, no. 21, sect. 27.
[3] A. Goetze in G, 28, 24.
[4] G, 12, 57.
[5] G, 12, 57 n. 52 (referring to §II, 13, no. 76).
[6] §II, 13, 47 ff.; §II, 25, *passim*; E. von Schuler in G, 28, 49.
[7] §I, 10, 216; but see G, 11, 23 n. 22; G, 12, 54 n. 13; G, 23, 54 f.; G, 24, 350 f.

throughout his reign, which must therefore have been short.[1] It has been claimed that, because his successors each had a queen, they, with Alluwamnash and Kharapshekish, must represent three generations;[2] but this does not necessarily follow, for in troubled times a *tawannannaš* might be succeeded by her sister-in-law, as occurred in the case of Kali, the queen of Murshilish I. Their filiation is quite unknown.

Arnuwandash is followed immediately in the lists by the wives and children of Shuppiluliumash. This section of the lists thus forms the bridge between the Old Kingdom and the Empire, to be described in later chapters. The period has come to be known, for no very adequate reason, as the Middle Kingdom.

The moderate successes achieved by Telepinush, especially the friendly relations which he established with Kizzuwadna, appear to have been shortlived. During the reigns of his successors the power of Mitanni reached its peak under Saustatar and a Mitannian empire became established over the whole of northern Syria.[3] Kizzuwadna, it seems, again became subject to Mitanni, for we have the record of a lawsuit brought before Saustatar by Niqmepa, king of Alalakh, against a certain Shunashshura, who, from his name alone, is thought to have been a king of Kizzuwadna, predecessor of the king of the same name who concluded a well-known treaty with Shuppiluliumash.[4] Such a lawsuit implies a vassal relationship of both parties to the Mitannian king.[5] This situation must have lasted throughout the reigns of Alluwamnash and Khantilish II; but under Zidantash II, apparently, Hittite fortunes again began to rise. As already mentioned, we assign to him the treaty of peace concluded by one of his name with a king of Kizzuwadna named Pelliya (II)[6] (the

[1] G, 11, 21, The case of Khuzziyash I is similar.

[2] G, 12, 57.

[3] On the date of Saustatar, one generation after Parattarna, see *C.A.H.* I³, pt. 1, pp. 289 f., and §II, 21, 284 n. 4. If so, it must be accepted that *a-bu a-ba a-bi-ia* in §II, 29, 38, l. 8 means no more than 'my ancestor'; see §II, 21, 285 f. n. 4, against G, 12, 66 n. 138 and §II, 15, 168 n. 47. This is no more difficult than to suppose that Kurtiwaza (see *C.A.H.* II³, pt. 2, ch. XVII, sect. III) was mistaken about the number of generations involved.

[4] G, 29, no. 14 and p. 7.

[5] For this very reason the two fragments of Hittite treaties with a Shunashshura (G, 21, nos. 36 b. and 94) can hardly be assigned to this king, for the subordinate partner was always required to renounce his right to an independent foreign policy. Cf. §I, 15, 121 f.; G, 12, 72; G, 18, 46; G, 28, 31 f. (Goetze); §II, 24, 242 ff.

[6] See above, p. 661. It should perhaps be mentioned here that if, after all, the more usual dating of the Mitannian Empire of Parattarna and Saustatar to the second half of the fifteenth century should prove to be correct (e.g. G, 12, 66 ff.; §II, 15,

use in it of the royal title 'My Sun' points to a later period than that of Zidantash I, though it is still the earliest instance of the usage).[1] The only clauses preserved consist of mutual agreements to restore certain towns (unnamed) captured in the preceding war and not to rebuild others which had been destroyed; but if the document is rightly assigned, we may infer that Zidantash waged a successful war, resulting in the return of Kizzuwadna to the Hittite camp. The moment was indeed favourable for him. This is the time when Egyptian armies under Tuthmosis III began again to establish their ascendancy in Syria and to drive back the Mitannian forces to the east of the Euphrates. The reassertion of Egyptian power could only be of advantage to the Hittites at this time, and so it was that a Hittite king—presumably Zidantash or Khuzziyash—is reported to have sent tribute to the pharaoh on his return from the great Syrian campaign of his thirty-third year, 1471 B.C. Eight years later the tribute was renewed.[2]

It must have been at approximately this time that the kings of Khatti and Egypt drew up an agreement over the transfer of some of the population of the northern city of Kurushtama into Egyptian territory. This 'treaty' is twice referred to in later documents as the earliest bond of friendship between the two countries, but the circumstances surrounding its conclusion are obscure.[3]

Between Khuzziyash II and Shuppiluliumash we have to place not only the couples Tudkhaliash–Nikkal-mati and Arnuwandash–Ashmu-Nikkal but also at least one other king, possibly two or more. The evidence is inconclusive and at the time of writing it is not possible to reconstruct a line of kings which has any claim to finality.

The Arnuwandash of the king-lists and his queen, Ashmu-Nikkal, figure in a number of contemporary documents. Their seal is impressed on a land deed which is undoubtedly older than Shuppiluliumash on archaeological grounds, as is another seal impression bearing the name of the queen alone.[4] *Both* appear to have been children of Tudkhaliash and his queen,

168 n. 47), it would be possible to equate this Pelliya with the partner of Idrimi. But it is difficult to believe that this Hurrian empire could have flourished at the very time when Tuthmosis III was in control of most of Syria without some reference to the Egyptians appearing in the Alalakh tablets.

[1] G, 17, 116 f.; G, 13, 88 f.
[2] §II, 3, sects. 485 and 525; §II, 15, 152 and 173 n. 144.
[3] G, 16, 60 ff.; §II, 10, 209 ff.; §II, 14, 98; §II, 15, 164.
[4] §II, 13, 33; §II, 11, 71; §II, 26, 234 ff.; G, 12, 58.

Nikkal-mati[1]—hardly a case of brother–sister marriage, in view of the concise statement in a later treaty that such marriages were forbidden, but one which suggests rather that in certain circumstances the queenship might pass to some one other than the king's wife.[2] They are associated on the documents with one Tudkhaliash the *tuḫkantiš*, probably 'heir designate'[3] and son of Arnuwandash, who appears to have succeeded his father as king, if an allusion to a Tudkhaliash who ascended the throne of his father Arnuwandash may be taken to refer to him rather than to a king at the end of the empire.[4] We therefore enter his name conjecturally in the line of kings, assuming an omission in the king-lists. Another son, Ashmi-Sharruma, evidently did not come to the throne:[5] this would require a special explanation if Tudkhaliash was not his elder brother.

The preamble to the treaty between Murshilish II and Talmi-Sharruma of Aleppo, where the previous relations of the contracting parties are briefly summarized,[6] mentions, between Murshilish I and Shuppiluliumash, a Tudkhaliash and a Khattushilish, without indicating their relationship either to each other or to the latter's successor. The text describes dealings between this Khattushilish and countries such as Mitanni, Ashtata and Nukhashshe, which did not exist before the fifteenth century B.C., and cannot therefore be referring back to events in the time of Khattushilish I, as has been proposed.[7] This Khattushilish (II) must therefore be included in the line of kings. Whether the Tudkhaliash who precedes him in the treaty is the father of Arnuwandash or the former *tuḫkantiš* of the texts has yet to be determined.

A work entitled 'The Deeds of Shuppiluliumash' composed by his son, Murshilish II, has been reconstructed out of many fragments.[8] It begins in the time of the father of Shuppiluliumash,

[1] §II, 13, seals 60 and 77; G, 12, 57, n. 52.

[2] G, 15, 387 n. 27; §II, 13, 37. But cf. G, 6, vol. III, 231; A, 24, 105; A, 12, 39 n. 90.

[3] The objection to this translation of *tuḫkantiš* (cf. §II, 28, 37) is no longer valid, since *K.Bo.* IV, no. 10 has been proved to belong to the reign of Tudkhaliash IV (A, 20, 40 ff.).

[4] G, 12, 58 n. 60; G, 20, 8–10; cf. A, 5, 30. The fact that we have a late copy of the text in question does not prove anything about the date either of the original text or of the succession of Tudkhaliash son of Arnuwandash mentioned in the colophon.

[5] G, 23, 66 (List 'C', 6) and 55–6.

[6] §II, 9, 59 ff.; §II, 17, 213 ff.

[7] So A, 24, 110 f. Cf. A, 10, 74; A, 28, 107.

[8] Edited in §II, 14.

described as 'my grandfather', but the name of the grandfather is nowhere mentioned except in 'Fragment 2', which contains the words 'Tudkhaliash, my grandfather'. It thus follows from the inclusion of this fragment in the 'Deeds' that another Tudkhaliash has to be entered in the line between Khattushilish II and Shuppiluliumash, for it is clear from this work that Shuppiluliumash succeeded his father directly.[1] Some confirmation of this may indeed be found in the 'affair of Tudkhaliash the younger', an episode of which we learn incidentally in a prayer of Murshilish II.[2] This 'Tudkhaliash the younger', who had apparently held the appointment of heir designate to the throne, was assassinated together with his brothers by a group of officers, including Shuppiluliumash himself, who had sworn allegiance to him. Had he been actually king, the text would surely have given him the title. Tudkhaliash his father, however, must have been king, and the natural assumption is that this Tudkhaliash was the king under whom he held his appointment and the immediate predecessor of Shuppiluliumash. Certain sacrificial lists which give the sequence Khattushilish–Tudkhaliash–Shuppiluliumash–Murshilish have also been adduced in favour of this view.[3]

It has recently been shown, however, that a genealogy of the later king Khattushilish III, which has often been misinterpreted, describes him as son of Murshilish (II), grandson of Shuppiluliumash, and 'great-grandson of Khattushilish, the great king, offspring of the king of Kussar, (who was) singled out by the gods'.[4] This, the only translation which is grammatically sound, can only mean that Shuppiluliumash was the son (and immediate successor) of Khattushilish II, and the evidence cited in the preceding paragraph needs to be re-examined. In fact there is no proof that 'Fragment 2' is part of the 'Deeds of Shuppiluliumash'; it contains some mutilated lines referring to Telepinush and a woman Harapshitish (a bye-form of Harapshilish?), which suggests that the 'grandfather Tudkhaliash' to whom it refers should be either the husband of Nikkal-mati or the *tuḫkantiš* and that the author of the text should be an earlier king than Murshilish II. The episode of Tudkhaliash the younger is also inconclusive, for it does not necessarily follow from the text that the assassination resulted immediately in the accession of Shuppiluliumash. The latter may have acted in the interests of his father, perhaps a

[1] §II, 14, 120.
[2] §II, 10, 164 ff. The text is damaged and many details are obscure.
[3] G, 23, 58.
[4] A, 10, 75.

younger brother of the older Tudkhaliash. Or alternatively, if the heir designate were a minor at the time of his father's death, it is possible that his uncle might have been accepted as king in his place, though there is nothing in the law of Telepinush (above, p. 669) explicitly covering such a case; the assassination would then have served to secure the accession of Shuppiluliumash himself on the death of his own father, Tudkhaliyash in the mean time having come to manhood. Thirdly, the sacrificial lists do not necessarily cite consecutive kings. Arnuwandash, who intervened between Shuppiluliumash and Murshilish II, is certainly omitted, and it is more than likely that the earlier kings Khattushilish and Tudkhaliash in these lists are the same two great monarchs of Hittite history, Khattushilish I and Tudkhaliash, whose names precede that of Khattushilish II in the Aleppo treaty.[1]

Other evidence, once regarded as fundamental in this problem, has been invalidated by the discovery of a second Shuppiluliumash (written *Šu-up-pi-lu-li-ia-ma-aš*) who reigned at the very end of the Empire.[2] Within the walls of Boğazköy itself there stands a badly weathered hieroglyphic inscription carved on the face of the rock and known today as the Nişantaş.[3] It is an inscription of a Shuppiluliumash, and though the purport of its text can no longer be read, it is at least clear that it opens with the genealogy 'Shuppiluliumash, son of Tudkhaliash, grandson of Khattushilish'. Recent study of this inscription has shown that the further generation 'great-grandson of Tudkhaliash', which was formerly thought to follow here, was in reality a misreading.[4] Without it the genealogy tallies exactly with the known ancestry of Shuppiluliumash II, who was son of Tudkhaliash IV and grandson of Khattushilish III, and it has now been shown that the more elaborate 'aedicula' enclosing the name of the author, Shuppiluliumash, proves that the inscription must be assigned to the later king, rather than to his illustrious predecessor, as was formerly supposed.[5] Similarly a document stating that 'Shuppiluliyama' was preceded on the throne by his brother is certainly to be assigned to Shuppiluliumash II and has no bearing on the issue.[6]

[1] So A, 24, 111 and A, 10, 77.
[2] §11, 20, 70 ff.; G, 12, 57.
[3] §11, 1, 63–4 and pl. 25.
[4] A, 9, 81.
[5] A, 22, 227–30.
[6] G, 23, 55 ff.; §11, 11, 68; §11, 20, 74 ff. Yet the brother still appears in the scheme advocated by A. Kammenhuber in A, 12, 41 ff.

We opt therefore, with some reserve, for the following stemma:[1]

Tudkhaliash II = Nikkal-mati

| Arnuwandash I | | Ashmu-Nikkal |

| Tudkhaliash III | Khattushilish II | Ashmi-Sharruma |

Tudkaliash the younger — Shuppiluliumash I

TABLE 3. *Descendants of Tudkhaliash II*

The name of the father of Tudkhaliash II is nowhere given and he may well have been the founder of a new dynasty. It is a well-established fact that the New Empire shows many significant changes in the character of the monarchy.[2] The peculiar demo-cratic (or oligarchic) institutions of the Old Kingdom are no longer found; the authority of the king appears to be absolute, conforming to a more 'oriental' pattern. Above all, it has now been demonstrated that the dynasty exhibits strongly Hurrian characteristics. The gods of the (royal) house appear in a Hurrian context with a Hurrian singer.[3] The *interpretatio hurritica* of the Anatolian pantheon so strikingly and uniquely embodied in the sculptures of Yazilikaya[4] and the proliferation of Hurrian cults under the later kings can be attributed to the same cause. The army of the empire, which owed much of its strength to its pro-ficiency in chariot-warfare, had adopted an elaborate régime of horse-training laid down by a Hurrian named Kikkuli.[5] Many of the later kings, queens and princes are even known to have borne Hurrian personal names; such a name would be replaced by a Hittite 'throne-name' when a prince succeeded or was appointed to a kingdom.[6] Now the earliest of these Hurrian names are those of the queens Nikkal-mati and Ashmu-Nikkal and of the latter's son, Ashmi-Sharruma. Nikkal-mati could, indeed, have been a Hurrian princess, but it is difficult to believe that she alone could have been responsible for the profound penetration of Hittite civilization by Hurrian ideas under the empire. These features seem rather to point to a Hurrian origin for the dynasty itself. In any case, the names of their queens seem by their Hurrian character

[1] Following H. G. Güterbock in A, 10, 77.
[2] G, 13, 88 ff.; G, 28, 29 ff.　　　[3] G, 15, 388.
[4] G, 13, 142; G, 15, 391.
[5] G, 13, 119; G, 28, 29 f.
[6] G, 15, 386 ff.; G, 28, 24; §II, 14, 120 ff.

to link Tudkhaliash and Arnuwandash firmly to the dynasty of Shuppiluliumash.

The narrative of the Aleppo treaty states in effect that some time after the conquest of Aleppo by Murshilish I[1] the king of Aleppo defected to the side of Mitanni (also called Hanigalbat).[2] For this 'sin' Tudkhaliash, when he 'arose' (*i-lu-ú*),[3] attacked and defeated both Aleppo and Mitanni and made peace with Aleppo. According to the treaty with Shunashshura (II)[4] Kizzuwadna also 'belonged to the Land of Hatti' during the reign of the grandfather of Shuppiluliumash, and therefore by implication previously. The king of Kizzuwadna at this time might still have been Pelliya II, or alternatively his presumed successor, Paddatishshu, whose treaty with an unnamed Hittite king, in the Akkadian language, is extant.[5]

Syria was dominated by Tuthmosis III for the last 21 years of his reign, 1471–1450 B.C., and the Egyptians appear to have maintained their suzerainty there, if somewhat precariously, until about the tenth year of his successor, Amenophis II, *c.* 1440 B.C.[6] The Hittite resurgence under Tudkhaliash must have followed immediately on their retirement from the scene—if it was not already responsible for the revolt of Aleppo which took place on the accession of Amenophis II[7] (for it is not certain that Aleppo was ever again under Egyptian control).

This Tudkhaliash, moreover, evidently began the reconquest of the west, for he is said to have made war on Arzawa (the satellite kingdom of Wilusa remaining neutral).[8] The account of this campaign may well be contained in the so-called 'Annals of Tudkhaliash', a text which has hitherto always been attributed to the late king Tudkhaliash IV.[9] The appearance of a king of the

---

[1] See above, ch. VI, sect. IV.

[2] This defection is related as if it occurred during the reign of Tudkhaliash. But the event can hardly be anything but the earlier conquest of Syria by Saustatar, which would otherwise be passed over in silence. It is suggested that the verb *ittaṣḥar* be taken as a pluperfect (indicated by the asyndeton). The new fragment (§II, 17) has at last established the identity of Mitanni with Hanigalbat; cf. §II, 12, 72 ff.; G, 16, 26; §II, 27, 35 ff.

[3] Taken as evidence that he was a usurper in §II, 29, 82 n. 6; but the modern lexicons show that the verb can be used of any king.

[4] §II, 29, 90 (5–7); G, 8, 58; G, 10, 36 ff.; G, 12, 58; §II, 9, 66; §II, 11, 69.

[5] G, 21, no. 30; §I, 15, 112 ff.

[6] *C.A.H.* I[3], pt. 1, pp 229 f.; §II, 15, 155 ff.

[7] *C.A.H.* I[3], pt. 1, p. 230; §II, 27, 38.   [8] §II, 7, 50 (B 9 ff.).

[9] G, 21, no. 85 and 123 (8); translation in G, 8, 121 f. These pieces must then be separated from the fragment G, 21, no. 123(6), translated *ibid.* 120 f., which clearly belongs to the later period. Cf. *C.A.H.* II[3], pt. 2, ch. XXIV, sect. IV.

Hurrians at the end of this broken text has always been an enigma;[1] in the light of fuller knowledge we can say it would have been an impossibility at the time of Tudkhaliash IV, when the kingdom of Mitanni had been destroyed and its territory incorporated into the empire of Assyria.[2] The fragment describes four successive campaigns. Of the first only the end is preserved, containing part of a list of countries conquered. Among these are Arzawa and its satellites, Khapalla and the Land of the River Shekha, also Wallarimma, which has western associations. This could be the campaign referred to in the treaty mentioned above. The next campaign is directed against twenty-two countries which are apparently summed up in the following lines as the 'Land of Assuwa'. These names have been much discussed, especially the last two, *Wilušiya* and *Taruiša*, for which an identification with Ilios and Troia has been proposed,[3] with some plausibility. Obviously, however, if the text belongs to this early period, *Wilušiya* cannot be also identical with Wilusa, since this country is said to have been neutral at the time. Very few of the other names in this list occur elsewhere and none can be located with certainty. The comprehensive name Assuwa is generally regarded as the prototype of the Roman 'Asia', which is first attested as the name for a region in the vicinity of Sardis. Assuwa was almost certainly in the west. This campaign seems to represent the farthest penetration westwards of any Hittite king. During the absence of Tudkhaliash in the west the Kaska-folk rose and devastated the Hittite homeland. The king on his return to Khattusha was obliged to set out immediately against them and defeated them in a pitched battle at Tiwara (not located). This is the third campaign, which was completed the following year. After a year's interval, in which there was no campaigning, the king set out eastwards apparently to quell a rebellion in the country of Ishuwa, which was supported by the king of the Hurrians. Only a few broken lines of this passage are preserved, but it is clear that it led to the reconquest of Ishuwa, a country situated in the great bend of the Euphrates, south of the Murad Su (Arsanias).[4] Obviously this is not the same incident as that which occurred at the beginning of the reign of the Assyrian king,

---

[1] G, 1, 87.

[2] The credit for this observation belongs to Dr Edmund I. Gordon.

[3] G, 8, 105 ff., with earlier literature, especially §II, 2. Assuwa might then, after all, be the 'Isy which sent gifts to Tuthmosis III (§II, 15, 290 and §II, 2, 11 ff.).

[4] G, 8, 40 ff.

Tukulti-Ninurta I, in which the Assyrians captured 28,800 Hittites 'from the other side of the Euphrates'.[1]

The 'Annals of Tudkhaliash' is only one of a large group of texts which exhibit certain archaic features of language and orthography. Hitherto this has been largely discounted as a criterion for dating, on the assumption that the scribes of the last decades of the Empire deliberately adopted an archaizing style. At the time of writing, however, there is an increasing tendency to back-date the whole of this group of texts to the fifteenth century.[2] If this movement gains general acceptance, Hittite history will be greatly altered, for the group includes such important historical documents as the 'Joint Annals' of Tudkhaliash and Arnuwandash,[3] the Indictment of the rebellious vassal, Madduwattash, in western Anatolia,[4] and the similar rescript against Mita of Pakhkhuwa, a trouble-maker in the far north-east.[5] They reveal Hittite kings claiming authority over wide areas of Anatolia, even over Alashia (Cyprus), an authority which is being eroded by adventurers whom the Hittites are unable to control. The present *History* cannot fully take cognizance of this development and treats these texts in the traditional way as reflecting the situation at the end of the thirteenth century, just before the collapse of the empire.[6] It should be noted, however, that if the higher dating of these texts should be eventually established, the reference to the activities of the 'man of Ahhiyā' in the Madduwattash text would become the earliest allusion to the Ahhiyawa people, usually identified in some way with the Mycenaean Greeks.[7]

The campaigns of 'Tudkhaliash' in Syria and the west in any case reveal him to have been an energetic and successful ruler. The question arises: was he the predecessor or (if the stemma here adopted is correct) the successor of Arnuwandash I? If the 'Joint Annals', which refer to the reign of Tudkhaliash, could be securely assigned to this period, it would be clear that the restorer of Hittite ascendancy, at least in the west, was Tudkhaliash II, since in this text his son, Arnuwandash, appears as co-regent with him. If, however, we disregard this evidence, we can only attempt to answer this question by comparing the political conditions under

[1] As suggested in G, 5, 160. Cf. *C.A.H.* 11³, pt. 2, ch. xxiv, sect. iv.

[2] So principally H. Otten (A, 23–5), O. Carruba (A, 2) and P. Houwink ten Cate (A, 11); opposed by A. Kammenhuber (A, 13–14).

[3] G, 21, no. 86. Cf. A, 11, 80; A, 16, 216.

[4] G, 21, no. 89. Cf. A, 25; A, 11, 58.

[5] G, 21, no. 88. Cf. A, 11, 58, 80–1.

[6] *C.A.H.* 11³, pt. 2, ch. xxiv, sect. iv.

[7] G, 16, 46 ff. *C.A.H.* 11³, pt. 2, ch. xxi (*a*), 27, with bibliography p. 38.

Arnuwandash, in so far as they are revealed by the few texts bearing the names of Arnuwandash and Ashmu-Nikkal. We learn from them that he too had trouble with the Kaska-folk and many of the central Hittite cult-centres were ravaged by the enemy.[1] However, the oaths of fealty sworn to him and his family by military commanders in the provinces of Kalashma, Shappa, Kishshiya, and other places doubtless in the same area,[2] and the elaborate royal seal by which state documents were ratified under the joint authority of the king and the queen, give an impression of order and stability. A fragmentary treaty thought to date from this reign on linguistic grounds records that the cities of Ura and Mutamutassa were subjected to Hittite suzerainty,[3] and another fragment is part of a treaty with the men of Ura themselves.[4] Ura was an important emporium for sea-borne trade with Ugarit and Egypt, near the mouth of the river Calycadnus.[5] It would seem therefore that the Hittites had at least regained control of part of the south coast of the peninsula. But these documents are silent about the situation farther east, in Syria, and about that in western Anatolia.

Now this period, when Kizzuwadna 'belonged to the land of Khatti' and the Hittite king was in alliance with Aleppo, is one possible dating for the treaty concluded by an Arnuwandash with certain individuals of Ishmirikka.[6] This curious document apparently records the resettlement of these men, natives of Ishmi-rikka, in various cities of Kizzuwadna,[7] prominent among which are Washshuganni, otherwise known as the capital of Mitanni, and Urushsha, a Kizzuwadnean border-town. It implies not only that Kizzuwadna had acquired part of the territory of Mitanni to the east of the Euphrates, but also that the whole country was under the effective control of the Hittite king. If this dating is correct, the conqueror of Aleppo (and presumably also of Arzawa) would necessarily be Tudkhaliash I. We might suppose that Tudkhaliash in defeating Mitanni actually captured its capital city and handed over the whole territory he had conquered to the king of Kizzuwadna with whom he was in close alliance. Yet this is not quite the impression created by the text. Kizzuwadna at this time, though friendly, was still powerful and independent

[1] G, 21, no. 277; translated G, 26, 399. New fragments: see G, 28, 43 n. 47.
[2] G, 21, no. 175; translated §11, 26, 223 ff.
[3] A, 15, XVI, no. 47; A, 23, 56–7.
[4] G, 21, no. 99; A, 18, 227; A, 23, 60.   [5] A, 23, 58 ff.; A, 6, 48.
[6] G, 21, no. 87; G, 10, 43 ff. and 76 ff.; G, 12, 58; §11, 11, 70; G, 8, 53–4; A, 16.   [7] A different interpretation is given in A, 16.

and it is difficult to imagine that the Hittite king could settle the people of Ishmirikka in its cities purely on his own authority; the matter would require the consent of the king of Kizzuwadna and would have been the subject of a special agreement or treaty. We are therefore inclined to concur with those scholars who would ascribe this treaty to Arnuwandash III, towards the end of the thirteenth century. At that time Kizzuwadna had long been incorporated in the Hittite kingdom and the second of the above conditions was thus fulfilled. Mitanni had also by then ceased to exist as a kingdom, and during a period of Assyrian weakness, following the murder of Tukulti-Ninurta I, it appears to have fallen for a time under the domination of the Hittites.[1] A well-known passage in the annals of Murshilish II is most naturally taken to imply that, on the disappearance of Kizzuwadna as a kingdom, its name came to be used as a mere geographical expression for northern Syria, including Carchemish.[2] The use of the name in the Ishmirikka Treaty could well be the same. The attribution of the treaty to Arnuwandash II, son of Shuppiluliumash,[3] is less probable, since at that time the treaties with the allied kings of Mitanni and Kizzuwadna would still have been in force.

The above considerations may eventually have to be discounted, for the Ishmirikka treaty is one of the group of texts with archaistic features.[4] It could then be adduced to prove that Arnuwandash I dominated an empire in north Syria and therefore the conqueror of Aleppo was his father, Tudkhaliyash II. If, however, as suggested, the text is to be regarded as late, we are left in doubt: the conqueror of Aleppo could be Tudkhaliash III (the former *tuḫkantiš*). We leave this question undecided.

We do not know what became of the kingdom of Mitanni during this period of its eclipse, but with the accession of Artatama I, *c.* 1430 B.C., its fortunes began to revive. In face of the upstart Hittite power the kings of Mitanni and Egypt drew together. The initiative came from Mitanni, towards the end of the reign of Amenophis II, in the form of a mission of peace, the like of which 'had never been heard of' at the Egyptian court 'since the time of men and gods'.[5] Subsequently messengers from the Egyptian court approached Artatama with proposals for a marriage-alliance, to which he eventually acceded, sending his daughter to become the wife of the young king, Tuthmosis IV, and so inaugurating a series of diplomatic marriages by which the two

---

[1] §11, 23, 6.   [2] §11, 8, 307 f., retracted G, 10, 19 f.

[3] §11, 5, 85 ff.   [4] A, 16, *passim*; A, 11, 61.   [5] §11, 15, 161.

dynasties became linked in alliance. In the eyes of the Syrian princelings this new union tipped the scales against the Hittites and some time during the reign of Khattushilish II first Aleppo, then Kizzuwadna shifted allegiance to the king of Mitanni.[1]

The Hittite king was unequal to the situation, which rapidly deteriorated. We learn of this incidentally from the preamble to an edict of the following century.[2] The failure of the Hittites to restore the situation in Syria was the signal for a general revolt. The province called the 'Lower Country' (roughly the modern plain of Konya)[3] was invaded and occupied by the armies of Arzawa, as far as Tuwanuwa (Tyana) and Uda (Hyde). From the south-east the people of Armatana sacked Hittite territory as far as the city of Kizzuwadna, otherwise known as Kumanni, probably Comana Cappadociae.[4] This seems to imply that when Kizzuwadna went over to the enemy, Khattushilish had retaliated by seizing the city which gave the country its name, together with some territory in the Taurus; the location of Armatana is uncertain. The plain of Malatya, as far west as modern Gürün (ancient Tegarama) fell to the people of Ishuwa. The 'Upper Country' (the upper valleys of the Kızıl Irmak and the Euphrates) was overrun by Azzi-Khayasha, a barbarous country in the far north-east, so that the religious centre, Shamu-kha, became a frontier outpost.[5] The province of Kashshiya or Kishshiya, still securely held by garrison-commanders under Arnuwandash I, fell to invaders from Arawanna, perhaps in the north-west.[6] Nearer home, the Kaska tribes yet again sacked the cities of the homeland, reaching as far as Nenashsha (possibly classical Nanassos on the Halys).[7] Finally even the capital, Khattusha, was raided and burnt. It must have seemed the end of the Hittite kingdom.

The aggrandizement of Mitanni and Arzawa at this time is shown by the correspondence conducted by their kings with Amenophis III towards the end of his reign.[8] Tushratta of Mitanni, whose sister was already married to the pharaoh when he came to the throne, addresses him as his brother, that is, as an equal.[9] His first letter was accompanied by gifts of booty

[1] §II, 9, 60 ff.; G, 19, 61; G, 1, 26 ff.; G, 10, 36 ff. (5–7).
[2] G, 21, no. 58; G, 10, 21 ff.; §II, 14, 119; G, 1, 29 n. 1.
[3] G, 8, 63 ff.   [4] G, 10, 9 ff.; G, 8, 44; but cf. A, 16, 13 n. 28.
[5] See above, p. 664.   [6] G, 14, 46.
[7] G, 22, 35. For an approximate location of all these areas, see Map 6.
[8] §II, 18, nos. 17–30 (Mitanni), 31–2 (Arzawa). On the date of these letters see §II, 4, 7 ff.; §II, 16, 10 f.; §II, 15, 174 ff.; also *C.A.H.* II³, pt. 2, ch. XVII, sect. 1.
[9] G, 18, 48.

captured by him from the Hittites.[1] The two letters in Hittite between the pharaoh and Tarkhundaradu, the king of Arzawa,[2] do not show the same familiar style of address, but they reveal that negotiations were in train for the dispatch of an Arzawan princess as wife to the Egyptian king, a union which would doubtless have resulted in relations similar to those subsisting between Egypt and Mitanni if it had ever come to fruition.[3]

For the story of the Hittite counter-attack against the invasions just described we are dependent on the 'Deeds of Shuppiluliumash' mentioned above.[4] Since this is not a history but a biography, it opens at the moment when the young Shuppiluliumash was first entrusted by his father with the command of troops in the field. Such was the genius of the man, however, that this moment of his 'coming to manhood'[5] was in fact the turning point in the fortunes of the Hittites, as is recognized explicitly in the edict of Khattushilish III from which the account of the preceding disasters has been taken. The biography does not mark regnal years, but we may infer that it covers only the last year or two of the reign, for the old king is already ailing. On at least two occasions he falls ill and is obliged to send out his son in command. Thus we have no means of estimating how many years the kingdom had survived the loss of its most important provinces.

Unfortunately the sections of the 'Deeds' which treated this early period when Shuppiluliumash was operating under his father's command are so badly mutilated that no consecutive narrative can be extracted from them.

The main scene of these operations appears to be in the northeast—the 'Upper Country'—and the war is directed against the Kaska tribes and Azzi-Khayasha. The town of Arziya is raided and recaptured. Shamukha is a base, to which prisoners are brought and from which sorties are made. Evidently the Azzian attack which made Shamukha into an outpost had been repulsed before the narrative opens. The Azzians at first avoid battle, but eventually their king, Karannish (Krannish) or Lannish, is forced to give battle at Kummakha, probably modern Kemah. The text breaks off here, but the battle must have resulted in a Hittite

---

[1] §II, 18, no. 17 (36 ff.). This letter may well date from before the accession of Shuppiluliumash.

[2] A, 26, 328 ff. (new edition of §II, 18, nos. 31–2).

[3] G, 1, 27 n. 1.

[4] See pp. 672 f.

[5] *šarā išparzašta*: see G, 10, 23 and G, 11, 24, l. 14.

victory, for it was the father of Shuppiluliumash who appointed the first vassal-king of Azzi-Khayasha, a certain Mariyash.[1]

References to other parts of the country are sporadic and disconnected. The town of Shallapa, an outpost on the road to Arzawa,[2] is attacked and burnt by the Hittites. Its recapture would have been the first step in the counter-attack against Arzawa, which still held Tuwanuwa. There is a reference to Mount Nanni, which cannot be located. More important is the passage describing the relief of the provinces of Kashshiya and the Khulana river. Kashshiya, as we have seen, had been overrun by the people of Arawanna; here, however, the enemies are the countries of Masha and Kammala. Since Masha has western connexions, this passage is a pointer to the general location of these countries.[3]

The section of the 'Deeds' which must have described the death of Tudkhaliash and the accession of Shuppiluliumash is lost. So short is the gap, however, that we may suppose the transition received only a brief mention in the narrative. None the less, the prayer mentioned above suggests that the death of the old king precipitated a crisis. This is the 'affair of Tudkhaliash the younger' which weighed heavily on the conscience of future generations. As already mentioned, the heir designate was assassinated by a group of officers and Shuppiluliumash was placed on the throne. The text is damaged and precise details are obscure, but the general situation is tolerably clear: an outstanding leader who had led the army to victory was carried to power by the military. Once in sole command, Shuppiluliumash showed himself not only a brilliant general but also a shrewd statesman of unusual ability. The stage was set for an expansion of Hittite power which raised the kingdom in one generation to a status of equality with the leading nations of the Near Eastern world.

III. TROY VI

The Sixth Settlement ushered in a new era distinguished by a culture of its own, with widespread innovations in almost all fields of human endeavour. Though some earlier elements evidently survived, a break with the past on the site is obvious and there can be no doubt that we must postulate the arrival of a fresh human stock. Whence the new masters came is still a mystery, but there is every reason to believe that they formed part of the movement that at the same time swept over the Greek

[1] §II, 7, 128–9 (53 ff.); §II, 6, 3.   [2] See above, p. 662.   [3] G, 14, 46 f.

mainland, overpowered the bearers of Early Helladic culture, and established Middle Helladic culture at what is taken to mark the beginning of the Middle Bronze Age. Progress and development in the two areas followed different lines. On the mainland of Greece the newcomers after a time came under steadily increasing Minoan cultural influence which ultimately in the Late Bronze Age gave rise to Mycenaean civilization. Their kinsmen who settled in the Troad, on the other hand, in their greater isolation clung tenaciously to their own way of life, which they maintained relatively pure and not fundamentally affected by foreign contacts, to the very end of the Sixth Settlement.

The Trojan branch excelled in architecture: three successive fortification walls were erected, each reconstruction surpassing its predecessor in size and magnificence.[1] The last, with a circuit of some six hundred yards, enclosed a citadel about two hundred and twenty-five yards long with at least four gates. The interior rose in a series of concentric terraces to the summit of the hill on which presumably stood the royal palace. The lower terraces were occupied by large, generously-spaced, free-standing houses, presumably the residences of the king's courtiers and favourite companions. Wooden columns set on shaped stone bases were a feature in many of these buildings. Great care was taken in the fitting and dressing of stone blocks especially in the fortress walls, and masonry in some sections almost attained the classical Greek excellence.

Another remarkable difference from the preceding settlements is represented by a cemetery which yielded remains of some two hundred cinerary urns, many of which contained the cremated bones of adults and the unburned bones of children. The cemetery, which lay outside the citadel and is attributable to the final phase of Troy VI, demonstrates that the practice of cremation was established at Troy at least as early as the beginning of the thirteenth century B.C.

Little metal has survived, but gold, electrum, silver and true bronze occur in competently executed ornaments and implements. Some of these together with objects of stone, ivory and bone were no doubt imported from Mycenaean centres; others may have been worked at Troy. Most of these pieces as well as the whorls and other objects of terracotta represent new types or forms that were rare in the Trojan Early Bronze Age. Grey Minyan Ware, which had no local antecedents, is the characteristic and predominant pottery through the whole life of the Sixth Settlement. At the outset it is virtually indistinguishable from the like ware of

[1] See Plate 131 (*a*) and (*b*).

the Helladic mainland, but modifications of fabric and shapes make their appearance in the later phases.

The layer of Troy VI in the central area of the citadel was almost entirely cut away in Hellenistic or Roman times when a broad open square was laid out about the Temple of Athena. Along the periphery, however, deposits of debris exceeding seventeen feet in depth have been found. Eight successive strata have been recognized and the chronological series of other objects and pottery they produced, showing gradual development and change, may be taken to establish the fact that the settlement lasted through a long period of time. For convenience it may be divided arbitrarily into an Early, Middle, and Late Sub-period.

External relations were principally with the Aegean. Imported Matt-painted Ware appears in the Early Sub-period and more commonly in the Middle. Mycenaean wares of Late Helladic I and II are found in the Middle Sub-period, and fabrics of Late Helladic IIIa become fairly numerous in the Late Sub-period, with elements of Late Helladic IIIb and Cypriote White Slip II Wares arriving before the end of the final phase. These correlations place the lower chronological limit of the Sixth Settlement some time within only a few years of 1300 B.C. The upper limit, which depends on the dating of Minyan and Matt-painted wares in the Helladic area, is not so closely fixed, but may provisionally be set at about 1900–1800 B.C., with the possibility of a considerable margin of error.

Although the Sixth Settlement was thus contemporary with the early and the greater part of the late stage of the Hittite Empire in Central Anatolia, not a single object of any kind whatsoever that can definitely be called Hittite has ever been recognized in strata of Troy VI, nor have any certainly identified Trojan objects yet been recovered in the Anatolian Hittite layers. This negative evidence is not conclusive in precluding the possibility that relations were maintained between the two areas. A trade route to Cyprus was open, and there may well have been communications with Central Asia Minor by way of Cilicia.

In its final phase, VI*h*, the Sixth Settlement was overthrown by a great upheaval which dislodged the superstructure of the fortification walls and evidently ruined most of the large houses inside the citadel. There is no evidence of an accompanying fire, and the disaster was surely the work of a violent earthquake, which probably occurred sometime in the first quarter of the thirteenth century.

CHAPTER XVI

THE ARCHAEOLOGICAL EVIDENCE OF THE SECOND MILLENNIUM B.C. ON THE PERSIAN PLATEAU

THE second millennium B.C. remains one of the most poorly known of all of the archaeological periods on the Persian plateau. Older excavations[1] and limited surveys,[2] summarized in several important articles and books,[3] have yielded scattered information about pottery styles and burial practices. The limited nature of this information has encouraged a renewal of field work relating to the second millennium during the past decade.[4] As a result, there is now sufficient new evidence to permit a tentative restructuring of some aspects of the interpretative problems involved, particularly in regard to the western and northern border areas of the plateau. In these areas many of the cultural patterns dating to the early second millennium had their inception in the third millennium, and had disappeared, or had been greatly modified, by the end of the first quarter of the second millennium. Many of the cultural patterns which then developed were in turn terminated in the third quarter of the millennium by the onset of the new ethnic movements and major political changes of the beginning Iron Age.

I. THE LATE THIRD AND EARLY SECOND MILLENNIA B.C.

During the late third and early second millennia B.C the Persian plateau was divided into distinct cultural areas as indicated by the distribution of ceramic tradition:[5] the Gurgan Grey Ware in Gurgan province in the north-east; the Giyān IV–III Painted Ware in eastern Luristān; and, between the two, the Yanik

[1] §1; 3; 5; 15; 39; 40 and 43; §III, 1; 2 and 10.
[2] G, 1; 2; 6; 7; 14; 16 and 19 to 24; §1, 3, 5 ff.; G, 25, 19 f. and 41 ff.; §III, 21.
[3] E.g. G, 3; 4; 8; 12; 13 and 17.
[4] G, 14; §1, 7 to 10; 12; 16; 19; 20; A, 3; 7, and §1, 44; A, 21; §III, 3 to 7; 13 to 16; 18 to 20; A, 5; 13; 14 and 20.
[5] The term 'ceramic tradition' is preferred to 'culture' since the evidence often consists only of pottery.

Early Bronze Age Wares[1] in central Persia and eastern Azarbāyjān. In the south local painted pottery traditions are currently being brought to light in Seistān and Kirmān.[2]

NORTH-EASTERN PERSIA: THE GURGAN GREY WARE

In north-eastern Persia, a grey pottery ceramic tradition, formed either from the indigenous painted pottery tradition, or with elements added, perhaps from the west,[3] has been found at the excavated sites of Shāh Tepe, Tureng Tepe, and Yarim Tepe, as well as at a number of unexcavated sites in the Gurgan plain. It also occurs at the site of Tepe Hisar which lies on the plateau not far from the upper end of the Shāhrūd pass.[4] The major occupational phases of these sites date to the latter half of the third millennium B.C. It seems quite possible, as suggested by the excavator of Yarim Tepe, that the Bronze Age occupation of Yarim Tepe and the III*b* occupation at Hisar came to an end at the same time as the results of raids originating from the east.[5] Tepe Hisar was then reoccupied (III*c*), while the occupation of the more western Gurgan sites, Tureng Tepe and Shāh Tepe, continued without interruption. The later stage of this occupation is known chiefly through burials and hoards found at these three sites, with only scattered and fragmentary mudbrick walls to represent the contemporary architecture. The pottery of this late stage is a further development of an earlier burnished grey ware. Vessels are often decorated with criss-crossed lines, or chevrons, executed in a fine pattern-burnishing technique. Tall bottles, vessels with open trough spouts placed at the rim, and canteens with perforated shoulder lugs occur as major forms. Vessels with short, unbridged, horizontal spouts made their appearance, as did occasional vessels of burnished orange ware. Many of these shapes, and the orange ware, became common in the following Iron Age.[6] Alabaster objects—cylindrical and spouted jars, offering tables on pedestal stands, miniature columns and large disks with handles, were common. There was a great increase in

---

[1] A Persian variant of a broader ceramic pattern variously called 'Trans-Caucasian Copper Age' (§1, 27), 'East Anatolian E.B.A. Culture' (§1, 6), and 'Kuro-Araxes Aeneolithic' (§1, 33).   [2] A, 11; 21.

[3] G, 12, 50 f.; §1, 3, 242; §1, 41, 137; §1, 30, 77 for Anatolian connexions; D. Stronach, on the basis of Yarim Tepe evidence, favours local development. Cf. §1, 20, 88 f.   [4] G, 1; §1, 3; 19; 20; 39; 40 and 43.

[5] Information from D. Stronach; §1, 16, 271.

[6] Spouted vessels: §1, 39, pl. cxvi, H 502, H 420; §1, 40, pl. xli, H 3511; §1, 3, pl. lix, 474*a*, *b*, 475. Orange ware: §1, 40, pl. xli, H 3509, H 3315. Cf. §11, 18; §iii, 1, and University Museum Philadelphia Collection.

the availability of metals, and graves contain copper[1] blades with bent tangs, terminal buttons and ridge-stops, circular copper stamp-seals, axe-adzes, roll-headed pins, and 'wands' with figures cast at the top. Gold, silver and lead were used for vessels and small objects, while carnelian, amber and agate were made into beads. The variety of fine materials and objects provides an indication of great local prosperity. The typology of the objects suggests trade contacts reaching from the Indus Valley and perhaps even China in the east[2] to Mesopotamia and central Anatolia in the west.[3]

Although a terminal date of 1900/1800 B.C. is commonly accepted for the Gurgan Grey Ware,[4] certain bits of evidence make it necessary to question the validity of this conclusion. First, the eroded condition of the topmost deposits at Hisar, Shāh, and Tureng Tepe required a precision of excavation technique which was unavailable at the time of the original excavations. The site reports provide inadequate documentation for this final occupation and leave in doubt the correct stratigraphic context of important artifacts and hoards. Second, moderate quantities of amber, dating to the Hisar IIIc period, seem most likely to have been connected with the general amber trade which flourished in the Aegean, southern Russia and the Caucasus between 1650 and 1450 B.C.[5] Third, the representation of what appears to be a six-spoked, wheeled chariot on a cylinder seal attributed to Hisar IIIb context should indicate a date of eighteenth century or slightly earlier for the end of the IIIb period.[6] Fourth, several typological parallels (notably a copper mattock and compartmented copper seals) link Hisar IIIb and c with the terminal and post-Harappan cultures at Mohenjo-daro and Chanhu-daro in the Indus valley.[7] Since current carbon-14 dating suggests that the Harappan culture did not end until early in the second millennium, the parallels with Chanhu-daro argue for an even later date for the post-Harappan contacts.[8] Finally, there are typological similarities between the Hisar IIIc pottery and the

---

[1] Current analyses of Hisar objects confirm the virtual absence of tin-bronze.

[2] §1, 36, 199, 209, 220; §1, 30, 77, 80; §1, 42, 58, 60, 94; §1, 41, 137; §1, 32.

[3] §1, 22, 240 ff.; §1, 34, 117 ff.; G, 12, 50 ff.

[4] §1, 3, 306 ff.; §1, 22, 242; G, 18, 451; §1, 34, 122, cf. §1, 29 for a date of c. 1550 B.C.; §1, 31 for 1250–1000 B.C. See §1, 4, 189 ff. for current dating of the Indian evidence.

[5] §1, 28, 47 ff. Unfortunately, the seal appears to be lost.

[6] §1, 14, 188; §1, 13, 726 f.   [7] §1, 26, 122; §1, 36, 176 ff.; §1, 4, 189 ff.

[8] §1, 17, 277 and A, 4, 306. Cf. §1, 26, 121 f. Recent research suggests that all dates in the 2000 B.C. range may be 200 or more years too late. Cf. §1, 37.

pottery of Iron Age I as found at Khorvin, Marlik, Tepe Sialk and other sites.[1] Other parallels occur between metal objects; for example, spearheads with bent tangs.[2] The parallels are close enough to indicate some cultural continuity, although the beginning of Iron Age I cannot be placed earlier than 1350 ± 50 years on present evidence.[3] No one has yet satisfactorily explained how this continuity survives the hiatus of 500 or more years created by ending Hisar IIIc at 1900/1800 B.C. The five points of evidence listed above, while admittedly insufficient for the establishment of firm dating, nevertheless, indicate that the question is still far from settled. The determination of the length of the hiatus following the end of the Gurgan Grey Ware and the appearance of the Iron Age ceramics of northern Persia thus remains one of the most important problems to be resolved in the understanding of events taking place during the middle second millennium in the northern part of the country.

With the notable exception of Tureng Tepe,[4] the occupation of the Gurgan sites seems to have ended abruptly, and was followed by an hiatus, the historical nature of which remains unknown. It has been suggested that the cause of abandonment may have been the intrusion into the area of nomadic tribesmen from Central Asia who temporarily destroyed town life while they either settled on new open sites or moved on to the south. The fact that Yarim Tepe and Tepe Hisar, the easternmost settlements, were the first destroyed may indicate the eastern origin of the newcomer.[5] Tepe Hisar, at least, would appear to have recovered from the initial attack which burned the IIIb town,[6] only to be overwhelmed along with the remaining Gurgan sites at the end of the IIIc period.[7] Depending upon the dates assigned to the end of Hisar IIIc and to the beginning of the Iron Age, the hiatus may have been 700 years (1900–1200 B.C.), 300 years (1600–1300 B.C.), or even non-existent. The resolution of this problem, which requires additional field work, will have a major impact on the general interpretation of cultural developments in the north, since the question of the relationship between the Gurgan ceramics and the ceramics of the Iron Age is directly involved.

In regard to the hiatus problem we have noted that a number

[1] §II, 18.   [2] §III, 15, fig. 44. Cf. §1, 40, pls. L, LI.
[3] See below, pp. 712 ff.   [4] §1, 19; 20; A, 6 to 8.   [5] See above, p. 687 n. 6.
[6] The Hisar IIIb level at Yarim Tepe has a carbon-14 date of 2166 ± 249 B.C. (P-508), 5730 half-life. Cf. §1, 16.
[7] The Hisar IIIc level at Tureng Tepe has a carbon-14 date of 1920 ± 200 B.C. (Gif 485), half-life unspecified. Cf. A, 6, 16 ff.

of techniques and artifact types indicate important continuities in cultural traditions between the Bronze and Iron Age grey ware cultures. The nature of some of these overlaps, such as pattern burnishing, pottery shapes, and various specialized forms of metal objects, suggests that the hiatus may not represent a very great cultural disruption after all.[1] The nature of this disruption must be examined, since the ultimate reconstruction of events in the north in the second millennium depends upon an understanding of the significance of the typological relationships which are evident. Two hypotheses present themselves: (1) a continuous internal development within the region, involving only the displacement during the early second millennium of the Gurgan people from their earlier centre westward to north central Persia; or (2) the intrusion of distinct but related foreign groups into the north central area sometime after the dispersal of the Gurgan people. In the first instance, the Gurgan Grey Ware is seen as the local outcome of the evolution under various stimuli of the north-eastern painted pottery cultures,[2] with a subsequent displacement westward producing the grey pottery tradition of Iron Age I.[3] If this hypothesis should prove correct it would indicate the existence in northern Persia of a cultural area which was essentially stable in terms of its ceramic tradition from some time in the third millennium until well into the first millennium (thus paralleling the situation in Luristān as described below). Factors promoting change in this situation would have been foreign trade contacts and the intrusion of additional groups, probably Indo-European in many cases, who would have been absorbed with little observable impact on the basic pattern of existing material culture.

In contrast with the first hypothesis, the second envisages a series of foreign but related groups following one another into Persia from the Caucasus, Anatolia, or Central Asia. Such groups would have been represented by the remains of Hisar II and III, Marlik, Sialk A and B, Hasanlu V and possibly IV, and so on. The general thrust of movement would have been either from the north-west eastward across northern Persia toward Central Asia and Pakistan with offshoots southward into west central and southern Persia, or around the Caspian Sea into eastern Persia, or both.[4] In this interpretation the material culture of the various sites would still exhibit a close typological similarity, but such

---

[1] §II, 18; §III, 23; §III, 16; §III, 19, 42 ff.
[2] See above, p. 687 n. 3. Cf. §I, 20, 88 f.   [3] §II, 18; A, 8, 38.
[4] G, 3, 60 ff.; G, 5, 2 ff.; §I, 22, 197; §I, 25; §I, 31; §III, 15, 37 f.

similarity would have been due to earlier shared traditions outside Persia, rather than to a continuous development within the country, and some of the culture-bearers would have been Indo-European.

Map. 7. Major second millennium sites on the Persian plateau.

Whichever interpretative hypothesis may ultimately prove correct there are very clear connexions to be considered both with the west and the east. In the west many specific typological parallels link the grey ware cultures of Persia to Anatolia, the Aegean and Central Europe where related material is often, but not always, associated with Indo-European speaking peoples. At the very least there are strong contacts and shared traditions in metal working and pottery making, and probably architecture as well.[1] On the other hand, the Gurgan Grey Ware spread eastward into

[1] G, 18, 404 ff.; §1, 25; §III, 22 and 23.

Soviet Turkmenistān where it occurs in the Namazga V Culture.[1] The original direction of movement of the Gurgan Grey Ware must, therefore, also involve the date of origin and direction of spread of the Namazga V Culture. At present the latter is dated by comparison with the former and hence does not provide independent evidence on the question. The Namazga V Culture evolved into a later local culture, Namazga VI, which spread eastward to the Murghāb region where it flourished until displaced by a painted pottery culture at the end of the second millennium. At this time those local peoples who were not absorbed by the newcomers probably moved south into Afghanistān, Pakistān, and India.[2]

CENTRAL WESTERN PERSIA: THE GIYĀN IV–III PAINTED WARE

A second ceramic tradition existed on the Persian plateau from the middle third until the early first millennium B.C. This was the Giyān IV–III tradition located in Luristān in the Zagros mountain-zone which intervenes between lowland Mesopotamia and the central Persian plateau. The early stage of this ceramic, represented by the Giyān IV style of painted pottery, has been found in the area from Nihāvand south to Burūjird, including the area south-east of Harsīn: the Khawa, Chawari and Alishtar plains. It probably also extended as far north as Godin Tepe in the Kangavār valley. The Giyān IV style appears to have originated under the influence of the Susa D type of Elamite painted pottery which has been found by surface survey from Malayer in Luristān south and south-west into Khūzistān where it occurs at Susa in the second half of the third millennium B.C.[3] The terminal stage of the Giyān IV style lasted into the first quarter of the second millennium and formed the transition to the following Giyān III style as seen in graves at Tepe Giyān and nearby Tepe Jamshidi.[4] Since the two styles have elements which are both similar and distinct, the established names Giyān IV and III may usefully be retained as designations for the periods during which those

[1] G, 9; 10; 11 and 15; §1, 23 and 24. A, 12, 178 gives 2100±50 B.C. for the end of Namazga IV, and (p. 186) 1030±60 B.C. for the end of Namazga VI. Two dates are available for Namazga V: 2075±100 B.C. (Berlin 717) and 2170±110 B.C. (Berlin 716). Half-life unspecified.

[2] G, 10, 76; A, 5 reports grey pottery cemeteries of Iron Age date which appear to have relations with the Gurgan Grey Ware. [3] §II, 5, 82–3.

[4] §1, 15, pls. 30–4; §1, 22, 232 includes graves 115, 112, 107, 105, 103, 101, 106 and 100 at Giyān and 15, 10–6 at Tepe Jamshidi in a terminal Giyān Ic phase. §II, 5, 70 ff. makes graves 115, 112, 110–100 and Tepe Jamshidi graves 10–8 a transitional IV–III phase.

styles were in vogue, although the material taken as a whole appears to represent a single tradition which may best be indicated by the term Giyān IV–III Painted Ware.

With the beginning of the Giyān III period, the characteristic globular jars of period IV became more bag-like with bulging lower bodies and a ridged instead of a curved shoulder. Decoration in both monochrome and polychrome (black on a cream shoulder zone with red body) occurs in geometric patterns such as bands of cross-hatching, solid bands, and wavy lines in various horizontal combinations. The style of decoration and the metal objects found in graves 11 to 15 at Tepe Jamshidi suggest that these graves fall late in the Giyān IV period, although the small jars are said to be identical with some in the Musée du Louvre,[1] classic Giyān IV vessels. To the period of transition to Giyān III belong two stone-built tombs at Tepe Jamshidi (8 and 9) which contain polychrome tripod vessels. The appearance of this new vessel type suggests a foreign influence in the area, perhaps originating in Anatolia where tripods have a much older history at Troy and elsewhere. Whether such influence was in the form of new trade contacts by way of north-western Persia, or whether it represents a new element in the population cannot be determined on present evidence. It has been suggested that contacts with central Anatolia may be indicated by the occurrence at Kültepe in *Kārum* II of socketed bronze spearheads with well-developed mid-ribs, and pottery painted with wavy lines, birds and sun motifs.[2] Two small juglets with handles found in Giyan grave 108 provide a parallel with similar juglets in Palestine and Syria dated to the Middle Bronze Age, and to a grave of Late Bronze Age date at Yanik Tepe in Azarbāyjān.[3] An early Giyān III cylinder seal from Tepe Jamshidi (grave 3) is Old Elamite–Old Babylonian in type and should date to 1600 B.C. or slightly earlier,[4] thus indicating that the Giyān IV style had already evolved into the III style prior to 1600 B.C.[5]

The late Giyān IV style is also attested in the Rumishgan valley to the south-west of Tepe Giyān where excavations by Erich Schmidt uncovered a building level of the period at the site of Kamtarlan II. Here sherds, said to be comparable with the pottery of grave 102 at Tepe Giyān, were associated with a cylinder

---

[1] §II, 5, 72 ff., cf. §I, 22, 232.   [2] §II, 5, 83 ff.
[3] G, 18, 463 dates these to later than 2000 B.C. Cf. §I, 15, pl. 31, 108 and §I, 9, pl. XLIV, 29 grave A6, pp. 141, 147.
[4] Information from E. Porada. Cf. §I, 18, pl. 34, 13–15 and §I, 15, pl. 74, 12.
[5] G, 18, 462 ff.; §I, 22, 235; §II, 5, 83 ff.

seal of Gutian type.[1] On the northern slope of nearby Kamtarlan I were found three child burials in jars of Giyān IV type, placed among the stone-built houses. At Chigha Sabz in the same region a burial of a man with silver rings and Giyān IV pots (which were a modified version of Giyān grave 13, pot 1) was found, slightly more than three metres below the surface.

The Giyān IV style also seems to have exerted some influence northward through Kurdistān to southern Azarbāyjān, perhaps in connexion with Anatolian trade passing north through the western Zagros. At Hasanlu the little-known Painted Orange Ware of period VII, dated by carbon-14 to the late third millennium, seems to have been influenced in both shape and painting style by Giyān IV.[2]

At the beginning of the second millennium, the Giyān IV–III Painted Ware spread outward from its established area in the Kangavār valley at Godin Tepe (III), and in the Nihāvand valley at Tepe Giyān, to the south and west through most of Luristān 'though in the west, in particular, there are regional variations which are difficult to date'.[3] The major sites at which Giyān III-related materials occur include Tepe Giyān, Tepe Bad Hora, Tepe Jamshidi, Godin Tepe, Cheshme Mahi, Kamtarlan II, Chigha Sabz, Surkh Dom, Tepe Gūrān, Tang-i-Hamamlan and Kuran Buzan.[4] Classic Giyān III style pottery is said to be found most frequently in eastern Luristān south-east of Harsīn. Survey work suggests that in the largest plains there was a tendency for the number of sites to decrease in comparison with earlier periods and for the population to group itself into cities; the biggest of these cities is reported as being Girairan in the Alishtar plain. Smaller sites of the later III, and the parallel 'Giyān II' period (see below), were usually placed by a pass or on a high natural bluff in the smaller valleys.[5] Some of the 'boulder cities' along the Saimarreh river date to this period, while others belong to the Iron Age. 'There seems also to have been a substantial nomadic population in the higher valleys and the first graveyards appear along the banks of the Badavar with no apparent sites attached.'[6]

The classic pottery of the period as found in Tepe Giyān III

---

[1] Information from M. van Loon. Cf. §II, 14, fig. 17.
[2] §I, 21, fig. 22; §I, 22, 233; cf. §III, 21 for geography.
[3] Information from C. Goff and §I, 44, 390.
[4] §I, 15; §I, 44; §II, 10; G, 14; G, 19; §III, 18.
[5] Information from C. Goff; §II, 5, 151–4.
[6] Information from C. Goff; §III, 18, 167.

is painted in a technique similar to that found in central Anatolia around 1900 B.C. This polychrome painting technique became widespread in north-western Persia following the decline of the Yanik E.B.A. Ware (see below), and persisted in central Persia until the beginning of the Iron Age. The Giyān III vessels are generally red, often with a bright red slip, with designs painted either directly on the surface in black or on a white slip which covers the upper part of the body. Geometric patterns consist largely of stripes, wavy lines and squares in various combinations. Vessel shapes are generally bag-like, often with ridged carinations or handles, or both, and occur with tripod vessels which have concave sides and rounded feet. Sometimes a small cup or two was placed on the upper rim of a tripod vessel as in Giyān graves 84 and 98; the use of similar rim-cups is attested in the late third millennium at Susa (D) and Tepe Gawra (VI).[1] The graves at Tepe Giyān were simple inhumations, whereas the stone tombs at Tepe Jamshidi contained multiple burials of three individuals. These burials were accompanied by copper/bronze pins with flat or conical heads, spiral rings, flat triangular knife blades (each with a rivet set into a short tang), and a hammered axe-head. Grave 3 at Jamshidi, which was found eighty centimetres higher in the fill than the stone tombs, contained the previously mentioned haematite cylinder seal bearing the Old Elamite–Old Babylonian motif of the god with a mace. The motif on this seal has been compared with a seal impression on a Babylonian tablet of the reign of Samsuiluna (1749–1712 B.C.).[2] It is of interest to recall that the first historical mention of the Kassites is in the reign of this same king.[3] The contents of these burials are remarkable mainly for the fact that the custom of building stone tombs is documented in this part of Persia for the first time, and for the first appearance of deep tripod vessels. The form of the tombs may have been used earlier in periods which are poorly known archaeologically, or they may have been introduced along with the tripods from the west where they were already in use in the Early Bronze Age.[4] The innovation in any event seems to have been adopted into the existing cultural pattern without causing any radical changes.

Period III graves at Tepe Giyān may be divided into two typo-

[1] Musée du Louvre; G, 18, fig. 91, 24.
[2] §1, 15, 99, 100, pl. 74, cf. §11, 14, vol. 1, 54, 55, vol. 11, 469, 475.
[3] See above, ch. v, sect. vi.
[4] G, 18, 80 ff.; G, 3, 67 f.; §111, 10, 100 f.; §11, 9, fig. 2; *C.A.H.* 1³, pt. 2, ch. xviii, sects. iii, iv; §1, 27.

logical groups: III *a* and III *b*.[1] The III *a* graves are characterized by the presence of deep red pottery tripods painted with wide and narrow bands of black. Accompanying bowls and jars are decorated with hanging semi-circles and wavy lines. Well-made copper or bronze vessels were placed in the graves along with knife blades with rivets in the tangs (which probably once held wooden handles), straight pins and simple beads. The III *b* group of graves offers a variant pattern with absence of metal objects and the replacement of the deep tripod by a shallow tripod dish. This replacement, which appeared to have a chronological significance at Tepe Giyān, may now be seen to have been only a local event, as both high and low tripods occur together in later context at Kamtarlan II and Chigha Sabz.[2] The low tripod form would thus seem to be at best a late addition to the assemblage rather than a replacement for the higher form. The difference in value of the objects placed in these grave groups could reflect differing social positions as much as chronological range. Other vessels in the III *b* group are of a yellow-buff ware painted with black bands or wavy lines and hanging concentric loops along the rim. Similar sherds have been published from Bakati in the Alishtar plain south-west of Tepe Giyān.[3]

In south-western Luristān excavations in the Rumishgan and Hulailan plains have uncovered occupations of Giyān III type. At Kamtarlan II a flat Giyān IV habitation site is overlain by a Giyān III cemetery. The middle strata of this cemetery produced eight burials, mostly of individuals in graves covered with stone slabs. Over one woman's grave these slabs formed a gabled roof, on top of which there was a jar with finger-impressed ridges and lions in relief flanking a short spout, vaguely reminiscent, it is said, of an Isin-Larsa vat from the Diyālā.[4] Inside the tomb there were both high and low tripods and toggle pins. Both toggle pins and an animal in relief have been found in Bronze Age context at Dinkha Tepe in recent excavations (see below). The tombs of men at Kamtarlan II contained dagger blades with pierced tangs and, in one case, a simple axe. All of the tombs contained pins and concave-sided cylindrical cups with disk bases. One tomb was a collective burial; the funerary furniture included thirty-

---

[1] III*a* graves: 99–90, 84–6 from −7·30 to −6·10 m.; III*b* graves; 89–87, and 83 from −6·50 to −6·10 m. Grave 88 contains a bronze blade and is atypical in this respect. But cf. the new evidence of Godin III which has a date of 1967 ± 124 B.C. (Gak 1071), 5730 half-life. See A, 23, 49 n. 37.

[2] Information from M. van Loon.   [3] G, 24, pl. xv, 1.

[4] §II, 12, fig. 8, p. 124; cf. §II, 2, frontispiece, pl. 128 *b*.

three pottery vessels, one of which has a disk base and is reminiscent of an Old Babylonian–Old Assyrian–Khabur shape.[1] Other
vessels included a pitcher painted with a kind of owl's face, bowls
with groups of radial lines at four points on the rim,[2] high tripods
with sagging base and pierced lugs, a square tripod and a tripod
with cup on the rim (as in Giyān grave 98). The common pottery
included bag-shaped pots with ridges,[3] and bands of paint, and
low tripods. Five more burials contained both high and low
tripods; Giyān III pottery lay just below these graves. One of
the lower graves contained a bronze jug with riveted handle.

At Chigha Sabz twenty-seven burials in the upper two metres
of the deposit contained pottery of Giyān IV–III type. One of
these graves contained two low tripods, one of which rested on
booted human feet. Five of the burials appear to belong properly
to Giyān III. These graves contained two dagger blades with
pierced tangs (for rivets), two elaborate axes like one inscribed
with the name of the nineteenth century B.C. Elamite ruler Attakhushu,[4] a concave-sided cylindrical bronze cup with convex base,
a toggle pin, a low tripod, and high tripods (some of which had
vertically pierced lugs). At Surkh Dom scattered graves containing low and high tripods of Giyān III type also occurred.

NORTH-WESTERN PERSIA: THE YANIK EARLY BRONZE AGE WARE

During the third millennium the Gurgan Grey Ware and the
earliest Giyān IV–III Culture were separated by the intrusion
south-eastward from eastern Anatolia and southern Transcaucasia
of the Yanik pottery which is characterized by the presence of a
light or dark grey-to-black burnished surface. The pottery is
handmade in shapes tending toward squared rims and pointed
bases and frequently has a metallic sheen. It is, however, quite
distinct from the thin, fine grey ware of Gurgan. In its earlier
stages (E.B. I at Yanik Tepe) it was decorated with elaborate
incised geometric patterns which are filled with a white paste.
Later (E.B. II at Yanik Tepe), the incised patterns gave way to
plain burnishing associated with 'Nahcevan lugs', impressed
dimples and occasional applied designs.[5] Peoples using these
types of pottery occupied the whole of northern Azarbāyjān around
the northern half of Lake Reẓā'īyeh (formerly Urmia) as indicated by their surface remains and the excavated levels of Geoy

[1] §II, 12, fig. 4, p. 123.
[2] G, 18, fig. 85, T. 139, T. 154; §I, 35.
[3] §II, 12, fig. 5, p. 123.
[4] §I, 38, pl. 49b.
[5] For Nahcevan lugs see §I, 6, 168 f.

Tepe (K period) near Reẓā'īyeh and at Yanik Tepe (E.B. I and II) near Tazekand south-west of Tabrīz, in the Trialeti region near Tiflis, in the middle Araxes Valley around Erivan, and on the plain of Erzurum.[1]

At Yanik Tepe nine building levels of round houses represent the early architecture of the E.B. I occupation. The houses were joined together by radial walls and were usually entered through the roof. This type of house is also known from Shengavit and Eilar in the Caucasus and from Beth Yeraḥ IV in Palestine and provides an important link, along with pottery, between the three areas.[2] In the later, or E.B. II stage at Yanik Tepe the round houses were replaced by rectangular ones. This architectural shift, however, was not reflected in the ceramics, for the incised ware had already gone out of style before the architecture changed.[3] Both round and rectangular houses were furnished with benches, ovens and hearths and plastered work-benches with grooves for draining the surface. The later houses had exterior, ground-level doorways and wooden staircases to the roof. At Geoy Tepe pottery similar to the plain ware, with the 'Nahcevan lug' (a perforated round lug found at Nahcevan in Soviet Armenia) has been found in period K, along with a flat-tanged copper spearhead, copper rings with overlapping ends, and two racquet pins. An analysis of the metal from Geoy Tepe shows that it was copper with arsenic added—a finding which suggests that the period ended before 2000 B.C. at which time tin-bronze appeared in the general region.[4]

This Yanik tradition is now known to have moved southward along the eastern side of the Mount Alvand alignment of the Zagros into the Hamadān plain where it is known from over a dozen sites.[5] These sites, recently discovered by survey work, include two large ones which seem to have been occupied only by users of this pottery, while Godin Tepe (IV) near Kangavār represents a similar occupation.[6] A few unstratified sherds of the ware have also been found on the surface at Tepe Giyan where it probably occurs as an import, and at least one sherd has been found in a probable Susa D context at Susa.[7] At Malayer a stratum of Yanik E.B.A. Wares is reported to underlie sherds of Susa D type,[8] a circumstance which suggests that the maximum

---

[1] §I, 5, 34 ff.; §I, 7 to 10; information from C. A. Burney and field observations by the author.　　[2] §I, 2.　　[3] §I, 9, 142; §I, 10, 59.

[4] §I, 5, 61 f., 193, fig. 121, 1203, 1204, 1207; §I, 33, 6.

[5] Information from T. C. Young, Jr.; §III, 21, 232, 235.　　[6] §I, 44, 390.

[7] Information on Giyān from L. Levine. An incised white-filled grey ware sherd of Yanik type is preserved in the Susa D sherd collection at the Musée des Antiquités Nationales, St Germain, Paris.　　[8] §II, 5, 82–3.

expansion southward may have been in the middle third millennium. At Godin Tepe the Yanik occupation is immediately overlain by the Giyān IV–III Painted Ware which suggests that by the end of the millennium the Yanik tradition was already on the wane and beginning to disappear. In western Azarbāyjān at Geoy Tepe the terminal date has been placed around 2050 B.C. on the basis of parallels in eastern Anatolia.[1] This date is supported by the absence of tin-bronze, by the presence of an imported K period dimple-impressed black sherd and what appear to be degenerate Nahcevan lugs in period VII at Hasanlu (c. 2170 ± 138 B.C., average of five carbon-14 dates),[2] and by what appears to be an imported piece of period VII Painted Orange Ware in Geoy Tepe K$_3$.[3] The date of the end of the occupation at Yanik Tepe is probably around the same time.[4] A piece of polychrome ware of second millennium type is said to occur in a terminal level of E.B. II, while a sherd of Painted Orange Ware has been found in good E.B. II context at Sūmūch Tepe halfway down the road from Yanik Tepe to Bonāb on the east side of Lake Reẓā'īyeh.

The movement of these Yanik E.B.A. Wares into Persia in the third millennium would appear to have been part of a general expansion of peoples centred in eastern Anatolia and southern Transcaucasia. In this expansion the southward movement of the Yanik pottery onto the Persian plateau provides an eastern parallel to the western movement of the related Khirbet Karak Wares into northern Syria and Palestine.[5]

Following the Yanik occupation the archaeological record of this area of Persia is little known until the later second millennium. Yanik Tepe itself was apparently abandoned during this period. At Geoy Tepe on the west side of Lake Reẓā'īyeh a few sherds of buff pottery with club-like rims (period G) have been attributed to the end of the third millennium.[6] This material is followed by a red, cream and black polychrome pottery which has close connexions with the 'Cappadocian Ware' of Alişar Hüyük in central Anatolia. This polychrome pottery represents the early second millennium occupation of the western shore of Lake Reẓā'īyeh from Geoy Tepe northward to Khoi. In this area several sites have yielded sherds of this type to survey teams. At Kara Tepe

[1] §1, 6, 207. [2] See §1, 22, 248 for actual dates.

[3] §1, 5, fig. 12, 1249; §III, 9, 193–4; but cf. §1, 37 on carbon-14 dates.

[4] C. A. Burney in a letter of September 1966 indicates a date of 2500 B.C. or later, but remains undecided as to how late.

[5] *C.A.H.* 1³, pt. 2, ch. xv, sects. I and VII.

[6] G material also occurs in D period. The division is said to be 'convenient', §1, 5, 63 ff.

just north of Shāpūr painted ware (exposed by earth hauling activities) overlies the Yanik E.B.A. levels. The nature of the cultural occupation of eastern Azarbāyjān in this period is as yet unclear.

The polychrome pottery at Geoy Tepe occurs in D and C periods which are best treated as a single period D–C with an early (early D) and a late (late D and C) phase. Early D–C polychrome is characterized by loops and wavy lines in matt black and white paint applied to polished red carinated bowls.[1] These bowls, in contrast with those which follow, tend to be deep with straight sides and slightly everted rims. A related bichrome ware also occurs which consists of a matt black paint placed on a polished red-brown slip.[2] Both types are decorated with patterns of wavy lines placed between straight lines arranged as zigzags, hanging triangles, or loops. Variants occur with black and white paint on red ground, black and red paint on red ground, and white paint on red ground.[3] These patterns appear to have been derived from certain forms of Cappadocian and Trialeti Ware, although the shapes are different. The Cappadocian Ware came to an end around 1900 B.C. in central Anatolia while the Trialeti Ware, found in Soviet Georgia, has been dated to between 1550 and 1450 B.C.[4] A dating between these two extremes seems probable for the Geoy Tepe early polychrome which certainly represents influences moving toward Persia from Anatolia and/or Caucasia. A unique polychrome sherd in early D–C context combines the polychrome technique with a motif of cross-hatched triangles alternating with birds as found on the monochrome Dinkha 'Khabur' Ware (as described below),[5] indicating contact with the Ushnu area south-west of Lake Reẓā'īyeh.

Beginning in early D–C at Geoy Tepe, and characterizing late D–C, is a polychrome pottery known also from mid-second millennium and Iron Age I deposits at Dinkha Tepe. The characteristic form is a carinated bowl with a rolled rim, a tall-necked globular jar, or a globular jar with thickened rim—all forms which appear in plain burnished grey and red ware in Iron Age I at Hasanlu (V) and Dinkha Tepe. Usually the body of the vessel is slipped red or red-brown, with a cream-white band around the shoulder or on the rim, and designs in black and red. The most common patterns are triangles and lozenges, cross-hatched, solid, or

[1] §1, 5, figs. 19, 59; 20, 57; 21, 84; pp. 93, 94, 96.
[2] §1, 5, figs. 20, 1640; 21, 505, 876; 22, 1053, 1056; pp. 94, 96, 98.
[3] §1, 5, figs, 20, 430; 22, 1046; 24, 945; pp. 92, 94, 99.
[4] G, 18, figs. 287, 289, 290.   [5] §1, 5, fig. 24, 735, p. 92.

with dots in the centre of the open figure. Other patterns include chequer-boards with alternate solid squares and dots. One of these sherds, as already mentioned, was found in the upper E.B. II fill at Yanik Tepe. An almost identical sherd made into a disk occurs in a mixed second–first millennium context at Alişar Hüyük.[1] Other sherds of polychrome ware which may be related to this Azarbāyjān material occur in Syria in second millennium context and need to be studied together with the Anatolian material before much can be said about their relationships.[2]

Associated with the later polychrome levels at Geoy Tepe are four stone-built tombs with multiple burials and a number of simple inhumations.[3] Tombs A and J appear to belong to the period of the later polychrome due to their respective depths while B and H could belong to the earlier stage. None of the tombs, however, actually contained polychrome pottery. Tomb J contained a toggle pin of a special type with a torsion shaft identical with several found at Dinkha Tepe.[4] The tombs, which are somewhat earlier than a number of overlying inhumation graves, are rectangular chambers built of small stone slabs and roofed over with large slabs. They were collective and contained two to four individuals, a practice paralleled in the somewhat earlier Tepe Jamshidi tombs, at Dinkha Tepe, and in the Late Bronze Age Talish tombs.[5] Grave furniture consisted of paste beads in shapes characteristic of the second and early first millennia at Nuzi and Hasanlu, carinated bowls of red polished pottery, and rare bangles and simple pins which analysis shows to be a 5 per cent tin-bronze.[6] The actual date of these tombs is not yet certain but several typological parallels with Dinkha artifacts suggest[7] the possibility that it may be between about 1750 and 1550 B.C.

SOUTHERN PERSIA: THE QAL'EH-SHOGA PAINTED WARES

In southern Persia the archaeological record for the second millennium in Fars and Kirmān remains very fragmentary. In Fars proper, the end of the third and possibly the early second millennium is known only through Qal'eh Ware—a ceramic assemblage reported from soundings at the sites of Tell-i-Shoga (II), Tell-i-Taimuran (IV) and Tell-i-Qal'eh (II).[8] The pottery exhibits a reddish-to-yellowish firing range and is painted with a

---

[1] §1, 9, pl. xliv, 21, cf. §11, 17, fig. 508, e1812.
[2] Collection of the Institute of Archaeology, London; §1, 35.
[3] §1, 5, 101 ff.   [4] In 1966. §1, 5, fig. 29, 1217, p. 107.
[5] G, 18, 415, 417, 420.   [6] §1, 5, 107, 193, no. 1217.
[7] See below, pp. 703 ff. [8] G, 25, 42 f., pls. 52, 53 and 57; §1, 22, 246.

brown-to-black paint with designs consisting of wavy lines, cross-hatched fish, and swimming birds—all reminiscent of Susa D and Giyān IV motifs. Large bowls with ring bases and flat rims, and globular jars with short necks suggest a similar connexion. A full assemblage of associated artifacts has yet to be excavated for this culture which seems to represent a local development with limited outside influence. As in the case of the Giyān IV–III pottery, the basic wares of Fars seems to have continued more or less undisturbed during the second millennium with the gradual evolution of one local style into another. The later style in the area has been termed Shoga Ware and has been found at Tell-i-Shoga (I), Tell-i-Qal'eh (I), Tell-i-Taimuran (III), Tell-i-Kamin, Tell-i-Darvazah and seven other sites.[1] The pottery shapes include cylindrical goblets, cups, bowls, spherical vases, and tripods made of poorly baked coarse paste with a pinkish-to-yellowish surface painted with red-brown or brown-black paint. Patterns are geometric and consist of fine lines combined with traditional elements such as zigzags, loops, birds and fish. A bronze ribbed macehead and a copper or bronze spherical goblet on a high ring base are the only metal objects reported. The ceramic material appears to be the typological counterpart of the Giyān III style with perhaps some elements of Giyān II. Shoga Ware has been dated to 2000–1600 B.C.,[2] but may, in fact, have persisted through the later second millennium in a manner similar to that of the Giyān IV–III tradition, until interrupted by the intrusions of the early Iron Age.

For Kirmān, current work at Tepe Yahyā will establish a local sequence and help date the painted stone ware of the Mashiz phase at Tell-i-Iblīs, which is later than the Aliābad phase dated by carbon-14 to 2869 ± 57 B.C.[3] Recent excavations in Baluchistān in the Bampur area and at Shahr-i-Sokhta in Seistān are also producing new information on this time range.[4]

II. CERAMIC PATTERNS OF THE MIDDLE SECOND MILLENNIUM

During the middle of the second millennium the polychrome tradition of the north-west which first appeared at Geoy Tepe spread south-eastward into central Persia, probably along routes followed earlier by the E.B.A. Wares, and established itself at

[1] G, 25, 42 ff., pls. 54–7. [2] §II, 16, Chronological Table.
[3] §I, 11, 16–17; cf. §I, 37 on carbon-14 dates.
[4] §I, 12, 41; A, 21.

Tepe Sakkizābād.[1] Yanik Tepe was reoccupied or at least used as a cemetery, and tumulus-building groups appeared in the Persian Talish area.[2] In the Ushnu and Solduz valleys at the south-west corner of Lake Reżā'īyeh, Dinkha Painted Ware represented the eastern end of the related Khabur ware cultures of northern Mesopotamia, while to the south the Giyān IV–III tradition continued parallel to a limited and localized Giyān II pottery. In the far south the Qal'eh Shoga Wares, or some variants, probably continued. In Gurgan the hiatus between the early and the late second millennium effectively blacked out town life.

SOUTH-WESTERN AZARBĀYJĀN: THE DINKHA PAINTED WARE

Test excavations at Hasanlu (producing period VI on the Citadel mound), and at Dinkha Tepe have revealed a culture characterized by painted wheelmade and incised handmade pottery.[3] Small cups or jars with disk or ring bases, globular bodies and low curved necks were a common form. The pottery is usually yellowish in colour with a firing range from red to a greenish-yellow. Often the vessels are decorated either with simple bands or with a combination of bands and triangles filled with cross-hatching.[4] The triangles sometimes alternate with solid double-axe patterns, birds, dots or circles with spokes (wheels?) or stick trees similar to designs seen on the older and younger Khabur Ware at Ashur, Tell Billa, Kültepe, Tell Brak, Chagar Bazar and elsewhere in Mesopotamia and southern Anatolia between 1900 and 1200 B.C.[5] Medium-sized storage jars normally are painted with simple parallel bands of red or brown paint or are left plain, whereas small drinking vessels are often decorated with the more elaborate patterns. Large pithoi of red or yellow-buff colour are decorated with numerous combinations of applied horizontal strips which are often incised with diagonal or criss-crossed lines or finger impressions, and bands of comb-incised wavy or straight lines. A certain amount of coarse handmade pottery also occurs, along with a number of sherds of what appears to be imported burnished light grey ware of a type also found in limited quantities at Chagar Bazar and Brak in similar context. These grey ware sherds require comparative technical study across the area of northern Mesopotamia and Persia before they can be interpreted, but their distribution between, and their qualitative resemblance to, the fine grey Minyan ware of the Aegean area on the one hand, and the fine Hisar grey ware on the other, is most striking.

[1] §II, 16, 14–16, 43–4.   [2] G, 18, fig. 31, pp. 404 ff.
[3] Cf. §III, 9, 193–5; §II, 3.   [4] G, 24, pls. XXI, 1; XXII, 1–20.   [5] §II, 7.

Preliminary excavations at Dinkha Tepe have shown that the initial settlement was associated with what appears to be a massive mud-brick structure which apparently went out of use in the second quarter of the second millennium B.C., to judge from carbon-14 dates for the stratum immediately overlying (1612 ± 61 B.C., P-1233; 1623 ± 61 B.C., P-1430; 1756 ± 68 B.C., P-1431; 5730 half-life).[1] An area of the northern edge of the site was investigated in 1936 and again in 1966 and 1968.[2] The excavations yielded quantities of plain and painted sherds associated with several levels of houses built of large square mudbricks set on free-standing foundations of large boulders packed with smaller stones and topped by a levelling course of small river cobbles. The whole was then plastered with mud plaster. Small objects recovered from the site included votive wall-cone fragments (uninscribed),[3] fragments of fenestrated offering stands, a painted plaque fragment with the head of a human figure, and 'andiron' or 'horns of consecration' fragments of a type also known from Boğazköy.[4] Three tombs were found among the houses,[5] two with sides of uncut stones and roof of flat stone slabs. All three tombs contained multiple burials. Of particular interest among the contents were bronze and silver toggle pins, a bronze sub-triangular arrowhead with flat rectangular mid-rib and tang, a bronze sword blade with wooden hilt set over a tang, a round gold pendant with incised and embossed star pattern, a gold crescent pendant, a pair of gold strip-twisted earrings, a bronze spool, and other small bronze objects. With the exception of rare toggle pins these objects no longer occur in the overlying Iron Age I tombs. Among the pottery was a bird or animal effigy dish with three compartments and rim sherds with human faces recalling similar pieces from Alişar Hüyük and Boğazköy,[6] a double bowl, and a tripod vessel made of three small jars joined together at the side, each with a single leg. Two small vases with disk bases were converted into tripods through the addition of bent legs, a technique also used in the contemporary polychrome vases at Sakkizābād.[7] As at Geoy Tepe D–C, none of the tombs contained any of the contemporary painted pottery but were furnished instead with ordinary plain ware of the period.

In broad terms the date of this later material at Dinkha Tepe is established by its stratigraphic position at Hasanlu as period VI.

---

[1] See §1, 37 on carbon-14 dates.   [2] G, 24, 367 ff.; §11, 3.
[3] G, 24, pl. xxi, 13, p. 374.   [4] G, 18, fig. 184, 1.
[5] §11, 3; G, 24, 374–5, fig. 104.   [6] G, 18, figs. 182, 30; 193, 4.
[7] G, 24, pls. xxi, 2; xxx, 4, cf. §11, 16, pl. 69.

The underlying period VII is dated by comparative typology and carbon-14 to the late third millennium, while the overlying period V is dated by the same methods to the late second millennium.[1] The oldest radiocarbon date so far available for period V at Hasanlu reads 1217 ± 126 B.C. (P-198, 5730 half-life).[2] The range of one probable error makes it wise to consider a beginning-date of 1350 B.C. as a working-date for the start of Iron Age I in the north, especially in view of the probable correction-factor of one hundred years as suggested by the information already noted above.[3] The typology of objects in the tomb which included the gold star and crescent pendants referred to, and the the strip-twisted earrings, suggests a date around 1500 B.C. The first two objects are found together at Tell el-'Ajjūl in Palestine and also occur at Nuzi and elsewhere. The strip-twisted earrings are common in Cyprus and are found all the way to Ireland in connexion with trade in gold.[4] The tomb itself is cut from the surface on which stands one of the last major buildings of the Bronze Age. The house had been burned and produced a radiocarbon date of 1555 ± 52 B.C. (P-1232, 5730 half-life) from internal floor debris. Following this disaster there was a short re-occupation of the area with some additional wall construction and then final abandonment before the accumulation of Iron Age I trash over the area and its use as a cemetery. The final level of the short re-occupation produced a carbon-14 date of 1434 ± 52 B.C. (P-1231, 5730 half-life), indicating that the terminal date of the occupation lay no later than the late fifteenth century B.C. and possibly as much as a century and a half earlier given the correction factor indicated by known age samples. An end of about 1550 would correspond to the date already suggested in northern Mesopotamia for the end of the older Khabur ware.[5] Such a dating raises the question whether some hiatus intervenes before the appearance of the Iron Age materials, or whether the date of that latter event should be moved back to some date even earlier than 1350. The question is important but must remain open pending publication and study of the new material.

Some contact between Dinkha Tepe and Geoy Tepe D–C is indicated through the occurrence at Geoy Tepe of several incised sherds of Dinkha type and the occurrence at Dinkha of sherds of Geoy late D–C polychrome type. At Dinkha the best preserved

[1] §I, 22, 233, 248; see §I, 37 on carbon-14 dates.
[2] Dinkha dates for this period: 1146 ± 37 B.C., P-1475; 1243 ± 73 B.C., P-1449; 1302 ± 57 B.C., P-1474; 5730 half-life. Cf. §I, 37.
[3] §I, 37.   [4] §II, 6, and occur at Marlik.   [5] §II, 7.

of these sherds have come from the stratum above the earlier second millennium structure while others, probably not *in situ*, turn up in early Iron Age I trash. This polychrome ware at Geoy Tepe is associated with vessel types of the local Iron Age I (Hasanlu V) culture, for bowls of plain burnished red or grey of Iron Age shape and fabric occur along with the polychrome. In fact several of the shapes of these plain ware vessels are simply polychrome forms without the polychrome. A further polychrome–Iron Age I connexion is indicated by the occurrence of a free-standing horizontal spouted vessel with a very small short spout on a polychrome vessel from Kızıl Vank which has been dated to 1450–1350 B.C. on typological grounds.[1] This vessel and the accompanying long necked polychrome vessel are related to two vessels found in Iron Age I graves (one at Hasanlu and one at Dinkha). They represent a terminal stage of the polychrome ware placed in burnished grey ware graves, a fact which suggests a persistence of the polychrome tradition in western Azarbāyjān until the third quarter of the second millennium. The alleged presence of iron slag in D–C context at Geoy Tepe is also relevant to this late dating, since an iron finger ring has been found in one Hasanlu V grave.[2] The whole situation suggests that the polychrome culture of north-western Azarbāyjān was already in contact with a Hasanlu V type culture in the middle second millennium which has yet to be located, or else perhaps implies that the Hasanlu V burnished grey ware assemblage grew out of the D–C mixed polychrome and plain ware assemblage through the loss of polychrome decoration. A whole range of new questions is thus raised which cannot be answered at present.

NORTH-EASTERN AZARBĀYJĀN: THE YANIK TEPE LATE BRONZE AGE CEMETERY AND TALISH TOMBS

At the north-east corner of Lake Reẓā'īyeh, Yanik Tepe was used during the later second millennium as a cemetery area (dated by the excavator to between 1500 and 1100 B.C.).[3] Graves contain handmade pottery of a rather drab grey colour. Shapes include the one-handled juglet with tall neck of a type found in the Middle Bronze Age in Palestine and at Tepe Giyān as already noted,[4] as well as two-handled kraters. A carinated red-slipped bowl of Geoy D–C and Hasanlu V type occurs. The burial of a woman contained a necklace of carnelian, agate and frit beads, bronze rings and bronze toggle-pins. The latter are also common in

[1] G, 18, fig. 270, 4, 5.   [2] §1, 5, 199 ff.
[3] §1, 9, 147.   [4] See above, p. 693 n. 3.

the Geoy D–C tombs and at Dinkha Tepe, but occur only rarely in Hasanlu V. Dating to the earlier period of this cemetery, but culturally distinct from it are the stone tombs and tanged bronze weapons found at Khoja-Dawud-Köprü and Chir-Chir in the Talish region further east.[1] Weapons with simple tangs, found also at Geoy and Dinkha Tepe, apparently precede the introduction of the more elaborate forms with cast handles, lappet-flanged grips, etc., which are typical of the Iron Age.[2] Grey pottery is known from survey work to have a distribution over much of north-eastern Azarbāyjān and the Talish,[3] but whether any of it represents the later second millennium occupation in the area remains to be seen.

CENTRAL PERSIA: THE SAKKIZĀBĀD POLYCHROME WARE

The polychrome tradition stemming from the Cappadocian Ware of Anatolia by way of north-western Persia penetrated in the middle second millennium (?c. 1600 B.C.) to central Persia where it has been found by commercial excavations at the site of Sakkiz-ābād some 66 km. south-west of Qazvīn.[4] The site lies at the end of the geographic corridor leading into central Persia by way of the Mianeh and Zenjan valleys. In this respect Sakkizābād perhaps occupies a position not unlike that held by the later Sialk B settlement near Kāshān which may also have had some Anatolian connexions.

Only the pottery is known in any quantity from Sakkizābād. The majority of vessels, presumably from graves, are of a buff ware with a red slipped and burnished body, a cream slipped shoulder zone and geometric designs in brown-black paint. Patterns are linear around the exterior and include zigzags and meanders, lozenges and triangles. Rotating interior patterns also occur in various swastika-like forms. Rims are often decorated around the inside by solid painted hanging triangles. Bowls with everted rims and cups with single handles and flat bases are common. Occasional double-handled jars and tripods are known. Some design elements and shapes appear to be distantly related to Giyān III materials, while the method of making the tripod from a small vase duplicates that at Dinkha Tepe as already mentioned. Several of the shapes of this pottery are repeated in the Iron Age grey ware[5] found at the site, showing the existence of some cultural continuity into the later period (an interesting if distinct parallel to the Geoy D–C and Hasanlu V situation). A

---

[1] G, 18, figs. 222, 224, pl. LIX. [2] §III, 8, 11 and 12.
[3] Information from T. C. Young, Jr. [4] §II, 16. [5] §II, 16, 43.

similar overlap may have occurred in the Tepe Sialk area where one or two vessels in Sialk A indicate contact with Sakkizābād.[1] In general the Sakkizābād pottery appears to have points of contact with the Dinkha Culture, Geoy D–C, and perhaps Giyān II. Considering the close relationship to the succeeding Iron Age materials at Sakkizābād, the evidence would indicate a date of about 1600 to about 1350 B.C. or a little later for the polychrome ware.

CENTRAL WESTERN PERSIA: THE GIYĀN II POTTERY

The unique character within Persia of the Giyān II pottery as found at Tepe Giyān and Godin, combined with its affinities to the Dinkha Ware of south-western Azarbāyjān (and its obvious typological connexion with the Khabur wares of northern Mesopotamia), and the painted kraters which appeared in northern Palestine in the sixteenth century B.C.[2] suggest that the Giyān II pottery represents the south-easternmost extension of this general Khabur ware arc.

The Giyān II graves fall into three distinct groups for the purpose of dating. Group II a follows stratigraphically directly upon the Giyān III graves at Tepe Giyān and consists of six graves (82, 81, 76, 74, 73, 72) from 5·50 to 4·30 metres below the surface. The graves contain material which closely resembles, and is probably partly contemporary with Dinkha Painted Ware. Bronze toggle-pins with conical heads, flat-rimmed bowls with radial lines painted on the rims, simple banded decoration, double axe patterns, birds placed between cross-hatched triangles in rows, and cross-hatched triangles in rows are all parallels. If the late Dinkha pottery dates in part to about 1500 B.C., as seems to be the case, this Giyān II a group of graves must also date to that time range. Such a date would fit acceptably with the evidence for the Giyān III stratum at the site as already presented.

A second grave group, II b, consists of six important graves (79, 77, 75, 71, 65, 64) at a slightly higher level (from 4·60 to 4·0 metres) which contain painted pottery similar to II a but with the addition of painted kraters. Each krater has a ring base and two vertical side handles. The 'classic' form of this vessel is decorated with two registers of panelled patterns placed above the carinated shoulder. The standard designs include radiating 'sun' symbols, birds, and cross-hatched panels painted in black on a fabric which has a firing range from reddish through yellow-buff

[1] §III, 10, pls. XXXVII, S444; XL, S476.
[2] §II, 8, 200; §II, 4, frontispiece, pls. VIII, 1; v, 1, 2, cf. §I, 15, pls. 21–4.

to a greyish cast. These patterns are, as far as is known at present, unique in Persia, and may have been inspired by painted wares farther west where they have been compared to pottery introduced to Palestine from the north in the sixteenth century.[1] Whether the Palestinian and Persian materials reflect a southward movement at either end of the Mesopotamian arc (as was previously seen in the parallel occurrences of Khirbet Karak and Yanik wares) from a more central point of origin, or whether the Persian styles moved westward towards Palestine as has also been suggested[2] cannot be determined in the absence of more precise dating than is currently available.

These II*b* krater graves are the richest of the Giyān II period and contain, along with the elaborately painted kraters, excellent metalwork which includes a variety of ribbed and tanged bronze blades, a long sword-blade with tang for the attachment of a handle, and a short knife with ring handle. The absence of cast hilts parallels the situation in northern Persia in this same period. The ring-handled knife, a unique find, is probably an import from the far north. Knives of this general type spread westward to the Caucasus from the Minusinsk region where they were being used at least as early as 1300 B.C.[3] Personal jewellery in the graves includes a round pendant with embossed star design of the type already noted in the Dinkha tomb, at Marlik, and in fourteenth-century Nuzi.[4] In general, therefore, the typological parallels suggest a date of about 1500–1400 B.C. for this range of grave materials.

Finally there is a third grave group, II*c*, consisting of nine graves ranging in depth from 4·10 to 3·40 metres below surface which are characterized by the disappearance of the krater form and the introduction of chaliciform goblets of a type which commonly occur in Assyria from about 1400 to 1200 B.C.[5] These goblets appear just at the end of the period of the use of kraters as shown by three graves (66, 63, 61) in which a degenerate form of the krater still occurs along with the goblets. In the remaining six graves (69, 62, 60, 43, and 40) the painted goblets occur without the krater. These graves mark the end of the painting traditions of the second millennium and are followed in period I$_4$ at Tepe Giyān by unpainted goblets dating to about 1200–1000 B.C.[6] A cylinder seal found in grave 68 at Tepe Giyān is of a

[1] See preceding note. [2] G, 3, 68 f.; G, 4.
[3] §II, 11, ill. 19; §I, 28, 563 f., figs. 387, 389.
[4] §III, 15, fig. 71; §II, 15, pl. 127, B1.
[5] §II, 1, fig. 11, p. 61. [6] §II, 18, 68.

type also known at Nuzi, the style of which in Persia lasted until the early Iron Age at Dinkha, Marlik, Hassan Zamini and Agha Evlar.[1] Similar seals are known from a thirteenth-century context in Palestine.[2] The Giyān seal is, in fact, associated with a carinated bowl which is typically Iron Age in type. The depth of the grave is such that it can be at best only late in period II. The general group of II *c* graves thus appears to date to between 1400 and 1200 B.C. and represents a strong contact with the Assyrian area in this period.

When Tepe Giyān was first excavated and stood alone in the area, it gave the impression that the Giyān II pottery followed the Giyān IV–III Painted Ware as a regional phenomenon.[3] Fieldwork carried out since in Luristān suggests, however, that the actual development was more complex. There is considerable evidence to the effect that outside of Tepe Giyan the Giyan IV–III tradition maintained itself in variant forms down to the Iron Age in much of Luristān, and that Giyān II influence was relatively limited. The dating of the earliest Giyān III materials rests primarily upon the fact that they underlie the Giyān II strata at Tepe Giyān, that they contain a seal of a type dating to between 1750 and 1600 B.C., and that a type of dagger found at Chigha Sabz is also known elsewhere with an inscription of the prince Attakhushu on it. In addition it may be added that the characteristic red bowls decorated with hanging concentric loops occur also at Trialeti in Kurgan XV which has been dated to about 1550–1400 B.C., and at Ališar Hüyük in the 'post-Hittite' period.[4] On the other hand, the date of the later Giyān III variants elsewhere in Luristān is much later, reaching the beginning of the Iron Age around 1200 B.C. or sometime thereafter. Giyān III relationships are found in pottery from Tepe Gūrān in the Hulailan plain in settlement level I and Tombs 9, 11, and 15.[5] Tomb 11 has Giyān III type tripods and metal objects of Giyān II type. The decoration on the tripods includes bands of hatching and hatched triangles—common themes in Giyān II pottery. This tomb has been dated to 1315 ± 124 B.C.[6] and provides important evidence indicating the persistence of Giyān III types after 1600 B.C. Similar pottery is reported from Cheshme Mahi where it is said to have been found with a sword of Iron Age I type and a 'Gilgamesh'

---

[1] §1, 15, pl. 38, 4; cf. §III, 16, 311 ff., G 18, 404.
[2] Information from Y. Yadin.
[3] G, 3, 68 f. But cf. now A, 23, 21 ff.
[4] G, 18, fig. 291, 4; §II, 17, figs. 434, 1; 437, 17; cf. §1, 20, pl. XXVIII, 19.
[5] Information from H. Thrane.   [6] 5730 half-life.

standard.[1] Other such standards are known to have come from this site which consists largely of an unpainted ceramic deposit which is thought to be late second millennium on the basis of survey information.[2]

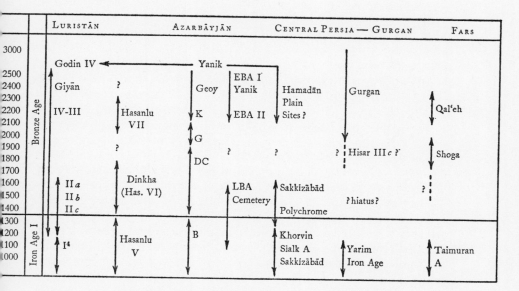

TABLE 4. *Approximate correlations for ceramic traditions during the second millennium* B.C. *on the Persian plateau*

Elsewhere in Luristān, the Giyān II pottery is less easily distinguished from the lingering Giyān IV–III Ware. At Bad Hora, north of the Hamadān–Kirmānshāh road, three graves belong to this late II group with pottery decorated with cross-hatched and solid double-axe patterns, and a dagger with an open crescent lying over the blade—a type the presence of which indicates the beginning of Iron Age influence in the area from the north.[3] The classic Giyān II*b* panelled ware seems to have been restricted largely to the area around Tepe Giyān, while elements of the II*a* and II*c* groups (the banded wares being referred to sometimes as 'Khabur Ware') seem to have spread into other parts of Luristān.

At Tepe Gūrān the main link with Giyān II lies in the general

[1] §II, 10, 20–1. For a summary of art-historical literature on the so-called 'Luristān Bronzes' see §III, 18; and G 18, 477 ff.

[2] §II, 5, 123–4.   [3] See below, p. 712 n. 5.

use of chaliciform pedestalled cups in layer P–R (called III–IV in the first report).[1] Otherwise the only indication of Giyān II influence in the basically Giyān III pottery of the Hulailan area lies in scattered finds of painted Giyān II goblets. Survey results suggest that sites like Tepe Jamshidi and Mauyilbak on the big plains were abandoned at the end of the Giyān II period and that there was then a general shift of the population into the mountains.[2] Such a shift, and the eventual break-up of the Giyān cultural patterns, was almost certainly brought about by the military campaigns of the Elamite rulers against the Kassites in this area in the late thirteenth and twelfth centuries.[3]

III. END OF THE BRONZE AGE CULTURES,
c. 1350–1150 B.C.

With the beginning of Iron Age I in northern Persia, a new stage of development is reached on the plateau which forms the proto-historic background of the Median and Achaemenian dynasties.[4] This change brought to an end all of the second millennium cultures which have been under discussion. North central Persia and the Talish area were occupied by people who used burnished grey pottery in some way related to the earlier Gurgan Grey Ware, and who manufactured masses of cast bronze weapons and small objects. Characteristic of this culture were short swords of bronze with an extension of the hilt in the form of a crescent overlapping the blade. Often the hilt was inlaid with wood or other material and was lapped-flanged.[5] Large cemeteries of tombs built of uncut rocks and large stone slabs are common. Important sites included Hassan Zamini, Agha Evlar, Marlik, Khorvin, and Sialk A, and a number of small sites, all in the north central part of the plateau.[6] In the east the sites of the Gurgan plain are reoccupied for the first time since the beginning of the hiatus which followed the disappearance of the Gurgan Grey Ware. The reoccupation is evidenced at Hotu Cave where it has been dated by carbon-14 to around 1000 B.C. (1105 ± 278 (P-44), 1085 ± 237 (P-33), 1023 ± 381 (P-41)) using the old solid carbon method of dating (calculated to a 5730 year half-life), and at Yarim Tepe with its more reliable date of 986 ± 61 B.C. (P-507) using current gas methods. In the west the grey pottery cultures

[1] Information from H. Thrane; G, 14. [2] Information from C. Goff.
[3] C.A.H. II³, pt. 2, ch. XXXI, sect. I; ch. XXXII, sect. II.
[4] §III, 23; §III, 9. [5] §III, 8.
[6] G, 18, figs. 30, 217, 221, pl. LVIII, pp. 404–15; §III, 10; 15; 16; 19 and 20.

established themselves at Geoy Tepe (B), Hasanlu (V) and Dinkha Tepe (Iron Age cemetery) sometime around 1350± 50 B.C.[1] To the south-west the influence of these new groupings began to appear in period I at Tepe Giyān, at Bad Hora, and at Tang-i-Hamamlan. Somewhat later Iron Age materials in Luristān have been reported from Mauyilbak, Tepe Gūrān, Kamtarlan I and II, Chigha Sabz, Surkh Dom, Tang-i-Hamamlan, Kuran Buzan, Derecht-i-Tabir, Tepe War Kabud, Tepe Kawali and Bābā Jān and are currently being studied.[2] The research done on the Iron Age in this area is still too recent and incomplete to allow any real interpretation of events other than to observe that the new Iron Age materials appear to flood into the area after the decline of the Giyān IV–III and II traditions. In the far south in Fars the lingering Bronze Age pattern of painted pottery cultures was also apparently broken up as indicated by the appearance of burnished grey wares in the Tell-i-Taimuran A Culture, although at what date this change took place is not yet established.[3]

The outstanding problems concerning this remarkable and relatively rapid spread of grey pottery making and bronze working through Persia at the end of the second millennium are three: (1) the nature of the origin of the craft traditions represented by ceramics and metallurgy; (2) the factors that led to the sudden expansion of these traditions; and (3) the date at which this process began. Although these problems are complicated by the historical inferences drawn from external historical sources and comparative linguistics, the immediate archaeological problem is the study of the known remains themselves in order to develop whatever relationships and patterns may exist. These patterns may then be viewed in terms of inferred historical events which in many instances will not have had much of an impact on the material remains. Thus, in regard to the question of the origins of these craft traditions we have already indicated the possible answers in pointing to the presence of foreign parallels on the one hand which give rise to a migration hypothesis and, on the other, to the excellent precedents already available in the earlier Gurgan Grey Ware as seen at Tepe Hisar. In addition, older techniques and styles (still relatively unknown to us) were probably adopted from the vanquished polychrome and painted ware users of the middle second millennium. Both interpretations, however, suffer from a lack of full data as to the cultural patterns of the sites being

[1] §III, 9; §II, 3; §I, 5, 141 ff.; §II, 18.
[2] G, 24; G, 14; §III, 18; §II, 16; 13; 14; information from M. van Loon.
[3] G, 25, 44, pl. 60.

compared, and from the need to jump long distances in order to make the comparisons. Thus it is impossible at present either to substantiate a migration into Persia at this moment in time along a specific route, or to document the steps of an internal development. The problem must be left open for solution by future field-work.

Similarly the second question does not yet lend itself readily to discussion. In view of the fact that a complex of new features appears to be involved in the spread of the grey pottery, and not just the technique of reduction firing, it would seem safe to conclude that at the very least some shifting of population was taking place on the northern plateau, whether entering from outside or stirring from within.[1] This shift was from the central north toward the west and south where we see the disappearance of the polychrome tradition at Geoy, the painted pottery at Dinkha and Hasanlu, the Giyān IV–III and II pottery of Luristān, and the painted ware cultures of Fars. In part this shift into the western Zagros may have been encouraged by the decline of Mitanni in the north and the collapse of the Kassites in the south of Mesopotamia—events which must have affected the political stability of adjacent allies.

The question involving the date of the beginning of this Iron Age expansion can be partly answered. In the east the carbon-14 dates suggest the reoccupation of the ancient town sites between 1100 and 900 B.C. In Luristān a similar range of time is suggested for the major impact of the Iron Age Cultures coming from the north central regions by the general typological dating of the Giyān IV–III and II materials and a single carbon date from Tepe Gūrān for a later stage of Giyān III–II material at 1315 ± 124 B.C. as already noted, and by the typology of newly excavated Iron Age material at sites already mentioned. In the north the available evidence appears to support an earlier date than in either the east or south-west, although how much earlier is problematical. Carbon-14 dates from Hasanlu previously suggested a range from 1250 to 1000 B.C. but may have to be corrected to something like 1400 to 1100.[2] Therefore, a working date of 1350 ± 50 B.C. for the beginning of the period would probably be realistic. Such a date would place the Hasanlu and Marlik occupations at the end of the range formerly proposed for the Talish area tombs. The excavations at the former sites and at Yanik Tepe have produced numerous parallels for special objects such as lappet-flanged dagger hilts and specialized arrowhead types, which suggest a

---

[1] Cf. §III, 23.   [2] §III, 9 n. 7; §I, 37.

close connexion between the whole group, and which support the proposal already made that the Talish materials probably ought, in part at least, to be lowered in date from the middle second millennium to the later second and even first millennium.[1] The main basis for dating these Talish sites in the past has been the presence of three badly preserved cylinder seals of the so-called 'Mitannian' type dated to 1450–1350 B.C.[2] Some caution in accepting this date is necessitated as a result of the discovery of comparable seals at Marlik and Dinkha Tepe in Iron Age I context, and in a late Giyān II grave as previously noted. These seals and the associated weapon types show that a new cultural development took place in the north sometime around 1350 ± 50 B.C. with considerable contact with Mesopotamia. The various artifacts recently excavated from the Royal Tombs at Marlik Tepe—gold jewellery with elaborate granulation, gold pendants with embossed stars, mosaic glass, cylinder seals, and beads—show the rich development which occurred in this part of the Persian plateau in this period.[3] Within the framework of such contacts many of the techniques found later over the whole country may have been introduced from the west or may have been taken over from local artisans. The precise dating and direction of movement of these new developments remains to be discovered. That Iron I is older in the north than elsewhere in Persia, and that its beginning falls in the range of 1350 ± 50 B.C., seems clear. The Marlik Royal Tombs, which represent the high point of this early Iron Age culture with its extraordinary wealth of bronze weapons, gold and silver vessels, personal jewellery and effigy vessels, are followed by the Iron Age riches of Hasanlu IV, the Zendan-i-Suleimān, the Sialk B cemetery, Bābā Jān, Godin II, and Nūsh-i-Jān,[4] all of which indicate the lines of the protohistoric development culminating in the great arts of the Achaemenian period that followed.

[1] §III, 17.   [2] G, 18, 408–15.   [3] §III, 15 and 16.
[4] §III, 4 to 7 and 10; A, 5; 1; 13; 18; 19 and 23.

BIBLIOGRAPHY

ABBREVIATIONS

Abh. Berlin (*München* etc.). *Abhandlungen der Preussischen* (*Bayerischen* etc.) *Akademie der Wissenschaften, Phil.-hist. Klasse*

Abh. Mainz. Abhandlungen der Preussischen Akademie der Wissenschaften, Math.-naturwiss. Klasse

Acta Arch. Acta Archaeologica

Acta Or. Acta Orientalia

Ägyptol. Abh. Ägyptologische Abhandlung

Ägyptol. Forsch. Ägyptologische Forschungen

A.I.A.R.S. Acta Instituti Atheniensis Regni Sueciae

A.I.R.R.S. Acta Instituti Romani Regni Sueciae

A.J. Antiquaries Journal

A.J.A. American Journal of Archaeology

A.J.S.L. American Journal of Semitic Languages and Literatures

Alte Or. Der Alte Orient

A.M.I. Archäologische Mitteilungen aus Iran

An. Or. Analecta Orientalia

Anc. Egypt. Ancient Egypt (continued as *Ancient Egypt and the East*)

A.N.E.P. The Ancient Near East in Pictures

A.N.E.T. Ancient Near Eastern Texts relating to the Old Testament

Ann. Arch. Anthr. Annals of Archaeology and Anthropology (Liverpool)

Ann. Arch. de Syrie. Annales Archéologiques de Syrie

Ann. A.S.O.R. Annual of the American Schools of Oriental Research

Ann. Inst. philol. hist. or. Annuaire de l'Institut de philologie et d'histoire orientales (later *Annuaire...orientales et slaves*)

Ann. Mus. Guimet. Annales du Musée Guimet

Ann. P.E.F. Annual of the Palestine Exploration Fund

Ann. Serv. Annales du Service des Antiquités de l'Égypte

Antiq. Antiquity

A.O.S. American Oriental Series; American Oriental Society

Arch. Anz. Archaeologischer Anzeiger. Beiblatt zum *Jahrbuch des deutschen Archäologischen Instituts*

Arch. Delt. Ἀρχαιολογικόν Δελτίον

Arch. Eph. (Ἀρχ. Ἐφ.) Ἀρχαιολογική Ἐφημερίς

Arch. f. äg. Arch. Archiv für ägyptische Archäologie

Arch. f. Keil. Archiv für Keilschriftforschung

Arch. f. Or. Archiv für Orientforschung

Arch. hist. dr. or. Archives d'histoire du droit oriental

Arch. Orient. Archiv Orientální

Arch. Reports. Archaeological Reports of the Society for Hellenic Studies

Arkæol. Kunsthist. Medd. Dan. Vid. Selsk. Kongelige Danske Videnskabernes Selskab, Arkæologisk-kunsthistoriske Meddelelser

A.R.M.T. Archives Royales de Mari (translation vols)

A.S. Atene. Annuario della scuola archeologica di Atene e delle missioni italiane in oriente

A. St. Anatolian Studies

Ath. Mitt. Athenische Mitteilungen, Mitteilungen des deutschen archäologischen Instituts, Athenische Abteilung

B.A. Beiträge zur Assyriologie

B.C.H. Bulletin de Correspondance hellénique

B.d'A. Boll. d'Arte

B.E. Babylonian Expedition of the University of Pennsylvania

Bibl. Aeg. Bibliotheca Aegyptiaca

B.I.C.S. Bulletin of the Institute of Classical Studies of the University of London

B.I.N. Babylonian inscriptions in the collection of J. B. Nies, Yale University

Bi. Ar. Biblical Archaeologist

Bi. Or. Bibliotheca Orientalis

B.M. Quart. British Museum Quarterly

B.P.I. Bullettino di Paletnologia Italiana

B.S.A. Annual of the British School of Archaeology at Athens

B.S.A. Egypt. British School of Archaeology, Egypt

B.S.A.W. Berichte der sächsischen Akademie der Wissenschaft

B.S.R. Papers of the British School at Rome

Bull. A.S.O.R. Bulletin of the American Schools of Oriental Research

Bull. Inst. d'Ég. Bulletin de l'Institut d'Égypte

Bull. Inst. fr. Caire. Bulletin de l'Institut français d'archéologie orientale, Le Caire

Bull. M.M.A. Bulletin of the Metropolitan Museum of Art (New York)

Bull. S.O.A.S. Bulletin of the School of Oriental and African Studies

Bull. Soc. fr. égyptol. Bulletin de la Société française d'Égyptologie

C.A.D. The Assyrian Dictionary of the Oriental Institute of the University of Chicago

C.A.H. Cambridge Ancient History

Cah. H.M. Cahiers d'histoire mondiale (See J. W. H.)

C.C.G. Cairo Museum, Catalogue Général des Antiquités Égyptiennes

Chron. d'Ég. Chronique d'Égypte

Cl. Phil. Classical Philology

Cl. Rh. Clara Rhodos

C.-R. Ac. Inscr. B.-L. Comptes-Rendus de l'Académie des Inscriptions et Belles-Lettres

C.-R. Rencontr. Assyriol. Internat. Compte-Rendu de la 1re (2e, 3e...) Rencontre assyriologique Internationale

E.E.F. Egypt Exploration Fund

E.E.S. Egypt Exploration Society

Eph. Arch. Ephemeris Archaiologike (Ἐφημερὶς Ἀρχαιολογική)

E.R.A. Egyptian Research Account

Flles Inst. Fr. Caire. Fouilles de l'Institut français du Caire

Forsch. u. Fortschr. Forschungen und Fortschritte

G.J. Geographical Journal

Harv. Stud. Class. Phil. Harvard Studies in Classical Philology

H.U.C.A. Hebrew Union College Annual

I.E.J. Israel Exploration Journal

Ill. Ldn News. Illustrated London News

Inst. fr., Bibl. d'Étude. Institut français, Bibliothèque d'Étude (Le Caire)

Ist. Mitt. Istanbuler Mitteilungen, Deutsches Archäologisches Institut, Abteilung Istanbul

J.A.O.S. *Journal of the American Oriental Society*

J.A.R.C.E. *Journal of the American Research Center in Egypt*

J. as. *Journal asiatique*

J.C.S. *Journal of Cuneiform Studies*

J.d.I. *Jahrbuch des deutschen archäologischen Instituts*

J.E.A. *Journal of Egyptian Archaeology*

J.E.O.L. *Jaarbericht van het Vooraziatisch-Egyptisch Genootschap,* '*Ex Oriente Lux*'

J.E.S.H.O. *Journal of the Economic and Social History of the Orient*

J.H.S. *Journal of Hellenic Studies*

J.J.P. *Journal of Juristic Papyrology*

J.K.P.K. *Jahrbuch der königlich-preussischen Kunstsammlungen*

J.N.E.S. *Journal of Near Eastern Studies*

J.P.O.S. *Journal of the Palestine Oriental Society*

J.R.A.S. *Journal of the Royal Asiatic Society*

J.R.H. *Journal of Religious History*

J.S.O.R. *Journal of the Society of Oriental Research*

J.S.S. *Journal of Semitic Studies*

J.W.H. *Journal of World History* (See *Cah.* H. M.)

K.Bo. *Keilschrifttexte aus Boghazköi*

K. Chr. Κρητικὰ Χρονικά

K.F. *Kleinasiatische Forschungen*

L.S.S. *Leipziger semitistische Studien*

M.A.O.G. *Mitteilungen der Altorientalischen Gesellschaft*

Marb. W. Pr. *Marburger Winckelmann-Programm*

M.C.S. *Manchester Cuneiform Studies*

M.D.A.I. *Mitteilungen des deutschen archäologischen Instituts*

M.D.O.G. *Mitteilungen der Deutschen Orient-Gesellschaft*

Mél. Dussaud. *Mélanges Syriens offerts à M. R. Dussaud*

Mél. Maspero. *Mélanges Maspero* (*Mém. Inst. fr.* 66–8)

Mém. Ac. Inscr. B.-L. *Mémoires de l'Académie des Inscriptions et Belles-Lettres*

Mém. D.P. *Mémoires de la Délégation en Perse*

Mém. Inst. fr. Caire. *Mémoires publiés par les membres de l'institut français d'archéologie orientale du Caire*

Mitt. deutsch. Inst. Kairo. *Mitteilungen des deutschen Instituts für ägyptische Altertumskunde in Kairo*

Mitt. Inst. Or. *Mitteilungen des Instituts für Orientforschung*

M.J. *Museum Journal, University of Pennsylvania*

M.M.A. *Metropolitan Museum of Art*

M.S.L. *Materialien zum Sumerischen Lexikon*

M.V.A[e].G. *Mitteilungen der vorderasiatisch-ägyptischen Gesellschaft*

Nachr. Göttingen. *Nachrichten von der Gesellschaft der Wissenschaften zu Göttingen, Phil.-hist. Klasse*

O.E.C.T. *Oxford Editions of Cuneiform Texts*

O.I.C. *Oriental Institute Communications*

O.I.P. *Oriental Institute Publications*

O.L.Z. *Orientalistische Literaturzeitung*

Op. Arch. *Opuscula Archaeologica., Acta Instituti Romani Regni Sueciae*

Op. Ath. *Opuscula Atheniensia. Acta Instituti Atheniensis Regni Sueciae*

Or. *Orientalia*

Or. antiq. *Oriens antiquus*

P.B.S.   *University of Pennsylvania. The University Museum. Publications of the Babylonian Section*

P.E.F.   *Quarterly Statement of the Palestine Exploration Fund*

P.E.Q.   *Palestine Exploration Quarterly*

P.J.B.   *Palästina Jahrbuch*

P.P.S.   *Proceedings of the Prehistoric Society*

Prähist. Zeitschr.   *Prähistorische Zeitschrift*

Proc. Amer. Philosoph. Soc.   *Proceedings of the American Philosophical Society*

P.S.B.A.   *Proceedings of the Society of Biblical Archaeology*

Publ. Inst. fr. Caire.   *Publications de l'Institut français d'archéologie orientale du Caire*

Publ. M.M.A.   *Publications of the Metropolitan Museum of Art, Department of Egyptian Art*

Publ. M.M.A.E.E.   *Publications of the Metropolitan Museum of Art, Egyptian Expedition*

P.W.   Pauly-Wissowa-Kroll-Mittelhaus, *Real-encyclopädie der classischen Altertums-wissenschaft*

Q.D.A.P.   *Quarterly of the Department of Antiquities of Palestine*

R.A.   *Revue d'assyriologie et d'archéologie orientale*

Rec. trav.   *Recueil de travaux relatifs à la philologie et à l'archéologie égyptiennes et assyriennes*

Rev. arch.   *Revue archéologique*

Rev. bibl.   *Revue biblique*

Rev. d'égyptol.   *Revue d'égyptologie*

Rev. du Caire.   *Revue du Caire*

Rev. Ég. anc.   *Revue de l'Égypte ancienne*

Rev. ét. gr.   *Revue des études grecques*

R.H.A.   *Revue hittite et asianique*

R.L.A.   *Reallexikon der Assyriologie*

R.S.O.   *Rivista degli Studi Orientali*

S.A.O.C.   *Oriental Institute of the University of Chicago, Studies in Ancient Oriental Civilization*

Sitzungsb. Berlin (München etc.).   *Sitzungsberichte der Preussischen (Bayerischen etc.) Akademie der Wissenschaften*

Soc. Prom. Hell. Studies.   *Society for the Promotion of Hellenic Studies*

Soviet Anth. and Arch.   *Soviet Anthropology and Archaeology*

Stud. Cl. e Or.   *Studi Classici e Orientali*

Trans. Amer. Philosoph. Soc.   *Transactions of the American Philosophical Society*

U.E.   *Ur Excavations*

U.E.T.   *Ur Excavations: Texts*

Unters.   *Untersuchungen zur Geschichte und Altertumskunde Ägyptens* (ed. K. Sethe, later H. Kees)

Urk.   *Urkunden des ägyptischen Altertums*

We. Or.   *Die Welt des Orients*

W.O.   Wilcken, *Griechische Ostraka aus Aegypten und Nubien*

W.V.D.O.G.   *Wissenschaftliche Veröffentlichungen der Deutschen Orient-Gesell-schaft*

W.Z.K.M.   *Wiener Zeitschrift für die Kunde des Morgenlandes*

Y.O.S.   *Yale Oriental Series*

Z.A.   *Zeitschrift für Assyriologie und vorderasiatische Archäologie*

Z.Ä.S.   *Zeitschrift für ägyptische Sprache und Altertumskunde*

Z.A.W.   Zeitschrift für alttestamentliche Wissenschaft
Z.D.M.G. Zeitschrift der Deutschen Morgenländischen Gesellschaft
Z.D.P.V. Zeitschrift des Deutschen Palästina-Vereins
Z. Sar.   Zeitschrift der Savigny-Stiftung für Rechtsgeschichte, romanistische Abteilung
Z.V.F.M. Zeitschrift für die vergleichende Forschung von Menschen

BIBLIOGRAPHY

CHAPTER I

G. GENERAL

1. *Archives royales de Mari* (*A.R.M.T.* texts in transliteration and translation), I–XIII. Paris, 1950–64.
2. Dossin, G. 'Les archives économiques du Palais de Mari.' In *Syria*, 20 (1939), 97–113.
3. Dossin, G. 'Les archives épistolaires du Palais de Mari.' In *Syria*, 19 (1938), 105–26.
4. Gelb, I. J. *Hurrians and Subarians* (*S.A.O.C.* 22). Chicago, 1944.
5. Goetze, A. 'On the Chronology of the Second Millennium B.C.' In *J.C.S.* 11 (1957), 63–73.
6. Kupper, J.-R. *Les nomades en Mésopotamie au temps des rois de Mari*. Paris, 1957.
7. Landsberger, B. 'Assyrische Königsliste und "Dunkles Zeitalter".' In *J.C.S.* 8 (1954), 31–45, 47–73, 106–33.
8. Wiseman, D. J. *The Alalakh Tablets* (*Occasional Publications of the British Institute of Archaeology at Ankara*, 2). London, 1953.

I. SHAMSHI-ADAD I

1. Borger, R. 'Šamši-Adad I. und seine Nachfolger.' In *Handbuch der Orientalistik*, Erste Abt., Ergänzungsband V, Heft I (Leiden, 1961), 9 ff.
2. Dossin, G. 'Les noms d'années et d'éponymes dans les "Archives de Mari".' In *Studia Mariana* (Leiden, 1950), 51–61.
3. Dossin, G. 'Šamši-Addu Ier, roi d'Assyrie (1726–1694 av. J.-C.).' In *Bulletin de l'Académie Royale de Belgique, Classe des Lettres*, 1948, 59–70.
4. Gadd, C. J. 'Tablets from Chagar Bazar and Tall Brak.' In *Iraq*, 7 (1940), 22–66.
5. Goossens, G. *Het ontstaan van het Assyrisch rijk* (*Mededeelingen van de Koninklijke vlaamse Academie van België, Klasse der Letteren*, XXII, 3). Brussels, 1960.
6. Laessøe, J. *The Shemshāra Tablets. A Preliminary Report*. Copenhagen, 1959.
7. Lewy, H. 'The Synchronism Assyria–Ešnunna–Babylon.' In *We. Or.* II, 5/6 (1959), 438–53.
8. von Soden, W. *Herrscher im Alten Orient*. Berlin–Göttingen–Heidelberg, 1954.

II. MARI

1. Birot, M. 'Textes économiques de Mari.' In *R.A.* 47 (1953), 121–30, 161–74; 49 (1955), 15–31; 50 (1956), 57–72.
2. Dossin, G. 'L'inscription de fondation de Iaḥdun-Lim, roi de Mari.' In *Syria*, 32 (1955), 1–28.

3. Kupper, J.-R. 'Baḫdi-Lim, préfet du palais de Mari.' In *Bulletin de l'Académie Royale de Belgique, Classe des Lettres*, 1954, 572–87.

4. Kupper, J.-R. 'Un gouvernement provincial dans le royaume de Mari.' In *R.A.* 41 (1947), 149–83.

5. Leemans, W. F. *Foreign Trade in the Old Babylonian Period.* Leiden, 1960.

6. Lewy, H. 'The Historical Background of the Correspondence of Baḫdi-Lim.' In *Or.* 25 (1956), 324–52.

7. Munn-Rankin, J. M. 'Diplomacy in Western Asia in the Early Second Millennium B.C.' In *Iraq*, 18 (1956), 68–110.

8. Parrot, A. *Mission archéologique de Mari*, II: *Le Palais.* 3 parts (*Inst. fr. d'Arch. de Beyrouth, Biblioth. arch. et hist.* 68–70). Paris, 1958–9.

9. Thureau-Dangin, F. 'Iaḫdunlim, roi de Ḫana.' In *R.A.* 33 (1936), 49–54.

10. Thureau-Dangin, F. 'Textes de Mâri.' In *R.A.* 33 (1936), 169–79.

III. ESHNUNNA, IAMKHAD, QATNA AND OTHER STATES

1. Dossin, G. 'Aplaḫanda, roi de Carkémiš.' In *R.A.* 35 (1938), 115–21.

2. Dossin, G. 'Iamḫad et Qatanum.' In *R.A.* 36 (1939), 46–54.

3. Dossin, G. 'Une lettre de Iarîm-Lim, roi d'Alep, à Iašûb-Iaḫad, roi de Dîr.' In *Syria*, 33 (1956), 63–9.

4. Dossin, G. 'Le royaume d'Alep au XVIIIe siècle avant notre ère d'après les "Archives de Mari".' In *Bulletin de l'Académie Royale de Belgique, Classe des Lettres*, 1952, 229–39.

5. Dossin, G. 'Le royaume de Qatna au XVIIIe siècle avant notre ère d'après les "Archives royales de Mari".' In *Bulletin de l'Académie Royale de Belgique, Classe des Lettres*, 1954, 417–25.

6. Jacobsen, Th. 'Historical Data.' In *O.I.P.* 43 (Chicago, 1940), 116–200.

7. Smith, S. 'Yarim-Lim of Yamḥad.' In *R.S.O.* 32 (1957), 155–84.

8. Tocci, Fr. M. *La Siria nell'età di Mari.* Rome, 1960.

IV. THE HURRIANS c. 1800 B.C.

1. O'Callaghan, R. T. *Aram Naharaim (An. Or. 26)*, ch. III. Rome, 1948.

V. THE BENJAMINITES AND OTHER NOMADS, AND THE HABIRU

1. Borger, R. 'Das Problem der 'apīru ("Ḫabiru").' In *Z.D.P.V.* 74 (1958), 121–32.

2. Bottéro, J. *Le problème des Ḫabiru à la 4e Rencontre assyriologique internationale (Cahiers de la Société Asiatique*, 12). Paris, 1954.

3. Dossin, G. 'Les Bédouins dans les textes de Mari.' In *L'antica società beduina* (Rome, 1959), 35–51.

4. Dossin, G. 'Benjaminites dans les textes de Mari.' In *Mélanges syriens offerts à M. R. Dussaud* (Paris, 1939), 981–96.

5. Gelb, I. J. 'The Early History of the West Semitic Peoples.' In *J.C.S.* 15 (1961), 27–47.

6. Kupper, J.-R. 'Le rôle des nomades dans l'histoire de la Mésopotamie ancienne.' In *Journ. of the Economic and Social History of the Orient*, II, 2 (1959), 113–27.

7. Kupper, J.-R. 'Sutéens et Ḫapiru.' In *R.A.* 55 (1961), 197–200. See especially p. 197 n. 2 for recent bibliography on the Habiru.

VI. HAMMURABI'S CONQUESTS IN THE NORTH, AND THE DECLINE
OF THE EASTERN AMORITE STATES

1. Lewy, H. 'On Some Problems of Kassite and Assyrian Chronology.' In
   Annuaire de l'Inst. de Philologie et d'Histoire orientales et slaves, XIII, 1953
   (Brussels, 1955), 241–91.
2. Nougayrol, J. 'Documents du Ḫabur.' In *Syria*, 37 (1960), 205–9.
3. Thureau-Dangin, F. 'La chronologie de la première dynastie babylonienne'
   (*Mém. Ac. inscr. B.-L.*, 43, 2). Paris, 1942.

VII. THE 'GREAT KINGSHIP' OF ALEPPO

1. Albright, W. F. 'Further Observations on the Chronology of Alalakh.' In
   Bull. A.S.O.R. 146 (1957), 26–34.
2. Alt, A. *Die Herkunft der Hyksos in neuer Sicht* (*B.S.A.W.* 101/6). Berlin,
   1954.
3. Goetze, A. 'Alalaḫ and Hittite Chronology.' In *Bull. A.S.O.R.* 146 (1957),
   20–6.
4. Nagel, W. and Strommenger, E. 'Alalaḫ und Siegelkunst.' In *J.C.S.* 12
   (1958), 109–23.
5. Otten, H. 'Vorläufiger Bericht über die Ausgrabungen in Boğazköy im Jahre
   1957.' In *M.D.O.G.* 91 (1958), 73–84.
6. Smith, S. *Alalakh and Chronology.* London, 1940.
7. Speiser, E. A. 'The Alalakh Tablets.' In *J.A.O.S.* 74 (1954), 18–25.
8. Wiseman, D. J. 'Abban and Alalaḫ.' In *J.C.S.* 12 (1958), 124–9. (See
   amendment in *J.C.S.* 13 (1959), 94–7, 132.)
9. Wiseman, D. J. 'Ration Lists from Alalakh VII.' In *J.C.S.* 13 (1959), 19–33.
10. Woolley, L. *Alalakh. An Account of the Excavations at Tell Atchana in the
    Hatay, 1937–1949.* Oxford, 1955.
11. Woolley, L. *A Forgotten Kingdom.* London, 1953.

VIII. DEVELOPMENT OF THE HURRIAN STATES

See bibliography for § VII.

IX. HURRIAN ELEMENTS IN ART AND RELIGION

1. Güterbock, H. G. 'The Hurrian Element in the Hittite Empire.' In *Cah.
   H.M.* II, 2 (1954), 383–94.
2. Hrouda, B. 'Die Churriter als Problem archäologischer Forschung.' In
   Archaeologia Geographica, 7 (1958), 14–19.
3. Speiser, E. A. 'The Hurrian Participation in the Civilizations of Mesopotamia,
   Syria and Palestine.' In *Cah. H.M.* I, 2 (1953), 311–27.
4. Thureau-Dangin, F. 'Tablettes hurrites provenant de Mari.' In *R.A.* 36
   (1939), 1–28.

A. ADDENDA

1. Birot, M. 'Les lettres de Iasîm-Sumû.' In *Syria*, 41 (1964), 25 ff.
2. Burke, M. L. 'Lettres de Numušda-naḫrâri et de trois autres correspondants
   à Idiniatum.' In *Syria*, 41 (1964), 67 ff.
3. Finet, A. 'Iawi-Ilâ, roi de Talḫayûm.' In *Syria*, 41 (1964), 117 ff.

4. Huffmon, H. B. *Amorite Personal Names in the Mari Texts: A Structural and Lexical Study*. Baltimore, 1965.
5. Klengel, H. *Geschichte Syriens im 2. Jahrtausend v. u. Z. Teil 1—Nordsyrien*. Berlin, 1965.
6. Kupper, J.-R. 'Correspondance de Kibri-Dagan.' In *Syria*, 41 (1964), 105 ff.
7. Mayrhofer, M. *Die Indo-Arier im Alten Vorderasien*. Wiesbaden, 1966.
8. Van Seters, J. *The Hyksos. A New Investigation*. New Haven and London, 1966.

CHAPTER II

G. GENERAL

1. Berlin Museum, *Aegyptische Inschriften aus den Königlichen Museen zu Berlin*, I, II. Leipzig, 1901, 1913.
2. British Museum, *Hieroglyphic Texts from Egyptian Stelae, etc. in The British Museum* (edited by P. D. Scott-Moncrieff, H. R. Hall, I. E. S. Edwards, T. G. H. James). 9 parts. London, 1911–70.
3. Drioton, É. and Vandier, J. *L'Égypte* ('*Clio*': *Introduction aux études historiques. Les peuples de l'orient méditerranéen*, II). Ed. 3. Paris, 1952.
4. Evers, H. G. *Staat aus dem Stein. Denkmäler, Geschichte und Bedeutung der ägyptischen Plastik während des mittleren Reichs*. 2 vols. Munich, 1929.
5. Gardiner, A. H. *The Royal Canon of Turin*. Oxford, 1959
6. Gauthier, H. *Le livre des rois d'Égypte*, I, II (*Mém. Inst. fr. Caire*, 17, 18). Cairo, 1907, 1912.
7. Griffith, F. Ll. *Hieratic Papyri from Kahun and Gurob*. 2 vols. London, 1898.
8. Hayes, W. C. *The Scepter of Egypt*. Parts I and II. New York, 1953, 1959.
9. Helck, W. *Untersuchungen zu Manetho und den ägyptischen Königslisten* (*Unters*. 18). Berlin, 1956.
10. Lange, H. O. and Schäfer, H. *Grab- und Denksteine des mittleren Reichs im Museum von Kairo* (*C.C.G.* nos. 20001–780). 4 vols. Berlin, 1902–25.
11. Meyer, E. *Aegyptische Chronologie* (*Abh. Berlin*, 1904, 1). Berlin, 1904.
12. Meyer, E. *Nachträge zur aegyptischen Chronologie* (*ibid.* 1907, III). Berlin, 1908.
13. Meyer, E. *Geschichte des Altertums*, I, 2 (ed. 5); II, 1 (ed. 2). Stuttgart and Berlin, 1926, 1928.
14. Petrie, W. M. F. *A History of Egypt from the Earliest Kings to the XVIth Dynasty*. Ed. 11. London, 1924.
15. Porter, B. and Moss, R. L. B. *Topographical Bibliography of Ancient Egyptian Hieroglyphic Texts, Reliefs, and Paintings*. 7 vols. Oxford, 1927–51.
16. Prisse d'Avennes, E. *Monuments égyptiens: Bas-reliefs, peintures, inscriptions, etc., d'après les dessins exécutés sur les lieux*. Paris, 1847.
17. Rowe, A. *A Catalogue of Egyptian Scarabs, Scaraboids, Seals, and Amulets in the Palestine Archaeological Museum* (Government of Palestine, Department of Antiquities). Cairo, 1936.
18. Säve-Söderbergh, T. *Ägypten und Nubien. Ein Beitrag zur altägyptischer Aussenpolitik*. Lund, 1941.
19. Sethe, K. *Urkunden der 18. Dynastie* (*Urkunden des aegyptischen Altertums*, IV). 4 parts. Leipzig, 1906–9.
20. Stock, H. *Studien zur Geschichte und Archäologie der 13. bis 17. Dynastie Ägyptens...* (*Ägyptol. Forsch.* 12). Glückstadt, 1942.
21. Vandier, J. 'Quelques nouvelles hypothèses sur la fin du moyen empire égyptien.' In *Journ. des Savants*, Oct.–Dec. 1944, 154–68.

22. Vandier, J. *Manuel d'archéologie égyptienne.* 5 vols. Paris, 1952–69.
23. Waddell, W. G. *Manetho, with an English Translation (The Loeb Classical Library).* London and Cambridge (Mass.), 1940.
24. Weill, R. *La fin du moyen empire égyptien. Étude sur les monuments et l'histoire de la période comprise entre la XIIe et la XVIIIe dynastie.* 2 vols. Paris, 1918.
25. Weill, R. 'Notes sur *La fin du moyen empire égyptien.*' In *J. as.* 202 (1923), 118–30.
26. Weill, R. 'Compléments pour *La fin du moyen empire égyptien.*' In *Bull. Inst. fr. Caire,* 32 (1932), 7–52.
27. Winlock, H. E. *The Rise and Fall of the Middle Kingdom in Thebes.* New York, 1947.
28. Yoyotte, J. 'Égypte ancienne.' In *Histoire universelle.* 1. *Des origines à l'Islam (Encyclopédie de la Pléiade).* Paris, 1956.

I. THE LAST YEARS OF THE TWELFTH DYNASTY

1. Brunton, G. 'A Monument of Amenemhet IV.' In *Ann. Serv.* 39 (1939), 177–85.
2. Daressy, G. 'Deux grandes statues de Ramsès II d'Héracléopolis.' In *Ann. Serv.* 17 (1917), 33–8.
3. Donadoni, S. 'Testi geroglifici di Madinet Madi.' In *Or.* 16 (1947), 333–52, 506–24.
4. Dunand, M. 'Les Égyptiens à Beyrouth.' In *Syria,* 9 (1928), 300–2.
5. Dunham, D. and Janssen, J. M. A. *Second Cataract Forts,* 1. *Semna–Kumma.* Boston, 1960.
6. Edgerton, W. F. 'Chronology of the Twelfth Dynasty.' In *J.N.E.S.* 1 (1942), 307–14.
7. Gardiner, A. H., Peet, T. E. and Černý, J. *The Inscriptions of Sinai.* 2 parts. London (*E.E.S.*), 1952, 1955.
8. Habachi, L. 'Khatâ'na-Qantir: Importance.' In *Ann. Serv.* 52 (1954), 443–559.
9. Hall, H. R. 'A Sphinx of Amenemhet IV.' In *B. M. Quart.* 2 (1927), 87–8.
10. Hayes, W. C. 'Notes on the Government of Egypt in the Late Middle Kingdom.' In *J.N.E.S.* 12 (1953), 31–9.
11. Jéquier, G. *Deux pyramides du moyen empire (Service des Antiquités de l'Égypte; Fouilles à Saqqarah,* xiv). Cairo, 1933.
12. Jéquier, G. *Douze ans de fouilles dans la nécropole memphite, 1924–1936 (Mémoires de l'Université de Neuchâtel,* xv). Neuchâtel, 1940.
13. Montet, P. *Byblos et l'Égypte; quatre campagnes de fouilles à Gebeil, 1921–1922–1923–1924.* 2 vols. Paris, 1928–9.
14. Moret, A. 'Note sur deux monuments égyptiens trouvés en Syrie.' In *C.-R. Ac. Inscr. B.-L.* 1928, 34–7.
15. Naumann, R. 'Der Tempel des mittleren Reichs in Medinet Mādi.' In *Mitt. deutsch. Inst. Kairo,* 8 (1939), 185–9, pl. 30.
16. Naville, E. *Goshen and the Shrine of Saft-el-Henneh (1885) (E.E.F.* 5th Memoir). London, 1887.
17. Newberry, P. E. 'Co-regencies of Ammenemes III, IV, and Sebknofru.' In *J.E.A.* 29 (1943), 74–5.
18. Parker, R. A. *The Calendars of Ancient Egypt (S.A.O.C.* 26). Chicago, 1950.
19. Petrie, W. M. F. *Kahun, Gurob, and Hawara.* London, 1890.

20. Petrie, W. M. F., Wainwright, G. A. and Mackay, E. *The Labyrinth, Gerzeh and Mazghuneh* (*British School of Archaeology in Egypt and Egyptian Research Account*, 18th Year). London, 1912.
21. Pillet, M. 'Rapport sur les travaux de Karnak (1923–1924).' In *Ann. Serv.* 24 (1924), 53–88.
22. Vogliano, A. *Secondo rapporto degli scavi...nella zona di Mādīnet Māḍi* (*Campagna inverno e primavera 1936—XIV*) (*Pubblicazioni della Regia Università di Milano*). Milan, 1937.
23. Wilson, J. A. 'The Egyptian Middle Kingdom at Megiddo.' In *A.J.S.L.* 58 (1941), 225–36.

II. THE DECLINE AND FALL OF THE MIDDLE KINGDOM: THE THIRTEENTH AND FOURTEENTH DYNASTIES

1. Albright, W. F. 'An Indirect Synchronism between Egypt and Mesopotamia, cir. 1730 B.C.' In *Bull. A.S.O.R.* 99 (1945), 9–18.
2. Albright, W. F. 'Northwest-Semitic Names in a List of Egyptian Slaves from the Eighteenth Century B.C.' In *J.A.O.S.* 74 (1955), 222–33.
3. Alliot, M. *Rapport sur les fouilles de Tell Edfou (1933)* (*Flles Inst. fr. Caire*, 10, part 2). Cairo, 1935.
4. Barsanti, A. 'Stèle inédite au nom du roi Radadouhotep Doudoumes.' In *Ann. Serv.* 9 (1908), 1–2, pl. 1.
5. von Beckerath, J. 'Notes on the Viziers 'Ankhu and 'Iymeru in the Thirteenth Egyptian Dynasty.' In *J.N.E.S.* 17 (1958), 263–8.
6. Breasted, J. H. 'The Monuments of Sudanese Nubia.' In *A.J.S.L.* 25 (1908–9), 1–110.
7. Capart, J. 'Deuxième rapport sommaire sur les fouilles...à el-Kab.' In *Ann. Serv.* 38 (1938), 623–40.
8. Capart, J. (ed.) *Fouilles d'El-Kab* (*Fondation Égyptologique Reine Élisabeth*). Brussels, 1940.
9. Chevrier, H. 'Rapport sur les travaux de Karnak (Novembre 1926–Mai 1927).' In *Ann. Serv.* 27 (1927), 134–53.
10. Cottevieille-Giraudet, R. *Rapport sur les fouilles de Médamoud, 1931: Les monuments du moyen empire* (*Flles Inst. fr. Caire*, 9). Cairo, 1933.
11. Debono, F. 'Expédition archéologique royale au désert oriental (Keft-Kosseir). Rapport préliminaire sur la campagne 1949.' In *Ann. Serv.* 51 (1951), 59–91.
12. Dunham, D. and Janssen, J. M. A. *Second Cataract Forts*, 1. *Semna-Kumma*. Boston, 1960.
13. Edwards, I. E. S. 'A Statuette of Mery-ankh-Re Mentuhotep.' In *Cahiers d'histoire égyptienne*, série III, fasc. 1 (1950), 42–6.
14. Engelbach, R. 'Notes of Inspection, April 1921.' In *Ann. Serv.* 21 (1921), 188–96.
15. Hayes, W. C. *A Papyrus of the Late Middle Kingdom in the Brooklyn Museum* [*Papyrus Brooklyn 35. 1446*]. Brooklyn, 1955.
16. Junker, H., *Die Ägypter* (*Die Völker des antiken Orients: Geschichte der führenden Völker*, III). Freiburg, 1933.
17. Kees, H. 'Zu einigen Fachausdrücken der altägyptischen Provinzialverwaltung.' In *Z.Ä.S.* 70 (1934), 83–91.
18. Kees, H. 'Tanis: Ein kritischer Überblick zur Geschichte der Stadt.' In *Nachr. Göttingen*, 1944, 145–82.

19. Lacau, P. 'Le roi ⊙𝄞 𓏏 ⌣𝄞 ⌣𝄞.' In *Bull. Inst. fr. Caire*, 30 (1931), 881–96.

20. Lacau, P. *Une stèle juridique de Karnak* (*Supplément aux Ann. Serv.* Cahier no. 13). Cairo, 1949.

21. Leclant, J. 'Fouilles et travaux en Égypte, 1955–57.' In *Or.* 27 (1958), 75–101.

22. Lythgoe, A. M. 'The Egyptian Expedition, 1914. Excavations at Lisht.' In *Bull. M.M.A.* 10 (1915), February, Supplement.

23. Macadam, M. F. L. 'A Royal Family of the Thirteenth Dynasty.' In *J.E.A.* 37 (1951), 20–8, pl. 6.

24. de Morgan, J. *Fouilles à Dahchour, Mars–Juin 1894.* Vienna, 1895.

25. Naville, E. *The XIth Dynasty Temple at Deir el-Bahari* (*E.E.F.* 28th, 30th, and 32nd Memoirs). 3 vols. London, 1907–13.

26. Newberry, P. E. 'A Stela Dated in the Reign of Ab-aa.' In *P.S.B.A.* 25 (1903), 130–4.

27. Otto, E. *Topographie des thebanischen Gaues* (*Unters.* 16). Berlin, 1952.

28. Posener, G. 'Les Asiatiques en Égypte sous les XIIe et XIIIe Dynasties.' In *Syria*, 34 (1957), 145–63.

29. Ranke, H. 'Ein Wesir der 13. Dynastie.' In *Mém. Inst. fr. Caire*, 66 (1943), 361–5.

30. Reisner, G. A. *Excavations at Kerma* (*Harvard African Studies*, 5–6). Cambridge (Mass.), 1923.

31. Reisner, G. A. 'Clay Sealings of Dynasty XIII from Uronarti Fort.' In *Kush*, 3 (1955), 26–69.

32. Säve-Söderbergh, T. 'The Hyksos Rule in Egypt.' In *J.E.A.* 37 (1951), 53–71.

33. Scharff, A. 'Ein Rechnungsbuch des königlichen Hofes der 13. Dynastie.' In *Z.Ä.S.* 57 (1922), 51–68.

34. Steindorff, G. 'Die blaue Königskrone.' In *Z.Ä.S.* 53 (1917), 59–74.

35. Tylor, J. J. *The Tomb of Sebeknekht* (*Wall Drawings and Monuments of El Kab*). London, 1896.

36. Vercoutter, J. 'Tôd (1945–1949). Rapport succinct des fouilles.' In *Bull. Inst. fr. Caire*, 50 (1952), 69–87, pls. 1–9.

37. Weill, R. 'Les successeurs de la XIIe Dynastie à Médamoud.' In *Rev. Ég. anc.* 2 (1929), 144–71.

38. Weill, R. 'Sekhemre-Souaztaoui Sebekhotep à Elkab. Un nouveau roi, Sekhemre-Sankhtaoui Neferhotep, à Elkab et à Karnak.' In *Rev. d'égyptol.* 4 (1940), 218–20.

39. Weill, R. 'Un grand dépositoire d'offrandes du moyen empire à Éléphantine.' In *Rev. d'égyptol.* 7 (1950), 188–90.

40. Wente, E. F. *American Research Center in Egypt, Newsletter* no. 25 (26 June, 1957).

41. Winlock, H. E. 'The Tombs of the Kings of the Seventeenth Dynasty at Thebes.' In *J.E.A.* 10 (1924), 217–77.

III. THE HYKSOS INFILTRATION AND THE FOUNDING OF THE FIFTEENTH DYNASTY

1. Bonnet, H. *Reallexikon der ägyptischen Religionsgeschichte.* Berlin, 1952.

2. Borchardt, L. *Die Mittel zur zeitlichen Festlegung von Punkten der ägyptische Geschichte und ihre Anwendung* (*Quellen und Forschungen zur Zeitbestimmung ägyptischen Geschichte*, 2). Cairo, 1935.

3. Emery, W. B. 'A Masterpiece of Egyptian Military Architecture of 3900 years ago: The Great Castle of Buhen in the Sudan.' In *Ill. Ldn. News*, no. 6267, vol. 235 (12 Sept. 1959), 232–3, 249–51.

4. Engberg, R. M. *The Hyksos Reconsidered (S.A.O.C. 18)*. Chicago, 1939.

5. Farina, G. *Il papiro dei re restaurato (Pubblicazioni egittologiche del R. Museo di Torino)*. Rome, 1938,

6. Gardiner, A. H. 'The Defeat of the Hyksos by Kamōse: The Carnarvon Tablet, No. 1.' In *J.E.A.* 3 (1916), 95–110.

7. Gardiner, A. H. 'Davies's Copy of the Great Speos Artemidos Inscription.' In *J.E.A.* 32 (1946), 43–56.

8. Gunn, B. and Gardiner, A. H. 'New Renderings of Egyptian Texts. II. The Expulsion of the Hyksos.' In *J.E.A.* 5 (1918), 36–56.

9. Habachi, L. 'Preliminary Report on the Kamose Stela and Other Inscribed Blocks Found...at Karnak.' In *Ann. Serv.* 53 (1955), 195–202.

10. Junker, H. 'Pḥrnfr.' In *Z.Ä.S.* 75 (1939), 63–84.

11. Kees, H. *Der Götterglaube im alten Ägypten*. Ed. 2. Berlin, 1956.

12. Labib, P. *Die Herrschaft der Hyksos in Ägypten und ihr Sturz*. Glückstadt, Hamburg, New York, 1936.

13. Möller, G. *Hieratische Paläographie. I. Bis zum Beginn der achtzehnten Dynastie*. Ed. 2. Leipzig, 1927.

14. Montet, P. *Le Drame d'Avaris: Essai sur la pénétration des Sémites en Égypte*. Paris, 1941.

15. Newberry, P. E. *Egyptian Antiquities, Scarabs: An Introduction to the Study of Egyptian Seals*, etc. (*Institute of Archaeology of the University of Liverpool*). London, 1908.

16. Parker, R. A. 'The Duration of the Fifteenth Dynasty according to the Turin Papyrus.' In *J.E.A.* 28 (1942), 68.

17. Ricke, H. 'Der "Hohe Sand in Heliopolis".' In *Z.Ä.S.* 71 (1935), 107–11.

18. Säve-Söderbergh, T. 'A Buhen Stela from the Second Intermediate Period (Khartūm No. 18).' In *J.E.A.* 35 (1949), 50–8.

19. Säve-Söderbergh, T. Review of H. E. Winlock, *The Rise and Fall of the Middle Kingdom in Thebes*. In *Bi. Or.* 6 (1949), 85–90.

20. Säve-Söderbergh, T. 'The Nubian Kingdom of the Second Intermediate Period.' In *Kush*, 4 (1956), 54–61.

21. Säve-Söderbergh, T. Review of Drioton, É. and Vandier, J., *L'Égypte*, ed. 3 In *Bi. Or.* 13 (1956), 118–23.

22. Sethe, K. 'Neue Spuren der Hyksos in Inschriften der 18. Dynastie.' In *Z.Ä.S.* 47 (1910), 73–86.

23. Sethe, K. *Urkunden des alten Reichs (Urk. I)*. Leipzig, 1933.

24. Steindorff, G. 'Skarabäen mit Namen von Privatpersonen....' In *Ann. Serv.* 36 (1936), 161–86, pls. 1–5.

25. Vandier, J. *La religion égyptienne* ('*Mana*': *Introduction à l'histoire des religions*, I. *Les anciennes religions orientales*). Ed. 2. Paris, 1949.

26. Yeivin, S. 'Yaʻqobʻel.' In *J.E.A.* 45 (1959), 16–18.

IV. THE HYKSOS KHYAN AND HIS SUCCESSORS

1. Breasted, J. H. *A History of Egypt from the Earliest Times to the Persian Conquest*. Ed. 2. London, 1927.

2. Carter, H. 'Report on the Tomb of Zeser-ka-Ra Amenhetep I ....' In *J.E.A.* 3 (1916), 147–54.

3. Chace, A. B., Manning, H. P. and Bull, L. *The Rhind Mathematical Papyrus. British Museum 10057 and 10058.* 2 vols. Oberlin, 1927, 1929.

4. Daressy, G. 'Notes et remarques.' In *Rec. trav.* 16 (1894), 42–60.

5. Daressy, G. 'Un poignard du temps des rois pasteurs.' In *Ann. Serv.* 7 (1906), 115–20.

6. Dawson, W. R. 'A Bronze Dagger of the Hyksos Period.' In *J.E.A.* 11 (1925), 216–17.

7. Hammad, M. 'Découverte d'une stèle du roi Kamose.' In *Chron. d'Ég.* 30 (1955), 198–208.

8. Lacau, P. 'Une stèle du roi "Kamosis" 𓊪𓅓𓏏𓄿 .' In *Ann. Serv.* 39 (1939), 245–71.

V. THE RECOVERY OF THE THEBAN KINGDOM: THE SEVENTEENTH DYNASTY TO THE DEATH OF SEQENENRE II

1. von Bissing, F. W. *Ein thebanischer Grabfund aus dem Anfang des neuen Reichs.* Berlin, 1900.

2. Capart, J. and Gardiner, A. H. *Le Papyrus Léopold II aux Musées royaux d'art et d'histoire de Bruxelles et le Papyrus Amherst à la Pierpont Morgan Library de New York.* New York and Brussels, 1939.

3. Capart, J., Gardiner, A. H. and van de Walle, B. 'New Light on the Rames-side Tomb-Robberies.' In *J.E.A.* 22 (1936), 169–93.

4. Daressy, G. *Statues de divinités* (*C.C.G.* nos. 38001–9384). 2 vols. Cairo, 1905–6.

5. Drioton, É. 'Notes diverses.' In *Ann. Serv.* 45 (1947), 53–92.

6. Gardiner, A. H. *Hieratic Papyri in the British Museum. Third Series, Chester Beatty Gift.* 2 vols. London, 1935.

7. Gauthier, H. 'Deux sphinx du moyen empire originaires d'Edfou.' In *Ann. Serv.* 31 (1931), 1–6.

8. Harari, I. 'Portée de la stèle juridique de Karnak.' In *Ann. Serv.* 51 (1951), 273–97.

9. Helck, W. *Zur Verwaltung des mittleren und neuen Reichs* (*Probleme der Ägyptologie*, edited by H. Kees, 3). Leiden–Cologne, 1958.

10. *Hieroglyphic Texts from Egyptian Stelae, etc., in the British Museum* (edited by H. R. Hall and others). 9 vols. London, 1911–70.

11. Lefebvre, G. *Romans et contes égyptiens de l'époque pharaonique. Traduction avec introduction, notices et commentaire.* Paris, 1949.

12. Lichtheim, M. 'The Songs of the Harpers.' In *J.N.E.S.* 4 (1945), 178–212.

13. Peet, T. E. *The Great Tomb Robberies of the Twentieth Dynasty.* 2 vols. Oxford, 1930.

14. Säve-Söderbergh, T. *On Egyptian Representations of Hippopotamus Hunting* (*Horae Soederblomianae*, 3). Uppsala, 1953.

15. Smith G. E. *The Royal Mummies* (*C.C.G.* nos. 61051–100). Cairo, 1912.

16. Steindorff, G. and Wolf, W. *Die thebanische Gräberwelt* (*Leipziger ägyptologische studien*, 4). Glückstadt, 1936.

17. Vandier, J. *Mo'alla. La tombe d'Ankhtifi et la tombe de Sébekhotep.* Cairo, 1950.

18. van de Walle, B. 'Antiquités égyptiennes.' In *Les antiquités égyptiennes, grecques, étrusques, romaines et gallo-romaines du Musée de Mariemont* (Brussels, 1952), 15–61, pls. 1–18.

19. Weill, R. 'Remise en position chronologique et conditions historiques de la XIIe Dynastie égyptienne.' In *J. as.* 234 (1943–5 [1947]), 131–49.
20. Winlock, H. E. 'On Queen Tetisheri, Grandmother of Ahmose I.' In *Anc. Egypt,* 1921, 14–16.

VI. THE PAN-GRAVE PEOPLE

1. Barguet, P. 'Quelques tombes du massif nord de la nécropole de Tôd.' In *Bull. Inst. fr. Caire,* 50 (1952), 17–31.
2. Brunton, G. *Qau and Badari,* III (*B.S.A. Egypt,* 1926). London, 1930.
3. Brunton, G. *Mostagedda and the Tasian Culture* (*British Museum Expedition to Middle Egypt,* 1st and 2nd years, 1928, 1929). London, 1937.
4. Firth, C. M. *The Archaeological Survey of Nubia Report for 1908–1909,* I (*Ministry of Finance, Egypt: Survey of Egypt*). Cairo, 1912.
5. Gardiner, A. H. *Ancient Egyptian Onomastica.* 3 vols. Oxford, 1947.
6. Garstang, J. 'An Ivory Sphinx from Abydos.' In *J.E.A.* 14 (1928), 46–7.
7. Junker, H. *Bericht über die Grabungen der Akademie der Wissenschaften in Wien auf den Friedhöfen von el-Kubanieh-Nord, Winter 1910–1911* (*Denkschriften der Akademie der Wissenschaften in Wien,* Phil.-hist. Klasse, 64). Vienna and Leipzig, 1920.
8. Junker, H. *Toschke. Bericht über die Grabungen der Akademie der Wissenschaften in Wien auf dem Friedhof von Toschke* (*Nubien*) *im Winter 1911– 1912* (*ibid.* 68). Vienna and Leipzig, 1926.
9. Kirwan, L. P. Review of G. Brunton, *Mostagedda and the Tasian Culture.* In *J.E.A.* 25 (1939), 107–9.
10. Lefébure, E. 'Le bucrane.' In *Sphinx,* 10 (1906), 67–129.
11. Petrie, W. M. F. *Diospolis Parva: The Cemeteries of Abadiyeh and Hu, 1898–9* (*E.E.F.,* 20th Memoir). London, 1901.
12. Petrie, W. M. F. *Gizeh and Rifeh* (*B.S.A. Egypt and E.R.A.,* 13th Year). London, 1907.
13. Posener, G. ' ⟨hieroglyphs⟩, et ⟨hieroglyphs⟩.' In *Z.Ä.S.* 83 (1958), 38–43.
14. Posener, G. 'Pour une localisation du pays Koush au Moyen Empire.' In *Kush,* 6 (1958), 39–68.
15. Reisner, G. A. *The Archaeological Survey of Nubia, Bulletin No. 4.* Cairo, 1909.
16. Wainwright, G. A. *Balabish* (*E.E.S.,* 37th Memoir). London, 1920.
17. Weigall, A. E. P. *A Report on the Antiquities of Lower Nubia* (*The First Cataract to the Sudan Frontier*) *and their Condition in 1906–7* (*Egypt: Department of Antiquities*). Oxford, 1907.

A. ADDENDA

1. Arnold, D. 'Bemerkungen zu den Königsgräbern der frühen 11. Dynastie von El-Târif.' In *Mitt. deutsch. Inst. Kairo,* 23 (1968), 26–37.
2. von Beckerath, J. 'Die Könige mit dem Thronnamen *Sḥm-rꜥ ḫw-tꜣwj.*' In *Z.Ä.S.* 84 (1959), 81–5.
3. von Beckerath, J. 'Ein neuer König des späten Mittleren Reiches.' In *Z.Ä.S.* 88 (1962), 4–5.
4. von Beckerath, J. *Untersuchungen zur politischen Geschichte der zweiten Zwischenzeit in Ägypten* (*Ägyptol. Forsch.* 23). Glückstadt, 1965.
5. Gardiner, Sir Alan H. *Egypt of the Pharaohs.* Oxford, 1961.

6. Giveon, R. 'A Sealing of Khayan from the Shephela of Southern Palestine.' In *J.E.A.* 51 (1965), 202–4.
7. Helck, W. *Die Beziehungen Ägyptens zu Vorderasien im 3. und 2. Jahrtausend v. Chr.* (*Ägyptol. Abh.* 5). Wiesbaden, 1962.
8. Hinze, F. 'Das Kerma-Problem.' In *Z.Ä.S.* 91 (1964), 79–86.
9. Hornung, E. *Untersuchungen zur Chronologie und Geschichte des Neuen Reiches* (*Ägyptol. Abh.* 11). Wiesbaden, 1964.
10. Kitchen, K. A. 'Byblos, Egypt and Mari in the Early Second Millennium B.C.' In *Or.* 36, fasc. 1 (1967), 39–54.
11. van Seters, J. *The Hyksos, a New Investigation.* New Haven and London, 1966.

CHAPTER III

G. GENERAL

1. Albright, W. F. 'The Excavation of Tell Beit Mirsim. I. The Pottery of the First Three Campaigns.' In *Ann. A.S.O.R.* 12. New Haven, 1932.
2. Albright, W. F. 'The Excavation of Tell Beit Mirsim. IA. The Bronze Age Pottery of the Fourth Campaign.' In *Ann. A.S.O.R.* 13 (1933), 55 ff.
3. Albright, W. F. 'The Excavation of Tell Beit Mirsim. II. The Bronze Age.' In *Ann. A.S.O.R.* 17 (1938).
4. Guy, P. L. O. and Engberg, R. M. *Megiddo Tombs* (*O.I.P.* 33). Chicago, 1938.
5. Kenyon, K. M. *Amorites and Canaanites* (Schweich Lectures of the British Academy, 1963). London, 1966.
6. Kenyon, K. M. *Archaeology in the Holy Land.* London, 1960.
7. Kenyon, K. M. *Excavations at Jericho*, I. London, 1960.
8. Kenyon, K. M. *Excavations at Jericho*, II. London, 1965.
9. Loud, G. *Megiddo*. II. *Seasons of 1935–39* (*O.I.P.* 62). Chicago, 1948.
10. Macdonald, E., Starkey, J. L. and Harding, L. *Beth-pelet*, II. London, 1932.
11. Petrie, W. M. F. *Ancient Gaza*, I. London, 1931.
12. Petrie, W. M. F. *Ancient Gaza*, II. London, 1932.
13. Petrie, W. M. F. *Ancient Gaza*, III. London, 1933.
14. Petrie, W. M. F. *Ancient Gaza*, IV. London, 1933.
15. Petrie, W. M. F. *City of Shepherd Kings*; and Mackay, E. J. H. and Murray, M. A. *Ancient Gaza*, V. London, 1952.
16. Petrie, W. M. F. *Beth-pelet*, I. London, 1930.
17. Sellin, E. and Watzinger, C. *Jericho* (*W.V.D.O.G.* 22). Leipzig, 1913.
18. Tufnell, O. *Lachish*. IV. *The Bronze Age*. Oxford, 1958.

I. MIDDLE BRONZE AGE I

1. Dunand, M. 'Byblos au temps du Bronze Ancien et la Conquête Amorite. In *Rev. bibl.* 59 (1952), 82 ff.
2. Dunand, M. *Fouilles de Byblos*, I. Paris, 1939.
3. Dunand, M. *Fouilles de Byblos*, II. Paris, 1954, 1958.
4. Gray, J. *The Canaanites.* London, 1964.
5. Kenyon, K. M. 'Some notes on the Early and Middle Bronze Age strata of Megiddo.' In *Eretz-Israel*, 5 (1958), 51* ff.
6. Mallowan, M. E. L. 'Excavations at Brak and Chagar Bazar.' In *Iraq*, 9 (1947), 1 ff.

7. Mesnil du Buisson, Comte du. 'Compte rendu de la quatrième campagne de fouilles a Mishrifé–Qatna.' In *Syria*, 11 (1930), 146 ff.

8. Montet, P. *Byblos et l'Égypte*. Paris, 1928 and 1929.

9. Ory, J. 'Excavations at Rās el 'Ain.' In *Q.D.A.P.* 4 (1935) and 5 (1936), 111 f.

10. Schaeffer, C. F. A. 'Les fouilles de Minet-el-Beida et de Ras Shamra (quatrième campagne).' In *Syria*, 14 (1933), 93 ff.

11. Schaeffer, C. F. A. 'Les fouilles de Ras Shamra–Ugarit (neuvième campagne).' In *Syria*, 19 (1938), 193 ff., 313 ff.

12. Schaeffer, C. F. A. *Ugaritica*, ii. Paris, 1949.

13. Vaux, R. de et Stève, A.-M. 'La première campagne de fouilles a Tell el-Fār'ah, près Naplouse'. In *Rev. bibl.* 54 (1947), 394 ff.

II. MIDDLE BRONZE AGE II

1. Ben-dor, I. 'Palestinian Alabaster Vases.' In *Q.D.A.P.* 11 (1945), 93 ff.

2. Loud, G. *The Megiddo Ivories* (*O.I.P.* 52). Chicago, 1939.

III. MIDDLE BRONZE AGE II: SITES

1. Albright, W. F. 'The Chronology of a South Palestinian City, Tell el-'Ajjûl.' In *A.J.S.L.* 55 (1938), 337 ff.

2. *Archives royales de Mari*, vi. Paris, 1954.

3. Ben-dor, I. 'A Middle Bronze-Age Temple at Nahariya.' In *Q.D.A.P.* 14 (1950), 1 ff.

4. Dothan, M. 'The excavations at Nahariyah: preliminary report (seasons 1954/55).' In *I.E.J.* 6 (1956), 14 ff.

5. Duncan, J. G. *Corpus of Palestinian Pottery*. London, 1930.

6. Garstang, J. 'Jericho; city and necropolis.' In *Ann. Arch. Anthr.* 19 (1932), 3 ff.

7. Garstang, J. 'Jericho; city and necropolis. Third Report.' In *Ann. Arch. Anthr.* 20 (1933), 3 ff.

8. Garstang, J. 'Jericho; city and necropolis. Fourth Report.' In *Ann. Arch. Anthr.* 21 (1934), 99 ff.

9. Grant, E. and Wright, G. E. *Ain Shems Excavations*, v. Haverford, Pennsylvania, 1939.

10. Grant, E. *Beth Shemesh*. Haverford, Pennsylvania, 1929.

11. Kenyon, K. M. *Digging up Jericho*. London, 1957.

12. Kenyon, K. M. 'Excavations at Jericho, 1953.' In *P.E.Q.* 1953, 81 ff.

13. Kenyon, K. M. 'Excavations at Jericho, 1956'. In *P.E.Q.* 1956, 67 ff.

14. Kenyon, K. M. 'Excavations at Jericho, 1957–8. In *P.E.Q.* 1960, 88 ff.

15. Knudtzon, J. A. *Die el-Amarna Tafeln*. Leipzig, 1915.

16. Macalister, R. A. S. *The Excavation of Gezer*, i. London, 1912.

17. Macalister, R. A. S. *The Excavation of Gezer*, iii. London, 1912.

18. Mackenzie, D. *Excavations at Ain Shems*. *Ann. P.E.F.* (1912–13).

19. May, H. G. *Oxford Bible Atlas*. London, 1962.

20. Pritchard, J. B. (ed.). *Ancient Near-Eastern Texts relating to the Old Testament*. Ed. 2. Princeton, 1955.

21. Vaux, R. de. 'La troisième campagne de fouilles à Tell el-Fār'ah, près Naplouse.' In *Rev. bibl.* 58 (1951), 393 ff.

22. Vaux, R. de. 'Les fouilles de Tell el-Fār'ah, près Naplouse. Cinquième campagne.' In *Rev. bibl.* 62 (1955), 541 ff.

23. Vaux, R. de. 'Les fouilles de Tell el-Fār'ah, près Naplouse. Sixième Campagne.' In *Rev. bibl.* 64 (1957), 552 ff.
24. Vaux, R. de. 'Les fouilles de Tell el-Fār'ah, près Naplouse. Rapport préliminaire sur les 7e, 8e, 9e Campagnes, 1958–1960.' In *Rev. bibl.* 69 (1962), 212 ff.
25. Wright, G. E. *Shechem.* New York, 1965.
26. Yadin, Y. 'Hyksos fortifications and the battering-ram.' In *Bull. A.S.O.R.* 137 (1955), 23 ff.
27. Yadin, Y. *Hazor—Exploration of a Biblical City.* An Archaeological Exhibition arranged by the Anglo-Israel Exploration Society at the British Museum. London, 1958
28. Yadin, Y. 'Excavations at Hazor 1957.' In *I.E.J.* 8 (1958), 1 ff.
29. Yadin, Y. 'Excavations at Hazor 1958.' In *I.E.J.* 9 (1959), 74 ff.
30. Yadin, Y. *Hazor,* I. Jerusalem, Israel, 1958.
31. Yadin, Y. *Hazor,* II. Jerusalem, Israel, 1960.

CHAPTER IV(*a*)

G. GENERAL

1. Blegen, C. W. 'Athens and the Early Age of Greece.' In *Athenian Studies presented to William Scott Ferguson (Harv. Stud. Class. Phil.,* suppl. 1. Cambridge, Mass., 1940), 1–9.
2. Blegen, C. W. 'Preclassical Greece—A Survey.' In *B.S.A.* 46 (1951), 16–24.
3. Bossert, H. Th. *The Art of Ancient Crete.* London, 1937.
4. Fimmen, D. *Die kretisch-mykenische Kultur* (2nd ed.). Leipzig and Berlin, 1924.
5. Frankfort, H. *Studies in Early Pottery of the Near East.* II. *Asia, Europe and the Aegean, and their Earliest Interrelations (Royal Anthropological Institute. Occasional Papers,* no. 8). London, 1927.
6. Hall, H. R. *The Civilization of Greece in the Bronze Age.* London, 1928.
7. Marinatos, S. 'La marine créto-mycénienne.' In *B.C.H.* 57 (1933), 170–235.
8. Marinatos, S. and Hirmer, M. *Crete and Mycenae.* London, 1960.
9. Matz, F. 'Die Ägäis.' In *Handbuch der Archäologie,* II (Munich, 1954), 179–308.
10. Matz, F. *Kreta, Mykene, Troja.* Stuttgart, 1956.
11. Matz, F. *The Art of Crete and Early Greece.* Baden-Baden and New York, 1962.
12. Schachermeyr, F. *Die ältesten Kulturen Griechenlands.* Stuttgart, 1955.
13. Schachermeyr, F. 'Prähistorische Kulturen Griechenlands.' In *P.W.* 22, 2, cols. 1350–1548.
14. Vermeule, E. *Greece in the Bronze Age.* Chicago, 1964.
15. Wace, A. J. B. 'The Early Age of Greece.' In *A Companion to Homer,* ed. A. J. B. Wace and F. H. Stubbings (London, 1962), 337–43.
16. Wace, A. J. B. 'The History of Greece in the Third and Second Millenniums B.C.' In *Historia,* 2 (1953/4), 74–94.
17. Wace, A. J. B. 'The Prehistoric Exploration of the Greek Mainland.' In *B.C.H.* 70 (1946), 628–38.
18. Wace, A. J. B. and Blegen, C. W. 'Pottery as Evidence for Trade and Colonization in the Aegean Bronze Age.' In *Klio,* 32 (1939), 131–47.
19. Zervos, Chr. *L'art des Cyclades du début à la fin de l'âge du bronze, 2500–1100 avant notre ère.* Paris, 1957.

II. THE ARCHAEOLOGICAL EVIDENCE

1. Akurgal, E. 'Bayraklı Kazısı: Ön rapor.' In *Ankara Üniversitesi Dil ve Tarih-Coğrafya Facültesi Dergisi*, 8 (1950), 1–51; German text, 52–97.
2. Atkinson, T. D. and others. *Excavations at Phylakopi in Melos* (*Soc. Prom. Hell. Studies, Suppl. Paper*, no. 4). London, 1904.
3. Bernabò-Brea, L. (ed.). *Poliochni, città preistorica nell'isola di Lemnos*, 1. Rome, 1964.
4. Blegen, C. W. 'An Early Tholos Tomb in Western Messenia.' In *Hesperia*, 23 (1954), 158–62.
5. Blegen, C. W. 'Hyria.' In *Commemorative Studies in Honor of Theodore Leslie Shear* (*Hesperia*, suppl. 8, 1949), 39–42.
6. Blegen, C. W. *Korakou, a Prehistoric Settlement near Corinth*. Boston and New York, 1921.
7. Blegen, C. W. *Prosymna, the Helladic Settlement Preceding the Argive Heraeum*. Cambridge, 1937.
8. Blegen, C. W. *Troy and the Trojans*. London and New York, 1963.
9. Blegen, C. W. *Zygouries, A Prehistoric Settlement in the Valley of Cleonae*. Cambridge, Mass., 1928.
10. Blegen, C. W. and Wace, A. J. B. 'Middle Helladic Tombs.' In *Symbolae Osloenses*, 9 (1930), 28–37.
11. Blegen, C. W. and others. *Troy. Excavations conducted by the University of Cincinnati, 1932–1938*. III. *The Sixth Settlement*. Princeton, 1953. Reviewed by K. Bittel in *Gnomon*, 28 (1956), 241–52.
12. Boehlau, J. and Schefold, K. *Larisa am Hermos*. III. *Die Kleinfunde*. Berlin, 1942.
13. Bossert, E.-M. 'Zur Datierung der Gräber von Arkesine auf Amorgos.' In *Festschrift für Peter Goessler, Tübinger Beiträge zur Vor- und Frühgeschichte* (Stuttgart, 1954), 23–34.
14. Buck, R. J. 'Middle Helladic Mattpainted Pottery.' In *Hesperia*, 33 (1964), 231–313.
15. Bulle, H. *Orchomenos*. I. *Die älteren Ansiedelungsschichten*. Munich, 1907.
16. Caskey, J. L. 'Houses of the Fourth Settlement at Lerna.' In *Charisterion Orlandos*, III, 144–52. Athens, 1965.
17. Caskey, J. L. Preliminary reports on excavations at Lerna. In *Hesperia*, 23 (1954), 3–30; 24 (1955), 25–49; 25 (1956), 147–73; 26 (1957), 142–62; 27 (1958), 125–44.
18. Caskey, J. L. Preliminary reports on excavations in Ceos. In *Hesperia*, 31 (1962), 263–83; 33 (1964), 314–35; 35 (1966), 363–76; *Archaeology*, 13 (1960), 290; 15 (1962), 223–6; 16 (1963), 284–5; 17 (1964), 227–80; *Arch. Delt.* 16 (1961), 251–2; 17 (1962), 275–8; 19 (1964), 413–19; 20 (1965), 527–33; 22 (1967), 470–9; 23 (1968), 389–93.
19. Childe, V. G. 'On the Date and Origin of Minyan Ware.' In *J.H.S.* 35 (1915), 196–207.
20. Coleman, J. E. 'Middle Bronze Age Burials on Ceos' (abstract). In *A.J.A.* 69 (1965), 167.
21. Dawkins, R. M. and Droop, J. P. 'The Excavations at Phylakopi in Melos.' In *B.S.A.* 17 (1910–11), 1–22.
22. Dörpfeld, W. *Alt-Ithaka*. Munich, 1927.
23. Dörpfeld, W. *Alt-Olympia*. Berlin, 1935.

24. Dor, L., Jannoray, J., van Effenterre, H. and van Effenterre, M. *Kirrha, étude de préhistoire phocidienne*. Paris, 1960. See also review in *A.J.A.* 66 (1962), 211.

25. Evangelides, D. ''Ηπειρωτικαὶ ἔρευναι. ι. ʽΗ ἀνασκαφὴ τῆς Δωδώνης, 1935.' In *Epeirotika Chronika*, 10 (1935), 192–260.

26. Farnsworth, M. and Simmons, I. 'Coloring Agents for Greek Glazes.' In *A.J.A.* 67 (1963), 389–96.

27. Forsdyke, E. J. *Catalogue of the Greek and Etruscan Vases in the British Museum. i, i. Prehistoric Aegean Pottery*. London, 1925.

28. Forsdyke, E. J. 'The Pottery Called Minyan Ware.' In *J.H.S.* 34 (1914), 126–56.

29. Frödin, O. and Persson, A. W. *Asine, Results of the Swedish Excavations, 1922–1930*. Stockholm, 1938.

30. Furumark, A. *The Mycenaean Pottery*. Stockholm, 1941. Particularly pp. 102, 214–35.

31. Gallet de Santerre, H. *Délos primitive et archaïque*. Paris, 1958.

32. Goldman, H. *Excavations at Eutresis in Boeotia*. Cambridge, Mass., 1931.

33. Heurtley, W. A. *Prehistoric Macedonia*. Cambridge, 1939.

34. Hiller v. Gaertringen, F. *Thera, Untersuchungen, Vermessungen und Ausgrabungen in den Jahren 1895–1902*. III. *Stadtgeschichte von Thera*. Berlin, 1904.

35. Holland, L. B. 'Primitive Aegean Roofs.' In *A.J.A.* 24 (1920), 323–41.

36. Holmberg, E. J. *The Swedish Excavations at Asea in Arcadia*. Lund, 1944.

37. Hood, S. Notices of excavations at Emporio in Chios. In *J.H.S.* 74 (1954), 163; *Arch. Reports, 1954*, 20.

38. Hope Simpson, R. and Lazenby, J. F. 'Notes from the Dodecanese.' In *B.S.A.* 57 (1962), 154–75.

39. Hope Simpson, R. and Lazenby, J. F. 'The Kingdom of Peleus and Achilles.' In *Antiq.* 33 (1959), 102–5.

40. Hopf, M. 'Nutzpflanzen vom lernäischen Golf.' In *Jahrb. des röm.-germ. Zentralmuseums Mainz*, 9 (1962), 1–19.

41. Hopf, M. 'Pflanzenfunde aus Lerna/Argolis.' In *Der Züchter*, 31 (1961), 239–47.

42. Hutchinson, R. W. *Prehistoric Crete*. Harmondsworth, 1962.

43. Jannoray, J. and van Effenterre, H. 'Fouilles de Krisa.' In *B.C.H.* 61 (1937), 299–326; 62 (1938), 110–48.

44. Karo, G. *Die Schachtgräber von Mykenai*. Munich, 1930/3.

45. Keramopoullos, A. D. 'Θηβαϊκά.' In *Arch. Delt.* 3 (1917), 1–503.

46. Lamb, W. *Excavations at Thermi in Lesbos*. Cambridge, 1936.

47. Marinatos, S. Notice of excavations in the region of Pylus. In *Ergon*, 1954, 41–3.

48. Marinatos, S. 'The Volcanic Destruction of Minoan Crete.' In *Antiq.* 13 (1939), 425–39.

49. Mastrokostas, E. 'The Wall of the Dymaeans.' In *Archaeology*, 15 (1962), 133–4; *Ergon* (1962), 171–5; *Arch. Delt.* 18 (1963), 111–14.

50. McDonald, W. A. and Hope Simpson, R. 'Further Exploration in Southwestern Peloponnese: 1962–1963.' In *A.J.A.* 68 (1964), 229–45.

51. McDonald, W. A. and Hope Simpson, R. 'Prehistoric Habitation in Southwestern Peloponnese.' In *A.J.A.* 65 (1961), 221–60.

52. Milojčić, V. 'Ausgrabungen in Thessalien.' In *Neue deutsche Ausgrabungen im Mittelmeergebiet und im vorderen Orient*, ed. E. Boehringer (Deutsches Archäologisches Institut. Berlin, 1959), 225–36.

53. Milojčić, V. 'Ergebnisse der deutschen Ausgrabungen in Thessalien (1953–1958).' In *Jahrb. des röm.-germ. Zentralmuseums Mainz*, 6 (1959), 1–56.

54. Milojčić, V. *Samos.* 1. *Die prähistorische Siedlung unter dem Heraion, Grabung 1953 und 1955.* Bonn, 1961.

55. Müller, K. *Tiryns, die Ergebnisse der Ausgrabungen des Instituts.* III. *Die Architektur der Burg und des Palastes.* Augsburg, 1930.

56. Müller, V. 'Development of the "Megaron" in Prehistoric Greece.' In *A.J.A.* 48 (1944), 342–8.

57. Mylonas, G. E. *Ancient Mycenae.* Princeton, 1957.

58. Mylonas, G. E. *Grave Circle B of Mycenae (Studies in Mediterranean Archaeology*, VII, ed. P. Åström). Lund, 1964.

59. Mylonas, G. E. *Mycenae and the Mycenaean Age.* Princeton, 1966.

60. Mylonas, G. E. *Προϊστορικὴ Ἐλευσίς.* Athens, 1932.

61. Mylonas, G. E. 'The Cult of the Dead in Helladic Times.' In *Studies Presented to D. M. Robinson*, 1 (St Louis, 1951), 64–105.

62. Persson, A. W. 'Rapport préliminaire sur les fouilles d'Asine, 1922–1924, part II.' In *Bull. de la Soc. Royale des Lettres de Lund*, 1924–5, 58–93.

63. Platon, N. and Stasinopoulou-Touloupa, E. Report of discoveries in Thebes. in *Ill. Ldn. News*, 28 Nov. 1964, 859–61; 5 Dec. 1964, 896–7.

64. Renaudin, L. 'Vases préhelléniques de Théra à l'École française d'Athènes.' In *B.C.H.* 46 (1922), 113–59.

65. Rhomaios, K. A. *'Ἐκ τοῦ προϊστορικοῦ Θέρμου.'* In *Arch. Delt.* 1 (1915), 225–79.

66. Rhomaios, K. A. *'Ἔρευναι ἐν Θέρμῳ.'* In *Arch. Delt.* 2 (1916), 179–89.

67. Roux, G. and Courbin, P. Reports of excavations in agora and cemetery of Argos. In *B.C.H.* 78 (1954), 158–73, 175–83.

68. Rubensohn, O. 'Die prähistorischen und frühgeschichtlichen Funde auf dem Burghügel von Paros.' In *Ath. Mitt.* 42 (1917), 1–98.

69. Säflund, G. *Excavations at Berbati, 1936–1937.* Stockholm, 1965.

70. Schachermeyr, F. 'Forschungsbericht über die Ausgrabungen und Neufunde zur ägäischen Frühzeit 1957–1960.' In *Arch. Anz.* 1962, 105–382, particularly 210–20.

71. Scholes, K. 'The Cyclades in the Later Bronze Age: a Synopsis.' In *B.S.A.* 51 (1956), 9–40.

72. Soteriades, G. 'Fouilles préhistoriques en Phocide.' In *Rev. ét. gr.* 25 (1912), 253–99.

73. Soteriades, G. *'Προϊστορικὰ ἀγγεῖα Χαιρωνείας καὶ Ἐλατείας.'* In *Eph. Arch.* 1908, 63–96.

74. Sperling, J. 'Explorations in Elis, 1939.' In *A.J.A.* 46 (1942), 77–89.

75. Taylour, Lord William. *Mycenaean Pottery in Italy and Adjacent Areas.* Cambridge, 1958.

76. Taylour, Lord William. Notices of excavations at Ayios Stephanos in Laconia. In *B.C.H.* 84 (1960), 692–3; *Arch. Reports, 1959–60*, 9–10; *1960–1, 32–3; 1963–4*, 9–10.

77. Theochares, D. R. *'Ἐκ τῆς προϊστορίας τῆς Εὐβοίας καὶ τῆς Σκύρου.'* In *Archeion Euboïkôn Meletôn*, 6 (1959), 279–328.

78. Threpsiades, J. and Travlos, J. *'Ἀνασκαφικαὶ ἔρευναι ἐν Μεγάροις.'* In *Praktika* 1934, 39–57.

79. Tsountas, Chr. *Αἱ προϊστορικαὶ ἀκροπόλεις Διμηνίου καὶ Σέσκλου.* Athens, 1908.

80. Tsountas, Chr. *'Κυκλαδικά*, II.' In *Eph. Arch.* (1899), 73–134.

81. Valmin, M. N. *The Swedish Messenia Expedition*. Lund, 1938.
82. Verdelis, N. ''Ἀνασκαφὴ Πτελεοῦ.' In *Praktika* 1951, 129–54; 1952, 164–85; (1953), 120–32.
83. Vollgraff, W. 'Arx Argorum.' In *Mnemosyne*, 56 (1928), 315–28.
84. Vollgraff, W. Notice of excavations on the Aspis, Argos. In *B.C.H.* 28 (1904), 364–99; 30 (1906), 5–45; 31 (1907), 139–84.
85. Vollgraff, W. Notice of excavations on the Larissa, Argos. In *B.C.H.* 52 (1928), 476–9.
86. Wace, A. J. B. *Mycenae. An Archaeological History and Guide*. Princeton, 1949.
87. Wace, A. J. B. and Blegen, C. W. 'The Pre-Mycenaean Pottery of the Mainland.' In *B.S.A.* 22 (1916–17, 1917–18), 175–89.
88. Wace, A. J. B. and Thompson, M. S. *Prehistoric Thessaly*. Cambridge, 1912.
89. Waterhouse, H. and Hope Simpson, R. 'Prehistoric Laconia: Parts I and II.' In *B.S.A.* 55 (1960), 67–107; 56 (1961), 114–75.
90. Weichert, C. 'Neue Ausgrabungen in Milet.' In *Neue deutsche Ausgrabungen im Mittelmeergebiet und im vorderen Orient*, ed. E. Boehringer (Deutsches Archäologisches Institut, Berlin, 1959), 181–96.
91. Welter, G. *Aigina*. Berlin, 1938.
92. Wide, S. 'Aphidna in Nordattika.' In *Ath. Mitt.* 21 (1896), 385–409.
93. Yalouris, N. 'Δοκιμαστικαὶ ἔρευναι εἰς τὸν κόλπον τῆς Φειᾶς Ἠλείας.' In *Eph. Arch.* 1957 (1961), 31–43.

III. THE PEOPLE:
QUESTIONS OF RACE, LANGUAGE AND CHRONOLOGY

1. Åberg, N. *Bronzezeitliche und früheisenzeitliche Chronologie*. IV, *Griechenland*. Stockholm, 1933.
2. Angel, J. L. 'Human Biological Changes in Ancient Greece, with Special Reference to Lerna.' In *Year Book of the American Philosophical Society*, 1957, 266–70.
3. Angel, J. L. 'Human Biology, Health, and History in Greece from First Settlement until Now.' In *Year Book of the American Philosophical Society*, 1954, 168–72.
4. Angel, J. L. 'The People of Lerna' (abstract). In *A.J.A.* 62 (1958), 221.
5. Åström, P. 'Remarks on Middle Minoan Chronology.' In *Kretika Chronika*, 15–16 (1963), 137–50.
6. Bisson de la Roque, F., Contenau, G. and Chapouthier, F. *Le Trésor de Tôd* (Documents de fouilles de l'Institut français d'archéologie orientale du Caire, XI). Cairo, 1953.
7. Brice, W. C. *Inscriptions in the Minoan Linear Script of Class A*. London, 1961.
8. Buck, C. D. 'The Language Situation in and about Greece in the Second Millennium B.C.' In *Cl. Phil.* 21 (1926), 1–26.
9. Caskey, J. L. 'The Early Helladic Period in the Argolid.' In *Hesperia*, 29 (1960), 285–303.
10. Chadwick, J. ''Η γέννησις τῆς Ἑλληνικῆς γλώσσης.' In 'Ἐπιστημονικὴ Ἐπετηρὶς τῆς Φιλοσοφικῆς Σχολῆς τοῦ Πανεπιστημίου 'Ἀθηνῶν, 12 (1961–2), 531–44.
11. Chadwick, J. ''Η πρώτη Ἑλληνικὴ γραφή.' In 'Ἐπιστημονικὴ Ἐπετηρὶς τῆς Φιλοσοφικῆς Σχολῆς τοῦ Πανεπιστημίου 'Ἀθηνῶν, 12 (1961–2), 515–30.

12. Childe, V. G. *The Dawn of European Civilization* (6th ed.). London, 1957.
13. Fick, A. *Vorgriechische Ortsnamen als Quelle für die Vorgeschichte Griechenlands.* Göttingen, 1905.
14. Goetze, A. *Kleinasien (Handbuch der Altertumswissenschaft*, III, 1, 3, 3, 1, 2nd ed.). Munich, 1957.
15. Haley, J. B. and Blegen, C. W. 'The Coming of the Greeks.' In *A.J.A.* 32 (1928), 141–54.
16. Harland, J. P. 'The Peloponnesos in the Bronze Age.' In *Harv. Stud. Class. Phil.* 34 (1923), 1–62.
17. Hopkins, C. 'The Early History of Greece. 1. The Origin of the Middle Helladic Culture.' In *Yale Classical Studies*, 2 (1931), 117–36.
18. Kantor, H. J. 'The Aegean and the Orient in the Second Millennium B.C.' In *A.J.A.* 51 (1947), 1–103 (=*Arch. Inst. of America*, monograph no. 1, Bloomington, 1947).
19. Kohler, E. L. and Ralph, E. K. 'C-14 Dates for Sites in the Mediterranean Area.' In *A.J.A.* 65 (1961), 357–67.
20. Kretschmer, P. *Einleitung in die Geschichte der griechischen Sprache.* Göttingen, 1896.
21. Landsberger, B. 'Assyrische Königsliste und "Dunkles Zeitalter".' In *J.C.S.* 8 (1954), 31–45, 47–73, 106–33.
22. Mellaart, J. 'The End of the Early Bronze Age in Anatolia and the Aegean.' In *A.J.A.* 62 (1958), 9–33.
23. Mylonas, G. E. 'The Luvian Invasions of Greece.' In *Hesperia*, 31 (1962), 284–309.
24. Myres, J. L. *Who Were the Greeks?* (*University of California, Sather Classical Lectures*, VI). Berkeley, 1930.
25. Nagy, G. 'Greek-like Elements in Linear A.' In *Greek, Roman, and Byzantine Studies*, 4 (1963), 181–211.
26. Nilsson, M. P. *Homer and Mycenae.* London, 1933.
27. Nilsson, M. P. *The Minoan-Mycenaean Religion and its Survival in Greek Religion.* Lund, 1927.
28. Palmer, L. R. *Mycenaeans and Minoans* (2nd. ed.). London, 1965.
29. Pendlebury, J. D. S. *Aegyptiaca.* Cambridge, 1930.
30. Pendlebury, J. D. S. 'Egypt and the Aegean.' In *Studies presented to D. M. Robinson*, 1 (St Louis, 1951), 184–97.
31. Pendlebury, J. D. S. *The Archaeology of Crete.* London, 1939.
32. Persson, A. W. *New Tombs at Dendra Near Midea.* Lund, 1942.
33. Pope, M. *Aegean Writing and Linear A (Studies in Mediterranean Archaeology*, VIII, ed. P. Åström). Lund, 1964.
34. Pugliese Carratelli, G. *Le epigrafi di Haghia Triada in lineare A.* Salamanca, 1963 (*Minos*, suppl. vol. 3).
35. Schachermeyr, F. 'Luwier auf Kreta?' In *Kadmos*, 1 (1962), 27–39.
36. Seyrig, H. 'Note sur le trésor de Tôd.' In *Antiquités syriennes*, 5 ser. (1958), 124–30 (=*Syria*, 31 (1954), 218–24); correction, *ibid.* v–vi.
37. Smith, S. 'Middle Minoan I–II and Babylonian Chronology.' In *A.J.A.* 49 (1945), 1–24.
38. Starr, C. G. *The Origins of Greek Civilization.* New York, 1961.
39. Vandier, J. 'A propos d'un dépôt de provenance asiatique trouvé à Tôd.' In *Syria*, 18 (1937), 174–82.
40. Vercoutter, J. *Essai sur les relations entre Égyptiens et Préhellènes.* Paris, 1954.
41. Vercoutter, J. *L'Égypte et le monde égéen préhellénique.* Cairo, 1956.

A. ADDENDA

1. Blegen, C. W. 'The Middle Helladic Period.' In *Corinth* 13, *The North Cemetery* (Princeton, 1964), 1–12.
2. Carpenter, R. *Discontinuity in Greek Civilization*, the J. H. Gray Lectures for 1965. Cambridge, 1966. Reprinted with an Afterword, The Norton Library, New York, 1968.
3. Caskey, J. L. 'Crises in the Minoan–Mycenaean World.' In *Proc. Amer. Philosoph. Soc.* 113 (1969), 433–49.
4. Erich, R. W. (ed.). *Chronologies in Old World Archaeology*. Chicago and London, 1965.
5. Gejvall, N.-G. *Lerna*, 1. Princeton, 1969.
6. Hammond, N. G. L. *Epirus*. Oxford, 1967.
7. Hammond, N. G. L. 'Tumulus-burial in Albania, The Grave Circles of Mycenae, and The Indo-Europeans.' In *B.S.A.* 62 (1967), 77–105.
8. Marinatos, S. *Excavations at Thera (1967 Season)*. Athens, 1968.
9. Marinatos, S. *Excavations at Thera II (1968 Season)*. Athens, 1969.
10. McDonald, W. A. and Hope Simpson, R. 'Further Explorations in South-western Peloponnese: 1964–1968.' In *A.J.A.* 73 (1969), 123–77.
11. Mylonas, G. E. *Eleusis*. Princeton, 1961.
12. Ninkovich, D. and Heezen, B. C. 'Santorini Tephra.' In *Colston Papers*, 17 (1965), 413–53.
13. Popham, M. R. and Sackett, L. H. (eds.). *Excavations at Lefkandi, Euboea, 1964–66*. Athens and London, 1968.
14. Renfrew, C. 'Crete and the Cyclades before Radamanthus.' In *Kretika Chronika*, 18 (1964), 107–41.
15. Sackett, L. H., Hankey, V., Howell, R. J., Jacobsen, T. W. and Popham, M. R. 'Prehistoric Euboea: Contributions toward a Survey.' In *B.S.A.* 61 (1966), 33–112.
16. Schachermeyr, F. *Die minoische Kultur des alten Kreta*. Stuttgart, 1964.
17. Touloupa, E. and Simeonoglou, S. Preliminary reports on excavations in Thebes, in *Arch. Delt.* 19, B2 (1964), 194–7; 20, B2 (1965), 230–9; 21, B1 (1966), 177–94.

CHAPTER IV(*b*)

G. GENERAL

1. Bossert, H. Th. *Altkreta*. Ed. 3. Berlin, 1937.
2. École Française d'Athènes. *Études Crétoises*, I–XII. Paris, 1928–62.
3. Evans, A. J. *The Palace of Minos at Knossos*, I–IV and Index. London, 1921–36.
4. Marinatos, Sp. and Hirmer, M. *Kreta und das Mykenische Hellas*. Munich, 1960.
5. Matz, F. 'Die Aegaeis.' In *Handbuch der Archaeologie*, II. Munich, 1954.
6. Matz, F. *Kreta, Mykene, Troia. Die Minoische und die Homerische Welt*. Stuttgart, 1956.
7. Nilsson, M. P. *The Minoan-Mycenaean Religion*. Ed. 2. Lund, 1950.
8. Pendlebury, J. D. S. *The Archaeology of Crete*. London, 1939.
9. Pernier, L. and Banti, L. *Il Palazzo Minoico di Festos*, I. Rome, 1935; II. 1951.
10. Schachermeyr, F. *Die minoische Kultur des alten Kreta*. Stuttgart, 1964.
11. Zervos, Chr. *L'Art de la Crète*. Paris, 1956.

IV. CHRONOLOGY

1. Alexiou, St. 'Ein Frühminoisches Grab bei Lebena.' In *Arch. Anz.* (1958), 1 ff.
2. Alexiou, St. '(Lebena).' In *B.C.H.* 84 (1960), 844 ff.
3. Åström, P. 'Remarks on Middle Minoan Chronology.' In *K.Chr.* 15/16 (1961/62), 137 ff. (The conclusions of Åström cannot be accepted by the present writer.)
4. Hutchinson, R. W. 'Minoan Chronology Reviewed.' In *Antiq.* 28 (1954), 153 ff.
5. Levi, D. 'L'Archivio di Cretule a Festos.' In *A.S. Atene*, 35/36 (1957/58), 136 ff.
6. Levi, D. 'Per una Nuova Classificazione della Civiltà Minoica.' In *La Parola del Passato*, 71 (1960), 81 ff.
7. Matz, F. 'Zur Aegaeischen Chronologie der Frühen Bronze-zeit.' In *Historia*, 1 (1950), 173 ff.
8. Platon, N. 'Χρονολογία τῶν Μινωϊκῶν 'Ανακτόρων τῆς Φαίστου.' In *K.Chr.* 3 (1949), 150 ff.
9. Platon, N. 'La Chronologie Minoenne.' In Chr. Zervos, *L'Art de la Crète*. Paris, 1956. Pp. 509 ff.

V. THE EVIDENCE OF THE MONUMENTS

1. Fiandra, E. 'I periodi struttivi del primo palazzo di Festos.' In *K.Chr.* 15/16 (1961/62), 112 ff.
2. Fimmen, D. *Die Kretisch-Mykenische Kultur*. Ed. 2. Leipzig/Berlin, 1928.
3. Gallet de Santerre, H. 'Mallia. Aperçu Historique.' In *K.Chr.* 3 (1949), 363.
4. Hood, S. 'Archaeology in Greece, 1959.' In *Arch. Reports* for 1959/60, 1960/1.
5. Kenna, V. E. G. *Cretan Seals*. Oxford, 1960.
6. Kirsten, E. and Grundmann, K. 'Die Grabung auf der Charakeshöhe bei Monastiraki.' In Matz, F. *Forschungen auf Kreta*, Berlin, 1942. Pp. 27 ff.
7. Levi, D. '(Phaistos).' In *B.d'A.* 36 (1951), 335 ff.; 37 (1952), 320 ff.; 38 (1953), 252 ff.; 40 (1955), 141 ff.; 41 (1956), 238 ff.; *A.S. Atene* 30/32 (1955), 388 ff.; 35/36 (1958), 7 ff.; 39/40 (1963), 8 ff. (Kamilari); 377 ff.
8. Mackenzie, D. 'The Pottery of Knossos.' In *J.H.S.* 23 (1903), 157 ff.
9. Matz, F. *Die Frühkretischen Siegel*. Berlin, 1928.
10. Platon, N. 'Τὸ 'Ιερὸν Μαζᾶ καὶ τὰ Μινωϊκὰ 'Ιερὰ Κορυφῆς.' In *K.Chr.* 5 (1951), 96 ff.
11. Platon, N. 'Τὰ Μινωϊκὰ Οἰκιακὰ 'Ιερά.' In *K.Chr.* 7 (1954), 428 ff.
12. Xanthudides, St. *The Vaulted Tombs of Mesara*. London, 1924.

VI. HISTORICAL CONCLUSIONS

1. Alexiou, St. 'Η Μινωϊκὴ Θεὰ μεθ' 'Υψωμένων Χειρῶν. Iraklion, Crete, 1958.
2. Alexiou, St. 'Ζητήματα τοῦ Προϊστορικοῦ Βίου Κρητομηκηναϊκῶν 'Εμπορίων.' In *Eph. Arch.* 1953/4 (1958), 135 ff.
3. Chapouthier, F. *Le Trésor de Tôd*. Cairo, 1953.
4. Dossin, G. 'Les Archives Économiques au Palais de Mari.' In *Syria*, 20 (1939), 97 ff.
5. Kantor, H. *The Aegaean and the Orient in the Second Millennium B.C.* Bloomington, 1949.
6. Marinatos, Sp. 'La Marine Créto-Mycénienne.' In *B.C.H.* 57 (1933), 170 ff.

7. Matz, F. 'Göttererscheinung und Kultbild im Minoischen Kreta.' In *Abh. Mainz*, 1958, 7.
8. Starr, Ch. G. 'The Myth of the Minoan Thalassokracy.' In *Historia*, 3 (1953), 282 ff.
9. Vercoutter, J. *L'Égypte et le Monde Égéen Préhellénique*. Cairo, 1956.

CHAPTER IV(*c*)

G. GENERAL

1. Bossert, H. T. *Alt-Syrien*. Tübingen, 1951.
2. Casson, S. *Ancient Cyprus*. London, 1937
3. Charles, R.-P. *Le Peuplement de Chypre dans l'antiquité. Étude anthropologique*. École Française d'Athènes (Études Chypriotes, II). Paris, 1962.
4. Daniel, J. F. Review of S. Casson, *Ancient Cyprus*. In *A.J.A.* 43 (1939), 354–7.
5. Daniel, J. F. Review of E. Sjöqvist, *Problems of the Late Cypriote Bronze Age*. In *A.J.A.* 46 (1942), 286–93.
6. Dikaios, P. *A Guide to the Cyprus Museum*, 3rd ed. Nicosia, 1961.
7. Dussaud, R. 'Kinyras. Étude sur les anciens cultes chypriotes'. In *Syria*, 27 (1950), 57–81.
8. Gjerstad, E. and others. *The Swedish Cyprus Expedition. Finds and results of the excavations in Cyprus, 1927–1931*, I, II and III. Stockholm, 1934–7.
9. Helbaek, H. 'Late Cypriote Vegetable Diet at Apliki.' In *Op. Ath.* 4 (1963), 171–86.
10. Hill, Sir George. *A History of Cyprus*, I. Cambridge, 1940.
11. Karageorghis, V. 'Ten years of Archaeology in Cyprus, 1953–1962.' In *A.A.* (1963), pp. 498–600.
12. Karageorghis, V. 'Chronique des fouilles et découvertes archéologiques à Chypre.' In *B.C.H.* 83 (1959), 336–61; 84 (1960), 242–99; 85 (1961), 256–315; 86 (1962), 327–414; 87 (1963), 325–87; 88 (1964), 289–379.
13. Karageorghis, V. *Treasures in the Cyprus Museum*. Nicosia, 1962.
14. Murray, A. S., Smith, A. H. and Walters, H. B. *Excavations in Cyprus*. London, 1900.
15. Myres, J. L. and Ohnefalsch-Richter, M. *A Catalogue of the Cyprus Museum*. Oxford, 1899.
16. Myres, J. L. *Handbook of the Cesnola Collection of Antiquities from Cyprus*. New York, 1914.
17. Schaeffer, C. F. A. *Missions en Chypre, 1932–1935*. Paris, 1936.
18. Schaeffer, C. F. A. *Stratigraphie Comparée et Chronologie de l'Asie Occidentale*. Oxford, 1948.
19. Sjöqvist, E. *Reports on Excavations in Cyprus*. Stockholm, 1940. (Revised reprint from *The Swedish Cyprus Expedition*, I.)
20. Trendall, A. D., Stewart, J. R. and others. *Handbook to the Nicholson Museum*. 2nd ed. Sydney, 1948.

VII. THE NATURE OF THE MIDDLE CYPRIOT PERIOD

1. Åström, P. *The Middle Cypriote Bronze Age*. Lund, 1957.
2. Åström, P. 'Remarks on Middle Minoan Chronology.' In *Kretika Chronika*, 15–16 (i) (1963), 137–50.

3. Gjerstad, E. *Studies on Prehistoric Cyprus.* Uppsala, 1926.
4. Grace, V. 'A Cypriote Tomb and Minoan Evidence for its Date.' In *A.J.A.* 44 (1940), 10–52.
5. Stewart, J. R. 'The Early Cypriote Bronze Age.' In the *Swedish Cyprus Expedition*, IV, part 1a, 205–401. Lund, 1962.
6. Stewart, J. R. 'The Tomb of the Seafarer at Karmi in Cyprus.' In *Op. Ath.* IV (1963), 197–204.

VIII. MIDDLE CYPRIOT SETTLEMENT

1. Åström, P. 'A Middle Cypriote Tomb from Galinoporni.' In *Op. Ath.* 3 (1960), 123–33.
2. Catling, H. W. 'Patterns of Settlement in Bronze Age Cyprus.' In *Op. Ath.* IV (1963), 129–69.
3. Dikaios, P. 'The Excavations at Vounous-Bellapais in Cyprus, 1931–32.' In *Archaeologia*, 88 (1938), 1–174.
4. Gardner, E. A. and others. 'Excavations in Cyprus, 1887–88. Paphos, Leontari, Amargetti.' In *J.H.S.* 9 (1888), 147–271.
5. Masson, O. 'Kypriaka. I. Recherches sur les antiquités de Tamassos.' In *B.C.H.* 88 (1964), 199–238.
6. Myres, J. L. 'Excavations in Cyprus in 1894.' In *J.H.S.* 17 (1897), 134–73.
7. Myres, J. L. 'Excavations in Cyprus, 1913.' In *B.S.A.* 41 (1940–5), 53–98.
8. Stewart, E. and Stewart, J. R. *Vounous, 1937–8.* Lund, 1950.

IX. MIDDLE CYPRIOT DEVELOPMENTS IN MATERIAL CULTURE

1. Åström, P. and Wright, G. R. H. 'Two Bronze Age Tombs at Dhenia in Cyprus.' In *Op. Ath.* IV (1963), 225–76.
2. Åström, P. 'Red-on-Black ware.' In *Op. Ath.* 5 (1965), 59–88.
3. Hennessy, J. B. *Stephania: A Middle and Late Bronze Age Cemetery in Cyprus.* London, n.d.
4. Hogarth, D. G. *Devia Cypria.* London, 1899.
5. Sjöqvist, E. *Problems of the Late Cypriote Bronze Age.* Stockholm, 1940.

X. CYPRUS AND HER NEIGHBOURS IN THE
MIDDLE BRONZE AGE

1. Catling, H. W. and Karageorghis, V. 'Minoika in Cyprus.' In *B.S.A.* 55 (1960), 109–27.
2. Dossin, G. 'Les archives économiques du Palais de Mari.' In *Syria*, 20 (1939), 97–113.
3. Popham, M. 'Two Cypriot Sherds from Crete.' In *B.S.A.* 58 (1963), 89–93.
4. Seton-Williams, V. 'A Painted Pottery of the Second Millennium from Southern Turkey and Northern Syria.' In *Iraq*, 15 (1953), 56–68.
5. Seton-Williams, V. 'Cilician Survey.' In *A.S.* 4 (1954), 121–74.

CHAPTER V

G. GENERAL

1. *A.N.E.P.* Pritchard, J. B. (ed.). *The Ancient Near East in Pictures*. Princeton, 1954.
2. *A.N.E.T.* Pritchard, J. B. (ed.). *Ancient Near-Eastern Texts relating to the Old Testament*. Ed. 2. Princeton, 1955.
3. *A.R.M.T. Archives royales de Mari* (texts in transliteration and translation, vols. I–IX; vol. XV, répertoire analytique des tomes I–IX). Paris, 1950–60.
4. Böhl, F. M. Th. *Opera minora* ('King Hammurabi of Babylon in the setting of his time', pp. 339 ff.). Groningen–Djakarta, 1953.
5. *C.A.D. The Assyrian Dictionary*. Chicago, 1956– .
6. Contenau, G. *La Divination chez les Assyriens et les Babyloniens*. Paris, 1940.
7. Driver, G. R. and Miles, J. C. *The Babylonian Laws*, vols. I, II. Oxford, 1952, 1955.
8. Ebeling, E., Meissner, B. and Weidner, E. F. *Die Inschriften der altassyrischen Könige (Altorientalische Bibliothek*, I). Leipzig, 1926.
9. Ebeling, E., Meissner, B. and Weidner, E. F. *Reallexikon der Assyriologie*, I–III. Berlin and Leipzig, 1932.
10. Edzard, D. O. *Die 'zweite Zwischenzeit' Babyloniens*. Wiesbaden, 1957.
11. Falkenstein, A. and Soden, W. von. *Sumerische und Akkadische Hymnen und Gebete*. Zürich–Stuttgart, 1953.
12. Figulla, H. and Martin, W. J. *Letters and Documents of the Old Babylonian Period (U.E.T.* v). London and Philadelphia, 1953.
13. Frankfort, H. *Cylinder Seals*. London, 1939.
14. Frankfort, H. *The Art and Architecture of the Ancient Orient*. Harmondsworth, 1954.
15. Gadd, C. J. *Ideas of Divine Rule in the Ancient East*. London, 1948.
16. Gadd, C. J. and Legrain, L. *Royal Inscriptions (U.E.T.* I). London and Philadelphia, 1928.
17. Gelb, I. J. *Glossary of Old Akkadian*. Chicago, 1957.
18. King, L. W. *The Letters and Inscriptions of Hammurabi, King of Babylon*, I–III. London, 1898–1900.
19. King, L. W. *Chronicles concerning Early Babylonian Kings*, I–II. London, 1907.
20. King, L. W. *History of Babylon*. London, 1915.
21. Knudtzon, J. A. *Die el-Amarna Tafeln (Vorderasiatische Bibliothek*, 2). Leipzig, 1915.
22. Kramer, S. N. *The Sumerians: their History, Culture, and Character*. Chicago, 1963.
23. Kupper, J.-R. *Les Nomades en Mésopotamie au temps des rois de Mari*. Paris, 1957.
24. Parrot, A. *Sumer*. London, 1960.
25. Smith, S. *Early History of Assyria*. London, 1928.
26. Soden, W. von *Assyrisches Handwörterbuch*. Wiesbaden, 1959– .
27. Thureau-Dangin, F. 'La chronologie de la Première Dynastie babylonienne.' In *Mém. Ac. Inscr. B.-L.* 43 (1942), 229 ff.
28. Woolley, C. L. *Alalakh: an Account of the Excavations at Tell Atchana*. Oxford, 1955.
29. Yadin, Yigael *The Art of Warfare in Biblical Lands*, I, II. New York–Toronto–London, 1963.

I. EVENTS OF HAMMURABI'S REIGN

1. Baqir, Taha. 'Date-formulae and date-lists from Harmal.' In *Sumer*, 5 (1949), 34 ff.
2. Dossin, G. 'Les archives épistolaires du palais de Mari.' In *Syria*, 19 (1938), 105 ff.
3. Dossin, G. 'Les archives économiques du palais de Mari.' In *Syria*, 20 (1939), 97 ff.
4. Edzard, D. O. 'Eine Inschrift des Kudurmabuk von Larsa aus Nippur.' In *Arch. f. Or.* 20 (1963), 159 ff.
5. Finkelstein, J. J. 'The antediluvian kings; a University of California tablet.' In *J.C.S.* 17 (1963), 39 ff.
6. Frankfort, H., Lloyd, Seton and Jacobsen, T. *The Gimilsin Temple and the Palace of the Rulers at Tell Asmar* (*O.I.P.* 43). Chicago, 1940.
7. Jacobsen, T. *The Sumerian King-list* (*Assyriological Studies*, no. 11). Chicago, 1939.
8. Kraus, F. R. 'Kazallu und andere nordbabylonische Kleinstaaten vor der Zeit des Hammurabi.' In *Arch. f. Or.* 16 (1952–3), 319 ff.
9. Kupper, J.-R. 'Nouvelles lettres de Mari relatives à Hammurabi de Babylone.' In *R.A.* 42 (1948), 35 ff.
10. Læssøe, J. 'The Shemshara Tablets.' In *Arkæol. Kunsthist. Medd. Dan. Vid. Selsk.* 4, no. 3 (1959).
11. Langdon, S. *The Weld-Blundell Collection*, vol. II. (*O.E.C.T.* 2). Oxford, 1923.
12. Lewy, H. 'The synchronism Assyria–Eshnunna–Babylon.' In *W.O.* II (1954–9), 438 ff.
13. Morgan, B. E. 'The destruction of Mari by Hammurabi.' In *M.C.S.* 1 (1951), 35 ff.
14. Morgan, B. E. 'Dated texts and date-formulae of some First Dynasty kings.' In *M.C.S.* 3 (1953), 16 ff.
15. Morgan, B. E. 'Dated texts of the reign of Hammurabi.' In *M.C.S.* 3 (1953), 36 ff.
16. Munn-Rankin, J. M. 'Diplomacy in Western Asia in the early second millennium B.C.' In *Iraq*, 18 (1956), 68 ff.
17. Schorr, M. *Urkunden des altbabylonischen Zivil- und Prozessrechts.* Leipzig, 1913.
18. Smith, S. 'A preliminary account of the tablets from Atchana.' In *A.J.* 19 (1939), 38 ff.
19. Wiseman, D. J. *The Alalakh Tablets.* London, 1953.

II. PERSONAL RULE OF HAMMURABI

1. Alexander, J. B. *Early Babylonian Letters and Economic Texts* (*B.I.N.* VII). New Haven, 1943.
2. Cuq, E. *Études sur le droit babylonien.* Paris, 1929.
3. Driver, G. R. *Letters of the First Babylonian Dynasty* (*O.E.C.T.* III). Oxford, 1924.
4. Driver, G. R. and Miles, J. 'The Laws of Eshnunna.' In *Arch. Orient.* 17 (1949), 174 ff.
5. Eilers, W. *Die Gesetzesstele Chammurabis* (*Alte Or.* 31, 3/4). Leipzig, 1932.
6. Finkelstein, J. J. 'Ammiṣaduqa's Edict and the Babylonian "Law Codes".' In *J.C.S.* 15 (1961), 91 ff.

7. Fish, T. 'Letters of Ḥammurabi to Šamaš-ḫazir.' In *M.C.S.* 1 (1951), 1 ff., 12 f.
8. Goetze, A. *The Laws of Eshnunna* (*Ann. A.S.O.R.* 31). New Haven, 1956.
9. Koschaker, P. 'Neue keilschriftliche Rechtsurkunden aus der el-Amarna Zeit.' In *Abh. Leipzig*, 39 (1928), no. 5.
10. Kraus, F. R. *Ein Edikt des Königs Ammi-ṣaduqa von Babylon.* Leiden, 1958.
11. Kraus, F. R. 'Ein zentrales Problem des altmesopotamischen Rechtes: was ist der Codex Ḥammu-rabi?' In *Genava*, N.S. 8 (1960), 283 ff.
12. Kupper, J.-R. 'Un gouvernement provincial dans le royaume de Mari.' In *R.A.* 41 (1947), 149 ff.
13. Kupper, J.-R. 'Baḫdi-Lim, préfet du palais à Mari.' In *Bulletin de l'Académie Royale de Belgique*, Classe de lettres, 1954, 572 ff.
14. Landsberger, B. 'Die babylonischen Termini für Gesetz und Recht.' In *Symbolae . . . P. Koschaker dedicatae* (Leiden, 1939), 219 ff.
15. Speiser, E. A. 'Cuneiform law and the History of Civilization.' In *Proc. Amer. Philosoph. Soc.* 107 (1963), 536 ff.
16. Steele, F. R. *Nuzi Real Estate Transactions* (*Amer. Orient. Ser.* 25). New Haven, 1943.
17. Steele, F. R. 'The Code of Lipit-Ishtar.' In *A.J.A.* 52 (1948), 425 ff.
18. Thureau-Dangin, F. 'La correspondance de Ḥammurapi avec Šamaš-ḫâṣir.' In *R.A.* 21 (1924), 1 ff.
19. Ungnad, A. *Babylonische Briefe aus der Zeit der Ḥammurapi-Dynastie.* Leipzig, 1914.
20. Wiseman, D. J. 'The Laws of Hammurabi again.' In *J.S.S.* 7 (1962), 161 ff.

III. ECONOMIC CONDITIONS

1. Balkan, K. 'Babilde Feodalizm Araştırmaları' (summary by Güterbock, H. G., 'Untersuchungen zum Feudalsystem in Babylonien'). In *Arch. f. Or.* 15 (1945–51), 130 f.
2. Bilgiç, Emin. 'Asurca vesikalara göre Etilerden önce Anadolu'da maden ekonomisi.' In *Sumeroloji Arştırmaları* (1941), 913 ff.
3. Falkenstein, A. *Zu den Inschriftfunden der Grabung in Uruk-Warka 1960–1961* (*Baghdader Mitteilungen*, 2). Berlin, 1963.
4. Garelli, P. *Les Assyriens en Cappadoce.* Paris, 1963.
5. Gelb, I. J. *Hurrians and Subarians* (*S.A.O.C.* 22). Chicago, 1944.
6. Goetze, A. *Kleinasien.* Ed. 2. München, 1957.
7. Harris, R. 'The organization and administration of the Cloister in ancient Babylonia.' In *J.E.S.H.O.* 6 (1963), 121 ff.
8. Jean, Ch. F. 'Redevance perçue par l'État sur la vente de produits des domaines royaux sous Samsu-iluna.' In *R.A.* 24 (1927), 1 ff.
9. Jean, Ch. F. *Larsa d'après les textes cunéiformes.* Paris, 1931
10. Klíma, J. 'Le droit élamite au IIe millénaire av. n. è.' In *Arch. Orient.* 31 (1963), 287 ff.
11. Kohler, J., Peiser, F. E., Ungnad, A. and Koschaker, P. *Hammurabis Gesetz*, I–VI. Leipzig, 1904–23.
12. Koschaker, P. *Rechtsvergleichende Studien zur Gesetzgebung Hammurapis, Königs von Babylon.* Leipzig, 1917.
13. Koschaker, P. 'Zur staatlichen Wirtschaftsverwaltung in altbabylonischer Zeit.' In *Z.A.* 47 (1942), 135 ff.
14. Kraus, F. R. 'Le rôle des temples depuis la troisième dynastie d'Ur jusqu'à la première dynastie de Babylone.' In *Cah. H.M.* 1 (1954), 518 ff.

15. Kraus, P. 'Altbabylonische Briefe.' In *M.V.A.G.* 35, 2 (1931), 1 Teil, and 36, 1 (1932), 11 Teil.
16. Leemans, W. F. *The Old-Babylonian Merchant.* Leiden, 1950.
17. Leemans, W. F. *Foreign Trade in the Old Babylonian Period.* Leiden, 1960.
18. Limet, H. *Le Travail du Métal au Pays de Sumer.* Paris, 1960.
19. Meissner, B. 'Warenpreise im alten Babylonien.' In *Abh. Berlin,* 1936, no. 1.
20. Mendelsohn, I. *Slavery in the Ancient Near East.* New York, 1949.
21. San Nicolò, M. 'Parerga Babylonica XII.' In *Arch. Orient.* 6 (1934), 179 ff.
22. Smith, S. 'The king's share.' In *J.R.A.S.* 1926, 436 ff.
23. Speiser, E. A. 'On the alleged *namru* "fair(-skinned)".' In *Or.* N.S. 23 (1954), 235 f.

IV. SOCIAL CONDITIONS

1. Böhl, F. M. Th. 'Die Tochter des Königs Nabonid.' In *Symbolae... P. Koschaker dedicatae* (Leiden, 1939), 151 ff.
2. Boyer, G. 'Introduction bibliographique à l'histoire du droit suméro-akkadien.' In *Arch. hist. dr. or.* 2 (1938), 63 ff.
3. Boyer, G. et Szlechter, E. 'Introduction bibliographique à l'histoire du droit suméro-akkadien, 11.' In *Rev. internat. des Droits de l'Antiquité* (Bruxelles), 111, 3 (1956), 41 ff.
4. David, M. *Die Adoption im altbabylonischen Recht.* Leipzig, 1927.
5. Diamond, A. S. 'An eye for an eye.' In *Iraq,* 19 (1957), 151 ff.
6. Dossin, G. 'L'article 142/143 du Code de Hammurabi.' In *R.A.* 42 (1948), 113 ff.
7. Dossin, G. 'Šamši-Addu Ier roi d'Assyrie.' In *Bulletin de l'Acad. Royale de Belgique,* Classe de lettres, 34 (1948), 59 ff.
8. Falkenstein, A. 'Ein sumerischer "Gottesbrief".' In *Z.A.* 44 (1938), 1 ff.
9. Falkenstein, A. *Die neusumerischen Gerichtsurkunden,* 1–111. München, 1956, 1957.
10. Falkenstein, A. 'Ein sumerischer Brief an den Mondgott.' In *Studia Biblica et Orientalia edita a Pontificio Instituto Biblico.* Roma, 1959, vol. 111, Oriens antiquus, 69 ff.
11. Gadd, C. J. 'En-an-e-du.' In *Iraq,* 13 (1951), 27 ff.
12. Gadd, C. J. 'Two sketches from the life at Ur.' In *Iraq,* 25 (1963), 177 ff.
13. Harris, R. 'On the process of secularization under Hammurapi.' In *J.C.S.* 15 (1961), 117 ff.
14. Jean, Ch. F. 'Lettres de Mari, IV, transcrites et traduites.' In *R.A.* 42 (1948), 53 ff.
15. Jean, Ch. F. 'L'armée du royaume de Mari.' In *R.A.* 42 (1948), 135 ff.
16. Klíma, J. 'La position successorale de la fille dans la Babylonie ancienne.' In *Arch. Orient.* 18 (1950), 150 ff.
17. Klíma, J. 'Bibliographisches zum Keilschriftrecht.' In *J.J.P.* (no. 1) vol. 6 (1952), 153 ff., (no. 11) vols. 7–8 (1953–4), 295 ff., (no. 111) vols. 9–10 (1955–6), 431 ff., (no. IV) vols. 11–12 (1957–8), 195 ff.
18. Kraus, F. R. *Nippur und Isin nach altbabylonischen Rechtsurkunden (J.C.S. 3).* New Haven, 1951.
19. Kupper, J.-R. '(w)ašibu.' In *R.A.* 45 (1951), 125 ff.
20. Lacheman, E. R. 'Note on the word *ḫupšu* at Nuzi.' In *Bull. A.S.O.R.* 86 (1942), 36 f.
21. Lacheman, E. R. 'Nuzi personal names.' In *J.N.E.S.* 8 (1949), 48 ff.

22. Landsberger, B. 'Zu den Frauenklassen des Kodex Hammurabi.' In *Z.A.* 30 (1915–16), 67 ff.
23. Landsberger, B. 'Studien zu den Urkunden aus der Zeit des Ninurta-tukul-Aššur.' In *Arch. f. Or.* 10 (1935–6), 140 ff.
24. Landsberger, B. *Die Serie* ana ittišu (*M.S.L.* 1). Rome, 1937.
25. Landsberger, B. 'Remarks on the archive of the soldier Ubarum.' In *J.C.S.* 9 (1955), 121 ff.
26. Lautner, J. G. *Die richterliche Entscheidung und die Streitbeendigung im altbabylonischen Prozessrechte.* Leipzig, 1922.
27. Lautner, J. G. *Altbabylonische Personenmiete und Erntearbeiterverträge.* Leiden, 1936.
28. Leemans, W. F. *Legal and Economic Records from the Kingdom of Larsa.* Leiden, 1954.
29. Legrain, L. *Business Documents of the Third Dynasty of Ur (U.E.T.* III). London and Philadelphia, 1947.
30. Matouš, L. 'Les contrats de partage de Larsa provenant des archives d'Iddin-Amurrum.' In *Arch. Orient.* 17 (1949), 142 ff.
31. Matouš, L. 'Quelques remarques sur les récentes publications de textes cunéiformes économiques et juridiques.' In *Arch. Orient.* 27 (1959), 438 ff.
32. Mendelsohn, I. 'The Canaanite term for "free proletarian".' In *Bull. A.S.O.R.* 83 (1941), 36 ff.
33. Neugebauer, O. *Mathematische Keilschrifttexte,* Erster Teil. Berlin, 1935.
34. Nougayrol, J. 'Textes hépatoscopiques de l'époque ancienne conservées au Musée du Louvre.' In *R.A.* 40 (1945–6), 56 ff.
35. Nougayrol, J. 'Un chef-d'œuvre inédit de la littérature babylonienne.' In *R.A.* 45 (1951), 169 ff.
36. O'Callaghan, R. T. *Aram-Naharaim (An. Or.* 26). Rome, 1948.
37. Praag, A. van. *Droit matrimonial assyro-babylonien.* Amsterdam, 1945.
38. Scheil, V. *Mémoires de la Mission archéologique de Perse,* tome 24. Paris, 1933.
39. Sollberger, E. 'Sur la chronologie des rois d'Ur et quelques problèmes connexes.' In *Arch. f. Or.* 17 (1954–6), 10 ff.
40. Thureau-Dangin, F. 'La ville ennemie de Marduk.' In *R.A.* 29 (1932), 109 ff.
41. Thureau-Dangin, F. *Textes mathématiques babyloniens.* Leiden, 1938.
42. Ungnad, A. 'Besprechungskunst und Astrologie in Babylonien.' In *Arch. f. Or.* 14 (1941–4), 251 ff.
43. Walther, A. *Das altbabylonische Gerichtswesen (L.S.S.* VI, 4–6). Leipzig, 1915.
44. Yadin, Yigael. 'Hyksos fortifications and the battering-ram.' In *Bull. A.S.O.R.* 137 (1955), 23 ff.
45. Zimmern, H. *Akkadische Fremdwörter.* Leipzig, 1917.

V. CULTURAL CONDITIONS

1. Barrelet, M.-T. 'Une peinture de la Cour 106 du Palais de Mari.' In *Studia Mariana* (ed. A. Parrot, Leiden, 1950), 9 ff.
2. Bauer, Theo. 'Eine Sammlung von Himmelsvorzeichen.' In *Z.A.* 43 (1936), 308 ff.
3. Boissier, A. *Mantique babylonienne et mantique hittite.* Paris, 1935.
4. Burke, M. 'Une réception royale au Palais de Mari.' In *R.A.* 53 (1959), 139 ff.
5. Civil, M. 'Prescriptions médicales sumériennes.' In *R.A.* 54 (1960), 57 ff.
6. Civil, M. 'Une nouvelle prescription médicale sumérienne.' In *R.A.* 55 (1961), 91 ff.

7. Dossin, G. 'Le panthéon de Mari.' In *Studia Mariana* (ed. A. Parrot, Leiden, 1950), 41 ff.

8. Falkenstein, A. *Die Haupttypen der sumerischen Beschwörung* (*L.S.S.*, n.F. 1). Leipzig, 1931.

9. Falkenstein, A. 'Der "Sohn des Tafelhauses".' In *We. Or.* 1 (1947–52), 172 ff.

10. Falkenstein, A. 'Ein sumerisches Kultlied auf Samsu'iluna.' In *Arch. Orient.* 17 (1949), 212 ff.

11. Falkner, M. 'Altorientalische Altertümer in den Museen: Kansas City.' In *Arch. f. Or.* 18 (1957–8), 167, with Abb. 3.

12. Fine, H. A. *Studies in Middle Assyrian Chronology and Religion*. Cincinnati, 1955.

13. Finet, A. 'Les médicins au royaume de Mari.' In *Ann. Inst. philol. hist. or.* 14 (1954–7), 123 ff.

14. Finkelstein, J. J. 'Mesopotamian Historiography.' In *Proc. Amer. Philosoph. Soc.* 107 (1963), 461 ff.

15. Frank, K. *Babylonische Beschwörungsreliefs* (*L.S.S.* III, no. 3). Leipzig, 1908.

16. Gadd, C. J. 'Tablets from Chagar Bazar and Tall Brak.' In *Iraq*, 7 (1940), 22 ff.

17. Gadd, C. J. *Teachers and Students in the Oldest Schools*. London, 1956.

18. Gadd, C. J. and Kramer, S. N. *Literary and Religious Texts*, first part (*U.E.T.* VI). London and Philadelphia, 1963.

19. Hallo, W. W. 'Royal hymns and Mesopotamian Unity.' In *J.C.S.* 17 (1963), 112 ff.

20. Köcher, F. and Oppenheim, A. L. 'The Old-Babylonian Omen-text VAT 7525.' In *Arch. f. Or.* 18 (1957–8), 62 ff.

21. Kramer, S. N. 'Sumerian Literature; a general survey.' In Wright, E. G. (ed.), *The Bible and the Ancient Near East; Essays in Honor of William Foxwell Albright*. London, 1961.

22. Kraus, F. R. 'Altmesopotamisches Lebensgefühl.' In *J.N.E.S.* 19 (1960), 117 ff.

23. Kupper, J.-R. *L'Iconographie du dieu Amurru* (Acad. R. Belgique, cl. lettres, *Mémoires*, LV, 1). Bruxelles, 1961.

24. Kupper, J.-R. 'L'opinion publique à Mari.' In *Iraq*, 25 (1963), 190 f.

25. Lambert, M. 'La littérature sumérienne à propos d'ouvrages récents.' In *R.A.* 55 (1961), 177 ff. and *R.A.* 56 (1962), 81 ff. (suite): 'Additions et corrections', *ibid.* 214.

26. Matouš, L. 'Zu den Ausdrücken für "Zugaben" in den vorsargonischen Grundstückkaufurkunden.' In *Arch. Orient.* 22 (1954), 434 ff.

27. Neugebauer, O. *Vorlesungen über Geschichte der antiken mathematischen Wissenschaften*, Erster Teil. Berlin, 1934.

28. Nougayrol, J. 'Note sur la place des "présages historiques" dans l'extispicine babylonienne.' In *École pratique des Hautes Études*: Annuaire 1944–5, 5 ff.

29. Oppenheim, A. L. 'Zur keilschriftlichen Omenliteratur.' In *Or.* N.S. 5 (1936), 199 ff.

30. Oppenheim, A. L. 'The archives of the Palace of Mari. II. A review article.' In *J.N.E.S.* 13 (1954), 141 ff

31. Parrot, A. 'Les fouilles de Mari; troisième campagne (hiver 1935–6).' In *Syria*, 18 (1937), 54 ff.

32. Parrot, A. 'Les fouilles de Mari; quatrième campagne (hiver 1936–7).' In *Syria*, 19 (1938), 1 ff.

33. Parrot, A. *Mission archéologique de Mari. II. Le Palais.* Paris, 1958.
34. Schmokel, H. 'Ḫammurabi und Marduk.' In *R.A.* 53 (1959), 183 ff.
35. Schott, A. 'Die Anfänge Marduks als eines assyrischen Gottes.' In *Z.A.* 43 (1936), 318 ff.
36. Schwenzner, W. 'Das Nationalheiligtum des assyrischen Reiches: die Bauge-schichte des Aššur-Tempels Eḫursagkurkurra.' In *Arch. f. Or.* 8 (1932–3), 113 ff.
37. Sjöberg, Åke. 'Ein Selbstpreis des Königs Ḫammurabi von Babylon.' In *Z.A.* 54 (1961), 51 ff.
38. Streck, M. *Assurbanipal und die letzten assyrischen Könige.* I Teil. Leipzig, 1916.
39. Strommenger, E. *Das Menschenbild in der altmesopotamischen Rundplastik von Mesilim bis Hammurapi (Baghdader Mitteilungen,* 1). Berlin, 1960.
40. Weidner, E. F. 'Studien zur Zeitgeschichte Tukulti-Ninurtas I.' In *Arch. f. Or.* 13 (1939–41), 109 ff.
41. Weidner, E. F. *Die Inschriften Tukulti-Ninurtas I und seiner Nachfolger (Arch. f. Or.* Beiheft 12). Graz, 1959.

VI. THE SUCCESSORS OF HAMMURABI

1. Chiera, E. *Legal and Administrative Documents from Nippur (P.B.S.* VIII, 1). Philadelphia, 1914.
2. Frankfort, H., Jacobsen, T. and Preusser, C. *Tell Asmar and Khafaje: the First Season's Work in Eshnunna (O.I.C.* 13). Chicago, 1932.
3. Goetze, A. 'Thirty tablets from the reigns of Abi-ešuḫ and Ammī-ditānā.' In *J.C.S.* 2 (1948), 73 ff.
4. Goetze, A. 'The year-names of Abī-ešuḫ.' In *J.C.S.* 5 (1951), 98 ff.
5. Goetze, A. 'An Old-Babylonian Itinerary.' In *J.C.S.* 7 (1953), 51 ff.
6. Landsberger, B. 'Assyrische Königsliste und "Dunkles Zeitalter".' In *J.C.S.* 8 (1954), 31 ff., 47 ff., 106 ff.
7. Langdon, S. and Fotheringham, J. K. *The Venus Tablets of Ammizaduga.* London, 1928.
8. Leemans, W. F. Review of G, 12 (Figulla and Martin, *Letters and documents of the Old-Babylonian Period).* In *Bi. Or.* 12 (1955), 112 ff.
9. Leemans, W. F. 'Tablets from Bad-tibira, and Samsuiluna's reconquest of the south.' In *J.E.O.L.* 15 (1957–8), 214 ff.
10. Morgan, Barbara E. 'Dated texts and date-formulae of the reign of Ammi-zaduga.' In *M.C.S.* 2 (1952), 31 ff.
11. Morgan, Barbara E. 'Dated texts and date-formulae of the reign of Ammi-ditana.' In *M.C.S.* 2 (1952), 44 ff.
12. Morgan, Barbara E. 'Dated texts and date-formulae of the reign of Sam-suiluna.' In *M.C.S.* 3 (1953), 56 ff.
13. Morgan, Barbara E. 'Dated tablets of the reign of Abiešuḫ.' In *M.C.S.* 3 (1953), 72 ff.
14. Morgan, Barbara E. 'Dated texts and date-formulae of the reign of Sam-suditana.' In *M.C.S.* 3 (1953), 76 ff.
15. Poebel, A. *Babylonian Legal and Business Documents from the time of the First Dynasty of Babylon (B.E.* vi, part 2). Philadelphia, 1909.
16. Poebel, A. 'Eine sumerische Inschrift Samsuilunas über die Erbauung der Festung Dur-Samsuiluna.' In *Arch. f. Or.* 9 (1933–4), 241 ff.
17. Poebel, A. *Miscellaneous Studies (Assyriological Studies,* 14). Chicago, 1947.

18. Stephens, Ferris J. *Votive and Historical Texts from Babylonia and Assyria* (*Y.O.S.* Babylonian Texts, IX). New Haven, 1937.
19. Thureau-Dangin, F. 'L'inscription bilingue B de Samsu-iluna.' In *R.A.* 39 (1942–4), 5 ff.

VII. BEGINNINGS OF THE KASSITE DYNASTY

1. Balkan, Kemal. *Kassitenstudien.* 1. *Die Sprache der Kassiten.* New Haven, 1954.
2. Clay, A. T. *Babylonian Records in the Library of J. Pierpont Morgan*, part IV. New Haven, 1923.
3. Feigin, S. I. and Landsberger, B. 'The date-list of the Babylonian king Samsuditana.' In *J.N.E.S.* 14 (1955), 137 ff.
4. Finkelstein, J. J. 'The year-dates of Samsuditana.' In *J.C.S.* 13 (1959), 39 ff.
5. Fossing, P. *Glass vessels before glass-blowing.* Copenhagen, 1940.
6. Gadd, C. J. 'Une donnée chronologique.' In *C.-R. Rencontr. assyriol. internat.* 2 (1951), 70 f.
7. Gadd, C. J. and Thompson, R. C. 'A middle-Babylonian chemical text.' In *Iraq*, 3 (1936), 87 ff.
8. Grayson, A. K. and Lambert, W. G. 'Akkadian Prophecies.' In *J.C.S.* 18 (1964), 7 ff.
9. Güterbock, H. G. 'Die historische Tradition und ihre literarische Gestaltung bei Babyloniern und Hethitern bis 1200,' Erster Teil. In *Z.A.* 42 (1934), 1 ff.
10. Harden, D. B. 'Glass and Glazes.' In Singer, C. *et al. A History of Technology*, vol. II. Oxford, 1957.
11. Hayes, W. C. *The Scepter of Egypt*, part II. Cambridge, Mass., 1959.
12. Jaritz, K. 'Quellen zur Geschichte der Kaššû-Dynastie.' In *Mitt. Inst. Or.* 6 (1958), 187 ff.
13. Lucas, A. and Harris, J. R. *Ancient Egyptian Materials and Industries.* 4th ed. London, 1962.
14. Moore, H. 'Reproductions of an ancient Babylonian glaze.' In *Iraq*, 10 (1948), 26 ff.
15. Nougayrol, J. 'Documents du Habur.' In *Syria*, 37 (1960), 205 ff.
16. Smith, S. Chronological note, in *C.-R. Rencontr. assyriol. internat.* 2 (1951), 67 ff.
17. Thompson, R. C. *A Dictionary of Assyrian Chemistry and Geology.* Oxford, 1936.
18. Thureau-Dangin, F. and Dhorme, E. 'Cinq jours de fouilles à 'Ashârah.' In *Syria*, 5 (1924), 265 ff.

CHAPTER VI

G. GENERAL

1. Cavaignac, E. *Le problème hittite.* Paris, 1936.
2. Cavaignac, E. *Les Hittites.* L'ancien orient illustré, no. 3. Paris, 1950.
3. Delaporte, L. *Les Hittites.* L'évolution de l'humanité. Paris, 1936.
4. Garstang, J. and Gurney, O. R. *The Geography of the Hittite Empire.* Occasional Publications of the British Institute of Archaeology at Ankara, no. 5. London, 1959.

5. Goetze, A. *Das Hethiter-Reich.* Alte Or., 27, 2. Leipzig, 1928.
6. Goetze, A. *Kizzuwatna.* Y.O.S., Researches, vol. XXII. New Haven, 1940.
7. Goetze, A. *Kleinasien.* Kulturgeschichte des alten Orients, Abschnitt III, 1. Ed. 2. München, 1957. (Part of I. Müller, *Handbuch der Altertumswissenschaft.*)
8. Gurney, O. R. *The Hittites.* Pelican Books. Ed. 3. London, 1961.
9. Walser, G. (ed.) *Neuere Hethiterforschung. Historia, Einzelschriften.* Heft 7. Wiesbaden, 1964.

I. SOURCES

1. Laroche, E. 'La bibliothèque de Hattusa.' In *Arch. Orient.* 17 (1949), 7 ff.
2. Laroche, E. 'Catalogue des textes hittites.' In *R.H.A.* XIV/58–XVI/62 (1956–8).

II. LANGUAGES AND RACES

1. Forrer, E. 'Die acht Sprachen der Boghazköi-Inschriften.' In *Sitzungsb. Berlin,* 1919, 1029–41.
2. Forrer, E. 'Die Inschriften und Sprachen des Hatti-Reiches.' In *Z.D.M.G.* 76 (1922), 174 ff.
3. Friedrich, J. 'Zur Verwandschaftsverhältnis von Keilhethitisch, Luwisch, Paläisch und Bildhethitisch.' In *Gedenkschrift P. Kretschmer.* Wien, 1956.
4. Goetze, A. 'The Cultures of Early Anatolia.' In *Proc. Amer. Philosoph. Soc.* 97 (1953), 214 ff.
5. Goetze, A. 'The theophorous elements of the Anatolian proper names from Cappadocia.' In *Language,* 29 (1953), 263 ff.
6. Goetze, A. 'Some groups of Anatolian proper names.' In *Language,* 30 (1954), 349 ff.
7. Goetze, A. 'The linguistic continuity of Anatolia as shown by its proper names.' In *J.C.S.* 8 (1954), 74 ff.
8. Goetze, A. 'Suffixes in "Kanishite" proper names.' In *R.H.A.* XVIII/66–7 (1960), 45 ff.
9. Güterbock, H. G. 'Notes on Luwian Studies.' In *Or.* n.s. 25 (1956), 113 ff.
10. Güterbock, H. G. 'Towards a definition of the term "Hittite".' In *Oriens,* 10 (1957), 233 ff.
11. Güterbock, H. G. Review of M. Riemschneider, *Die Welt der Hethiter,* in *O.L.Z.* 51 (1956), 513 ff.
12. Güterbock, H. G. 'Kanes and Nesa: two forms of one Anatolian place-name?' In *Eretz-Israel,* 5 (1958), 46 ff.
13. Landsberger, B. 'Kommt *ḫattum* "Hettiterland" und *ḫattī'um* "Hettiter" in den Kültepe-tafeln vor?' In *Arch. Orient.* 18 (1–2), 329 ff., with corrections, *ibid.* (3), 321 ff.
14. Mellaart, J. 'The end of the Early Bronze Age in Anatolia and the Aegean.' In *A.J.A.* 62 (1958), 9 ff.
15. Palmer, L. R. 'Luwian and Linear A.' In *Transactions of the Philological Society* (London), 1958, 75 ff.
16. Sommer, F. *Hethiter und Hethitisch.* Stuttgart, 1947.
17. Sturtevant, E. H. and Hahn, E. A. *A Comparative Grammar of the Hittite Language.* Ed. 2. New Haven and London, 1951.

III. ORIGIN OF THE KINGDOM OF KHATTUSHA

1. Balkan, K. *Observations on the Chronological Problems of the Karum Kaniš.* Ankara, 1955.
2. Balkan, K. *Letter of King Anum-hirbi of Mama to King Warshama of Kanish.* Ankara, 1957.
3. Goetze, A. 'On the chronology of the second millennium B.C.' In *J.C.S.* 11 (1957), 53 ff.
4. Güterbock, H. G. 'Die historische Tradition und ihre literarische Gestaltung bei Babyloniern und Hethitern.' Zweiter Teil: 'Hethiter.' In *Z.A.* 44 (1938), 45 ff.
5. Mellaart, J. 'Anatolian chronology in the early and middle Bronze Age.' In *A.St.* 7 (1957), 55 ff.
6. Osten, H. H. von der. *The Alishar Hüyük, seasons of 1930–32,* I–III. *O.I.P.* XXVIII–XXX. Chicago, 1937.
7. Otten, H. 'Zu den Anfängen der hethitischen Geschichte.' In *M.D.O.G.* 83 (1951), 33 ff.
8. Özgüç, T. *Ausgrabungen in Kültepe, 1948.* T.T.K. Yayınlarından, series v, no. 10. Ankara, 1950.
9. Özgüç, T. and N. *Ausgrabungen in Kültepe, 1949.* T.T.K. Yayınlarından, series v, no. 12. Ankara, 1953.
10. Özgüç, T. 'The dagger of Anitta.' In *Belleten,* xx/77 (1956), 33 ff.
11. Özgüç, T. *Kültepe-Kanis.* T.T.K. Yayınlarından, series v, no. 19. Ankara 1959.
12. Schmidt, E. F. *The Alishar Hüyük, seasons of 1928 and 1929,* I–II. *O.I.P.* XIX–XX. Chicago, 1932–3.

IV. THE OLD HITTITE KINGDOM

1. Albright, W. F. 'Further observations on the chronology of Alalakh.' In *Bull. A.S.O.R.* 146 (1957), 26 ff.
2. Cornelius, F. 'Zur Chronologie von Alalakh VII.' In *R.H.A.* XVIII/66 (1960), 19 ff.
3. Falkner, M. 'Studien zur Geographie des alten Mesopotamiens.' In *Arch. f. Or.* 18 (1957), 1 ff.
4. Forrer, E. *Die Boghazköi-Texte in Umschrift. W.V.D.O.G.* 41, 42 (1922–6).
5. Goetze, A. 'Die historische Einleitung des Aleppo-Vertrages.' In *M.A.O.G.* 4 (1928–9), 59 ff.
6. Goetze, A. 'Alalaḫ and Hittite Chronology.' In *Bull. A.S.O.R.* 146 (1957), 20 ff.
7. Güterbock, H. C. 'The Hurrian element in the Hittite empire.' In *J.W.H.* 2 (1954), 383 ff.
8. Hardy, R. S. 'The Old Hittite Kingdom.' In *A.J.S.L.* 58 (1941), 177 ff.
9. Landsberger, B. 'Assyrische Königsliste und "Dunkles Zeitalter".' In *J.C.S.* 8 (1954), 31 ff. and 106 ff.
10. Otten, H. 'Die hethitischen "Königslisten" und die altorientalische Chronologie.' In *M.D.O.G.* 83 (1951), 47 ff.
11. Otten, H., *apud* K. Bittel, 'Vorläufiger Bericht über die Ausgrabungen in Boğazköy im Jahre 1957.' In *M.D.O.G.* 91 (1958), 78 ff.
12. Smith, S. *Alalakh and Chronology.* London, 1940.
13. Sommer, F. and Falkenstein, A. *Die hethitisch-akkadische Bilingue des Hattušili I (Labarna II).* Abh. München, n.F. 16. München, 1938.

14. Sturtevant, E. H. and Bechtel, G. *A Hittite Chrestomathy*. Philadelphia, 1935.
15. Wiseman, D. J. *The Alalakh Tablets*. Occasional Publications of the British Institute of Archaeology at Ankara, no. 2. London, 1953.

V. EARLY HITTITE SOCIETY

1. Friedrich, J. *Die hethitischen Gesetze*. Leiden, 1959.
2. Güterbock, H. G. 'Authority and Law in the Hittite Kingdom.' In *J.A.O.S.* Supplement 17 (1954), 16 ff.
3. Macqueen, J. G. 'Hattian Mythology and Hittite Monarchy.' In *A.St.* 9 (1959), 171 ff.
4. Planhol, F. X. de. 'Limites antique et actuelle des cultures arbustives méditerranéennes en Asie Mineure.' In *Bulletin de l'Association de géographes français*, no. 239–40 (1954), 4 ff.
5. Schuler, E. von. 'Die Würdenträgereide des Arnuwanda.' In *Or.* n.s. 25 (1956), 209 ff.

A. ADDENDA

1. Bilgiç, E. 'Die Ortsnamen der "kappadokischen" Urkunden im Rahmen der alten Sprachen Anatoliens.' In *Arch. f. Or.* 15 (1945–51), 1 ff.
2. Bittel, K. *Die Ruinen von Boğazköy*. Berlin and Leipzig, 1937.
3. Bittel, K. 'Vorläufiger Bericht über die Ausgrabungen in Boğazköy im Jahre 1956.' In *M.D.O.G.* 89 (1957), 5 ff.
4. Bossert, H. T. 'Die Göttin Hepat in den hieroglyphen-hethitischen Texten.' In *Belleten*, xv/59 (1951), 315 ff.
5. Bossert, H. T. 'Schreibstoff und Schreibgeraet der Hethiter.' In *Belleten*, xvi/61 (1952), 9 ff.
6. Bossert, H. T. 'GIŠ. ḪUR.' In *Bi. Or.* 9 (1952), 172 ff.
7. Cavaignac, E. 'La place du Palâ et du Tumanna.' In *R.H.A.* iii/22 (1936), 178 ff.
8. Cornelius, F. 'Hethitische Reisewege.' In *R.H.A.* xiii/57 (1955), 49 ff.
9. Cornelius, F. 'Zur hethitischen Geographie: die Nachbarn des Hethiterreiches.' In *R.H.A.* xvi/62 (1958), 1 ff.
10. Cornelius, F. 'Geographie des Hethiterreiches.' In *Or.* n.s. 27 (1958), 225 ff., 373 ff.
11. Cornelius, F. 'Die Annalen des Hattušiliš I.' In *Or.* n.s. 28 (1959), 292 ff.
12. Fischer, F. *Boğazköy-Hattuša*, iv. *Die hethitische Keramik von Boğazköy*. *W.V.D.O.G.* 75. Berlin, 1963.
13. Fischer, F. 'Boğazköy und die Chronologie der altassyrischen Handelsniederlassungen.' In *Istanbuler Mitteilungen*, 15 (1965), 1 ff.
14. Forrer, E. O. 'The Hittites in Palestine.' In *P.E.F.* 68 (1936), 190 ff. and 69 (1937), 100 ff.
15. Gamkrelidze, T. V. 'The Akkado-Hittite syllabary and the problem of the origins of the Hittite script.' In *Arch. Orient.* 29 (1961), 406 ff.
16. Garelli, P. *Les Assyriens en Cappadoce*. Paris, 1963.
17. Garstang, J. 'Hittite military roads in Asia Minor.' In *A.J.A.* 47 (1943), 35 ff.
18. Gelb, I. J. *Hurrians and Subarians*. Chicago, 1944.
19. Goetze, A. 'Bemerkungen zu dem hethitischen Text AO. 9608 des Louvre.' In *R.H.A.* i/1 (1930), 18 ff.
20. Goetze, A. Review of §iii, 6. In *J.A.O.S.* 59 (1939), 510 ff.
21. Goetze, A. 'The roads of northern Cappadocia in Hittite times.' In *R.H.A.* xv/61 (1957), 91 ff.
22. Goetze, A. Review of G, 4. In *J.C.S.* 14 (1960), 43 ff.

23. Goetze, A. Review of *K.Bo.* x. In *J.C.S.* 16 (1962), 24 ff.
24. Güterbock, H. G. 'The north-central area of Hittite Anatolia.' In *J.N.E.S.* 20 (1961), 85 ff.
25. Güterbock, H. G. 'Sargon of Akkad mentioned by Hattušili I of Hatti.' In *J.C.S.* 18 (1964), 1 ff.
26. Güterbock, T. M. *Guide to the Ruins at Boğazkale* (*Boğazköy*). Privately printed, 1966.
27. Haase, R. 'Über Noxalhaftung in der hethitischen Rechtssammlung.' In *Arch. Orient.* 29 (1961), 419 ff.
28. Imparati, F. *I Hurriti*. Florence, 1964.
29. Imparati, F. 'L'autobiografia di Hattušili I.' In *Stud. Cl. e Or.* 13 (1964), 1 ff.
30. Jacobsen, T. 'Primitive Democracy in Ancient Mesopotamia.' In *J.N.E.S.* 2 (1943), 159 ff.
31. Kammenhuber, A. 'Die hethitische Geschichtsschreibung.' In *Saeculum*, 9 (1958), 136 ff.
32. Klengel, H. *Geschichte Syriens*, 1. Berlin, 1965.
33. Klengel, H. 'Die Rolle der Ältesten im Kleinasien der Hethiterzeit.' In *Z.A.* n.F. 23 (1965), 223 ff.
34. Klengel, H. Review of *C.A.H.* II³, ch. VI. In *O.L.Z.* 61 (1966), 458 ff.
35. Korošec, V. 'Einige Beiträge zum hethitischen Sklavenrecht.' In *Festschrift Paul Koschaker* (Weimar, 1939), III, 127 ff.
36. Laroche, E. *Les hiéroglyphes hittites*. Paris, 1960.
37. Laroche, E. Review of G, 9. In *Bi. Or.* 23 (1966), 59 f.
38. Lewy, H. 'Neša.' In *J.C.S.* 17 (1963), 103 f.
39. Lewy, J. 'Hatta, Hattu, Hatti, Hattuša and "Old Assyrian" Hattum.' In *Arch. Orient.* 18 (3), (1950), 366 ff.
40. Lewy, J. 'On some institutions of the Old Assyrian Empire.' In *H.U.C.A.* 27 (1956), 1 ff.
41. Lewy, J. 'Apropos of a recent study in Old Assyrian chronology.' In *Or.* n.s. 26 (1957), 12 ff.
42. Lewy, J. 'Old Assyrian evidence concerning Kuššara and its location.' In *H.U.C.A.* 33 (1962), 45 ff.
43. Orthmann, W. *Boğazköy-Hattuša*, III. *Frühe Keramik von Boğazköy*. *W.V.D.O.G.* 74. Berlin, 1963.
44. Otten, H. 'Die altassyrischen Texte aus Boğazköy.' In *M.D.O.G.* 89 (1957), 68 ff.
45. Otten, H. 'Das Hethiterreich.' In H. Schmökel, *Kulturgeschichte des alten Orients*. Stuttgart, 1961.
46. Otten, H. 'Der Weg des hethitischen Staates zum Grossreich.' In *Saeculum*, 15 (1964), 115 ff.
47. Otten, H. 'Hethiter, Hurriter und Mitanni.' In *Fischer Weltgeschichte*, 3 (1966), 102 ff.
48. Otten, H. 'Die hethitischen historischen Quellen und die altorientalische Chronologie.' In *Akademie der Wissenschaften und der Literatur* (Mainz), *Abh. der Geistes- und Sozialwissenschaftlichen Klasse* (1968), 101 ff.
49. Saporetti, C. 'L'autobiografia di Hattušili, II, versione accadica.' In *Stud. Cl. e Or.* 14 (1965), 77 ff.
50. Schuler, E. von. *Die Kaškäer*. Berlin, 1965.
51. Toynbee, A. *A Study of History*, vol. XI (Historical Atlas and Gazetteer). Oxford, 1959.
52. Wainwright, G. A. 'The Cappadocian Symbol.' In *A.St.* 6 (1956), 137 ff.

CHAPTER VII

G. GENERAL

1. Cameron, G. G. *History of Early Iran*. Chicago, 1936.
2. Dhorme, E. 'Elam.' In *Supplément au Dictionnaire de la Bible*, II, cols. 920 ff. Paris, 1934.
3. D'yakonov, M. M. *Očerk istorii drevnego Irana* [Outline of the history of ancient Iran]. Moscow, 1961.
4. Edzard, D. O. *Die 'Zweite Zwischenzeit' Babyloniens*. Wiesbaden, 1957.
5. Ghirshman, R. *L'Iran des origines à l'Islam*. Paris, 1951.
6. Huart, C. and Delaporte, L. *L'Iran antique—Élam et Perse et la civilisation iranienne*. Paris, 1943.
7. König, F. W. *Geschichte Elams*. Leipzig, 1931.
8. König, F. W. 'Elam (Geschichte).' In *R.L.A.* II, 324 ff. Berlin/Leipzig, 1938.
9. Lambert, M. 'Littérature élamite.' In *L'Histoire générale des littératures*, 36 ff. Paris, 1961.
10. Mayer, R. 'Die Bedeutung Elams in der Geschichte des alten Orients.' In *Saeculum*, 7 (1956), 198 ff.
11. *Mém. D.P.* = *Mémoires de la Délégation en Perse*, vols. I–XIII, Paris, 1900–1912; *Mémoires de la Mission archéologique de Susiane*, vol. XIV, Paris, 1913; *Mémoires de la Mission archéologique de Perse*, vols. XV–XXVIII, Paris, 1914–1939; *Mémoires de la Mission archéologique en Iran*, vols. XXIX–XXXIII, Paris, 1943–53.
12. Soden, W. von 'Sumer, Babylon und Hethiter bis zur Mitte des zweiten Jahrtausends v. Chr.' In *Propyläen-Weltgeschichte*, 525–609. Berlin, 1961.

I. THE DYNASTY OF THE 'GRAND REGENT' RULERS IN ELAM

1. *Archives royales de Mari (A.R.M.T.)*. Vol. II: *Lettres diverses, transcrites et traduites par Charles-F. Jean*, Paris, 1950; vol. VI: *Correspondance de Baḫdi-Lim préfet du palais de Mari, transcrite et traduite par J.-R. Kupper*, Paris, 1954.
2. Dossin, G. 'Les archives économiques du palais de Mari.' In *Syria*, 20 (1939), 97 ff.
3. Hallo, W. W. *Early Mesopotamian Royal Titles: A Philologic and Historical Analysis*. New Haven, 1957.
4. Hinz, W. 'Die elamischen Inschriften des Hanne.' In *Volume in Honour of S. H. Taqizadeh*, 105 ff. London, 1962.
5. Hinz, W. 'Elamica.' In *Or*. n.s. 32 (1963), 1 ff.
6. Hüsing, G. *Die einheimischen Quellen zur Geschichte Elams*. I. Teil: *Altelamische Texte*. Leipzig, 1916.
7. Jaritz, K. 'Quellen zur Geschichte der Kaššū-Dynastie.' In *Mitt. Inst. Or*. 6 (1958), 187 ff.
8. König, F. W. *Corpus Inscriptionum Elamicarum*. 1. *Die altelamischen Texte. Tafeln*. Hannover, [1923].
9. König, F. W. 'Mutterrecht und Thronfolge im alten Elam.' In *Festschrift der Nationalbibliothek in Wien*, 529 ff. Wien, 1926.
10. Koschaker, P. 'Göttliches und weltliches Recht nach den Urkunden aus Susa. Zugleich ein Beitrag zu ihrer Chronologie.' In *Or*. n.s. 4 (1935), 38 ff.
11. Laessøe, J. *The Shemshāra Tablets—A Preliminary Report*. Copenhagen, 1959.

12. Munn-Rankin, J. M. 'Diplomacy in Western Asia in the Early Second Millennium B.C.' In *Iraq*, 18 (1956), 68 ff.
13. Rutten, M. 'Archéologie susienne. Deux fragments de tablette provenant de Suse au nom de Şiwepalarhuhpak.' In *Mém. D.P.* 31, 151 ff.
14. Scheil, V. 'Passim.' In *R.A.* 22 (1925), 141 ff.
15. Scheil, V. 'Raptim.' In *R.A.* 23 (1926), 35 ff.
16. Scheil, V. 'La division du pouvoir à Suse.' In *R.A.* 25 (1928), 31 ff.
17. Scheil, V. 'Documents et arguments.' In *R.A.* 26 (1929), 1 ff.
18. Scheil, V. 'Kutir Naḫḫunte I.' In *R.A.* 29 (1932), 67 ff.
19. Scheil, V. 'Siruktuḫ–Sirtuḫ.' In *R.A.* 33 (1936), 152.
20. Streck, M. *Assurbanipal und die letzten assyrischen Könige bis zum Untergange Niniveh's.* (*Vorderasiatische Bibliothek* 7, II.) Leipzig, 1916.
21. *Studia Mariana*, publiées sous la direction de André Parrot. Leiden, 1950.
22. Ungnad, A. 'Zur Geschichte der Nachbarstaaten Babyloniens zur Zeit der Hammurapi-Dynastie. 1. Elam. In *B.A.* VI, Heft 5 (1909), 1 ff.
23. Weidner, E. F. 'Historisches Material in der babylonischen Omina-Literatur.' In *M.A.O.G.* 4 (1928/9), 226 ff.

II. LEGAL LIFE IN OLD ELAM

1. Cuq, E. 'Les actes juridiques susiens.' In *R.A.* 28 (1931), 43 ff.
2. Cuq, E. 'Le droit élamite d'après les actes juridiques de Suse.' In *R.A.* 29 (1932), 149 ff.
3. Dossin, G. 'Un cas d'ordalie par le Dieu Fleuve d'après une lettre de Mari.' In *Festschrift P. Koschaker*, 112 ff. Leiden, 1939.
4. Klíma, J. 'Zur Entziehung des Erbrechtes nach den akkadischen Urkunden aus Susa.' In *Festschrift J. Rypka*, 128 ff. Prag, 1956.
5. Klíma, J. 'Donationes mortis causa nach den akkadischen Rechtsurkunden aus Susa.' In *Festschrift J. Friedrich*, 229 ff. Heidelberg, 1959.
6. Klíma, J. 'Untersuchungen zum elamischen Erbrecht. (Auf Grund der akkadischen Urkunden aus Susa.)' In *Arch. Orient.* 28 (1960), 5 ff.
7. Koschaker, P. Review of V. Scheil, 'Actes juridiques susiens' [*Mém. D.P.* 22, 1930]. In *O.L.Z.* 35 (1932), cols. 318 ff.
8. Koschaker, P. 'Fratriarchat, Hausgemeinschaft und Mutterrecht in Keilschrift-texten.' In *Z.A.* 31 (1933), 1 ff.
9. Koschaker, P. 'Randnotizen zu neueren keilschriftlichen Rechtsurkunden.' In *Z.A.* 33 (1936), 196 ff.
10. Leemans, W. F. '*Kidinnu*. Un symbole de droit divin babylonien.' In *Festschrift J. Ch. van Oven*, 36 ff. Leiden, 1946.
11. Meyer, L. de. 'Une famille susienne du temps des *sukkalmaḫḫu*.' In *Iranica Antiqua*, 1 (1961), 8 ff.
12. Oppenheim, L. 'Studien zu den altbabylonischen Stadtrechten.' In *Or.* n.s. 4 (1935), 145 ff.
13. Oppenheim, L. 'Der Eid in den Rechtsurkunden aus Susa.' In *W.Z.K.M.* 43 (1936), 241 ff.
14. San Nicolò, M. *Beiträge zur Rechtsgeschichte im Bereiche der keilschriftlichen Rechtsquellen.* Oslo, 1931.
15. San Nicolò, M. 'Eid' in *R.L.A.* II, 305 ff. Berlin/Leipzig, 1938.
16. Scheil, V. 'Fraternité et solidarité à Suse, au temps de Sirukduḫ.' In *Festschrift P. Koschaker*, 106 ff. Leiden, 1939.

17. Szlechter, R. 'Le colonat partiaire à Suse et le code de Hammurapi.' In *R.A.* 55 (1961), 113 ff.

18. Yusifov, Yu. B. 'Ělamskie dolgovie dokumenti iz Suz' [Elamite debt documents from Susa]. In *Vestnik Drevney Istorii*, 2 (1959), 45 ff.

19. Yusifov, Yu. B. 'Kuplya-prodaža nedvižimogo imuščestva i častnoe zemle-vladenie v Ělame (II tysyačeletie do n.ě.)' [Purchase and sale of estates and private land-ownership in Elam (2nd millennium B.C.)]. In *Klio*, 38 (1960), 5 ff.

20. Yusifov, Yu. B. 'On Private Landownership in Elam in the Second Millennium B.C.' (*XXV International Congress of Orientalists, Papers presented by the U.S.S.R. Delegation.*) Moscow, 1960. Pp. 1 ff.

A. ADDENDA

1. König, F. W. 'Geschwisterehe in Elam.' In *R.L.A.* III, 224 ff. Berlin, 1964.

2. König, F. W. *Die elamischen Königsinschriften.* (*Arch. f. Or.*, Beiheft 16.) Graz, 1965.

3. Lambert, M. 'Cylindres de Suse des premiers temps des *Sukal-mah.*' In *Iranica Antiqua*, 6 (1966), 34 ff.

4. Yusifov, Yu. B. 'Khramovoe khozyaystvo v Ělame' [Church economy in Elam]. In *Klio*, 46 (1965), 5 ff.

5. Yusifov, Yu. B. 'Dogovor o *bratstve* v Ělame' [A treaty about *brothership* in Elam]. In *Vestnik Drevney Istorii*, 1966 (4), 3 ff.

6. Yusifov, Yu. B. *Ělam—Social'no-ěkonomičeskaya Istoriya* [Social and Economic History of Elam]. Moscow, 1968.

CHAPTER VIII

G. GENERAL

1. Breasted, J. H. *A History of Egypt from the Earliest Times to the Persian Conquest.* Ed. 2. London, 1927.

2. Drioton, E. and Vandier, J. *L'Égypte* ('*Clio*': *Introduction aux études historiques. Les peuples de l'orient méditerranéen*, II). Ed. 4. Paris, 1962.

3. Gardiner, Sir A. *Egypt of the Pharaohs.* Oxford, 1961.

4. Kees, H. *Ancient Egypt. A Cultural Topography.* London, 1961.

5. Lucas, A. *Ancient Egyptian Materials and Industries.* Ed. 4 (revised and enlarged by J. R. Harris). London, 1962.

6. Porter, B. and Moss, R. L. B. *Topographical Bibliography of Ancient Egyptian Hieroglyphic Texts, Reliefs and Paintings.* 7 vols. (vol. 1 rev. in 2 pts.). Oxford, 1927–64.

7. Sethe, K. *Urkunden der 18. Dynastie* (*Urk.* IV). Leipzig, 1906–9.

8. Vandier, J. *Manuel d'archéologie égyptienne.* 5 vols. Paris, 1952–69.

I. THE CAMPAIGNS OF KAMOSE

1. Chevrier, H. 'Rapport sur les travaux de Karnak (1934–1935).' In *Ann. Serv.* 35 (1935), 97–121.

2. Gardiner, A. H. 'Davies's Copy of the great Speos Artemidos Inscription.' In *J.E.A.* 32 (1946), 43–56.

3. Gardiner, A. H. 'The Defeat of the Hyksos by Kamōse: The Carnarvon Tablet, No. 1.' In *J.E.A.* 3 (1916), 95–110.

4. Gunn, B. and Gardiner, A. H. 'New Renderings of Egyptian Texts. II. The Expulsion of the Hyksos.' In *J.E.A.* 5 (1918), 36–56.

5. Habachi, L. 'Preliminary Report on Kamose Stela and Other Inscribed Blocks found... at Karnak.' In *Ann. Serv.* 53 (1955), 195–202.

6. Hammad, M. 'Découverte d'une stèle du roi Kamose.' In *Chron. d'Ég.* 30 (1955), 198–208.

7. Helck, W. *Die Beziehungen Ägyptens zu Vorderasien im 3. und 2. Jahrtausend v. Chr. (Ägyptol. Abh.* 5). Wiesbaden, 1962.

8. Lacau, P. 'Une Stele du roi "Kamosis" .' In *Ann. Serv.* 39 (1939), 245–71.

9. Montet, P. 'La stèle du roi Kamose.' In *C.-R. Ac. Inscr. B.-L.*, 1956, 112–20.

10. Peet, T. E. *The Great Tomb Robberies of the Twentieth Egyptian Dynasty.* 2 vols. Oxford, 1930.

11. Säve-Söderbergh, T. 'The Hyksos Rule in Egypt.' In *J.E.A.* 37 (1951), 53–71.

12. Säve-Söderbergh, T. *On Egyptian Representations of Hippopotamus Hunting as a Religious Motive (Horae Soederblomianae,* 3). Uppsala, 1953.

13. Winlock, H. E. *The Rise and Fall of the Middle Kingdom in Thebes.* New York, 1947.

14. Winlock, H. E. 'The Tombs of the Kings of the Seventeenth Dynasty.' In *J.E.A.* 10 (1924), 217–77.

II. THE EXPULSION OF THE HYKSOS BY AMOSIS

1. Breasted, J. H. *Ancient Records of Egypt: Historical Documents,* II. Chicago, 1906.

2. Epstein, C. 'A new appraisal of some lines from a long-known papyrus.' In *J.E.A.* 49 (1963), 49–56.

3. Gardiner, A. H. *Ancient Egyptian Onomastica.* 3 vols. Oxford, 1947.

4. Meyer, E. *Geschichte des Altertums,* II, 1. *Die Zeit der ägyptischen Grossmacht.* Ed. 2. Stuttgart and Berlin, 1928.

5. Sethe, K. *Urkunden der 18. Dynastie,* I (Translation). Leipzig, 1914.

6. Waddell, W. G. *Manetho* (The Loeb Classical Library). London and Cambridge (Mass.), 1940.

III. THE PRINCE OF KUSH AND THE REOCCUPATION OF NUBIA

1. Barns, J. W. B. 'Four Khartoum Stelae.' In *Kush,* 2 (1954), 19–25.

2. Emery, W. B. 'A Preliminary Report on the Excavations of the Egypt Exploration Society at Buhen 1957–8.' In *Kush,* 7 (1959), 7–14.

3. Emery, W. B. 'A Preliminary Report on the Excavations of the Egypt Exploration Society at Buhen 1958–59.' In *Kush,* 8 (1960), 7–10.

4. Gauthier, H. 'Les "fils royaux de Kouch" et le personnel administratif de l'Éthiopie.' In *Rec. trav.* 39 (1921), 179–238.

5. Griffith, F. Ll. 'Oxford Excavations in Nubia.' In *Ann. Arch. Anthr.* 8 (1921), 1–18, 65–104.

6. Gunn, B. 'A Middle Kingdom stela from Edfu.' In *Ann. Serv.* 29 (1929), 5–14.

7. Habachi, L. 'The first two Viceroys of Kush and their Family.' In *Kush,* 7 (1959), 45–62.

8. Posener, G. 'Pour une localisation du pays Koush au Moyen Empire.' In *Kush*, 6 (1958), 39–65.
9. Randall-MacIver, D. and Woolley, C. L. *Buhen* (University of Pennsylvania, Eckley B. Coxe Junior Expedition to Nubia, vols. 7 and 8). 2 vols. Philadelphia, 1911.
10. Reisner, G. A. 'The Viceroys of Nubia.' In *J.E.A.* 6 (1920), 28–55, 73–88.
11. Säve-Söderbergh, T. *Aegypten und Nubien. Ein Beitrag zur Geschichte altägyptischer Aussenpolitik.* Lund, 1941.
12. Säve-Söderbergh, T. 'A Buhen stela from the Second Intermediate Period (Khartūm no. 18).' In *J.E.A.* 35 (1949), 50–8.
13. Säve-Söderbergh, T. 'The Nubian Kingdom of the Second Intermediate Period.' In *Kush*, 4 (1956), 54–61.
14. Säve-Söderbergh, T. 'The Paintings in the Tomb of Djehuty-hetep at Debeira.' In *Kush*, 8 (1960), 25–44.
15. Säve-Söderbergh, T. 'Preliminary Report of the Scandinavian Joint Expedition.' In *Kush*, 10 (1962), 76–105.
16. Säve-Söderbergh, T. 'Preliminary Report of the Scandinavian Joint Expedition.' In *Kush*, 11 (1963), 47–69.
17. Vercoutter, J. 'New Egyptian texts from the Sudan.' In *Kush*, 4 (1956), 66–82.
18. Weigall, A. E. P. *A Report on the Antiquities of Lower Nubia (The First Cataract to the Sudan Frontier) and their Condition in 1906–7.* Oxford, 1907.

IV. REUNION AND REORGANIZATION UNDER AMOSIS I

1. Aldred, C. *New Kingdom Art in Ancient Egypt.* Ed. 2. London, 1961.
2. Ayrton, E. R., Currelly, C. T. and Weigall, A. E. P. *Abydos.* Part III. London (E.E.S.), 1904.
3. Chevrier, H. 'Rapport sur les travaux de Karnak (1935–1936).' In *Ann. Serv.* 36 (1936), 131–57.
4. Deines, H. von. '"Das Gold der Tapferkeit", eine militarisches Auszeichnung oder eine Belohnung?' In *Z.Ä.S.* 79 (1954), 83–6.
5. Gardiner, A. H. *The Inscription of Mes. A Contribution to the Study of Egyptian Judicial Procedure (Unters. 4, 3).* Leipzig, 1905.
6. Gardiner, A. H., Peet, T. E. and Černý, J. *The Inscriptions of Sinai.* 2 parts. London (E.E.S.), 1952, 1955.
7. Mond, Sir R. and Myers, O. H. *The Bucheum.* 3 vols. London (E.E.S.), 1934.
8. Mond, Sir R. and Myers, O. H. *The Temples of Armant.* 2 vols. London (E.E.S.), 1940.
9. Randall-MacIver, D. and Mace, A. C. *El Amrah and Abydos.* London (E.E.S.), 1902.
10. Smith, W. S. *The Art and Architecture of Ancient Egypt (The Pelican History of Art).* Harmondsworth, 1958.
11. Vernier, E. *Bijoux et orfèvreries (C.C.G. nos. 52001–53855).* 2 vols. Cairo, 1927.

V. THREE ROYAL LADIES

1. Bissing, F. W. von. *Ein thebanischer Grabfund aus dem Anfang des neuen Reichs.* Berlin, 1900.
2. Černý, J. *Ancient Egyptian Religion* (Hutchinson's University Library). London, 1952.

3. Drioton, É. 'Un document sur la vie chère à Thèbes au début de la XVIIIe dynastie.' In *Bull. soc. fr. égyptol.* 12 (1953), 10–19.
4. Erman, A. 'Teti der Kleine.' In *Z.Ä.S.* 38 (1900), 150.
5. Gauthier, H. *Le livre des rois d'Égypte*, II (*Mém. Inst. fr. Caire*, 18). Cairo, 1912.
6. Kees, H. 'Das Gottesweib Ahmes-Nofretere als Amonspriester.' In *Or.* 23 (1954), 57–63.
7. Lacau, P. *Stèles du Nouvel Empire* (*C.C.G.* nos. 34001–34189). Cairo, 1909–57.
8. Murray, M. A. 'Queen Tety-shery.' In *Anc. Egypt*, 1934, 6, 65–9.
9. Sander-Hansen, C. E. *Das Gottesweib des Amun* (*Det Kongelige Danske Videnskabernes Selskab*, Historisk-filologiske Skrifter, Bind 1, nr. 1). Copenhagen, 1940.
10. Winlock, H. E. 'On Queen Tetisheri, Grandmother of Ahmose I.' In *Anc. Egypt*, 1921, 14–16.

VI. CONSOLIDATION UNDER AMENOPHIS I

1. Barguet, P. *Le Temple d'Amon-Re à Karnak* (*Publ. Inst. fr. Caire. Recherches d'arch., phil., hist.*, 21). Cairo, 1962.
2. Bates, O. *The Eastern Libyans*. London, 1914.
3. Borchardt, L. *Die altägyptische Zeitmessung*. (E. von Bassermann-Jordan, *Die Geschichte der Zeitmessung und der Uhren*, vol. 1.) Berlin and Leipzig, 1920.
4. Brunner, H. 'Mitanni in einem ägyptischen Text vor oder um 1500.' In *Mitt. Inst. Or.* 4 (1956), 323–7.
5. Carter, H. 'Report on the Tomb of Zeser-ka-ra Amenhetep I, discovered by the Earl of Carnarvon in 1914.' In *J.E.A.* 3 (1916), 147–54.
6. Černý, J. 'Le culte d'Amenophis Ier chez les ouvriers de la Nécropole thébaine.' In *Bull. Inst. fr. Caire*, 27 (1927), 159–203.
7. Clarke, S. 'El-Kâb and its Temples.' In *J.E.A.* 8 (1922), 16–40.
8. Fischer, H. G. 'A God and a General of the Oasis on a stela of the Late Middle Kingdom.' In *J.N.E.S.* 16 (1957), 223–35.
9. Gauthier, H. *Dictionnaire des noms géographiques contenus dans les textes hiéroglyphiques*. 7 vols. Cairo, 1922–31.
10. Habachi, L. 'Four Objects belonging to Viceroys of Kush and Officials associated with them.' In *Kush*, 9 (1961), 210–225.
11. Hayes, W. C. *The Scepter of Egypt*. 2 vols. New York, 1953, 1959.
12. Hölscher, W. *Libyer und Ägypter*. (*Ägyptol. Forsch.* 4.) Glückstadt–Hamburg–New York, 1937.
13. Lange, K. and Hirmer, M. *Egypt. Architecture, Sculpture, Painting in Three Thousand Years*. 4th ed. London, 1968.
14. Petrie, W. M. F. *Abydos*. Part I. London (E.E.S.), 1902.
15. Werbrouck, M. 'Quelques monuments d'Amenophis Ier à El-Kab.' In Capart, J., *Fouilles de El-Kab. Documents*, III (Brussels, 1954), 99–102.
16. Winlock, H. E. *Excavations at Deir el Bahri 1911–1931*. New York, 1942.
17. Winlock, H. E. 'A Restoration of the reliefs from the Mortuary Temple of Amenhotep I.' In *J.E.A.* 4 (1917), 11–15.
18. Yoyotte, J. 'Egypte ancienne.' In *Histoire Universelle*. I. *Des origines à l'Islam* (*Encyclopédie de la Pléiade*). Paris, 1956.

A. ADDENDA

1. Redford, D. B. *History and Chronology of the Eighteenth Dynasty of Egypt.* Toronto, 1967.
2. Van Seters, J. *The Hyksos.* New Haven and London, 1966.
3. Stadelmann, R. 'Ein Beitrag zum Brief des Hyksos Apophis.' In *Mitt. deutsch. Inst. Kairo*, 20 (1965), 62–9.
4. Vandersleyen, C. 'Deux nouveaux fragments de la stelè d'Amosis relatant une tempête.' In *Rev. d'égyptol.* 20 (1968), 127–34.
5. Vandersleyen, C. 'Une tempête sons le règne d'Amosis.' In *Rev. d'égyptol.* 19 (1967), 123–59.

CHAPTER IX

I. THE RULE OF THE MILITARY KING

1. Breasted, J. H. *Ancient Records of Egypt: Historical Documents (Ancient Records,* 2nd series), 2: *The Eighteenth Dynasty.* Chicago, 1906.
2. Breasted, J. H. *A History of Egypt from the Earliest Times to the Persian Conquest.* Ed. 2. London, 1927.
3. Drioton, É. and Vandier, J. *L'Égypte* ('*Clio.' Les peuples de l'Orient méditerranéen*, 2). Ed. 3. Paris, 1952.
4. Edgerton, W. F. 'The Government and the Governed in the Egyptian Empire.' In *J.N.E.S.* 6 (1947), 152–60.
5. Gardiner, A. H. 'Davies's Copy of the Great Speos Artemidos Inscription.' In *J.E.A.* 32 (1946), 43–56.
6. Habachi, L. 'Two Graffiti at Sehēl from the Reign of Queen Hatshepsut.' In *J.N.E.S.* 16 (1957), 88–104.
7. Helck, H.-W. *Der Einfluss der Militärführer in der 18. ägyptischen Dynastie* (*Unters.* 14). Leipzig, 1939.
8. Helck, H.-W. *Zur Verwaltung des mittleren und neuen Reichs* (*Probleme der Ägyptologie*, edited by H. Kees, III). Leiden-Cologne, 1958.
9. Meyer, E. *Geschichte des Altertums.* II, 1: *Die Zeit der ägyptischen Grossmacht.* Ed. 2. Stuttgart and Berlin, 1928.
10. Säve-Söderbergh, T. *The Navy of the Eighteenth Egyptian Dynasty* (*Uppsala Universitets Arsskrift* 1946, 6). Uppsala, 1946.
11. Yoyotte, J. 'Égypte ancienne'. In *Histoire universelle*, I: *Des origines à l'Islam* (*Encyclopédie de la Pléiade*). Paris, 1956.

II. THE TUTHMOSIDE SUCCESSION

1. Aldred, C. 'The End of the El-'Amārna Period.' In *J.E.A.* 43 (1957), 30–41.
2. Aldred, C. 'Year Twelve at El-'Amārna.' In *J.E.A.* 43 (1957), 114–17.
3. Aldred, C. 'Two Theban Notables during the Later Reign of Amenophis III.' In *J.N.E.S.* 18 (1959), 113–20.
4. Barguet, P. 'L'obélisque de Saint-Jean-de-Latran dans le temple de Ramsès II á Karnak.' In *Ann. Serv.* 50 (1950), 269–80.
5. Barguet, P. 'L'emplacement, dans Karnak, de l'obélisque de Saint-Jean de Latran.' In *Rev. arch.* 6e série, 37 (1951), 1–4.
6. Campbell, E. F. 'The Amarna Letters and the Amarna Period.' In *Bi. Ar.* 23 (1960), 2–22.

7. Chevrier, H. 'Rapport[s] sur les travaux de Karnak, 1926–1939, 1947–1954.' In *Ann. Serv.* 26–39 (1926–39) and 46–53 (1947–55), *passim*.

8. Daressy, G. 'La chapelle d'Uazmès.' In *Ann. Serv.* 1 (1900), 97–108.

9. Davies, Nina de G. and Norman de G. *The Tombs of Menkheperresonb, Amenmosĕ, and Another (Nos. 86, 112, 42, 226)* (*E.E.S.*, The Theban Tombs Series, 5th memoir). London, 1933.

10. Doresse, M. and J. 'Le culte d'Aton sous la XVIIIe dynastie avant le schisme amarnien.' In *J. as.* 233 (1941–2), 181–99.

11. Edel, E. 'Die Stelen Amenophis' II. aus Karnak und Memphis mit dem Bericht über die asiatischen Feldzüge des Königs.' In *Z.D.P.V.* 69 (1953), 97–176.

12. Edgerton, W. F. *The Thutmosid Succession* (*S.A.O.C.* 8). Chicago, 1933.

13. Engelbach, R. 'Material for a Revision of the History of the Heresy Period of the XVIIIth Dynasty.' In *Ann. Serv.* 40 (1940), 133–65.

14. Fakhry, A. 'A Note on the Tomb of Kheruef at Thebes.' In *Ann. Serv.* 42 (1943), 447–508.

15. Gardiner, A. H. 'Regnal Years and Civil Calendar in Pharaonic Egypt.' In *J.E.A.* 31 (1945), 11–28.

16. Gardiner, A. H. 'The So-called Tomb of Queen Tiye.' In *J.E.A.* 43 (1957), 10–25.

17. Gauthier, H. *Le Livre des rois d'Égypte*, II (*Mém. Inst. fr. Caire*, 18). Cairo, 1912.

18. Hassan, S. 'A Representation of the Solar Disk with Human Hands and Arms....' In *Ann. Serv.* 38 (1938), 53–61.

19. Hayes, W. C. *Royal Sarcophagi of the XVIII Dynasty* (*Princeton Monographs in Art and Archaeology: Quarto Series*, 19). Princeton, 1935.

20. Hayes, W. C. 'Inscriptions from the Palace of Amenhotep III.' In *J.N.E.S.* 10 (1951), 35–56, 82–111, 156–83, 231–42.

21. Hayes, W. C. *The Scepter of Egypt*. 2 parts. New York, 1953, 1959.

22. Hayes, W. C. 'Varia from the Time of Hatshepsut.' In *Mitt. deutsch. Inst. Kairo*, 15 (1957), 78–90.

23. Helck, H. W. 'Die Sinai-Inschrift des Amenmose.' In *Mitt. Inst. Or.* 2 (1954), 189–207.

24. Helck, H. W. 'Die Berufung des Vezirs Wśr.' In *Ägyptol. Studien Hermann Grapow zum 70. Geburtstag gewidmet* (Berlin, 1955), 107–17.

25. Helck, H. W. 'Eine Stele des Vizekönigs Wśr-St.t.' In *J.N.E.S.* 14 (1955), 22–31.

26. Helck, H. W. *Untersuchungen zu Manetho und den ägyptischen Konigslisten* (*Unters.* 18). Berlin, 1956.

27. Knudtzon, J. A. *Die el-Amarna-Tafeln* (*Vorderasiatische Bibliothek*). 2 vols. Leipzig, 1908, 1915.

28. Meyer, E. *Aegyptische Chronologie* (*Abh. Berlin*, 1904). Berlin, 1904.

29. Parker, R. A. 'The Lunar Dates of Thutmose III and Ramesses II.' In *J.N.E.S.* 16 (1957), 39–43.

30. Pendlebury, J. D. S. *Tell el-Amarna*. London, 1935.

31. Pendlebury, J. D. S. 'Summary Report on the Excavations at Tell el-'Amarnah. 1935–1936.' In *J.E.A.* 22 (1936), 194–8.

32. Pendlebury, J. D. S. *The City of Akhenaten*. Part III (*E.E.S.*, 44th Memoir). 2 vols. London, 1951.

33. Petrie, W. M. F. *Six Temples at Thebes*. London, 1897.

34. Porter, B. and Moss, R. L. B. *Topographical Bibliography of Ancient Egyptian Hieroglyphic Texts, Reliefs, and Paintings*. 7 vols. Oxford, 1927–51.

35. Porter, B. and Moss, R. L. B. *Ibid.* Ed. 2 of volume I. *The Theban Necropolis.* Part I. Private Tombs. Oxford, 1960.

36. Roeder, G. 'Thronfolger und König Smench-ka-Rê.' In *Z.Ä.S.* 83 (1958), 43–74.

37. Sauneron, S. 'La tradition officielle relative à la XVIIIe dynastie d'après un ostracon de la Vallée des Rois.' In *Chron. d'Ég.* 26 (1951), 46–9.

38. Säve-Söderbergh, T. *Ägypten und Nubien. Ein Beitrag zur Geschichte altägyptischer Aussenpolitik.* Lund, 1941.

39. Schott, S. 'Zum Krönungstag der Königin Hatschepsut.' In *Nachr. Göttingen,* 1955, Nr. 6, 195–219.

40. Sethe, K. *Die Thronwirren unter den Nachfolgern Königs Thutmosis' I., ihr Verlauf und ihre Bedeutung (Unters.* I, 1). Leipzig, 1896.

41. Sethe, K. *Das Hatschepsut-Problem noch einmal untersucht (Abh. Berlin,* 1932, Nr. 4). Berlin, 1932.

42. Sethe K. and Helck, W. *Urkunden der 18. Dynastie (Urk.* IV). 22 Hefte. Leipzig and Berlin, 1906–58.

43. Simpson, W. K. 'Reshep in Egypt.' In *Or.* 29 (1960), 63–74.

44. Smith, G. E. *The Royal Mummies (C.C.G.* nos. 61051–100). Cairo, 1912.

45. Smith, W. S. *The Art and Architecture of Ancient Egypt (Pelican History of Art).* Harmondsworth, 1958.

46. Steindorff, G. and Seele, K. C. *When Egypt Ruled the East.* Ed. 2. Chicago, 1957.

47. Varille, A. 'Toutankhamon, est-il fils d'Aménophis III et de Satamon?' In *Ann. Serv.* 40 (1941), 651–7.

48. Waddell, W. G. *Manetho, with an English Translation (The Loeb Classical Library).* London and Cambridge (Mass.), 1940.

49. Wilson, J. A. *Egyptian Texts.* In *A.N.E.T.* Princeton, 1950.

50. Wilson, J. A. *The Culture of Ancient Egypt.* Chicago, 1956.

51. Winlock, H. E. 'Notes on the Reburial of Tuthmosis I.' In *J.E.A.* 15 (1929), 56–68.

52. Winlock, H. E. *Excavations at Deir el Baḥri 1911–1931.* New York, 1942.

53. Yoyotte, J. 'À propos de l'obélisque unique.' In *Kêmi,* 14 (1957), 81–91.

III. THE POWER OF AMUN

1. Blackman, A. M. 'On the Position of Women in the Ancient Egyptian Hierarchy.' In *J.E.A.* 7 (1921), 8–30.

2. Bonnet, H. *Reallexikon der ägyptischen Religionsgeschichte.* Berlin, 1952.

3. Caminos, R. A. *Late-Egyptian Miscellanies (Brown Egyptological Studies,* 1). London, 1954.

4. Campbell, C. *The Miraculous Birth of Amon-hotep III and other Egyptian Studies.* Edinburgh, 1912.

5. Černý, J. 'Questions addressées aux oracles.' In *Bull. Inst. fr. Caire,* 35 (1935), 41–8.

6. Davies, N. de G. *The Rock Tombs of el Amarna (Archaeological Survey of Egypt.* Memoirs 13–18). 6 vols. London, 1903–8.

7. Davies, N. de G. *The Tomb of Puyemrê at Thebes (Pub. M.M.A.E.E. Robb de Peyster Tytus Memorial Series,* vols. II, III). 2 vols. New York, 1922–3.

8. Davies, N. de G. *The Tomb of Rekh-mi-Rēʿ at Thebes (Pub. M.M.A.E.E.* 11). New York, 1943.

9. Desroches-Noblecourt, C. 'Deux grands obélisques précieux d'un sanctuaire à Karnak. Les Egyptiens ont-ils érigé des obélisques d'électrum?' In *Rev. d'égyptol.* 8 (1951), 47–61.

10. Erichsen, W. *Papyrus Harris I, Hieroglyphische Transkription* (*Bibl. Aeg.* v). Brussels, 1933.

11. Erman, A. *Die Religion der Ägypter, ihr Werden und Vergehen in vier Jahrtausende.* Berlin and Leipzig, 1934.

12. Gardiner, A. H. 'Ramesside Texts Relating to the Taxation and Transport of Corn.' In *J.E.A.* 27 (1941), 19–73.

13. Gardiner, A. H. The Wilbour Papyrus (*The Brooklyn Museum*). 4 vols. Oxford, 1941–52.

14. Gardiner, A. H. *Ancient Egyptian Onomastica.* 3 vols. Oxford, 1947.

15. Gardiner, A. H. *Ramesside Administrative Documents* (*The Griffith Institute, Ashmolean Museum*, Oxford). London, 1948.

16. Gardiner, A. H. 'Tuthmosis III returns Thanks to Amūn.' In *J.E.A.* 38 (1952), 6–23.

17. Gardiner, A. H. 'Some Reflections on the Nauri Decree.' In *J.E.A.* 38 (1952), 24–33.

18. Griffith, F. Ll. 'The Abydos Decree of Seti I at Nauri.' In *J.E.A.* 13 (1927), 193–208.

19. Gunn, B. and Gardiner, A. H. 'New Renderings of Egyptian Texts.' II. The Expulsion of the Hyksos.' In *J.E.A.* 5 (1918), 36–56.

20. Kees, H. *Ägypten* (W. Otto (ed.), *Handbuch der Altertumswissenschaft*, III, part 1, no. 3. *Kulturgeschichte des alten Orients*, 1). Munich, 1933.

21. Kees, H. 'Ein Sonnenheiligtum im Amonstempel von Karnak.' In *Or.* 18 (1949), 427–42.

22. Kees, H. *Das Priestertum im ägyptischen Staat vom neuen Reich bis zur Spätzeit* (*Probleme der Ägyptolgie*, 1). 2 vols. Leiden–Cologne, 1953, 1958.

23. Kees, H. *Der Götterglaube im alten Ägypten.* Ed. 2. Berlin, 1956.

24. Kees, H. 'Wêbpriester der 18. Dynastie in Trägendienst bei Prozessionen.' In *Z.Ä.S.* 85 (1960), 45–56.

25. Lefebvre, G. *Histoire des grands prêtres d'Amon de Karnak jusqu'à la XXIe Dynastie.* Paris, 1929.

26. Posener, G. *Dictionnaire de la civilisation égyptienne.* Paris, 1959.

27. Reisner, G. A. 'The Viceroys of Ethiopia.' In *J.E.A.* 6 (1920), 28–55, 73–88.

28. Sander-Hansen, C. E. *Das Gottesweib des Amun* (*Det Kongelige Danske Videnskabernes Selskab*, Historisk-filologiske Skrifter, Bind 1, Nr. 1). Copenhagen, 1940.

29. Sandman, M. *Texts from the Time of Akhenaten* (*Bibl. Aeg.* VIII). Brussels, 1938.

30. Sauneron, S. *Les prêtres de l'ancienne Égypte* ('Le Temps qui Court.' *Éditions du Seuil*). Bourges, 1957.

31. Schaedel, H. D. *Die Listen des grossen Papyrus Harris, ihre wirtschaftliche und politische Ausdeutung* (*Leipsiger ägyptol. St.*, Heft 6). Glückstadt, 1936.

32. Sethe, K. 'Die Berufung eines Hohenpriesters des Amon unter Ramses II.' In *Z.Ä.S.* 44 (1907), 30–5.

33. Shorter, A. W. *An Introduction to Egyptian Religion. An Account of Religion in Egypt during the Eighteenth Dynasty.* London, 1931.

34. Vandier, J. *La religion égyptienne* ('Mana': *Introduction à l'histoire des religions* 1. *Les anciennes religions orientales*, 1). Ed. 2. Paris, 1949.

35. Varille, A., Christophe, L.-A., Barguet, P. and Leclant, J. *Karnak I* and *Karnak-Nord III–IV (Flles. Inst. fr. Caire,* 19, 23, 25). Cairo, 1943–51.
36. Werbrouck, M. *Le temple d'Hatshepsout à Deir el Bahari (Fondation Égyptologique Reine Élisabeth).* Brussels, 1949.

IV. HATSHEPSUT'S EXPEDITIONS

1. Ballard, G. A. 'The Great Obelisk Lighter of 1550 B.C.' In *The Mariner's Mirror,* 27 (1941), 290–306.
2. Ballard, G. A. 'The Egyptian Obelisk Lighter.' *Ibid.* 33 (1947), 158–64.
3. Bell, C. D. J. 'The Obelisk Barge of Hatshepsut.' In *Anc. Egypt,* 1934, 107–14.
4. Brunner-Traut, E. 'Die Krankheit der Fürstin von Punt.' In *We. Or.* [10] (1957), 307–11.
5. Fairman, H. W. and Grdseloff, B. 'Texts of Hatshepsut and Sethos I inside Speos Artemidos.' In *J.E.A.* 33 (1947), 12–33.
6. Fakhry, A. 'A New Speos from the Reign of Hatshepsut and Tuthmosis III at Beni-Ḥasan.' In *Ann. Serv.* 39 (1939), 709–23.
7. Faulkner, R. O. 'Egyptian Seagoing Ships.' In *J.E.A.* 26 (1940), 3–9.
8. Gardiner, A. H., Peet, T. E. and Černy, J. *The Inscriptions of Sinai.* Ed. 2 (*E.E.S.,* 45th Memoir). 2 vols. London, 1952, 1955.
9. Ghalioungi, P. 'Sur deux formes d'obésité représentées dans l'Égypte ancienne.' In *Ann. Serv.* 49 (1949), 303–16.
10. Kuentz, C. *Obélisques* (CCG, nos. 1308–15, 17001–36). Cairo, 1932.
11. Lacau, P. 'L'or dans l'architecture égyptienne.' In *Ann. Serv.* 53 (1955), 221–50.
12. Legrain, G. and Naville, E. 'L'aile nord du pylone d'Aménôphis III à Karnak.' In *Ann. Mus. Guimet,* 30 (1902), 1–22.
13. Lucas, A. 'Cosmetics, Perfumes, and Incense in Ancient Egypt.' In *J.E.A.* 16 (1930), 41–53.
14. Lucas, A. *Ancient Egyptian Materials and Industries.* Ed. 3. London, 1948.
15. Naville, E. *The Temple of Deir el Bahari (E.E.F.,* 12th–14th, 16th, 19th, 27th, 29th Memoirs). 7 vols. London, 1894–1908.
16. Newberry, P. E. 'Notes on Seagoing Ships.' In *J.E.A.* 28 (1942), 64–6.
17. Posener, G. 'Le canal du Nil à la Mer Rouge avant les Ptolemées.' In *Chron. d'Ég.* 13 (1938), 258–73.
18. Ruffer, M. A. *Studies in the Palaeopathology of Egypt.* Chicago, 1921.
19. Säve-Söderbergh, T. *Four Eighteenth Dynasty Tombs (Private Tombs at Thebes,* 1). Oxford, 1957.
20. Sethe, K. 'Ein bisher unbeachtet gebliebene Episode der Puntexpedition der Königin Hatschepsowet.' In *Z.Ä.S.* 42 (1905), 91–9.
21. Sølver, C. V. 'The Egyptian Obelisk-Ships.' In *The Mariner's Mirror,* 26 (1940), 237–56.
22. Sølver, C. V. 'Egyptian Obelisk-Ships.' *Ibid.* 33 (1947), 39–43.
23. Steuer, R. O. 'Stactē in Egyptian Antiquity.' In *J.A.O.S.* 63 (1943), 279–84.
24. Vandier, J. *Manuel d'archéologie égyptienne.* 5 vols. Paris, 1952–69.
25. Varille, A. 'Description sommaire du sanctuaire oriental d'Amon-Rê à Karnak.' In *Ann. Serv.* 50 (1950), 137–72.
26. Watermann, U. and R. *Über die rätsvolle Gestalt der Königin von Punt.* In *Homo (Z.V.F.M.* (Göttingen)), 8 (1957), 149–51.

V. THE SPORTING TRADITION

1. Buck, A. de. 'Een sportief egyptisch Koning.' In *Jaarbericht...'Ex Oriente Lux'*, no. 6 (1939), 9–14.
2. Chard, T. 'An Early Horse Skeleton.' In *The Journal of Heredity*, 28 (1937), 317–19.
3. Davies, N. de G. 'The Work of the Graphic Branch of the Expedition.' In *Bull. M.M.A.* 30 (1935), November, sect. II, 46–57.
4. Desroches-Noblecourt, C. 'Un petit monument commémoratif du roi athlète.' In *Rev. d'égyptol.* 7 (1950), 37–46.
5. Drioton, É. 'Notes Diverses. 15.—Deux scarabées commémoratifs d'Aménophis III.' In *Ann. Serv.* 45 (1947), 85–92.
6. Emery, W. B. 'A Masterpiece of Egyptian Military Architecture of 3900 Years Ago: The Great Castle of Buhen in the Sudan—New Discoveries, including the Earliest Horse known in Egypt.' In *Ill. Ldn. News*, no. 6267, vol. 235 (12 Sept. 1959), 232, 233, 249–51.
7. Hassan, S. 'The Great Limestone Stela of Amenhotep II.' In *Ann. Serv.* 37 (1937), 129–34.
8. Klebs, L. *Die Reliefs und Malereien des neuen Reiches. 1. Szenen aus dem Leben des Volkes (Abh. Heidelberg*, 9 (1924), 1–193).
9. Lansing, A. and Hayes, W. C. 'The Museum's Excavations at Thebes.' In *Bull. M.M.A.* 32 (1937), January, sect. II, 4–39.
10. Mond, R. and Myers O. H. *Temples of Armant: A Preliminary Survey.* 2 vols. London, 1940.
11. Newberry, P. E. 'The Elephant's Trunk called its *drt* (*drt*) "*Hand*".' In *J.E.A.* 30 (1944), 75.
12. Reisner, G. A. and M. B. 'Inscribed Monuments from Gebel Barkal. Part 2. The Granite Stela of Thutmosis III.' In *Z.Ä.S.* 69 (1933), 24–39.
13. Säve-Söderbergh, T. 'The Hyksos Rule in Egypt.' In *J.E.A.* 37 (1951), 53–71.
14. Säve-Söderbergh, T. 'The Nubian Kingdom of the Second Intermediate Period.' In *Kush*, 4 (1956), 54–61.
15. Schulman, A. R. 'Egyptian Representations of Horsemen and Riding in the New Kingdom.' In *J.N.E.S.* 16 (1957), 263–71.
16. Varille, A. 'La grande stèle d'Aménophis II à Giza.' In *Bull. Inst. fr. Caire*, 41 (1942), 31–8.
17. Walle, B. van de. 'Les rois sportifs de l'ancienne Égypte.' In *Chron. d'Ég.* 13 (1938), 234–57.
18. Wilson, J. A. 'Ceremonial Games of the New Kingdom.' In *J.E.A.* 17 (1931), 211–20.
19. Winlock, H. E. *The Rise and Fall of the Middle Kingdom in Thebes.* New York, 1947.
20. Winlock, H. E. *The Treasure of Three Egyptian Princesses (Pub. M.M.A., Department of Egyptian Art*, vol. 10). New York, 1948.

VI. AMENOPHIS III'S DISPLAY

1. Aldred, C. *New Kingdom Art in Ancient Egypt during the Eighteenth Dynasty, 1590 to 1315 B.C.* London, 1951.
2. Aldred, C. 'The Beginning of the el-'Amārna Period.' In *J.E.A.* 45 (1959), 19–33.

3. Anonymous. 'Les fouilles.' In *Chron. d'Ég.* 9 (1934), 65–84.

4. Baedeker, K. *Egypt and the Sûdân: Handbook for Travellers.* Ed. 8 (edited by G. Steindorff). Leipzig, 1929.

5. Davis, T. M., Maspero, G. and Newberry, P. E. *The Tomb of Iouiya and Touiyou* (*Theodore M. Davis' Excavations: Bibân el Molûk*). London, 1907.

6. Engelbach, R. 'A "Kirgipa" Commemorative Scarab of Amenophis III presented by His Majesty King Farouk I to the Cairo Museum.' In *Ann. Serv.* 40 (1941), 659–61.

7. Giorgini, M. S. 'Soleb.' In *Kush*, 6 (1958), 82–98; 7 (1959), 154–70.

8. Glanville, S. R. K. 'Amenophis III and his Successors in the XVIIIth Dynasty.' In W. Brunton, *Great Ones of Ancient Egypt* (London, 1929), 105–39.

9. Griffith, F. Ll. 'Stela in Honour of Amenophis III and Taya from Tell el-'Amarnah.' In *J.E.A.* 12 (1926), 1–2.

10. Guentch-Ogloueff, M. 'Le culte solaire sous la XVIIIe dynastie avant le schisme amarnien.' In *J. as.* 234 (1943–45 (publ. 1947)), 414–15.

11. Krieger, P. 'Le scarabée du mariage d'Aménophis III avec la reine Tiy trouvé dans le palais royal d'Ugarit.' In C. F.-A. Schaeffer, *Ugaritica*, 3 (*Mission de Ras Shamra*, 8 [Paris, 1956]), 221–6.

12. Lansing, A. 'Excavations at the Palace of Amenhotep III at Thebes.' In *Bull. M.M.A.* 13 (1918), March. Supplement, 8–14.

13. Lansing, A. 'A Commemorative Scarab of Amen-hotpe III.' In *Bull. M.M.A.* 31 (1936), 12–14.

14. Mercer, S. A. B. *The Tell el-Amarna Tablets.* 2 vols. Toronto, 1939.

15. Möller, G. 'Das Dekret des Amenophis, des Sohnes des Hapu.' In *Sitzungsb. Berlin*, 47 (1910), 932–48.

16. Newberry, P. E. *Egyptian Antiquities: Scarabs* (*University of Liverpool, Institute of Archaeology*). London, 1906.

17. Pillet, M. *Thèbes. Karnak et Louxor* (*Les Villes d'Art Célèbres*). Paris, 1928.

18. Quibell, J. E. *Tomb of Yuaa and Thuiu* (*C.C.G.* nos. 51001–191). Cairo, 1908.

19. Ranke, H. 'Istar als Heilgöttin in Ägypten.' In *Studies presented to F. Ll. Griffith* (*E.E.S.* London, 1932), 412–18.

20. Robichon, C. and Varille, A. *Le temple du scribe royal Amenhotep, fils de Hapou*, 1 (*Flles. Inst. fr. Caire*, 11). Cairo, 1936.

21. Rowe, A. 'Newly-Identified Monuments in the Egyptian Museum Showing the Deification of the Dead....' In *Ann. Serv.* 40 (1940), 1–50.

22. Rowe, A. 'Inscriptions on the Model Coffin containing the Lock of Hair of Queen Tyi.' In *Ann. Serv.* 40 (1941), 623–7.

23. Schäfer, H. 'Das Simonsche Holzköpfchen der Königin Teje.' In *Z.Ä.S.* 68 (1932), 81–6.

24. Seidl, E. *Einführung in die ägyptische Rechtsgeschichte bis zum Ende des neuen Reiches.* 1. *Juristischer Teil* (*Ägyptol. Forsch.* 10). Gluckstadt–Hamburg– New York, 1939.

25. Sethe, K. 'Amenhotep, der Sohn des Hapu.' In *Aegyptiaca* (*Festschrift für Georg Ebers*. Leipzig, 1897), 107–16.

26. Shorter, A. W. 'Historical Scarabs of Tuthmosis IV and Amenophis III.' In *J.E.A.* 17 (1931), 23–5.

27. Smith G. E. and Dawson, W. R. *Egyptian Mummies.* New York, 1924.

28. Varille, A. 'L'inscription dorsale du colosse méridional de Memnon.' In *Ann. Serv.* 33 (1933), 85–94; 'Notes complémentaires....' *Ibid.* 34 (1934), 9–16.

29. Varille, A. 'Fragments d'une colosse d'Aménophis III donnant une liste de pays africains (Louvre A 18 et A 19).' In *Bull. Inst. fr. Caire*, 35 (1935), 161–71.

30. Varille, A. 'Fragments de socles colossaux provenant du temple funéraire d'Aménophis III avec representations de peuples étrangers.' In *Bull. Inst. fr. Caire*, 35 (1935), 173–9.

31. Varille, A. 'Nouvelles listes géographiques d'Amenophis III à Karnak.' In *Ann. Serv.* 36 (1936), 202–14.

32. Weigall, A. E. P. *A Guide to the Antiquities of Upper Egypt from Abydos to the Sudan Frontier.* London, 1910.

33. Wolf, W. 'Vorläufer der Reformation Echnatons.' In *Z.Ä.S.* 59 (1924), 109–19.

34. Yoyotte, J. 'Le bassin de Djâroukha.' In *Kêmi*, 15 (1959), 23–33.

VII. THE NUBIAN GOLD TRADE

1. Arkell, A. J. 'Varia Sudanica.' In *J.E.A.* 36 (1950), 24–40.
2. Černý, J. 'Graffiti at the Wadi el-'Allâḳi.' In *J.E.A.* 33 (1947), 52–7.
3. Emery, W. B. 'The Work of an Egyptian Master Castle-Architect of 3900 Years ago revealed in new excavations at Buhen, in the Sudan.' In *Ill. Ldn. News*, 21 June 1958, 1049–51.
4. Emery, W. B. 'A Preliminary Report on the Excavations of the Egypt Exploration Society at Buhen 1957–8.' In *Kush*, 7 (1959), 7–14.
5. Fairman, H. W. 'The Four Ages of Amarah West: New Findings in a Unique Site.' In *Ill. Ldn. News*, no. 5687, vol. 212 (17 April 1948), 439–41.
6. Fakhry, A. *The Inscriptions of the Amethyst Quarries at Wadi el Hudi (Service des Antiquités de l'Égypte: The Egyptian Deserts).* Cairo, 1952.
7. Gauthier, H. 'Les "Fils royaux de Kouch" et le personnel administratif de l'Éthiopie.' In *Rec. trav.* 39 (1921), 179–238.
8. Habachi, L. 'The Graffiti and Work of the Viceroys of Kush in the Region of Aswan.' In *Kush*, 5 (1957), 13–36.
9. Habachi, L. 'The First Two Viceroys of Kush and their Family.' In *Kush*, 7 (1959), 45–62.
10. Junker, H. 'The First Appearance of the Negroes in History.' In *J.E.A.* 7 (1921), 121–32.
11. Posener, G. 'Pour une localisation du pays Koush au Moyen Empire.' In *Kush*, 6 (1958), 39–68.
12. Posener, G. 𓈖𓏏𓏤𓎡 et 𓈖𓏏𓏤𓎡. In *Z.Ä.S.* 83 (1958), 38–43.
13. Säve-Söderbergh, T. 'A Buhen Stela from the Second Intermediate Period (*Kharṭûm No.* 18).' In *J.E.A.* 35 (1949), 50–8.
14. Vercoutter, J. 'New Egyptian Texts from the Sudan.' In *Kush*, 4 (1956), 66–82.
15. Vercoutter, J. 'The Gold of Kush. Two Gold-Washing Stations at Faras East.' In *Kush*, 7 (1959), 120–53.
16. Wolf, W. 'Amenhotep, Vizekönig von Nubien.' In *Z.Ä.S.* 59 (1924), 157–8.

VIII. THE CIVIL SERVICE

1. Boeser, P. A. A. *Beschreibung der aegyptischen Sammlung des niederländischen Reichsmuseum der Altertümer in Leiden.* Vol. 6. The Hague, 1913.
2. Brunner, H. *Altägyptische Erziehung.* Wiesbaden, 1957.

768 BIBLIOGRAPHY

3. Brunner, H. 'Die Methode des Anfängerunterrichts im alten Ägypten und ihre Bedeutung.' In *Festschrift für Eduard Spranger* (Tübingen, 1957), 207–18.

4. Černý, J. 'Les ostraca hiératiques, leur intérêt et la nécessité de leur étude.' In *Chron. d'Ég.* 6 (1931), 212–24.

5. Drioton, É. 'La pédagogie au temps des Pharaons.' In *Rev. des Conférences françaises en Orient*, 13 (1949), 193–9.

6. Dunham, D. 'Three Inscribed Statues in Boston.' In *J.E.A.* 15 (1929), 164–6.

7. Erman, A. 'Aus dem Grabe eines Hohenpriesters von Memphis.' In *Z.Ä.S.* 33 (1895), 18–24.

8. Erman, A. *Die ägyptischen Schülerhandschriften (Abh. Berlin*, 1925, Nr. 2). Berlin, 1925.

9. Erman, A. *The Literature of the Ancient Egyptians. Poems, Narratives, and Manuals of Instruction, from the Third and Second Millennia B.C.* Translated into English by Aylward M. Blackman. London, 1927.

10. Erman A. and Ranke, H. *Aegypten and aegyptische Leben im Altertums.* Tubingen, 1923.

11. Faulkner, R. O. Review of N. de G. Davies, *The Tomb of Rekh-mi-Rēʿ at Thebes.* In *J.E.A.* 31 (1945), 114–15.

12. Faulkner, R. O. 'Egyptian Military Organisation.' In *J.E.A.* 39 (1953), 32–47.

13. Faulkner, R. O. 'The Installation of the Vizier.' In *J.E.A.* 41 (1955), 18–29.

14. Gabra, S. *Les conseils de fonctionnaires dans l'Égypte pharaonique. Scènes de récompenses royales aux fonctionnaires (Service des Antiquités de l'Égypte).* Cairo, 1929.

15. Gardiner, A. H. *The Inscription of Mes. A Contribution to the Study of Egyptian Judicial Procedure (Unters.* 4, 3). Leipzig, 1905.

16. Gardiner, A. H. 'Four Papyri of the 18th Dynasty from Kahun.' In *Z.Ä.S.* 43 (1906), 27–47.

17. Gardiner, A. H. *Late-Egyptian Miscellanies (Bibl. Aeg.* 7). Brussels, 1937.

18. Gardiner, A. H. 'The Harem at Miwēr.' In *J.N.E.S.* 12 (1953), 145–9.

19. Gardiner, A. H. *Egyptian Grammar: Being an Introduction to the Study of Hieroglyphs.* Ed. 3. London, 1957.

20. Hayes, W. C. 'A Statue of the Herald Yamu-nedjeh in the Egyptian Museum, Cairo, and some biographical Notes on its Owner. In *Ann. Serv.* 33 (1933), 6–16.

21. Hayes, W. C. *A Papyrus of the Late Middle Kingdom in the Brooklyn Museum (The Brooklyn Museum: Publications of the Department of Egyptian Art).* Brooklyn, 1955.

22. Hayes, W. C. 'A Selection of Tuthmoside Ostraca from Dēr el Baḥri.' In *J.E.A.* 46 (1960), 29–52.

23. Helck, W. 'Die Opferstiftung des *Śn-mwt*.' In *Z.Ä.S.* 85 (1960), 23–24.

24. Otto, E. 'Prolegomena zur Frage der Gesetzgebung und Rechtssprechungen in Ägypten.' In *Mitt. deutsch. Inst. Kairo*, 14 (1956), 150–9.

25. Otto, E. 'Bildung und Ausbildung im alten Ägypten.' In *Z.Ä.S.* 81 (1956), 41–8.

26. Pflüger, K. 'The Edict of King Haremhab.' In *J.N.E.S.* 5 (1946), 260–8.

27. Posener, G. *Catalogue des ostraca hiératiques littéraires de Deir el Médineh (Documents de Flles. Inst. fr. Caire*, 1 and 18). 2 vols. Cairo, 1934–52.

28. Roeder, G. *Aegyptische Inschriften aus den Königlichen Museen zu Berlin.* Band II. Leipzig, 1913, 1914, 1924.
29. Seidl, E. Review of W. Helck, *Zur Verwaltung des Mittleren und Neuen Reiches.* In *Z.D.M.G.* 109 (1959), 403–6.
30. Sethe K., *Die Einsetzung des Veziers unter der 18. Dynastie. Inschrift im Grabe des Rekh-mi-reʿ zu Schech Abd el Gurna (Unters. 5, 2).* Leipzig, 1909.
31. Spiegelberg, W. *Studien und Materialen zum Rechtswesen des Pharaonenreiches der Dynast. XVIII–XXI.* Hannover, 1892.
32. Spiegelberg, W. 'Ein Gerichtsprotokoll aus der Zeit Thutmosis' IV.' In *Z.Ä.S.* 63 (1928), 105–15.
33. Volten, A. *Studien zum Weisheitsbuch des Anii (Kongelige-Danske Videnskaberneʒ Selskab.* Hist.-filol. Meddelelser, 23, no. 3). Copenhagen, 1937.
34. van de Walle, B.. *La transmission des textes littéraires égyptiens (avec une Annexe de G. Posener).* Brussels, 1948.
35. Wilson, J. A. 'The Oath in Ancient Egypt.' In *J.N.E.S.* 7 (1948), 129–56.

IX. THE ARMY, NAVY, AND POLICE FORCE

1. Bonnet, H. *Die Waffen der Völker des alten Orients.* Leipzig, 1926.
2. *The Cambridge Ancient History.* Volume II. *The Egyptian and Hittite Empires to c. 1000 B.C.* Ed. 1 reprinted with corrections. Cambridge, 1926.
3. Christophe, L. 'La stèle de l'an III de Ramsès IV au Ouâdi Hammâmât (No. 12). In *Bull. Inst. fr. Caire,* 48 (1949), 1–38.
4. Christophe, L. 'L'organisation de l'armée égyptienne à l'époque ramesside.' In *Rev. du Caire,* 39 (1957), 387–405.
5. Christophe, L. *The Army in Ancient Egypt (Centre de Documentation et d'études ...Publications culturelles).* Cairo, [1958?].
6. Davies, N. de G. *The Tombs of Two Officials of Tuthmosis the Fourth (E.E.S., The Theban Tomb Series,* 3rd memoir). London, 1923.
7. Davies, N. de. G. *The Tomb of Ḳen-Amūn at Thebes (Pub. M.M.A.E.E.,* 5). 2 vols. New York, 1930.
8. Davies, N. de G. and Faulkner, R. O. 'A Syrian Trading Venture to Egypt.' In *J.E.A.* 33 (1947), 40–6.
9. von Deines, H. '"Das Gold der Tapferkeit," eine militärische Auszeichnung.' In *Z.Ä.S.* 79 (1954), 83–6.
10. Erman A. and Schäfer H. 'Zwei Rekrutenaushebungen in Abydos aus dem mittleren Reich.' In *Z.Ä.S.* 38 (1900), 42–5.
11. Faulkner, R. O. 'Egyptian Military Standards.' In *J.E.A.* 27 (1941), 12–18.
12. Faulkner, R. O. 'The Battle of Megiddo.' In *J.E.A.* 28 (1942), 2–15.
13. Faulkner, R. O. 'The Euphrates Campaign of Tuthmosis III.' In *J.E.A.* 32 (1946), 39–42.
14. Glanville, S. R. K. 'Records of a Royal Dockyard of the Time of Tuthmosis III: Papyrus British Museum 10056.' In *Z.Ä.S.* 66 (1930), 105–21; 68 (1932), 7–41.
15. Hickmann, H. *La trompette dans l'Égypte ancienne (Supplément aux Ann. Serv., Cahier No.* 1). Cairo, 1946.
16. von Komorzýnski, E. 'Die Trompete als Signalinstrument im altägyptischen Heer.' In *Arch. f. äg. Arch.* 1 (1938), 155–7.
17. Marx, E. 'Egyptian Shipping of the Eighteenth and Nineteenth Dynasties.' In *The Mariner's Mirror,* 32 (1946), 21–34.

18. Moret, A. *The Nile and Egyptian Civilization* (*The History of Civilization*, edited by C. K. Ogden). London, 1927.
19. Schäfer, H. 'Zum Ehrengold.' In *Z.Ä.S.* 70 (1934), 10–13.
20. Schulman, A. R. *The Military Establishment of the Egyptian Empire* (*A Dissertation... for the Degree of Master of Arts, Dept. of Oriental Languages and Civilizations, The University of Chicago*). Chicago, 1958.
21. Sethe, K. 'Eine ägyptische Expedition nach dem Libanon im 15. Jahrhundert v. Chr.' In *Sitzungsb. Berlin*, 1906, 356–63.
22. Sethe, K. 'Altägyptische Ordensauszeichnungen.' In *Z.Ä.S.* 48 (1910), 143–5.
23. Sølver, C. V. 'Egyptian Shipping of about 1500 B.C.' In *The Mariner's Mirror*, 22 (1936), 430–69.
24. Wolf, W. *Die Bewaffnung des altägyptischen Heeres*. Leipzig, 1926.

X. THE EMPLOYMENT AND SOURCES OF LABOUR

1. Allen, T. G. *The Egyptian Book of the Dead. Documents in the Oriental Institute Museum at the University of Chicago* (*O.I.P.* 82). Chicago, 1960.
2. Bakir, Abd el-M. *Slavery in Pharaonic Egypt* (*Supplément aux Ann. Serv., Cahier* no. 18). Cairo, 1952.
3. Bruyère, B. *Rapport(s) sur les fouilles de Deir el Médineh* (1922–1951) (*Flles. Inst. fr. Caire*, 1–8, 10, 14–16, 20, 21, 26). Cairo, 1924–53.
4. Černý, J. 'Le culte d'Aménophis Ier chez les ouvriers de la nécropole thébaine.' In *Bull. Inst. fr. Caire*, 27 (1927), 159–203.
5. Černý, J. 'L'identité des "Serviteurs dans la Place de Vérité" et des ouvriers de la nécropole royale de Thèbes.' In *Rev. Ég. anc.* 2 (1929), 200–9.
6. Černý, J. 'Semites in Egyptian Mining Expeditions to Sinai.' In *Arch Orient.* 7 (1935), 384–9.
7. Černý, J. *Catalogue des ostraca hiératiques non littéraires de Deir el Médineh*, nos. 1–456 (*Documents de Flles. Inst. fr. Caire*, 3–7). Cairo, 1935–51.
8. Černý, J. *Paper and Books in Ancient Egypt* (*Lecture delivered at University College, London, May 29, 1947*). London, 1952.
9. Černý, J. 'Prices and Wages in Egypt in the Ramesside Period.' In *J.W.H.* [Paris], 1 (1954), 903–21.
10. Černý, J., Bruyère, B. and Clère, J. J. *Répertoire onomastique de Deir el-Médineh* (*Documents de Flles. Inst. fr. Caire*, 12). Cairo, 1949.
11. 'Corvée.' In *The Encyclopaedia Britannica*, Ed. 11 (1910–11), vol. 7, 209–10.
12. Davies, Nina de G. and Gardiner, A. H. *The Tomb of Amenemhēt* (*No. 82*) (*E.E.F. The Theban Tombs Series*, 1st Memoir). London, 1915.
13. Davies, Norman de G. 'The Graphic Work of the Expedition at Thebes.' In *Bull. M.M.A.* 23 (1928), December, sect. II, 37–48.
14. Debono, F. *Pics en pierre de Sérabit el-Khadim* (*Sinaï*) *et d'Égypte*. In *Ann. Serv.* 46 (1947), 265–85.
15. Deines, H. von. 'Die Nachrichten über das Pferd und den Wagen in den ägyptischen Texten.' In *Mitt. Inst. Or.* 1 (1953), 3–15.
16. Donner, H. 'Die Herkunft des ägyptischen Wortes 𓏲𓏲𓄿𓆑 = Pferd.' In *Z.Ä.S.* 80 (1955), 97–103.
17. Edgerton, W. F. 'The Nauri Decree of Seti I. A Translation and Analysis of the Legal Portion.' In *J.N.E.S.* 6 (1947), 219–30.
18. Erman A. and Grapow, H. *Wörterbuch der aegyptischen Sprache*. 7 vols. Leipzig, 1926–63.

19. Gardiner, A. H. 'A Lawsuit arising from the Purchase of Two Slaves.' In *J.E.A.* 21 (1935), 140–6.
20. Gardiner, A. H. 'Horus the Beḥdetite.' in *J.E.A.* 30 (1944), 23–60.
21. Glanville, S. R. K. *Daily Life in Ancient Egypt* (*Routledge Introductions to Modern Knowledge*, no. 16). London, 1930.
22. Hartmann, F. *L'agriculture dans l'ancienne Égypte*. Paris, 1923.
23. Hayes, W. C. *Ostraka and Name Stones from the Tomb of Sen-Mūt (no. 71) at Thebes (Pub. M.M.A.E.E.* 15). New York, 1942.
24. Helck, W. and Otto, E. *Kleines Wörterbuch der Aegyptologie*. Wiesbaden, 1956.
25. Kees, H. 'Darstellung eines Geflügelhofes der Ramessidenzeit.' In *Z.Ä.S.* 75 (1939), 85–9.
26. Kees, H. *Das alte Agypten. Eine kleine Landeskunde*. Ed. 2. Berlin, 1958.
27. Kuény, G. 'Scènes apicoles dans l'ancienne Égypte.' In *J.N.E.S.* 9 (1950), 84–93.
28. Legrain, G. 'Notes d'inspection: I. Les stèles d'Aménôthès IV à Zernik et à Gebel Silsileh.' In *Ann. Serv.* 3 (1902), 259–66.
29. Posener, G. 'Une liste de noms propres étrangers sur deux ostraca hiératiques du Nouvel Empire.' In *Syria*, 18 (1937), 181–97.
30. Shorter, A. W. *Everyday Life in Ancient Egypt*. London [1932].
31. Smith, W. S. *A History of Egyptian Sculpture and Painting in the Old Kingdom* (*M.F.A.*, Boston). Ed. 2. Cambridge (Mass.), 1949.
32. Speleers, L. *Les figurines funéraires égyptiennes* (*Fondation Universitaire de Belgique*). Brussels, 1923.
33. Steindorff, G. 'Eine ägyptische Liste syrischer Sklaven.' In *Z.Ä.S.* 38 (1900), 15–18.
34. Wilson, J. A. 'The Artist of the Egyptian Old Kingdom.' In *J.N.E.S.* 6 (1947), 231–49.
35. Wolf, W. 'Papyrus Bologna 1086. Ein Beitrag zur Kulturgeschichte des neuen Reiches.' In *Z.Ä.S.* 65 (1930), 89–97.
36. Wolf, W. *Die Kunst Aegyptens: Gestalt und Geschichte*. Stuttgart, 1957.

XI. TAXATION, COMMERCE, AND EXCHANGE

1. Berger, S. 'A Note on some Scenes of Land-Measurement.' In *J.E.A.* 20 (1934), 54–6.
2. Borchardt, L. 'Statuen von Feldmessern.' In *Z.Ä.S.* 42 (1905), 70–2.
3. Cartland, B. M. 'Egyptian Weights and Balances.' In *Bull. M.M.A.* 12 (1917), 85–90.
4. Davies, N. de G. 'The Graphic Work of the Expedition.' In *Bull. M.M.A.* 21 (1926), March, part II, 41–51.
5. Fakhry, A. 'Baḥria and Farafra Oases.' In *Ann. Serv.* 39 (1939), 627–42.
6. Fakhry, A. *Baḥria Oasis* (*Service des Antiquités de l'Égypte. The Egyptian Deserts*, 1). Cairo, 1942.
7. Fakhry, A. *Siwa Oasis, its History and Antiquities* (*ibid.* [II?]). Cairo, 1944.
8. Gardiner, A. H. *The Chester Beatty Papyri, No. 1. The Library of A. Chester Beatty. Description of a Hieratic Papyrus....* London, 1931.
9. Glanville, S. R. K. *Weights and Balances in Ancient Egypt* (*Royal Institution of Great Britain*, Meeting of 8 Nov. 1935). London, 1936.
10. Griffith, F. Ll. 'The Teaching of Amenophis the Son of Kanakht, Papyrus B.M. 10474.' In *J.E.A.* 12 (1926), 191–231.

11. Kantor, H. J. *The Aegean and the Orient in the Second Millennium* B.C. (*The Archaeological Institute of America, Monograph* No. 1). Bloomington, 1948.
12. Köster, A. 'Zur Seefahrt der alten Ägypter.' In *Z.Ä.S.* 58 (1923), 125–32.
13. Peet, T. E. 'The Egyptian Words for "Money", "Buy", and "Sell".' In *Griffith Studies* (London, 1932), 122–7.
14. Peet, T. E. 'The Unit of Value šᶜty in Papyrus Bulaq 11.' In *Mél. Maspero*, 1 (Cairo, 1935–8), 185–99.
15. Pendlebury, J. D. S. *Aegyptiaca: A Catalogue of Egyptian Objects in the Aegean Area*. Cambridge, 1930.
16. Pendlebury, J. D. S. 'Egypt and the Aegean in the Late Bronze Age.' In *J.E.A.* 16 (1930), 75–92.
17. Schäfer, H. 'Altägyptische Geldgewichte.' In *Z.Ä.S.* 43 (1906), 70–1.
18. Théodoridès, A. 'À propos de Pap. Lansing 4, 8–5, 2 et 6, 8–7, 5.' In *Rev. Internationale des Droits de l'Antiquité*, 3ème série, 5 (1958), 65–119.
19. Vercoutter, J. *L'Egypte et le monde égéen préhellenique* (*Inst. fr., Bibl. d'Étude*, 22). Cairo, 1956.
20. Weigall, A. E. P. *Weights and Balances* (*C.C.G.* nos. 31271–670). Cairo, 1908.
21. Weill, R. 'L'unité de valeur ℺⏦ *shat* et le Papyrus de Boulaq No. 11.' In *Rev. Ég. anc.* 1 (1927), 45–87 (see also 243–4).
22. Wolf, W. *Die Welt der Ägypter* (*Grosse Kulturen der Frühzeit*, edited by H. T. Bossert). Stuttgart, 1955.

XII. BUILDING AND THE STATE MONOPOLY OF STONE

1. Badawy, A. 'La maison mitoyenne de plan uniforme dans l'Égypte pharaonique.' In *Bull. Faculty of Arts* (Cairo Univ.), 15 (1954), part II, 1–58.
2. Badawy, A. 'Orthogonal and Axial Town Planning in Egypt.' In *Z.Ä.S.* 85 (1959), 1–12.
3. Barguet, P. 'La structure du temple Ipet-sout d'Amon à Karnak du Moyen-Empire à Aménophis II.' In *Bull. Inst. fr. Caire*, 52 (1953), 145–55.
4. Borchardt, L. 'Zur Geschichte des Luqsortempels.' In *Z.Ä.S.* 34 (1896), 122–38.
5. Borchardt, L. *Zur Baugeschichte des Amonstempel von Karnak* (*Unters.* 5, 1). Leipzig, 1905.
6. Borchardt, L. *Ägyptische Tempel mit Umgang* (*Beiträge zur ägyptischen Bauforschung und Altertumskunde*, II). Cairo, 1938.
7. Caminos, R. A. 'Surveying Gebel el-Silsilah.' In *J.E.A.* 41 (1955), 51–5.
8. Capart, J. and Werbrouck, M. *Thebes, the Glory of a Great Past*. English translation by W. E. Caldwell. Brussels, 1926.
9. Clarke, S. and Engelbach, R. *Ancient Egyptian Masonry: The Building Craft*. London, 1930.
10. Daressy, G. 'Inscriptions des carrières de Tourah et Mâsarah.' In *Ann. Serv.* 11 (1911), 257–68.
11. Davies, N. de G. *The Town House in Ancient Egypt*. In Metropolitan Museum Studies, 1 (New York, 1929), 233–55.
12. Desroches, C. 'Un modèle de maison citadine du Nouvel Empire (Musée du Louvre: No. E. 5357).' In *Rev. d'égyptol.* 3 (1938), 17–25.
13. Engelbach, R. *The Aswân Obelisk, with some Remarks on the Ancient Engineering* (*Service des Antiquités de l'Égypte*). Cairo, 1922.
14. Engelbach, R. *The Problem of the Obelisks, from a Study of the Unfinished Obelisk at Aswan*. New York, 1923.

15. Gauthier, H. *Dictionnaire des noms géographiques contenus dans les textes hiéroglyphiques* (*La Société royale de géographie d'Egypte*). 7 vols. Cairo, 1925–31.

16. Gorringe, H. H. *Egyptian Obelisks*. New York, 1882.

17. Hayes, W. C. *The Burial Chamber of the Treasurer Sobk-mosĕ from er Rizeiḳāt* (*M.M.A. Papers*, no. 9). New York, 1939.

18. Hölscher U. and Anthes, R. *The Temples of the Eighteenth Dynasty. The Excavations of Medinet Habu*, 2 (*O.I.P.*, 41). Chicago, 1939.

19. Janssen, J. 'Een bezoek aan den Gebel Silsilah.' In *J.E.O.L.* 10 (1945–8), 337–8, pl. 21.

20. Lacau, P. 'La chapelle rouge d'Hatshepsowet (Sanctuaire de la Barque) au temple de Karnak.' In *Annuaire du Collège de France*, 40 (1943), 79–81, 99–102.

21. Lacau, P. 'Deux magasins à encens du temple de Karnak.' In *Ann. Serv.* 52 (1952), 185–98.

22. Legrain, G. 'Rapport sur les travaux exécutés à Karnak.' In *Ann. Serv.* 5 (1904), 1–43.

23. Legrain, G. 'Au pylône d'Harmhabi à Karnak (Xe pylône).' In *Ann. Serv.* 14 (1914), 13–44.

24. Legrain, G. 'Le logement et transport des barques sacrées et des statues des dieux dans quelques temples égyptiens.' In *Bull. Inst. fr. Caire* 13 (1917), 1–76.

25. Lepsius, C. R. *Denkmaeler aus Aegypten und Aethiopien, Text* (edited by E. Naville). 5 vols. Leipzig, 1897–1913.

26. Macadam, M. F. L. 'Gleanings from the Bankes Mss.' In *J.E.A.* 32 (1946), 57–64.

27. Nelson, H. H. *Key Plans Showing Locations of Theban Temple Decorations* (*O.I.P.* 56). Chicago, 1941.

28. Otto, E. *Topographie des thebanischen Gaues* (*Unters.* 16). Berlin, 1952.

29. Petrie, W. M. F. *A History of Egypt*, II. *The XVIIth and XVIIIth Dynasties*. 7th edition. London, 1924.

30. Ricke, H. 'Eine Inventartafel aus Heliopolis im Turiner Museum.' In *Z.Ä.S.* 71 (1935), 111–33.

31. Ricke, H. 'Ein Tempel mit Pfeilerumgang Thutmoses' III und Hatschepsuts in Karnak.' In *Ann Serv.* 37 (1937), 71–8.

32. Ricke, H. 'Der Tempel "Lepsius 16" in Karnak.' In *Ann Serv.* 38 (1938), 357–68; 39 (1939), 607–8.

33. Ricke, H. *Der Totentempel Thutmoses' III. Baugeschichtliche Untersuchungen* (*Beiträge zur ägyptischen Bauforschung und Altertumskunde*, III, 1). Cairo, 1939.

34. Ricke, H. *Das Kamutef-Heiligtum Hatschepsut's und Thutmoses' III in Karnak. Bericht über eine Ausgrabung vor dem Muttempelbezirk* (*ibid.* III, 2). Cairo, 1954.

35. Robichon C. and Varille, A. *En Égypte: Cent soixante-cinq photographies*. Paris, 1937.

36. Schäfer, H. 'Die angebliche Basilikenhalle des Tempel von Luksor.' In *Z.Ä.S.* 61 (1926), 52–7.

37. Sethe, K. *Die Bau- und Denkmalsteine der alten Ägypter und ihre Namen* (*Sitzungsb. Berlin*, 1933, 22). Berlin, 1933.

38. Varille, A. 'Un colosse d'Aménophis III dans les carrières d'Assouan.' In *Rev. d'égyptol.* 2 (1935), 173–6.

39. Vercoutter, J. 'Excavations at Sai 1955–7. A Preliminary Report.' In *Kush*, 6 (1958), 144–69.

40. Vyse, H. *The Pyramids of Gizeh*. Vol. 3. London, 1842.
41. Winlock, H. E. 'The Museum's Excavations at Thebes.' In *Bull. M.M.A.* 27 (1932), March, sect. II, 4–37.
42. Winlock, H. E. 'New Egyptian Rooms.' In *Bull. M.M.A.* 30 (1935), 176–8.

XIII. TOMB DEVELOPMENT

1. Bucher, P. *Les textes des tombes de Thoutmosis III et d'Aménophis II* (*Mém. Inst. fr. Caire*, 60). Cairo, 1932.
2. Carter, H. 'Report on the Tomb of Zeser-ka-Ra Amenhetep I, discovered by the Earl of Carnarvon in 1914.' In *J.E.A.* 3 (1916), 147–54.
3. Carter, H. 'A Tomb Prepared for Queen Hatshepsuit and Other Recent Discoveries at Thebes.' In *J.E.A.* 4 (1917), 130–58.
4. Carter, H. and Gardiner, A. H. 'The Tomb of Ramesses IV and the Turin Plan of a Royal Tomb.' In *J.E.A.* 4 (1917), 130–58.
5. Carter, H. and Mace, A. C. *The Tomb of Tut·ankh·Amen*. Vol. 1. London, New York, Toronto, and Melbourne, 1923.
6. Carter, H., Newberry, P. E. and Maspero, G. *The Tomb of Thoutmôsis IV* (*Theodore M. Davis' Excavations: Bibân el Molûk*). London, 1904.
7. Černý, J. *Ancient Egyptian Religion* (*Hutchinson's University Library: World Religions*). London, 1952.
8. Davies, Nina M. 'Some Representations of Tombs from the Theban Necropolis.' In *J.E.A.* 24 (1938), 25–40.
9. Davies, Norman de G. *The Tomb of Nakht at Thebes* (*Pub. M.M.A.E.E. Robb de Peyster Tytus Memorial Series*, 1). New York, 1917.
10. Davies, Norman de G. *A Corpus of Inscribed Egyptian Funerary Cones* (edited by M. F. L. Macadam). Oxford, 1937.
11. Drioton, E. 'Croyances et coutumes funéraires de l'ancienne Égypte' (Éditions de *La Revue du Caire*). Cairo, 1943.
12. Grapow, H. 'Studien zu den thebanischen Königsgräbern.' In *Z.Ä.S.* 72 (1936), 12–39.
13. Grapow, H. 'Zum Alter des Buches Amduat und der Sonnenlitanei.' In *Z.Ä.S.* 75 (1939), 134.
14. Hayes, W. C. 'A Writing-palette of the Chief Steward Amenhotpe and some Notes on its Owner.' In *J.E.A.* 24 (1938), 9–24.
15. Hermann, A. *Die Stelen der thebanischen Felsgräber der 18. Dynastie* (*Ägyptol. Forsch.* 11). Glückstadt, 1940.
16. Legrain, G. 'Fragments de canopes' and 'Seconde note sur des fragments de canopes.' In *Ann. Serv.* 4 (1903), 138–49; 5 (1904), 139–41.
17. Maciver, D. R. and Mace, A. C. *El Amrah and Abydos, 1899–1901* (E.E.F. Special Extra Publication). London, 1902.
18. Peet, T. E. Review of H. E. Winlock, *The Tomb of Queen Meryet-Amūn at Thebes*. In *J.E.A.* 20 (1934), 122–3.
19. Piankoff, A. 'Les differents "livres" dans les tombes royales du Nouvel Empire.' In *Ann. Serv.* 40 (1940), 283–9.
20. Piankoff, A. *The Tomb of Ramesses VI* (*Bollingen Series*, XL, vol 1. *Egyptian Religious Texts and Representations*). New York, 1954.
21. Piankoff, A. 'Les tombeaux de la Vallée des Rois avant et apres l'hérésie amarnienne.' In *Bull. Soc. fr. égyptol.*, nos. 28–9 (mars-juillet 1959), 7–14.
22. Schott, S. 'Die Schrift der verborgenen Kammer in Königsgräbern der 18. Dynastie.' In *Nachr. Göttingen*, 1958, Nr. 4, 315–72.

23. Steindorff, G. and Wolf, W. *Die thebanische Gräberwelt* (*Leipziger ägyptol. St.* 4). Glückstadt, 1936.
24. Wegner, M. 'Stilentwickelung der thebanischen Beamtengräber.' In *Mitt. deutsch. Inst. Kairo*, 4 (1933), 38–164.
25. Winlock, H. E. 'The Tomb of Queen Inhapi.' In *J.E.A.* 17 (1931), 107–10.
26. Winlock, H. E. *The Tomb of Queen Meryet-Amūn at Thebes* (*Pub. M.M.A.E.E.* 6). New York, 1932.

XIV. ART

1. Aldred, C. 'Amenophis Redivivus.' In *Bull. M.M.A.* n.s. 14 (1955–6), 114–21.
2. Aldred, C. 'The Beginning of the el-'Amarna Period.' In *J.E.A.* 45 (1959), 19–33.
3. Baud, M. *Les dessins ébauchés de la nécropole thébaine* (*au temps du Nouvel Empire*) (*Mém. Inst. fr. Caire*, 63). Cairo, 1935.
4. von Bissing, F. W. *Denkmäler ägyptischer Skulptur.* 3 vols. Munich, 1911–14.
5. Borchardt, L. *Der Porträtkopf der Königin Teje* (*Ausgrabungen der Deutschen Orient-Gesellschaft in Tell el-Amarna*, 1). Leipzig, 1911.
6. Borchardt, L. *Statuen and Statuetten von Königen und Privatleuten* (*C.C.G.* nos. 1–1294). 5 parts (Part 5 by A. Volten). Berlin, 1911–36.
7. Bothmer, B. V. 'Block Statues of the Egyptian Middle Kingdom.' In *The Brooklyn Museum Bull.* 20 (1959), 11–26.
8. Brunner-Traut, E. *Die altägyptischen Scherbenbilder* (*Bildostraka*) *der deutschen Museen und Sammlungen.* Wiesbaden, 1956.
9. Budge E. A. W. (ed.). *Egyptian Sculptures in the British Museum* (*The British Museum, Dept. of Egyptian and Assyrian Antiquities*). London, 1914.
10. Capart, J. *Documents pour servir à l'étude de l'art égyptien.* 2 vols. Paris, 1927, 1931.
11. Černý, J. 'A Note on the "Repeating of Births".' In *J.E.A.* 15 (1929), 194–8.
12. Chassinat, É. 'Une statuette d'Aménôthès III.' In *Bull. Inst. fr. Caire*, 7 (1910), 169–72.
13. Daressy, G. *Fouilles de la Vallée des Rois* (*C.C.G.* nos. 24001–990). Cairo, 1902.
14. Daressy, G. *Statues de divinités* (*C.C.G.* nos. 38001–9384). 2 vols. Cairo, 1905–6.
15. Davies, Nina M. *Ancient Egyptian Paintings* (*Special Publication of the Oriental Institute of the University of Chicago*). 3 vols. Chicago, 1936.
16. Davies, Norman de G. 'Egyptian Drawings on Limestone Flakes.' In *J.E.A.* 4 (1917), 234–40.
17. Dessene, A. *Le sphinx: Étude iconographique* I. *Des origines à la fin du second millénaire* (*Bibl. Écoles fr. d'Athènes et de Rome*, 196). Paris, 1957.
18. Edgerton, W. F. 'Two Notes on the Flying Gallop.' In *J.A.O.S.* 56 (1936), 178–88.
19. Fechheimer, H. *Kleinplastik der Ägypter* (*Die Kunst des Östens*, III). Berlin, 1922.
20. Fechheimer, H. *Die Plastik der Ägypter* (*ibid.* I). 2nd printing. Berlin, 1923.
21. [Gardiner, A. H.] 'Three Engraved Plaques in the Collection of the Earl of Carnarvon.' In *J.E.A.* 3 (1916), 73–5.
22. Hall, H. R. 'The Statues of Sennemut and Menkheperrēʿsenb in the British Museum.' In *J.E.A.* 14 (1928), 1–2.

776 BIBLIOGRAPHY

23. Hall, H. R. 'Some Wooden Figures of the Eighteenth and Nineteenth Dynasties in the British Museum.' In *J.E.A.* 15 (1929), 236–8; 16 (1930), 39–40.

24. Hayes, W. C. 'Minor Art and Family History in the Reign of Amun-ḥotpe III.' In *Bull. M.M.A.*, n.s. 6 (1948), 272–9.

25. Jéquier, G. *Les temples memphites et thébains (L'architecture et la décoration dans l'ancienne Égypte*, 1). Paris, 1920.

26. Kayser, H. *Die Tempelstatuen ägyptischer Privatleute im mittleren und im neuen Reich (Dissert. z. Erlang. d. Doktorwürde, Univ. Heidelberg).* Heidelberg, 1936.

27. Keimer, L. 'Remarques sur les "cuillers a fard" du type dit à la nageuse.' In *Ann. Serv.* 52 (1952), 59–72.

28. Lacau, P. *Stèles du Nouvel Empire (C.C.G. nos. 34001–189).* Cairo, 1909–57.

29. Lange, K. and Hirmer, M. *Egypt: Architecture, Sculpture and Painting in Three Thousand Years.* London, 1956.

30. Legrain, G. *Statues et statuettes des rois et particuliers (C.C.G. nos. 42001–250).* 3 vols. Cairo, 1906–14.

31. Mekhitarian, A. *Egyptian Painting (The Great Centuries of Painting:* Éditions d'Art Albert Skira). Geneva–Paris–New York, 1954.

32. Mogensen, M. *La collection égyptienne (La Glyptothèque Ny Carlsberg).* Copenhagen, 1930.

33. Montet, P. *Les reliques de l'art syrien dans l'Égypte du nouvel empire (Publications de la Faculté des Lettres, Univ. de Strasbourg*, 76). Paris, 1937.

34. Nagel, G. *La céramique du Nouvel Empire à Deir el Médineh (Documents de Flles. Inst. fr. Caire*, 10). Cairo, 1938.

35. Naville, E. *Das aegyptische Todtenbuch der XVIII. bis XX. Dynastie.* 3 vols. Berlin, 1886.

36. Naville, E. *The Funeral Papyrus of Iouyia (Theodore M. Davis' Excavations: Bibân el Molûk).* London, 1908.

37. Newberry, P. E. 'A Glass Chalice of Tuthmosis III.' In *J.E.A.* 6 (1920), 155–60.

38. Phillips, D. W. *Ancient Egyptian Animals. A Picture Book (M.M.A.).* New York, 1942.

39. Riefstahl. E. *Patterned Textiles in Pharaonic Egypt (Brooklyn Institute of Arts and Sciences).* New York, 1944.

40. Schäfer, H. 'Ägyptische Zeichnungen auf Scherben.' In *J.K.P.K.* 37 (1916), 23–51.

41. Schäfer, H. and Andrae, W. *Die Kunst des alten Orients.* Berlin, 1925.

42. Scharff, A. 'Zwei Rundbildwerke der Königin Hatschepsut.' In *Berichte aus den preussischen Kunstsammlungen*, 52 (1931), 28–34.

43. Scharff, A. *Ägypten.* In W. Otto (ed.), *Handbuch der Archäologie*, 1 *(Handbuch der Altertumswissenschaft*, VI). Munich, 1939.

44. Schiaparelli, E. *La tomba intatta dell'architetto Cha (Relazione...Missione archaeologia italiana in Egitto*, 1903–20, II). Turin, [1927].

45. Schwaller de Lubicz, R. A. *Le temple de l'homme: Apet du Sud à Louqsor.* Vol. II (plates). Paris, 1957.

46. Schweitzer, U. *Löwe und Sphinx im alten Ägypten (Ägyptol. Forsch.* 15). Glückstadt, 1948.

47. Smith, W. S. *Ancient Egypt as Represented in the Museum of Fine Arts, Boston.* 4th edition. Boston, 1960.

48. Spiegelberg, W. 'Die Inschriften des grossen Skarabäus in Karnak.' In *Z.Ä.S.* 66 (1931), 44–5.

49. Vandier d'Abbadie, J. *Catalogue des ostraca figurés de Deir el Médineh* (*nos. 2001 à 2733*) (*Documents de Flles. Inst. fr. Caire*, 11). Cairo, 1937–46.

50. Vandier d'Abbadie, J. 'Cuillères à fards de l'Égypte ancienne.' In *Recherches* [Paris], October, 1952, no. 2, 20–9.

51. Wallis, H. *Egyptian Ceramic Art; The MacGregor Collection*. London, 1898.

52. Wallis, H. *Egyptian Ceramic Art*. London, 1900.

53. Winlock, H. E. 'The Egyptian Expedition (1925–1931).' In *Bull. M.M.A.* 23–6 (1928–32), sect. 11.

54. Winlock, H. E. 'A Granite Sphinx of Hatshepsut.' In *Bull. M.M.A.* 30 (1935), 159–60.

55. Wreszinski, W. *Atlas zur altaegyptischen Kulturgeschichte*. Part 11. Leipzig, 1935.

A. ADDENDA

1. Hornung, E. *Untersuchungen zur Chronologie und Geschichte des Neuen Reiches* (*Ägyptol. Abh.* 11). Wiesbaden, 1964.

2. Hornung, E. 'Neue Materialien zur ägyptischen Chronologie.' In *Z.D.M.G.* 117 (1967), 11–16.

3. Nims, C. F. *Thebes of the Pharaohs*. London, 1965.

4. Nims, C. F. 'The Date of Dishonoring Hatshepsut.' In *Z.Ä.S.* 93 (1966), 97–100.

5. Parker, R. A. 'Once Again the Coregency of Thutmose III and Amenhotep II.' In *Studies in Honor of John A. Wilson* (*S.A.O.C.* 35). Chicago, 1969.

6. Redford, D. B. 'The Coregency of Tuthmosis III and Amenophis II.' In *J.E.A.* 51 (1965), 107–36.

7. Redford, D. B. *History and Chronology of the Eighteenth Dynasty in Egypt: Seven Studies*. Toronto, 1967.

8. Riefstahl, E. *Thebes in the Time of Amunhotep III*. Oklahoma, 1964.

CHAPTER X

G. GENERAL

1. Breasted, J. H. *Ancient Records of Egypt*. 5 vols. Chicago, 1906.

2. *C.A.D. The Assyrian Dictionary*. Chicago, 1956–.

3. Contenau, G. *Manuel d'archéologie orientale*. 4 vols. Paris, 1927–47.

4. *C.T. Cuneiform Texts in the British Museum*. London, 1896–.

5. Drioton, E. and Vandier, J. *Les peuples de l'Orient méditerranéen*. 11. *L'Egypte*. Clio: Introduction aux études historiques. Ed. 3. Paris, 1952.

6. Dussaud, R. *Topographie historique de la Syrie antique et médiévale*. Paris, 1927.

7. EA. The Amarna Letters, as numbered in G, 16.

8. Ebeling, E., Meissner, B. and Weidner, E. F. (eds.). *Reallexikon der Assyriologie*, I–III. Berlin and Leipzig, 1932–.

9. Frankfort, H. *The Art and Architecture of the Ancient Orient*. Harmondsworth, 1954.

10. Gelb, I. J. 'The early history of the West Semitic peoples.' In *J.C.S.* 15 (1961), 27 ff.

11. Gelb, I. J. *Hurrians and Subarians* (*S.A.O.C.* 22). Chicago, 1944.

12. Götze, A. *Hethiter, Churriter und Assyrer*. Oslo, 1936.

13. Goetze, A. 'On the Chronology of the Second Millennium B.C.' In *J.C.S.* 11 (1957), 53 ff., 63 ff.

778 BIBLIOGRAPHY

14. Helck, W. *Die Beziehungen Ägyptens zu Vorderasien im 3. und 2. Jahrtausend vor Chr.* Aegyptologische Abhandlungen 5. Wiesbaden, 1962.
15. *K.Bo. Keilschrifttexte aus Boghazköi*, 1–. Leipzig and Berlin, 1916–.
16. Knudtzon, J. A. *Die el-Amarna Tafeln.* (*Vorderasiatische Bibliothek* 2.) Leipzig, 1915.
17. *K.U.B. Keilschrifturkunden aus Boghazköi*, 1–. Berlin, 1921–.
18. Luckenbill, D. D. *Ancient Records of Assyria and Babylonia.* 2 vols. Chicago, 1926.
19. Meissner, B. *Babylonien und Assyrien.* 2 vols. Heidelberg, 1920, 1925.
20. Meyer, E. *Geschichte des Altertums* II, 1: *Die Zeit der ägyptischen Grossmacht.* Ed. 2. Stuttgart and Berlin, 1928.
21. O'Callaghan, R. T. *Aram Naharaim: A Contribution to the History of Upper Mesopotamia in the Second Millennium* B.C. (*An. Or.* 26). Rome, 1948.
22. Pallis, S. A. *The Antiquity of Iraq. A Handbook of Assyriology.* Copenhagen, 1956.
23. Pritchard, J. B. *The Ancient Near East in Pictures.* Princeton, 1954.
24. Pritchard, J. B. (ed.). *Ancient Near-Eastern Texts relating to the Old Testament.* Ed. 2. Princeton, 1955.
25. Scharff, A. and Moortgat, A. *Aegypten und Vorderasien im Altertum.* Munich, 1950.
26. Schmökel, H. *Keilschriftforschung und Alte Geschichte Vorderasiens: Handbuch der Orientalistik*, ed. B. Spuler, Bde. 2, 3. Abschnitt. Leiden, 1957.
27. Sethe, K. and Helck, W. *Urkunden der 18. Dynastie* (*Urk.* IV), 22 Hefte. Leipzig and Berlin, 1906–.
28. Smith, Sidney. *Alalakh and Chronology.* London, 1940.
29. Smith, Sidney. *Early History of Assyria to 1000* B.C. London, 1928.
30. Smith, W. Stevenson. *Interconnections in the Ancient Near East.* New Haven and London, 1965.

I. SYRIA IN THE SIXTEENTH CENTURY B.C.

1. Albright, W. F. *From the Stone Age to Christianity.* Ed. 2. Baltimore, 1957.
2. Albright, W. F. 'The land of Damascus between 1850 and 1750.' In *Bull. A.S.O.R.* 83 (1941), 30 ff.
3. Albright, W. F. 'New Light on the History of Western Asia in the Second Millennium B.C.' In *Bull. A.S.O.R.* 77 (Feb. 1940), 20 ff.; 78 (April 1940), 23 ff.
4. Albright, W. F. 'Palestine in the Earliest Historical Period.' In *J.P.O.S.* 15 (1935), 193 ff.
5. Albright, W. F. 'Some Important Recent Discoveries: Alphabetic Origins and the Idrimi Statue.' In *Bull. A.S.O.R.* 118 (1950), 11 ff.
6. Albright, W. F. 'A Prince of Taanach in the Fifteenth Century B.C.' In *Bull. A.S.O.R.* 95 (1944), 30 ff.
7. Alt, A. 'Die Wege der Pharaonenheere in Palästina und Syrien.' In *Z.D.P.V.* 60 (1937), 183 ff.; 61 (1938), 26 ff.
8. Benedict, W. C. 'Urartians and Hurrians.' In *J.A.O.S.* 80 (1960), 100 ff.
9. Brunner, H. 'Mitanni in einem ägyptischen Text vor oder um 1500.' In *Mitt. Inst. Or.* 4 (1956), 323 ff.
10. Chiera, E. and Speiser, E. A. 'A new factor in the history of the Ancient Near East.' In *Ann. A.S.O.R.* 6 (1926), 75 ff.

11. Clay, A. T. 'The so-called Fertile Crescent and Desert Bay.' In *J.A.O.S.* 44 (1924), 186 ff.

12. du Mesnil du Buisson, Comte. 'Qatna: ville des greniers des Hourri-Mitanniens.' In *Bull. Inst. fr. Caire*, 36 (1936–7), 175 ff.

13. du Mesnil du Buisson, Comte. 'Les ruines d'el Mishrifé (l'ancienne Qatna): deuxième campagne de fouilles, 1927.' In *Syria*, 8 (1927), 277 ff.

14. Dumont, A. 'Indo-Iranian Names from Mitanni, Nuzi and Syrian Documents.' In *J.A.O.S.* 67 (1947), 251 ff.

15. Engberg, R. M. *The Hyksos Reconsidered*. (*S.A.O.C.* 18.) Chicago, 1939.

16. Friedrich, J. 'Aus verschiedenen Keilschriftsprachen, 1–2, 3–4.' In *Or.* n.s. 9 (1940), 205 ff., 348 ff.

17. Gadd, C. J. 'Tablets from Chagar Bazar and Tall Brak, 1937–38.' In *Iraq*, 7 (1940), 22 ff.

18. Gardiner, A. H. *Ancient Egyptian Onomastica*. 3 vols. Oxford, 1947.

19. Gelb, I. J. 'New Light on Hurrians and Subarians.' In *Studi Orientalistici in onore di Giorgio Levi della Vida*, vol. 1, 378 ff. Rome, 1956.

20. Gelb, I. J., Purves, P. M. and McRae, A. A. *Nuzi Personal Names* (*O.I.P.* 57). Chicago, 1943.

21. Gibson, J. C. L. 'Observations on some important ethnic terms in the Pentateuch.' In *J.N.E.S.* 20 (1961), 217 ff.

22. Goetze, A. 'Cilicians.' In *J.C.S.* 16 (1962), 48 ff.

23. Goetze, A. *Kizzuwadna and the Problem of Hittite Geography* (*Y.O.S.* Researches, vol. 22). New Haven, 1941.

24. Goetze, A. *Kleinasien* (*Kulturgeschichte des alten Orients*, III, 1). Ed. 2. Munich, 1957.

25. Goetze, A. Review of I. J. Gelb, *Hurrians and Subarians*. In *J.N.E.S.* 5 (1946), 165 ff.

26. Goetze, A. Review of H. G. Güterbock and H. Otten, *Keilschrifturkunden aus Boghazköi: Zehntes Heft*. In *J.C.S.* 16 (1962), 24 ff.

27. Goetze, A. Review of S. Smith, *The Statue of Idri-mi*. In *J.C.S.* 4 (1950), 226 ff.

28. Güterbock, H. G. 'The Hurrian Element in the Hittite Empire.' In *Cah. H.M.* 2 (1954), 383 ff.

29. Güterbock, H. G. 'The Song of Ullikummi.' In *J.C.S.* 5 (1951), 135 ff.; 6 (1952), 8 ff.

30. Hauschild, R. *Über die frühesten Arier im Alten Orient* (*Berichte über die Verhandlungen der sächsischen Akademie der Wissenschaft*, 106, 6). Berlin, 1962.

31. Hrouda, B. 'Waššukanni, Urkiš, Šubat-Enlil.' In *M.D.O.G.* 90 (1958), 22 ff.

32. Imparati, F. *I Hurriti*. Florence, 1964.

33. Kupper, J.-R. *Les nomades en Mésopotamie aux temps des rois de Mari*. Paris, 1957.

34. Laessøe, J. 'The Shemshara Tablets.' *Arkæol. Kunsthist. Medd. Dan. Vid. Selsk.* 4, no. 3 (1959).

35. Laessøe, J. and Knudsen, E. E. 'An Old Babylonian Letter from a Hurrian environment.' In *Z.A.* 55 (1962), 131 ff.

36. Lesný, V. 'The language of the Mitanni chieftains: a third branch of the Aryan group.' In *Arch. Orient.* 4 (1932), 257 ff.

37. Lewy, J. 'Studies in the Historic Geography of the Ancient Near East.' In *Or.* n.s. 21 (1952), 265 ff., 393 ff.

38. Maisler, B. 'Canaan and the Canaanites.' In *Bull. A.S.O.R.* 102 (1946), 7 ff.
39. Matouš, L. 'Einige Bemerkungen zum Beduinenproblem im alten Mesopotamien.' In *Arch. Orient.* 26 (1958), 631 ff.
40. Meyer, G. R. 'Noch einige Mitanni-Namen aus Drehem und Djoḫa.' In *Arch. f. Or.* 13 (1939–41), 147 ff.
41. Mironov, N. D. 'Aryan Vestiges in the Near East.' In *Acta Or.* 11 (1933), 140 ff.
42. Moscati, S. *The Face of the Ancient Orient.* London, 1960.
43. Müller, W. Max. *Asien und Europa, nach altägyptischen Denkmäler.* Leipzig, 1893.
44. O'Callaghan, R. T. 'New light on the *maryannu* as "chariot-warriors".' In *Jahrb. f. kleinasiatische Forschung*, 1 (1950), 309 f.
45. Otten, H. 'Ein althethitischer Vertrag mit Kizzuvatna.' In *J.C.S.* 5 (1951), 129 ff.
46. Pézard, M. *Qadesh: Mission archéologique à Tell Nebi Mend, 1921–1922 (Bibliothèque archéologique et historique*, 15). Paris, 1931.
47. Pfeiffer, R. H. and Speiser, E. A. *One Hundred New Selected Nuzi Texts (Ann. A.S.O.R.* 16). New Haven, 1936.
48. Pohl, A. Art. 'Ḫurriti' in *Enciclopedia Cattolica*, vol. 6, col. 1511 f. Vatican, 1951.
49. Schaeffer, C. F. A. *Stratigraphie comparée et chronologie de l'Asie occidentale.* London, 1948.
50. Schaeffer, C. F. A. *Ugaritica.* 4 vols. Paris, 1939–62.
51. Schmökel, H. *Die ersten Arier im Alten Orient.* Leipzig, 1938.
52. Smith, Sidney. 'The "Hurrian" Language.' In *Antiq.* 16 (1942), 320 ff.
53. Smith, Sidney. 'A Preliminary Account of the Tablets from Atchana.' In *A.J.* 19 (1939), 38 ff.
54. Smith, Sidney. *The Statue of Idri-mi.* London, 1949.
55. Speiser, E. A. 'Ethnic Movements in the Near East in the 2nd millennium B.C: The Hurrians and their connections with the Ḫabiru and the Hyksos.' In *Ann. A.S.O.R.* 13 (1933), 13 ff.
56. Speiser, E. A. *Excavations at Tepe Gawra*, vol. 1. Philadelphia, 1935.
57. Speiser, E. A. 'The Hurrian Participation in the Civilizations of Mesopotamia, Syria and Palestine.' In *Cah. H.M.* 1, 2 (1953), 311 ff.
58. Speiser, E. A. *An Introduction to Hurrian (Ann. A.S.O.R.* 20). New Haven, 1941.
59. Speiser, E. A. 'A letter of Shaushatar and the date of the Kirkuk tablets.' In *J.A.O.S.* 49 (1929), 269 ff.
60. Thureau-Dangin, F. 'Tablettes hourrites provenant de Mari.' In *R.A.* 36 (1939), 1 ff.
61. Tocci, F. M. *La Siria nell'età di Mari* (Studi Semitici, 3). Rome, 1960.
62. Unger, M. F. *Israel and the Aramaeans of Damascus.* London, 1957.
63. Ungnad, A. *Subartu: Beiträge zur Kulturgeschichte und Völkerkunde Vorderasiens.* Berlin, Leipzig, 1936.
64. Van Liere, W. J. 'Urkiš, centre religieux hurrite retrouvé dans la haute Jézireh syrienne.' In *Ann. Arch. de Syrie*, 7 (1957), 91 ff.
65. Virolleaud, Ch. 'Les tablettes cunéiformes de Mishrifé-Kaṭna.' In *Syria*, 9 (1928), 90 ff.
66. Weidner, E. F. *Politische Dokumente aus Kleinasien.* Leipzig, 1923.
67. Wiseman, D. J. *The Alalakh Tablets.* London, 1953.

68. Woolley, C. L. *Alalakh: an Account of the Excavations at Tell Atchana.* Oxford, 1955.
69. Woolley, C. L. *A Forgotten Kingdom.* Harmondsworth, 1953.

II. THE KASSITES AND THEIR NEIGHBOURS

1. Andrae, W. *Das wiedererstandene Assur.* Leipzig, 1938.
2. Balkan, K. *Kassitenstudien. 1. Die Sprache der Kassiten.* American Oriental Society Publ. no. 37. New Haven, 1954.
3. Balkan, K. 'Kas tarihinin ana hatları.' In *Belleten*, 12 (1948), 723 ff.
4. Baqir, Taha. *Iraq Government Excavations at ʿAqar Qūf, 1942–1943.* Supplement to *Iraq*, 1944.
5. Baqir, Taha. *Iraq Government Excavations at ʿAqar Qūf, 1943–1944.* Supplement to *Iraq*, 1945.
6. Baqir, Taha. 'Iraq Government Excavations at ʿAqar Qūf. Third Interim Report, 1944–5.' In *Iraq*, 8 (1946), 73 ff.
7. Bilabel, F. *Geschichte Vorderasiens und Aegyptens vom 16.–11. Jahrhundert v. Chr.* (Bibl. der Klassischen Altertumswissenschaft III, 1). Heidelberg, 1927.
8. Borger, R. *Einleitung in die assyrischen Königsinschriften. Teil I: Das zweite Jahrtausend v. Chr. Handbuch der Orientalistik*, Ergänzungsband V. Leiden, 1961.
9. Cameron, G. G. *History of Early Iran.* Chicago, 1936.
10. Clay, A. T. *Documents from the Temple Archives at Nippur...dated in the reigns of Kassite Rulers* (*B.E.* vols. 14, 15). Philadelphia, 1906.
11. Clay, A. T. *Personal Names of the Cassite Period* (*Y.O.S.* 1). New Haven, 1912.
12. Delitzsch, F. *Die Sprache der Kossäer.* Leipzig, 1904.
13. Delitzsch, F. *Wo lag das Paradies?* Leipzig, 1881.
14. Dougherty. R. P. *The Sealand of Ancient Arabia* (*Y.O.S.* Researches, vol. 19). New Haven, 1932.
15. Ebeling, E. *Bruchstücke einer mittelassyrischen Vorschriftensammlung für die Akklimatisierung und Trainierung von Wagenpferden* (*Deutsche Akademie d. Wissenschaften zu Berlin, Institut für Orientforschung*, Nr 7). Berlin, 1951.
16. Ebeling, E. 'Die Eigennamen der mittelassyrischen Rechts- und Geschäftsurkunden.' In *M.A.O.G.* 13 (1939), Heft 1, 1 ff.
17. Ebeling, E., Meissner, B. and Weidner, E. F. *Die Inschriften der altassyrischen Könige.* Leipzig, 1926.
18. El Wailly, F. 'Synopsis of Royal Sources of the Kassite Period.' In *Sumer*, 10 (1954), 43 ff.
19. Fine, F. A. *Studies in Middle Assyrian Chronology and Religion.* Cincinnati, 1955.
20. Friedrich, J. 'Zum Subaräischen und Urartäischen.' In *An. Or.* 12 (1935), 122 ff.
21. Goetze, A. 'The Kassites and Near Eastern Chronology.' In *J.C.S.* 18 (1964), 97 ff.
22. Güterbock, H. G. 'Die historische Tradition und ihre literarische Gestaltung bei Babyloniern u. Hethitern bis 1200.' In *Z.A.* 44 (1938), 45 ff.
23. Jaritz, K. 'Die kassitischen Sprachreste.' In *Anthropos*, 52 (1957), 850 ff.
24. Jaritz, K. 'Die Kulturreste der Kassiten.' In *Anthropos*, 55 (1960), 17 ff.
25. Jaritz, K. 'Quellen zur Geschichte der Kaššû-Dynastie.' In *Mitt. Inst. Or.* 6 (1958), 187 ff.

26. Jirku, A. *Geschichte Palästina-Syriens im orientalischen Altertum.* Aalen, 1963.
27. King, L. W. *Babylonian Boundary Stones and Memorial Tablets in the British Museum.* London, 1912.
28. King, L. W. *Chronicles concerning Early Babylonian Kings.* 2 vols. London, 1907.
29. King, L. W. *A History of Babylon.* London, 1915.
30. Kraus, F. R. *Wandel und Kontinuität in der sumerisch-babylonischen Kultur.* Leiden, 1954.
31. Landsberger, B. 'Assyrische Königsliste und "dunkles Zeitalter".' In *J.C.S.* 8 (1954), 31 ff., 47 ff., 106 ff.
32. Lewy, H. 'Miscellanea Nuziana 1. An Assyro-Nuzian synchronism.' In *Or.* n.s. 28 (1959), 4 ff.
33. Lewy, H. 'On some problems of Kassite and Assyrian Chronology.' In *Mélanges Isidore Levy* (*Annuaire de l'Institut de Philologie et d'Histoire orientales et slaves,* 13 (1955)), 241 ff.
34. Levy, S. J., Baqir, T. and Kramer, S. N. 'Fragments of a diorite statue of Kurigalzu in the Iraq Museum.' In *Sumer,* 4 (1948), 1 ff.
35. Messerschmidt, L. and Schroeder, O. *Keilschrifttexte aus Assur historischen Inhalts.* 2 vols. Leipzig, 1911 and 1922.
36. Oppenheim, A. L. 'Ein Beitrag zum Kassitenproblem.' In *Miscellanea Orientalia dedicata Antonio Deimel* (*An. Or.* 12, 266 ff.). Rome, 1935.
37. Poebel, A. 'The Assyrian King List from Khorsabad.' In *J.N.E.S.* 1 (1942) 247 ff., 460 ff.; 2 (1943), 56 ff.
38. Radau, H. *Letters to Cassite Kings.* (*B.E.* vol. 17, part 1.) Philadelphia, 1908.
39. Ross, A. D. C. 'A Note on Kassite Phonology.' In *Bull. S.O.A.S.* 8 (1935–7), 1196 ff.
40. Schmidtke, F. *Der Aufbau der babylonischen Chronologie.* Orbis Antiquus, Heft 7. Münster, 1952.
41. Smith, S. 'The chronology of the Kassite dynasty.' In *C.-R. Rencontre assyriol. internat.* 2 (1951), 67 ff.
42. Steinmetzer, Fr. X. *Die babylonische* kudurru (*Grenzsteine*) *als Urkundenform.* Paderborn, 1922.
43. Steinmetzer, Fr. X. *Über die Grundbesitz in Babylonien zur Kassitenzeit. Alte Or.* no. 19, 1/2. Leipzig, 1919.
44. von Soden, W. 'Zweisprachigkeit in der geistigen Kultur Babyloniens.' In *Sitzungsberichte d. deutschen Akad. d. Wiss., phil.-hist. Kl.,* 235 Bd., 1 Abh. (Vienna, 1960), 9 ff.
45. Waschow, H. 'Babylonische Briefe aus der Kassitenzeit.' In *M.A.O.G.* 10, Heft 1. Leipzig, 1936.
46. Weidner, E. F. 'Die grosse Königsliste aus Assur.' In *Arch. f. Or.* 3 (1926), 66 ff.
47. Weissbach, F. H. *Babylonische Miscellen* (*W.V.D.O.G.* 4). Leipzig, 1903.
48. Weissbach, F. H. Art. Κοσσαῖοι. In *P.W.* Bd. 11, col. 1499 ff.
49. Woolley, Sir Leonard. *The Kassite Period and the Period of the Assyrian Kings* (*U.E.* 8). London and Philadelphia, 1965.

III. THE EGYPTIAN CHALLENGE

1. Abel, F.-M. 'Le littoral palestinien et ses ports.' In *Rev. bibl.* 11 (1914), 556 ff.
2. Aharoni, Y. 'Zephath of Thutmose.' In *I.E.J.* 9 (1959), 110 ff.

3. Alt, A. 'Das Institut im Jahre 1928: Die Reise.' In *P.J.B.* 25 (1929), 27 ff.
4. Alt, A. *Kleine Schriften zur Geschichte des Volkes Israel.* 3 vols. Munich, 1959.
5. Alt, A. 'Neue Berichte über Feldzüge von Pharaonen des Neuen Reiches nach Palästina.' In *Z.D.P.V.* 70 (1954), 33 ff.
6. Astour, M. C. 'Place Names from the Kingdom of Alalakh in the North Syrian List of Thutmose III: A Study in Historical Topography.' In *J.N.E.S.* 22 (1963), 220 ff.
7. Boreux, Ch. *Musée National du Louvre; Département des antiquités égyptiennes: Guide-catalogue sommaire.* 2 vols. Paris, 1932.
8. Botti, Giuseppe. 'A Fragment of the Story of a Military Expedition of Tuthmosis III to Syria.' In *J.E.A.* 41 (1955), 64 ff.
9. Braidwood, R. J. 'Report on two sondages on the coast of Syria, south of Tartous.' In *Syria*, 21 (1940), 183 ff.
10. Christophe, L.-A. 'Notes géographiques à propos des campagnes de Thoutmosis III.' In *Rev. d'égyptol.* 6 (1950), 89 ff.
11. Davies, N. de G. *The Tomb of Menkheperrasonb, Amenmose and another (E.E.S., Theban Tombs Series,* no. 5). London, 1932.
12. Drower, M. S. 'The Inscriptions.' In Sir Robert Mond and O. H. Myers, *Temples of Armant*, vol. 1 (*E.E.S., Excavation Memoirs*, 43). London 1940.
13. Dunand, M. and Saliby, N. 'A la recherche de Simyra.' In *Ann. Arch. de Syrie*, 7 (1957), 3 ff.
14. Dunand, M., Bouni, A. and Saliby, N. 'Fouilles de Tell Kazel: Rapport préliminaire.' In *Ann. Arch. de Syrie*, 14 (1964), 3 ff.
15. Erman, Adolf. *Die Literatur der Aegypter.* Leipzig, 1923.
16. Faulkner, R. O. 'The Battle of Megiddo.' In *J.E.A.* 28 (1942), 2 ff.
17. Faulkner, R. O. 'The Euphrates Campaign of Tuthmosis III.' In *J.E.A.* 32 (1946), 39 ff.
18. Février, H. 'Les origines de la marine phénicienne.' In *Revue d'histoire de la philosophie et d'histoire générale de la civilisation*, n.s. fasc. 10 (1935), 97 ff.
19. Fox, Penelope. *Tutankhamun's Treasure.* Oxford, 1951.
20. Gardiner, A. H. 'The Ancient Military Road between Egypt and Palestine.' In *J.E.A.* 6 (1920), 99 ff.
21. Gardiner, A. H. *Late Egyptian Stories. Bibliotheca Aegyptiaca*, 1. Brussels, 1932.
22. Glanville, S. R. K. 'Records of a Royal Dockyard in the time of Tuthmosis III: Papyrus British Museum 10056.' In *Z.Ä.S.* 66 (1931), 105 ff.; 68 (1932), 7 ff.
23. Goetze, A. 'The Syrian Town of Emar.' In *Bull. A.S.O.R.* 147 (1957), 22 ff.
24. Grapow, H. *Studien zu den Annalen Thutmosis des Dritten und zu ihnen verwandten historischen Berichten des Neuen Reiches (Abh. Berlin*, 1947). Berlin, 1949.
25. Hallo, W. 'The Road to Emar.' In *J.C.S.* 18 (1964), 57 ff.
26. Harris, J. R. *Lexicographical Studies in Ancient Egyptian Minerals (Deutsche Akademie der Wissenschaften zu Berlin, Institut für Orientforschung, Veröffentlichung*, Nr 54). Berlin, 1961.
27. Helck, W. *Der Einfluss der Militärführer in der 18. ägyptischen Dynastie (Unters.* 14). Leipzig, 1939.
28. Helck, W. *Urkunden der 18. Dynastie: Übersetzung zu den Heften 17–22.* Berlin, 1961.
29. Kees, H. *Ancient Egypt: A Cultural Topography.* London, 1961.

30. Lucas, A. *Ancient Egyptian Materials and Industries*. Ed. 4, revised by J. R. Harris. London, 1962.
31. Naville, E. *The Temple of Deir el Bahari*. 7 vols. E.E.F. London, 1894–1908.
32. Nelson, H. H. *The Battle of Megiddo*. Chicago, 1913.
33. Noth, M. 'Der Aufbau der Palästinaliste Thutmosis' III.' In *Z.D.P.V.* 61 (1938), 26 ff.
34. Noth, M. 'Die Annalen Thutmosis III als Geschichtsquelle.' In *Z.D.P.V.* 66 (1943), 156 ff.
35. Porter, B. and Moss, R. L. B. *A Topographical Bibliography of ancient Egyptian Hieroglyphic Texts*. 7 vols. Oxford, 1927–51.
36. Reisner, G. A. and Reisner, M. B. 'Inscribed Monuments from Gebel Barkal II: The Granite Stela of Thutmosis III.' In *Z.Ä.S.* 69 (1933), 24 ff.
37. Säve-Söderbergh, T. *The Navy of the Eighteenth Egyptian Dynasty*. *Uppsala Universitets Årsskrift* 1946, 6. Uppsala and Leipzig, 1946.
38. Sethe, K. 'Eine ägyptische Expedition nach dem Libanon im 15. Jahrhundert vor Chr.' In *Sitzungsb. Berlin*, 1906, 356 ff.
39. Simons, J. *The Geographical and Topographical Texts of the Old Testament*. Leiden, 1959.
40. Simons, J. *Handbook for the Study of Egyptian Topographical Lists*. Leiden, 1937.
41. Steindorff, G. and Seele, K. C. *When Egypt Ruled the East*. Ed. 3. Chicago, 1963.
42. Wilson, J. A. *The Culture of Ancient Egypt*. Chicago, 1956.
43. Winlock, H. E. *The Rise and Fall of the Middle Kingdom at Thebes*. New York, 1947.
44. Wreszinski, W. *Atlas zur altägyptischen Kulturgeschichte*. 3 vols. Leipzig, 1923–40.
45. Yeivin, S. 'A New Source for the History of Palestine and Syria.' In *J.P.O.S.* 14 (1934), 194 ff.

IV. THE BALANCE OF POWER

1. Abel, F.-M. *Géographie de la Palestine*. 2 vols. Paris, 1938–67.
2. Aharoni, Y. 'Some geographical remarks concerning the campaigns of Amenhotep II.' In *J.N.E.S.* 19 (1960), 177 ff.
3. Andrae, W. *Die Stelenreihen in Assur* (*W.V.D.O.G.* 24). Leipzig, 1913.
4. Badawi, A. 'Die neue historische Stela Amenophis' II.' In *Ann. Serv.* 42 (1943), 1 ff.
5. Baqir, Taha. 'Aqar-Quf (Dur Kurigalzu).' In *Sumer*, 17 (1961), 3 ff.
6. Carter, H., Newberry, P. E. and Maspero, G. *The Tomb of Thoutmôsis IV* (*Theodore M. Davis' Excavations in Bibân el Molûk*). London, 1904.
7. Edel, E. 'Die Stelen Amenophis' II aus Karnak und Memphis mit dem Bericht über die asiatischen Feldzüge des Königs.' In *Z.D.P.V.* 69 (1953), 97 ff.
8. Forrer, E. 'The Hittites in Palestine.' In *P.E.Q.* 69 (1937), 100 ff.
9. Gadd, C. J. *History and Monuments of Ur*. London, 1929.
10. Gadd, C. J. and Legrain, L. *Royal Inscriptions* (*U.E.T.* 1). London and Philadelphia, 1928.
11. Götze, A. 'Die Pestgebete des Muršiliš.' In *K.F.* 1 (1929), 204 ff.
12. Gurney, O. *The Hittites*. Ed. 2. Harmondsworth, 1964.

13. Güterbock, H. G. 'The Deeds of Suppiluliuma as told by his son, Mursili II.' In *J.C.S.* 10 (1956), 41 ff., 75 ff., 107 ff.
14. Hassan, Selim. 'The Great Limestone Stela of Amenhotep II.' In *Ann. Serv.* 37 (1937), 129 ff.
15. Hickmann, H. 'Ägypten und Vorderasien im musikalischen Austausch.' In *Z.D.M.G.* 111 (1961), 23 ff.
16. Jaritz, K. 'The Kassite King Ātanaḫ-Šamaš.' In *J.S.S.* 2 (1957), 321 ff.
17. Jordan, J. 'Die Innin-Tempel Karaindasch's.' In *Abh. Berlin*, 1st Prelim. Report, 31 ff. Berlin, 1939.
18. Kitchen, K. 'Theban Topographical Lists, Old and New.' In *Or.* n.s. 34 (1965), 1 ff.
19. Kuschke, A. 'Beiträge zur Siedlungsgeschichte der Bika.' In *Z.D.P.V.* 70 (1954), 104 ff.; 74 (1958), 81 ff.
20. Maisler, B. 'Die westliche Linie des Meerweges.' In *Z.D.P.V.* 58 (1935), 78 ff.
21. Oppenheim, A. L. 'Etude sur la topographie de Nuzi.' In *R.A.* 35 (1938), 136 ff.
22. Scheil, V. 'Documents et Arguments.' In *R.A.* 26 (1929), 1 ff.
23. Ungnad, A. 'Schenkungsurkunde des Kurigalzu mâr Kadašman-Ḫarbe.' In *Arch. f. Keil.* 1 (1923), 29 ff.
24. Varille, A. 'Nouvelles Listes géographiques d'Amenophis III à Karnak.' In *Ann. Serv.* 36 (1936), 202 ff.
25. Von der Osten, H. H. *Svenska Syrenexpedition 1952–53: I. Die Grabung von Tell es-Salihiyeh.* Lund, 1956.
26. Vikentiev, V. 'La traversée de l'Oronte.' In *Bull. Inst. d'Ég.* 30 (1949), 251 ff.

V. THE EGYPTIANS IN RETENU

1. Aharoni, Y. 'The Land of 'Amqi.' In *I.E.J.* 3 (1953), 153 ff.
2. Albright, W. F. *The Archaeology of Palestine.* Revised ed. Harmondsworth, 1960.
3. Albright, W. F. 'The chronology of a South Palestinian city, Tell el-'Ajjūl.' In *A.J.S.L.* 55 (1938), 337 ff.
4. Albright, W. F. 'Cuneiform Material for Egyptian Prosopography.' In *J.N.E.S.* 5 (1946), 7 ff.
5. Albright, W. F. 'Egypt and the early history of the Negeb.' In *J.P.O.S.* 4 (1924), 131 ff.
6. Albright, W. F. 'The Excavation of Tell Beit Mirsim: II. The Bronze Age.' In *Ann. A.S.O.R.* 17 (1938).
7. Albright, W. F. 'An unrecognised Amarna Letter from Ugarit.' In *Bull. A.S.O.R.* 95 (1944), 30 ff.
8. Albright, W. F. *Yahweh and the Gods of Canaan.* London, 1968.
9. Albright, W. F. and Rowe, Alan. 'A Royal Stele of the New Empire from Galilee.' In *J.E.A.* 14 (1928), 281 ff.
10. Burchardt, Max. *Die altkanaanäischen Fremdworte und Eigennamen im Ägyptischen.* 2 vols. Leipzig, 1909, 1910.
11. Davies, Nina M. and Davies, N. de G. 'The Tomb of Amenmose.' In *J.E.A.* 26 (1914), 131 ff.
12. Davies, N. de G. *The Rock Tombs of El-Amarna* (E.E.S. *Archaeological Survey of Egypt*, Memoirs 13–18). 6 vols. London, 1903–8.
13. Davies, N. de G. *The Tomb of Rekh-mi-Reʿ at Thebes* (*Pub. M.M.A.E.E.* 11). New York, 1943.

14. Davies, N. de G. *The Tombs of Two Officials of Tuthmosis the Fourth* (*E.E.S.*, *Theban Tombs Series*, no. 3). London, 1923.
15. Dunand, M. *Fouilles de Byblos*. 2 vols. Paris, 1939, 1954–8.
16. Edwards, I. E. S. 'A Relief of Qudshu-Astarte-Anath in the Winchester College Collection.' In *J.N.E.S* 15 (1955), 49 ff.
17. Farmer, H. G. 'The Music of Ancient Egypt.' In *The Oxford History of Music: I. Ancient and Oriental Music*, 255 ff. Ed. E. Wellesz. London/ New York/Toronto, 1957.
18. Faulkner, R. O. 'A Syrian Trading Venture to Egypt.' In *J.E.A.* 33 (1947), 40 ff.
19. Gardiner, A. H. *Egyptian Hieratic Texts I, Literary Texts of the New Kingdom: Part I. The Papyrus Anastasi and the Papyrus Koller*. Leipzig, 1911.
20. Gardiner, A. H. 'Thutmosis III returns Thanks to Amun.' In *J.E.A.* 38 (1952), 6 ff.
21. Grdseloff, B. *Les débuts du culte de Rechef en Égypte*. Cairo, 1940.
22. Hayes, W. C. *The Scepter of Egypt: A Background for the Study of the Egyptian Antiquities in the Metropolitan Museum of Art*. 2 vols. Cambridge, Mass. 1953, 1959.
23. Helck, W. 'Die ägyptische Verwaltung in den syrischen Besitzungen.' In *M.D.O.G.* 92 (1960), 1 ff.
24. Hickmann, H. Art. 'Ägyptische Musik' in *Allgemeine Enzyklopädie der Musik*, cols. 92–6. Kassel and Basel, 1949.
25. Horn, S. H. 'Scarabs from Shechem.' In *J.N.E.S.* 21 (1962), 1 ff.
26. Janssen, Jac. J. 'Eine Beuteliste von Amenophis II.' In *J.E.O.L.* 17 (1963), 141 ff.
27. Kenyon, K. M. *Archaeology in the Holy Land*. London, 1961.
28. Klebs, Luise. *Reliefs und Malereien des neuen Reiches, I: Szenen aus dem Leben des Volkes* (*Abh. Heidelberg*, 9). Heidelberg, 1934.
29. Lambdin, T. O. 'The *Miši* people of the Byblian Amarna Letters.' In *J.C.S.* 7 (1953), 75 ff.
30. Leclant, J. 'Astarté à cheval d'après les représentations égyptiennes.' In *Syria*, 37 (1960), 1 ff.
31. Leclant, J. 'Découverte de monuments égyptiens ou égyptisants hors de la vallée du Nil, 1955–1960.' In *Or.* n.s. 30 (1961), 391 ff.
32. Loud, Gordon. *Megiddo II: Seasons of 1935–39* (*O.I.P.* 62). Chicago,1948.
33. Montet, P. *Byblos et l'Egypte: Quatre campagnes de fouilles à Gebeil*, 1921, 1922, 1923, 1924. 2 vols. Paris, 1928.
34. Munn-Rankin, J. M. 'Diplomacy in Western Asia in the Early Second Millennium B.C.' In *Iraq*, 18 (1956), 68 ff.
35. Muhammad, M. Abdul Kader. 'The administration of Syro-Palestine during the New Kingdom.' In *Ann. Serv.* 56 (1959), 105 ff.
36. Petrie, W. M. F. *Ancient Gaza* (*Tell el-Ajjul*) (*Publ. of the Eg. Research Acct. and School of Archaeology in Egypt*). 4 parts. London, 1931–4.
37. Petrie, W. M. F. *Tell el Amarna*. London, 1894.
38. Pritchard, J. B. *The Bronze Age Cemetery at Gibeon* (*University of Pennsylvania, Museum Monographs*). Philadelphia, 1963.
39. Rowe, A. *A Catalogue of Scarabs in the Palestine Archaeological Museum*. Cairo, 1936.
40. Rowe, A. *The History and Topography of Beth-Shan*. Philadelphia, 1930.
41. Säve-Söderbergh, T. *Ägypten und Nubien: Ein Beitrag zur Geschichte altägyptischer Aussenpolitik*. Lund, 1941.

42. Schulman, A. *Military Rank, Title and Organisation in the Egyptian New Kingdom* (*Münchener aegyptologische Studien*, 6). Munich, 1966.
43. Simpson, W. K. 'Reshep in Egypt.' In *Or.* n.s. 29 (1960), 63 ff.
44. Smith, Sidney and Gadd, C. J. 'A Cuneiform Vocabulary of Egyptian Words.' In *J.E.A.* 11 (1925), 230 ff.
45. Spiegelberg, W. 'Grabstein eines syrischen Söldners aus Tell Amarna.' In *Z.Ä.S.* 36 (1898), 126 ff.
46. Tufnell, O. *Lachish IV: The Bronze Age.* London, 1958.
47. Vandier, J. *La religion égyptienne* ('*Mana*': *Introduction à l'histoire des religions: I. Les anciennes religions orientales*, 1). Ed. 2. Paris, 1949.
48. Winlock, H. E. *The Treasure of Three Egyptian Princesses* (*Publ. M.M.A., Department of Egyptian Art*, 20). New York, 1948.
49. Woolley, C. L. 'The Egyptian Temple at Byblos.' In *J.E.A.* 7 (1921), 200 ff.
50. Yadin, Y., Aharoni, Y., Amiran, R. and others. *Hazor: The James A. Rothschild Expedition at Hazor.* 4 vols. Jerusalem, 1958–65.
51. Yeivin, S. 'The Third District in Tuthmosis III's List of Palestino-Syrian Towns.' In *J.E.A.* 36 (1950), 51 ff.

VI. THE AMARNA AGE

1. Albright, W. F. 'The Egyptian Correspondence of Abi-Milki, Prince of Tyre.' In *J.E.A.* 23 (1937), 190 ff.
2. Astour, M. 'Second Millennium B.C. Cypriot and Cretan Onomastica Reconsidered.' In *J.A.O.S.* 84 (1964), 241 ff.
3. Bass, G. F. *Cape Gelidoniya: a Bronze Age Shipwreck* (*Trans. Am. Philosoph. Soc.* n.s. 57, part 8). Philadelphia, 1967.
4. Buchholz, H.-G. 'Der Kupferhandel des zweiten vorchristlichen Jahrtausends im Spiegel der Schriftforschung.' In *Minoica: Festschrift zum 80. Geburtstag von Joh. Sundwall*, 92 ff. Berlin, 1958.
5. Campbell, E. F. *The Chronology of the Amarna Letters.* Baltimore, 1964.
6. Carter, Howard and Mace, A. C. *The Tomb of Tut-ankh-Amen.* 3 vols. London, New York, Toronto and Melbourne, 1923.
7. Casson, S. A. *Ancient Cyprus, its art and archaeology.* London, 1937.
8. Černý, J. *Ancient Egyptian Religion.* London, 1952.
9. Dossin, G. 'Une nouvelle lettre d'El-Amarna.' In *R.A.* 31 (1934), 125 ff.
10. Edzard, D. O. 'Die Beziehungen Babyloniens und Ägyptens in der mittelbabylonischen Zeit und das Gold.' In *J.E.S.H.O.* 3 (1960), 38 ff.
11. Eissfeldt, O. 'Die Ausgrabungen in Ras Shamra.' In *Arch. f. Or.* 14 (1941–4), 371 ff.
12. Eissfeldt, O. *Kleine Schriften* (eds. R. Sellheim and F. Maass). 3 vols. Tübingen, 1962–6.
13. Engelbach, R. 'A 'Kirgipa' commemorative scarab of Amenophis III presented by H.M. King Farouk I to the Cairo Museum.' In *Ann. Serv.* 40 (1941), 659 ff.
14. Epstein, Clare. *Palestinian Bichrome Ware.* Leiden, 1966.
15. Hall, H. R. 'Egypt and the External World in the Time of Akhenaten.' In *J.E.A.* 7 (1921), 39 ff.
16. Hill, Sir George. *A History of Cyprus.* 4 vols. Cambridge, 1940–52.
17. Kitchen, K. A. 'Aegean Place-names in a List of Amenophis III.' In *Bull. A.S.O.R.* 181 (1966), 23 f.

18. Kitchen, K. A. *Suppiluliuma and the Amarna Pharaohs. A Study in Relative Chronology* (*Liverpool monographs in Archaeology and Oriental Studies*). Liverpool, 1962.

19. Knudtzon, J. A. 'Weitere Studien zu den El-Amarna Tafeln.' In *B.A.* 4 (1899), 279 ff.

20. Knudtzon, J. A. *Die zwei Arzawa-briefe: die ältesten Urkunden in Indogermanischer Sprache.* Leipzig, 1902.

21. Korošec, V. *Hethitische Staatsverträge* (*Leipziger Rechtswissenschaftliche Studien*, Heft 60). Leipzig, 1931.

22. Korošec, V. 'Les Hittites et leurs vassaux syriens à la lumière des nouveaux textes d'Ugarit' (*P.R.U.* iv). In *R.H.A.* 66 (1960), 65 ff.

23. Kühne, Cord. 'Zum Status der Syro-Palästinischen Vassalen des Neuen Reiches.' In *Andrews University Seminary Studies* i (Mich., U.S.A., 1963), 71 ff.

24. Meissner, B. and von Soden, W. *Akkadisches Handwörterbuch.* Wiesbaden, 1959-.

25. Mercer, S. A. B. *The Tell-el-Amarna Tablets.* 2 vols. Toronto, 1939.

26. Müller, W. Max. 'Das Land Alašia.' In *Z.Ä.* 10 (1895), 257 ff.

27. Nougayrol, J. 'Guerre et Paix à Ugarit.' In *Iraq*, 25 (1963), 110 ff.

28. Oberhummer, E. Art. 'Kypros' in *P.W.* 23, 59 ff.

29. Peet, T. E. and Woolley, C. L. and others. *The City of Akhenaten*, i–iii (*E.E.S.*, *Excavation Memoirs* 38, 40 and 44). London, 1923, 1933, 1951.

30. *P.R.U. Le Palais Royal d'Ugarit*, ii–v (*Mission de Ras Shamra*, vii, vi, ix, xi). Ed. C. F. A. Schaeffer. Paris, 1957–65.

31. Quiring, H. 'Die Abkunft des Tutankhamon.' In *Klio*, 38 (1960), 53 ff.

32. Quiring, H. 'Vorphönizischer Königspurpur und *uqnû*-Stein.' In *Forsch. u. Fortschr.* 21–23 (1945–7), 98 ff.

33. Ranke, H. 'Istar als Heilgöttin in Ägypten.' In *Studies presented to F. Ll. Griffith*, 412 ff. London, 1932.

34. Riedel, W. 'Das Archiv Amenophis' IV.' In *O.L.Z.* 42 (1934), 145 ff.

35. Riedel, W. *Untersuchungen zu den Amarna-Briefen.* Tübingen, 1920.

36. Rost, L. 'Die ausserhalb von Bogazköy gefundene hethitische Briefe.' In *Mitt. Inst. Or.* 4 (1956), 328 ff., 334 ff.

37. Sayce, A. H. 'The Discovery of the Tell el Amarna Tablets.' In *A.J.S.L.* 33 (1917), 89 f.

38. Schachermeyr, F. 'Zum ältesten Namen von Kypros.' In *Klio*, 17 (1921), 230 ff.

39. Schaeffer, C. F. A. *Enkomi-Alasia: nouvelles missions en Chypre.* Paris, 1952.

40. Singer, C., Holmyard, E. J. and Hall, A. R. *A History of Technology*, vol. i. Oxford, 1955.

41. Stadelmann, R. *Syrisch-palestinensische Gottheiten in Aegypten* (Probleme der Ägyptologie, 5). Leiden, 1967.

42. Van der Meer, P. 'The Chronological Determination of the Mesopotamian Letters in the El-Amarna Archives.' In *J.E.O.L.* 15 (1957–8), 74 ff.

43. Virolleaud, C. 'Les Inscriptions cunéiformes de Ras Shamra.' In *Syria*, 10 (1929), 304 ff.

44. Virolleaud, C. 'Lettres et documents administratifs de Ras Shamra V: Les fouilles et la ville d'Alašia.' In *Syria*, 21 (1940), 267 ff.

45. von Soden, W. 'Zu den Amarnabriefen aus Babylon und Assur.' In *Or.* n.s. 21 (1952), 426 ff.

46. Wainwright, G. 'Alashia = Alasa; and Asy.' In *Klio*, 14 (1915), 1 ff.

47. Wright, G. E. 'The Archaeology of Palestine.' In *The Bible and the Ancient Near East: Essays in Honor of William Foxwell Albright*, 73 ff. London, 1961.

VII. WARFARE AND SOCIETY

1. Albright, W. F. 'Abram the Hebrew. A New Archaeological Interpretation.' In *Bull. A.S.O.R.* 163 (1961), 36 ff.
2. Albright, W. F. 'Syrien, Phönizien und Palästina.' In *Historia Mundi*, ed. Fritz Kern, II: *Grundlagen und Entfaltung der ältesten Hochkulturen*, 331 ff. Bern, 1953.
3. Albright, W. F. 'Two letters from Ugarit.' In *Bull. A.S.O.R.* 82 (1941), 43 ff.
4. Alt, A. 'Bemerkungen zu den Verwaltungsurkunden von Ugarit und Alalakh.' In *We. Or.* II (1957), 7 ff., 234 ff., 338 ff.
5. *A.R.M.T.* Les *Archives Royales de Mari* (texts in transliteration and translation), I–IX. Paris, 1950–60.
6. Astour, M. 'Les étrangers à Ugarit et le status juridique des Ḫabiru.' In *R.A.* 53 (1959), 70 ff.
7. Bittel, K., Heere, W. and Otten, H. 'Die hethitischen Grabfünde von Osman-kayasi.' In *Boğazköy–Ḫattusa*, II, 60 ff. Berlin, 1958.
8. Bottéro, J. *Le Problème des Ḫabiru*. Paris, 1954.
9. Cassin, E. *L'adoption à Nuzi*. Paris, 1958.
10. Cazelles, H. 'Hébreux, Ubru et Ḫapiru.' In *Syria*, 35 (1958), 198 ff.
11. Davies, N. de G. and Gardiner, A. H. *The Tomb of Huy, Viceroy of Nubia in the reign of Tut'ankhamūn* (no. 40) (*E.E.S.*, *Theban Tombs Series*, no. 4). London, 1926.
12. Driver, G. R. *Canaanite Myths and Legends*. Edinburgh, 1956.
13. Dussaud, R. *Les Découvertes de Ras Shamra (Ugarit) et l'Ancien Testament*. Ed. 2. Paris, 1941.
14. Ebert, Max (ed.) *Reallexikon der Vorgeschichte*. 13 vols. Berlin, 1927–8.
15. Evans, G. '"Gates" and "Streets": Urban Institutions in Old Testament Times.' In *J.R.H.* 2 (1962), 1 ff.
16. Goetze, A. 'Warfare in Asia Minor.' In *Iraq*, 25 (1963), 124 ff.
17. Gordon, C. H. 'The Dialect of the Nuzu Tablets.' In *Or.* n.s. 7 (1938), 215 ff.
18. Gordon, C. H. 'Nuzu Tablets relating to theft.' In *Or.* n.s. 5 (1936), 305 ff.
19. Gordon, C. H. 'Observations on the Akkadian Tablets from Ugarit.' In *R.A.* 50 (1956), 127 ff.
20. Gordon, C. H. 'Parallèles nouziens aux lois et coutumes de l'Ancien Testament.' In *Rev. bibl.* 44 (1925), 34 ff.
21. Gordon, C. H. 'The Status of Woman Reflected in the Nuzi Tablets.' In *Z.A.* 43 (1936), 146 ff.
22. Gordon, C. H. and Lacheman, E. R. 'The Nuzu menology.' In *Arch. Orient.* 10 (1938), 51 ff.
23. Gordon, D. H. 'Swords, Rapiers and Horseriders.' In *Antiq.* 27 (1953), 67 ff.
24. Gordon, M. B. 'The hippiatric texts from Ugarit.' In *Annals of Medical History*, 4 (1942), 406 ff.
25. Gray, John. *The Canaanites* (*Ancient Peoples and Places*, vol. 38). London, 1964.
26. Gray, John. 'Feudalism in Ugarit and Ancient Israel.' In *Z.A.W.* 64 (1952), 49 ff.

27. Gray, M. P. 'The Ḫâbiru-Hebrew Problem in the Light of the Source Material available at present.' In *H.U.C.A.* 29 (1958), 135 ff.

28. Hančar, Fr. *Das Pferd in prähistorischer und früher historischer Zeit.* Vienna, 1955.

29. Hanfmann, G. M. A. 'A Near Eastern Horseman.' In *Syria*, 38 (1961), 243 ff.

30. Hutchinson, R. W. *Prehistoric Crete.* Harmondsworth, 1962.

31. Kammenhuber, A. *Hippologia Hethitica.* Wiesbaden, 1961.

32. Kinal, F. 'Zur Geschichte der Zähmung des Pferdes im alten Vorderasien.' In *Belleten*, 17 (no. 66, 1953), 193 ff.

33. Klíma, Josef. 'Die Stellung der ugaritischen Frau.' In *Arch. Orient.* 25 (1957), 313 ff.

34. Klíma, Josef. 'Untersuchungen zum ugaritischen Erbrecht.' In *Arch. Orient.* 24 (1956), 356 ff.

35. Korošeč, V. 'Keilschriftrecht.' In *Handbuch der Orientalistik*, ed. B. Spuler, I, Ergänzungsband III: Orientalisches Recht. 49 ff. Leiden, 1964.

36. Koschaker, P. 'Drei Rechtsurkunden aus Arrapḫa.' In *Z.A.* 48 (1944), 161 ff.

37. Koschaker, P. 'Neue keilschriftliche Rechtsurkunden aus der el-Amarna Zeit.' *Abh. Leipzig* 39, no. 5. Leipzig, 1928.

38. Lewy, H. 'The Nuzian feudal system.' In *Or.* 11 (1942), 1 ff., 209 ff., 297 ff.

39. Liverani, M. *La Storia di Ugarit nell' età degli archivi politici (Studi Semitici,* 6). Rome, 1962.

40. Lorimer, H. L. *Homer and the Monuments.* Oxford, 1950.

41. Maag, V. 'Syrien-Palästina.' In *Kulturgeschichte des Alten Orients*, ed. H. Schmökel, 448 ff. Stuttgart, 1961.

42. McEwan, C. W. (*et al.*). *Soundings at Tell Fakhariyah.* O.I.P. 79. Chicago, 1958.

43. Mallowan, M. E. L. 'The Excavations at Tall Chagar Bazar and an Archaeological Survey of the Habur region: Second Campaign, 1936.' In *Iraq*, 4 (1937), 91 ff.

44. Mellink, Machteld. 'A Hittite Figurine from Nuzi.' In *Vorderasiatische Archäologie: Studien u. Aufsätze* (Festschrift A. Moortgat), ed. K. Bittel, W. Heinrich, B. Hrouda and W. Nagel. Berlin, 1965.

45. Mendelsohn, I. 'New Light on the Ḫupšu.' In *Bull. A.S.O.R.* 139 (1955), 9 ff.

46. Mendelsohn, I. 'On Corvée Labor in Ancient Canaan and Israel.' In *Bull. A.S.O.R.* 167 (1962), 31 ff.

47. Mendelsohn, I. 'On Slavery in Alalakh.' In *I.E.J.* 5 (1955), 65 ff.

48. Mendelsohn, I. 'Samuel's Denunciation of Kingship in the Light of the Akkadian Documents from Ugarit.' In *Bull. A.S.O.R.* 143 (1956), 17 ff.

49. Mendelsohn, I. *Slavery in the Ancient Near East.* New York, 1949.

50. Moscati, S. *Historical Art in the Ancient Near East (Studi Semitici,* 8). Rome, 1963.

51. Pfeiffer, R. *The Archives of Shilwateshub, Son of the King.* Harvard Semitic Studies, IX (*Excavations at Nuzi*, II). Cambridge, Mass. 1932.

52. Piggott, Stuart. *Prehistoric India, to 1000 B.C.* Harmondsworth, 1950.

53. Pritchard, J. B. 'Syrians as pictured in the paintings of the Theban Tombs.' In *Bull. A.S.O.R.* 122 (1951), 36 ff.

54. Purves, P. M. 'A commentary on Nuzi real property in the light of recent studies.' In *J.N.E.S.* 4 (1945), 68 ff.

55. Rainey, A. F. 'Family Relationships in Ugarit.' In *Or.* n.s. 34 (1965), 10 ff.
56. Rainey, A. F. 'The Military Personnel of Ugarit.' In *J.N.E.S.* 24 (1965), 17 ff.
57. Salonen, A. *Hippologia Accadica. Suomalaisen Tiedeakatemian Toimituksia,* Sarja–Ser. B nide–Tom. 100. Helsinki, 1956.
58. Salonen, A. *Die Landfahrzeuge des alten Mesopotamien nach sumerisch-akkadischen Quellen. Suomalaisen Tiedeakatemian Toimituksia,* Sarja–Ser. B nide–Tom. 72, 3. Helsinki, 1951.
59. Schachermeyr, F. 'Streitwagen und Streitwagenbild im alten Orient und bei den mykenischen Griechen.' In *Anthropos,* 46 (1951), 705 ff.
60. Speiser, E. A. 'New Kirkuk Tablets relating to Family Laws.' In *Ann. A.S.O.R.* 10 (1928–9), 1 ff.
61. Starr, R. F. S. *Nuzi. Report on the Excavations at Yorghan Tepa near Kirkuk.* 2 vols. (text and plates). Cambridge, Mass. 1937–39.
62. Steele, F. R. *Nuzi Real Estate Transactions (A.O.S.* 25). Philadelphia, 1943.
63. Sukenik, Y. 'The composite bow of the Canaanite goddess Anath.' In *Bull. A.S.O.R.* 107 (1947). 11 ff.
64. Thureau-Dangin, F. 'Trois contrats de Ras-Shamra.' In *Syria,* 18 (1937), 246 ff.
65. Toombs, L. E. and Wright, G. E. 'The Fourth Campaign at Balâṭah (Shechem).' In *Bull. A.S.O.R.* 169 (1963), 1 ff.
66. van Liere, W. J. 'Capitals and citadels of Bronze and Iron Age Syria in their relationship to Land and Water.' In *Ann. Arch. de Syrie,* 13 (1963), 109 ff.
67. van Selms, A. *Marriage and Family Life in Ugaritic Literature.* London, 1954.
68. Virolleaud, Ch. 'Cinq tablettes accadiennes de Ras-Shamra.' In *R.A.* 38 (1941), 1 ff.
69. Virolleaud, Ch. 'Fragments d'un traité phénicien de thérapeutique hippologique.' In *Syria,* 15 (1934), 75 ff.
70. Virolleaud, Ch. 'Les villes et les corporations du royaume d'Ugarit.' In *Syria,* 21 (1940), 123 ff.
71. Woolley, C. L. (*et al.*). *Carchemish: Report on the excavations on behalf of the British Museum.* 3 vols. London, 1921–52.
72. Yadin, Y. *The Art of Warfare in Biblical Lands in the Light of Archaeological Discovery.* London, 1963.
73. Yadin, Y. 'Hyksos Fortifications and the Battering Ram.' In *Bull. A.S.O.R.* 137 (1955), 23 ff.
74. Yeivin, S. 'Canaanite and Hittite Strategy in the Second Half of the Second Millennium B.C.' In *J.N.E.S.* 9 (1950), 101 ff.
75. Zeuner, F. *A History of Domesticated Animals.* London, 1963.

VIII. COMMERCE AND INDUSTRY

1. Albright, W. F. *The Proto-Sinaitic Inscriptions and their Decipherment (Harvard Theol. Studies,* 22). Cambridge, Mass., 1966.
2. Albright, W. F. *The Vocalization of the Egyptian Syllabic Orthography (A.O.S.* 5). New Haven, 1934.
3. Anati, E. *Palestine before the Hebrews.* London, 1963.
4. Andrae, W. *Die jüngere Ischtartempel in Assur (W.V.D.O.G.* 58). Leipzig, 1935.
5. Astour, M. 'New Evidence on the Last Days of Ugarit.' In *A.J.A.* 69 (1965), 253 ff.

6. Astour, M. 'The Origins of the terms "Canaan", "Phoenician" and "Purple".' In *J.N.E.S.* 24 (1965), 346 ff.
7. Barnett, R. D. *A Catalogue of the Nimrud Ivories*. London, 1957.
8. Barnett, R. D. 'Early Shipping in the Near East.' In *Antiq.* 32 (1958), 220 ff.
9. Barnett, R. D. 'Phoenician and Syrian Ivory-carving.' In *P.E.Q.* 1939, 4 ff.
10. Barrois, A. G. *Manuel d'archéologie biblique*. 2 vols. Paris, 1939, 1953.
11. Bauer, Hans. *Der Ursprung des Alphabets (Alte Or.* 36 Bd. 1/2). Leipzig, 1937.
12. Bossert, H. *Alt-Syrien*. Tübingen, 1951.
13. Brentjes, B. 'Der Elefant im alten Orient.' In *Klio*, 39 (1961), 8 ff.
14. Buchholz, H. G. 'Keftiubarren u. Erzhandel im zweiten vorchristlichen Jahrtausend.' In *Prähist. Zeitschr.* 37 (1959), 1 ff.
15. Cassin, E. 'Nouvelles données sur les relations familières à Nuzi.' In *R.A.* 53 (1963), 113 ff.
16. Černý, J. 'Semites in Egyptian Mining Expeditions to Sinai.' In *Arch. Or.* 7 (1935), 384 ff.
17. Charlesworth, M. P. *Trade Routes and Commerce of the Roman Empire*. Ed. 2. Cambridge, 1926.
18. Childe, V. G. 'The Final Bronze Age in the Near East and in Temperate Europe.' In *P.P.S.* n.s. 14 (1948), 177 ff.
19. Contenau, G. 'Drogues de Canaan, d'Amurru et jardins botaniques.' In *Mél. Dussaud*, vol. 1 (1939), 11 ff.
20. Cross, D. *Movable Property in the Nuzi Documents (A.O.S.* 10). New Haven, 1937.
21. Cross, F. M. and Lambdin, Thos. O. 'An Ugaritic Abecedary and the Origins of the Proto-Canaanite Script.' In *Bull. A.S.O.R.* 160 (1960), 21 ff.
22. Culican, W. *The First Merchant Venturers*. London, 1966.
23. Dhorme, E. 'Le déchiffrement des inscriptions pseudo-hiéroglyphiques de Byblos.' In *Syria*, 25 (1946–8), 1 ff.
24. Diringer, D. *The Alphabet*. Ed. 2. London, 1949.
25. Driver, G. R. *Semitic Writing: From Pictograph to Alphabet* (Schweich Lectures of the British Academy, 1944). London, 1948.
26. Dunand, M. *Byblia Grammata: Documents et recherches sur le développement de l'écriture en Phénicie*. Paris, 1945.
27. Edel, E. 'Neues Material zur Beurteilung der syllabischen Orthographie des Aegyptischen.' In *J.N.E.S.* 8 (1949), 44 ff.
28. Edgerton, W. F. 'Egyptian Phonetic Writing from its invention to the close of the Nineteenth Dynasty.' In *J.A.O.S.* 60 (1940), 473 ff.
29. Evans, Sir Arthur. *The Palace of Minos*. 5 vols. London, 1921–35.
30. Faulkner, R. O. 'Egyptian Seagoing Ships.' In *J.E.A.* 26 (1941), 3 ff.
31. Février, J. G. 'Les origines de la marine phénicienne.' In *Rev. d'histoire de la philosophie et d'histoire générale de la civilisation*, 3 (1935), 97 ff.
32. Flight, J. W. 'The History of Writing in the Near East.' In *The Haverford Symposium on Archaeology and the Bible*, 111 ff., 1938.
33. Forbes, R. J. *Studies in Ancient Technology*. 9 vols. Leiden 1955–1964.
34. Frankfort, H. 'The Origin of the Bit-Ḫilani.' In *Iraq*, 14 (1952), 120 ff.
35. Frost, Honor. 'Rouad, ses récifs et mouillages: prospection sous-marine.' In *Ann. Arch. de Syrie*, 14 (1964), 66 ff.
36. Frost, Honor. *Under the Mediterranean*. London, 1963.
37. Gardiner, A. H. 'The Egyptian Origin of the Semitic Alphabet.' In *J.E.A.* 3 (1916), 5 ff.

38. Gardiner, Sir Alan. 'Once again the Proto-Sinaitic Inscriptions.' In *J.E.A.* 48 1962, 45 ff.
39. Gardiner, A. H., Peet, T. E. and Černý, J. *The Inscriptions of Sinai.* Ed. 2. (*E.E.S., Excavation Memoirs,* 45.) 2 vols. London, 1952, 1955.
40. Garelli, P. *Les Assyriens en Cappadoce* (*Bibliothèque archéologique et historique de l'Institut français d'archéol. d'Istanbul,* xix). Paris, 1963.
41. Gelb, I. J. *A Study of Writing.* London, 1952.
42. Goetze, A. and Levy, S. 'Fragment of the Gilgamesh Epic from Megiddo.' In '*Atiqot,* 2 (1959), 121 ff.
43. Gordon, Cyrus H. 'The Ugaritic "ABC".' In *Or.* n.s. 19 (1950), 374 ff.
44. Hamilton, R.W. 'Excavations at Tell Abu Hawām.' In *Q.D.A.P.* 8 (1938), 21 ff.
45. Harris, Zellig S. *A Grammar of the Phoenician Language* (*Amer. Oriental Society,* vol. 8). 1936.
46. Herdner, A. 'A-t-il existé une variété palestinienne de l'écriture cunéiforme alphabétique?' In *Syria,* 25 (1946–8), 165 ff.
47. Heurtley, W. A. 'A Palestinian Vase-Painter of the Sixteenth Century B.c.' In *Q.D.A.P.* 8 (1938), 21 ff.
48. Hillers, D. R. 'An alphabetic cuneiform inscription from Taanach.' In *Bull. A.S.O.R.* 173 (1964), 45 ff.
49. Hrouda, Barthel. *Die bemalte Keramik des zweiten Jahrtausends in Nord-mesopotamien und Nordsyrien* (*Abteilung Istanbul d. deutschen archaeol. Instituts: Istanbuler Forschungen,* 19). Berlin, 1957.
50. Jensen, L. B. 'Royal Purple of Tyre.' In *J.N.E.S.* 22 (1963), 104 ff.
51. Kantor, H. 'The Aegean and the Orient in the Second Millennium B.c.' In *A.J.A.* 51 (1947), 1 ff.
52. Landsberger, B. *Sam'al: Studien zur Entdeckung der Ruinenstaette Karatepe* (Turkish Historical Soc. Publ. vii ser., no. 16). Ankara, 1948.
53. Leemans, W. F. *Foreign Trade in the Old Babylonian Period* (*Studi et documenta ad iura orientalia antiqui pertinentia,* 6). Leiden, 1960.
54. Lehmann-Hartleben, K. 'Die antiken Hafenanlagen des Mittelmeeres.' In *Klio,* 14 (1923), 43 ff.
55. Loud, G. *The Megiddo Ivories* (O.I.P. 52). Chicago, 1939.
56. Mallon, A. 'L'origine égyptienne de l'alphabet phénicien.' In *B.I.F.A.O.* 30 (1931), 131 ff.
57. Mallowan, M. E. L. 'White-painted Subartu Pottery.' In *Mél. Dussaud,* vol. 2 (1939), 891 ff.
58. Merrillees, R. 'Opium Trade in the Bronze Age Levant.' In *Antiq.* 36 (1962), 287 ff.
59. Nougayrol, J. 'Nouveaux textes accadiens de Ras-Shamra.' In *C.-R. Ac. Inscr. B.-L.* 163 ff., 1960.
60. Otten, H. 'Neue Quellen zum Ausklang des Hethitischen Reiches.' In *M.D.O.G.* 94 (1963), 1 ff.
61. Platon, N. and Stassinopoulou-Touloupa, E. 'Oriental Seals from the Palace of Cadmus: unique discoveries in Boeotian Thebes.' In *Ill. Ldn News,* 28 Nov. 1964, 859 ff.
62. Poidebard, A. *Un grand port disparu: Recherches aériennes et sous-marines,* 1934–1936. Paris, 1939.
63. Rainey, A. F. 'Foreign Business Agents in Ugarit.' In *I.E.J.* 4 (1963), 313 ff.
64. Revere, R. B. '"No Man's Coast": Ports of Trade in the Eastern Mediter-ranean.' In *Trade and Market in the Early Empires,* ed. K. Polanyi, C. M. Arensberg and Harry W. Pearson. Glencoe, Ill., 1957.

65. Riefstahl, E. *Patterned Textiles in Pharaonic Egypt.* Brooklyn Museum, 1944.
66. Sasson, J. 'Canaanite Maritime Involvement in the Second Millennium B.C.' In *J.A.O.S.* 86 (1966), 126 ff.
67. Schaeffer, C. F. A. 'Les fouilles de Ras Shamra-Ugarit: huitième campagne.' In *Syria*, 18 (1937), 125 ff.
68. Schaeffer, C. F. A. 'Les fouilles de Ras Shamra-Ugarit: neuvième campagne (printemps 1937). Rapport sommaire.' In *Syria*, 19 (1938), 313 ff.
69. Schaeffer, C. F. A. 'Les fouilles de Ras Shamra-Ugarit: dixième et onzième campagnes (automne et hiver 1938–1939).' In *Syria*, 20 (1939), 277 ff.
70. Schaeffer, C. F. A. 'Neue Entdeckungen in Ugarit.' In *Arch. f. Or.* 20 (1963), 206 ff.
71. Schaeffer, C. F. A. 'La pourpre à Ugarit.' In *Ann. Arch. de Syrie*, 1 (1950), 188 ff.
72. Schaeffer, C. F. A. 'Résumé des résultats de la XIXe campagne de fouilles à Ras Shamra-Ugarit, 1955.' In *Ann. Arch. de Syrie*, 7 (1957), 35 ff.
73. Schulman, A. 'Egyptian Representations of Horsemen and Riding in the New Kingdom.' In *J.N.E.S.* 16 (1957), 263 ff.
74. Smith, Sidney. 'The Ship Tyre.' In *P.E.Q.*, 1953, 97 ff.
75. Spekke, A. *The Ancient Amber Routes and the Geographical Discovery of the Eastern Baltic.* Stockholm, 1957.
76. Sprengling, M. *The Alphabet: its Rise and Development from the Sinai Inscriptions (O.I.C.* 12). Chicago, 1931.
77. Stubbings, F. *Mycenaean Pottery from the Levant.* Cambridge, 1951.
78. Thureau-Dangin, F. 'Un comptoir de laine-pourpre à Ugarit.' In *Syria*, 15 (1934), 137 ff.
79. Thureau-Dangin, F. 'Vocabulaires de Ras Shamra.' In *Syria* 12 (1931), 234 ff.
80. Ullmann, B. 'The Origin and Development of the Alphabet.' In *A.J.A.* 31 (1927), 311 ff.
81. Vercoutter, J. *L'Égypte et le monde égéen préhellénique (Inst. français d'archéol. Orient: Bibliothèque d'étude*, 22). Cairo, 1956.
82. Wainwright, G. A. 'Asiatic Keftiu.' In *A.J.A.* 56 (1952), 196 ff.
83. Welker, Marian. 'The painted pottery of the Near East in the second millennium B.C. and its chronological background.' In *Trans. Amer. Philosoph. Soc.* 1948.
84. —— 'Chronique de fouilles en Grèce en 1955.' In *B.C.H.* 80 (1956), 219 ff.

IX. RELIGION, ART AND LITERATURE

1. Amiran, R. B. K. 'A Seal from Brak: Expression of Consecutive Movement.' In *Iraq*, 18 (1956), 57 ff.
2. Astour, M. C. *Hellenosemitica.* Leiden, 1965.
3. Barnett, R. D. 'The Epic of Kumarbi and the Theogony of Hesiod.' In *J.H.S.* 45 (1945), 100 f.
4. Beran, T. 'Die Babylonische Glyptik der Kassitenzeit.' In *Arch. f. Or.* 18 (1958), 257 ff.
5. Bisi, A. M. *Il Grifone. Storia di un motivo iconografico nell'antico oriente mediterraneo (Studi Semitici*, 13). Rome, 1965.
6. Bittel, K. 'Nur hethitische oder auch hurritische Kunst?' In *Z.A.* 49 (1950), 256 ff.
7. Crowfoot, J. W. and Grace, M. *Early Ivories from Samaria: Samaria-Sebaste*, vol. II. London, 1938.

8. Danmanville, J. 'Aperçus sur l'art hittite à propos de l'iconographie d'IŠTAR-Šaušga.' In *R.H.A.* 20, 70 (1962), 37 ff.

9. Danmanville, J. 'Un roi hittite honore Ishtar de Šamuḫa.' In *R.H.A.* 14, 59 (1956), 39 ff.

10. de Mertzenfeld, C. 'Ivoires syriens.' In *Mél. Dussaud*, vol. 11 (1939), 587 ff.

11. Dumézil, G. *Les dieux des Indo-Européens.* Paris, 1952.

12. Dussaud, R. *L'art phénicien du IIᵉ millénaire.* Paris, 1949.

13. Dussaud, R. *Prélydiens, Hittites et Achéens.* Paris, 1953.

14. Erlenmeyer, M.-L. and Erlenmeyer, H. 'Einige syrische Siegel mit ägäischen Bildelementen.' In *Arch. f. Or.* 21 (1966), 32 ff.

15. Frankfort, H. *Cylinder Seals.* London, 1939.

16. Friedrich, J. 'Churritische Märchen und Sagen in hethitischer Sprache.' In *Z.A.* 49 (1949), 213 ff.

17. Friedrich, J. 'Der churritische Mythus vom Schlangendämon Ḫedammu.' In *Arch. Orient.* 17 (1949), 230 ff.

18. Furlani, G. 'La religione degli Hurriti (Subarei, Mitannici).' In *Storia delle Religioni*, ed. P. Tacchi-Venturi, 1. 241 ff. Turin, 1949.

19. Gardiner, Alan H. 'The Astarte Papyrus.' In *Studies presented to F. Ll. Griffith*, 74 ff. London, 1932.

20. Gordon, C. H. 'The Glyptic Art of Nuzu.' In *J.N.E.S.* 7 (1948), 261 ff.

21. Gordon, C. H. *Ugaritic Literature.* Rome 1949.

22. Güterbock, H. G. 'The Hittite version of the Hurrian Kumarbi Myths: Oriental Forerunners of Hesiod.' In *A.J.A.* 52 (1948), 123 ff.

23. Güterbock, H. G. *Kumarbi: Mythen vom churritischen Kronos (Istanbuler Schriften, 16).* Zürich and New York, 1946.

24. Hrouda, B. 'Die Churriter als Problem archäologischer Forschung.' In *Archaeologia Geographica*, 7 (1958), 14 ff.

25. Kantor, H. J. 'Syro-Palestinian Ivories.' In *J.N.E.S.* 15 (1956), 153 ff.

26. Laroche, E. 'Elements de Haruspicine Hittite.' In *R.H.A.* 12 (1952), 19 ff.

27. Laroche, E. 'Le panthéon de Yazilikaya.' In *J.C.S.* 6 (1952), 115 ff.

28. Laroche, E. 'Recherches sur les noms des dieux hittites.' In *R.H.A.* 7, 46 (1946–7), 7 ff.

29. Laroche, E. 'Teššub, Ḫebat et leur cour.' In *J.C.S.* 2 (1948), 113 ff.

30. Matthiae, P. *Ars Syra.* Centro di Studi Semitici, Rome, serie archeologica, 4. Rome, 1962.

31. Montet, P. *Les reliques de l'art syrien dans l'Egypt du Nouvel Empire.* Strasbourg, 1937.

32. Moortgat, A. *Die bildende Kunst des alten Orients und die Bergvölker.* Berlin, 1932.

33. Moortgat, A. 'Nur hethitische oder auch churrische Kunst?' In *Z.A.* 48 (1949), 152 ff.

34. Moortgat, A. *Vorderasiatische Rollsiegel.* Berlin, 1940.

35. Moscati, S. (ed.). *Le antiche divinità semitiche (Studi Semitici, 1).* Rome, 1958.

36. Nougayrol, J. *Cylindres-sceaux et empreintes de cylindres trouvés en Palestine (au cours des fouilles régulières).* Paris, 1939.

37. Parker, B. 'Cylinder Seals from Palestine.' In *Iraq*, 11 (1949), 1 ff.

38. Parrot, J. and Nougayrol, J. 'Un document de fondation hurrite.' In *R.A.* 42 (1948), 1 ff.

39. Porada, E. *Seal Impressions of Nuzi. Ann. A.S.O.R.* 24 (1944–5). New Haven, 1945.

40. Safadi, Hisham. 'Zur Identifizierung des Elfenbeinkopfes aus Ras-Shamra.' In *Ann. Arch. de Syrie*, 13 (1963), 97 ff.

41. Schaeffer, C. F. A. 'Les fouilles de Ras Shamra–Ugarit. Quinzième, seizième, et dix-septième campagnes (1951, 1952, et 1953).' In *Syria*, 31 (1954), 14 ff.

42. Seyrig, H. 'Acquisitions et inédits du Louvre: Antiquités syriennes 86: quelques cylindres syriens.' In *Syria*, 40 (1960), 253 ff.

43. Seyrig, H. 'Cylindre représentant une tauromachie.' In *Syria*, 33 (1956), 169 ff.

44. Thieme, P. 'The "Aryan" gods of the Mitanni treaties.' In *J.A.O.S.* 80 (1960), 301 ff.

45. Thureau-Dangin, F., Barrois, A., Dossin, G. and Dunand, M. *Arslan Tash* (*Bibliothèque archéologique et historique*, tome XVI). Paris, 1931.

46. Ungnad, A. 'Das hurritische Fragment des Gilgamesch-Epos.' In *Z.A.* 35 (1924), 133 ff.

47. Van Buren, E. D. 'The Cylinder Seals from Brak.' In *Iraq*, 11 (1949), 59 ff.

48. Van Buren, E. D. 'The esoteric significance of Kassite glyptic art.' In *Or.* n.s. 24 (1955), 345 ff.

49. Vieyra, M. 'Ištar de Ninive.' In *R.A.* 51 (1957), 83 ff., 130 ff.

50. von Oppenheim, Max Freiherr. *Tell Halaf: 3. Die Bildwerke*. Ed. A. Moortgat. Berlin, 1955.

A. ADDENDA

1. Aharoni, Y. 'Anaharath.' In *J.N.E.S.* 26 (1967), 212 ff.

2. Aharoni, Y. *The Land of the Bible: a Historical Geography*. Trs. A. F. Rainey. London, 1968.

3. Amadasi, M. G. *L'iconografia del carro da guerra in Siria e Palestina* (*Studi Semitici*, 17). Rome, 1965.

4. Artzi, Pinḥas. 'Some unrecognized Syrian Amarna Letters (EA 260, 317, 318).' In *J.N.E.S.* 27 (1968), 163 ff.

5. Astour, M. C. 'The Partition of Mukiš–Nuḫašše–Nii by Suppiluliuma. A Study in the Political Geography of the Amarna Age.' In *Or.* n.s. 38 (1969), 381 ff.

6. Beck, C. W. and Southard, G. C. 'The provenience of Mycenaean amber.' In *Atti e Memorie del I° Congresso Internazionale di Micenologia, Roma 1967* (*Incunabula Graeca* 25: 1–3). 3 vols. Rome, 1968.

7. Bietak, Manfred. 'Bericht über die erste und zweite Kampagne der österreichischen Ausgrabungen auf Tell Ed-Dabʿa.' In *M.D.A.I.* Abt. Kairo, 23 (1968), 79 ff.

8. Brinkmann, J. A. 'Ur: "The Kassite Period and the Period of the Assyrian Kings".' In *Or.* n.s. 38 (1969), 310 ff.

9. Buccellati, G. *Cities and Nations of Ancient Syria* (*Studi Semitici*, 26). Rome, 1967.

10. Carruba, E. 'Die Chronologie der hethitischen Texte und die hethitische Geschichte der Grossreichzeit.' Suppl. 1 to *Z.D.M.G.* (1969), 226 ff.

11. Cecchini, S. *La ceramica di Nuzi* (*Studi Semitici*, 15). Rome, 1965.

12. Crossland, R. 'Archaic Forms in the Maduwattas Text.' In *C.-R. Rencontr. Assyriol. Internat.* 3 (1954), 158 ff.

13. de Vaux, R. 'Le problème des Ḫapiru après quinze années.' In *J.N.ES.* 27 (1968), 221 ff.

14. Dietrich, M. and Loretz, O. 'Die soziale Struktur von Alalaḫ und Ugarit.' In *We. Or.* III (1966), 188 ff.

15. Edel, E. *Die Ortsnamenlisten aus dem Totentempel Amenophis III* (*Bonner biblische Beiträge*, 25). Bonn, 1966.
16. Epstein, C. ' "That Wretched Enemy of Kadesh." ' In *J.N.E.S.* 22 (1963), 242 ff.
17. Garelli, P. *Le Proche-Orient Asiatique. Des origines aux invasions des Peuples de la Mer* (*La Nouvelle Clio*, 2). Paris, 1969.
18. Gimbutas, Marija. *Bronze Age Cultures in Central and Eastern Europe*. The Hague, 1965.
19. Giveon, R. 'Thutmosis IV and Asia.' In *J.N.E.S.* 28 (1969), 54 ff.
20. Hachmann, R. and Kuschke, A. *Bericht über die Ergebnisse der Ausgrabungen in Kamid-el-Loz* (*Libanon*) *in den Jahren 1963 u. 1964.* Bonn, 1966.
21. Helck, W. 'Zur staatlichen Organisation Syriens im Beginn der 18. Dynastie.' In *Arch. f. Or.* 22 (1968/9), 27 ff.
22. Hornung, Erick. 'Neue Materialien zur ägyptischen Chronologie.' In *Z.D.M.G.* 117 (1967), 11 ff.
23. Hornung, Erick. *Untersuchungen zur Chronologie und Geschichte des Neuen Reiches* (Ägyptol. Abh., 11). Wiesbaden, 1964.
24. Kammenhuber, A. *Die Arier im Vorderen Orient*. Heidelberg, 1968.
25. Kammenhuber, A. 'Konsequenzen aus neueren Datierungen hethitischer Texte.' In *Or.* 38 (1969), 548 ff.
26. Kitchen, K. A. 'Interrelations of Egypt and Syria.' In *La Siria nel Tardo Bronzo*, ed. M. Liverani (Orientis Antiqui Collectio ix) (Rome, 1969), 77 ff.
27. Kitchen, K. A. Review of E. Edel, *Die Ortsnamenlisten aus dem Totentempel Amenophis III*. In *Bi. Or.* 26 (1969), 198 ff.
28. Klengel, Horst. *Geschichte Syriens im 2. Jahrtausend v.u.Z.*, vols. 1, 2. Deutsche Akad. d. Wissenschaften zu Berlin; Inst. für Orientforschung, Veröffentlichungen 40. Berlin, 1965–9.
29. Landsberger, B. and Tadmor, H. 'Fragments of Clay Liver Models from Hazor.' In *I.E.J.* 14 (1965), 201 ff.
30. Laroche, E. *Les noms des Hittites* (*Études linguistiques* 4). Paris, 1966.
31. Malamat, A. 'Campaigns of Amenhotep II and Thutmose IV to Canaan.' In *Studies in the Bible, Scripta Hierosolymita*, viii (Jerusalem, 1961), 218 ff.
32. Malamat, A. 'Syrien-Palästina in der zweiten Hälfte des 2. Jahrtausends.' In *Fischer Weltgeschichte: Die altorientalischen Reiche*, ii, ed. E. Cassin, J. Bottéro and J. Vercoutter (Frankfurt, 1966), 177 ff.
33. Mayrhofer, M. *Die Indo-Arier im alten Vorderasien*. Wiesbaden, 1966.
34. Mazar, B. 'The Middle Bronze Age in Palestine.' In *I.E.J.* 18 (1968), 65 ff.
35. Merrillees, R. S. *The Cypriote Bronze Age Pottery found in Egypt* (*Studies in Mediterranean Archaeology*, ed. P. Åström, 18). Lund, 1968.
36. Merrillees, R. S. Review of Lena Åström, *Studies in the Arts and Crafts of the Late Cypriote Bronze Age*. In *P.E.Q.* 1968, 64 ff.
37. Muntingh, L. M. 'The Social and Legal Status of a Free Ugaritic Female.' In *J.N.E.S.* 26 (1967), 102 ff.
38. Nougayrol, J., Laroche, E., Virolleaud, C. and Schaeffer, C. F. A. *Ugaritica*, v. (*Mission de Ras Shamra*, 16). Paris, 1968.
39. Oppenheim, A. L. 'Essay on Overland Trade in the First Millennium B.C.' In *J.C.S.* 21 (1969), 236 ff.
40. Otten, H. *Die hethitischen Quellen und die altorientalische Chronologie* (In Akad. d. Wiss. und Literatur zu Mainz: *Abh. der Geistes u. Sozialwiss. Kl.* 1968, nr. 3). Weisbaden, 1968.

41. Parr, P. J. 'The Origin of the Rampart Fortifications of Middle Bronze Age Palestine and Syria.' In *Z.D.P.V.* 84 (1968), 18 ff.
42. Porada, E. 'Cylinder Seals from Thebes.' In *A.J.A.* 69 (1965), 173.
43. Rausing, G. *The Bow. Some Notes on its Origin and Development* (*Acta Archaeologia Lundensia* no. 6). Bonn and Lund, 1967.
44. Redford, D. B. *History and Chronology of the Eighteenth Dynasty of Egypt: Seven Studies.* Toronto, 1967.
45. Sasson, J. M. 'A Sketch of North Syrian Economic Relations in the Middle Bronze Age.' In *J.E.S.H.O.* 9 (1966), 161 ff.
46. Schmökel, H. 'Die theophoren Personennamen Babyloniens und Assyriens.' In *J.E.O.L.* 19 (1967), 468 ff.
47. Scott, R. B. Y. 'The scale-weights from Ophel.' In *P.E.Q.* 1965, 128 ff.
48. Skaist, A. 'The Authority of the Brother at Arrapḫa and Nuzi.' In *J.A.O.S.* 89 (1969), 10 ff.
49. Van Seters, J. *The Hyksos. A New Investigation.*
50. Ward, W. A. (ed.). *The Role of the Phoenicians in the Interaction of Mediterranean Civilisations.* Beirut, 1968.
51. Yeivin, Sh. 'Amenophis II's Asiatic Campaigns.' In *J.A.R.C.E.* 6 (1967), 119 ff.

CHAPTER XI

G. GENERAL

1. Albright, W. F. 'The Excavation of Tell Beit Mirsim. I. The Pottery of the First Three Campaigns.' In *Ann. A.S.O.R.* 12 (1932).
2. Albright, W. F. 'The Excavation of Tell Beit Mirsim. IA. The Bronze Age Pottery of the Fourth Campaign.' In *Ann. A.S.O.R.* 13 (1933), 55 ff.
3. Albright, W. F. 'The Excavation of Tell Beit Mirsim. II. The Bronze Age.' In *Ann. A.S.O.R.* 17 (1938).
4. Buhl, M.-L. and Holm-Nielsen, S. *Shiloh. The Pre-Hellenistic Remains.* Copenhagen, 1969.
5. FitzGerald, G. M. *The Four Canaanite Temples of Beth-shan.* Part II. *The Pottery.* Philadelphia, 1930.
6. Garstang, J. 'Jericho: City and Necropolis. Fourth Report.' In *Ann. Arch. Anthr.* 21 (1934), 99 ff.
7. Grant, E. and Wright, G. E. *Ain Shems Excavations.* IV. (*Pottery*). Haverford, Pennsylvania. 1939.
8. Guy, P. L. O. and Engberg, R. M. *Megiddo Tombs* (*O.I.P.* 33). Chicago 1938.
9. Hamilton, R. W. 'Excavations at Tell Abu Hawām.' In *Q.D.A.P.* 4 (1935), 1 ff.
10. Hankey, V. 'Mycenaean Pottery in the Middle East.' In *B.S.A.* 62 (1967), 107 ff.
11. Harding, G. L. 'Four Tomb Groups from Jordan.' In *Ann. P.E.F.* 6 (1953).
12. James, F. W. *The Iron Age at Beth-shan* (University of Pennsylvania, Museum Monographs). Philadelphia, 1966.
13. Kenyon, K. M. 'Excavations in Jerusalem, 1961.' In *P.E.Q.* 1962, 72 ff.
14. Kenyon, K. M. 'Excavations in Jerusalem, 1962.' In *P.E.Q.* 1963, 7 ff.
15. Kenyon, K. M. 'Excavations in Jerusalem, 1964.' In *P.E.Q.* 1965, 9 ff.
16. Kenyon, K. M. 'Some notes on the History of Jericho in the 2nd Millennium B.C.' In *P.E.Q.* 1951, 101 ff.

17. Kenyon, K. M. *Excavations at Jericho*, I–II. London, 1960, 1965.
18. Kenyon, K. M. *Digging up Jericho*. London, 1957.
19. Kenyon, K. M. 'Excavations at Jericho, 1954.' In *P.E.Q.* 1954, 45 ff.
20. Kenyon, K. M. 'The Middle and Late Bronze Age Strata at Megiddo.' In *Levant*, I (1969), 25 ff.
21. Kenyon, K. M. 'Some Notes on the Early and Middle Bronze Age Strata at Megiddo.' In *Eretz-Israel*, 5 (1958), 51* ff.
22. Kenyon, K. M. *Archaeology in the Holy Land*. London, 1960.
23. Knutzon, J. A. *Die el-Amarna Tafeln*. Leipzig, 1915.
24. Lapp, P. W. 'Taanach by the Waters of Megiddo.' In *Bi. Ar.* 30 (1967), 2 ff.
25. Loud, G. *Megiddo*. II. *Seasons of 1935–39 (O.I.P. 62)*. Chicago, 1948.
26. Macalister, R. A. S. *The Excavation of Gezer*, I–III. London, 1912.
27. Macdonald, E., Starkey, J. L. and Harding, L. *Beth-pelet*, II. London, 1932.
28. Petrie, W. M. F. *Beth-pelet*, I, London, 1930.
29. Petrie, W. M. F. *Ancient Gaza*, I–IV. London, 1931–34.
30. Pritchard, J. B. *Ancient Near-Eastern Texts Relating to the Old Testament*. Ed. 2. Princeton, 1955.
31. Pritchard, J. B. *Winery, Defenses, and Soundings at Gibeon* (University of Pennsylvania, Museum Monographs). Philadelphia, 1964.
32. Pritchard, J. B. *The Bronze Age Cemetery at Gibeon* (University of Pennsylvania, Museum Monographs). Philadelphia, 1963.
33. Rowe, A. *The Topography and History of Beth-shan*. Philadelphia, 1930.
34. Saller, S. J. *The Jebusite Burial Place. The Excavations of Dominus Flevit (Mount Olivet, Jerusalem)*, Part II. Jerusalem, 1964.
35. Stubbings, F. H. *Mycenaean Pottery from the Levant*. Cambridge, 1951.
36. Tufnell, O., Inge, C. H. and Harding, L. *Lachish*. II. *The Fosse Temple*. Oxford, 1940.
37. Tufnell, O. *Lachish*. IV. *The Bronze Age*. Oxford, 1958.
38. Vaux, R. de. 'Les fouilles de Tell el-Fâr'ah, près Naplouse.' In *Rev. bibl.* 58 (1951), 393 ff.; 62 (1955), 541 ff.; 64 (1957), 552 ff.
39. Wright, G. E. *Shechem. The Biography of a Biblical City*. New York, 1965.
40. Yadin, Y. (*et al.*). *Hazor*, I–IV. Jerusalem, 1958–61.
41. Yadin, Y. 'Excavations at Hazor, 1958.' In *I.E.J.* 9 (1959), 74 ff.

CHAPTER XII

G. GENERAL

1. Bossert, H. Th. *Altkreta*. Ed. 3. Berlin, 1937.
2. École Française d'Athènes. *Études Crétoises*, I–XI. Paris, 1928–59.
3. Evans, A. J. *The Palace of Minos at Knossos*, I–IV and Index. London, 1921–36.
4. Marinatos, Sp. and Hirmer, M. *Kreta und das Mykenische Hellas*. Munich, 1960.
5. Matz, F. 'Die Aegaeis.' In *Handbuch der Archaeologie*, II. Munich, 1954.
6. Matz, F. *Kreta, Mykene, Troia. Die Minoische und die Homerische Welt*. Stuttgart, 1956.
7. Matz, F. *Crete and Early Greece. The Prelude to Greek Art*. London, 1962.
8. Nilsson, M. P. *The Minoan-Mycenaean Religion*. Ed. 2. Lund, 1950.
9. Pendlebury, J. D. S. *The Archaeology of Crete*. London, 1939.
10. Pernier, L. and Banti, L. *Il Palazzo Minoico di Festos*. I, 1935. II, Rome, 1951.
11. Zervos, Chr. *L'Art de la Crète*. Paris, 1956.

I. CHRONOLOGY

1. Alexiou, St. 'Νέα Στοιχεῖα διὰ τὴν Ὑστέραν Αἰγαιακὴν Χρονολογίαν καὶ Ἱστορίαν.' In *K.Chr.* 6 (1952), 9 ff.
2. Marinatos, Sp. 'The Volcanic Destruction of Minoan Crete.' In *Antiq.* 13 (1939), 425 ff.
3. Vermeule-Townsend, E. 'The Fall of Knossos and the Palace Style.' In *A.J.A.* 67 (1963), 195 ff.

II. THE EVIDENCE OF THE MONUMENTS

1. Biesantz, H. *Kretisch-Mykenische Siegelbilder. Stilgeschichtliche und Chronologische Untersuchungen.* Marburg/Lahn, 1954.
2. Dessenne, A. *Le Sphinx.* Paris, 1957.
3. Hood, M. S. F. 'Tholos Tombs of the Aegaean.' In *Antiq.* 34 (1960), 166 ff.
4. Kenna, V. E. G. *Cretan Seals.* Oxford, 1960.
5. Platon, N. 'Συμβολὴ εἰς τὴν Σπουδὴν τῆς Μινωϊκῆς Τοιχογραφίας.' In *K.Chr.* 13 (1958), 319 f.
6. Rodenwaldt, G. *Tiryns,* II. Athens, 1912. Pp. 144 ff.

III. HISTORICAL CONCLUSIONS

1. Alexiou, St. 'Ζητήματα τοῦ Προϊστορικοῦ Βίου Κρητομυκηναϊκὸν Ἐμπόριον.' In *Ephem. Arch.* 1953/54, part III (1961), 135 ff.
2. Blegen, C. W. 'A Chronological Problem.' In *Minoica, Festschrift für J. Sundwall.* 1958. Pp. 61 ff.
3. Bernabò Brea, L. and Cavalier, L. 'Civiltà Preistoriche delle Isole Eolie.' In *B.P.I.* n.s. 19 (1956), 7 ff.
4. Buchholz, H. G. 'Der Kupferhandel im 2. vorchr. Jahrtausend im Spiegel der Schriftforschung.' In *Minoica.* 1958. Pp. 92 ff.
5. Buchholz, H. G. *Zur Herkunft der Kretischen Doppelaxt.* Munich, 1959.
6. Buchholz, H. G. 'Keftiubarren und Erzhandel im 2. vorchr. Jahrtausend.' In *Prähist. Zeitschr.* 37 (1959), 1 ff.
7. Dunbabin, T. J. 'Minos and Daidalos in Sicily.' In *B.S.R.* 16 (1948), 1 ff.
8. Furumark, A. 'The Settlement at Ialysos and the Aegean History at 1550/1400 B.C.' In *Op. Arch.* 6 (1950), 150 ff.
9. Hood, M. S. F. 'Late Minoan Warrior Graves from A.Ioannis and the Hospital Site at Knossos.' In *B.S.A.* 47 (1952), 243 ff.
10. Hood, M. S. F. 'Another Warrior-Grave at A.Ioannis near Knossos.' In *B.S.A.* 51 (1956), 81 ff.
11. Hood, M. S. F. 'The Date of the Linear-B-Tablets from Knossos.' In *Antiquity,* 35 (1961), 4 ff.
12. Hood, M. S. F. 'The Knossos Tablets. A Complete Version.' In *Antiq.* 36 (1962), 38 ff.
13. Kantor, A. *The Aegaean and the Orient in the Second Millennium.* Bloomington, 1949.
14. Malten, L. 'Elysion und Rhadamanthys.' In *J.d.I.* 28 (1913), 35 ff.
15. Marinatos, Sp. 'Some General Notes on the Minoan Written Documents.' In *Minos,* 1 (1951), 39 ff.
16. Matz, F. 'Zu den Sphingen von Yerkapu in Boghazköy.' In *Marb. W. Pr.* 1957, 1 ff.

17. Matz, F. 'Göttererscheinung und Kultbild im Minoischen Kreta.' In *Abh. Mainz*. 1958, 7.
18. Matz, F. 'Minoischer Stiergott?' In *K.Chr*. 15/16 (1961/62), 215 ff.
19. Monaco, G. 'Scavi nella Zona Micenea di Ialiso (Trianda) 1935/36.' In *Cl.Rh*. 10 (1941), 43 ff.
20. Palmer, L. R. and Boardman, J. *On the Knossos Tablets*. Oxford, 1963.
21. Reusch. H. 'Zum Wandschmuck des Thronsaals in Knossos.' In *Minoica*. 1958. Pp. 334 ff.
22. Wace, A. J. B. and Blegen, C. W. 'Pottery as Evidence for Trade and Colonization.' In *Klio*, 32 (1939), 131 ff.
23. Weickert, C. and others. 'Die Ausgrabungen beim Athena Tempel in Milet.' In *Ist. Mitt*. 7 (1957), 102 ff.; 9/10 (1959/60), 1 ff.

CHAPTER XIII

(*a*) LITERACY IN MINOAN AND MYCENAEAN LANDS

G. GENERAL

1. Baumbach, L. *Studies in Mycenaean Inscriptions and Dialect, 1953–1964*. Rome, 1968.
2. Brice, W. C. *Inscriptions in the Minoan Linear Script of Class A*. London, 1961.
3. Evans, A. J. *Scripta Minoa* I. Oxford, 1909.
4. Evans, A. J. *Scripta Minoa* II. Oxford, 1952.
5. Evans, A. J. *The Palace of Minos* I–IV and Index. Oxford, 1921–36.
6. Kenna, V. E. G. *Cretan Seals*. Oxford, 1960.
7. Landau, O. *Mykenisch-griechische Personennamen*. Göteborg, 1958.
8. Morpurgo, A. *Mycenaeae Graecitatis Lexicon*. Rome, 1963.
9. Palmer, L. R. *The Interpretation of Mycenaean Greek Texts*. Oxford, 1963.
10. Palmer, L. R. and Boardman, J. *On the Knossos Tablets*. Oxford, 1963.
11. Ventris, M. and Chadwick, J. *Documents in Mycenaean Greek*. Cambridge, 1959. (New edition in course of preparation.)

Journals and other Serials

12. *Minos*. Two fascicles in each volume:
   Vols. 1–3 (1951–5): *Investigaciones y materiales para el estudio de los textos paleocretenses* (Theses et Studia Philologica Salmanticensia, 4, 6, 8). Universidad, Salamanca.
   Vols. 4–8.1 (1956–63), 8.2– (1967–): *Revista de filología egea*. Universidad, Salamanca.
   Supplements.
13. *Kadmos: Zeitschrift für vor- und frühgriechische Epigraphik*. Berlin, Two fascicles in each (annual) volume: Vol. 1 (1962)–.
14. *Incunabula Graeca*. Centro di studi miceni, Università, Rome. Vol. 1 (1961)–45 (1970) and continuing. Monographs, texts; also volumes containing various short studies, the latter being called Studi Micenei ed Egeo-Anatolici, with numbers in the Incunabula series, and other numbers of their own (viz. Fasc. 1 [1966]–12 [1970] and continuing).

15. *Minutes of the Minoan Linear B Seminar of the Institute of Classical Studies of the University of London*. Several issues each year, beginning 1954: detailed lists of the issues, Grumach, *Bibliographie* (1963), p. 165, and Supplement 1 (1967), p. 44.

International Colloquia: Proceedings

16. Gif, France: April 1956
    Etudes mycéniennes: Actes du Colloque international sur les textes mycéniens, ed. M. Lejeune (Colloques internationaux du Centre national de la recherche scientifique, Sciences Humaines, 1). Paris, 1956.
17. Pavia, Italy: September 1958
    Atti del 2° Colloquio internazionale di studi minoico-micenei, ed. P. Meriggi. *Athenaeum*, N.S. 36 (1958), fasc. 4 (pp. 295–436). Università, Pavia, 1958.
18. 'Wingspread', Racine, Wisconsin, USA: September 1961
    Mycenaean Studies: Proceedings of the Third International Colloquium for Mycenaean Studies, ed. E. L. Bennett, Jr. Madison, Wis., 1964.
19. Cambridge, Eng.: April 1965
    Proceedings of the Cambridge Colloquium on Mycenaean Studies, ed. L. R. Palmer and J. Chadwick. Cambridge, 1966.
20. Brno, Czechoslovakia: April 1966
    Studia Mycenaea: Proceedings of the Mycenaean Symposium, ed. A. Bartoněk. Amsterdam, 1968.

I. THE PHAESTUS DISK

1. Barnett, R. D. *C.A.H.* II[2] (1969), ch. XXVIII, pp. 6–7.
2. Davaras, C. 'Zur Herkunft des Diskos von Phaistos.' In *Kadmos* VI (1967), 101–5.
3. Davis, Simon. 'Remarks on the Phaistos Disk.' In *Studi Micenei ed Egeo-Anatolici*, fasc. 2 (*Incunabula Graeca* 18) (1967), 114–17.
4. Della Seta, A. 'Il disco di Phaestos.' In *Rendiconti della reale Accademia dei Lincei*, series 5, 18 (1909), 297–367.
5. Evans, Arthur J. *Scripta Minoa*, 1 (1909), 22–8, 273–93 (includes standard numbering of signs). Virtually *the editio princeps*.
6. Evans, Arthur J. *Palace of Minos at Knossos*. 4 vols. in 6 parts, plus Index. London, 1921–36. Vol. 1, 647–68; other refs. in Index 115 s.v. 'Phaistos Disk'.
7. Grumach, E. 'Die Korrekturen des Diskus von Phaistos.' In *Kadmos*, 1 (1962), 16–26.
8. Grumach, E. *Bibliographie der kretisch-mykenischen Epigraphik* (1963), 23–30. Supplement, 1 (1967), 8–9.
9. Kober, A. E. 'The Minoan Scripts, Fact and Theory.' In *A.J.A.* 52 (1948), 87–8.
10. Kretschmer, P. 'Die antike Punktierung und der Diskus von Phaistos.' In *Minos*, 1 (1951), 7–25.
11. Ktistopoulos, K. D. "Ὁ δίσκος τῆς Φαιστοῦ.' Athens, 1948.
12. Lejeune, M. In *Revue de l'enseignement supérieur*, fascs. 1–2 of 1967, 66.
13. Mackay, A. L. 'On the Type-Fount of the Phaistos Disc.' Department of Crystallography, Birkbeck College, University of London, 1964.
14. Marinatos, S. 'La marine créto-mycénienne.' In *B.C.H.* 57 (1933), 186–7.

15. Marinatos, S. and Hirmer, M. *Crete and Mycenae.* London 1960, New
    York n.d. Plates 72 and 73 (among the best photographs); p. 142, with
    references.
16. Mellink, M. J. 'Lycian Wooden Huts and Sign 24 on the Phaistos Disk.' In
    Kadmos, 3 (1964), 1–7.
17. Meyer, Eduard. 'Der Diskus von Phaestos und die Philister von Kreta.' In
    Sitzungsb. Berlin, phil.-hist. Kl., 1909, 1022–9.
18. Pernier, L. 'Il disco di Phaestos con caratteri pittografici.' In *Ausonia,* 3 (1908,
    pub. 1909), 271–302. Formally the *editio princeps;* see also Evans
    (1909.)
19. Pernier, L. and Banti, L. *Il Palazzo di Festòs,* Vol. I. Rome, 1935, pp. 419–
    25 (bibliography to 1935, p. 24). Vol. II. Rome, 1951, pp. 392, 402.
20. Reinach, A. J. 'Le disque de Phaistos et les peuples de la mer.' In *Rev. Arch.*
    série 4, vol. 15 (1910), 1–65.
21. Schwartz, B. In *J.N.E.S.* 18 (1959), 105–12, 222–8, with *Nestor,* p. 532,
    and (by B. V. Gwynn) *Nestor,* pp. 541–2.

Bronze Axe from Arkalokhori, etc.

22. Grumach, *Bibliographie* (1963), 30–1; Supplement, 1 (1967), 9.
23. Marinatos, S. 'Ausgrabungen und Funde auf Kreta 1934/5.' In *Arch. Anz.*
    (1935), 248–54.
24. Vermeule, E. D. T. 'A Gold Minoan Double Axe.' In *Bulletin of the Museum
    of Fine Arts,* Boston, 57 (1959), 8–10.

Limestone Block from Mallia

25. Grumach, *Bibliographie* (1963), 31.
26. Chapouthier, F. 'Une inscription hiéroglyphique sur pierre.' In *C.-R. Ac.
    Inscr. B.-L.* (1937), pp. 277–8.
27. Chapouthier, F. 'Inscription hiéroglyphique minoenne gravée sur un bloc de
    calcaire.' In *B.C.H.* 62 (1938), 104–9.
28. Kober, A. E. In *A.J.A.* 52 (1948), 88.

11. SIGNS AND MARKS NOT SPOKEN
Potters' Marks

1. Grumach, *Bibliographie* (1963), 64–5, 96–8; Supplement 1 (1967), 29.
2. Caskey, J. L. 'Inscriptions and Potters' Marks from Ayia Irini in Keos.' In
   Kadmos 9 (1970), 107–17.

Masons' Marks

3. Grumach, *Bibliographie* (1963), 60–4, 96; Supplement 1 (1967), 17, 29.
4. Evans, A. J. *Palace of Minos* (1921–1935), index s.v.
5. Graham, J. W. *The Palaces of Crete.* Princeton, N.J., 1962. Pages 154–5.
6. Sakellarakis, J. 'Masons' marks from Arkhanes.' In W. C. Brice, ed., *Europa:
   Festschrift für E. Grumach.* Berlin, 1967. Pages 277–88.

Seals and Signets

7. Grumach, E. *Bibliographie* (1963), 16–23 passim; Supplement (1967), 5–8
   passim.

8. Betts, J. H. 'New Light on Cretan Bureaucracy.' In *Kadmos* 6 (1967), 15–40.
9. Grumach, E. 'Neue Schriftsiegel der Sammlung Metaxas, Herakleion.' In *Kadmos*, 6 (1967), 6–14.
10. Kenna, V. E. G. 'Ancient Crete and the Use of the Cylinder Seal.' In *A.J.A.* 72 (1968), 321–36.
11. Wiencke, M. H. 'Further Seals and Sealings from Lerna.' In *Hesperia* 38 (1969), 500–52.

III. SCRIPTS
Pictographic

1. Grumach, *Bibliographie* (1963), 17–20, 31–3; Supplement, 5–6, 10.
2. Kober, A. E. 'The Minoan Scripts: Fact and Theory.' In *A.J.A.* 52 (1948), 83–7.
3. Erlenmeyer, H. 'Hieroglyphisch-hethitische und ägäische Schriftsiegel.' In *Kadmos* 5 (1966), 118–20.
4. Grumach, E. and Sakellarakis, J. 'Die neuen Hieroglyphensiegel vom Phourni (Archanes) I.' In *Kadmos* 5 (1966), 109–14.

Numerals

5. Grumach, *Bibliographie* (1963), 67–9 (Weights, measures, accounts); Supplement (1967), 18.
6. Bennett, E. L., Jr. 'Fractional Quantities in Minoan Bookkeeping.' In *A.J.A.* 54 (1950), 204–22.

Linear A

7. Grumach, *Bibliographie* (1963), 33–49, 73–4; Supplement (1967), 10–14, 20–1.

IV. EVIDENCE ABOUT SURVIVAL
End of Literacy

1. Grumach, *Bibliographie* (1963), 70–2, 98–103; Supplement (1967), 30–1.
2. Dow, S. 'Minoan Writing.' In *A.J.A.* 58 (1954), 108–29.
3. Dow, S. 'Literacy: The Palace Bureaucracies, the Dark Age, Homer.' In P. W. Lehmann, ed., *A Land Called Crete*. Northampton, Mass., 1968. Pages 109–47.

Cyprus

4. Grumach, *Bibliographie* (1963), 103–4, 120–7.
5. Catling, H. W. *C.A.H.* II² 1966, ch. XXII (*b*), 62–4, 76–7 (bibliography).

Writing in Homer

6. Jeffery, L. H. 'Writing.' In A. J. B. Wace – F. H. Stubbings, eds., *A Companion to Homer*. London, 1962. Pages 555–9.

(*b*) THE LINEAR B TABLETS AS HISTORICAL DOCUMENTS

References to Linear B tablets are given in accordance with the internationally accepted system. The main collections of inscriptions are in course of being re-edited. The Thebes tablets are still in process of publication.

Cnossus (KN): A new edition by J. Chadwick, J. T. Killen and J.-P. Olivier is in preparation at Cambridge. Older edition: Chadwick, J. and Killen, J. T., *The Knossos Tablets in Transcription* (3rd ed.). London, 1964.

Mycenae (MY): Olivier, J.-P., *The Mycenae Tablets IV*. Leiden, 1969.

Pylus (PY): A new edition by E. L. Bennett and J.-P. Olivier is in preparation at Rome. Older editions: Bennett, E. L., *The Pylos Tablets: texts of the inscriptions found 1939–1954*. Princeton, 1955; Gallavotti, C. and Sacconi, A., *Inscriptiones Pyliae*. Rome, 1961.

G. GENERAL

1. Baumbach, L. (editor). *Studies in Mycenaean Inscriptions and Dialect 1953–1964*. Rome, 1968.
2. Bennett, E. L. (ed.). *The Mycenae Tablets II. Transactions of the American Philosophical Society* (Philadelphia), 48 (1958), Part 1.
3. Bennett, E. L. 'Tentative identifications of the hands of the scribes of the Pylos tablets.' In *Athenaeum*, 46 (1958), 328–33.
4. Chadwick, J. 'The Organization of the Mycenaean Archives.' In *Studia Mycenaea* (Brno, 1968), 11–21.
5. Chadwick, J. and Killen, J. T. *A Mycenaean Industry*. Cambridge (in preparation).
6. Duhoux, Y. 'Le groupe lexical de δίδωμι en mycénien.' In *Minos*, 9 (1968), 81–108.
7. Landau, O. *Mykenisch-griechische Personennamen*. Göteborg, 1958.
8. Lejeune, M. 'Les forgerons de Pylos.' In *Historia*, 10 (1961), 409–34.
9. Marinatos, S. 'Βασιλικὰ μυρεψεῖα καὶ ἀρχεῖα ἐν Μυκήναις.' In Πρακτικὰ τῆς Ἀκαδημίας Ἀθηνῶν, 33 (1958), 161–73.
10. Morpurgo, A. *Mycenaeae Graecitatis Lexicon*. Rome, 1963.
11. Olivier, J.-P. *Les Scribes de Cnossos*. Rome, 1967.
12. Palmer, L. R. *The Interpretation of Mycenaean Greek texts*. Oxford, 1963.
13. Palmer, L. R. and Boardman, J. *On the Knossos Tablets*. Oxford, 1963.
14. Ventris, M. and Chadwick, J. *Documents in Mycenaean Greek*. Cambridge, 1956. (New edition in course of preparation.)

CHAPTER XIV

G. GENERAL

1. Dow, S. 'The Greeks in the Bronze Age.' In *Rapports du XIe congrès international des sciences historiques, Stockholm, 1960*, 1–34.
2. Evans, A. J. *The Palace of Minos*. London, 1922–37.

3. Fimmen, D. *Die kretisch-mykenische Kultur*. Leipzig and Berlin, 1921.
4. Furumark, A. *The Chronology of Mycenaean Pottery*. Stockholm, 1941.
5. Furumark, A. *The Mycenaean Pottery*. Stockholm, 1941.
6. Karo, G. 'Mykenische Kultur.' In *P.W.* Suppl. VI (1935), 584 ff.
7. Matz, F. *Die Ägäis*. In *Handbuch der Archäologie*, 2, 1 (1950), vol. 2, 179 ff.
8. Mylonas, G. E. 'H 'ἀκρόπολις τῶν Μυκηνῶν.' In 'Αρχ. 'Εφ. 1958, 153 ff.
9. Mylonas, G. E. *Ancient Mycenae*. London, 1957.
10. Nilsson, M. P. *The Mycenaean Origin of Greek Mythology*. Cambridge, 1932.
11. Nilsson, M. P. *Homer and Mycenae*. London, 1933.
12. Tsountas, C. and Manatt, J. I. *The Mycenaean Age*. London, 1897.
13. Wace, A. J. B. *Mycenae. An archaeological history and guide*. Princeton, 1949.
14. Wace, A. J. B. and Stubbings, F. H. (edd.). *A Companion to Homer*. London, 1962.

I. THE NATURE OF THE EVIDENCE

1. Lolling, H. G. *Das Kuppelgrab bei Menidi*. Athens, 1880.
2. Mylonas, G. E. 'The Cult of the Dead in Helladic Times.' In *Studies presented to David M. Robinson*, 1, 64 ff. St Louis, 1951–3.
3. Mylonas, G. E. 'The Tombs of the Seven against Thebes.' In *Ill. Ldn News*, 12 Sept. 1953, 402 f.
4. Wolters, P. 'Vasen aus Menidi.' In *Jahrb. d. Deutsch. Archaeol. Inst.*: (*a*) 13 (1898), 13 ff.; (*b*) 14 (1899), 103 ff.

II. THE SHAFT GRAVES AT MYCENAE

1. Angel, J. L. 'Kings and Commoners' [summary of a paper]. In *A.J.A.* 61 (1957), 181.
2. Childe, V. G. *The Dawn of European Civilisation*. Ed. 5. London, 1950.
3. Karo, G. *Die Schachtgräber von Mykenai*. Munich, 1930–3.
4. Rowe, K. R. 'A Possible M.H. Fortification Wall [at Mycenae].' In *B.S.A.* 49 (1954), 248–53.
5. Schliemann, H. *Mycenae*. New York, 1880.

III. THE EGYPTIAN CONNEXION

1. Lorimer, H. L. *Homer and the Monuments*. London, 1950.
2. Nilsson, M. P. 'The Prehistoric Migrations of the Greeks.' In A.I.A.R.S. 4° ser. II (1953), 1–8; also in A.I.A.R.S. 8° ser. II. 3 (*M. P. Nilsson opuscula selecta*, vol. II), 467–78.
3. Persson, A. W. *New Tombs at Dendra*. Lund, 1942.
4. Schachermeyr, F. 'Streitwagen und Streitwagenbild im alten Orient und bei den mykenischen Griechen.' In *Anthropos*, 46 (1951), 705 ff.
5. Schachermeyr, F. 'Welche geschichtliche Ereignisse führten zur Entstehung der mykenischen Kultur?' In *Arch. Orient.* 17 (1949), 331 ff.
6. Stone, J. F. S. *Wessex before the Celts*. London, 1958.

IV. DANAUS AND THE HYKSOS

1. Bérard, J. 'Les Hyksos et la légende d'Io.' In *Syria*, 29 (1952), 1 ff.
2. Engberg, R. M. *The Hyksos Reconsidered* (*S.A.O.C.* 18). Chicago, 1939.
3. Galling, K. 'Hyksosherrschaft und Hyksoskultur.' In *Ztschr. d. deutschen Palästinavereins*, 62 (1939–40), 89 ff.

4. Holland, L. B. 'The Danaoi.' In *Harv. Stud. Class. Phil.* 39 (1928), 59 ff.

5. O'Callaghan, R. T. 'New Light on the *Maryannu....*' In *Jb. für kleinasiatische Forschung*, 1 (1950), 309 ff.

6. Säve-Söderbergh, T. 'The Hyksos Rule in Egypt.' In *J.E.A.* 37 (1951), 53 ff.

7. Wolf, W. 'Der Stand der Hyksosfrage.' In *Z.D.M.G.* N.F. 8 (83) (1929), 67 ff.

VI. THE PROGRESS OF MYCENAEAN SETTLEMENT

1. Atkinson, T. D. (*et al.*). *Excavations at Phylakopi in Melos* (*Soc. Prom. Hell. Stud. Suppl. Paper no. 4*). London, 1904.

2. Blegen, C. W. 'An Early Tholos Tomb in W. Messenia.' In *Hesperia*, 23 (1954), 158–62.

3. Blegen, C. W. *Prosymna: the Helladic Settlement Preceding the Argive Heraeum.* Cambridge, 1937.

4. Blegen, C. W. (*et al.*). *Troy.* 4 vols. Princeton 1950–8.

5. Caskey, J. L. 'Royal Shaft Graves at Lerna.' In *Archaeology*, 13 (1960), 130–3.

6. Daux, G. 'Chronique des fouilles en 1957.' In *B.C.H.* 82 (1958).

7. Dawkins, R. M. and Droop, J. P. 'Excavations at Phylakopi in Melos, 1911.' In *B.S.A.* 17 (1912), 1–22.

8. Dörpfeld, W. 'Alt-Pylos I.' In *Ath. Mitt.* 33 (1908), 295–317.

9. Dörpfeld, W. 'Tiryns, Olympia, Pylos.' In *Ath. Mitt.* 32 (1907), 1–15.

10. Furumark, A. 'Ialysos and Aegean History.' In *A.I.R.R.S.* 15 (1950), 150–271.

11. Hankey, V. 'Late Helladic Tombs at Khalkis.' In *B.S.A.* 42 (1952), 49–95.

12. Hood, M. S. F. '*Tholos* Tombs of the Aegean.' In *Antiq.* 34 (1960), 166 ff.

13. Jacopi, G. 'Nuovi scavi nella necropoli micenea di Jalisso.' In *Ann. della R. Scuola archeol. di Atene*, 13–14 (1934), 253–345.

14. Jacopi, G. 'Sepolcreto miceneo di Calavarda.' In *Clara Rhodos*, 6–7 (1926), 133–50.

15. Kenney, E. J. A. 'The Ancient Drainage of the Copaïs.' In *Liverpool Annals of Arch. and Anth.* 22 (1935), 189–206.

16. Keramopoullos, A. D. "Η οἰκία τοῦ Κάδμου." In 'Αρχ. 'Εφ. 1909, 57–122.

17. 'Kourouniotis, K. 'Ανασκαφὴ θολωτοῦ τάφου ἐν Βόλῳ.' In 'Αρχ. 'Εφ. 1906, 211 ff.

18. Maiuri, A. 'Jalisos: la necropoli micenea.' In *Ann. della R. Scuola archeol. di Atene*, 6–7 (1926), 86–251.

19. Maiuri, A. 'Le necropole micenee dell'isola di Rodi.' In *Ann. della R. Scuola archeol. di Atene*, 6–7 (1926), 251–6.

20. Monaco, G. 'Scavi nella zona micenea di Jaliso (1935–36).' In *Clara Rhodos*, 10 (1941), 41 ff.

21. Müller, K. 'Alt-Pylos II.' In *Athenische Mitteilungen d. Deutschen Archäol. Instituts*, 34 (1909), 269–328.

22. Orlandos, A. K. (ed.). Τὸ ἔργον τῆς 'Αρχαιολογικῆς 'Εταιρείας (Athens 1954– , annual publication).

23. Page, D. L. *History and the Homeric Iliad.* Berkeley and Los Angeles, 1959.

24. Persson, A. W. *The Royal Tombs at Dendra near Midea.* Lund, 1931.

25. Platon, N. "Ο τάφος τοῦ Σταφύλου." In Κρητικὰ Χρονικά, 3 (1949), 534–73.

26. Reusch, H. *Die zeichnerische Rekonstruktion des Frauenfrieses im böotischen Theben.* (*Abh. d. deutschen Akad. d. Wissenschaften Berlin. Klasse für Sprachen, Literatur, u. Kunst. 1955, no. 1*)

27. Schliemann, H. *Bericht über meine Ausgrabungen im böotischen Orchomenos.* 1881.
28. Staïs, V. [Report on excavations at Thoricus.] In Πρακτικὰ τῆς ᾿Αρχαιολ. ῾Εταιρείας, 1893, 12 ff.
29. Stubbings, F. H. *Mycenaean Pottery from the Levant.* Cambridge, 1951.
30. Taylour, Lord William D. *Mycenaean Pottery in Italy and Adjacent Areas.* Cambridge, 1958.
31. Tsountas, C. ῎Ερευναὶ ἐν τῇ Λακωνικῇ καὶ ὁ τάφος τοῦ Βαφείου.᾿ In ᾿Αρχ. ᾿Εφ. 1889, 129 ff.
32. Vermeule, E. T. 'New Excavations in W. Greece.' In *Boston Univ. Graduate Journal,* 9 (1961), 73–84, 119–127.
33. Wace, A. J. B. *Chamber Tombs at Mycenae.* London, 1932 [=*Archaeologia* 82].
34. Wace, A. J. B. 'Ephyraean Ware.' In *B.S.A.* 51 (1956), 123–7.
35. Wace, A. J. B. (*et al.*). 'Mycenae.' In *B.S.A.* 24 (1919–21), 185–209.
36. Wace, A. J. B. (*et al.*). 'Excavations at Mycenae.' In *B.S.A.* 25 (1921–3).
37. Wace, A. J. B. and Blegen, C. W. 'Pottery as Evidence for Trade and Colonisation....' In *Klio,* 32 (1939), 131–47.
38. Wace, A. J. B. 'The Tholos Tombs at Mycenae: Structural Analysis.' In Persson, A. W., *The Royal Tombs at Dendra,* 140 ff.
39. Weickert, C. 'Die Ausgrabung beim Athena-Tempel in Milet.' In *Istanbuler Mitt.* 7 (1957), 102–32; 9/10 (1959/60), 1–96.

VII. THE FIRST HEROIC AGE

1. Chadwick, H. M. *The Heroic Age.* Cambridge, 1912.
2. Myres, J. L. *Who were the Greeks?* Berkeley, 1930.

IX. HERACLES AND EARLY MYCENAEAN HISTORY

1. Caskey, J. L. 'Excavations at Lerna.' In *Hesperia,* 27 (1958), 125–44.
2. Guthrie, W. K. C. *The Greeks and Their Gods.* London, 1950.
3. Leonhard, W. *Hettiter und Amazonen.* Leipzig, Berlin, 1911.

X. THE MAINLAND AND CRETE

1. Chadwick, J. *The Decipherment of Linear B.* Cambridge, 1958.
2. Dunbabin, T. J. 'Minos and Daidalos in Sicily.' In *Papers of the British School at Rome,* 1948, 8 ff.
3. Hood, M. S. F. 'Late Minoan Warrior Graves...at Knossos.' In *B.S.A.* 47 (1952), 243–77.
4. Hutchinson, R. W. *Prehistoric Crete.* Harmondsworth, 1962.
5. Mylonas, G. E. 'Athens and Minoan Crete.' In *Harv. Stud. Class. Phil.* Suppl. 1 (1940).
6. Palmer, L. R. *Mycenaeans and Minoans.* London, 1961.
7. Pendlebury, J. D. S. *The Archaeology of Crete.* London, 1939.
8. Severyns, A. *Grèce et proche-orient avant Homère.* Brussels, 1960.
9. Starr, C. G. *The Origins of Greek Civilisation.* New York, 1961. Chs. 1 and 2.
10. Ventris, M. G. F. and Chadwick, J. *Documents in Mycenaean Greek.* Cambridge, 1956.

A. ADDENDA

1. Hammond, N. G. L. 'Tumulus-burial in Albania, the Grave Circles of Mycenae, and the Indo-Europeans.' In *B.S.A.* 62 (1967), 77–105.
2. Higgins, R. *Minoan and Mycenaean Art.* London, 1967.
3. Hope Simpson, R. *A Gazetteer and Atlas of Mycenaean Sites* (B.I.C.S. Suppl. 16). London, 1965.
4. Marinatos, S. 'A gold treasure from the realm of Nestor.' In *Ill. Ldn News*, 4 Dec. 1965, 32.
5. Mylonas, G. E. *Mycenae and the Mycenaean Age.* Princeton, 1966.
6. Ninkovich, D. and Heezen, B. C. 'Santorini Tephra.' In *Colston Papers*, 17 (1965), 413–53.
7. Van Seters, J. *The Hyksos.* New Haven, 1966.

CHAPTER XV

G. GENERAL

1. Cavaignac, E. *Le problème hittite.* Paris, 1936.
2. Cavaignac, E. *Les Hittites.* L'ancien Orient illustré, no. 3. Paris, 1950.
3. Cornelius, F. 'Die Chronologie des vorderen Orients im 2. Jahrtausend v. Chr.' In *Arch. f. Or.* 17 (1954–6), 294 ff.
4. Cornelius, F. 'Chronology, eine Erwiderung.' In *J.C.S.* 12 (1958), 101 ff.
5. Delaporte, L. *Les Hittites.* L'évolution de l'humanité. Paris, 1936.
6. Ebeling, E., Meissner, B. and Weidner, E. (ed.). *Reallexikon der Assyriologie.* Berlin, 1928– .
7. Forrer, E. *Die Boghazköi-Texte in Umschrift. W.V.D.O.G.* 41, 42 (1922–6).
8. Garstang, J. and Gurney, O. R. *The Geography of the Hittite Empire.* Occasional Publications of the British Institute of Archaeology at Ankara, no. 5. London, 1959.
9. Goetze, A. *Das Hethiter-Reich. Alte Or.* 27, 2. Leipzig, 1928.
10. Goetze, A. *Kizzuwatna. Y.O.S.* Researches, vol. XXII. New Haven, 1940.
11. Goetze, A. 'The problem of chronology and early Hittite history.' In *Bull. A.S.O.R.* 122 (1951), 18 ff.
12. Goetze, A. 'On the chronology of the second millennium B.C.' In *J.C.S.* 11 (1957), 53 ff.
13. Goetze, A. *Kleinasien.* Kulturgeschichte des alten Orients, Abschnitt III, 1. Ed. 2. München, 1957. (Part of I. Müller, *Handbuch der Altertumswissenschaft.*)
14. Goetze, A. Review of G, 8. In *J.C.S.* 14 (1960), 43 ff.
15. Güterbock, H. G. 'The Hurrian Element in the Hittite Empire.' In *J.W.H.* 2 (1954), 383 ff.
16. Gurney, O. R. *The Hittites.* Pelican Books. Revised, 1964.
17. Gurney, O. R. 'Hittite Kingship.' In Hooke, S. H., *Myth, Ritual, and Kingship.* Oxford, 1958.
18. Korošec, V. *Hethitische Staatsverträge.* Leipzig, 1931.
19. Landsberger, B. 'Assyrische Königsliste und "Dunkles Zeitalter".' In *J.C.S.* 8 (1954), 31 ff. and 106 ff.
20. Laroche, E. 'Chronologie hittite, état des questions.' In *Anadolu*, 2 (1955), 1 ff.
21. Laroche, E. 'Catalogue des textes hittites.' In *R.H.A.* XIV/58–XVI/62 (1956–8).

22. Mayer, L. A. and Garstang, J. *Index of Hittite Names*. British School of Archaeology in Jerusalem, Supplementary Papers, no. 1. London, 1923.

23. Otten, H. 'Die hethitischen Königslisten und die altorientalische Chronologie.' In *M.D.O.G.* 83 (1951), 47 ff.

24. Otten, H. 'Das Hethiterreich.' In H. Schmökel, *Kulturgeschichte des alten Orients*. Stuttgart, 1961.

25. Otten, H. 'Der Weg des hethitischen Staates zum Grossreich.' In *Saeculum*, 15 (1964), 115 ff.

26. Pritchard, J. B. *Ancient Near Eastern Texts relating to the Old Testament*, ed. 2. Princeton, 1955.

27. Rowton, M. B. 'The date of Hammurabi.' In *J.N.E.S.* 17 (1958), 97 ff.

28. Walser, G. (ed.). *Neuere Hethiterforschung*. Historia, Einzelschriften, Heft 7. Wiesbaden, 1964.

29. Wiseman, D. J. *The Alalakh Tablets*. Occasional Publications of the British Institute of Archaeology at Ankara, no. 2. London, 1953.

I. THE OLD HITTITE KINGDOM (*continued*)

1. Alp, S. *Zur Lesung von manchen Personennamen auf den hieroglyphenhethitischen Siegeln und Inschriften*. Ankara, 1950.

2. Carruba, O. Review of Friedrich, *Die hethitischen Gesetze*. In *Kratylos*, 7 (1962), 155 ff.

3. Dovgyalo, G. I. 'O perekhode k nasledovaniyu tsarskoĭ vlasti po otsovsko-pravovomu printsipu (po materialam khettskikh klinopisnykh istochnikov XVII–XIII vv. do n. é).' [On the transition to succession to kingship by patrilineal law (based on Hittite cuneiform sources of the XVIIth to XIIIth centuries B.C.).] In *Sovetskaya Etnografiya*, 6 (1963), 72 ff.

4. Friedrich, J. *Die hethitischen Gesetze*. Leiden, 1959.

5. Goetze, A. 'The linguistic continuity of Anatolia as shown by its proper names.' In *J.C.S.* 8 (1954), 74 ff.

6. Goetze, A. 'Some groups of ancient Anatolian proper names.' In *Language*, 30 (1954), 349 ff.

7. Goetze, A. 'Suffixes in "Kanishite" proper names.' In *R.H.A.* XVII/66–7 (1960), 45 ff.

8. Güterbock, H. G. Review of §1, 4. In *J.C.S.* 15 (1961), 62 ff.

9. Güterbock, H. G. 'Further notes on the Hittite Laws.' In *J.C.S.* 16 (1962), 17 ff.

10. Hardy, R. S. 'The Old Hittite Kingdom.' In *A.J.S.L.* 58 (1941), 177 ff.

11. Koschaker, P. Review of Sommer and Falkenstein, *Die hethitisch-akkadische Bilingue des Ḫattušili I*. In *Z. Sav.* 60 (1940), 242 ff.

12. Liverani, M. 'Hurri e Mitanni.' In *Or. antiq.* 1 (1962), 253 ff.

13. Macqueen, J. G. 'Hattian Mythology and Hittite Monarchy.' In *A. St.* 9 (1959), 171 ff.

14. Menabde, E. A. 'De l'ordre de succession dans l'empire hittite.' In XXV Congrès International des Orientalistes, Conférences présentées par la Délégation de l'U.R.S.S. Moscow, 1960.

15. Meyer, G. R. 'Zwei neue Kizzuwatna-Verträge.' In *Mitt. Inst. Or.* 1 (1953), 108 ff.

16. Otten, H. 'Ein althethitischer Vertrag aus Kizzuwatna.' In *J.C.S.* 5 (1951), 129 ff.

17. Smith, S. *The Statue of Idrimi*. Occasional Publications of the British Institute of Archaeology at Ankara, no. 1. London, 1949.
18. Sturtevant, E. H. and Bechtel, J. *A Hittite Chrestomathy*. Philadelphia, 1935.
19. van der Meer, P. *The Chronology of Western Asia and Egypt*, ed. 2. Leiden 1955.

II. THE MIDDLE HITTITE KINGDOM

1. Bittel, K. and Güterbock, H. G. *Boğazköy, neue Untersuchungen*. *Abh. Berlin*, 1935.
2. Bossert, H. T. *Asia*. Istanbul, 1946.
3. Breasted, J. H. *Ancient Records of Egypt*. Chicago, 1906.
4. Cavaignac, E. *Subbiluliuma et son temps*. Paris, 1932.
5. Cavaignac, E. 'L'Arnuwandas d'Ismirikka.' In *Arch. Orient.* 17 (1949), 85–7.
6. Forrer, E. 'Hajasa-Azzi.' In *Caucasica*, 9 (1931), 1 ff.
7. Friedrich, J. 'Staatsverträge des Hatti-Reiches, 2. Teil.' In *M.V.A.G.* 34.1 (1930).
8. Goetze, A. 'Die Lage von Kizwatnaš.' In *Z.A.* n.F. 2 (1925), 305 ff.
9. Goetze, A. 'Die historische Einleitung des Aleppo-Vertrages.' In *M.A.O.G.* 4 (1928–9), 59 ff.
10. Goetze, A. 'Die Pestgebete des Muršiliš.' In *K.F.* 1 (1930), 161 ff.
11. Goetze, A. 'The Predecessors of Šuppiluliumaš of Hatti.' In *J.A.O.S.* 72 (1952), 67 ff.
12. Gelb, I. J. *Hurrians and Subarians*. Chicago, 1944.
13. Güterbock, H. G. *Siegel aus Boğazköy*, 1. Berlin, 1940.
14. Güterbock, H. G. 'The Deeds of Suppiluliuma as told by his son, Mursili II.' In *J.C.S.* 10 (1956), 41 ff. and 75 ff.
15. Helck, W. *Die Beziehungen Aegyptens zu Vorderasien im 3. und 2. Jahrtausend v. Chr.* Wiesbaden, 1962.
16. Kitchen, K. A. *Suppiluliuma and the Amarna Pharaohs*. Liverpool, 1962.
17. Klengel, H. 'Ein neues Fragment zur historischen Einleitung des Talmišarruma Vertrages.' In *Z.A.* n.F. 22 (1964), 213 ff.
18. Knudtzon, J. A. *Die El-Amarna Tafeln*. Leipzig, 1915.
19. Kronasser, H. 'Die Umsiedelung der schwarzen Gottheit.' In *Sitzungsb. Wien*, 241/3 (1963), 1 ff.
20. Laroche, E. 'Suppiluliuma II.' In *R.A.* 47 (1953), 70 ff.
21. Lewy, H. 'On Some Problems of Kassite and Assyrian Chronology.' In *Ann. Inst. phil. hist. or.* tome 13 (1953), 241 ff. Brussels, 1955.
22. O'Callaghan, R. T. *Aram-Naharaim*. *An. Or.* 26. Rome, 1948.
23. Otten, H. 'Neue Quellen zum Ausklang des hethitischen Reiches.' In *M.D.O.G.* 94 (1963), 1 ff.
24. Petschow, H. 'Zur Noxalhaftung im hethitischen Recht.' In *Z.A.* n.F. 21 (1962), 237 ff.
25. Riemschneider, K. K. 'Die hethitischen Landschenkungsurkunden.' In *Mitt. Inst. Or.* 6 (1958), 321 ff.
26. Schuler, E. von. 'Die Würdenträgereide des Arnuwanda.' In *Or.* n.s. 25 (1956), 209 ff.
27. Smith, S. *Alalakh and Chronology*. London, 1940.
28. Sommer, F. *Die Ahhijavā-Urkunden*. *Abh. München*, n.F. 6. München, 1932.
29. Weidner, E. F. *Politische Dokumente aus Kleinasien*. Boghazköi-Studien 8–9. Leipzig 1923.

III. TROY

See Bibliography to C.A.H. ɪɪ³, pt. 2, ch. xxɪ.

A. ADDENDA

1. Beran, T. *Boğazköy-Hattuša*, v. *Die hethitische Glyptik von Boğazköy*, 1. Teil. *W.V.D.O.G.* 76. Berlin, 1967.
2. Carruba, O. 'Die Chronologie der hethitischen Texte und die hethitische Geschichte der Grossreichszeit.' In *Z.D.M.G.* Suppl. I (xvɪɪ. Deutscher Orientalistentag), 1969, 226 ff.
3. Cornelius, F. 'Der Text des Hattušilis III, geographisch erläutert.' In *R.H.A.* xvɪɪ/65 (1959), 104 ff.
4. Cornelius, F. 'Neue Aufschlüsse zur hethitischen Geographie.' In *Or.* n.s. 32 (1963), 233 ff.
5. Goetze, A. Review of *K. Bo.* x. In *J.C.S.* 16 (1962), 24 ff.
6. Goetze, A. 'Cilicians.' In *J.C.S.* 16 (1962), 48 ff.
7. Güterbock, H. G. Review of §1, 1. In *Oriens*, 6 (1953), 152 ff.
8. Güterbock, H. G. 'Sargon of Akkad mentioned by Hattušili I of Hatti.' In *J.C.S.* 18 (1964), 1 ff.
9. Güterbock, H. G. 'The Hittite conquest of Cyprus reconsidered.' In *J.N.E.S.* 26 (1967), 73 ff.
10. Güterbock, H. G. 'The predecessors of Suppiluliuma again.' In *J.N.E.S.* 29 (1970), 73 ff.
11. Houwink ten Cate, Philo H. J. *The Records of the Early Hittite Empire* (*c. 1450–1380 B.C.*) Publications de l'Institut historique et archéologique de Stamboul, no. xxvɪ. Istanbul, 1970.
12. Kammenhuber, A. *Die Arier im Vorderen Orient*. Heidelberg, 1968.
13. Kammenhuber, A. 'Konsequenzen aus neueren Datierungen hethitischer Texte: Pferdetrainingsanweisungen eine Erfindung der Hethiter.' In *Or.* n.s. 38 (1969), 548 ff.
14. Kammenhuber, A. 'Die Vorgänger Šuppiluliumas I. Untersuchungen zu einer neueren Geschichtsdarstellung H. Ottens.' In *Or.* n.s. 39 (1970), 278 ff.
15. *K.Bo.*, *Keilschrifttexte aus Boghazköi*, 1–xvɪɪ. Leipzig and Berlin, 1916–69.
16. Kempinsky, A. and Košak, S. 'Der Išmeriga-Vertrag.' In *W.O.* 5 (1970), 191 ff.
17. Klengel, H. *Geschichte Syriens im 2. Jahrtausend v. u. Z.* Berlin, 1965 and 1969.
18. Klengel, H. 'Die Rolle der "Ältesten" (LÚᴹᴱˢ ŠU. GI) im Kleinasien der Hethiterzeit.' In *Z.A.* n.F. 23 (1965), 223 ff.
19. Landsberger, B. *Sam'al*. Ankara, 1948.
20. Laroche, E. 'Un point d'histoire: Ulmi-Teššub.' In *R.H.A.* vɪɪɪ/48 (1947–8), 40 ff.
21. Otten, H. 'Hethiter, Hurriter und Mitanni.' In *Fischer Weltgeschichte*, 3 (1966). 102 ff.
22. Otten, H. 'Zur Datierung und Bedeutung des Felsheiligtums von Yazilikaya.' In *Z.A.* n. F. 24 (1967), 222 ff.
23. Otten, H. 'Ein hethitischer Vertrag aus dem 15./14. Jahrhundert v. Chr. (*K.Bo.* xvɪ 47).' In *Ist. Mitt.* 17 (1967), 55 ff.
24. Otten, H. 'Die hethitischen historischen Quellen und die altorientalische Chronologie.' In Akademie der Wissenschaften und der Literatur (Mainz), *Abh. der Geistes- und Sozialwissenschaftlichen Klasse*, 1968, 101 ff.
25. Otten, H. *Sprachliche Stellung und Datierung des Madduwatta-textes*. Studien zu den Boğazköy-Texte, Heft 11. Wiesbaden, 1969.

26. Rost, L. 'Die ausserhalb von Boğazköy gefundenen hethitischen Briefe.' In *Mitt. Inst. Or.* 4 (1956), 328 ff.
27. Schuler, E. von. *Die Kaškäer.* Berlin, 1965.
28. Schuler, E. von. 'Beziehungen zwischen Syrien und Anatolien in der späten Bronzezeit.' In *La Siria nel tardo bronzo* (Orientis Antiqui Collectio, ix). Rome, 1969.

CHAPTER XVI

G. GENERAL

1. Arne, T. J. 'La Steppe turkomane et ses antiquités.' In *Geografiska Annaler* (1935).
2. Fairservis, W. F. Jr. *Archaeological Studies in the Seistan Basin.* New York, 1961.
3. Ghirshman, R. *Iran.* Baltimore, 1954.
4. Ghirshman, R. 'Iranian Pre-Sassanian Art Cultures.' In *Encyclopedia of World Art*, 7, 247 ff. London, 1963.
5. Ghirshman, R. *The Art of Ancient Iran.* New York, 1965.
6. Godard, A. *Les Bronzes du Luristan.* Paris, 1931.
7. Herzfeld, E. 'Bericht über archäologische Beobachtungen im südlichen Kurdistan und im Luristan.' In *A.M.I.* 1 (1929), 65 ff.
8. Herzfeld, E. *Iran in the Ancient East.* New York, 1941.
9. Masson, V. M. and M. E. 'Archaeological Cultures of Central Asia of the Aeneolithic and Bronze Ages.' In *Cah. H.M.* 5 (1959), 15 ff.
10. Masson, V. M. *Drevnezemledeltcheskaya kultura Margiani.* Moscow–Leningrad, 1959. (French summary by R. Ghirshman, *Iranica antiqua*, 4 (1964), 69 ff.)
11. Masson, V. M. 'The Historical Position of Central Asian Civilization.' In *Soviet Anth. and Arch.* 3 (1964), 3 ff.
12. McCown, D. E. *The Comparative Stratigraphy of Early Iran.* Chicago, 1942.
13. McCown, D. E. 'The Relative Stratigraphy and Chronology of Iran.' In *Relative Chronologies in Old World Archeology* (R. W. Ehrich, ed.), Chicago, 1954, 56 ff.
14. Meldgaard, J., Mortensen, P. and Thrane, H. 'Excavations at Tepe Guran, Luristan.' In *Acta Arch.* 34 (1964), 97 ff.
15. Mongait, A. *Archaeology in the U.S.S.R.* Moscow, 1959.
16. de Morgan, J. J. *Mission scientifique en Perse.* iv. *Recherches archéologiques.* Paris, 1896.
17. Porada, E. *Ancient Iran.* New York, 1965.
18. Schaeffer, C. F. A. *Stratigraphie comparée et chronologie de l'Asie occidentale.* London, 1948.
19. Schmidt, E. F. *Flights Over Ancient Cities of Iran.* Chicago, 1940.
20. Stein, Sir A. 'Archaeological Reconnaissances in Southern Persia.' In *G.J.* 83 (1934), 119 ff.
21. Stein, Sir A. 'An Archaeological Tour in Ancient Persis.' In *G.J.* 86 (1935), 489 ff.
22. Stein, Sir A. *Archaeological Reconnaissances in Northwest India and Southeast Iran.* London, 1937.
23. Stein, Sir A. 'An Archaeological Journey in Western Iran.' In *G.J.* 92 (1938), 313 ff.
24. Stein, Sir A. *Old Routes of Western Iran.* London, 1940.
25. Vanden Berghe, L. *Archéologie de l'Iran ancien.* Leiden, 1959.

I. THE LATE THIRD AND EARLY SECOND MILLENNIA B.C.

1. Antonini, C. S. 'Preliminary Notes on the Excavation of the Necropolises found in Western Pakistan.' In *East and West*, 14 (1963), 13 ff.
2. Amiran, R. 'Yanik Tepe, Shengavit, and the Khirbet Kerak Ware.' In *A. St.* 15 (1965), 165 ff.
3. Arne, T. J. *Excavations at Shah Tepe, Iran.* Stockholm, 1945.
4. Banerjee, N. R. 'The Iron Age in India.' In *Indian Prehistory: 1964* (V. N. Misra and M. S. Mate, eds.), 177 ff. Poona, 1965.
5. Brown, T. B. *Excavations in Azerbaijan, 1948.* London, 1951.
6. Burney, C. A. 'Eastern Anatolia in the Chalcolithic and Early Bronze Age.' In *A. St.* 8 (1958), 157 ff.
7. Burney, C. A. 'Circular Buildings Found at Yanik Tepe in North-west Iran.' In *Antiq.* 35 (1961), 237 ff.
8. Burney, C. A. 'Excavations at Yanik Tepe, North-west Iran.' In *Iraq*, 23 (1961), 138 ff.
9. Burney, C. A. 'Excavations at Yanik Tepe, Azerbaijan, 1961.' In *Iraq*, 24 (1962), 134 ff.
10. Burney, C. A. 'The Excavations at Yanik Tepe, Azerbaijan, 1962.' In *Iraq*, 25 (1963), 54 ff.
11. Caldwell, J. and Shahmirzadi, S. M. *Tal-i-Iblis.* Illinois State Museum Preliminary Report 7. Springfield, Illinois, 1966.
12. de Cardi, B. 'The Bampur Sequence in the 3rd Millennium B.C.' In *Antiq.* 41 (1967), 33 ff.
13. Childe, V. G. 'Wheeled Vehicles.' In *A History of Technology*, vol. 1 (C. Singer, E. J. Holmyard and A. R. Hall, eds.). Oxford, 1954.
14. Childe, V. G. 'The First Waggons and Carts—from the Tigris to the Severn.' In *P.P.S.* 17 (1951), 177 ff.
15. Contenau, G. and Ghirshman, R. *Fouilles du Tépé Giyan, près de Néhavend, 1931 et 1932.* Paris, 1935.
16. Crawford, V. E. 'Beside the Kara Su.' In *Bull. M.M.A.* 23 (1963), 263 ff.
17. Dales, G. F. 'A Suggested Chronology for Afghanistan, Baluchistan, and the Indus Valley.' In *Chronologies in Old World Archaeology* (R. W. Ehrich, ed.), Chicago, 1965, 257–84.
18. Delaporte, L. *Catalogue des cylindres, cachets et pierres gravées de style oriental du Musée du Louvre.* Paris, 1920–3.
19. Deshayes, J. 'Rapport préliminaire sur les deux premières campagnes de fouilles à Tureng Tépé.' In *Syria*, 40 (1963), 85 ff.
20. Deshayes, J. 'Rapport préliminaire sur les troisième et quatrième campagnes de fouilles à Tureng Tépé.' In *Iranica antiqua*, 5 (1965), 83 ff.
21. Dyson, R. H. Jr. 'Iran, 1957: Iron Age Hasanlu.' In *University Museum Bulletin* (Philadelphia), 20 (1958), 25–32.
22. Dyson, R. H. Jr. 'Problems in the Relative Chronology of Iran, 6000–2000 B.C.' In *Chronologies in Old World Archaeology* (R. W. Ehrich, ed.), Chicago, 1965, 215 ff.
23. Frumkin, G. 'Archaeology in Soviet Central Asia, v. The Deltas of the Oxus and Jaxartes.' In *Central Asian Review*, 13 (1964), 69 ff.
24. Frumkin, G. 'Archaeology in Soviet Central Asia, VII. Turkmenistan.' In *Central Asian Review*, 14 (1965), 71 ff.
25. Ghirshman, R. 'Notes sur les peuples et l'art de l'Iran préhistorique.' In *Revue des Arts Asiatiques*, 10 (1936), 33 ff.

26. Ghosh, A. 'The Indus Civilization: its Origins, Authors, Extent and Chronology.' In *Indian Prehistory: 1964* (V. N. Misra and M. S. Mate, eds.), Poona, 1965, 113 ff.

27. Gimbutas, M. 'The Indo-Europeans: Archeological Problems.' In *American Anthropologist*, 65 (1963), 815 ff.

28. Gimbutas, M. *Bronze Age Cultures in Central and Eastern Europe*. The Hague, 1965.

29. Gordon, Col. D. H. 'The Chronology of the Third Cultural Period at Tepe Hissar.' In *Iraq*, 13 (1951), 40 ff.

30. Gordon, Col. D. H. *The Prehistoric Background of Indian Culture*. Bombay, 1960.

31. Heine-Geldern, R. 'Archaeological Traces of the Vedic Aryans.' In *Journ. of the Indian Society of Oriental Art*, 4 (1936), 87 ff.

32. Heine-Geldern, R. 'The Coming of the Aryans and the end of the Harappan Civilization.' In *Man*, 56 (1956), 136 ff.

33. Kushnareva, K. K. and Chubinishvili, T. N. 'The Historical Significance of the Southern Caucasus in the Third Millennium B.C.E.' In *Soviet Anth. and Arch.* 2 (1963/4), 3 ff.

34. Mallowan, M. E. L. *Early Mesopotamia and Iran*. London, 1965.

35. Mallowan, M. E. L. 'Excavations at Tell Chagar Bazar.' In *Iraq*, 3 (1936), 1 ff.

36. Piggot, S. 'Dating the Hissar Sequence—the Indian Evidence.' In *Antiq*. 17 (1943), 169 ff.

37. Rainey, F. and Ralph, E. K. 'Archeology and its New Technology. In *Science*, 153 (1966), 1481 ff.

38. Pope, A. U. *A Survey of Persian Art*, vol. IV. Oxford, 1938.

39. Schmidt, E. F. 'The Tepe Hissar Excavations.' In *M.J.* 23 (1933), no. 4.

40. Schmidt, E. F. *Excavations at Tepe Hissar (Damghan)*. Philadelphia, 1937.

41. Ward, L. 'The Relative Chronology of China through the Han Period.' In *Relative Chronologies in Old World Archeology* (R. W. Ehrich, ed.), Chicago, 1954, 130 ff.

42. Wheeler, Sir M. *The Indus Civilization*. London, 1962.

43. Wulsin, F. 'Excavations at Tureng Tepe.' *Suppl. to the Bull. Amer. Inst. Persian Art and Arch.* New York, 1932.

44. Young, T. C. Jr. and Smith, P. E. L. 'Research in the Prehistory of Central Western Iran.' In *Science*, 153 (1966), 386 ff.

II. CULTURAL PATTERNS OF THE MIDDLE SECOND MILLENNIUM

1. Carter, T. H. 'Excavations at Tell al-Rimah, 1964.' In *Bull. A.S.O.R.* 178 (1965), 40 ff.

2. Delougaz, P. *Pottery from the Diyala Region* (O.I.P. 63). Chicago, 1952.

3. Dyson, R. H. Jr. 'Excavations at Dinkha Tepe, 1966.' In *Iran*, 5 (1967).

4. Epstein, C. M. *Palestinian Bichrome Ware*. Leiden, 1966.

5. Goff, C. *New Evidence of Cultural Development in Luristan in the Late Second and Early First Millennia*. Thesis, Univ. of London (Inst. of Archaeology), 1966.

6. Hawkes, C. 'Gold Earrings of the Bronze Age, East and West.' In *Folklore*, 72 (1961), 438 ff.

7. Hrouda, B. *Die bemalte Keramik des zweiten Jahrtausends in Nordmesopotamien und Nordsyrien*. Berlin, 1957.

8. Kenyon, K. *Archaeology in the Holy Land.* London and New York, 1960.
9. Lloyd, S. *Early Anatolia.* Baltimore, 1956.
10. Maleki, Y. 'Une Fouille en Luristan.' In *Iranica antiqua*, 4 (1964), 1 ff.
11. Phillips, E. D. *The Royal Hordes.* London, 1965.
12. Pope, A. U. 'A Note on some Pottery from the Holmes Luristan Expedition.' In *Bull. Amer. Inst. Persian Art and Arch.* 4 (1936), 120 ff.
13. Pope, A. U. 'The Second Holmes Expedition to Luristan.' In *Bull. Amer. Inst. Persian Art and Arch.* 5 (1938), 205 ff.
14. Porada, E. and Buchanan, B. *Corpus of Ancient Near-Eastern Seals in North American Collections*, 1. Washington, 1948.
15. Starr, R. F. S. *Nuzi*, vol. II. Cambridge, Mass., 1937.
16. Vanden Berghe, L. *Art Iranien ancien.* Brussels, 1966.
17. Von der Osten, H. H. *The Alishar Hüyük, season of 1930–32*, part II. Chicago, 1937.
18. Young, T. C. Jr. 'A Comparative Ceramic Chronology for Western Iran, 1500–500 B.C.' In *Iran*, 3 (1965), 53 ff.

III. END OF THE BRONZE AGE CULTURES, *c.* 1350–1150 B.C.

1. Coon, C. S. 'Excavations in Hotu Cave, Iran, 1951, a Preliminary Report.' In *Proc. Amer. Philos. Soc.* 96 (1952), 231 ff.
2. Coon, C. S. *The Seven Caves.* New York, 1957.
3. Crawford, V. E. 'Hasanlu, 1960.' In *Bull. M.M.A.* 20 (1961), 85–94.
4. Dyson, R. H. Jr. 'Where the Golden Bowl of Hasanlu was found.' In *Ill. Ldn News*, 236 (1960), 132 ff.
5. Dyson, R. H. Jr. 'The Golden Bowl and the Silver Cup.' In *Ill. Ldn News*, 236 (1960), 250 f.
6. Dyson, R. H. Jr. 'Excavating the Mannaean Citadel of Hasanlu.' In *Ill. Ldn News*, 239 (1961), 534 ff.
7. Dyson, R. H. Jr. 'In the City of the Golden Bowl: New Excavations at Hasanlu.' In *Ill. Ldn News*, 245 (1964), 372 ff.
8. Dyson, R. H. Jr. 'Notes on Weapons and Chronology in Northern Iran around 1000 B.C.' In *Nomads and Dark Ages* (M. Mellink, ed.), Istanbul, 1964, 32 ff.
9. Dyson, R. H. Jr. 'Problems of Protohistoric Iran as seen from Hasanlu.' In *J.N.E.S.* 24 (1965), 193 ff.
10. Ghirshman, R. *Fouilles de Sialk, près de Kashan, 1933, 1934, 1937*, vol. II. Paris, 1939.
11. Maxwell-Hyslop, R. 'Daggers and Swords in Western Asia.' In *Iraq*, 8 (1946), 1 ff.
12. Maxwell-Hyslop, R. and Hodges, H. W. M. 'A Note on the Significance of the Technique of "Casting on" as applied to a group of Daggers from Northwest Persia.' In *Iraq*, 26 (1964), 50 ff.
13. Muscarella, O. W. 'Hasanlu 1964.' In *Bull. M.M.A.* 25 (1966), 121 ff.
14. Negahban, E. O. 'A Brief Report on the Excavations of Marlik Tepe and Pileh Qal'eh.' In *Iran*, 2 (1964), 13 ff.
15. Negahban, E. O. *A Preliminary Report on Marlik Excavations.* Tehran, 1964.
16. Negahban, E. O. 'Notes on some Objects from Marlik.' In *J.N.E.S.* 24 (1965), 309 ff.
17. Sulimirski, T. 'Scythian Antiquities in Western Asia.' In *Artibus Asiae*, 17 (1954), 282 ff.

18. Thrane, H. 'Archaeological Investigations in Western Luristan.' In *Acta Arch.* 35 (1965), 153 ff.

19. Vanden Berghe, L. *La Nécropole de Khūrvīn.* Istanbul, 1964.

20. Vanden Berghe, L. 'Le mystérieux Luristan livre ses secrets.' In *Trésors de l'ancien Iran,* Musée Rath, Geneva, 1966, 23 ff.

21. Young, T. C. Jr. 'Survey in Western Iran, 1961.' In *J.N.E.S.* 25 (1966), 228 ff.

22. Young, T. C. Jr. 'Thoughts on the Architecture of Hasanlu IV.' In *Iranica antiqua,* 6 (1966), 48 ff.

23. Young, T. C. Jr. 'The Iranian Migration into the Zagros.' In *Iran,* 5 (1967), 11 ff.

A. ADDENDA

1. Boehmer, R. M. 'Forschungen am Zendan-i Suleiman in Persisch-Aserbeidschan 1958–1964.' In *Arch. Anz.* 82 (1967–68), 573 ff.

2. Caldwell, J. (ed.). *Investigations at Tal-i-Iblis.* Illinois State Museum Preliminary Report 9. Springfield, Illinois, 1967.

3. de Cardi, B. 'Bampur: a Third Millennium Site in Persian Baluchistan.' In *Archaeologia viva,* 1 (1968), 151 ff.

4. Dales, G. F. 'A Review of the Chronology of Afghanistan, Baluchistan and the Indus Valley.' In *A.J.A.* 72 (1968), 305 ff.

5. Dani, A. H. (ed.). 'Timargarha and Gandhara Grave Culture.' In *Ancient Pakistan,* vol. III (1967).

6. Deshayes, J. 'New Evidence for the Indo-Europeans from Tureng Tepe, Iran.' In *Archaeology,* 22 (1967), 10 ff.

7. Deshayes, J. 'Rapport préliminaire sur la sixième campagne de fouilles à Tureng Tépé (1965).' In *Iranica antiqua,* 6 (1966), 1 ff.

8. Deshayes, J. 'Tureng Tepe and the Plain of Gorgan in the Bronze Age.' In *Archaeologia viva,* 1 (1968), 35 ff.

9. Dyson, R. H. Jr. 'Annotations and Corrections of the Relative Chronology of Iran, 1968.' In *A.J.A.* 72 (1970), 308 ff.

10. Hakemi, A. 'Gilan-Mazanderan—Kaluraz and the Civilization of the Mardes.' In *Archaeologia viva,* 1 (1968), 63 ff.

11. Lamberg-Karlovsky, C. C. 'Tepe Yahyā.' In *Iran,* 7 (1969), 184 ff.

12. Masson, V. M. 'The Urban Revolution in Southern Turkmenia.' In *Antiquity,* 167 (1968), 178 ff.

13. Meade, C. G. 'Excavations at Bābā Jān 1967.' In *Iran,* 7 (1969), 115 ff.

14. Meade, C. G. 'Luristan in the First Half of the First Millennium B.C.' In *Iran,* 6 (1968), 105 ff.

15. Muscarella, O. W. 'Excavations at Dinkha Tepe, 1966.' In *Bull. M.M.A.* 27 (1968), 187 ff.

16. Muscarella, O. W. 'The Tumuli at Se Girdan.' In *Bull. M.M.A.* 28 (1969), 5 ff.

17. Nicol, M. B. 'Darvāzeh Tepe.' In *Iran,* 7 (1969), 172.

18. Stronach, D. 'Excavations at Tepe Nūsh-i Jān, 1967.' In *Iran,* 7 (1969), 1 ff.

19. Stronach, D. 'Tepe Nūsh-i Jān.' In *Bull. M.M.A.* 27 (1968), 177 ff.

20. Thrane, H. 'Tepe Guran and the Luristan Bronzes.' In *Archaeology,* 23 (1970), 27 ff.

21. Tosi, M. 'Excavations at Shahr-i Sokhta.' In *East and West,* 18 (1968), 9 ff.

22. Vanden Berghe, L. 'La nécropole de Kalleh Nisar.' In *Archaeologia,* 32 (1970), 64 ff.

23. Young, T. C. Jr. *Excavations at Godin Tepe; First Progress Report.* Occasional Paper no. 17, Royal Ontario Museum, Toronto, 1969.

CHRONOLOGICAL TABLES

(A) EGYPT
Kings from the Thirteenth to the Eighteenth Dynasties

THIRTEENTH DYNASTY: 1786–1633 B.C.
(Selected Kings)

Sekhemre Khutowy Ammenemes Sobkhotpe I	5+x years	Khaneferre Sobkhotpe IV	8+x years
Sekhemkare Ammenemes Senbuef	3+x years	Khaankhre Sobkhotpe V	
		Mersekhemre Neferhotep II	
Sehetepibre (II) Ammenemes	1 year c. 1770–1769 B.C.	Khahetepre Sobkhotpe VI	4 years 9 months
Sankhibre Ameny Inyotef Ammenemes		Sekhemre Sankhtowy Neferhotep III	
Hetepibre Amu Sihornedjheryotef		Wahibre Yayebi	10 years 9 months
Sobkhotpe II, son of Mentuhotpe		Merneferre Iy	23 years 9 months
Renseneb	4 months	Merhetepre Ini	2 years 2 months
Awibre Hor		Djedneferre Dudimose I (Tutimaios)	c. 1674 B.C.
Sedjefakare Kay Ammenemes			
Khutowyre Ugaf	2 years 4 months		
Seneferibre Sesostris IV		Djedhetepre Dudimose II	
Userkare Khendjer	4+x years	Sewahenre Senebmiu	
Semenkhkare, 'the General'	3+x years	Meryankhre Mentuhotpe	Upper Egyptian rulers and vassals of the Hyksos
Sekhemre Wadjkhau Sobkemsaf I	7 years	Djedankhre Mentuemsaf	
Sekhemre Sewadjtowy Sobkhotpe III	3 years 2 months	Menkhaure Senaayeb	
Khasekhemre Neferhotep I	11 years c. 1740–1730 B.C.	Nehsy	

FOURTEENTH DYNASTY: 1786–c. 1603 B.C.

'Seventy-six kings of Xoïs', who reigned together 184 years, according to the Africanus version of Manetho. Many of their names are preserved in columns VIII–X of the Turin Canon. Few monuments.

FIFTEENTH DYNASTY: 1674–1567 B.C.

Mayebre Sheshi	[1 ?]3 years	Auserre Apophis I	40+x years
Meruserre Yakubher	8 years	Aqenenre Apophis II	
Seuserenre Khyan		Asehre Khamudy (?)	

SIXTEENTH DYNASTY: c. 1684–1567 B.C.

A succession of eight Hyksos chieftains probably contemporary with the 'Great Hyksos' of the Fifteenth Dynasty and including some or all of the following rulers:

Anather	Ahetepre
Semqen	Sekhaenre
Khauserre	Amu
Seket	Nebkhepeshre Apophis (III ?)

SEVENTEENTH DYNASTY: c. 1650–1567 B.C.

First Group

Sekhemre Wahkhau Rehotpe	—	Sankhenre Mentuhotpe VI	1 year
Sekhemre Wepmaat Inyotef V, 'the Elder'	3 years	Sewadjenre Nebiryerawet I	6 years
		Neferkare(?) Nebiryerawet II	x months
Sekhemre Heruhirmaat Inyotef VI	x months	Semenmedjat(?)re	—
Sekhemre Shedtowy Sobkemsaf II	16 years	Seuserenre (Userenre ?)	12 years
		Sekhemre Shedwast	—
Sekhemre Sementowy Thuty	1 year		

Second Group

Nubkheperre Inyotef VII	3+x years	Seqenenre Tao II, 'the Brave'	—
Senakhtenre	—	Wadjkheperre Kamose	3+x years
Seqenenre Tao I, 'the Elder'	—		

EIGHTEENTH DYNASTY: 1567–1320 B.C.

Nebpehtyre Amosis	1570–1546 B.C.	Nebmare Amenophis III	1417–1379 B.C.
Djeserkare Amenophis I	1546–1526 B.C.	Neferkheprure Amenophis IV (Akhenaten)	1379–1362 B.C.
Akheperkare Tuthmosis I	1525–c. 1512 B.C.		
Akheperenre Tuthmosis II	c. 1512–1504 B.C.	(Ankhkheprure) Smenkhkare (3)*	1364–1361 B.C.
Makare Hatshepsut	1503–1482 B.C.		
Menkheperre Tuthmosis III (21)*	1504–1450 B.C.	Nebkheprure Tutankhamun	1361–1352 B.C.
Akheprure Amenophis II	1450–1425 B.C.	Kheperkheprure Ay	1352–1348 B.C.
Menkheprure Tuthmosis IV	1425–1417 B.C.	Djeserkheprure Horemheb	1348–1320 B.C.

* Years of co-regency with his predecessor.

(B) WESTERN ASIA 1792–1390 B.C.

DATE	BABYLONIA		I. LARSA / II. SEALAND KINGS	I. ESHNUNNA / II. MITANNI	ELAM (see also p. 272, Table 2)	ASSYRIA	I. MARI / II. KHANA	ALEPPO	KHATTI	DATE
	BABYLON	KASSITE DYNASTY								
1792	Hammurabi (43) 1792–1750		I. Larsa: Rim-Sin I (defeated in 1763)	I. Eshnunna: Dadusha	Sirukdukh I	Shamshi-Adad I (rule ends in 1781)	I. Mari: Zimrilim (defeated by Hammurabi of Babylon)	Hammurabi I	Anitta	1792
				Ibalpiel II (son) c. 1784–?	Shimut-wartash Siwe-palar-khuppak	Ishme-Dagan I (40?) (son) 1780–1741?				
1750	Samsuiluna (38) 1749–1712		Rim-Sin II (nephew) (// Samsuiluna)	Silli-Sin '(// Hammurabi of Babylon)	Kuduzulush I	Mut-Ashkur (son) 1740?–?	II. Khana: (sequence of kings uncertain)	Abbael I (son)		1750
			II. Sea Country: Ilima-ilu	Iqish-Tishpak	Kutir-Nahhunte I	Rimu[sh?] (name uncertain) Asinum (grandson of Shamshi-Adad I?) Anarchy: 8 usurpers from Puzur-Sin to Adasi				
				Anni (or Thuni) ?–1727						
	Abieshu' (28) 1711–1684	Gandash (16)					Isharlim			
1700		Agum I (22) (son)	Itti-ili-nibi		Lila-ir-tash Temti-agun I	Belu-bani (10) (son of Adasi) 1700–1691	Isikh-Dagan	Iarimlim II (son)	(Tudkhaliash I?)	1700
	Ammiditana (37) 1683–1647	Kashtiliyash I (22) (son)	Damiq-ilishu (26)		Tan-Uli	Libaia (17) 1690–1674	Kashtiliash	Niqmiepu' I (son) Irkabtum (son)	(PU-Sharruma ?)	
						Sharma-Adad I (12) 1673–1662	Sunukhrammu	Hammurabi II	Labarnash (son)	
1650	Ammisaduqa (21) 1646–1626	Ushshi (8) (son)	Ishkibal (15)		Temti-khalki	Iptar(?)-Sin (12) 1661–1650	Ammimadar (son)	Iarimlim III	Khattushiliish I (son)	1650
		Abirattash (brother)	Sushshi (24) (brother)		Kuk-nashur II	Bazaia (28) 1649–1622	Hammurapi'			
		(Kashtiliiash II?)			Kutir-Shilkhakha I					
	Samsuditana	Urzigurumash	Gulkishar (55)		Temti-raptash	Lullaia (6)				

Chronological table (kings, with regnal years in parentheses and absolute dates B.C.). Time runs from left (earliest) to right (latest); approximate date divisions at 1550, 1500, 1450, 1390.

Date	Babylon	(Sealand)	II. Mitanni	Elam	Assyria	Syria	Hatti
1600–1550	Tiptakzi Agum II (son of Urzi-gurumash)	Peshgaldara-mash (50)	(Kirta?) Shuttarna I (son)	Atta-merra-khalki Pala-ishshan	[...] 1601–1599 Erishum III (13) 1598–1586 Shamshi-Adad II (6) 1585–1580 Ishme-Dagan II (16) 1579–1564 Shamshi-Adad III (16) 1563–1548	(Sharrael?) Abbael II (son) Ilimilimma I	Khantilish I (brother-in-law) Zidantash I (son)
1550–1500		Adarakalamma (28)	Parattarna	Kuh-kirwash	Ashur-nirari I (26) 1547–1522 Puzur-Ashur III (24) 1521–1498	Idrimi (son)	Ammunash (son) Khuzziyash I (short reign) Telepinush
1500–1450	Burnaburiash I (A missing king) Kashtiliash III (son of Burna-buriash I) Ulamburiash (brother) Agum III (son of Kash-tiliash III)	Ekurduanna (26) Melamkurkurra (7) Ea-gamil (9)	(Parsatatar?) Saustatar (son)	Kuk-Nahhunte Kutir-Nah-hunte II	Enlil-nasir I (13) 1497–1485 Nur-ili (12) 1484–1473 Ashur-shaduni (one month) Ashur-rabi I (20) 1472–1453	(Adad-nirari?) Niqmiepu' II (Niqmepa) (son of Idrimi) Ilimilimma II (son)	Alluwamnash Khantilish II (short reign) Zidantash II Khuzziyash II
1450–1390	(A missing king?) Kadashman-kharbe I Karaindash Kurigalzu I (son of Kadashman-kharbe I)		Artatama Shuttarna II (son) Artashshumara (son)		Ashur-nadin-ahhe I (20) 1452–1433 Enlil-nasir II (6) 1432–1427 Ashur-nirari II (7) 1426–1420 Ashur-bel-nisheshu (9) 1419–1411 Ashur-rim-nisheshu (8) 1410–1403 Ashur-nadin-ahhe II (10) 1402–1393		Tudkhaliash II Arnuwandash I (son) Tudkhaliash III (son) Khattushilish II (brother)

(C) CRETE, THE AEGEAN ISLANDS AND MAINLAND GREECE

(Note: Items in *italics* refer to legendary events. Datings are given by centuries and are not to be regarded as precise.   F.H.S.)

B.C.	CRETE	AEGEAN ISLANDS	MAINLAND GREECE
1700	MIDDLE MINOAN III begins: ('New era' in Crete) *Minos*	'*Thalassocracy of Minos*' Increased Minoan influence in Melos, Thera, Ceos (import or imitation of pottery; frescoes of Minoan style, etc.) *?Minoan conquest of Ceos* Minoan settlement at Trianda (Rhodes)	A few MIDDLE MINOAN III imports in the Argolid
1600	Great earthquake disaster at Cnossus LATE MINOAN IA begins		*Danaus, Cadmus, ?Pelops* SHAFT-GRAVES of Mycenae Earliest beehive tombs at Karditsa (Thessaly) and Koryphasion (Messenia) *Pelias at Iolcus; Neleus to Messenia* LATE HELLADIC I (MYCENAEAN I) begins Establishment of Mycenaean centres in Greece *Perseids at Mycenae ? Siege of Calydon* First Helladic traders in Eastern & Central Mediterranean *Voyage of Argo*
		Minoan trade & ? settlement at Miletus	
		Volcanic destruction of Minoan settlement on Thera	

TABLE (C) (*cont.*)

B.C.	CRETE	AEGEAN ISLANDS	MAINLAND GREECE
1500	LATE MINOAN IB begins		LATE HELLADIC II begins
	Destruction of Zakro, Mallia, Phaestus, etc.	Final volcanic cataclysm of Thera	
c. 1450	LATE MINOAN II at Cnossus: Helladic influence & ?Helladic conquest at Cnossus Linear B script	Minoan settlement at Trianda (Rhodes) destroyed	First palace at Mycenae
		Mycenaean (LATE HELLADIC II) settlement in Rhodes (*Heraclids*), and perhaps also at Miletus	*?Orchomenus destroyed by Thebes* *Thebes and Argolid at war (the 'Seven')*
	Daedalus at Cnossus *Attica becomes tributary to Crete:* *Theseus at Cnossus*		*Synoecism of Attica under Theseus*
	Minos in Sicily		
1400	Destruction of Minoan palace at Cnossus LATE MINOAN III begins		LATE HELLADIC IIIA begins *Establishment of Pelopids in Argolid*
			Destruction & rebuilding of palace, etc. at Mycenae
		Expansion of Mycenaean influence in the Aegean islands	Myc. trade expands in Cyprus, Syria, Palestine, Egypt (Tell el Amarna) *Sack of Thebes by Epigoni* (? later)

INDEX TO MAPS

The Arabic definite article (Al-, El-, etc.) has been disregarded as an element in the alphabetical arrangement of place-names. For example, Al-'Ubaid is to be found under 'U'.

GENERAL INDEX

The Arabic definite article (Al-, El- etc.) has been disregarded as an element in the alphabetical arrangement of place-names. For example, El-Amarna is to be found under 'A'.

Apart from the above, the order of main headings is strictly alphabetical by letters, e.g. Tanis, Tan-Rukhuratir, Tanturah, Tan-Uli.

Bold figures indicate main references; italic figures indicate maps, plans, illustrations, tables, etc.

law, current in Elam, 275; occupation of Assyria, 37; occupation of Mari, 29; scribes, 438; suzerainty over Susiana, 275; words, 482

Babylonian Period, Early *or* Old, 190, 196, 210, 211, 212, 214, 216, 217, 256, 257, 270, 280; religion of, 210; literature of, 212–13

Bacchylides, a Greek poet, 628

Badakhshān, in Afghanistān, 480

Badrah, *see* Dēr

baetyls, 540

Baghdad (Map 3), 61

Baḥrain island, *see* Tilmun

Bahrīya oasis, in Egypt, 292, 387

Bakhtyari, modern, *see* Anshan

Baki (Qūbān, *q.v.*), in Nubia, 348

Balāṭa (Shechem, *q.v.*), in Palestine, 111

Balīkh river (Map 5), 2, 9, 24, 27, 184

El-Ballās, in Upper Egypt, 68, 305

bāmāh (high-place), 110, 536, 544

Bampur, in Persia (Map 7), 702

Barga, kingdom of, in Syria (Map 5), 430

Barrāmīya-Sukori gold mines, in Upper Egypt, 350

barter, trade by, 574

Bashan, in Syria, 452

battering-rams, 115, 245

Bayburt, modern, in Armenia, 232

Bayraklı (Old Smyrna), in Anatolia, 132

Beblem *or* Bebnem, Asiatic ruler of Egypt, 54

bedawin (Bedouin, beduin; *see also* nomads), 25, 263, 316, 347, 425, 434, 473, 509; princes of Palestine and Syria, 55; Tuthmosis III and, 458

Bedouin (beduin), *see* bedawin

bee-keeping in Egypt, 373

Beersheba, in Southern Palestine, 113

Beirut, in Lebanon, 42, 484

Bēli (Elamite litigant), 273, 283

Bellerophon story, Homer's, 607–8

Bener, an Egyptian court official, 50

Benē-sim'āl ('Sons of the North'), 26

Beni Hasan, in Middle Egypt, 55, 399; desert village near, 332

Benjaminites (Iaminites, 'Sons of the South'), 9, 10, 24–8, 25 n(1)

Beon *or* Bnon of Egypt, 59, 60

Berlin: genealogy of Memphite priests, 58; Museum, 62, 344

Beruta (Beirut), in Lebanon (Maps 5(14) and 6), 42, 484

Bethel, in Palestine, 547, 555

Beth-shan (Beisan), in Palestine (Map 4), 101, 538–40, 556

Beth-shemesh, in Palestine (Map 4), 113, 547–8, 555

Beth Yerah (Khirbet Karak), in Palestine, 114

Beycesultan, in Western Anatolia, 149; palace, 164

Bichrome ware, 532

Bīga island, near Aswān, 349

billeting of troops and messengers in Egypt, 384

Biqā, the (plain of Coele-Syria, in valley of Litani), 430, 436, 452, 457–61 *passim*, 472–5 *passim*

Birgalzu, in Elam, 271

Biridashwa (significant name), 419

Bīsra, near Asyūt in Middle Egypt, 304

Black Punctured ware, 174

Black Slip ware, 172

Blaene district, in Anatolia, 231

Blue Crown, the (of Egypt), 51 and n(8)

Bnon *or* Beon of Egypt, 59, 60

boat-handling, 336

Boeotia, in Greece (Map 1), 122

Boğazköy (ancient Khattusha, *q.v.*), in Anatolia, 31, 32, 40, 41, 170, 228, 232–4 *passim*, 239, 420, 484, 513, 665, 704; *res gestae* of Khattushilish, *q.v.*, 31–3 *passim*, 37; rituals, 40

Bologna, in Italy, 51

Book of the Dead, 301, 403 n(3), 404, 406

Book of What-is-in-the-Underworld (*ᵓImy-Dēt*), 402

booty secured by Egyptians in war, distribution of, 371

Boreas (Greek god), 438

Bothrosschicht, 122

bowmen, royal, of Egypt, 335–6

bows and arrows (*see also* archery), 333–6 *passim*, 496–7

bows, composite, 335, 336, 364, 497

Brauron, in Greece (Map 1(28)), 123, 132

bridge of boats on Orontes, 460

British Museum (London), 53, 70, 306, 369, 408, 453

Bronze Age, Middle (*see also* Bronze Ages), 77–164, 228; in Anatolia, 228; in Cyprus, 141–64; in Greece and Aegean islands, 117–40; in Palestine, 77–116 *passim* (I, 78–88 *passim*; II, 88–116 *passim*)

Bronze Ages: Early, 77, 121, 122, 132, 139, 165–6, 170, 171, 228, 230, 231; Intermediate (E.B.-M.B.), 77–88, 90, 93, 97, 98, 103, 107, 113, 117; Middle, *see next above*; Late, 87, 166, 167, 171–2, 228

Brooklyn Museum (New York), 47, 49